LEAGUE
Publications Ltd

RUGBY LEAGUE 2001-02
Rising from the Ashes

League Publications Ltd

First published in Great Britain in 2001 by
League Publications Ltd
Wellington House
Briggate
Brighouse
West Yorkshire HD6 1DN

A CIP catalogue record for this book is available from the British Library
ISBN 1-901347-09-5

Designed and Typeset by League Publications Limited
Printed by ColourBooks Ltd, Dublin, Eire

Contributing Editor	Tim Butcher
Contributors	Martyn Sadler
	Gareth Walker
	Mike Latham
	Malcolm Andrews
	John Drake
	Raymond Fletcher
Statistics, production and design	Daniel Spencer
Pictures	Andy Howard
	Vicky Matthers
	Andrew Varley
	Col Whelan
	Graham Lynch
	Ken Brown

CONTENTS

Acknowledgments   8
Foreword   9
Introduction   12

1. Personalities of 2001   **15**
Rob Burrow   16
Stuart Fielden   17
Paul Sculthorpe   18
Jason Smith   19
Neil Turley   20

2. The 2001 Season   **21**
December 2000   22
January   26
February   31
March   35
April   42
Challenge Cup Final   50
May   54
June   60
July   67
August   74
September   78

3. Super League Play-offs 2001   **81**
Play-offs week by week   82
Super League Grand Final   91

4. NFP 2001   **113**
NFP Season   114
NFP Play-offs   130
NFP Grand Final   134

5. International 2001   **137**
The Ashes Series   138
Home Internationals   154
Trans-Tasman Test   160
International round-up   163
The Origin Game   167
Season Down Under   169

6. Statistical review 2001   **193**
Super League Players 1996-2001   195
Super League VI club by club   203
Super League VI round by round   228
Super League VI
Opta Index Analysis   246
NFP 2001 club by club   260
NFP 2001 round by round   280
Challenge Cup 2001
round by round   304
International scoreboard   310
2002 Fixtures   313
2001 Awards   317
2001 Statistical round-up   318

ACKNOWLEDGEMENTS

Rugby League 2001/2002 is the sixth in League Publications Ltd's annual series of Rugby League Yearbooks and again would not have been possible without the hard work and inspiration of a number of individuals.

We couldn't even begin the yearbook without the enthusiasm, hard work and dedication of all the contributors to Rugby League Express and Rugby League World who provide such a tremendous service to the game of Rugby League.

So too to those hardy souls who plough the touchlines of playing fields throughout the land to bring us some exceptional action photography throughout the year, in particular League Express staff photographer Andy Howard and Varley Picture Agency.

Special mentions for Gareth Walker, League Express editor Martyn Sadler, Malcolm Andrews, the undisputed king of trivia, Raymond Fletcher and Mike Latham, who have contributed so much to the writing of this book, and to Opta Index, who compiled the Opta Index Analysis in our burgeoning statistical section.

The statistical review was once again put together with loving care by Daniel Spencer, who has also single-handedly designed the book this year.

Tim Butcher, Contributing Editor

FOREWORD

When the history of Rugby League in the 21st Century eventually comes to be written, I suspect that the 2001 season may come to be seen as a turning point in the game, both in this country and internationally.

After the financial and organisational shortcomings of the 2000 Lincoln World Cup, the year 2001 was a year for the game to rebuild, and that process seems to have begun with some success.

St Helens' stunning 20-18 World Club Challenge victory over Brisbane Broncos at Bolton's Reebok Stadium set the tone on a cold January night, and we had some sparkling football, both in Super League and in the Northern Ford Premiership, with a host of new, young stars coming to the fore, with some of them playing a key role in representative games later in the season.

The Rugby Football League began to implement its World Class Performance Programme, designed to ensure a throughput of young players who would form the bedrock of the future of the game, while the urgency of that task was emphasised by a number of leading stars unfortunately opting to take up tempting financial offers to play rugby union, and, in several cases, gaining an almost automatic route into domestic international rugby union teams.

Apart from Saints' victory against Brisbane, the other highlights of the season included the Silk Cut Challenge Cup final in April, held for the first time at Twickenham. St Helens ground out a slightly disappointing 13-6 win against Bradford Bulls. But the Bulls gained their own reward in October, when more than 60,000 fans packed out Old Trafford to see the Bulls give a devastating display in hammering Wigan to defeat.

Finally the Australians came to England, after they had initially cancelled their tour, limiting it to three Tests, in an Ashes Series that would be sponsored by Guinness. Great Britain, coached for the first time by an Australian, in David Waite, won the first Test, but couldn't win the second or third, although the evidence of the third game suggests that the day may not be too far away when the Ashes will return to this country. Sadly, Australian coach Chris Anderson suffered a heart attack during the Third Test, and had to be detained in hospital for several days after the game.

One of the good things that happened during the autumn, while the Ashes series was taking place, was that the Rugby League International Federation made Russia its eleventh full member, finally recognising the great work that has been taking place in that country for the last ten years, which culminated in the Europa Cup in September, as big crowds in Tatarstan saw the England Students win an exciting international tournament.

Foreword

This is the sixth edition of this annual handbook that attempts to chart the Rugby League year. We cover the professional game in Great Britain, as well as giving you details of the international season, and the Australian NRL season. We have given you the match facts for every Super League, Challenge Cup and Northern Ford Premiership game, so that you can chart the achievements of your favourite team or player. And we give a brief résumé of the season for five players who we judge to have made the biggest impact on Rugby League domestically in 2001.

In fact this book contains a whole host of information that no serious Rugby League fan can really afford to be without, and we hope you will enjoy many happy hours of reading about this sport that is such a vital part of its community, and of the lives of so many people who live in the towns that have professional clubs, as well as a growing number of fans who live outside the traditional Rugby League heartland.

League Publications produces the weekly newspaper 'Rugby League Express', as well as the monthly glossy magazine 'Rugby League World' and the website 'totalrugbyleague.com'. If you are buying this book, we also hope that you either read our other products already, or you will take the trouble to check them out.

But whether you do or not, you can rest assured that, with your support, this wonderful sport will continue to grow and prosper, and will have a great future, both domestically and internationally.

Martyn Sadler
Chairman, League Publications Limited

INTRODUCTION

2001 was in many ways a typical Rugby League year - dramatic, heartbreaking, joyous, exhilarating, thrilling, controversial.

It was the year that Rugby League celebrated the return of Great Britain-Australia Ashes series with the visit of the 19th Kangaroos. That tour was already tinged with controversy even before it started, with world events in the wake of the 11th September outrage threatening to scupper the most eagerly awaited match-up in Rugby League for decades.

The Kangaroos came, but on a shortened tour that involved just a three-match Test series that revived international Rugby League and gave us all real hope that Great Britain was on the way to regaining its place at the top of the international ladder. And that, despite the Australians demonstrating skill levels and courage arguably greater than any other touring side before them.

And yet with 20 minutes of the Test series to go, Great Britain were in with a definite chance of taking their first series for 31 years.

Nobody remembers losers for too long, but we won't quickly forget the effort and heart from a Lions side that was prepared for the first time, controversially, by an Australian coach.

This was the year that the Rugby League Challenge Cup final was played at Twickenham for the first time, before it heads back to Edinburgh in 2002.

And what a triumph that proved to be for St Helens coach Ian Millward, chosen as coach of the year at the end of season Super League awards.

Saints finished off a magnificent treble of Super League Championship, World Club Challenge and Challenge Cup. If there was one single event that raised the spirits of British Rugby League fans, it was on that night at the Reebok Stadium, when Saints came from behind to stun the Brisbane Broncos.

And if ever we needed confirmation that Rugby League is the greatest game in the world it came in the two Challenge Cup semi-finals, where St Helens, Leeds, Bradford and Warrington produced two magnificent games as if to order, because huge TV audiences were tuned in.

We saw thrilling regular domestic league seasons in both the top-flight competitions, providing two Grand Finals to savour at Spotland and Old Trafford, and success for Widnes Vikings and Bradford Bulls, both coached by young English coaches.

Brian Noble had a hard act to follow after the departure to Canberra of coach Matthew Elliott, who led the Bulls to their Championship in 1997.

But not only did Noble match that, but the huge Grand Final victory over their nearest rivals Wigan killed any arguments that Bradford Bulls weren't the

Champion side of 2001.

What a prospect we now have on the first night in February, when the Bulls and NRL Premiers Newcastle Knights clash in next year's World Club Challenge.

With the return of so many brilliant Kangaroos, the McAlpine Stadium in Huddersfield is sure to be packed to the rafters on that night.

It was also the year when a great name of Rugby League, who had World Club Challenge glory themselves only twelve years ago, returned to the top flight. Neil Kelly guided the Widnes Vikings to a win in the NFP Grand Final at Spotland to give Widnes their big chance in Super League. Meanwhile Huddersfield Giants, despite having their best season in Super League, were relegated to the NFP.

Rugby League has developed a thick skin over the years, but in 2001 the sport came under heavy fire from the media establishment for simply being Rugby League.

The death of the game was widely predicted by a coterie of national newspaper columnists

But Rugby League answered its critics in its own inimitable style, with the Super League play-offs and the international game reaching spectacular new heights.

Record crowds for both the NFP and Super League Grand Finals spoke for themselves.

2001 was also the year when the phrase "play Rugby League and see the world" was introduced.

Tours to the USA, South Africa, Russia, Australia, New Zealand and Fiji, plus jaunts across the Channel into France, provided opportunities for League players like never before.

It was the year of the first English Origin game – a venture the powers considered so successful they decided to hold two next year. And it was a year when Wales almost mastered England on a fine night in Wrexham.

Who could argue that it hasn't been a rollercoaster twelve months?

Certainly not supporters of Wakefield, who survived in Super League despite having league points deducted for a salary cap breach the year before.

Not supporters of Warrington, who saw the club hit by tragedy, but had a team that could still be relied upon to cock a snook at the top-five clubs.

What about Leigh Centurions fans, whose side waltzed to the NFP Minor Premiership before being beaten when it mattered in the play-offs by rivals Oldham and Widnes.

Or British Rugby League supporters, who saw Great Britain master the Kangaroos one week, humbled the next, and come within an inch of taking the decider.

What a way to finish a season!

It left us all breathless, mentally drained, and asking for more, more, more.

We hope you enjoy looking back over the year 2001 with us. And, if you are ready for 2002, you can find your club's fixtures for next season at the back of this yearbook. Hold on tight!

Tim Butcher
Editor, Totalrugbyleague.com

13

1
PERSONALITIES OF 2001

Rob Burrow

Leeds Rhinos supporters who enjoy parties might find themselves holding one on 6 April every year, given the significance of what happened on that day in 2001.

It was a Friday night, and Leeds were playing Hull at Headingley. The Rhinos had won two of their opening three Super League games, and they were hosting Hull, who also were coming into the game after winning two of their three opening Super League fixtures.

After 36 minutes a little bloke wearing number 29 came on the field for Leeds, taking the place of prop forward Darren Fleary. Rob Burrow, at the age of 18 easily the smallest man to have played in Super League in 2001, was making his debut for the Rhinos. He didn't score a try, but from that point onwards his career took off.

As it happened, the Rhinos went down 16-18 to Hull, in a game that would signal the departure of coach Dean Lance, with Daryl Powell taking over for the following week's trip to Warrington. That was the game in which Burrow made his starting debut for the Rhinos, scoring the only try in Leeds' 36-6 defeat, and gaining the nomination as the League Express Man of the Match for the Rhinos. The description of Burrow's try by League Express reporter Nathan Ashurst told us much about the playing style of this little jewel in the Headingley crown: "From the resulting scrum, nippy scrum-half Burrow collected and sped across the Wire line, throwing dummy after dummy, which eventually saw him cross."

Burrow would mesmerise defences a few more times in 2001 with his brilliant footwork, and he would go on to appear 17 times in Super League VI, scoring seven tries and 16 goals. Burrow would also captain the Great Britain Academy side to victory in New Zealand, before putting up a valiant struggle against the Australian under-19 side in two Tests Down Under.

Voted Super League Young Player of the Year, Burrow also toured South Africa with the England under-21 squad, and was recommended by Australian skipper Brad Fittler as a player who would surely have a bright international future for Great Britain. A bright future surely awaits the game's newest young star.

Stuart Fielden

Bradford Bulls prop forward Stuart Fielden was voted the Super League Young Player of the Year in 2000, but he really came of age in 2001 as a member of the most fearsome pack in Super League, as the Bulls swept to a wonderful Grand Final victory over the Wigan Warriors at Old Trafford.

But it didn't stop there. Fielden continued the good work with Great Britain, in November's Guinness Ashes Series against Australia, when he was picked out by knowledgeable observers as belonging in the very top echelon of world class prop forwards.

Great Britain coach David Waite rated Fielden as "one of the best young props in the international game" after the third Test, and leading Australian pundits cited Fielden's name when suggesting that Great Britain are back in business as big-time challengers to Australia's domination of the world game.

Fielden, 22, played 32 times for the Bulls during the 2001 season. But the nature of the modern game is such that he only made starting appearances three times, instead taking to the field usually after 20 minutes to help pulverise opposition defences and shore up the Bulls' formidable defence.

Widely rated as the outstanding Great Britain forward in the Ashes series, Fielden is an intelligent observer of the game, who isn't fooled by his own growing publicity.

"It's very flattering for people to say those things about me, but I thought I had one of my worst games, and I don't see myself as one of the best young props in the world," he said, after the third Ashes Test at Wigan, while others were singing his praises.

With an attitude like that, Fielden is likely to be a fixture for Great Britain for many years to come.

Paul Sculthorpe

Paul Sculthorpe won the Tetley's Super League Man of Steel Award in 2001, and it's fair to say that he was the only realistic candidate for the award, so clearly did his performances stand out during Super League VI.

Sculthorpe played 31 games for St Helens in 2001, scoring 273 points from 27 tries and 82 goals, and a solitary field goal. He scored his field goal in the World Club Challenge against the Brisbane Broncos in January at the Reebok Stadium, as the British Super League V Champions completely surprised the Australian NRL Champions with a 20-18 victory on a cold night at Bolton's Reebok Stadium.

Sculthorpe was a tower of strength for the whole season for St Helens, whether playing at loose forward or at stand-off half, and taking over the goalkicking for the injured Sean Long.

But he saved his most memorable performance for the First Guinness Test in the autumn Ashes Series against Australia. Sculthorpe had a blinder that day, scoring two tries and two more field goals from stand-off half, as Great Britain shocked the Australians with a 20-12 scoreline, as the on-off Ashes series exploded into life on its opening day.

Sadly, Great Britain were unable to repeat that success in the two remaining Tests, but Sculthorpe had done enough to cement his reputation as one of the outstanding stars of World Rugby League. After his Test performances Sculthorpe could walk into virtually any Australian NRL club, although Saints fans would no doubt cause a riot at any suggestion that one of their most brilliant stars would ever leave the most successful club in the Super League era.

Jason Smith

When he was in England for the Lincoln World Cup in November 2000, Rugby League International Federation Chairman John McDonald predicted that Jason Smith would prove to be the best overseas signing in Super League during the 2001 season.

Any Hull fan will tell you that McDonald was spot on with his forecast.

A jubilant Hull FC chief executive Shane Richardson swooped to sign Smith when it became obvious that he was likely to leave NRL club Parramatta at the end of the 2000 season, and it soon became clear that Richardson and his coach Shaun McRae saw Smith as the most vital piece in the jigsaw as they continued to rebuild the fortunes of the once great club on the Humber.

The degree of their success can be judged by the fact that Hull finished third in the Super League table, although they went out of the play-offs at home to St Helens, on a night when it was no coincidence that Smith was absent through injury.

A gifted ballplayer with tremendous co-ordination, one of the main weapons in Smith's armoury is a devastating inside pass, done so naturally and so late that defenders find it difficult to deal with. Any weakness in defences Smith is sure to exploit, as he organises his second-rowers who are usually running inside him. And Smith is one of the toughest defenders in the game, always managing to repay aggression with aggression of his own, but never being out of control.

Smith also has a strong kicking game, having landed several '40-20's during the season, and his all round game enables him to take the pressure off other players.

During the season he played 29 games for Hull, scoring six tries but, more importantly, bringing to the club a sense of direction and belief that trophy-winning days are just around the corner.

19

Neil Turley

Any player who can score 56 tries from 32 games must be a very special player.

Neil Turley, Leigh Centurions' fullback during the 2001 season, did just that, causing most pundits to suggest that the young fullback, signed from Wigan during the close season, should be plying his trade in Super League.

Turley, however, has declared that he prefers to stick with his hometown club, and Leigh fans can feel very fortunate that the young star, who won a host of awards (Player of the Year, Young Player of the Year) at the Northern Ford Premiership awards night, will still be with the club in the 2002 season.

It was no coincidence that the Centurions bombed out of the NFP play-offs in the Major Semi-final at home to Widnes Vikings when Turley was absent through injury. And Turley will no doubt be the key player for the Centurions as they try to emulate the Vikings' feat of gaining promotion to Super League at the end of the 2002 NFP season.

Leigh had signed Turley from Wigan after he suffered a confidence-draining knee injury, and both the club and the player thought he would gradually ease his way into the side. Instead he set off like a house on fire, and continued that way, eventually scoring a record number of tries in a season for a fullback, beating a record previously held by the great Salford and Great Britain star Paul Charlton, and scoring a record number of tries for any player in the Northern Ford Premiership since the advent of summer rugby.

But Turley really came to prominence when he was the only NFP player to be selected in The Origin Game, coming on as a substitute to score a sparkling try in Lancashire's 36-24 victory at Headingley.

And to cap off a great season, the Centurions fullback toured South Africa with the England under-21 squad, scoring five tries in the first Test against the South African Rhinos, as England ran up a century of points. He is surely a player to watch in 2002.

2
THE 2001 SEASON

DECEMBER 2000
Home fires burning

The start of the Northern Ford Premiership season at the beginning of December - seemingly confirming a drift back to the winter season for the game outside Super League, did its bit to lift the gloom brought on by New Zealand's thrashing of England in the World Cup semi-finals.

The best news of all for League expansionists, Gateshead Thunder were back, starting like Sheffield Eagles had had to do eleven months earlier, at the bottom of the Rugby League, and a healthy crowd turned out at the Thunderdome to see their re-incarnation, a highly respectable 18-nil defeat by Hull KR.

But the campaign to get international Rugby League on track had taken a body blow. A World Cup involving 16 teams had been an ambitious project and after a scheduling of matches which left a lot to be desired, added to the coldest and wettest four weeks in living memory, the tournament wasn't the success it should have been. Indeed, the shortfall in the projected profits were to have repercussions long into the year 2001.

As the World Cup came to a close, with a big crowd on hand at Old Trafford to see Australia retain their crown, beating New Zealand 40-12 in the final, the World Cup's organisers were still claiming a profit of over one million pounds would be pumped back into the game.

But when the tournament was first planned, a figure of ten million had been forecast and with Rugby League taking a malicious pounding from the national press, morale within the game was low.

Super League Europe chairman Chris Caisley took the opportunity to give a massive thumbs down to the growing clamour for a home internationals series. "People have to accept that the strength of our competition lies in our club game," he said.

Caisley's thoughts led to a massive backlash from the League public, with the Mailbag page of League Express inundated with letters from all parts of the country decrying the lack of leadership and ambition within the game.

The criticism stung Caisley, who as chairman of Bradford Bulls as well as Super League, wrote to League Publications banning any of its magazines from covering the club's games claiming that the club was presented 'in a negative and detrimental fashion.'

The World Cup wasn't a total failure in everyone's eyes. Australia's achievement of winning their sixth successive World Cup was voted the fourth best sporting achievement of the year in a poll organised by the BBC.

For some nations - France, Papua New Guinea and Wales - the World Cup had

Rob Burrow in action during his Leeds first team debut against Halifax on Boxing Day

been a resounding success; interest in the Ireland team had grown steadily and the quarter-final between England and Ireland had given a glimpse of what a home international series could create.

But with Super League having already published their fixture schedule, there was little room left in 2001, and a home international series never happened.

On the playing side, the experience of England's World Cup persuaded Bradford's Mike Forshaw to retire from representative football and Ireland's Kevin Campion, due to sign for Warrington Wolves from Brisbane Broncos for Super League VI, had such a cold and wet four weeks during November, he decided Auckland would be a better option.

As the NFP got underway, Super League clubs were gearing up for 2001 with a number of high-profile signings. Leeds Rhinos unveiled Auckland's Aussie hooker Robbie Mears to join their two other high-profile overseas signings - former Kangaroos Brett Mullins and Bradley Clyde - and said, because of his English grandparents, he would make himself available for Great Britain at the end of the season.

Reports were surfacing that Keiron Cunningham was to move from St Helens to join the Welsh Rugby Union. "These are just Chinese whispers that are getting out of control," said Saints boss Ian Millward.

Another former Kangaroo, Mike Hancock was set to join Salford despite a reported attempt by Auckland Warriors to make him renege.

As compensation for Campion's change of

mind, Kevin Walters was announced as a Wolves signing, the 33 year old Brisbane and Australia stand-off coming out of retirement to head for England, and he was unveiled this month along with former Junior Kiwi and New Zealand Maori World Cup centre David Kidwell, from Parramatta.

Ambitious Hull brought Lee Jackson home from Headingley, while Dennis Moran joined Parramatta teammate Jim Dymock at London Broncos, who were clearly gearing up for a tilt at the title.

Wakefield Trinity Wildcats - widely tipped for the wooden spoon after having to offload most of their big-name players at the end of a financially ruinous Super League V - signed Australians Ben Rauter and Dane Dorahy.

NFP Grand Final man of the match Mick Higham made his debut for St Helens in the Boxing Day friendly at Wigan, despite Halifax Blue Sox claiming they had already signed the player from Leigh Centurions. Wigan, fielding a team of youngsters, won the game 40-20.

The Higham saga was to spill over into the New Year with the case eventually going against Halifax, but the episode was an indication that the Rugby Football League, still without a chief executive since the departure of Neil Tunnicliffe earlier that year, was lacking leadership.

Political talk centred on the coming together of Super League Europe, the Rugby Football League and BARLA before a new boss could be named.

The RFL initially accepted Halifax's registration of Higham and then withdrew it 24 hours later.

By the end of the month, Halifax coach Gary Mercer had signed old boy Johnny Lawless from Huddersfield to fill the gap left by Paul Rowley who had already headed in the opposite direction to the McAlpine Stadium.

In other Boxing Day friendlies, Leeds Rhinos, with a tiny young bloke called Rob Burrow playing at scrum-half, with Clyde in the pack, beat Halifax - fielding new signings Shayne McMenemy, from Oldham; Stuart Donlan from Leigh and Adam Hughes from Wakefield - 38-34, Wakefield hammered a virtual Castleford reserve side 38-2 at the Jungle; and Salford City Reds won at Warrington 36-20, with Andy Coley making his first appearance for the Reds after signing from Swinton Lions, alongside former Wakefield players Warren Jowitt and Francis Maloney.

In this month, Leeds received an almighty shock when the club was found guilty of "unconscious racism" against winger Paul Sterling at an industrial tribunal. The club had to pay Sterling over six thousand pounds for loss of earnings and £10,000 for injury to his feelings, plus offer him a contract for the new season. Sterling didn't play Rugby League in 2001

At the start of the month, the 2001 Silk Cut Challenge Cup got underway. The reach of rugby's most prestigious club knockout has widened in recent years and 95 teams were involved in the 2001 competition.

That's an impressive statistic by any measure, and the playing standards were as high as ever from the very first skirmishes on the far-flung playing fields of Britain.

The chance was there in the first two rounds for amateur clubs to take a step towards a lucrative and glorious clash against professional opposition in January, with the NFP teams, plus the two French challengers due then to enter.

In the previous year's competition, the Army was the surprise package, forcing its way to a third round clash against professionals Rochdale. This year, Cumberland champions Wath Brow knocked them out at the first call, and the RAF also fell in the opening round at home to Conference Premier Division Heworth.

Which left the Royal Navy to fly the Armed Forces flag, which they did with honour in an 18-6 win over Oldham club Waterhead, eventually meeting their match in the second round, but only just, against Eccles, going down by the narrowest of margins, 12-13 at Portsmouth.

Eccles had already accounted for the Rugby League Conference Lionhearts in round one. This was the first year that the burgeoning summer Rugby League Conference was invited to play in the Cup, and their 25-16 defeat was an extremely creditable result against tough opposition.

Newcastle University stunned Hunslet Warriors from the Yorkshire League and destined for the National Conference with a 36-22 win that emphasised the potential of League's other nation-wide competition, the Student Rugby League. Student Champions Leeds Met University repeated the trick, with a 20-10 win in Bradford against Clayton.

London Skolars also made their mark with an 18-10 win over Warrington side Crosfields, and Bangor Vikings did Northern Ireland proud, going down with honour at York club New Earswick All Blacks 36-20.

The Welsh Students came back late against Conference club Askam but the men from the Furness Peninsula just held on for a 18-15 win; while Glasgow Bulls, the Scottish champions - found the challenge of playing out of season too much, getting a 72-0 hammering at Wigan Rose Bridge.

In the second round, Conference Premiers Thornhill just ended Leeds Mets' progress by 18-10 while Leigh Miners Rangers showed their class with a 51-8 beating of Newcastle University. With London Skolars going down 28-10 at East Leeds, that left only northern clubs alive into the New Year.

2001 SILK CUT CHALLENGE CUP ROUND ONE RESULTS

Clayton 10 Leeds Met University 20; Cottingham 2 Hensingham 17; Dewsbury Moor 17 Eastmoor 18; East Leeds 14 Elland 12; Eccles 25 RLC Lionhearts 16; Hull Dockers 28 West Bowling 4; Leigh East 10 Shaw Cross Sharks 15; London Skolars 18 Crosfields 10; Milford Marlins 16 Wigan St Judes 26; Millom 34 Normanton 8; Newcastle University 36 Hunslet Warriors 22; New Earswick All Blacks 36 Bangor Vikings 20; Queensbury 24 Charleston Knights 0; RAF 12 Heworth 32; Rochdale Mayfield 32 Castleford Panthers 16; Royal Navy 18 Waterhead 6; Sheffield Hillsborough Hawks 10 Featherstone Lions 18; Siddal 28 Dewsbury Celtic 8; Thatto Heath Crusaders 24 Keighley Albion 22; Wath Brow 41 Army 6; Welsh Students 15 Askam 18; Widnes St Maries 38 Blackbrook 18; Wigan Rose Bridge 72 Glasgow Bulls 0; York Acorn 0 Halton Simms Cross 18

2001 SILK CUT CHALLENGE CUP ROUND TWO RESULTS

Askam 12 Millom 2; East Leeds 28 London Skolars 10; Eastmoor Dragons 0 West Hull 34; Halton Simms Cross 8 Shaw Cross Sharks 0; Heworth 12 Featherstone Lions 10; New Earswick All Blacks 11 Thatto Heath Crusaders 7; Newcastle University 8 Leigh Miners Rangers 51; Rochdale Mayfield 15 Dudley Hill 10; Royal Navy 12 Eccles 13; Saddleworth Rangers 0 Oldham St Annes 30; Siddal 22 Hull Dockers 12; Skirlaugh 16 Oulton Raiders 38; Thornhill Trojans 18 Leeds Met University 10; Walney Central 4 Queensbury 13; Wath Brow Hornets 8 Castleford Lock Lane 11; Wigan Rosebridge 26 Redhill 8; Wigan St Judes 15 Widnes St Maries 9; Wigan St Patricks 4 Ideal Isberg 3; Woolston Rovers 32 Hensingham 11

JANUARY
Fantasy football!

The month of January was a good one for British Rugby League as St Helens entered the history books after an outstanding 20-18 win over NRL champions Brisbane Broncos in the World Club Challenge.

The club and its supporters had been unhappy at the decision of Super League Europe to play the one-off game at a neutral venue, but all that was forgotten on that glorious Friday night at the Reebok Stadium in Bolton.

After experiencing the end of British involvement in the World Cup at the semi-final stage, this was just the result the game in this country needed on the verge of Super League VI, as Saints joined Widnes and three-times-winners Wigan in the roll of honour in the seventh World Club Challenge game.

"It was a very important win, not just for me and the team, and but for the game as a whole," said Saints' skipper Chris Joynt.

"We needed a massive lift, to get the great game of Rugby League on the move again.

"If you read any rugby union article it's all positive about their game, and yet when you read a report in the national press about Rugby League there are three lines on the game, and the rest focuses on minor political squabbles.

"If this win helps everyone involved with Rugby League in this country to take a more positive view of our game, then that will be a great outcome.

"We were always confident, because we have found at the club that you gain the habit of winning, and we never doubted our ability to do that.

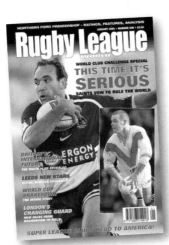

"We are a team that is focused, and everybody is pulling in the same direction.

"We are a confident team too, but in my opinion it's the people who write about the game who need to share that confidence, and should focus on the good things about Rugby League."

For Sean Long, the win was a sweet experience. When he made his first appearance in a Saints jersey against Cronulla in the World Club Championship, they crashed to a 48-8 defeat at Knowsley Road.

Saints went on to concede 50 points at home to Penrith before embarking on a disastrous trip down under. There, they conceded a total of 130 points in defeats against

Sean Long races away from the clutches of Gorden Tallis

Cronulla, Auckland and Penrith, before the curtain was brought down with a humbling 12-66 defeat at the hands of the Broncos in the quarter-final.

In 2000 St Helens had been hammered 44-6 by Melbourne Storm.

And ten weeks before the match-up with the Broncos, Long had trooped off the Reebok with his hopes of England World Cup glory in tatters after the Kiwis' 49-6 semi-final romp.

Yet Long picked himself up, dusted himself down, and quickly learnt the lessons.

In a team of heroes, led magnificently from the front by official man-of-the-match Joynt, Long produced a masterful performance in what was, especially considering it was both sides' first game of the new season, a memorable game of great quality.

Just four minutes after half-time, as the Broncos opened up an 18-6 lead, visions of a Storm-type demolition appeared in some minds. But less than six minutes later, a Long-inspired revival had miraculously whipped Saints back on level terms and created a momentum they never lost.

Long's piercing angled run for a try of deceptive skill hauled Saints back into a compelling contest after Michael DeVere's foul on Peter Shiels gave the back-

27

to-back English champions a foothold in the Broncos' 20-metre area.

Then, as hail stones lashed the players from a wintry Bolton sky, Long sparked another brilliant move, sending Paul Newlove powering through Wendell Sailor's attempted challenge down the left channel, before captain fantastic Joynt popped up on the inside to complete a stunning 60-metre move.

Joynt's opposite number, Gorden Tallis, was placed on report for a heavy challenge over the dead-ball line, an act borne out of frustration, with the RFL agreeing afterwards to take no action, and Long's third goal had Saints back on level terms.

The final 30 minutes produced some wonderful Rugby League as Saints' defence somehow resisted everything the Broncos could throw at them. Newlove and Martyn, twice, came up with crucial interceptions, and Paul Wellens was outstanding at the back, belying his tender years with a performance of great maturity.

Paul Sculthorpe and Keiron Cunningham confirmed their ranking as world class players in that crucial phase, as the Broncos' best attacking efforts were repulsed in a sterling defensive effort.

Sculthorpe, who typified Saints' resolve with a great one-on-one effort on Sailor, proved to be the match-winner.

Again, the score came on the back of a slip in discipline, as Lote Tuqiri was penalised for a foul on Kevin Iro. Long eschewed the chance to try his luck from wide out on the right, fully 40-metres out. The decision was justified as, after Saints attacked the left-sided Broncos defence, play was expertly switched to the middle where Cunningham set up Sculthorpe for a cool 15-metre field goal with six minutes remaining.

Long added the coup de grace with a perfectly struck one-pointer from 25 metres, with 67 seconds left.

There had been little hint of the drama to follow as the Broncos, despite a disappointing kicking game, opened up what appeared to be a decisive 12-point lead.

Stand-off Shaun Berrigan, who was the Broncos' stand-out player alongside hooker Luke Priddis, burrowed over from dummy-half

---

Friday 26th January 2001

WORLD CLUB CHALLENGE

ST HELENS 20 BRISBANE BRONCOS 18

SAINTS: 1 Paul Wellens; 2 Sean Hoppe; 3 Kevin Iro; 4 Paul Newlove; 5 Anthony Sullivan; 20 Tommy Martyn; 7 Sean Long; 10 David Fairleigh (D); 9 Keiron Cunningham; 12 Sonny Nickle; 11 Chris Joynt (C); 8 Peter Shiels (D); 13 Paul Sculthorpe. Subs: 15 Tim Jonkers for Shiels (17); 16 Vila Matautia for Nickle (17); 18 John Stankevitch for Fairleigh (26); 19 Anthony Stewart for Sullivan (26); Shiels for Matautia (34); Fairleigh for Stankevitch (39); Nickle for Shiels (56); Matautia for Fairleigh (66); Fairleigh for Joynt (69); Shiels for Nickle (69); Joynt for Matautia (76).
Tries: Sculthorpe (19), Long (48), Joynt (50); **Goals:** Long 3; **Field goals:** Sculthorpe, Long.
BRONCOS: 1 Darren Lockyer; 5 Wendell Sailor; 3 Stuart Kelly; 4 Michael DeVere; 2 Lote Tuqiri; 6 Shaun Berrigan; 7 Scott Prince; 8 Shane Webcke; 9 Luke Priddis; 10 Petero Civoniceva; 11 Gorden Tallis (C); 12 Dane Carlaw; 13 Phillip Lee. Subs: 14 Chris Walker not used; 15 Shane Walker for Webcke (34); 16 Ashley Harrison for Lee (56); 17 Brad Meyers for Civoniceva (16); Civoniceva for Carlaw (29); Webcke for S Walker (41); Carlaw for Civoniceva (54); Civoniceva for Meyers (62); S Walker for Prince (65); Lee for Webcke (67); Webcke for Civoniceva (70); Prince for S Walker (76).
Tries: Berrigan (8), Lee (30), Meyers (44); **Goals:** DeVere 3.
On report: Tallis (50) - late tackle (no case to answer).
League Express Men of the Match:
Saints: Sean Long; *Broncos:* Luke Priddis.
Penalty count: 7-4; **Half-time:** 6-12; **Referee:** Stuart Cummings (England); **Attendance:** 16,041 *(at the Reebok Stadium, Bolton).*

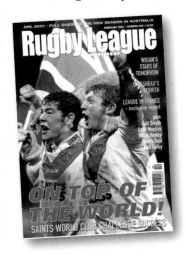

for an eighth-minute try in his side's first attack, and he was denied a second with 63 seconds remaining of the first half on the intervention of the video referee.

The Broncos' loose forward, Phillip Lee, had scored their second try after half-an-hour when Sailor's drive gave them the field position, and Priddis, Berrigan and Meyers combined expertly in a devastating move that showed the NRL Champions, fielding ten of their Grand Final side, at their best.

Berrigan's earlier disappointment appeared to have been allayed when Brad Meyers went over on the angle four minutes after the re-start from Tallis' expert assist, with DeVere adding his third conversion.

Long had been instrumental in Saints drawing level in the first half. After his raking kick, Long followed up to make the crucial tackle on Lockyer, who lost the ball in attempting to clear his lines. Long took full advantage of the slip by sending Sculthorpe over out wide.

"It is an incredible feeling, and we always knew that we were nowhere near as bad as last year's result implied," said Long.

"The fact that everyone wrote us off did wind us up, but the Aussies underestimated us, and that motivated us even more. They were all thinking they would win easily, and were a bit arrogant in their approach, not taking us seriously.

"What a great night for us and for Great Britain."

Saints had already proved that their two big close-season signings - David Fairleigh and Peter Shiels were going to be great value, but other Super League clubs were just getting ready for the new season.

Bradford Bulls signed huge Australian centre Graham Mackay from rivals Leeds and, after several weeks of negotiations, Bobbie Goulding eventually secured a two-year deal with Salford City Reds, breaking a thumb on his debut in an end of the month friendly with Wigan - who unveiled new signings Adrian Lam and David Furner, with Harvey Howard still to arrive.

Batley coach Jon Sharp joined Huddersfield as assistant to Tony Smith who had released the unlucky Nick Fozzard after he broke his arm again in training.

Steve Anderson arrived at Headingley from Melbourne Storm to take up the post of Technical, Performance and Development Director two weeks after the Rhinos had lost 16-14 to Castleford Tigers in the New Year's Day friendly at Headingley, new Cas halfback Mitch Healey looking the part.

While the Wildcats Academy team was in Australia defeating the Central Queensland Development side, the fraud squad paid a visit to Belle Vue to investigate the club's financial dealings.

And the month ended with the RFL desperately trying to mediate after the Blue Sox threatened to sue St Helens for £100,000 for allegedly inducing Mick Higham to break a three-year contract he signed in September

By the time the clubs from the Northern Ford Premiership entered the fray in the third round of the Challenge Cup, there was some real quality amateur opposition left standing and a few nervous club chairmen around the north of England.

29

January

Askam - at the time struggling at the bottom of the Conference first division - landed a plum draw against neighbouring professionals Barrow Border Raiders, a tie which really captured the imagination of the public on the Furness peninsula.

One of the biggest crowds for years gathered at Craven Park to see the Raiders run in three late tries for a distorted scoreline of 40-16 after a super show from the local amateurs.

Wigan St Judes were well in the game at the Thunderdome, 14-10 down at the break, before going down 34-20 to the Rugby Football League's newest club, Gateshead; West Hull put in a superb performance to limit high-flying Leigh to 28-5 at Hilton Park; up in Cumbria, Oldham St Annes actually led Whitehaven at the break but two Haven tries, while St Annes were down to twelve men, turned the game and the professionals finished 34-16 winners. Oulton Raiders also pushed York all the way at the Huntington Stadium before exiting the Cup, 24-12.

But pride of place went to Conference side Woolston, coached by former Great Britain forward John Fieldhouse, who travelled to NFP strugglers Chorley Lynx quietly confident of causing an upset. The confidence was well placed as pocket battleship Lee Westwood led them to a 22-8 win at Victory Park.

The January weather badly affected the NFP with the third week of the month completely wiped out by frost and snow, which re-opened the debate on the timing of the playing season.

The game received a three-year World Class Performance grant of £4.5 million designed to improve England's showing on the world sporting stage and Sir Rodney Walker denied that he was to step down as RFL Chairman, after being charged by the government with securing a new national stadium after plans for the re-building of Wembley Stadium fell into disarray.

St Helens celebrate their stunning World Club Challenge victory over Brisbane

FEBRUARY
League goes West

After Saints' heroics in the World Club Challenge at the end of January, Leeds Rhinos wrapped up one of Rugby League's more exotic excursions by winning the inaugural Sunshine State Challenge held in Jacksonville, Florida on the first weekend of February.

In a one-day event played at the grid iron Alltel Stadium in the city on the north east coast of Florida, Leeds beat Halifax Blue Sox 18-10 and then Huddersfield Giants 28-0 in an adventure warmly received by Leeds chief executive Gary Hetherington.

"I have been quite amazed at the amount of interest and quality media coverage that has been generated, even on national television and newspapers," was his reaction.

The result was a turnout of six and a half thousand people to see what was essentially pre-season training run for the British sides, and that had Hetherington calling for a five-year strategy to develop the game in the USA, culminating in the staging of the World Club Challenge in Jacksonville.

For the record, Huddersfield beat the USA Tomahawks 22-8 in the other semi-final.

Back at home, it was announced that Great Britain would play France the week before the First Test against Australia in October, and that Ireland and Scotland would travel to France in the summer to play France on consecutive Tuesday nights.

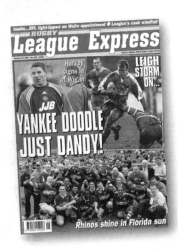

Rhinos shine in Florida sun

But a proposed European Competition involving English, French and Russian clubs, floated by the French Federation, was never heard of again.

The RFL also revealed that an "Area of Origin" game would be staged in June as a step on the Great Britain representative ladder.

Australian David Waite, who was already installed as Technical Director at the RFL, was appointed as coach to Great Britain after interviews involving former GB bosses Mal Reilly and Andy Goodway, and England coach John Kear

Meanwhile Hull boss Shaun McRae stepped down as Scotland coach because of the uncertainty surrounding the future of the home nations. Billy McGinty took over the job, while Swinton coach Mike Gregory replaced Mal Reilly as Great Britain Academy coach after Reilly resigned in disgust at the appointment of Waite to the national job.

Incredibly, when the fourth round draw of the Silk Cut Challenge Cup was made, amateur giant-killers Woolston were paired with Super League neighbours Warrington Wolves, a classic David v Goliath encounter that drew a crowd of over 6,000 to Wilderspool on the second weekend of February. Woolston played with tremendous spirit despite going down 48-6, with giant Wolves centre Ian Sibbit getting a hat-trick of tries.

There were also some gritty performances from NFP sides against Super League opponents in round four, with Dewsbury Rams losing 18-4 to Castleford Tigers after two tries in the last ten minutes; Keighley falling 20-34 at Cougar Park to Hull FC, for whom Tony Smith's senior debut lasted three minutes before he was sent off for a high tackle on winger Craig Horne (for which he received a one-match ban); and Featherstone Rovers hanging on for dear life at Huddersfield Giants before losing 28-6.

Leeds Rhinos shot to a record 106-10 win at Swinton Lions, with Iestyn Harris breaking the Leeds' goals-in-a-match record with 17 from 18 attempts, surpassing Lewis Jones's 13 against Blackpool in August 1956.

It was Leeds' biggest victory since a 102-0 win at Coventry on 12 April, 1913, but it was at a price as new hooker Robbie Mears suffered a broken collar bone just before half-time of the tie. It was the first time in his career that he had broken a bone.

That week, the Rhinos dismissed speculation over the future of Kevin Sinfield, who had yet to sign a new contract for the end of 2001, but Keith Senior did sign a one-year extension to his contract to keep him at Headingley until 2004

It is the two BBC TV games that will be best remembered from round four. On the Saturday, St Helens won a monster clash with arch-rivals Wigan at Knowsley Road with skipper Chris Joynt leading from the front, and scoring his 100th try for the club to gain a sensational 22-8 win.

"'The team that once dominated Rugby League is now cast in the role of bridesmaid," wrote Mike Latham, as the new Wigan halfback pairing of Adrian Lam and Matthew Johns failed to click.

"It's really disappointing," was coach Frank Endacott's immediate reaction. "We came here prepared to win but they beat us in every area of the game. It's early days yet and it's certainly not the end of the world."

Pundits reckon Wigan's exit could have cost them a cool million, but the days when any club could guarantee a march to the final had obviously gone.

Saints coach Ian Millward took the risk of

Inspirational St Helens skipper Chris Joynt in action against Wigan in the Challenge Cup

bringing back Paul Wellens only two weeks after he had fractured an eye socket in the World Club Challenge, but Wellens played the whole game, while Wigan withdrew Kris Radlinski at half-time with a deadleg. Saints' win was all the more impressive as they lost Paul Sculthorpe with a broken jaw in the opening stages of the game.

The following day there was even more drama as Leigh Centurions became the first NFP side for four years to beat Super League opposition when they topped Salford City Reds 16-12.

It was a remarkable win as the City Reds looked to be in the box seat at 12-0 at half-time, as the superior strength and fitness of the Reds produced two tries for Warren Jowitt.

But Leigh, who were at the top of the NFP table with the only 100 per cent record, came out after the break and gave their big city opponents a real football lesson. Tries to Paul Anderson and Neil Turley brought the Centurions to within two points and with nine minutes to go, Adam Bristow scoring the winning try. It was just reward for some magnificent rugby in the second 40 minutes, spearheaded by former Salford stand-off Simon Svabic.

" We believed we could beat Salford from the beginning," said Leigh coach Paul Terzis.

Leigh fancied their chances when they travelled to Warrington for the next round, but they eventually fell to defeat, losing 20-10, in front of a near full house at Wilderspool.

Leeds had a tougher task in round five, having to travel down the road to the Jungle to meet the Castleford Tigers, whose coach Stuart Raper was being heavily tipped to become the successor to John Lang at Cronulla at the end of the season

The Saturday TV game showed the Rhinos at their best as they marched to a 42-12 win, with young England international Kevin Sinfield scoring twice in a man-of-the-match display.

The Tigers were rocked when halfback Mitch Healey strained a hamstring in the warm-up and had to withdraw, with hooker Aaron Raper having to fill in at scrum-half. Leeds' star signing Brett Mullins also took an injury - tearing a bicep during a highly impressive Leeds display.

Leeds prop Jamie Mathiou looks for a way through the Castleford defence

St Helens were expected to have few problems at Whitehaven but, with six of their big names missing, and Vila Matautia sent off just after half-time, they were relieved to come away from the Recreation Ground with a 34-22 win.

The Bulls looked to have a trickier passage when they drew arch-rivals Halifax at the Shay, but they blew the Blue Sox away 68-18, scoring eleven tries in front of the Sunday Grandstand cameras. Scott Naylor and Tevita Vaikona both collected two tries each and Henry Paul kicked nine goals, with Paul Deacon kicking three after Henry went off

French Cup holders Villeneuve Leopards became the first French team to reach the quarter-finals of the Challenge Cup as they beat Rochdale Hornets 26-19 at a snowbound Spotland, three second-half tries to man of the match Artie Shead, Chad Dillinger and Gilles Cornut winning them the tie.

The individual try-scoring feat of the fifth round was by Huddersfield's former Northern Eagles winger Andrew Frew, who scored four in the second half as the Giants pulled away from Doncaster Dragons to win 38-24.

There was a high-quality thriller at the Boulevard as Lee Jackson inspired a Hull comeback from 16-0 down after 20 minutes to edge the London Broncos 30-20. Jackson's second try with six minutes to go sealed it for the Black and Whites.

And Wakefield Trinity Wildcats proved too strong for Oldham at Boundary Park. Tries in a seven-minute spell in the second half from Tony Tatupu and two from Waisale Sovatabua gave Wakefield a 26-6 win.

MARCH
The sparks fly

The sixth season of Super League was the most eagerly anticipated yet in the wake of St Helens' win over Brisbane and the impending Ashes Series - the first since 1994 - at the end of the year.

Every year Super League is billed as more competitive, and this year there was an air of confidence about the prediction.

The seeded fixture format devised by Super League Europe had bolted eight games onto the home and away series with the top six from 2000 having to play each other at least once again, likewise for the bottom six.

That meant a greater chance of some of the lesser teams making a genuine tilt for the top-five play-offs. Among those were Hull and London, who had both strengthened considerably.

The Broncos had shipped in some of the biggest names in the game in New Zealand captain Richie Barnett and former Kangaroos Jason Hetherington and Jim Dymock. Centre Tony Martin had returned from Melbourne, seasoned NRL men Nigel Roy, Dennis Moran and Michael Gillett had come to the capital to chance their arm.

Hull had already showed they meant business this year with their win over London in the Cup. Lee Jackson was still a matchwinner; Tony Smith was there to give them fire up the middle, and in Parramatta's Jason Smith they were reckoned to have the best overseas signing of them all.

With the additions of David Fairleigh and Peter Shiels from Newcastle, St Helens looked better than ever and destined to secure their crown as the big-match specialists and, though Wigan had already gone out of the Cup, the class of David Furner, Adrian Lam and Matthew Johns was expected to make them into the side to beat.

The Bulls had beefed up even more with the capture of Kiwi giant prop Joe Vagana and former Manly back-rower Daniel Gartner, and Leeds had recruited big names in Bradley Clyde, Brett Mullins and the already injured Robbie Mears.

Salford City Reds were confident they could shake off their also-rans tag with the addition of Bobbie Goulding, Mike Hancock, Francis Maloney and Warren Jowitt; and Halifax Blue

Sox had their usual uncompromising look about them, with Paul Davidson to add a bit more spice.

Warrington Wolves, with Kevin Walters; Castleford Tigers, with Mitch Healey, and the previous year's wooden spoonists, Huddersfield Giants, with Paul Rowley and Brandon Costin from Canberra, had all recruited strongly. Only Wakefield Trinity Wildcats were looking weaker, on paper at least.

But the paper talk was about to stop. The opening weekend provided some big clashes right across the board, and Super League VI kicked off in explosive fashion at Wigan on Friday 2nd March.

Explosive was the only word available as Wigan beat the Wolves 34-6 in a crackerjack of a match that boiled over more than once.

Two players – Toa Kohe-Love for a high tackle, and Tawera Nikau - were dismissed, two more were sin-binned and a string of fiery incidents were put on report by referee Steve Ganson.

RFL Director of Rugby Greg McCallum promised he would study the game 'frame by frame'. That week Kohe-Love (high tackle on Steve Renouf) copped a two-match ban. Wolves prop Danny Nutley and Wigan's Mick Cassidy were both suspended for two matches, both for 'striking'. Nikau escaped suspension or a fine after being found guilty of a late tackle, classed as a 'technical offence' that was not deemed worthy of further punishment.

The two clubs escaped with severe reprimands for the series of brawls and a new charge of "behaviour in any way contrary to the true spirit of the game" was promised to be introduced for players who get involved in fights.

It was almost forgotten that Alfie Langer had played a blinder, and his opposite, Adrian Lam, had won the game with his two tries just before half-time.

Saturday had replaced Sunday as Sky TV's second live Rugby League night this year and there was an intriguing first game up with the Rhinos' visit to the Valley to take on the highly-fancied Broncos.

It proved to be the comeback of the season. London raced into an 18-0 lead after 20 minutes on a freezing cold night. A cover tackle by winger Karl Pratt prevented Dennis Moran making it 24-0 before the Rhinos got down to business.

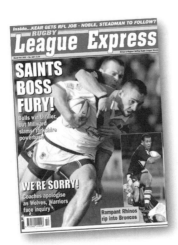

Moran left the field injured as Chev Walker scored the first of Leeds' nine tries, Pratt getting two and Keith Senior a hat-trick as Leeds won 50-18.

Again Leeds had injury worries as scrum-half Ryan Sheridan limped off with a hamstring problem to joining Brett Mullins, Brad Clyde and Robbie Mears on the casualty list.

In the clash of the 1999 Grand Finalists, Valley Parade had a big crowd inside to see the Bulls draw first blood with a 31-24 win over St Helens, with Shane Rigon, signed from Sydney City, scoring a decisive try hat-trick

After the game, Saints coach Ian Millward launched a verbal attack on Bulls and Super

Wigan's Kris Radlinski brought down by Warrington's Ian Sibbit during an
explosive Super League VI opener

League Europe chairman Chris Caisley.

"They have the powerbase over this side of the Pennines. This is where the
game is based, Chris Caisley is always there when they hand out the trophies,
but he never shakes our hand."

"I have an excellent relationship with the St Helens club and they congratulated
us on our win today," said Caisley in reply. Millward was also having to contend
with reports that Keiron Cunningham's move to rugby union was a done deal.

Wakefield-Castleford games have always been close in Super League and the
round one match-up this year was the same. The Tigers won at Belle Vue 22-17,
with two tries from Michael Smith – given a last chance by coach Stuart Raper –
securing the points.

Martin Moana was Halifax's gamestar as he scored two tries in the 34-10 win
over Huddersfield Giants at the McAlpine Stadium. "We beat ourselves," was
Giants coach Tony Smith's call after the game as he realised the size of the task
facing him for 2001.

Hull raced into an 18-0 lead at home to the Salford City but it need late tries
from Paul King and Gareth Raynor to secure a 46-34 win as Francis Maloney
scored two tries on his Reds Super League debut.

Back to the Silk Cut Challenge Cup on the second weekend in March and Warrington Wolves proved there was still a big gap between the French game and Super League as they ended Villeneuve's interest at Wilderspool by 32-0.

Wolves coach Darryl Van de Velde had moved Lee Briers to fullback to accommodate the arrival of Kevin Walters and his hat-trick set up Warrington for an eventually comfortable passage into the semi-finals.

Wakefield Trinity Wildcats put up sterner opposition than Halifax had the round before, but there was no stopping the Bulls machine as it went on to record a 38-0 win at Belle Vue, Henry Paul collecting his second successive sponsors' man of the match award.

On the Friday night, St Helens - with their big guns back - blitzed Huddersfield Giants in the second half at Knowsley Road to go through 54-16, despite the Giants taking a 10-4 lead early on. Sean Long was once again in sparkling form, notching 22 points with two tries and seven goals.

The Saturday game on BBC couldn't have been much more exciting as the fourth semi-finalist, Leeds Rhinos, came through a trial of fire at the Boulevard, winning 20-18, coming back from 10-0 down. Only a magnificent tackle by Karl Pratt and Keith Senior on Chris Smith in the last minute prevented Hull snatching a dramatic late win after 80 minutes of pulsating action. Coach Dean Lance admitted Brad Clyde was not a hundred per cent fit but he looked back to his best with a two-try gamestar performance.

Warrington's Super League year had got off to a traumatic start at Wigan, with two suspensions already to contend with, and things got dramatically worse as the month wore on. It emerged that one of their players, late to emerge as first-choice hooker Dave Highton, had failed a drugs test. That was in the same week that Kevin Walters decided he had had enough of Britain and was to return to Brisbane.

In the second round of Super League, Hull dealt them another blow at Wilderspool as Jason Smith inspired the Black and Whites to a 32-20 win to maintain their 100 per cent record. It wasn't as close as the final scoreline looked, with Hull on top from the moment that Deon Bird scored in the first minute of the game, and at one stage Hull led 32-8. "I'm not at all happy with our discipline and we lacked enthusiasm at times," said Wolves coach Darryl Van de Velde.

On a freezing Friday night Brian Noble's Bulls beat Salford 40-6. The Reds trailed by only four points on the half-hour mark after Warren Jowitt replied to Stuart Spruce's opening score. But two tries to Jamie Peacock either side of half-time virtually decided a highly competitive game.

It looked like being a long fruitless season for Wakefield as they went down to Leeds Rhinos at Headingley 42-14, with Kiwi centre Tonie Carroll scoring four barnstorming tries as the Wildcats hung in at half-time, level at 8-all. "Keep backing us at 500 to one because you will make a fortune," was Wakefield coach John Harbin's advice, although he looked to have lost the services of Tony Tatupu with a knee ligament injury.

Also on the Friday night – with Leeds, Wigan and St Helens all opting to stage

Paul Anderson goes on the rampage as the Bulls dump Wakefield out of the Challenge Cup

their home games at that time throughout the season - the Giants got a bit closer to St Helens at Knowsley Road. They even outplayed the Champions for long spells, but eventually fell to a 44-22 defeat, winger Steve Hall's try five minutes from time settling the issue, after Aussie winger Andrew Frew had again collected a couple of tries

The day after, 23 year old Wigan reserve Phil Jones, the former Lancashire Lynx stand-off, stepped up to fill the shoes of the injured Matthew Johns at Castleford and mesmerised the Tigers with a hat-trick man of the match performance that had commentators asking how many more young talented English players were being denied a chance to shine by Aussie imports.

Wigan won a highly competitive game 24-8 with Jones' 66th minute hat-trick try the killer for Cas, who were already suffering injury disruption, with Mitch Healey failing a fitness test, Adrian Vowles playing stand-off with Danny Orr at scrum-half, and then losing Lee Harland, Dean Sampson and Aaron Raper to injury in the first half.

Sunday night proved a huge disappointment for London supporters as the Blue Sox maintained their hundred per cent start with a 16-11 grind of a win at the Shay.

Jamie Bloem's two late penalties took Halifax home, with Brett Goldspink producing a towering display up front for the home side.

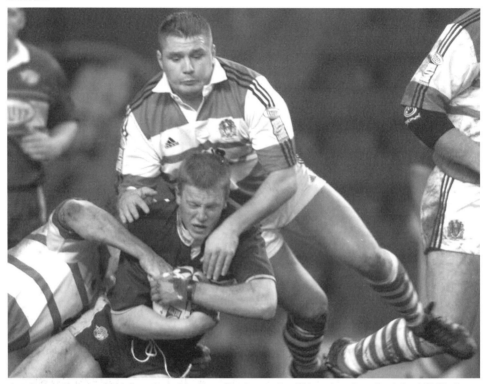

Leeds debutant Jon Liddell grounded by Terry Newton as the Rhinos lose heavily at the JJB Stadium

On the weekend of round three of Super League, RFL chairman Sir Rodney Walker admitted he was concerned about the targeting of League players by rugby union, after reports surfaced of a plan by the England union coach to sign League players to draft straight into his side. "Clearly Henry Paul is one of those players, and we estimate that there could be as many a dozen in total," said Walker. "We are treating the situation seriously and we are watching it very carefully". Walker denied that any talks had taken place between the RFL and the RFU about merging the two sports.

Walker also had to admit that the 2000 World Cup had failed to deliver anything like the profits that had been predicted before the tournament began the previous October. "The outcome is beginning to look very disappointing," said Sir Rodney. Gate income and commercial sponsorship was below projections and some sponsors were reportedly disputing payment.

On the field, the game of the weekend was at JJB Stadium, where two unbeaten sides - Wigan and Leeds – clashed. The Rhinos were missing Keith Senior, who broke a thumb the previous Friday against Wakefield, Matt Diskin (shoulder), Robbie Mears, Ryan Sheridan and Brad Clyde and handed a debut to teenage scrum-half Jon Liddell at hooker. The Rhinos, with a Challenge Cup semi-final to come in a week's time were 20-0 down at half-time, the Warriors again hardly missing the still-injured Matthew Johns. Adrian Lam had a hand or touch in all Wigan's seven tries and Andy Farrell scored a try and kicked seven goals in a 42-6 win.

On the Sunday the Bulls joined Wigan at the top of the table but their visit to the McAlpine Stadium wasn't the formality that everyone expected.

Huddersfield led 10-8 at the break thanks to an Andrew Frew try and three Steve McNamara goals and it took all the Bulls' renowned power to go on and win the game after Tevita Vaikona gave them the lead after half-time. "We're sitting on the bottom with no points but once we get a couple of wins we'll start to grow, and I feel that's not too far away," said Giants coach Tony Smith.

Huddersfield's long-term prospects didn't improve as Wakefield got off the mark with a convincing 30-14 win over Halifax Blue Sox at Belle Vue. The returned Brad Davis at last made his debut and he and Willie Poching spearheaded the Trinity win as Martin Pearson's seven goals proved crucial.

Lacking Andrew Dunemann for most of the match - he broke his jaw after twelve minutes – the Blue Sox lost direction. The defeat – the first of the season – proved too much for Mercer the coach, who resigned the position that week, insisting he would stay on as a player. His assistant, Aussie Steve Linnane, took up the reins.

Hull lost their perfect start when Castleford Tigers took a point off them at the Boulevard and it took a Lee Jackson try off a ricocheted kick five minutes from time to snatch an 18-18 draw. Mark Lennon made his first senior start at scrum-half which allowed Danny Orr to produce something like his best at stand-off as the Tigers led 12-0 and 18-12 before the Airlie Birds levelled.

Salford got off the mark at the Willows with a 39-14 win over the troubled Wolves, who were without the injured Alfie Langer. Nick Pinkney scored two outstanding winger's tries, the first a 70-metre effort after only three minutes of the game, the second a 90-metre interception ten minutes from time. Francis Maloney was also a double try-scorer for the Reds.

And there was real excitement at the Valley as Keiron Cunningham denied the Broncos with two dummy-half tries in the last eight minutes to wrap up St Helens' 20-18 win. "The best team lost by far," said a relieved Saints coach Ian Millward after the game.

It was a fine end for St Helens to a week in which they were forced to pay Aussie halfback Darrell Trindall £45,000 in compensation after sacking him the previous April.

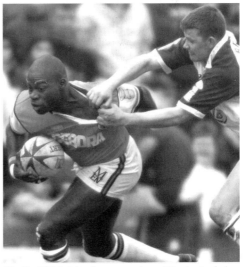

Martin Offiah tries to escape from Warrington's Lee Briers as the City Reds get off the mark

SUPER LEAGUE TABLE - *Sunday 25th March*

	P	W	D	L	F	A	D	PTS
Wigan Warriors	3	3	0	0	100	20	80	6
Bradford Bulls	3	3	0	0	101	44	57	6
Hull FC	3	2	1	0	96	72	24	5
Leeds Rhinos	3	2	0	1	98	74	24	4
St Helens	3	2	0	1	88	71	17	4
Halifax Blue Sox	3	2	0	1	64	51	13	4
Castleford Tigers	3	1	1	1	48	59	-11	3
Wakefield T Wildcats	3	1	0	2	61	78	-17	2
Salford City Reds	3	1	0	2	79	100	-21	2
London Broncos	3	0	0	3	47	86	-39	0
Huddersfield Giants	3	0	0	3	46	108	-62	0
Warrington Wolves	3	0	0	3	40	105	-65	0

APRIL
Tragic Wolves

Twickenham doesn't have the aura of Wembley but the determination of the four sides going into the semi-finals of the Silk Cut Challenge Cup as March turned to April began was plain to see.

The result was two superb matches widely appreciated by huge audiences watching the games on BBC TV.

In the Saturday semi-final Leeds and St Helens produced a match of unbearable excitement at the JJB Stadium, with Saints victorious 27-22.

As Raymond Fletcher noted in League Express: "Every succeeding minute was followed by more all-out attack and quick-to-respond defence from both sides," as St Helens came back to stop the Rhinos making their third Cup final in succession.

Tommy Martyn landed what everyone thought was the winning field goal in the last minute of a wonderful Silk Cut Challenge Cup semi-final.

"Time was clicking on, we'd looked up at the stand clock and saw there was only a minute left," explained Martyn.

"So get a drop goal over and we've got it sewn up. I did that and we were going back to play what we thought was our last set of six when we saw the clock then showed that there was five minutes left. A few of the players were upset about that."

Saints showed their character to finish in even greater style as they came up with a glorious match-clinching try in the last few seconds. Once again they kept the ball alive as the seconds ticked away to leave the opposition devastated, Paul Sculthorpe finishing it all off with an almost casual romp to the line.

St Helens coach Ian Millward said with a hint of irony afterwards: "We don't have a gameplan - we just go out and play. Off the cuff rugby, that's all we do. It's pretty easy to coach these guys."

Saints had taken a 6-0 lead after Sculthorpe intercepted Barrie McDermott's blind offload and raced 50 metres for a shock try goaled by Sean Long.

It was a stunning blow, but Leeds responded superbly when, from close to their own line, Kevin Sinfield launched Chev Walker on a 90-metre raid. As the cover came across he handed on to his winger Francis Cummins, who whipped the ball inside just as he was tackled into touch. It went to Brett Mullins and the experienced fullback slowed the tempo down just a little as he moved inside looking for more support. He found it in Mark Calderwood, who went in between the posts.

Saints hooker Keiron Cunningham took the man of the match award for a typical non-stop display, highlighted by several punishing runs. Sean Long made

Struck by tragedy - Warrington's Lee Briers in action against Bradford in the Challenge Cup semi-final

a major contribution to victory – one try, a hand and foot in two others and three goals.

Saints held a 16-6 interval lead, Long and Martyn adding further tries before Leeds' tremendous second-half comeback. They came out all fired up and scored a try within a minute. Walker again set it up with a powerful run down the left and from the position gained Karl Pratt forced his way over.

Long pegged Leeds back with a penalty goal in the 50th minute, but four minutes later Kevin Sinfield spliced open a tight defence with an outrageous dummy to saunter through for a try.

Harris banged over the goal to make it 18-16 to Saints, who widened the gap again when Paul Newlove squeezed in at the left corner off Joynt's pass in the 61st minute. But two minutes later Leeds were level. Pratt, enjoying his switch from wing to scrum-half, put in a neat kick for Mullins to touch down and Harris added the equalising goal to set up the frantic finish.

The last tension-packed ten minutes began with a tremendous Martyn 40-20. Within the next five tackles Martyn had dived over for what seemed like the match-winning try only for the video replay to show he had dropped the ball. Martyn admitted he felt like crawling into a hole, but he stayed on top to put everything right with his 20-metre field goal and part in the final try.

One blot on an otherwise fast and furious game was the eye injury to St Helens forward Peter Shiels following a punch from McDermott, which earned the Ireland prop a four-match ban.

The expected one-sided semi-final at the McAlpine the following day turned out to be a belter too.

The Cup-holders, Bradford Bulls, had to produce a devastating 21-point barrage in the space of 13 minutes to finally break a wonderful effort from the Wolves.

With the match tied at 18-18, Henry Paul gave the Bulls the impetus for their compelling finish with a left-footed field goal. Then, as prop Paul Anderson produced two awesome surges down centre-field, tries by Stuart Spruce, Scott Naylor and Robbie Paul earned the Bulls their final date at Twickenham.

The Wolves' Lee Briers - proving himself a big-match performer, won the Silk Cut award for a brilliant individual display, completing a deserved hat-trick with the final act of a wonderful game.

After Michael Withers opened the scoring from a Paul Deacon bomb, the man who'd dropped it, Rob Smyth, supplied the perfect response, finishing off a flowing move in the right corner - capped by Toa Kohe-Love's sensational pass out of the back door - that Briers brilliantly converted. Then Allan Langer put through a bouncing kick that Tevita Vaikona was unable to hold and Briers acrobatically pounced for the touchdown.

Henry Paul pulled back two points with a penalty midway through the half before the Bulls brought on Robbie Paul, who took the field with a bandage above his left eye. Robbie's impact was immediate as he exploded into life from dummy half fully 40-metres out as Tawera Nikau, at marker, slipped after an off-the-ball incident with James Lowes.

His searing acceleration took him between two trailing defenders and he wrong-footed the last man, Alan Hunte, for a brilliant try. Henry tagged on the goal and the Bulls had the lead again before the Wolves drew level, deservedly, at the interval as Briers hit a penalty from in front of the posts.

After the break Nikau had a try controversially disallowed for offside on the last tackle after a Langer kick as referee Cummings declined the video referee option. In response, Henry Paul and Scott Naylor took on the Warrington defence and Lowes brilliantly committed the close-range cover before ushering Jamie Peacock though a gap. Henry Paul added the goal and the Bulls were 18-12 in front.

But the Wolves kept in a pulsating contest as Briers pulled another rabbit out of his box of tricks. After successive penalties kept the Wolves pounding the Bulls line, Langer and Andrew Gee threw the ball to the left and Briers used Nikau as a foil before arcing through to score an outstanding try wide out. Briers' nerves were up to the test as he tied the scores with the testing conversion.

But Henry Paul regained the lead for the Bulls with his sweetly-struck field goal and the Bulls finally established some daylight when Henry's raking kick forced Jamie Stenhouse to back-track and the young Wolves winger lost possession in Pryce's challenge, Spruce swooping to grab the loose ball and score a converted try.

Bradford's late scoring burst gave a final score-line of 37-22 that was so cruel for the Wolves.

Hull had talked a good game and came out of March with five out of six points but their first big test of the Super League year came on the Friday of Round Four when they travelled to Headingley.

In incessant rain and mud, the two served up a great game, as Leeds gave debuts to two more of their youngsters in Andy Kirk and Rob Burrow as they went down 18-16. Half the Leeds side was under 20 years of age and in the end they found the guile of Jason Smith just too much, despite the return from injury of Robbie Mears, and the sight of Brett Mullins leaving the field on quarter time with a hamstring injury did little for the South Stand's morale.

The Rhinos lead 12-10 at the break but tries to Matt Crowther and Deon Bird gave Hull a six-point advantage before Burrow created a try for Francis Cummins just after the hour, creating a nail-biting last quarter.

The post-match press conference gave no clue that Rhinos coach Dean Lance would the next day agree "to an early termination of his contract by mutual consent", which a club press statement claimed. Leeds chief executive Gary Hetherington ruled out the appointment from anyone outside the club and early that week, former player Daryl Powell, the club's Director of Youth Development, was given a three-year contract to do the coaching job.

The mystery surrounding the timing of Lance's departure was as nothing compared to the tragedies that were unfolding at Warrington.

On the Thursday following the Wolves' Cup exit, Tawera Nikau was hit by an unimaginable personal tragedy when he returned home to find his wife had committed suicide. To compound the sadness, Lee Briers older brother Brian that same day lost a long battle against cancer.

There was a minute's silence before Warrington's game against Castleford at the Jungle the following Saturday and a flat game ended in a Castleford victory, 18-0, with Nikau absent, but Briers playing on, and Gary Mercer making his second Wolves debut after his move from Halifax.

Elsewhere, the Bulls and Wigan kept up their perfect records.

Bradford had it tough in a 24-6 win over London at Valley Parade - with Michael Withers' Cup final appearance in doubt as he broke a hand. Wigan had a heck of a battle in another Friday night mudbath at the Shay, with Halifax going down 20-10 in Steve Linnane's first game in charge. Warriors hooker Terry Newton was outstanding with two tries, the second of which scuppered the Blue Sox fightback led by the irrepressible Paul Davidson

Saints continued collecting the league points as they beat the battling Wildcats 24-0 at

Wakefield's Martin Pearson on the burst as the Wildcats inflict a first defeat of the season on the Bulls

Knowsley Road, with Peter Shiels, Tommy Martyn and Sean Hoppe all absent.

And Bobbie Goulding kicked six goals from as many attempts as two late tries from Mike Hancock and Malcolm Alker condemned Huddersfield to another defeat, the Reds coming out 28-14 on top at the Willows.

Bank Holiday weekend's can often make or break a team's season and by the end of Good Friday several of the top clubs must have been thinking along similar lines.

On the Thursday night, Wakefield entertained Bradford Bulls and provided the biggest shock of the season to date, winning 16-12.

The Bulls had beaten the Wildcats at Belle Vue by 38-0 in the Cup and after eleven minutes looked to be en route to another routine win when they led 10-0. But that was as good as it got for unbeaten Bradford as Willie Poching led Trinity in an astonishing comeback. Winger Neil Law got over twice before the break and sub David March, with his first touch of the ball sealed the win just after the hour when he raced in from 30 metres. "Tactical genius, wasn't it," quipped Trinity coach John Harbin. "Now I know what heaven is like."

Wigan also lost their hundred per cent Super League record when they drew 22-22 with St Helens in the Good Friday derby, as Saints proved again they could never be written off until the final whistle.

At 22-12 in the lead with ten minutes left on the clock the Warriors were on course to take full revenge for their Cup exit at Knowsley Road two months before.

But tries to Dwayne West and Paul Sculthorpe and a goal by Long levelled and the record JJB Stadium crowd was spellbound as Andy Farrell had two chances to steal the points with a long-range penalty, and then an equally ambitious field goal attempt. And then as the hooter sounded John Stankevitch pulled a field goal attempt wide. "We're never beaten till the bell goes," said Saints coach Ian Millward.

Hull kept their unbeaten record by 30-14 in a controversial game - the first of four scheduled league matches with Halifax - at the Boulevard.

Hull chief executive Shane Richardson labelled the Blue Sox "the most cynical sports team in Britain" and labelled Paul Davidson as "the equivalent of a villain in a very ordinary pantomime. Everything you could do wrong on a rugby field, they do it."

Leeds sunk to seventh place in the table as Warrington ended their own winless record with a superb 36-6 win in the televised game on Easter Thursday. It was an inauspicious start for Daryl Powell's coaching career as the Wolves cast off their off-field troubles in style, Ian Sibbit getting a try hat-trick.

London Broncos also got off the mark as Friday 13th proved to be lucky for them, relegating Huddersfield to inglorious isolation at the foot of the table with a 43-12 win at the Valley. It was one-way traffic for most of the game with Dennis Moran at the heart of the increasingly impressive London attack.

Salford entered the top-five as Bobbie Goulding produced one of his command performances to help the Reds beat Castleford 24-22 at the Jungle - Salford's first win there since 1992. Mike Hancock created a try for former Cas player Francis Maloney in the 76th minute that gave Salford a six point lead, and there was great excitement as Darren Rogers went in at the other end of the field with only two minutes remaining. But Danny Orr couldn't convert from the touchline.

Easter Monday threw up the clash of the season so far in Wigan's visit to Bradford.

Henry Paul created two tries as the Bulls raced into a 20-0 lead at the break before resisting a Wigan comeback to win 35-24 to move one point clear at the top of the Super League table.

Andy Farrell became only the second player in history, after the legendary Jim Sullivan, to score over 2,000 points for Wigan with the second of his four conversions. But the Bulls had laid down a marker for the year.

Hull finally lost their unbeaten record, but only just, as they went down 38-34 at St Helens.

Saints led 24-10 at half-time and 38-16 with eleven minutes to go. But Hull rattled the champions with three tries in five minutes from Steve Prescott, Jason Smith and Paul Parker, all converted by Matt Crowther, to set up a tense final five minutes, Paul Newlove's two second-half tries proving vital.

Leeds gave Daryl Powell his first win, a 32-22 success over the Tigers, with Marcus St Hilaire scoring a hat-trick of tries. Cas led 12-0 at one stage through two Darren Rogers tries but sub Danny Ward came off the bench to play a blinder and set up the Rhinos' win. 'We've forgotten how to win games," said Tigers coach Stuart Raper.

London Broncos made it four out of four points for the weekend with a hard-fought 14-12 win over Salford at the Willows. And Warrington continued their revival with a 32-20 win over Halifax at the Shay, Martin Masella crashing over for the winning try nine minutes from time.

But Huddersfield Giants' woes continued when they lost 24-16 at home to Wakefield. The Wildcats blitzed them with three tries early on and then, after a fightback brought the Giants to within two points, Waisale Sovatabua intercepted a Steve McNamara pass in the last seconds to seal the win. The Giants were now four points adrift at the bottom.

After Round Seven, the Giants were still point-less despite a gutsy show at Wigan.

After gleaning only one point from four over Easter, Frank Endacott made six changes to his starting 13 and it proved too good for the Giants, the Warriors running out 37-8 winners.

Irishman Brian Carney made his Wigan debut and scored two tries.

The win meant by the end of the weekend they were at the top of the table on points difference as the Bulls were held to thrilling 24-24 draw by Hull at the Boulevard.

The game provided conclusive proof that Hull had arrived amongst the elite. The Bulls certainly held nothing back despite being seven days away from the Challenge Cup final and led 24-12 after 51 minutes. But converted tries to Tony

Hull's Gareth Raynor charges in to the Bradford defence during a thrilling Boulevard draw

Grimaldi and Matt Crowther capped a superb comeback.

Stuart Spruce suffered a shoulder injury in the second half - it was to be his last appearance in a Bradford shirt.

It took two pieces of brilliance from Iestyn Harris to secure a 19-14 Leeds win at the Willows that kept them their top five spot. Harris scored a superb solo try midway through the second half and went on to add a crucial field goal with 14 minutes remaining. After Mike Hancock had narrowed the deficit to one point, Karl Pratt confirmed the win with a try in the left corner.

Wakefield came down with a bump at Belle Vue as London Broncos - with Richie Barnett at his brilliant best - beat them hands down 38-10. "Life goes on," shrugged John Harbin after game. "I'll still have to do the washing up tomorrow."

Warrington's wonder-show continued as they hammered St Helens at Wilderspool on the Friday night 56-22, shaking off another hammer blow with the loss for the season of Steve Georgallis, who ruptured his Achilles tendon in the Easter Monday win at Halifax. Allan Langer was brilliant again as Anthony Sullivan in particular showed pre-Cup final nerves. Coach Ian Millward had rested Sean Long, Sean Hoppe, David Fairleigh and Kevin Iro, starting Paul Wellens at scrum-half, and was left sweating after Paul Newlove was sent off by referee Bob Connolly for a high tackle on Toa Kohe-Love. He escaped punishment that week.

It didn't put the Kiwi off as he scored a hat-trick - at the time rumours suggested that he had already signed for St Helens for 2002 - as did Alan Hunte.

A Danny Orr penalty on the hour mark got the Tigers back to winning ways as they beat Halifax 34-24 at the Jungle, Michael Smith - a real revelation for Cas in 2001 - scoring the clinching try seven minutes from time.

It was almost ironic that on the last weekend of April, Rugby League was to stage the Challenge Cup final at Twickenham

Throughout the month an incessant stream of anti-League propaganda in the guise of serious journalism had been churned out in national newspapers. The RFL met with its union counterpart after RFU officials had been discovered making direct telephone calls to young League players contracted to RFL clubs. The meeting was brokered by Sport England, who had been alerted to the fact that the RFU could be using the money it had given it in grants to lure League players to their game.

RFL Director of Rugby Greg McCallum denounced the RFU's "pillaging" of Rugby League talent.

The RFU denied any of the accusations which led McCallum to announce: "The dismissive comments we received from the RFU at the weekend we know aren't true, and we have evidence to suggest that what we allege is actually happening."

Hull that month concluded a new four-year contract with 18 year old Great Britain hopeful Richard Horne.

SUPER LEAGUE TABLE - *Sunday 22nd April*

	P	W	D	L	F	A	D	PTS
Wigan Warriors	7	5	1	1	203	95	108	11
Bradford Bulls	7	5	1	1	196	114	82	11
Hull FC	7	4	2	1	202	164	38	10
St Helens	7	4	1	2	194	183	11	9
Leeds Rhinos	7	4	0	3	171	164	7	8
Castleford Tigers	7	3	1	3	144	139	5	7
London Broncos	7	3	0	4	148	144	4	6
Salford City Reds	7	3	0	4	157	169	-12	6
Warrington Wolves	7	3	0	4	164	181	-17	6
Wakefield T Wildcats	7	3	0	4	111	168	-57	6
Halifax Blue Sox	7	2	0	5	142	167	-25	4
Huddersfield Giants	7	0	0	7	96	240	-144	0

CHALLENGE CUP FINAL
History makers

The Challenge Cup continued on its sojourn as for the second year it had to find a home for its final away from the still undemolished Wembley stadium.

This year the Cup roadshow alighted back in London, at Twickenham, which had staged its first Rugby League match the previous October with the World Cup game between England and Australia.

The great bastion of rugby union failed to evoke the magic of Wembley, or Murrayfield, and as if by pre-ordination, the 2001 Final will not be remembered too fondly.

On a grey dreary afternoon, St Helens secured their eighth Challenge Cup in the 100th final, 104 years after being defeated by Batley in the very first final at Headingley.

It wasn't a classic final, for sure, but then the horrible rainy weather had a big part to play in that.

But there was so much to admire in a game that held the attention throughout, with Sean Long, coach Ian Millward and Paul Sculthorpe the pivotal figures in St Helens' defeat of Bradford Bulls.

The history and prestige of the Lance Todd Trophy inspired Long to a man of the match Cup-winning performance.

"I remember Wigan playing Hull at Wembley (in 1985) and watching Brett Kenny winning the trophy," said Long. "I thought that was something special and something I'd like to do. I spoke to Tommy Martyn (who won the Lance Todd award in St Helens' 1997 defeat of Bradford) early in the week, and he said it was one of the best feelings you'll have in your life if you do it. I thought I'll soak it in tonight and have a crack."

Long's halfback partner Martyn played a major supporting role in the win, completing the duo's party piece to touch down the first of Long's two try-making kicks.

Bradford were only too aware of the duo's well-rehearsed act, but could do nothing about it. Their anxiety to prevent it cost Shane Rigon an early spell in the sin bin, when the Bradford centre obstructed Martyn as he chased Long's first kick into the in-goal area.

St Helens ignored a likely two points from the penalty, took a tap, and within the next set

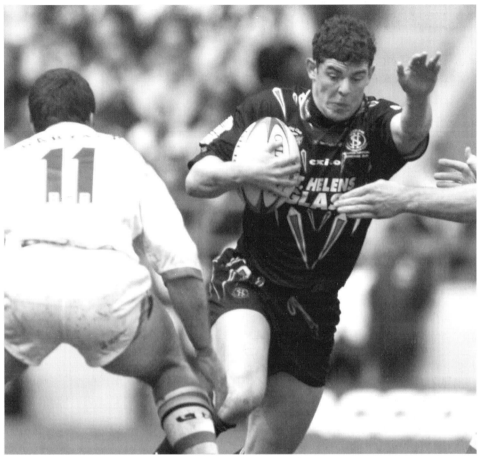

Daniel Gartner moves in to tackle Paul Wellens

of six Long put in another short kick. This time the ball rebounded off the base of the post, but Saints retained possession as Paul Sculthorpe dived on it.

Long was determined to get it right, and immediately put in another short kick. This time Martyn shot in for the opening score after 11 minutes. The video referee confirmed he was onside and Long tagged on the goal.

Fifteen minutes later the persistent Long put in yet another short kick, which ricocheted off Daniel Gartner's leg for Keiron Cunningham to swoop for another try. Again the video referee had to be satisfied before Long popped over the conversion.

That made it 12-2 and Long had been mainly responsible for all the St Helens points, and their only other score was to be a Martyn field goal in the 37th minute. Long was denied a hat-trick of try-making kicks late in the game when the video referee ruled against Tim Jonkers' touchdown attempt after Henry Paul had fumbled the ball over his own line.

Although the rain-sodden pitch limited the running chances of the teams' many exciting attackers, Long always threatened danger with his short, scudding dashes, and made one of the best clear-cut breaks in the first half. He also pulled off a vital tackle to stop Rigon breaking well clear after intercepting.

Coach Millward had also positioned Long on the right wing in defence to negate Henry Paul's kicking game, which had effectively won the Bulls the Cup the year before at Murrayfield. It worked perfectly as the renowned Bulls attack was snuffed out, Henry's three penalty goals all that Saints would allow them.

Long was an overwhelming winner of the Lance Todd Trophy. He justified the bookmakers' ranking as a 13-2 joint favourite, with Robbie Paul, by picking up 17 votes. The only other nominees were four colleagues way down the list: Martyn and Paul Sculthorpe with three votes, David Fairleigh with two, and Chris Joynt with one.

Sculthorpe had missed out on England's World Cup game against Australia at Twickenham through injury, and eight weeks before the final had undergone surgery to the jaw he broke in the victory over Wigan in round four of the Cup. He produced a marvellous effort, providing tremendous inspiring go-forward against the mighty Bulls pack, combining with back-row colleagues Chris Joynt and Peter Shiels to lead Saints' defensive effort.

For Millward the game was another tactical triumph. Saints' kicking game was spot-on, their handling skills and confidence intact, and their defensive effort was composed and secure. Saints showed tremendous confidence, resolve and self-belief; qualities instilled into them by Millward.

Captain fantastic Joynt, Martyn, Vila Matautia, Paul Newlove, Anthony Sullivan and Keiron Cunningham all completed a hat-trick of Cup-winners' medals against the Bulls, having played in the 1996 and 1997 finals, while Bulls captain Robbie Paul and prop Brian McDermott tasted defeat for a third time against Saints.

Heavy rain swirled around the stadium, drenching all the fans in the lower tiers, well before kick-off, but the elements mercifully relented for the pre-match rituals, and there was even a glint of sunshine and blue skies as the game unfolded on a patched-up pitch.

Australian Michael Withers was back in the Bulls starting line-up, just three

Henry Paul faces up to Tommy Martyn

St Helens celebrate their Challenge Cup Final win over Bradford

weeks after fracturing a hand against London. Withers replaced Stuart Spruce, whose damaged shoulder, suffered the previous Saturday against Hull, was to end his Bradford career.

The Paul brothers ran and tackled their hearts out (a combined total of 30 drives and 48 tackles) but neither tested Saints under the high ball, and the Bulls' kicking game was several notches below that of Saints. Mike Forshaw was excellent in the pack, providing consistent go-forward and topping the tackle count with 29, and Daniel Gartner produced a huge, if unspectacular effort. But it was all to no avail, as Saints again triumphed on the big occasion. The back-row trio of Joynt, Sculthorpe and Shiels combined for 92 tackles, Joynt leading the way with 35, and Martyn made 20, a superb effort. Saints had never won at Bradford in six years of Super League, but they had won every game between the two that really mattered.

Saturday 28th April 2001

CHALLENGE CUP FINAL

BRADFORD BULLS 6 ST HELENS 13

BULLS: 5 Michael Withers; 2 Tevita Vaikona; 20 Scott Naylor; 15 Shane Rigon; 3 Leon Pryce; 6 Henry Paul; 1 Robbie Paul (C); 8 Joe Vagana; 9 James Lowes; 22 Brian McDermott; 19 Jamie Peacock; 11 Daniel Gartner; 12 Mike Forshaw. Subs: 10 Paul Anderson for Vagana (19); 29 Stuart Fielden for McDermott (23); 14 Lee Gilmour for Naylor (62); 7 Paul Deacon for Lowes (70); McDermott for Gartner (50); Vagana for Anderson (57).
Goals: H Paul 3.
Sin bin: Rigon (10) - obstruction off the ball on Martyn.
SAINTS: 1 Paul Wellens; 2 Sean Hoppe; 3 Kevin Iro; 4 Paul Newlove; 5 Anthony Sullivan; 20 Tommy Martyn; 7 Sean Long; 12 Sonny Nickle; 9 Keiron Cunningham; 10 David Fairleigh; 11 Chris Joynt (C); 8 Peter Shiels; 13 Paul Sculthorpe. Subs: 16 Vila Matautia for Nickle (20); 15 Tim Jonkers for Fairleigh (33); 17 Steve Hall for Newlove (52); 19 Anthony Stewart not used; Nickle for Matautia (33BB, rev 37); Fairleigh for Matautia (47BB).
Tries: Martyn (12), Cunningham (26); **Goals:** Long 2;
Field goal: Martyn.
League Express Men of the Match:
Bulls: Mike Forshaw; *Saints:* Sean Long.
Penalty count: 9-10; **Half-time:** 4-13;
Referee: Russell Smith (Castleford);
Attendance: 68,250 *(at Twickenham).*

And with this win they secured a treble that is unlikely to be matched: the Super League crown, the World Club Champions title, and the Challenge Cup.

"Nobody has done what we have done or achieved this before, and we are going to be in the history books forever," said Saints hooker Keiron Cunningham. "It is just fantastic."

MAY
A Frank farewell

On the day after the Cup final, London Broncos crept into the top five with a 20-12 win against Wigan Warriors in front of their biggest crowd of the season.

Frank Endacott said: "They ambushed us good, but we never played well enough to win that game. Our ball control in the second half was 57 per cent and you won't even beat an under-10s team with that." Tony Martin scored the winning try, pouncing on a spilled Dennis Moran kick behind the Wigan line.

Round Eight continued on Monday and into Wednesday, with the Bulls and Hull both stealing a march on Wigan.

On the Monday night Hull, who the week before had banned four supporters for life following bad language and unruly behaviour during the game against Bradford, travelled to Huddersfield where they pulled off a routine victory over the Giants, with Jason Smith supervising matters and Paul Cooke and Richard Horne combining well at halfback.

Leeds made it three in a row with a 38-26 win at Halifax - who gave a debut to on-loan Rhino Dean Lawford - with Robbie Mears starting to show the consistency that had made him a key player at Auckland in the NRL the year before. Two second-half tries from Keith Senior decided the game.

And also on the Monday night - it wasn't a Bank Holiday - two late Justin Brooker tries gave Wakefield their fourth win of the season, with a young prop called Keith Mason catching the eye. Salford's injury list was beginning to look critical, as Warren Jowitt was ruled out for the rest of the season with a dislocated shoulder.

On the Wednesday night, the Bulls bounced back from their Cup final disappointment with a resounding victory over Warrington at Valley Parade. They didn't score a try at Twickenham but put nine past the Wolves with three spectacular efforts from Tevita Vaikona the highlight. Henry Paul - thought to almost certainly be leaving the Bulls at the end of the season for Canberra - kicked eight goals to take him to 35 successful consecutive kicks - past the world record of 30 set by Daryl Halligan for Canterbury Bulldogs. Tawera Nikau was one of Warrington's best of the night after making a surprise return from a four-match absence following the funeral of his wife in New Zealand. Former Leeds Rhino Graham Mackay also made a huge impact in his first game for the Bulls, scoring a typical bullocking try.

St Helens' Challenge Cup success had taken more out of them than they thought. On the following Friday they went to Leeds for a Round Nine game and were sent reeling by the rampant Rhinos 74-26. Saints were missing only three players from

Castleford's Danny Orr looks for support as the battling Tigers go down at home to the Bulls

the Cup-winning team - Paul Wellens, Tommy Martyn and Paul Newlove - but they were swept aside as Tonie Carroll scored another Headingley four-timer, Francis Cummins collected a hat-trick and Iestyn Harris scored 26 points to pass the 2,000 points in a career barrier.

The win moved Leeds into fourth place, three points clear of Saints in fifth and well in touch of the Bulls on top with 15 points.

But Bradford only just kept top spot as, looking tired and jaded, they edged Castleford at the Jungle 24-22. Henry Paul missed the first of his conversion attempts to end his record run, but his 68th minute penalty goal proved the difference between the two sides as Cas fought back from 22-8 down, with halves Danny Orr and Mark Lennon outstanding.

Wigan were back to their best as a fluent eight-try display blew away Wakefield Trinity Wildcats at the JJB Stadium 50-6. Andy Farrell kicked nine goals from ten attempts, plus a try, and young hooker Mark Smith had a fine game, with Terry Newton switching to the back row. Young prop Ricky Bibey made his debut from the bench.

Warrington made it four wins from five with a 26-16 win over the Giants at Wilderspool in a forgettable game and Steve Linnane won his first game in charge at the Halifax Blue Sox as they beat Salford 30-18 at the Shay to lift the Colin Dixon Memorial Trophy.

Danny Tickle and Damian Gibson hold up Sonny Nickle during a bad-tempered affair at Knowsley Road

It ended a six-match losing run and left Huddersfield six points adrift at the bottom of the table.

And in one of the more significant games of the round, Hull beat London 19-14 at the Boulevard to keep second spot and suggest it would be them making the play-offs at the end of the season, not the Broncos.

Hull led 19-8 going into the final quarter with Paul Broadbent putting in a mighty effort in the pack, but a Michael Gillett try on 67 minutes, set up by Richie Barnett and converted by Brett Warton, meant an exciting finish. There wasn't enough to stop the Broncos' four-match winning run coming to an end.

Round Ten proved to be Frank Endacott's last game in charge at Wigan as the Warriors lost at Salford, a Graham Holroyd field goal with three minutes left on the clock effectively ending his tenure.

A sensational Nick Pinkney hat-trick in a second half in which Wigan's rookie prop Ricky Bibey was dismissed for a high tackle on Michael Hancock, was the highlight of a memorable Reds performance that produced a shock 31-30 scoreline. The following day Endacott was the former Wigan coach and within a couple of days Castleford boss Stuart Raper was taking his chair in the office. "I think it is a good appointment and I wish him the very best," said Frank, whose genuine and affable nature had made the Super League a richer place. Bibey got one match.

One of the downsides of winning the Challenge Cup in the modern era is having to catch up in the league and St Helens certainly had it rough at the start of May, fronting Castleford Tigers and Halifax in the space of two days.

On the Wednesday Paul Sculthorpe guided them to a 36-16 win over Castleford Tigers, who gave a debut to former Leeds and Sheffield hooker Andy Speak. And on the Friday they had to produce another comeback in a fiery game against the Blue Sox.

Sonny Nickle was sent off on the 60th minute for a high tackle on Jamie Thackray and Vila Matautia, who had already served a four-match ban after his send off in the Cup at Whitehaven and was talking of quitting the game because of his unfair treatment at the hands of the Disciplinary, was on report for a spear tackle on the same player.

Nickle got two matches, and both Matautia and Paul Davidson (after an incident that fractured Saints' Wayne McDonald's jaw) were cleared by the RFL of any foul play.

It was only a last-minute Sean Hoppe try that won Saints the two points.

On the same night the Bulls put on another majestic display to beat the Rhinos at Headingley 33-14, with Michael Withers, now seemingly established at fullback after the injury to Stuart Spruce, in superb form, scoring two tries to help build a 20-2 half-time lead. The introduction of Rob Burrow in the second half pepped up the Rhinos but they were second best.

Hull kept within a point of Bradford at the summit with an under-par 30-22 win at Belle Vue after Wakefield had shot into a 12-0 lead. Young guns Paul Cooke and Paul King, with two second-half tries, got the Black and Whites out of jail.

It got worse for the Giants as they squandered a 20-6 half-time lead over the Tigers at the McAlpine to equal the worst ever start to Super League - ten straight losses (Castleford in 1997). "I still think a victory is not far off," said Giants boss Tony Smith. Dean Sampson spent plenty of time in the blood-bin but still scored a hat-trick as he led Castleford to a 46-26 win, in what turned out to be Stuart Raper's last game in charge at the Jungle.

London remained sixth as Jim Dymock scored twice in a 38-16 win at the Valley over Warrington.

Stuart Raper could hardly have got his Wigan coaching career off to a better start than he did at the Boulevard in the Saturday game of Round Eleven.

Denis Betts, with two tries, and Gary Connolly, who scored one, looked like new men as Hull were put to the sword 46-10.

Hull were being linked that weekend to Aussie stars Craig Greenhill at Penrith and Jamie Ainscough at St George Illawarra, with skipper Tony Grimaldi already signed for Canterbury Bulldogs for 2002. They were missing Luke Felsch who was out with medial ligament damage incurred at Wakefield the week before but there were no excuses as they fell to their first defeat at the Boulevard in Super League VI.

Bradford had already put the Blue Sox through the grinder on the Friday night with a 64-12 mauling after leading 40-0 at the break. Injury-hit Halifax - with Academy forward Andrew Brocklehurst on debut from the bench - weren't that bad either but the Bulls just blew them away with power, pace and invention.

Richard Marshall takes on Tonie Carroll, as the Giants, despite scoring 46 points, lose again

Tevita Vaikona was the main tormentor and Leon Pryce, about to sign a new long-term contract with the Bulls, collected a hat-trick. Henry Paul kicked ten goals.

There were also try hat-tricks for Paul Wellens and Anthony Stewart as St Helens hammered Salford 66-16 at Knowsley Road. The Reds were by this stage looking less and less likely to make the play-offs with injures to Bobbie Goulding, Warren Jowitt, Kris Tassell, Steve Blakeley, Mike Hancock and Graham Holroyd being compounded by the loss of Paul Southern with cruciate damage.

London Broncos were serious contenders and they proved it with a 25-12 win against the fifth-placed side for the past two season, Castleford Tigers.

There was no Richie Barnett but Dennis Moran was at his best, a key figure in midfield yet again, as the Broncos pulled away in the second half.

There was plenty of controversy as the Wildcats battled to their fifth win of the season, a 30-24 success over the Wolves at Wilderspool. Rookie ref Richard Silverwood copped some flak for disallowing two home tries in the closing minutes. "That's not the headline," blasted Wolves coach Darryl Van de Velde.

"The headline is poor defence," citing a missed one-on-one tackle by Jon Clarke - who was on debut after signing from London - that let in Martin Pearson for the winning try.

The Huddersfield Giants put on their best attacking show of the season at Headingley to rack up 46 points. Sadly for them, Leeds Rhinos scored 52. "A mixture of sublime and ridiculous", wrote Phil Caplan in League Express.

Meanwhile St Helens had to dismiss further reports that they had agreed a £400,000 fee for the sale of Keiron Cunningham to the Welsh RU.

Only one game in Round Twelve was played on the Spring Bank Holiday Monday and it turned out to be one of the most momentous of the season. Not because of the result, as St Helens beat Huddersfield at the McAlpine 44-26.

It was the game Sean Long was taken out late by Aussie stand-off Brandon Costin. It looked an innocuous challenge as Long kicked downfield but it was the end of Long's season, as he'd sustained serious cruciate damage.

The Giants lost Graham Appo for the season too through an accidental ankle injury, but that was hardly likely to affect Huddersfield's Championship chances - this was their record 12th straight defeat in Super League VI. Costin was suspended for three matches.

There was bad news for London too the day before as Jason Hetherington looked in danger of missing the rest of the season after damaging knee ligaments in a 14-12 home win over Halifax on the Sunday.

The Broncos led by eight points until Oliver Marns' converted try brought the Blue Sox to within two points.

Leeds got their defence back into shape with a 38-16 win over the Wildcats at Belle Vue. The Rhinos led 20-0 at the break, and Iestyn Harris scored two tries in a virtuoso performance.

Hull got back to winning form as Jason Smith led them to a 32-16 win over the Wolves at the Boulevard, Stanley Gene getting a decisive try 13 minutes from time.

Stuart Raper masterminded Wigan's 54-12 win against his old club, the Tigers, at the JJB on the Friday. Raper admitted to mixed emotions as his new side hammered the Tigers with nine tries, as Andy Farrell racked up another 22 points.

And the Bulls remained three points clear with a 42-10 home win over Salford, Lee Gilmour getting his first hat-trick for Bradford.

SUPER LEAGUE TABLE - *Monday 28th May*

	P	W	D	L	F	A	D	PTS
Bradford Bulls	12	10	1	1	415	196	219	21
Hull FC	12	8	2	2	337	276	61	18
Wigan Warriors	12	8	1	3	395	174	221	17
St Helens	12	8	1	3	388	341	47	17
Leeds Rhinos	12	8	0	4	387	301	86	16
London Broncos	12	7	0	5	259	215	44	14
Wakefield T Wildcats	12	5	0	7	217	332	-115	10
Castleford Tigers	12	4	1	7	252	304	-52	9
Warrington Wolves	12	4	0	8	280	353	-73	8
Salford City Reds	12	4	0	8	254	369	-115	8
Halifax Blue Sox	12	3	0	9	248	333	-85	6
Huddersfield Giants	12	0	0	12	224	462	-238	0

JUNE
Saints' Long road

St Helens' chances of making it three Super League Championships in a row looked to have been severely dented with the loss of Sean Long for the season and when Bradford came to visit on the first Saturday of June, they were also lacking hernia-victim Tommy Martyn. The Bulls, who had been in awesome form since the two had met in the Challenge Cup final, were widely expected to go six points clear of their main rivals with a comfortable enough win.

But the Saints outplayed them in sensational style, at half-time leading 28-10 and then soaking up a terrific comeback to within two points, before pulling away to 38-26 with late tries for Peter Shiels and Paul Sculthorpe – playing an absolute blinder at stand-off in his 100th game for the Saints.

"It was just another game to be honest," was Ian Millward's reaction. "They didn't hand out any trophies tonight."

"We lost the battle, but there are plenty of more battles to come and I am confident we can bounce back," said Brian Noble.

Sculthorpe finished with two tries and even took over the kicking mantle from Long, converting five goals in a wonderful game.

Saints' win gave Hull a big chance to close in on the Bulls and they moved to within a point with a 36-24 win at Salford. It was a third consecutive defeat for the Reds as Tony Smith, back from injury, scored a hat-trick of tries to take the Airlie Birds home.

Wigan sank to fifth after coming out the worse in an astounding game at Wilderspool, Warrington winning 47-38.

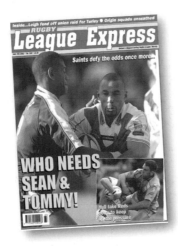

The Wolves were 12-0 down after seven minutes but by half-time had taken a massive 34-18 advantage. Twenty-three point Lee Briers and Alfie Langer ran the show from halfback and there were towering performances from Wigan old boy Jon Clarke at hooker and the ubiquitous Gary Mercer. It was a first defeat for Wigan under Stuart Raper.

But on the same night the London Broncos missed their chance to put pressure on the top-five when they went down 36-12 at Headingley.

The Broncos suffered the massive blow of losing Richie Barnett before the game when he strained a hamstring during the pre-match warm-up. Iestyn Harris played only the first 65 minutes but it was enough to get him the gamestar award as he mesmerised the Broncos, now lacking Barnett and Jason Hetherington. Chev Walker's try a minute before the break effectively wrapped up the game, making it 28-6 half-time.

Huddersfield fans were still wondering where their first win was coming from as the Blue Sox completed a comfortable eight-try 40-8 win over their neighbours at the Shay. The Giants gave former Halifax players Graeme Hallas and Toby Green debuts but with Andrew Dunemann – at the end of a week in which he signed a new-two-year contract with the Blue Sox - and Gavin Clinch re-united at halfback, they were 14-0 up in as many minutes.

The Cas-Wakefield re-match didn't disappoint as a disputed Richard Gay try two minutes from time secured a 26-22 win for the Tigers. Castleford coach Graham Steadman was more than happy to take his first win in charge at the Jungle but admitted: "We had a little bit of luck and Richard Gay capitalised on it." Cas were without five first team regulars and Wakefield had a patched up look too, but it didn't prevent a rip-roaring derby.

With the first 'Origin game' in midweek having been hailed a success (see separate chapter) press reports about Iestyn Harris's departure to rugby union resurfaced and, despite Gary Hetherington rubbishing the story, Leeds fans feared their captain's exit at the end of the season.

Warrington had yet another blow when hooker David Highton was suspended until April 30 2002 after pleading guilty to taking a steroid, although it was admitted he had taken the product in good faith.

And at Bradford, James Lowes and Brian McDermott signed contract extensions but it emerged that Henry Paul had yet to pledge his future to the club, with speculation mounting that he would leave the Bulls at the end of the season.

Henry wasn't letting the uncertainty get to him as he kicked eleven goals and scored a try in the Bulls' 78-18 Valley Parade hammering of the Giants.

Five tries in the opening 13 minutes decided the game, with Graham Mackay ending up with a try hat-trick.

In sixth spot the Broncos were falling off the pace but they gave St Helens a big test at Knowsley Road on the Friday night before losing 22-14. The Champions had to come from behind to snatch the points. Tries to skipper Chris Joynt and Steve Hall and a couple of match-winning tackles from Paul Wellens and Mick Higham were crammed into the last twelve action-packed minutes of a high quality match. Paul Sculthorpe was missing after having stitches in his upper lip after the Origin game and winger Tony Stewart was named at stand-off on the teamsheet.

Toa Kohe-Love was sent off for the second time in the season for a high tackle on Francis Maloney as the Reds ended their three-match losing run, beating the Wolves at the Willows 26-18. With Darren Brown the latest to join the casualty list, it was a welcome change of fortune for the Reds and their coach John Harvey. Kohe-Love was suspended for four games.

A dramatic try from Stuart Donlan seven minutes from time decided a cracking Sunday night game at the Shay, Halifax beating the Wildcats 26-20.

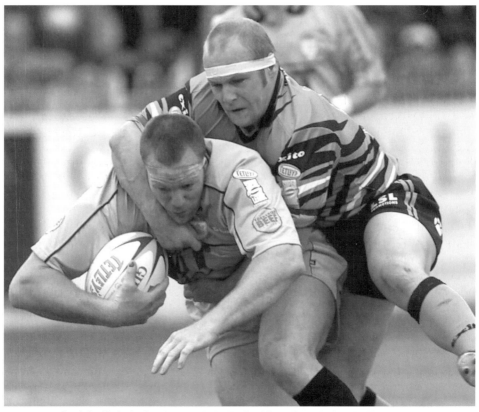

Castleford's Andy Speak grounds Hull's Paul Broadbent during the Tigers' win

Wakefield fans were livid at the loss of Dane Dorahy on half-time with concussion thanks to a Jim Gannon challenge that was put on report, with the big Aussie copping a three-match ban, reduced to two on appeal.

Trinity led 12-0 but by the break the Blue Sox had taken a 14-12 lead, with three tries, the third to Damian Gibson in his 100th appearance in a Blue Sox shirt. A Martin Pearson penalty just after the hour looked to have clinched it for the Wildcats, but Donlan's try, and a late Danny Tickle penalty gave the Blue Sox the points.

Castleford dealt Hull a blow with a 33-26 win in the Saturday night game at the Jungle. With Danny Orr injured, young Aussie Mark Lennon took his chance at scrum-half, with Mitch Healey moving to stand-off, and showed terrific pace for a try after only five minutes.

Hull, without Jason Smith, looked lost at times and did well to make a game of it after going down 24-10 six minutes into the second half.

The big game of the weekend was at Headingley on the Friday night, when Wigan beat Leeds 36-18, with Chris Chester getting his first start of the season, filling in for Matthew Johns at stand-off. With so many players backing up from the Origin game it was excellent fare, with Andy Farrell and Adrian Lam outstanding as the Warriors came back from a 12-10 half-time deficit. "It was a big game and I was as pumped up as the players," confessed Wigan coach Stuart Raper, who lost Gary Connolly with a dislocated shoulder.

As the action on the field continued to improve, the off-field state of the game came under fire again.

In an amazing attack on Sir Rodney Walker in League Express by former RFL president Ronnie Teeman, the chairman of the RFL was urged to quit. The criticism came on the back of rumours that the 2000 World Cup had in fact lost a considerable amount of money, instead of making the profit still forecast at the start of the year. There were even stories that the Samoan Rugby League had abandoned the game completely because it had received none of the monies it had been promised, This proved to be erroneous, but the expected development bonanza on the back of the World Cup was clearly no going to happen.

Meanwhile, a new Labour government had brought a new Sports Minister in Sheffield MP Richard Caborn, the first Rugby League supporter to hold the position.

On the field, Super League clubs rejected a proposal to bring Britain in line with Australia, and immediately institute the twelve changes from four subs rule; Jamie Ainscough was being strongly tipped to join Wigan for 2002, and Widnes Vikings coach Neil Kelly was the latest to be tipped for the Warrington Wolves' coaching job. Darryl Van de Velde was to return Down Under at the end of the season, but was to stay on to ease the transition to the new coach before the end of the season.

As the second half of the 28-game home and away season began reports emerged that Wakefield Wildcats, at the time next to bottom of the table on ten points, were on the brink of being deducted six league points for breaching the salary cap in 2000.

But you wouldn't have guessed they had any worries as Wakefield pushed St Helens all the way before they won 36-26 in a cracking game at Belle Vue. The returned Paul Sculthorpe eventually wrapped it up with his third try in the final minute. And the siege mentality was setting in at Belle Vue. "Nobody is going to get us," said coach John Harbin.

While Huddersfield were losing, it didn't matter how many points the Wildcats lost. The Giants slumped to their 17th straight defeat (including two at the end of Super League V) by 24-32 to Salford, but there were signs that things were finally coming together at the McAlpine. A 78th minute penalty from Francis Maloney finished them off, after Stuart Littler scored two crucial first-half tries.

The Tigers - giving a debut to on-loan signing Simon Lewis from the Bulls - suffered a double blow at Wilderspool. Not only did they go down 30-16 to Super League VI's enigma side, they lost Darren Rogers – filling in admirably for the injured Mike Eagar at centre - with a broken hand. A 72nd minute Jon Clarke try was the clincher.

The Friday TV game gladdened the hearts of Leeds fans as a young Rhinos side showed plenty of character to beat Hull 15-6 at the Boulevard, with Iestyn Harris an inspiration. Hull had Roosters prop Scott Logan on debut and led 6-0 at the break, but Danny Ward snapped an impromptu field goal a minute after the turnaround and it inspired the young Rhinos, a superb late Francis Cummins try sealing the win as Leeds leapfrogged Hull into fourth place in the table.

Wigan reached 50 for the third successive home game, beating Halifax 50-18 as Andy Farrell's third goal took him past 1,000 in his career. Steve Renouf finished with a hat-trick in a one-sided encounter.

It was one-way traffic too at Welford Road Leicester where London's biggest 'home' crowd of the year saw the Bulls hammer them 42-0. Marvin Golden and Mat Toshack had joined the Broncos injury list and the raw London talent given their chance – BARLA youth tourist Iain Morrison was on debut – was blown away by the most powerful side in Super League VI.

And then almost suddenly, there was a four-point gap between Bradford and the rest.

With a home banker to come on the Sunday against Wakefield, the Bulls could watch on with satisfaction on the Friday night as Wigan finally got the edge on Saints with a 29-28 success.

That week Wigan chairman Maurice Lindsay had negotiated a higher salary cap for his club for the 2002 season, although both Leeds and Huddersfield were rumoured to be about to reduce its wage bill by signing the out of favour Simon Haughton.

Saints out-scored Wigan five tries to four and the kicking of Andy Farrell proved pivotal, none more so than the monster field goal he converted on the stroke of half-time to send the Warriors in 21-12 to the good.

In the end Wigan were hanging on for dear life as Saints came back to within a point and the cover tackle by Brian Carney on Anthony Sullivan on the 72nd minute was probably the tackle of the season.

The result meant Wigan leapfrogged Saints into second but were four points adrift of the Bulls as Wakefield fell to 62-10 defeat on the Sunday, Henry Paul netting 20 points with a try and eight goals. Lesley Vainikolo was revealed in League Express the day after as a Bulls target for 2002.

Iestyn Harris pulled out of Leeds' game with Warrington on the Friday night because of the birth of his first child as the Rhinos sneaked a draw when Robbie Mears ducked and darted over for a try four minutes from time. The game was littered with 22 penalties, with referee Bob Connolly coming in for some stick from Leeds coach Daryl Powell.

Steve Prescott left it even later for Hull at Halifax as he launched a 41-metre field goal in the first minute of added time to gain a precious 27-26 win that put Hull back in fourth spot.

Cas Tigers got revenge on Salford Reds with a 26-18 win at the Willows in one of the least memorable games of the year.

And the Giants' losing run was over at last, as they notched a 22-all draw with the ailing Broncos.

The last four minutes at the McAlpine were probably the most action-packed of the year.

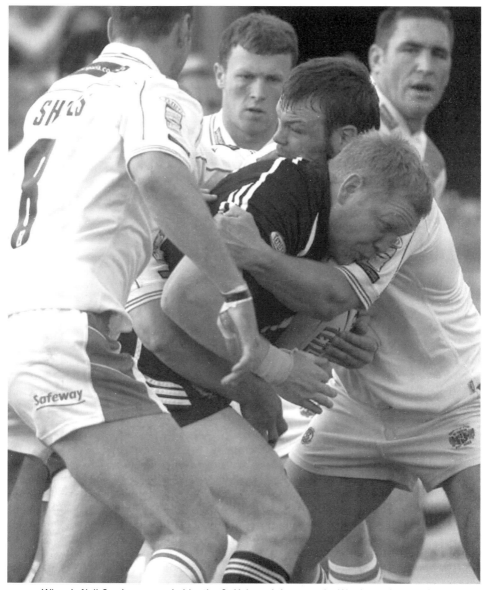

Wigan's Neil Cowie surrounded by the St Helens defence as the Warriors edge a thriller

London, who gave debuts to Paul Sykes and Rob Parker, on-loan from Bradford, were heading for victory poised at 18-10 before Paul Reilly twisted over from close range, Brandon Costin converting.

Within two minutes Costin's wayward pass landed in the arms of Dennis Moran who raced 50 metres for what had to be the winning try, even though Brett Warton's kick hit the post and bounced out.

Incredibly, Costin then sent in David Atkins at the other end and, as cool as a cucumber, converted the try from ten metres inside the touchline.

Significantly, the Giants had Stanley Gene (on loan from Hull) and Troy Stone (the former Hunter Mariners captain) on debut.

The Giants' draw with the Broncos had fired them with hope that they could escape relegation, and with the NFP shake-up involving mostly clubs with credible Super League cases, that was distinct possibility come the end of the season.

But going into Round 17, with twelve matches left to play, a yawning gap still existed between them and Wakefield in eleventh spot. So the Giants' visit to Belle Vue on that Sunday had added significance and their 38-22 win, with Stanley Gene and Troy Stone, on their full debuts, was a genuine four-pointer for Tony Smith's side. On-form stand-off Brandon Costin scored twice as Huddersfield beat their nearest rivals - the last team they had beaten in Super League the previous September.

The mood at Belle Vue was becoming increasingly nervous, with Super League Europe's auditors still waiting for some convincing arguments as to why they shouldn't have six league points docked for their salary cap breach of 2000.

Warrington Wolves were without Allan Langer who was performing miracles for Queensland in the State of Origin but they kept the play-off spots in sight with a 34-22 win over Halifax at Wilderspool. Blue Sox were missing Gavin Clinch, injured in Ireland's midweek hammering by France.

Hull got their first win in Super League over St Helens at the eighth attempt in the Saturday game. Shaun McRae's side - lacking Lee Jackson, Paul King and Adam Maher, and with Tony Smith playing with delayed concussion - came back from 16-8 down after 27 minutes of an action-packed encounter to lead 30-24 just after the hourmark, and held on to win 34-28. Tommy Martyn returned for Saints after a hernia operation and Chris Joynt set a club record with his 87th consecutive appearance, but the Champions suffered another blow with the loss of Paul Newlove for the season with a ruptured Achilles tendon.

Leeds missed the chance to move into fourth at the Jungle where the Tigers just held on after holding an 18-point lead to beat the Rhinos 28-26. Cas's only try of the second half - from on-loan Simon Lewis - was enough to hold off the Iestyn Harris-inspired Rhinos.

Martin Offiah scored his 500th career try (including those scored Down Under) as he went over just before half-time in Salford's shock 37-14 win over the Broncos at the Valley.

London gave a debut to France winger Sylvain Houles as they frantically tried to fill the injury gap.

But the big game of the weekend was at the JJB Stadium where Wigan announced their intentions with a 44-30 win over the Bulls. Kris Radlinski was again outstanding in a brilliant team performance, scoring a hat-trick, and hooker Terry Newton was fast gaining support for the Great Britain hooking spot with some brilliant dummy-half work. Wigan led 33-12 after Radlinski's third. but Bradford, with a try-double from Michael Withers, came back strongly in a week where they had to scotch rumours that Kiwi prop Joe Vagana was unhappy in England and set to return home.

SUPER LEAGUE TABLE - *Sunday 1st July*

	P	W	D	L	F	A	D	PTS
Bradford Bulls	17	13	1	3	653	306	347	27
Wigan Warriors	17	12	1	4	592	315	277	25
Hull FC	17	11	2	4	466	402	64	24
St Helens	17	11	1	5	540	470	70	23
Leeds Rhinos	17	10	1	6	506	407	99	21
Castleford Tigers	17	8	1	8	381	426	-45	17
Warrington Wolves	17	7	1	9	433	479	-46	15
London Broncos	17	7	1	9	321	374	-53	15
Salford City Reds	17	7	0	10	391	487	-96	14
Halifax Blue Sox	17	5	0	12	380	472	-92	10
Wakefield T Wildcats	17	5	0	12	317	520	-203	10
Huddersfield Giants	17	1	1	15	334	656	-322	3

JULY
Club Great Britain

Round 18 opened on a moving night for Bradford Bulls, who were given the chance to say farewell to fullback Stuart Spruce, who had played such a big part in the Bulls revolution in Super League. A shoulder operation meant the former Great Britain player's season was ended and he was the subject of a special tribute at Valley Parade after Bulls' game with Hull.

First v third should have been a tight contest, but the Bulls, who that week confirmed they had signed Lesley Vainikolo, made Hull look ordinary in a 40-0 win. The Paul brothers shared four tries – Robbie's second his 100th for the Bulls as Henry became the first player to pass 100 goals in Super League this season – against a Hull side missing Steve Prescott and winger Gareth Raynor, who had starred in their win the week before over St Helens.

Saints got full revenge for their pre-Cup final hammering at Warrington as Paul Sculthorpe led the rout in a 70-16 win at Knowsley Road.

Sculthorpe kicked eleven goals from a dozen attempts and scored two of Saints' twelve tries for a 30-point haul to confirm his standing as the brightest star in the English game.

Coach Ian Millward's vision of a team of multi-skilled players, each capable of filling several roles, often in the same game, was borne out again, as Keiron Cunningham joined skipper Chris Joynt on the sidelines.

The Huddersfield Giants' revival continued, even in defeat. Super League's bottom club repeatedly had high-flying Wigan Warriors rattled at the McAlpine before going down 48-24. They led twice early on, were level at half-time and Wigan made it a flattering scoreline with two tries in the last three minutes. Even after Wigan had gone 36-12 ahead Huddersfield hit back to be only 12 points behind going into the last six minutes.

Brandon Costin took over the captaincy of Huddersfield's injury-hit side and led by example. He grabbed an early first try and pulled off a lightning interception late on when he raced 70 metres to set up a try for Paul Reilly. Four goals added to Costin's major contribution.

Wigan - whose stand-off Matthew Johns was reportedly a target for Cronulla coach designate Chris Anderson - were also well under-strength, but they still had plenty of other stars to pull them round when things got rocky. Andy Farrell led the way with an inspiring performance that brought him 24 points from two tries and eight goals.

Wildcats coach John Harbin claimed that he had cheated the fans who made the long trek to the capital, after his side's seventh successive defeat, London winning 26-6 at the Valley.

London's Jim Dymock held by Wakefield's Gary Price during the Broncos' 26-6 win

The Broncos, who hadn't a win in their last five games, seemed to have found a stop-gap solution to the absence of Jason Hetherington, with stand-in Glen Air taking the gamestar award.

At the Shay, Halifax dealt a cruel blow to the Tigers' play-off hopes with late tries to Johnny Lawless and Adam Hughes securing a 22-16 win in another cliff-hanger.

The Tigers, seeking their fifth win in their last six games, were 10-2 up at the break, but Andrew Dunemann inspired a terrific Blue Sox comeback with Hughes' 77th minute try sealing it.

And Leeds got their play-off aspirations back on track with a comprehensive ten-try 56-6 demolition of an out-of-sorts Salford Reds.

Karl Pratt and Bradley Clyde were back in the Rhinos starting line-up, and Kevin Sinfield celebrated his new four-year contract with a quality midfield performance which included eight goals, as Iestyn Harris struggled gamely to overcome a knee injury.

When Harris left the fray in the 52nd minute - allowing the next outstanding talent, Danny McGuire, to make his debut - the job was done at 38-6.

St Helens coach Ian Millward got Round 19 off to a bang with an amazing outburst after Saints' 46-24 victory over top-five rivals Leeds Rhinos at Knowsley Road.

Millward launched a scathing attack on Leeds prop Barrie McDermott, after he had clashed with Saints' Australian forward David Fairleigh in the first minute of Friday's match.

He warned that players risked being dragged into court. "McDermott lashed out at Fairleigh and he got away with it," blasted Millward. "He should at least have been put in the sin bin and told to calm down. Had he connected cleanly, that could have been a bad situation.

"And I think there are two players in the British game, in Barrie McDermott and Harvey Howard, who are prime candidates to have that happen to them. Barrie has got it in for Australians."

Leeds boss Gary Hetherington blasted back: "We're very disappointed with the comments that were made and particularly that he chose to air these views to a packed press conference. The fact that he also chose to single out two individual players and make very damaging accusations about them is not only damaging to the players concerned, but also the game as a whole."

On the field Saints – with Tommy Martyn at the top of his game - were irresistible, particularly in the third quarter, when three tries in eight minutes sapped the resistance of obdurate Leeds.

That the first two came when the hosts were down to twelve men, Chris Joynt cooling his heels in the sin bin after one interference at the play-the-ball too many, said much for the Champions' unwavering self-belief. The so-called fringe players drafted in, like John Stankevitch, Tim Jonkers and Wayne McDonald, were able to effortlessly slot into the well-worn groove, as Paul Sculthorpe scored a try hat-trick and kicked seven goals.

Saints need to keep winning as Hull bounced back from the blow to their morale at Bradford, with a late, late 24-20 win at London. The Airlie Birds were trailing by two points going into the last two minutes when rookie referee Richard Silverwood awarded them their 13th and most decisive penalty of a pulsating game.

Shaun McRae admitted after that he was trying to get a message to skipper Tony Grimaldi to take two points, which would have given them a share of the spoils. Grimaldi and Jason Smith, however, believed that their side were down by four and opted to run the ball.

As the Hull coach was preparing to give the pair a roasting back in the dressing room, Smith picked the ball up from acting halfback to cross the whitewash for Steve Prescott to convert his fourth goal.

Wigan almost stumbled at Wakefield but emerged with a scratchy 29-23 success. Andy Farrell's 64th minute try and goal finally put Wigan back in the lead and set them up for the win.

Halifax coach Steve Linnane didn't know whether to laugh or cry after his side recovered from 20-8 down at Salford to earn their second away victory of the season and move above the Reds in the Super League table. "It was a coach's nightmare," said Linnane after the 50-24 win.

July

Tony Smith's nightmare was turning into a dream though as his Giants registered their second win of the season in style – a 52-10 mauling of Warrington at the McAlpine.

It was the Giants' first home win of the Super League season and narrowed the gap at the bottom of the table to five points. Captain Brandon Costin was a clear gamestar with a 24-point haul but it was a terrific team performance by Smith's side.

League Express reporter Mike Latham couldn't find one candidate for the Wolves' man of the match award.

At the other end of the table Bradford celebrated becoming the first club to have one million fans pass through the turnstiles in the Super League era by proving there was no shortage of life at Valley Parade without the Paul brothers.

With their prized Kiwi halfback pairing still on the plane back from New Zealand after the previous Friday's Anzac Test, and Leon Pryce coming in from the wing to partner Paul Deacon at halfback, Bradford overcame a little uncertainty and an early Castleford try to hit back with seven of their own and comfortably maintain their 100% home record with a 44-4 win.

In mid-July, with Bradford the centre of national media attention because of race riots in the city, it was revealed that Henry Paul was set to switch codes. Several potential targets for a replacement had already been mentioned Down Under - including the Roosters' explosive State of Origin centre Matt Sing.

St Helens remained determined to hang on to international hooker, Keiron Cunningham, despite continued speculation linking him with a move to rugby union.

Reports suggested that Cunningham and his international teammate, Iestyn Harris, would both be unveiled by the Welsh Rugby Union in the next few days, as part of a £1million raid on League.

Saints confirmed that they have knocked back two big money offers from Swansea RUFC, but despite being braced for further bids, they remained defiant.

Meanwhile, after union official Peter Wheeler had claimed in an interview with an Australian newspaper that top Super League clubs had been in discussions to switch their operations to rugby union, Hull chief executive Shane Richardson, also a Super League board member, made some forthright comments: "Those people who have had discussions with him, no matter who they are, should show the balls to stand up and tell people what they're doing. I don't want to be sitting in the same room as people (who are talking to rugby union), while we're discussing how to move our game forward. If you don't have Rugby League in your heart, go and form a basketball team, or form a volleyball team, but don't talk to me about forming a hybrid game with rugby union."

By the end of the month the RFL had put together a joint initiative with Super League (Europe) to create 'Club Great Britain' - a funding arm to boost elite players' contracts, effectively putting them on central contracts and reducing the chances of the game losing its key international players to union. The first beneficiary of the new initiative was expected to be St Helens star Cunningham.

Meanwhile RFL chairman Sir Rodney Walker said: "We are looking forward to

Salford's Francis Maloney on the charge during the City Reds' 70-4 defeat at Wigan

the publication of our Strategic Planning report in August which we believe will be the launch pad for a bright future for our game."

Walker had appointed Nigel Wood, who had quit as chief executive of struggling Halifax, to write the wide-ranging report which was to map out the game's future.

John Harvey quit as head coach of Salford City Reds, following their 70-4 mauling at Wigan on the Friday night of Round 20.

The Australian met with Reds chief executive David Tarry the following morning, and tendered his resignation and was succeeded until the end of the season by his assistant, Steve McCormack, who, at 28, became the youngest head coach in Super League.

The Warriors ran in twelve tries and Andy Farrell, who scored two of them, added eleven goals from just about every angle with some perfectly struck kicking.

Another coach, Darryl Van de Velde, due to leave at the end of the season, was just one game away from departure after watching his side lose 31-28 at home to the Broncos. On the Warrington board's instructions, he had to deliver his post-match verdict from the bowels of the stadium as a peaceful protest by frustrated Wolves fans, calling for his immediate removal, took place behind the main stand.

71

July

It was a game that the Wolves, slumping to their third successive loss in a run that had seen them finally fall off the play-off pace, should have won. The Broncos had Dewsbury centre Dan Potter on loan and another loanee, Bradford's Paul Sykes, sealed the game for them with a late field goal.

Bradford found Leeds a tough nut to crack at Valley Parade but came through with a 44-22 win after a magnificent game, which had Bulls coach Brian Noble in combative mood.

"I'm sick and tired of hearing about rugby union," he said at the beginning of the post-match press conference. "I'm not an outspoken person but I feel I've had an absolute gutful of negative comments about Rugby League. I think the obituary columns are a little bit premature.

"We've seen another magnificent spectacle today. It was absolutely fantastic. And it gets better and better. I don't want to talk about rugby union again. We've all got a responsibility to promote the game of Rugby League."

It seemed to be a major blow to the Bulls when Michael Withers pulled out with a groin strain but Leon Pryce stepped in at fullback and played his best game for a long time, finishing Leeds off with a length of the field try in the 73rd minute.

Dean Sampson's 400th appearance in a Castleford shirt was marked with a 20-14 victory but the prop and his teammates were fortunate to bring Huddersfield Giants' renaissance to a halt.

Tigers coach Graham Steadman pleaded guilty to Giants counterpart Tony Smith's accusation that the hosts had got out of jail at The Jungle, after Huddersfield's enterprising brand of rugby failed to earn the reward of two Super League points.

After the Giants had left the field, Sampson's colleagues stayed on the pitch to hail 'Diesel' as he embarked on a lap of honour with his four-year-old son Joseph.

Hull and St Helens stayed neck and neck in the table with wins. Keiron Cunningham scored two tries a Saints won 46-22 at Halifax and a 24-point haul from fullback Steve Prescott cemented Hull's fourth place while opening up a five-point lead over their closest rivals, Leeds Rhinos.

As we entered the last weekend of July, confusion reigned as to Wakefield's exact points-total in Super League as Super League Europe deducted four points for their 2000 Salary Cap breach, but then, according to the club, re-instated them until an appeal could be heard by the RFL.

It made Trinity's 18-19 loss at home to Warrington all the harder to take - a tenth successive defeat for the Wildcats in what was Darryl Van de Velde's last match in charge of the Wolves.

Lee Briers' 77th minute field goal that made it 19-12 to Warrington proved to be the vital point.

When asked how he felt about it being his last match in charge, Van de Velde abruptly replied. "I've finished the press conference and I'm going home mate."

Warrington still didn't have a coach. The favourite for the job, Neil Kelly, had opted to stay with NFP Champions Widnes as they looked certain to be in Super League the following year.

Wakefield's Paul March tackled by Warrington's Dean Busby during the Wolves' one-point win

Fortunately for Wakefield the Giants were losing, narrowly, again, this time a 32-26 home defeat to Leeds. A Tonie Carroll hat-trick helped the Rhinos re-establish their four-point advantage over London on the edge of the top five, but not before a few heartstopping scares against the resurgent Giants.

Wigan completed a perfect ten wins out of ten since Hull entered Super League in 1998 as Steve Renouf and Brian Carney took centre stage. Former Australian Test great Renouf was still in prime attacking form at the veteran stage of his career while the charismatic Carney, who learned the ropes of Rugby League in two years under Shaun McRae at Gateshead and at Hull, was emerging as a genuine Test hopeful.

Tony Rea's London Broncos had Richie Barnett back and were still nicely poised for the play-offs after a 40-10 win over the Tigers at the Valley, with Paul Sykes having a blinder on the wing.

New Salford coach Steve McCormack couldn't look back with any great fondness on his first match in charge of the City Reds, a 56-18 thrashing by St Helens.

Saints ran in ten tries against three and had two further efforts ruled out for forward passes, in a match that was marred by a high tackle by Gary Broadbent on reserve hooker Mick Higham, which broke the youngster's jaw. Broadbent received a five-match ban.

And Tevita Vaikona scored a memorable hat-trick as the Bulls maintained their two-point lead at the top of the Super League after a full-blooded West Yorkshire derby on a glorious summer's evening at the Shay, Bradford beating local rivals Halifax 52-28.

SUPER LEAGUE TABLE - *Sunday 29th July*

	P	W	D	L	F	A	D	PTS
Bradford Bulls	21	17	1	3	833	360	473	35
Wigan Warriors	21	16	1	4	775	378	397	33
St Helens	21	15	1	5	758	550	208	31
Hull FC	21	13	2	6	550	514	36	28
Leeds Rhinos	21	12	1	8	640	529	111	25
London Broncos	21	10	1	10	438	442	-4	21
Castleford Tigers	21	9	1	11	431	546	-115	19
Warrington Wolves	21	8	1	12	506	650	-144	17
Halifax Blue Sox	21	7	0	14	502	620	-118	14
Salford City Reds	21	7	0	14	453	719	-266	14
Wakefield T Wildcats	21	5	0	16	380	642	-262	10
Huddersfield Giants	21	2	1	18	450	766	-316	5

AUGUST
Wildcats feel the heat

Steve Anderson quit his post at Headingley to become the new chief at Warrington and watching his first game he must have thought he'd landed on a goldmine.

The Bulls had looked stronger than ever since their defeat at Wigan in Round 17 racking up 180 points in a four-match winning run that not one person would have predicted would have ended at Wilderspool in Round 22. But it did. "If only Warrington could be a club in turmoil more frequently, the Wolves would be already qualified for the play-offs," wrote Nathan Ashurst in League Express.

Coach-less and skipper-less – Allan Langer had decided he'd had enough and gone home with Darryl Van de Velde - in the run-up the game, trepidation proved too much for many of the Wolves fans who couldn't face turning up to witness the expected slaughter.

The Wolves won 18-14, Rob Smyth's scintillating effort a minute from time finally breaking the deadlock between the two sides.

The Saturday night defeat for the Bulls meant Wigan, who had already gained their two points the night before with a 46-18 home win over London, moved level on points at the top.

The Broncos' play-off hopes were left hanging by a thread after they were blown away in the final quarter, Kris Radlinski's second try, on the hour, sparking Wigan's impressive late flourish.

Saints – who'd confirmed the signing of Newcastle winger Darren Albert for 2002 - missed their chance to get within two points of the Bulls and Wigan when they were stunned by the Tigers in the Friday night TV game at the Jungle.

Castleford, whose second defeat of St Helens in 12 Super League matches revived hopes of a play-off place, played the last 26 minutes without both their Australian halfbacks – Mark Lennon and Mitch Healey - who had been key figures in the exhilarating fightback.

St Helens almost snatched victory when Paul Sculthorpe lunged over with the big screen showing only eleven seconds left. But referee Karl Kirkpatrick ruled he had lost the ball.

More confusion surrounded Wakefield's points deduction as Super League Europe handed their case onto the RFL for another hearing. But the official ruling was that the points came off, which left them on six, only one above the revived Giants.

Wakefield's 26-16 defeat at Salford – with Michael Hancock turning the game with two pieces of class, despite playing with a virus - gave reds coach Steve McCormack his first victory, a late Stuart Littler try finally killing off a brave

Wakefield fightback.

Wakefield could breathe a small sigh of relief as the Giants – giving a debut off the bench to on-loan Maori international Martin Moana - went down at Hull 36-16, with scrum-half Richard Horne producing a superb performance, including a stunning opportunist try.

Leeds stayed six points clear of London in the last play-off berth with a 36-18 win over Halifax – who had Paul Davidson, back for his first game since a three-match ban, sent off in the second half for a challenge on Keith Senior. He escaped suspension.

Ryan Sheridan was back for his first home start of the campaign, while Karl Pratt filled in superbly for Iestyn Harris, who was that week announced as a signing for the Welsh Rugby Union, the day after Keiron Cunningham pledged his future to St Helens. The Welsh RU did themselves no credit by petulantly claiming that Cunningham had never proved his Welsh ancestry. League Express published a copy of his grandfather's birth certificate the following Monday.

By the start of Round 23, every team had met each other home and away and the extra six games threw up some mighty matches. And the vagaries of the draw meant that Leeds, although six points clear with six games to go, were expected to slip to sixth, with London Broncos taking their place.

That Saturday Leeds - without Anthony Farrell who was suspended for one game after being found guilty of illegal use of his knees on Halifax Blue Sox's Andrew Dunemann - lost to the Bulls 34-6 at Headingley.

At Knowsley Road the night before, Saints produced another display out of the top drawer to re-affirm their desire to retain their Super League crown, Keiron Cunningham playing a pivotal role in a five-try 30-16 success over their oldest and most bitter rivals Wigan.

The Wolves stuck to their new policy on youth which had proved so successful against the Bulls with Dave Alstead starting at fullback and Gary Hulse handed his full debut at scrum-half, whilst Paul Smith - recently signed on loan from Dewsbury - made the bench. It worked as they beat Castleford 27-12.

The RFL looked kindly in Wakefield's salary cap transgressions and reduced their points-deduction from four to two. But the breathing space was wiped out that Sunday as they sank to defeat in London – who welcomed back Jason Hetherington from a ten-match absence with a knee injury - this time by 44-18, while the Giants got the better of Salford, 35-14, with Brandon Costin again the gamestar, with a try, seven goals and a field goal.

With NFP Champions Widnes Vikings having that week been told that they would be promoted to Super League, the pressure was on.

Hull completed their third victory from three starts against the Blue Sox - helped by the dismissal of Paul Davidson for the second time in as many matches following a foul on Richard

Horne. This time Davidson was suspended for five matches and fined £250 for the 'deliberate use of the forearm to the neck of an opponent'.

Bradford Bulls coach Brian Noble's assessment of the Friday night game summed up the Bulls' 27-14 Round 24 win over champions St Helens, a result that made a fourth-place finish for Saints look almost inevitable: "It was a fantastic game of rugby. It had everything – atmosphere, speed, controversial decisions and great tries from both teams."

It was certainly an extraordinary game in that Bradford's victory was built on six penalty goals by Henry Paul, plus three field goals from Paul Deacon. Paul also added two conversions. St Helens looked shattered after scoring three tries to two.

On the Saturday Leeds made their play-off place secure with a 17-10 win at the Jungle – coming back from 10-2 down, in the week that the Rhinos appointed Malcolm Reilly as assistant to Daryl Powell. Cas gave a debut to on-loan Hull KR back-rower Chris Charles from the bench, while

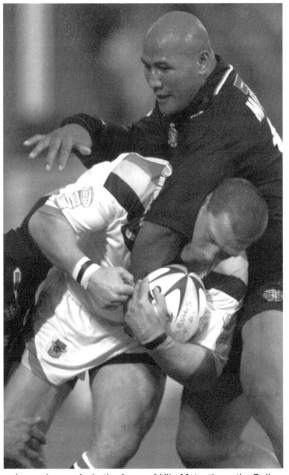

James Lowes feels the force of Vila Matautia as the Bulls defeat the Saints at Valley Parade for the second time in 2001

Gary Mercer made a second debut for Leeds after joining them from Warrington.

Wakefield finally put an end to the longest run of defeats in the club's history – 12 straight losses - and collected two vital points with a 23-20 win over Salford at Belle Vue. A 77th minute field goal from Martin Pearson finally ended a stunning Reds comeback and brought the points home to Wakefield.

The Giants' four-year hold on their Super League place was looking increasingly tenuous after the Blue Sox beat them 19-12 at the Shay.

A late field goal by Danny Tickle secured a hat-trick of wins for the Blue Sox over their local rivals in a bad tempered affair. Giants hooker Paul Rowley was suspended for three-matches after being spotted on video using knees in a tackle on Andrew Dunemann, reduced to one game on appeal.

Hull just about killed off London's play-off hopes with a 28-12 home win led by 20-point man of the match Steve Prescott and Paul King, who had just signed a new four-year deal at Boulevard. Hull also announced that they had signed Wolves centre Toa Kohe-Love for 2002.

The Kiwi was dropped for Warrington's visit to Wigan as Steve Anderson looked to the future by fielding thee more trialists in Steve Thomas, David Whittle and David Bates, from Leeds, Leigh and Castleford respectively. Wigan won 28-12 in another fiery encounter between the two clubs.

The play-off spots were decided by the end of Round 25 when the Giants turned the Broncos over at the Valley 21-12. Leeds lost to Wigan too, 38-18, but they were safe in fifth, six points clear of the Broncos, with a hugely superior points difference.

Andy Farrell broke the Super League points in a season record set by Sean Long (352) in 2000 with his first of seven successful conversions at Headingley. That week the Rhinos announced they had captured the NRL's top pointscorer, Ben Walker from Northern Eagles, for 2002.

The crowd at the Valley of less than 2,000 was the worst of the season and the following week it emerged that Richard Branson was keen to offload ownership of the London club, with a bizarre plan to relocate to Leigh being mooted.

Damian Gibson, playing against the club he had signed for for 2002, grabbed a crucial try and Stuart Donlan and Daryl Cardiss a brace apiece as the Blue Sox completed a hat-trick of wins over the Reds. A game of 13 tries produced another huge scoreline of 41-30.

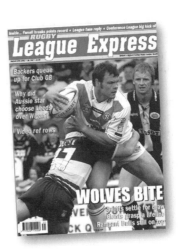

A Wilderspool crowd of just under 8,000 was richly entertained as Warrington and Saints drew 28-28. The Wolves had Anthony Swann and Kevin Crouthers on trialist debuts, while youngsters John Kirkpatrick, Dave McConnell and John Braddish were given their first senior chance by Ian Millward.

At Valley Parade the Bulls, inspired by the brilliant Henry Paul, blasted their way into a 38-2 lead minutes before half-time and ran out 56-30 winners over the Tigers –who had learned that skipper Adrian Vowles was to join Leeds the next season.

And on the Bank Holiday Monday Hull beat Wakefield at Belle Vue for he second time in the year, this time by 30-18. "We won the toss and they went to the video screen, so we knew we were in trouble then!" said Wakefield coach John Harbin after a number of close calls went against the Wildcats.

SUPER LEAGUE TABLE - *Monday 27th August*

	P	W	D	L	F	A	D	PTS
Bradford Bulls	25	20	1	4	964	428	536	41
Wigan Warriors	25	19	1	5	903	456	447	39
Hull FC	25	17	2	6	676	576	100	36
St Helens	25	16	2	7	856	649	207	34
Leeds Rhinos	25	14	1	10	717	629	88	29
London Broncos	25	11	1	13	524	555	-31	23
Warrington Wolves	25	10	2	13	591	732	-141	22
Castleford Tigers	25	10	1	14	511	672	-161	21
Halifax Blue Sox	25	9	0	16	596	730	-134	18
Salford City Reds	25	8	0	17	543	834	-291	16
Wakefield T Wildcats •	25	6	0	19	455	762	-307	10
Huddersfield Giants	25	4	1	20	534	847	-313	9

• *Deducted two points for breach of salary cap rules*

SEPTEMBER
Giants fall

Salford hooker Malcolm Alker broke the Super League record for tackles made in a season, when he made the first of his 43 tackles during the Reds' Round 26 50-12 home defeat by London Broncos.

Alker tackled Broncos fullback Richie Barnett after one minute 13 seconds, taking him to 943 tackles for the season, surpassing the previous Super League record of 942 held by former Gateshead Thunder and Hull forward Luke Felsch.

A magical try from Brett Dallas turned the game of the weekend at the JJB on Friday evening Wigan's way and left the Warriors still in contention for the Minor Premiership after a 16-10 win over the Bulls. Wigan moved level on points at the top of Super League after their second home win over the Bulls in a game far different in character to their 44-30 success back in June.

It capped a marvellous week for the Warriors, after, with the help of Club GB, they secured the services for another five years of Kris Radlinski.

Hull backed up from a battle against other relegation candidates Wakefield the previous Monday and edged an increasingly desperate Giants outfit 36-30 at the McAlpine; while Leeds brought down the curtain on Super League VI at Headingley, beating Warrington – who had PNG international Tom O'Reilly on trial - 16-12 in a mistake-ridden contest.

The inspiration of the brilliant Keiron Cunningham and a hat-trick from full-debutant Dave McConnell were central to a comfortable 44-20 St Helens defeat of Castleford Tigers.

And Wakefield moved three points clear of the Giants at the bottom with a crucial 23-10 win at the Shay. Martin Pearson's eleven-point contribution from the boot proved crucial.

The tension was almost too much to bear at Belle Vue the following Saturday as Huddersfield just about deserved their 21-19 win over the Wildcats, to set up a white knuckle final round.

Welsh international Hefin O'Hare's 63rd minute converted try made it 18-13 to Huddersfield and they stayed ahead in a tense finish with a Brandon Costin penalty and Ben Kusto field goal stretching the lead before David March's try two minutes from time set up a nail-biting finish.

Henry Paul broke records in Bradford Bulls' 84-12 demolition of Warrington Wolves at Wilderspool – a club record defeat for Warrington. His ten goals and a try helped him to break his own club records for goals and points in a season.

Cas fought back magnificently after being down 28-6 in the second half to fall 30-22 to Wigan at the Jungle; and the Broncos again made the most of the adversity at the club to record a stunning 46-8 victory over the Blue Sox. "Maybe Virgin should have announced their decision to offload the club earlier in the season" wrote Neil Fissler in his match report in League Express. The Broncos future was settled when minority shareholder David Hughes bought the club, with Virgin staying on as major sponsors, but the search was on again for a new home.

Hull easily accounted for Salford by 40-8 at the Boulevard; and Leeds proved they might not be just making up the numbers in the play-offs after all, with a surprise 23-18 win at Knowsley Road, condemning Saints to a fourth place finish. It marked the end of Robbie Mears' English career as he had his jaw broken in a late tackle by Sonny Nickle. Nickle was banned for six months, later amended to nine matches. Mears decided to return home less than a year into his two-year contract.

The last regular round of Super League VI was overshadowed by the horrific attacks on the World Trade Centre and the Pentagon in the USA, and a minute's silence was held before every match as a mark of respect and solidarity.

Wakefield coach John Harbin piloted his side to a nerve-wracking 32-24 victory at Salford City Reds to avoid finishing at the bottom of Super League.

Trinity looked in danger of dropping into the Northern Ford Premiership when Salford led 24-14 after 43 minutes.

But a last half hour of madness by the home side resulting in Russell Smith working overtime led them to losing three key players sent off: Stuart Littler, ex-Wildcat Bobbie Goulding and Graham Holroyd. Trinity centre Justin Brooker was also red-carded in the mayhem, leaving Harbin to muse: "There was certainly a lot of traffic coming past the dug out!"

David March sent the Wildcats fans delirious with a final try in injury-time.

The Giants beat London Broncos 28-24 on the same afternoon, but it wasn't enough for them to avoid the drop, with Giants coach Tony Smith, who had done a fine job in turning the team around in 2001, saying it would "be crazy to let a team, a backer, and a club like this go."

But go they did, even though Wakefield had failed their Super League points assessment. As the autumn rolled on the Wakefield club was in disarray, with star men Willie Poching and Ryan Hudson signing for local rivals Leeds and Castleford respectability, and John Harbin moving to the chief executive job at Dewsbury.

The Bulls' 62-18 thrashing of injury-hit Leeds Rhinos – with another young gun, Gareth Morton, on debut - wrapped up the Minor Premiership with a record 1,120 points.

Wigan dealt a big blow to St Helens with a 40-6 hammering, with David Furner the standout in an awesome team display; Warrington beat Castleford to seventh spot in the table, beating them at the Jungle 31-28; and Hull beat Halifax for the fourth time in 2001 by 20-16, the Black and Whites' seventh consecutive win.

Bradford's Jamie Peacock takes on Leeds duo Keith Senior and Kevin Sinfield as the Bulls seal the Minor Premiership with a big win at Valley Parade

In September the long awaited findings of the Strategic Planning Committee were presented to the clubs. When the RFL Council came to accept the plan, only ten of its original 100-plus recommendations were approved, with Super League rejecting a 10-team league, opting instead to stick at twelve. However, a decision was taken to split the current two divisions into three by incorporating another two lower divisions in a five-division National League structure by 2003.

Sir Rodney Walker announced he would quit the chairmanship of the RFL in January as the board was to be replaced by directors with no club interests.

But nothing could deflect the attention from the most exciting yet of Super League's play-off series.

SUPER LEAGUE FINAL TABLE - *Sunday 16th September*

	P	W	D	L	F	A	D	PTS
Bradford Bulls	28	22	1	5	1120	474	646	45
Wigan Warriors	28	22	1	5	989	494	495	45
Hull FC	28	20	2	6	772	630	142	42
St Helens	28	17	2	9	924	732	192	36
Leeds Rhinos	28	16	1	11	774	721	53	33
London Broncos	28	13	1	14	644	603	41	27
Warrington Wolves	28	11	2	15	646	860	-214	24
Castleford Tigers	28	10	1	17	581	777	-196	21
Halifax Blue Sox	28	9	0	19	630	819	-189	18
Salford City Reds	28	8	0	20	587	956	-369	16
Wakefield T Wildcats ●	28	8	0	20	529	817	-288	14
Huddersfield Giants	28	6	1	21	613	926	-313	13

● *Deducted two points for breach of salary cap rules*

3
SUPER LEAGUE PLAY-OFFS 2001

Qualifying Play-off

WIGAN WARRIORS 27..**HULL FC 24**

at the JJB Stadium, Friday 21st September

Wigan Warriors took the victory and Hull FC the plaudits after a pulsating play-off.

As the Warriors moved to within one game of the Grand Final, Hull FC contemplated a home tie the following Friday after a mighty effort that came within a whisker of achieving their first ever Super League win over the Warriors.

The Hull effort was even more remarkable considering they lost their two key playmakers for half of this game, and for the rest of the season.

The former Wigan halfback Tony Smith quit the action at half-time with a groin injury, while the outstanding Jason Smith was forced off early in the second half with a dislocated elbow.

Despite those blows, Hull simply refused to lie down and the Warriors were relieved to hear the final hooter.

The kicking of Andy Farrell, as so often, proved the difference between the two sides with the try-count ending at four-apiece. Farrell landed six goals from as many attempts, including a superb touch-line effort to Brian Carney's first-half try and a similar effort, though from the opposite wing, to Denis Betts's try with 15 minutes remaining. Farrell also ended the scoring with a close-range field goal seven minutes from time and helped the Warriors recover from a poor start with a close-range try.

Matt Crowther, who kicked four from five for Hull, saw his conversion attempt to Maiden's first-half try rebound from a post while Jason Smith pulled an early field goal attempt wide.

"I thought we answered the critics that reckoned we were the pretenders," said Hull coach Shaun McRae. "We are now contenders."

Hull skipper Tony Grimaldi and his second-row partner Adam Maher were both in inspirational form for Hull, getting through a mountain of defensive work and constantly driving the ball forward. Paul King, Paul Cooke and Richard Horne, switched to halfback in the second half, were other stand-outs with Lee Jackson and Logan Campbell making big impacts off the bench.

Jason Smith and King carved out a third-minute try for Cooke as Hull started impressively and Mick Cassidy made an important tackle on Cooke to prevent the Warriors falling further behind while Jason Smith was off-target with a one-pointer.

Wigan drew level when Terry Newton's smart work from the ruck sent Farrell bursting over after Adrian Lam had been held up by Grimaldi, and then Carney fought off the attentions of three defenders after quick hands by Lam and Gary Connolly to open up a 12-6 lead midway through the first half.

Crowther reduced the arrears with a confidently struck 40-metre penalty before David Maiden grabbed a superb, equalising try. Jason Smith's high kick to the corner was struck with stunning accuracy and Maiden timed his run and leap to perfection to claim the touchdown.

Hull thoroughly deserved to go in on level terms at the break but Kris

Tony Grimaldi hauls down Wigan's Matthew Johns as Hull go close at the JJB Stadium

Radlinski's opportunist try, with less than two minutes remaining gave the Warriors a six-point buffer.

Wigan moved further ahead when Farrell potted a penalty after Scott Logan was placed on report for a high tackle on Matthew Johns, until Horne's slick pass sent Luke Felsch over in David Furner's tackle.

The Warriors had Neil Cowie placed on report for a high shot, although he escaped a ban, receiving a fine instead, before Betts made a vital interception on halfway to set up an attack that ended when he took Farrell's pass to fight his way over in the left corner.

At 26-18 Wigan looked safe but still Hull refused to concede defeat and Cooke's deflected kick created a try for Jackson that made for a tense closing ten minutes broken only by Farrell's one-pointer.

Elimination Play-off
ST HELENS 38 ....**LEEDS RHINOS 30**

at Knowsley Road, Saturday 22nd September

Champions St Helens' dogged determination and the "foot of God" was just enough to eliminate Leeds Rhinos in a pulsating play-off.

When St Helens were under pressure near their own line midway through the second half, Tommy Martyn saw a spare ball on the field and quick-wittedly kicked it inside so that the referee had to hold up play while it was removed. The brief stoppage gave the Saints' defence a few extra seconds to regroup and Martyn later laughed off any suggestion of gamesmanship by saying: "It was the foot of God!"

Martyn's action - for which he later apologised - copped him a fair amount of criticism, but the Saints were just about the best side on the night.

"It was a very brave performance," said Saints coach Ian Millward. "We were struggling with injuries again and I'm very proud of the way they conducted themselves. Players like Edmondson, Jonkers, Stankevitch and Cruckshank, they are not what you think of as part of a back to back championship team. There's no big money players there."

Mark Edmondson, in particular, made a big impact with his powerful running after going on as a 55th minute substitute. But the two key players were the experienced Keiron Cunningham and Paul Sculthorpe, on his 24th birthday. Both scored two tries and set off countless other attacks.

Test hooker Cunningham was on the teamsheet at loose forward and Test second row Sculthorpe at stand-off, but they popped up all over the place.

Leeds' Jamie Mathiou leaves the St Helens field in despair as the Rhinos' season comes to an end

Leeds' 18 year old scrum-half Rob Burrow confirmed his ranking as the discovery of the season with another outstanding performance as he scored one try and created two others. His try gave Leeds a shock lead after only six minutes.

Later in the game one of Burrow's inimitable dashes had Saints dithering before he sent in Mark Calderwood between the posts. Burrow was like a bad itch in the St Helens side and the irritation got worse in the last minute when he backed up a powerful break by Barrie McDermott from halfway to put Senior clear for a superb score. Burrow's fifth goal capped his major contribution.

Leeds coach Daryl Powell joined in the praise of Burrow, but stopped short of backing the increasing calls for him to be pitched into the Ashes series.

After Burrow's early try, St Helens hit back with touchdowns from Hall and Sculthorpe before they were rocked again.

Burrow had equalised with a penalty when Hay sent Francis Cummins through to put Leeds 12-8 ahead. Quick tries from Cunningham and Sculthorpe, who goaled one, swept St Helens back in front, only for Leeds to draw level. The impressive Matt Diskin, another of Leeds' promising youngsters, squeezed in from a play-the-ball and Burrow added the goal.

That should have been it for the first half, but Leeds infringed in the last seconds and Sculthorpe banged over a 40-metre penalty to make it 20-18 and give Saints a psychological half-time boost. Within two minutes of the restart Cunningham grabbed his second try. Sculthorpe tagged on the goal and added a penalty after Vila Matautia and Gary Mercer were sent to the sin bin for fighting. Mercer was also put on report for the alleged spear tackle which sparked off the fight

The Saints were on a roll now and Cunningham's long pass enabled Martyn to put Kevin Iro over. Sculthorpe's goal gave them a 16-point lead after 47 minutes, but Leeds were far from finished and Calderwood's try put the Saints back on red alert.

They responded with Hall's second try to clinch victory, although Leeds' brilliant final try was a timely reminder of their part in a thrilling game.

Elimination Semi-final

HULL FC 20..**ST HELENS 24**

at the Boulevard, Friday 28th September

SAINTS had to battle like champions desperate to hang on to a title they had held for two years despite being badly wounded and rocked with a series of punishing blows. And the way Hull fought back to level the scores after going 20-6 down early in the second half made this a match to remember.

Hull, too, were badly hit by injuries with key players Tony and Jason Smith ruled out and David Maiden being a late withdrawal. Then there was Paul Cooke, who had played with a broken wrist for several months, giving it one last shot before having an operation. The youngster again held nothing back in an outstanding performance.

In the 23rd minute Cooke's long pass opened the way for Steve Prescott to put in Gareth Raynor for the first of his two tries. Cooke formed an impressive halfback pairing with Richard Horne, as the youngsters more than made up for the absence of the two Smiths.

Horne also tormented the Saints with well-placed kicks and Tony Grimaldi and Deon Bird both followed up to two of them to grab touchdowns in Hull's rousing fightback. The scrum-half's big contribution was well noted by Great Britain coach David Waite, who immediately drafted him into the national squad after the match.

It was quite a day for halfbacks as Paul Sculthorpe stood out for St Helens, calling on all of his big match experience to pull the Saints through several rocky

Vila Matautia meets Hull duo Adam Maher and Paul Broadbent as the Saints march on

patches. The first came after Raynor's try had put Hull 6-4 in front. Within six minutes he had seized back the initiative to dummy and power past two defenders for a try to which he added the goal that gave St Helens a 10-6 interval lead.

The big debate after the game was whether St Helens' Anthony Stewart should have been ruled in touch shortly before Tommy Martyn scored the match-winning try four minutes from the end. The video seemed to show Stewart's head over the line after he had been tackled by Horne, but touch judge Steve Wright's flag stayed down and within the set of six St Helens broke away for the vital score.

Another talking point was whether St Helens forward David Fairleigh should have played after injuring his shoulder two weeks before. Fairleigh went on in the 18th minute and lasted only 17 minutes before doing further damage to the shoulder and came off.

Hull had most of the play in the first quarter, when Paul Broadbent was prominent, but all they had to show for it was a Matt Crowther penalty goal and it was St Helens substitute John Kirkpatrick who opened the try-scoring within two minutes of going on following a break by Kevin Iro.

Mike Forshaw swamped by the Wigan defence as the Bulls charge to Old Trafford

Hull's breakthrough came with Gareth Raynor's 23rd minute try, before Sculthorpe's touchdown put the Saints back on top and they seemed to take complete control early in the second half, as Hull fell to two tries scored straight from play-the-balls.

Keiron Cunningham charged in for the first and then John Stankevitch powered over.

Fourteen points behind and with only 23 minutes left, Hull should have been out of it. But they fired back with the same ferocity that had rocked Wigan Warriors a week earlier. Their three tries-in-eleven minutes scoring burst began with Grimaldi snapping up Horne's short kick. That was quickly followed by Raynor's second touchdown and when Bird touched down Horne's towering kick, the video referee kept everyone in suspense for ages before awarding the try. 20-20 with just twelve tension-packed minutes left.

Yet again Hull had St Helens on the rack without being able to finish them off, and after Prescott's field goal attempt went wide the Saints almost inevitably came roaring back for Sean Hoppe to send in Martyn for the match-winning try.

Qualifying Semi-final

BRADFORD BULLS 24 ....**WIGAN WARRIORS 18**

at Valley Parade, Sunday 30th September

The Bulls took the shortest possible route to the Tetley's Super League Grand Final as they maintained their 100 percent record at the Valley Parade home they had made a fortress.

The Warriors now faced a final eliminator against St Helens for the right to earn revenge for this defeat against the Bulls.

At Valley Parade the Bulls had been invincible with 16 wins from 16 games but the Warriors outscored them by three tries to two despite the Bulls dominating much of the possession and field position.

Henry Paul, making what proved to be his final home appearance for the Bulls, was in brilliant kicking form, landing two conversions and six penalties and failing at goal on just one occasion. Brother Robbie scored two first-half tries with James Lowes, Mike Forshaw and Michael Withers also having top games.

Terry O'Connor put in a heroic effort in the Warriors pack with Denis Betts, David Furner and Terry Newton producing huge tackling stints.

The Warriors welcomed back Paul Johnson after injury for David Hodgson, though hamstring victim Brett Dallas was still an absentee. Chris Chester came into the 17 on the bench.

Two penalties in quick succession, the first for a Terry Newton high tackle, the second for offside, gave Henry Paul the opportunity to boot the Bulls into a sixth-minute lead. It was the Bulls' marksman's 200th goal of a record-breaking season.

Then, after Mike Forshaw's surging run, Robbie Paul dummied to pass to the right and cut through on the arc to score his first try. Brother Henry converted for an 8-0 lead and then landed the angled 22-metre penalty for a 10-0 lead after 24 minutes.

From nowhere, the Warriors grabbed a lifeline as Steve Renouf intercepted Robbie Paul's long pass and galloped over unopposed from 20 metres, Andy Farrell kicking the conversion.

But Radlinski then knocked on in another Wigan attack and the Bulls regained the initiative. Henry Paul, Naylor and Withers combined in a sweeping attack that had the Warriors back-pedalling and Withers again linked into the attack to send Robbie over for his second try. Henry added his fourth goal and the Bulls were 16-6 ahead.

But Wigan broke the onslaught on the back of a Farrell penalty kick to touch, as Newton and Adrian Lam combined to get Radlinski over on the left for his 29th try of the season.

Farrell, though, was unable to convert and also pulled a 39th-minute penalty attempt wide but, even so, the Warriors could hardly believe their fortune to go in at the break trailing by only six points, such had been the Bulls dominance.

Henry Paul's boot stretched the Bulls lead to 22-10 within twelve minutes of the re-start as the ace marksman calmly potted three penalties, two against Newton for high tackles and the first for offside.

Newton had gone desperately close to a try from dummy-half before Farrell pulled Wigan back to within ten points with a 40-metre penalty.

Radlinski kept the Warriors in the contest with a ball-and-all tackle on Shane Rigon, sent through by the tireless Forshaw, and that proved crucial as Wigan replied in stunning style.

Farrell did the damage with a piercing cross-field run and Hodgson collected his flung-out pass to dart for the corner and dive over under Leon Pryce's despairing tackle. Farrell landed the goal from the touch-line to leave the Warriors just four points behind with 13 minutes left.

As the rain continued to pour down it was Henry Paul who provided the final scoring act of the game after a controversial decision against Farrell for alleged ball stealing on Jamie Peacock in a two-man tackle. Paul kicked his eighth goal from nine attempts to give the Bulls a six-point cushion with nine minutes remaining.

"There is a hell of a lot of improvement to come at Old Trafford," said Bradford boss Brian Noble.

Final Eliminator
WIGAN WARRIORS 44...ST HELENS 10
at the JJB Stadium, Saturday 6th October

Wigan learned the lessons of their defeat at Valley Parade as they made it one game too far for Ian Millward's gallant Saints side.

The treble champions showed the effects of a long, tiring campaign and the absence of key players through injuries as they suffered their first defeat in twelve knockout games under Millward. The results of playing five more competitive games than their opponents in a season that began with their World Club Championship success over Brisbane nearly nine months ago were there for all to see.

For the Warriors, halfbacks Matthew Johns and Adrian Lam assumed a midfield dominance that they never achieved against the Bulls a week before. Terry Newton's brilliant approach play and tireless work at hooker and the kicking and footballing skills of captain Andrew Farrell, playing in a wider attacking role, allied to far better discipline from the side, took the Warriors through.

After an even start, when the Warriors produced some big defence with the scores locked at 6-6, the game turned with two Wigan tries in a decisive four-minute spell.

Lam and Johns combined brilliantly to unlock the Saints defence and fullback Kris Radlinski was at Johns' shoulder to scoot over from 20 metres, despite Tommy Martyn's despairing cover tackle, for his 31st try of the season.

Newton then cut through to score from dummy-half for another converted try and, with Farrell tagging on a penalty on the stroke of half-time, after Kevin Iro was penalised at the play-the-ball, the Warriors had a commanding 20-6 lead.

The Warriors began in ominously fluent style, David Furner, put through by Johns' superb inside pass having a try chalked off by the video referee for a fumble by Steve Renouf at the play-the-ball in the build-up, before Farrell's break and fine inside pass sent Lam galloping over.

But Saints, attacking their supporters massed at the north stand end, pulled level when Iro burst over from dummy-half. With Martyn also going close down the left and Chris Joynt and Paul Sculthorpe almost engineering something down the right, Saints were well in the game at that stage.

Write a Saints comeback off at your peril was the theme at half-time. But it was the Warriors that secured their Old Trafford date when Newton brilliantly committed two defenders with a searing break and Lam went over on the angle for his second try. When, three minutes later, Johns scored the try his own efforts deserved, again off Newton's superb approach play, the game was in the bag.

Farrell, who ended with a 16-point haul from the boot, broke Frano Botica's club record for points in a season with his sixth successful attempt. Botica amassed 423 points for Wigan in 1992-93 and Farrell ended the game with 429 with two games, the Grand Final and the Australian Tests still to come.

Though Sculthorpe fought his way over for Saints from dummy-half for a second try and his 31st of the season, the game was beyond the visitors.

Brian Carney completed Wigan's night with two fine tries. Carney showed exceptional finishing speed to power onto Renouf's pass 30 metres out and race down the left touchline before reacting first to Farrell's precise chip to the corner. Farrell missed at goal for the only time attempting to convert Carney's second but concluded the scoring with a penalty seven minutes from the end.

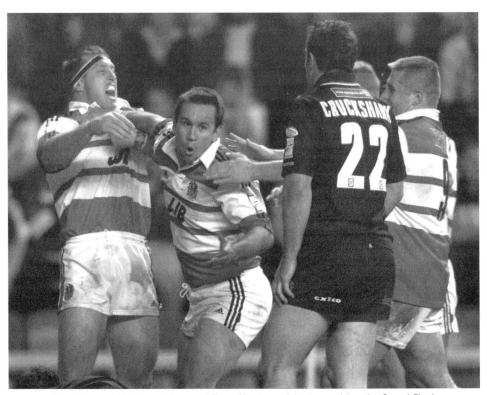

David Furner, Matthew Johns and Terry Newton celebrate reaching the Grand Final

SUPER LEAGUE GRAND FINAL
Dreams come true

It was the night that Bradford Bulls and their coach Brian Noble took hold of the "big match chokers" tag and threw it right back into the faces of the critics.

After the final whistle of a stunningly one-sided Tetley's Super League Grand Final at Old Trafford, Noble threw an imaginary gorilla off his back as he saluted the celebrating Bulls fans.

The Bulls had been beaten four times in five previous finals in the summer era, including a heartbreaking 6-8 defeat against Saints at Old Trafford in 1999 and the 13-6 Challenge Cup Final reverse to the Saints earlier in the year.

But they showed all the power, flair and ruthlessness they displayed week in week out to finish as minor premiers as they hammered the Warriors 37-6 in the first Grand Final to be played in rain-free conditions.

It was a dream come true for Noble, in the first year of his tenure as head coach at the Bulls after patiently learning his trade under the mentorship of Brian Smith and Matthew Elliott.

Literally a dream come true.

In the week leading up to the game, Noble and fullback Michael Withers both dreamed that Withers would score a hat-trick of tries and win the Harry Sunderland Trophy as the man of the match. And that's exactly what happened.

"Mike came to me during the week and said he'd dreamed he was man of the match after scoring three tries," said Noble. "I told him we are in for a good day because I'd had the same dream. I thought there is something spooky going on here."

Nicknamed 'The Ghost' for his knack of appearing out of nowhere to score, Withers was as solid as a rock in defence and devastating on attack as he scored the first Grand Final hat-trick.

Withers became the fourth Australian to win the trophy, along with John Dorahy (Hull KR 1984), Les Boyd (Warrington 1986) and Greg Mackey (Hull 1991), all in the days of the old Premiership Final.

Henry Paul tries to halt a charging Kris Radlinski

"I'm honoured to be alongside them," said Withers.

The former Australia Junior Player of the Year acknowledged Noble's faith in him after the Bulls coach had to find someone to replace Stuart Spruce, injured early in the season. Spruce had been in top form and Noble admitted: "It was never going to be smooth losing a player of Stuart Spruce's calibre. I had a few options, but Michael Withers was the first one I had in mind to take over at fullback. I had a word with him and said it would give him more freedom and space. He is also a very tough defender and great catcher of the ball."

Withers' hat-trick, which built the Bulls' 26-0 half-time lead, was the highlight of the Grand Final but he also produced three vital second-half tackles when Wigan made a late burst for respectability.

Adrian Lam looked a likely scorer when he slipped through, only for Withers to bring him down. Then Steve Renouf was wrapped up in full cry, and even in the last minutes, when Withers could have been excused for relaxing, he epitomised the Bradford spirit by going low to stop Paul Johnson close to the line.

His hat-trick was a genuine one, with the three tries coming in quick succession during a 20-minute first half scoring burst that shattered Wigan. The first came in the eleventh minute. Bradford were already 8-0 up when Henry Paul broke through from halfway and was tackled five metres short of the line. Withers was the first at the play-the-ball, and quick off the mark to charge through two attempted tackles to touch down.

Sixteen minutes later Withers followed up a terrific attack from halfway by Scott Naylor and Tevita Vaikona to take the latter's pass and go in between the posts. Wigan fans claimed a forward pass, but referee Stuart Cummings awarded the try.

Another four minutes and Withers had done it once more. This time the two Pauls and Stuart Fielden were involved in the build up before Withers provided the finishing touch. Henry Paul banged over the goal and Bradford were 26-0 up.

It was all over. Wigan supporters were stunned to silence.

Withers' performance was out of the top drawer, but he was pushed all the way by Henry Paul for the Harry Sunderland Trophy.

Paul, playing in his last Rugby League match - his 100th for the Bulls - before switching to rugby union, kicked six goals, including a towering field goal, plus a succession of inspiring attacking raids, made him a strong contender for the award. But in one of the closest ever contests for a big match individual award Withers just edged home with 15 votes to Paul's 13. The only other one to be considered was James Lowes, who picked up four after a display that would have won him the honour in many other years.

Hat-trick hero Michael Withers brought to ground

Henry was almost tearful as he mopped up the adulation of the Bradford supporters among a record Super League crowd of 60,164.

"It's hard to sum up my eight years playing Rugby League in this country, but I've certainly got no regrets," he said. "It isn't just the victories, but it's the mates I've played with. It's fantastic to be able to wear a winners' ring, but it's seeing the smiles on the boys' faces that really sums it up. It's been a great day for the club here at Old Trafford, and it's a shame to leave now, because there are big things on the horizon for this team."

Henry admitted that the lack of international opportunity in League played a major part in him leaving the sport.

"The club side of Rugby League is great, but they do need to do some work on the international side of the game," he said. "If there had been more international competition it might have influenced my decision to go to rugby union. A series involving Australia, New Zealand and Great Britain would have been great. The Tri-Series was fantastic in 1999, and I do think we should put international Rugby League ahead of club Rugby League."

The 2001 Grand Final ranked up there with Paul's very best Rugby League days.

"I hate to compare wins in different years, but Wembley in 1995 (with Wigan) was very special. I scored a try, I was such a young kid and it was fantastic, but tonight ranks alongside it. The Bradford fans were just fantastic. They made such a lot of noise, and they helped us tremendously."

Henry's brother Robbie was also influential behind a go-forward pack that punched huge holes in the Warriors rearguard and had them on the back foot from the off. Two players who had almost been written off as has-beens had the games of their lives. James Lowes enjoyed one of his finest hours with a beguiling mixture of craft, energy and opportunism and the block-busting Scott Naylor, at right centre, was unstoppable. Their efforts raised the rest of the Bradford team to their very best too.

"People talk about tactics but they are flesh and blood these blokes," said Noble, pointing to his players as they celebrated on the Old Trafford turf. "This game is about players and I am a privileged man, I get to work with them week in, week out. They deserved this because they worked harder than anyone else, scored more tries and conceded less. So we're tough and we can play footie. I think that we just killed the gorilla."

But the Warriors players trooped off, several contemplating having made their final appearance in a Wigan jersey, the retiring Neil Cowie and departing Matthew Johns and Steve Renouf for three.

"It was an abject Wigan performance as they were destroyed around the rucks, their first and second markers unable to contend with the tide of Bulls pressure and, one dimensional in attack, they might easily have been nilled, such was the dominance of the Bulls defence." wrote Mike Latham in League Express.

"I am very disappointed and so are the players," said Stuart Raper, the coach who had come to the Warriors when Frank Endacott had been sacked in mid-season. "But give Bradford credit. They were outstanding in the first half when the game was won and lost.

Joe Vagana tries to shake off the attentions of Denis Betts

Super League Grand Final

"It was a first taste of the big occasion for me but it has left a bitter taste right now. It has made me more determined to work harder in the close season to build on this and go one step better next year."

From the moment Henry opened the scoring with a penalty from halfway, Wigan were paddling up-river. In the first set of the game, the Warriors were penalised for Harvey Howard not being square at the ruck and Henry Paul calmly potted the goal - laying to rest another theory; that he could only kick goals because of the 'short' Valley Parade pitch.

On the back of an incessant Bulls barrage, Lowes dived over from dummy-half for a converted try on nine minutes. Withers' hat-trick, two conversions and another penalty goal made it 26-0 at the break but it could have been more.

"At half-time I told them to have pride in their own performance as well as the jerseys and if Bradford could score 26 points in a half then so could we," Raper said. "But it was always catch-up and although we played better Rugby League in the second half, the game was gone."

Wigan made one breakthrough as Lam, involved in the previous two plays, used Terry O'Connor as a foil and squirmed over despite the attentions of three Bulls defenders.

Andy Farrell's hopes of kicking the four goals he needed to break Frano Botica's club record for goals in a season had disappeared as he left the field with a corked thigh, his run of 48 successive scoring games over, and David Furner deputised as kicker to land the conversion.

But Lam's try served only to increase the Bulls' desire to finish on a high and, two minutes later, after Brett Dallas couldn't collect Vagana's offload, Naylor and Gartner combined to get Fielden over on the left.

Robbie Paul left the action suffering with cramp but it merely gave Paul Deacon the chance of a brief cameo and the Wigan-born halfback didn't disappoint. After Henry Paul succeeded with his second field goal attempt, to extend his Bulls seasonal club records to 213 goals and 457 points, Deacon stabbed through a perfectly-weighted kick from 20 metres out and Graham Mackay beat the Wigan defence to the touchdown. This was farewell time for the Australian, too, and he was allowed to add the conversion for the perfect send-off, as he, and Daniel Gartner, completed Grand Final wins on both sides of the world.

The Bulls captain, Robbie Paul, had scored a hat-trick and been the man of the match in a losing cause in the 1996 Challenge Cup Final and he was ecstatic as he went up for the presentation of the trophy.

The Bulls were the Champion side of 2001. No-one could argue with that.

Saturday 13th October 2001

SUPER LEAGUE GRAND FINAL

BRADFORD BULLS 37 WIGAN WARRIORS 6

BULLS: 5 Michael Withers; 2 Tevita Vaikona; 20 Scott Naylor; 23 Graham Mackay; 3 Leon Pryce; 6 Henry Paul; 1 Robbie Paul (C); 8 Joe Vagana; 9 James Lowes; 22 Brian McDermott; 11 Daniel Gartner; 19 Jamie Peacock; 12 Mike Forshaw. Subs: 29 Stuart Fielden for McDermott (21BB, rev 65); 10 Paul Anderson for Vagana (22); 15 Shane Rigon for Pryce (40); 7 Paul Deacon for R Paul (69); Fielden for Gartner (72); Anderson for Vagana (74).
Tries: Lowes (9), Withers (11, 27, 31), Fielden (65), Mackay (72); **Goals:** H Paul 5, Mackay;
Field goal: H Paul.
WARRIORS: 1 Kris Radlinski; 2 Brett Dallas; 4 Gary Connolly; 3 Steve Renouf; 5 Brian Carney; 6 Matthew Johns; 7 Adrian Lam; 8 Terry O'Connor; 9 Terry Newton; 20 Harvey Howard; 11 Mick Cassidy; 14 David Furner; 13 Andy Farrell (C). Subs: 15 Paul Johnson for Carney (12BB); 10 Neil Cowie for Howard (17); 12 Denis Betts for O'Connor (32); 19 Chris Chester for Farrell (59); O'Connor for Cowie (55); Howard for Newton (64); Cowie for Cassidy (72).
Try: Lam (63); **Goal:** Furner.
League Express Men of the Match:
Bulls: Michael Withers; *Warriors:* Adrian Lam.
Penalty count: 6-7; **Half-time:** 26-0;
Referee: Stuart Cummings (Widnes);
Attendance: 60,164 *(at Old Trafford, Manchester).*

SUPER
LEAGUE
SEASON
ROUND BY ROUND

ROUND 1

ROUND 2

ROUND 3

Wigan's David Furner falls under pressure from Castleford's Lee Harland as the Warriors tame the Tigers

ABOVE: Bradford's Scott Naylor tries to shake off St Helens' Paul Newlove during the first Super League match at the Bulls' new home at Valley Parade
BELOW: Castleford's Jon Wells wrapped up by the Hull defence during a thrilling draw at The Boulevard

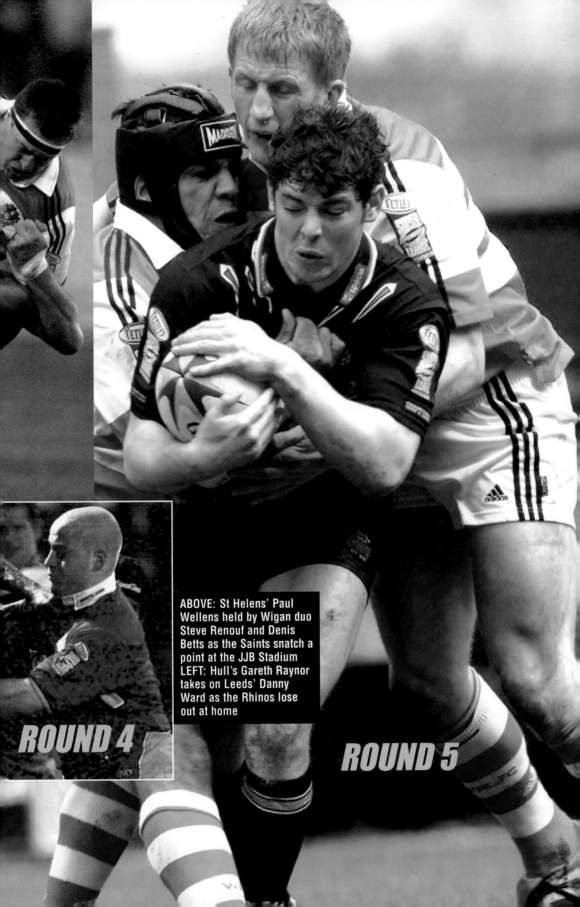

ABOVE: St Helens' Paul Wellens held by Wigan duo Steve Renouf and Denis Betts as the Saints snatch a point at the JJB Stadium
LEFT: Hull's Gareth Raynor takes on Leeds' Danny Ward as the Rhinos lose out at home

ROUND 4

ROUND 5

ROUND 7

LEFT: Warrington's Martin Masella hauled down against St Helens as the Wolves give Saints a mauling

BELOW: Leeds' Tonie Carroll collared by St Helens' Kevin Iro as the Saints suffer a Challenge Cup hangover

ROUND 9

Bradford's Brian McDermott offloads under pressure from Wigan's David Furner as the Bulls produce a Bank Holiday victory

ROUND 6

ROUND 8

ABOVE: London's Richie Barnett tries to break through the Wigan defence as the Broncos stun the Warriors
BELOW: Wigan's woe goes on as Salford's Darren Brown takes the ball up during the City Reds' one-point victory

ROUND 10

ROUND 11

Wakefield's Justin Brooker loses the ball under pressure from Warrington's Toa Kohe-Love as the Wildcats claw the Wolves

ROUND 12

ROUND 14

ABOVE: London's Jason Hetherington tries to shake off Halifax's Stuart Donlan as the Broncos scrape past the Blue Sox
RIGHT: Leeds' Chev Walker engulfed by Wigan trio Terry Newton, Andy Farrell and Harvey Howard as the Warriors take apart the Rhinos at Headingley

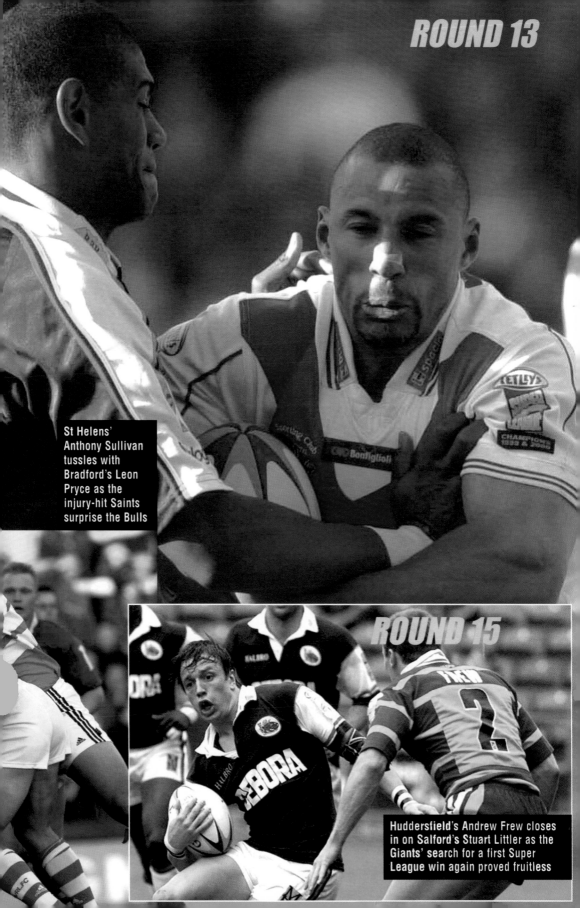

St Helens'
Anthony Sullivan
tussles with
Bradford's Leon
Pryce as the
injury-hit Saints
surprise the Bulls

ROUND 15

Huddersfield's Andrew Frew closes
in on Salford's Stuart Littler as the
Giants' search for a first Super
League win again proved fruitless

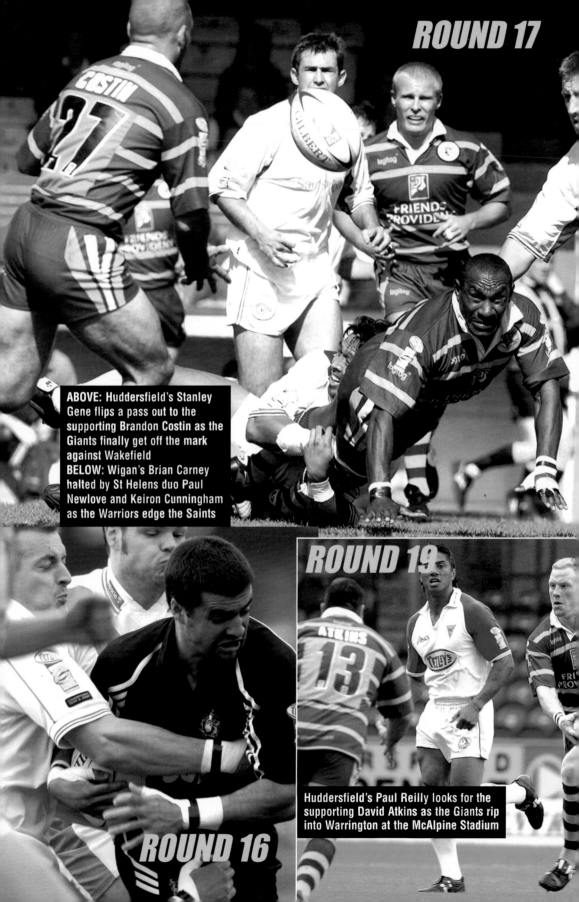

ROUND 17

ABOVE: Huddersfield's Stanley Gene flips a pass out to the supporting Brandon Costin as the Giants finally get off the mark against Wakefield
BELOW: Wigan's Brian Carney halted by St Helens duo Paul Newlove and Keiron Cunningham as the Warriors edge the Saints

ROUND 19

Huddersfield's Paul Reilly looks for the supporting David Atkins as the Giants rip into Warrington at the McAlpine Stadium

ROUND 16

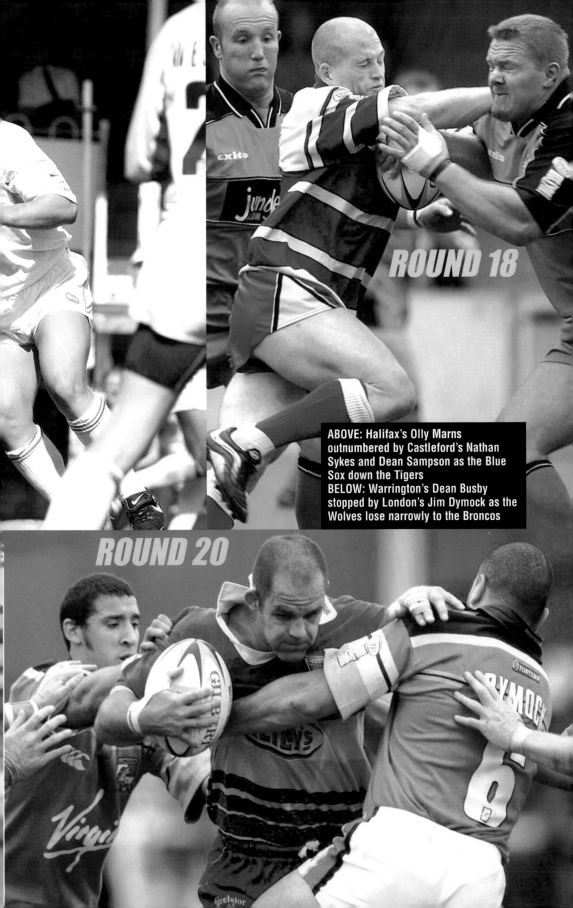

ROUND 18

ABOVE: Halifax's Olly Marns outnumbered by Castleford's Nathan Sykes and Dean Sampson as the Blue Sox down the Tigers
BELOW: Warrington's Dean Busby stopped by London's Jim Dymock as the Wolves lose narrowly to the Broncos

ROUND 20

ROUND 21

Wigan's Harvey Howard feels the force of Hull duo David Maiden and Tony Grimaldi as the Warriors ease home

ROUND 24

Hull's Steve Craven in thick of the action duri side's win against Lon

Halifax's Phil Hassan comes in for some close attention from the Salford defence as the Blue Sox win a high-scoring affair at The Willows

Leeds' Chev Walker on the burst against Warrington as the Rhinos clinch a play-off spot

ROUND 26

ROUND 25

ROUND 22

Castleford's Adrian Vowles takes on Sonny Nickle and David Fairleigh during the Tigers' nailbiting home win over St Helens

ROUND 23

Bradford's Tevita Vaikona crashes through the despairing challenges of Leeds pair Mark Calderwood and Keith Senior as the Bulls run riot against the Rhinos

RIGHT: Huddersfield coach Tony Smith consoles Steve McNamara as the Giants are relegated despite defeating London

BELOW: Wakefield trio Waisale Sovatabua, Julian O'Neill and Neil Law celebrate Super League survival as the Wildcats win away at Salford

Bradford's Robbie Paul falls to the challenge of Warrington's Martin Masella as the Bulls hammer the Wolves at Wilderspool

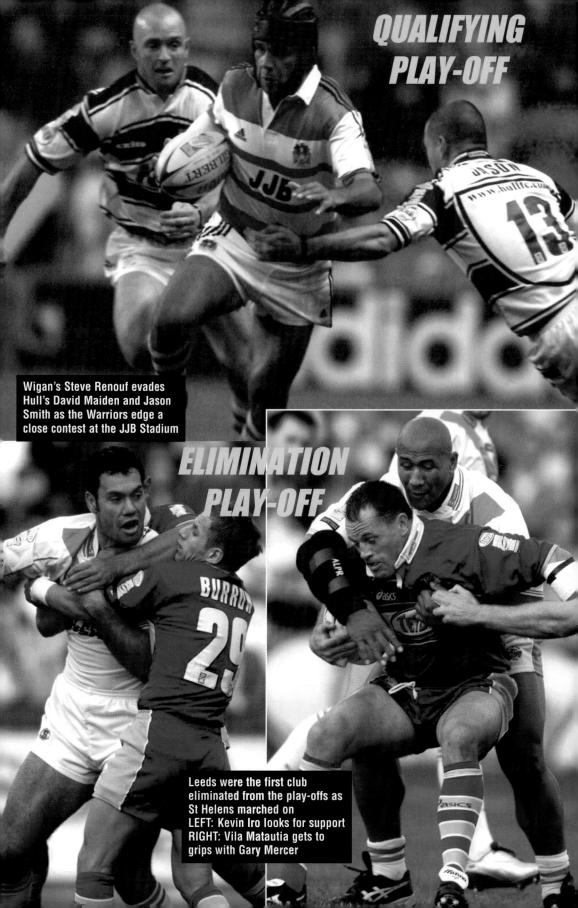

QUALIFYING
PLAY-OFF

Wigan's Steve Renouf evades
Hull's David Maiden and Jason
Smith as the Warriors edge a
close contest at the JJB Stadium

ELIMINATION
PLAY-OFF

Leeds were the first club
eliminated from the play-offs as
St Helens marched on
LEFT: Kevin Iro looks for support
RIGHT: Vila Matautia gets to
grips with Gary Mercer

Bradford's Graham Mackay meets Wigan's Andy Farrell as the Bulls become the first team to reach Old Trafford and the Grand Final

QUALIFYING SEMI-FINAL

ELIMINATION SEMI-FINAL

Luke Felsch tries to break free from the challenge of St Helens' Tim Jonkers as Hull bow out of the play-offs

St Helens trio Kevin Iro, Keiron Cunningham and David Fairleigh halt Wigan's Terry O'Connor as the Saints' two-year reign as Super League champions comes to an end

FINAL ELIMINATOR

GRAND FINAL

GRAND FINAL

BRADFORD BULLS 37
WIGAN WARRIORS 6

CLOCKWISE, FROM TOP LEFT:
Stuart Fielden brought down
by Neil Cowie; No way through
for Andy Farrell; Henry Paul
skips away from Terry Newton

4
NORTHERN FORD PREMIERSHIP 2001

NORTHERN FORD PREMIERSHIP SEASON
Centurions conquer all

LEIGH CENTURIONS finished the regular Northern Ford Premiership season nine points ahead of their nearest rivals after a campaign of consistency and excellence under coach Paul Terzis.

With Neil Turley, Simon Svabic and Simon Baldwin prominent on their long list of influential contributors, the Centurions were undefeated at Hilton Park in the league and scored well over 1,000 points.

The season started in spectacular fashion; crucial away wins at title challengers Widnes and Oldham in front of big crowds in the opening weeks were followed by the Centurions dumping Super League side Salford out of the Challenge Cup with a memorable, televised 16-12 win at Hilton Park.

Terzis's side went on to win their first twelve NFP games before Doncaster Dragons ended their undefeated run at Belle Vue, but between then and the end of the season the Centurions lost only once more - at Rochdale in mid-June.

Turley was, quite simply, the star of the competition, finishing with 55 tries in all competitions in his first full season, while Svabic ended the campaign as the top goal and pointscorer in the Premiership.

They were aided by the Centurions running up some huge scores during the course of the season - the side scored 40 points or more in half of their Premiership fixtures.

Turley and Svabic were joined by Baldwin in the NFP All Stars team, while prop Dave Bradbury, back-rower Adam Bristow and centre Paul Anderson also had tremendous seasons.

Simon Baldwin

WIDNES VIKINGS secured second place on the final day of the season, making great strides in the aftermath of Neil Kelly replacing David Hulme as coach mid-way through the campaign.

Kelly took charge following Hulme's departure in March, and after bringing key members from his Grand Final-winning side at Dewsbury with him in the shape of Richard Agar, Sean Richardson and Matt Long, lost just one game in charge, at Leigh in early April.

After that game the Vikings finished the league campaign with twelve straight victories, including crucial wins against top-four contenders Oldham, Rochdale and Featherstone.

115

Phil
Cantillon

Hooker Phil Cantillon was a shining light throughout and finished the season with more tries than any other forward in the history of the British game - 48 in all competitions.

Prop Simon Knox was also a tireless worker and grew stronger with the arrival of Long and Richardson, while in the backs, another Kelly signing, Craig Weston, formed an outstanding centre partnership with fellow Aussie Jason Demetriou.

Wingers Damian Munro and Chris Percival shared 41 tries between them, while Chris McKinney, Steve Gee and Tommy Hodgkinson were all the epitome of the unsung hero in the back row.

With their average attendance up to almost 4,000, the feel-good factor finally returned to Widnes in 2001, and in Kelly the Vikings' supporters found themselves a new figurehead to lead them into Super League.

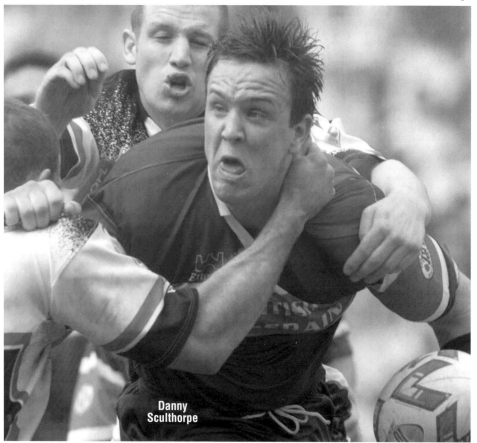

Danny
Sculthorpe

ROCHDALE HORNETS were undoubtedly the competition's biggest improvers, as under rookie coach Martin Hall they progressed from 13th place in 2000 to third in 2001, despite Hall taking over the reins just three weeks before the start of the season.

Hall endured a shaky start as Hornets lost five of their opening seven league games, the last of which was a 48-0 thumping at Leigh that left them in 16th place.

But that appeared to be a turning point as they quickly recorded three stunning results - beating full-strength Doncaster, Dewsbury and Keighley sides within a month.

Hall added to an already talented squad with the shrewd acquisitions of Doncaster trio Latham Tawhai, James Bunyan and Joe Berry, and Hornets lost just twice more in the Premiership, at Hull KR and Widnes.

Hornet's pivotal figure was undoubtedly young ball-handling prop Danny Sculthorpe, who was deservedly nominated for the NFP Player of the Year award, while powerful winger Marlon Billy surpassed just about everybody's expectations in breaking Hornets' 66-year old tries in a season record with 31.

Captain Brendan O'Meara and a rejuvenated Matt Calland formed arguably the strongest centre partnership in the Premiership, and hooker Darren Robinson scored 20 tries and Danny Wood over 300 points.

Neil Roden

Hornets were separated from fourth-placed **OLDHAM** only by points difference, after the Roughyeds lost at Hull KR in the final league game of the season. But overall it was another outstanding year for Mike Ford and the Roughyeds, who came undefeated through a spell of seven games in 21 days in April and May.

That came after Ford's side had endured a shaky spell in March, losing three out of four games, and then an Easter to forget, going down to crucial defeats against top-four rivals Rochdale and Widnes in the space of four days.

Ford himself played a lesser part during the league campaign, allowing young halfback Neil Roden to display his talents during their marathon 21-day run.

Roden's former Wigan Alliance teammate Phil Farrell had an immense season in the second row, and gained selection for the NFP All Stars Team to go along with his Young Player of the Year nomination.

Generally, the pack was Oldham's strength, with hookers John Hough and Keith Brennan both playing key roles and Kiwi Bryan Henare arriving from St Helens to help fill the considerable void left by Shayne McMenemy's early departure to Halifax.

Veteran prop Leo Casey was again a model of consistency and effort, while the kicking of centre Pat Rich was a prominent feature throughout.

Richard Chapman

In fifth place for the third consecutive year were **FEATHERSTONE ROVERS**, who looked a good bet for the top four before losing a handful of crucial games in the second half of the season.

Narrow defeats against Widnes and particularly Rochdale ultimately cost Peter Roe's side a place in the elite quartet, but they again proved to be one of the strongest and most consistent sides in the Premiership.

After beginning the season with just three points from their opening four games, they soon established themselves among the competition's front-runners.

Goal-kicking scrum-half Jamie Rooney was again their key figure in the middle of the park; his performances earning him a brief spell at Super League neighbours Castleford Tigers after the end of the NFP season.

Rooney was well supported by hooker Richard Chapman and loose forward Paul Darley, who both enjoyed productive seasons in the pack alongside the likes of Neil Lowe and Danny Evans.

Out wide, wingers Jamie Stokes and Matt Bramald amassed 42 tries between them, while Australian fullback Michael Rhodes was a constant rock at the back.

An injury to signing Danny Seal just four games into his Featherstone career was certainly a hindrance in the closing weeks of the league season and then the play-offs, and another telling statistic was that Rovers defeated a side from the top four just once.

Barry
Eaton

Last year's Champions **DEWSBURY RAMS** suffered from a mid-season exodus to Widnes that saw coach Kelly and several important players depart, and never really recovered, although they did string together an impressive run of results late in the league campaign.

Eleven games into the season the Rams looked on course to eclipse 2000's Grand Final win, sitting second on the league ladder with just one defeat.

But a comprehensive 44-26 defeat at Rochdale raised doubts in Kelly's mind about the state of his squad ("the atmosphere in the changing room and at training is not the same as it was last year," Kelly said after that match), and he had departed for Widnes before their next league game at home to Barrow.

Sean Richardson, Richard Agar and Matt Long soon followed to the Auto Quest Stadium, and the Rams - now under Kelly's assistant Roy Sampson - lost seven games in the space of ten matches.

But they did recover to record four straight wins, including two vital victories against Doncaster, to help them to sixth place, with centre Dan Potter and the ever-reliable Barry Eaton and Adrian Flynn key figures.

Flynn again finished as the club's top try-scorer, while stand-off Mark Cain, the returning Kevin Crouthers, Eaton, Potter and hooker Richard Pachniuk all reached double figures.

Chris
Charles

HULL KINGSTON ROVERS finished as strongly as anyone with seven wins from their last eight games after a season of genuine improvement under another coach who took over at short notice last November, Gary Wilkinson.

Rovers' seventh-place finish was based around their solid form at Craven Park - they lost just two games at home all season, to Doncaster and Sheffield.

But they often struggled on their travels, not least at the leading clubs, as they failed to beat any of the top eight clubs away from home in the regular season.

Club captain Whetu Taewa was typically prominent on a week-to-week basis, and was Rovers' leading scorer with 16. But the side's lack of pointscoring prowess was illustrated by the fact that only two other players - Jimmy Walker and Bob Everitt - reached double figures, and they scored fewer points than all but six Premiership teams.

But that didn't prevent them from being touted as possible Grand Finalists come the play-offs, and with loose forward Chris Charles and smart Wilkinson acquisitions Craig Murdock and Rob Wilson all influential, they improved as the season unfolded.

Wilson and Charles helped form an impressive pack alongside the likes of industrious trio Mike Dixon, Richard Slater and Rich Hayes, and with several talented youngsters on the fringes of the first team they could look forward to the new campaign with a certain amount of justified optimism.

121

Martin Wood

KEIGHLEY COUGARS enjoyed, and suffered, a rollercoaster of a season - beginning it challenging for the Minor Premiership, losing almost their entire first team squad mid-term, and then recovering with a group of young, enthusiastic players guiding them into a play-off place.

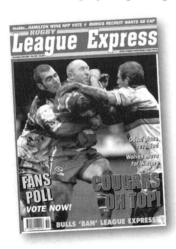

Coach Steve Deakin was one constant during the turmoil, and emerged from the mid-season wreckage with credit after building a side from virtually nothing that gave Featherstone a real scare in the play-offs.

Deakin was again installed as Cougars' coach in October, after the club finally hit rock bottom and relaunched after going into liquidation.

Those days seemed a long way away nine games into the league season in 2001, when the Cougars sat top of the Premiership, undefeated. Even after defeat to Rochdale, they recovered and recorded a super away win at Widnes in late March.

But that is when it all began to fall apart. Deakin's playmaker Martin Wood sustained a serious knee injury and was ruled out for the season, while halfback partner Nathan Antonik was also sidelined.

The Cougars lost four games on the trot, owner Hami Patel withdrew his financial investment, and almost all of the club's high profile stars departed.

It left Deakin with a considerable mountain to climb, but he constructed a competitive team made up of amateurs and fringe players, and with halfback Paul Ashton, back-rower Rob Roberts and Cougar icon Jason Ramshaw all playing key roles, they ended the season positively.

WORKINGTON TOWN were only denied a play-off place when Hull KR defeated Oldham on the final day of the league season, with a horrendous May - they lost four games out of five - playing a significant part in their disappointment.

Town coach Gary Murdock was also hit by the absence of influential halfback Tane Manihera in vital fixtures.

When Manihera did play Town showed signs of becoming a Premiership force, and they had a pack that could match it with any other on their day.

Kiwi Matt Sturm was probably their most consistent figure, a tower of strength in the front row, while skilful loose forward Anthony Samuel and livewire young hooker Carl Sice were also stand-out performers.

Strong-running winger Graeme Lewthwaite collected 33 tries in a highly profitable campaign on the flanks, but no other player scored more than nine tries - an illustration of Town's lack of resources out wide.

And the fact that they won just three times against top-eight opposition also dented their play-off aspirations.

Anthony Samuel

Rob
Purdham

Their West Cumbrian neighbours **WHITEHAVEN** recovered from a horror start to conclude the season in positive fashion under coach Paul Cullen.

Haven lost their first five league games under Cullen, including narrow and disappointing defeats to Swinton and Barrow, leaving them just two places off the foot of the Premiership.

But Cullen gradually began to exert his influence despite the most severe injury list in the NFP, and six games undefeated helped them start to climb the table.

In the end, narrow defeats against Rochdale and Oldham in the closing weeks of the campaign cost them a play-off place.

Perhaps the biggest plus points to come out of the season surrounded the progression of several local young stars, headed by Rob Purdham, Dean Vaughan and Spencer Miller. Purdham's form was such that by November he had earned selection as the England under-21s stand-off.

Cullen's side was made up predominantly of locally-born youngsters, while two of the senior players, top try-scorer David Seeds and the outstanding Aaron Lester, provided guidance and experience.

Such was the progress that the side made under Cullen that in their final game of the year they won 24-20 away at Featherstone, despite being without no less than ten first team players.

SHEFFIELD EAGLES continued their own development since reforming, but their inconsistency ensured they were always struggling to make up ground on the leading eight.

They started the season in highly convincing fashion with a comfortable defeat of Batley and then a superb win away at Featherstone. But Mark Aston's side won just one of their ensuing seven league games, and during the remainder of the campaign they occupied a top-eight place for just three weeks, during April.

They were, however, rewarded for off-field activities with their NFP Club of the Year award, and could find several reasons to be optimistic on the field.

Back-rower Richard Goddard attained a place in the All Stars Team as reward for his influential performances in a mainly young side, and was the club's top try, goal and pointscorer.

Aston spent much of the year looking to develop young halfbacks to take over his own mantle in the centre of the field, and both Scott Rhodes and Gavin Brown displayed several flashes to illustrate their credentials.

Australian second-rower Heath Cruckshank was a considerable loss, to St Helens, after an excellent start to the season, but Steve Hill and Jon Bruce were willing workers up front throughout, and Neil Kite and Andy Poynter found themselves among the tries out wide.

Scott Rhodes

DONCASTER DRAGONS were another side hit by mass player-defections half-way through the year, a factor that severely dented their play-off aspirations.

Even then, they recovered to become the first side to defeat Leigh, but a desperately disappointing end to the season - in which they lost their last six games - confined them to twelfth place.

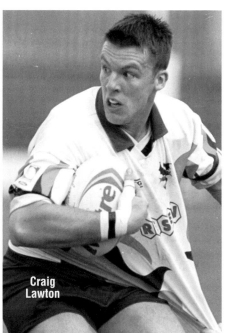

Craig Lawton

St John Ellis' side started the campaign as genuine top-four contenders, and won six of their opening seven fixtures.

But losing the likes of Craig Weston, Latham Tawhai, Joe Berry, Asa Amone, James Bunyan and Joe Berry was always going to hit the Dragons hard.

To their credit they did regroup somewhat mid-season, and with Kiwi stand-off Paul Mansson typically involved, they recorded outstanding back-to-back wins against Widnes (away) and then Leigh.

But a five-match suspension to Mansson during the run-in proved costly, and despite the emergence of youngsters Johnny Woodcock and Craig Lawton, they fell short of the coveted top eight by some distance in the end.

BATLEY BULLDOGS had three coaches during the course of the season, and that uncertainty didn't help during a campaign in which they were only in the top half of the table for one week.

They started under rookie John Sharp, but his early exit to become assistant at Huddersfield led to David Ward being re-installed, and then him passing the reins onto another young coach, Paul Storey.

Storey's arrival introduced some stability at Mount Pleasant, and the Bulldogs produced some promising performances in the later stages of the season.

Aussie scrum-half and Batley favourite Glen Tomlinson was an ever-present during the course of the season, and at times recaptured his brilliant best form, not least during March when he was named as the Rugby League World Player of the Month.

Incisive fullback Craig

Craig Lingard

Lingard also confirmed his status as one of the competition's leading players with 19 tries in 24 starts, but the Bulldogs found scoring hard to come by elsewhere, despite a number of quality performances in the three-quarters from Danny Maun and Davide Longo.

Hooker Andy Heptinstall was another consistent performer, as was prop Paul Hicks, but the Bulldogs inability to beat sides above them in the table regularly, ensured they were never really in the running to make the play-offs.

Neither were **BARROW BORDER RAIDERS**, whose coach Paul Charlton paid the price for some disappointing results and the lack of a top-eight challenge with his job near the end of the season.

Three consecutive defeats got the Border Raiders off on the wrong foot, and they were never in the top half of the Premiership table, despite the efforts of scrum-half Darren Holt, hooker Anthony Murray and back-rower Matt Leigh.

Holt again amassed plenty of points with the boot, but his effectiveness as an attacking force was often limited by the options around him.

Murray and Leigh both arrived from Lancashire and didn't let anyone down, finishing with eleven tries each.

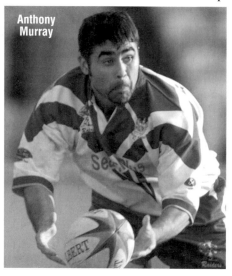

Anthony Murray

But perhaps the biggest success story of the season was brilliant young three-quarter Adrian Gardner, whose form and 16 tries were rewarded firstly with an Academy Tour Down Under and then a move to Super League club St Helens.

Of the other locally-based players, loose forward Brett McDermott never gave anything less than 100 per cent, Mike Whitehead produced some big performances in the pack and winger Glen Hutton scored some excellent tries.

But overall it was a season to forget on most fronts in Barrow, and it is now hoped new coach Cameron Bell can inspire a revival.

SWINTON LIONS also parted company with their coach at the end of the campaign, after Mike Gregory decided he had taken a somewhat depleted side as far as he could.

The Lions decided not to retain a number of high-profile players and instead look more to youth, and initially it looked as thought Great Britain Academy coach Gregory could make a go of it, as they surprisingly won their opening three games.

But a run of seven consecutive defeats followed, and - stirring wins against Featherstone, Keighley and Dewsbury apart - it rarely got any better.

One bright spot was young goal-kicking centre Mick Nanyn, whose strong performances out wide earned him a place in the NFP All Stars Team and a nomination for the Young Player of the Year.

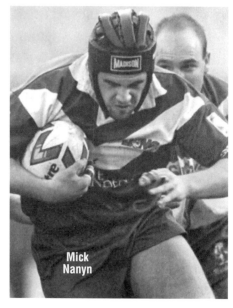

Mick Nanyn

He found support in hard-working hooker Rob Barraclough, second-rower Paul Smith and prop Lee Hansen, while veteran Australian Phil Veivers rolled back the years with a handful of outstanding performances.

Those three victories listed above, as well as a one-point defeat of Doncaster, proved that the Lions could challenge most sides when they hit top form and performed as a unit.

But unfortunately for Gregory, that didn't happen on enough occasions, although his tenure at Gigg Lane ended with a Veivers-inspired, memorable 42-16 win at the Rams on the final day of the season.

HUNSLET HAWKS also turned to youth after being forced to release a string of established players through financial restrictions, and their principal reasons to be cheerful centred around their talented young stars, notably second-rower Craig Ibbotson and stand-off Jermaine Coleman.

For coach David Plange, it was a far cry from working with the Grand Final-winning squad of 1999, but the former Castleford winger showed both his coaching versatility and his loyalty by remaining at the South Leeds Stadium and coaxing some gutsy performances out of his young charges.

The make-up of the squad ensured that this was never going to be a play-offs campaign, and wins were hard to come by for the Hawks.

But there were a few highlights among the gloom, notably an early-season defeat of Sheffield and a comprehensive win over Barrow in June.

Alongside Ibbotson and Coleman, former Leeds Rhinos youngsters George Raynor and Michael Wainwright shared the honour of Hawks' top try-scorers, while centre Iain Higgins was an ever-present and clubman Mick Coyle as consistent as always.

Dave Jessey and Tony Howcroft also impressed, and the Hawks are hoping that their long list of youngsters with first team experience will form the backbone of their side in coming years under new coach Roy Sampson.

GATESHEAD THUNDER's first season in the NFP was a largely disappointing affair, but a couple of wins towards the end of the season gave them real hope for next year, and they achieved their main objective in surviving.

It took the Thunder until their 22nd league game to record their first Premiership victory, when a Jim Carlton hat-trick helped them to an emphatic 40-12 win at Hunslet, and they followed that up the following weekend by beating York at home.

But those were the only two wins in a long season, and during the first half of the campaign Andy Kelly's side copped some heavy defeats, notably at Featherstone.

The club's famous Thunder Army stayed loyal, and were a welcome and refreshing sight at the various Premiership grounds they visited, although after an opening home game crowd of over 2,000 against Hull KR, attendances at the Thunderdome dwindled dramatically late on.

Mickey Johnson

On the field, second-rower Carlton was certainly a stand-out performer, finishing as the top try-scorer, while former Sheffield halfback Carl Briggs made a significant impact after joining the club.

Another reason to be optimistic could be found in the line of young Geordies who progressed into the first team, with Paul Thorman crossing for nine tries and fellow Academy products Stephen Rutherford and Stephen Bradley also impressing.

And former Sheffield fullback Mickey Johnson didn't gain the recognition he deserved for an excellent season at the back.

The bottom two of the competition was again made up of York and **CHORLEY LYNX**, with the Wasps this time collecting the unwanted wooden spoon after a year of turmoil.

The Lynx also had a few afternoons to forget, but they have long term plans in place to turn around recent disappointments, and at least avoided bottom place this time.

Experienced New Zealander Graeme West took over the reins at Victory Park at the beginning of the season, but with a squad comprising primarily of young fringe players and a handful of amateurs, it was always going to be a stern task for the former Wigan coach to make an immediate impact.

Eleven straight league defeats and a Challenge Cup exit at the hands of amateurs Woolston painted a pretty gloomy picture early one, but when they did record their first victory, they did it in style, thumping York 78-8.

Former Wigan Alliance halfback Stuart Fisher scored five tries and kicked nine goals for a club record 38 points in that game, and three weekends later the Lynx beat Gateshead as well.

But in their closing 13 games they conceded 50 points or more on no less than ten occasions, and the season rapidly escalated into one that couldn't finish quickly enough.

Second-rower Phil Harrison was a willing worker throughout, while winger Paul Wilcock caught the eye in the final weeks and captain Ian Talbot put in some excellent performances in difficult circumstances.

December saw a promising-looking squad starting the campaign for **YORK**, but many of their players soon left amid a financial crisis, and coach Lee Crooks even had to pull on the boots to avoid a potentially crippling fine at their lowest point.

With the likes of Kiwi Michael Smith, halfbacks Paddy Handley and Gareth Stephens and fullback Jamie Benn in their side they had a strong look about them early on, but financial difficulties set in, the big names all left the club along with a score of others, and the Wasps were left battling to make it to the end of the season.

Their sole Premiership win of the year came in February against Gateshead, one of the two games that the gallant Crooks was forced to turn out in.

But other than that, an early draw against Hunslet and a Cup win against amateurs Oulton, there was very little to smile about at the Huntington Stadium in 2001.

Prop Andy Hutchinson was one of the many heroes who provided effort and guts on a weekly basis, with club captain Alan Pallister and stand-off Gareth Oulton two others that ensured this famous club fulfilled their fixtures.

But in doing so, they found themselves on the end of a few cricket scores, with Featherstone, Rochdale and Widnes all topping 90 points.

The Wasps ended up conceding almost 1,500 points in the Premiership, but the dignity with which a Rugby League great such as Crooks handled himself during incredible adversity will not be forgotten.

NORTHERN FORD PREMIERSHIP PLAY-OFFS
Leigh fall at Final hurdle

LEIGH CENTURIONS 14 ....**OLDHAM 15**
OLDHAM stunned Minor Premiers Leigh Centurions by inflicting their first defeat of the season at Hilton Park, with Keith Brennan's field goal proving to be the difference between the sides.

The Roughyeds established a 9-0 half-time lead, with substitute hooker John Hough crossing after half an hour and Pat Rich kicking two goals.

The Centurions roared back after the interval, with tries from Neil Turley, Paul Anderson and Michael Watts giving them the lead inside the final quarter of a pulsating game.

But just moments after Watts' try, Roughyeds' fullback Mark Sibson responded with a superb score to nudge his side back in front, and with player-coach Mike Ford playing a key role, Oldham hung on in a dramatic finale.

WIDNES VIKINGS 34 ....**ROCHDALE HORNETS 24**
TWO moments of magic from Richard Agar and Phil Cantillon helped the Vikings to a thrilling victory over Rochdale Hornets at the Auto Quest.

Hornets led 14-6 at one stage following early tries from David Stephenson and impressive hooker Darren Robinson, and were only two points behind with 17 minutes remaining at 22-20.

But then a towering 40-20 from Agar set the platform for a Matt Long try, before Cantillon secured the win with an opportunist score late on.

Scrum-half Martin Crompton was highly influential for the Vikings, laying on three tries with his astute distribution.

ELIMINATION SEMI-FINALS

FEATHERSTONE ROVERS 28 ....KEIGHLEY COUGARS 24
KEIGHLEY COUGARS fell at the first hurdle of the play-offs but not before giving Featherstone Rovers an almighty scare at Lionheart Stadium.

The young Cougars outfit fought back from a 22-8 half-time deficit to come within four points of the home side with minutes remaining, with much-travelled second-rower Rob Roberts crossing twice.

Roberts' second gave the Cougars hope of a sensational late victory, but Peter Roe's side - with two-try scrum-half Jamie Rooney typically immersed in the action - held out under extensive pressure in the closing stages.

DEWSBURY RAMS 6 ....HULL KINGSTON ROVERS 19
HULL KINGSTON ROVERS marched into the second weekend of the play-offs with a superb win at Champions Dewsbury.

In an outstanding Rovers team performance, a tremendous display from loose forward Chris Charles and two tries from fullback Bob Everitt were central to their win, as the Rams crashed out of the competition on its opening weekend.

Rovers led 10-2 at the break following an early score from hooker Mike Dixon and Everitt's first.

A second from the fullback stretched the lead to 18-2, and Barry Eaton's late try was little more than consolation.

WEEKEND TWO
MINOR SEMI-FINALS

LEIGH CENTURIONS 26..FEATHERSTONE ROVERS 10
AN outstanding first-half performance from the Centurions saw them sew up a place in the Major Semi-finals.

Tries from Adam Bristow, Neil Turley and Dave Bradbury helped them establish a commanding 22-0 half-time lead, and although Rovers responded bravely in the second period, the Centurions booked a showdown with Widnes Vikings for a place in the Grand Final.

Rovers did improve markedly after the break, with Andy Bastow and Richard Thaler tries giving them a glimmer of hope going into the closing quarter, but two goals from Simon Svabic ensured the Centurions were always far enough ahead.

ROCHDALE HORNETS 21 ....HULL KINGSTON ROVERS 14
HULL KINGSTON ROVERS' gallant bid for the Grand Final was ended at Spotland as Hornets produced a clinical second-half performance.

The sides were locked at 4-all at half-time after an opening period dominated for long spells by Rovers.

But Gary Wilkinson's side failed to convert superior possession and field position into points, and tries from Marlon Billy, James Bunyan and Danny Wood just saw Hornets through.

Widnes coach Neil Kelly celebrates reaching the Grand Final with Martin Crompton

Even then Rovers - one of the form teams in the competition late in the season - scored late tries through Whetu Taewa and Richard Slater, but they weren't enough to prevent Hornets from progressing.

WEEKEND THREE
MAJOR SEMI-FINALS

LEIGH CENTURIONS 18 ....**WIDNES VIKINGS 26**
THE Vikings secured their place in the Grand Final by defeating Minor Premiers Leigh for the first time in the season in front over 6,000 supporters at Hilton Park.

The home side held a 12-4 interval lead following tries from Chris Morley and Alan Hadcroft, after dominating long periods of the opening half, despite being without star fullback Neil Turley through injury.

But the Vikings roared back after half-time, with winger Chris Percival's second try and a brace from Damian Munro giving them the lead. Richard Agar nudged them seven points in front with a well-taken field goal, before Centurions' substitute Phil Kendrick dragged the home side back into the game with a 73rd minute try.

Simon Knox was the unlikely candidate to edge the Vikings further in front with their second one-pointer, before Chris McKinney crossed to seal the game for Neil Kelly's side in the dying stages.

"We felt at half-time that although we had very little possession and we had to do a lot of work, we just need some ball in good positions, as we had shown in the first half we could score," Vikings' coach Neil Kelly said.

"It was a great game and the right result."

Oldham's Jason Clegg takes on the Rochdale defence in a Major Semi-final thriller

ROCHDALE HORNETS 32 ....OLDHAM 39

OLDHAM player-coach Mike Ford and substitute hooker John Hough combined to instigate the most amazing of comebacks, as the Roughyeds fought back from 18 points behind with twelve minutes remaining to win a classic semi-final at Spotland.

Hornets led 32-14 after 67 minutes, and at that stage had scored six tries to one, including Marlon Billy's effort, which broke Rochdale's 66-year-old club record.

But the emergence of Ford and Hough from the bench inspired the Roughyeds, and four late, late tries completed the incredible turnaround.

Hornets led 24-12 at the interval through tries from Danny Sculthorpe, Sean Cooper, Darren Robinson, Matt Calland and Billy, but four goals from the impeccable boot of Pat Rich just kept Oldham within sight.

Eight points after the break from Danny Wood looked to have confirmed Hornets' place in the Grand Final, but the kicking of Rich - who finished the game with nine goals from nine attempts - just kept his side in it.

Ford stepped off the bench on 67 minutes and, with second-rower Bryan Henare crossing twice in the last seven minutes, the Roughyeds powered home against a devastated Hornets outfit.

"Pat Rich won us the football game," Ford said after the game.

"Every week he's mithering for footballs to practise with. They scored one more try than us, but Pat's kicking won it for us."

NORTHERN FORD PREMIERSHIP GRAND FINAL
Vikings plunder title

WIDNES VIKINGS achieved the primary objective of their Super League dream by beating Oldham in the Northern Ford Premiership Grand Final at Spotland.

The Vikings were comprehensive winners against an Oldham side that failed to reach the heights of their outstanding play-off wins at Leigh and Rochdale, scoring five tries to lead 24-4 with six minutes remaining.

Hooker Phil Cantillon completed a wondrous season by scoring a try in a Man of the Match performance, while the win represented a second successive Grand Final win for coach Neil Kelly, who took over at the Auto Quest Stadium mid-season.

When Kelly took over in March, a third successive defeat, at home to Keighley, left the Vikings clinging to the eighth and last play-off place with just 15 points from 13 games.

Yet four months later, after an extraordinary run of 17 wins in 18 games, the Vikings could contemplate a return to the big stage.

The level of experience in Kelly's Vikings' side proved too much for the Roughyeds, none of whose players had played in a Grand Final before they walked out at Spotland on one of the hottest days of the year.

"It was just as good second time around," said Kelly after the game. "To do it with a different club was even more satisfying. Winning is a special experience and everyone at the club can feel really proud. Hopefully, it will lead to what it didn't lead to for Dewsbury last year. But we have done our job and now it is up to other people to do theirs.

"My predecessor (David Hulme) deserves credit for laying the foundations and the players for turning the season around. We had a tremendous run and played some tremendous football."

No way through the Oldham defence for Chris Percival

Mike Ford, the Oldham player-coach, playing the final game of his distinguished career, was proud of his players' efforts and felt they would gain from the experience.

"They are all pretty gutted at the moment," he said. "The sad thing is that we never gave ourselves a chance to win the game.

"At half-time, losing 10-4, we hadn't played well but we still felt it could be our day. The commitment and effort of the players was brilliant but we didn't play well on the day and credit to Widnes. We got a terrific reaction from the fans and we are proud of what we achieved but there is only one winner and that is Widnes."

The near 9,000 crowd set a new record for a NFP Grand Final and the concept of the play-offs had now been embraced fully by the NFP family. The supporters of both clubs, plus many neutrals, made for a terrific atmosphere and a colourful backdrop.

Saturday 28th July 2001

NORTHERN FORD PREMIERSHIP GRAND FINAL

OLDHAM 14 WIDNES VIKINGS 24

OLDHAM: 1 Mark Sibson; 2 Joey Hayes; 3 Anthony Gibbons; 4 Pat Rich; 5 Joe McNicholas; 6 David Gibbons; 7 Neil Roden; 8 Leo Casey; 9 Keith Brennan; 10 Paul Norton; 11 Phil Farrell; 12 Bryan Henare; 13 Kevin Mannion. Subs: 14 Mike Ford for Mannion (27); 15 Jason Clegg for Casey (18); 16 John Hough for Brennan (44); 17 Danny Guest for Norton (40BB, rev 54); Mannion for Henare (66); Guest for Clegg (73).
Tries: Brennan (9), Ford (74), Mannion (80); **Goal:** Rich.
VIKINGS: 1 Paul Atcheson; 2 Damian Munro; 3 Craig Weston; 4 Jason Demetriou; 5 Chris Percival; 6 Richard Agar; 7 Martin Crompton; 8 Simon Knox; 9 Phil Cantillon; 10 Stephen Holgate; 11 Steve Gee; 12 Sean Richardson; 13 Tommy Hodgkinson. Subs: 14 Andy Craig for Percival (65); 15 Chris McKinney for Gee (41); 16 Joe Faimalo for Knox (32); 17 Matthew Long for Holgate (23); Knox for Long (49BB, rev 61); Holgate for Long (74).
Tries: Gee (17), Demetriou (38, 60), Cantillon (50), Munro (69); **Goals:** Weston 2.
League Express Men of the Match:
Oldham: Jason Clegg; *Vikings:* Phil Cantillon.
Penalty count: 8-5; **Half-time:** 4-10;
Referee: Steve Ganson (St Helens);
Attendance: 8,974 *(at Spotland, Rochdale).*

The Vikings started the better, and Craig Weston kicked the Vikings into an early lead after Oldham skipper Leo Casey gave away a penalty.

But the Roughyeds, in virtually their first attack, took the lead. David Gibbons hoisted a high ball to the right wing and, when Chris Percival failed to gather, hooker Keith Brennan nipped in for an unconverted score.

The Vikings regained the lead when loose forward Tommy Hodgkinson switched an attack to the left and Steve Gee took Simon Knox's pass to force his way over, despite the attentions of three defenders. And Widnes secured a six-point interval lead when, after a scampering run down the middle by Cantillon, Richard Agar's cut-out pass sent Jason Demetriou over in the right corner.

Ford had come off the bench to inspire his side and his shrewd kicking game certainly posed Widnes problems. From one kick, Damian Munro dropped the ball close to his own line and Widnes conceded a penalty that out of form kicker Pat Rich failed to convert.

Cantillon's try, ten minutes after the restart, was the killer. After Ford, attempting to take Joey Hayes' rushed pass from dummy-half, knocked on to concede a scrum ten metres out, Cantillon brought out his party trick, burrowing over from dummy-half after a Knox charge.

Ten minutes later, from another scrum after Mark Sibson hacked clear Weston's raking kick, Paul Atcheson received from Agar and fed the impressive Demetriou for his second, Weston adding his second goal.

Widnes's third try of the half also came from a scrum, this time after Rich fumbled Agar's towering kick under pressure. Atcheson again joined the line and, when his pass rebounded off an Oldham player in a three-man tackle, Munro swooped on the loose ball and tapped ahead before gathering to romp over.

The Roughyeds did manage two consolations, Ford grabbing his first try of the season after combining well with Kevin Mannion down the short side before repaying the compliment by providing the rangy Oldham loose forward with the Roughyeds' third try in the last minute.

But there was no catching Widnes and the club that was World Champion just over ten years before, was back for a tilt at the big time.

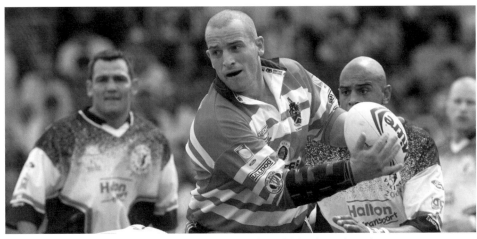

Paul Norton looks for support as Sean Richardson closes in

5
INTERNATIONAL SCENE

THE ASHES SERIES 2001
Closer and closer

IT was the tour that almost never happened.

Seven years since their last tour to Europe, the 19th Kangaroos were due to revive the greatest of sporting contests, a three-match Ashes series between Great Britain and Australia.

And then, in the space of a few hours, the whole world of trans-continental travel came to a juddering halt. Within a month, the airspace between Australia and Europe was to become a warzone.

On October 8 the Australian Rugby League team was sitting at Port Moresby airport having beaten Papua New Guinea 54-12 the previous day. On a television on the wall, CNN is reporting that bombing in the so-called War On Terror has started in Afghanistan.

Rumours about the seven-match English leg of the tour being in jeopardy were, by then, almost a month old. Officials had been "monitoring the situation" since the September 11 terrorist attacks in New York City and Washington. In the lead-up to Brisbane's NRL preliminary final against Parramatta on September 23, Broncos prop Shane Webcke had become the first player to express serious concern about leaving the southern hemisphere.

On their arrival back in Sydney, Melbourne prop Robbie Kearns was the most outspoken of the players. "I'm really worried about going and I might have to consider my own position if the tour goes ahead," he told a group of journalists outside the arrivals hall, before offering the immortal line that landmarks such as "the Eiffel Tower" will be terrorist targets."

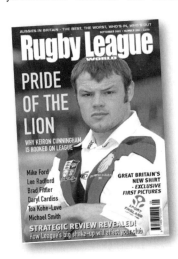

The next day, team manager Darrell Bampton conducted a straw poll of the players. The vote is never made public, but there are varying reports to suggest the vote is 16-8, or 19-5, in favour. Those against include Brad Fittler, Andrew Johns, Darren Lockyer, Webcke and Kearns.

Within 24 hours, with the 16 in favour given the chance to speak to their families, the vote is 12-12. On Wednesday, October 10, the Australian Rugby League called a media conference at their offices at 165 Phillip Street, Sydney, and the 2001 Kangaroo Tour was called off.

The blow to Rugby League was almost

incalculable, with some reports putting a financial shortfall for the RFL of over two million pounds.

In the days ahead, the Australian players would be labelled "scared", the ARL "spineless" and the decision "disgraceful" and "a victory for terrorism".

It was the greatest Rugby League imbroglio since Super League, and there were conflicting versions of why the Kangaroo Tour was scrapped. One was the ARL led the way, deciding that they did not want to shoulder the supposed risk - including insurance issues - of sending the players on tour. The other had at least some players more worried about working on their suntans than going to England.

Captain Brad Fittler copped the brunt of the backlash.

The day after his fiancée, Maria Liarris, implored him from the back of the Daily Telegraph not to tour, it was called off.

Less than a week after saying he would not play for Australia again, Fittler was packing his bags.

ARL Chairman Colin Love defended the original decision. "If we were in the same situation again, we would do the same thing," he said, pointing out that other Australian companies had suspended international travel for executives at the time. "Maybe with hindsight we could have delayed."

The original board vote against travelling was 5-3, with Love and chief executive Geoff Carr abstaining. The change of heart, after the players changed theirs, was not unanimous.

A factor in the affair may have been money. RFL Director of Rugby Greg McCallum admitted at a media conference shortly after the tour was revived that there was ill-feeling between Phillip Street and Red Hall over last year's World Cup, and that a "line in the sand" needed to be drawn under the issue.

Wigan Chairman Maurice Lindsay, who was rightly credited with getting the tour back on in the holiday absence of RFL chairman Sir Rodney Walker, subsequently increased the ARL's guarantee, but Love stated: "I can give you a cast-iron guarantee that financial considerations played absolutely no role in our original decision, or the subsequent decision."

It was Lindsay who met with Greg McCallum, Nigel Wood, David Waite and Gary Hetherington and hatched the plan for a shortened tour. All the club games would be cancelled and the first Test at Huddersfield put back eight days to shorten the Aussies' stay.

When the ARL asked for more information, the British High Commissioner in Australia,

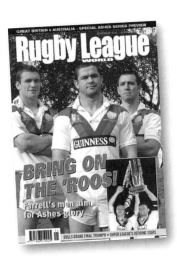

Great Britain debutant Paul King looks for a gap against France

Friday 26th October 2001

FRANCE 12 GREAT BRITAIN 42

FRANCE: 1 Renaud Guigue (Avignon); 2 Michael Van Snick (Villeneuve); 3 Gilles Cornut (Villeneuve); 4 Arnaud Dulac (St Gaudens); 5 Sylvain Houles (London Broncos); 6 Laurent Frayssinous (Villeneuve); 7 Fabien Devecchi (Toulouse) (C); 8 Romain Gagliazzo (Villeneuve); 9 Vincent Wulf (Villeneuve); 10 Frederic Teixido (Limoux); 11 Aurelin Cologni (UTC); 12 Adel Fellous (UTC); 13 Laurent Carrasco (Villeneuve). Subs (all used): 14 Romain Sort (Villeneuve); 15 Julien Gerin (St Gaudens); 16 David Collado (Villeneuve); 17 Eric Anselme (St Gaudens).
Tries: Sort (44), Frayssinous (56); **Goals:** Frayssinous 2.
GREAT BRITAIN: 1 Kris Radlinski (Wigan Warriors); 2 Paul Wellens (St Helens); 3 Paul Johnson (Wigan Warriors); 4 Gary Connolly (Wigan Warriors); 5 David Hodgson (Wigan Warriors); 6 Lee Briers (Warrington Wolves); 7 Paul Deacon (Bradford Bulls); 8 Terry O'Connor (Wigan Warriors); 9 Kevin Sinfield (Leeds Rhinos); 10 Barrie McDermott (Leeds Rhinos); 11 Chris Joynt (St Helens); 12 Paul King (Hull FC); 13 Andrew Farrell (Wigan Warriors) (C). Subs (all used): 14 Richard Horne (Hull FC); 15 Mike Forshaw (Bradford Bulls); 16 Stuart Fielden (Bradford Bulls); 17 Paul Anderson (Bradford Bulls).
Tries: Radlinski (2), Joynt (5, 8), Wellens (10), Briers (31), Deacon (48), King (75); **Goals:** Farrell 6, Briers.
League Express Men of the Match:
France: Laurent Frayssinous; *Great Britain:* Chris Joynt.
Penalty count: 6-1; **Half-time:** 0-30;
Referee: Robert Connolly (England);
Attendance: 10,000 *(at Stade Armandie, Agen).*

Alistair Goodlad, became involved. He sent the Consul General in Sydney to a media conference on Wednesday, October 17. The tour was back on, albeit without Shane Webcke, who was the only player who still refused to travel.

The whole Rugby League world breathed a sigh of relief.

THE WARM-UPS

The warm-up game against the French on October 26th was nowhere near a true Test for the Lions.

Great Britain blitzed France in the opening ten minutes of the first international between the two countries since 1994.

With nine minutes on the clock the

Lions were 24-0 up and the game was over. But Waite chose to make several substitutions and positional changes that disrupted the rhythm and the French fought back to 'draw' the second half 12-12.

"I don't think we were ruthless enough," Waite admitted after the game. "We need to develop a bit more killer."

Waite denied his use of Kevin Sinfield and Mike Forshaw at hooker was an attempt to throw a dummy to the Aussies.

"We have nothing up our sleeves for Australia," he said. "You can't hide anything in this game."

That stunning opening nine minutes in which Britain scored four unanswered tries laid the platform for a 42-12 victory. Great Britain debutants Paul Wellens, Lee Briers, Paul Deacon and Paul King all crossed for tries, while St Helens' second-rower Chris Joynt was outstanding, scoring twice and causing the French all kinds of problems throughout.

The Australians unveiled their latest generation of stars in their 54-12 win over Papua New Guinea in Port Moresby, with five of the six new caps selected to tour on debut - winger Nathan Blacklock, centre Mark Gasnier and reserves Jason Ryles, Jamie Lyon and Braith Anasta. All but prop Ryles ended up scoring points.

The World Cup holders led only 18-6 at half-time, but in the final 25 minutes proved they are packed with talent. St George Illawarra's Blacklock performed a backflip after his second try and even booted a couple of goals. Clubmate Gasnier - nephew of the all-time Kangaroo great Reg Gasnier - was commanding out wide, flicking the ball to Blacklock in the first half and bagging a try of his own with five minutes to go.

Bulldogs five-eighth Braith Anasta only managed a goal but showed more than a glimpse of his undoubted pedigree along with Ryles, who relished the unexpectedly hard going up front.

As it turned out, with the First Test being put back a week, it was to be Australia's last game for more than a month.

Sunday 7th October 2001

PAPUA NEW GUINEA 12 AUSTRALIA 54

PNG: 1 John Wilshere (Brisbane Easts); 2 Alfred Songoro (Central Comets); 3 Eddie Aila (Wynnum-Manly); 4 Chris Purkilil (Rabaul Gurias); 5 Marcus Bai (Melbourne); 6 Stanley Tepend (Enga Mioks); 7 Tom O'Reilly (Warrington); 8 David Westley (Parramatta); 9 Mark Mom (C) (Brisbane Easts); 10 Mikaili Aizure (Goroka Lahanis); 11 Raymond Karl (Enga Mioks); 12 Stanley Gene (Huddersfield); 13 Duncan Naawi (Wynnum-Manly). Subs (all used): 14 Nigel Hukula (Goroka Lahanis); 15 Chris Lome (Port Moresby); 16 John Waka (Rabaul Gurias); 17 Michael Marum (Rabaul Gurias).
Tries: Aizure (39), Wilshere (52); **Goals:** Wilshere 2.
AUSTRALIA: 1 Darren Lockyer (Brisbane); 2 Nathan Blacklock (St George Illawarra); 3 Mark Gasnier (St George Illawarra); 4 Matt Gidley (Newcastle); 5 Lote Tuqiri (Brisbane); 6 Trent Barrett (St George Illawarra); 7 Craig Gower (Penrith); 8 Jason Stevens (Sharks); 9 Danny Buderus (Newcastle); 10 Robbie Kearns (Melbourne); 11 Brad Meyers (Brisbane); 12 Dane Carlaw (Brisbane); 13 Brad Fittler (C) (Sydney). Subs (all used): 14 Petero Civoniceva (Brisbane); 15 Jason Ryles (St George Illawarra); 16 Braith Anasta (Bulldogs); 17 Jamie Lyon (Parramatta).
Tries: Gower (10), Blacklock (18, 64), Lyon (36, 53), Tuqiri (44, 78), Lockyer (48), Gidley (59), Gasnier (75);
Goals: Lockyer 4, Blacklock 2, Anasta.
League Express Men of the Match:
PNG: Raymond Karl; *Australia:* Jamie Lyon.
Penalty count: 2-1; **Half-time:** 6-18;
Referee: Bill Harrigan (Australia); **Attendance:** 13,000 (capacity) *(at Lloyd Robson Oval, Port Moresby)*.

FIRST GUINNESS TEST
GREAT BRITAIN 20 ....AUSTRALIA 12

Paul Sculthorpe spearheaded Great Britain's thrilling first Guinness Test victory with an outstanding individual contribution, capped by the match-clinching try with less than five minutes remaining of a pulsating game.

Not for nothing was the brilliant St Helens star the Man of Steel for 2001 and he showed all the qualities that made him such a clear choice for that prestigious award as Great Britain emulated their feats of 1990 and 1994 in winning the first Test of the series.

Hopes were high that this time Great Britain could finish the job and secure a first Ashes series victory since Frank Myler's side down under in 1970 and a first success on home soil for 42 years.

Sculthorpe's winning try came with Australia firmly scenting a famous comeback after recovering from 0-13 down to trail by only a point after Andrew Johns and Adam MacDougall had scored converted tries in a devastating six-minute spell. Then Lote Tuqiri had a try disallowed for a forward pass by Jamie Lyon.

Lyon's first Ashes Test then got worse as he lost the ball, in Sculthorpe's tackle, in the first tackle of a set as the Kangaroos desperately tried to clear their lines. Sculthorpe took full advantage, taking Mike Forshaw's pass and showing great strength and vision to burrow his way through a mass of defenders for a try that skipper Andrew Farrell nervelessly converted.

The McAlpine crowd went mad and Sculthorpe's confidently-struck field goal, with under two minutes left, was merely the icing on the cake.

It was a major triumph for David Waite, who had been a member of the 1973 Kangaroos that won the series 2-1 after losing the first Test at Wembley.

Given the boost of an opportunist Jamie Peacock try inside 119.5 seconds, Britain were inspired. Farrell and Sculthorpe led from the front, their kicking game spot-on, and Gary Connolly produced an awesome display in the centre, coming up with some awesome defensive hits, while Kris Radlinski was another hero at the back.

Harried into uncharacteristic errors by the ferocity of the British defence, the world champions, who suffered their first defeat in 13 internationals, were stung.

The Great Britain side on the official teamsheet was of a different composition to that announced during the week with Kevin Sinfield at scrum-half, Mike Forshaw at hooker and Richard Horne on the bench. Paul Johnson, instead of Keith Senior, was listed on the wing.

There were no such machinations in the Australian line-up, which was as anticipated on a chilly November afternoon for the first Ashes Test in Huddersfield since 1937. Then, despite losing the third game at Fartown before a crowd of only 9,093, Great Britain already had their eighth successive series victory in the bag.

Farrell, captaining Britain for the 15th successive time, Connolly, Barrie McDermott and Chris Joynt were the players remaining from the last proper Ashes series, in 1994, between the countries with Brad Fittler, the Australian

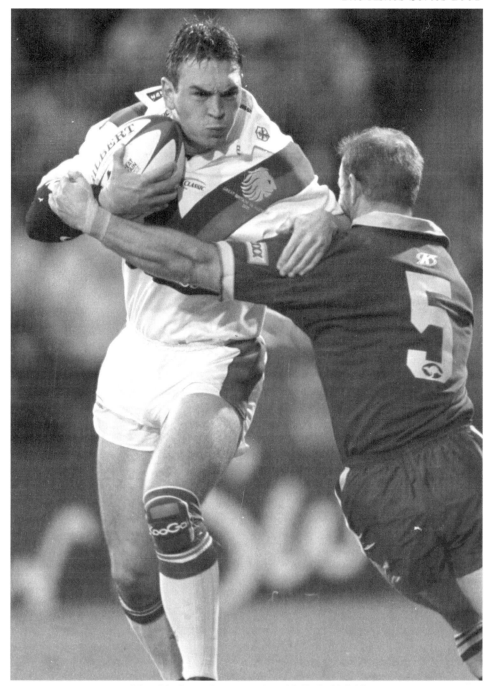

Adam MacDougall gets to grips with Kevin Sinfield

captain in his farewell Test series, the sole Australian survivor.

Britain got the perfect start as Peacock grabbed a sensational opening try after just 86 seconds. Peacock was quickly out of the defensive line as Darren Lockyer attempted a clearance kick and charged down the effort. Connolly reacted first to the loose ball and, as the cover closed in, flipped out a perfect inside pass for the supporting Peacock to romp over. Farrell tagged on the conversion and the home side had a 6-0 lead.

The Australians were clearly rattled and their prop, Jason Stevens, was fortunate to stay on the field after appearing to stamp on the grounded Terry O'Connor before playing the ball. O'Connor was forced to the blood bin with a cut chin before returning to the fray in the second half, and Stevens was banned for one match the following week.

Tuqiri was clearly targeted by Farrell and Sculthorpe with raking kicks, and looked uncertain under the barrage. After Sculthorpe pulled a field goal attempt wide, Lockyer was pinned behind his own line as Britain attempted to build on their great start.

At the other end, Radlinski was outstanding under an aerial barrage, making a 50-metre kick return from Andrew Johns's kick only for the supporting Johnson to unluckily spill the ball on halfway. Joynt typified the British resolve with a crucial try-saving tackle on Jason Ryles midway through the first half.

Sculthorpe was then pulled up for ball-reefing on Lockyer to set up a Kangaroo attack but Michael Vella lost the ball in a shuddering tackle from Mike Forshaw, another British hero.

Sculthorpe then scored the second British try with 13 minutes remaining of a breathtaking first half. Taking Farrell's pass, he cut between two defenders from 20 metres out and then straightened up to brush off Lockyer's despairing tackle. Farrell added the goal and Great Britain, well worthy of their 12-0 interval lead, might have gone into the dressing sheds with an even bigger advantage but Sinfield had a field goal attempt charged down while Farrell failed with a 48-metre penalty shot after Connolly was felled by Fittler's swinging arm.

As the British dominated the start of the second half, Sculthorpe received from Sinfield and potted a 20-metre field goal to extend their lead to 13-0 after 50 minutes. It might have been more, Farrell failing with a similar effort from 25 metres while Sculthorpe, after a brilliant 40-20 kick, saw his pass intercepted by Fittler. Joynt almost burrowed over from dummy-half as the Kangaroos hung on.

But the warning signs were flashing as Radlinski pulled off a crucial try-saving tackle on Danny Buderus who had gathered Fittler's angled kick on the run and looked a certain scorer. And the Kangaroos finally put it together when halfbacks Johns and Barrett shipped the ball to the left on half way and Lyon and Tuqiri combined to send Johns scampering over for a converted try.

Six minutes later, the lead was just one point after Barrett sent Matthew Gidley down the right and the backflip pass was perfect for MacDougall to fly over, despite the attempts of the covering Radlinski and Stuart Fielden. The video referee confirmed the grounding and Johns's second goal flew between the sticks.

Britain rallied when Farrell kicked through for Sculthorpe, the ball bouncing off his back

Man of the Match Paul Sculthorpe held up

behind the Australian line with Tuqiri just beating Radlinski to the vital touchdown.

But with nine minutes remaining the McAlpine crowd was hushed as Tuqiri, receiving from Lyon after Fittler had created an overlap on the left, burst inside for what looked to be the clinching try only for groans to turn to relieved cheers as referee Connolly ruled the pass forward.

Britain survived and found enough in the tank to come back. Lyon, on the first tackle, lost the ball in Sculthorpe's tackle close to his own line and, after Sinfield went close, Sculthorpe went over for a try that will live long in the memory. Farrell's third goal and Sculthorpe's second one-pointer, from Forshaw's pass, confirmed the British triumph.

FIRST GUINNESS TEST

GREAT BRITAIN 20 AUSTRALIA 12
Sunday 11th September
at McAlpine Stadium, Huddersfield

GREAT BRITAIN: 1 Kris Radlinski (Wigan Warriors); 2 Leon Pryce (Bradford Bulls); 3 Gary Connolly (Wigan Warriors); 5 Keith Senior (Leeds Rhinos); 4 Paul Johnson (Wigan Warriors); 6 Paul Sculthorpe (St Helens); 9 Kevin Sinfield (Leeds Rhinos); 8 Terry O'Connor (Wigan Warriors); 15 Mike Forshaw (Bradford Bulls); 10 Barrie McDermott (Leeds Rhinos); 11 Chris Joynt (St Helens); 12 Jamie Peacock (Bradford Bulls); 13 Andrew Farrell (Wigan Warriors) (C). Subs: 14 Paul Wellens (St Helens) not used; 7 Richard Horne (Hull FC); 16 Paul Anderson (Bradford Bulls); 17 Stuart Fielden (Bradford Bulls).
Tries: Peacock (2), Sculthorpe (27, 76); **Goals:** Farrell 3; **Field goals:** Sculthorpe 2.
AUSTRALIA: 1 Darren Lockyer (Brisbane Broncos); 5 Adam MacDougall (Newcastle Knights); 3 Matthew Gidley (Newcastle Knights); 4 Jamie Lyon (Parramatta Eels); 2 Lote Tuqiri (Brisbane Broncos); 6 Trent Barrett (St George-Illawarra); 7 Andrew Johns (Newcastle Knights); 8 Jason Stevens (Sharks); 9 Danny Buderus (Newcastle Knights); 10 Robbie Kearns (Melbourne Storm); 11 Dane Carlaw (Brisbane Broncos); 12 Ben Kennedy (Newcastle Knights); 13 Brad Fittler (Sydney Roosters) (C). Subs (all used); 14 Braith Anasta (Canterbury Bulldogs); 15 Michael Vella (Parramatta Eels); 16 Petero Civoniceva (Brisbane Broncos); 17 Jason Ryles (St George-Illawarra).
Tries: Johns (57), MacDougall (63); **Goals:** Johns 2.
On report: Stevens (5) - stamping on O'Connor.
League Express Men of the Match:
Great Britain: Paul Sculthorpe; *Australia:* Andrew Johns.
Penalty count: 8-3; **Half-time:** 12-0;
Referee: Robert Connolly (England); **Attendance:** 21,758.

SECOND GUINNESS TEST

GREAT BRITAIN 12 ....AUSTRALIA 40

If Great Britain bridged the gap with their shock first Guinness Test win, then Australia blew it wide open again in the second.

It was a re-run of the many thrashings Britain have suffered since they last won the Ashes in 1970. At 40-0 it looked as if it was going to be the worst horror show of all. But with 25 minutes left Britain, to their credit, scrambled back to score the final 12 points.

The Kangaroos were unrecognisable from Huddersfield only six days earlier. And so were Britain, who had been so full of confidence and now looked hesitant and unsure.

Andrew Johns in particular showed a vast improvement to live up to his reputation as the world's best player. His 20-point haul came from two tries and six goals, while he had a big hand in two other touchdowns, despite aggravating a rib cartilage injury in the first half.

With Great Britain coach David Waite dispensing with a specialist halfback for the second match running, Johns's scrum-half craft was totally dominating. His flickering runs, astute handling and decisive support play were a joy to watch.

Johns was in at the beginning of the move that led to the first try after only six minutes, when he linked with Robbie Kearns to send Brad Fittler sidestepping past Kris Radlinski. He was involved twice in the next try, which he scored himself, but he would be the first to give most of the credit to Lote Tuqiri. The big winger had been targeted as vulnerable under a high kick in the first Test, but the same tactic rebounded on Great Britain with shattering effect when they tried it again at Bolton. Tuqiri fielded one easily enough not far from his own line in the 18th minute, and then set off on the sort of run with which Eric Grothe and Wendell Sailor used to terrify British defences. It took him deep into enemy territory before handing on to Johns, who exchanged passes with Darren Lockyer before completing the magnificent 95-metre raid.

Johns' second try came two minutes after the interval, and made a monkey of Britain's defence as he held off three challengers to plunge in from close range. Johns was running the show now, and nine minutes later his long pass opened the way for Matthew Gidley to send in Adam MacDougall near the corner flag. Things went from bad to worse for Great Britain when Ben Kennedy went in for Australia's seventh try in the 55th minute, and Johns added his sixth goal. Johns' second try was bad enough for British fans to suffer, MacDougall's could not have been more simple, but Kennedy's was like suffering an horrific flashback of the 1980s when the likes of Les Boyd and Wayne Pearce brushed aside the feeblest of tackling attempts to rampage through.

The Aussies virtually shut up shop when it got to 40-0, but they had already done enough to show that Huddersfield was just a bad dream for them. Fittler was back to his best, leading his team in great style and finding plenty of support.

Lockyer was another Australian to shake off the lethargy of the first Test, the fullback adding impetus to their attack every time he linked up. Eight minutes after he had backed up to send in Johns for the second try, Lockyer went on his

Jamie Lyon tries to break free from Jamie Peacock

SECOND GUINNESS TEST

GREAT BRITAIN 12 AUSTRALIA 40
Saturday 17th November 2001
at Reebok Stadium, Bolton

GREAT BRITAIN: 1 Kris Radlinski (Wigan Warriors); 2 Leon Pryce (Bradford Bulls); 3 Gary Connolly (Wigan Warriors); 4 Keith Senior (Leeds Rhinos); 5 Paul Johnson (Wigan Warriors); 6 Paul Sculthorpe (St Helens); 7 Kevin Sinfield (Wigan Warriors); 8 Terry O'Connor (Wigan Warriors); 9 Mike Forshaw (Bradford Bulls); 10 Barrie McDermott (Leeds Rhinos); 11 Chris Joynt (St Helens); 12 Jamie Peacock (Bradford Bulls); 13 Andrew Farrell (Wigan Warriors (C). Subs (all used): 14 Paul Wellens (St Helens); 15 Richard Horne (Hull FC); 16 Paul Anderson (Bradford Bulls); 17 Stuart Fielden (Bradford Bulls).
Tries: Sculthorpe (69), Pryce (79); **Goals:** Farrell 2.
AUSTRALIA: 1 Darren Lockyer (Brisbane Broncos); 5 Adam MacDougall (Newcastle Knights); 3 Matthew Gidley (Newcastle Knights); 4 Jamie Lyon (Parramatta Eels); 2 Lote Tuqiri (Brisbane Broncos); 6 Trent Barrett (St George-Illawarra); 7 Andrew Johns (Newcastle Knights); 17 Jason Ryles (St George-Illawarra); 9 Danny Buderus (Newcastle Knights); 10 Robbie Kearns (Melbourne Storm); 11 Dane Carlaw (Brisbane Broncos); 12 Ben Kennedy (Newcastle Knights); 13 Brad Fittler (Sydney Roosters) (C). Subs (all used): 14 Braith Anasta (Canterbury Bulldogs); 15 Michael Vella (Parramatta Eels); 16 Petero Civoniceva (Brisbane Broncos); 17 Brad Meyers (Brisbane Broncos).
Tries: Fittler (6), Johns (18, 42), Lockyer (26), Anasta (34), MacDougall (53), Kennedy (55); **Goals:** Johns 6.
League Express Men of the Match:
Great Britain: Andrew Farrell; *Australia:* Andrew Johns.
Penalty count: 3-3; **Half-time:** 0-24;
Referee: Bill Harrigan (Australia); **Attendance:** 22,152.

own to dance through for another. He should also have scored earlier, when he sliced through only to lose the ball as he stretched out for the touchdown.

Braith Anasta had a similar hit and miss late in the first half. On for the injured Tuqiri, the rising young star outjumped Leon Pryce to collect Gidley's high kick and bring it down for Australia's fourth try. But four minutes later Anasta just failed to get another touchdown when he chased Lockyer's kick through and dived ahead of hesitant home fullback Radlinski, only for the video replay to clearly show he had failed to connect.

It mattered little. The 24-0 scoreline told its own story. Not since Australia had led 31-8 at half-time on the way to the record 50-12 victory in 1963 had one side so dominated the first half, and Britain did at least score two tries then. This time they never looked like scoring before the interval.

There were real fears that the record books and Britain's defence was going to be torn to shreds in the second half, when Australia's three quick tries made it 40-0 after 55 minutes. But mercifully, an easing off of Australia's intent and a spirited reply by Britain avoided any such embarrassment.

Paul Sculthorpe finally broke through for a try in the 69th minute. It was similar to his second in the first Test as he charged in from close range, but there was no repeat of the wild joy that followed the late match-clincher at Huddersfield. Just a wry smile from Britain's hero of the week, who was never allowed to repeat the wonderful performance that had demolished Australia.

Britain did at least keep going to the very last seconds, and they had the small satisfaction of completing the scoring when Paul Wellens slipped through to send Pryce racing 20 metres to the corner. Andrew Farrell's second goal, a terrific effort from near touch, made it 12 points in the last eleven minutes to give Britain just a glimmer of hope that they could carry on where they left off in the decider.

Farrell's performance epitomised Britain's overall display. Their captain put in plenty of effort and never gave up but there was nothing but doom, gloom and despondency in the press the next day.

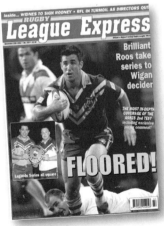

Andrew Johns and Brad Fittler celebrate Australia's Ashes victory

THIRD GUINNESS TEST

GREAT BRITAIN 8...AUSTRALIA 28

BRAD FITTLER brought the curtain down on his illustrious test career by leading Australia to victory in the third and deciding Guinness Ashes Test before a capacity crowd at Wigan's JJB Stadium.

Fittler, who set the seal on this hard-fought game with the conversion to Trent Barrett's second try, could have hardly anticipated the drama that would follow from the Kangaroos' late decision to tour. Defeat in the first Test to a Great Britain side that did just about everything right, with the Australians looking decidedly under-cooked, was swiftly put right by the Kangaroos' stunning second Test romp. The third Test was an altogether tighter affair, and the home side, after a committed and brave performance, could feel hard done by after losing by a 20-point margin.

The shock over the condition of coach Chris Anderson - who suffered a heart attack in the first half of the game and was rushed to Wigan Infirmary - was still filtering through as Fittler put into words the weight of expectation that he carried as Kangaroo captain.

"The mood is still very sombre," he explained.

"Not just about Chris, but the hardest thing about being Australian is that you don't feel jubilation like other teams do when you win. It's just relief at not being beaten."

Fittler, who brought his 39-Test career to a close, saw at first hand that the new breed of Australian stars is in the making, led by the brilliant Trent Barrett, who climaxed an outstanding display with a late two-try burst. Darren Lockyer, wonderfully positioned at the back and a devastating counter-attacker, Adam MacDougall, who produced a superb winger's game, and Andrew Johns took him close for individual honours, with Danny Buderus another star Australian performer.

It was a courageous effort by David Waite's Great Britain side, and the coach was left to reflect on what difference a fit Sean Long, Keiron Cunningham, Adrian Morley and Terry Newton might have made, had they been available for the series. As Waite pointed out, if Great Britain had capitalised on a couple of opportunities, especially early in the second half, then Australia's fear of losing might have been tested to the full. There was no disgrace in losing the way they did, when a patriotic 25,011 crowd at the splendidly appointed and atmospheric JJB stadium saw an authentic Ashes Test in the best traditions.

On a mild, still and dry evening, the British could hardly have made a more impressive start. Paul Deacon, drafted in to add some creativity at halfback, set the tone with an inch-perfect high kick to the right, and Nathan Blacklock, in for the injured Lote Tuqiri, after gathering the ball ten metres from his own line, was unceremoniously bundled into touch by Leon Pryce and Stuart Fielden.

From the scrum, Deacon fed Andrew Farrell and Gary Connolly's cut-out pass was gathered above his head by Paul Johnson, who cut inside MacDougall's challenge for a fine try wide out on the left. Though Farrell's conversion attempt rebounded out off an upright, the British captain added a penalty in the seventh minute after Jason Stevens, back from suspension, was caught offside.

Paul Sculthorpe, kicking out on the full 20 metres out, came up with the first British error but, despite two mighty MacDougall charges, the home defence held firm under their first severe test. Keith Senior and Johnson came up with a determined double tackle to halt MacDougall by the flag after Buderus and Matthew Gidley combined, and Johns was wide with a 23-metre penalty attempt after 12 minutes when Bill Harrigan pinged the Great Britain defence for offside.

When Johns put in a wicked, bouncing kick, the cool Paul Wellens brilliantly took the ball by his own posts despite the presence of the on-rushing Ben Kennedy and Gidley. Finally, though, the pressure paid off for the Kangaroos when, after Pryce lost the ball 20 metres from his own line, in a double tackle by Stevens and Buderus, Johns kicked through with inch-perfect precision for Lockyer to claim the touchdown before the ball ran dead. The video referee confirmed the score and Johns' first goal brought parity.

Two minutes later, the Australians attacked from deep, Buderus's inside pass releasing the elegant Lockyer 60 metres out, but as Blacklock came up in support to take the scoring pass with 20 metres to go, referee Harrigan, brilliantly positioned, disallowed the score for a forward pass. It was a marginal decision.

The British defence was far more cohesive and determined than at the Reebok Stadium, but the sheer weight of the Kangaroos pressure was unrelenting. Throwing the ball wide at every opportunity, with the outstanding Johns the general and Barrett increasingly involved, the Kangaroos went for the decisive try. Wellens was a rock at the back and the British forwards got through a huge tackling stint as the onslaught continued. As the home side was pinned back time and again, Sculthorpe tried to relieve the pressure with a '40-20' but

Stuart Fielden tries to break away

the ball again went into touch on the full.

Finally the breakthrough came, as Barrett slipped out a perfectly disguised short ball that Kennedy took at pace and raced down the right channel from halfway. As Wellens came across, Gidley was in support to take the inside pass and dart over, despite the covering attempts of Johnson and Fielden. Johns converted off a post and the Australians had a 12-6 lead at the break, though Great Britain could be well satisfied with their efforts.

Just before the hooter, the British side rallied, Jamie Peacock's 50-metre run, halted by a Lockyer tackle, rousing the patriotic crowd. Then Lockyer had to pat the ball dead, under pressure from Senior, after Sculthorpe's weighted kick. Deacon kicked to the corner but Johns came up with the ball with the home fans hollering that he was offside after Blacklock had competed in mid-air with Pryce. Then Farrell cross-kicked to the right and Pryce gathered the ball at full speed, only to lose possession in a double tackle by Blacklock and Jamie Lyon.

News of Anderson's condition was relayed to the media at the break, and no sooner had the second half got underway than the Ashes were in the bag for the

Dejected Great Britain skipper Andy Farrell leaves the field

THIRD GUINNESS TEST

GREAT BRITAIN 8 AUSTRALIA 28
Saturday 24th November 2001 at JJB Stadium, Wigan

GREAT BRITAIN: 1 Paul Wellens (St Helens); 2 Leon Pryce (Bradford Bulls); 3 Gary Connolly (Wigan Warriors); 4 Keith Senior (Leeds Rhinos); 5 Paul Johnson (Wigan Warriors); 6 Paul Sculthorpe (St Helens); 7 Paul Deacon (Bradford Bulls); 17 Terry O'Connor (Wigan Warriors); 9 Mike Forshaw (Bradford Bulls); 10 Barrie McDermott (Leeds Rhinos); 11 Chris Joynt (St Helens); 8 Stuart Fielden (Bradford Bulls); 13 Andrew Farrell (Wigan Warriors) (C). Subs (all used): 16 Paul Anderson (Bradford Bulls); 14 Kevin Sinfield (Leeds Rhinos); 12 Jamie Peacock (Bradford Bulls); 15 David Hodgson (Wigan Warriors).
Try: Johnson (3); **Goals:** Farrell 2.
AUSTRALIA: 1 Darren Lockyer (Brisbane Broncos); 2 Adam MacDougall (Newcastle Knights); 3 Matthew Gidley (Newcastle Knights); 4 Jamie Lyon (Parramatta Eels); 5 Nathan Blacklock (St George-Illawarra); 6 Trent Barrett (St George-Illawarra); 7 Andrew Johns (Newcastle Knights); 8 Jason Stevens (Sharks); 9 Danny Buderus (Newcastle Knights); 10 Robbie Kearns (Melbourne Storm); 11 Dane Carlaw (Brisbane Broncos); 12 Ben Kennedy (Newcastle Knights); 13 Brad Fittler (Sydney Roosters) (C). Subs (all used): 14 Braith Anasta (Canterbury Bulldogs); 15 Brad Meyers (Brisbane Broncos); 16 Petero Civoniceva (Brisbane Broncos); 17 Jason Ryles (St George-Illawarra).
Tries: Lockyer (15), Gidley (28), Meyers (42), Barrett (67, 74); **Goals:** Johns 3, Fittler.
League Express Men of the Match:
Great Britain: Keith Senior; *Australia:* Trent Barrett.
Penalty count: 4-2; **Half-time:** 6-12; **Referee:** Bill Harrigan (Australia); **Attendance:** 25,011 (capacity).

Kangaroos. With just 90 seconds on the clock, Brad Meyers glided over for a third try after Johns and Barrett unlocked the home defence with a combination of deceptive simplicity, Barrett, after feigning to pass once, supplying the inside ball for the try assist. Johns potted the goal and the game looked over.

But the British rallied again and enjoyed their best spell of the game, peppering the Australian defence. Farrell reduced the arrears with his second penalty after three separate fights had broken out following a scrum awarded to the home side after a disallowed try to Pryce. Blacklock had lost the ball in Pryce's tackle, with Sculthorpe also involved. The Bulls winger hacked ahead and claimed the touchdown, only for the video referee

to rule that the ball had also come off Sculthorpe in the melee. Harrigan swiftly quelled the disturbance, without recourse to even the sin bin, and there was no further trouble.

A minute after Farrell's goal, Great Britain almost got the try they yearned, but MacDougall came up with a crucial tackle, stretching to haul down Johnson after Farrell sent Senior cutting through down a left channel that was becoming increasingly fruitful. MacDougall surpassed that effort with another fine defensive effort to deny Senior. Then Connolly, seeking his first Test try, kicked ahead and claimed a touchdown as the ball rebounded off a post only to be denied by Lockyer's despairing hack to safety. If Lockyer had got to the ball a mere split second later it would have been a try and the whole game could have changed.

In the next set Farrell, probing for an opening close to the line, was thwarted by a copybook Kennedy tackle, the stand-out Australian second row throwing everything into a grasping clutch at the British captain's legs.

But the Kangaroos sealed the Test and the series 13 minutes from time. Gidley had already passed up one chance, just failing to grasp the ball with the line open after MacDougall brilliantly knocked back Johns's kick to the corner. But Stevens then caught out the home defence with a bomb to the corner, MacDougall leaping high to pat the ball back for Barrett to collect on the bounce and score. Johns missed the conversion, and then almost created a try for Braith Anasta that was disallowed for a knock-on by Lyon as he challenged for the high ball.

But six minutes from the end Barrett wrapped up the game with an archetypal stand-off's try, supporting when Robbie Kearns slipped the brilliant Lockyer through a gap. Fittler was allowed to add the conversion from in front of the posts and that was the Ashes trophy on its way back to Australia.

Waite, speaking after the game, felt there were plenty of positives for the future of Great Britain as an international force, despite a heroic defeat.

"We're hurting at the moment, and we need to be," said Waite.

"It was a committed and courageous effort in difficult circumstances. The captain and the young players - and our captain is a young player - I'm sure will have reaffirmed their commitment to chase the prize. And I'd like to be here to see that."

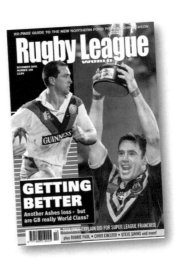

HOME INTERNATIONALS
Mixed blessing

In a packed domestic season culminating in an Ashes Series, there was little room left for the Home International competition that had been demanded in the wake of the 2000 World Cup.

But the home nations did get a run-out each in the summer, with mixed results.

FRANCE 56...IRELAND 16

France took a step towards its international rehabilitation against a threadbare and almost totally out-gunned Ireland side.

Ten tries to three - the score didn't come any where near their 82-0 win against Russia last year - summed up the French domination, and just after the break they looked like breaking the record against a proud but exhausted Ireland side. The French Federation had lost half-a-dozen of its best players to cash-happy union clubs, but it didn't affect the national team one little bit, as a young side combined strength, speed and flamboyance in equal proportion.

That was best illustrated by their fifth try just before the half-time hooter that gave France an unassailable 28-4 lead. Jerome Guisset started it off on the halfway line with a tremendous pass out of the tackle. Vincent Wulf was on hand to take the ball on and lay Roman Gagliazzo off with another short ball. The Villeneuve prop charged down the middle and fed supporting skipper Fabien Devecchi, who shot in under the posts.

The high-profile Irish withdrawals after the previous weekend's Super League battles devalued the exercise as makeshift reorganisations were forced on the Irish coaching staff Andy Kelly and Steve O'Neill. Wigan Alliance prop Martin McLoughlin was called up at quarter to midnight on Sunday, and managed to make the Monday morning flight to the South of France after the rest of the team. Loose forward Mark O'Connell was flown in from Cork Bulls as cover, though he sat out the game as 18th man.

McLoughlin started as sub but played most of the game and never gave up trying, taking a heap of punishment from the French pack, and ended up as a makeshift left winger.

Gateshead Thunder stand-off Scott Dyson also had a good stint on the left wing, and at one point played scrum-half with Gavin Clinch off the field. London Skolars' Gavin Gordon – the youngest ever Ireland international back in 1995 –

made the even bigger step up from the TotalRL.com Conference before picking up an injury. Saints forward Tim Jonkers spent most of the second half in the right centre position.

"Full credit to the lads on the bench," was the reaction of a disappointed O'Neill, after he witnessed his side go down to their biggest ever defeat in their eleventh international. "We have got to hold our heads high, because we had 17 people out there who wanted to represent Ireland."

Of that there could be no doubt. Clinch was a good example. He limped off half way through the second half, and could have every excuse for sitting out the remainder of the game. But he chose to get back on as quickly as he could to help the cause, though he was clearly only firing on three cylinders.

Tuesday 26th June 2001

FRANCE 56 IRELAND 16

FRANCE: 1 Renaud Guigue (Avignon); 5 Michael Van Snick (Villeneuve); 3 Sylvain Houles (UTC); 4 Arnaud Dulac (St Gaudens); 2 Patrick Noguera (Pia); 6 Laurent Frayssinous (Villeneuve); 7 Fabien Devecchi (Toulouse) (C); 8 Jerome Guisset (Warrington Wolves); 9 Vincent Wulf (Villeneuve); 10 Romain Gagliazzo (Villeneuve); 11 Pascal Jampy (UTC); 12 Jerome Vincent (Toulouse); 13 Laurent Carrasco (Villeneuve); Subs (all used); 15 Frederic Teixido (Limoux); 15 Artie Shead (Villeneuve); 16 Romain Sort (Villeneuve); 17 Gilles Cornut (Villeneuve).
Tries: Van Snick (4), Frayssinous (10, 77), Dulac (21), Shead (27), Devecchi (40), Gigue (42), Houles (46), Jampy (59), Vincent (67); **Goals:** Dulac 6, Frayssinous 2
IRELAND: 1 Damian Munro (Widnes); 2 Rob Smyth (Warrington); 4 Richard Smith (Wakefield); 3 Francis Cummins (Leeds); 5 Mark Forster (Widnes); 6 Gavin Clinch (Halifax); 7 Liam Bretherton (Leigh); 8 Neil Harmon (Salford); 9 Johnny Lawless (Halifax); 10 Barrie McDermott (Leeds) (C); 11 David Bradbury (Leigh); 12 Tim Jonkers (St Helens); 13 Shayne McMenemy (Halifax); Subs (all used); 14 Gavin Gordon (North London); 15 Scott Dyson (Gateshead Thunder); 16 Martin McLoughlin (Wigan); 17 Mick Slicker (Huddersfield).
Tries: Forster (2), McDermott (53), Bradbury (69);
Goals: Clinch 2
League Express Men of the Match:
France: Jerome Vincent; *Ireland:* David Bradbury.
Penalty count: 2-7; **Half-time:** 28-4; **Referee:** Bob Connolly (England); **Attendance:** 2,006 *(at Stadium Municipale, Albi).*

Barrie McDermott takes the ball up

The pack – in temperatures approaching 30 degrees Celsius, despite the evening kick-off - ran their blood to water, in particular Johnny Lawless, Dave Bradbury, skipper Barrie McDermott and Neil Harmon. Harmon was out on his feet after the first half hour, but returned to take up the charge again, and had the legs to break out of his own '20' on a 40-metre charge that had the crowd on their feet half-way through the second half.

McDermott and Bradbury both got their reward with second-half tries – the Leigh man's coming after supporting clubmate Liam Bretherton's break on the inside. Bretherton was another who stood out in a mighty effort.

No-one could have predicted the rout when Mark Forster – who became the most capped League international for Ireland with his ninth appearance – registered a try in the 82nd second of the match. Forster was to hobble off in the tenth minute, and by that time France had scored twice to take a 12-4 lead. And it was exhibition stuff from then on.

FRANCE 20 ....SCOTLAND 42

SCOTLAND created history in Lezignan last July, with their first-ever victory over France.

And in further landmarks for the game, the Scots rattled up their highest ever score and Matt Crowther set a new record as his country's top points and goals-in-a-match scorer – his try and seven goals taking him past his own previous record set against Wales in 1999.

It was a dream night for coach Billy McGinty, who had lost several high-profile Super League players from his squad just 36 hours before the game.

Like Ireland the previous week, the Scots suffered from injury-enforced withdrawals that meant McGinty and manager George Fairbairn travelled with the bare minimum of 17 players.

The situation wasn't helped when scrum-half Scott Rhodes missed the Monday morning flight because of passport problems. He eventually arrived at the team hotel after a nightmare 16-hour journey that meant he missed the crucial last training session.

But from the minute this international kicked off at the picturesque Lezignan stadium, Scotland slipped into gear and cruised along as though they were at full strength and had been playing together forever.

"The preparation was disrupted, but the lads went out and played with pride and passion, and that's what international rugby is all about," beamed McGinty. "You have to play with your heart on your sleeve and give your all because it's not just another game, it's something special.

"I'm so proud. We are starting to get some youngsters in the squad who are passionate about playing for Scotland.

"Gareth Morton, when he filled in the registration form, he had to put down who else he might qualify for, but he just put Scotland, and left the options box empty. He is Scottish through and through."

The chief playmaker was Castleford's Adrian Vowles, playing out of position at stand-off but finding himself immediately in control and displaying a kicking game that, by his own admission, has sadly been shackled at the Tigers.

He created four of Scotland's tries, three of them from superbly-weighted kicks that took advantage of the huge in-goal areas. "Adrian was great, he created a lot for us out wide, and all four props were outstanding," McGinty added.

"But it was a tremendous team effort. They [France] have come off a

---

Tuesday 3rd July 2001

FRANCE 20 SCOTLAND 42

FRANCE: 1 Renaud Guigue (Avignon); 2 Patrick Noguera (Pia); 3 Sylvain Houles (UTC); 4 Arnaud Dulac (St Gaudens); 5 Michael Van Snick (Villeneuve); 6 Laurent Frayssinous (Villeneuve); 7 Fabien Devecchi (Toulouse) (C); 8 Jerome Guisset (Warrington); 9 Vincent Wulf (Villeneuve); 10 Romain Gagliazzo (Villeneuve); 11 Pascal Jampy (UTC); 12 Artie Shead (Villeneuve); 13 Laurent Carrasco (Villeneuve); Subs (all used); 14 Frederic Teixido (Limoux); 15 Eric Anselme (St Gaudens); 16 Romain Sort (Villeneuve); 17 Gilles Cornut (Villeneuve).
Tries: Sort (20), Jampy (51), Houles (59), Van Snick (70); **Goals:** Dulac 2.
SCOTLAND: 1 Jason Flowers (Castleford); 2 Danny Arnold (Salford); 3 David Maiden (Hull); 4 Iain Higgins (Hunslet); 5 Matt Crowther (Hull); 6 Adrian Vowles (Castleford); 7 Scott Rhodes (Sheffield); 8 Wayne McDonald (St Helens); 9 Mike Dixon (Hull KR); 10 Scott Cram (London); 11 Darren Shaw (Castleford) (C); 12 Artie Fletcher (Hull); 13 Neil Lowe (Featherstone); Subs (all used); 14 Nathan Graham (Dewsbury); 15 Gareth Morton (Leeds); 16 Ryan McDonald (Dewsbury); 17 Joe Berry (Rochdale).
Tries: Maiden (5), Arnold (11, 39), Flowers (13, 67), Lowe (55), Crowther (79); **Goals:** Crowther 7.
League Express Men of the Match:
France: Pascal Jampy; *Scotland:* Adrian Vowles.
Penalty count: 5-6; **Half-time:** 6-22; **Referee:** Ian Smith (England); **Attendance:** 3,161 *(at Stade du Moulin, Lezignan).*

Laurent Frayssinous gets to grips with Adrian Vowles

successful tour, they have a lot of match fitness and are very close as a group having been on tour. They know all the plays, all the patterns.

"Our lads played on Sunday, some came out with injuries, but they all wanted to play."

Scotland's first try came after just five minutes, when Vowles hoisted a cross-field kick towards the corner that fullback Renaud Guigue struggled with, and David Maiden pounced for the vital touch.

That, and Matt Crowther's goal, settled any early nerves. The Scots were clearly psyched up, talking and encouraging each other non-stop.

The French offered a brief threat when Fabien Devecchi brought Romain Sort onto a flat pass to score, but at 6-22 at the break the game was gone.

WALES 33 ....ENGLAND 42

International Rugby League was widely predicted to suffer another body blow in Wrexham in July.

It didn't. This was Rugby League at its vibrant best, better than could be expected on a mid-season Tuesday night. With Wales weakened by the withdrawal of six Super League players on the eve of the match, their coach Neil Kelly had to spend most of Monday ringing around for players, rather than making final preparations on the training paddock.

But the sun shone down on Rugby League, literally, as the tidy Racecourse Ground provided a brilliant backdrop to a bright and buzzing occasion.

What chance did Wales have to push England all the way?

After 20 minutes it appeared that the patched up side in red and green were the only ones taking the Test trial business seriously as they led 16-nil, with England having hardly touched the ball. It was a first-half performance that evoked memories of the World Cup semi-final against Australia the previous November, as Wales hung onto their lead for an hour before the power and speed of the all-Super League England line-up opened them up, three tries in seven minutes putting them into an unassailable lead.

"I'm thrilled," said Kelly. "We had no right to expect a performance like that. It just goes to show what putting a Welsh shirt on means."

It meant a lot to Lee Briers. The Wolves stand-off may only have been a fringe Great Britain candidate at 8 o'clock that night, but by 20 past the hour he had thrown down a claim for the Ashes number six shirt, mesmerising England with an array of tactical kicking that reminded the crowd of his former Wolves teammate Alfie Langer.

And when he dummied and side-stepped through from 20 metres for Wales' third try, the question: "Who needs Iestyn Harris" was going through the minds of one or two Welsh folk, who were able to watch the apparently union-bound Leeds star, whose commitment to the Welsh Rugby League cause could never be questioned, acting as his side's water-carrier.

Briers' brilliance was achieved on the back of a mighty effort from the Wales pack, with props Keith Mason - who on this showing became a cert' for the England under-21 side at the end of the season - and Dave Whittle playing out of their skins, and Keiron Cunningham - skipper for the night - playing out of position at loose forward, but doing the usual damage around the rucks.

Tuesday 31st July 2001

WALES 33 ENGLAND 42

WALES: 1 Mark Lennon (Castleford); 2 Damian Gibson (Halifax); 3 Martin Pearson (Wakefield); 4 Jason Critchley (Whitehaven); 5 Jason Lee (Halifax); 6 Lee Briers (Warrington); 7 Barry Eaton (Dewsbury); 8 Keith Mason (Wakefield); 9 Ian Watson (Widnes); 10 David Whittle (Leigh); 11 Chris Morley (Leigh); 12 Dean Busby (Warrington); 13 Keiron Cunningham (St Helens) (C); Subs (all used); 14 Paul Atcheson (Widnes); 15 Steffan Hughes (London); 16 Gareth Dean (Wigan); 17 Gareth Price (St Helens).
Tries: Lee (4, 35), Gibson (12), Briers (15), Morley (70), Atcheson (73); **Goals:** Briers 4; **Field goal:** Briers
ENGLAND: 1 Paul Wellens (St Helens); 2 Leon Pryce (Bradford); 3 Kris Radlinski (Wigan); 4 Keith Senior (Leeds); 5 Chev Walker (Leeds); 6 Paul Sculthorpe (St Helens); 7 Paul Deacon (Bradford); 8 Paul Anderson (Bradford); 9 Terry Newton (Wigan); 10 Brian McDermott (Bradford); 11 Jamie Peacock (Bradford); 12 Kevin Sinfield (Leeds); 13 Andy Farrell (Wigan) (C); Subs (all used); 10 Karl Pratt (Leeds); 11 Paul King (Hull); 12 Nathan Sykes (Castleford); 13 Lee Radford (Bradford).
Tries: Peacock (23), Sculthorpe (27, 61, 66), Farrell (49), Radford (53), Pratt (59), Wellens (76); **Goals:** Farrell 5.
League Express Men of the Match:
Wales: Keith Mason; *England:* Paul King.
Penalty count: 4-4; **Half-time:** 23-10;
Referee: Thierry Alibert (France);
Attendance: 6,373 *(at the Racecourse Ground, Wrexham).*

Keith Mason moves in to tackle Brian McDermott

Add to that the scampering darting runs of Castleford fullback Mark Lennon, and Wales were just too much of a handful for England.

After trailing 23-10 at the break, England re-grouped and won supremacy, but the writing had already been posted on the wall between the 23rd and 26th minutes of the game, when the Welsh defence showed definite signs of exhaustion as, first, Jamie Peacock was sent through a gap on the right by clubmate Paul Deacon, and then Paul Sculthorpe took the same route to the try-line, fending a weary-looking Mason off on his way.

Without the ball for most of the first half, England had to control possession after the break to have a shout, and that they did excellently.

The result was a marauding pack which made the space for Terry Newton to display his destructive skills from dummy-half.

159

TRANS-TASMAN TEST
Changing of the guard

NEW ZEALAND 10 ....**AUSTRALIA 28**

It was the Face of Future Australia on display in the New Zealand capital of Wellington in July in the annual Trans-Tasman Test. And the new-look Aussies caught the confident Kiwis napping.

The Kiwis were hopeful of an upset at the ground they call 'The Cake Tin' under new coach Gary Freeman. The man who had played more Tests for New Zealand than any other (46, including a world record run of 37 consecutive appearances) never went into a match thinking he couldn't win.

And so it was as he took over the reins of the Kiwis in 2001.

He'd orchestrated a big win against the Frenchmen a month before the Trans-Tasman clash. And the locals were buoyed by the return from England of the Paul brothers, Robbie and Henry, for what would ultimately be their last Test together.

Emotionally, at least, the Kiwis were ready for the world champions.

But it was a case of the changing of the guard for the visitors.

Andrew Johns at last got his chance in his rightful place at scrum-half (after playing 14 of his 17 previous internationals in the unfamiliar role of hooker). And he was teamed with the exciting stand-off Trent Barrett.

The pair was probably the difference between the two sides.

Johns was especially devastating - giving credence to claims that he was the world's best player.

He turned in such a superb display that it was hard to realise that it was only his second game in almost three months after being sidelined with chronic groin and rib injuries.

To make way for Barrett, veteran skipper Brad Fittler had moved to loose forward. His experience would be vital, with no less than five Test debutants in the green and gold.

Winger Lote Tuqiri (although he did play for Fiji in the World Cup), hooker Danny Buderus, and the Brisbane forward trio of Brad Meyers, Dane Carlaw and Petero Civoniceva were in their maiden Test for Australia.

The Aussies defended grimly for the first ten minutes and then switched on.

Johns made a wonderful break, flicked the ball back to the trailing Barrett, who kicked behind the defence. Centre Matthew Gidley stormed onto the ball, toed it ahead and won the race to touch down.

A couple of penalty goals stretched the lead to 10.

Test debutant Dane Carlaw looks for support

Then within moments of Robbie Kearns coming on as a substitute he slipped a great offload to Barrett who in turn sent Darren Lockyer on an uninterrupted run for the line. One of the touch judges reckoned the pass from Barrett had been forward but English referee Russell Smith overruled him.

It was 16-nil after just 22 minutes and the result for Australia was never again in jeopardy.

Trans-Tasman Test

The Kiwis briefly embarked on a mini-revival after the break, with the Paul brothers combining with centre David Vaealiki for Robbie Paul to score after handling twice.

But it was a mere aberration.

The Australians hit back immediately with a try to Tuqiri, off a masterful kick by Johns.

All that remained were late tries to each side - some more magic from the Australian halfback combination leading to a Barrett try and a consolation touchdown to Kiwi winger Francis Meli a couple of minutes from full-time.

The result was a relief for Brad Fittler who had experienced a horror fortnight leading up to the Test.

Allan Langer had come back from England and spoiled Fittler's State of Origin farewell. And then the Northern Eagles rained on his parade as he 'celebrated' his 250th senior club game.

"The nightmare is over," Fittler said after the Test. "I went into this game thinking I was a hoodoo. But it's all turned out okay.

"We won it with our great defence. And I'm a very relieved man."

Fittler knew that evening that he would never again play stand-off at Test level.

"After the way Trent Barrett played in partnership with Joey Johns, it's obvious I've played my last game in the No 6 jumper," smiled Fittler. "But I couldn't be happier for Trent."

And what about the real surprise selection - that of Buderus as hooker?

Friday 13th July 2001

TRANS-TASMAN TEST

NEW ZEALAND 10 AUSTRALIA 28

NEW ZEALAND: 1 Robbie Paul (Bradford); 2 Clinton Toopi (Warriors); 3 Nigel Vagana (Bulldogs); 4 David Vaealiki (Eels); 5 Francis Meli (Warriors); 6 Henry Paul (Bradford); 7 Stacey Jones (Warriors); 8 Nathan Cayless (Eels) (C); 9 Richard Swain (Storm); 10 Craig Smith (Dragons); 11 Ruben Wiki (Raiders); 12 Stephen Kearney (Storm); 13 Monty Betham (Warriors). Subs: 14 Logan Swann (Warriors); 15 Jerry Seu Seu (Warriors); 16 Ali Lauiti'iti (Warriors); 17 David Solomona (Eels).
Tries: R Paul (50), Meli (77); **Goal:** H Paul.
AUSTRALIA: 1 Darren Lockyer (Broncos); 2 Lote Tuqiri (Broncos); 3 Ryan Girdler (Panthers); 4 Matthew Gidley (Knights); 5 Wendell Sailor (Broncos); 6 Trent Barrett (Dragons); 7 Andrew Johns (Knights); 8 Shane Webcke (Broncos); 9 Danny Buderus (Knights); 10 Jason Stevens (Sharks); 11 Bryan Fletcher (Roosters); 12 Brad Meyers (Broncos); 13 Brad Fittler (Roosters) (C). Subs: 14 Adam MacDougall (Knights); 15 Robbie Kearns (Storm); 16 Dane Carlaw (Broncos); 17 Petero Civoniceva (Broncos).
Tries: Gidley (11), Lockyer (22), Tuqiri (54), Barrett (69); **Goals:** Girdler 5, Johns.
League Express Men of the Match
New Zealand: Craig Smith; *Australia:* Andrew Johns.
Half-time: 0-16; **Referee:** Russell Smith (England); **Video referee:** Neville Kesha (NZ); **Attendance:** 26,580 at WestpacTrust Stadium, Wellington.

He hadn't even played State of Origin. But he was one of the real success stories of the night and played himself into the Kangaroo squad for Britain with his slick work at dummy half and his stoic defence.

The Kiwi forwards tried hard and Wigan-bound Craig Smith gave them some backbone. But the New Zealanders did seem to be missing some 'mongrel' in both attack and defence.

There was one unpleasant incident, when Kiwi winger Clinton Toopi hit Meyers with a rugged high tackle that ended the Bronco's night. The effects of the concussion kept Meyers out of action for several weeks and it was only at the end of the season that he fully regained the confidence necessary to win him a spot in the Kangaroo squad.

The disappointed Freeman came away realising he had to realign his sights onto the Kiwis' 2002 tour of Britain.

And, like in his playing days, he will settle for nothing less than victory over the British.

INTERNATIONAL ROUND-UP

Rugby League in 2001 produced more opportunities for overseas travel than at any time in its history.

The Army made a historic tour of New Zealand, winning both Tests against the NZ Army team, three Super League sides played in the inaugural Sunshine State Challenge in Florida and in the summer there were tours at various levels to Australia, Fiji, New Zealand, the United States and Russia. And to cap it off England under-21s played two games against the Rhinos in South Africa.

Before the 2001 England Academy Tour left for New Zealand and Australia to embark on a programme which included two Tests against each of the host nations, Nick Halafihi, Director of Player Performance at Red Hall, described its purpose as to establish a benchmark of where we stand against the best in the world.

The first game took place in the storm-tossed city of Wellington, where the Academy squad comprehensively defeated the Junior Kiwis, 30-8, and in so doing notched their first ever Test win south of the equator at Academy level.

A week later, in perfect conditions at Rugby League Park, Christchurch, they proved it was no fluke with a staggering 72-16 second Test victory. It was achieved by a much changed side, after coach Mike Gregory insisted that all 22 players in the party should be given the opportunity to show their wares in Test football.

The Australians were always likely to be a different proposition, but at a dimly-lit Wynnum in Brisbane, the Academy pushed them all the way before going down 18-12. But the Aussies were in no mood to let it happen a second time, dominating virtually throughout to win the second Test to win 44-22.

ENGLAND ACADEMY TOUR SQUAD: Dwayne Barker (Leeds Rhinos); Neil Baxter (Salford City Reds); Shaun Briscoe (Wigan Warriors); Andrew Brocklehurst (Halifax Blue Sox); Robert Burrow (Leeds Rhinos) (C); Andrew Crabtree (Wigan Warriors); Eorl Crabtree (Huddersfield Giants); Adrian Gardner (Barrow Border Raiders); Gareth Hock (Wigan Warriors); Nicky Johnson (Bradford Bulls); Jamie Langley (Bradford Bulls); Richard Mathers (Leeds Rhinos); Danny McGuire (Leeds Rhinos); Matt McGuire (Hull FC); Gareth Morton (Leeds Rhinos); Steve Musgrave (Hull FC); Vinny Myler (Bradford Bulls); Jason Netherton (Leeds Rhinos); Shaun O'Loughlin (Wigan Warriors); Jon Wilkins (Hull Kingston Rovers); Alex Wilkinson (Bradford Bulls); Kirk Yeaman (Hull FC)

ENGLAND ACADEMY TOUR 2001

v NZ Northern Districts	Won	40-18
v New Zealand	Won	30-8
v New Zealand	Won	72-16
v Australia	Lost	12-18
v Australia	Lost	22-44

With just one win from its programme of games Down Under, it would be easy to condemn the Combined Youth under-16s tourists as failures. But the tourists went into their one and only Test, played at Carlaw Park, within four days of nding in New Zealand. Their one win came in Brisbane against South East Queensland.

The England under-21s side demanded the opportunity to take on their New Zealand and Australian counterparts following their successful tour to South Africa in November.

John Kear's young team arrived back to the UK having twice demolished the full South African side, winning 112-6 in Pretoria and then 74-14 in Johannesburg a week later.

The under-21s basically swept aside all before them in South Africa, running in 33 tries in the space of the two Tests. The South Africans - made up entirely of home-based players - lacked the experience and know-how of the Rhinos teams that have competed in the last two World Cups, and John Kear's youngsters were ruthless in their execution.

The management was impressed by the tour's Premiership contingent. Neil Turley, Rob Purdham and Paul Salmon were all among the tries, with Turley crossing five times in Johannesburg, while prop Danny Sculthorpe rose to the role of vice captain. All had won their place after the NFP under-21s had beaten their Super League counterparts 27-20 in a trial at Widnes in October.

ENGLAND UNDER-16'S COMBINED YOUTH 2001: Brad Attwood (Queensbury/Halifax Blue Sox); Paul Ballard (Hindley/Wigan Warriors); Kevin Brown (Thatto Heath/St Helens); Paul Burns (Wigan St Pats/High Wigan Warriors); John Clough (Pilkingtons/Salford City Reds); Ben Feehan (Newsome/Huddersfield Giants); Peter Fox (Acorn/Leeds Rhinos); Scott Gandy (Woolston/Wigan Warriors); James Graham (Thatto Heath/St Helens); Kieron Hersnip (Hindley/Salford City Reds); Daniel Hill West (Hull/Hull FC); Graeme Horne (West Hull/High Hull FC); Philip Joseph (Newsome/Huddersfield Giants); Martin Kenyon (Hindley/Wigan Warriors); Christopher Lodge (Newsome/Huddersfield Giants); Jamie Maxfield (Abraham Guest High/Wigan Warriors); Liam McGovern (Halton Hornets/St Helens); Chris Melling (Hindley/Wigan Warriors); Barry Pugh (Ulverston); Stephen Rowlands (Halton Hornets/St Helens); Nicholas Scruton (Churwell/Leeds Rhinos); Craig Vines (Stanley Rangers/Leeds Rhinos)

COMBINED YOUTH UNDER-16S TOUR 2001		
v New Zealand	Lost	4-20
v Queensland Southern Division	Lost	6-38
v South East Queensland	Won	32-30
v Cronulla	Lost	18-28
v Wests Tigers	Lost	20-28

Mark Edmondson on the charge for England Under-21s against South Africa

● The summer and autumn tours had technical Director David Waite putting Great Britain's defeat in the Ashes series in perspective.

"We have re-written history," he said.

"It's the most successful year Rugby League has ever had in history. Winning Down Under at 16s, winning in New Zealand times two at 18s, taking the Australian Schoolboys as close as they did, and the 21s had a record score. We have, I think, a rejuvenated, positive group of players that has represented Great Britain in an Ashes series. And for those who doubted we should have an Ashes series, you should have a look at yourselves, because I thought that was a terrific contest in very, very difficult circumstances."

ENGLAND UNDER-21s TOURISTS 2001: Ryan Hudson (C) (Wakefield Trinity Wildcats); Danny Sculthorpe (VC) (Rochdale Hornets); Rob Burrow (Leeds Rhinos); Mark Calderwood (Leeds Rhinos); Mark Edmondson (St Helens); Richard Fletcher (Hull FC); Martin Gleeson (St Helens); Mick Higham (St Helens); Tim Jonkers (St Helens); Keith Mason (Wakefield Trinity Wildcats); Danny McGuire (Leeds Rhinos); Rob Parker (Bradford Bulls); Rob Purdham (Whitehaven); Paul Salmon (Barrow Border Raiders); Mark Smith (Wigan Warriors); John Stankevitch (St Helens); Chris Thorman (Huddersfield Giants); Neil Turley (Leigh Centurions); Chev Walker (Leeds Rhinos); Danny Ward (Leeds Rhinos); Ben Westwood (Wakefield Trinity Wildcats)

FIRST TEST, PRETORIA
ENGLAND U-21 112....................................SOUTH AFRICA 6
England: T-Turley 5, Calderwood 4, McGuire 3, Purdham 2, Edmondson 2, Salmon, Burrow, Walker, Smith; G-Burrow 16
T-Louw; G-O'Shea

SECOND TEST, GERMISTON, JOHANNESBURG
ENGLAND U-21 74....................................SOUTH AFRICA 14
England: T-McGuire 3, Fletcher 2, Gleeson 2, Calderwood 2, Westwood, Turley, Walker, Burrow; G-Burrow 9, Fletcher, Thorman
South Africa: T-Gendall, Jonker; G-Van der Merwe 2, O'Shea

BARLA's Young Lions also toured Australia in August and won their first 'Test' matches against the Australian Emerging States in Melbourne, losing only one game out of seven matches - against the same side a week later 28-12.

But the Lions finished their amazing Australian tour four days later by snatching victory in their last match, beating the NSW Combined High Schools 26-16 at Cabramatta.

BARLA YOUNG LIONS AUSTRALIA TOUR PARTY 2001: David Agnew (Kells); Dale Asquith (Milford); Dean Bragg (Kells); Kevin Brown (Eastmoor Dragons); Craig Calvert (Wath Brow Hornets); David Dickinson (Kells); Sean Dickinson (Dudley Hill); Jonathon Grayshon (West Bowling); Jon Hepworth (Castleford Panthers); John Ledger (Hull Dockers); Craig McAvoy (Hensingham); Martin Meadows (Leigh East); Dexter Miller (Kells); Glenn Osborn (Kingston Warriors); Ryan Robb (Kells); Darrell Rowlands (Leigh Miners Rangers); Greg Rowley (Maryport); Lee Rowley (Leigh East); Carl Rudd (Wath Brow Hornets); David Rushton (Hindpool Tigers); Mark Troughton (Wath Brow Hornets); Richard Varkulis (Leigh Miners Rangers); Stephen Wallace (Seaton Pack Horse); Simon Warhurst (Leigh East); Asa Watson (Wigan St Patricks); Paul White (Queensbury)

● BARLA under-21s made history with a first match at that level with USA. BARLA won 62-14 in the match played in Philadelphia.

The North West Counties youth touring team also enjoyed another highly successful trip down under.

The under-15s development squad came back unbeaten with seven wins and a draw from eight matches, while the under-16s finished with three wins, one draw and five defeats from nine games.

NWC UNDER-15s: Hardman (West Bank), Edwards (St Judes), Johnson (St Judes), Speakman (St Patricks), Ballard (Ashton Bears), Coyle (St Patricks), Roby (Blackbrook), Hayes (Leigh East), Parkinson (Ince St Williams), Bibey (Leigh Miners Rangers), Jarvis (Crosfields), Hart Woolston),Allen (Halton Hornets). Subs: Gwilliam (Blackbrook), Irvine (Ashton Bears), Pilling (Ashton Bears), Smith (Parkside Golborne), Lacey (Pilkington Recs).
NWC UNDER-16s: Hartley (Leigh Miners Rangers), Higginson (Leigh Miners Rangers), Lloyd (Wigan St Judes), Taylor (Wigan St Judes), West(Leigh Miners Rangers), Forber (Thatto Heath), Collins (Waterhead), Sharples (Royton Tigers), McDonald (Halton Hornets), Brown (Langworthy Reds), Dootson(Leigh East), Jones (Leigh Miners Rangers), Corcoran (Royton Tigers). Subs: Boland (Wigan St Judes), Terry (Thatto Heath), Tindall (Royton Tigers), Thompson (Langworthy Reds), Milligan (Blackbrook), Jarvis (Crosfields), Smith (Parkside Golborne).

RANCE also enjoyed a mid-summer tour to the South Pacific, losing to New Zealand (36-0) and tying the series in Papua New Guinea (27-16, 24-34)

STUDENT RUGBY LEAGUE again extended the boundaries of Rugby League with a ground-breaking competition in the former Soviet state of Tatarstan.

Described as the Student game's "biggest adventure yet", the Europa Cup saw teams from all of the four home nations travel to the city of Kazan, the capital of Tatarstan, about 12,000 kilometres east of Moscow, in early September to compete against teams from Russia, Tatarstan and a guest side from New South Wales.

The students who arrived in Kazan were instantly transformed into celebrities and over 16,000 people turned up to watch the opening ceremony which featured the game between Tatarstan and Ireland, the hosts displaying skills that belied their emerging nation status in a 38-12 win.

For the record, England brought the curtain down on an immensely successful competition by winning the final against the host nation by 36-14.

STUDENT EUROPA CUP 2001

Group A

	P	W	D	L	F	A	D	PTS
England	2	2	0	0	68	22	46	4
Tatarstan	2	1	0	1	50	42	8	2
Ireland	2	0	0	2	22	76	-54	0

GROUP A RESULTS: England 38 Ireland 10; Tatarstan 38 Ireland 12; Tatarstan 12 England 30

Group B

	P	W	D	L	F	A	D	PTS
Wales	2	1	1	0	39	28	11	3
Scotland	2	1	0	1	46	35	11	2
Russia	2	0	1	1	36	58	-22	1

GROUP B RESULTS: NSW 20 Wales 49; Russia 16 Scotland 38; NSW 42 Scotland 18; Wales 20 Russia 20; Wales 19 Scotland 8; NSW 24 Russia 24

SEMI-FINALS: Tatarstan 26 Wales 10; England 13 Scotland 12

FINAL: England 36 Tatarstan 14

June 2
FRANCE 24 (Michael Van Snick, Jerome Vincent, Arnaud Dulac, Pascal Jampy tries; Freddy Banquet 4 goals) d. **SOUTH ISLAND 18** (Gafa Tuiloma, Raymond Hubbard, Aaron Whittaker tries; Hubbard 3 goals) at Rugby League Park, Christchurch. Referee: Darryn Hopewell Crowd: 3000

June 6
FRANCE 28 (Nicolas Picolo, Renaud Guigue, David Berthezene, Fabien Devecchi, Sylvain Houles tries; Freddy Banquet 4 goals) d. **CENTRAL DISTRICTS 26** (Chris Faifua, Mark Graham, Willie Puohotaua, Pat Nanai tries; Tenga Pickering 4, David Collingwood goals) at Palmerston North. Referee: Gareth Kemp Crowd: 2000

June 10 - Test match
NEW ZEALAND 36 (Willie Talau 2, Stephen Kearney, Tasesa Lavea, Motu Tony, Monty Betham, Stacey Jones tries; Lavea 4 goals) d. **FRANCE 0** at Ericsson Stadium. Referee: Tim Mander (Australia) Crowd: 4500
New Zealand: Motu Tony, Francis Meli, Clinton Toopi, Willie Talau, Henry Faafili, Tasesa Lavea, Stacey Jones, Nathan Cayless), Richard Swain, Ali Lauitiiti, Stephen Kearney, Ruben Wiki, Henry Perenara Interchange: Monty Betham, Jerry Seu Seu, Matt Rua, David Vaealiki
France: Freddy Banquet, Renaud Guigue, Gilles Cornut, Arnaud Dulac, Sylvain Houles, Laurent Frayssinous, Fabien Devecchi), Romain Gagliazzo, Vincent Wulf, Artie Shead Jerome Vincent, Gael Tallec, Laurent Carrasco Interchange: Romain Sort, Eric Anselme, Pascal Jampy, Michael van Snick

June 13
FRANCE 40 (Arnaud Dulac 3, Sylvain Houles 3, Renaud Guigue, Patrice Benausse tries; Benausse 4 goals) d. **NORTHERN DISTRICTS 16** (Frank Peresi 2, Joe Rau tries, Joe Flavell 2 goals) at Huntly.

June 17 - Test match
FRANCE 27 (Frederic Banquet 2, Vincent Wulf, Sylvain Houles, Jean-Christophe Borlin tries, Banquet 3 goals, field goal) d. **PAPUA NEW GUINEA 16** (John Wilshere, Michael Marum, Stanley Tepend tries, Wilshere 2 goals). At Lloyd Robson Oval, Port Moresby. Attendance: 15,000 (capacity).
PNG: David Buko, John Wilshere, Eddie Aila, Chris Purkilil, Alfred Songoro, Stanley Tepend, Nime Kapo, Makaili Aizure, Michael Marum, John Waka, Raymond Karl, Duncan Naawi, Mark Mom (c). Interchange: Tarzan Malaguna, James Kops, Joe Sipa, Charlie Joe
France: Frederic Banquet, Renaud Guigue, Sylvain Houles, Arnaud Dulac, Michael Van-snick, Laurent Frayssinous, Fabien Devecchi, Romain Gagliazzo, Vincent Wulf, Frederic Teixido, Jerome Vincent, Gael Tallec, Laurent Carrasco. Interchange: Gilles Cornut, Pascal Jampy, Romain Sort, Artie Shead

June 20 - Test match
PAPUA NEW GUINEA 34 (Michael Mundo 3, David Buko, Joe Sipa, Tarzan Malaguna tries; John Wilshere 5 goals) d. **FRANCE 24** (Romain Sort 2, Laurent Frayssinous, Michael Van-Snick tries; Freddy Banquet 4 goals). At Sir Danny Leahy Rugby League Ground, Goroka. Attendance: 12,000
PNG: David Buko, John Wilshere (c), Eddie Aila, Alfred Songoro, Chris Purkilil, Stanley Tepend, Nime Kapo, Tarzan Malaguna, Michael Marum, Michael Mondo, Raymond Karl, Joe Sipa, Duncan Naawi. Interchange: Eric Aba, James Kops, Charlie Joe, Lawrence Goive
France: Frederic Banquet, Renaud Guigue, Sylvain Houles, Arnaud Dulac, Michael Van-Snick, Laurent Frayssinous, Fabien Devecchi (c), Romain Gagliazzo, Vincent Wulf, Frederic Teixido, Jerome Vincent, Gael Tallec, Laurent Carrasco; Interchange: Gilles Cornut, Pascal Jampy, Romain Sort, Artie Shead

THE ORIGIN GAME
The Origin-al

There were widely contrasting views about the merits of the revived War of the Roses in early June – rebranded the 'The Origin Game'.

"Exhilarating," proclaimed one headline, "Phoney War," said another.

In fact, it was a bit of both. Ten, mostly spectacular, tries kept the biggest county game crowd (10,253) for 35 years well entertained. But nine of them were scored in a first half that lacked the fierce intensity of Australia's State of Origin, which it was supposed to copy.

It was also promoted as a Test trial, and on that score Great Britain coach David Waite had no doubts about its value. "I learned a great deal from it," said Waite. "It left me wishing there was another one, because they warmed to their task and some players really contributed to a great game of football. At half-time I hoped they would improve their defence in the second half, and they did.

"I thought the first 20 minutes of the second half was a very important period, and some people really put their hands up. It was a tribute to the players over the 80 minutes. Their attitude to the game was terrific."

Any doubts that this game wasn't for real soon vanished, as both defences tightened up in the second half, with Lancashire battling to hold on to their 28-24 interval lead before Paul Johnson's 74th minute try clinched a 36-24 victory.

A look in at the dressing rooms would also have been an insight to the players' commitment. They were more like casualty wards, and Yorkshire captain James Lowes, one of several injured players, spoke up for them when he said there was plenty of intensity.

"You could see that on the field and the fact that players didn't want to come off when they were injured shows how much it meant to them," said Lowes.

After Yorkshire had led 18-6, Lancashire came back with an incredible four tries in nine minutes to lead 28-18, before a Lowes try and Francis Maloney goal completed the first-half scoring.

The use of five substitutes and twelve interchanges per team irritated the fans, but the substitute to make the biggest impact was Neil Turley. The Leigh Centurions star was the only Northern Ford Premiership player on view, and was soon standing fair comparison with the Super League players. He had a hand in one try, and then slipped through for his 46th touchdown of the season.

Established Test fullback Kris Radlinski looked certain to retain his place against Australia after winning the man of the match, the choice made by Britain coach Waite and a manager from each county. Radlinski produced his top Wigan form with a well-taken try and a big say in another. The Wigan fullback became the inaugural winner of the Roy Powell Medal, named in honour of the former

The Origin Game

Great Britain and Yorkshire forward who died suddenly and prematurely two years before, which was presented to Radlinski by Roy's widow Helen and his son Lewis.

Waite must also have been impressed with Wigan centre Paul Johnson, who gave a powerful display of hard running and distributive skills. He combined both assets to set up first-half tries for Paul Deacon and Paul Sculthorpe, before showing his alertness to score the late match-clinching try after Chev Walker dropped the ball behind his own line when trying to field Andy Farrell's kick.

Ironically, it had been two Lancashire blunders that led to Yorkshire taking an early 12-0 lead.

First, Chris Joynt lost the ball in a tackle, and from the position gained Stuart Fielden forced his way over. Then Lancashire-Londoner Dominic Peters failed to take Tony Smith's high kick, and the halfback snapped up the ball to race clear.

Lancashire's Paul Sculthorpe finds himself with nowhere to go against Yorkshire

Tuesday 5th June 2001

THE ORIGIN GAME

YORKSHIRE 24 LANCASHIRE 36

YORKSHIRE: 1 Daryl Cardiss (Halifax); 2 Leon Pryce (Bradford); 3 Chev Walker (Leeds); 4 Keith Senior (Leeds); 5 David Hodgson (Wigan); 6 Danny Orr (Castleford); 7 Tony Smith (Hull); 8 Brian McDermott (Bradford); 9 James Lowes (Bradford) (C); 10 Stuart Fielden (Bradford); 11 Jamie Peacock (Bradford); 12 Lee Radford (Bradford); 13 Lee Gilmour (Bradford). Subs (all used): 14 Francis Cummins (Leeds); 15 Francis Maloney (Salford); 16 Paul King (Hull); 17 Darren Fleary (Leeds); 18 Paul Anderson (Bradford).
Tries: Fielden (4), Smith (11), Senior (18), Lowes (39);
Goals: Orr 3, Maloney.
LANCASHIRE: 1 Kris Radlinski (Wigan); 2 Paul Wellens (St Helens); 3 Paul Johnson (Wigan); 4 Gary Connolly (Wigan); 5 Dominic Peters (London); 6 Lee Briers (Warrington); 7 Paul Deacon (Bradford); 8 Terry O'Connor (Wigan); 9 Keiron Cunningham (St Helens); 10 Barrie McDermott (Leeds); 11 Chris Joynt (St Helens); 12 Paul Sculthorpe (St Helens); 13 Andy Farrell (Wigan) (C). Subs (all used): 14 Neil Turley (Leigh); 15 Terry Newton (Wigan); 16 Kevin Sinfield (Leeds); 17 Tim Jonkers (St Helens); 18 Andy Coley (Salford).
Tries: Deacon (16, 25), Radlinski (27), Sculthorpe (30), Turley (34), Johnson (74); **Goals:** Farrell 6.
League Express Men of the Match:
Yorkshire: James Lowes; *Lancashire:* Paul Johnson.
Penalty count: 3-1; **Half-time:** 24-28; **Referee:** Robert Connolly (Wigan); **Attendance:** 10,253 *(at Headingley,*

Deacon opened the Lancashire scoring, when he touched down following great play by Johnson and Radlinski. But Keith Senior replied with a try for Yorkshire, and Danny Orr added his third goal.

Then came the amazing Lancashire comeback, as Deacon, Radlinski, Paul Sculthorpe and Turley ripped in for tries. Farrell added three goals, and suddenly Lancashire were ten points ahead.

Lowes' converted try just before the interval kept Yorkshire well in the game, and set the stage for a far more intense second half.

Although there was not the spectacular movement of the first half – Turley's try followed a bewildering bout of eleven passes – it enhanced the game's credibility.

168

SEASON DOWN UNDER
Rabbitohs hop back

What a season Down Under! Newcastle finally came of age in a unified competition. A Brian Smith-coached club again faltered at the final hurdle. Finger-pointing, the likes of which we've never before seen. Drugs. Sackings and defections. A comeback that silenced the critics.

For what more could you ask?

Well, try South Sydney for size. The Pride of the League won against all odds, topping the headliners for 2001.

Souths have always been making headlines since they were one of the first clubs to defect from rugby union in 1908 and helped start the new code of Rugby League in Australia.

They won the inaugural Premiership that year. And in the next nine decades they added another 19 for a record unequalled in the game.

Then came the unthinkable. The Rabbitohs were axed from the NRL Premiership at the end of the 1999 season, high-profile victims of the political machinations that followed the peace in the Super League war and demands that there be only 14 teams in future competitions.

The NRL hierarchy hoped the Souths problem would be quietly swept under the carpet. But the game's leadership did not count on the stubbornness of Souths' president George Piggins, the former World Cup hooker and self-made millionaire.

He ignored early legal advice that the Rabbitohs could never hope to win a court case, rallied the fans, found money to pay the lawyers and fought on.

Even an original court loss did not deter the doughty Piggins. He engaged in more fund-raising and appealed. He was again defying logic which, in the words of a famous Aussie saying, suggested Souths had two chances - 'Buckley's and Nunn'. No chance whatsoever!

On July 6, 2001, Piggins was vindicated. Souths beat the NRL. The Appeals Court ruled that the Rabbitohs should not have been kicked out of the competition.

Legally, the judges did not have the power to reinstate the club. That was an entirely different legal problem. But within hours of their judgment being handed down, NRL chief executive David Moffett had called a media conference to announce that the Rabbitohs would be part of the Premiership race in 2002.

The newspapers carried pages upon pages of stories about King George and his Court. Craig Coleman, coach when Souths were kicked out, would be again at the helm. The 1995 World Cup back-rower Adam Muir would be their captain.

EMBARRASSMENT FOR TIGERS

But as the backroom boys at Redfern set about building a new team from nothing, the Premiership went on as usual.

It had already been hit by two scandals - headlines the game could ill-afford.

Two players from Wests Tigers - controversial scrum-half Craig Field and the unassuming centre Kevin McGuinness - had tested positive to banned recreational drugs. The pair had been caught in an out-of- season test after a club party, with Field showing traces of cocaine and McGuinness ecstasy. Both were suspended for six months. McGuinness was to later have his suspension cut to four months on an appeal. Field's appeal at the same time was dismissed.

The Tigers may have thought their problems couldn't get any worse.

But they did.

After a match against Wests at Townsville in late March, several players made allegations against former international winger John Hopoate. He was accused of poking his opponents in the backside with a finger.

Videos of the incidents proved his guilt and Hoppa was suspended for 12 matches for contrary conduct. He parted company with Wests but, suitably contrite, bobbed up late in the season with the Northern Eagles.

On the field, the players were turning in some razzle-dazzle performances. It was a season of record pointscoring, with an average of almost 50 points per game. Four times a side racked up more than 60 points in a game, with the biggest thrashing being Melbourne Storm's 64-0 success over Wests Tigers (it was a forgetful year for Wests).

The Parramatta Eels, under coach Brian Smith, had their best season since their most recent Premiership in 1986. They finished a whopping five points clear of the rest when winning the Minor Premiership and amassed a massive 839 points in the season proper, the most by any club in the history of the game.

Jason Taylor

They topped the half-century five times (66-12 over Wests Tigers, 54-28 against Penrith Panthers, 50-22 over Canberra Raiders, a 62-0 whitewash of the North Queensland Cowboys and 56-12 over the New Zealand Warriors in the first round of the finals' series).

The greatest 'buy' of the season proved to be veteran halfback Jason Taylor.

Discarded by the Northern Eagles, Taylor had written to Smith in the off-season asking for one last chance to prove he could still make it in top company.

Make it? He was a vital cog in the Parramatta juggernaut, scoring 265 points and, in the process, becoming the greatest pointscorer in the history of the Australian Premiership. His 2,117 points topped the previous best of 2,034 set by Darryl Halligan only twelve months earlier.

Danny Buderus looks for a way through the Parramatta defence

NIGHT OF KNIGHTS

Such was Parramatta's superior form over the season that the Eels went into the Grand Final against Newcastle as red-hot favourites.

But it took Andrew Johns and his team of Novocastrians less than half a game to prove the pundits terribly wrong in the first Grand Final held under lights.

What a Night! What a Night of Nights! What a Night of Knights!

In doing so, the Knights laid to rest a criticism that had dogged them for the previous four years.

In 1997 they had won a Premiership. But that was under the ARL banner in the split competition during the Super League War. And the critics were always quick to point out that the Brisbane Broncos had won the alternative competition that season and had followed it up with another victory twelve months later when peace unified the Premiership race once more.

This time there could be no pedantic questioning of the Knight's credentials.

The match seemed as good as over at the break with Newcastle ahead 24-0. The Knights had played an almost perfect first half, with just one error. The Eels, on the other hand, coughed up possession with simple unforced mistakes.

The Newcastle party gets underway in the Knights' dressing room

One of the Parramatta errors led to the first try. Fullback Brett Hodgson threw a pass to Nathan Hindmarsh, who wasn't expecting it. After all, he was surrounded by Newcastle players just 20 metres out from his own tryline.

The Knights pounced on the loose ball. Moments later Andrew Johns was grassed half a metre short. And from the next play-the-ball Parramatta centre Jamie Lyon fell for a decoy run by barnstorming Ben Kennedy as Bill Peden took advantage of the slightest of gaps to bulldoze his way over. He planted the ball down on a giant Knights logo painted into the area behind the northern tryline. There were less than four minutes on the clock.

Three minutes later a charge-down of an attempted clearing kick saw Kennedy in possession close to the tryline. And in the blink of an eyelid his second-row partner Steve Simpson, lurking out in the centres, was over. Peden then scored again in an almost identical position to his first try, with Kennedy involved in the lead-up.

It was 18-nil after 22 minutes and the Parramatta players were shaking their heads in disbelief.

Eels substitute Andrew Ryan got across the line a few minutes later. But video replays showed he had not been able to ground the ball for a try. From the ensuing six, winger Luke Burt over-ran a poor Nathan Hindmarsh pass when he looked certain to score. And with this mistake Parramatta's hopes of getting back into the game were clearly dashed.

To rub salt into the wound, Kennedy scored himself after yet another fine burst by Johns had seen the Newcastle captain brought down near the line.

The 24-point lead at half-time was a record for a grand final.

The Knights were fired up as they left the field. The Eels, on the other hand, trooped off with heads bowed.

But coach Smith reminded his players that the lowly Wests Tigers had come back from a 24-point deficit to beat Newcastle earlier in the season.

It was nip and tuck for the first 15 minutes of the second half.

Newcastle fullback Robbie O'Davis had a try disallowed by the video referees after losing the ball over the line. Then his opposite number Brett Hodgson capitalised on a break by PJ Marsh to run 30 metres and score under the posts.

The Parramatta spirits were lifted. But they were soon dashed again when Timana Tahu touched down wide out. Yet the Eels refused to give up and were to snare another three tries - two to young Kangaroo hopeful Lyon and a second to Hodgson.

But it was much too late.

When the restart of play came after Hodgson's second try there were just 25 seconds left. It was time for just one frantic effort with winger Jason Moodie desperately kicking when cornered near the halfway line, only to see the ball veer off into touch.

The side that had set the standard all season had been found wanting in the final showdown.

Coach Michael Hagan won himself a place in the record books as only the fourth coach since World War II to have won a Premiership in his first season at the helm of a senior side. He followed in the footsteps of Tom McMahon (Wests) in 1952, Leo Nosworthy (Balmain) in 1969 and Phil Gould (Canterbury) in 1988.

"I never dreamed of getting this far so early in my career," Hagan explained.

Johns won the Clive Churchill Medal as Man of the Match. Joey's pride was obvious as he received the medal from the widow of the man they dubbed 'The Little Master'. Johns said he was even more proud because Churchill was, like him, a Newcastle boy.

The Newcastle skipper thoroughly deserved his award. Yet it was the pack of forwards that laid the foundations for the victory.

None played better than Kennedy. He admitted later he had gone out too hard and was feeling it late in the match when the Eels were storming home. But his display ensured he would be one of the first picked in the Kangaroo squad less than twelve hours later. He had received a 'wake-up call' from the selectors mid-season when they dropped him from the NSW State of Origin after a few ordinary displays.

Simpson, his unfashionable second-row partner, also stood tall with a sensational game. He scored one try, had another that looked okay disallowed and saved a certain four-pointer with an incredible ball and all tackle.

For the losers, captain Nathan Cayless tried hard and World Cup star Nathan Hindmarsh led the tackle-count with 38 and the forward hit-ups with 19. Lyon was the best of the backs in both attack and defence in a display that won him a Test berth with the Kangaroos.

HEADS ROLL

Parramatta's neighbours in Sydney's west, the Penrith Panthers, will remember 2001 as a season of woe. Semi-finalists the previous season, they finished with the competition's most despised trophy, the wooden spoon, as they were regularly humiliated by opposition sides.

The Panthers conceded an incredible 847 points, the third worst by any club in the history of the Australian game. As a result heads rolled. Coach Royce Simmons was shown the door after eight years at the helm (receiving his marching orders after a 60-18 drubbing by Newcastle in the final round). And several top officials followed, with Hull and former Gateshead chief executive Shane Richardson returning to Australia to join his old mate John Lang, who had moved from the Sharks as Simmons' replacement as coach.

Simmons wasn't the first coach to go. There were mid-season exits by Tim Sheens (Cowboys) and Chris Anderson (Storm). At least Anderson had a job awaiting him - the replacement for Lang at the Sharks.

Graham Murray was axed by the Sydney Roosters after their defeat by Newcastle in the first week of the play-offs - this despite the fact that Murray, the former Leeds Rhinos' hero, had only twelve months earlier steered the Roosters to their first grand final in 20 years. The knives were sharp at Bondi Junction!

With the season over, Mal Meninga finally stood down from the Raiders, after sharing coaching duties for the season with his replacement, former Bradford Bulls mentor Matthew Elliott.

As far as the clubs themselves were concerned, the merger of Manly and North Sydney into the Northern Eagles was finally dissolved, with Manly taking over control of the side for 2002. The Northern Eagles name would remain - but Norths would be having nothing more to do with running the club.

On the playing front, Test wingers Mat Rogers and Wendell Sailor accepted massive offers to switch to rugby union for the 2002 season while the usual end-of-season exodus to England continued, led by internationals Darren Britt, Quentin Pongia, Lesley Vainikolo, Wayne Bartrim and Craig Greenhill.

ORIGIN FAIRYTALE

Souths' return may have grabbed the headlines off the field, but as far as the action on the pitch was concerned nothing could match the fairytale return from across the world of Allan Langer for a State of Origin triumph.

After the previous year's record drubbing at the hands of the Blues, the Queensland chiefs turned to supercoach Wayne Bennett in an effort to restore the Maroons' pride.

He shocked everyone with a team of rookies to take on the might of NSW in the first encounter, the last held at Lang Park, before a multi-million-dollar upgrade of 'The Cauldron'. Bennett chose a monstrous pack of forwards and gambled on ten newcomers being able to rise to the occasion. Adding to the emotions was a pre-match talk to the Queenslanders by the 'Emperor of Lang Park' Wally Lewis, who had personally presented the newcomers with their first State of Origin strip.

It worked. In the second set of six tackles a shell-shocked NSW kicked straight down the throat of Queensland fullback Darren Lockyer. He grabbed the ball with delight, 20 metres from his line, took it to the defence and flicked a perfect pass to Lote Tuqiri, who sliced through the opposing three-quarters on a 50-metre burst. Tuqiri beat NSW fullback Mark Hughes, and when Adam MacDougall managed to reach him, returned the ball to a trailing Lockyer who scored. The clock showed just 1min 47sec.

It set the scene for the whole match.

The Queenslanders went on to win 34-16 - the biggest victory by Queensland in the most recent twelve seasons of Origin clashes. And it was only when the Maroons' tired defence slipped down a notch late in the game that the Blues were able to score a couple of tries to make the score a little more respectable.

It was a different matter in Origin II at Sydney's Stadium Australia.

Queensland had lost several players from the side that had triumphed five weeks earlier. The most worrying loss was that of captain Gorden Tallis to a career-threatening neck injury.

And the NSW players were keen for revenge. The forwards - those of them who remained after the selectors' purge and the newcomers eager to make amends - muscled up from the start and dictated the trend of play. They gave their halves Trent Barrett and Brad Fittler the momentum to get the Blues' attack moving.

And when referee Bill Harrigan mercifully blew the whistle for full-time, they had exorcised the demons from the first game with a decisive 26-8 victory. It was the second biggest winning margin by the Blues in Origin history, topped only by the 56-16 victory in last year's final clash.

Queensland had more injury worries for the third encounter.

It was then that Bennett played his trump card - he brought Alfie Langer home. Most of the media was highly critical of Bennett's decision to recall Langer. The little genius hadn't played in the Origin cauldron since 1998. And his

Queensland - State Of Origin Winners 2001

most recent appearance in an NRL game was in early 1999.

The so-called experts lined up to query the wisdom of flying him halfway across the world from Warrington to provide experience to a young Queensland side that had been thoroughly outplayed in the second clash.

One who did agree with Bennett's bold move was another supercoach, Jack Gibson.

"Champion players have a way of making critics eat their words," Gibson warned before the match.

And Langer certainly did. He scored one try himself and had a hand in at least three others in the Maroons' eight-try romp, to win 40-14.

No way through for Shane Webcke

"This has to be the best day of my life," the Wolves scrum-half said after the game. "It was great to come to play with these blokes, especially with Wayne Bennett coaching. It shows fairytales do come true."

Bennett did not agree.

"I'm not a great believer in fairytales," he said. "And I'm not sure one happened tonight. But I'm glad he [Langer] got the finish he deserved. It wasn't the right way he finished in 1998.

"And now the fans realise what a great player Allan Langer was...and still is. It was no gamble bringing him home...not ever. He's a champion."

It didn't look as if the gamble had paid off in the opening minutes of the game when Queensland had a disastrous start. Big prop John Buttigieg dropped the ball in the first tackle of the match, when crunched by three NSW forwards.

And from the ensuing scrum the Blues put on a rehearsed move. Ryan Girdler went in and away from opposing centre Paul Bowman, dummied towards winger Adam MacDougall, palmed off Darren Smith with a no-nonsense fend and was over to score in the corner.

The clock showed just 38 seconds - the fastest try in Origin history, beating one by Robbie Ross two years earlier by two seconds.

But that was as good it got for NSW.

The Queenslanders exploded and by half-time they were comfortably in the lead, 28-8. And when Langer scored 13 minutes into the second half, the game was out of NSW's reach.

There was to be no fairytale ending to Brad Fittler's Origin career although he tried all evening to rally his troops.

As for Langer, this, too, was to be his last hurrah at Origin level.

"That's it for me," he said. "That's the end."

FIRST ASHES TEST

SECOND ASHES TEST

GREAT BRITAIN 12
AUSTRALIA 40

CLOCKWISE, FROM RIGHT:
Brad Fittler offloads under
pressure from Terry O'Connor;
Ben Kennedy celebrates
scoring; Andrew Johns
crashes past Kris Radlinski to
touch down; Stuart **Fielden**
held up by Danny **Buderus**

THIRD ASHES TEST

GREAT BRITAIN 8
AUSTRALIA 28

CLOCKWISE, FROM TOP:
The champagne flows as the Australian side celebrate their Ashes Series success; Nowhere to go for Andy Farrell; Paul Anderson goes on the rampage

INTERNATIONALS

WALES...........................33
ENGLAND 42

Keiron Cunningham tries to find a way past Brian McDermott and Paul King

FRANCE 12
GREAT BRITAIN 42

LEFT: Paul Anderson carries the French defence forward
RIGHT: Kevin Sinfield tackled by Arnaud Dulac

INTERNATIONALS

FRANCE 56
IRELAND 16

Francis Cummins looks for a
gap in the French defence

FRANCE 20
SCOTLAND 42

Wayne McDonald sets off on a
marauding run

NEW ZEALAND 10
AUSTRALIA 28

Robbie Paul fends off the
tackle of Andrew Johns

PAPUA NEW GUINEA 12
AUSTRALIA 54

LEFT: Lote Tuqiri dumped by
the Papua New Guinean
defence
RIGHT: PNG fans enjoy the
occasion

INTERNATIONAL

England's Mark Calderwood in the thick of the action during the Under-21s' tour to South Africa

NEW ZEALAND 36
FRANCE 0

Ali Lauitiiti held by the French defence

RIGHT: Action from the first international between the USA and Great Britain at junior age level, as BARLA Great Britain defeated the Junior Tomahawks in Philadelphia

SUNSHINE STATE CHALLENGE

The Huddersfield defence puts a stop to this USA attack during the inaugural Sunshine State Challenge in Jacksonville, Florida. The tournament was eventually won by Leeds Rhinos, who beat the Giants 28-0 in the final

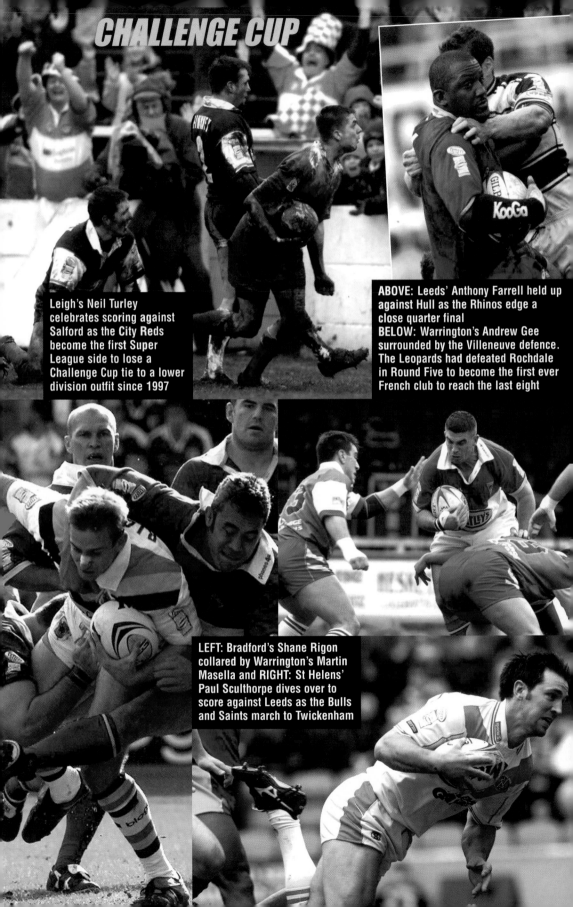

CHALLENGE CUP

Leigh's Neil Turley celebrates scoring against Salford as the City Reds become the first Super League side to lose a Challenge Cup tie to a lower division outfit since 1997

ABOVE: Leeds' Anthony Farrell held up against Hull as the Rhinos edge a close quarter final

BELOW: Warrington's Andrew Gee surrounded by the Villeneuve defence. The Leopards had defeated Rochdale in Round Five to become the first ever French club to reach the last eight

LEFT: Bradford's Shane Rigon collared by Warrington's Martin Masella and **RIGHT:** St Helens' Paul Sculthorpe dives over to score against Leeds as the Bulls and Saints march to Twickenham

BRADFORD BULLS 6
ST HELENS 13

CLOCKWISE, FROM LEFT: Tommy Martyn beats Henry Paul to the ball to score the opening try; Mike Forshaw faces up to Keiron Cunningham; Chris Joynt lifts the Challenge Cup

CHALLENGE CUP FINAL

NFP PLAY-OFFS

LEFT: Featherstone's Gavin Swinson meets Keighley duo Andy Rice and Rob Roberts
RIGHT: Hull KR's Chris Charles tackled by Dewsbury's Andy Fisher and Barry Eaton

RIGHT: Leigh's David Bradbury in action against Widnes. The Centurions carried off the Minor Premiership and the Trans-Pennine Cup but were ultimately denied a Grand Final spot by the Vikings in the play-offs

NFP SEASON

ABOVE: Rochdale's Brendan O'Meara in action against Whitehaven. The Hornets were the big NFP improvers of 2001, finishing third in the table and coming close to reaching the Grand Final, only to be denied by a late rally from local rivals

Adam Bristow and Andy Fairclough celebrate the Centurions' Trans-Pennine Final win over Keighley

OLDHAM 14
WIDNES VIKINGS 24

**ABOVE: Tommy Hodgkinson takes on the Oldham defence
LEFT: Mark Sibson tries to escape from Craig Weston**

NFP GRAND FINAL

Widnes celebrate winning the NFP title

NORTHERN DEALERS

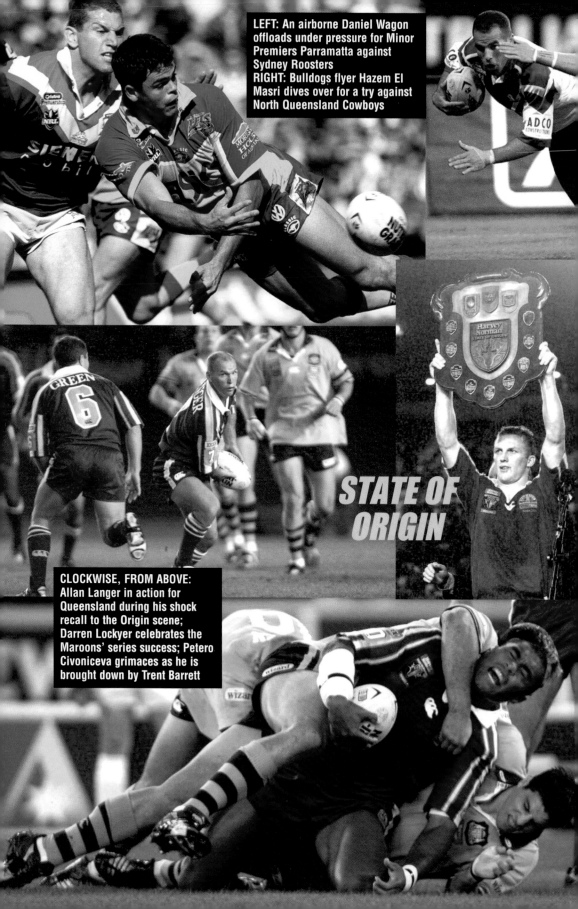

LEFT: An airborne Daniel Wagon offloads under pressure for Minor Premiers Parramatta against Sydney Roosters
RIGHT: Bulldogs flyer Hazem El Masri dives over for a try against North Queensland Cowboys

STATE OF ORIGIN

CLOCKWISE, FROM ABOVE: Allan Langer in action for Queensland during his shock recall to the Origin scene; Darren Lockyer celebrates the Maroons' series success; Petero Civoniceva grimaces as he is brought down by Trent Barrett

NRL SEASON

ABOVE: Brisbane's Lote Tuqiri tries to keep his balance following a break against St George-Illawarra
LEFT: Chris McKenna plunges through the Brisbane defence to touch down for a Sharks try

NRL GRAND FINAL

NEWCASTLE KNIGHTS 30
PARRAMATTA EELS 24

Newcastle's players start the celebrations after the Knights' stunning Grand Final victory over Parramatta

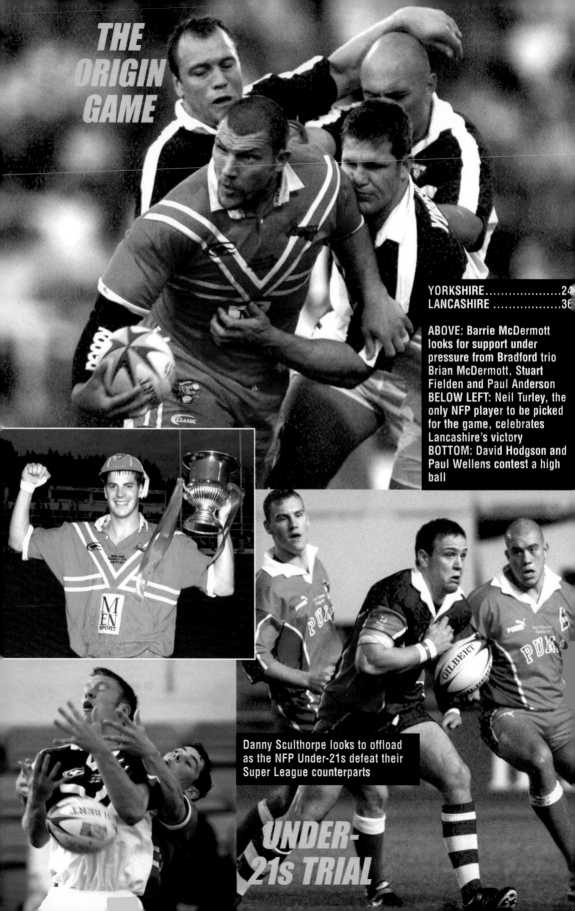

THE ORIGIN GAME

YORKSHIRE	24
LANCASHIRE	36

ABOVE: Barrie McDermott looks for support under pressure from Bradford trio Brian McDermott, Stuart Fielden and Paul Anderson
BELOW LEFT: Neil Turley, the only NFP player to be picked for the game, celebrates Lancashire's victory
BOTTOM: David Hodgson and Paul Wellens contest a high ball

Danny Sculthorpe looks to offload as the NFP Under-21s defeat their Super League counterparts

UNDER-21s TRIAL

STUDENT EUROPA CUP

Rugby League is set for a bright future in the former Soviet Union following the hugely successful Student Europa Cup, which was held in the city of Kazan. Over 16,000 people turned up to watch the opening ceremony which featured the game between hosts Tatarstan and Ireland. The tournament was eventually won by England, who defeated Tatarstan 34-16 in the final.

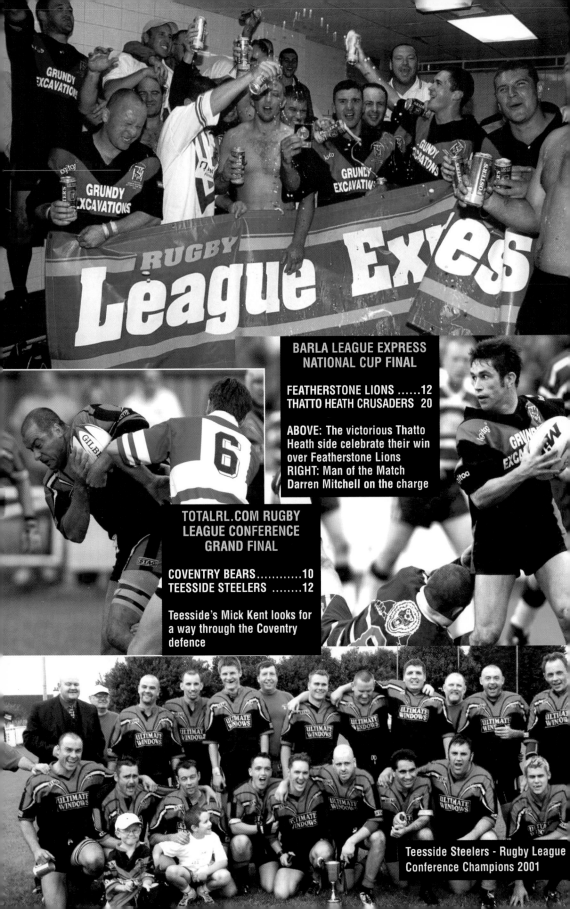

RUGBY League Exes

BARLA LEAGUE EXPRESS NATIONAL CUP FINAL

FEATHERSTONE LIONS 12
THATTO HEATH CRUSADERS 20

ABOVE: The victorious Thatto Heath side celebrate their win over Featherstone Lions
RIGHT: Man of the Match Darren Mitchell on the charge

TOTALRL.COM RUGBY LEAGUE CONFERENCE GRAND FINAL

COVENTRY BEARS............10
TEESSIDE STEELERS 12

Teesside's Mick Kent looks for a way through the Coventry defence

Teesside Steelers - Rugby League Conference Champions 2001

6
STATISTICAL REVIEW

SUPER LEAGUE PLAYERS
1996-2001

Super League Players 1996-2001

PLAYER	CLUB	YEAR	APP	TRIES	GOALS	FG	PTS
Darren Abram	Oldham	1996-97	25(2)	11	0	0	44
Darren Adams	Paris	1996	9(1)	1	0	0	4
Guy Adams	Huddersfield	1998	1(2)	0	0	0	0
Phil Adamson	St Helens	1999	(1)	0	0	0	0
Glen Air	London	1998-2001	57(13)	27	0	1	109
Neil Alexander	Salford	1998	(1)	0	0	0	0
Malcolm Alker	Salford	1997-2001	92(1)	23	0	1	93
Chris Allen	Castleford	1996	(1)	0	0	0	0
Gavin Allen	London	1996	10	0	0	0	0
John Allen	Workington	1996	20(1)	6	0	0	24
Ray Allen	London	1996	5(3)	3	0	0	12
Richard Allwood	Gateshead	1999	(4)	0	0	0	0
Sean Allwood	Gateshead	1999	3(17)	1	0	0	4
David Alstead	Warrington	2000-01	5(10)	0	0	0	0
Asa Amone	Halifax	1996-97	32(7)	10	0	0	40
Grant Anderson	Castleford	1996-97	15(6)	3	0	0	12
Paul Anderson	Bradford	1997-2001	54(47)	21	0	0	84
	Halifax	1996	5(1)	1	0	0	4
Paul Anderson	Sheffield	1999	3(7)	1	0	0	4
	St Helens	1996-98	2(28)	4	1	0	18
Eric Anselme	Halifax	1997	(2)	0	0	0	0
Graham Appo	Huddersfield	2001	7	4	0	0	16
Colin Armstrong	Workington	1996	11(2)	1	0	0	4
Richard Armswood							
	Workington	1996	5(1)	1	0	0	4
Danny Arnold	Salford	2001	6(12)	5	0	0	20
	Huddersfield	1998-2000	55(7)	26	0	0	104
	Castleford	2000	(4)	0	0	0	0
	St Helens	1996-97	40(1)	33	0	0	132
Martin Aspinwall	Wigan	2001	(6)	0	0	0	0
Mark Aston	Sheffield	1996-99	67(6)	6	243	6	516
Paul Atcheson	St Helens	1998-2000	58(4)	18	0	0	72
	Oldham	1996-97	40	21	0	0	84
David Atkins	Huddersfield	2001	26(1)	4	0	0	16
Warren Ayres	Salford	1999	2(9)	1	2	0	8
Jerome Azema	Paris	1997	(1)	0	0	0	0
David Baildon	Hull	1998-99	26(2)	4	0	0	16
Simon Baldwin	Sheffield	1999	7(15)	2	0	0	8
	Halifax	1996-98	41(15)	16	0	1	65
Rob Ball	Wigan	1998-2000	3(4)	0	0	0	0
Michael Banks	Bradford	1998	(1)	0	0	0	0
Frederic Banquet							
	Paris	1996	16(2)	7	4	0	36
Lee Bardauskas	Castleford	1996-97	(2)	0	0	0	0
Craig Barker	Workington	1996	(2)	0	0	0	0
Danny Barnes	Halifax	1999	2	0	0	0	0
Richie Barnett	London	2001	17	10	0	0	40
David Barnhill	Leeds	2000	20(8)	5	0	0	20
Paul Barrow	Warrington	1996-97	1(10)	1	0	0	4
Scott Barrow	St Helens	1997-2000	9(13)	1	0	0	4
Steve Barrow	London	2000	2	0	0	0	0
	Hull	1998-99	4(17)	1	0	0	4
	Wigan	1996	(8)	3	0	0	12
Ben Barton	Huddersfield	1998	1(6)	1	0	0	4
Danny Barton	Salford	2001	1	0	0	0	0
Greg Barwick	London	1996-97	30(4)	21	110	2	306
David Bastian	Halifax	1996	(2)	0	0	0	0
David Bates	Castleford	2001	(2)	0	0	0	0
	Warrington	2001	1(2)	0	0	0	0
Nathan Batty	Wakefield	2001	1(1)	0	0	0	0
Russell Bawden	London	1996-97	25(16)	7	0	0	28
Neil Baxter	Salford	2001	1	0	0	0	0
Neil Baynes	Salford	1999-2001	44(14)	4	0	0	16
	Wigan	1996-98	(10)	1	0	0	4
Robbie Beazley	London	1997-99	48(15)	13	0	0	52
Dean Bell	Leeds	1996	1	1	0	0	4
Mark Bell	Wigan	1998	22	12	0	0	48
Paul Bell	Leeds	2000	1	0	0	0	0
Troy Bellamy	Paris	1997	5(10)	0	0	0	0
Adrian Belle	Huddersfield	1998	10(2)	0	0	0	0
	Oldham	1996	19	8	0	0	32
Jamie Benn	Castleford	1998, 2000	3(8)	1	15	0	34
Andy Bennett	Warrington	1996	6(5)	1	0	0	4
Mike Bennett	St Helens	2000-01	1(10)	0	0	0	0
John Bentley	Huddersfield	1999	13(4)	3	0	0	12
	Halifax	1996, 1998	22(3)	24	0	0	96
Phil Bergman	Paris	1997	20(1)	14	0	0	56
Joe Berry	Huddersfield	1998-99	25(14)	3	0	0	12
Roger Best	London	1997-98	1(5)	1	0	0	4
Mike Bethwaite	Workington	1996	17(3)	1	0	0	4
Denis Betts	Wigan	1998-2000	82(24)	33	0	0	132
Ricky Bibey	Wigan	2001	(4)	0	0	0	0
Chris Birchall	Bradford	2000	(1)	0	0	0	0
Deon Bird	Hull	2000-01	37(6)	20	0	0	80
	Gateshead	1999	19(3)	13	0	0	52
	Paris	1996-97	30	12	2	0	52
Richie Blackmore							
	Leeds	1997-2000	63	25	0	0	100
Steve Blakeley	Salford	1997-2001	89(3)	21	224	2	534
	Warrington	2000	4(3)	1	9	0	22
Ian Blease	Salford	1997	(1)	0	0	0	0
Jamie Bloem	Halifax	1998-2000	65(17)	20	79	0	238
Vea Bloomfield	Paris	1996	4(14)	3	0	0	12
Pascal Bomati	Paris	1996	17(1)	10	0	0	40
Simon Booth	Hull	1998-99	15(9)	2	0	0	8
	St Helens	1996-97	10(4)	1	0	0	4
Steve Booth	Huddersfield	1998-99	16(4)	2	3	0	14
Alan Boothroyd	Halifax	1997	2(3)	0	0	0	0
Frano Botica	Castleford	1996	21	5	84	2	190
Hadj Boudebza	Paris	1996	(2)	0	0	0	0
David Boughton	Huddersfield	1999	26(1)	4	0	0	16
David Bouveng	Halifax	1997-99	66(2)	19	0	0	76
Tony Bowes	Huddersfield	1998	3(2)	0	0	0	0
Radney Bowker	St Helens	2001	(1)	0	0	0	0
David Boyle	Bradford	1999-2000	36(13)	15	0	1	61
David Bradbury	Hudds-Sheff	2000	21(2)	1	0	0	4
	Salford	1997-99	23(10)	6	0	0	24
	Oldham	1996-97	19(6)	9	0	0	36
John Braddish	St Helens	2001	(1)	0	0	0	0
Graeme Bradley	Bradford	1996-98	62(1)	29	0	0	116
Darren Bradstreet							
	London	1999-2000	1(3)	0	0	0	0
Liam Bretherton	Wigan	1999	(5)	2	0	0	8
	Warrington	1997	(2)	0	0	0	0
Johnny Brewer	Halifax	1996	4(2)	2	0	0	8
Lee Briers	Warrington	1997-2001	106(11)	31	287	22	720
	St Helens	1997	3	0	11	0	22
Carl Briggs	Salford	1999	8(5)	3	0	1	13
	Halifax	1996	5(3)	1	0	0	4
Gary Broadbent	Salford	1997-2001	107	22	0	0	88
Paul Broadbent	Hull	2000-01	40(9)	3	0	0	12
	Halifax	1999	26(1)	2	0	0	8
	Sheffield	1996-98	63(1)	6	0	0	24
Andrew Brocklehurst							
	Halifax	2001	2(2)	0	0	0	0
Justin Brooker	Wakefield	2001	25	9	0	0	36
	Bradford	2000	17(4)	11	0	0	44
Darren Brown	Salford	1999-2001	47(9)	11	6	0	56
Gavin Brown	Leeds	1996-97	5(2)	1	2	0	8
Lee Brown	Hull	1999	(1)	0	0	0	0
Michael Brown	London	1996	(2)	0	0	0	0
Todd Brown	Paris	1996	8(1)	2	0	0	8
Adrian Brunker	Wakefield	1999	17	6	0	0	24
Justin Bryant	Paris	1996	4(1)	0	0	0	0
	London	1996	7(8)	1	0	0	4
James Bunyan	Huddersfield	1998-99	8(7)	2	0	0	8
Andy Burgess	Salford	1997	3(12)	0	0	0	0
Gary Burns	Oldham	1996	6	1	0	0	4
Paul Burns	Workington	1996	5(2)	1	0	0	4
Robert Burrow	Leeds	2001	11(6)	7	16	0	60
Dean Busby	Warrington	1999-2001	29(28)	6	0	0	24
	Hull	1998	8(6)	0	0	0	0
	St Helens	1996-98	1(7)	0	0	0	0
Ikram Butt	London	1996	5(1)	0	0	0	0
Shane Byrne	Huddersfield	1998-99	1(5)	0	0	0	0
Didier Cabestany							
	Paris	1996-97	20(6)	2	0	0	8
Mark Calderwood							
	Leeds	2001	20(8)	11	0	0	44
Matt Calland	Hull	1999	1	0	0	0	0
	Bradford	1996-98	44(5)	24	0	0	96
Dean Callaway	London	1999-2000	26(24)	12	0	0	48
Laurent Cambres							
	Paris	1996	(1)	0	0	0	0
Chris Campbell	Warrington	2000	7(1)	2	0	0	8
Logan Campbell	Hull	1998-99,					
		2001	70(13)	14	0	0	56
	Castleford	2000	14(2)	3	0	0	12
	Workington	1996	7(1)	1	0	0	4
Phil Cantillon	Leeds	1997	(1)	0	0	0	0
Daryl Cardiss	Halifax	1999-2000	69(3)	34	4	0	144
	Wigan	1996-98	12(6)	4	0	0	16
Dale Cardoza	Halifax	2001	3	1	0	0	4
	Huddersfield	2000-01	20(9)	11	0	0	44
	Sheffield	1998-99	11(7)	3	0	0	12
Paul Carige	Salford	1999	24(1)	7	0	0	28
Jim Carlton	Huddersfield	1999	3(11)	2	0	0	8
Brian Carney	Wigan	2001	18(5)	14	0	0	56
	Hull	2000	13(3)	7	0	0	28
	Gateshead	1999	3(2)	2	0	0	8
Martin Carney	Warrington	1997	(1)	0	0	0	0
Paul Carr	Sheffield	1996-98	45(5)	15	0	0	60
Bernard Carroll	London	1996	2(1)	1	0	0	4
Mark Carroll	London	1998	15(3)	1	0	0	4
Tonie Carroll	Leeds	2001	23(1)	22	0	0	88
Darren Carter	Workington	1996	10(3)	0	1	0	2
John Cartwright	Salford	1997	9	0	0	0	0
Garreth Carvell	Hull	2001	2(15)	0	0	0	0
	Leeds	1997-2000	(4)	0	0	0	0
	Gateshead	1999	4(4)	1	0	0	4
Garen Casey	Salford	1999	13(5)	3	23	0	58
Mick Cassidy	Wigan	1996-2001	132(22)	23	0	0	92
Chris Causey	Warrington	1997-99	(18)	0	0	0	0
Arnaud Cervello	Paris	1996	4	4	0	0	16
Gary Chambers	Warrington	1996-2000	65(28)	9	0	0	36
Pierre Chamorin	Paris	1996-97	27(3)	8	3	0	38
Chris Chapman	Leeds	1999	(1)	0	0	0	0

PLAYER	CLUB	YEAR	APP	TRIES	GOALS	FG	PTS
Damien Chapman							
	London	1998	6(2)	3	4	1	21
David Chapman	Castleford	1996-98	24(6)	8	0	0	32
Richard Chapman							
	Sheffield	1996	1	2	0	0	8
Chris Charles	Castleford	2001	1(4)	1	0	0	4
Andy Cheetham	Huddersfield	1998-99	30	11	0	0	44
Kris Chesney	London	1998	1(2)	0	0	0	0
Chris Chester	Wigan	1999-2001	21(22)	5	0	0	20
	Halifax	1996-99	47(14)	16	15	1	95
Lee Chilton	Workington	1996	10(3)	6	0	0	24
Gary Christie	Bradford	1996-97	4(7)	1	0	0	4
Dean Clark	Leeds	1996	11(2)	3	0	0	12
Des Clark	St Helens	1999	4	0	0	0	0
	Halifax	1998-99	35(13)	6	0	0	24
Greg Clarke	Halifax	1997	1(1)	0	0	0	0
John Clarke	Oldham	1996-97	27(4)	5	0	0	20
Jon Clarke	Warrington	2001	17(1)	4	0	0	16
	London	2000-01	19(11)	2	0	0	8
	Wigan	1997-99	13(10)	3	0	0	12
Ryan Clayton	Halifax	2000	(1)	0	0	0	0
Gavin Clinch	Halifax	1998-99,					
		2001	64	22	36	5	165
	Hudds-Sheff	2000	18(2)	5	0	1	21
	Wigan	1999	10(2)	4	12	0	40
Bradley Clyde	Leeds	2001	7(5)	1	0	0	4
Evan Cochrane	London	1996	5(1)	1	0	0	4
Andy Coley	Salford	2001	15(10)	4	0	0	16
Steve Collins	Hull	2000	28	17	0	0	68
	Gateshead	1999	20(4)	13	0	0	52
Wayne Collins	Leeds	1997	21	3	0	0	12
Gary Connolly	Wigan	1996-2001	133(3)	66	5	0	274
Mick Cook	Sheffield	1996	9(10)	2	0	0	8
Paul Cook	Huddersfield	1998-99	11(6)	2	13	0	34
	Bradford	1996-97	14(8)	7	38	1	105
Paul Cooke	Hull	1999-2001	43(16)	11	11	1	67
Ben Cooper	Huddersfield	2000-01	18(2)	2	0	0	8
Brandon Costin	Huddersfield	2001	25	15	33	1	127
Wes Cotton	London	1997-98	12	3	0	0	12
Phil Coussons	Salford	1997	7(2)	3	0	0	12
Alex Couttet	Paris	1997	1	0	0	0	0
Nick Couttet	Paris	1997	1	0	0	0	0
Jamie Coventry	Castleford	1996	1	0	0	0	0
Jimmy Cowan	Oldham	1996-97	2(8)	0	0	0	0
Will Cowell	Warrington	1998-2000	6(8)	1	0	0	4
Neil Cowie	Wigan	1996-2001	116(27)	10	0	1	41
Eorl Crabtree	Huddersfield	2001	(4)	0	0	0	0
Andy Craig	Halifax	1999	13(7)	1	3	0	10
	Wigan	1996	5(5)	2	0	0	8
Scott Cram	London	1999-2001	53(7)	3	0	0	12
Steve Craven	Hull	1998-2001	51(33)	4	0	0	16
Nicky Crellin	Workington	1996	(2)	0	0	0	0
Jason Critchley	Wakefield	2000	7(1)	4	0	0	16
	Castleford	1997-98	27(3)	11	0	0	44
Martin Crompton							
	Salford	1998-2000	30(6)	11	6	2	58
	Oldham	1996-97	36(1)	16	0	3	67
Paul Crook	Oldham	1996	4(9)	0	3	0	6
Lee Crooks	Castleford	1996-97	27(2)	2	14	0	36
Alan Cross	St Helens	1997	(2)	0	0	0	0
Kevin Crouthers	Warrington	2001	4	3	0	0	12
	London	2000	6(4)	1	0	0	4
	Wakefield	1999	4(4)	1	0	0	4
	Bradford	1997-98	3(9)	2	0	0	8
Matt Crowther	Hull	2001	23	10	69	0	178
	Hudds-Sheff	2000	10(4)	5	22	0	64
	Sheffield	1996-99	43(4)	22	10	0	108
Heath Cruckshank							
	St Helens	2001	1(12)	0	0	0	0
Paul Cullen	Warrington	1996	19	3	0	0	12
Francis Cummins							
	Leeds	1996-2001	139(7)	91	26	1	417
Keiron Cunningham							
	St Helens	1996-2001	149(2)	68	0	0	272
Andy Currier	Warrington	1996-97	(2)	1	0	0	4
Joe Dakuitoga	Sheffield	1996	6(3)	0	0	0	0
Brett Dallas	Wigan	2000-01	45	28	0	0	112
Paul Darbyshire	Warrington	1997	(6)	0	0	0	0
Maea David	Hull	1998	1	0	0	0	0
Paul Davidson	Halifax	2001	18(3)	5	0	0	20
	London	2000	6(10)	4	0	0	16
	St Helens	1998-99	27(16)	7	0	0	28
	Oldham	1996-97	17(18)	14	0	1	57
Gareth Davies	Warrington	1996-97	(1)	0	0	0	0
Wes Davies	Wigan	1998-2001	22(22)	11	0	0	44
Brad Davis	Wakefield	2001	14(3)	2	2	0	12
	Castleford	1997-2000	83	26	41	9	195
Matt Daylight	Hull	2000	17(1)	7	0	0	28
	Gateshead	1999	30	25	0	0	100
Paul Deacon	Bradford	1998-2001	52(42)	20	85	8	258
	Oldham	1997	(2)	0	0	0	0
Craig Dean	Halifax	1996-97	25(11)	12	1	1	51
Yacine Dekkiche	Hudds-Sheff	2000	11(3)	3	0	0	12
Martin Dermott	Warrington	1997	1	0	0	0	0
David Despin	Paris	1996	(1)	0	0	0	0
Fabien Devecchi	Paris	1996-97	17(10)	2	0	0	8
Matthew Diskin	Leeds	2001	4(10)	1	0	0	4
Paul Dixon	Sheffield	1996-97	5(9)	1	0	0	4
Gareth Dobson	Castleford	1998-2000	(10)	0	0	0	0
Michael Docherty							
	Hull	2000-01	(6)	0	0	0	0
Stuart Donlan	Halifax	2001	23(2)	11	0	0	44
Jason Donohue	Bradford	1996	(4)	0	0	0	0
Jeremy Donougher							
	Bradford	1996-99	40(21)	13	0	0	52
Justin Dooley	London	2000-01	37(18)	2	0	0	8
Dane Dorahy	Wakefield	2000-01	16(2)	4	19	1	55
Ewan Dowes	Leeds	2001	1(4)	0	0	0	0
Adam Doyle	Warrington	1998	9(3)	4	0	0	16
Rod Doyle	Sheffield	1997-99	52(10)	10	0	0	40
Damien Driscoll	Salford	2001	23(1)	1	0	0	4
John Duffy	Salford	2000	3(11)	0	1	1	3
	Warrington	1997-99	12(12)	0	0	0	0
Andrew Duncan	London	1997	2(4)	2	0	0	8
	Warrington	1997	(1)	0	0	0	0
Andrew Dunemann							
	Halifax	1999-2001	45	12	0	0	48
Matt Dunford	London	1997-98	18(20)	3	0	1	13
James Durkin	Paris	1997	(5)	0	0	0	0
Bernard Dwyer	Bradford	1996-2000	65(10)	14	0	0	56
Jim Dymock	London	2001	26	6	0	0	24
Leo Dynevor	London	1996	8(11)	5	7	0	34
Jason Eade	Paris	1997	9	4	0	0	16
Michael Eagar	Castleford	1999-2001	81	36	0	0	144
	Warrington	1998	21	6	0	0	24
Barry Eaton	Castleford	2000	1(4)	0	3	0	6
Cliff Eccles	Salford	1997-98	30(5)	1	0	0	4
Chris Eckersley	Warrington	1996	1	0	0	0	0
Steve Edmed	Sheffield	1997	15(1)	0	0	0	0
Mark Edmondson							
	St Helens	1999-2001	5(24)	1	0	0	4
Diccon Edwards	Castleford	1996-97	10(5)	1	0	0	4
Peter Edwards	Salford	1997-98	35(2)	4	0	0	16
Shaun Edwards	London	1997-2000	32(8)	16	1	0	66
	Bradford	1998	8(2)	4	0	0	16
	Wigan	1996	17(3)	12	1	0	50
Danny Ekis	Halifax	2001	(1)	0	0	0	0
Abi Ekoku	Bradford	1997-98	21(4)	6	0	0	24
	Halifax	1996	15(1)	5	0	0	20
Abderazak Elkhalouki							
	Paris	1997	(1)	0	0	0	0
Gareth Ellis	Wakefield	1999-2001	9(16)	4	0	0	16
Danny Ellison	Castleford	1998-99	7(16)	6	0	0	24
	Wigan	1996-97	15(1)	13	0	0	52
Patrick Entat	Paris	1996	22	2	0	0	8
Jason Erba	Sheffield	1997	1(4)	0	0	0	0
Paul Evans	Paris	1997	18	8	0	0	32
Richie Eyres	Warrington	1997	2(5)	0	0	0	0
	Sheffield	1997	2(3)	0	0	0	0
Esene Faimalo	Salford	1997-99	23(25)	2	0	0	8
	Leeds	1996	3(3)	0	0	0	0
Joe Faimalo	Salford	1998-2000	23(47)	7	0	0	28
	Oldham	1996-97	37(5)	7	0	0	28
Karl Fairbank	Bradford	1996	17(2)	4	0	0	16
David Fairleigh	St Helens	2001	26(1)	8	0	0	32
Jim Fallon	Leeds	1996	10	5	0	0	20
Danny Farrar	Warrington	1998-2000	76	13	0	0	52
Andy Farrell	Wigan	1996-2001	157	49	761	1	11729
Anthony Farrell	Leeds	1997-2001	99(23)	18	0	0	72
	Sheffield	1996	14(5)	5	0	0	20
Craig Farrell	Hull	2000-01	1(3)	0	0	0	0
Abraham Fatnowna							
	London	1997-98	7(2)	2	0	0	8
	Workington	1996	5	2	0	0	8
Vince Fawcett	Wakefield	1999	13(1)	2	0	0	8
	Warrington	1998	4(7)	1	0	0	4
	Oldham	1997	5	3	0	0	12
Danny Fearon	Huddersfield	2001	(1)	0	0	0	0
	Halifax	1999-2000	5(6)	0	0	0	0
Chris Feather	Wakefield	2001	(5)	0	0	0	0
Luke Felsch	Hull	2000-01	46(6)	7	0	0	28
	Gateshead	1999	28(1)	2	0	0	0
Leon Felton	St Helens	2001	1(1)	0	0	0	0
Jamie Field	Wakefield	1999-2001	44(31)	5	0	0	20
	Huddersfield	1998	15(5)	0	0	0	0
	Leeds	1996-97	3(11)	0	0	0	0
Jamie Fielden	Huddersfield	1998-2000	4(8)	0	0	0	0
Stuart Fielden	Bradford	1998-2001	38(59)	19	0	0	76
Lafaele Filipo	Workington	1996	15(4)	3	0	0	12
Salesi Finau	Warrington	1996-97	16(15)	8	0	0	32
Phil Finney	Warrington	1998	1	0	0	0	0
Matt Firth	Halifax	2000-01	12(2)	0	0	0	0
Andy Fisher	Wakefield	1999-2000	31(8)	4	0	0	16
Darren Fleary	Leeds	1997-2001	93(8)	2	0	0	8
Greg Fleming	London	1999-2001	64(1)	40	2	0	164
Richard Fletcher	Hull	1999-2001	4(29)	3	0	0	12
Greg Florimo	Halifax	2000	26	6	4	0	32
	Wigan	1999	18(2)	7	1	0	30

197

Super League Players 1996-2001

PLAYER	CLUB	YEAR	APP	TRIES	GOALS	FG	PTS
Jason Flowers	Castleford	1996-2001	119(19)	33	0	1	133
Stuart Flowers	Castleford	1996	(3)	0	0	0	0
Adrian Flynn	Castleford	1996-97	19(2)	10	0	0	40
Wayne Flynn	Sheffield	1997	3(5)	0	0	0	0
Adam Fogerty	Warrington	1998	4	0	0	0	0
	St Helens	1996	13	1	0	0	4
Paul Forber	Salford	1997-98	19(12)	4	0	0	16
Mike Ford	Castleford	1997-98	25(12)	5	0	3	23
	Warrington	1996	3	0	0	0	0
Jim Forshaw	Salford	1999	(1)	0	0	0	0
Mike Forshaw	Bradford	1997-2001	107(6)	23	0	0	92
	Leeds	1996	11(3)	5	0	0	20
Mark Forster	Warrington	1996-2000	102(1)	40	0	0	160
David Foster	Halifax	2000-01	4(9)	0	0	0	0
Nick Fozzard	Huddersfield	1998-2000	24(8)	2	0	0	8
	Leeds	1996-97	6(16)	3	0	0	12
David Fraisse	Workington	1996	8	0	0	0	0
Andrew Frew	Huddersfield	2001	26	15	0	0	60
Dale Fritz	Castleford	1999-2001	74(3)	6	0	0	24
David Furner	Wigan	2001	30(1)	13	5	0	62
David Furness	Castleford	1996	(1)	0	0	0	0
Mark Gamson	Sheffield	1996	3	0	0	0	0
Jim Gannon	Halifax	1999-2001	58(2)	13	0	0	52
Steve Garces	Salford	2001	(1)	0	0	0	0
Jean-Marc Garcia							
	Sheffield	1996-97	35(3)	22	0	0	88
Steve Gartland	Oldham	1996	1(1)	0	1	0	2
Daniel Gartner	Bradford	2001	26(1)	12	0	0	48
Richard Gay	Castleford	1996-2001	87(16)	38	0	0	152
Andrew Gee	Warrington	2000-01	33(1)	4	0	0	16
Stanley Gene	Huddersfield	2001	12(1)	8	0	0	32
	Hull	2000-01	5(23)	6	0	0	24
Steve Georgallis	Warrington	2001	5(1)	2	0	0	8
Shaun Geritas	Warrington	1997	(5)	1	0	0	4
Anthony Gibbons							
	Leeds	1996	9(4)	2	0	1	9
David Gibbons	Leeds	1996	3(4)	2	0	0	8
Scott Gibbs	St Helens	1996	9	3	0	0	12
Damian Gibson	Halifax	1998-2001	104(1)	39	0	0	156
	Leeds	1997	18	3	0	0	12
Ian Gildart	Oldham	1996-97	31(7)	0	0	0	0
Peter Gill	Leeds	1996-99	75(6)	20	0	0	80
Carl Gillespie	Halifax	1996-99	47(36)	13	0	0	52
Michael Gillett	London	2001	7(12)	6	2	0	28
Simon Gillies	Warrington	1999	28	6	0	0	24
Lee Gilmour	Bradford	2001	14(9)	7	0	0	28
	Wigan	1997-2000	44(39)	22	0	0	88
Marc Glanville	Leeds	1998-99	43(3)	5	0	0	20
Eddie Glaze	Castleford	1996	1	0	0	0	0
Paul Gleadhill	Leeds	1996	4	0	0	0	0
Mark Gleeson	Warrington	2000-01	2(2)	3	0	0	12
Martin Gleeson	Huddersfield	1999-2001	47(9)	18	0	0	72
Jonathan Goddard							
	Castleford	2000-01	(2)	0	0	0	0
Richard Goddard	Castleford	1996-97	11(3)	2	10	0	28
Brad Godden	Leeds	1998-99	47	15	0	0	60
Wayne Godwin	Castleford	2001	(6)	2	0	0	8
Marvin Golden	London	2001	17(2)	1	0	0	4
	Halifax	2000	20(2)	5	0	0	20
	Leeds	1996-99	43(11)	19	0	0	76
Brett Goldspink	Halifax	2000-01	44(3)	2	0	0	8
	Wigan	1999	6(16)	1	0	0	4
	St Helens	1998	19(4)	2	0	0	8
	Oldham	1997	13(2)	0	0	0	0
Luke Goodwin	London	1998	9(2)	3	1	1	15
	Oldham	1997	16(4)	10	17	2	76
Andy Gorski	Salford	2001	(1)	0	0	0	0
Bobbie Goulding	Salford	2001	21	0	29	2	60
	Wakefield	2000	12	3	25	3	65
	Huddersfield	1998-99	27(1)	3	65	4	146
	St Helens	1996-98	42(2)	9	210	4	460
Nathan Graham	Bradford	1996-98	17(28)	4	0	1	17
Brett Green	Gateshead	1999	10(2)	0	0	0	0
Toby Green	Huddersfield	2001	3(1)	1	0	0	4
Brandon Greenwood							
	Halifax	1996	1	0	0	0	0
Lee Greenwood	Halifax	2000-01	6(2)	5	0	0	20
	Sheffield	1999	1(1)	0	0	0	0
Jonathan Griffiths							
	Paris	1996	(4)	1	0	0	4
Andrew Grima	Workington	1996	2(9)	2	0	0	8
Tony Grimaldi	Hull	2000-01	56(1)	14	0	0	56
	Gateshead	1999	27(2)	10	0	0	40
Danny Grimley	Sheffield	1996	4(1)	1	0	0	4
Brett Grogan	Gateshead	1999	14(7)	3	0	0	12
Jerome Guisset	Warrington	2000-01	30(22)	7	0	0	28
Reece Guy	Oldham	1996	3(4)	0	0	0	0
Andy Haigh	St Helens	1996-98	20(16)	11	0	0	44
Carl Hall	Leeds	1996	7(2)	3	0	0	12
Martin Hall	Halifax	1998	2(10)	0	0	0	0
	Hull	1999	7	0	0	0	0
	Castleford	1998	(1)	0	0	0	0
	Wigan	1996-97	31(5)	7	6	0	40
Steve Hall	St Helens	1999-2001	36(22)	19	0	0	76

PLAYER	CLUB	YEAR	APP	TRIES	GOALS	FG	PTS
Graeme Hallas	Huddersfield	2001	1	0	0	0	0
	Hull	1998-99	30(10)	6	39	1	103
	Halifax	1996	11(4)	5	0	0	20
Danny Halliwell	Halifax	2000-01	5(3)	2	0	0	8
Jon Hamer	Bradford	1996	(1)	0	0	0	0
Andrew Hamilton							
	London	1997	1(7)	3	0	0	12
John Hamilton	St Helens	1998	3	0	0	0	0
Karle Hammond	Salford	2001	2(3)	1	0	0	4
	London	1999-2000	47	23	2	3	99
	St Helens	1996-98	58(8)	28	0	4	116
Anthony Hancock							
	Paris	1997	8(6)	1	0	0	4
Michael Hancock	Salford	2001	10(15)	7	0	0	28
Gareth Handford	Castleford	2001	7(2)	0	0	0	0
	Bradford	2000	1(1)	0	0	0	0
Paul Handforth	Wakefield	2000-01	5(7)	2	0	0	8
Paddy Handley	Leeds	1996	1(1)	2	0	0	8
Dean Hanger	Warrington	1999	7(11)	3	0	0	12
	Huddersfield	1998	20(1)	5	0	0	20
Lee Hansen	Wigan	1997	10(5)	0	0	0	0
Lionel Harbin	Wakefield	2001	(1)	0	0	0	0
Jeff Hardy	Hudds-Sheff	2000	20(5)	6	0	1	25
	Sheffield	1999	22(4)	7	0	0	28
Spencer Hargrave							
	Castleford	1996-99	(6)	0	0	0	0
Lee Harland	Castleford	1996-2001	107(21)	15	0	0	60
Neil Harmon	Salford	2001	6(5)	0	0	0	0
	Bradford	1998-2000	15(13)	2	0	0	8
	Huddersfield	1998	12	1	0	0	4
	Leeds	1996	10	1	0	0	4
Iestyn Harris	Leeds	1997-2001	111(7)	57	490	6	1214
	Warrington	1996	16	4	63	2	144
Karl Harrison	Hull	1999	26	2	0	0	8
	Halifax	1996-98	60(2)	2	0	0	8
Carlos Hassan	Bradford	1996	6(4)	2	0	0	8
Phil Hassan	Halifax	2000-01	25(4)	3	0	0	12
	Salford	1998	15	2	0	0	8
	Leeds	1996-97	38(4)	12	0	0	48
Tom Haughey	Wakefield	2001	2(6)	0	0	0	0
Simon Haughton	Wigan	1996-2001	62(42)	32	0	0	128
Andy Hay	Leeds	1997-2001	89(26)	33	0	0	132
	Sheffield	1996-97	17(3)	5	0	0	20
Adam Hayes	Hudds-Sheff	2000	2(1)	0	0	0	0
Joey Hayes	Salford	1999	9	2	0	0	8
	St Helens	1996-98	11(6)	7	0	0	28
Mitch Healey	Castleford	2001	20	4	0	0	16
Ricky Helliwell	Salford	1997-99	(2)	0	0	0	0
Bryan Henare	St Helens	2000-01	4(12)	1	0	0	4
Richard Henare	Warrington	1996-97	28(2)	24	0	0	96
Brad Hepi	Castleford	1999, 2001	9(21)	3	0	0	12
	Salford	2000	3(5)	0	0	0	0
	Hull	1998	15(1)	3	0	0	12
Ian Herron	Hull	2000	9	1	17	0	38
	Gateshead	1999	25	4	105	0	226
Jason Hetherington							
	London	2001	17	3	0	0	12
Gareth Hewitt	Salford	1999	2(1)	0	0	0	0
Andrew Hick	Hull	2000	9(9)	1	0	0	4
	Gateshead	1999	12(5)	2	0	0	8
Paul Hicks	Wakefield	1999	(1)	0	0	0	0
Darren Higgins	London	1998	5(6)	2	0	0	8
Iain Higgins	London	1997-98	1(7)	2	0	0	8
Mick Higham	St Helens	2001	1(1)	1	0	0	4
Chris Highton	Warrington	1997	1(1)	0	0	0	0
David Highton	Warrington	1998-2001	18(14)	2	0	0	8
Paul Highton	Salford	1998-2001	50(42)	8	0	0	32
	Halifax	1996-97	12(18)	2	0	0	8
Andy Hill	Huddersfield	1999	(4)	0	0	0	0
	Castleford	1999	4(4)	0	0	0	0
Howard Hill	Oldham	1996-97	22(12)	4	0	0	16
John Hill	Warrington	2001	(1)	0	0	0	0
Mark Hilton	Warrington	1996-2000	46(22)	1	0	0	4
Andy Hobson	Halifax	1998-2001	25(60)	5	0	0	20
Andy Hodgson	Wakefield	1999	14(2)	2	1	0	10
	Bradford	1997-98	8(2)	4	0	0	16
David Hodgson	Wigan	2000-01	27(12)	15	0	0	60
	Halifax	1999	10(3)	5	0	0	20
Darren Hogg	London	1996	(1)	0	0	0	0
Michael Hogue	Paris	1997	5(7)	0	0	0	0
Chris Holden	Warrington	1996-97	2(1)	0	0	0	0
Stephen Holgate	Halifax	2000	1(10)	0	0	0	0
	Hull	1999	1	0	0	0	0
	Wigan	1997-98	11(26)	2	0	0	8
	Workington	1996	19	3	0	0	12
Martyn Holland	Wakefield	2000-01	16(1)	1	0	0	4
Graham Holroyd	Salford	2000-01	27(6)	4	35	4	90
	Halifax	1999	24(2)	3	74	5	165
	Leeds	1996-98	40(26)	22	101	8	298
Sean Hoppe	St Helens	1999-2001	50(8)	21	0	0	84
Richard Horne	Hull	1999-2001	57(9)	23	12	0	116
John Hough	Warrington	1996-97	9	0	0	0	8
Sylvain Houles	London	2001	8(1)	6	0	0	24
	Hudds-Sheff	2000	5(2)	1	0	0	4

PLAYER	CLUB	YEAR	APP	TRIES	GOALS	FG	PTS
Harvey Howard	Wigan	2001	18(8)	1	0	0	4
	Bradford	1998	4(2)	1	0	0	4
	Leeds	1996	8	0	0	0	0
Kim Howard	London	1997	4(5)	0	0	0	0
Stuart Howarth	Workington	1996	(2)	0	0	0	0
Phil Howlett	Bradford	1999	5(1)	2	0	0	8
Ryan Hudson	Wakefield	2000-01	42(9)	11	0	1	45
	Huddersfield	1998-99	12(7)	0	0	0	0
Adam Hughes	Halifax	2001	8(8)	8	0	0	32
	Wakefield	1999-2000	43(3)	21	34	0	152
	Leeds	1996-97	4(5)	4	0	0	16
Ian Hughes	Sheffield	1996	9(8)	4	0	0	16
Steffan Hughes	London	1999-2001	1(13)	1	0	0	4
David Hulme	Salford	1997-99	53(1)	5	0	0	20
	Leeds	1996	8(1)	2	0	0	8
Paul Hulme	Warrington	1996-97	23(1)	2	0	0	8
Gary Hulse	Warrington	2001	5(1)	1	0	0	4
Alan Hunte	Warrington	1999-2001	83	49	0	0	196
	Hull	1998	21	7	0	0	28
	St Helens	1996-97	30(2)	28	0	0	112
Nick Hyde	Paris	1997	5(5)	1	0	0	4
Andy Ireland	Hull	1998-99	22(15)	0	0	0	0
	Bradford	1996	1	0	0	0	0
Kevin Iro	St Helens	1999-2001	76	39	0	0	156
	Leeds	1996	16	9	0	0	36
Andrew Isherwood	Wigan	1998-99	(5)	0	0	0	0
Olu Iwenofu	London	2000-01	2(1)	0	0	0	0
Chico Jackson	Hull	1999	(4)	0	0	0	0
Lee Jackson	Hull	2001	13(8)	5	1	0	22
	Leeds	1999-2000	28(24)	7	0	0	28
Michael Jackson	Sheffield	1998-99	17(17)	2	0	0	8
	Halifax	1996-97	27(6)	11	0	0	44
Paul Jackson	Wakefield	1999-2001	35(39)	2	0	0	8
	Huddersfield	1998	(11)	0	0	0	0
Wayne Jackson	Halifax	1996-97	17(5)	2	0	0	8
Andy James	Halifax	1996	(4)	0	0	0	0
Pascal Jampy	Paris	1996-97	3(2)	0	0	0	0
Mick Jenkins	Hull	2000	24	2	0	0	8
	Gateshead	1999	16	3	0	0	12
Ed Jennings	London	1998-99	1(2)	0	0	0	0
Matthew Johns	Wigan	2001	24	3	0	1	13
Andy Johnson	London	2000-01	24(21)	12	0	0	48
	Huddersfield	1999	5	1	0	0	4
	Wigan	1996-99	24(20)	19	0	0	76
Jason Johnson	St Helens	1997-99	2	0	0	0	0
Mark Johnson	Salford	1999-2000	22(9)	16	0	0	64
	Hull	1998	10(1)	4	0	0	16
	Workington	1996	4	4	0	0	16
Paul Johnson	Wigan	1996-2001	49(34)	44	0	0	176
David Jones	Oldham	1997	14(1)	5	0	0	20
Mark Jones	Warrington	1996	8(11)	2	0	0	8
Phil Jones	Wigan	1999-2001	14(7)	6	25	0	74
Jamie Jones-Buchanan	Leeds	1999-2001	(6)	0	0	0	0
Tim Jonkers	St Helens	1999-2001	17(46)	7	0	0	28
Warren Jowitt	Salford	2001	8	2	0	0	8
	Wakefield	2000	19(3)	8	0	0	32
	Bradford	1996-99	13(25)	5	0	0	20
Chris Joynt	St Helens	1996-2001	143(4)	54	0	0	216
Gregory Kacala	Paris	1996	7	1	0	0	4
Shaun Keating	London	1996	1(3)	0	0	0	0
Mark Keenan	Workington	1996	3(4)	1	0	0	4
Tony Kemp	Wakefield	1999-2000	15(5)	2	0	1	9
	Leeds	1996-98	23(2)	5	0	2	22
Shane Kenward	Wakefield	1999	28	6	0	0	24
	Salford	1998	1	0	0	0	0
Jason Keough	Paris	1997	2	1	0	0	4
Martin Ketteridge	Halifax	1996	7(5)	0	0	0	0
Ronnie Kettlewell	Warrington	1996	(1)	0	0	0	0
David Kidwell	Warrington	2001	12(10)	8	0	0	32
Dave King	Huddersfield	1998-99	11(17)	2	0	0	8
Paul King	Hull	1999-2001	42(23)	7	0	1	29
Andy Kirk	Leeds	2001	2(4)	0	0	0	0
John Kirkpatrick	St Helens	2001	3(3)	2	0	0	8
Wayne Kitchin	Workington	1996	11(6)	3	17	1	47
Ian Knott	Warrington	1996-2001	68(41)	24	18	0	132
Matt Knowles	Wigan	1996	(3)	0	0	0	0
Phil Knowles	Salford	1997	1	0	0	0	0
Simon Knox	Halifax	1999	(6)	0	0	0	0
	Salford	1998	1(1)	0	0	0	0
	Bradford	1996-98	9(19)	7	0	0	28
Toa Kohe-Love	Warrington	1996-2001	114(2)	69	0	0	276
Paul Koloi	Wigan	1997	1(2)	1	0	0	4
David Krause	London	1996-97	22(1)	7	0	0	28
Ben Kusto	Huddersfield	2001	21(4)	9	0	1	37
Adrian Lam	Wigan	2001	29	12	0	0	48
Mark Lane	Paris	1996	(2)	0	0	0	0
Allan Langer	Warrington	2000-01	47	13	4	0	60
Kevin Langer	London	1996	12(4)	2	0	0	8
Chris Langley	Huddersfield	2000-01	18(1)	3	0	0	12
Andy Last	Hull	1999-2001	2(4)	0	0	0	0
Dale Laughton	Huddersfield	2000-01	36(2)	4	0	0	16
	Sheffield	1996-99	48(22)	5	0	0	20
Jason Laurence	Salford	1997	1	0	0	0	0
Graham Law	Wakefield	1999-2001	25(20)	3	23	0	58
Neil Law	Wakefield	1999-2001	73	34	0	0	136
	Sheffield	1998	1(1)	1	0	0	4
Dean Lawford	Halifax	2001	1(1)	0	0	0	0
	Leeds	1997-2000	15(8)	2	3	0	14
	Huddersfield	1999	6(1)	0	6	1	13
	Sheffield	1996	9(5)	2	1	1	11
Johnny Lawless	Halifax	2001	27	6	0	0	24
	Hudds-Sheff	2000	19(6)	3	0	0	12
	Sheffield	1996-99	76(4)	11	0	0	44
Leroy Leapai	London	1996	2	0	0	0	0
Jim Leatham	Hull	1998-99	20(18)	4	0	0	16
	Leeds	1997	(1)	0	0	0	0
Andy Leathem	Warrington	1999	2(8)	0	0	0	0
	St Helens	1996-98	20(1)	1	0	0	4
Danny Lee	Gateshead	1999	16(2)	0	0	0	0
Jason Lee	Halifax	2001	10(1)	2	0	0	8
Mark Lee	Salford	1997-2000	25(11)	1	0	4	8
Robert Lee	Hull	1999	4(3)	0	0	0	0
Matthew Leigh	Salford	2000	(6)	0	0	0	0
Jim Lenihan	Huddersfield	1999	19(1)	10	0	0	40
Mark Lennon	Castleford	2001	19(9)	5	15	0	50
Gary Lester	Hull	1998-99	46	17	0	0	68
Stuart Lester	Wigan	1997	1(3)	2	0	0	8
Afi Leuila	Oldham	1996-97	17(3)	2	0	0	8
Simon Lewis	Castleford	2001	4	3	0	0	12
Jon Liddell	Leeds	2001	1	0	0	0	0
Jason Lidden	Castleford	1997	15(1)	7	0	0	28
Stuart Littler	Salford	1998-2001	55(12)	18	0	0	72
Peter Livett	Workington	1996	3(1)	0	0	0	0
Scott Logan	Hull	2001	11(4)	3	0	0	12
David Lomax	Huddersfield	2000-01	45(9)	4	0	0	16
	Paris	1997	19(2)	1	0	0	4
Dave Long	London	1999	(1)	0	0	0	0
Sean Long	St Helens	1997-2001	98(4)	63	406	5	1069
	Wigan	1996-97	1(5)	0	0	0	0
Davide Longo	Bradford	1996	1(3)	0	0	0	0
Gary Lord	Oldham	1996-97	28(12)	3	0	0	12
Paul Loughlin	Huddersfield	1998-99	34(2)	4	4	0	24
	Bradford	1996-97	36(4)	15	8	0	76
Karl Lovell	Hudds-Sheff	2000	14	5	0	0	20
	Sheffield	1999	22(4)	8	0	0	32
James Lowes	Bradford	1996-2001	151	66	0	2	266
Laurent Lucchese	Paris	1996	13(5)	2	0	0	8
Peter Lupton	London	2000-01	10(13)	2	2	0	12
Andy Lynch	Castleford	1999-2001	8(39)	3	0	0	12
Brad Mackay	Bradford	2000	24(2)	8	0	0	32
Graham Mackay	Bradford	2001	16(3)	12	1	0	50
	Leeds	2000	12(8)	10	2	0	44
Mateaki Mafi	Warrington	1996-97	7(8)	7	0	0	28
Brendan Magnus	London	2000	3	1	0	0	4
Mark Maguire	London	1996-97	11(4)	7	13	0	54
Adam Maher	Hull	2000-01	40(2)	13	0	0	52
	Gateshead	1999	21(5)	3	0	0	12
Lee Maher	Leeds	1996	4(1)	0	0	0	0
Shaun Mahony	Paris	1997	5	0	0	0	0
David Maiden	Hull	2000-01	32(10)	11	0	0	44
	Gateshead	1999	5(16)	8	0	0	32
Craig Makin	Salford	1999-2001	24(20)	2	0	0	8
Brady Malam	Wigan	2000	5(20)	1	0	0	4
Francis Maloney	Salford	2001	27	19	3	0	82
	Wakefield	2000	11	1	1	0	6
	Castleford	1998-99	43(4)	19	22	0	120
	Oldham	1996-97	39(2)	12	91	2	232
George Mann	Warrington	1997	14(5)	1	0	0	4
	Leeds	1996	11(4)	2	0	0	8
David March	Wakefield	1999-2001	44(7)	15	0	0	60
Paul March	Wakefield	1999-2001	32(23)	14	18	0	92
Nick Mardon	London	1997-98	14	2	0	0	8
Oliver Marns	Halifax	1996-2001	53(18)	23	0	0	92
Iain Marsh	Salford	1998-2001	1(4)	0	0	0	0
Lee Marsh	Salford	2001	(2)	0	0	0	0
Richard Marshall	Huddersfield	2000-01	35(14)	1	0	0	4
	Halifax	1996-99	38(34)	2	0	0	8
Jason Martin	Paris	1997	15(2)	3	0	0	12
Scott Martin	Salford	1997-99	32(18)	8	0	0	32
Tony Martin	London	1996-97, 2001	45(1)	16	50	1	165
Mick Martindale	Halifax	1996	(4)	0	0	0	0
Tommy Martyn	St Helens	1996-2001	104(14)	67	59	8	394
Dean Marwood	Workington	1996	9(6)	0	22	0	44
Martin Masella	Warrington	2001	10(14)	5	0	0	20
	Wakefield	2000	14(8)	4	0	0	16
	Leeds	1997-1999	59(5)	1	0	0	4
Colin Maskill	Castleford	1996	8	1	1	0	6
Keith Mason	Wakefield	2000-01	5(17)	0	0	0	0
Vila Matautia	St Helens	1996-2001	31(68)	9	0	0	36

199

Super League Players 1996-2001

PLAYER	CLUB	YEAR	APP	TRIES	GOALS	FG	PTS
Barrie-Jon Mather	Castleford	1998, 2000-01	39(1)	14	0	0	56
Jamie Mathiou	Leeds	1997-2001	31(82)	3	0	0	12
Terry Matterson	London	1996-98	46	15	90	6	246
Casey Mayberry	Halifax	2000	1(1)	0	0	0	0
Danny McAllister	Gateshead	1999	3(3)	1	0	0	4
	Sheffield	1996-97	33(7)	10	0	0	40
John McAtee	St Helens	1996	2(1)	0	0	0	0
Nathan McAvoy	Bradford	1998-2001	50(12)	31	0	0	124
	Salford	1997-98	36	15	0	0	60
Dave McConnell	St Helens	2001	3(1)	4	0	0	16
Robbie McCormack	Wigan	1998	24	2	0	0	8
Steve McCurrie	Warrington	1998-2001	69(26)	31	0	0	124
Barrie McDermott	Leeds	1996-2001	100(23)	17	0	0	68
Brian McDermott	Bradford	1996-2001	123(19)	29	0	0	116
Wayne McDonald	St Helens	2001	7(11)	4	0	0	16
	Hull	2000	5(8)	4	0	0	16
	Wakefield	1999	9(17)	8	0	0	32
Craig McDowell	Bradford	2000	(1)	0	0	0	0
Wes McGibbon	Halifax	1999	1	0	0	0	0
Billy McGinty	Workington	1996	1	0	0	0	0
Danny McGuire	Leeds	2001	(2)	0	0	0	0
Gary McGuirk	Workington	1996	(4)	0	0	0	0
Richard McKell	Castleford	1997-98	22(7)	2	0	0	8
Phil McKenzie	Workington	1996	4	0	0	0	0
Chris McKinney	Oldham	1996-97	4(9)	2	0	0	8
Shayne McMenemy	Halifax	2001	26	7	0	0	28
Andy McNally	Castleford	2001	(4)	0	0	0	0
Steve McNamara	Huddersfield	2001	26(1)	1	66	0	136
	Wakefield	2000	15(2)	2	32	0	72
	Bradford	1996-99	90(3)	14	348	7	759
Neil McPherson	Salford	1997	(1)	0	0	0	0
Duncan McRae	London	1996	11(2)	3	0	1	13
Derek McVey	St Helens	1996-97	28(4)	6	1	0	26
Dallas Mead	Warrington	1997	2	0	0	0	0
Robert Mears	Leeds	2001	23	6	0	0	24
Paul Medley	Bradford	1996-98	6(35)	9	0	0	36
Craig Menkins	Paris	1997	4(5)	0	0	0	0
Gary Mercer	Leeds	1996-97, 2001	40(2)	9	0	0	36
	Warrington	2001	18	2	0	0	8
	Halifax	1998-2001	73(2)	16	0	0	64
Tony Mestrov	London	1996-97, 2001	59(8)	4	0	0	16
	Wigan	1998-2000	39(39)	3	0	0	12
Keiran Meyer	London	1996	4	1	0	0	4
Simon Middleton	Castleford	1996-97	19(3)	8	0	0	32
Shane Millard	London	1998-2001	72(14)	11	1	0	46
Lee Milner	Halifax	1999	(1)	0	0	0	0
John Minto	London	1996	13	4	0	0	16
Martin Moana	Huddersfield	2001	3(3)	2	0	0	8
	Halifax	1996-2001	110(32)	61	0	1	245
Steve Molloy	Huddersfield	2000-01	26(20)	3	0	0	12
	Sheffield	1998-99	32(17)	3	0	0	12
Chris Molyneux	Huddersfield	2000-01	1(18)	0	0	0	0
	Sheffield	1999	1(2)	0	0	0	0
Adrian Moore	Huddersfield	1998-99	1(4)	0	0	0	0
Danny Moore	London	2000	7	0	0	0	0
	Wigan	1998-99	49(3)	18	0	0	72
Jason Moore	Workington	1996	(5)	0	0	0	0
Dennis Moran	London	2001	27	10	0	3	43
Willie Morganson	Sheffield	1997-98	18(12)	5	3	0	26
Paul Moriarty	Halifax	1996	3(2)	0	0	0	0
Adrian Morley	Leeds	1996-2000	95(14)	25	0	0	100
Chris Morley	Salford	1999	3(5)	0	0	0	0
	Warrington	1998	2(8)	0	0	0	0
	St Helens	1996-97	21(16)	4	0	0	16
Iain Morrison	London	2001	(1)	0	0	0	0
Gareth Morton	Leeds	2001	1	0	0	0	0
Wilfried Moulinec	Paris	1996	1	0	0	0	0
Mark Moxon	Huddersfield	1998-2001	20(5)	1	0	1	5
Brett Mullins	Leeds	2001	5(3)	1	0	0	4
Damian Munro	Halifax	1996-97	9(6)	8	0	0	32
Matt Munro	Oldham	1996-97	26(5)	8	0	0	32
Craig Murdock	Salford	2000	(2)	0	0	0	0
	Hull	1998-99	21(6)	8	0	2	34
	Wigan	1996-98	18(17)	14	0	0	56
Doc Murray	Warrington	1997	(2)	0	0	0	0
	Wigan	1997	6(2)	0	0	0	0
David Mycoe	Sheffield	1996-97	12(13)	1	0	0	4
Rob Myler	Oldham	1996-97	19(2)	6	0	0	24
Matt Nable	London	1997	2(2)	1	0	0	4
Brad Nairn	Workington	1996	14	4	0	0	16
Frank Napoli	London	2000	14(6)	2	0	0	8
Carlo Napolitano	Salford	2000	(3)	1	0	0	4
Jim Naylor	Halifax	2000	7(6)	2	0	0	8
Scott Naylor	Bradford	1999-2001	74(1)	31	0	0	124
	Salford	1997-98	23(1)	9	0	0	36
Mike Neal	Salford	1998	(1)	0	0	0	0
	Oldham	1996-97	6(4)	3	0	0	12
Jonathan Neill	Huddersfield	1998-99	20(11)	0	0	0	0
	St Helens	1996	1	0	0	0	0
Jason Netherton	Leeds	2001	(3)	0	0	0	0
Paul Newlove	St Helens	1996-2001	119	93	0	0	372
Terry Newton	Wigan	2000-01	57(2)	27	0	0	108
	Leeds	1996-1999	55(14)	4	0	0	16
Gene Ngamu	Huddersfield	1999-2000	29(2)	9	67	0	170
Sonny Nickle	St Helens	1999-2001	67(13)	11	0	0	44
	Bradford	1996-98	25(16)	9	0	0	36
Jason Nicol	Salford	2000-01	36(2)	7	0	0	28
Tawera Nikau	Warrington	2000-01	51	7	0	0	28
Rob Nolan	Hull	1998-99	20(11)	6	0	0	24
Paul Noone	Warrington	2000-01	15(13)	3	0	0	12
Paul Norman	Oldham	1996	(1)	0	0	0	0
Andy Northey	St Helens	1996-97	8(17)	2	0	0	8
Danny Nutley	Warrington	1998-2001	94(1)	3	0	0	12
Tony Nuttall	Oldham	1996-97	1(7)	0	0	0	0
Matt O'Connor	Paris	1997	11(4)	1	26	2	58
Terry O'Connor	Wigan	1996-2001	118(29)	6	0	0	24
David O'Donnell	Paris	1997	21	3	0	0	12
Martin Offiah	Salford	2000-01	41	20	0	2	82
	London	1996-99	29(3)	21	0	0	84
	Wigan	1996	8	7	0	0	28
Hefin O'Hare	Huddersfield	2001	5(1)	4	0	0	16
Hitro Okesene	Hull	1998	21(1)	0	0	0	0
Anderson Okiwe	Sheffield	1997	1	0	0	0	0
Jamie Olejnik	Paris	1997	11	8	0	0	32
Kevin O'Loughlin	Halifax	1997-98	2(4)	0	0	0	0
	St Helens	1997	(3)	0	0	0	0
Julian O'Neill	Wakefield	2001	24(1)	2	0	0	8
	St Helens	1997-2000	95(8)	5	0	0	20
Steve O'Neill	Gateshead	1999	1(1)	0	0	0	0
Tom O'Reilly	Warrington	2001	(1)	0	0	0	0
Chris Orr	Huddersfield	1998	19(3)	2	0	0	8
Danny Orr	Castleford	1997-2001	99(17)	43	239	2	652
Jason Palmada	Workington	1996	12	2	0	0	8
Junior Paramore	Castleford	1996	5(5)	3	0	0	12
Paul Parker	Hull	1999-2001	16(8)	8	0	0	32
Robert Parker	London	2001	9	1	0	0	4
	Bradford	2000	(4)	1	0	0	4
Wayne Parker	Halifax	1996-97	12(1)	0	0	0	0
Ian Parry	Warrington	2001	(1)	0	0	0	0
Jules Parry	Paris	1996	10(2)	0	0	0	0
Regis Pastre-Courtine	Paris	1996	4(3)	4	0	0	16
Andrew Patmore	Oldham	1996	8(5)	3	0	0	12
Henry Paul	Bradford	1999-2001	81(5)	29	350	6	822
	Wigan	1996-98	60	37	23	0	194
Junior Paul	London	1996	3	1	0	0	4
Robbie Paul	Bradford	1996-2001	120(11)	82	0	0	328
Danny Peacock	Bradford	1997-99	32(2)	15	0	0	60
Jamie Peacock	Bradford	1999-2001	49(25)	21	0	0	84
Martin Pearson	Wakefield	2001	21(1)	3	60	3	135
	Halifax	1997-98, 2000	55(6)	24	181	0	458
	Sheffield	1999	17(6)	9	36	2	110
Jacques Pech	Paris	1996	16	0	0	0	0
Mike Pechey	Warrington	1998	6(3)	2	0	0	8
Sean Penkywicz	Halifax	2000-01	3(17)	2	0	0	8
Julian Penni	Salford	1998-99	4	0	0	0	0
Lee Penny	Warrington	1996-2001	116(3)	49	0	0	196
Paul Penrice	Workington	1996	11(2)	2	0	0	8
Apollo Perelini	St Helens	1996-2000	103(16)	27	0	0	108
Mark Perrett	Halifax	1996-97	15(4)	4	0	0	16
Adam Peters	Paris	1997	16(3)	0	0	0	0
Dominic Peters	London	1998-2001	41(10)	9	0	0	36
Mike Peters	Warrington	2000	2(12)	1	0	0	4
	Halifax	2000	1	0	0	0	0
Willie Peters	Wigan	2000	29	15	5	6	76
	Gateshead	1999	27	11	1	6	52
Adrian Petrie	Workington	1996	(1)	0	0	0	0
Rowland Phillips	Workington	1996	22	1	0	0	4
Nathan Picchi	Leeds	1996	(1)	0	0	0	0
Ian Pickavance	Hull	1999	4(2)	2	0	0	8
	Huddersfield	1999	3(14)	0	0	0	0
	St Helens	1996-98	12(44)	6	0	0	24
James Pickering	Castleford	1999	1(19)	0	0	0	0
Nick Pinkney	Salford	2000-01	55	24	0	0	96
	Halifax	1999	26(2)	13	0	0	52
	Sheffield	1997-98	33	10	0	0	40
Michal Piscunov	Paris	1996	1(1)	1	0	0	4
Darryl Pitt	London	1996	2(16)	4	0	1	17
Andy Platt	Salford	1997-98	20(3)	1	0	0	4
Michael Platt	Salford	2001	1	0	0	0	0
Willie Poching	Wakefield	1999-2001	65(4)	20	0	0	80
Dan Potter	London	2001	1(3)	1	0	0	4
Craig Poucher	Hull	1999-2001	30(2)	4	0	0	16

PLAYER	CLUB	YEAR	APP	TRIES	GOALS	FG	PTS
Daio Powell	Sheffield	1999	13(1)	2	0	0	8
	Halifax	1997-98	30(3)	17	0	0	68
Daryl Powell	Leeds	1998-2000	49(30)	12	0	2	50
Karl Pratt	Leeds	1999-2001	48(7)	24	0	0	96
Steve Prescott	Hull	1998-99, 2001	62	27	113	3	337
	Wakefield	2000	22(1)	3	13	0	38
	St Helens	1996-97	32	15	17	0	94
Lee Prest	Workington	1996	(1)	0	0	0	0
Gareth Price	St Helens	1999	(11)	2	0	0	8
Gary Price	Wakefield	1999-2001	55(13)	11	0	0	44
Richard Price	Sheffield	1996	1(2)	0	0	0	0
Tony Priddle	Paris	1997	11(7)	3	0	0	12
Leon Pryce	Bradford	1998-2001	73(10)	39	0	0	156
Waine Pryce	Castleford	2000-01	13(11)	6	0	0	24
Andrew Purcell	Castleford	2000	15(5)	3	0	0	12
	Hull	1999	27	4	0	0	16
Scott Quinnell	Wigan	1996	6(3)	1	0	0	4
Lee Radford	Bradford	1999-2001	9(27)	3	0	0	12
	Hull	1998	(7)	2	0	0	8
Kris Radlinski	Wigan	1996-2001	149	90	1	0	362
Jean-Luc Ramondou	Paris	1996	1(1)	1	0	0	4
Craig Randall	Halifax	1999	8(11)	4	0	0	16
	Salford	1997-98	12(18)	4	0	0	16
Scott Ranson	Oldham	1996-97	19(2)	7	0	0	28
Aaron Raper	Castleford	1999-2001	48(4)	4	2	1	21
Ben Rauter	Wakefield	2001	15(6)	4	0	0	16
Gareth Raynor	Hull	2001	27	11	0	0	44
	Leeds	2000	(3)	0	0	0	0
Tony Rea	London	1996	22	4	0	0	16
Mark Reber	Wigan	1999-2000	9(9)	5	0	0	20
Alan Reddicliffe	Warrington	2001	1	0	0	0	0
Tahi Reihana	Bradford	1997-98	17(21)	0	0	0	0
Paul Reilly	Huddersfield	1999-2001	51(5)	8	0	0	32
Steve Renouf	Wigan	2000-01	55	40	0	0	160
Steele Retchless	London	1998-2001	98(5)	6	0	0	24
Scott Rhodes	Hull	2000	2	0	0	0	0
Phillipe Ricard	Paris	1996-97	2	0	0	0	0
Andy Rice	Huddersfield	2000-01	2(13)	1	0	0	4
Basil Richards	Huddersfield	1998-99	28(17)	1	0	0	4
Craig Richards	Oldham	1996	1	0	0	0	0
Andy Richardson	Hudds-Sheff	2000	(2)	0	0	0	0
Sean Richardson	Wakefield	1999	5(1)	0	0	0	0
	Castleford	1996-97	3(8)	1	0	0	4
Shane Rigon	Bradford	2001	14(11)	12	0	0	48
Craig Rika	Halifax	1996	2	0	0	0	0
Peter Riley	Workington	1996	7(5)	0	0	0	0
Leroy Rivett	Hudds-Sheff	2000	5(1)	1	0	0	4
	Leeds	1996-2000	39(15)	21	0	0	84
Jason Roach	Warrington	1998-99	29(7)	15	0	0	60
	Castleford	1997	7	4	0	0	16
Robert Roberts	Huddersfield	2001	(1)	0	0	0	0
	Halifax	2000	(3)	0	0	0	0
	Hull	1999	24(2)	4	13	4	46
Jason Robinson	Wigan	1996-2000	126(1)	87	0	1	349
Jeremy Robinson	Paris	1997	10(3)	1	21	0	46
Will Robinson	Hull	2000	22	4	0	0	16
	Gateshead	1999	28	9	0	0	36
Carl Roden	Warrington	1997	1	0	0	0	0
Darren Rogers	Castleford	1999-2001	80	46	0	0	184
	Salford	1997-98	42	16	0	0	64
Jamie Rooney	Castleford	2001	2(1)	0	6	0	12
Jonathan Roper	Castleford	2001	13	7	12	0	52
	Salford	2000	1(4)	1	3	0	10
	London	2000	4	0	0	0	0
	Warrington	1996-2000	75(8)	33	71	0	274
Scott Roskell	London	1996-97	30(2)	16	0	0	64
Steve Rosolen	London	1996-98	25(9)	10	0	0	40
Adam Ross	London	1996	(1)	0	0	0	0
Paul Round	Castleford	1996	(3)	0	0	0	0
Paul Rowley	Huddersfield	2001	24	3	0	0	12
	Halifax	1996-2000	107(3)	27	1	3	113
Nigel Roy	London	2001	28	10	0	0	40
Chris Rudd	Warrington	1996-98	31(17)	10	16	0	72
James Rushforth	Halifax	1997	(4)	0	0	0	0
Danny Russell	Huddersfield	1998-2000	50(13)	8	0	0	32
Ian Russell	Oldham	1997	1(3)	1	0	0	4
	Paris	1996	3	0	0	0	0
Richard Russell	Castleford	1996-98	37(4)	2	0	0	8
Robert Russell	Salford	1998-99	2(1)	0	1	0	2
Chris Ryan	London	1998-99	44(3)	17	10	0	88
Matt Salter	London	1997-99	14(34)	0	0	0	0
Ben Sammut	Hull	2000	20	4	67	0	150
	Gateshead	1999	26(2)	6	17	0	58
Dean Sampson	Castleford	1996-2001	117(14)	22	0	0	88
Paul Sampson	Wakefield	2000	17	8	0	0	32
Jason Sands	Paris	1996-97	28	0	0	0	0
Lokeni Savelio	Halifax	2000	2(11)	0	0	0	0
	Salford	1997-98	18(20)	0	0	0	0

PLAYER	CLUB	YEAR	APP	TRIES	GOALS	FG	PTS
Jonathan Scales	Halifax	2000	1	0	0	0	0
	Bradford	1996-98	46(4)	24	0	0	96
Andrew Schick	Castleford	1996-98	45(13)	10	0	0	40
Garry Schofield	Huddersfield	1998	(2)	0	0	0	0
Gary Schubert	Workington	1996	(1)	0	0	0	0
Matt Schultz	Hull	1998-99	23(9)	2	0	0	8
	Leeds	1996	2(4)	0	0	0	0
John Schuster	Halifax	1996-97	31	9	127	3	293
Paul Sculthorpe	St Helens	1998-2001	103(1)	45	82	3	347
	Warrington	1996-97	40	6	0	0	24
Mick Seaby	London	1997	3(2)	1	0	0	4
Danny Seal	Halifax	1996-99	8(17)	3	0	0	12
Anthony Seibold	London	1999-2000	33(19)	5	0	0	20
Keith Senior	Leeds	1999-2001	58	31	0	0	124
	Sheffield	1996-99	90(2)	40	0	0	160
Fili Seru	Hull	1998-99	37(1)	13	0	0	52
Darren Shaw	Castleford	2000-01	50(6)	1	0	0	4
	Sheffield	1998-99	51(1)	3	0	1	13
	London	1996	19(2)	3	0	0	12
Mick Shaw	Halifax	1999	5	1	0	0	4
	Leeds	1996	12(2)	7	0	0	28
Phil Shead	Paris	1996	3(2)	0	0	0	0
Richard Sheil	St Helens	1997	(1)	0	0	0	0
Kelly Shelford	Warrington	1996-97	25(3)	4	0	2	18
Ryan Sheridan	Leeds	1997-2001	98(6)	36	0	0	144
	Sheffield	1996	9(3)	5	0	1	21
Ian Sherratt	Oldham	1996	5(3)	1	0	0	4
Peter Shiels	St Helens	2001	22(1)	6	0	0	24
Gary Shillabeer	Huddersfield	1999	(2)	0	0	0	0
Ian Sibbit	Warrington	1999-2001	31(8)	16	0	0	64
Mark Sibson	Huddersfield	1999	2	2	0	0	8
Craig Simon	Hull	2000	23(2)	8	0	0	32
	Gateshead	1999	25(4)	6	0	0	24
Darren Simpson	Huddersfield	1998-99	17(1)	5	0	0	20
Robbie Simpson	London	1999	6(7)	0	0	0	0
Kevin Sinfield	Leeds	1997-2001	53(22)	11	41	1	127
Wayne Sing	Paris	1997	18(1)	2	0	0	8
Fata Sini	Salford	1997	22	7	0	0	28
Kelvin Skerrett	Halifax	1997-99	31(6)	2	0	0	8
	Wigan	1996	1(8)	0	0	0	0
Troy Slattery	Huddersfield	1999	3	1	0	0	4
Michael Slicker	Huddersfield	2001	1(14)	1	0	0	4
	Sheffield	1999	(3)	1	0	0	4
	Halifax	1997	2(5)	0	0	0	0
Ian Smales	Castleford	1996-97	10(8)	5	0	0	20
Chris Smith	Hull	2001	8	2	0	0	8
	St Helens	1998-2000	62(9)	26	0	0	104
	Castleford	1996-97	36(1)	12	0	0	48
Damien Smith	St Helens	1998	21(1)	8	0	0	32
Danny Smith	Paris	1996	10(2)	1	15	0	34
	London	1996	2(1)	1	0	0	4
Gary Smith	Castleford	2001	(1)	0	0	0	0
Hudson Smith	Bradford	2000	8(22)	2	0	0	8
	Salford	1999	23(2)	5	0	0	20
James Smith	Salford	2000	23(3)	6	0	0	24
Jamie Smith	Hull	1998-99	24(6)	6	12	0	48
	Workington	1996	5(3)	0	1	0	2
Jason Smith	Hull	2001	26	6	0	0	24
Kris Smith	London	2001	(1)	0	0	0	0
	Halifax	2001	(1)	0	0	0	0
Leigh Smith	Workington	1996	9	4	0	0	16
Mark Smith	Wigan	1999-2001	17(23)	4	0	0	16
Michael Smith	Castleford	1998, 2001	24(22)	16	0	0	64
	Hull	1999	12(6)	3	0	0	12
Paul Smith	Warrington	2001	(1)	0	0	0	0
	Castleford	1997-2000	6(37)	3	0	0	12
Paul Smith	London	1997	7(1)	2	0	0	8
Peter Smith	Oldham	1996	2	0	0	0	0
Richard Smith	Wakefield	2001	8(1)	1	0	0	4
	Salford	1997	(1)	1	0	0	4
Tony Smith	Hull	2001	23(1)	18	0	0	72
	Wigan	1997-2000	66(5)	46	0	0	184
	Castleford	1996-97	18(2)	10	0	0	40
Tony Smith	Workington	1996	9	1	0	0	4
Rob Smyth	Warrington	2000-01	26	6	11	0	86
	London	1998-2000	32(2)	9	15	0	66
	Wigan	1996	11(5)	16	0	0	64
Bright Sodje	Wakefield	2000	15	4	0	0	16
	Sheffield	1996-99	54	34	0	0	136
Alfred Songoro	Wakefield	1999	8(5)	4	0	0	16
Romain Sort	Paris	1997	(1)	0	0	0	0
Paul Southern	Salford	1997-2001	77(21)	4	13	0	42
Roy Southernwood	Wakefield	1999	1	0	0	0	0
	Halifax	1996	2	0	0	0	0
Waisale Sovatabua	Wakefield	2001	28	14	0	0	56
	Hudds-Sheff	2000	23(1)	8	0	0	32
	Sheffield	1996-99	56(11)	19	0	1	77
Yusef Sozi	London	2000-01	(5)	0	0	0	0
Andy Speak	Castleford	2001	4(4)	0	0	0	0
	Wakefield	2000	6(5)	2	0	0	8
	Leeds	1999	4	1	0	0	4
Ady Spencer	London	1996-99	8(36)	5	0	0	20

PLAYER	CLUB	YEAR	APP	TRIES	GOALS	FG	PTS
Stuart Spruce	Bradford	1996-2001	107(2)	57	0	0	228
Lee St Hilaire	Castleford	1997	4(2)	0	0	0	0
Marcus St Hilaire							
	Leeds	1996-2001	51(32)	25	0	0	100
Dylan Stainton	Workington	1996	2(3)	0	0	0	0
Mark Stamper	Workington	1996	(1)	0	0	0	0
John Stankevitch	St Helens	2000-01	21(26)	9	0	0	36
Gareth Stanley	Bradford	2000	1	1	0	0	4
Graham Steadman							
	Castleford	1996-97	11(17)	5	0	0	20
Jamie Stenhouse							
	Warrington	2000-01	9(3)	3	0	0	12
Gareth Stephens	Sheffield	1997-99	23(6)	2	0	0	8
David Stephenson							
	Hull	1998	11(7)	3	0	0	12
	Oldham	1997	10(8)	2	0	0	8
Francis Stephenson							
	Wigan	2001	2(9)	0	0	0	0
	Wakefield	1999-2000	50(1)	6	0	0	24
Paul Sterling	Leeds	1997-2000	79(12)	50	0	0	200
Paul Stevens	Oldham	1996	2(1)	0	0	0	0
	London	1996	(1)	0	0	0	0
Warren Stevens	Salford	2001	(8)	0	0	0	0
	Warrington	1996-99	15(20)	0	0	0	0
Anthony Stewart	St Helens	1997-2001	47(16)	25	0	0	100
Troy Stone	Huddersfield	2001	12(1)	1	0	0	4
Lynton Stott	Wakefield	1999	21	4	6	1	29
	Sheffield	1996-98	40(4)	15	0	0	60
Graham Strutton	London	1996	9(1)	2	0	0	8
Matt Sturm	Huddersfield	1998-99	46	8	0	0	32
Anthony Sullivan	St Helens	1996-2001	137(2)	105	0	0	420
Phil Sumner	Warrington	1996	(5)	0	0	0	0
Simon Svabic	Salford	1998-2000	13(5)	3	19	0	50
Anthony Swann	Warrington	2001	3	1	0	0	4
Willie Swann	Warrington	1996-97	25(2)	6	0	0	24
Nathan Sykes	Castleford	1996-2001	106(33)	3	0	0	12
Paul Sykes	London	2001	9	1	23	1	51
	Bradford	1999-2000	4(2)	2	0	0	8
Wayne Sykes	London	1999	(2)	0	0	0	0
Whetu Taewa	Sheffield	1997-98	33(7)	8	0	0	32
Alan Tait	Leeds	1996	3(3)	1	0	0	4
Ian Talbot	Wakefield	1999	9(5)	2	31	0	70
	Wigan	1997	3	1	0	0	4
Gael Tallec	Halifax	2000	5(19)	3	0	0	12
	Castleford	1998-99	19(21)	3	0	0	12
	Wigan	1996-97	8(12)	3	0	0	12
Joe Tamani	Bradford	1996	11(3)	4	0	0	16
Andrew Tangata-Toa							
	Huddersfield	1999	15	2	0	0	8
Kris Tassell	Salford	2000-01	35(10)	12	0	0	48
Shem Tatupu	Wigan	1996	(3)	0	0	0	0
Tony Tatupu	Wakefield	2000-01	20	2	0	0	8
	Warrington	1997	21(1)	6	0	0	24
Joe Taylor	Paris	1997	9(5)	2	0	0	8
Lawrence Taylor	Sheffield	1996	(1)	0	0	0	0
Frederic Teixido	Sheffield	1999	(4)	0	0	0	0
	Paris	1996-97	2(3)	1	0	0	4
Jason Temu	Hull	1998	13(2)	1	0	0	4
	Oldham	1996-97	25(3)	1	0	0	4
Paul Terry	London	1997	(1)	0	0	0	0
Jamie Thackray	Halifax	2000-01	4(19)	1	0	0	4
Giles Thomas	London	1997-99	1(2)	0	0	0	0
Steve Thomas	Warrington	2001	2	0	0	0	0
Alex Thompson	Sheffield	1997	4(11)	0	0	0	0
Bobby Thompson							
	Salford	1999	28	5	2	0	24
Chris Thorman	Huddersfield	2000-01	38(13)	10	2	0	44
	Sheffield	1999	5(13)	2	8	1	25
Tony Thorniley	Warrington	1997	(5)	0	0	0	0
Danny Tickle	Halifax	2000-01	19(14)	4	65	2	148
Kris Tickle	Warrington	2001	(1)	0	0	0	0
John Timu	London	1998-2000	57(3)	11	0	0	44
Kerrod Toby	London	1997	2(2)	0	0	0	0
Tulsen Tollett	London	1996-2001	105(5)	38	49	1	251
Glen Tomlinson	Wakefield	1999-2000	41(5)	8	0	0	32
	Hull	1998	5	1	0	0	4
	Bradford	1996-97	27(13)	12	0	0	48
Ian Tonks	Castleford	1996-2001	32(50)	11	13	0	70
Paul Topping	Oldham	1996-97	23(10)	1	19	0	42
Patrick Torreilles	Paris	1996	9(1)	1	25	0	54
Mat Toshack	London	1998-2001	71(18)	15	0	0	60
George Truelove	London	2000	5	1	0	0	4
Va'aiga Tuigamala							
	Wigan	1996	21	10	3	0	46
Fereti Tuilagi	St Helens	1999-2000	43(15)	21	0	0	84
	Halifax	1996-98	55(3)	27	0	0	108
Sateki Tuipulotu	Leeds	1996	6(3)	1	2	0	8
Darren Turner	Huddersfield	2000-01	15(8)	4	0	0	16
	Sheffield	1996-99	41(29)	15	0	0	60
Ian Turner	Paris	1996	1(1)	1	0	0	4
Gregory Tutard	Paris	1996	1(1)	0	0	0	0
Brendon Tuuta	Warrington	1998	18(2)	4	0	0	16
	Castleford	1996-97	41(1)	3	0	0	12
Mike Umaga	Halifax	1996-97	38(1)	16	5	0	74
Kava Utoikamanu							
	Paris	1996	6(3)	0	0	0	0
Joe Vagana	Bradford	2001	28(1)	2	0	0	8
Nigel Vagana	Warrington	1997	20	17	0	0	68
Tevita Vaikona	Bradford	1998-2001	86(2)	50	0	0	200
Eric Van Brussel							
	Paris	1996	2	0	0	0	0
Marcus Vassilakopoulos							
	Sheffield	1997-99	15(11)	3	10	2	34
	Leeds	1996-97	1(3)	0	0	0	0
Phil Veivers	Huddersfield	1998	7(6)	1	0	0	4
	St Helens	1996	(1)	1	0	0	4
Eric Vergniol	Paris	1996	14(1)	6	0	0	24
Adrian Vowles	Castleford	1997-2001	123	29	1	1	119
Mike Wainwright							
	Salford	2000-01	47(3)	5	0	0	20
	Warrington	1996-2000	55(10)	9	0	0	36
Chev Walker	Leeds	1999-2001	35(10)	16	0	0	64
Matt Walker	Huddersfield	2001	3(6)	0	0	0	0
Anthony Wall	Paris	1997	9	3	3	0	18
Mark Wallace	Workington	1996	14(1)	3	0	0	12
Kerrod Walters	Gateshead	1999	10(12)	2	1	0	10
Kevin Walters	Warrington	2001	1	0	0	0	0
Danny Ward	Leeds	1999-2001	5(22)	4	0	1	17
Phil Waring	Salford	1997-99	6(8)	2	0	0	8
Brett Warton	London	1999-2001	49(7)	14	133	0	322
Frank Watene	Wakefield	1999-2001	24(37)	6	0	0	24
Dave Watson	Sheffield	1998-99	41(4)	4	0	0	16
Ian Watson	Salford	1997	13(6)	5	3	4	34
	Workington	1996	4(1)	1	15	0	34
Kris Watson	Warrington	1996	11(2)	2	0	0	8
Jason Webber	Salford	2000	25(1)	10	0	0	40
Paul Wellens	St Helens	1998-2001	71(19)	31	9	1	143
Jon Wells	Castleford	1996-2001	92(13)	37	0	0	148
Dwayne West	St Helens	2000-01	5(13)	5	0	0	20
	Wigan	1999	1(1)	0	0	0	0
Craig Weston	Huddersfield	1998-99	46(1)	15	15	0	90
Ben Westwood	Wakefield	1999-2001	22(7)	4	1	0	18
Andrew Whalley	Workington	1996	(2)	0	0	0	0
David White	Wakefield	2000	(1)	0	0	0	0
Josh White	Salford	1998	18(3)	5	5	1	31
	London	1997	14(2)	8	0	1	33
Danny Whittle	Warrington	1998	(2)	0	0	0	0
David Whittle	Warrington	2001	1(2)	0	0	0	0
Stephen Wild	Wigan	2001	1(2)	0	0	0	0
Oliver Wilkes	Huddersfield	2000-01	1(6)	0	0	0	0
	Sheffield	1998	(1)	0	0	0	0
Alex Wilkinson	Bradford	2000-01	3(3)	1	0	0	4
Bart Williams	London	1998	5(3)	1	0	0	4
Craig Wilson	Hull	2000	2(16)	1	0	1	5
	Gateshead	1999	17(11)	5	0	1	21
George Wilson	Paris	1996	7(2)	3	0	0	12
Richard Wilson	Hull	1998-99	(13)	0	0	0	0
Scott Wilson	Warrington	1998-99	23(2)	6	0	0	24
Johan Windley	Hull	1999	2(2)	1	0	0	4
Paul Wingfield	Warrington	1997	5(3)	6	1	0	26
Michael Withers	Bradford	1999-2001	64(3)	48	0	1	193
Jeff Wittenberg	Huddersfield	1998	18(1)	1	0	0	4
	Bradford	1997	8(9)	4	0	0	16
Martin Wood	Sheffield	1997-98	24(11)	4	18	2	54
Paul Wood	Warrington	2000-01	2(22)	1	0	0	4
David Wrench	Leeds	1999-2001	7(17)	0	0	0	0
Craig Wright	Castleford	2000	1(9)	0	0	0	0
Nigel Wright	Huddersfield	1999	4(6)	1	0	0	4
	Wigan	1996-97	5(5)	2	0	1	9
Ricky Wright	Sheffield	1997-99	2(13)	0	0	0	0
Vincent Wulf	Paris	1996	13(4)	4	0	0	16
Andrew Wynyard							
	London	1999-2000	34(6)	4	0	0	16
Bagdad Yaha	Paris	1996	4(4)	2	4	0	16
Malakai Yasa	Sheffield	1996	1(3)	0	0	0	0
Kirk Yeaman	Hull	2001	(2)	0	0	0	0
Grant Young	London	1998-99	22(2)	2	0	0	8
Ronel Zenon	Paris	1996	(4)	0	0	0	0
Nick Zisti	Bradford	1999	6(1)	0	0	0	0

SUPER LEAGUE VI
Club by Club

---

17 October 2000 - Karl Harrison is appointed as coach Brian Noble's assistant for Super League VI

26 October 2000 - The Bulls sign Wigan utility Lee Gilmour for the 2001 season

8 November 2000 - Three-quarter Justin Brooker leaves for Wakefield Trinity Wildcats

10 November 2000 - The Bulls announce that they are to play at Bradford City's Valley Parade ground for the 2001 season as planning applications for redevelopment of Odsal are submitted

10 November 2000 - Australian second-rower Hudson Smith leaves the Bulls

14 November 2000 - Northern Eagles second-rower Daniel Gartner signs a two-year contract

16 November 2000 - Shane Rigon joins the Bulls from Sydney City on a two-year deal

18 November 2000 - Bradford appoint former player Bernard Dwyer as assistant coach

20 November 2000 - New Zealand International prop Joe Vagana signs a three-year contract

29 November 2000 - Mike Forshaw announces his retirement from International League

8 December 2000 - The Bulls write to League Express, banning the magazines from covering their games in 2001, claiming that they were continually presented "in a negative and detrimental fashion"

1 January 2001 - Bradford great Trevor Foster is awarded the MBE

17 January 2001 - The Bulls sign Australian three-quarter Graham Mackay from Leeds for his second spell with the club

25 February 2001 - The Bulls blow Halifax away 68-18 in their televised Challenge Cup Fifth Round tie

4 March 2001 - The Bulls open their Super League VI campaign with a tremendous 31-24 defeat of St Helens at Valley Parade in front of over 16,000 fans, with Shane Rigon scoring a hat-trick

10 March 2001 - A dispute between the Bulls and major sponsor Skylark emerges after the company fails to pay a six-figure instalment

11 March 2001 - Henry Paul inspires the Bulls to a 38-0 Challenge Cup quarter-final win at Wakefield after a weekend of speculation linking him to a move to rugby union

31 March 2001 - The Bulls overcome a spirited Warrington Wolves 39-22 to reach the Challenge Cup Final

KEY DATES - BRADFORD BULLS

16 April 2001 - Noble's side crash to an unexpected first defeat of the season, losing 16-12 at Wakefield

21 April 2001 - Fullback Stuart Spruce suffers a serious shoulder injury against Hull, ruling him out for the remainder of the season

28 April 2001 - The Bulls lose the 2001 Challenge Cup Final 13-6 against St Helens at Twickenham after a disappointing display

5 May 2001 - Henry Paul's record breaking run of 35 consecutive goal kicks finally ends at Castleford

11 May 2001 - The Bulls record a superb 33-14 win at Leeds at a packed Headingley

6 June 2001 - Brian McDermott and James Lowes sign contracts for the 2002 season, leaving just Henry Paul without a deal past the current campaign

10 June 2001 - The Bulls chalk up their biggest win of the season to date by thrashing Huddersfield Giants 78-18

4 July 2001 - The club reveals they have signed New Zealand wing sensation Lesley Vainikolo for 2002

12 July 2001 - Henry Paul's projected move to Canterbury Bulldogs collapses, raising hopes in Bradford that he will remain a Bull

25 July 2001 - The Bulls reject an audacious bid from Leeds for second-rower Jamie Peacock

4 August 2001 - Bradford crash to a shock 18-14 defeat at Warrington

9 September 2001 - Henry Paul breaks the club records for points and goals in a season in the 84-12 demolition of Warrington

13 September 2001 - Bulls conditioner Carl Jennings confirms he is to leave the club and join former Bradford coach Matthew Elliot at Canberra Raiders

15 September 2001 - Bradford claim the Super League Minor Premiership on the final day of the season by beating Leeds 62-18

30 September 2001 - The Bulls march into the Grand Final via the shortest route by beating Wigan 24-18 at Valley Parade

13 October 2001 - The Bulls are crowned Super League VI Champions after a stunning opening burst helps them towards a 37-6 win over Wigan in front of a record crowd at Old Trafford

15 October 2001 - Centre Scott Naylor signs a new two-year deal

24 October 2001 - Bradford announce the capture of Australian Brandon Costin from Huddersfield Giants, at the same time they finally release Shane Rigon for "personal reasons"

204

BRADFORD BULLS

DATE	FIXTURE	RESULT	SCORERS	LGE	ATT
11/2/01	Widnes (h) (CCR4)	W54-10	t:Withers(3),Naylor(2),Vaikona,Spruce,Lowes,McDermott,Anderson g:H Paul(7)	N/A	7,760
25/2/01	Halifax (a) (CCR5)	W18-68	t:Naylor(2),Vaikona(2),Lowes,R Paul,Forshaw,Gartner,Gilmour,Spruce, Withers g:H Paul(9),Deacon(3)	N/A	6,129
4/3/01	St Helens (h)	W31-24	t:Rigon(3),Spruce,H Paul g:H Paul(5) fg:H Paul	N/A	16,572
11/3/01	Wakefield (a) (CCQF)	W0-38	t:Lowes(2),Withers(2),H Paul,Spruce,Gartner g:H Paul(4),Deacon	N/A	6,500
16/3/01	Salford (a)	W6-40	t:Peacock(2),Spruce,Rigon,Lowes,Anderson,Withers g:H Paul(6)	3rd	4,355
25/3/01	Huddersfield (a)	W14-30	t:Deacon,Vaikona,Gartner,R Paul,Pryce g:Deacon(4),H Paul	2nd	6,648
1/4/01	Warrington (CCSF)	W39-22	t:R Paul(2),Withers,Peacock,Spruce,Naylor g:H Paul(7) fg:H Paul	N/A	13,856
8/4/01	London (h)	W24-6	t:Rigon,Lowes,Anderson,Pryce g:H Paul(4)	2nd	10,864
12/4/01	Wakefield (a)	L16-12	t:R Paul,Pryce g:Deacon(2)	3rd	4,729
16/4/01	Wigan (h)	W35-24	t:Vaikona,Pryce,Rigon,Gartner,R Paul g:H Paul(7) fg:H Paul	1st	16,247
21/4/01	Hull (a)	D24-24	t:Gartner(2),Forshaw g:H Paul(6)	2nd	7,518
28/4/01	St Helens (CCF)	L6-13	g:H Paul(3)	N/A	68,250
2/5/01	Warrington (h)	W56-24	t:Vaikona(3),Gilmour,Withers,Pryce,Naylor,Mackay,R Paul g:H Paul(8),Deacon(2)	1st	9,663
5/5/01	Castleford (a)	W22-24	t:H Paul,R Paul,Lowes g:H Paul(6)	1st	8,528
11/5/01	Leeds (h)	W14-33	t:Withers(2),Forshaw,Anderson,Vaikona g:H Paul(6) fg:H Paul	1st	18,242
18/5/01	Halifax (h)	W64-12	t:Pryce(3),Forshaw(2),Vaikona,Naylor,Gartner,R Paul,Gilmour,Fielden g:H Paul(10)	1st	11,691
27/5/01	Salford (h)	W42-10	t:Gilmour(3),Radford,Withers,Pryce,Rigon,Vaikona g:H Paul(5)	1st	10,907
2/6/01	St Helens (a)	L38-26	t:R Paul(2),Vaikona,Gilmour,Peacock g:H Paul(3)	1st	10,428
10/6/01	Huddersfield (h)	W78-18	t:Mackay(3),Rigon(2),Vaikona(2),Gartner,Peacock,Pryce,H Paul,McAvoy, Vagana,Withers g:H Paul(11)	1st	10,886
16/6/01	London (a)	W0-42	t:Rigon,Peacock,Fielden,Gartner,Withers,Vaikona,Deacon,Gilmour g:H Paul(5)	1st	5,259
24/6/01	Wakefield (h)	W62-10	t:Gartner,Withers,H Paul,Anderson,Rigon,McAvoy,R Paul,Vaikona, McDermott,Vagana g:H Paul(8),Deacon(3)	1st	11,298
29/6/01	Wigan (a)	L44-30	t:Withers(2),Anderson,Vaikona,McDermott g:H Paul(5)	1st	14,886
6/7/01	Hull (h)	W40-0	t:H Paul(2),R Paul(2),Deacon,Mackay,Withers g:H Paul(6)	1st	12,807
15/7/01	Castleford (h)	W44-4	t:Lowes(2),Naylor(2),Withers,Pryce,Deacon g:Deacon(8)	1st	9,287
22/7/01	Leeds (h)	W44-22	t:Pryce(2),Vaikona(2),McAvoy,Peacock,Gartner g:H Paul(7),Deacon	1st	15,106
29/7/01	Halifax (a)	W28-52	t:Vaikona(3),Mackay(2),R Paul,Gartner,Pryce,Anderson g:H Paul(8)	1st	5,982
4/8/01	Warrington (a)	L18-14	t:R Paul,Radford g:H Paul(3)	1st	4,929
11/8/01	Leeds (a)	W6-34	t:H Paul,Naylor,Vaikona,R Paul,Withers g:H Paul(7)	1st	13,712
17/8/01	St Helens (h)	W27-14	t:Withers,Mackay g:H Paul(8) fg:Deacon(3)	1st	13,805
26/8/01	Castleford (h)	W56-30	t:Withers(3),Vaikona,R Paul,Lowes,Gartner,Deacon,McAvoy g:H Paul(9),Deacon	1st	10,469
31/8/01	Wigan (h)	L16-10	t:Lowes g:H Paul(2) fg:Deacon,Lowes	1st	15,052
9/9/01	Warrington (a)	W12-84	t:Withers(3),Mackay(3),Pryce(2),Naylor(2),R Paul,H Paul,Rigon,Peacock g:H Paul(10),Deacon(4)	1st	8,393
15/9/01	Leeds (h)	W62-18	t:Naylor(2),R Paul(2),Withers(2),Forshaw,Gartner,Vaikona,Deacon,Lowes g:H Paul(9)	1st	12,863
30/9/01	Wigan (h) (QSF)	W24-18	t:R Paul(2) g:H Paul(8)	N/A	13,216
13/10/01	Wigan (GF)	W37-6	t:Withers(3),Lowes,Fielden,Mackay g:H Paul(5),Mackay fg:H Paul	N/A	60,164

	APP		TRIES		GOALS		FG		PTS		
	ALL	SL	ALL	SL	ALL	SL	ALL	SL	ALL	SL	
Paul Anderson	3(32)	2(28)	7	6	0	0	0	0	28	24	
Paul Deacon	11(20)	9(17)	6	6	29	25	4	4	86	78	
Stuart Fielden	3(29)	2(25)	3	3	0	0	0	0	12	12	
Mike Forshaw	31	26	6	5	0	0	0	0	24	20	
Daniel Gartner	30(1)	26(1)	14	12	0	0	0	0	56	48	
Lee Gilmour	16(11)	14(9)	8	7	0	0	0	0	32	28	
James Lowes	34	29	13	9	0	0	1	1	53	37	
Graham Mackay	16(3)	16(3)	12	12	1	1	0	0	50	50	
Nathan McAvoy	5(3)	5(3)	4	4	0	0	0	0	16	16	
Brian McDermott	33(1)	28(1)	3	2	0	0	0	0	12	8	
Scott Naylor	26	21	14	9	0	0	0	0	56	36	
Henry Paul	32(2)	27(2)	9	8	208	178	5	4	457	392	
Robbie Paul	27(7)	24(5)	23	20	0	0	0	0	92	80	
Jamie Peacock	31	26	8	7	0	0	0	0	32	28	
Leon Pryce	26(3)	25(2)	16	16	0	0	0	0	64	64	
Lee Radford	7(8)	6(8)	2	2	0	0	0	0	8	8	
Shane Rigon	17(13)	14(11)	12	12	0	0	0	0	48	48	
Stuart Spruce	11	7	6	2	0	0	0	0	24	8	
Joe Vagana	31(3)	28(1)	2	2	0	0	0	0	8	8	
Tevita Vaikona	32	27	25	22	0	0	0	0	100	88	
Alex Wilkinson	1(1)	1(1)	0	0	0	0	0	0	0	0	
Michael Withers	31	26	32	25	0	0	0	0	128	100	

LEAGUE RECORD
P28-W22-D1-L5
(1st, SL/Grand Final Winners, Champions)
F1120, A474, Diff+646
45 points.

CHALLENGE CUP
Runners Up

ATTENDANCES
Best - v St Helens (SL - 16,572)
Worst - v Widnes (CC - 7,760)
Total (SL, inc play-offs) - 185,681
Average (SL, inc play-offs) - 12,379
(Down by 2,971 on 2000)

TOP TACKLES	TOP CARRIES	TOP METRES	TOP BREAKS	TOP OFFLOADS	TOP BUSTS
James Lowes	Tevita Vaikona	Tevita Vaikona	Michael Withers	Mike Forshaw	Tevita Vaikona
695	377	3587	42	79	100

205

25 September 2000 - Castleford beat London Broncos to the signature of Cronulla Sharks scrum-half Mitch Healey, but part company with Australians Brad Davis and Andrew Purcell

30 October 2000 - Centre Logan Campbell parts company with the Tigers, signing for Hull FC on a 12-month contract

20 November 2000 - Castleford snap up former Warrington Wolves star Jon Roper

20 November 2000 - The Tigers announce the signing of 20-year-old unknown Mark Lennon from Australian club St George-Illawarra Dragons

13 December 2000 - Officials from the club meet with Wakefield Council to discuss plans for developing The Jungle

5 February 2001 - Speculation links Castleford coach Stuart Raper with a number of Super League clubs and a possible return to his former club Cronulla Sharks

11 February 2001 - Castleford overcome a valiant Dewsbury,18-4, to go through to the fifth round of the Silk Cut Challenge Cup

12 February 2001 - David Smart is appointed as the club's new media manager

25 February 2001 - The Tigers lose new signing Mitch Healey to a hamstring strain just 50 minutes before their Silk Cut Challenge Cup fifth round tie against Leeds Rhinos at the Jungle. With the dismissal of Dean Sampson in the 73rd minute for a late and high tackle, the Rhinos prove too strong, running out 42-12 victors

4 March 2001 - Healey aggravates his hamstring injury and is forced to leave the field during the Tiger's 22-17 victory over Wakefield Trinity Wildcats on the opening weekend of Super League VI

2 April 2001 - Castleford abandon plans to move to a new stadium in the town, instead opting for redevelopment of The Jungle

16 April 2001 - The Tigers suffer a setback when they receive news that Jon Roper will require surgery on an ankle injury

18 May 2001 - Stuart Raper leaves the club to take the vacant coaching position at Wigan after the Warriors part company with New Zealander Frank Endacott

20 May 2001 - The Tigers lose their first game under the guidance of coach Graham Steadman, going down 25-12 to London Broncos

25 May 2001 - Castleford suffer a nine-try hammering in a 54-12 defeat at the hands of Raper's Wigan Warriors

KEY DATES - CASTLEFORD TIGERS

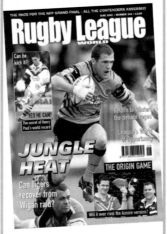

28 May 2001 - Danny Orr is included in the Yorkshire squad to face Lancashire at Headingley in the Origin game

10 June 2001 - The Tigers prevent Hull FC from going top of Super League with a 33-26 win

15 June 2001 - Mark Lennon signs a new one-and-a-half-year contract with the club

17 June 2001 - Darren Rogers suffers a compound fracture of the hand in the Tigers' 30-16 defeat against Warrington Wolves

30 June 2001 - Castleford almost throw away an 18-point lead but manage to hold on and defeat bitter rivals Leeds Rhinos 28-26

2 July 2001 - Australian hooker Aaron Raper leaves the club, but centre Michael Eagar signs a two-year extension to his contract that will keep him at Castleford until 2003

8 July 2001 - The Tigers' play-off aspirations are dealt a blow as they lose

22-16 against Halifax Blue Sox at The Shay

9 July 2001 - Lennon signs a further new deal with the club that will keep him at Castleford until the end of 2003

9 July 2001 - Caretaker coach Steadman loses the services of Barrie-Jon Mather, who is ruled out for the rest of the season with a shoulder injury

16 July 2001 - Mitch Healey confirms he is ready to delay his retirement in order to enjoy a final season at The Jungle

22 July 2001 - Tigers prop Dean Sampson makes his 400th appearance for the club in the 20-14 victory over Huddersfield Giants

3 August 2001 - Castleford record a memorable 28-26 victory over St Helens

12 August 2001 - The Tigers complete the signing of St George-Illawarra's star hooker Wayne Bartrim for 2002

3 September 2001 - Castleford beat off competition from Widnes Vikings to secure the services of London Broncos utility player Andy Johnson on a two-year contract

3 September 2001 - Dean Sampson and Tony Marchant are appointed as Tigers' Alliance and Academy coaches

10 September 2001 - Second-rower Dale Fritz agrees to a two-year extension to his contract that will keep him at the club until the end of the 2003 season

16 September 2001 - Castleford lose 31-28 to Warrington at The Jungle in the last game of the season, as captain Adrian Vowles plays his last game for the club before joining Leeds Rhinos

17 September 2001 - Jon Roper signs for Leigh Centurions

28 September 2001 - Castleford confirm Graham Steadman as head coach for 2002 and appoint Kiwi Gary Mercer as his assistant

CASTLEFORD TIGERS

DATE	FIXTURE	RESULT	SCORERS	LGE	ATT
11/2/01	Dewsbury (a) (CCR4)	W4-18	t:Healey,Sampson,Orr g:Orr(3)	N/A	3,384
24/2/01	Leeds (h) (CCR5)	L12-42	t:Rogers(2),Sykes	N/A	11,418
4/3/01	Wakefield (a)	W17-22	t:M Smith(2),Vowles,Mather g:Orr(3)	N/A	5,130
17/3/01	Wigan (h)	L8-24	t:Vowles g:Orr(2)	7th	7,214
25/3/01	Hull (a)	D18-18	t:Eagar(2),Orr g:Orr(3)	7th	7,640
7/4/01	Warrington (h)	W18-0	t:Wells,Orr g:Orr(5)	5th	6,293
13/4/01	Salford (h)	L22-24	t:Fritz,M Smith,Healey,Rogers g:Orr(3)	6th	6,816
16/4/01	Leeds (a)	L32-22	t:Rogers(2),Orr,Eagar g:Orr(3)	8th	15,039
22/4/01	Halifax (h)	W34-24	t:Eagar(2),Gay,Wells,M Smith g:Orr(7)	6th	6,483
5/5/01	Bradford (h)	L22-24	t:Orr,Wells,Gay g:Orr(5)	9th	8,528
9/5/01	St Helens (a)	L36-16	t:Wells,Gay,Tonks g:Orr(2)	9th	6,836
13/5/01	Huddersfield (a)	W26-46	t:Sampson(3),Tonks(2),Flowers(2),Wells,Orr g:Orr(5)	7th	3,453
20/5/01	London (h)	L12-25	t:Mather,Flowers g:Orr(2)	8th	6,142
25/5/01	Wigan (a)	L54-12	t:Eagar,Orr g:Orr(2)	8th	10,190
1/6/01	Wakefield (h)	W26-22	t:Sampson,Rogers,Pryce,Orr,Gay g:Orr(3)	7th	6,309
9/6/01	Hull (h)	W33-26	t:Wells(2),Lennon,Rogers,Tonks,M Smith g:Lennon(4) fg:Vowles	7th	6,952
17/6/01	Warrington (a)	L30-16	t:Lewis,Rogers g:Lennon(4)	7th	6,002
23/6/01	Salford (a)	W18-26	t:M Smith,Roper,Sampson,Healey g:Orr(5)	7th	3,530
29/6/01	Leeds (h)	W28-26	t:Pryce,Fritz,Lennon,Roper,Lewis g:Orr(4)	6th	10,625
8/7/01	Halifax (a)	L22-16	t:Lewis,Gay,Orr g:Orr(2)	7th	5,041
15/7/01	Bradford (a)	L44-4	t:Fritz	7th	9,287
22/7/01	Huddersfield (h)	W20-14	t:Orr,Healey,Roper,M Smith g:Orr,Roper	7th	5,698
28/7/01	London (a)	L40-10	t:Wells,Lennon g:Roper	7th	2,342
3/8/01	St Helens (h)	W28-26	t:Pryce,Fritz,Healey,Vowles,Harland g:Roper(4)	7th	7,054
12/8/01	Warrington (a)	L27-12	t:Rogers g:Rooney(4)	8th	5,235
18/8/01	Leeds (h)	L10-17	t:Eagar,Wells g:Lennon	7th	7,750
26/8/01	Bradford (h)	L56-30	t:Harland(2),Godwin,M Smith,Roper g:Roper(3),Rooney(2)	8th	10,469
31/8/01	St Helens (a)	L44-20	t:Lennon,Roper,Vowles,M Smith g:Lennon(2)	8th	7,680
9/9/01	Wigan (h)	L22-30	t:Roper,Charles,Lennon,M Smith g:Roper(3)	8th	7,546
16/9/01	Warrington (h)	L28-31	t:Pryce(2),Eagar,Godwin,Roper g:Lennon(4)	8th	6,019

	APP		TRIES		GOALS		FG		PTS	
	ALL	SL	ALL	SL	ALL	SL	ALL	SL	ALL	SL
David Bates	(2)	(2)	0	0	0	0	0	0	0	0
Chris Charles	1(4)	1(4)	1	1	0	0	0	0	4	4
Michael Eagar	22	20	8	8	0	0	0	0	32	32
Jason Flowers	13(6)	13(6)	3	3	0	0	0	0	12	12
Dale Fritz	25(2)	25(2)	4	4	0	0	0	0	16	16
Richard Gay	19(4)	18(4)	5	5	0	0	0	0	20	20
Jonathan Goddard	(1)	(1)	0	0	0	0	0	0	0	0
Wayne Godwin	(6)	(6)	2	2	0	0	0	0	8	8
Gareth Handford	7(4)	7(2)	0	0	0	0	0	0	0	0
Lee Harland	24(2)	22(2)	3	3	0	0	0	0	12	12
Mitch Healey	21	20	5	4	0	0	0	0	20	16
Brad Hepi	1(4)	1(4)	0	0	0	0	0	0	0	0
Mark Lennon	20(10)	19(9)	5	5	15	15	0	0	50	50
Simon Lewis	4	4	3	3	0	0	0	0	12	12
Andy Lynch	5(16)	3(16)	0	0	0	0	0	0	0	0
Barrie-Jon Mather	10	8	2	2	0	0	0	0	8	8
Andy McNally	(4)	(4)	0	0	0	0	0	0	0	0
Danny Orr	19(1)	17(1)	10	9	60	57	0	0	160	150
Waine Pryce	12(7)	12(7)	5	5	0	0	0	0	20	20
Aaron Raper	9	7	0	0	0	0	0	0	0	0
Darren Rogers	22	20	9	7	0	0	0	0	36	28
Jamie Rooney	2(1)	2(1)	0	0	6	6	0	0	12	12
Jonathan Roper	13(1)	13	7	7	12	12	0	0	52	52
Dean Sampson	23(2)	21(2)	6	5	0	0	0	0	24	20
Darren Shaw	25(4)	24(3)	0	0	0	0	0	0	0	0
Gary Smith	(1)	(1)	0	0	0	0	0	0	0	0
Michael Smith	10(17)	10(16)	10	10	0	0	0	0	40	40
Andy Speak	4(4)	4(4)	0	0	0	0	0	0	0	0
Nathan Sykes	20(3)	20(1)	1	0	0	0	0	0	4	0
Ian Tonks	6(9)	4(9)	4	4	0	0	0	0	16	16
Adrian Vowles	23	21	4	4	0	0	1	1	17	17
Jon Wells	30	28	9	9	0	0	0	0	36	36

LEAGUE RECORD
P28-W10-D1-L17
(8th, SL)
F581, A777, Diff-196
21 points.

CHALLENGE CUP
Round Five

ATTENDANCES
Best - v Leeds (CC - 11,418)
Worst - v Huddersfield (SL - 5,698)
Total (SL only) - 99,429
Average (SL only) - 7,102
(Down by 873 on 2000)

TOP TACKLES
Darren Shaw 619

TOP CARRIES
Michael Smith 445

TOP METRES
Michael Smith 3578

TOP BREAKS
Danny Orr 20

TOP OFFLOADS
Dean Sampson 61

TOP BUSTS
Michael Smith 120

19 August 2000 - Aussie prop Brett Goldspink agrees a new three-year deal

10 September 2000 - Halifax confirm the re-signing of Australian scrum-half Gavin Clinch from the Huddersfield Giants

20 September 2000 - Paul Rowley agrees to sign for neighbours Huddersfield after seven seasons with Halifax

21 September 2000 - Wakefield Trinity Wildcats centre Adam Hughes signs for the Blue Sox along with London Broncos forward Paul Davidson

23 September 2000 - Halifax fight against Leigh Centurions for the signatures of hooker Mick Higham and centre Stuart Donlan

1 October 2000 - Gary Mercer is offered a one-year deal to continue as coach of the Blue Sox, although he publicly expresses his desire for a two-year contract

17 November 2000 - Halifax's chief executive Nigel Wood registers Mike Higham and Stuart Donlan as Halifax players after a RFL tribunal, adjudicating between the Blue Sox and Leigh, said the two players were free agents

16 December 2000 - Halifax sign Oldham's back-row forward Shayne McMenemy, and are linked with Johnny Lawless, after confusion over Higham, who St Helens claim they have signed

26 December 2000 - The Rugby Football League accept Halifax's registration of Higham but withdraw it 24-hours later, and the hooker makes his debut for Saints in the Boxing Day friendly with Wigan

30 December 2000 - The Blue Sox sign Huddersfield hooker Johnny Lawless

6 January 2001 - Halifax decide to take

KEY DATES - HALIFAX BLUE SOX

legal action against St Helens after Higham signs for them 14 days after the RFL ruled Higham was a Halifax player

10 January 2001 - Halifax re-sign young hooker Matty Firth on a one-year deal

3 February 2001 - The Blue Sox fail to make the finals of the Florida Sunshine State Challenge as they lose 18-10 to Leeds in the semi-finals.

16 February 2001 - Jim Gannon signs a one-year extension to his contract, keeping him at the Blue Sox until the end of the 2002 season

24 February 2001 - Halifax's old ground Thrum Hall suffers an arson attack, and the main stand is destroyed

25 February 2001 - Halifax go out of the Challenge Cup with a poor display against Bradford, losing 18-68

2 March 2001 - Halifax make a positive start to the Super League season with a 34-10 win at Huddersfield

18 March 2001 - Halifax's bright start continues with a 16-11 win over the London Broncos in Round Two

25th March 2001 - Halifax lose Andrew Dunemann with a broken jaw and fractured cheekbone in their 34-14 defeat by Wakefield

30 March 2001 - Gary Mercer resigns as Halifax's player-coach, but vows to carry on playing for the Blue Sox

9 April 2001 - Mercer's assistant, Steve Linnane, is to coach the Blue Sox until September 2002, after the Australian signs a two-year deal. Mercer signs a playing contract at Warrington until the end of the season

15 April 2001 - Chief executive Wood admits there will be a delay in finishing the development of The Shay due to a lack of money

3 May 2001 - Halifax sign Keighley Cougars winger Jason Lee

24 May 2001- Shayne McMenemy signs a new two-year deal that will keep him at the club until the end of 2003

1 June 2001 - Andrew Dunemann will be staying with the club until the end of 2003 after signing a new two-year contract

23 June 2001 - Jamie Bloem is cleared of racism charges after allegedly saying something out of turn in an Alliance match against Salford

29 July 2001 - Stuart Donlan signs a three-year contract with the Blue Sox

3 August 2001 - Halifax secure Dale Cardoza on loan from Huddersfield in a swap deal that sees Martin Moana go to Huddersfield. Halifax also sign up Rochdale Hornets centre Matt Calland until the end of the season

12 August 2001 - Paul Davidson is sent off in the Blue Sox's match against Hull for the use of a forearm, only a week after his dismissal at Leeds

23 August 2001 - The club re-signs Daryl Cardiss on a new three-year deal

1 September 2001 - Hooker Johnny Lawless signs a new one-year deal and the Blue Sox release former Keighley duo Jason Lee and Chris Hartley

7 September 2001 - The Blue Sox get a huge boost as the council approves the selling of Thrum Hall to Asda, releasing the money they need to finish The Shay

10 September 2001 - The Blue Sox sign Australian centre Dave Woods and Robbie Beckett from Penrith Panthers, and Parramatta Eels player Callum Halpenny for 2002

28 September 2001 - Halifax release Matty Firth, along with Paul Davidson and Phil Hassan

HALIFAX BLUE SOX

DATE	FIXTURE	RESULT	SCORERS	LGE	ATT
11/2/01	Barrow (a) (CCR4)	W4-56	t:Hughes(3),Cardiss(3),McMenemy(2),Davidson,Greenwood,Bloem g:Hughes(6)	N/A	2,160
25/2/01	Bradford (h) (CCR5)	L18-68	t:Mercer,Dunemann,Clinch g:Bloem(3)	N/A	6,129
4/3/01	Huddersfield (a)	W10-34	t:Moana(2),McMenemy,Gibson,Gannon,Hughes g:Bloem(5)	N/A	4,401
18/3/01	London (h)	W16-11	t:Marns,Mercer g:Bloem(4)	4th	4,153
25/3/01	Wakefield (a)	L30-14	t:Cardiss(2),Goldspink g:Bloem	6th	3,147
6/4/01	Wigan (h)	L10-20	t:Cardiss g:Bloem(3)	7th	4,549
13/4/01	Hull (a)	L30-14	t:Cardiss,Davidson g:Bloem(2),Tickle	8th	7,160
16/4/01	Warrington (h)	L30-32	t:Hughes(2),Bloem(2),Gibson g:Tickle(5)	9th	4,889
22/4/01	Castleford (a)	L34-24	t:Cardiss(2),Marns,Tickle g:Tickle(4)	11th	6,483
30/4/01	Leeds (h)	L26-38	t:Marns,Lawless,Davidson,Bloem g:Tickle(5)	11th	6,471
6/5/01	Salford (h)	W30-18	t:Cardiss(2),McMenemy(2),Tickle g:Tickle(5)	10th	4,180
11/5/01	St Helens (a)	L32-26	t:Davidson,Cardiss,Lee,Donlan g:Tickle(5)	11th	6,986
18/5/01	Bradford (a)	L64-12	t:Donlan,Bloem g:Tickle(2)	11th	11,691
27/5/01	London (a)	L14-12	t:Hughes,Marns g:Tickle(2)	11th	2,584
3/6/01	Huddersfield (h)	W40-8	t:Gibson(2),Lee,McMenemy,Davidson,Lawless,Thackray,Marns g:Bloem(3),Tickle	10th	4,253
10/6/01	Wakefield (h)	W26-20	t:Moana(2),McMenemy,Gibson,Donlan g:Tickle(2),Bloem	8th	4,863
15/6/01	Wigan (a)	L50-18	t:Clinch,Davidson,Gibson g:Tickle(3)	10th	9,038
24/6/01	Hull (h)	L26-27	t:Cardiss(2),Marns g:Bloem(7)	10th	4,723
1/7/01	Warrington (a)	L34-22	t:Donlan(2),Hassan,Lawless g:Bloem(2),Tickle	10th	5,628
8/7/01	Castleford (h)	W22-16	t:Bloem,Marns,Lawless,Hughes g:Bloem(2),Tickle	10th	5,041
15/7/01	Salford (a)	W34-50	t:Cardiss(2),Gibson(2),Gannon(2),Dunemann,Penkywicz g:Tickle(7),Bloem(2)	9th	3,597
22/7/01	St Helens (a)	L22-46	t:Cardiss,Clinch,McMenemy,Gibson g:Tickle,Bloem,Clinch	9th	5,142
29/7/01	Bradford (h)	L28-52	t:Gannon,Gibson,Dunemann,Marns g:Bloem(5),Tickle	9th	5,982
3/8/01	Leeds (a)	L36-18	t:Donlan(2),Lawless g:Bloem(3)	10th	10,201
12/8/01	Hull (a)	L32-16	t:Gibson,Donlan,Gannon g:Tickle(2)	10th	5,620
19/8/01	Huddersfield (h)	W19-12	t:McMenemy,Tickle,Hughes g:Tickle(3) fg:Tickle	9th	4,328
26/8/01	Salford (a)	W30-41	t:Donlan(2),Cardiss(2),Cardoza,Gibson,Penkywicz g:Tickle(6) fg:Tickle	9th	3,649
2/9/01	Wakefield (h)	L10-23	t:Donlan,Gibson g:Tickle	9th	4,485
8/9/01	London (a)	L46-8	t:Greenwood g:Clinch(2)	9th	2,854
16/9/01	Hull (h)	L16-20	t:Hughes(2),Lawless g:Clinch(2)	9th	4,593

	APP		TRIES		GOALS		FG		PTS	
	ALL	SL	ALL	SL	ALL	SL	ALL	SL	ALL	SL
Jamie Bloem	15(9)	13(9)	6	5	44	41	0	0	112	102
Andrew Brocklehurst	2(2)	2(2)	0	0	0	0	0	0	0	0
Daryl Cardiss	23(2)	21(2)	19	16	0	0	0	0	76	64
Dale Cardoza	3	3	1	1	0	0	0	0	4	4
Gavin Clinch	28	26	3	2	5	5	0	0	22	18
Paul Davidson	18(5)	18(3)	6	5	0	0	0	0	24	20
Stuart Donlan	23(2)	23(2)	11	11	0	0	0	0	44	44
Andrew Dunemann	17	15	3	2	0	0	0	0	12	8
Danny Ekis	(1)	(1)	0	0	0	0	0	0	0	0
Matt Firth	8(1)	8(1)	0	0	0	0	0	0	0	0
David Foster	(1)	(1)	0	0	0	0	0	0	0	0
Jim Gannon	28	26	5	5	0	0	0	0	20	20
Damian Gibson	29	27	13	13	0	0	0	0	52	52
Brett Goldspink	25(2)	25	1	1	0	0	0	0	4	4
Lee Greenwood	4		2	1	0	0	0	0	8	4
Danny Halliwell	3(1)	3(1)	0	0	0	0	0	0	0	0
Phil Hassan	11(3)	11(3)	1	1	0	0	0	0	4	4
Andy Hobson	13(16)	11(16)	0	0	0	0	0	0	0	0
Adam Hughes	10(8)	8(8)	11	8	6	0	0	0	56	32
Dean Lawford	1(1)	1(1)	0	0	0	0	0	0	0	0
Johnny Lawless	29	27	6	6	0	0	0	0	24	24
Jason Lee	10(1)	10(1)	2	2	0	0	0	0	8	8
Oliver Marns	24	24	8	8	0	0	0	0	32	32
Shayne McMenemy	28	26	9	7	0	0	0	0	36	28
Gary Mercer	4	2	2	1	0	0	0	0	8	4
Martin Moana	14(8)	12(8)	4	4	0	0	0	0	16	16
Sean Penkywicz	2(18)	2(17)	2	2	0	0	0	0	8	8
Kris Smith	(1)	(1)	0	0	0	0	0	0	0	0
Jamie Thackray	3(16)	3(14)	1	1	0	0	0	0	4	4
Danny Tickle	15(11)	15(10)	3	3	58	58	2	2	130	130

LEAGUE RECORD
P28-W9-D0-L19
(9th, SL)
F630, A819, Diff-189
18 points.

CHALLENGE CUP
Round Five

ATTENDANCES
Best - v Leeds (SL - 6,471)
Worst - v London (SL - 4,153)
Total (SL only) - 67,652
Average (SL only) - 4,832
(Down by 882 on 2000)

TOP TACKLES
Johnny Lawless 712

TOP CARRIES
Jim Gannon 431

TOP METRES
Jim Gannon 2847

TOP BREAKS
Daryl Cardiss 17

TOP OFFLOADS
Brett Goldspink 58

TOP BUSTS
Daryl Cardiss 67

16 August 2000 - Tony Smith is unveiled as the Giants new coach

7 September 2000 - The club decides to drop Sheffield from their name and revert to being Huddersfield Giants

10 September 2000 - Gavin Clinch leaves to join Halifax Blue Sox

12 September 2000 - The club signs Australian half back Ben Kusto from Parramatta

14 September 2000 - Steve McNamara signs for the Giants from Wakefield Trinity Wildcats

18 September 2000 - Winger Andrew Frew joins from Australian club Northern Eagles, but Matt Crowther moves to Hull

20 September 2000 - Paul Rowley agrees to sign for Huddersfield from neighbours Halifax

21 September 2000 - The Giants release Johnny Lawless, Jim Carlton and Karl Lovell

1 October 2000 - Assistant coach Phil Veivers is sacked after four years at the McAlpine Stadium

5 October 2000 - Kiwi stand-off Gene Ngamu leaves the Giants, as the club signs Leeds' Alliance player Hefin O'Hare

10 October 2000 - The Giants sign Chris Langley from Bradford Bulls

14 October 2000 - Fijian International Waisale Sovatabua is released along with a string of Alliance players

18 October 2000 - Australian second-rower Dave Atkins signs a two-year contract at the McAlpine

9 November 2000 - Australian hooker Danny Russell is released

28 November 2000 - The Giants secure the signature of Australian utility-back Graham Appo on a one-year contract, but release Danny Arnold

15 December 2000 - The Giants sign a sponsorship deal with Friends Provident worth £100,000

8 January 2001 - Nick Fozzard confirms

KEY DATES - HUDDERSFIELD GIANTS

he will be leaving the club after breaking his forearm during the build-up for the Infirmary Cup against Halifax News

18 January 2001 - Jon Sharp quits as coach of Batley Bulldogs to join the Giants' backroom staff

11 February 2001 - The Giants make a winning start under Smith, beating NFP side Featherstone Rovers 28-6 in the Challenge Cup

14 February 2001 - The Giants unveil Australian Brandon Costin to complete their overseas quota

4 March 2001 - Halifax Blue Sox condemn the Giants to a Super League opening day defeat at the McAlpine, 10-34

9 March 2001 - The Giants' dreams of Twickenham are over as they are beaten 54-16 at St Helens in the Challenge Cup quarter-finals

16 April 2001 - Huddersfield fall to a 16-24 home defeat to Wakefield Trinity

Wildcats - a result that will have much more significance come the end of the season. Further bad news concerns Darren Turner, who plays his last game of the season, sustaining a serious knee injury

11 May 2001 - The Giants sign 22 year old prop Mick Slicker from Keighley Cougars

18 May 2001 - Graeme Hallas joins Slicker in making the move from Cougar Park to the McAlpine

28 May 2001 - Australian Graham Appo sustains a serious ankle injury in the game against St Helens, ending his season

10 June 2001 - The Giants season hits a new low with the 78-18 thrashing at the hands of Bradford - their 14th straight defeat

11 June 2001 - Australian prop Troy Stone joins the club from Sydney Bulldogs

17 June 2001 - Defeat at home to Salford equals the Super League record of 17 consecutive defeats, dating back to the end of the 2000 season

18 June 2001 - Stanley Gene arrives on loan from Hull until the end of the season

24 June 2001 - The Giants finally get off the mark when Brandon Costin's last-minute conversion grabs them a dramatic draw at home to London

1 July 2001 - Tony Smith collects his first Super League win as the Giants throw themselves a relegation lifeline by beating Wakefield 38-22 at Belle Vue

15 July 2001 - The gap at the bottom is closed to five as the Giants thrash Warrington 52-10

4 August 2001 - Smith adds Martin Moana to his squad for the crucial run-in

11 August 2001 - The Giants are now just a point behind Wakefield after beating Salford at home

25 August 2001 - Victory in London closes the gap to a point again, with just three games remaining

8 September 2001 - A thrilling 21-19 win at Belle Vue sends the Giants into the final round of Super League still with a chance of avoiding relegation

15 September 2001 - Despite a gutsy 28-24 win at home to London, the Giants are condemned to relegation by virtue of the Wildcats win at Salford

18 September 2001 - The Giants announce Tony Smith will remain with the club and they will operate with a full-time squad of 20 in the Northern Ford Premiership, although Australians Ben Kusto, Andrew Frew and David Lomax are released.

HUDDERSFIELD GIANTS

DATE	FIXTURE	RESULT	SCORERS	LGE	ATT
11/2/01	Featherstone (h) (CCR4)	W28-6	t:Frew,McNamara,Kusto,Appo,Cardoza g:McNamara(3),Thorman	N/A	2,527
25/2/01	Doncaster (h) (CCR5)	W38-24	t:Frew(4),Rowley,Kusto,Appo g:McNamara(5)	N/A	2,176
4/3/01	Halifax (h)	L10-34	t:Costin,Thorman g:McNamara	N/A	4,401
9/3/01	St Helens (a) (CCQF)	L54-16	t:Frew,Molloy,Rowley g:McNamara(2)	N/A	7,899
16/3/01	St Helens (a)	L44-22	t:Frew(2),Moxon,Costin g:McNamara(3)	12th	7,275
25/3/01	Bradford (h)	L14-30	t:Frew,Costin g:McNamara(3)	11th	6,648
8/4/01	Salford (a)	L28-14	t:Appo,Atkins g:McNamara(3)	11th	3,793
13/4/01	London (a)	L43-12	t:Appo,Lomax g:McNamara(2)	12th	2,894
16/4/01	Wakefield (h)	L16-24	t:Costin,Appo,Kusto g:McNamara(2)	12th	3,516
20/4/01	Wigan (a)	L37-8	t:O'Hare,Cardoza	12th	7,772
30/4/01	Hull (h)	L14-44	t:Kusto,O'Hare g:McNamara(3)	12th	3,859
6/5/01	Warrington (a)	L36-16	t:Lomax,Kusto g:McNamara(4)	12th	5,912
13/5/01	Castleford (h)	L26-46	t:Kusto,Gleeson,Frew,Cardoza g:McNamara(5)	12th	3,453
18/5/01	Leeds (a)	L52-46	t:Costin(2),Cooper,Rowley,Slicker,Gleeson,Kusto,Lomax g:McNamara(7)	12th	11,579
28/5/01	St Helens (h)	L26-44	t:Frew,Thorman,Appo,Laughton,Cardoza g:McNamara(3)	12th	3,559
3/6/01	Halifax (a)	L40-8	t:Marshall,Cardoza	12th	4,253
10/6/01	Bradford (a)	L78-18	t:Cardoza,Frew,Reilly g:McNamara(3)	12th	10,886
17/6/01	Salford (h)	L24-32	t:Thorman,Cardoza,McNamara,Molloy g:McNamara(4)	12th	2,721
24/6/01	London (h)	D22-22	t:Gene,Gleeson,Reilly,Atkins g:Costin(2),McNamara	12th	2,235
1/7/01	Wakefield (a)	W22-38	t:Costin(2),Rowley,Frew,Gene,Reilly,Atkins g:McNamara(5)	12th	2,847
8/7/01	Wigan (h)	L24-48	t:Frew,Costin,Langley,Reilly g:Costin(4)	12th	4,039
15/7/01	Warrington (h)	W52-10	t:Costin(2),Frew(2),Atkins,Kusto,Langley,Stone g:Costin(8),McNamara(2)	12th	3,203
22/7/01	Castleford (a)	L20-14	t:Frew,Kusto,Costin g:Costin	12th	5,698
29/7/01	Leeds (a)	L26-32	t:Kusto,Thorman,Langley,Costin g:McNamara(5)	12th	4,645
5/8/01	Hull (a)	L36-16	t:Gene(2),Kusto g:McNamara,Costin	12th	5,621
12/8/01	Salford (h)	W35-14	t:Moana(2),Gene,Costin,Gleeson g:Costin(7) fg:Costin	12th	2,815
19/8/01	Halifax (a)	L19-12	t:Rowley,Gene g:Costin(2)	12th	4,328
26/8/01	London (a)	W12-21	t:Green,Costin,Frew g:Costin(4) fg:Moxon	12th	1,800
1/9/01	Hull (h)	L30-36	t:Frew(3),Gleeson,Gene g:McNamara(4),Costin	12th	3,337
8/9/01	Wakefield (a)	W19-21	t:Gleeson,Molloy,O'Hare g:McNamara(2),Costin(2) fg:Kusto	12th	4,150
16/9/01	London (h)	W28-24	t:Gleeson(2),O'Hare,Reilly,Gene g:McNamara(3),Costin	12th	3,103

	APP		TRIES		GOALS		FG		PTS	
	ALL	**SL**	**ALL**	**SL**	**ALL**	**SL**	**ALL**	**SL**	**ALL**	**SL**
Graham Appo	9	7	6	4	0	0	0	0	24	16
David Atkins	29(1)	26(1)	4	4	0	0	0	0	16	16
Dale Cardoza	18(3)	15(3)	7	6	0	0	0	0	28	24
Ben Cooper	12(1)	9(1)	1	1	0	0	0	0	4	4
Brandon Costin	25	25	15	15	33	33	1	1	127	127
Earl Crabtree	(4)	(4)	0	0	0	0	0	0	0	0
Danny Fearon	(1)	(1)	0	0	0	0	0	0	0	0
Andrew Frew	29	26	21	15	0	0	0	0	84	60
Stanley Gene	12(1)	12(1)	8	8	0	0	0	0	32	32
Martin Gleeson	29	26	8	8	0	0	0	0	32	32
Toby Green	3(1)	3(1)	1	1	0	0	0	0	4	4
Graeme Hallas	1	1	0	0	0	0	0	0	0	0
Ben Kusto	24(4)	21(4)	11	9	0	0	1	1	45	37
Chris Langley	14(1)	14(1)	3	3	0	0	0	0	12	12
Dale Laughton	15(2)	12(2)	1	1	0	0	0	0	4	4
David Lomax	25(6)	22(6)	3	3	0	0	0	0	12	12
Richard Marshall	20(10)	20(7)	1	1	0	0	0	0	4	4
Steve McNamara	29(1)	26(1)	2	1	76	66	0	0	160	136
Martin Moana	3(3)	3(3)	2	2	0	0	0	0	8	8
Steve Molloy	15(13)	12(13)	3	2	0	0	0	0	12	8
Chris Molyneux	1(15)	1(12)	0	0	0	0	0	0	0	0
Mark Moxon	7(7)	7(4)	1	1	0	0	1	1	5	5
Hefin O'Hare	5(1)	5(1)	4	4	0	0	0	0	16	16
Paul Reilly	15	14	5	5	0	0	0	0	20	20
Andy Rice	1(5)	1(5)	0	0	0	0	0	0	0	0
Robert Roberts	(1)	(1)	0	0	0	0	0	0	0	0
Paul Rowley	27	24	5	3	0	0	0	0	20	12
Michael Slicker	1(14)	1(14)	1	1	0	0	0	0	4	4
Troy Stone	12(1)	12(1)	1	1	0	0	0	0	4	4
Chris Thorman	18(10)	15(10)	4	4	1	0	0	0	18	16
Darren Turner	(7)	(5)	0	0	0	0	0	0	0	0
Matt Walker	3(6)	3(6)	0	0	0	0	0	0	0	0
Oliver Wilkes	(2)	(1)	0	0	0	0	0	0	0	0

LEAGUE RECORD
P28-W6-D1-L21
(12th, SL)
F613, A926, Diff-313
13 points.

CHALLENGE CUP
Quarter Finalists

ATTENDANCES
Best - v Bradford (SL - 6,648)
Worst - v Doncaster (CC - 2,176)
Total (SL only) - 51,534
Average (SL only) - 3,681
(Up by 259 on 2000)

TOP TACKLES
David Atkins 824

TOP CARRIES
Brandon Costin 326

TOP METRES
Andrew Frew 2377

TOP BREAKS
Brandon Costin 20

TOP OFFLOADS
David Lomax 31

TOP BUSTS
Paul Reilly 83

8 September 2000 - Steve Prescott and Chris Smith both sign deals for the 2001 season

12 September 2000 - Hull announce the signings of England scrum half Tony Smith from Wigan

26 October 2000 - Logan Campbell returns to the club from Castleford Tigers

30 October 2000 - Hull agree to sell their Boulevard ground to Kingston Communications for £750,000 ahead of a proposed move to a new stadium in 2003

1 December 2000 - Lee Jackson returns to the club from Leeds Rhinos

25 February 2001 - Hull win a thrilling Challenge Cup fifth round tie against London Broncos, recovering from a 16-0 deficit to win 30-20

10 March 2001 - Despite a late rally Hull go out of the Challenge Cup at the quarter-final stage, losing 20-18 to Leeds in a televised clash at the Boulevard

15 March 2001 - Hull City soccer club are sold, removing the last barrier to a new £45 million shared stadium in the city

6 April 2001 - Hull sit third in the Super League season after a superb 18-16 win at Leeds

13 April 2001 - Shaun McRae's men are up to second after maintaining their

KEY DATES - HULL F.C.

unbeaten start to the season with a 30-14 win over Halifax

16 April 2001 - Hull suffer their first Super League defeat of the season, 38-34 at St Helens

30 April 2001 - Hull are top of Super League - if only for two days - after their 44-14 win at Huddersfield

10 May 2001 - Jason Smith is named as the Super League Player of the Month for April

30 May 2001 - Hull announce the immediate signing of Australian forward Scott Logan from Sydney City Roosters

13 June 2001 - Reports in Australia reveal that Hull have signed Penrith forward Craig Greenhill for the 2002 season

21 June 2001 - Hull confirm that they have signed Cronulla back-rower Sean Ryan on a two-year contract to begin next season

28 June 2001 - Steve Craven signs a new two-year deal

30 June 2001 - Hull leapfrog St Helens to third in the Super League table following a 34-28 defeat of Ian Millward's side

6 July 2001 - Hooker Lee Jackson is informed he requires an operation on a torn bicep

13 August 2001 - Hull announce the capture of Warrington centre Toa-Kohe Love on a two-year contract starting in 2002

15 August 2001 - The club announces that England International Paul King has signed a new four-year contract

1 September 2001 - Hull move back into the top three with a hard-fought 36-30 win at Huddersfield

3 September 2001 - Chief executive Shane Richardson denies reports in Australia linking him with a move to North Queensland Cowboys

12 September 2001 - Young stand-off Paul Cooke signs a new four-year deal

21 September 2001 - Hull lose out in the opening play-off game but impress in a 27-24 defeat away at Wigan

28 September 2001 - Saints bring an end to Hull's season when a late Tommy Martyn try sees them to a 24-20 win in a superb game at the Boulevard

29 October 2001 - Shane Richardson tells League Express he is unsure as to whether he will move to Australia and link-up with the Penrith Panthers

29 October 2001 - Steve Prescott signs a new two-year deal

5 November 2001 - Richardson is now linked with taking over as the NRL boss following the resignation of current incumbent David Moffett

12 November 2001 - Richardson confirms he is going home to take over as Penrith chief executive

HULL F.C.

DATE	FIXTURE	RESULT	SCORERS	LGE	ATT
11/2/01	Keighley (a) (CCR4)	W20-34	t:Prescott(2),Crowther,Bird,Campbell,Gene g:Crowther(3),Prescott(2)	N/A	4,401
25/2/01	London (h) (CCR5)	W30-20	t:Jackson(2),Campbell(2),Cooke g:Crowther(5)	N/A	6,701
4/3/01	Salford (h)	W46-34	t:T Smith,Horne,Cooke,J Smith,Crowther,Grimaldi,King,Raynor g:Crowther(7)	N/A	6,628
10/3/01	Leeds (h) (CCQF)	L18-20	t:Horne,T Smith,C Smith g:Crowther(3)	N/A	10,123
18/3/01	Warrington (a)	W20-32	t:Bird,Crowther,T Smith,Prescott,C Smith,Horne g:Crowther(4)	5th	7,577
25/3/01	Castleford (h)	D18-18	t:Jackson(2),Bird g:Crowther(3)	3rd	7,640
6/4/01	Leeds (h)	W16-18	t:T Smith(2),Crowther,Bird g:Crowther	3rd	12,693
13/4/01	Halifax (h)	W30-14	t:T Smith(2),Crowther,Grimaldi,Maher g:Crowther(5)	2nd	7,160
16/4/01	St Helens (a)	L38-34	t:Crowther,Felsch,Bird,Prescott,J Smith,Parker g:Crowther(5)	4th	10,479
21/4/01	Bradford (h)	D24-24	t:Grimaldi(2),Fletcher,T Smith g:Crowther(4)	3rd	7,518
30/4/01	Huddersfield (a)	W14-44	t:Raynor(2),Prescott,Jackson,Grimaldi,Bird,J Smith,Maiden g:Crowther(6)	1st	3,859
6/5/01	London (h)	W19-14	t:Bird(2),Horne g:Crowther(3) fg:King	2nd	6,554
12/5/01	Wakefield (a)	W22-30	t:Prescott(2),King(2),Raynor,Grimaldi g:Crowther(3)	2nd	3,876
19/5/01	Wigan (h)	L10-46	t:Maher(2) g:Crowther	2nd	7,581
27/5/01	Warrington (h)	W32-16	t:Bird(2),Parker,Gene,J Smith g:Crowther(6)	2nd	5,968
3/6/01	Salford (a)	W24-36	t:T Smith(3),Crowther,Prescott,Bird g:Crowther(6)	2nd	4,143
9/6/01	Castleford (a)	L33-26	t:Broadbent,Raynor,Maiden,King,Campbell g:Prescott(3)	3rd	6,952
15/6/01	Leeds (a)	L6-15	t:T Smith g:Prescott	5th	6,426
24/6/01	Halifax (a)	W26-27	t:T Smith,J Smith,Raynor,Prescott,C Smith g:Prescott(3) fg:Prescott	4th	4,723
30/6/01	St Helens (h)	W34-28	t:Cooke(2),Grimaldi,Broadbent,Maiden g:Prescott(7)	3rd	6,538
6/7/01	Bradford (a)	L40-0	No Scorers	4th	12,807
15/7/01	London (a)	W20-24	t:Crowther,Maiden,Grimaldi,J Smith g:Prescott(4)	4th	2,847
22/7/01	Wakefield (h)	W48-16	t:Horne(2),Prescott(2),Crowther,Bird,Grimaldi,King g:Prescott(8)	4th	6,240
27/7/01	Wigan (a)	L36-12	t:Raynor,Prescott g:Prescott(2)	4th	9,174
5/8/01	Huddersfield (h)	W36-16	t:Grimaldi,Horne,Felsch,Campbell,Bird,Fletcher,Cooke g:Crowther(4)	4th	5,621
12/8/01	Halifax (h)	W32-16	t:Bird(2),Maiden,Horne,Logan g:Prescott(6)	4th	5,620
19/8/01	London (h)	W28-12	t:T Smith(2),Prescott(2) g:Prescott(6)	3rd	5,710
27/8/01	Wakefield (a)	W18-30	t:T Smith(2),Logan,Prescott,Horne,Raynor g:Prescott(3)	3rd	3,518
1/9/01	Huddersfield (a)	W30-36	t:Prescott(2),Horne,Cooke,Logan,Craven g:Prescott(6)	3rd	3,337
9/9/01	Salford (h)	W40-8	t:T Smith(2),Grimaldi,Crowther,Cooke,Maiden,Jackson g:Prescott(4),Crowther,Jackson	3rd	6,262
16/9/01	Halifax (a)	W16-20	t:Crowther,Cooke,Raynor g:Crowther(4)	3rd	4,593
21/9/01	Wigan (a) (QPO)	L27-24	t:Cooke,Maiden,Felsch,Jackson g:Crowther(4)	N/A	9,103
28/9/01	St Helens (h) (ESF)	L20-24	t:Raynor(2),Grimaldi,Bird g:Crowther(2)	N/A	9,186

	APP		TRIES		GOALS		FG		PTS	
	ALL	SL	ALL	SL	ALL	SL	ALL	SL	ALL	SL
Deon Bird	27(1)	24(1)	16	15	0	0	0	0	64	60
Paul Broadbent	23(4)	20(4)	2	2	0	0	0	0	8	8
Logan Campbell	19(14)	17(13)	5	2	0	0	0	0	20	8
Garreth Carvell	2(17)	2(15)	0	0	0	0	0	0	0	0
Paul Cooke	25(3)	23(3)	9	8	0	0	0	0	36	32
Steve Craven	15(16)	15(13)	1	1	0	0	0	0	4	4
Matt Crowther	26	23	11	10	80	69	0	0	204	178
Michael Docherty	(4)	(4)	0	0	0	0	0	0	0	0
Craig Farrell	1	1	0	0	0	0	0	0	0	0
Luke Felsch	23(3)	21(3)	3	3	0	0	0	0	12	12
Richard Fletcher	1(11)	1(11)	2	2	0	0	0	0	8	8
Stanley Gene	1(12)	(10)	2	1	0	0	0	0	8	4
Tony Grimaldi	32	30	12	12	0	0	0	0	48	48
Richard Horne	26	23	10	9	0	0	0	0	40	36
Lee Jackson	16(8)	13(8)	7	5	1	1	0	0	30	22
Paul King	18(8)	17(6)	5	5	0	0	1	1	21	21
Andy Last	1(1)	1(1)	0	0	0	0	0	0	0	0
Scott Logan	11(4)	11(4)	3	3	0	0	0	0	12	12
Adam Maher	20	17	3	3	0	0	0	0	12	12
David Maiden	16(10)	15(8)	7	7	0	0	0	0	28	28
Paul Parker	4(6)	4(6)	2	2	0	0	0	0	8	8
Craig Poucher	3(1)	3(1)	0	0	0	0	0	0	0	0
Steve Prescott	26	25	17	15	55	53	1	1	179	167
Gareth Raynor	27	27	11	11	0	0	0	0	44	44
Chris Smith	11	8	3	2	0	0	0	0	12	8
Jason Smith	29	26	6	6	0	0	0	0	24	24
Tony Smith	26(1)	23(1)	19	18	0	0	0	0	76	72
Kirk Yeaman	(2)	(2)	0	0	0	0	0	0	0	0

LEAGUE RECORD
P28-W20-D2-L6
(3rd, SL/Elimination Semi Finalists)
F772, A630, Diff+142
42 points.

CHALLENGE CUP
Quarter Finalists

ATTENDANCES
Best - v Leeds (CC - 10.123)
Worst - v Halifax (SL - 5,620)
Total (SL, inc play-offs) - 100,652
Average (SL, inc play-offs) - 6,710
(Up by 767 on 2000)

TOP TACKLES
Tony Grimaldi 887

TOP CARRIES
Steve Craven 371

TOP METRES
Steve Craven 2809

TOP BREAKS
Deon Bird 27

TOP OFFLOADS
Jason Smith 47

TOP BUSTS
Steve Prescott 68

3 November 2000 - Paul Sterling wins his claim that he had been racially discriminated against by coach Dean Lance in an employment tribunal hearing

13 November 2000 - Chief executive Gary Hetherington refutes a claim that Lance is set to return down under in a development role with the Western Australian Rugby League

20 November 2000 - Rhinos' Kiwi centre Richie Blackmore signs for the New Zealand Warriors

1 December 2000 - Hooker Lee Jackson departs for Hull

10 December 2000 - The Rhinos unveil new hooker Robbie Mears in front of 3,000 supporters, along with other overseas signings Brad Clyde and Brett Mullins

15 December 2000 - An employment tribunal forces the Rhinos to reinstate Sterling in their squad for the 2001 season, as well ordering the club to pay substantial compensation for loss of earnings

27 December 2000 - The Rhinos announce that they will appeal against the Sterling decision

4 January 2001 - Australian Steve Anderson is appointed as the Rhinos' Technical, Performance and Development Director

17 January 2001 - Powerful Aussie three-quarter Graham Mackay joins Bradford

4 February 2001 - The Rhinos win the inaugural Sunshine State Challenge in Florida after defeating Halifax and Huddersfield

11 February 2001 - The Rhinos chalk up a club record 106-10 defeat of NFP side Swinton Lions in the fourth round of the Challenge Cup, but Australian hooker Mears suffers a broken collar bone

15 February 2001 - Keith Senior signs a one-year extension to his contract, which now runs until 2004

24 February 2001 - The Rhinos comprehensively defeat local rivals Castleford 42-12 at the Jungle in Challenge Cup Round Five

10 March 2001 - Leeds march into the Challenge Cup semi-finals, defeating Hull 20-18 in a thriller at the Boulevard

16 March 2001 - Keith Senior suffers a broken thumb against Wakefield, ruling him out of the Cup semi-final against St Helens

8 April 2001 - Head coach Dean Lance leaves the Rhinos by "mutual consent" following their home defeat to Hull

12 April 2001 - Daryl Powell is confirmed as the new Rhinos coach

KEY DATES - LEEDS RHINOS

4 May 2001 - Iestyn Harris records the 2,000th point of his career as the Rhinos thrash St Helens 74-16 at Headingley

11 June 2001 - Rhinos' chief executive Gary Hetherington states that the club will not sell Iestyn Harris to the Welsh Rugby Union following a report in Sunday Times

15 June 2001 - Harris inspires a crucial 15-6 win away at Hull

4 July 2001 - Kevin Sinfield rejects a move to rugby union and signs a new four-year contract with the Rhinos

2 August 2001 - Performance Director Steve Anderson leaves the club to take over a similar role at Warrington

8 August 2001 - Rhinos supporters' worst fears are realised as Harris confirms he has signed a lucrative deal with the Welsh Rugby Union

13 August 2001 - Australian Brett

Mullins sees a specialist to try and rectify the knee injury that has plagued his season

17 August 2001 - Veteran Kiwi Gary Mercer joins the club from Warrington Wolves

18 August 2001 - Former Great Britain boss Malcolm Reilly is unveiled as Daryl Powell's assistant

23 August 2001 - NRL top pointscorer Ben Walker is announced as the man to fill Harris' boots in 2002

7 September 2001 - Hooker Robbie Mears sees his season ended by a high tackle from St Helens' Sonny Nickle that leaves him with a broken jaw

14 September 2001 - Leeds sign loose forward Adrian Vowles from arch-rivals Castleford Tigers for 2002

22 September 2001 - The Rhinos season is over as they are beaten 38-30 in the Elimination Semi-final at St Helens, despite a gutsy performance

24 September 2001 - League Express reveal that Penrith Panthers forward Matt Adamson is Leeds' latest capture for the new season, signing a three-year contract

28 September 2001 - The Rhinos appoint Barrow's Stuart Wilkinson as the new player development manager and Steve Walsh as conditioner

6 October 2001 - The Rhinos terminate the contract of hooker Mears by mutual consent

8 October 2001 - Teenage sensation Rob Burrow is named as the Super League Young Player of the Year

10 October 2001 - Wayne McDonald joins the Rhinos from St Helens

12 October 2001 - Leeds agree a £35,000 fee with Wakefield Trinity Wildcats for back-rower Willie Poching

24 October 2001 - Fringe forward David Wrench is released

LEEDS RHINOS

DATE	FIXTURE	RESULT	SCORERS	LGE	ATT
11/2/01	Swinton (a) (CCR4)	W10-106	t:Farrell(2),Hay(2),Mullins(2),Sinfield(2),Sheridan(2),St Hilaire(2), Mears,Harris,Senior,McDermott,Pratt,Clyde g:Harris(17)	N/A	3,239
24/2/01	Castleford (a) (CCR5)	W12-42	t:Sinfield(2),Harris(2),Senior,Carroll,McDermott,Pratt g:Harris(5)	N/A	11,418
3/3/01	London (a)	W18-50	t:Senior(3),Walker(2),Pratt(2),Sinfield,Mathiou g:Harris(7)	N/A	4,045
10/3/01	Hull (a) (CCQF)	W18-20	t:Pratt(2),Clyde(2) g:Harris(2)	N/A	10,123
16/3/01	Wakefield (h)	W42-14	t:Carroll(4),Pratt(2),Cummins,Walker g:Harris(5)	1st	14,019
23/3/01	Wigan (a)	L42-6	t:Ward g:Harris	4th	12,321
31/3/01	St Helens (CCSF)	L22-27	t:Calderwood,Pratt,Sinfield,Mullins g:Harris(3)	N/A	16,416
6/4/01	Hull (h)	L16-18	t:Mears,Ward,Cummins g:Sinfield(2)	6th	12,693
12/4/01	Warrington (a)	L36-6	t:Burrow g:Harris	7th	5,871
16/4/01	Castleford (h)	W32-22	t:St Hilaire(3),Sinfield,Farrell,Cummins g:Harris(4)	5th	15,039
22/4/01	Salford (a)	W14-19	t:Walker,Harris,Pratt g:Harris(3) fg:Harris	5th	5,069
30/4/01	Halifax (a)	W26-38	t:Cummins(2),Senior(2),Mears,Harris g:Harris(7)	4th	6,471
4/5/01	St Helens (h)	W74-16	t:Carroll(4),Cummins(3),Senior(2),Pratt,Hay,Harris,Walker g:Harris(11)	4th	15,702
11/5/01	Bradford (h)	L14-33	t:Carroll,Burrow g:Harris(3)	5th	18,242
18/5/01	Huddersfield (h)	W52-46	t:St Hilaire(2),McDermott,Calderwood,Mears,Harris,Senior,Cummins, Farrell g:Harris(8)	5th	11,579
26/5/01	Wakefield (a)	W16-38	t:Harris(2),Senior,St Hilaire,Pratt,Cummins,Hay g:Harris(5)	5th	4,963
1/6/01	London (a)	W36-12	t:Cummins,Harris,Carroll,Sinfield,Walker,Calderwood g:Harris(6)	4th	10,535
8/6/01	Wigan (h)	L18-36	t:Pratt,Carroll,Burrow g:Harris(3)	5th	14,435
15/6/01	Hull (a)	W6-15	t:Calderwood,Senior g:Harris(3) fg:Ward	4th	6,426
22/6/01	Warrington (h)	D24-24	t:Burrow,Carroll,Calderwood,Mears g:Burrow(4)	5th	12,178
29/6/01	Castleford (a)	L28-26	t:Carroll,Farrell,McDermott,Harris g:Harris(3)	5th	10,625
6/7/01	Salford (h)	W56-6	t:Carroll(2),Calderwood(2),Ward,Cummins,McDermott,Clyde,Walker, Hay g:Sinfield(8)	5th	10,119
13/7/01	St Helens (a)	L46-24	t:Carroll(2),Hay,Cummins g:Sinfield(4)	5th	8,913
22/7/01	Bradford (a)	L44-22	t:McDermott,Mears,Senior g:Harris(5)	5th	15,106
29/7/01	Huddersfield (a)	W26-32	t:Carroll(3),Sinfield,Hay,Mullins g:Sinfield(3),Harris	5th	4,645
3/8/01	Halifax (h)	W36-18	t:Pratt(2),Calderwood,Sheridan,Hay,Carroll g:Sinfield(6)	5th	10,201
11/8/01	Bradford (h)	L6-34	t:Pratt g:Sinfield	5th	13,712
18/8/01	Castleford (a)	W10-17	t:Senior,Pratt,Calderwood g:Sinfield(2) fg:Cummins	5th	7,750
24/8/01	Wigan (h)	L18-38	t:Sinfield,Calderwood,Mears g:Burrow(2),Cummins	5th	11,585
31/8/01	Warrington (h)	W16-12	t:Walker,Senior,Cummins g:Burrow(2)	5th	10,291
7/9/01	St Helens (a)	W18-23	t:Burrow(2),Calderwood,Cummins g:Sinfield(3) fg:Sinfield	5th	7,592
15/9/01	Bradford (a)	L62-18	t:St Hilaire,Ward,Walker g:Burrow(3)	5th	12,863
22/9/01	St Helens (a) (EPO)	L38-30	t:Burrow,Cummins,Diskin,Calderwood,Senior g:Burrow(5)	N/A	8,467

	APP		TRIES		GOALS		FG		PTS		
	ALL	SL	ALL	SL	ALL	SL	ALL	SL	ALL	SL	LEAGUE RECORD
Robert Burrow	11(6)	11(6)	7	7	16	16	0	0	60	60	
Mark Calderwood	21(9)	20(8)	12	11	0	0	0	0	48	44	
Tonie Carroll	27(1)	23(1)	23	22	0	0	0	0	92	88	
Bradley Clyde	8(7)	7(5)	4	1	0	0	0	0	16	4	
Francis Cummins	33	29	16	16	1	1	1	1	67	67	
Matthew Diskin	7(10)	4(10)	1	1	0	0	0	0	4	4	
Ewan Dowes	1(4)	1(4)	0	0	0	0	0	0	0	0	
Anthony Farrell	26(1)	22(1)	5	3	0	0	0	0	20	12	
Darren Fleary	27(1)	23(1)	0	0	0	0	0	0	0	0	
Iestyn Harris	20(2)	16(2)	11	8	103	76	1	1	251	185	
Andy Hay	26(3)	22(3)	8	6	0	0	0	0	32	24	
Jamie Jones-Buchanan	(2)	(2)	0	0	0	0	0	0	0	0	
Andy Kirk	2(4)	2(4)	0	0	0	0	0	0	0	0	
Jon Liddell	1	1	0	0	0	0	0	0	0	0	
Jamie Mathiou	11(15)	11(11)	1	1	0	0	0	0	4	4	
Barrie McDermott	26(3)	22(3)	6	4	0	0	0	0	24	16	
Danny McGuire	(2)	(2)	0	0	0	0	0	0	0	0	
Robert Mears	24	23	7	6	0	0	0	0	28	24	
Gary Mercer	6	6	0	0	0	0	0	0	0	0	
Gareth Morton	1	1	0	0	0	0	0	0	0	0	
Brett Mullins	9(3)	5(3)	4	1	0	0	0	0	16	4	
Jason Netherton	(3)	(3)	0	0	0	0	0	0	0	0	
Karl Pratt	26	22	17	12	0	0	0	0	68	48	
Keith Senior	28	25	16	14	0	0	0	0	64	56	
Ryan Sheridan	8(2)	6(2)	3	1	0	0	0	0	12	4	
Kevin Sinfield	32(1)	28(1)	10	5	29	29	1	1	99	79	
Marcus St Hilaire	14(5)	14(2)	9	7	0	0	0	0	36	28	
Chev Walker	25(7)	24(4)	9	9	0	0	0	0	36	36	
Danny Ward	2(17)	2(17)	4	4	0	0	1	1	17	17	
David Wrench	7(16)	7(14)	0	0	0	0	0	0	0	0	

LEAGUE RECORD
P28-W16-D1-L11
(5th, SL/Elimination Play-Off)
F774, A721, Diff+53
33 points.

CHALLENGE CUP
Semi Finalists

ATTENDANCES
Best - v Bradford (SL - 18,242)
Worst - v Salford (SL - 10,119)
Total (SL only) - 180,330
Average (SL only) - 12,881
(Up by 141 on 2000)

TOP TACKLES
Robert Mears 658

TOP CARRIES
Barrie McDermott 352

TOP METRES
Barrie McDermott 2762

TOP BREAKS
Keith Senior 42

TOP OFFLOADS
Barrie McDermott 69

TOP BUSTS
Iestyn Harris 84

22 September 2000 - Paul Davidson leaves the club, signing for Halifax Blue Sox on a one-year deal

25 September 2000 - Auckland Warriors coach Mark Graham confirms he has been approached about the vacant coaching position at The Valley

13 October 2000 - Tony Rea stands down from his role as chief executive and succeeds John Monie as the Broncos' new coach

20 October 2000 - London unveil new signings, Wigan prop Tony Mestrov and Wests Tigers stand-off half Michael Gillett

4 December 2000 - Parramatta scrum-half Dennis Moran joins the Broncos on a two-year deal, to team up with former Aussie Test forward Jim Dymock

11 December 2000 - London announce that they are to are to repeat their 1999 experiment of playing their home fixture against the Bradford Bulls at Leicester RUFC's Welford Road ground.

27 December 2000 - Lionel Hurst, chairman of the Rugby League Conference, is appointed as the Broncos' new chief executive

29 January 2001 - Former Halifax and Leeds back Marvin Golden signs for the Broncos on a two-month trial

11 February 2001 - The Broncos defeat Batley Bulldogs 44-4 in the fourth round of the Challenge Cup and in the process break new ground by playing the fixture at Broadfield Stadium in Crawley, home of Rugby League Conference Champions Crawley Jets

25 February 2001 - The Broncos lose 20-30 to Hull FC in the fifth round of the Challenge Cup

24 March 2001 - Round Three of Super League VI, and London allow an 18-8 lead against St Helens to slip through their fingers, thanks to two tries in the final ten minutes by Keiron Cunningham. The Broncos lose the match 20-18

2 April 2001 - Chief executive Hurst makes a bid to stage one of this autumn's Ashes Test matches at the Valley.

15 April 2001 - The Broncos record their first victory of the season with a convincing 43-12 victory over bottom club Huddersfield Giants at the Valley

29 April 2001 - A virtuoso performance from Richie Barnett ensures the Broncos record a shock 20-12 victory over the Wigan Warriors at The Valley in front of 5,101 fans, their biggest crowd of the season so far

13 May 2001 - London maintain pressure on the top five, and make it five wins out of their last six with a well-deserved 38-16 victory over Warrington Wolves

KEY DATES - LONDON BRONCOS

27 May 2001 - It is feared Broncos skipper Jason Hetherington could miss the rest of the season after he damages knee ligaments during the 14-12 league defeat of Halifax Blue Sox

27 May 2001 - Broncos favourite Steele Retchless plays his 100th game for the club in the fixture against the Blue Sox

28 May 2001 - Winger Dominic Peters is a surprise inclusion in the Lancashire squad for the 'Origin' game against Yorkshire at Headingley in June

1 June 2001 - The Broncos go down 36-12 against Leeds Rhinos at Headingley after skipper Richie Barnett sustains an injury during the warm-up

16 June 2001 - London are hammered 42-0 by the Bradford Bulls in their "home" game at Leicester, in front of a crowd of 5,259

18 June 2001 - Bradford Bulls stars Paul Sykes and Rob Parker join the Broncos on loan

2 July 2001 - The Broncos snap up teenage French international Sylvain Houles on a two-month contract

16 July 2001 - The Broncos sign Dewsbury centre Dan Potter on loan until the end of the season

30 July 2001 - The Broncos announce that they have decided not to take up the second year options on the contracts of forwards Shane Millard and Justin Dooley

12 August 2001 - London welcome back hooker Jason Hetherington after a ten-match absence with a convincing 44-18 win over the Wakefield Trinity Wildcats at the Valley

3 September 2001 - It is revealed that directors of the Broncos' main sponsor Virgin want to sell their stake in the club, and have had talks with Leigh Centurions with a view to relocating the club at Leigh's Hilton Park.

3 September 2001 - Utility player Andy Johnson signs a two-year contract with Castleford Tigers

9 September 2001 - The Broncos play what will prove to be their last game at The Valley, but do so in style with a stunning 46-8 victory over Halifax Blue Sox

10 September 2001 - London Broncos owners the Virgin Group offer the club to Super League (Europe) together with an offer of £500,000 of sponsorship for the following season if the proposal is accepted

10 September 2001 - Nearly 500 concerned Broncos fans turn up at Floyd's Bar at the Valley pledging to "do whatever it takes" to maintain the Bronco's presence in South-East London

14 September 2001 - Ownership of the club is transferred to businessman David Hughes and Virgin Group, the Broncos' previous owners, promise £1 million of sponsorship over the next two years

16 September 2001 - Australian back Greg Fleming retires following London's 28-24 defeat at the hands of bottom club Huddersfield Giants on the final day of the season

11 October 2001 - London deny persistent rumours that star halfback Moran has signed for South Sydney

LONDON BRONCOS

DATE	FIXTURE	RESULT	SCORERS	LGE	ATT
11/2/01	Batley (h) (CCR4)	W44-6	t:Roy(2),Martin,Dymock,Gillett,Golden,Toshack,Retchless g:Warton(6)	N/A	1,204
25/2/01	Hull (a) (CCR5)	L30-20	t:Moran,Golden,Millard,Gillett g:Warton(2)	N/A	6,701
3/3/01	Leeds (h)	L18-50	t:Retchless,Hetherington,Millard g:Warton(3)	N/A	4,045
18/3/01	Halifax (a)	L16-11	t:Millard,Moran g:Warton fg:Moran	9th	4,153
24/3/01	St Helens (h)	L18-20	t:Martin(2),Moran,Hetherington g:Warton	10th	3,736
8/4/01	Bradford (a)	L24-6	t:Martin g:Martin	10th	10,864
13/4/01	Huddersfield (h)	W43-12	t:Golden,Dymock,Toshack,Roy,Gillett,Hetherington,Fleming g:Martin(7) fg:Moran	10th	2,894
16/4/01	Salford (a)	W12-14	t:Millard,Roy g:Martin(3)	10th	3,967
22/4/01	Wakefield (a)	W10-38	t:Fleming(2),Barnett(2),Dooley,Warton g:Martin(6),Warton	7th	2,547
29/4/01	Wigan (h)	W20-12	t:Tollett,Barnett,Fleming,Martin g:Martin(2)	5th	5,101
6/5/01	Hull (a)	L19-14	t:Roy,Gillett g:Warton(3)	6th	6,554
13/5/01	Warrington (h)	W38-16	t:Dymock(2),Barnett,Millard,Martin,Roy,Clarke g:Martin(5)	6th	3,796
20/5/01	Castleford (a)	W12-25	t:Roy,Moran,Cram,Toshack g:Martin(4) fg:Moran	6th	6,142
27/5/01	Halifax (h)	W14-12	t:Barnett,Johnson g:Martin(3)	6th	2,584
1/6/01	Leeds (a)	L36-12	t:Johnson,Roy g:Martin(2)	6th	10,535
8/6/01	St Helens (a)	L22-14	t:Moran,Toshack g:Warton(3)	6th	6,938
16/6/01	Bradford (h)	L0-42	No Scorers	6th	5,259
24/6/01	Huddersfield (a)	D22-22	t:Moran(2),Johnson,Roy g:Warton(3)	6th	2,235
1/7/01	Salford (h)	L14-37	t:Warton,Air g:Warton(3)	8th	2,941
8/7/01	Wakefield (h)	W26-6	t:Roy,Johnson,Air,Sykes g:Warton(4),Sykes	6th	2,153
15/7/01	Hull (h)	L20-24	t:Air,Houles,Moran,Dymock g:Warton(2)	6th	2,847
21/7/01	Warrington (a)	W28-31	t:Air(2),Houles(2),Dymock g:Warton(4),Sykes fg:Sykes	6th	4,249
28/7/01	Castleford (h)	W40-10	t:Air(2),Houles(2),Fleming,Gillett g:Sykes(8)	6th	2,342
3/8/01	Wigan (a)	L46-18	t:Air,Dooley,Toshack g:Sykes(3)	6th	8,244
12/8/01	Wakefield (h)	W44-18	t:Millard(2),Moran(2),Fleming,Martin,Air g:Sykes(8)	6th	2,126
19/8/01	Hull (a)	L28-12	t:Parker,Air g:Sykes(2)	6th	5,710
26/8/01	Huddersfield (h)	L12-21	t:Martin,Fleming g:Martin(2)	6th	1,800
2/9/01	Salford (a)	W12-50	t:Barnett(3),Dymock,Houles,Martin,Gillett,Potter g:Martin(9)	6th	2,618
8/9/01	Halifax (h)	W46-8	t:Gillett(2),Barnett(2),Moran,Cram,Roy,Toshack g:Martin(6),Fleming	6th	2,854
16/9/01	Huddersfield (a)	L28-24	t:Moran,Fleming,Toshack,Roy g:Warton(2),Gillett(2)	6th	3,103

	APP		TRIES		GOALS		FG		PTS	
	ALL	SL	ALL	SL	ALL	SL	ALL	SL	ALL	SL
Glen Air	8(9)	8(8)	10	10	0	0	0	0	40	40
Richie Barnett	17(1)	17	10	10	0	0	0	0	40	40
Jon Clarke	1(8)	1(6)	1	1	0	0	0	0	4	4
Scott Cram	25	23	2	2	0	0	0	0	8	8
Justin Dooley	13(17)	11(17)	2	2	0	0	0	0	8	8
Jim Dymock	28	26	7	6	0	0	0	0	28	24
Greg Fleming	18(1)	16(1)	8	8	1	1	0	0	34	34
Michael Gillett	9(12)	7(12)	8	6	2	2	0	0	36	28
Marvin Golden	19(2)	17(2)	3	1	0	0	0	0	12	4
Jason Hetherington	19	17	3	3	0	0	0	0	12	12
Sylvain Houles	8(1)	8(1)	6	6	0	0	0	0	24	24
Steffan Hughes	1(7)	1(6)	0	0	0	0	0	0	0	0
Olu Iwenofu	1	1	0	0	0	0	0	0	0	0
Andy Johnson	6(13)	6(13)	5	5	0	0	0	0	20	20
Peter Lupton	3(4)	3(4)	0	0	0	0	0	0	0	0
Tony Martin	21	19	9	8	50	50	0	0	136	132
Tony Mestrov	17(8)	17(7)	0	0	0	0	0	0	0	0
Shane Millard	28(1)	26(1)	7	6	0	0	0	0	28	24
Dennis Moran	29	27	11	10	0	0	3	3	47	43
Iain Morrison	(1)	(1)	0	0	0	0	0	0	0	0
Robert Parker	9	9	1	1	0	0	0	0	4	4
Dominic Peters	4(2)	4(2)	0	0	0	0	0	0	0	0
Dan Potter	1(3)	1(3)	1	1	0	0	0	0	4	4
Steele Retchless	29(1)	27(1)	2	1	0	0	0	0	8	4
Nigel Roy	30	28	12	10	0	0	0	0	48	40
Kris Smith	(1)	(1)	0	0	0	0	0	0	0	0
Yusef Sozi	(4)	(4)	0	0	0	0	0	0	0	0
Paul Sykes	9	9	1	1	23	23	1	1	51	51
Tulsen Tollett	7(1)	7(1)	1	1	0	0	0	0	4	4
Mat Toshack	18(6)	18(4)	7	6	0	0	0	0	28	24
Brett Warton	12(6)	10(6)	2	2	38	30	0	0	84	68

LEAGUE RECORD
P28-W13-D1-L14
(6th, SL)
F644, A603, Diff+41
27 points.

CHALLENGE CUP
Round Five

ATTENDANCES
Best - v Bradford (SL - 5,259)
Worst - v Batley (CC - 1,204)
Total (SL only) - 44,478
Average (SL only) - 3,177
(Down by 242 on 2000)

TOP TACKLES
Steele Retchless 837

TOP CARRIES
Shane Millard 423

TOP METRES
Nigel Roy 3263

TOP BREAKS
Richie Barnett 29

TOP OFFLOADS
Shane Millard 72

TOP BUSTS
Richie Barnett 119

19 September 2000 - Warren Jowitt and Francis Maloney sign from troubled Wakefield Trinity Wildcats

26 September 2000 - John Harvey signs a new one-year contract with the club

10 December 2000 - The Reds play down rumours from down under suggesting Michael Hancock could be set to turn his back on Salford and sign for Auckland

30 December 2000 - Reds' chief executive David Tarry tells League Express the club's finances won't stretch to signing Bobbie Goulding

5 January 2001 - Salford City Council agree in principle to a Joint Venture Agreement to build a new stadium at Barton

12 January 2001 - The Reds unveil new signing Bobbie Goulding after weeks of negotiations

24 January 2001 - Goulding suffers a broken thumb in the Reds' friendly with Wigan

5 February 2001 - Australian prop Damien Driscoll signs with the club

11 February 2001 - Salford are dumped out of the Challenge Cup by NFP side Leigh Centurions on live television

4 March 2001 - The Reds start Super League VI with a creditable 46-34 defeat at Hull

25 March 2001 - John Harvey's side record their first win of the season, beating Warrington 39-14 at Wilderspool, with Karle Hammond making his debut after joining from Widnes

15 April 2001 - The Reds move up to fifth in Super League with their third successive victory, beating Castleford 24-22 at the Jungle

30 April 2001 - Second-rower Warren Jowitt dislocates his shoulder in the

KEY DATES - SALFORD CITY REDS

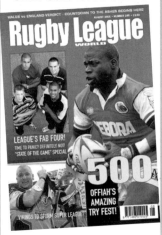

round eight defeat at Wakefield, and is ruled out for the remainder of the season

5 May 2001 - Danny Arnold joins from NFP side Oldham, while Andy Coley, Francis Maloney and Nick Pinkney all sign long-term deals with the Reds

13 May 2001 - The Reds stun Wigan 31-30 at the Willows, a result that ultimately leads to the sacking of Warriors' Frank Endacott

18 May 2001 - A Salford side without several injured players is beaten 66-16 at St Helens

13 June 2001 - Former Huddersfield and Bradford prop Neil Harmon joins the Reds on a performance-based contract

18 June 2001 - The Reds are linked with a move for disgraced Australian winger John Hopoate

1 July 2001 - League legend Martin Offiah scores his 500th career try in

Salford's 37-14 win in London

16 July 2001 - Press reports link the Reds with a move for Warrington's David Highton, who is currently serving a suspension after testing positive for steroids

21 July 2001 - John Harvey quits as Reds coach after the side loses 70-4 at Wigan. Salford immediately replace him with his assistant, Steve McCormack, who becomes Super League's youngest coach at the age of 28

29 July 2001 - McCormack's first game in charge ends in defeat, 18-56 at home to St Helens

5 August 2001 - The Reds record their first win under McCormack, defeating Wakefield Trinity Wildcats 25-16 at the Willows

12 August 2001 - Salford lose 35-14 at bottom club Huddersfield

23 August 2001 - The Reds announce the signing of Halifax utility-back Damian Gibson for the 2002 season

2 September 2001 - Hooker Malcolm Alker breaks the Super League record for most tackles in a season, his first in the game against London taking him past Luke Felsch's record of 942

16 September 2001 - Stuart Littler, Bobbie Goulding and Graham Holroyd are all sent off as the Reds lose at home to Wakefield on the final day of the season, their sixth straight loss

26 September 2001 - The Reds sign Australian prop/second-rower Darren Shaw from Castleford

7 October 2001 - Salford officials confirm the club has agreed terms with experienced Australian back-rower Darren Treacy, currently with St George Illawarra Dragons

8 October 2001 - Alker is presented with the Super League 'Hit Man' award at the Tetley's Man of Steel Dinner, in recognition of his tackling achievements during 2001

SALFORD CITY REDS

DATE	FIXTURE	RESULT	SCORERS	LGE	ATT
11/2/01	Leigh (a) (CCR4)	L16-12	t:Jowitt(2) g:Blakeley(2)	N/A	6,408
4/3/01	Hull (a)	L46-34	t:Maloney(2),Tassell,Highton,Pinkney,Offiah g:Goulding(5)	N/A	6,628
16/3/01	Bradford (h)	L6-40	t:Jowitt g:Goulding	11th	4,355
25/3/01	Warrington (a)	W14-39	t:Pinkney(2),Maloney(2),Offiah,Broadbent,Alker g:Goulding(5) fg:Holroyd	9th	6,147
8/4/01	Huddersfield (h)	W28-14	t:Tassell,Maloney,Hancock,Alker g:Goulding(6)	8th	3,793
13/4/01	Castleford (a)	W22-24	t:Maloney(2),Pinkney,Jowitt g:Goulding(4)	5th	6,816
16/4/01	London (h)	L12-14	t:Pinkney,Coley g:Goulding(2)	6th	3,967
22/4/01	Leeds (h)	L14-19	t:Littler,Hancock g:Goulding(2),Holroyd	8th	5,069
30/4/01	Wakefield (a)	L32-22	t:Maloney(2),Pinkney,Coley g:Holroyd(3)	9th	2,940
6/5/01	Halifax (a)	L30-18	t:Maloney(2),Blakeley,Wainwright g:Holroyd	11th	4,180
13/5/01	Wigan (h)	W31-30	t:Pinkney(3),Offiah,Hancock g:Holroyd(5) fg:Holroyd	8th	5,691
18/5/01	St Helens (a)	L66-16	t:Alker(2),Brown g:Maloney(2)	10th	7,837
27/5/01	Bradford (a)	L42-10	t:Littler,Arnold g:Blakeley	10th	10,907
3/6/01	Hull (h)	L24-36	t:Alker(2),Maloney,Hancock g:Blakeley(3),Goulding	11th	4,143
10/6/01	Warrington (h)	W26-18	t:Pinkney(2),Maloney,Highton g:Blakeley(5)	10th	4,963
17/6/01	Huddersfield (a)	W24-32	t:Littler(2),Alker,Coley,Blakeley g:Blakeley(5),Maloney	9th	2,721
23/6/01	Castleford (a)	L18-26	t:Offiah,Coley,Tassell g:Blakeley(3)	9th	3,530
1/7/01	London (a)	W14-37	t:Offiah(2),Wainwright,Blakeley,Tassell,Hammond g:Blakeley(6) fg:Goulding	9th	2,941
6/7/01	Leeds (a)	L56-6	t:Blakeley g:Blakeley	9th	10,119
15/7/01	Halifax (h)	L34-50	t:Arnold(3),Hancock,Pinkney,Tassell g:Goulding(3),Blakeley(2)	10th	3,597
20/7/01	Wigan (a)	L70-4	t:Pinkney	10th	8,085
29/7/01	St Helens (h)	L18-56	t:Broadbent,Arnold,Wainwright g:Holroyd(3)	10th	5,234
5/8/01	Wakefield (h)	W26-16	t:Nicol,Offiah,Hancock,Littler g:Holroyd(3),Blakeley fg:Goulding,Alker	9th	3,509
12/8/01	Huddersfield (a)	L35-14	t:Maloney(2),Littler g:Holroyd	9th	2,815
19/8/01	Wakefield (a)	L23-20	t:Nicol,Littler,Maloney g:Holroyd(4)	10th	2,376
26/8/01	Halifax (h)	L30-41	t:Littler(2),Holroyd,Pinkney,Blakeley,Maloney g:Holroyd(3)	10th	3,649
2/9/01	London (h)	L12-50	t:Driscoll,Maloney g:Holroyd(2)	10th	2,618
9/9/01	Hull (a)	L40-8	t:Littler g:Holroyd(2)	10th	6,262
16/9/01	Wakefield (h)	L24-32	t:Hancock,Baynes,Maloney,Littler g:Holroyd(4)	10th	4,264

	APP		TRIES		GOALS		FG		PTS	
	ALL	SL	ALL	SL	ALL	SL	ALL	SL	ALL	SL
Malcom Alker	29	28	7	7	0	0	1	1	29	29
Danny Arnold	6(12)	6(12)	5	5	0	0	0	0	20	20
Danny Barton	1	1	0	0	0	0	0	0	0	0
Neil Baxter	1	1	0	0	0	0	0	0	0	0
Neil Baynes	7(6)	7(5)	1	1	0	0	0	0	4	4
Steve Blakeley	21(2)	20(2)	5	5	29	27	0	0	78	74
Gary Broadbent	18	17	2	2	0	0	0	0	8	8
Darren Brown	8(8)	7(8)	1	1	0	0	0	0	4	4
Andy Coley	16(10)	15(10)	4	4	0	0	0	0	16	16
Damien Driscoll	23(1)	23(1)	1	1	0	0	0	0	4	4
Steve Garces	(1)	(1)	0	0	0	0	0	0	0	0
Andy Gorski	(1)	(1)	0	0	0	0	0	0	0	0
Bobbie Goulding	21	21	0	0	29	29	2	2	60	60
Karle Hammond	2(3)	2(3)	1	1	0	0	0	0	4	4
Michael Hancock	11(15)	10(15)	7	7	0	0	0	0	28	28
Neil Harmon	6(5)	6(5)	0	0	0	0	0	0	0	0
Paul Highton	19(7)	19(6)	2	2	0	0	0	0	8	8
Graham Holroyd	14(5)	13(5)	1	1	32	32	2	2	70	70
Warren Jowitt	9	8	4	2	0	0	0	0	16	8
Stuart Littler	23(3)	23(3)	11	11	0	0	0	0	44	44
Craig Makin	1(9)	1(8)	0	0	0	0	0	0	0	0
Francis Maloney	28	27	19	19	3	3	0	0	82	82
Iain Marsh	(3)	(3)	0	0	0	0	0	0	0	0
Lee Marsh	(2)	(2)	0	0	0	0	0	0	0	0
Jason Nicol	14(2)	14(2)	2	2	0	0	0	0	8	8
Martin Offiah	20	19	7	7	0	0	0	0	28	28
Nick Pinkney	28	27	14	14	0	0	0	0	56	56
Michael Platt	1	1	0	0	0	0	0	0	0	0
Paul Southern	12	11	0	0	0	0	0	0	0	0
Warren Stevens	(8)	(8)	0	0	0	0	0	0	0	0
Kris Tassell	13(6)	13(6)	5	5	0	0	0	0	20	20
Mike Wainwright	24(1)	23(1)	3	3	0	0	0	0	12	12

LEAGUE RECORD
P28-W8-D0-L20
(10th, SL)
F587, A956, Diff-369
16 points.

CHALLENGE CUP
Round Four

ATTENDANCES
Best - v Wigan (SL - 5,691)
Worst - v London (SL - 2,618)
Total (SL only) - 58,382
Average (SL only) - 4,170
(Down by 278 on 2000)

TOP TACKLES
Malcolm Alker 1050

TOP CARRIES
Andy Coley 318

TOP METRES
Andy Coley 2513

TOP BREAKS
Stuart Littler 26

TOP OFFLOADS
Michael Hancock 86

TOP BUSTS
Nick Pinkney 56

21 October 2000 - Ian Millward's father Bob slams reports down under that his son is set to take over as coach of St George Illawarra in 2002

23 October 2000 - The row over where Saints' World Club Challenge game with Brisbane Broncos will be played begins, after Super League confirm they want to stage the game at Wigan's JJB Stadium rather than Knowsley Road

9 November 2000 - Saints announce they will play their home games in Super League VI on Friday nights

20 November 2000 - St Helens' chief executive Mal Kay slams confirmation that the Brisbane game will be played at the JJB

24 November 2000 - Saints' officials admits problems over the town's proposed new stadium

4 December 2000 - The RFL confirm they will investigate both St Helens' and Halifax's claims that they have signed Leigh hooker Mick Higham

26 December 2000 - Higham debuts for Saints in the friendly against Wigan, although the RFL are still to investigate the transfer

8 January 2001 - Halifax claim they will seek £100,000 compensation for Higham

26 January 2001 - Saints stun reigning Australian Champions Brisbane Broncos by defeating them 20-18 in the World Club Challenge at the JJB Stadium

10 February 2001 - Millward's side dump arch-rivals Wigan out of the Challenge Cup with a stunning 22-8 victory at Knowsley Road in round four

4 March 2001 - Super League VI begins with a 31-24 defeat at Bradford Bulls

11 March 2001 - Millward reiterates that he is not seeking the St George Illawarra job

23 March 2001 - Saints reach an out-of-court settlement with Darrell Trindall, paying their former halfback £45,000 as compensation for his dismissal

24 March 2001 - Two late tries from Keiron Cunningham grab a late 20-18 victory at London

31 March 2001 - Saints reach the Challenge Cup Final with a 27-22 win over Leeds Rhinos at the JJB Stadium

20 April 2001 - Saints are trounced 56-22 at Warrington on the eve of the Challenge Cup Final

28 April 2001 - St Helens win the 2001 Challenge Cup by defeating Bradford Bulls 13-6 at Twickenham, Sean Long winning the Lance Todd Trophy

4 May 2001 - Saints suffer a Twickenham hangover and are thrashed 74-16 at Leeds

KEY DATES - ST HELENS

9 May 2001 - Tommy Martyn undergoes a hernia operation that is expected to keep him out for eight weeks

11 May 2001 - A dramatic last-minute Sean Long try secures victory over Halifax - Saints' second win in three days following victory over Castleford

28 May 2001 - Long is out for the season after seriously damaging his knee in a late tackle by Huddersfield's Brandon Costin

2 June 2001 - Saints shrug off the absences of Long and Martyn to beat Bradford 38-26 at Knowsley Road

22 June 2001 - Millward's side lose out to rivals Wigan by a point, courtesy of Andy Farrell's long-range field goal

30 June 2001 - Chris Joynt sets a new St Helens record of 87 consecutive appearances

3 July 2001 - Paul Newlove undergoes an Achilles tendon injury that rules him out for the remainder of the season

7 July 2001 - Saints announce that Australian prop David Fairleigh has signed a twelve-month extension to his contract

7 August 2001 - Keiron Cunningham gives St Helens and Rugby League in general a huge boost by turning his back on rugby union and signing a new four-year contract at Knowsley Road

10 August 2001 - Despite being without a number of stars, Saints gain revenge on Wigan with a 30-16 home win

1 September 2001 - Saints drop out of the top three following Hull's win at Huddersfield

2 September 2001 - Winger Anthony Sullivan is released by the club

5 September 2001 - Millward takes young Canterbury Bulldogs back Leon

Felton on trial until the end of the season

11 September 2001 - Sonny Nickle is hit with a six month suspension for a late high tackle on Leeds' Robbie Mears

14 September 2001 - Eric Hughes announces he is to step down as Saints' football operations manager at the end of the season

18 September 2001 - Nickle's suspension is changed to nine matches on appeal

22 September 2001 - Saints win their opening play-off game, beating Leeds 38-30 at Knowsley Road

25 September 2001 - Millward signs Great Britain Academy youngster Adrian Gardner from Barrow Border Raiders

26 September 2001 - Chris Joynt announce that he has signed a new three-year contract with the club

28 September 2001 - Saints' remarkable run continues as they hold off a Hull comeback to beat the Airlie Birds 24-20 in a thriller at the Boulevard

6 October 2001 - St Helens' bold bid to regain their Super League crown is ended at Wigan, where they lose 44-10 in the Final Eliminator

7 October 2001 - Millward rules star scrum-half Sean Long out of the Ashes series

8 October 2001 - Saints enjoy a memorable night at the annual Man of Steep Awards, with Paul Sculthorpe picking up the main prize and the Players' Player award, and Millward named as Coach of the Year

1 November 2001 - Jon Sharp is named as the man to replace Harry Bryant as Millward's assistant

ST HELENS

DATE	FIXTURE	RESULT	SCORERS	LGE	ATT
26/1/01	Brisbane (WCC)	W20-18	t:Sculthorpe,Long,Joynt g:Long(3) fg:Sculthorpe,Long	N/A	16,041
10/2/01	Wigan (h) (CCR4)	W22-8	t:Sullivan,Joynt,Jonkers,Stewart g:Long(3)	N/A	13,593
25/2/01	Whitehaven (a) (CCR5)	W22-34	t:Higham,Joynt,Wellens,Newlove,Hall,Martyn,McDonald g:Martyn(3)	N/A	4,750
4/3/01	Bradford (a)	L31-24	t:Newlove,Long,Fairleigh,Cunningham g:Long(4)	N/A	16,572
9/3/01	Huddersfield (h) (CCQF)	W54-16	t:Wellens(2),Long(2),Martyn,Joynt,Cunningham,Hall,Jonkers,Edmondson g:Long(7)	N/A	7,899
16/3/01	Huddersfield (h)	W44-22	t:Iro(2),Newlove,Jonkers,McDonald,Hoppe,Hall,Long g:Long(6)	6th	7,275
24/3/01	London (a)	W18-20	t:Cunningham(2),Hoppe,Joynt g:Long(2)	5th	3,736
31/3/01	Leeds (CCSF)	W22-27	t:Sculthorpe(2),Long,Martyn,Newlove g:Long(3) fg:Martyn	N/A	16,416
6/4/01	Wakefield (h)	W24-0	t:Iro,Newlove,Sullivan,Wellens g:Long(4)	4th	6,746
13/4/01	Wigan (a)	D22-22	t:Long,Iro,West,Sculthorpe g:Long(3)	4th	21,073
16/4/01	Hull (h)	W38-34	t:Stewart(2),Newlove(2),Cunningham,Hoppe,Wellens g:Long(5)	3rd	10,479
20/4/01	Warrington (a)	L56-22	t:Cunningham,Newlove,Hall,Jonkers g:Martyn(3)	4th	8,060
28/4/01	Bradford (CCF)	W6-13	t:Martyn,Cunningham g:Long(2) fg:Martyn	N/A	68,250
4/5/01	Leeds (a)	L74-16	t:Sullivan,Iro,Hall g:Long(2)	5th	15,702
9/5/01	Castleford (h)	W36-16	t:Stewart(2),Nickle,Long,Cunningham,Sullivan,Matautia g:Long(4)	5th	6,836
11/5/01	Halifax (h)	W32-26	t:Newlove(2),West,Cunningham,Sculthorpe,Hoppe g:Long(4)	4th	6,986
18/5/01	Salford (h)	W66-16	t:Stewart(3),Wellens(3),Sculthorpe,Joynt,Iro,Hall,Sullivan g:Long(11)	4th	7,837
28/5/01	Huddersfield (a)	W26-44	t:Sculthorpe(2),Newlove(2),Cunningham(2),Edmondson,Wellens g:Sculthorpe(5),Long	4th	3,559
2/6/01	Bradford (h)	W38-26	t:Joynt(2),Sculthorpe(2),Nickle,Stewart,Shiels g:Sculthorpe(5)	3rd	10,428
8/6/01	London (h)	W22-14	t:Fairleigh,Newlove,Joynt,Hall g:Wellens(3)	2nd	6,938
17/6/01	Wakefield (a)	W26-36	t:Sculthorpe(3),Iro,Shiels,Jonkers g:Sculthorpe(6)	2nd	4,157
22/6/01	Wigan (h)	L28-29	t:Fairleigh(2),Hoppe,Shiels,Newlove g:Sculthorpe(4)	3rd	13,830
30/6/01	Hull (a)	L34-28	t:Martyn(2),Newlove,Sculthorpe,Iro,Hall g:Sculthorpe(2)	4th	6,538
7/7/01	Warrington (h)	W70-16	t:McDonald(2),Hoppe(2),Sculthorpe(2),Stewart,Stankevitch,Martyn,Hall,Fairleigh,Higham g:Sculthorpe(11)	3rd	8,113
13/7/01	Leeds (h)	W46-24	t:Sculthorpe(3),Iro,Sullivan,Stankevitch,Martyn,Hoppe g:Sculthorpe(7)	3rd	8,913
22/7/01	Halifax (a)	W22-46	t:Sullivan(2),Cunningham(2),Martyn,Fairleigh,Sculthorpe,Matautia g:Sculthorpe(7)	3rd	5,142
29/7/01	Salford (a)	W18-56	t:Wellens(3),Hoppe(2),Cunningham,Martyn,Sculthorpe,Shiels,McDonald g:Sculthorpe(8)	3rd	5,234
3/8/01	Castleford (a)	L28-26	t:Hoppe(2),Shiels,Cunningham,Iro g:Sculthorpe(3)	3rd	7,054
10/8/01	Wigan (h)	W30-16	t:Wellens(2),Shiels,Sculthorpe,Jonkers g:Sculthorpe(5)	3rd	13,571
17/8/01	Bradford (a)	L27-14	t:Fairleigh(2),Stewart g:Sculthorpe	4th	13,805
26/8/01	Warrington (a)	D28-28	t:Cunningham(2),Martyn,Kirkpatrick,Wellens,Stankevitch g:Martyn,Wellens	4th	7,910
31/8/01	Castleford (h)	W44-20	t:McConnell(3),Hall,Stewart,Cunningham,Hoppe,Nickle g:Sculthorpe(6)	4th	7,680
7/9/01	Leeds (h)	L18-23	t:McConnell,Hoppe,Cunningham g:Sculthorpe(3)	4th	7,592
14/9/01	Wigan (a)	L40-6	t:Sculthorpe g:Sculthorpe	4th	15,235
22/9/01	Leeds (h) (EPO)	W38-30	t:Hall(2),Sculthorpe(2),Cunningham(2),Iro g:Sculthorpe(5)	N/A	8,467
28/9/01	Hull (a) (ESF)	W20-24	t:Kirkpatrick,Sculthorpe,Cunningham,Stankevitch,Martyn g:Sculthorpe(2)	N/A	9,186
6/10/01	Wigan (a) (FE)	L44-10	t:Iro,Sculthorpe g:Sculthorpe	N/A	19,260

	APP		TRIES		GOALS		FG		PTS	
	ALL	SL	ALL	SL	ALL	SL	ALL	SL	ALL	SL
Mike Bennett	1(4)	1(3)	0	0	0	0	0	0	0	0
Radney Bowker	(1)	(1)	0	0	0	0	0	0	0	0
John Braddish	(1)	(1)	0	0	0	0	0	0	0	0
Heath Cruckshank	1(12)	1(12)	0	0	0	0	0	0	0	0
Keiron Cunningham	34	29	22	20	0	0	0	0	88	80
Mark Edmondson	4(10)	4(9)	2	1	0	0	0	0	8	4
David Fairleigh	31(1)	26(1)	8	8	0	0	0	0	32	32
Leon Felton	1(1)	1(1)	0	0	0	0	0	0	0	0
Steve Hall	23(9)	21(7)	12	10	0	0	0	0	48	40
Bryan Henare	(2)	(1)	0	0	0	0	0	0	0	0
Mick Higham	3(11)	2(11)	2	1	0	0	0	0	8	4
Sean Hoppe	32(1)	27(1)	14	14	0	0	0	0	56	56
Kevin Iro	32	28	12	12	0	0	0	0	48	48
Tim Jonkers	13(24)	11(20)	6	4	0	0	0	0	24	16
Chris Joynt	32(2)	26(2)	9	5	0	0	0	0	36	20
John Kirkpatrick	3(3)	3(3)	2	2	0	0	0	0	8	8
Sean Long	16	11	8	4	64	46	1	0	161	108
Tommy Martyn	24	18	12	8	7	4	2	0	64	40
Vila Matautia	9(16)	8(13)	2	2	0	0	0	0	8	8
Dave McConnell	3(1)	3(1)	4	4	0	0	0	0	16	16
Mark McCully	(1)	0	0	0	0	0	0	0	0	0
Wayne McDonald	8(12)	7(11)	5	4	0	0	0	0	20	16
Paul Newlove	21	15	15	13	0	0	0	0	60	52
Sonny Nickle	28(3)	23(2)	3	3	0	0	0	0	12	12
Paul Sculthorpe	31	27	27	24	82	82	1	0	273	260
Peter Shiels	27(1)	22(1)	6	6	0	0	0	0	24	24
John Stankevitch	15(12)	14(8)	4	4	0	0	0	0	16	16
Anthony Stewart	25(7)	24(3)	12	11	0	0	0	0	48	44
Anthony Sullivan	26	20	8	7	0	0	0	0	32	28
Paul Wellens	35(1)	29(1)	15	12	4	4	0	0	68	56
Dwayne West	3(5)	2(5)	2	2	0	0	0	0	8	8

LEAGUE RECORD
P28-W17-D2-L9
(4th, SL/Final Eliminator)
F924, A732, Diff+192
36 points.

CHALLENGE CUP
Winners

ATTENDANCES
Best - v Wigan (SL - 13,830)
Worst - v Wakefield (SL - 6,746)
Total (SL, inc play-offs) - 131,691
Average (SL, inc play-offs) - 8,779
(Down by 51 on 2000)

TOP TACKLES
Tim Jonkers 656

TOP CARRIES
Paul Sculthorpe 429

TOP METRES
David Fairleigh 3344

TOP BREAKS
Keiron Cunningham 34

TOP OFFLOADS
Keiron Cunningham 77

TOP BUSTS
Keiron Cunningham 129

7 September 2000 - Trinity enter into a Company Voluntary Arrangement (CVA) and are forced end the contracts of six players - Steve McNamara, Francis Maloney, Tony Tatupu, Glen Tomlinson, Bright Sodje and Martin Masella. Tony Kemp resigns as coach, and Steve Prescott signs for Hull.

9 September 2000 - John Harbin is appointed as stand-in coach for the remaining two games of the season

19 September 2000 - Francis Stephenson and Adam Hughes join Wigan and Halifax respectively

20 September 2000 - The Wildcats receive the backing of the other Super League clubs to continue in the top flight, providing they produce a satisfactory business plan and receive the support of their creditors

22 September 2000 - Warren Jowitt and Francis Maloney sign for Salford

4 October 2000 - Trinity finally gain approval from their creditors for a CVA, allowing the club to start afresh financially. Steve Ferres returns to the club as recruitment director

12 October 2000 - The Wildcats re-sign Willie Poching and Gary Price, and Brad Davis agrees to return to the club from Castleford

10 November 2000 - John Harbin is confirmed as the Wildcats coach for the 2001 season

11 November 2000 - Julian O'Neill and Justin Brooker join, while Ryan Hudson agrees a new contract with the club

18 November 2000 - Harbin signs Martin Pearson, who had been released by Halifax Blue Sox earlier in the year

8 December 2000 - Australians Ben Rauter and Dane Dorahy are added to the squad

8 January 2001 - The Wildcats fail to raise the cash to buy the hospitality suite at the south end of Belle Vue

14 January 2001 - West Yorkshire Police confirm that an investigation has been launched by the fraud squad into 'financial irregularities' at Trinity

27 January 2001 - The Wildcats' Academy side defeats the Central Queensland development team 23-20 in Australia

11 March 2001 - Bradford Bulls dump the Wildcats out of the Cup, winning 38-0 at Belle Vue

24 March 2001 - Trinity get off the mark in Super League Round Three, defeating Halifax 30-14 at home

12 April 2001 - The Wildcats pull off the shock result of the season when they inflict Bradford Bulls' first defeat of the season, winning 16-12 at Belle Vue

KEY DATES - WAKEFIELD TRINITY WILDCATS

23 April 2001 - Eleven of their sacked players take Trinity to court, where an Industrial Tribunal finds the club guilty of unfair dismissal. However, the tribunal accepts the club doesn't have the funds to pay what the players are owed

20 May 2001 - The Wildcats' record a superb 30-24 win at Warrington, their fifth Super League victory in eleven games

29 June 2001 - Reports claim that Trinity could face a points penalty for breaching the salary cap in 2000

1 July 2001 - Huddersfield record their first win of the season by defeating the Wildcats 38-22 at Belle Vue

2 July 2001 - The Wildcats forward details of their expenditure for the 2000 season to Super League (Europe)

26 July 2001 - Trinity are docked four league points by Super League (Europe) after being found to have spent 71.1 percent of their income on players' salaries during 2000. The club

immediately indicates it will appeal against the decision

4 August 2001 - The RFL takes over the case on Super League (Europe)'s request

6 August 2001 - Ted Richardson steps down as Chairman of the club, with Tony Docherty appointed chief executive and charged with overseeing the establishment of a new board

9 August 2001 - Trinity's points deduction is reduced to two by the RFL, but the Wildcats signal their intentions to appeal again

19 August 2001 - The Wildcats end the longest losing sequence in the club's history when they overcome Salford City Reds 23-20 to stretch the gap between themselves and Huddersfield to three points with four games remaining

8 September 2001 - The Wildcats' fight against relegation goes to the final day of the season as they lose 21-19 at home to Huddersfield

15 September 2001 - Trinity secure safety with a dramatic, thrilling 32-24 win at Salford on the final day of the league season

19 September 2001 - It emerges that Trinity have failed Super League's Points Assessment Programme, again casting doubt on their future

21 September 2001 - Chief executive Tony Docherty resigns and Ted Richardson announces he will donate his shares to supporters' trust, with local MP David Hinchliffe a possible trustee

24 September 2001 - The club's supporters and shareholders rush to donate money to the Wildcats

3 October - Melbourne Storm announce that they have signed Trinity's 19 year old prop forward Keith Mason, with Trinity to receive a £35,000 transfer fee.

12 October 2001 - Leeds sign Willie Poching

WAKEFIELD T WILDCATS

DATE	FIXTURE	RESULT	SCORERS	LGE	ATT
11/2/01	Workington (a) (CCR4)	W6-56	t:Sovatabua(2),N Law(2),Price,Poching,Davis,Holland,Field,Brooker g:Pearson(8)	N/A	1,710
25/2/01	Oldham (a) (CCR5)	W6-26	t:Sovatabua(2),Field,Pearson,Tatupu g:Pearson(3)	N/A	3,071
4/3/01	Castleford (h)	L17-22	t:Sovatabua,Jackson g:Pearson(4) fg:Pearson	N/A	5,130
11/3/01	Bradford (h) (CCQF)	L0-38	No Scorers	N/A	6,500
16/3/01	Leeds (a)	L42-14	t:Sovatabua,Rauter g:Pearson(3)	8th	14,019
25/3/01	Halifax (h)	W30-14	t:Sovatabua,N Law,Hudson,Smith g:Pearson(7)	8th	3,147
6/4/01	St Helens (a)	L24-0	No Scorers	9th	6,746
12/4/01	Bradford (h)	W16-12	t:N Law(2),D March g:Pearson(2)	9th	4,729
16/4/01	Huddersfield (a)	W16-24	t:Rauter(2),Field,Sovatabua g:Pearson(4)	7th	3,516
22/4/01	London (h)	L10-38	t:Handforth g:Pearson(2),Westwood	10th	2,547
30/4/01	Salford (h)	W32-22	t:Price(2),Brooker(2),Field,Sovatabua g:P March (4)	7th	2,940
4/5/01	Wigan (a)	L50-6	t:D March g:Dorahy	8th	8,282
12/5/01	Hull (h)	L22-30	t:Hudson(2),N Law,D March g:Dorahy(3)	10th	3,876
20/5/01	Warrington (a)	W24-30	t:Sovatabua(2),Hudson,Field,Pearson g:Dorahy(5)	7th	6,231
26/5/01	Leeds (h)	L16-38	t:Brooker(2),Pearson g:Pearson(2)	7th	4,963
1/6/01	Castleford (a)	L26-22	t:Sovatabua,Watene,Dorahy g:Pearson(5)	9th	6,309
10/6/01	Halifax (a)	L26-20	t:O'Neill(2),Davis g:Pearson(4)	11th	4,863
17/6/01	St Helens (h)	L26-36	t:Sovatabua,Dorahy,Brooker,N Law,G Law g:Pearson(3)	11th	4,157
24/6/01	Bradford (a)	L62-10	t:Pearson,Price g:Pearson	11th	11,298
1/7/01	Huddersfield (h)	L22-38	t:N Law(2),Davis,Sovatabua g:Pearson(3)	11th	2,847
8/7/01	London (a)	L26-6	t:Brooker g:Pearson	11th	2,153
15/7/01	Wigan (h)	L23-29	t:Poching,P March,Dorahy g:Dorahy(5) fg:Dorahy	11th	4,011
22/7/01	Hull (a)	L48-16	t:Westwood,Brooker,Sovatabua g:Dorahy,Davis	11th	6,240
29/7/01	Warrington (h)	L18-19	t:Hudson,G Law,Ellis g:Dorahy(3)	11th	2,717
5/8/01	Salford (a)	L26-16	t:D March,Hudson,Field g:Dorahy,G Law	11th	3,509
12/8/01	London (a)	L44-18	t:N Law,Sovatabua,Ellis g:Pearson(3)	11th	2,126
19/8/01	Salford (h)	W23-20	t:N Law,Dorahy,Poching,Brooker g:Pearson(3) fg:Pearson	11th	2,376
27/8/01	Hull (h)	L18-30	t:Hudson(2),Ellis,Sovatabua g:Pearson	11th	3,518
2/9/01	Halifax (a)	W10-23	t:Westwood,Sovatabua,Rauter g:Pearson(5) fg:Pearson	11th	4,485
8/9/01	Huddersfield (h)	L19-21	t:Hudson,Brooker,D March g:Pearson(2),G Law fg:Hudson	11th	4,150
16/9/01	Salford (a)	W24-32	t:N Law(2),Ellis,Poching,D March g:Pearson(5),Davis	11th	4,264

	APP		TRIES		GOALS		FG		PTS	
	ALL	SL	ALL	SL	ALL	SL	ALL	SL	ALL	SL
Nathan Batty	1(1)	1(1)	0	0	0	0	0	0	0	0
Justin Brooker	28	25	10	9	0	0	0	0	40	36
Brad Davis	16(3)	14(3)	3	2	2	2	0	0	16	12
Dane Dorahy	14(2)	14(2)	4	4	19	19	1	1	55	55
Gareth Ellis	7(8)	7(7)	4	4	0	0	0	0	16	16
Chris Feather	(5)	(5)	0	0	0	0	0	0	0	0
Jamie Field	26(3)	23(3)	6	4	0	0	0	0	24	16
Paul Handforth	5(5)	5(5)	1	1	0	0	0	0	4	4
Lionel Harbin	(1)	(1)	0	0	0	0	0	0	0	0
Tom Haughey	3(8)	2(6)	0	0	0	0	0	0	0	0
Martyn Holland	17(1)	14(1)	1	0	0	0	0	0	4	0
Ryan Hudson	25(4)	25(1)	9	9	0	0	1	1	37	37
Paul Jackson	16(12)	15(10)	1	1	0	0	0	0	4	4
Graham Law	9(15)	9(14)	2	2	2	2	0	0	12	12
Neil Law	25	23	13	11	0	0	0	0	52	44
David March	18(3)	16(3)	6	6	0	0	0	0	24	24
Paul March	8(5)	7(5)	1	1	4	4	0	0	12	12
Keith Mason	5(16)	5(15)	0	0	0	0	0	0	0	0
Julian O'Neill	27(1)	24(1)	2	2	0	0	0	0	8	8
Martin Pearson	24(1)	21(1)	4	3	71	60	3	3	161	135
Willie Poching	24(1)	23(1)	4	3	0	0	0	0	16	12
Gary Price	16(8)	13(8)	4	3	0	0	0	0	16	12
Ben Rauter	17(6)	15(6)	4	4	0	0	0	0	16	16
Richard Smith	11(1)	8(1)	1	1	0	0	0	0	4	4
Waisale Sovatabua	31	28	18	14	0	0	0	0	72	56
Tony Tatupu	3(1)	2	1	0	0	0	0	0	4	0
Frank Watene	13(10)	11(9)	1	1	0	0	0	0	4	4
Ben Westwood	14(3)	14(3)	2	2	1	1	0	0	10	10

LEAGUE RECORD
P28-W8-D0-L20
(11th, SL)
F529, A817, Diff-288
14 points. *(deducted two points for breach of salary cap rules)*

CHALLENGE CUP
Quarter Finalists

ATTENDANCES
Best - v Bradford (CC - 6,500)
Worst - v Salford (SL - 2,376)
Total (SL only) - 51,108
Average (SL only) - 3,651
(Down by 964 on 2000)

TOP TACKLES
Ryan Hudson 673

TOP CARRIES
Julian O'Neill 382

TOP METRES
Waisale Sovatabua 2620

TOP BREAKS
Waisale Sovatabua 21

TOP OFFLOADS
Willie Poching 70

TOP BUSTS
Willie Poching 88

25 September 2000 - The Wolves sign former Wakefield star Martin Masella

25 September 2000 - Plans for a new stadium for the club are placed in jeopardy, as the deputy leader of Warrington Council writes to the government opposing the project

9 October 2000 - Warrington release veteran winger and long-serving player Mark Forster

13 October 2000 - Lee Briers signs a new two-year deal with the Wolves to keep him at Wilderspool until the end of the 2002 season

6 November 2000 - The club starts its own internal fraud investigation after claims that around £300,000 is owed to the Inland Revenue

13 November 2000 - Darryl Van de Velde denies reports that club captain Allan Langer wants to terminate his contract with the Wolves and return to Australia

13 November 2000 - Jon Roper moves across the Pennines to Castleford Tigers

17 November 2000 - Reports in Australia claim new signing Kevin Campion is rumoured to be having second thoughts about joining the Wolves

20 November 2000 - Alan Hunte changes codes temporarily, signing for Welsh rugby union team Pontypridd

12 December 2000 - Wolves announce the signing of New Zealand Maori star David Kidwell

18 December 2000 - Brisbane Broncos' 33 year old stand-off Kevin Walters comes out of retirement and signs for the Wolves on a two-year deal after Campion signs for Auckland

15 January 2001 - News surfaces that deputy Prime Minister John Prescott has ordered a public inquiry into whether plans for a new stadium should be granted

11 February 2001 - The Wolves defeat amateur side and near-neighbours Woolston Rovers 48-6 in the fourth round of the Silk Cut Challenge Cup in front of 6,008 fans

5 March 2001 - After the Wolves' 34-6 defeat at the hands of Wigan Warriors at the JJB Stadium, in their opening fixture of Super League VI, both clubs issue public apologies for a bad-tempered game in which the Wolves had two players dismissed

11 March 2001 - Warrington reach the semi-final of the Challenge Cup with a 32-0 win over French Cup-holders Villeneuve Leopards

12 March 2001 - Tesco and Carlsberg Tetley both agree in principal to ease the financial problems at Wilderspool by lending the Wolves around £250,000 each

17 March 2001 - Warrington are hit by the news that Kevin Walters will return to Australia after his family fail to settle in England

19 March 2001 - The Wolves face an anxious wait after it is revealed that one of their players, David Highton, has tested positive for drugs

1 April 2001 - Warrington put up a brave fight but are eventually overcome by Bradford 39-22 in the Silk Cut Challenge Cup semi-final at the McAlpine Stadium

KEY DATES - WARRINGTON WOLVES

6 April 2001 - The Warrington club is left in a state of shock after receiving news of the suicide of Tawera Nikau's wife Letitia, a day after the death of Lee Briers' older brother Brian, who loses his battle against cancer

12 April 2001 - A convincing 36-6 home victory for the Wolves over the Leeds Rhinos brings to an end their four match losing streak in Super League

16 April 2001 - Former star Gary Mercer is snapped up by the Wolves after he resigns as player-coach of Halifax Blue Sox

16 April 2001 - Australian star Steve Georgallis ruptures his Achilles tendon in the narrow 32-30 victory over the Halifax Blue Sox, ruling him out for the season

20 April 2001 - Coach Darryl Van de Velde pays a special tribute to his skipper Allan Langer after the Wolves demolish St Helens 56-22 at Wilderspool

21 April 2001 - The Wolves hold a public rally at the Parr Hall in Warrington town centre to outline plans for their new stadium

1 June 2001 - The Wolves stun the Wigan Warriors, fighting back from an early 12-0 deficit to defeat their rivals 47-38 in a thrilling match at Wilderspool

10 June 2001 - Warrington and New Zealand Maori international Toa-Kohe Love is sent off for the second time in Super League VI, after only 30 minutes of the match against Salford City Reds which the Wolves lose 26-18

22 June 2001 - Warrington's Australian scrum-half Allan Langer flies home to Brisbane to make a surprise appearance for Queensland in their State of Origin clash against New South Wales

1 July 2001 - Langer plays a major role in Queensland's 40-14 success over New South Wales in the third and deciding State of Origin encounter in Brisbane

8 July 2001 - Warrington crash to their heaviest defeat of the season so far, a 70-16 thrashing at the hands of St Helens

9 July 2001 - Warrington's Jon Clarke, on-

loan from the London Broncos, agrees to a full-time contract with the club that will keep him at Wilderspool until the end of 2002

15 July 2001 - The Wolves slump to a 52-10 defeat against bottom club Huddersfield

16 July 2001 - Australian prop Danny Nutley announces he is to leave the club at the end of the season to take up a two-year contract with Cronulla Sharks

29 July 2001 - Darryl Van de Velde steps down as coach after the Wolves 19-18 win at Wakefield

4 August 2001 - Newly-appointed Performance Director Steve Anderson gets off to a flying start as his Wolves pull off a shock 18-14 victory over table-toppers Bradford Bulls

12 August 2001 - Reports in the Australian media suggest Allan Langer quit the Wolves because the club fell behind on contract payments, and not because of an injured ankle

14 August 2001 - Gary Mercer leaves the Wolves and joins Leeds Rhinos

17 August 2001 - Leigh Centurions' Welsh international front-rower Dave Whittle joins Warrington on loan

20 August 2001 - Toa-Kohe-Love announces he is to leave the club, having signed a two-year contract with Hull FC

20 August 2001 - The Wolves take Western Samoan international Anthony Swann, 26, on trial as a possible replacement Kohe-Love

26 August 2001 - The Wolves draw 28-28 in an epic encounter against rivals St Helens

27 August 2001 - Lee Penny and Jerome Guisset both sign new deals with Warrington, as the club also announces the on-loan signing of Dewsbury Rams' Kevin Crouthers and the acquisition of Penrith Panthers utility player Sid Domic for 2002

9 September 2001 - Warrington go down to their heaviest defeat of the season with an 84-12 mauling by the Bradford Bulls at Wilderspool

10 September 2001 - Warrington's up-and-coming young centre Ian Sibbit agrees to join NRL side Melbourne Storm

10 September 2001 - The Wolves announce the signings of Papua New Guinea World Cup star Tom O'Reilly, Kiwi forward Matt Sturm and Australian centre Craig Weston

11 September 2001 - Tawera Nikau confirms he will leave the club at the end of the season and return home to New Zealand

11 September 2001 - Welsh international Dave Whittle rejects a contract to play with the Wolves

14 September 2001 - Warrington announce the signings of props Dale Laughton, 30, and Nick Fozzard, 24, on two-year contracts

24 September 2001 - The club announces the signing of 27 year-old Brisbane Broncos forward Darren Burns

1 November 2001 - Australian utility-back Leon Felton signs for the Wolves after an unsuccessful trial spell with St Helens

WARRINGTON WOLVES

DATE	FIXTURE	RESULT	SCORERS	LGE	ATT
11/2/01	Woolston (h) (CCR4)	W48-6	t:Sibbit(3),Knott,Stenhouse,Nikau,Walters,Kidwell,Noone g:Smyth(6)	N/A	6,008
25/2/01	Leigh (h) (CCR5)	W20-10	t:McCurrie(2),Langer,Guisset g:Briers(2)	N/A	8,844
2/3/01	Wigan (a)	L34-6	t:Sibbit g:Briers	N/A	11,318
11/3/01	Villeneuve (h) (CCQF)	W32-0	t:Briers(3),Smyth(2),Kidwell,Langer g:Briers(2)	N/A	4,805
18/3/01	Hull (h)	L20-32	t:Hunte(2),Briers,Georgallis g:Smyth(2)	10th	7,577
25/3/01	Salford (h)	L14-39	t:Kohe-Love(2),Smyth g:Smyth	12th	6,147
1/4/01	Bradford (CCSF)	L39-22	t:Briers(3),Smyth g:Briers(3)	N/A	13,856
7/4/01	Castleford (a)	L18-0	No Scorers	12th	6,293
12/4/01	Leeds (h)	W36-6	t:Sibbit(3),Kidwell,Kidwell,Georgallis,Kohe-Love g:Smyth(4)	11th	5,871
16/4/01	Halifax (a)	W30-32	t:Busby(2),Smyth(2),Hunte,Masella g:Briers(4)	11th	4,889
20/4/01	St Helens (h)	W56-22	t:Hunte(3),Kohe-Love(3),Sibbit(2),Smyth(2) g:Briers(8)	9th	8,060
2/5/01	Bradford (a)	L56-24	t:Mercer,Masella,Nikau,Briers g:Briers(4)	9th	9,663
6/5/01	Huddersfield (h)	W36-16	t:Hunte,Briers,Nikau,Kohe-Love,Sibbit,Guisset g:Briers(6)	7th	5,912
13/5/01	London (a)	L38-16	t:Hunte(2),Busby g:Briers(2)	9th	3,796
20/5/01	Wakefield (h)	L24-30	t:Smyth,Kidwell,Sibbit,Penny g:Briers(4)	9th	6,231
27/5/01	Hull (a)	L32-16	t:Kidwell(2),Wood g:Briers(2)	9th	5,968
1/6/01	Wigan (h)	W47-38	t:Briers(2),Kidwell,McCurrie,Hunte,Langer,Penny,Kohe-Love g:Briers(7) fg:Briers	8th	7,766
10/6/01	Salford (a)	L26-18	t:Penny(2),Clarke,Busby g:Smyth	9th	4,963
17/6/01	Castleford (h)	W30-16	t:Sibbit,McCurrie,Hunte,Clarke,Briers g:Briers(5)	8th	6,002
22/6/01	Leeds (a)	D24-24	t:McCurrie,Smyth,Penny,Masella g:Briers(4)	8th	12,178
1/7/01	Halifax (a)	W34-22	t:Hunte(2),Nikau,Kidwell,Smyth,Sibbit g:Briers(5)	7th	5,628
7/7/01	St Helens (a)	L70-16	t:Penny,Kidwell,McCurrie g:Briers(2)	8th	8,113
15/7/01	Huddersfield (a)	L52-10	t:Hunte,Masella g:Briers	8th	3,203
21/7/01	London (h)	L28-31	t:Smyth(2),Penny,Mercer,McCurrie g:Briers(4)	8th	4,249
29/7/01	Wakefield (a)	W18-19	t:Langer,Kohe-Love,Clarke g:Briers(3) fg:Briers	8th	2,717
4/8/01	Bradford (h)	W18-14	t:Gleeson,McCurrie,Smyth g:Smyth(3)	8th	4,929
12/8/01	Castleford (h)	W27-12	t:Kohe-Love(3),Hulse g:Briers(5) fg:Briers	7th	5,235
17/8/01	Wigan (a)	L28-12	t:Noone,Nikau g:Briers(2)	8th	9,692
26/8/01	St Helens (h)	D28-28	t:Crouthers(2),Penny,Kidwell,Kohe-Love g:Briers(3),Knott	7th	7,910
31/8/01	Leeds (a)	L16-12	t:Penny,Nikau,Swann	7th	10,291
9/9/01	Bradford (h)	L12-84	t:Crouthers,Knott g:Briers(2)	7th	8,393
16/9/01	Castleford (a)	W28-31	t:Gleeson(2),Clarke,Hunte,Masella g:Briers(5) fg:Briers	7th	6,019

	APP		TRIES		GOALS		FG		PTS		
	ALL	SL	ALL	SL	ALL	SL	ALL	SL	ALL	SL	
David Alstead	5(8)	5(7)	0	0	0	0	0	0	0	0	
David Bates	1(2)	1(2)	0	0	0	0	0	0	0	0	
Lee Briers	25(2)	23(1)	12	6	86	79	4	4	224	186	
Dean Busby	18(4)	14(4)	4	4	0	0	0	0	16	16	
Jon Clarke	17(1)	17(1)	4	4	0	0	0	0	16	16	
Kevin Crouthers	4	4	3	3	0	0	0	0	12	12	
Andrew Gee	8(1)	6(1)	0	0	0	0	0	0	0	0	
Steve Georgallis	8(2)	5(1)	2	2	0	0	0	0	8	8	
Mark Gleeson	2(1)	2(1)	3	3	0	0	0	0	12	12	
Jerome Guisset	20(9)	19(6)	2	1	0	0	0	0	8	4	
David Highton	12	9	0	0	0	0	0	0	0	0	
John Hill	(1)	(1)	0	0	0	0	0	0	0	0	
Gary Hulse	5(1)	5(1)	1	1	0	0	0	0	4	4	
Alan Hunte	28	26	16	16	0	0	0	0	64	64	
David Kidwell	15(11)	12(10)	10	8	0	0	0	0	40	32	
Ian Knott	5(3)	4(3)	2	1	1	1	0	0	10	6	
Toa Kohe-Love	21(2)	20(1)	13	13	0	0	0	0	52	52	
Allan Langer	23	19	4	2	0	0	0	0	16	8	
Martin Masella	13(14)	10(14)	5	5	0	0	0	0	20	20	
Steve McCurrie	17(10)	16(8)	8	6	0	0	0	0	32	24	
Gary Mercer	18	18	2	2	0	0	0	0	8	8	
Tawera Nikau	28	24	6	5	0	0	0	0	24	20	
Paul Noone	7(10)	7(8)	2	1	0	0	0	0	8	4	
Danny Nutley	25(2)	23(1)	0	0	0	0	0	0	0	0	
Tom O'Reilly	(1)	(1)	0	0	0	0	0	0	0	0	
Ian Parry	(1)	(1)	0	0	0	0	0	0	0	0	
Lee Penny	18(1)	16(1)	9	9	0	0	0	0	36	36	
Alan Reddicliffe	1	1	0	0	0	0	0	0	0	0	
Ian Sibbit	25(2)	21(2)	13	10	0	0	0	0	52	40	
Paul Smith	(1)	(1)	0	0	0	0	0	0	0	0	
Rob Smyth	26	22	14	11	17	11	0	0	90	66	
Jamie Stenhouse	9(4)	6(3)	1	0	0	0	0	0	4	0	
Anthony Swann	3	3	1	1	0	0	0	0	4	4	
Steve Thomas	2	2	0	0	0	0	0	0	0	0	
Kris Tickle	(1)	(1)	0	0	0	0	0	0	0	0	
Kevin Walters	4	1	1	0	0	0	0	0	4	0	
David Whittle	1(2)	1(2)	0	0	0	0	0	0	0	0	
Paul Wood	2(22)	2(20)	1	1	0	0	0	0	4	4	

LEAGUE RECORD
P28-W11-D2-L15
(7th, SL)
F646, A860, Diff-214
24 points.

CHALLENGE CUP
Semi Finalists

ATTENDANCES
Best - v Leigh (CC - 8,844)
Worst - v London (SL - 4,249)
Total (SL only) - 89,910
Average (SL only) - 6,422
(Down by 450 on 2000)

TOP TACKLES
Danny Nutley 726

TOP CARRIES
Alan Hunte 362

TOP METRES
Alan Hunte 2630

TOP BREAKS
Alan Hunte 26

TOP OFFLOADS
David Kidwell 40

TOP BUSTS
Alan Hunte 72

19 September 2000 - The Warriors sign prop Francis Stephenson from Wakefield

10 November 2000 - Wigan announce the signing of local-born prop Mark Hilton from Warrington

15 November 2000 - The club confirms that their home games in Super League VI will be staged on Friday nights, despite protests from supporters

5 January 2001 - The Warriors sign prop Harvey Howard from NRL club Brisbane Broncos following the collapse of Hilton's move, due to a broken arm

10 January 2001 - New signing Adrian Lam arrives in England

15 January 2001 - Chairman Maurice Lindsay dismisses newspaper speculation linking the club with a merger with rugby union club Leicester Tigers

10 February 2001 - The Warriors are dumped out of the Challenge Cup in Round Four, as they are defeated 22-8 by rivals St Helens at Knowsley Road

2 March 2001 - The Warriors kick off Super League VI with an explosive 34-6 defeat of Warrington in which two players are dismissed and two others sin-binned

13 April 2001 - A late Saints comeback earns them a 22-all draw on Good Friday in front of a JJB Stadium record crowd of 21,073

16 April 2001 - Skipper Andy Farrell scores his 2,000th point for Wigan in the defeat at Bradford

29 April 2001 - Wigan are blasted by coach Frank Endacott after a 20-12 defeat at London

13 May 2001 - The Warriors crash to a 31-30 defeat at Salford City Reds

14 May 2001 - Endacott is sacked

15 May 2001 - Castleford Tigers' coach

KEY DATES - WIGAN WARRIORS

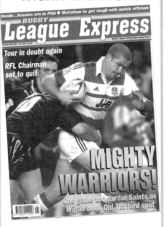

Stuart Raper is unveiled as the man to take charge of the Warriors

18 May 2001 - Raper wins his first game in charge of the Warriors, a stunning 46-10 victory at Hull

22 June 2001 - A long-range Farrell field goal proves to be the difference as Wigan edge out Saints at Knowsley Road 29-28

25 June 2001 - Chairman Lindsay defends Super League's decision to exempt Wigan from the salary cap for the 2002 season

29 June 2001 - Wigan close in on leaders Bradford by beating them 44-30 at the JJB

1 July 2001 - Reports emerge linking Cronulla Sharks with a move for Warriors' stand-off Matthew Johns, even though he is contracted to Wigan for a further season

29 July 2001 - A Sunday newspaper report quoting Wigan owner Dave Whelan as saying he is ready to establish a rugby union club in the town is played down by chairman Lindsay

28 August 2001 - The Warriors are given a huge boost with Kris Radlinski's decision to stay with the club and Rugby League, turning down a huge offer from union

31 August 2001 - Wigan throw the race for the Minor Premiership open again by beating Bradford 16-10

15 September 2001 - Despite having comfortably beaten Saints 40-6 a day earlier, Wigan miss out on the Minor Premiership on points difference when Bradford beat Leeds

21 September 2001 - The Warriors win their opening play-off game against Hull but only just, 27-24 at the JJB

30 September 2001 - The Warriors lose their Qualifying Semi-final against Bradford, going down 24-18 at Valley Parade

6 October 2001 - Wigan are in their second successive Grand Final by virtue of a comprehensive 44-10 home defeat of St Helens

13 October 2001 - A stunning first half sees Wigan trail Bradford 26-0 in the Grand Final, and they never recover, losing 37-6 at Old Trafford

WIGAN WARRIORS

DATE	FIXTURE	RESULT	SCORERS	LGE	ATT
10/2/01	St Helens (a) (CCR4)	L22-8	t:Connolly g:Farrell(2)	N/A	13,593
2/3/01	Warrington (h)	W34-6	t:Lam(2),Betts,Johnson,Hodgson,Renouf g:Farrell(5)	N/A	11,318
17/3/01	Castleford (a)	W8-24	t:Jones(3),Dallas g:Farrell(2),Jones(2)	2nd	7,214
23/3/01	Leeds (h)	W42-6	t:Renouf(2),Johnson(2),Farrell,Radlinski,Furner g:Farrell(7)	1st	12,321
6/4/01	Halifax (a)	W10-20	t:Newton(2),Farrell g:Farrell(4)	1st	4,549
13/4/01	St Helens (h)	D22-22	t:Radlinski(2),Renouf(2) g:Farrell(3)	1st	21,073
16/4/01	Bradford (a)	L35-24	t:Newton,Johns,Davies,Lam g:Farrell(4)	2nd	16,247
20/4/01	Huddersfield (h)	W37-8	t:Carney(2),Radlinski,Furner,Dallas,Jones g:Furner(4),Farrell(2) fg:Johns	1st	7,772
29/4/01	London (a)	L20-12	t:Johns,Radlinski g:Farrell(2)	1st	5,101
4/5/01	Wakefield (h)	W50-6	t:Radlinski(2),Lam,Renouf,Connolly,Furner,Farrell,Dallas g:Farrell(9)	3rd	8,282
13/5/01	Salford (a)	L31-30	t:Dallas,Lam,Furner,Hodgson g:Farrell(7)	3rd	5,691
19/5/01	Hull (a)	W10-46	t:Betts(2),Renouf(2),Furner,Radlinski,Dallas,Connolly g:Farrell(7)	3rd	7,581
25/5/01	Castleford (h)	W54-12	t:Radlinski(2),Newton(2),Johnson(2),Hodgson,Farrell,Jones g:Farrell(9)	3rd	10,190
1/6/01	Warrington (a)	L47-38	t:Radlinski(2),Johnson(2),Betts,Farrell g:Farrell(7)	5th	7,766
8/6/01	Leeds (a)	W18-36	t:Renouf(2),Lam,Farrell,Carney g:Farrell(8)	4th	14,435
15/6/01	Halifax (h)	W50-18	t:Renouf(3),Furner(2),Lam,Newton,Farrell,Hodgson g:Farrell(7)	3rd	9,038
22/6/01	St Helens (a)	W28-29	t:Radlinski(2),Furner,Farrell g:Farrell(6) fg:Farrell	2nd	13,830
29/6/01	Bradford (h)	W44-30	t:Radlinski(3),Carney,Renouf,Furner,Betts g:Farrell(8)	2nd	14,886
8/7/01	Huddersfield (a)	W24-48	t:Farrell(2),Radlinski(2),Newton,Hodgson,Howard,Furner g:Farrell(8)	2nd	4,039
15/7/01	Wakefield (h)	W23-29	t:Furner,Dallas,Renouf,Farrell,Johnson g:Farrell(4) fg:Farrell	2nd	4,011
20/7/01	Salford (h)	W70-4	t:Newton(3),Radlinski(3),Farrell(2),Cassidy,Johnson,Carney,Betts g:Farrell(11)	2nd	8,085
27/7/01	Hull (h)	W36-12	t:Carney(2),Renouf,Radlinski,Johnson,Farrell g:Farrell(6)	2nd	9,174
3/8/01	London (h)	W46-18	t:Radlinski(2),Farrell,Johnson,Furner,Chester,Renouf,Cassidy g:Farrell(7)	2nd	8,244
10/8/01	St Helens (a)	L30-16	t:Newton,Johnson g:Farrell(4)	2nd	13,571
17/8/01	Warrington (h)	W28-12	t:Dallas(2),Johnson,Hodgson,Carney g:Farrell(4)	2nd	9,692
24/8/01	Leeds (a)	W18-38	t:Newton(2),Connolly,Johnson,Lam,Farrell g:Farrell(7)	2nd	11,585
31/8/01	Bradford (h)	W16-10	t:Dallas,Radlinski g:Farrell(3) fg:Farrell(2)	2nd	15,052
9/9/01	Castleford (a)	W22-30	t:Lam,Radlinski,Renouf,Johnson,Connolly,Carney g:Farrell(3)	2nd	7,546
14/9/01	St Helens (h)	W40-6	t:Carney(2),Renouf,Furner,Newton,Betts,Hodgson g:Farrell(6)	2nd	15,235
21/9/01	Hull (h) (QPO)	W27-24	t:Farrell,Carney,Radlinski,Betts g:Farrell(5) fg:Farrell	N/A	9,103
30/9/01	Bradford (a) (QSF)	L24-18	t:Renouf,Radlinski,Hodgson g:Farrell(3)	N/A	13,216
6/10/01	St Helens (h) (FE)	W44-10	t:Lam(2),Carney(2),Radlinski,Newton,Johns g:Farrell(8)	N/A	19,260
13/10/01	Bradford (GF)	L37-6	t:Lam g:Furner	N/A	60,164

	APP		TRIES		GOALS		FG		PTS	
	ALL	SL	ALL	SL	ALL	SL	ALL	SL	ALL	SL
Martin Aspinwall	(6)	(6)	0	0	0	0	0	0	0	0
Denis Betts	11(21)	10(21)	8	8	0	0	0	0	32	32
Ricky Bibey	(4)	(4)	0	0	0	0	0	0	0	0
Brian Carney	18(5)	18(5)	14	14	0	0	0	0	56	56
Mick Cassidy	21(9)	21(8)	2	2	0	0	0	0	8	8
Chris Chester	6(6)	6(6)	1	1	0	0	0	0	4	4
Gary Connolly	16(1)	15(1)	5	4	0	0	0	0	20	16
Neil Cowie	19(13)	18(13)	0	0	0	0	0	0	0	0
Brett Dallas	25	24	9	9	0	0	0	0	36	36
Wes Davies	3(4)	3(3)	1	1	0	0	0	0	4	4
Andy Farrell	33	32	17	17	178	176	5	5	429	425
David Furner	31(1)	30(1)	13	13	5	5	0	0	62	62
Simon Haughton	1(6)	1(5)	0	0	0	0	0	0	0	0
David Hodgson	19(6)	19(6)	8	8	0	0	0	0	32	32
Harvey Howard	18(9)	18(8)	1	1	0	0	0	0	4	4
Matthew Johns	25	24	3	3	0	0	1	1	13	13
Paul Johnson	26(5)	25(5)	15	15	0	0	0	0	60	60
Phil Jones	4(4)	4(4)	5	5	2	2	0	0	24	24
Adrian Lam	30	29	12	12	0	0	0	0	48	48
Terry Newton	32	31	15	15	0	0	0	0	60	60
Terry O'Connor	27(3)	26(3)	0	0	0	0	0	0	0	0
Kris Radlinski	31	30	30	30	0	0	0	0	120	120
Steve Renouf	27	26	20	20	0	0	0	0	80	80
Mark Smith	3(11)	3(11)	0	0	0	0	0	0	0	0
Francis Stephenson	2(9)	2(9)	0	0	0	0	0	0	0	0
Stephen Wild	1(2)	1(2)	0	0	0	0	0	0	0	0

LEAGUE RECORD
P28-W22-D1-L5
(2nd, SL/Grand Final Runners Up)
F989, A494, Diff+495
45 points.

CHALLENGE CUP
Round Four

ATTENDANCES
Best - v St Helens (SL - 21,073)
Worst - v Huddersfield (SL - 7,772)
Total (SL, inc play-offs) - 188,725
Average (SL, inc play-offs) - 11,795
(Up by 466 on 2000)

TOP TACKLES
Terry Newton 647

TOP CARRIES
Andy Farrell 492

TOP METRES
Andy Farrell 3811

TOP BREAKS
Kris Radlinski 37

TOP OFFLOADS
Terry Newton 65

TOP BUSTS
Andy Farrell 80

SUPER LEAGUE VI
Round by Round

ROUND 1

Friday 2nd March 2001

WIGAN WARRIORS 34 WARRINGTON WOLVES 6

WARRIORS: 1 Kris Radlinski; 2 Brett Dallas; 15 Paul Johnson; 3 Steve Renouf; 23 David Hodgson; 6 Matthew Johns; 7 Adrian Lam; 8 Terry O'Connor; 9 Terry Newton; 10 Neil Cowie; 12 Denis Betts; 14 David Furner; 13 Andy Farrell (C). Subs: 11 Mick Cassidy for O'Connor (41); 17 Francis Stephenson (D) for Betts (42); 21 Mark Smith for Newton (55); 18 Wes Davies for Radlinski (67); O'Connor for Cowie (59); Betts for Johns (70).
Tries: Lam (24, 35), Betts (31), Johnson (43), Hodgson (65), Renouf (72); **Goals:** Farrell 5.
Sin bin: Cowie (45) - fighting.
WOLVES: 6 Lee Briers; 2 Rob Smyth; 4 Toa Kohe-Love; 16 Ian Sibbit; 1 Lee Penny; 14 Kevin Walters; 7 Allan Langer (C); 10 Danny Nutley; 9 David Highton; 12 Jerome Guisset; 11 Steve McCurrie; 20 Dean Busby; 13 Tawera Nikau. Subs: 15 Steve Georgallis for Busby (22BB); 3 David Kidwell for Georgallis (41); 24 Paul Noone for McCurrie (59); 5 Jamie Stenhouse for Penny (79); Busby for Guisset (53); Guisset for Nutley (68); Georgallis for Highton (68).
Try: Sibbit (2); **Goal:** Briers.
Sent off: Kohe-Love (28) - high tackle; Nikau (78) - striking.
Sin bin: Kidwell (45) - fighting.
On report: Brawls in the 45th and 78th minutes.
League Express Men of the Match:
Warriors: Adrian Lam; *Wolves:* Allan Langer.
Penalty count: 7-8; **Half-time:** 18-6;
Referee: Steve Ganson (St Helens); **Attendance:** 11,318.

Saturday 3rd March 2001

LONDON BRONCOS 18 LEEDS RHINOS 50

BRONCOS: 4 Greg Fleming; 5 Brett Warton; 2 Nigel Roy; 3 Tony Martin; 28 Marvin Golden; 27 Michael Gillett; 7 Dennis Moran; 10 Scott Cram; 9 Jason Hetherington (C); 18 Justin Dooley; 11 Shane Millard; 12 Steele Retchless; 13 Mat Toshack. Subs: 8 Tony Mestrov for Dooley (25); 15 Andy Johnson for Millard (58); 17 Glen Air for Moran (32); 21 Jon Clarke for Hetherington (78); Dooley for Cram (47); Cram for Mestrov (58BB, rev 69); Millard for Dooley (69).
Tries: Retchless (7), Hetherington (11), Millard (20); **Goals:** Warton 3.
RHINOS: 14 Marcus St Hilaire; 2 Karl Pratt; 3 Tonie Carroll; 4 Keith Senior; 5 Francis Cummins; 1 Iestyn Harris (C); 7 Ryan Sheridan; 8 Darren Fleary; 23 Matthew Diskin; 10 Barrie McDermott; 11 Andy Hay; 17 Anthony Farrell; 13 Kevin Sinfield. Subs: 15 Chev Walker for Cummins (12); 16 Mark Calderwood (D) for St Hilaire (19); 22 David Wrench for Farrell (66); 20 Jamie Mathiou for McDermott (26); McDermott for Fleary (54); Fleary for Sinfield (73).
Tries: Walker (29, 74), Senior (37, 61, 76), Pratt (47, 69), Sinfield (53), Mathiou (78); **Goals:** Harris 7.
League Express Men of the Match:
Broncos: Jason Hetherington; *Rhinos:* Keith Senior.
Penalty count: 3-6; **Half-time:** 18-12; **Referee:** Karl Kirkpatrick (Warrington); **Attendance:** 4,045.

Sunday 4th March 2001

BRADFORD BULLS 31 ST HELENS 24

BULLS: 28 Stuart Spruce; 2 Tevita Vaikona; 20 Scott Naylor; 15 Shane Rigon; 5 Michael Withers; 6 Henry Paul; 1 Robbie Paul (C); 8 Joe Vagana; 9 James Lowes; 22 Brian McDermott; 19 Jamie Peacock; 11 Daniel Gartner; 12 Mike Forshaw. Subs: 7 Paul Deacon not used; 10 Paul Anderson for Vagana (23); 16 Alex Wilkinson for Spruce (52); 29 Stuart Fielden for Peacock (22BB, rev 34); Peacock for McDermott (35); McDermott for Anderson (56); Vagana for Gartner (59).
Tries: Rigon (2, 49, 70), Spruce (27), H Paul (67); **Goals:** H Paul 5; **Field goal:** H Paul.
SAINTS: 1 Paul Wellens; 19 Anthony Stewart; 2 Sean Hoppe; 4 Paul Newlove; 5 Anthony Sullivan; 20 Tommy Martyn; 7 Sean Long; 8 Peter Shiels; 9 Keiron Cunningham; 10 David Fairleigh; 12 Sonny Nickle; 15 Tim Jonkers; 11 Chris Joynt (C). Subs: 14 Wayne McDonald for Nickle (30); 27 Bryan Henare for Shiels (80); 17 Steve Hall for Stankevitch (70); 18 John Stankevitch for Fairleigh (56); Fairleigh for Jonkers (65).
Tries: Newlove (13), Long (22), Fairleigh (34), Cunningham (47); **Goals:** Long 4.
League Express Men of the Match:
Bulls: Henry Paul; *Saints:* Keiron Cunningham.
Penalty count: 10-10; **Half-time:** 14-18; **Referee:** Russell Smith (Castleford); **Attendance:** 16,572.

HUDDERSFIELD GIANTS 10 HALIFAX BLUE SOX 34

GIANTS: 1 Paul Reilly; 2 Andrew Frew; 3 Martin Gleeson; 27 Brandon Costin (D); 4 Dale Cardoza; 6 Chris Thorman; 7 Ben Kusto; 12 Richard Marshall; 9 Paul Rowley; 10 Dale Laughton (C); 11 David Lomax; 13 David Atkins; 26 Steve McNamara. Subs: 17 Mark Moxon for Kusto (57); 8 Steve Molloy for Laughton (23); 18 Chris Molyneux for Lomax (32); 15 Darren Turner for Marshall (47); Laughton for Molloy (53); Lomax for Molyneux (60); Molyneux for Laughton (76BB).
Tries: Costin (18), Thorman (59); **Goal:** McNamara.
BLUE SOX: 1 Daryl Cardiss; 2 Jamie Bloem; 3 Damian Gibson; 4 Adam Hughes; 19 Oliver Marns; 6 Andrew Dunemann; 7 Gavin Clinch; 23 Brett Goldspink; 9 Johnny Lawless; 10 Jim Gannon; 16 Jamie Thackray; 12 Shayne McMenemy; 13 Martin Moana (C). Subs: 14 Danny Tickle for Clinch (24BB, rev 26); 15 Paul Davidson for Goldspink (27); 8 Andy Hobson for Thackray (27); 18 Stuart Donlan (D) for Cardiss (72); Goldspink for Davidson (58); Tickle for Moana (74).
Tries: McMenemy (3), Moana (14, 64), Gibson (27), Gannon (44), Hughes (80); **Goals:** Bloem 5.
League Express Men of the Match:
Giants: David Atkins; *Blue Sox:* Brett Goldspink.
Penalty count: 10-7; **Half-time:** 6-18;
Referee: Robert Connolly (Wigan); **Attendance:** 4,401.

HULL FC 46 SALFORD CITY REDS 34

HULL: 5 Matt Crowther; 2 Chris Smith; 6 Richard Horne; 23 Logan Campbell; 21 Gareth Raynor (D); 16 Paul Cooke; 7 Tony Smith; 8 Paul Broadbent; 9 Lee Jackson; 10 Luke Felsch; 11 Adam Maher; 12 Tony Grimaldi (C); 13 Jason Smith. Subs: 14 Stanley Gene for Jackson (49); 3 David Maiden for Grimaldi (49); 15 Paul King for Broadbent (20); 18 Steve Craven for Felsch (30); Grimaldi for J Smith (61); Broadbent for Craven (68).
Tries: T Smith (2), Horne (6), Cooke (10), J Smith (23), Crowther (56), Grimaldi (69), King (76), Raynor (79); **Goals:** Crowther 7.
CITY REDS: 1 Gary Broadbent; 2 Nick Pinkney; 3 Francis Maloney; 14 Kris Tassell; 5 Martin Offiah; 6 Steve Blakeley; 16 Bobbie Goulding (D); 15 Damian Driscoll (D); 9 Malcolm Alker; 10 Paul Southern; 11 Warren Jowitt; 12 Darren Brown (C); 23 Mike Wainwright. Subs: 18 Stuart Littler for Tassell (57); 24 Neil Baxter not used; 13 Paul Highton for Wainwright (32); 20 Andy Coley for Driscoll (32); Wainwright for Jowitt (72).
Tries: Tassell (20), Maloney (32, 59), Highton (38), Pinkney (48), Offiah (72); **Goals:** Goulding 5.
League Express Men of the Match:
Hull: Matt Crowther; *City Reds:* Bobbie Goulding.
Penalty count: 7-4; **Half-time:** 24-16;
Referee: Ian Smith (Oldham); **Attendance:** 6,628.

WAKEFIELD TRINITY WILDCATS 17 CASTLEFORD TIGERS 22

WILDCATS: 1 Martyn Holland; 2 Neil Law; 21 Tony Tatupu; 4 Justin Brooker; 5 Waisale Sovatabua; 6 Martin Pearson; 14 Paul March; 16 Julian O'Neill; 18 Ben Rauter; 8 Paul Jackson; 11 Jamie Field; 13 Gary Price (C); 25 Tom Haughey. Subs: 15 Ryan Hudson for Rauter (59); 10 Frank Watene for O'Neill (38); 17 Graham Law for March (49); 23 Paul Handforth for N Law (70); O'Neill for Watene (65).
Tries: Sovatabua (27), Jackson (78); **Goals:** Pearson 4; **Field goal:** Pearson.
TIGERS: 1 Richard Gay; 2 Jon Wells; 3 Michael Eagar; 4 Barrie-Jon Mather; 5 Darren Rogers; 6 Danny Orr; 7 Mitch Healey; 10 Dean Sampson; 9 Aaron Raper; 17 Andy Lynch; 11 Lee Harland; 15 Darren Shaw; 13 Adrian Vowles (C). Subs: 23 Michael Smith for Lynch (22); 20 Waine Pryce not used; 22 Mark Lennon for Healey (44); 19 Gareth Handford for Sampson (31); Sampson for Shaw (62); Lynch for Handford (68).
Tries: Vowles (48), M Smith (53, 70), Mather (73); **Goals:** Orr 3.
League Express Men of the Match:
Wildcats: Martin Pearson; *Tigers:* Adrian Vowles.
Penalty count: 6-7; **Half-time:** 9-0;
Referee: Stuart Cummings (Widnes); **Attendance:** 5,130.

ROUND 2

Friday 16th March 2001

LEEDS RHINOS 42 WAKEFIELD TRINITY WILDCATS 14

RHINOS: 6 Brett Mullins; 5 Francis Cummins; 3 Tonie Carroll; 4 Keith Senior; 2 Karl Pratt; 13 Kevin Sinfield; 1 Iestyn Harris (C); 8 Darren Fleary; 23 Matthew Diskin; 10 Barrie McDermott; 17 Anthony Farrell; 12 Bradley Clyde; 11 Andy Hay. Subs: 20 Jamie Mathiou for McDermott (26); 15 Chev Walker for Diskin (48); 16 Mark Calderwood for Farrell (49); 21 Jamie Jones-Buchanan for Senior (70); McDermott for Fleary (56); Farrell for Clyde (72).
Tries: Carroll (21, 32, 55, 61), Pratt (64, 70), Cummins (66), Walker (76); **Goals:** Harris 5.
WILDCATS: 1 Martyn Holland; 2 Waisale Sovatabua; 3 Richard Smith; 21 Tony Tatupu; 2 Neil Law; 14 Paul March; 6 Martin Pearson; 17 Frank Watene; 18 Ben Rauter; 8 Paul Jackson; 12 Willie Poching (C); 15 Ryan Hudson; 13 Gary Price. Subs: 17 Graham Law for Tatupu (15); 11 Jamie Field for Watene (26); 22 Keith Mason for Poching (36); 24 Chris Feather (D) for March (71); Watene for Jackson (59BB); Poching for Rauter (62); Rauter for Sovatabua (71).
Tries: Sovatabua (29), Rauter (45); **Goals:** Pearson 3.
League Express Men of the Match:
Rhinos: Tonie Carroll; *Wildcats:* Martin Pearson.
Penalty count: 6-5; **Half-time:** 8-8; **Referee:** Karl Kirkpatrick (Warrington); **Attendance:** 14,019.

SALFORD CITY REDS 6 BRADFORD BULLS 40

CITY REDS: 1 Gary Broadbent; 2 Nick Pinkney; 3 Francis Maloney; 4 Michael Hancock; 5 Martin Offiah; 6 Steve Blakeley; 16 Bobbie Goulding; 15 Damian Driscoll; 9 Malcolm Alker; 10 Paul Southern; 11 Warren Jowitt; 12 Darren Brown (C); 13 Paul Highton. Subs: 14 Kris Tassell for Jowitt (25); 20 Andy Coley for Driscoll (25); 7 Graham Holroyd for Blakeley (35); 18 Stuart Littler for Hancock (69); Driscoll for Coley (52BB); Jowitt for Southern (59); Southern for Brown (63).
Try: Jowitt (12); **Goal:** Goulding.
BULLS: 28 Stuart Spruce; 2 Tevita Vaikona; 20 Scott Naylor; 15 Shane Rigon; 5 Michael Withers; 6 Henry Paul; 1 Robbie Paul (C); 10 Paul Anderson; 9 James Lowes; 29 Stuart Fielden; 11 Daniel Gartner; 19 Jamie Peacock; 12 Mike Forshaw. Subs: 22 Brian McDermott for Fielden (25); 8 Joe Vagana for Anderson (31); 14 Lee Gilmour for Naylor (55); 7 Paul Deacon for R Paul (58); Fielden for Vagana (51); Anderson for McDermott (69).
Tries: Spruce (9), Rigon (23), Lowes (31), Peacock (33, 57), Anderson (72), Withers (75); **Goals:** H Paul 6.
Sin bin: Rigon (59) - obstruction.
League Express Men of the Match:
City Reds: Malcolm Alker; *Bulls:* Jamie Peacock.
Penalty count: 9-4; **Half-time:** 6-22;
Referee: Robert Connolly (Wigan); **Attendance:** 4,355.

ST HELENS 44 HUDDERSFIELD GIANTS 22

SAINTS: 1 Paul Wellens; 2 Sean Hoppe; 3 Kevin Iro; 4 Paul Newlove; 5 Anthony Sullivan; 20 Tommy Martyn; 7 Sean Long; 12 Sonny Nickle; 9 Keiron Cunningham; 10 David Fairleigh; 8 Peter Shiels; 11 Chris Joynt (C); 15 Tim Jonkers. Subs: 17 Steve Hall for Joynt (64); 18 John Stankevitch for Shiels (45); 19 Anthony Stewart for Newlove (70); 14 Wayne McDonald for Fairleigh (34); Fairleigh for Nickle (57).
Tries: Newlove (5), Iro (22, 63), Jonkers (32), McDonald (43), Hoppe (58), Hall (75), Long (80); **Goals:** Long 6.
GIANTS: 25 Ben Cooper; 2 Andrew Frew; 3 Martin Gleeson; 27 Brandon Costin; 4 Dale Cardoza; 6 Chris Thorman; 17 Mark Moxon; 8 Steve Molloy; 9 Paul Rowley; 10 Dale Laughton (C); 11 David Lomax; 13 David Atkins; 26 Steve McNamara. Subs: 18 Chris Molyneux for Laughton (24); 7 Ben Kusto for Moxon (31); 12 Richard Marshall for Molloy (33); 15 Darren Turner for Lomax (58); Molloy for Atkins (66); Laughton for Molyneux (67).
Tries: Moxon (27), Frew (33, 69), Costin (50); **Goals:** McNamara 3.
League Express Men of the Match:
Saints: David Fairleigh; *Giants:* Andrew Frew.
Penalty count: 7-4; **Half-time:** 16-12;
Referee: Ian Smith (Oldham); **Attendance:** 7,275.

Saturday 17th March 2001

CASTLEFORD TIGERS 8 WIGAN WARRIORS 24

TIGERS: 1 Richard Gay; 5 Darren Rogers; 3 Michael Eagar; 4 Barrie-Jon Mather; 2 Jon Wells; 13 Adrian Vowles (C); 6 Danny Orr; 10 Dean Sampson; 9 Aaron Raper; 8 Nathan Sykes; 16 Ian Tonks; 15 Darren Shaw; 11 Lee Harland. Subs: 22 Mark Lennon for Harland (13); 23 Michael Smith for Raper (19); 12 Dale Fritz for Tonks (56); 19 Gareth Handford for Sampson (40); Tonks for Shaw (58); Shaw for Vowles (73).
Try: Vowles (48); **Goals:** Orr 2.
WARRIORS: 1 Kris Radlinski; 2 Brett Dallas; 15 Paul Johnson; 3 Steve Renouf; 23 David Hodgson; 22 Phil Jones; 7 Adrian Lam; 8 Terry O'Connor; 9 Terry Newton; 10 Neil Cowie; 12 Denis Betts; 14 David Furner; 13 Andy Farrell (C). Subs: 4 Gary Connolly for Renouf (67); 17 Francis Stephenson for Cowie (31); 21 Mark Smith for Newton (54); 16 Simon Haughton for Farrell (26); Cowie for O'Connor (44BB, rev 58, rev 73); Newton for Betts (72).
Tries: Jones (10, 42, 66), Dallas (33); **Goals:** Farrell 2, Jones 2.
League Express Men of the Match:
Tigers: Adrian Vowles; *Warriors:* Phil Jones.
Penalty count: 13-7; **Half-time:** 2-14;
Referee: Stuart Cummings (Widnes); **Attendance:** 7,214.

Sunday 18th March 2001

WARRINGTON WOLVES 20 HULL FC 32

WOLVES: 6 Lee Briers; 2 Rob Smyth; 16 Ian Sibbit; 3 David Kidwell; 22 Alan Hunte; 15 Steve Georgallis; 7 Allan Langer (C); 8 Andrew Gee; 9 David Highton; 12 Jerome Guisset; 20 Dean Busby; 24 Paul Noone; 13 Tawera Nikau. Subs: 1 Lee Penny for Noone (51); 5 Jamie Stenhouse for Sibbit (63); 21 Paul Wood for Masella (55); 18 Martin Masella for Guisset (25); Guisset for Busby (70); Sibbit for Langer (75).
Tries: Briers (12), Georgallis (38), Hunte (67, 74); **Goals:** Smyth 2.
HULL: 1 Steve Prescott; 2 Chris Smith; 6 Richard Horne; 4 Deon Bird; 5 Matt Crowther; 13 Jason Smith; 7 Tony Smith; 8 Paul Broadbent; 9 Lee Jackson; 10 Luke Felsch; 11 Adam Maher; 12 Tony Grimaldi (C); 3 David Maiden. Subs: 14 Stanley Gene for Jackson (46BB); 18 Steve Craven for Broadbent (28); 20 Garreth Carvell for Broadbent (75); 23 Logan Campbell for Maiden (63); Broadbent for Craven (45); Craven for Felsch (52); Felsch for Craven (69).
Tries: Bird (1), Crowther (7), T Smith (27), Prescott (48), C Smith (54), Horne (62); **Goals:** Crowther 4.
League Express Men of the Match:
Wolves: Allan Langer; *Hull:* Jason Smith.
Penalty count: 8-11; **Half-time:** 8-16;
Referee: Russell Smith (Castleford); **Attendance:** 7,577.

HALIFAX BLUE SOX 16 LONDON BRONCOS 11

BLUE SOX: 1 Daryl Cardiss; 2 Jamie Bloem; 3 Damian Gibson; 4 Adam Hughes; 19 Oliver Marns; 6 Andrew Dunemann; 7 Gavin Clinch; 23 Brett Goldspink; 9 Johnny Lawless; 10 Jim Gannon; 12 Shayne McMenemy; 11 Gary Mercer; 13 Martin Moana (C). Subs: 14 Danny Tickle for Hughes (24); 15 Paul Davidson for Goldspink (37); 8 Andy Hobson for Gannon (52); 16 Jamie Thackray for McMenemy (52); Goldspink for Davidson (62); McMenemy for Goldspink (62).
Tries: Marns (30), Mercer (64); **Goals:** Bloem 4.
BRONCOS: 23 Richie Barnett; 2 Nigel Roy; 4 Greg

Fleming; 3 Tony Martin; 28 Marvin Golden; 27 Michael Gillett; 7 Dennis Moran; 10 Scott Cram; 9 Jason Hetherington (C); 18 Justin Dooley; 11 Shane Millard; 12 Steele Retchless; 13 Mat Toshack. Subs: 8 Tony Mestrov for Toshack (33); 15 Andy Johnson for Gillett (32); 5 Brett Warton for Hetherington (24); 22 Yusef Sozi for Dooley (60); Hetherington for Cram (71); Dooley for Sozi (77).
Tries: Millard (36), Moran (55); **Goal:** Warton;
Field goal: Moran.
League Express Men of the Match:
Blue Sox: Brett Goldspink; *Broncos:* Dennis Moran.
Penalty count: 10-6; **Half-time:** 4-4;
Referee: Steve Ganson (St Helens); **Attendance:** 4,153.

ROUND 3

Friday 23rd March 2001

WIGAN WARRIORS 42 LEEDS RHINOS 6

WARRIORS: 1 Kris Radlinski; 2 Brett Dallas; 15 Paul Johnson; 3 Steve Renouf; 23 David Hodgson; 22 Phil Jones; 7 Adrian Lam; 8 Terry O'Connor; 9 Terry Newton; 10 Neil Cowie; 12 Denis Betts; 14 David Furner; 13 Andy Farrell (C). Subs: 16 Simon Haughton for Betts (22); 20 Harvey Howard for Cowie (28); 21 Mark Smith for Haughton (60); 18 Wes Davies for Howard (65); Cowie for O'Connor (55); O'Connor for Furner (74).
Tries: Farrell (15), Renouf (19, 66), Radlinski (34), Johnson (50, 72), Furner (61); **Goals:** Farrell 7.
RHINOS: 6 Brett Mullins; 5 Francis Cummins; 3 Tonie Carroll; 15 Chev Walker; 2 Karl Pratt; 13 Kevin Sinfield; 1 Iestyn Harris (C); 8 Darren Fleary; 26 Jon Liddell (D); 10 Barrie McDermott; 20 Jamie Mathiou; 17 Anthony Farrell; 11 Andy Hay. Subs: 21 Jamie Jones-Buchanan for McDermott (15); 16 Mark Calderwood for Carroll (37); 18 Danny Ward for Mathiou (24); 24 Ewan Dowes (D) for Ward (63); McDermott for Fleary (51); Mathiou for Walker (56BB).
Try: Ward (56); **Goal:** Harris.
League Express Men of the Match:
Warriors: Adrian Lam; *Rhinos:* Karl Pratt.
Penalty count: 8-7; **Half-time:** 20-0; **Referee:** Russell Smith (Castleford); **Attendance:** 12,321.

Saturday 24th March 2001

LONDON BRONCOS 18 ST HELENS 20

BRONCOS: 23 Richie Barnett; 2 Nigel Roy; 3 Tony Martin; 4 Greg Fleming; 28 Marvin Golden; 6 Jim Dymock; 7 Dennis Moran; 18 Justin Dooley; 9 Jason Hetherington (C); 10 Scott Cram; 11 Shane Millard; 12 Steele Retchless; 15 Andy Johnson. Subs: 8 Tony Mestrov for Cram (29); 13 Mat Toshack for Millard (25); 5 Brett Warton for Golden (53BB, rev 60); 22 Yusef Sozi for Dooley (58); Millard for Hetherington (35BB, rev 46); Cram for Mestrov (51); Warton for Moran (60).
Tries: Martin (12, 15), Johnson (20), Hetherington (65); **Goal:** Warton.
SAINTS: 1 Paul Wellens; 2 Sean Hoppe; 3 Kevin Iro; 4 Paul Newlove; 17 Steve Hall; 20 Tommy Martyn; 7 Sean Long; 12 Sonny Nickle; 9 Keiron Cunningham; 10 David Fairleigh; 11 Chris Joynt (C); 8 Peter Shiels; 13 Paul Sculthorpe. Subs: 14 Wayne McDonald for Fairleigh (35); 15 Tim Jonkers for Nickle (22); 18 John Stankevitch for Joynt (63); 19 Anthony Stewart for Shiels (79); Fairleigh for McDonald (58).
Tries: Hoppe (39), Joynt (53), Cunningham (74, 78); **Goals:** Long 2.
League Express Men of the Match:
Broncos: Richie Barnett; *Saints:* Paul Newlove.
Penalty count: 5-9; **Half-time:** 12-4;
Referee: Ian Smith (Oldham); **Attendance:** 3,736.

Sunday 25th March 2001

HUDDERSFIELD GIANTS 14 BRADFORD BULLS 30

GIANTS: 25 Ben Cooper; 2 Andrew Frew; 3 Martin Gleeson; 27 Brandon Costin; 21 Graham Appo; 6 Chris Thorman; 17 Mark Moxon; 8 Steve Molloy; 9 Paul Rowley; 10 Dale Laughton (C); 11 David Lomax; 13 David Atkins; 26 Steve McNamara. Subs: 18 Chris Molyneux for Laughton (20BB, rev 39); 7 Ben Kusto for Moxon (20); 12 Richard Marshall for Molloy (29); 15 Darren Turner for Lomax (57); Molloy for Laughton (69).
Tries: Frew (19), Costin (78); **Goals:** McNamara 3.
BULLS: 28 Stuart Spruce; 2 Tevita Vaikona; 14 Lee Gilmour; 5 Michael Withers; 3 Leon Pryce; 1 Robbie Paul (C); 7 Paul Deacon; 8 Joe Vagana; 9 James Lowes; 22 Brian McDermott; 19 Jamie Peacock; 11 Daniel Gartner; 15 Shane Rigon. Subs: 6 Henry Paul for Lowes (40); 10 Paul Anderson for Vagana (21); 29 Stuart Fielden for McDermott (21); 18 Lee Radford for Rigon (54); McDermott for Anderson (39BB, rev 54); Vagana for Gartner (66).
Tries: Deacon (15), Vaikona (43), Gartner (48), R Paul (53), Pryce (73); **Goals:** Deacon 4, H Paul.
League Express Men of the Match:
Giants: Andrew Frew; *Bulls:* Robbie Paul.
Penalty count: 9-10; **Half-time:** 10-8; **Referee:** Karl Kirkpatrick (Warrington); **Attendance:** 6,648.

WARRINGTON WOLVES 14 SALFORD CITY REDS 39

WOLVES: 1 Lee Penny; 2 Rob Smyth; 16 Ian Sibbit; 4 Toa Kohe-Love; 22 Alan Hunte; 6 Lee Briers; 15 Steve Georgallis; 8 Andrew Gee; 9 David Highton; 10 Danny Nutley; 19 Ian Knott; 24 Paul Noone; 13 Tawera Nikau (C). Subs: 3 David Kidwell for Penny (15); 21 Paul Wood for Gee (26); 18 Martin Masella for Gee (66); 12 Jerome Guisset for Knott (35); Gee for Wood (40); Wood for Nutley (71).
Tries: Kohe-Love (8, 14), Smyth (29); **Goal:** Smyth.
CITY REDS: 1 Gary Broadbent; 2 Nick Pinkney; 3 Francis Maloney; 14 Kris Tassell; 5 Martin Offiah; 7 Graham Holroyd; 16 Bobbie Goulding (C); 15 Damian Driscoll; 9 Malcolm Alker; 10 Paul Southern; 11 Warren Jowitt; 13 Paul Highton; 23 Mike Wainwright. Subs: 12 Darren Brown for Wainwright (24); 4 Michael Hancock for Southern (31); 20 Andy Coley for Driscoll (18); 24 Karle Hammond (D) for Hancock (65); Wainwright for Jowitt (60).
Tries: Pinkney (3, 69), Offiah (25), Broadbent (34), Maloney (44, 55), Alker (64); **Goals:** Goulding 5;
Field goal: Holroyd.
League Express Men of the Match:
Wolves: Danny Nutley; *City Reds:* Nick Pinkney.
Penalty count: 5-7; **Half-time:** 14-14;
Referee: Stuart Cummings (Widnes); **Attendance:** 6,147.

HULL FC 18 CASTLEFORD TIGERS 18

HULL: 1 Steve Prescott; 2 Chris Smith; 6 Richard Horne; 4 Deon Bird; 5 Matt Crowther; 13 Jason Smith; 7 Tony Smith; 8 Paul Broadbent; 9 Lee Jackson; 10 Luke Felsch; 11 Adam Maher; 12 Tony Grimaldi (C); 3 David Maiden. Subs: 20 Garreth Carvell for Felsch (50); 23 Logan Campbell for Prescott (24); 14 Stanley Gene for C Smith (ht); 18 Steve Craven for Broadbent (31); Broadbent for Craven (60).
Tries: Bird (30), Jackson (38, 75); **Goals:** Crowther 3.
TIGERS: 1 Richard Gay; 2 Jon Wells; 4 Barrie-Jon Mather; 3 Michael Eagar; 5 Darren Rogers; 6 Danny Orr; 22 Mark Lennon; 8 Nathan Sykes; 26 Brad Hepi (D2); 19 Gareth Handford; 16 Ian Tonks; 15 Darren Shaw; 13 Adrian Vowles (C). Subs: 12 Dale Fritz for Hepi (10); 23 Michael Smith for Tonks (24); 17 Andy Lynch for Handford (32); 20 Waine Pryce for Shaw (62); Handford for Lynch (66); Shaw for Sykes (72).
Tries: Eagar (12, 24), Orr (52); **Goals:** Orr 3.
League Express Men of the Match:
Hull: Deon Bird; *Tigers:* Danny Orr.
Penalty count: 7-7; **Half-time:** 12-12;
Referee: Steve Ganson (St Helens); **Attendance:** 7,640.

WAKEFIELD TRINITY WILDCATS 30
HALIFAX BLUE SOX 14

WILDCATS: 1 Martyn Holland; 2 Neil Law; 3 Richard Smith; 4 Justin Brooker; 5 Waisale Sovatabua; 6 Martin Pearson; 7 Brad Davis; 16 Julian O'Neill; 18 Ben Rauter; 10 Frank Watene; 15 Ryan Hudson; 12 Willie Poching (C); 11 Jamie Field. Subs: 17 Graham Law for Poching (65); 8 Paul Jackson for Watene (20); 14 Paul March for Rauter (70); 25 Tom Haughey for Hudson (75).
Tries: Sovatabua (8), N Law (16), Hudson (25), Smith (65); **Goals:** Pearson 7.
Sin bin: O'Neill (35) - punching & (56) - late tackle.
BLUE SOX: 1 Daryl Cardiss; 2 Jamie Bloem; 3 Damian Gibson; 20 Danny Halliwell; 19 Oliver Marns; 6 Andrew Dunemann; 7 Gavin Clinch; 23 Brett Goldspink; 9 Johnny Lawless; 10 Jim Gannon; 11 Gary Mercer; 12 Shayne McMenemy; 13 Martin Moana (C). Subs: 14 Danny Tickle for Dunemann (12BB); 15 Paul Davidson for Halliwell (59); 16 Jamie Thackray for Gannon (31); 8 Andy Hobson for Goldspink (31); Gannon for Thackray (54); Goldspink for Hobson (56).
Tries: Cardiss (28, 74), Goldspink (61); **Goal:** Bloem.
Sin bin: McMenemy (12) - obstruction;
Hobson (35) - punching.
League Express Men of the Match:
Wildcats: Brad Davis; *Blue Sox:* Daryl Cardiss
Penalty count: 10-7; **Half-time:** 20-4;
Referee: Robert Connolly (Wigan); **Attendance:** 3,147.

ROUND 4

Friday 6th April 2001

HALIFAX BLUE SOX 10 WIGAN WARRIORS 20

BLUE SOX: 1 Daryl Cardiss; 20 Danny Halliwell; 2 Jamie Bloem; 3 Damian Gibson; 19 Oliver Marns; 13 Martin Moana (C); 7 Gavin Clinch; 8 Andy Hobson; 9 Johnny Lawless; 23 Brett Goldspink; 10 Jim Gannon; 15 Paul Davidson; 12 Shayne McMenemy. Subs: 14 Danny Tickle for Hobson (29); 16 Jamie Thackray for McMenemy (29); 17 Sean Penkywicz for Hobson (73); 18 Stuart Donlan not used; Hobson for Thackray (43); McMenemy for Goldspink (50); Goldspink for McMenemy (63).
Try: Cardiss (52); **Goals:** Bloem 3.
WARRIORS: 1 Kris Radlinski; 2 Brett Dallas; 3 Steve Renouf; 15 Paul Johnson; 23 David Hodgson; 6 Matthew Johns; 7 Adrian Lam; 17 Francis Stephenson; 9 Terry Newton; 8 Terry O'Connor; 12 Denis Betts; 14 David Furner; 13 Andy Farrell (C). Subs: 18 Wes Davies not used; 11 Mick Cassidy for Betts (40); 16 Simon Haughton for Howard (48); 20 Harvey Howard for Stephenson (26); Stephenson for O'Connor (44BB, rev 63); Howard for Haughton (63); Haughton for Howard (75).
Tries: Newton (1, 65), Farrell (29); **Goals:** Farrell 4.
On report: Haughton (63) - high tackle.
League Express Men of the Match:
Blue Sox: Paul Davidson; *Warriors:* Terry Newton.
Penalty count: 10-5; **Half-time:** 2-14; **Attendance:** 4,549; **Referee:** Karl Kirkpatrick (Warrington).

LEEDS RHINOS 16 HULL FC 18

RHINOS: 6 Brett Mullins; 16 Mark Calderwood; 28 Andy Kirk (D); 15 Chev Walker; 5 Francis Cummins; 13 Kevin Sinfield (C); 2 Karl Pratt; 8 Darren Fleary; 9 Robert Mears; 18 Danny Ward; 17 Anthony Farrell; 12 Bradley Clyde; 11 Andy Hay. Subs: 14 Marcus St Hilaire for Mullins (23); 29 Robert Burrow (D) for Fleary (36); 24 Ewan Dowes for Ward (47); 22 David Wrench for Clyde (58); Fleary for Farrell (40BB, rev 65); Ward for Dowes (72).
Tries: Mears (17), Ward (39), Cummins (62);
Goals: Sinfield 2.
HULL: 4 Deon Bird; 21 Gareth Raynor; 3 David Maiden; 23 Logan Campbell; 5 Matt Crowther; 16 Paul Cooke; 7 Tony Smith; 8 Paul Broadbent; 9 Lee Jackson; 10 Luke Felsch; 11 Adam Maher; 12 Tony Grimaldi (C); 13 Jason Smith. Subs: 18 Steve Craven for Felsch (29); 14 Stanley Gene for Cooke (45BB, rev 67); 20 Garreth Carvell for Craven (62); 26 Paul Parker for Raynor (73); Felsch for Broadbent (50); Gene for Grimaldi (73).
Tries: T Smith (5, 32), Crowther (48), Bird (57);
Goal: Crowther.
League Express Men of the Match:
Rhinos: Robert Mears; *Hull:* Jason Smith.
Penalty count: 4-3; **Half-time:** 12-10; **Referee:** Stuart Cummings (Widnes); **Attendance:** 12,693.

ST HELENS 24 WAKEFIELD TRINITY WILDCATS 0

SAINTS: 19 Anthony Stewart; 17 Steve Hall; 3 Kevin Iro; 4 Paul Newlove; 5 Anthony Sullivan; 13 Paul Sculthorpe (C); 7 Sean Long; 12 Sonny Nickle; 9 Keiron Cunningham; 10 David Fairleigh; 14 Wayne McDonald; 18 John Stankevitch; 15 Tim Jonkers. Subs: 16 Vila Matautia for McDonald (26); 11 Chris Joynt for Fairleigh (55); 21 Dwayne West for Stankevitch (57); 1 Paul Wellens for Cunningham (49); McDonald for Matautia (48); Matautia for Long (74).
Tries: Iro (12), Newlove (15), Sullivan (51), Wellens (78); **Goals:** Long 4.
WILDCATS: 1 Martyn Holland; 5 Waisale Sovatabua; 4 Justin Brooker; 3 Richard Smith; 2 Neil Law; 6 Martin Pearson; 7 Brad Davis; 16 Julian O'Neill; 18 Ben Rauter; 10 Frank Watene; 15 Ryan Hudson; 11 Jamie Field; 12 Willie Poching (C). Subs: 8 Paul Jackson for Watene (35); 17 Graham Law for Davis (41); 19 Gareth Ellis for Rauter (59); 22 Keith Mason for Pearson (69); Watene for O'Neill (59).
League Express Men of the Match:
Saints: Sonny Nickle; *Wildcats:* Jamie Field.
Penalty count: 7-3; **Half-time:** 16-0;
Referee: Robert Connolly (Wigan); **Attendance:** 6,746.

Saturday 7th April 2001

CASTLEFORD TIGERS 18 WARRINGTON WOLVES 0

TIGERS: 1 Richard Gay; 2 Jon Wells; 3 Michael Eagar; 4 Barrie-Jon Mather; 5 Darren Rogers; 6 Danny Orr; 7 Mitch Healey; 15 Darren Shaw; 9 Aaron Raper; 19 Gareth Handford; 12 Dale Fritz; 11 Lee Harland; 13 Adrian Vowles (C). Subs: 26 Brad Hepi for Shaw (61); 23 Michael Smith for Vowles (8); 17 Andy Lynch for Handford (53); 22 Mark Lennon for Healey (63); Handford for Raper (72).
Tries: Wells (20), Orr (34); **Goals:** Orr 5.
WOLVES: 22 Alan Hunte; 2 Rob Smyth; 4 Toa Kohe-Love; 16 Ian Sibbit; 5 Jamie Stenhouse; 6 Lee Briers; 7 Allan Langer (C); 8 Andrew Gee; 9 David Highton; 10 Danny Nutley; 20 Dean Busby; 25 Gary Mercer (D2); 15 Steve Georgallis. Subs: 3 David Kidwell for Sibbit (66); 18 Martin Masella for Nutley (21); 11 Steve McCurrie for Georgallis (52); 12 Jerome Guisset not used; Nutley for Masella (50).
On report: Nutley (14) – late, high tackle.
League Express Men of the Match:
Tigers: Danny Orr; *Wolves:* David Highton.
Penalty count: 8-5; **Half-time:** 16-0;
Referee: Ian Smith (Oldham); **Attendance:** 6,293.

Sunday 8th April 2001

BRADFORD BULLS 24 LONDON BRONCOS 6

BULLS: 28 Stuart Spruce; 3 Leon Pryce; 20 Scott Naylor; 15 Shane Rigon; 5 Michael Withers; 6 Henry Paul; 1 Robbie Paul (C); 8 Joe Vagana; 9 James Lowes; 22 Brian McDermott; 19 Jamie Peacock; 18 Lee Radford; 12 Mike Forshaw. Subs: 7 Paul Deacon for R Paul (53); 10 Paul Anderson for McDermott (20); 29 Stuart Fielden for Vagana (20); 14 Lee Gilmour for Radford (26); Vagana for Anderson (60); McDermott for Peacock (75).
Tries: Rigon (4), Lowes (27), Anderson (30), Pryce (43);
Goals: H Paul 4.
BRONCOS: 23 Richie Barnett; 2 Nigel Roy; 3 Tony Martin; 4 Greg Fleming; 28 Marvin Golden; 6 Jim Dymock; 17 Glen Air; 8 Tony Mestrov; 9 Jason Hetherington (C); 10 Scott Cram; 11 Shane Millard; 12 Steele Retchless; 13 Mat Toshack. Subs: 20 Steffan Hughes for Hetherington (24BB, rev 31); 21 Jon Clarke for Toshack (17); 5 Brett Warton for Mestrov (66); 18 Justin Dooley for Retchless (45); Toshack for Clarke (43); Retchless for Air (76); Hughes for Toshack (79).
Try: Martin (49); **Goal:** Martin.
Sin bin: Millard (55) - lying on.
League Express Men of the Match:
Bulls: Henry Paul; *Broncos:* Jim Dymock.
Penalty count: 7-4; **Half-time:** 18-0; **Referee:** Colin Morris (Huddersfield); **Attendance:** 10,864.

SALFORD CITY REDS 28 HUDDERSFIELD GIANTS 14

CITY REDS: 1 Gary Broadbent; 2 Nick Pinkney; 3 Francis Maloney; 14 Kris Tassell; 5 Martin Offiah; 6 Steve Blakeley; 16 Bobbie Goulding (C); 15 Damian Driscoll; 9 Malcolm Alker; 10 Paul Southern; 11 Warren Jowitt; 13 Paul Highton; 23 Mike Wainwright. Subs: 12 Darren

Brown for Wainwright (46); 4 Michael Hancock for Highton (52); 20 Andy Coley for Driscoll (24); 6 Graham Holroyd for Maloney (64); Driscoll for Southern (68).
Tries: Tassell (2), Maloney (59), Hancock (73), Alker (79); **Goals:** Goulding 6.
GIANTS: 25 Ben Cooper; 2 Andrew Frew; 3 Martin Gleeson; 27 Brandon Costin; 21 Graham Appo; 6 Chris Thorman; 7 Ben Kusto; 8 Steve Molloy; 9 Paul Rowley; 10 Dale Laughton (C); 11 David Lomax; 13 David Atkins; 26 Steve McNamara. Subs: 18 Chris Molyneux for Laughton (34); 12 Richard Marshall for Lomax (50); 4 Dale Cardoza for Gleeson (67); 15 Darren Turner for Molloy (25); Molloy for Molyneux (67).
Tries: Appo (31), Atkins (34); **Goals:** McNamara 3.
League Express Men of the Match:
City Reds: Bobbie Goulding; *Giants:* Steve McNamara.
Penalty count: 8-8; **Half-time:** 8-10;
Referee: Steve Ganson (St Helens); **Attendance:** 3,793.

ROUND 5

Thursday 12th April 2001

WAKEFIELD TRINITY WILDCATS 16 BRADFORD BULLS 12

WILDCATS: 1 Martyn Holland; 2 Neil Law; 3 Richard Smith; 4 Justin Brooker; 5 Waisale Sovatabua; 6 Martin Pearson; 17 Graham Law; 16 Julian O'Neill; 18 Ben Rauter; 10 Frank Watene; 15 Ryan Hudson; 12 Willie Poching (C); 11 Jamie Field. Subs: 9 David March for Field (61); 8 Paul Jackson for Watene (30); 25 Tom Haughey for N Law (34); 22 Keith Mason for O'Neill (58); Field for G Law (76).
Tries: N Law (16, 21), D March (62); **Goals:** Pearson 2.
BULLS: 28 Stuart Spruce; 16 Alex Wilkinson; 14 Lee Gilmour; 15 Shane Rigon; 3 Leon Pryce; 1 Robbie Paul (C); 7 Paul Deacon; 8 Joe Vagana; 9 James Lowes; 22 Brian McDermott; 19 Jamie Peacock; 18 Lee Radford; 12 Mike Forshaw. Subs: 29 Stuart Fielden for McDermott (23); 11 Daniel Gartner for Radford (50); 10 Paul Anderson for Vagana (23); 6 Henry Paul for Deacon (52); Vagana for Anderson (66); Deacon for Spruce (70).
Tries: R Paul (6), Pryce (11); **Goals:** Deacon 2.
League Express Men of the Match:
Wildcats: Willie Poching; *Bulls:* Robbie Paul.
Penalty count: 6-3; **Half-time:** 10-12;
Referee: Peter Taberner (Wigan); **Attendance:** 4,729.

WARRINGTON WOLVES 36 LEEDS RHINOS 6

WOLVES: 22 Alan Hunte; 2 Rob Smyth; 16 Ian Sibbit; 4 Toa Kohe-Love; 5 Jamie Stenhouse; 15 Steve Georgallis; 7 Allan Langer (C); 18 Martin Masella; 9 David Highton; 10 Danny Nutley; 11 Steve McCurrie; 25 Gary Mercer; 20 Dean Busby. Subs: 17 Dave Alstead for Stenhouse (70); 3 David Kidwell for McCurrie (26); 21 Paul Wood for Nutley (67); 12 Jerome Guisset for Masella (31); Masella for Guisset (56); McCurrie for Kidwell (66).
Tries: Hunte (12), Sibbit (33, 65, 77), Kidwell (37), Georgallis (61), Kohe-Love (69); **Goals:** Smyth 4.
RHINOS: 5 Francis Cummins; 16 Mark Calderwood; 28 Andy Kirk; 15 Chev Walker; 14 Marcus St Hilaire; 2 Karl Pratt; 29 Robert Burrow; 8 Darren Fleary; 9 Robert Mears; 17 Anthony Farrell; 11 Andy Hay; 12 Bradley Clyde; 13 Kevin Sinfield (C). Subs: 1 Iestyn Harris for Pratt (51); 18 Danny Ward for Farrell (32); 22 David Wrench for Hay (67); 24 Ewan Dowes for Fleary (48BB, rev 74); Farrell for Ward (64); Pratt for Mears (66).
Try: Burrow (55); **Goal:** Harris.
League Express Men of the Match:
Wolves: Danny Nutley; *Rhinos:* Robert Burrow.
Penalty count: 9-6; **Half-time:** 16-0;
Referee: Robert Connolly (Wigan); **Attendance:** 5,871.

Friday 13th April 2001

WIGAN WARRIORS 22 ST HELENS 22

WARRIORS: 1 Kris Radlinski; 2 Brett Dallas; 15 Paul Johnson; 3 Steve Renouf; 23 David Hodgson; 6 Matthew Johns; 7 Adrian Lam; 8 Terry O'Connor; 9 Terry Newton; 10 Neil Cowie; 12 Denis Betts; 14 David Furner; 13 Andy Farrell (C). Subs: 20 Harvey Howard for Cowie (24); 11 Mick Cassidy for Betts (41); 21 Mark Smith for Newton (64); 18 Wes Davies not used; Cowie for O'Connor (44); Betts for Howard (61); Newton for Cowie (72BB).
Tries: Radlinski (21, 68), Renouf (50, 57);
Goals: Farrell 3.
SAINTS: 1 Paul Wellens; 17 Steve Hall; 3 Kevin Iro; 4 Paul Newlove; 5 Anthony Sullivan; 13 Paul Sculthorpe; 7 Sean Long; 10 David Fairleigh; 9 Keiron Cunningham; 12 Sonny Nickle; 15 Tim Jonkers; 8 Peter Shiels; 11 Chris Joynt (C). Subs: 16 Vila Matautia for Nickle (25BB, rev 32); 18 John Stankevitch for Shiels (56); 19 Anthony Stewart for Nickle (63); 21 Dwayne West for Joynt (67BB, rev 72); Matautia for Fairleigh (32); Fairleigh for Shiels (48BB, rev 54); Fairleigh for Matautia (56); Matautia for Jonkers (75).
Tries: Long (13), Iro (32), West (71), Sculthorpe (76);
Goals: Long 3.
League Express Men of the Match:
Warriors: Steve Renouf; *Saints:* Paul Sculthorpe.
Penalty count: 8-6; **Half-time:** 8-12; **Referee:** Stuart Cummings (Widnes); **Attendance:** 21,073.

LONDON BRONCOS 43 HUDDERSFIELD GIANTS 12

BRONCOS: 23 Richie Barnett; 2 Nigel Roy; 3 Tony Martin; 4 Greg Fleming; 28 Marvin Golden; 6 Jim Dymock; 7 Dennis Moran; 8 Tony Mestrov; 9 Jason Hetherington (C); 10 Scott Cram; 11 Shane Millard; 12 Steele Retchless; 13 Mat Toshack. Subs: 5 Brett Warton for Moran (68); 18 Justin Dooley for Mestrov (30); 21 Jon Clarke for Millard (69); 27 Michael Gillett for Hetherington (49BB, rev 61); Gillett for Dymock (62); Mestrov for Barnett (75).
Tries: Golden (3), Dymock (5), Toshack (9), Roy (49), Gillett (54), Hetherington (64), Fleming (79);
Goals: Martin 7; **Field goal:** Moran.
GIANTS: 21 Graham Appo; 25 Ben Cooper; 27 Brandon Costin; 4 Dale Cardoza; 2 Andrew Frew; 6 Chris Thorman; 7 Ben Kusto; 8 Steve Molloy; 9 Paul Rowley; 10 Dale Laughton (C); 11 David Lomax; 13 David Atkins; 26 Steve McNamara. Subs: 22 Eorl Crabtree (D) for Molloy (17); 12 Richard Marshall for McNamara (46); 17 Mark Moxon for Kusto (63); 18 Chris Molyneux for Laughton (33); McNamara for Crabtree (58); Marshall for McNamara (68); Laughton for Cardoza (66BB, rev 70); Molloy for Molyneux (71BB); Cardoza for Atkins (78BB).
Tries: Appo (26), Lomax (40); **Goals:** McNamara 2.
League Express Men of the Match:
Broncos: Dennis Moran; *Giants:* Graham Appo.
Penalty count: 11-11; **Half-time:** 18-12;
Referee: Russell Smith (Castleford); **Attendance:** 2,894.

HULL FC 30 HALIFAX BLUE SOX 14

HULL: 4 Deon Bird; 21 Gareth Raynor; 6 Richard Horne; 23 Logan Campbell; 5 Matt Crowther; 16 Paul Cooke; 7 Tony Smith; 8 Paul Broadbent; 9 Lee Jackson; 10 Luke Felsch; 11 Adam Maher; 12 Tony Grimaldi (C); 13 Jason Smith. Subs: 14 Stanley Gene for Fletcher (67); 19 Richard Fletcher for Grimaldi (htBB, rev 50); 20 Garreth Carvell for Felsch (64); 18 Steve Craven for Broadbent (27); Fletcher for Cooke (50); Felsch for Craven (70).
Tries: Crowther (2), T Smith (18, 44), Grimaldi (57), Maher (75); **Goals:** Crowther 5.
Sin bin: Raynor (23) - interference at the play-the-ball; Bird (39) - fighting.
BLUE SOX: 1 Daryl Cardiss; 20 Danny Halliwell; 2 Jamie Bloem; 4 Adam Hughes; 19 Oliver Marns; 13 Martin Moana (C); 7 Gavin Clinch; 8 Andy Hobson; 9 Johnny Lawless; 23 Brett Goldspink; 10 Jim Gannon; 15 Paul Davidson; 12 Shayne McMenemy. Subs: 14 Danny Tickle for Goldspink (31); 16 Jamie Thackray for Hobson (30); 17 Sean Penkywicz for Lawless (64); 18 Stuart Donlan for Moana (75).
Tries: Cardiss (20), Davidson (68);
Goals: Bloem 2, Tickle.
Sin bin: Bloem (39) - fighting.
League Express Men of the Match:
Hull: Luke Felsch; *Blue Sox:* Daryl Cardiss.
Penalty count: 10-8; **Half-time:** 10-10;
Referee: Ian Smith (Oldham); **Attendance:** 7,160.

CASTLEFORD TIGERS 22 SALFORD CITY REDS 24

TIGERS: 1 Richard Gay; 2 Jon Wells; 3 Michael Eagar; 4 Barrie-Jon Mather; 5 Darren Rogers; 6 Danny Orr; 7 Mitch Healey; 8 Nathan Sykes; 9 Aaron Raper (C); 19 Gareth Handford; 12 Dale Fritz; 15 Darren Shaw; 11 Lee Harland. Subs: 26 Brad Hepi for Sykes (58); 23 Michael Smith for Handford (25); 10 Dean Sampson for Shaw (50); 22 Mark Lennon for Healey (32BB, rev 40); Sykes for Fritz (75); Lennon for Hepi (77).
Tries: Fritz (10), M Smith (28), Healey (48), Rogers (78); **Goals:** Orr 3.
On report: Gay (46) - unsighted incident.
CITY REDS: 14 Kris Tassell; 2 Nick Pinkney; 3 Francis Maloney; 18 Stuart Littler; 5 Martin Offiah; 6 Steve Blakeley; 16 Bobbie Goulding (C); 15 Damian Driscoll; 9 Malcolm Alker; 10 Paul Southern; 11 Warren Jowitt; 13 Paul Highton; 23 Mike Wainwright. Subs: 12 Darren Brown for Wainwright (27); 20 Andy Coley for Driscoll (24); 7 Graham Holroyd for Highton (65); 4 Michael Hancock for Coley (54); Driscoll for Southern (57); Coley for Driscoll (71).
Tries: Maloney (18, 76), Pinkney (38), Jowitt (67);
Goals: Goulding 4.
League Express Men of the Match:
Tigers: Mitch Healey; *City Reds:* Bobbie Goulding.
Penalty count: 8-4; **Half-time:** 8-12;
Referee: Steve Ganson (St Helens); **Attendance:** 6,816.

ROUND 6

Monday 16th April 2001

BRADFORD BULLS 35 WIGAN WARRIORS 24

BULLS: 28 Stuart Spruce; 2 Tevita Vaikona; 20 Scott Naylor; 15 Shane Rigon; 3 Leon Pryce; 6 Henry Paul; 1 Robbie Paul (C); 8 Joe Vagana; 9 James Lowes; 22 Brian McDermott; 19 Jamie Peacock; 11 Daniel Gartner; 12 Mike Forshaw. Subs: 10 Paul Anderson for Vagana (20); 7 Paul Deacon for Lowes (76); 29 Stuart Fielden for Gartner (16BB, rev 34); 14 Lee Gilmour for Pryce (63); Vagana for McDermott (48); Fielden for Vagana (55); McDermott for Gartner (66BB); Vagana for Anderson (69).
Tries: Vaikona (7), Pryce (27), Rigon (30), Gartner (56), R Paul (62); **Goals:** H Paul 7; **Field goal:** H Paul.
WARRIORS: 1 Kris Radlinski; 2 Brett Dallas; 15 Paul Johnson; 3 Steve Renouf; 23 David Hodgson; 6 Matthew Johns; 7 Adrian Lam; 10 Neil Cowie; 9 Terry Newton; 8 Terry O'Connor; 12 Denis Betts; 14 David Furner; 13 Andy Farrell (C). Subs: 18 Wes Davies for Renouf (38); 17 Francis Stephenson for O'Connor (28); 11 Mick Cassidy for Betts (43BB, rev 70); 20 Harvey Howard for Cowie (21); O'Connor for Stephenson (54); Cowie for Howard (56); Stephenson for Cowie (68).
Tries: Newton (49), Johns (54), Davies (64), Lam (71);
Goals: Farrell 4.
League Express Men of the Match:
Bulls: Henry Paul; *Warriors:* Adrian Lam.
Penalty count: 5-8; **Half-time:** 20-0; **Referee:** Russell Smith (Castleford); **Attendance:** 16,247.

HUDDERSFIELD GIANTS 16 WAKEFIELD TRINITY WILDCATS 24

GIANTS: 21 Graham Appo; 2 Andrew Frew; 27 Brandon Costin; 4 Dale Cardoza; 3 Martin Gleeson; 6 Chris Thorman; 7 Ben Kusto; 12 Richard Marshall; 9 Paul Rowley; 10 Dale Laughton (C); 11 David Lomax; 13 David Atkins; 26 Steve McNamara. Subs: 8 Steve Molloy for Laughton (25); 18 Chris Molyneux for Marshall (32); 15 Darren Turner for Lomax (50); 17 Mark Moxon not used; Laughton for Molloy (53).
Tries: Costin (30), Appo (34), Kusto (52);
Goals: McNamara 2.
WILDCATS: 1 Martyn Holland; 3 Richard Smith; 25 Tom Haughey; 4 Justin Brooker; 5 Waisale Sovatabua; 6 Martin Pearson; 9 David March; 16 Julian O'Neill; 18 Ben Rauter; 10 Frank Watene; 15 Ryan Hudson; 12 Willie Poching (C); 11 Jamie Field. Subs: 8 Paul Jackson for Watene (33); 19 Gareth Ellis for Poching (33); 23 Paul Handforth for Rauter (68); 27 Lionel Harbin (D) for Field (56); Watene for O'Neill (59).
Tries: Rauter (5, 16), Field (12), Sovatabua (79);
Goals: Pearson 4.
League Express Men of the Match:
Giants: Ben Kusto; *Wildcats:* Martyn Holland.
Penalty count: 7-6; **Half-time:** 10-18;
Referee: Steve Ganson (St Helens); **Attendance:** 3,516.

LEEDS RHINOS 32 CASTLEFORD TIGERS 22

RHINOS: 5 Francis Cummins; 16 Mark Calderwood; 15 Chev Walker; 4 Keith Senior; 14 Marcus St Hilaire; 1 Iestyn Harris (C); 29 Robert Burrow; 8 Darren Fleary; 2 Karl Pratt; 20 Jamie Mathiou; 17 Anthony Farrell; 11 Andy Hay; 13 Kevin Sinfield. Subs: 18 Danny Ward for Fleary (25); 22 David Wrench for Farrell (51); 28 Andy Kirk for Hay (71); 12 Bradley Clyde not used; Fleary for Mathiou (51); Farrell for Ward (54); Mathiou for Farrell (69).
Tries: St Hilaire (29, 32, 51), Sinfield (38), Farrell (59), Cummins (70); **Goals:** Harris 4.
TIGERS: 1 Richard Gay; 2 Jon Wells; 3 Michael Eagar; 4 Barrie-Jon Mather; 5 Darren Rogers; 6 Danny Orr; 7 Mitch Healey; 8 Nathan Sykes; 9 Aaron Raper (C); 19 Gareth Handford; 15 Darren Shaw; 12 Dale Fritz; 11 Lee Harland. Subs: 23 Michael Smith for Handford (27); 17 Andy Lynch for Sykes (54); 22 Mark Lennon for Gay (72); 26 Brad Hepi for Fritz (72); Handford for Shaw (61).
Tries: Rogers (5, 19), Orr (56), Eagar (74); **Goals:** Orr 3.
League Express Men of the Match:
Rhinos: Karl Pratt; *Tigers:* Michael Eagar.
Penalty count: 5-6; **Half-time:** 16-12;
Referee: Ian Smith (Oldham); **Attendance:** 15,039.

ST HELENS 38 HULL FC 34

SAINTS: 1 Paul Wellens; 2 Sean Hoppe; 3 Kevin Iro; 4 Paul Newlove; 19 Anthony Stewart; 20 Tommy Martyn; 7 Sean Long; 12 Sonny Nickle; 9 Keiron Cunningham; 14 Wayne McDonald; 10 David Fairleigh; 11 Chris Joynt (C); 13 Paul Sculthorpe. Subs: 16 Vila Matautia for Nickle (25); 15 Tim Jonkers for McDonald (28); 21 Dwayne West for Joynt (62); 18 John Stankevitch for Matautia (50); McDonald for Cunningham (64); Joynt for Hoppe (73).
Tries: Stewart (9, 17); Cunningham (32), Hoppe (38), Newlove (54, 62), Wellens (57); **Goals:** Long 5.
HULL: 1 Steve Prescott; 21 Gareth Raynor; 4 Deon Bird; 23 Logan Campbell; 5 Matt Crowther; 16 Paul Cooke; 6 Richard Horne; 18 Steve Craven; 15 Paul King; 10 Luke Felsch; 11 Adam Maher; 12 Tony Grimaldi (C); 13 Jason Smith. Subs: 19 Richard Fletcher for Maher (25); 14 Stanley Gene for King (25); 20 Garreth Carvell for Craven (31BB, rev 59); 26 Paul Parker for Campbell (59); King for Gene (40); Carvell for Felsch (73).
Tries: Crowther (14), Felsch (27), Bird (50), Prescott (69), J Smith (72), Parker (74); **Goals:** Crowther 5.
League Express Men of the Match:
Saints: Keiron Cunningham; *Hull:* Jason Smith.
Penalty count: 8-3; **Half-time:** 24-10;
Referee: Robert Connolly (Wigan); **Attendance:** 10,479.

SALFORD CITY REDS 12 LONDON BRONCOS 14

CITY REDS: 14 Kris Tassell; 2 Nick Pinkney; 3 Francis Maloney; 18 Stuart Littler; 4 Michael Hancock; 6 Steve Blakeley; 16 Bobbie Goulding (C); 10 Paul Southern; 9 Malcolm Alker; 15 Damian Driscoll; 11 Warren Jowitt; 13 Paul Highton; 23 Mike Wainwright. Subs: 12 Darren Brown for Jowitt (28); 20 Andy Coley for Driscoll (20); 17 Craig Makin for Southern (62); 7 Graham Holroyd for Blakeley (57); Jowitt for Highton (55).
Tries: Pinkney (48), Coley (78); **Goals:** Goulding 2.
BRONCOS: 23 Richie Barnett; 2 Nigel Roy; 3 Tony Martin; 4 Greg Fleming; 28 Marvin Golden; 6 Jim Dymock; 7 Dennis Moran; 8 Tony Mestrov; 9 Jason Hetherington (C); 10 Scott Cram; 11 Shane Millard; 12 Steele Retchless; 13 Mat Toshack. Subs: 5 Brett Warton not used; 18 Justin Dooley for Mestrov (28); 21 Jon Clarke for Hetherington (67); 27 Michael Gillett for Millard (49); Mestrov for Dooley (67); Hetherington for Dymock (77).
Tries: Millard (35), Roy (66); **Goals:** Martin 3.
League Express Men of the Match:
City Reds: Bobbie Goulding; *Broncos:* Richie Barnett
Penalty count: 7-7; **Half-time:** 2-8; **Referee:** Stuart Cummings (Widnes); **Attendance:** 3,967.

HALIFAX BLUE SOX 30 WARRINGTON WOLVES 32

BLUE SOX: 18 Stuart Donlan; 19 Oliver Marns; 14 Danny Tickle; 4 Adam Hughes; 3 Damian Gibson; 1 Daryl Cardiss; 7 Gavin Clinch; 23 Brett Goldspink; 9 Johnny Lawless; 10 Jim Gannon; 12 Shayne McMenemy; 15 Paul Davidson; 13 Martin Moana (C). Subs: 2 Jamie Bloem for Goldspink (31); 8 Andy Hobson for Davidson (48); 17 Sean Penkywicz not used; 20 Danny Halliwell not used; Goldspink for Gannon (60); Davidson for Moana (64); Gannon for Hobson (68); Moana for Lawless (74).
Tries: Hughes (3, 33), Gibson (24), Bloem (52, 78); **Goals:** Tickle 5.
WOLVES: 22 Alan Hunte; 2 Rob Smyth; 4 Toa Kohe-Love; 16 Ian Sibbit; 5 Jamie Stenhouse; 6 Lee Briers; 7 Allan Langer (C); 18 Martin Masella; 9 David Highton; 10 Danny Nutley; 20 Dean Busby; 25 Gary Mercer; 15 Steve Georgallis. Subs: 11 Steve McCurrie for Georgallis (12); 3 David Kidwell for Busby (13BB, rev 22); 21 Paul Wood for Nutley (65); 17 David Alstead not used; Kidwell for McCurrie (60).
Tries: Busby (6, 75), Smyth (27, 45), Hunte (59), Masella (71); **Goals:** Briers 4.
League Express Men of the Match:
Blue Sox: Gavin Clinch; *Wolves:* Dean Busby.
Penalty count: 5-5; **Half-time:** 18-12;
Referee: Peter Taberner (Wigan); **Attendance:** 4,889.

ROUND 7

Friday 20th April 2001

WARRINGTON WOLVES 56 ST HELENS 22

WOLVES: 22 Alan Hunte; 2 Rob Smyth; 16 Ian Sibbit; 4 Toa Kohe-Love; 5 Jamie Stenhouse; 6 Lee Briers; 7 Allan Langer (C); 18 Martin Masella; 9 David Highton; 10 Danny Nutley; 11 Steve McCurrie; 25 Gary Mercer; 20 Dean Busby. Subs: 3 David Kidwell for Busby (29); 8 Andrew Gee for Masella (23); 21 Paul Wood for Nutley (71); 17 David Alstead for Smyth (71); Masella for Nutley (49); Nutley for Gee (60).
Tries: Hunte (5, 67, 73), Kohe-Love (19, 39, 50), Sibbit (22, 63), Smyth (27, 43); **Goals:** Briers 8.
SAINTS: 19 Anthony Stewart; 21 Dwayne West; 17 Steve Hall; 4 Paul Newlove; 5 Anthony Sullivan; 20 Tommy Martyn; 1 Paul Wellens; 14 Wayne McDonald; 9 Keiron Cunningham; 12 Sonny Nickle; 8 Peter Shiels; 11 Chris Joynt (C); 13 Paul Sculthorpe. Subs: 15 Tim Jonkers for Nickle (36); 16 Vila Matautia for McDonald (26); 18 John Stankevitch for Matautia (52); 23 Mike Bennett for Sculthorpe (72); Matautia for Stankevitch (60); McDonald for Cunningham (61).
Tries: Cunningham (2), Newlove (7), Hall (15), Jonkers (79); **Goals:** Martyn 3.
Sent off: Newlove (29) - high tackle on Kohe-Love.
League Express Men of the Match:
Wolves: Allan Langer; *Saints:* Keiron Cunningham.
Penalty count: 8-7; **Half-time:** 28-16;
Referee: Robert Connolly (Wigan); **Attendance:** 8,060.

WIGAN WARRIORS 37 HUDDERSFIELD GIANTS 8

WARRIORS: 1 Kris Radlinski; 2 Brett Dallas; 23 David Hodgson; 4 Gary Connolly; 5 Brian Carney (D); 6 Matthew Johns; 7 Adrian Lam; 17 Francis Stephenson; 21 Mark Smith; 10 Neil Cowie; 11 Mick Cassidy; 16 Simon Haughton; 13 Andy Farrell (C). Subs: 8 Terry O'Connor for Stephenson (31); 14 David Furner for Farrell (41); 22 Phil Jones for Lam (60); 15 Paul Johnson for Connolly (60); Stephenson for Cowie (45BB, rev 50).
Tries: Carney (7, 54), Radlinski (31), Furner (45), Dallas (64), Jones (78); **Goals:** Farrell 2, Furner 4;
Field goal: Johns.
GIANTS: 25 Ben Cooper; 3 Martin Gleeson; 4 Dale Cardoza; 27 Brandon Costin; 5 Hefin O'Hare (D); 7 Ben Kusto; 17 Mark Moxon; 8 Steve Molloy; 9 Paul Rowley; 12 Richard Marshall; 13 David Atkins; 11 David Lomax; 26 Steve McNamara (C). Subs: 10 Dale Laughton for Molloy (23); 18 Chris Molyneux for Marshall (29); 6 Chris Thorman for Lomax (55); 14 Andy Rice for Atkins (67); Marshall for McNamara (48BB, rev 62); Molloy for Molyneux (58); Lomax for Laughton (74).
Tries: O'Hare (39), Cardoza (61).
League Express Men of the Match:
Warriors: Kris Radlinski; *Giants:* Dale Cardoza.
Penalty count: 6-4; **Half-time:** 12-4;
Referee: Ian Smith (Oldham); **Attendance:** 7,772.

Saturday 21st April 2001

HULL FC 24 BRADFORD BULLS 24

HULL: 1 Steve Prescott; 21 Gareth Raynor; 6 Richard Horne; 4 Deon Bird; 5 Matt Crowther; 16 Paul Cooke; 7 Tony Smith; 8 Paul Broadbent; 15 Paul King; 18 Steve Craven; 10 Luke Felsch; 12 Tony Grimaldi (C); 13 Jason Smith. Subs: 23 Logan Campbell for Bird (35); 19 Richard Fletcher for Broadbent (34); 20 Garreth Carvell for Craven (59); 9 Lee Jackson for King (30); King for Felsch (67).
Tries: Grimaldi (13, 68), Fletcher (45), T Smith (77); **Goals:** Crowther 4.
BULLS: 28 Stuart Spruce; 14 Lee Gilmour; 20 Scott Naylor; 15 Shane Rigon; 3 Leon Pryce; 6 Henry Paul; 1 Robbie Paul (C); 8 Joe Vagana; 9 James Lowes; 22 Brian McDermott; 19 Jamie Peacock; 11 Daniel Gartner; 12 Mike Forshaw. Subs: 29 Stuart Fielden for McDermott (14BB, rev 25); 10 Paul Anderson for Vagana (23); 7 Paul Deacon for Gilmour (33); 18 Lee Radford for Rigon (55); Vagana for Anderson (57); Fielden for Gartner (69); Anderson for McDermott (74).
Tries: Gartner (13, 64), Forshaw (51); **Goals:** H Paul 6.
League Express Men of the Match:
Hull: Steve Prescott; *Bulls:* Henry Paul.
Penalty count: 5-4; **Half-time:** 8-10;
Referee: Stuart Cummings (Widnes); **Attendance:** 7,518.

Sunday 22nd April 2001

CASTLEFORD TIGERS 34 HALIFAX BLUE SOX 24

TIGERS: 1 Richard Gay; 22 Mark Lennon; 2 Jon Wells; 3 Michael Eagar; 5 Darren Rogers; 6 Danny Orr; 7 Mitch Healey; 8 Nathan Sykes; 9 Aaron Raper; 10 Dean Sampson (C); 12 Dale Fritz; 15 Darren Shaw; 11 Lee Harland. Subs: 26 Brad Hepi for Fritz (73); 23 Michael Smith for Sampson (25); 17 Andy Lynch for Sykes (50); 20 Waine Pryce for Healey (19); Sampson for Shaw (52); Sykes for Sampson (68).
Tries: Eagar (6, 37), Gay (14), Wells (55), M Smith (73); **Goals:** Orr 7.
BLUE SOX: 18 Stuart Donlan; 3 Damian Gibson; 14 Danny Tickle; 4 Adam Hughes; 19 Oliver Marns; 1 Daryl Cardiss; 7 Gavin Clinch; 10 Jim Gannon; 9 Johnny Lawless; 23 Brett Goldspink; 12 Shayne McMenemy; 15 Paul Davidson; 13 Martin Moana (C). Subs: 2 Jamie Bloem for Goldspink (31); 26 Danny Ekis (D) for Lawford (59); 25 Dean Lawford (D) for Hughes (17); 17 Sean Penkywicz for Lawless (56); Davidson for Goldspink (50); Goldspink for McMenemy (68).
Tries: Cardiss (10, 46), Marns (29), Tickle (34); **Goals:** Tickle 4.
League Express Men of the Match:
Tigers: Danny Orr; *Blue Sox:* Daryl Cardiss.
Penalty count: 8-4; **Half-time:** 18-18; **Referee:** Karl Kirkpatrick (Warrington); **Attendance:** 6,483.

WAKEFIELD TRINITY WILDCATS 10 LONDON BRONCOS 38

WILDCATS: 1 Martyn Holland; 28 Nathan Batty (D); 20 Ben Westwood; 4 Justin Brooker; 5 Waisale Sovatabua; 6 Martin Pearson; 23 Paul Handforth; 16 Julian O'Neill; 9 David March; 10 Frank Watene; 15 Ryan Hudson; 12 Willie Poching (C); 18 Ben Rauter. Subs: 22 Keith Mason for O'Neill (20); 8 Paul Jackson for Watene (19); 25 Tom Haughey for Rauter (51); 19 Gareth Ellis for March (51); March for Pearson (53BB); O'Neill for Mason (68); Watene for Poching (77).
Try: Handforth (79); **Goals:** Pearson 2, Westwood.
BRONCOS: 23 Richie Barnett (C); 2 Nigel Roy; 3 Tony Martin; 4 Greg Fleming; 28 Marvin Golden; 6 Jim Dymock; 7 Dennis Moran; 8 Tony Mestrov; 21 Jon Clarke; 10 Scott Cram; 11 Shane Millard; 12 Steele Retchless; 13 Mat Toshack. Subs: 1 Tulsen Tollett for Moran (47BB); 5 Brett Warton for Clarke (67); 18 Justin Dooley for Clarke (16BB, rev 46); 27 Michael Gillett for Millard (59); Dooley for Mestrov (51); Mestrov for Cram (67); Moran for Dymock (73); Clarke for Toshack (79).
Tries: Fleming (4, 20), Dooley (34), Barnett (57, 67) Warton (75); **Goals:** Martin 6, Warton.
League Express Men of the Match:
Wildcats: Paul Handforth; *Broncos:* Richie Barnett.
Penalty count: 6-6; **Half-time:** 4-20;
Referee: Steve Ganson (St Helens); **Attendance:** 2,547.

SALFORD CITY REDS 14 LEEDS RHINOS 19

CITY REDS: 7 Graham Holroyd; 2 Nick Pinkney; 3 Francis Maloney; 18 Stuart Littler; 24 Neil Baxter (D); 6 Steve Blakeley; 16 Bobbie Goulding (C); 10 Paul Southern; 9 Malcolm Alker; 15 Damian Driscoll; 11 Warren Jowitt; 13 Paul Highton; 23 Mike Wainwright. Subs: 12 Darren Brown for Highton (34); 4 Michael Hancock for Baxter (49); 20 Andy Coley for Driscoll (24); 22 Karle Hammond for Goulding (51); Highton for Southern (67); Driscoll for Jowitt (78).
Tries: Littler (50), Hancock (74);
Goals: Goulding 2, Holroyd.
Sin bin: Jowitt (20) - punching.
RHINOS: 5 Francis Cummins; 14 Marcus St Hilaire; 15 Chev Walker; 4 Keith Senior; 2 Karl Pratt; 1 Iestyn Harris (C); 29 Robert Burrow; 8 Darren Fleary; 9 Robert Mears; 20 Jamie Mathiou; 11 Andy Hay; 17 Anthony Farrell; 13 Kevin Sinfield. Subs: 7 Ryan Sheridan for Burrow (53); 16 Mark Calderwood for St Hilaire (47); 3 Tonie Carroll for Farrell (32); 12 Bradley Clyde for Mathiou (26); Farrell for Fleary (70).
Tries: Walker (33), Harris (59), Pratt (80);
Goals: Harris 3; **Field goal:** Harris.
League Express Men of the Match:
City Reds: Andy Coley; *Rhinos:* Iestyn Harris.
Penalty count: 11-9; **Half-time:** 4-8;
Referee: Russell Smith (Castleford); **Attendance:** 5,069.

ROUND 8

Sunday 29th April 2001

LONDON BRONCOS 20 WIGAN WARRIORS 12

BRONCOS: 23 Richie Barnett; 2 Nigel Roy; 3 Tony Martin; 4 Greg Fleming; 28 Marvin Golden; 1 Tulsen Tollett; 7 Dennis Moran; 8 Tony Mestrov; 9 Jason Hetherington (C); 10 Scott Cram; 13 Mat Toshack; 12 Steele Retchless; 6 Jim Dymock. Subs: 5 Brett Warton for Golden (54); 18 Justin Dooley for Mestrov (12BB, rev 34); 27 Michael Gillett for Tollett (71); 21 Jon Clarke not used; Dooley for Mestrov (47); Mestrov for Dymock (59BB, rev 70); Mestrov for Dooley (75).
Tries: Tollett (22), Barnett (28), Fleming (34), Martin (62); **Goals:** Martin 2.
On report: Dooley - suspected high tackle.
WARRIORS: 1 Kris Radlinski; 2 Brett Dallas; 3 Steve Renouf; 15 Paul Johnson; 5 Brian Carney; 6 Matthew Johns; 7 Adrian Lam; 8 Terry O'Connor; 9 Terry Newton; 10 Neil Cowie; 11 Mick Cassidy; 14 David Furner; 13 Andy Farrell (C). Subs: 12 Denis Betts for Newton (47); 16 Simon Haughton for O'Connor (59); 20 Harvey Howard for Cowie (30); 4 Gary Connolly not used; Cowie for Howard (57); Newton for Cassidy (65); O'Connor for Cowie (75).
Tries: Johns (10), Radlinski (37); **Goals:** Farrell 2.
On report: Incident after dangerous tackle midway through the second half.
League Express Men of the Match:
Broncos: Richie Barnett; *Warriors:* Brian Carney.
Penalty count: 7-9; **Half-time:** 16-12; **Referee:** Karl Kirkpatrick (Warrington); **Attendance:** 5,101.

Monday 30th April 2001

HALIFAX BLUE SOX 26 LEEDS RHINOS 38

BLUE SOX: 1 Daryl Cardiss; 3 Damian Gibson; 18 Stuart Donlan; 14 Danny Tickle; 19 Oliver Marns; 25 Dean Lawford; 7 Gavin Clinch; 23 Brett Goldspink; 9 Johnny Lawless; 10 Jim Gannon; 12 Shayne McMenemy; 15 Paul Davidson; 13 Martin Moana (C). Subs: 17 Sean Penkywicz for Lawless (19); 8 Andy Hobson for Goldspink (27); 2 Jamie Bloem for Lawford (55); 4 Adam Hughes for Moana (71); Lawless for Clinch (61); Goldspink for Hobson (64).
Tries: Marns (25), Lawless (52), Davidson (63), Bloem (78); **Goals:** Tickle 5.
RHINOS: 5 Francis Cummins; 16 Mark Calderwood; 3 Tonie Carroll; 4 Keith Senior; 14 Marcus St Hilaire; 1 Iestyn Harris (C); 2 Karl Pratt; 8 Darren Fleary; 9 Robert Mears; 20 Jamie Mathiou; 11 Andy Hay; 17 Anthony Farrell; 13 Kevin Sinfield. Subs: 12 Bradley Clyde for Hay (20BB, rev 35); 10 Barrie McDermott for Mathiou (23); 15 Chev Walker for Farrell (70); 29 Robert Burrow not used; Clyde for Fleary (35); Mathiou for Hay (55); Fleary for McDermott (66).
Tries: Cummins (4, 16), Mears (14), Senior (43, 46), Harris (68); **Goals:** Harris 7.
On report: Dangerous tackle involving Pratt and Harris.
League Express Men of the Match:
Blue Sox: Sean Penkywicz; *Rhinos:* Robert Mears.
Penalty count: 10-8; **Half-time:** 8-18;
Referee: Ian Smith (Oldham); **Attendance:** 6,471.

HUDDERSFIELD GIANTS 14 HULL FC 44

GIANTS: 25 Ben Cooper; 2 Andrew Frew; 4 Dale Cardoza; 27 Brandon Costin; 5 Hefin O'Hare; 7 Ben Kusto; 17 Mark Moxon; 8 Steve Molloy; 9 Paul Rowley; 18 Chris Molyneux; 11 David Lomax; 13 David Atkins; 26 Steve McNamara (C). Subs: 22 Eorl Crabtree for Molyneux (20); 10 Dale Laughton for Molloy (28); 6 Chris Thorman for Moxon (47); 14 Andy Rice for Laughton (51); Molloy for Lomax (66); Molyneux for Crabtree (66).
Tries: Kusto (18), O'Hare (80); **Goals:** McNamara 3.
HULL: 1 Steve Prescott; 21 Gareth Raynor; 23 Logan Campbell; 4 Deon Bird; 5 Matt Crowther; 16 Paul Cooke; 6 Richard Horne; 8 Paul Broadbent; 9 Lee Jackson; 18 Steve Craven; 10 Luke Felsch; 12 Tony Grimaldi (C); 13 Jason Smith. Subs: 3 David Maiden for Smith (60); 15 Paul King for Broadbent (31); 19 Richard Fletcher for Jackson (45); 20 Garreth Carvell for Craven (54); Broadbent for Felsch (68).
Tries: Prescott (15), Raynor (22, 32), Jackson (27), Grimaldi (46), Bird (51), J Smith (58), Maiden (76);
Goals: Crowther 6.
League Express Men of the Match:
Giants: Ben Kusto; *Hull:* Jason Smith.
Penalty count: 5-6; **Half-time:** 8-20;
Referee: Robert Connolly (Wigan); **Attendance:** 3,859.

WAKEFIELD TRINITY WILDCATS 32 SALFORD CITY REDS 22

WILDCATS: 1 Martyn Holland; 5 Waisale Sovatabua; 3 Richard Smith; 4 Justin Brooker; 2 Neil Law; 14 Paul March; 23 Paul Handforth; 16 Julian O'Neill; 15 Ryan Hudson; 8 Paul Jackson; 11 Jamie Field; 13 Gary Price; 12 Willie Poching (C). Subs: 22 Keith Mason for O'Neill (20); 17 Graham Law for P March (49BB, rev 54); 9 David March for Field (53); 20 Ben Westwood for Smith (73); Field for Mason (65); G Law for Price (67).
Tries: Price (17, 30), Field (23), Sovatabua (53), Brooker (75, 80); **Goals:** P March 4.
CITY REDS: 7 Graham Holroyd; 2 Nick Pinkney; 30 Jason Nicol; 3 Francis Maloney; 18 Stuart Littler; 22 Karle Hammond; 6 Steve Blakeley; 10 Paul Southern; 9 Malcolm Alker (C); 15 Damian Driscoll; 11 Warren Jowitt; 13 Paul Highton; 23 Mike Wainwright. Subs: 12 Darren Brown for Jowitt (20); 20 Andy Coley for Driscoll (25); 4 Michael Hancock for Highton (49); 25 Lee Marsh (D) for Hammond (60); Driscoll for Southern (63).
Tries: Maloney (10, 34), Pinkney (58), Coley (70);
Goals: Holroyd 3.
Sin bin: Holroyd (23) - lying on.
League Express Men of the Match:
Wildcats: Ryan Hudson; *City Reds:* Andy Coley.
Penalty count: 2-3; **Half-time:** 16-10;
Referee: Stuart Cummings (Widnes); **Attendance:** 2,940.

Wednesday 2nd May 2001

BRADFORD BULLS 56 WARRINGTON WOLVES 24

BULLS: 5 Michael Withers; 2 Tevita Vaikona; 20 Scott Naylor; 14 Lee Gilmour; 3 Leon Pryce; 6 Henry Paul; 1 Robbie Paul (C); 8 Joe Vagana; 9 James Lowes; 22 Brian McDermott; 11 Daniel Gartner; 18 Lee Radford; 12

Mike Forshaw. Subs: 7 Paul Deacon for Lowes (14BB, rev 25); 10 Paul Anderson for Vagana (20); 23 Graham Mackay (D2) for Naylor (55); 29 Stuart Fielden for McDermott (22); McDermott for Gartner (39); Deacon for H Paul (40); H Paul for Deacon (64).
Tries: Gilmour (7), Withers (10), Pryce (17), Vaikona (40, 68, 70), Naylor (45), Mackay (78), R Paul (80);
Goals: H Paul 8, Deacon 2.
Sin bin: Fielden (65) – fighting.
WOLVES: 22 Alan Hunte; 2 Rob Smyth; 16 Ian Sibbit; 4 Toa Kohe-Love; 17 David Alstead; 6 Lee Briers; 7 Allan Langer (C); 8 Andrew Gee; 9 David Highton; 10 Danny Nutley; 11 Steve McCurrie; 25 Gary Mercer; 13 Tawera Nikau. Subs: 3 David Kidwell for McCurrie (33); 18 Martin Masella for Gee (14BB, rev 23); 21 Paul Wood for Gee (76); 12 Jerome Guisset for Nutley (74); Masella for Nutley (30); Nutley for Gee (42BB, rev 49); Nutley for Masella (50); McCurrie for Kidwell (55).
Tries: Mercer (26), Masella (49), Nikau (57), Briers (74);
Goals: Briers 4.
Sin bin: Gee (65) – fighting.
League Express Men of the Match:
Bulls: Tevita Vaikona; *Wolves:* Tawera Nikau.
Penalty count: 8-8; **Half-time:** 24-6;
Referee: Ian Smith (Oldham); **Attendance:** 9,663.

Wednesday 9th May 2001

ST HELENS 36 CASTLEFORD TIGERS 16

SAINTS: 19 Anthony Stewart; 17 Steve Hall; 3 Kevin Iro; 2 Sean Hoppe; 5 Anthony Sullivan; 1 Paul Wellens; 7 Sean Long; 10 David Fairleigh; 9 Keiron Cunningham; 25 Mark Edmondson; 8 Peter Shiels; 11 Chris Joynt (C); 13 Paul Sculthorpe. Subs: 15 Tim Jonkers for Matautia (55); 21 Dwayne West for Long (73); 12 Sonny Nickle for Fairleigh (20); 16 Vila Matautia for Edmondson (30); Edmondson for Joynt (61); Matautia for Cunningham (75).
Tries: Nickle (28), Stewart (32, 69), Long (41), Cunningham (43), Sullivan (58), Matautia (80);
Goals: Long 4.
TIGERS: 14 Jason Flowers; 1 Richard Gay; 2 Jon Wells; 3 Michael Eagar; 5 Darren Rogers; 6 Danny Orr; 22 Mark Lennon; 10 Dean Sampson (C); 12 Dale Fritz; 19 Gareth Handford; 15 Darren Shaw; 16 Ian Tonks; 11 Lee Harland. Subs: 21 Andy McNally (D) for Rogers (75); 20 Waine Pryce for Lennon (74); 17 Andy Lynch for Handford (25); 27 Andy Speak (D) for Tonks (19); Tonks for Speak (28); Speak for Shaw (58).
Tries: Wells (7), Gay (56), Tonks (65); **Goals:** Orr 2.
League Express Men of the Match:
Saints: Paul Sculthorpe; *Tigers:* Danny Orr.
Penalty count: 6-10; **Half-time:** 6-10;
Referee: Ian Smith (Oldham); **Attendance:** 6,836.

ROUND 9

Friday 4th May 2001

LEEDS RHINOS 74 ST HELENS 16

RHINOS: 5 Francis Cummins; 15 Chev Walker; 3 Tonie Carroll; 4 Keith Senior; 14 Marcus St Hilaire; 1 Iestyn Harris (C); 2 Karl Pratt; 8 Darren Fleary; 9 Robert Mears; 20 Jamie Mathiou; 17 Anthony Farrell; 11 Andy Hay; 13 Kevin Sinfield. Subs: 10 Barrie McDermott for Fleary (24); 12 Bradley Clyde for Mathiou (30); 16 Mark Calderwood for Cummins (49BB, rev 60); 22 David Wrench for Senior (50BB, rev 51); Fleary for Farrell (58); Mathiou for McDermott (62); Wrench for Hay (68); Hay for Clyde (74).
Tries: Senior (11, 79), Carroll (19, 23, 38, 70), Pratt (33), Cummins (35, 66, 77), Hay (43), Harris (58), Walker (64); **Goals:** Harris 11.
SAINTS: 19 Anthony Stewart; 17 Steve Hall; 3 Kevin Iro; 2 Sean Hoppe; 5 Anthony Sullivan; 13 Paul Sculthorpe; 7 Sean Long; 12 Sonny Nickle; 9 Keiron Cunningham; 10 David Fairleigh; 11 Chris Joynt (C); 8 Peter Shiels; 15 Tim Jonkers. Subs: 18 John Stankevitch for Joynt (24BB, rev 40); 16 Vila Matautia for Nickle (30); 14 Wayne McDonald for Matautia (52); 21 Dwayne West for Hoppe (73); Nickle for Fairleigh (52); Matautia for Joynt (69).
Tries: Sullivan (7), Iro (30), Hall (55); **Goals:** Long 2.
League Express Men of the Match:
Rhinos: Iestyn Harris; *Saints:* Sean Long.
Penalty count: 8-3; **Half-time:** 32-10;
Referee: Robert Connolly (Wigan); **Attendance:** 15,702.

WIGAN WARRIORS 50
WAKEFIELD TRINITY WILDCATS 6

WARRIORS: 1 Kris Radlinski; 2 Brett Dallas; 4 Gary Connolly; 3 Steve Renouf; 5 Brian Carney; 6 Matthew Johns; 7 Adrian Lam; 8 Terry O'Connor; 21 Mark Smith; 10 Neil Cowie; 9 Terry Newton; 14 David Furner; 13 Andy Farrell (C). Subs: 26 Ricky Bibey (D) for Cowie (28); 11 Mick Cassidy for Newton (41); 12 Denis Betts for Bibey (56); 23 David Hodgson for Carney (13); Cowie for O'Connor (41); O'Connor for Cowie (66).
Tries: Radlinski (9, 78), Lam (23), Renouf (35), Connolly (45), Furner (54), Farrell (62), Dallas (73);
Goals: Farrell 9.
WILDCATS: 1 Martyn Holland; 5 Waisale Sovatabua; 4 Justin Brooker; 3 Richard Smith; 2 Neil Law; 14 Paul March; 23 Paul Handforth; 8 Paul Jackson; 9 David March; 11 Jamie Field; 15 Ryan Hudson; 12 Willie Poching (C); 13 Gary Price. Subs: 22 Keith Mason for Field (49); 26 Dane Dorahy for Holland (16); 24 Chris Feather for Jackson (56); 17 Graham Law for P March (41); Field for Price (62).
Try: D March (67); **Goal:** Dorahy.

League Express Men of the Match:
Warriors: Adrian Lam; *Wildcats:* Ryan Hudson.
Penalty count: 9-6; **Half-time:** 18-0; **Referee:** Karl Kirkpatrick (Warrington); **Attendance:** 8,282.

Saturday 5th May 2001

CASTLEFORD TIGERS 22 BRADFORD BULLS 24

TIGERS: 1 Richard Gay; 2 Jon Wells; 3 Michael Eagar; 4 Barrie-Jon Mather; 5 Darren Rogers; 6 Danny Orr; 22 Mark Lennon; 8 Nathan Sykes; 9 Aaron Raper (C); 19 Gareth Handford; 15 Darren Shaw; 12 Dale Fritz; 11 Lee Harland. Subs: 10 Dean Sampson for Sykes (28); 23 Michael Smith for Raper (23); 16 Ian Tonks for Handford (53); 14 Jason Flowers for Shaw (65).
Tries: Orr (48), Wells (61), Gay (74); **Goals:** Orr 5.
On report: Fritz (38) – spear tackle.
BULLS: 5 Michael Withers; 2 Tevita Vaikona; 23 Graham Mackay; 14 Lee Gilmour; 3 Leon Pryce; 6 Henry Paul; 1 Robbie Paul (C); 8 Joe Vagana; 9 James Lowes; 22 Brian McDermott; 19 Jamie Peacock; 18 Lee Radford; 12 Mike Forshaw. Subs: 10 Paul Anderson for Vagana (22); 29 Stuart Fielden for McDermott (22); 26 Paul Sykes not used; 27 Robert Parker not used; McDermott for Anderson (54); Vagana for Forshaw (62); Anderson for Vagana (71).
Tries: H Paul (13), R Paul (44), Lowes (52);
Goals: H Paul 6.
League Express Men of the Match:
Tigers: Danny Orr; *Bulls:* Henry Paul.
Penalty count: 11-12; **Half-time:** 2-8;
Referee: Stuart Cummings (Widnes); **Attendance:** 8,528.

Sunday 6th May 2001

WARRINGTON WOLVES 36 HUDDERSFIELD GIANTS 16

WOLVES: 22 Alan Hunte; 2 Rob Smyth; 4 Toa Kohe-Love; 16 Ian Sibbit; 17 David Alstead; 6 Lee Briers; 7 Allan Langer (C); 8 Andrew Gee; 9 David Highton; 10 Danny Nutley; 11 Steve McCurrie; 25 Gary Mercer; 13 Tawera Nikau. Subs: 21 Paul Wood for Nutley (69); 20 Dean Busby for McCurrie (20); 3 David Kidwell for Nikau (54); 12 Jerome Guisset for Gee (66); McCurrie for Highton (25).
Tries: Hunte (10), Briers (27), Nikau (36), Kohe-Love (55), Sibbit (68), Guisset (79); **Goals:** Briers 6.
GIANTS: 21 Graham Appo; 2 Andrew Frew; 27 Brandon Costin; 4 Dale Cardoza; 3 Martin Gleeson; 6 Chris Thorman; 7 Ben Kusto; 8 Steve Molloy; 9 Paul Rowley; 12 Richard Marshall; 13 David Atkins; 11 David Lomax; 26 Steve McNamara (C). Subs: 17 Mark Moxon for Thorman (56); 18 Chris Molyneux for Marshall (46); 14 Andy Rice for Lomax (48); 22 Eorl Crabtree for Molloy (16); Marshall for Crabtree (56); Crabtree for Molyneux (57).
Tries: Lomax (19), Kusto (31); **Goals:** McNamara 4.
League Express Men of the Match:
Wolves: Danny Nutley; *Giants:* David Atkins.
Penalty count: 13-6; **Half-time:** 16-16;
Referee: Russell Smith (Castleford); **Attendance:** 5,912.

HULL FC 19 LONDON BRONCOS 14

HULL: 1 Steve Prescott; 21 Gareth Raynor; 6 Richard Horne; 4 Deon Bird; 5 Matt Crowther; 16 Paul Cooke; 7 Tony Smith; 8 Paul Broadbent; 9 Lee Jackson; 18 Steve Craven; 10 Luke Felsch; 12 Tony Grimaldi (C); 13 Jason Smith. Subs: 23 Logan Campbell for Horne (13); 19 Richard Fletcher for Broadbent (50); 20 Garreth Carvell for Felsch (65); 15 Paul King for Craven (29); Broadbent for T Smith (73).
Tries: Horne (11), Bird (35, 51); **Goals:** Crowther 3;
Field goal: King.
Sin bin: Prescott (59) – fighting.
On report: King (65) – possible dangerous play.
BRONCOS: 23 Richie Barnett (C); 5 Brett Warton; 3 Tony Martin; 2 Nigel Roy; 28 Marvin Golden; 1 Tulsen Tollett; 7 Dennis Moran; 8 Tony Mestrov; 9 Jason Hetherington; 10 Scott Cram; 13 Mat Toshack; 12 Steele Retchless; 6 Jim Dymock. Subs: 11 Shane Millard for Golden (22); 27 Michael Gillett for Dymock (66); 18 Justin Dooley for Cram (18); 21 Jon Clarke for Hetherington (44).
Tries: Roy (33), Gillett (67); **Goals:** Warton 3.
Sin bin: Dooley (59) – fighting.
On report: Dymock (57) – high tackle.
League Express Men of the Match:
Hull: Paul Broadbent; *Broncos:* Richie Barnett.
Penalty count: 6-3; **Half-time:** 12-6;
Referee: Steve Ganson (St Helens); **Attendance:** 6,554.

HALIFAX BLUE SOX 30 SALFORD CITY REDS 18

BLUE SOX: 1 Daryl Cardiss; 19 Oliver Marns; 3 Damian Gibson; 18 Stuart Donlan; 28 Jason Lee (D); 7 Gavin Clinch; 27 Matt Firth; 23 Brett Goldspink (C); 9 Johnny Lawless; 10 Jim Gannon; 12 Shayne McMenemy; 15 Paul Davidson; 14 Danny Tickle. Subs: 13 Martin Moana for Gibson (50); 8 Andy Hobson for Goldspink (5BB, rev 8); 16 Jamie Thackray for Davidson (48); 17 Sean Penkywicz for Lawless (27); Hobson for Goldspink (38BB, rev 48); Davidson for Gannon (62); Hobson for Thackray (66); Lawless for McMenemy (70).
Tries: Cardiss (4, 23), McMenemy (7, 21), Tickle (34);
Goals: Tickle 5.
CITY REDS: 7 Graham Holroyd; 2 Nick Pinkney; 30 Jason Nicol; 3 Francis Maloney; 4 Michael Hancock; 12 Darren Brown (C); 6 Steve Blakeley; 10 Paul Southern; 9 Malcolm Alker; 15 Damian Driscoll; 20 Andy Coley; 13 Paul Highton; 23 Mike Wainwright. Subs: 26 Danny Arnold (D) for Blakeley (70); 18 Stuart Littler for Driscoll (24); 19 Warren Stevens (D) for Southern (67); 21 Iain Marsh for Driscoll (72); Driscoll for Highton (63).

Tries: Maloney (43, 71), Blakeley (45), Wainwright (79);
Goal: Holroyd.
League Express Men of the Match:
Blue Sox: Brett Goldspink; *City Reds:* Francis Maloney.
Penalty count: 7-9; **Half-time:** 28-0; **Referee:** Richard Silverwood (Dewsbury); **Attendance:** 4,180.

ROUND 10

Friday 11th May 2001

LEEDS RHINOS 14 BRADFORD BULLS 33

RHINOS: 5 Francis Cummins; 15 Chev Walker; 3 Tonie Carroll; 4 Keith Senior; 14 Marcus St Hilaire; 1 Iestyn Harris (C); 9 Robert Mears; 8 Darren Fleary; 23 Matthew Diskin; 20 Jamie Mathiou; 17 Anthony Farrell; 11 Andy Hay; 13 Kevin Sinfield. Subs: 10 Barrie McDermott for Mathiou (21); 16 Mark Calderwood for Hay (55); 29 Robert Burrow for Diskin (55); 22 David Wrench for Farrell (59); Mathiou for McDermott (49BB, rev 64); Mathiou for Fleary (64); Diskin for Sinfield (74).
Tries: Carroll (43), Burrow (66); **Goals:** Harris 3.
Sin bin: Mathiou (80) - professional foul.
BULLS: 5 Michael Withers; 2 Tevita Vaikona; 23 Graham Mackay; 14 Lee Gilmour; 3 Leon Pryce; 6 Henry Paul; 1 Robbie Paul (C); 8 Joe Vagana; 9 James Lowes; 22 Brian McDermott; 19 Jamie Peacock; 11 Daniel Gartner; 12 Mike Forshaw. Subs: 10 Paul Anderson for Vagana (20); 29 Stuart Fielden for McDermott (20); 18 Lee Radford for Gartner (29BB, rev 47); 7 Paul Deacon for R Paul (63); McDermott for Anderson (36BB, rev 50); Vagana for Anderson (62); McDermott for Vagana (71); Radford for Gartner (73).
Tries: Withers (6, 17), Forshaw (35), Anderson (54), Vaikona (75); **Goals:** H Paul 6; **Field goal:** H Paul.
Sin bin: Fielden (32) - dissent.
League Express Men of the Match:
Rhinos: Iestyn Harris; *Bulls:* Henry Paul.
Penalty count: 10-7; **Half-time:** 2-20; **Referee:** Stuart Cummings (Widnes); **Attendance:** 18,242.

ST HELENS 32 HALIFAX BLUE SOX 26

SAINTS: 19 Anthony Stewart; 21 Dwayne West; 3 Kevin Iro; 4 Paul Newlove; 5 Anthony Sullivan; 1 Paul Wellens; 7 Sean Long; 12 Sonny Nickle; 9 Keiron Cunningham; 14 Wayne McDonald; 10 David Fairleigh; 11 Chris Joynt (C); 13 Paul Sculthorpe. Subs: 15 Tim Jonkers for McDonald (17BB); 2 Sean Hoppe for Stewart (50); 16 Vila Matautia for Nickle (52); 24 Mick Higham for Matautia (64); Nickle for Fairleigh (57); Fairleigh for Joynt (64); Joynt for West (74).
Tries: West (10), Newlove (38, 40), Cunningham (64), Sculthorpe (76), Hoppe (80); **Goals:** Long 4.
Sent off: Nickle (60) - alleged high tackle on Thackray.
Sin bin: Nickle (23) - late tackle on Clinch.
On report: Matautia (58) - alleged spear tackle on Thackray.
BLUE SOX: 1 Daryl Cardiss; 19 Oliver Marns; 3 Damian Gibson; 18 Stuart Donlan; 28 Jason Lee; 7 Gavin Clinch; 27 Matt Firth; 23 Brett Goldspink (C); 9 Johnny Lawless; 10 Jim Gannon; 12 Shayne McMenemy; 15 Paul Davidson; 14 Danny Tickle. Subs: 8 Andy Hobson for Goldspink (28); 13 Martin Moana for McMenemy (49); 16 Jamie Thackray for Gannon (57); 17 Sean Penkywicz for Firth (67); Goldspink for Hobson (53).
Tries: Davidson (4), Cardiss (20), Lee (28), Donlan (73);
Goals: Tickle 5.
League Express Men of the Match:
Saints: Tim Jonkers; *Blue Sox:* Danny Tickle.
Penalty count: 7-7; **Half-time:** 16-18; **Referee:** Karl Kirkpatrick (Warrington); **Attendance:** 6,986.

Saturday 12th May 2001

WAKEFIELD TRINITY WILDCATS 22 HULL FC 30

WILDCATS: 26 Dane Dorahy; 5 Waisale Sovatabua; 4 Justin Brooker; 3 Richard Smith; 2 Neil Law; 12 Willie Poching (C); 23 Paul Handforth; 16 Julian O'Neill; 9 David March; 8 Paul Jackson; 13 Gary Price; 18 Ben Rauter; 15 Ryan Hudson. Subs: 17 Graham Law for Price (27); 22 Keith Mason for O'Neill (30); 25 Tom Haughey for Rauter (66); 6 Martin Pearson for March (51); O'Neill for Mason (55).
Tries: N Law (8), D March (14), Hudson (36, 73);
Goals: Dorahy 3.
HULL: 1 Steve Prescott; 21 Gareth Raynor; 23 Logan Campbell; 4 Deon Bird; 5 Matt Crowther; 16 Paul Cooke; 7 Tony Smith; 8 Paul Broadbent; 9 Lee Jackson; 10 Luke Felsch; 11 Adam Maher; 12 Tony Grimaldi (C); 13 Jason Smith. Subs: 15 Paul King for Felsch (22); 18 Steve Craven for Broadbent (28); 19 Richard Fletcher for Maher (66); 26 Paul Parker for Campbell (58BB, rev 67); Broadbent for King (62); Parker for J Smith (72).
Tries: Prescott (22, 70), Raynor (32), King (47, 52), Grimaldi (57); **Goals:** Crowther 3.
League Express Men of the Match:
Wildcats: Paul Jackson; *Hull:* Paul Cooke.
Penalty count: 4-6; **Half-time:** 16-10;
Referee: Steve Ganson (St Helens); **Attendance:** 3,876.

Sunday 13th May 2001

HUDDERSFIELD GIANTS 26 CASTLEFORD TIGERS 46

GIANTS: 21 Graham Appo; 2 Andrew Frew; 27 Brandon Costin; 4 Dale Cardoza; 3 Martin Gleeson; 6 Chris Thorman; 7 Ben Kusto; 10 Dale Laughton; 9 Paul Rowley; 12 Richard Marshall; 13 David Atkins; 11 David Lomax; 26 Steve McNamara (C). Subs: 20 Chris Langley for Appo (44); 18 Chris Molyneux not used; 14 Andy

Rice for Atkins (32); 22 Eorl Crabtree for Laughton (24BB, rev 40); Crabtree for Laughton (58BB); Atkins for Lomax (51); Appo for Langley (58); Lomax for Marshall (62).
Tries: Kusto (6), Gleeson (34), Frew (36), Cardoza (79); **Goals:** McNamara 5.
TIGERS: 14 Jason Flowers; 1 Richard Gay; 3 Michael Eagar; 2 Jon Wells; 20 Waine Pryce; 6 Danny Orr; 22 Mark Lennon; 8 Nathan Sykes; 12 Dale Fritz; 10 Dean Sampson; 15 Darren Shaw; 11 Lee Harland; 13 Adrian Vowles (C). Subs: 23 Michael Smith for Harland (44); 16 Ian Tonks for Sampson (34BB, rev 53); 21 Andy McNally for Pryce (75); 27 Andy Speak for Shaw (63); Tonks for Sampson (57BB, rev 62); Tonks for Sykes (62).
Tries: Sampson (9, 27, 77), Tonks (46, 58), Flowers (50, 61), Wells (65), Orr (72); **Goals:** Orr 5.
League Express Men of the Match:
Giants: Ben Kusto; *Tigers:* Dean Sampson.
Penalty count: 5-7; **Half-time:** 20-8; **Referee:** Richard Silverwood (Dewsbury); **Attendance:** 3,453.

LONDON BRONCOS 38 WARRINGTON WOLVES 16

BRONCOS: 23 Richie Barnett (C); 28 Marvin Golden; 3 Tony Martin; 1 Tulsen Tollett; 2 Nigel Roy; 6 Jim Dymock; 7 Dennis Moran; 10 Scott Cram; 9 Jason Hetherington; 18 Justin Dooley; 11 Shane Millard; 12 Steele Retchless; 13 Mat Toshack. Subs: 8 Tony Mestrov for Dooley (27); 15 Andy Johnson for Barnett (78); 19 Dominic Peters for Dymock (69); 21 Jon Clarke for Tollett (72); Dooley for Mestrov (53); Mestrov for Cram (68).
Tries: Barnett (6), Millard (29), Martin (37), Dymock (50, 68), Roy (58), Clarke (74); **Goals:** Martin 5.
WOLVES: 22 Alan Hunte; 2 Rob Smyth; 4 Toa Kohe-Love; 16 Ian Sibbit; 17 David Alstead; 6 Lee Briers; 7 Allan Langer (C); 8 Andrew Gee; 11 Steve McCurrie; 10 Danny Nutley; 25 Gary Mercer; 20 Dean Busby; 13 Tawera Nikau. Subs: 5 Jamie Stenhouse for Alstead (61); 3 David Kidwell for Nikau (62); 12 Jerome Guisset for Gee (39); 23 Mark Gleeson for McCurrie (24); McCurrie for Gleeson (58); Gleeson for Nutley (76).
Tries: Hunte (18, 63), Busby (77); **Goals:** Briers 2.
League Express Men of the Match:
Broncos: Jim Dymock; *Wolves:* Allan Langer.
Penalty count: 5-3; **Half-time:** 16-6;
Referee: Robert Connolly (Wigan); **Attendance:** 3,796.

SALFORD CITY REDS 31 WIGAN WARRIORS 30

CITY REDS: 1 Gary Broadbent; 2 Nick Pinkney; 3 Francis Maloney; 18 Stuart Littler; 5 Martin Offiah; 12 Darren Brown (C); 7 Graham Holroyd; 10 Paul Southern; 9 Malcolm Alker; 15 Damian Driscoll; 30 Jason Nicol; 4 Michael Hancock; 23 Mike Wainwright. Subs: 26 Danny Arnold not used; 13 Paul Highton for Southern (30); 20 Andy Coley for Driscoll (22); 21 Iain Marsh not used; Southern for Hancock (51); Driscoll for Nicol (57); Nicol for Driscoll (77).
Tries: Offiah (6), Hancock (18), Pinkney (44, 47, 71); **Goals:** Holroyd 5; **Field goal:** Holroyd.
WARRIORS: 1 Kris Radlinski; 2 Brett Dallas; 4 Gary Connolly; 3 Steve Renouf; 23 David Hodgson; 6 Matthew Johns; 7 Adrian Lam; 8 Terry O'Connor; 21 Mark Smith; 10 Neil Cowie; 9 Terry Newton; 14 David Furner; 13 Andy Farrell (C). Subs: 26 Ricky Bibey for Cowie (25); 11 Mick Cassidy for O'Connor (57); 12 Denis Betts for Newton (48); 15 Paul Johnson for Renouf (52).
Tries: Dallas (11), Lam (21), Furner (38), Hodgson (67); **Goals:** Farrell 7.
Sent off: Bibey (51) - swinging arm on Hancock.
League Express Men of the Match:
City Reds: Nick Pinkney; *Warriors:* Adrian Lam.
Penalty count: 12-6; **Half-time:** 12-22;
Referee: Russell Smith (Castleford); **Attendance:** 5,691.

ROUND 11

Friday 18th May 2001

BRADFORD BULLS 64 HALIFAX BLUE SOX 12

BULLS: 5 Michael Withers; 2 Tevita Vaikona; 20 Scott Naylor; 14 Lee Gilmour; 3 Leon Pryce; 6 Henry Paul; 1 Robbie Paul (C); 8 Joe Vagana; 9 James Lowes; 22 Brian McDermott; 19 Jamie Peacock; 11 Daniel Gartner; 12 Mike Forshaw. Subs: 10 Paul Anderson for Vagana (23); 29 Stuart Fielden for McDermott (23); 18 Lee Radford for Gartner (57); 7 Paul Deacon for Lowes (40); McDermott for Anderson (57); Anderson for McDermott (73).
Tries: Pryce (9, 11, 79), Vaikona (19), Naylor (22), Forshaw (24, 75), Gartner (27), R Paul (31), Gilmour (59), Fielden (72); **Goals:** H Paul 10.
On report: Anderson (47) – high tackle.
BLUE SOX: 18 Stuart Donlan; 19 Oliver Marns; 3 Damian Gibson; 13 Martin Moana; 28 Jason Lee; 7 Gavin Clinch; 27 Matt Firth; 8 Andy Hobson; 17 Sean Penkywicz; 16 Jamie Thackray; 10 Jim Gannon (C); 15 Paul Davidson; 14 Danny Tickle. Subs: 2 Jamie Bloem for Penkywicz (20); 4 Adam Hughes for Thackray (28); 21 Phil Hassan for Hobson (30); 29 Andrew Brocklehurst (D) for Hassan (55); Penkywicz for Firth (29BB, rev 61); Thackray for Davidson (62).
Tries: Donlan (49), Bloem (68); **Goals:** Tickle 2.
League Express Men of the Match:
Bulls: Tevita Vaikona; *Blue Sox:* Gavin Clinch.
Penalty count: 11-8; **Half-time:** 40-0; **Referee:** Russell Smith (Castleford); **Attendance:** 11,691.

LEEDS RHINOS 52 HUDDERSFIELD GIANTS 46

RHINOS: 5 Francis Cummins; 16 Mark Calderwood; 15 Chev Walker; 4 Keith Senior; 14 Marcus St Hilaire; 1 Iestyn Harris (C); 29 Robert Burrow; 8 Darren Fleary; 9 Robert Mears; 10 Barrie McDermott; 3 Tonie Carroll; 17 Anthony Farrell; 22 David Wrench. Subs: 20 Jamie Mathiou for Fleary (25); 11 Andy Hay for Walker (40); 6 Brett Mullins for Calderwood (47); 13 Kevin Sinfield for Farrell (71); Fleary for McDermott (58); McDermott for Fleary (68).
Tries: McDermott (8), St Hilaire (18, 60), Calderwood (25), Mears (28), Harris (30), Senior (33), Cummins (43), Farrell (68); **Goals:** Harris 8.
GIANTS: 25 Ben Cooper; 2 Andrew Frew; 27 Brandon Costin; 4 Dale Cardoza; 3 Martin Gleeson; 6 Chris Thorman; 7 Ben Kusto; 10 Dale Laughton (C); 9 Paul Rowley; 12 Richard Marshall; 11 David Lomax; 13 David Atkins; 26 Steve McNamara. Subs: 8 Steve Molloy for Laughton (24); 28 Michael Slicker (D) for Lomax (27); 18 Chris Molyneux for Molloy (45); 20 Chris Langley not used; Laughton for Slicker (58); Lomax for Marshall (58); Slicker for Molyneux (72).
Tries: Costin (3, 46), Cooper (11), Rowley (39), Slicker (51), Gleeson (53), Kusto (76), Lomax (78);
Goals: McNamara 7.
League Express Men of the Match:
Rhinos: Keith Senior; *Giants:* Ben Cooper.
Penalty count: 6-6; **Half-time:** 34-16;
Referee: Steve Ganson (St Helens); **Attendance:** 11,579.

ST HELENS 66 SALFORD CITY REDS 16

SAINTS: 19 Anthony Stewart; 2 Sean Hoppe; 3 Kevin Iro; 4 Paul Newlove; 5 Anthony Sullivan; 1 Paul Wellens; 7 Sean Long; 25 Mark Edmondson; 9 Keiron Cunningham; 10 David Fairleigh; 8 Peter Shiels; 11 Chris Joynt (C); 13 Paul Sculthorpe. Subs: 17 Steve Hall for Joynt (61); 15 Tim Jonkers for Fairleigh (30); 22 Heath Cruckshank (D) for Edmondson (35BB, rev 57); 24 Mick Higham for Cunningham (72); Fairleigh for Shiels (44); Cruckshank for Edmondson (68BB); Edmondson for Iro (71).
Tries: Stewart (11, 38, 62), Wellens (16, 18, 79), Sculthorpe (24), Joynt (27), Iro (47), Hall (70), Sullivan (80); **Goals:** Long 11.
CITY REDS: 1 Gary Broadbent; 2 Nick Pinkney; 3 Francis Maloney; 18 Stuart Littler; 5 Martin Offiah; 12 Darren Brown (C); 22 Karle Hammond; 10 Paul Southern; 9 Malcolm Alker; 15 Damian Driscoll; 30 Jason Nicol; 13 Paul Highton; 23 Mike Wainwright. Subs: 26 Danny Arnold for Hammond (31); 19 Warren Stevens for Highton (70); 20 Andy Coley for Driscoll (25); 21 Iain Marsh for Broadbent (56); Driscoll for Southern (34).
Tries: Alker (51, 75), Brown (55); **Goals:** Maloney 2.
League Express Men of the Match:
Saints: Paul Wellens; *City Reds:* Malcolm Alker.
Penalty count: 1-2; **Half-time:** 36-0;
Referee: Robert Connolly (Wigan); **Attendance:** 7,837.

Saturday 19th May 2001

HULL FC 10 WIGAN WARRIORS 46

HULL: 1 Steve Prescott; 21 Gareth Raynor; 4 Deon Bird; 6 Richard Horne; 5 Matt Crowther; 16 Paul Cooke; 7 Tony Smith; 8 Paul Broadbent; 9 Lee Jackson; 18 Steve Craven; 11 Adam Maher; 12 Tony Grimaldi (C); 13 Jason Smith. Subs: 15 Paul King for Broadbent (15); 23 Logan Campbell for Horne (35); 14 Stanley Gene for Craven (45BB, rev 67); 19 Richard Fletcher for Grimaldi (54); Grimaldi for Cooke (67); Gene for Jackson (73); Cooke for Maher (77).
Tries: Maher (22, 28); **Goal:** Crowther.
WARRIORS: 1 Kris Radlinski; 2 Brett Dallas; 4 Gary Connolly; 3 Steve Renouf; 23 David Hodgson; 6 Matthew Johns; 7 Adrian Lam; 8 Terry O'Connor; 9 Terry Newton; 10 Neil Cowie; 12 Denis Betts; 14 David Furner; 13 Andy Farrell (C). Subs: 20 Harvey Howard for Cowie (28); 11 Mick Cassidy for O'Connor (54); 15 Paul Johnson for Betts (60); 21 Mark Smith for Newton (67); Cowie for Howard (67); Betts for Furner (74).
Tries: Furner (3), Betts (14, 18), Renouf (51, 66), Radlinski (53), Dallas (61), Connolly (80);
Goals: Farrell 7.
League Express Men of the Match:
Hull: Steve Prescott; *Warriors:* Gary Connolly.
Penalty count: 3-4; **Half-time:** 10-18; **Referee:** Stuart Cummings (Widnes); **Attendance:** 7,581.

Sunday 20th May 2001

WARRINGTON WOLVES 24
WAKEFIELD TRINITY WILDCATS 30

WOLVES: 22 Alan Hunte; 2 Rob Smyth; 4 Toa Kohe-Love; 16 Ian Sibbit; 1 Lee Penny; 6 Lee Briers; 7 Allan Langer (C); 18 Martin Masella; 26 Jon Clarke (D); 10 Danny Nutley; 11 Steve McCurrie; 20 Dean Busby; 13 Tawera Nikau. Subs: 17 David Alstead for Penny (60); 21 Paul Wood for McCurrie (68); 12 Jerome Guisset for Masella (19); 3 David Kidwell for McCurrie (26); McCurrie for Nikau (61).
Tries: Smyth (9), Kidwell (35), Sibbit (39), Penny (55); **Goals:** Briers 4.
WILDCATS: 26 Dane Dorahy; 2 Neil Law; 17 Graham Law; 4 Justin Brooker; 5 Waisale Sovatabua; 12 Willie Poching (C); 6 Martin Pearson; 16 Julian O'Neill; 9 David March; 8 Paul Jackson; 11 Jamie Field; 18 Ben Rauter; 15 Ryan Hudson. Subs: 22 Keith Mason for O'Neill (40); 13 Gary Price for Rauter (62); 23 Paul Handforth for Poching (55); 20 Ben Westwood not used; O'Neill for Mason (69).
Tries: Sovatabua (4, 50), Hudson (19), Field (47), Pearson (57); **Goals:** Dorahy 5.
League Express Men of the Match:
Wolves: Steve McCurrie; *Wildcats:* Willie Poching.
Penalty count: 11-7; **Half-time:** 18-10; **Referee:** Richard Silverwood (Dewsbury); **Attendance:** 6,231.

CASTLEFORD TIGERS 12 LONDON BRONCOS 25

TIGERS: 1 Richard Gay; 5 Darren Rogers; 3 Michael Eagar; 4 Barrie-Jon Mather; 2 Jon Wells; 6 Danny Orr; 7 Mitch Healey; 8 Nathan Sykes; 12 Dale Fritz; 10 Dean Sampson; 15 Darren Shaw; 11 Lee Harland; 13 Adrian Vowles (C). Subs: 23 Michael Smith for Shaw (40); 16 Ian Tonks for Sampson (53BB, rev 70); 22 Mark Lennon for Mather (40); 14 Jason Flowers for Gay (23); Shaw for Sykes (51); Tonks for Vowles (73).
Tries: Mather (27), Flowers (74); **Goals:** Orr 2.
BRONCOS: 2 Nigel Roy; 28 Marvin Golden; 3 Tony Martin; 1 Tulsen Tollett; 19 Dominic Peters; 6 Jim Dymock; 7 Dennis Moran; 10 Scott Cram; 9 Jason Hetherington (C); 18 Justin Dooley; 11 Shane Millard; 12 Steele Retchless; 13 Mat Toshack. Subs: 8 Tony Mestrov for Dooley (25); 15 Andy Johnson for Retchless (60); 17 Glen Air not used; 26 Peter Lupton for Dymock (79); Dooley for Mestrov (54); Mestrov for Cram (75); Retchless for Johnson (76).
Tries: Roy (19), Moran (55), Cram (65), Toshack (79);
Goals: Martin 4; **Field goal:** Moran.
League Express Men of the Match:
Tigers: Michael Smith; *Broncos:* Dennis Moran.
Penalty count: 7-5; **Half-time:** 6-8;
Referee: Ian Smith (Oldham); **Attendance:** 6,142.

ROUND 12

Friday 25th May 2001

WIGAN WARRIORS 54 CASTLEFORD TIGERS 12

WARRIORS: 1 Kris Radlinski; 18 Wes Davies; 4 Gary Connolly; 15 Paul Johnson; 23 David Hodgson; 6 Matthew Johns; 7 Adrian Lam; 8 Terry O'Connor; 9 Terry Newton; 10 Neil Cowie; 12 Denis Betts; 14 David Furner; 13 Andy Farrell (C). Subs: 11 Mick Cassidy for Farrell (8BB, rev 10); 22 Phil Jones for Johns (25); 20 Harvey Howard for Cowie (28); 21 Mark Smith for Newton (65); Cassidy for Betts (54); Cowie for O'Connor (58); Betts for Jones (69).
Tries: Hodgson (6), Radlinski (14, 80), Newton (18, 48), Farrell (35), Jones (43), Johnson (60, 64);
Goals: Farrell 9.
TIGERS: 14 Jason Flowers; 22 Mark Lennon; 2 Jon Wells; 3 Michael Eagar; 5 Darren Rogers; 6 Danny Orr; 7 Mitch Healey; 8 Nathan Sykes; 12 Dale Fritz; 10 Dean Sampson; 11 Lee Harland; 15 Darren Shaw; 13 Adrian Vowles (C). Subs: 16 Ian Tonks for Sampson (26BB, rev 37); 23 Michael Smith for Shaw (49); 20 Waine Pryce for Eagar (52); 17 Andy Lynch for Harland (65); Tonks for Sykes (37); Sykes for Sampson (65); Sampson for Sykes (76BB).
Tries: Eagar (51), Orr (57); **Goals:** Orr 2.
League Express Men of the Match:
Warriors: Andy Farrell; *Tigers:* Adrian Vowles.
Penalty count: 6-5; **Half-time:** 22-0; **Referee:** Stuart Cummings (Widnes); **Attendance:** 10,190.

Saturday 26th May 2001

WAKEFIELD TRINITY WILDCATS 16 LEEDS RHINOS 38

WILDCATS: 26 Dane Dorahy; 2 Neil Law; 17 Graham Law; 4 Justin Brooker; 5 Waisale Sovatabua; 12 Willie Poching (C); 6 Martin Pearson; 16 Julian O'Neill; 9 David March; 8 Paul Jackson; 11 Jamie Field; 18 Ben Rauter; 15 Ryan Hudson. Subs: 13 Gary Price for Rauter (27); 14 Paul March for Field (61); 10 Frank Watene for O'Neill (22BB, rev 46); 3 Richard Smith for Dorahy (73); Rauter for D March (46); Field for O'Neill (71BB); Watene for Jackson (71).
Tries: Brooker (45, 60), Pearson (52); **Goals:** Pearson 2.
RHINOS: 5 Francis Cummins; 16 Mark Calderwood; 15 Chev Walker; 4 Keith Senior; 14 Marcus St Hilaire; 1 Iestyn Harris (C); 2 Karl Pratt; 8 Darren Fleary; 9 Robert Mears; 10 Barrie McDermott; 11 Andy Hay; 12 Bradley Clyde; 13 Kevin Sinfield. Subs: 29 Robert Burrow for Sinfield (61); 20 Jamie Mathiou for Fleary (29); 22 David Wrench for McDermott (32); 23 Matthew Diskin for Mears (72); McDermott for Clyde (49); Sinfield for McDermott (74).
Tries: Senior (2), St Hilaire (8), Pratt (19), Cummins (35), Harris (43, 79), Hay (68); **Goals:** Harris 5.
League Express Men of the Match:
Wildcats: Willie Poching; *Rhinos:* Iestyn Harris.
Penalty count: 5-6; **Half-time:** 0-20;
Referee: Robert Connolly (Wigan); **Attendance:** 4,963.

Sunday 27th May 2001

LONDON BRONCOS 14 HALIFAX BLUE SOX 12

BRONCOS: 23 Richie Barnett; 19 Dominic Peters; 3 Tony Martin; 2 Nigel Roy; 28 Marvin Golden; 6 Jim Dymock; 7 Dennis Moran; 8 Tony Mestrov; 9 Jason Hetherington (C); 10 Scott Cram; 11 Shane Millard; 12 Steele Retchless; 13 Mat Toshack. Subs: 15 Andy Johnson for Millard (49BB, rev 61); 18 Justin Dooley for Mestrov (24); 27 Michael Gillett for Mestrov (69); 1 Tulsen Tollett not used; Mestrov for Dooley (44); Dooley for Hetherington (61); Mestrov for Dooley (76).
Tries: Barnett (9), Johnson (51); **Goals:** Martin 3.
BLUE SOX: 3 Damian Gibson; 19 Oliver Marns; 18 Stuart Donlan; 4 Adam Hughes; 28 Jason Lee; 13 Martin Moana (C); 6 Andrew Dunemann; 23 Brett Goldspink; 9 Johnny Lawless; 10 Jim Gannon; 15 Paul Davidson; 12 Shayne McMenemy; 14 Danny Tickle. Subs: 2 Jamie Bloem for Davidson (28); 16 Jamie Thackray for Hobson

(66); 8 Andy Hobson for Goldspink (28); 21 Phil Hassan not used; Davidson for McMenemy (54); Goldspink for Bloem (60); McMenemy for Moana (68).
Tries: Hughes (12), Marns (80); **Goals:** Tickle 2.
League Express Men of the Match:
Broncos: Richie Barnett; *Blue Sox:* Andrew Dunemann.
Penalty count: 9-8; **Half-time:** 6-4; **Referee:** Richard Silverwood (Dewsbury); **Attendance:** 2,584.

HULL FC 32 WARRINGTON WOLVES 16

HULL: 1 Steve Prescott; 21 Gareth Raynor; 4 Deon Bird; 26 Paul Parker; 5 Matt Crowther; 16 Paul Cooke; 13 Jason Smith; 15 Paul King; 9 Lee Jackson; 18 Steve Craven; 11 Adam Maher; 12 Tony Grimaldi (C); 3 David Maiden. Subs: 23 Logan Campbell for Maher (70); 20 Garreth Carvell for Docherty (65); 27 Michael Docherty for King (30); 14 Stanley Gene for Maiden (55); King for Craven (52); Docherty for Jackson (77).
Tries: Parker (9), Bird (32, 54), Gene (67), J Smith (72); **Goals:** Crowther 6.
WOLVES: 22 Alan Hunte; 2 Rob Smyth; 4 Toa Kohe-Love; 3 David Kidwell; 5 Jamie Stenhouse; 6 Lee Briers; 7 Allan Langer (C); 12 Jerome Guisset; 26 Jon Clarke; 10 Danny Nutley; 11 Steve McCurrie; 25 Gary Mercer; 13 Tawera Nikau. Subs: 17 David Alstead not used; 21 Paul Wood for Guisset (33); 18 Martin Masella for Nutley (26BB, rev 37); 20 Dean Busby not used; Guisset for Nikau (58); Nikau for Wood (70).
Tries: Kidwell (15, 26), Wood (65); **Goals:** Briers 2.
Sin bin: Clarke (51) – dissent.
On report: Guisset (5) – late tackle.
League Express Men of the Match:
Hull: Jason Smith; *Wolves:* David Kidwell.
Penalty count: 17-8; **Half-time:** 14-10;
Referee: Russell Smith (Castleford); **Attendance:** 5,968.

BRADFORD BULLS 42 SALFORD CITY REDS 10

BULLS: 5 Michael Withers; 2 Tevita Vaikona; 20 Scott Naylor; 14 Lee Gilmour; 3 Leon Pryce; 6 Henry Paul; 1 Robbie Paul (C); 8 Joe Vagana; 9 James Lowes; 22 Brian McDermott; 11 Daniel Gartner; 18 Lee Radford; 15 Shane Rigon. Subs: 7 Paul Deacon for R Paul (49); 23 Graham Mackay for Radford (39); 10 Paul Anderson for McDermott (22); 29 Stuart Fielden for Vagana (22); Vagana for Anderson (60); McDermott for Gartner (60).
Tries: Radford (5), Withers (10), Pryce (13), Gilmour (39, 48, 76), Rigon (43), Vaikona (80); **Goals:** H Paul 5.
CITY REDS: 1 Gary Broadbent; 2 Nick Pinkney; 3 Francis Maloney; 18 Stuart Littler; 5 Martin Offiah; 12 Darren Brown (C); 6 Steve Blakeley; 15 Damian Driscoll; 9 Malcolm Alker; 20 Andy Coley; 30 Jason Nicol; 13 Paul Highton; 23 Mike Wainwright. Subs: 26 Danny Arnold for Highton (40); 19 Warren Stevens for Nicol (43); 17 Craig Makin for Driscoll (50); 21 Iain Marsh for Wainwright (68); Driscoll for Stevens (65); Stevens for Makin (73).
Tries: Littler (31), Arnold (56); **Goal:** Blakeley.
League Express Men of the Match:
Bulls: Lee Gilmour; *City Reds:* Malcolm Alker.
Penalty count: 6-4; **Half-time:** 22-4; **Referee:** Karl Kirkpatrick (Warrington); **Attendance:** 10,907.

Monday 28th May 2001

HUDDERSFIELD GIANTS 26 ST HELENS 44

GIANTS: 21 Graham Appo; 2 Andrew Frew; 4 Dale Cardoza; 6 Chris Thorman; 3 Martin Gleeson; 27 Brandon Costin; 7 Ben Kusto; 10 Dale Laughton (C); 9 Paul Rowley; 12 Richard Marshall; 11 David Lomax; 26 Steve McNamara; 13 David Atkins. Subs: 8 Steve Molloy for Marshall (30); 28 Michael Slicker for Laughton (20BB, rev 53); 18 Chris Molyneux for Molloy (54); 25 Ben Cooper for McNamara (61); Marshall for Lomax (50); Molloy for Appo (67); Lomax for Laughton (65BB); Slicker for Molyneux (72).
Tries: Frew (6), Thorman (33), Appo (49), Laughton (60), Cardoza (72); **Goals:** McNamara 3.
Sin bin: Costin (13) - late challenge on Long.
On report: Costin (13) - same late challenge.
SAINTS: 19 Anthony Stewart; 2 Sean Hoppe; 3 Kevin Iro; 4 Paul Newlove; 5 Anthony Sullivan; 1 Paul Wellens; 7 Sean Long; 25 Mark Edmondson; 9 Keiron Cunningham; 10 David Fairleigh; 8 Peter Shiels; 11 Chris Joynt (C); 13 Paul Sculthorpe. Subs: 15 Tim Jonkers for Long (15); 16 Vila Matautia for Shiels (18BB, rev 27); 17 Steve Hall for Joynt (57); 22 Heath Cruckshank for Edmondson (30); Edmondson for Cruckshank (56); Matautia for Fairleigh (61); Fairleigh for Cunningham (71).
Tries: Sculthorpe (9, 13), Newlove (23, 58), Cunningham (28, 52), Edmondson (64), Wellens (74); **Goals:** Long, Sculthorpe 5.
League Express Men of the Match:
Giants: Andrew Frew; *Saints:* Paul Sculthorpe.
Penalty count: 5-7; **Half-time:** 10-22;
Referee: Ian Smith (Oldham); **Attendance:** 3,559.

ROUND 13

Friday 1st June 2001

CASTLEFORD TIGERS 26
WAKEFIELD TRINITY WILDCATS 22

TIGERS: 14 Jason Flowers; 1 Richard Gay; 2 Jon Wells; 5 Darren Rogers; 20 Waine Pryce; 6 Danny Orr; 7 Mitch Healey; 19 Gareth Handford; 27 Andy Speak; 10 Dean Sampson; 16 Ian Tonks; 12 Dale Fritz; 13 Adrian Vowles (C). Subs: 23 Michael Smith for Tonks (24); 15 Darren Shaw for Handford (24); 22 Mark Lennon for Speak (55); 17 Andy Lynch for Sampson (27BB, rev 40); Tonks for Shaw (36BB, rev 66).
Tries: Sampson (25), Rogers (27), Pryce (40), Orr (74), Gay (78); **Goals:** Orr 3.
WILDCATS: 6 Martin Pearson; 2 Neil Law; 20 Ben Westwood; 4 Justin Brooker; 5 Waisale Sovatabua; 26 Dane Dorahy; 7 Brad Davis; 16 Julian O'Neill; 18 Ben Rauter; 8 Paul Jackson; 12 Willie Poching (C); 15 Ryan Hudson; 11 Jamie Field. Subs: 13 Gary Price for Poching (36); 17 Graham Law for Hudson (74); 10 Frank Watene for O'Neill (30); 22 Keith Mason for Jackson (75); Poching for Davis (64); O'Neill for Watene (60).
Tries: Sovatabua (12), Watene (33), Dorahy (65); **Goals:** Pearson 5.
League Express Men of the Match:
Tigers: Danny Orr; *Wildcats:* Dane Dorahy.
Penalty count: 6-5; **Half-time:** 18-12; **Referee:** Karl Kirkpatrick (Warrington); **Attendance:** 6,309.

LEEDS RHINOS 36 LONDON BRONCOS 12

RHINOS: 5 Francis Cummins; 15 Chev Walker; 3 Tonie Carroll; 4 Keith Senior; 14 Marcus St Hilaire; 1 Iestyn Harris (C); 2 Karl Pratt; 8 Darren Fleary; 9 Robert Mears; 10 Barrie McDermott; 11 Andy Hay; 22 David Wrench; 13 Kevin Sinfield. Subs: 20 Jamie Mathiou for McDermott (27); 16 Mark Calderwood for Carroll (40); 29 Robert Burrow for Harris (65); 23 Matthew Diskin for Wrench (67); McDermott for Fleary (53).
Tries: Cummins (6), Harris (13), Carroll (23), Sinfield (25), Walker (39), Calderwood (63); **Goals:** Harris 6.
BRONCOS: 2 Nigel Roy; 19 Dominic Peters; 3 Tony Martin; 1 Tulsen Tollett; 28 Marvin Golden; 27 Michael Gillett; 7 Dennis Moran; 8 Tony Mestrov; 11 Shane Millard; 18 Justin Dooley; 12 Steele Retchless (C); 13 Matt Toshack; 6 Jim Dymock. Subs: 15 Andy Johnson for Retchless (32); 20 Steffan Hughes for Mestrov (69); 26 Peter Lupton for Gillett (72); 17 Glen Air for Millard (73); Retchless for Johnson (52).
Tries: Johnson (38), Roy (59); **Goals:** Martin 2.
Sin bin: Hughes (76) - interference at play the ball.
League Express Men of the Match:
Rhinos: Iestyn Harris; *Broncos:* Shane Millard.
Penalty count: 15-7; **Half-time:** 28-6;
Referee: Ian Smith (Oldham); **Attendance:** 10,535.

WARRINGTON WOLVES 47 WIGAN WARRIORS 38

WOLVES: 22 Alan Hunte; 2 Rob Smyth; 3 David Kidwell; 4 Toa Kohe-Love; 1 Lee Penny; 6 Lee Briers; 7 Allan Langer (C); 12 Jerome Guisset; 26 Jon Clarke; 10 Danny Nutley; 11 Steve McCurrie; 25 Gary Mercer; 13 Tawera Nikau. Subs: 17 David Alstead for Hunte (74); 21 Paul Wood for Guisset (32); 18 Martin Masella for Nutley (66); 20 Dean Busby for McCurrie (37); McCurrie for Mercer (55); Mercer for Nikau (67).
Tries: Kidwell (16), McCurrie (20), Briers (24, 59), Hunte (26), Langer (29), Penny (38), Kohe-Love (78);
Goals: Briers 7; **Field goal:** Briers.
WARRIORS: 1 Kris Radlinski; 23 David Hodgson; 15 Paul Johnson; 4 Gary Connolly; 18 Wes Davies; 13 Andy Farrell (C); 7 Adrian Lam; 10 Neil Cowie; 9 Terry Newton; 8 Terry O' Connor; 12 Denis Betts; 11 Mick Cassidy; 14 David Furner. Subs: 20 Harvey Howard for Cowie (25BB, rev 34); 21 Mark Smith for Newton (59); 5 Brian Carney for Davies (66); 19 Chris Chester for Betts (62); Howard for Cowie (59); Betts for Cassidy (75).
Tries: Radlinski (3, 71), Johnson (6, 69), Betts (32), Farrell (48); **Goals:** Farrell 7.
League Express Men of the Match:
Wolves: Gary Mercer; *Warriors:* David Furner.
Penalty count: 6-3; **Half-time:** 34-18;
Referee: Stuart Cummings (Widnes); **Attendance:** 7,766.

Saturday 2nd June 2001

ST HELENS 38 BRADFORD BULLS 26

SAINTS: 19 Anthony Stewart; 2 Sean Hoppe; 3 Kevin Iro; 4 Paul Newlove; 5 Anthony Sullivan; 13 Paul Sculthorpe; 1 Paul Wellens; 12 Sonny Nickle; 9 Keiron Cunningham; 10 David Fairleigh; 8 Peter Shiels; 11 Chris Joynt (C); 15 Tim Jonkers. Subs: 24 Mick Higham not used; 17 Steve Hall for Joynt (58); 22 Heath Cruckshank not used; 25 Mark Edmondson for Nickle (26); Nickle for Fairleigh (34); Fairleigh for Edmondson (49); Edmondson for Nickle (68); Joynt for Edmondson (78).
Tries: Joynt (7, 40), Nickle (17), Sculthorpe (30, 73), Stewart (33), Shiels (78); **Goals:** Sculthorpe 5.
BULLS: 5 Michael Withers; 2 Tevita Vaikona; 20 Scott Naylor; 14 Lee Gilmour; 3 Leon Pryce; 6 Henry Paul; 1 Robbie Paul (C); 8 Joe Vagana; 9 James Lowes; 22 Brian McDermott; 19 Jamie Peacock; 11 Daniel Gartner; 12 Mike Forshaw. Subs: 15 Shane Rigon for Gartner (60); 23 Graham Mackay for Naylor (49); 10 Paul Anderson for Vagana (20); 29 Stuart Fielden for McDermott (20); Vagana for Anderson (62).
Tries: Vaikona (3), Gilmour (13), R Paul (50, 57), Peacock (55); **Goals:** H Paul 3.
Sin bin: Naylor (16) - dissent.
League Express Men of the Match:
Saints: Paul Sculthorpe; *Bulls:* Robbie Paul.
Penalty count: 7-4; **Half-time:** 28-10;
Referee: Robert Connolly (Wigan); **Attendance:** 10,428.

Sunday 3rd June 2001

HALIFAX BLUE SOX 40 HUDDERSFIELD GIANTS 8

BLUE SOX: 1 Daryl Cardiss; 19 Oliver Marns; 3 Damian Gibson; 18 Stuart Donlan; 28 Jason Lee; 6 Andrew Dunemann; 7 Gavin Clinch; 23 Brett Goldspink (C); 9 Johnny Lawless; 10 Jim Gannon; 12 Shayne McMenemy; 15 Paul Davidson; 14 Danny Tickle. Subs: 2 Jamie Bloem for Tickle (49); 8 Andy Hobson for Goldspink (29); 13 Martin Moana for Gibson (49); 16 Jamie Thackray for Hobson (60); Goldspink for Davidson (55); Davidson for Gannon (65); Gibson for Cardiss (70).
Tries: Lee (4), McMenemy (9), Gibson (14, 39), Davidson (49), Lawless (63), Thackray (78), Marns (80);
Goals: Tickle, Bloem 3.
GIANTS: 25 Ben Cooper; 2 Andrew Frew; 4 Dale Cardoza; 29 Graeme Hallas (D); 3 Martin Gleeson; 6 Chris Thorman; 7 Ben Kusto; 8 Steve Molloy; 26 Steve McNamara (C); 10 Dale Laughton; 11 David Lomax; 12 Richard Marshall; 13 David Atkins. Subs: 28 Michael Slicker for Molloy (19); 14 Andy Rice for Laughton (62); 30 Toby Green (D) for Laughton (34BB, rev 41); 5 Hefin O'Hare for Hallas (50); Molloy for Slicker (50BB, rev 61); Green for Cooper (56).
Tries: Marshall (24), Cardoza (68).
League Express Men of the Match:
Blue Sox: Andrew Dunemann; *Giants:* Ben Kusto.
Penalty count: 5-10; **Half-time:** 18-4; **Referee:** Richard Silverwood (Dewsbury); **Attendance:** 4,253.

SALFORD CITY REDS 24 HULL FC 36

CITY REDS: 1 Gary Broadbent; 2 Nick Pinkney; 3 Francis Maloney; 18 Stuart Littler; 5 Martin Offiah; 6 Steve Blakeley; 16 Bobbie Goulding; 15 Damian Driscoll; 9 Malcolm Alker; 20 Andy Coley; 30 Jason Nicol; 12 Darren Brown (C); 23 Mike Wainwright. Subs: 4 Michael Hancock for Nicol (20); 13 Paul Highton for Driscoll (30); 19 Warren Stevens not used; 26 Danny Arnold for Maloney (69).
Tries: Alker (2, 60), Maloney (16), Hancock (44);
Goals: Goulding, Blakeley 3.
Sin bin: Hancock (57) – striking out in the tackle.
HULL: 1 Steve Prescott; 21 Gareth Raynor; 4 Deon Bird; 26 Paul Parker; 5 Matt Crowther; 13 Jason Smith; 7 Tony Smith; 18 Steve Craven; 9 Lee Jackson; 15 Paul King; 11 Adam Maher; 12 Tony Grimaldi (C); 3 David Maiden. Subs: 14 Stanley Gene for Maher (19BB, rev 28); 23 Logan Campbell for Maiden (13BB, rev 28); 27 Michael Docherty for Craven (41); 16 Paul Cooke for Docherty (61); Gene for Jackson (44); Craven for Maher (70); Campbell for Grimaldi (78).
Tries: T Smith (11, 29, 61), Crowther (21), Prescott (25), Bird (74); **Goals:** Crowther 6.
Sin bin: J Smith (57) – striking out in the tackle.
League Express Men of the Match:
City Reds: Malcolm Alker; *Hull:* Tony Smith.
Penalty count: 6-9; **Half-time:** 10-24;
Referee: Steve Ganson (St Helens); **Attendance:** 4,143.

ROUND 14

Friday 8th June 2001

LEEDS RHINOS 18 WIGAN WARRIORS 36

RHINOS: 5 Francis Cummins; 15 Chev Walker; 3 Tonie Carroll; 4 Keith Senior; 14 Marcus St Hilaire; 1 Iestyn Harris (C); 2 Karl Pratt; 8 Darren Fleary; 9 Robert Mears; 10 Barrie McDermott; 11 Andy Hay; 22 David Wrench; 13 Kevin Sinfield. Subs: 17 Anthony Farrell for McDermott (24); 23 Matthew Diskin for Wrench (61); 29 Robert Burrow for Pratt (61); 16 Mark Calderwood not used; McDermott for Fleary (49); Wrench for Farrell (73).
Tries: Pratt (9), Carroll (37), Burrow (73); **Goals:** Harris 3.
WARRIORS: 1 Kris Radlinski; 15 Paul Johnson; 3 Steve Renouf; 4 Gary Connolly; 23 David Hodgson; 19 Chris Chester; 7 Adrian Lam; 8 Terry O'Connor; 9 Terry Newton; 20 Harvey Howard; 11 Mick Cassidy; 14 David Furner; 13 Andy Farrell (C). Subs: 10 Neil Cowie for Howard (11BB, rev 30); 12 Denis Betts for Cassidy (27); 5 Brian Carney for Connolly (36); 21 Mark Smith for Newton (43BB, rev 53); Cowie for O'Connor (30); O'Connor for Howard (57); Cassidy for Cowie (69); Smith for Johnson (72).
Tries: Lam (12), Renouf (46, 79), Farrell (60), Carney (65); **Goals:** Farrell 8.
League Express Men of the Match:
Rhinos: Robert Mears; *Warriors:* Andy Farrell.
Penalty count: 6-6; **Half-time:** 12-10; **Referee:** Russell Smith (Castleford); **Attendance:** 14,435.

ST HELENS 22 LONDON BRONCOS 14

SAINTS: 1 Paul Wellens; 17 Steve Hall; 2 Sean Hoppe; 4 Paul Newlove; 5 Anthony Sullivan; 3 Kevin Iro; 19 Anthony Stewart; 10 David Fairleigh; 9 Keiron Cunningham; 12 Sonny Nickle; 8 Peter Shiels; 11 Chris Joynt (C); 15 Tim Jonkers. Subs: 25 Mark Edmondson for Nickle (25); 24 Mick Higham for Edmondson (53); 22 Heath Cruckshank for Nickle (76); 6 Radney Bowker (D) for Joynt (79); Nickle for Joynt (34BB); Joynt for Iro (46BB, rev 59); Joynt for Hall (61); Hall for Iro (73).
Tries: Fairleigh (36), Newlove (55), Joynt (68), Hall (75);
Goals: Wellens 3.
BRONCOS: 5 Brett Warton; 28 Marvin Golden; 1 Tulsen Tollett; 2 Nigel Roy; 15 Andy Johnson; 26 Peter Lupton; 7 Dennis Moran; 8 Tony Mestrov; 11 Shane Millard; 18 Justin Dooley; 12 Steele Retchless; 13 Mat Toshack; 6 Jim Dymock (C). Subs: 19 Dominic Peters for Golden (21); 17 Glen Air for Dooley (28); 20 Steffan Hughes for Mestrov (35BB, rev 49); 27 Michael Gillett for Warton (70); Dooley for Millard (64); Millard for Air (70); Hughes for Mestrov (74).
Tries: Moran (32), Toshack (44); **Goals:** Warton 3.
League Express Men of the Match:
Saints: David Fairleigh; *Broncos:* Dennis Moran.
Penalty count: 9-3; **Half-time:** 6-8;

Referee: Stuart Cummings (Widnes); **Attendance**: 6,938.

Saturday 9th June 2001

CASTLEFORD TIGERS 33 HULL FC 26

TIGERS: 14 Jason Flowers; 1 Richard Gay; 2 Jon Wells; 5 Darren Rogers; 20 Waine Pryce; 7 Mitch Healey; 22 Mark Lennon; 8 Nathan Sykes; 27 Andy Speak; 10 Dean Sampson; 11 Lee Harland; 12 Dale Fritz; 13 Adrian Vowles (C). Subs: 23 Michael Smith for Harland (24); 15 Darren Shaw for Speak (32); 16 Ian Tonks for Sampson (36); 21 Andy McNally for Gay (39); Speak for Sykes (60BB, rev 75); Harland for Tonks (70).
Tries: Lennon (5), Rogers (13), Wells (21, 72), Tonks (41), M Smith (46); **Goals:** Lennon 4; **Field goal:** Vowles.
HULL: 1 Steve Prescott; 21 Gareth Raynor; 4 Deon Bird; 26 Paul Parker; 2 Chris Smith; 16 Paul Cooke; 7 Tony Smith; 18 Steve Craven; 9 Lee Jackson; 8 Paul Broadbent; 20 Garreth Carvell; 12 Tony Grimaldi (C); 3 David Maiden. Subs: 14 Stanley Gene for Jackson (57); 23 Logan Campbell for Fletcher (40); 15 Paul King for Broadbent (26); 19 Richard Fletcher for Carvell (34); Broadbent for Craven (63).
Tries: Broadbent (10), Raynor (23), Maiden (48), King (54), Campbell (76); **Goals:** Prescott 3.
League Express Men of the Match:
Tigers: Adrian Vowles; *Hull:* Steve Prescott.
Penalty count: 3-5; **Half-time:** 16-10; **Referee:** Karl Kirkpatrick (Warrington); **Attendance:** 6,952.

Sunday 10th June 2001

BRADFORD BULLS 78 HUDDERSFIELD GIANTS 18

BULLS: 5 Michael Withers; 2 Tevita Vaikona; 23 Graham Mackay; 15 Shane Rigon; 3 Leon Pryce; 6 Henry Paul; 7 Paul Deacon; 8 Joe Vagana; 1 Robbie Paul (C); 22 Brian McDermott; 11 Daniel Gartner; 19 Jamie Peacock; 12 Mike Forshaw. Subs: 4 Nathan McAvoy for Deacon (40); 14 Lee Gilmour for Peacock (56); 10 Paul Anderson for Vagana (23); 29 Stuart Fielden for McDermott (15); Vagana for Anderson (51); McDermott for Fielden (57).
Tries: Mackay (2, 42, 66), Rigon (4, 31), Gartner (7), Peacock (10), Pryce (13), H Paul (29), Vaikona (40, 47), McAvoy (68), Vagana (71), Withers (77);
Goals: H Paul 11.
GIANTS: 1 Paul Reilly; 2 Andrew Frew; 4 Dale Cardoza; 3 Martin Gleeson; 5 Hefin O'Hare; 26 Steve McNamara (C); 17 Mark Moxon; 28 Michael Slicker; 9 Paul Rowley; 10 Dale Laughton; 12 Richard Marshall; 11 David Lomax; 14 Andy Rice. Subs: 13 David Atkins for Laughton (25); 7 Ben Kusto for Gleeson (17); 16 Oliver Wilkes for Rice (11); 18 Chris Molyneux for Slicker (ht); Laughton for Atkins (63); Slicker for Molyneux (58).
Tries: Cardoza (27), Frew (57), Reilly (63);
Goals: McNamara 3.
League Express Men of the Match:
Bulls: Graham Mackay; *Giants:* Andrew Frew.
Penalty count: 5-4; **Half-time:** 44-6;
Referee: Ian Smith (Oldham); **Attendance:** 10,886.

HALIFAX BLUE SOX 26
WAKEFIELD TRINITY WILDCATS 20

BLUE SOX: 1 Daryl Cardiss; 19 Oliver Marns; 3 Damian Gibson; 18 Stuart Donlan; 28 Jason Lee; 6 Andrew Dunemann; 7 Gavin Clinch; 23 Brett Goldspink (C); 9 Johnny Lawless; 8 Andy Hobson; 10 Jim Gannon; 12 Shayne McMenemy; 14 Danny Tickle. Subs: 21 Phil Hassan not used; 2 Jamie Bloem for Hobson (17); 16 Jamie Thackray for Gannon (77); 13 Martin Moana for Tickle (17); Hobson for Goldspink (55); Tickle for Moana (71).
Tries: Moana (25, 51), McMenemy (30), Gibson (36), Donlan (77); **Goals:** Bloem, Tickle 2.
Sin bin: Bloem (29) - retaliation.
On report: Gannon (35) - alleged late challenge on Dorahy.
WILDCATS: 6 Martin Pearson; 5 Waisale Sovatabua; 20 Ben Westwood; 17 Graham Law; 2 Neil Law; 26 Dane Dorahy; 7 Brad Davis; 16 Julian O'Neill; 18 Ben Rauter; 10 Frank Watene; 12 Willie Poching (C); 15 Ryan Hudson; 11 Jamie Field. Subs: 19 Gareth Ellis for G Law (77); 13 Gary Price for Watene (14BB, rev 30); 8 Paul Jackson for O'Neill (22BB, rev 40); 23 Paul Handforth for Rauter (69); Price for Dorahy (35); Jackson for Watene (41); Watene for O'Neill (69).
Tries: Davis (3), O'Neill (15, 43); **Goals:** Pearson 4.
Sin bin: Field (29) - striking;
Watene (78) - late tackle on Clinch.
On report: Watene (78) - same late tackle.
League Express Men of the Match:
Blue Sox: Shayne McMenemy; *Wildcats:* Martin Pearson.
Penalty count: 5-3; **Half-time:** 14-12; **Referee:** Robert Connolly (Wigan); **Attendance:** 4,863.

SALFORD CITY REDS 26 WARRINGTON WOLVES 18

CITY REDS: 1 Gary Broadbent; 2 Nick Pinkney; 3 Francis Maloney; 18 Stuart Littler; 5 Martin Offiah; 6 Steve Blakeley; 16 Bobbie Goulding (C); 15 Damian Driscoll; 9 Malcolm Alker; 20 Andy Coley; 13 Paul Highton; 4 Michael Hancock; 23 Mike Wainwright. Subs: 17 Craig Makin for Highton (72); 19 Warren Stevens for Driscoll (36); 26 Danny Arnold for Maloney (69); 27 Steve Garces (D) for Hancock (79).
Tries: Pinkney (6, 27), Maloney (35), Highton (57);
Goals: Blakeley 5.
Sin bin: Hancock (39) - ball stealing.
WOLVES: 22 Alan Hunte; 2 Rob Smyth; 4 Toa Kohe-Love; 3 David Kidwell; 1 Lee Penny; 13 Tawera Nikau; 7 Allan Langer (C); 12 Jerome Guisset; 26 Jon Clarke; 10 Danny Nutley; 11 Steve McCurrie; 25 Gary Mercer; 20 Dean Busby. Subs: 17 David Alstead not used; 16 Ian Sibbit for McCurrie (74); 21 Paul Wood for Nutley (39); 18 Martin Masella for McCurrie (54); Nutley for Wood (58); McCurrie for Busby (63).
Tries: Penny (11, 18), Clarke (42), Busby (54);
Goal: Smyth.
Sent off: Kohe-Love (30) - head tackle on Maloney.
League Express Men of the Match:
City Reds: Malcolm Alker; *Wolves:* Jon Clarke.
Penalty count: 10-8; **Half-time:** 18-8; **Referee:** Richard Silverwood (Dewsbury); **Attendance:** 4,963.

ROUND 15

Friday 15th June 2001

HULL FC 6 LEEDS RHINOS 15

HULL: 1 Steve Prescott; 2 Chris Smith; 4 Deon Bird; 23 Logan Campbell; 21 Gareth Raynor; 6 Richard Horne; 7 Tony Smith; 18 Steve Craven; 15 Paul King; 8 Paul Broadbent; 11 Adam Maher; 12 Tony Grimaldi (C); 13 Jason Smith. Subs: 9 Lee Jackson for King (51); 28 Scott Logan (D) for Broadbent (28); 3 David Maiden for Raynor (65); 29 Kirk Yeaman not used; Broadbent for Logan (51BB, rev 61); King for Craven (62); Broadbent for Logan (72).
Try: T Smith (18); **Goal:** Prescott.
RHINOS: 5 Francis Cummins; 15 Chev Walker; 3 Tonie Carroll; 4 Keith Senior; 14 Marcus St Hilaire; 1 Iestyn Harris (C); 29 Robert Burrow; 24 Ewan Dowes; 9 Robert Mears; 10 Barrie McDermott; 11 Andy Hay; 22 David Wrench; 13 Kevin Sinfield. Subs: 16 Mark Calderwood for St Hilaire (40); 18 Danny Ward for McDermott (32); 23 Matthew Diskin for Wrench (30); 27 Jason Netherton (D) for Wrench (8BB, rev 19); McDermott for Dowes (50); Netherton for Mears (55); Dowes for Ward (70).
Tries: Calderwood (60), Senior (77); **Goals:** Harris 3;
Field goal: Ward.
League Express Men of the Match:
Hull: Tony Smith; *Rhinos:* Iestyn Harris.
Penalty count: 7-5; **Half-time:** 6-0;
Referee: Ian Smith (Oldham); **Attendance:** 6,426.

WIGAN WARRIORS 50 HALIFAX BLUE SOX 18

WARRIORS: 18 Wes Davies; 5 Brian Carney; 15 Paul Johnson; 3 Steve Renouf; 23 David Hodgson; 6 Matthew Johns; 7 Adrian Lam; 8 Terry O'Connor; 9 Terry Newton; 20 Harvey Howard; 11 Mick Cassidy; 14 David Furner; 13 Andy Farrell (C). Subs: 10 Neil Cowie for Howard (29); 12 Denis Betts for Johnson (44); 21 Mark Smith for Farrell (68); 22 Phil Jones for Carney (20); Howard for O'Connor (51BB).
Tries: Lam (6), Furner (8, 37), Newton (16), Renouf (19, 55, 66), Farrell (30), Hodgson (50); **Goals:** Farrell 7.
BLUE SOX: 1 Daryl Cardiss; 19 Oliver Marns; 3 Damian Gibson; 18 Stuart Donlan; 28 Jason Lee; 6 Andrew Dunemann (C); 7 Gavin Clinch; 8 Andy Hobson; 9 Johnny Lawless; 16 Jamie Thackray; 15 Paul Davidson; 2 Jamie Bloem; 14 Danny Tickle. Subs: 13 Martin Moana for Thackray (23); 30 Kris Smith (D) for Bloem (23); 17 Sean Penkywicz for Davidson (49BB, rev 59); 21 Phil Hassan for Lee (47); Thackray for Hobson (57); Penkywicz for Smith (59); Bloem for Tickle (69).
Tries: Clinch (33), Davidson (63), Gibson (74);
Goals: Tickle 3.
League Express Men of the Match:
Warriors: Adrian Lam; *Blue Sox:* Paul Davidson.
Penalty count: 7-10; **Half-time:** 36-8; **Referee:** Karl Kirkpatrick (Warrington); **Attendance:** 9,038.

Saturday 16th June 2001

LONDON BRONCOS 0 BRADFORD BULLS 42

BRONCOS: 5 Brett Warton; 15 Andy Johnson; 14 Olu Iwenofu; 1 Tulsen Tollett; 2 Nigel Roy; 26 Peter Lupton; 7 Dennis Moran; 8 Tony Mestrov; 11 Shane Millard; 18 Justin Dooley; 20 Steffan Hughes; 12 Steele Retchless; 6 Jim Dymock (C). Subs: 17 Glen Air for Dooley (16BB, rev 32); 22 Yusef Sozi for Hughes (34); 27 Michael Gillett for Mestrov (33); 31 Iain Morrison (D) for Millard (61); Air for Moran (52); Mestrov for Sozi (62); Millard for Dymock (77).
Sin bin: Dooley (37) - interference at play the ball.
BULLS: 5 Michael Withers; 2 Tevita Vaikona; 3 Leon Pryce; 23 Graham Mackay; 15 Shane Rigon; 6 Henry Paul; 1 Robbie Paul (C); 8 Joe Vagana; 9 James Lowes; 22 Brian McDermott; 11 Daniel Gartner; 19 Jamie Peacock; 12 Mike Forshaw. Subs: 7 Paul Deacon for R Paul (42BB); 10 Paul Anderson for McDermott (21); 14 Lee Gilmour for Peacock (19); 29 Stuart Fielden for Vagana (21); McDermott for Forshaw (ht); Vagana for Anderson (48).
Tries: Rigon (3), Peacock (11), Fielden (25), Gartner (44), Withers (48), Vaikona (68), Deacon (71), Gilmour (78); **Goals:** H Paul 5.
League Express Men of the Match:
Broncos: Peter Lupton; *Bulls:* Daniel Gartner.
Penalty count: 4-11; **Half-time:** 0-16;
Referee: Robert Connolly (Wigan);
Attendance: 5,259 *(at Welford Road, Leicester).*

Sunday 17th June 2001

HUDDERSFIELD GIANTS 24 SALFORD CITY REDS 32

GIANTS: 1 Paul Reilly; 2 Andrew Frew; 4 Dale Cardoza; 3 Martin Gleeson; 20 Chris Langley; 6 Chris Thorman; 7 Ben Kusto; 8 Steve Molloy; 9 Paul Rowley; 10 Dale Laughton; 13 David Atkins; 11 David Lomax; 26 Steve McNamara (C). Subs: 12 Richard Marshall for Molloy (30); 28 Michael Slicker for Laughton (26BB, rev 52); 31 Matt Walker (D) for Lomax (37); 17 Mark Moxon for Cardoza (43BB, rev 75); Molloy for Marshall (56); Lomax for Walker (69); Slicker for Laughton (74); Walker for Molloy (76).
Tries: Thorman (28), Cardoza (39), McNamara (46), Molloy (65); **Goals:** McNamara 4.
Sin bin: Rowley (78) – fighting.
On report: Brawl incident (78).
CITY REDS: 1 Gary Broadbent; 2 Nick Pinkney; 3 Francis Maloney; 18 Stuart Littler; 5 Martin Offiah; 6 Steve Blakeley; 16 Bobbie Goulding (C); 8 Neil Baynes; 9 Malcolm Alker; 17 Craig Makin; 20 Andy Coley; 4 Michael Hancock; 13 Paul Highton. Subs: 15 Damian Driscoll for Baynes (17); 28 Neil Harmon (D) for Baynes (65); 26 Danny Arnold for Broadbent (73); 14 Kris Tassell for Makin (18); Baynes for Driscoll (47).
Tries: Littler (10, 35), Alker (24), Coley (55), Blakeley (59); **Goals:** Blakeley 5, Maloney.
Sin bin: Blakeley (78) – fighting.
On report: Brawl incident (78).
League Express Men of the Match:
Giants: Paul Reilly; *City Reds:* Michael Hancock.
Penalty count: 6-11; **Half-time:** 12-18; **Referee:** Richard Silverwood (Dewsbury); **Attendance:** 2,721.

WARRINGTON WOLVES 30 CASTLEFORD TIGERS 16

WOLVES: 22 Alan Hunte; 2 Rob Smyth; 3 David Kidwell; 16 Ian Sibbit; 17 David Alstead; 6 Lee Briers; 7 Allan Langer (C); 12 Jerome Guisset; 26 Jon Clarke; 10 Danny Nutley; 11 Steve McCurrie; 25 Gary Mercer; 13 Tawera Nikau. Subs: 20 Dean Busby for Nikau (37); 21 Paul Wood for Nutley (34); 18 Martin Masella for Wood (60); 24 Paul Noone for McCurrie (48); Nikau for Busby (69).
Tries: Sibbit (6), McCurrie (11), Hunte (29), Clarke (72), Briers (79); **Goals:** Briers 5.
TIGERS: 14 Jason Flowers; 20 Waine Pryce; 2 Jon Wells; 5 Darren Rogers; 28 Simon Lewis (D); 7 Mitch Healey; 22 Mark Lennon; 15 Darren Shaw; 27 Andy Speak; 8 Nathan Sykes; 11 Lee Harland; 12 Dale Fritz; 13 Adrian Vowles (C). Subs: 21 Andy McNally for Sykes (64); 16 Ian Tonks for Shaw (24); 23 Michael Smith for Harland (26); 17 Andy Lynch for Rogers (65); Shaw for Speak (51); Harland for Vowles (55).
Tries: Lewis (3), Rogers (40); **Goals:** Lennon 4.
Sin bin: Fritz (62) - dissent.
League Express Men of the Match:
Wolves: Jerome Guisset; *Tigers:* Mitch Healey.
Penalty count: 8-7; **Half-time:** 16-14;
Referee: Stuart Cummings (Widnes); **Attendance:** 6,002.

WAKEFIELD TRINITY WILDCATS 26 ST HELENS 36

WILDCATS: 6 Martin Pearson; 5 Waisale Sovatabua; 4 Justin Brooker; 20 Ben Westwood; 2 Neil Law; 26 Dane Dorahy; 7 Brad Davis; 16 Julian O'Neill; 18 Ben Rauter; 8 Paul Jackson; 12 Willie Poching (C); 15 Ryan Hudson; 11 Jamie Field. Subs: 10 Frank Watene for O'Neill (31); 13 Gary Price for Hudson (36); 17 Graham Law for Poching (50); 23 Paul Handforth for Rauter (77); O'Neill for Watene (60); Hudson for Field (74).
Tries: Sovatabua (2), Dorahy (23), Brooker (45), N Law (58), G Law (70); **Goals:** Pearson 3.
On report: Watene (41) - high tackle on Stewart.
SAINTS: 19 Anthony Stewart; 2 Sean Hoppe; 3 Kevin Iro; 4 Paul Newlove; 5 Anthony Sullivan; 13 Paul Sculthorpe; 1 Paul Wellens; 12 Sonny Nickle; 9 Keiron Cunningham; 10 David Fairleigh; 8 Peter Shiels; 11 Chris Joynt (C); 15 Tim Jonkers. Subs: 17 Steve Hall not used; 22 Heath Cruckshank for Fairleigh (35); 24 Mick Higham for Wellens (47); 25 Mark Edmondson for Nickle (24); Fairleigh for Cruckshank (51); Nickle for Edmondson (61).
Tries: Iro (10), Sculthorpe (20, 32, 80), Shiels (52), Jonkers (64); **Goals:** Sculthorpe 6.
Sin bin: Newlove (38) - holding down.
League Express Men of the Match:
Wildcats: Willie Poching; *Saints:* Paul Sculthorpe.
Penalty count: 10-10; **Half-time:** 12-16;
Referee: Russell Smith (Castleford); **Attendance:** 4,157.

ROUND 16

Friday 22nd June 2001

LEEDS RHINOS 24 WARRINGTON WOLVES 24

RHINOS: 5 Francis Cummins; 15 Chev Walker; 3 Tonie Carroll; 4 Keith Senior; 16 Mark Calderwood; 2 Karl Pratt; 29 Robert Burrow; 8 Darren Fleary; 9 Robert Mears; 10 Barrie McDermott; 11 Andy Hay; 17 Anthony Farrell; 13 Kevin Sinfield (C). Subs: 18 Danny Ward for McDermott (30); 12 Bradley Clyde for Farrell (52); 23 Matthew Diskin for Pratt (58); 14 Marcus St Hilaire not used; McDermott for Fleary (56); Fleary for Ward (66).
Tries: Burrow (2), Carroll (33), Calderwood (50), Mears (76); **Goals:** Burrow 4.
Sin bin: Senior (44) - interference at play the ball.
WOLVES: 22 Alan Hunte; 2 Rob Smyth; 3 David Kidwell; 16 Ian Sibbit; 1 Lee Penny; 6 Lee Briers; 7 Allan Langer (C); 12 Jerome Guisset; 26 Jon Clarke; 10 Danny Nutley; 11 Steve McCurrie; 25 Gary Mercer; 13 Tawera Nikau. Subs: 20 Dean Busby for McCurrie (31); 18 Martin Masella for Nutley (43); 21 Paul Wood for Masella (69); 24 Paul Noone not used; McCurrie for Nikau (66); Masella for Guisset (73BB, rev 75).
Tries: McCurrie (9), Smyth (16), Penny (27), Masella (62); **Goals:** Briers 4.
Sin bin: Guisset (32) - interference at play the ball; Briers (49) - dissent.
League Express Men of the Match:

Rhinos: Robert Burrow; *Wolves:* Jon Clarke.
Penalty count: 11-11; **Half-time:** 14-18;
Referee: Robert Connolly (Wigan); **Attendance:** 12,178.

ST HELENS 28 WIGAN WARRIORS 29

SAINTS: 19 Anthony Stewart; 17 Steve Hall; 3 Kevin Iro; 4 Paul Newlove; 5 Anthony Sullivan; 13 Paul Sculthorpe; 1 Paul Wellens; 12 Sonny Nickle; 9 Keiron Cunningham; 10 David Fairleigh; 11 Chris Joynt (C); 8 Peter Shiels; 2 Sean Hoppe. Subs: 15 Tim Jonkers for Nickle (30); 22 Heath Cruckshank not used; 24 Mick Higham for Joynt (36BB, rev 41); 25 Mark Edmondson not used; Nickle for Hoppe (48); Hoppe for Shiels (57); Higham for Nickle (75).
Tries: Hoppe (22), Fairleigh (28, 63), Shiels (53), Newlove (68); **Goals:** Sculthorpe 4.
WARRIORS: 1 Kris Radlinski; 5 Brian Carney; 15 Paul Johnson; 3 Steve Renouf; 23 David Hodgson; 6 Matthew Johns; 7 Adrian Lam; 8 Terry O'Connor; 9 Terry Newton; 20 Harvey Howard; 11 Mick Cassidy; 14 David Furner; 13 Andy Farrell (C). Subs: 10 Neil Cowie for Howard (23); 12 Denis Betts for Cassidy (25); 19 Chris Chester for Johns (36); 18 Wes Davies not used; Cassidy for O'Connor (36); Howard for Cowie (66); Cowie for Cassidy (74).
Tries: Furner (4), Farrell (8), Radlinski (38, 57);
Goals: Farrell 6; **Field goal:** Farrell.
On report: Howard (15) - leading with forearm.
League Express Men of the Match:
Saints: David Fairleigh; *Warriors:* Kris Radlinski.
Penalty count: 11-8; **Half-time:** 12-21; **Referee:** Russell Smith (Castleford); **Attendance:** 13,830.

Saturday 23rd June 2001

SALFORD CITY REDS 18 CASTLEFORD TIGERS 26

CITY REDS: 1 Gary Broadbent; 2 Nick Pinkney; 3 Francis Maloney; 18 Stuart Littler; 5 Martin Offiah; 6 Steve Blakeley; 16 Bobbie Goulding (C); 8 Neil Baynes; 9 Malcolm Alker; 15 Damian Driscoll; 20 Andy Coley; 4 Michael Hancock; 13 Paul Highton. Subs: 14 Kris Tassell for Maloney (16); 17 Craig Makin for Baynes (75); 26 Danny Arnold for Baynes (33); 28 Neil Harmon for Driscoll (4BB, rev 47); Baynes for Coley (60); Harmon for Driscoll (61); Coley for Hancock (67).
Tries: Offiah (37), Coley (50), Tassell (78);
Goals: Blakeley 3.
TIGERS: 22 Mark Lennon; 20 Waine Pryce; 2 Jon Wells; 18 Jonathan Roper; 28 Simon Lewis; 6 Danny Orr; 7 Mitch Healey; 8 Nathan Sykes; 27 Andy Speak; 10 Dean Sampson; 23 Michael Smith; 12 Dale Fritz; 13 Adrian Vowles (C). Subs: 11 Lee Harland for Smith (26); 14 Jason Flowers for Vowles (33); 15 Darren Shaw for Speak (40BB, rev 72); 16 Ian Tonks for Sykes (30); Sykes for Tonks (47); Tonks for Sampson (52); Smith for Flowers (60BB); Sampson for Tonks (70).
Tries: M Smith (3), Roper (14), Sampson (24), Healey (65); **Goals:** Orr 5.
League Express Men of the Match:
City Reds: Malcolm Alker; *Tigers:* Dale Fritz.
Penalty count: 6-5; **Half-time:** 6-16; **Referee:** Richard Silverwood (Dewsbury); **Attendance:** 3,530.

Sunday 24th June 2001

HUDDERSFIELD GIANTS 22 LONDON BRONCOS 22

GIANTS: 1 Paul Reilly; 2 Andrew Frew; 4 Dale Cardoza; 3 Martin Gleeson; 20 Chris Langley; 27 Brandon Costin; 7 Ben Kusto; 8 Steve Molloy; 9 Paul Rowley; 12 Richard Marshall; 13 David Atkins; 31 Matt Walker; 26 Steve McNamara (C). Subs: 32 Troy Stone (D) for Molloy (22); 28 Michael Slicker for Marshall (29); 11 David Lomax for Walker (50); 33 Stanley Gene (D) for Atkins (34); Molloy for Stone (59BB, rev 75); Atkins for McNamara (64BB); Marshall for Slicker (70).
Tries: Gene (46), Gleeson (65), Reilly (76), Atkins (80);
Goals: Costin 2, McNamara.
BRONCOS: 30 Paul Sykes (D); 26 Peter Lupton; 15 Andy Johnson; 2 Nigel Roy; 5 Brett Warton; 27 Michael Gillett; 7 Dennis Moran; 8 Tony Mestrov; 17 Glen Air; 12 Steele Retchless; 11 Shane Millard; 29 Robert Parker (D); 6 Jim Dymock (C). Subs: 14 Olu Iwenofu not used; 22 Yusef Sozi not used; 18 Justin Dooley for Air (26); 20 Steffan Hughes for Mestrov (28BB, rev 49); Hughes for Mestrov (60BB, rev 69); Hughes for Mestrov (75BB); Air for Sykes (40).
Tries: Johnson (17), Moran (38, 78), Roy (62);
Goals: Warton 3.
League Express Men of the Match:
Giants: Stanley Gene; *Broncos:* Dennis Moran.
Penalty count: 9-9; **Half-time:** 0-12;
Referee: Ian Smith (Oldham); **Attendance:** 2,235.

BRADFORD BULLS 62
WAKEFIELD TRINITY WILDCATS 10

BULLS: 5 Michael Withers; 2 Tevita Vaikona; 20 Scott Naylor; 14 Lee Gilmour; 4 Nathan McAvoy; 6 Henry Paul; 1 Robbie Paul (C); 8 Joe Vagana; 9 James Lowes; 22 Brian McDermott; 11 Daniel Gartner; 18 Lee Radford; 15 Shane Rigon. Subs: 7 Paul Deacon for H Paul (55); 3 Leon Pryce for Withers (47); 10 Paul Anderson for McDermott (24); 29 Stuart Fielden for Vagana (24); Vagana for Anderson (60); McDermott for Radford (71).
Tries: Gartner (7), Withers (8), H Paul (20), Anderson (29), Rigon (39), McAvoy (43), R Paul (48), Vaikona (62), McDermott (74), Vagana (78);
Goals: H Paul 8, Deacon 3.
WILDCATS: 6 Martin Pearson; 2 Neil Law; 20 Ben Westwood; 4 Justin Brooker; 5 Waisale Sovatabua; 26 Dane Dorahy; 7 Brad Davis; 22 Keith Mason; 18 Ben Rauter; 8 Paul Jackson; 19 Gareth Ellis; 17 Graham Law; 13 Gary Price (C). Subs: 11 Jamie Field for G Law (32); 24 Chris Feather for Jackson (49); 10 Frank Watene for Mason (33); 9 David March for Rauter (74); Mason for Watene (60).
Tries: Pearson (23), Price (53); **Goal:** Pearson.
League Express Men of the Match:
Bulls: James Lowes; *Wildcats:* Martin Pearson.
Penalty count: 9-7; **Half-time:** 32-4;
Referee: Peter Taberner (Wigan); **Attendance:** 11,298.

HALIFAX BLUE SOX 26 HULL FC 27

BLUE SOX: 1 Daryl Cardiss; 19 Oliver Marns; 21 Phil Hassan; 18 Stuart Donlan; 3 Damian Gibson; 6 Andrew Dunemann; 7 Gavin Clinch; 8 Andy Hobson; 9 Johnny Lawless; 23 Brett Goldspink (C); 15 Paul Davidson; 12 Shayne McMenemy; 2 Jamie Bloem. Subs: 5 Lee Greenwood not used; 17 Sean Penkywicz for Hobson (22); 13 Martin Moana for Davidson (62); 29 Andrew Brocklehurst not used; Hobson for Goldspink (45); Goldspink for Hobson (71); Davidson for McMenemy (71).
Tries: Marns (6), Cardiss (11, 25); **Goals:** Bloem 7.
HULL: 1 Steve Prescott; 2 Chris Smith; 23 Logan Campbell; 4 Deon Bird; 21 Gareth Raynor; 6 Richard Horne; 7 Tony Smith; 8 Paul Broadbent; 15 Paul King; 10 Luke Felsch; 11 Adam Maher; 12 Tony Grimaldi (C); 13 Jason Smith. Subs: 9 Lee Jackson for King (9); 28 Scott Logan for Maher (17); 3 David Maiden for Jackson (32); 18 Steve Craven for Broadbent (27); Broadbent for Craven (73).
Tries: T Smith (16), J Smith (19), Raynor (36), Prescott (40), C Smith (70); **Goals:** Prescott 3;
Field goal: Prescott.
Sin bin: Felsch (59) - dissent.
League Express Men of the Match:
Blue Sox: Daryl Cardiss; *Hull FC:* Steve Prescott.
Penalty count: 12-10; **Half-time:** 20-22;
Referee: Stuart Cummings (Widnes); **Attendance:** 4,723.

ROUND 17

Friday 29th June 2001

CASTLEFORD TIGERS 28 LEEDS RHINOS 26

TIGERS: 22 Mark Lennon; 20 Waine Pryce; 2 Jon Wells; 18 Jonathan Roper; 28 Simon Lewis; 6 Danny Orr; 7 Mitch Healey; 8 Nathan Sykes; 15 Darren Shaw; 10 Dean Sampson; 11 Lee Harland; 12 Dale Fritz; 13 Adrian Vowles (C). Subs: 17 Andy Lynch for Sykes (34); 14 Jason Flowers for Lennon (40); 27 Andy Speak for Shaw (60); 16 Ian Tonks for Sampson (38BB, rev 73); Sykes for Lynch (51); Shaw for Speak (67).
Tries: Pryce (16), Fritz (20), Lennon (25), Roper (40), Lewis (55); **Goals:** Orr 4.
RHINOS: 5 Francis Cummins; 14 Marcus St Hilaire; 3 Tonie Carroll; 15 Chev Walker; 16 Mark Calderwood; 1 Iestyn Harris (C); 29 Robert Burrow; 8 Darren Fleary; 9 Robert Mears; 10 Barrie McDermott; 11 Andy Hay; 17 Anthony Farrell; 13 Kevin Sinfield. Subs: 18 Danny Ward for McDermott (21); 12 Bradley Clyde for Fleary (51); 23 Matthew Diskin for Ward (63); 28 Andy Kirk not used; McDermott for Farrell (51).
Tries: Farrell (28), Carroll (50, 58), McDermott (66), Harris (72); **Goals:** Harris 3.
Sin bin: Walker (34) – holding down.
League Express Men of the Match:
Tigers: Dale Fritz; *Rhinos:* Iestyn Harris.
Penalty count: 8-6; **Half-time:** 24-6;
Referee: Steve Ganson (St Helens); **Attendance:** 10,625.

WIGAN WARRIORS 44 BRADFORD BULLS 30

WARRIORS: 1 Kris Radlinski; 2 Brett Dallas; 15 Paul Johnson; 3 Steve Renouf; 5 Brian Carney; 6 Matthew Johns; 7 Adrian Lam; 10 Neil Cowie; 9 Terry Newton; 20 Harvey Howard; 11 Mick Cassidy; 14 David Furner; 13 Andy Farrell (C). Subs: 17 Francis Stephenson for Howard (24BB, rev 49); 12 Denis Betts for Furner (14BB, rev 17); 19 Chris Chester for Johns (71); 23 David Hodgson for Newton (74); Betts for Cassidy (22); Stephenson for Cowie (51); Cassidy for Stephenson (66); Cowie for Howard (71).
Tries: Radlinski (2, 37, 54), Carney (23), Renouf (42), Furner (67), Betts (79); **Goals:** Farrell 8.
On report: Johnson (59) - high tackle on McDermott.
BULLS: 5 Michael Withers; 2 Tevita Vaikona; 23 Graham Mackay; 14 Lee Gilmour; 3 Leon Pryce; 6 Henry Paul; 1 Robbie Paul (C); 22 Brian McDermott; 9 James Lowes; 8 Joe Vagana; 11 Daniel Gartner; 19 Jamie Peacock; 15 Shane Rigon. Subs: 7 Paul Deacon for Rigon (56); 18 Lee Radford for Gartner (41); 29 Stuart Fielden for Vagana (21); 10 Paul Anderson for McDermott (21); McDermott for Anderson (52); Vagana for Radford (68); Anderson for McDermott (72BB).
Tries: Withers (7, 74), Anderson (40), Vaikona (57), McDermott (61); **Goals:** H Paul 5.
League Express Men of the Match:
Warriors: Kris Radlinski; *Bulls:* Michael Withers.
Penalty count: 7-5; **Half-time:** 20-12;
Referee: Russell Smith (Castleford); **Attendance:** 14,886.

Saturday 30th June 2001

HULL FC 34 ST HELENS 28

HULL: 1 Steve Prescott; 2 Chris Smith; 23 Logan Campbell; 4 Deon Bird; 21 Gareth Raynor; 7 Tony Smith; 6 Richard Horne; 18 Steve Craven; 12 Tony Grimaldi (C); 10 Luke Felsch; 20 Garreth Carvell; 28 Scott Logan; 13 Jason Smith. Subs: 16 Paul Cooke for T Smith (22); 8 Paul Broadbent for Carvell (33); 3 David Maiden for Craven (60); 5 Matt Crowther not used; T Smith for Horne (70).
Tries: Grimaldi (19), Cooke (38, 44), Broadbent (48), Maiden (61); **Goals:** Prescott 7.
SAINTS: 1 Paul Wellens; 19 Anthony Stewart; 3 Kevin Iro; 4 Paul Newlove; 5 Anthony Sullivan; 20 Tommy Martyn; 13 Paul Sculthorpe; 12 Sonny Nickle; 9 Keiron Cunningham; 16 Vila Matautia; 11 Chris Joynt (C); 2 Sean Hoppe; 18 John Stankevitch. Subs: 25 Mark Edmondson for Matautia (4BB, rev 6); 17 Steve Hall for Newlove (30); 15 Tim Jonkers for Nickle (33); 24 Mick Higham for Cunningham (61); Edmondson for Matautia (16BB, rev 33); Nickle for Matautia (51); Edmondson for Stankevitch (63); Stankevitch for Hoppe (76).
Tries: Newlove (1), Sculthorpe (14), Martyn (27, 76), Iro (56), Hall (73); **Goals:** Sculthorpe 2.
On report: Matautia (38) - high tackle on Prescott.
League Express Men of the Match:
Hull: Jason Smith; *Saints:* Sean Hoppe.
Penalty count: 11-6; **Half-time:** 16-16;
Referee: Stuart Cummings (Widnes); **Attendance:** 6,538.

Sunday 1st July 2001

LONDON BRONCOS 14 SALFORD CITY REDS 37

BRONCOS: 30 Paul Sykes; 5 Brett Warton; 15 Andy Johnson; 2 Nigel Roy; 34 Sylvain Houles (D); 6 Jim Dymock (C); 7 Dennis Moran; 10 Scott Cram; 17 Glen Air; 8 Tony Mestrov; 11 Shane Millard; 12 Steele Retchless; 29 Robert Parker. Subs: 18 Justin Dooley for Mestrov (21); 20 Steffan Hughes for Air (37); 22 Yusef Sozi for Dooley (72); 14 Olu Iwenofu not used; Air for Millard (49); Mestrov for Cram (53); Millard for Hughes (63); Cram for Johnson (65BB).
Tries: Warton (12), Air (15); **Goals:** Warton 3.
CITY REDS: 1 Gary Broadbent; 2 Nick Pinkney; 3 Francis Maloney; 18 Stuart Littler; 5 Martin Offiah; 6 Steve Blakeley; 16 Bobbie Goulding (C); 20 Andy Coley; 9 Malcolm Alker; 28 Neil Harmon; 13 Paul Highton; 23 Mike Wainwright; 14 Kris Tassell. Subs: 4 Michael Hancock for Highton (23); 8 Neil Baynes for Harmon (16); 26 Danny Arnold for Coley (69); 22 Karle Hammond for Harmon (67); Harmon for Baynes (40); Highton for Hancock (49).
Tries: Wainwright (21), Offiah (29, 35), Blakeley (38), Tassell (61), Hammond (68); **Goals:** Blakeley 6;
Field goal: Goulding.
League Express Men of the Match:
Broncos: Glen Air; *City Reds:* Gary Broadbent.
Penalty count: 7-9; **Half-time:** 12-24; **Referee:** Karl Kirkpatrick (Warrington); **Attendance:** 2,941.

WARRINGTON WOLVES 34 HALIFAX BLUE SOX 22

WOLVES: 22 Alan Hunte; 2 Rob Smyth; 3 David Kidwell; 16 Ian Sibbit; 1 Lee Penny; 13 Tawera Nikau (C); 6 Lee Briers; 12 Jerome Guisset; 26 Jon Clarke; 21 Paul Wood; 11 Steve McCurrie; 25 Gary Mercer; 20 Dean Busby. Subs: 17 David Alstead for Penny (65); 18 Martin Masella for Wood (27); 24 Paul Noone for Mercer (13BB); 19 Ian Knott for McCurrie (54); Wood for Guisset (64); McCurrie for Busby (72); Guisset for Masella (74).
Tries: Nikau (3), Kidwell (14), Smyth (21), Hunte (41, 63), Sibbit (57); **Goals:** Briers 5.
Sin bin: Sibbit (67) - fighting.
BLUE SOX: 3 Damian Gibson; 19 Oliver Marns; 18 Stuart Donlan; 21 Phil Hassan; 5 Lee Greenwood; 13 Martin Moana; 6 Andrew Dunemann; 23 Brett Goldspink (C); 9 Johnny Lawless; 10 Jim Gannon; 15 Paul Davidson; 12 Shayne McMenemy; 14 Danny Tickle. Subs: 17 Sean Penkywicz for Goldspink (35); 2 Jamie Bloem for Marns (15); 8 Andy Hobson for Penkywicz (43); 16 Jamie Thackray for Goldspink (71); Goldspink for Tickle (48); Marns for Moana (62).
Tries: Donlan (33, 76), Hassan (61), Lawless (73);
Goals: Tickle, Bloem 2.
Sin bin: Davidson (67) - fighting.
On report: Gannon (19) - high shot on Noone.
League Express Men of the Match:
Wolves: David Kidwell; *Blue Sox:* Andrew Dunemann.
Penalty count: 6-7; **Half-time:** 16-6;
Referee: Ian Smith (Oldham); **Attendance:** 5,628.

WAKEFIELD TRINITY WILDCATS 22
HUDDERSFIELD GIANTS 38

WILDCATS: 6 Martin Pearson; 2 Neil Law; 20 Ben Westwood; 4 Justin Brooker; 5 Waisale Sovatabua; 26 Dane Dorahy; 7 Brad Davis; 16 Julian O'Neill; 18 Ben Rauter; 8 Paul Jackson; 15 Ryan Hudson; 12 Willie Poching (C); 13 Gary Price. Subs: 19 Gareth Ellis for Dorahy (70); 11 Jamie Field for Hudson (48); 17 Graham Law for Davis (56); 22 Keith Mason for O'Neill (32); O'Neill for Jackson (59); Hudson for Rauter (76).
Tries: Davis (22), N Law (39, 71), Sovatabua (75);
Goals: Pearson 3.
GIANTS: 1 Paul Reilly; 20 Chris Langley; 33 Stanley Gene; 3 Martin Gleeson; 2 Andrew Frew; 27 Brandon Costin; 7 Ben Kusto; 8 Steve Molloy; 9 Paul Rowley; 32 Troy Stone; 13 David Atkins; 31 Matt Walker; 26 Steve McNamara (C). Subs: 6 Chris Thorman for Rowley (36); 11 David Lomax for Molloy (28); 12 Richard Marshall for Stone (30BB, rev 41); 28 Michael Slicker for Walker (48); Molloy for Slicker (55); Marshall for McNamara (56BB, rev 63); Marshall for Stone (64BB, rev 72); Marshall for Molloy (77).
Tries: Rowley (6), Costin (19, 47), Frew (34), Gene (44), Reilly (60), Atkins (80); **Goals:** McNamara 5.
On report: Reilly (68) - high tackle.
League Express Men of the Match:
Wildcats: Willie Poching; *Giants:* Stanley Gene.
Penalty count: 13-5; **Half-time:** 12-18; **Referee:** Richard

Silverwood (Dewsbury); **Attendance:** 2,847.

ROUND 18

Friday 6th July 2001

BRADFORD BULLS 40 HULL FC 0

BULLS: 5 Michael Withers; 2 Tevita Vaikona; 23 Graham Mackay; 20 Scott Naylor; 4 Nathan McAvoy; 6 Henry Paul (C); 7 Paul Deacon; 22 Brian McDermott; 9 James Lowes; 8 Joe Vagana; 14 Lee Gilmour; 19 Jamie Peacock; 12 Mike Forshaw. Subs: 1 Robbie Paul for Deacon (57); 15 Shane Rigon for Gilmour (48); 29 Stuart Fielden for McDermott (25); 10 Paul Anderson for Vagana (25); McDermott for Anderson (67); Vagana for Peacock (71).
Tries: Deacon (15), Mackay (20), H Paul (42, 70), R Paul (60, 75), Withers (79); **Goals:** H Paul 6.
Sin bin: Fielden (64) – fighting.
On report: Brawl incident (64).
HULL: 5 Matt Crowther; 2 Chris Smith; 23 Logan Campbell; 4 Deon Bird; 26 Paul Parker; 6 Richard Horne; 7 Tony Smith; 18 Steve Craven; 12 Tony Grimaldi (C); 10 Luke Felsch; 11 Adam Maher; 28 Scott Logan; 13 Jason Smith. Subs: 16 Paul Cooke for Bird (53); 8 Paul Broadbent for Craven (21); 3 David Maiden for Maher (53); 20 Gareth Carvell for Logan (40); Craven for Broadbent (62); Logan for Felsch (72).
Sin bin: J Smith (64) – fighting.
On report: Brawl incident (64).
League Express Men of the Match:
Bulls: Henry Paul; *Hull:* Tony Smith.
Penalty count: 8-5; **Half-time:** 12-0;
Referee: Ian Smith (Oldham); **Attendance:** 12,807.

LEEDS RHINOS 56 SALFORD CITY REDS 6

RHINOS: 5 Francis Cummins; 15 Chev Walker; 3 Tonie Carroll; 4 Keith Senior; 16 Mark Calderwood; 1 Iestyn Harris (C); 2 Karl Pratt; 17 Anthony Farrell; 9 Robert Mears; 10 Barrie McDermott; 11 Andy Hay; 12 Bradley Clyde; 13 Kevin Sinfield. Subs: 18 Danny Ward for McDermott (10BB, rev 26); 20 Jamie Mathiou for Farrell (32); 30 Danny McGuire (D) for Harris (52); 23 Matthew Diskin for Carroll (57); Farrell for Clyde (58); Ward for McDermott (59); McDermott for Mathiou (70).
Tries: Carroll (14, 36), Ward (25), Cummins (27), Calderwood (38, 68), McDermott (43), Clyde (51), Walker (58), Hay (74); **Goals:** Sinfield 8.
CITY REDS: 1 Gary Broadbent; 2 Nick Pinkney; 3 Francis Maloney; 18 Stuart Littler; 5 Martin Offiah; 6 Steve Blakeley; 16 Bobbie Goulding (C); 20 Andy Coley; 9 Malcolm Alker; 28 Neil Harmon; 13 Paul Highton; 14 Kris Tassell; 23 Mike Wainwright. Subs: 4 Michael Hancock for Harmon (19); 8 Neil Baynes for Highton (29); 26 Danny Arnold for Broadbent (31); 30 Jason Nicol for Maloney (52); Harmon for Baynes (50); Highton for Coley (59); Maloney for Wainwright (70BB).
Try: Blakeley (11); **Goal:** Blakeley.
League Express Men of the Match:
Rhinos: Karl Pratt; *City Reds:* Kris Tassell.
Penalty count: 8-8; **Half-time:** 28-6; **Referee:** Russell Smith (Castleford); **Attendance:** 10,119.

Saturday 7th July 2001

ST HELENS 70 WARRINGTON WOLVES 16

SAINTS: 19 Anthony Stewart; 17 Steve Hall; 2 Sean Hoppe; 3 Kevin Iro; 5 Anthony Sullivan; 20 Tommy Martyn; 1 Paul Wellens; 12 Sonny Nickle; 24 Mick Higham; 14 Wayne McDonald; 10 David Fairleigh; 18 John Stankevitch; 13 Paul Sculthorpe (C). Subs: 22 Heath Cruckshank for McDonald (28); 15 Tim Jonkers for Nickle (32); 25 Mark Edmondson for Cruckshank (38); 23 Mike Bennett for Martyn (67); McDonald for Fairleigh (65).
Tries: Stewart (4), McDonald (7, 72), Hoppe (18, 31), Stankevitch (27), Martyn (40), Sculthorpe (44, 68), Hall (49), Fairleigh (54), Higham (80); **Goals:** Sculthorpe 11.
WOLVES: 22 Alan Hunte; 2 Rob Smyth; 3 David Kidwell; 16 Ian Sibbit; 1 Lee Penny; 6 Lee Briers; 7 Allan Langer (C); 12 Jerome Guisset; 26 Jon Clarke; 10 Danny Nutley; 20 Dean Busby; 25 Gary Mercer; 13 Tawera Nikau. Subs: 11 Steve McCurrie for Busby (20); 24 Paul Noone for Mercer (34BB, rev 58); 21 Paul Wood for Nutley (41); 18 Martin Masella for Guisset (51).
Tries: Penny (35), Kidwell (41), McCurrie (76);
Goals: Briers 2.
Sin bin: Nikau (39) - dissent.
League Express Men of the Match:
Saints: Paul Sculthorpe; *Wolves:* None.
Penalty count: 10-6; **Half-time:** 34-6;
Referee: Robert Connolly (Wigan); **Attendance:** 8,113.

Sunday 8th July 2001

HUDDERSFIELD GIANTS 24 WIGAN WARRIORS 48

GIANTS: 1 Paul Reilly; 2 Andrew Frew; 4 Dale Cardoza; 3 Martin Gleeson; 20 Chris Langley; 27 Brandon Costin (C); 7 Ben Kusto; 32 Troy Stone; 30 Toby Green; 12 Richard Marshall; 11 David Lomax; 31 Matt Walker; 33 Stanley Gene. Subs: 18 Chris Molyneux for Stone (47); 8 Steve Molloy for Walker (28); 6 Chris Thorman for Frew (67); 34 Danny Fearon (D) for Molloy (54); Stone for Green (52); Walker for Marshall (70); Molloy for Molyneux (72BB).
Tries: Frew (4), Costin (15), Langley (66), Reilly (74);
Goals: Costin 4.
WARRIORS: 1 Kris Radlinski; 2 Brett Dallas; 15 Paul Johnson; 23 David Hodgson; 5 Brian Carney; 22 Phil Jones; 7 Adrian Lam; 10 Neil Cowie; 9 Terry Newton; 20 Harvey Howard; 11 Mick Cassidy; 14 David Furner; 13 Andy Farrell (C). Subs: 17 Francis Stephenson for Cowie (27); 12 Denis Betts for Cassidy (30); 26 Ricky Bibey for Howard (54); 24 Martin Aspinwall (D) for Furner (61); Cassidy for Lam (68); Cowie for Stephenson (72).
Tries: Newton (9), Hodgson (33), Howard (47), Farrell (51, 77), Furner (53), Radlinski (60, 79); **Goals:** Farrell 8.
League Express Men of the Match:
Giants: Brandon Costin; *Warriors:* Andy Farrell.
Penalty count: 8-11; **Half-time:** 12-12;
Referee: Steve Ganson (St Helens); **Attendance:** 4,039.

LONDON BRONCOS 26 WAKEFIELD TRINITY WILDCATS 6

BRONCOS: 30 Paul Sykes; 28 Marvin Golden; 34 Sylvain Houles; 2 Nigel Roy; 5 Brett Warton; 6 Jim Dymock (C); 7 Dennis Moran; 10 Scott Cram; 17 Glen Air; 8 Tony Mestrov; 11 Shane Millard; 12 Steele Retchless; 29 Robert Parker. Subs: 15 Andy Johnson for Cram (33); 18 Justin Dooley for Mestrov (27); 20 Steffan Hughes for Dymock (79); 35 Kris Smith (D) for Warton (78BB); Cram for Millard (62); Mestrov for Retchless (67); Millard for Dooley (75).
Tries: Roy (33), Johnson (45), Air (47), Sykes (80);
Goals: Warton 4, Sykes.
WILDCATS: 6 Martin Pearson; 4 Justin Brooker; 20 Ben Westwood; 17 Graham Law; 5 Waisale Sovatabua; 12 Willie Poching (C); 7 Brad Davis; 10 Frank Watene; 9 David March; 8 Paul Jackson; 11 Jamie Field; 13 Gary Price; 15 Ryan Hudson. Subs: 16 Julian O'Neill for Watene (22BB, rev 64); 1 Martyn Holland for Pearson (34); 18 Ben Rauter for Price (61); 22 Keith Mason for Jackson (30); Price for Poching (69).
Try: Brooker (11); **Goal:** Pearson.
On report: Westwood (78) - striking.
League Express Men of the Match:
Broncos: Glen Air; *Wildcats:* Brad Davis.
Penalty count: 11-7; **Half-time:** 8-6; **Referee:** Stuart Cummings (Widnes); **Attendance:** 2,153.

HALIFAX BLUE SOX 22 CASTLEFORD TIGERS 16

BLUE SOX: 1 Daryl Cardiss; 19 Oliver Marns; 21 Phil Hassan; 18 Stuart Donlan; 3 Damian Gibson; 6 Andrew Dunemann; 7 Gavin Clinch; 23 Brett Goldspink (C); 9 Johnny Lawless; 10 Jim Gannon; 2 Jamie Bloem; 15 Paul Davidson; 12 Shayne McMenemy. Subs: 4 Adam Hughes for Hassan (15); 8 Andy Hobson for Goldspink (30); 31 David Foster for Davidson (35BB, rev 48); 14 Danny Tickle for Bloem (64); Goldspink for Hobson (62).
Tries: Bloem (45), Marns (51), Lawless (68), Hughes (77); **Goals:** Bloem 2, Tickle.
Sin bin: Gannon (39) - interference.
On report: Davidson (29) - taking out Orr off the ball.
TIGERS: 22 Mark Lennon; 1 Richard Gay; 2 Jon Wells; 18 Jonathan Roper; 28 Simon Lewis; 6 Danny Orr; 7 Mitch Healey; 8 Nathan Sykes; 15 Darren Shaw; 10 Dean Sampson; 11 Lee Harland; 12 Dale Fritz; 13 Adrian Vowles (C). Subs: 14 Jason Flowers for Lennon (71); 27 Andy Speak for Shaw (48); 16 Ian Tonks for Vowles (27BB, rev 37); 23 Michael Smith for Harland (27BB); Tonks for Sampson (60); Shaw for Sykes (60BB).
Tries: Lewis (9), Gay (17), Orr (63); **Goals:** Orr 2.
League Express Men of the Match:
Blue Sox: Andrew Dunemann; *Tigers:* Dean Sampson.
Penalty count: 8-10; **Half-time:** 2-10; **Referee:** Richard Silverwood (Dewsbury); **Attendance:** 5,041.

ROUND 19

Friday 13th July 2001

ST HELENS 46 LEEDS RHINOS 24

SAINTS: 19 Anthony Stewart; 17 Steve Hall; 3 Kevin Iro; 2 Sean Hoppe; 5 Anthony Sullivan; 20 Tommy Martyn; 1 Paul Wellens; 12 Sonny Nickle; 9 Keiron Cunningham; 10 David Fairleigh; 14 Wayne McDonald; 18 John Stankevitch; 13 Paul Sculthorpe (C). Subs: 11 Chris Joynt for McDonald (22); 15 Tim Jonkers for Stewart (25); 25 Mark Edmondson for Fairleigh (34BB, rev 40); 24 Mick Higham for Martyn (70); McDonald for Nickle (56); Edmondson for Iro (76).
Tries: Iro (7), Sullivan (24), Sculthorpe (33, 55, 59), Stankevitch (51), Martyn (69), Hoppe (77);
Goals: Sculthorpe 7.
Sin bin: Joynt (45) - interference at the play-the-ball.
RHINOS: 5 Francis Cummins (C); 15 Chev Walker; 3 Tonie Carroll; 4 Keith Senior; 16 Mark Calderwood; 13 Kevin Sinfield; 2 Karl Pratt; 10 Barrie McDermott; 9 Robert Mears; 20 Jamie Mathiou; 11 Andy Hay; 17 Anthony Farrell; 12 Bradley Clyde. Subs: 18 Danny Ward for McDermott (31); 6 Brett Mullins for Calderwood (56); 22 David Wrench for Farrell (61); 23 Matthew Diskin for Pratt (71); McDermott for Mathiou (54).
Tries: Hay (36), Cummins (39), Carroll (63, pen, 73);
Goals: Sinfield 4.
League Express Men of the Match:
Saints: Tommy Martyn; *Rhinos:* Andy Hay.
Penalty count: 9-10; **Half-time:** 16-12;
Referee: Stuart Cummings (Widnes); **Attendance:** 8,913.

Sunday 15th July 2001

BRADFORD BULLS 44 CASTLEFORD TIGERS 4

BULLS: 5 Michael Withers; 2 Tevita Vaikona; 20 Scott Naylor; 15 Shane Rigon; 4 Nathan McAvoy; 3 Leon Pryce; 7 Paul Deacon; 8 Joe Vagana; 9 James Lowes (C); 22 Brian McDermott; 11 Daniel Gartner; 19 Jamie Peacock; 12 Mike Forshaw. Subs: 14 Lee Gilmour for Rigon (54); 18 Lee Radford for Gartner (56); 10 Paul Anderson for Vagana (22); 29 Stuart Fielden for McDermott (15); Vagana for Anderson (49); Rigon for Withers (66).
Tries: Withers (17), Lowes (23, 31), Pryce (33), Deacon (54), Naylor (59, 76); **Goals:** Deacon 8.
TIGERS: 14 Jason Flowers; 1 Richard Gay; 2 Jon Wells; 18 Jonathan Roper; 20 Waine Pryce; 7 Mitch Healey; 22 Mark Lennon; 8 Nathan Sykes; 15 Darren Shaw; 10 Dean Sampson; 11 Lee Harland; 12 Dale Fritz; 13 Adrian Vowles (C). Subs: 24 Jonathan Goddard for Sykes (65); 17 Andy Lynch for Sampson (24); 26 Wayne Godwin (D) for Shaw (68); 23 Michael Smith for Wells (40); Sampson for Lynch (50).
Try: Fritz (12).
League Express Men of the Match:
Bulls: Paul Deacon; *Tigers:* Dale Fritz.
Penalty count: 5-9; **Half-time:** 26-4;
Referee: Steve Ganson (St Helens); **Attendance:** 9,287.

HUDDERSFIELD GIANTS 52 WARRINGTON WOLVES 10

GIANTS: 1 Paul Reilly; 2 Andrew Frew; 3 Martin Gleeson; 33 Stanley Gene; 20 Chris Langley; 27 Brandon Costin (C); 7 Ben Kusto; 32 Troy Stone; 9 Paul Rowley; 8 Steve Molloy; 11 David Lomax; 13 David Atkins; 26 Steve McNamara. Subs: 4 Dale Cardoza for Gene (64); 6 Chris Thorman for Costin (64); 12 Richard Marshall for Molloy (26); 31 Matt Walker for Stone (33); Stone for Lomax (51BB, rev 72); Molloy for Marshall (69); Marshall for McNamara (79).
Tries: Atkins (3), Costin (22, 54), Frew (39, 77), Kusto (43), Langley (63), Stone (69); **Goals:** Costin 8, McNamara 2.
WOLVES: 22 Alan Hunte; 2 Rob Smyth; 3 David Kidwell; 16 Ian Sibbit; 1 Lee Penny; 6 Lee Briers; 7 Allan Langer (C); 12 Jerome Guisset; 26 Jon Clarke; 10 Danny Nutley; 25 Gary Mercer; 20 Dean Busby; 13 Tawera Nikau. Subs: 21 Paul Wood for Nutley (53); 4 Toa Kohe-Love for Kidwell (21); 18 Martin Masella for Guisset (59); 11 Steve McCurrie for Nikau (22); Kidwell for McCurrie (45); Nikau for Busby (78).
Tries: Hunte (56), Masella (67); **Goal:** Briers.
League Express Men of the Match:
Giants: Brandon Costin; *Wolves:* None.
Penalty count: 16-6; **Half-time:** 20-0;
Referee: Ian Smith (Oldham); **Attendance:** 3,203.

LONDON BRONCOS 20 HULL FC 24

BRONCOS: 30 Paul Sykes; 5 Brett Warton; 34 Sylvain Houles; 2 Nigel Roy; 19 Dominic Peters; 6 Jim Dymock (C); 7 Dennis Moran; 10 Scott Cram; 17 Glen Air; 8 Tony Mestrov; 11 Shane Millard; 12 Steele Retchless; 29 Robert Parker. Subs: 15 Andy Johnson for Millard (31); 18 Justin Dooley for Mestrov (12); 26 Peter Lupton not used; 36 Dan Potter not used; Mestrov for Cram (52); Millard for Dooley (55); Cram for Mestrov (73).
Tries: Air (21), Houles (44), Moran (61), Dymock (66);
Goals: Warton 2.
HULL: 1 Steve Prescott; 21 Gareth Raynor; 6 Richard Horne; 4 Deon Bird; 5 Matt Crowther; 16 Paul Cooke; 7 Tony Smith; 18 Steve Craven; 15 Paul King; 10 Luke Felsch; 11 Adam Maher; 12 Tony Grimaldi (C); 13 Jason Smith. Subs: 8 Paul Broadbent for Craven (32); 23 Logan Campbell for Maiden (60); 28 Scott Logan for Felsch (48); 3 David Maiden for King (23); Craven for Broadbent (68).
Tries: Crowther (26), Maiden (34), Grimaldi (53), J Smith (78); **Goals:** Prescott 4.
League Express Men of the Match:
Broncos: Dennis Moran; *Hull:* Jason Smith.
Penalty count: 5-13; **Half time:** 6-12; **Referee:** Richard Silverwood (Dewsbury); **Attendance:** 2,847.

WAKEFIELD TRINITY WILDCATS 23
WIGAN WARRIORS 29

WILDCATS: 1 Martyn Holland; 2 Neil Law; 4 Justin Brooker; 20 Ben Westwood; 5 Waisale Sovatabua; 12 Willie Poching (C); 26 Dane Dorahy; 16 Julian O'Neill; 9 David March; 8 Paul Jackson; 11 Jamie Field; 13 Gary Price; 15 Ryan Hudson. Subs: 19 Gareth Ellis for Field (75); 18 Ben Rauter for Hudson (67); 22 Keith Mason for O'Neill (63); 14 Paul March for Poching (26); Hudson for D March (72); O'Neill for Jackson (72).
Tries: Poching (2), P March (49), Dorahy (55);
Goals: Dorahy 5; **Field goal:** Dorahy.
WARRIORS: 1 Kris Radlinski; 2 Brett Dallas; 15 Paul Johnson; 3 Steve Renouf; 5 Brian Carney; 6 Matthew Johns; 22 Phil Jones; 10 Neil Cowie; 9 Terry Newton; 20 Harvey Howard; 11 Mick Cassidy; 14 David Furner; 13 Andy Farrell (C). Subs: 17 Francis Stephenson for Cowie (29); 12 Denis Betts for Cassidy (33); 26 Ricky Bibey for Howard (53); 23 David Hodgson not used; Cowie for Stephenson (68).
Tries: Furner (6), Dallas (19), Renouf (42), Farrell (64), Johnson (78); **Goals:** Farrell 4; **Field goal:** Farrell.
League Express Men of the Match:
Wildcats: Dane Dorahy; *Warriors:* Andy Farrell.
Penalty count: 3-6; **Half-time:** 10-12; **Referee:** Karl Kirkpatrick (Warrington); **Attendance:** 4,011.

SALFORD CITY REDS 34 HALIFAX BLUE SOX 50

CITY REDS: 1 Gary Broadbent; 2 Nick Pinkney; 3 Francis Maloney; 18 Stuart Littler; 5 Martin Offiah; 6 Steve Blakeley; 16 Bobbie Goulding (C); 20 Andy Coley; 9 Malcolm Alker; 28 Neil Harmon; 30 Jason Nicol; 4 Michael Hancock; 23 Mike Wainwright. Subs: 8 Neil Baynes for Harmon (25); 14 Kris Tassell for Nicol (21); 26 Danny Arnold for Offiah (11); 13 Paul Highton for Baynes (50); Nicol for Coley (58); Harmon for Hancock (62).

Tries: Hancock (4), Pinkney (26), Tassell (31), Arnold (34, 45, 77); **Goals:** Blakeley 2, Goulding 3.
BLUE SOX: 1 Daryl Cardiss; 19 Oliver Marns; 4 Adam Hughes; 18 Stuart Donlan; 3 Damian Gibson; 6 Andrew Dunemann; 7 Gavin Clinch; 23 Brett Goldspink (C); 9 Johnny Lawless; 10 Jim Gannon; 12 Shayne McMenemy; 2 Jamie Bloem; 13 Martin Moana. Subs: 14 Danny Tickle for Bloem (32); 8 Andy Hobson for Goldspink (32); 17 Sean Penkywicz for McMenemy (65); 21 Phil Hassan for Marns (65); Bloem for Moana (50); Goldspink for Hobson (65); Hobson for Gannon (77BB).
Tries: Cardiss (20, 79), Gibson (39, 71), Gannon (49, 66), Dunemann (57), Penkywicz (74);
Goals: Bloem 2, Tickle 7.
League Express Men of the Match:
City Reds: Danny Arnold; *Blue Sox:* Gavin Clinch.
Penalty count: 7-5; **Half-time:** 20-14;
Referee: Peter Taberner (Wigan); **Attendance:** 3,597.

ROUND 20

Friday 20th July 2001

WIGAN WARRIORS 70 SALFORD CITY REDS 4

WARRIORS: 1 Kris Radlinski; 2 Brett Dallas; 15 Paul Johnson; 3 Steve Renouf; 5 Brian Carney; 19 Chris Chester; 6 Matthew Johns; 10 Neil Cowie; 9 Terry Newton; 20 Harvey Howard; 11 Mick Cassidy; 14 David Furner; 13 Andy Farrell (C). Subs: 8 Terry O'Connor for Cowie (46); 12 Denis Betts for Furner (50); 17 Francis Stephenson for Howard (53); 23 David Hodgson for Dallas (59); Dallas for Carney (70); Furner for Hodgson (79); Carney for Betts (80BB).
Tries: Cassidy (1), Johnson (6), Newton (15, 27, 72), Farrell (18, 24), Radlinski (29, 43, 60), Carney (34), Betts (58); **Goals:** Farrell 11.
CITY REDS: 1 Gary Broadbent; 2 Nick Pinkney; 3 Francis Maloney; 18 Stuart Littler; 26 Danny Arnold; 6 Steve Blakeley; 16 Bobbie Goulding (C); 15 Damian Driscoll; 9 Malcolm Alker; 20 Andy Coley; 13 Paul Highton; 30 Jason Nicol; 23 Mike Wainwright. Subs: 4 Michael Hancock for Coley (30); 14 Kris Tassell for Nicol (28); 28 Neil Harmon for Driscoll (7BB, rev 26); 7 Graham Holroyd for Blakeley (59); Nicol for Hancock (52); Harmon for Driscoll (54BB); Coley for Highton (60); Hancock for Wainwright (73).
Try: Pinkney (80).
League Express Men of the Match:
Warriors: Kris Radlinski; *City Reds:* Nick Pinkney.
Penalty count: 5-3; **Half-time:** 46-0;
Referee: Russell Smith (Castleford); **Attendance:** 8,085.

Saturday 21st July 2001

WARRINGTON WOLVES 28 LONDON BRONCOS 31

WOLVES: 22 Alan Hunte; 2 Rob Smyth; 4 Toa Kohe-Love; 16 Ian Sibbit; 1 Lee Penny; 6 Lee Briers; 7 Allan Langer (C); 12 Jerome Guisset; 26 Jon Clarke; 10 Danny Nutley; 25 Gary Mercer; 20 Dean Busby; 13 Tawera Nikau. Subs: 21 Paul Wood for Nutley (66); 24 Paul Noone for McCurrie (78); 18 Martin Masella for Guisset (26); 11 Steve McCurrie for Mercer (37BB, rev 53); McCurrie for Busby (55); Busby for Masella (66).
Tries: Smyth (8, 54), Penny (19), Mercer (21), McCurrie (68); **Goals:** Briers 4.
BRONCOS: 30 Paul Sykes; 34 Sylvain Houles; 36 Dan Potter (D); 2 Nigel Roy; 5 Brett Warton; 6 Jim Dymock (C); 7 Dennis Moran; 10 Scott Cram; 17 Glen Air; 8 Tony Mestrov; 11 Shane Millard; 12 Steele Retchless; 29 Robert Parker. Subs: 15 Andy Johnson for Dooley (68); 18 Justin Dooley for Mestrov (25); 4 Greg Fleming for Warton (55); 13 Mat Toshack for Millard (52); Mestrov for Cram (72); Millard for Mestrov (77).
Tries: Dymock (14), Air (24, 29), Houles (52, 59);
Goals: Warton 4, Sykes; **Field goal:** Sykes.
League Express Men of the Match:
Wolves: Lee Briers; *Broncos:* Paul Sykes.
Penalty count: 6-5; **Half-time:** 18-18;
Referee: Robert Connolly (Wigan); **Attendance:** 4,249.

Sunday 22nd July 2001

BRADFORD BULLS 44 LEEDS RHINOS 22

BULLS: 3 Leon Pryce; 2 Tevita Vaikona; 20 Scott Naylor; 23 Graham Mackay; 4 Nathan McAvoy; 6 Henry Paul; 7 Paul Deacon; 8 Joe Vagana; 9 James Lowes (C); 29 Stuart Fielden; 11 Daniel Gartner; 19 Jamie Peacock; 12 Mike Forshaw. Subs: 1 Robbie Paul for Deacon (54); 10 Paul Anderson for Vagana (22); 14 Lee Gilmour for Naylor (67); 18 Lee Radford for Gartner (27BB, rev 46); Vagana for Anderson (59); Deacon for H Paul (78); Radford for Forshaw (78).
Tries: Pryce (11, 73), Vaikona (42, 75), McAvoy (56), Peacock (72), Gartner (79); **Goals:** H Paul 7, Deacon.
Sin bin: Lowes (1) – fighting.
RHINOS: 5 Francis Cummins; 15 Chev Walker; 3 Tonie Carroll; 4 Keith Senior; 16 Mark Calderwood; 1 Iestyn Harris (C); 2 Karl Pratt; 20 Jamie Mathiou; 9 Robert Mears; 10 Barrie McDermott; 11 Andy Hay; 12 Bradley Clyde; 13 Kevin Sinfield. Subs: 7 Ryan Sheridan for Pratt (40); 18 Danny Ward for McDermott (18BB, rev 30); 6 Brett Mullins for Hay (49); 22 David Wrench for Clyde (62); Ward for McDermott (49BB, rev 55); Ward for Mathiou (65).
Tries: McDermott (37), Mears (48), Senior (52);
Goals: Harris 5.
Sin bin: Mathiou (1) – fighting.
On report: Mathiou (44) – high tackle.
League Express Men of the Match:
Bulls: Leon Pryce; *Rhinos:* Robert Mears.

Penalty count: 9-9; **Half-time:** 18-10; **Referee:** Stuart Cummings (Widnes); **Attendance:** 15,106.

HULL FC 48 WAKEFIELD TRINITY WILDCATS 16

HULL: 1 Steve Prescott; 21 Gareth Raynor; 6 Richard Horne; 4 Deon Bird; 5 Matt Crowther; 16 Paul Cooke; 7 Tony Smith; 18 Steve Craven; 15 Paul King; 10 Luke Felsch; 28 Scott Logan; 12 Tony Grimaldi (C); 13 Jason Smith. Subs: 8 Paul Broadbent for Felsch (25); 23 Logan Campbell for Logan (59); 26 Paul Parker for Crowther (68); 3 David Maiden for Broadbent (47); Felsch for King (59); King for Craven (75).
Tries: Horne (7, 73), Crowther (20), Bird (39), Grimaldi (42), Prescott (50, 77), King (76); **Goals:** Prescott 8.
WILDCATS: 1 Martyn Holland; 2 Neil Law; 4 Justin Brooker; 20 Ben Westwood; 5 Waisale Sovatabua; 14 Paul March; 26 Dane Dorahy; 16 Julian O'Neill; 9 David March; 8 Paul Jackson; 11 Jamie Field; 13 Gary Price (C); 15 Ryan Hudson. Subs: 25 Tom Haughey for Price (27); 7 Brad Davis for Dorahy (54); 22 Keith Mason for O'Neill (54); 17 Graham Law for D March (70); Dorahy for P March (74); O'Neill for Jackson (74).
Tries: Westwood (27), Brooker (67), Sovatabua (79);
Goals: Dorahy, Davis.
League Express Men of the Match:
Hull: Steve Prescott; *Wildcats:* Jamie Field.
Penalty count: 8-5; **Half-time:** 20-6; **Referee:** Karl Kirkpatrick (Warrington); **Attendance:** 6,240.

CASTLEFORD TIGERS 20 HUDDERSFIELD GIANTS 14

TIGERS: 14 Jason Flowers; 2 Jon Wells; 18 Jonathan Roper; 3 Michael Eagar; 20 Waine Pryce; 6 Danny Orr; 7 Mitch Healey; 10 Dean Sampson (C); 15 Darren Shaw; 23 Michael Smith; 11 Lee Harland; 12 Dale Fritz; 13 Adrian Vowles. Subs: 1 Richard Gay for Orr (54); 22 Mark Lennon for Flowers (52); 17 Andy Lynch for Smith (27BB, rev 44); 25 David Bates not used; Lynch for Harland (56); Orr for Shaw (68); Flowers for Wells (70).
Tries: Orr (16), Healey (45), Roper (59), M Smith (67);
Goals: Orr, Roper.
GIANTS: 1 Paul Reilly; 2 Andrew Frew; 33 Stanley Gene; 3 Martin Gleeson; 20 Chris Langley; 27 Brandon Costin; 7 Ben Kusto; 32 Troy Stone; 9 Paul Rowley; 12 Richard Marshall; 13 David Atkins; 11 David Lomax; 26 Steve McNamara (C). Subs: 6 Chris Thorman for Atkins (68); 4 Dale Cardoza for McNamara (57BB, rev 79); 8 Steve Molloy for Marshall (26); 31 Matt Walker for Stone (35); Stone for Lomax (50); Marshall for Molloy (65); Lomax for Walker (73).
Tries: Frew (9), Kusto (14), Costin (49); **Goal:** Costin.
League Express Men of the Match:
Tigers: Mitch Healey; *Giants:* Brandon Costin.
Penalty count: 11-10; **Half-time:** 6-10; **Referee:** Richard Silverwood (Dewsbury); **Attendance:** 5,698.

HALIFAX BLUE SOX 22 ST HELENS 46

BLUE SOX: 1 Daryl Cardiss; 2 Jamie Bloem; 21 Phil Hassan; 18 Stuart Donlan; 3 Damian Gibson; 6 Andrew Dunemann; 7 Gavin Clinch; 23 Brett Goldspink (C); 9 Johnny Lawless; 8 Andy Hobson; 12 Shayne McMenemy; 10 Jim Gannon; 14 Danny Tickle. Subs: 4 Adam Hughes for Hobson (21); 13 Martin Moana for Tickle (54); 17 Sean Penkywicz for Bloem (66); 19 Oliver Marns not used; Hobson for Goldspink (51); Goldspink for Hobson (72); Bloem for McMenemy (80).
Tries: Cardiss (28), Clinch (58), McMenemy (68), Gibson (76); **Goals:** Tickle, Bloem, Clinch.
Sin bin: McMenemy (22) - foul on Hall.
SAINTS: 1 Paul Wellens; 17 Steve Hall; 2 Sean Hoppe; 3 Kevin Iro; 5 Anthony Sullivan; 13 Paul Sculthorpe; 20 Tommy Martyn; 14 Wayne McDonald; 9 Keiron Cunningham; 10 David Fairleigh; 11 Chris Joynt (C); 15 Tim Jonkers; 18 John Stankevitch. Subs: 12 Sonny Nickle for McDonald (22); 8 Peter Shiels for Hall (33BB, rev 40); 16 Vila Matautia for Nickle (56); 24 Mick Higham for Iro (66); Shiels for Joynt (53); McDonald for Fairleigh (70); Joynt for Cunningham (76).
Tries: Sullivan (5, 79), Cunningham (11, 52), Martyn (17), Fairleigh (24), Sculthorpe (35), Matautia (61);
Goals: Sculthorpe 7.
League Express Men of the Match:
Blue Sox: Gavin Clinch; *Saints:* Keiron Cunningham.
Penalty count: 6-6; **Half-time:** 6-30;
Referee: Peter Taberner (Wigan); **Attendance:** 5,142.

ROUND 21

Friday 27th July 2001

WIGAN WARRIORS 36 HULL FC 12

WARRIORS: 1 Kris Radlinski; 2 Brett Dallas; 15 Paul Johnson; 3 Steve Renouf; 5 Brian Carney; 19 Chris Chester; 6 Matthew Johns; 10 Neil Cowie; 9 Terry Newton; 20 Harvey Howard; 11 Mick Cassidy; 14 David Furner; 13 Andy Farrell (C). Subs: 17 Francis Stephenson for Howard (53); 12 Denis Betts for Furner (26BB, rev 35); 8 Terry O'Connor for Cowie (25); 24 Martin Aspinwall for Chester (63); Betts for Cassidy (51); Cowie for Carney (71); Cassidy for Newton (74).
Tries: Renouf (4), Radlinski (29), Carney (35, 47), Johnson (59), Farrell (69); **Goals:** Farrell 6.
HULL: 1 Steve Prescott; 21 Gareth Raynor; 6 Richard Horne; 4 Deon Bird; 5 Matt Crowther; 16 Paul Cooke; 7 Tony Smith; 18 Steve Craven; 15 Paul King; 28 Scott Logan; 3 David Maiden; 12 Tony Grimaldi (C); 13 Jason Smith. Subs: 20 Garreth Carvell for T Smith (41); 23 Logan Campbell for King (30); 26 Paul Parker for J Smith (63); 27 Michael Docherty for Logan (67); King for Craven (55BB, rev 71); King for Grimaldi (72).

Tries: Raynor (12), Prescott (32); **Goals:** Prescott 2.
League Express Men of the Match:
Warriors: Steve Renouf; *Hull:* Scott Logan.
Penalty count: 9-7; **Half-time:** 20-12;
Referee: Ian Smith (Oldham); **Attendance:** 9,174.

Saturday 28th July 2001

LONDON BRONCOS 40 CASTLEFORD TIGERS 10

BRONCOS: 23 Richie Barnett; 30 Paul Sykes; 4 Greg Fleming; 2 Nigel Roy; 34 Sylvain Houles; 6 Jim Dymock (C); 7 Dennis Moran; 8 Tony Mestrov; 17 Glen Air; 10 Scott Cram; 11 Shane Millard; 12 Steele Retchless; 29 Robert Parker. Subs: 13 Mat Toshack for Cram (30); 15 Andy Johnson for Barnett (64); 18 Justin Dooley for Mestrov (24); 27 Michael Gillett for Dymock (75); Cram for Millard (61); Mestrov for Cram (76).
Tries: Fleming (1), Air (34, 66), Houles (71, 75), Gillett (79); **Goals:** Sykes 8.
TIGERS: 14 Jason Flowers; 2 Jon Wells; 18 Jonathan Roper; 3 Michael Eagar; 20 Waine Pryce; 7 Mitch Healey; 22 Mark Lennon; 8 Nathan Sykes; 12 Dale Fritz; 10 Dean Sampson; 11 Lee Harland; 23 Michael Smith; 13 Adrian Vowles (C). Subs: 6 Danny Orr for Flowers (41); 17 Andy Lynch for Sampson (50BB, rev 58); 24 Jonathan Goddard not used; 26 Wayne Godwin for Harland (22); Harland for Smith (52); Flowers for Godwin (67); Smith for Sykes (75).
Tries: Wells (42), Lennon (56); **Goal:** Roper.
League Express Men of the Match:
Broncos: Paul Sykes; *Tigers:* Danny Orr.
Penalty count: 7-4; **Half time:** 14-0;
Referee: Stuart Cummings (Widnes); **Attendance:** 2,342.

Sunday 29th July 2001

HUDDERSFIELD GIANTS 26 LEEDS RHINOS 32

GIANTS: 1 Paul Reilly; 2 Andrew Frew; 33 Stanley Gene; 3 Martin Gleeson; 20 Chris Langley; 27 Brandon Costin; 6 Chris Thorman; 32 Troy Stone; 9 Paul Rowley; 12 Richard Marshall; 13 David Atkins; 11 David Lomax; 26 Steve McNamara (C). Subs: 7 Ben Kusto for Rowley (38BB); 28 Michael Slicker for Stone (28); 8 Steve Molloy for Lomax (24); 31 Matt Walker for Marshall (54); Stone for Slicker (30BB, rev 39); Rowley for Thorman (52); Stone for Slicker (62); Lomax for Atkins (67BB, rev 78); Slicker for Molloy (76).
Tries: Kusto (40), Thorman (46), Langley (67), Costin (73); **Goals:** McNamara 5.
Sin bin: Thorman (33) - holding down.
RHINOS: 5 Francis Cummins (C); 6 Brett Mullins; 3 Tonie Carroll; 4 Keith Senior; 16 Mark Calderwood; 2 Karl Pratt; 7 Ryan Sheridan; 18 Danny Ward; 9 Robert Mears; 10 Barrie McDermott; 22 David Wrench; 20 Jamie Mathiou; 13 Kevin Sinfield. Subs: 23 Matthew Diskin for Mears (66); 15 Chev Walker for Wrench (56); 11 Andy Hay for McDermott (24); 1 Iestyn Harris for Sheridan (53); McDermott for Ward (51); Wrench for Mullins (70).
Tries: Carroll (20, 41, 65), Sinfield (23), Hay (36), Mullins (60); **Goals:** Sinfield 3, Harris.
League Express Men of the Match:
Giants: Troy Stone; *Rhinos:* Tonie Carroll.
Penalty count: 5-8; **Half-time:** 10-18;
Referee: Robert Connolly (Wigan); **Attendance:** 4,645.

WAKEFIELD TRINITY WILDCATS 18 WARRINGTON WOLVES 19

WILDCATS: 1 Martyn Holland; 20 Ben Westwood; 4 Justin Brooker; 17 Graham Law; 5 Waisale Sovatabua; 14 Paul March; 26 Dane Dorahy; 16 Julian O'Neill; 9 David March; 10 Frank Watene; 11 Jamie Field; 12 Willie Poching (C); 15 Ryan Hudson. Subs: 19 Gareth Ellis for Field (66); 7 Brad Davis for P March (40); 22 Keith Mason for Watene (53); 24 Chris Feather for O'Neill (66); P March for Westwood (71).
Tries: Hudson (39), G Law (48), Ellis (79);
Goals: Dorahy 3.
Sin bin: Westwood (54) - fighting.
On report: Brawl (54).
WOLVES: 22 Alan Hunte; 5 Jamie Stenhouse; 4 Toa Kohe-Love; 16 Ian Sibbit; 1 Lee Penny; 6 Lee Briers; 7 Allan Langer (C); 12 Jerome Guisset; 26 Jon Clarke; 18 Martin Masella; 25 Gary Mercer; 20 Dean Busby; 13 Tawera Nikau. Subs: 21 Paul Wood for Masella (26); 24 Paul Noone for Nikau (68); 17 David Alstead for Hunte (68); 11 Steve McCurrie for Busby (40); Masella for Wood (58); Nikau for Clarke (72BB); Hunte for Stenhouse (74).
Tries: Langer (17), Kohe-Love (32), Clarke (65);
Goals: Briers 3; **Field goal:** Briers.
Sin bin: Kohe-Love (54) - fighting; Hunte (54) - fighting.
On report: Brawl (54); Nikau – high tackle (60).
League Express Men of the Match:
Wildcats: Willie Poching; *Wolves:* Jon Clarke.
Penalty count: 10-5; **Half-time:** 6-12; **Referee:** Richard Silverwood (Dewsbury); **Attendance:** 2,717.

HALIFAX BLUE SOX 28 BRADFORD BULLS 52

BLUE SOX: 1 Daryl Cardiss; 19 Oliver Marns; 21 Phil Hassan; 18 Stuart Donlan; 3 Damian Gibson; 7 Gavin Clinch; 27 Matt Firth; 23 Brett Goldspink (C); 9 Johnny Lawless; 10 Jim Gannon; 12 Shayne McMenemy; 2 Jamie Bloem; 6 Andrew Dunemann. Subs: 8 Andy Hobson for Goldspink (25); 13 Martin Moana for Clinch (3BB, rev 8); 17 Sean Penkywicz not used; 14 Danny Tickle for Bloem (46); Moana for Lawless (55); Goldspink for Hobson (55); Bloem for Cardiss (65).
Tries: Gannon (23), Gibson (27), Dunemann (40), Marns (64); **Goals:** Bloem 5, Tickle.

BULLS: 5 Michael Withers; 2 Tevita Vaikona; 20 Scott Naylor; 23 Graham Mackay; 3 Leon Pryce; 6 Henry Paul; 1 Robbie Paul (C); 8 Joe Vagana; 9 James Lowes; 22 Brian McDermott; 11 Daniel Gartner; 19 Jamie Peacock; 12 Mike Forshaw. Subs: 7 Paul Deacon for H Paul (52); 10 Paul Anderson for Vagana (20); 14 Lee Gilmour for Peacock (65); 15 Shane Rigon for Gartner (50); Vagana for Anderson (54); H Paul for R Paul (60); Anderson for McDermott (72BB).
Tries: R Paul (3), Gartner (14), Pryce (32), Vaikona (36, 49, 80), Anderson (46), Mackay (66, 79); **Goals:** H Paul 8.
Sin bin: Pryce (75) - holding down.
League Express Men of the Match:
Blue Sox: Jim Gannon; *Bulls:* Tevita Vaikona.
Penalty count: 9-9; **Half-time:** 22-24;
Referee: Russell Smith (Castleford); **Attendance:** 5,982.

SALFORD CITY REDS 18 ST HELENS 56

CITY REDS: 1 Gary Broadbent; 2 Nick Pinkney; 14 Kris Tassell; 18 Stuart Littler; 26 Danny Arnold; 7 Graham Holroyd; 16 Bobbie Goulding (C); 15 Damian Driscoll; 9 Malcolm Alker; 13 Paul Highton; 4 Michael Hancock; 20 Andy Coley; 23 Mike Wainwright. Subs: 3 Francis Maloney not used; 6 Steve Blakeley for Holroyd (63); 30 Jason Nicol for Hancock (21); 28 Neil Harmon for Highton (20); Hancock for Coley (41); Coley for Harmon (72).
Tries: Broadbent (8), Arnold (51), Wainwright (63);
Goals: Holroyd 3.
On report: Broadbent (79) - high tackle.
SAINTS: 1 Paul Wellens; 17 Steve Hall; 3 Kevin Iro; 2 Sean Hoppe; 5 Anthony Sullivan; 13 Paul Sculthorpe; 20 Tommy Martyn; 12 Sonny Nickle; 9 Keiron Cunningham; 10 David Fairleigh; 18 John Stankevitch; 8 Peter Shiels; 11 Chris Joynt (C). Subs: 16 Vila Matautia for Nickle (41); 14 Wayne McDonald for Fairleigh (25); 24 Mick Higham for Cunningham (53); 15 Tim Jonkers for Sullivan (41); Nickle for Sculthorpe (73).
Tries: Cunningham (2), Hoppe (12, 31), Wellens (15, 22, 71), Martyn (20), Sculthorpe (40), Shiels (43), McDonald (62); **Goals:** Sculthorpe 8.
League Express Men of the Match:
City Reds: Malcolm Alker; *Saints:* Paul Sculthorpe.
Penalty count: 4-8; **Half-time:** 6-38; **Referee:** Karl Kirkpatrick (Warrington); **Attendance:** 5,234.

ROUND 22

Friday 3rd August 2001

CASTLEFORD TIGERS 28 ST HELENS 26

TIGERS: 14 Jason Flowers; 2 Jon Wells; 18 Jonathan Roper; 3 Michael Eagar; 20 Waine Pryce; 7 Mitch Healey; 22 Mark Lennon; 23 Michael Smith; 15 Darren Shaw; 10 Dean Sampson; 11 Lee Harland; 12 Dale Fritz; 13 Adrian Vowles (C). Subs: 5 Darren Rogers not used; 1 Richard Gay for Lennon (30); 8 Nathan Sykes for Harland (26); 17 Andy Lynch for Sampson (50); Harland for Healey (54); Sampson for Sykes (59); Sykes for Lynch (75).
Tries: Pryce (18), Fritz (26), Healey (30), Vowles (32), Harland (60); **Goals:** Roper 4.
SAINTS: 19 Anthony Stewart; 17 Steve Hall; 3 Kevin Iro; 18 John Stankevitch; 2 Sean Hoppe; 20 Tommy Martyn; 1 Paul Wellens; 12 Sonny Nickle; 9 Keiron Cunningham; 10 David Fairleigh; 11 Chris Joynt (C); 8 Peter Shiels; 13 Paul Sculthorpe. Subs: 16 Vila Matautia for Nickle (29); 14 Wayne McDonald for Fairleigh (49); 23 Mike Bennett for Stewart (77); 15 Tim Jonkers for Matautia (51); Fairleigh for Shiels (60); Matautia for McDonald (75); Shiels for Joynt (78).
Tries: Hoppe (7, 67), Shiels (11), Cunningham (58), Iro (70); **Goals:** Sculthorpe 3.
League Express Men of the Match:
Tigers: Adrian Vowles; *Saints:* Keiron Cunningham.
Penalty count: 6-2; **Half time:** 22-10; **Referee:** Karl Kirkpatrick (Warrington); **Attendance:** 7,054.

LEEDS RHINOS 36 HALIFAX BLUE SOX 18

RHINOS: 5 Francis Cummins (C); 6 Brett Mullins; 3 Tonie Carroll; 4 Keith Senior; 16 Mark Calderwood; 2 Karl Pratt; 7 Ryan Sheridan; 20 Jamie Mathiou; 9 Robert Mears; 10 Barrie McDermott; 11 Andy Hay; 17 Anthony Farrell; 13 Kevin Sinfield. Subs: 8 Darren Fleary for Mathiou (25); 18 Danny Ward for McDermott (31); 22 David Wrench for Farrell (58); 28 Andy Kirk for Mullins (68); Mathiou for Ward (55); McDermott for Fleary (62).
Tries: Calderwood (12), Pratt (29, 39), Sheridan (32), Hay (42), Carroll (44); **Goals:** Sinfield 6.
Sin bin: Mathiou (60) - altercation.
BLUE SOX: 2 Jamie Bloem; 19 Oliver Marns; 21 Phil Hassan; 18 Stuart Donlan; 3 Damian Gibson; 7 Gavin Clinch; 6 Andrew Dunemann (C); 23 Brett Goldspink; 27 Matt Firth; 10 Jim Gannon; 9 Johnny Lawless; 15 Paul Davidson; 12 Shayne McMenemy. Subs: 1 Daryl Cardiss for Davidson (23); 17 Sean Penkywicz for Dunemann (29); 8 Andy Hobson for Goldspink (56BB, rev 71); 16 Jamie Thackray for Penkywicz (65); Davidson for Bloem (40); Bloem for Cardiss (58).
Tries: Donlan (6, 16), Lawless (74); **Goals:** Bloem 3.
Sent off: Davidson (65) - foul play.
Sin bin: Gannon (60) - altercation.
On report: McMenemy (67) - high tackle.
League Express Men of the Match:
Rhinos: Andy Hay; *Blue Sox:* Shayne McMenemy.
Penalty count: 9-11; **Half-time:** 26-12;
Referee: Steve Ganson (St Helens); **Attendance:** 10,201.

WIGAN WARRIORS 46 LONDON BRONCOS 18

WARRIORS: 1 Kris Radlinski; 2 Brett Dallas; 15 Paul Johnson; 3 Steve Renouf; 5 Brian Carney; 6 Matthew Johns; 7 Adrian Lam; 8 Terry O'Connor; 9 Terry Newton; 20 Harvey Howard; 11 Mick Cassidy; 14 David Furner; 13 Andy Farrell (C). Subs: 10 Neil Cowie for Howard (27BB, rev 58); 12 Denis Betts for Cassidy (30); 19 Chris Chester for Cassidy (66); 24 Martin Aspinwall for Johnson (72); Cassidy for O'Connor (37); Cassidy for Newton (68); Cowie for Lam (74).
Tries: Farrell (1), Johnson (19), Radlinski (21, 60), Furner (29), Chester (67), Renouf (77), Cassidy (80);
Goals: Farrell 7.
BRONCOS: 23 Richie Barnett; 30 Paul Sykes; 4 Greg Fleming; 2 Nigel Roy; 3 Tony Martin; 6 Jim Dymock (C); 7 Dennis Moran; 8 Tony Mestrov; 17 Glen Air; 12 Steele Retchless; 11 Shane Millard; 13 Mat Toshack; 29 Robert Parker. Subs: 34 Sylvain Houles for Johnson (75); 15 Andy Johnson for Retchless (36); 18 Justin Dooley for Mestrov (25); 27 Michael Gillett for Millard (66); Mestrov for Dooley (74); Retchless for Toshack (74).
Tries: Air (5), Dooley (47), Toshack (54); **Goals:** Sykes 3.
League Express Men of the Match:
Warriors: Kris Radlinski; *Broncos:* Robert Parker.
Penalty count: 4-4; **Half-time:** 24-8;
Referee: Ian Smith (Oldham); **Attendance:** 8,244.

Saturday 4th August 2001

WARRINGTON WOLVES 18 BRADFORD BULLS 14

WOLVES: 1 Lee Penny; 2 Rob Smyth; 4 Toa Kohe-Love; 16 Ian Sibbit; 22 Alan Hunte; 13 Tawera Nikau (C); 26 Jon Clarke; 12 Jerome Guisset; 23 Mark Gleeson; 18 Martin Masella; 25 Gary Mercer; 11 Steve McCurrie; 24 Paul Noone. Subs: 27 Gary Hulse not used; 21 Paul Wood for Masella (35); 17 David Alstead for Penny (39BB, rev 43); 28 Gary Chambers not used; Alstead for Penny (50); Masella for McCurrie (62); McCurrie for Noone (69).
Tries: Gleeson (14), McCurrie (54), Smyth (79);
Goals: Smyth 3.
BULLS: 5 Michael Withers; 2 Tevita Vaikona; 20 Scott Naylor; 23 Graham Mackay; 4 Nathan McAvoy; 6 Henry Paul; 1 Robbie Paul (C); 8 Joe Vagana; 9 James Lowes; 22 Brian McDermott; 11 Daniel Gartner; 15 Shane Rigon; 12 Mike Forshaw. Subs: 14 Lee Gilmour for McAvoy (50); 3 Leon Pryce for H Paul (57); 18 Lee Radford for McDermott (55); 10 Paul Anderson for Vagana (25); Vagana for Anderson (58); H Paul for Gartner (72).
Tries: R Paul (24), Radford (71); **Goals:** H Paul 3.
League Express Men of the Match:
Wolves: Mark Gleeson; *Bulls:* Robbie Paul.
Penalty count: 6-3; **Half-time:** 8-10;
Referee: Stuart Cummings (Widnes); **Attendance:** 4,929.

Sunday 5th August 2001

HULL FC 36 HUDDERSFIELD GIANTS 16

HULL: 1 Steve Prescott; 21 Gareth Raynor; 23 Logan Campbell; 4 Deon Bird; 5 Matt Crowther; 16 Paul Cooke; 6 Richard Horne; 18 Steve Craven; 15 Paul King; 28 Scott Logan; 3 David Maiden; 12 Tony Grimaldi (C); 13 Jason Smith. Subs: 20 Garreth Carvell for Cooke (37BB, rev 46); 10 Luke Felsch for Craven (29); 17 Craig Poucher not used; 19 Richard Fletcher for Maiden (50); Craven for Logan (56); Maiden for King (63).
Tries: Grimaldi (4), Horne (17), Felsch (38), Campbell (43), Bird (51), Fletcher (74), Cooke (78);
Goals: Crowther 4.
GIANTS: 1 Paul Reilly; 2 Andrew Frew; 33 Stanley Gene; 3 Martin Gleeson; 20 Chris Langley; 27 Brandon Costin; 7 Ben Kusto; 32 Troy Stone; 9 Paul Rowley; 12 Richard Marshall; 13 David Atkins; 11 David Lomax; 26 Steve McNamara (C). Subs: 31 Matt Walker for Molloy (58); 28 Michael Slicker for Lomax (34BB); 35 Martin Moana (D) for McNamara (27BB, rev 46); 8 Steve Molloy for Stone (29); Stone for Marshall (47); Moana for McNamara (53); Lomax for Stone (73); Marshall for Atkins (78).
Tries: Gene (11, 68), Kusto (55);
Goals: McNamara, Costin.
Sin bin: Frew (37) – holding down.
League Express Men of the Match:
Hull: Richard Horne; *Giants:* Ben Kusto.
Penalty count: 10-6; **Half-time:** 16-6;
Referee: Russell Smith (Castleford); **Attendance:** 5,621.

SALFORD CITY REDS 26
WAKEFIELD TRINITY WILDCATS 16

CITY REDS: 14 Kris Tassell; 2 Nick Pinkney; 3 Francis Maloney; 18 Stuart Littler; 5 Martin Offiah; 7 Graham Holroyd; 16 Bobbie Goulding (C); 15 Damian Driscoll; 9 Malcolm Alker; 28 Neil Harmon; 20 Andy Coley; 30 Jason Nicol; 23 Mike Wainwright. Subs: 4 Michael Hancock for Nicol (20); 6 Steve Blakeley for Holroyd (76); 8 Neil Baynes for Harmon (10); 19 Warren Stevens for Driscoll (32BB, rev 52); Nicol for Hancock (41); Harmon for Baynes (61); Hancock for Coley (66).
Tries: Nicol (4), Offiah (9), Hancock (38), Littler (74);
Goals: Holroyd 3, Blakeley; **Field goals:** Goulding, Alker.
WILDCATS: 1 Martyn Holland; 5 Waisale Sovatabua; 4 Justin Brooker; 17 Graham Law; 20 Ben Westwood; 14 Paul March; 26 Dane Dorahy; 16 Julian O'Neill; 9 David March; 10 Frank Watene; 11 Jamie Field; 12 Willie Poching (C); 15 Ryan Hudson. Subs: 8 Paul Jackson for Watene (21); 13 Gary Price for Poching (48); 19 Gareth Ellis not used; 7 Brad Davis for Dorahy (41); Watene for O'Neill (51).
Try: D March (27), Hudson (51), Field (60);
Goals: Dorahy, G Law.
League Express Men of the Match:
City Reds: Michael Hancock; *Wildcats:* Ryan Hudson.
Penalty count: 2-3; **Half-time:** 16-6;
Referee: Robert Connolly (Wigan); **Attendance:** 3,509.

ROUND 23

Friday 10th August 2001

ST HELENS 30 WIGAN WARRIORS 16

SAINTS: 19 Anthony Stewart; 2 Sean Hoppe; 18 John Stankevitch; 3 Kevin Iro; 17 Steve Hall; 13 Paul Sculthorpe; 1 Paul Wellens; 12 Sonny Nickle; 9 Keiron Cunningham; 16 Vila Matautia; 10 David Fairleigh; 8 Peter Shiels; 11 Chris Joynt (C). Subs: 14 Wayne McDonald for Cruckshank (58); 15 Tim Jonkers for Matautia (16); 22 Heath Cruckshank for Nickle (33); 29 Dave McConnell not used; Nickle for Joynt (54); Matautia for Nickle (77).
Tries: Shiels (18), Wellens (23, 27), Sculthorpe (38), Jonkers (75); **Goals:** Sculthorpe 5.
Sin bin: Iro (65) - fighting.
WARRIORS: 1 Kris Radlinski; 2 Brett Dallas; 15 Paul Johnson; 3 Steve Renouf; 5 Brian Carney; 6 Matthew Johns; 7 Adrian Lam; 8 Terry O'Connor; 9 Terry Newton; 10 Neil Cowie; 14 David Furner; 11 Mick Cassidy; 13 Andy Farrell (C). Subs: 16 Simon Haughton for Cassidy (54); 17 Francis Stephenson for Cowie (30); 12 Denis Betts for Johns (42); 23 David Hodgson for Carney (77); Cowie for Stephenson (59); Cassidy for O'Connor (70).
Tries: Newton (9), Johnson (52); **Goals:** Farrell 4.
Sin bin: Renouf (65) - fighting.
League Express Men of the Match:
Saints: Paul Sculthorpe; *Warriors:* Terry Newton.
Penalty count: 6-10; **Half-time:** 22-8; **Referee:** Stuart Cummings (Widnes); **Attendance:** 13,571.

Saturday 11th August 2001

LEEDS RHINOS 6 BRADFORD BULLS 34

RHINOS: 5 Francis Cummins (C); 15 Chev Walker; 3 Tonie Carroll; 4 Keith Senior; 16 Mark Calderwood; 2 Karl Pratt; 7 Ryan Sheridan; 20 Jamie Mathiou; 9 Robert Mears; 10 Barrie McDermott; 11 Andy Hay; 8 Darren Fleary; 13 Kevin Sinfield. Subs: 18 Danny Ward for McDermott (23BB, rev 35); 22 David Wrench for Mathiou (28); 28 Andy Kirk for Senior (35BB, rev 40); 23 Matthew Diskin for Hay (37); Mathiou for Fleary (57); Ward for McDermott (67); Kirk for Diskin (71).
Try: Pratt (53); **Goal:** Sinfield.
BULLS: 5 Michael Withers; 2 Tevita Vaikona; 20 Scott Naylor; 23 Graham Mackay; 3 Leon Pryce; 6 Henry Paul; 7 Paul Deacon; 22 Brian McDermott; 9 James Lowes (C); 8 Joe Vagana; 19 Jamie Peacock; 11 Daniel Gartner; 12 Mike Forshaw. Subs: 10 Paul Anderson for Vagana (23BB, rev 46); 4 Nathan McAvoy for Naylor (43); 1 Robbie Paul for Deacon (48); 15 Shane Rigon for Gartner (54); Deacon for Lowes (56BB, rev 72); Gartner for Pryce (64); Anderson for McDermott (68); McDermott for Vagana (76).
Tries: H Paul (4), Naylor (14), Vaikona (17), R Paul (64), Withers (67); **Goals:** H Paul 7.
League Express Men of the Match:
Rhinos: Karl Pratt; *Bulls:* Daniel Gartner.
Penalty count: 12-6; **Half-time:** 0-20; **Referee:** Russell Smith (Castleford); **Attendance:** 13,712.

Sunday 12th August 2001

HUDDERSFIELD GIANTS 35 SALFORD CITY REDS 14

GIANTS: 1 Paul Reilly; 2 Andrew Frew; 3 Martin Gleeson; 27 Brandon Costin (C); 20 Chris Langley; 6 Chris Thorman; 7 Ben Kusto; 32 Troy Stone; 9 Paul Rowley; 12 Richard Marshall; 33 Stanley Gene; 35 Martin Moana; 13 David Atkins. Subs: 11 David Lomax for Frew (50); 28 Michael Slicker for Stone (36BB, rev 56); 26 Steve McNamara for Reilly (49BB, rev 63); 8 Steve Molloy for Marshall (30); Marshall for Molloy (65); Slicker for Marshall (75); Molloy for Atkins (78).
Tries: Gene (8), Moana (35, 40), Costin (41), Gleeson (44); **Goals:** Costin 7; **Field goal:** Costin.
CITY REDS: 26 Danny Arnold; 2 Nick Pinkney; 3 Francis Maloney; 18 Stuart Littler; 5 Martin Offiah; 7 Graham Holroyd (C); 6 Steve Blakeley; 15 Damian Driscoll; 9 Malcolm Alker; 28 Neil Harmon; 14 Kris Tassell; 30 Jason Nicol; 23 Mike Wainwright. Subs: 4 Michael Hancock for Tassell (30); 8 Neil Baynes for Harmon (23); 19 Warren Stevens for Baynes (68); 12 Darren Brown for Driscoll (40); Tassell for Offiah (40); Harmon for Nicol (73).
Tries: Littler (6), Maloney (58, 62); **Goal:** Holroyd.
League Express Men of the Match:
Giants: Brandon Costin; *City Reds:* Graham Holroyd.
Penalty count: 8-7; **Half-time:** 20-4;
Referee: Ian Smith (Oldham); **Attendance:** 2,815.

LONDON BRONCOS 44
WAKEFIELD TRINITY WILDCATS 18

BRONCOS: 23 Richie Barnett; 30 Paul Sykes; 4 Greg Fleming; 2 Nigel Roy; 3 Tony Martin; 6 Jim Dymock; 7 Dennis Moran; 18 Justin Dooley; 9 Jason Hetherington (C); 10 Scott Cram; 11 Shane Millard; 12 Steele Retchless; 29 Robert Parker. Subs: 8 Tony Mestrov for Dooley (51); 15 Andy Johnson for Millard (62); 17 Glen Air for Hetherington (25); 27 Michael Gillett for Dymock (59); Hetherington for Moran (71); Dooley for Cram (76).
Tries: Millard (20, 53), Fleming (32), Martin (36), Air (56), Moran (59, 70); **Goals:** Sykes 8.
WILDCATS: 1 Martyn Holland; 5 Waisale Sovatabua; 6 Martin Pearson; 19 Gareth Ellis; 2 Neil Law; 17 Graham Law; 7 Brad Davis; 16 Julian O'Neill; 23 Paul Handforth;

8 Paul Jackson; 11 Jamie Field; 12 Willie Poching (C); 13 Gary Price. Subs: 22 Keith Mason for Jackson (28); 24 Chris Feather for O'Neill (28); 26 Dane Dorahy for Price (54); 28 Nathan Batty for Holland (73); Jackson for Mason (57); O'Neill for G Law (68).
Tries: N Law (44), Sovatabua (63), Ellis (80);
Goals: Pearson 3.
Sin bin: Ellis (16) - professional foul.
League Express Men of the Match:
Broncos: Shane Millard; *Wildcats:* Neil Law.
Penalty count: 10-9; **Half-time:** 18-4;
Referee: Steve Ganson (St Helens); **Attendance:** 2,126.

WARRINGTON WOLVES 27 CASTLEFORD TIGERS 12

WOLVES: 17 David Alstead; 2 Rob Smyth; 4 Toa Kohe-Love; 16 Ian Sibbit; 22 Alan Hunte; 6 Lee Briers; 27 Gary Hulse (D); 18 Martin Masella; 26 Jon Clarke; 10 Danny Nutley; 11 Steve McCurrie; 12 Jerome Guisset; 13 Tawera Nikau (C). Subs: 21 Paul Wood for Nutley (7); 29 Paul Smith (D) for McCurrie (64); 19 Ian Knott for Smyth (20); 24 Paul Noone for Masella (24); Nutley for Wood (17); Masella for Noone (56).
Tries: Hulse (9), Kohe-Love (16, 55, 62);
Goals: Briers 5; **Field goal:** Briers.
TIGERS: 14 Jason Flowers; 20 Waine Pryce; 2 Jon Wells; 3 Michael Eagar; 5 Darren Rogers; 18 Jonathan Roper; 27 Jamie Rooney (D); 8 Nathan Sykes; 15 Darren Shaw; 10 Dean Sampson; 23 Michael Smith; 12 Dale Fritz; 13 Adrian Vowles (C). Subs: 11 Lee Harland for Smith (40); 22 Mark Lennon for Pryce (55); 25 David Bates (D) for Sampson (51); 1 Richard Gay for Flowers (73); Smith for Shaw (60); Shaw for Sykes (70).
Try: Rogers (41); **Goals:** Rooney 4.
League Express Men of the Match:
Wolves: Jerome Guisset; *Tigers:* Jamie Rooney.
Penalty count: 3-8; **Half-time:** 14-6;
Referee: Robert Connolly (Wigan); **Attendance:** 5,235.

HULL FC 32 HALIFAX BLUE SOX 16

HULL: 1 Steve Prescott; 21 Gareth Raynor; 23 Logan Campbell; 4 Deon Bird; 24 Craig Farrell; 16 Paul Cooke; 6 Richard Horne; 28 Scott Logan; 15 Paul King; 10 Luke Felsch; 3 David Maiden; 12 Tony Grimaldi (C); 13 Jason Smith. Subs: 20 Garreth Carvell for Grimaldi (72); 7 Tony Smith for King (49BB, rev 55); 18 Steve Craven for Logan (23); 19 Richard Fletcher for J Smith (14BB, rev 19); T Smith for Farrell (57); Fletcher for Felsch (57); Logan for Craven (61); Grimaldi for J Smith (75).
Tries: Maiden (15), Bird (21, 72), Horne (39), Logan (66); **Goals:** Prescott 6.
On report: J Smith (55) – high tackle.
BLUE SOX: 3 Damian Gibson; 32 Dale Cardoza (D); 21 Phil Hassan; 18 Stuart Donlan; 28 Jason Lee; 27 Matt Firth; 7 Gavin Clinch (C); 8 Andy Hobson; 9 Johnny Lawless; 10 Jim Gannon; 15 Paul Davidson; 12 Shayne McMenemy; 2 Jamie Bloem. Subs: 14 Danny Tickle for Bloem (23BB, rev 73); 17 Sean Penkywicz for Hassan (50); 4 Adam Hughes for Hobson (34); 19 Oliver Marns not used; Hobson for Lawless (60); Lawless for Firth (68); Firth for Penkywicz (75).
Tries: Gibson (33), Donlan (43), Gannon (53);
Goals: Tickle 2.
Sent off: Davidson (28) – use of forearm.
Sin bin: Gannon (24) – holding down.
League Express Men of the Match:
Hull: Paul King; *Blue Sox:* Gavin Clinch.
Penalty count: 11-9; **Half-time:** 20-6; **Referee:** Richard Silverwood (Dewsbury); **Attendance:** 5,620.

ROUND 24

Friday 17th August 2001

BRADFORD BULLS 27 ST HELENS 14

BULLS: 5 Michael Withers; 2 Tevita Vaikona; 20 Scott Naylor; 23 Graham Mackay; 3 Leon Pryce; 6 Henry Paul; 7 Paul Deacon; 22 Brian McDermott; 9 James Lowes (C); 8 Joe Vagana; 19 Jamie Peacock; 11 Daniel Gartner; 12 Mike Forshaw. Subs: 10 Paul Anderson for McDermott (31); 29 Stuart Fielden for Vagana (28); 1 Robbie Paul for Lowes (33); 15 Shane Rigon for Gartner (36); Gartner for Naylor (69); McDermott for Anderson (74).
Tries: Withers (65), Mackay (73); **Goals:** H Paul 8;
Field goals: Deacon 3.
Sin bin: Pryce (39) - dissent.
SAINTS: 1 Paul Wellens; 19 Anthony Stewart; 2 Sean Hoppe; 3 Kevin Iro; 5 Anthony Sullivan; 13 Paul Sculthorpe (C); 20 Tommy Martyn; 12 Sonny Nickle; 9 Keiron Cunningham; 16 Vila Matautia; 10 David Fairleigh; 8 Peter Shiels; 18 John Stankevitch. Subs: 14 Wayne McDonald for Matautia (16); 15 Tim Jonkers for Shiels (5); 22 Heath Cruckshank for Nickle (30); 17 Steve Hall for McDonald (66); Nickle for Cruckshank (48); Matautia for Iro (76).
Tries: Fairleigh (9, 79), Stewart (39); **Goal:** Sculthorpe.
Sin bin: McDonald (35) – holding down.
League Express Men of the Match:
Bulls: Henry Paul; *Saints:* David Fairleigh.
Penalty count: 8-3; **Half-time:** 8-10;
Referee: Robert Connolly (Wigan); **Attendance:** 13,805.

WIGAN WARRIORS 28 WARRINGTON WOLVES 12

WARRIORS: 1 Kris Radlinski; 5 Brian Carney; 23 David Hodgson; 15 Paul Johnson; 2 Brett Dallas; 19 Chris Chester; 7 Adrian Lam; 8 Terry O'Connor; 9 Terry Newton; 20 Harvey Howard; 11 Mick Cassidy; 14 David Furner; 13 Andy Farrell (C). Subs: 10 Neil Cowie for Howard (29); 22 Phil Jones for Chester (68); 12 Denis Betts for Cassidy (58); 24 Martin Aspinwall for Johnson (31); Howard for O'Connor (50); O'Connor for Cowie (74); Cassidy for Betts (75BB).
Tries: Dallas (10, 41), Johnson (14), Hodgson (28), Carney (50); **Goals:** Farrell 4.
Sin bin: Howard (59) - punching; Newton (70) - fighting.
On report: Howard (17) - leading with the elbow.
WOLVES: 1 Lee Penny; 31 Steve Thomas (D); 3 David Kidwell; 16 Ian Sibbit; 22 Alan Hunte; 6 Lee Briers; 27 Gary Hulse; 32 David Whittle (D); 26 Jon Clarke; 10 Danny Nutley; 12 Jerome Guisset; 13 Tawera Nikau (C); 24 Paul Noone. Subs: 21 Paul Wood for Guisset (31); 11 Steve McCurrie for Whittle (17); 19 Ian Knott for Noone (70); 30 David Bates (D) for Nutley (57); Whittle for Wood (57); Guisset for McCurrie (65).
Tries: Noone (31), Nikau (77); **Goals:** Briers 2.
Sin bin: Whittle (70) - fighting.
League Express Men of the Match:
Warriors: Terry O' Connor; *Wolves:* Paul Noone.
Penalty count: 9-12; **Half-time:** 16-6;
Referee: Steve Ganson (St Helens); **Attendance:** 9,692.

Saturday 18th August 2001

CASTLEFORD TIGERS 10 LEEDS RHINOS 17

TIGERS: 14 Jason Flowers; 2 Jon Wells; 18 Jonathan Roper; 3 Michael Eagar; 5 Darren Rogers; 7 Mitch Healey; 22 Mark Lennon; 8 Nathan Sykes; 15 Darren Shaw; 10 Dean Sampson (C); 23 Michael Smith; 12 Dale Fritz; 11 Lee Harland. Subs: 27 Jamie Rooney for Healey (60); 19 Chris Charles (D) for Sampson (19); 17 Andy Lynch for Shaw (75); 1 Richard Gay for Roper (57); Sampson for Sykes (51); Sykes for Harland (64).
Tries: Eagar (36), Wells (43); **Goal:** Lennon.
RHINOS: 5 Francis Cummins (C); 15 Chev Walker; 3 Tonie Carroll; 4 Keith Senior; 16 Mark Calderwood; 2 Karl Pratt; 7 Ryan Sheridan; 8 Darren Fleary; 9 Robert Mears; 10 Barrie McDermott; 17 Anthony Farrell; 31 Gary Mercer (D2); 13 Kevin Sinfield. Subs: 18 Danny Ward for Fleary (52); 22 David Wrench for Farrell (68); 28 Andy Kirk not used; 20 Jamie Mathiou for McDermott (25); McDermott for Mathiou (60); Mathiou for Mercer (78).
Tries: Senior (46), Pratt (61), Calderwood (63);
Goals: Sinfield 2; **Field goal:** Cummins.
League Express Men of the Match:
Tigers: Michael Smith; *Rhinos:* Karl Pratt.
Penalty count: 8-7; **Half-time:** 6-2; **Referee:** Karl Kirkpatrick (Warrington); **Attendance:** 7,750.

Sunday 19th August 2001

HULL FC 28 LONDON BRONCOS 12

HULL: 1 Steve Prescott; 21 Gareth Raynor; 23 Logan Campbell; 6 Richard Horne; 17 Craig Poucher; 16 Paul Cooke; 7 Tony Smith; 28 Scott Logan; 15 Paul King; 8 Paul Broadbent; 3 David Maiden; 12 Tony Grimaldi (C); 13 Jason Smith. Subs: 9 Lee Jackson for King (65); 18 Steve Craven for Broadbent (20BB, rev 34); 10 Luke Felsch for Logan (30); 29 Kirk Yeaman (D) for Poucher (76); Logan for Maiden (54); Craven for Broadbent (54); Broadbent for Felsch (74).
Tries: T Smith (28, 75), Prescott (33, 42);
Goals: Prescott 6.
BRONCOS: 23 Richie Barnett; 30 Paul Sykes; 4 Greg Fleming; 2 Nigel Roy; 3 Tony Martin; 6 Jim Dymock; 7 Dennis Moran; 18 Justin Dooley; 9 Jason Hetherington (C); 10 Scott Cram; 11 Shane Millard; 12 Steele Retchless; 29 Robert Parker. Subs: 8 Tony Mestrov for Dooley (50); 15 Andy Johnson for Mestrov (67); 17 Glen Air for Hetherington (39); 13 Mat Toshack for Millard (25); Millard for Cram (75).
Tries: Parker (48), Air (55); **Goals:** Sykes 2.
League Express Men of the Match:
Hull: Steve Prescott; *Broncos:* Richie Barnett.
Penalty count: 10-6; **Half-time:** 12-0;
Referee: Ian Smith (Oldham); **Attendance:** 5,710.

WAKEFIELD TRINITY WILDCATS 23 SALFORD CITY REDS 20

WILDCATS: 26 Dane Dorahy; 5 Waisale Sovatabua; 4 Justin Brooker; 19 Gareth Ellis; 2 Neil Law; 6 Martin Pearson; 7 Brad Davis; 16 Julian O'Neill; 9 David March; 22 Keith Mason; 11 Jamie Field; 12 Willie Poching (C); 15 Ryan Hudson. Subs: 8 Paul Jackson for Mason (30); 10 Frank Watene for O'Neill (70); 13 Gary Price for Field (17BB, rev 53); 14 Paul March for Davis (72).
Tries: N Law (23), Dorahy (25), Poching (32), Brooker (56); **Goals:** Pearson 3; **Field goal:** Pearson.
CITY REDS: 14 Kris Tassell; 2 Nick Pinkney; 3 Francis Maloney; 18 Stuart Littler; 5 Martin Offiah; 7 Graham Holroyd (C); 6 Steve Blakeley; 28 Neil Harmon; 9 Malcolm Alker; 8 Neil Baynes; 30 Jason Nicol; 20 Andy Coley; 23 Mike Wainwright. Subs: 4 Michael Hancock for Baynes (19); 12 Darren Brown for Nicol (45); 17 Craig Makin for Harmon (31); 26 Danny Arnold for Pinkney (41BB, rev 56); Baynes for Makin (56).
Tries: Nicol (9), Littler (59), Maloney (65);
Goals: Holroyd 4.
Sin bin: Blakeley (22) - interference at the play the ball.
League Express Men of the Match:
Wildcats: Julian O'Neill; *City Reds:* Kris Tassell.
Penalty count: 5-9; **Half-time:** 16-10; **Referee:** Stuart Cummings (Widnes); **Attendance:** 2,376.

HALIFAX BLUE SOX 19 HUDDERSFIELD GIANTS 12

BLUE SOX: 3 Damian Gibson; 19 Oliver Marns; 21 Phil Hassan; 18 Stuart Donlan; 28 Jason Lee; 6 Andrew Dunemann; 7 Gavin Clinch; 23 Brett Goldspink (C); 9 Johnny Lawless; 10 Jim Gannon; 14 Danny Tickle; 29 Andrew Brocklehurst; 12 Shayne McMenemy. Subs: 27 Matt Firth for Dunemann (15); 4 Adam Hughes for Marns (28); 8 Andy Hobson for Goldspink (57); 17 Sean Penkywicz for Brocklehurst (33); Brocklehurst for Gannon (75); Goldspink for Penkywicz (77).
Tries: McMenemy (10), Tickle (23), Hughes (44);
Goals: Tickle 3; **Field goal:** Tickle.
GIANTS: 1 Paul Reilly; 2 Andrew Frew; 3 Martin Gleeson; 6 Chris Thorman; 20 Chris Langley; 27 Brandon Costin (C); 7 Ben Kusto; 32 Troy Stone; 9 Paul Rowley; 12 Richard Marshall; 13 David Atkins; 26 Steve McNamara; 33 Stanley Gene. Subs: 8 Steve Molloy for Marshall (29); 11 David Lomax for Atkins (50); 28 Michael Slicker for Stone (29); 31 Matt Walker for Molloy (59); Stone for Slicker (50); Marshall for Stone (73BB, rev 77); Atkins for McNamara (73).
Tries: Rowley (30), Gene (54); **Goals:** Costin 2.
On report: Gene (34) - high tackle.
League Express Men of the Match:
Blue Sox: Brett Goldspink; *Giants:* Paul Rowley.
Penalty count: 12-10; **Half-time:** 14-8;
Referee: Russell Smith (Castleford); **Attendance:** 4,328.

ROUND 25

Friday 24th August 2001

LEEDS RHINOS 18 WIGAN WARRIORS 38

RHINOS: 5 Francis Cummins (C); 15 Chev Walker; 3 Tonie Carroll; 4 Keith Senior; 16 Mark Calderwood; 13 Kevin Sinfield; 7 Ryan Sheridan; 8 Darren Fleary; 9 Robert Mears; 10 Barrie McDermott; 31 Gary Mercer; 17 Anthony Farrell; 22 David Wrench. Subs: 27 Jason Netherton for Wrench (24); 20 Jamie Mathiou for McDermott (25); 29 Robert Burrow for Sheridan (40); 18 Danny Ward for Netherton (44); McDermott for Fleary (54); Fleary for Farrell (73).
Tries: Sinfield (18), Calderwood (48), Mears (54);
Goals: Cummins, Burrow 2.
WARRIORS: 1 Kris Radlinski; 2 Brett Dallas; 4 Gary Connolly; 15 Paul Johnson; 23 David Hodgson; 19 Chris Chester; 7 Adrian Lam; 8 Terry O'Connor; 9 Terry Newton; 20 Harvey Howard; 14 David Furner; 11 Mick Cassidy; 13 Andy Farrell (C). Subs: 10 Neil Cowie for Howard (23); 12 Denis Betts for Cassidy (29); 5 Brian Carney for Hodgson (70); 24 Martin Aspinwall for Connolly (74); Howard for O'Connor (57); Cassidy for Newton (69).
Tries: Connolly (28), Johnson (31), Lam (37), Newton (41, 61), Farrell (63); **Goals:** Farrell 7.
Sin bin: Connolly (46) - professional foul.
League Express Men of the Match:
Rhinos: Kevin Sinfield; *Warriors:* Terry Newton.
Penalty count: 6-7; **Half-time:** 6-18;
Referee: Ian Smith (Oldham); **Attendance:** 11,585.

Sunday 26th August 2001

LONDON BRONCOS 12 HUDDERSFIELD GIANTS 21

BRONCOS: 23 Richie Barnett; 28 Marvin Golden; 3 Tony Martin; 4 Greg Fleming; 2 Nigel Roy; 6 Jim Dymock; 7 Dennis Moran; 18 Justin Dooley; 9 Jason Hetherington (C); 10 Scott Cram; 11 Shane Millard; 13 Mat Toshack; 15 Andy Johnson. Subs: 12 Steele Retchless for Dooley (20); 17 Glen Air for Hetherington (31); 27 Michael Gillett for Cram (35); 36 Dan Potter not used; Cram for Johnson (52); Hetherington for Millard (68); Johnson for Cram (77).
Tries: Martin (39), Fleming (43); **Goals:** Martin 2.
GIANTS: 25 Ben Cooper; 2 Andrew Frew; 35 Martin Moana; 3 Martin Gleeson; 20 Chris Langley; 27 Brandon Costin (C); 17 Mark Moxon; 32 Troy Stone; 30 Toby Green; 12 Richard Marshall; 13 David Atkins; 33 Stanley Gene; 26 Steve McNamara. Subs: 8 Steve Molloy for Marshall (28); 28 Michael Slicker for Stone (33BB, rev 48); 6 Chris Thorman for Gene (60); 11 David Lomax for Moana (58); Marshall for Molloy (63).
Tries: Green (2), Costin (34), Frew (79); **Goals:** Costin 4;
Field goal: Moxon.
Sin bin: Cooper (8) - professional foul.
League Express Men of the Match:
Broncos: Dan Potter; *Giants:* Brandon Costin.
Penalty count: 10-8; **Half time:** 8-16;
Referee: Stuart Cummings (Widnes); **Attendance:** 1,800.

WARRINGTON WOLVES 28 ST HELENS 28

WOLVES: 1 Lee Penny; 34 Kevin Crouthers (D); 3 David Kidwell; 4 Toa Kohe-Love; 33 Anthony Swann (D); 6 Lee Briers; 27 Gary Hulse; 18 Martin Masella; 26 Jon Clarke; 30 David Bates; 13 Tawera Nikau (C); 12 Jerome Guisset; 19 Ian Knott. Subs: 11 Steve McCurrie not used; 24 Paul Noone for Knott (57); 32 David Whittle for Bates (17); 10 Danny Nutley for Masella (17); Masella for Whittle (56); Knott for Briers (67); Bates for Masella (71).
Tries: Penny (5), Crouthers (19, 47), Kidwell (36), Kohe-Love (72); **Goals:** Briers 3, Knott.
Sin bin: Nikau (33) - interference at the play the ball; Nutley (65) - fighting.
On report: Penny (12) - high tackle on Stewart; Nikau (27) - late challenge on Martyn.
SAINTS: 19 Anthony Stewart; 30 John Kirkpatrick (D); 2 Sean Hoppe; 23 Mike Bennett; 17 Steve Hall; 20 Tommy Martyn (C); 1 Paul Wellens; 16 Vila Matautia; 9 Keiron Cunningham; 12 Sonny Nickle; 10 David Fairleigh; 18 John Stankevitch; 15 Tim Jonkers. Subs: 14 Wayne McDonald for Matautia (22); 29 Dave McConnell (D) for Martyn (31); 22 Heath Cruckshank for Nickle (53); 31 John Braddish (D) for Bennett (50); Matautia for Cruckshank (73).
Tries: Martyn (8), Kirkpatrick (23), Cunningham (28, 67), Wellens (43), Stankevitch (56); **Goals:** Martyn, Wellens.
Sin bin: McDonald (65) - fighting.
League Express Men of the Match:

Wolves: Jerome Guisset; *Saints:* Keiron Cunningham.
Penalty count: 8-10; **Half-time:** 18-16;
Referee: Russell Smith (Castleford); **Attendance:** 7,910.

BRADFORD BULLS 56 CASTLEFORD TIGERS 30

BULLS: 5 Michael Withers; 2 Tevita Vaikona; 23 Graham Mackay; 14 Lee Gilmour; 3 Leon Pryce; 6 Henry Paul; 1 Robbie Paul (C); 10 Paul Anderson; 9 James Lowes; 22 Brian McDermott; 11 Daniel Gartner; 19 Jamie Peacock; 12 Mike Forshaw. Subs: 7 Paul Deacon for H Paul (ht); 15 Shane Rigon for Mackay (55); 29 Stuart Fielden for McDermott (29); 4 Nathan McAvoy for Withers (49); McDermott for Anderson (57); H Paul for Gartner (68).
Tries: Vaikona (6), R Paul (14), Lowes (21), Gartner (25), Withers (33, 38, 41), Deacon (74), McAvoy (78);
Goals: H Paul 9, Deacon.
TIGERS: 22 Mark Lennon; 1 Richard Gay; 2 Jon Wells; 3 Michael Eagar; 5 Darren Rogers; 18 Jonathan Roper; 27 Jamie Rooney; 17 Andy Lynch; 15 Darren Shaw; 10 Dean Sampson (C); 23 Michael Smith; 12 Dale Fritz; 11 Lee Harland. Subs: 20 Waine Pryce for Eagar (51); 19 Chris Charles for Smith (34BB, rev 52); 14 Jason Flowers for Rooney (43); 26 Wayne Godwin for Lynch (22); Lynch for Sampson (46); Charles for Shaw (69).
Tries: Harland (4, 59), Godwin (54), M Smith (61), Roper (67); **Goals:** Rooney 2, Roper 3.
Sin bin: Wells (25) - holding down.
League Express Men of the Match:
Bulls: Henry Paul; *Tigers:* Lee Harland.
Penalty count: 9-6; **Half-time:** 38-8;
Referee: Steve Ganson (St Helens); **Attendance:** 10,469.

SALFORD CITY REDS 30 HALIFAX BLUE SOX 41

CITY REDS: 14 Kris Tassell; 2 Nick Pinkney; 3 Francis Maloney; 18 Stuart Littler; 5 Martin Offiah; 6 Steve Blakeley; 16 Bobbie Goulding (C); 8 Neil Baynes; 9 Malcolm Alker; 15 Damian Driscoll; 30 Jason Nicol; 20 Andy Coley; 7 Graham Holroyd. Subs: 4 Michael Hancock for Baynes (29); 17 Craig Makin for Driscoll (25); 13 Paul Highton for Makin (48); 26 Danny Arnold for Tassell (60); Baynes for Nicol (54).
Tries: Littler (13, 78), Holroyd (16), Pinkney (19), Blakeley (44), Maloney (80); **Goals:** Holroyd 3.
BLUE SOX: 3 Damian Gibson; 21 Phil Hassan; 32 Dale Cardoza; 18 Stuart Donlan; 28 Jason Lee; 27 Matt Firth; 7 Gavin Clinch; 23 Brett Goldspink (C); 9 Johnny Lawless; 10 Jim Gannon; 14 Danny Tickle; 29 Andrew Brocklehurst; 12 Shayne McMenemy. Subs: 1 Daryl Cardiss for Hassan (25); 4 Adam Hughes for Cardoza (75); 8 Andy Hobson for Brocklehurst (45); 17 Sean Penkywicz for Goldspink (30); Goldspink for McMenemy (45); McMenemy for Firth (60); Hassan for Lee (62BB).
Tries: Cardoza (2), Donlan (24, 33), Cardiss (28, 53), Gibson (66), Penkywicz (72); **Goals:** Tickle 6;
Field goal: Tickle.
League Express Men of the Match:
City Reds: Andy Coley; *Blue Sox:* Gavin Clinch.
Penalty count: 9-5; **Half-time:** 18-25; **Referee:** Karl Kirkpatrick (Warrington); **Attendance:** 3,649.

Monday 27th August 2001

WAKEFIELD TRINITY WILDCATS 18 HULL FC 30

WILDCATS: 26 Dane Dorahy; 2 Neil Law; 19 Gareth Ellis; 4 Justin Brooker; 5 Waisale Sovatabua; 6 Martin Pearson; 7 Brad Davis; 16 Julian O'Neill; 9 David March; 22 Keith Mason; 11 Jamie Field; 12 Willie Poching (C); 15 Ryan Hudson. Subs: 20 Ben Westwood for Law (1); 18 Ben Rauter for Field (54); 10 Frank Watene for O'Neill (71); 8 Paul Jackson for Mason (60); Law for Dorahy (41); Field for Poching (67).
Tries: Ellis (4), Hudson (34, 61), Sovatabua (45);
Goal: Pearson.
HULL: 1 Steve Prescott; 17 Craig Poucher; 23 Logan Campbell; 6 Richard Horne; 21 Gareth Raynor; 16 Paul Cooke; 7 Tony Smith; 8 Paul Broadbent; 15 Paul King; 28 Scott Logan; 3 David Maiden; 12 Tony Grimaldi (C); 13 Jason Smith. Subs: 29 Kirk Yeaman for Jackson (76); 18 Steve Craven for Logan (31); 10 Luke Felsch for Broadbent (23); 9 Lee Jackson for King (56); Logan for Maiden (65BB); Broadbent for Felsch (75); King for Craven (75).
Tries: Logan (7), T Smith (22, 42), Prescott (38), Horne (53), Raynor (75); **Goals:** Prescott 3.
League Express Men of the Match:
Wildcats: Brad Davis; *Hull:* Jason Smith.
Penalty count: 6-6; **Half-time:** 8-16;
Referee: Robert Connolly (Wigan); **Attendance:** 3,518.

ROUND 26

Friday 31st August 2001

LEEDS RHINOS 16 WARRINGTON WOLVES 12

RHINOS: 5 Francis Cummins (C); 15 Chev Walker; 3 Tonie Carroll; 4 Keith Senior; 16 Mark Calderwood; 2 Karl Pratt; 29 Robert Burrow; 8 Darren Fleary; 9 Robert Mears; 10 Barrie McDermott; 17 Anthony Farrell; 31 Gary Mercer; 13 Kevin Sinfield. Subs: 18 Danny Ward for McDermott (33); 11 Andy Hay for Farrell (40); 20 Jamie Mathiou for Fleary (51); 30 Danny McGuire not used; Farrell for Mercer (62); McDermott for Ward (64).
Tries: Walker (21), Senior (33), Cummins (48);
Goals: Burrow 2.
Sin bin: Mathiou (78) - altercation.
WOLVES: 1 Lee Penny; 34 Kevin Crouthers; 33 Anthony Swann; 4 Toa Kohe-Love; 22 Alan Hunte; 13 Tawera Nikau (C); 27 Gary Hulse; 21 Paul Wood; 26 Jon Clarke; 10 Danny Nutley; 12 Jerome Guisset; 24 Paul Noone; 19 Ian Knott. Subs: 18 Martin Masella for Wood (12); 11 Steve McCurrie for Knott (12BB); 32 David Whittle for Guisset (13BB, rev 15); 35 Tom O'Reilly (D) for Hulse (49); Whittle for Nutley (35); Nutley for Masella (49); Masella for McCurrie (65); McCurrie for Whittle (76).
Tries: Penny (54), Nikau (66), Swann (72).
Sin bin: Nutley (78) - altercation.
League Express Men of the Match:
Rhinos: Tonie Carroll; *Wolves:* Paul Noone.
Penalty count: 8-8; **Half-time:** 8-0;
Referee: Robert Connolly (Wigan); **Attendance:** 10,291.

ST HELENS 44 CASTLEFORD TIGERS 20

SAINTS: 19 Anthony Stewart; 30 John Kirkpatrick; 3 Kevin Iro; 2 Sean Hoppe; 17 Steve Hall; 13 Paul Sculthorpe; 1 Paul Wellens; 10 David Fairleigh; 9 Keiron Cunningham; 12 Sonny Nickle; 11 Chris Joynt (C); 18 John Stankevitch; 29 Dave McConnell. Subs: 14 Wayne McDonald for Matautia (62); 15 Tim Jonkers for Iro (53); 22 Heath Cruckshank for Stankevitch (26); 16 Vila Matautia for Fairleigh (26); Matautia for Nickle (69).
Tries: Hall (7), Stewart (16), Cunningham (20), McConnell (23, 63, 78), Hoppe (52), Nickle (58);
Goals: Sculthorpe 6.
TIGERS: 14 Jason Flowers; 1 Richard Gay; 2 Jon Wells; 18 Jonathan Roper; 5 Darren Rogers; 13 Adrian Vowles (C); 22 Mark Lennon; 8 Nathan Sykes; 15 Darren Shaw; 10 Dean Sampson; 23 Michael Smith; 12 Dale Fritz; 11 Lee Harland. Subs: 20 Waine Pryce for Flowers (36); 19 Chris Charles for Smith (27); 17 Andy Lynch for Harland (50); 26 Wayne Godwin for Sykes (66); Smith for Sampson (ht).
Tries: Lennon (33), Roper (48), Vowles (67), M Smith (73); **Goals:** Lennon 2.
League Express Men of the Match:
Saints: Dave McConnell; *Tigers:* Mark Lennon.
Penalty count: 7-7; **Half-time:** 22-4; **Referee:** Richard Silverwood (Dewsbury); **Attendance:** 7,680.

WIGAN WARRIORS 16 BRADFORD BULLS 10

WARRIORS: 1 Kris Radlinski; 2 Brett Dallas; 4 Gary Connolly; 3 Steve Renouf; 15 Paul Johnson; 6 Matthew Johns; 7 Adrian Lam; 8 Terry O'Connor; 9 Terry Newton; 20 Harvey Howard; 11 Mick Cassidy; 14 David Furner; 13 Andy Farrell (C). Subs: 10 Neil Cowie for Howard (23); 5 Brian Carney for Dallas (75); 23 David Hodgson for Johnson (41); 12 Denis Betts for Cassidy (26); Cassidy for Johns (59BB); Howard for O'Connor (62); O'Connor for Cowie (78).
Tries: Dallas (52), Radlinski (55); **Goals:** Farrell 3;
Field goals: Farrell 2.
BULLS: 5 Michael Withers; 2 Tevita Vaikona; 20 Scott Naylor; 14 Lee Gilmour; 3 Leon Pryce; 6 Henry Paul; 7 Paul Deacon; 22 Brian McDermott; 9 James Lowes (C); 8 Joe Vagana; 11 Daniel Gartner; 19 Jamie Peacock; 12 Mike Forshaw. Subs: 10 Paul Anderson for Vagana (24); 29 Stuart Fielden for McDermott (24); 1 Robbie Paul for Lowes (ht); 15 Shane Rigon for Gilmour (64); Vagana for Anderson (59); McDermott for Gartner (69).
Try: Lowes (18); **Goals:** H Paul 2;
Field goals: Deacon, Lowes.
League Express Men of the Match:
Warriors: Brett Dallas; *Bulls:* James Lowes.
Penalty count: 4-6; **Half-time:** 2-8; **Referee:** Stuart Cummings (Widnes); **Attendance:** 15,052.

Saturday 1st September 2001

HUDDERSFIELD GIANTS 30 HULL FC 36

GIANTS: 1 Paul Reilly; 2 Andrew Frew; 35 Martin Moana; 3 Martin Gleeson; 20 Chris Langley; 27 Brandon Costin; 17 Mark Moxon; 32 Troy Stone; 30 Toby Green; 12 Richard Marshall; 13 David Atkins; 33 Stanley Gene; 26 Steve McNamara (C). Subs: 28 Michael Slicker for Stone (23); 6 Chris Thorman for Gene (25BB, rev 35); 11 David Lomax for Moana (53BB); 36 Robert Roberts (D) for McNamara (33BB, rev 63); Stone for Slicker (44); Thorman for Moxon (63); Moana for Marshall (70).
Tries: Gleeson (25), Frew (44, 60, 80), Gene (66);
Goals: McNamara 4, Costin.
HULL: 1 Steve Prescott; 5 Matt Crowther; 23 Logan Campbell; 3 David Maiden; 21 Gareth Raynor; 6 Richard Horne; 7 Tony Smith; 8 Paul Broadbent; 15 Paul King; 10 Luke Felsch; 28 Scott Logan; 12 Tony Grimaldi (C); 16 Paul Cooke. Subs: 20 Gareth Carvell for Grimaldi (63); 18 Steve Craven for Broadbent (25); 22 Andy Last for Horne (79); 17 Craig Poucher not used; Broadbent for Felsch (51).
Tries: Prescott (2, 62), Horne (29), Cooke (32), Logan (70), Craven (72); **Goals:** Prescott 6.
Sin bin: Logan (43) - ball stealing.
League Express Men of the Match:
Giants: Stanley Gene; *Hull:* Steve Prescott.
Penalty count: 13-10; **Half-time:** 10-18;
Referee: Russell Smith (Castleford); **Attendance:** 3,337.

Sunday 2nd September 2001

HALIFAX BLUE SOX 10
WAKEFIELD TRINITY WILDCATS 23

BLUE SOX: 1 Daryl Cardiss; 32 Dale Cardoza; 21 Phil Hassan; 18 Stuart Donlan; 3 Damian Gibson; 27 Matt Firth; 7 Gavin Clinch; 23 Brett Goldspink (C); 9 Johnny Lawless; 8 Andy Hobson; 10 Jim Gannon; 14 Danny Tickle; 12 Shayne McMenemy. Subs: 16 Jamie Thackray for Goldspink (25); 29 Andrew Brocklehurst for Penkywicz (49); 17 Sean Penkywicz for Hobson (25); 28 Jason Lee for Cardoza (55); Goldspink for Firth (49).
Tries: Donlan (60), Gibson (72); **Goal:** Tickle.
WILDCATS: 2 Neil Law; 5 Waisale Sovatabua; 4 Justin Brooker; 19 Gareth Ellis; 20 Ben Westwood; 6 Martin Pearson; 7 Brad Davis; 16 Julian O'Neill; 9 David March; 22 Keith Mason; 13 Gary Price (C); 11 Jamie Field; 15 Ryan Hudson. Subs: 14 Paul March for D March (78); 10 Frank Watene for O'Neill (44BB, rev 52); 18 Ben Rauter for Hudson (44); 17 Graham Law for Westwood (79); Watene for Mason (68).
Tries: Westwood (18), Sovatabua (39), Rauter (77);
Goals: Pearson 5; **Field goal:** Pearson.
League Express Men of the Match:
Blue Sox: Gavin Clinch; *Wildcats:* Martin Pearson.
Penalty count: 10-9; **Half-time:** 2-16;
Referee: Steve Ganson (St Helens); **Attendance:** 4,485.

SALFORD CITY REDS 12 LONDON BRONCOS 50

CITY REDS: 14 Kris Tassell; 2 Nick Pinkney; 3 Francis Maloney; 18 Stuart Littler; 26 Danny Arnold; 6 Steve Blakeley; 16 Bobbie Goulding (C); 8 Neil Baynes; 9 Malcolm Alker; 15 Damian Driscoll; 20 Andy Coley; 30 Jason Nicol; 7 Graham Holroyd. Subs: 4 Michael Hancock for Coley (15); 13 Paul Highton for Baynes (32); 28 Neil Harmon for Driscoll (29); 23 Mike Wainwright for Blakeley (43); Coley for Hancock (62); Baynes for Harmon (71).
Tries: Driscoll (25), Maloney (79); **Goals:** Holroyd 2.
BRONCOS: 23 Richie Barnett; 34 Sylvain Houles; 3 Tony Martin; 4 Greg Fleming; 2 Nigel Roy; 27 Michael Gillett; 7 Dennis Moran; 10 Scott Cram; 9 Jason Hetherington (C); 12 Steele Retchless; 11 Shane Millard; 13 Mat Toshack; 6 Jim Dymock. Subs: 17 Glen Air for Moran (64); 18 Justin Dooley for Cram (26); 28 Marvin Golden for Roy (70); 36 Dan Potter for Millard (66); Cram for Retchless (51).
Tries: Dymock (2), Houles (11), Barnett (32, 54, 75), Martin (61), Gillett (70), Potter (73); **Goals:** Martin 9.
League Express Men of the Match:
City Reds: Kris Tassell; *Broncos:* Richie Barnett.
Penalty count: 8-6; **Half-time:** 6-18; **Referee:** Karl Kirkpatrick (Warrington); **Attendance:** 2,618.

ROUND 27

Friday 7th September 2001

ST HELENS 18 LEEDS RHINOS 23

SAINTS: 1 Paul Wellens; 17 Steve Hall; 2 Sean Hoppe; 3 Kevin Iro; 30 John Kirkpatrick; 13 Paul Sculthorpe; 20 Tommy Martyn; 10 David Fairleigh; 29 Dave McConnell; 12 Sonny Nickle; 11 Chris Joynt (C); 8 Peter Shiels; 9 Keiron Cunningham. Subs: 16 Vila Matautia for Fairleigh (2); 18 John Stankevitch for Matautia (29); 15 Tim Jonkers for McConnell (52); 32 Leon Felton (D) for Shiels (72); Matautia for Nickle (56); Nickle for Matautia (75).
Tries: McConnell (4), Hoppe (56), Cunningham (68);
Goals: Sculthorpe 3.
On report: Nickle (24) - late challenge on Mears.
RHINOS: 5 Francis Cummins (C); 15 Chev Walker; 3 Tonie Carroll; 4 Keith Senior; 16 Mark Calderwood; 2 Karl Pratt; 29 Robert Burrow; 8 Darren Fleary; 9 Robert Mears; 10 Barrie McDermott; 17 Anthony Farrell; 31 Gary Mercer; 13 Kevin Sinfield. Subs: 22 David Wrench for Pratt (23); 20 Jamie Mathiou for Mears (25); 18 Danny Ward for McDermott (30); 30 Danny McGuire for Mercer (78); McDermott for Fleary (55); Fleary for Ward (72).
Tries: Burrow (11, 37), Calderwood (14), Cummins (60);
Goals: Sinfield 3; **Field goal:** Sinfield.
Sin bin: McDermott (78) - interference.
League Express Men of the Match:
Saints: Keiron Cunningham; *Rhinos:* Robert Burrow.
Penalty count: 8-7; **Half-time:** 6-18;
Referee: Ian Smith (Oldham); **Attendance:** 7,592.

Saturday 8th September 2001

LONDON BRONCOS 46 HALIFAX BLUE SOX 8

BRONCOS: 23 Richie Barnett; 34 Sylvain Houles; 2 Nigel Roy; 4 Greg Fleming; 3 Tony Martin; 27 Michael Gillett; 7 Dennis Moran; 12 Steele Retchless; 9 Jason Hetherington (C); 10 Scott Cram; 11 Shane Millard; 13 Mat Toshack; 6 Jim Dymock. Subs: 26 Peter Lupton for Moran (55); 18 Justin Dooley for Cram (29); 28 Marvin Golden for Barnett (60); 36 Dan Potter for Hetherington (68); Cram for Dooley (69); Hetherington for Gillett (76).
Tries: Moran (14), Cram (18), Gillett (30, 72), Roy (36), Barnett (47, 54), Toshack (69); **Goals:** Martin 6, Fleming.
BLUE SOX: 1 Daryl Cardiss; 19 Oliver Marns; 3 Damian Gibson; 18 Stuart Donlan; 5 Lee Greenwood; 12 Shayne McMenemy; 7 Gavin Clinch; 8 Andy Hobson; 9 Johnny Lawless; 10 Jim Gannon; 15 Paul Davidson; 23 Brett Goldspink (C); 21 Phil Hassan. Subs: 4 Adam Hughes for Cardiss (ht); 20 Danny Halliwell for Davidson (55); 17 Sean Penkywicz for Hassan (45); 16 Jamie Thackray for Hobson (29); Hobson for Goldspink (57); Davidson for Thackray (68).
Try: Greenwood (58); **Goals:** Clinch 2.
League Express Men of the Match:
Broncos: Richie Barnett; *Blue Sox:* Paul Davidson.
Penalty count: 6-8; **Half-time:** 22-4; **Referee:** Karl Kirkpatrick (Warrington); **Attendance:** 2,854.

WAKEFIELD TRINITY WILDCATS 19
HUDDERSFIELD GIANTS 21

WILDCATS: 2 Neil Law; 5 Waisale Sovatabua; 4 Justin Brooker; 19 Gareth Ellis; 20 Ben Westwood; 6 Martin Pearson; 7 Brad Davis; 16 Julian O'Neill; 9 David March; 22 Keith Mason; 13 Gary Price (C); 11 Jamie Field; 15 Ryan Hudson. Subs: 12 Willie Poching for Price (37); 10 Frank Watene for Mason (36); 18 Ben Rauter for Field (68); 17 Graham Law for Pearson (71); Mason for Watene (68).

Tries: Hudson (5), Brooker (49), D March (78);
Goals: Pearson 2, G Law; **Field goal:** Hudson.
Sin bin: March (27) - fighting.
On report: O'Neill and Mason (75) - spear tackle.
GIANTS: 5 Hefin O'Hare; 2 Andrew Frew; 33 Stanley
Gene; 3 Martin Gleeson; 20 Chris Langley; 27 Brandon
Costin; 7 Ben Kusto; 32 Troy Stone; 9 Paul Rowley; 12
Richard Marshall; 13 David Atkins; 11 David Lomax; 26
Steve McNamara (C). Subs: 6 Chris Thorman for O'Hare
(27BB, rev 50); 28 Michael Slicker for Molloy (60); 35
Martin Moana for Atkins (47); 8 Steve Molloy for Stone
(27); Stone for Lomax (44BB, rev 68); Thorman for
McNamara (62); Stone for Marshall (70); Molloy for
Slicker (78).
Tries: Gleeson (2), Molloy (27), O'Hare (63);
Goals: McNamara 2, Costin 2; **Field goal:** Kusto.
Sin bin: Atkins (27) - fighting.
League Express Men of the Match:
Wildcats: Brad Davis; *Giants:* Ben Kusto.
Penalty count: 11-11; **Half-time:** 6-12;
Referee: Stuart Cummings (Widnes); **Attendance:** 4,150.

Sunday 9th September 2001

WARRINGTON WOLVES 12 BRADFORD BULLS 84

WOLVES: 1 Lee Penny; 34 Kevin Crouthers; 33 Anthony
Swann; 3 David Kidwell; 22 Alan Hunte; 19 Ian Knott; 26
Jon Clarke; 18 Martin Masella; 11 Steve McCurrie; 10
Danny Nutley; 12 Jerome Guisset; 24 Paul Noone; 13
Tawera Nikau (C). Subs: 16 Ian Sibbit for Noone (18); 6
Lee Briers for Knott (25); 27 Gary Hulse for Clarke (64);
30 David Bates for Masella (31); Knott for Sibbit (44).
Tries: Crouthers (32), Knott (69); **Goals:** Briers 2.
BULLS: 5 Michael Withers; 2 Tevita Vaikona; 20 Scott
Naylor; 23 Graham Mackay; 3 Leon Pryce; 6 Henry Paul;
1 Robbie Paul (C); 22 Brian McDermott; 9 James Lowes;
8 Joe Vagana; 11 Daniel Gartner; 19 Jamie Peacock; 12
Mike Forshaw. Subs: 10 Paul Anderson for Vagana (27);
29 Stuart Fielden for McDermott (27); 15 Shane Rigon
for Forshaw (45); 7 Paul Deacon for R Paul (51);
McDermott for Gartner (54); R Paul for H Paul (64).
Tries: R Paul (10), H Paul (13), Withers (15, 43, 79),
Mackay (17, 20, 37), Pryce (24, 72), Naylor (46, 75),
Rigon (60), Peacock (67); **Goals:** H Paul 10, Deacon 4.
League Express Men of the Match:
Wolves: David Bates; *Bulls:* Henry Paul.
Penalty count: 4-8; **Half-time:** 6-44;
Referee: Robert Connolly (Wigan); **Attendance:** 8,393.

HULL FC 40 SALFORD CITY REDS 8

HULL: 1 Steve Prescott; 21 Gareth Raynor; 23 Logan
Campbell; 3 David Maiden; 5 Matt Crowther; 16 Paul
Cooke; 7 Tony Smith; 8 Paul Broadbent; 15 Paul King;
10 Luke Felsch; 28 Scott Logan; 12 Tony Grimaldi (C);
13 Jason Smith. Subs: 20 Garreth Carvell for Logan
(58); 9 Lee Jackson for King (21); 17 Craig Poucher for
Prescott (67); 18 Steve Craven for Broadbent (27BB, rev
48); King for Felsch (56); Felsch for Carvell (66).
Tries: T Smith (31, 79), Grimaldi (39), Crowther (41),
Cooke (43), Maiden (63), Jackson (69);
Goals: Prescott 4, Crowther, Jackson.
CITY REDS: 1 Gary Broadbent; 2 Nick Pinkney; 3 Francis
Maloney; 18 Stuart Littler; 26 Danny Arnold; 7 Graham

Holroyd; 16 Bobbie Goulding (C); 8 Neil Baynes; 9
Malcolm Alker; 15 Damian Driscoll; 13 Paul Highton; 30
Jason Nicol; 23 Mike Wainwright. Subs: 4 Michael
Hancock for Nicol (26); 14 Kris Tassell for Highton (57);
19 Warren Stevens for Makin (43BB, rev 66); 17 Craig
Makin for Baynes (28); Baynes for Driscoll (55); Highton
for Broadbent (68).
Try: Littler (78); **Goals:** Holroyd 2.
League Express Men of the Match:
Hull: Lee Jackson; *City Reds:* Mike Wainwright.
Penalty count: 11-10; **Half-time:** 12-4;
Referee: Russell Smith (Castleford); **Attendance:** 6,262.

CASTLEFORD TIGERS 22 WIGAN WARRIORS 30

TIGERS: 1 Richard Gay; 2 Jon Wells; 3 Michael Eagar;
18 Jonathan Roper; 5 Darren Rogers; 7 Mitch Healey; 22
Mark Lennon; 8 Nathan Sykes; 15 Darren Shaw; 23
Michael Smith; 19 Chris Charles; 12 Dale Fritz; 13 Adrian
Vowles (C). Subs: 20 Waine Pryce for Gay (70); 28 Gary
Smith (D) for Healey (62); 26 Wayne Godwin for M
Smith (25BB, rev 32); 17 Andy Lynch for Sykes (40);
Godwin for Lynch (59); Lynch for Charles (66).
Tries: Roper (22), Charles (54), Lennon (58), M Smith
(69); **Goals:** Roper 3.
WARRIORS: 1 Kris Radlinski; 2 Brett Dallas; 4 Gary
Connolly; 3 Steve Renouf; 15 Paul Johnson; 19 Chris
Chester; 7 Adrian Lam; 8 Terry O'Connor; 9 Terry
Newton; 20 Harvey Howard; 12 Denis Betts; 11 Mick
Cassidy; 13 Andy Farrell (C). Subs: 10 Neil Cowie for
Howard (33); 5 Brian Carney for Dallas (11); 29 Stephen
Wild (D) for O'Connor (56); 21 Mark Smith for Newton
(70); Dallas for Radlinski (23); Howard for Cassidy (70).
Tries: Lam (4), Radlinski (15), Renouf (26), Johnson
(41), Connolly (44), Carney (65); **Goals:** Farrell 3.
League Express Men of the Match:
Tigers: Michael Smith; *Warriors:* Gary Connolly.
Penalty count: 8-6; **Half-time:** 8-16;
Referee: Steve Ganson (St Helens); **Attendance:** 7,546.

ROUND 28

Friday 14th September 2001

WIGAN WARRIORS 40 ST HELENS 6

WARRIORS: 4 Gary Connolly; 5 Brian Carney; 15 Paul
Johnson; 3 Steve Renouf; 23 David Hodgson; 6 Matthew
Johns; 7 Adrian Lam; 8 Terry O'Connor; 9 Terry Newton;
20 Harvey Howard; 14 David Furner; 29 Stephen Wild;
13 Andy Farrell (C). Subs: 10 Neil Cowie for Howard
(27); 21 Mark Smith for Lam (41BB, rev 46); 12 Denis
Betts for Wild (47); 24 Martin Aspinwall for Johnson
(66); Howard for O'Connor (52BB, rev 72); Smith for
Newton (58); Johnson for Lam (79).
Tries: Renouf (7), Carney (12, 31), Furner (15), Newton
(29), Betts (55), Hodgson (68); **Goals:** Farrell 6.
Sin bin: Johns (27) - lying on.
SAINTS: 1 Paul Wellens; 17 Steve Hall; 3 Kevin Iro; 2
Sean Hoppe; 32 Leon Felton; 13 Paul Sculthorpe; 20
Tommy Martyn; 16 Vila Matautia; 29 Dave McConnell; 25
Mark Edmondson; 8 Peter Shiels; 22 Heath Cruckshank;
11 Chris Joynt (C). Subs: 14 Wayne McDonald for
Matautia (26); 30 John Kirkpatrick for Hall (31); 15 Tim

Jonkers for Edmondson (32); 24 Mick Higham for
McConnell (41); Matautia for Cruckshank (59); Hall for
Kirkpatrick (63); Cruckshank for Joynt (68BB);
Edmondson for Shiels (68BB).
Try: Sculthorpe (40); **Goal:** Sculthorpe.
League Express Men of the Match:
Warriors: David Furner; *Saints:* Paul Wellens.
Penalty count: 9-10; **Half-time:** 28-6; **Referee:** Stuart
Cummings (Widnes); **Attendance:** 15,235.

Saturday 15th September 2001

BRADFORD BULLS 62 LEEDS RHINOS 18

BULLS: 5 Michael Withers; 2 Tevita Vaikona; 20 Scott
Naylor; 23 Graham Mackay; 3 Leon Pryce; 6 Henry Paul;
1 Robbie Paul (C); 22 Brian McDermott; 9 James Lowes;
8 Joe Vagana; 11 Daniel Gartner; 19 Jamie Peacock; 12
Mike Forshaw. Subs: 10 Paul Anderson for Vagana (28);
29 Stuart Fielden for McDermott (24); 15 Shane Rigon
for Gartner (65); 7 Paul Deacon for R Paul (40); Vagana
for Anderson (61); Anderson for Fielden (68).
Tries: Naylor (4, 35), Forshaw (10), Gartner (12),
Vaikona (15), R Paul (20, 30), Deacon (56), Withers (61,
64), Lowes (79); **Goals:** H Paul 9.
RHINOS: 5 Francis Cummins (C); 14 Marcus St Hilaire;
15 Chev Walker; 4 Keith Senior; 16 Mark Calderwood;
13 Kevin Sinfield; 29 Robert Burrow; 8 Darren Fleary; 17
Anthony Farrell; 10 Barrie McDermott; 22 David Wrench;
31 Gary Mercer; 25 Gareth Morton (D). Subs: 24 Ewan
Dowes for Fleary (26); 27 Jason Netherton for Farrell
(56); 18 Danny Ward for McDermott (15); 28 Andy Kirk
for St Hilaire (66); McDermott for Dowes (53); Fleary for
Ward (65).
Tries: St Hilaire (33), Ward (46), Walker (55);
Goals: Burrow 3.
League Express Men of the Match:
Bulls: James Lowes; *Rhinos:* Robert Burrow.
Penalty count: 11-7; **Half-time:** 38-8;
Referee: Robert Connolly (Wigan); **Attendance:** 12,863.

Sunday 16th September 2001

HUDDERSFIELD GIANTS 28 LONDON BRONCOS 24

GIANTS: 1 Paul Reilly; 5 Hefin O'Hare; 3 Martin Gleeson;
33 Stanley Gene; 20 Chris Langley; 27 Brandon Costin; 7
Ben Kusto; 12 Richard Marshall; 9 Paul Rowley; 32 Troy
Stone; 13 David Atkins; 11 David Lomax; 26 Steve
McNamara (C). Subs: 8 Steve Molloy for Lomax (25); 28
Michael Slicker for Stone (30BB, rev ht); 35 Martin
Moana for Marshall (55); 6 Chris Thorman for Langley
(19BB); Lomax for Molloy (48); Marshall for Atkins (71);
Slicker for Lomax (75); Molloy for Stone (72).
Tries: O'Hare (6), Gleeson (13, 49), Reilly (24), Gene
(36); **Goals:** McNamara 3, Costin.
BRONCOS: 5 Brett Warton; 28 Marvin Golden; 2 Nigel
Roy; 4 Greg Fleming; 34 Sylvain Houles; 27 Michael
Gillett; 7 Dennis Moran; 10 Scott Cram; 9 Jason
Hetherington; 12 Steele Retchless; 11 Shane Millard; 13
Mat Toshack (C); 6 Jim Dymock. Subs: 3 Tony Martin
not used; 18 Justin Dooley for Cram (25); 26 Peter
Lupton for Warton (60); 36 Dan Potter for Retchless
(28); Cram for Dooley (50).
Tries: Moran (2), Fleming (53), Toshack (64), Roy (67);
Goals: Warton 2, Gillett 2.
League Express Men of the Match:

Huddersfield's Chris Langley faces up to London's Jim Dymock during his side's Round 28 win over the Broncos,
a win which ultimately wasn't enough to save the Giants from Super League relegation

Super League VI - Round by Round

Giants: Troy Stone; *Broncos:* Jim Dymock.
Penalty count: 5-4; **Half-time:** 22-6;
Referee: Ian Smith (Oldham); **Attendance:** 3,103.

SALFORD CITY REDS 24
WAKEFIELD TRINITY WILDCATS 32

CITY REDS: 26 Danny Arnold; 29 Michael Platt (D); 3 Francis Maloney; 18 Stuart Littler; 4 Michael Hancock; 7 Graham Holroyd; 16 Bobbie Goulding (C); 15 Damian Driscoll; 9 Malcolm Alker; 8 Neil Baynes; 31 Danny Barton (D); 13 Paul Highton; 23 Mike Wainwright. Subs: 25 Lee Marsh for Gorski (54); 32 Andy Gorski (D) for Barton (27); 19 Warren Stevens for Makin (47); 17 Craig Makin for Driscoll (44); Makin for Stevens (67).
Tries: Hancock (13), Baynes (27), Maloney (35), Littler (43); **Goals:** Holroyd 4.
Sent off: Littler (52) - tripping; Goulding (60) - fighting; Holroyd (80) - tripping.
Sin bin: Alker (33) - fighting.
WILDCATS: 2 Neil Law; 5 Waisale Sovatabua; 4 Justin Brooker; 19 Gareth Ellis; 20 Ben Westwood; 6 Martin Pearson; 7 Brad Davis; 16 Julian O'Neill; 9 David March; 10 Frank Watene; 11 Jamie Field; 12 Willie Poching (C); 15 Ryan Hudson. Subs: 8 Paul Jackson for Watene (41); 18 Ben Rauter for Poching (72); 17 Graham Law for N Law (62); 13 Gary Price for Hudson (43).
Tries: Ellis (16), Poching (40), N Law (47, 61), D March (80); **Goals:** Pearson 5, Davis.
Sent off: Brooker (60) - fighting.
Sin bin: Pearson (33) - fighting.
League Express Men of the Match:
City Reds: Michael Hancock; *Wildcats:* Neil Law.
Penalty count: 13-8; **Half-time:** 18-14;
Referee: Russell Smith (Castleford); **Attendance:** 4,264.

CASTLEFORD TIGERS 28 WARRINGTON WOLVES 31

TIGERS: 2 Jon Wells; 20 Waine Pryce; 3 Michael Eagar; 18 Jonathan Roper; 5 Darren Rogers; 7 Mitch Healey; 22 Mark Lennon; 17 Andy Lynch; 15 Darren Shaw; 10 Dean Sampson; 23 Michael Smith; 12 Dale Fritz; 13 Adrian Vowles (C). Subs: 25 David Bates for Lynch (23); 28 Gary Smith not used; 19 Chris Charles for Fritz (57); 26 Wayne Godwin for Shaw (32); Shaw for Sampson (54); Sampson for Shaw (65).
Tries: Pryce (11, 49), Eagar (38), Godwin (42), Roper (80); **Goals:** Lennon 4.
WOLVES: 22 Alan Hunte; 36 Alan Reddicliffe (D); 34 Kevin Crouthers; 4 Toa Kohe-Love; 31 Steve Thomas; 6 Lee Briers; 27 Gary Hulse; 18 Martin Masella; 23 Mark Gleeson; 10 Danny Nutley; 12 Jerome Guisset; 24 Paul Noone; 13 Tawera Nikau (C). Subs: 37 John Hill (D) for Masella (30); 38 Ian Parry (D) for Hill (59); 26 Jon Clarke for Guisset (32); 39 Kris Tickle (D) for Thomas (50); Masella for Noone (48); Hill for Masella (71).
Tries: Gleeson (16, 71), Clarke (35), Hunte (60), Masella (64); **Goals:** Briers 5; **Field goal:** Briers.
Sin bin: Clarke (67) - obstruction.
League Express Men of the Match:
Tigers: Michael Smith; *Wolves:* Lee Briers.
Penalty count: 7-6; **Half-time:** 8-14;
Referee: Peter Taberner (Wigan); **Attendance:** 6,019.

HALIFAX BLUE SOX 16 HULL FC 20

BLUE SOX: 1 Daryl Cardiss; 19 Oliver Marns; 4 Adam Hughes; 18 Stuart Donlan; 3 Damian Gibson; 7 Gavin Clinch; 17 Sean Penkywicz; 8 Andy Hobson; 9 Johnny Lawless; 23 Brett Goldspink (C); 15 Paul Davidson; 10 Jim Gannon; 12 Shayne McMenemy. Subs: 2 Jamie Bloem for Goldspink (24); 14 Danny Tickle for Marns (41); 16 Jamie Thackray for Hobson (24); 22 Ryan Clayton not used; Goldspink for Thackray (67); Hobson for Tickle (67).
Tries: Hughes (12, 49), Lawless (63); Clinch 2.
HULL: 5 Matt Crowther; 21 Gareth Raynor; 3 David Maiden; 4 Deon Bird; 17 Craig Poucher; 16 Paul Cooke; 22 Andy Last; 8 Paul Broadbent; 9 Lee Jackson; 10 Luke Felsch; 11 Adam Maher; 19 Richard Fletcher; 12 Tony Grimaldi (C). Subs: 23 Logan Campbell for Maher (53); 24 Craig Farrell not used; 26 Paul Parker for Poucher (44); 27 Michael Docherty for Broadbent (30); Broadbent for Grimaldi (58).
Tries: Crowther (9), Cooke (51), Raynor (70);
Goals: Crowther 4.
Sin bin: Felsch (46) - leading with forearm.
League Express Men of the Match:
Blue Sox: Johnny Lawless; *Hull:* Paul Cooke.
Penalty count: 9-12; **Half-time:** 8-8;
Referee: Steve Ganson (St Helens); **Attendance:** 4,593.

PLAY-OFFS

Friday 21st September 2001

QUALIFYING PLAY-OFF

WIGAN WARRIORS 27 HULL FC 24

WARRIORS: 1 Kris Radlinski; 5 Brian Carney; 4 Gary Connolly; 3 Steve Renouf; 23 David Hodgson; 6 Matthew Johns; 7 Adrian Lam; 8 Terry O'Connor; 9 Terry Newton; 20 Harvey Howard; 11 Mick Cassidy; 14 David Furner; 13 Andy Farrell (C). Subs: 10 Neil Cowie for Howard (28); 12 Denis Betts for Cassidy (30); 29 Stephen Wild for O'Connor (77); 24 Martin Aspinwall not used; Howard for O'Connor (58); O'Connor for Cowie (71); Cassidy for Howard (76).
Tries: Farrell (13), Carney (19), Radlinski (38), Betts (65); **Goals:** Farrell 5; **Field goal:** Farrell.
On report: Cowie (58) - high tackle.
HULL: 1 Steve Prescott; 21 Gareth Raynor; 6 Richard Horne; 3 David Maiden; 5 Matt Crowther; 16 Paul Cooke;

7 Tony Smith; 8 Paul Broadbent; 15 Paul King; 10 Luke Felsch; 11 Adam Maher; 12 Tony Grimaldi (C); 13 Jason Smith. Subs: 9 Lee Jackson for King (14BB, rev 21); 4 Deon Bird for T Smith (41); 28 Scott Logan for Broadbent (21); 23 Logan Campbell for J Smith (44); Jackson for King (50BB, rev 67); Broadbent for Felsch (59); Jackson for Logan (67).
Tries: Cooke (3), Maiden (34), Felsch (56), Jackson (70); **Goals:** Crowther 4.
On report: Logan (48) - high tackle.
League Express Men of the Match:
Warriors: Terry Newton; *Hull:* Tony Grimaldi.
Penalty count: 10-7; **Half-time:** 18-12;
Referee: Russell Smith (Castleford); **Attendance:** 9,103.

Saturday 22nd September 2001

ELIMINATION PLAY-OFF

ST HELENS 38 LEEDS RHINOS 30

SAINTS: 1 Paul Wellens; 17 Steve Hall; 3 Kevin Iro; 2 Sean Hoppe; 19 Anthony Stewart; 13 Paul Sculthorpe; 20 Tommy Martyn; 16 Vila Matautia; 24 Mick Higham; 18 John Stankevitch; 11 Chris Joynt (C); 8 Peter Shiels; 9 Keiron Cunningham. Subs: 25 Mark Edmondson for Shiels (55); 15 Tim Jonkers for Matautia (19BB, rev 32); 30 John Kirkpatrick for Wellens (76); 22 Heath Cruckshank for Higham (25); Jonkers for Cruckshank (53); Shiels for Matautia (61BB, rev 77); Cruckshank for Stankevitch (71).
Tries: Hall (12, 70), Matautia (18, 33), Cunningham (30, 42), Iro (47); **Goals:** Sculthorpe 5.
Sin bin: Matautia (44) - fighting.
RHINOS: 5 Francis Cummins (C); 15 Chev Walker; 3 Tonie Carroll; 4 Keith Senior; 16 Mark Calderwood; 13 Kevin Sinfield; 29 Robert Burrow; 8 Darren Fleary; 23 Matthew Diskin; 10 Barrie McDermott; 17 Anthony Farrell; 31 Gary Mercer; 11 Andy Hay. Subs: 18 Danny Ward for McDermott (33); 14 Marcus St Hilaire for

Wigan's Mick Cassidy on the charge during the Warriors' Qualifying Play-Off victory over Hull

Carroll (66); 22 David Wrench for Hay (58); 20 Jamie Mathiou for Fleary (50); McDermott for Ward (56).
Tries: Burrow (6), Cummins (24), Diskin (37), Calderwood (57), Senior (79); **Goals:** Burrow 5.
Sin bin: Mercer (44) - fighting.
On report: Mercer (44) - spear tackle.
League Express Men of the Match:
Saints: Keiron Cunningham; *Rhinos:* Robert Burrow.
Penalty count: 11-8; **Half-time:** 20-18;
Referee: Stuart Cummings (Widnes); **Attendance:** 8,467.

Friday 28th September 2001

ELIMINATION SEMI-FINAL

HULL FC 20 ST HELENS 24

HULL: 1 Steve Prescott; 21 Gareth Raynor; 4 Deon Bird; 23 Logan Campbell; 5 Matt Crowther; 16 Paul Cooke; 6 Richard Horne; 8 Paul Broadbent; 15 Paul King; 10 Luke Felsch; 11 Adam Maher; 28 Scott Logan; 12 Tony Grimaldi (C). Subs: 18 Steve Craven for Broadbent (30); 19 Richard Fletcher for Maher (53); 9 Lee Jackson for King (40); 26 Paul Parker not used; King for Craven (68); Broadbent for Felsch (74).
Tries: Raynor (23, 61), Grimaldi (57), Bird (68);
Goals: Crowther 2.
On report: Logan (26) - high tackle.
SAINTS: 1 Paul Wellens; 17 Steve Hall; 3 Kevin Iro; 2 Sean Hoppe; 19 Anthony Stewart; 13 Paul Sculthorpe; 20 Tommy Martyn; 8 Peter Shiels; 9 Keiron Cunningham; 16 Vila Matautia; 11 Chris Joynt (C); 18 John Stankevitch; 15 Tim Jonkers. Subs: 25 Mark Edmondson for Cruckshank (57); 10 David Fairleigh for Matautia (18); 30 John Kirkpatrick for Stewart (14BB, rev 29); 22 Heath Cruckshank for Fairleigh (35); Kirkpatrick for Hall (29); Matautia for Cruckshank (68).
Tries: Kirkpatrick (16), Sculthorpe (29), Cunningham (43), Stankevitch (50), Martyn (76); **Goals:** Sculthorpe 2.
League Express Men of the Match:

244

Hull: Richard Horne; *Saints:* Paul Sculthorpe.
Penalty count: 6-4; **Half-time:** 6-10;
Referee: Robert Connolly (Wigan); **Attendance:** 9,186.
Sunday 30th September 2001

QUALIFYING SEMI-FINAL

BRADFORD BULLS 24 WIGAN WARRIORS 18

BULLS: 5 Michael Withers; 2 Tevita Vaikona; 20 Scott
Naylor; 23 Graham Mackay; 3 Leon Pryce; 6 Henry Paul;
1 Robbie Paul (C); 8 Joe Vagana; 9 James Lowes; 22
Brian McDermott; 11 Daniel Gartner; 19 Jamie Peacock;
12 Mike Forshaw. Subs: 15 Shane Rigon for Gartner
(54BB); 29 Stuart Fielden for Vagana (25); 10 Paul
Anderson for McDermott (25); 7 Paul Deacon for R Paul
(63); Vagana for Anderson (59); McDermott for Fielden
(70).
Tries: R Paul (12, 30); **Goals:** H Paul 8.
WARRIORS: 1 Kris Radlinski; 5 Brian Carney; 4 Gary
Connolly; 3 Steve Renouf; 15 Paul Johnson; 6 Matthew
Johns; 7 Adrian Lam; 8 Terry O'Connor; 9 Terry Newton;
20 Harvey Howard; 11 Mick Cassidy; 14 David Furner;
13 Andy Farrell (C). Subs: 10 Neil Cowie for Howard
(34); 19 Chris Chester not used; 23 David Hodgson for
Connolly (4BB, rev 41); 12 Denis Betts for Cassidy
(11BB, rev 56); Hodgson for Connolly (50BB, rev 70);
Howard for O'Connor (56); Betts for Cowie (64);
O'Connor for Howard (73).
Tries: Renouf (25), Radlinski (36), Hodgson (67);
Goals: Farrell 3.
League Express Men of the Match:
Bulls: Henry Paul; *Warriors:* Terry O'Connor.
Penalty count: 14-11; **Half-time:** 16-10;
Referee: Russell Smith (Castleford); **Attendance:** 13,216.

Saturday 6th October 2001

FINAL ELIMINATOR

WIGAN WARRIORS 44 ST HELENS 10

WARRIORS: 1 Kris Radlinski; 2 Brett Dallas; 3 Steve
Renouf; 4 Gary Connolly; 5 Brian Carney; 6 Matthew
Johns; 7 Adrian Lam; 8 Terry O'Connor; 9 Terry Newton;
20 Harvey Howard; 11 Mick Cassidy; 14 David Furner;
13 Andy Farrell (C). Subs: 10 Neil Cowie for Howard
(24); 15 Paul Johnson for Dallas (30); 19 Chris Chester
for Furner (72); 12 Denis Betts for O'Connor (36);
O'Connor for Cassidy (65); Howard for Cowie (70).
Tries: Lam (10, 46), Radlinski (28), Newton (32), Johns
(49), Carney (57, 68); **Goals:** Farrell 8.
SAINTS: 1 Paul Wellens; 17 Steve Hall; 2 Sean Hoppe; 3
Kevin Iro; 19 Anthony Stewart; 13 Paul Sculthorpe; 20
Tommy Martyn; 10 David Fairleigh; 9 Keiron
Cunningham; 16 Vila Matautia; 8 Peter Shiels; 18 John
Stankevitch; 11 Chris Joynt (C). Subs: 25 Mark
Edmondson for Martyn (70); 15 Tim Jonkers for Matautia
(17); 24 Mick Higham for Cunningham (5BB, rev 9); 22
Heath Cruckshank for Stankevitch (48); Matautia for
Fairleigh (52); Higham for Joynt (64); Fairleigh for
Matautia (65BB); Matautia for Cruckshank (76).
Tries: Iro (18), Sculthorpe (53); **Goal:** Sculthorpe.
League Express Men of the Match:

Robbie Paul looks for a gap in the Wigan
defence as Bradford seal the Super League
Championship with a 37-6 Grand Final win

Warriors: Terry Newton; *Saints:* Paul Sculthorpe.
Penalty count: 9-8; **Half-time:** 20-6; **Referee:** Stuart
Cummings (Widnes); **Attendance:** 19,260.
Saturday 13th October 2001

GRAND FINAL

BRADFORD BULLS 37 WIGAN WARRIORS 6

BULLS: 5 Michael Withers; 2 Tevita Vaikona; 20 Scott
Naylor; 23 Graham Mackay; 3 Leon Pryce; 6 Henry Paul;
1 Robbie Paul (C); 8 Joe Vagana; 9 James Lowes; 22
Brian McDermott; 11 Daniel Gartner; 19 Jamie Peacock;
12 Mike Forshaw. Subs: 29 Stuart Fielden for
McDermott (21BB, rev 65); 10 Paul Anderson for
Vagana (22); 15 Shane Rigon for Pryce (40); 7 Paul
Deacon for R Paul (69); Vagana for Anderson (53);
Fielden for Gartner (72); Anderson for Vagana (74).
Tries: Lowes (9), Withers (11, 27, 31), Fielden (65),
Mackay (72); **Goals:** H Paul 5, Mackay;
Field goal: H Paul.
WARRIORS: 1 Kris Radlinski; 2 Brett Dallas; 4 Gary
Connolly; 5 Steve Renouf; 5 Brian Carney; 6 Matthew
Johns; 7 Adrian Lam; 8 Terry O'Connor; 9 Terry Newton;
20 Harvey Howard; 11 Mick Cassidy; 14 David Furner;
13 Andy Farrell (C). Subs: 15 Paul Johnson for Carney
(12BB); 10 Neil Cowie for Howard (17); 12 Denis Betts
for O'Connor (32); 19 Chris Chester for Farrell (59);
O'Connor for Cowie (55); Howard for Newton (64);
Cowie for Cassidy (72).
Try: Lam (63); **Goal:** Furner.
League Express Men of the Match:
Bulls: Michael Withers; *Warriors:* Adrian Lam.

Anthony Stewart under pressure from Harvey Howard as St Helens' two-year Super
League title reign comes to an end with a Final Eliminator loss to Wigan

245

SUPER LEAGUE VI
Opta Index Analysis

SUPER LEAGUE VI TOP PERFORMERS *(BY CATEGORY)*

TACKLES
Malcolm Alker	Salford City Reds	..1050
Tony Grimaldi	Hull FC	887
Steele Retchless	London Broncos	837
David Atkins	Huddersfield Giants	..824
Danny Nutley	Warrington Wolves	..726
Johnny Lawless	Halifax Blue Sox	712
Shane Millard	London Broncos	701
James Lowes	Bradford Bulls	695
Ryan Hudson	Wakefield Wildcats	..673
Shayne McMenemy	Halifax Blue Sox	671

TACKLES MADE *(% Success)*
Paul March	Wakefield Wildcats	..97.2
Sonny Nickle	St Helens	......96.8
Andy Lynch	Castleford Tigers	..96.7
Robert Mears	Leeds Rhinos	..........96.6
David March	Wakefield Wildcats	96.4
Scott Cram	London Broncos	....96.3
Luke Felsch	Hull FC	....................96.1
Lee Radford	Bradford Bulls	........96.1
Terry O'Connor	Wigan Warriors	....95.9
Robert Burrow	Leeds Rhinos	..........95.8

CARRIES
Andy Farrell	Wigan Warriors	492
Michael Smith	Castleford Tigers	445
Jim Gannon	Halifax Blue Sox	431
Paul Sculthorpe	St Helens	429
Terry O'Connor	Wigan Warriors	427
Shane Millard	London Broncos	423
Paul Wellens	St Helens	422
Justin Dooley	London Broncos	417
David Fairleigh	St Helens	408
Nigel Roy	London Broncos	400

METRES MADE
Andy Farrell	Wigan Warriors	3811
Terry O'Connor	Wigan Warriors	3689
Tevita Vaikona	Bradford Bulls	3587
Michael Smith	Castleford Tigers	..3578
David Fairleigh	St Helens	3344
Nigel Roy	London Broncos	3263
Keiron Cunningham	St Helens	3160
Paul Sculthorpe	St Helens	3058
Paul Wellens	St Helens	2980
Jamie Peacock	Bradford Bulls	2965

CLEAN BREAKS
Keith Senior	Leeds Rhinos	42
Michael Withers	Bradford Bulls	42
Robbie Paul	Bradford Bulls	37
Kris Radlinski	Wigan Warriors	37
Tevita Vaikona	Bradford Bulls	36

Andy Farrell	Wigan Warriors	35
Steve Renouf	Wigan Warriors	34
Keiron Cunningham	St Helens	34
Paul Sculthorpe	St Helens	32
Kevin Iro	St Helens	30

OFFLOADS
Michael Hancock	Salford City Reds	86
Mike Forshaw	Bradford Bulls	79
Keiron Cunningham	St Helens	77
Shane Millard	London Broncos	72
Jim Dymock	London Broncos	71
Willie Poching	Wakefield Wildcats	70
Barrie McDermott	Leeds Rhinos	69
Kevin Sinfield	Leeds Rhinos	67
Tevita Vaikona	Bradford Bulls	66
David Furner	Wigan Warriors	65
Terry Newton	Wigan Warriors	65

TACKLE BUSTS
Keiron Cunningham	St Helens	129
Michael Smith	Castleford Tigers	120
Richie Barnett	London Broncos	119
Tevita Vaikona	Bradford Bulls	100
Paul Wellens	St Helens	94
Willie Poching	Wakefield Wildcats	88
Iestyn Harris	Leeds Rhinos	84
Paul Reilly	Huddersfield Giants	..83
Andy Farrell	Wigan Warriors	80
Keith Senior	Leeds Rhinos	76
Waisale Sovatabua	Wakefield Wildcats	76

40/20s
Dennis Moran	London Broncos	9
Mitch Healey	Castleford Tigers	8
Lee Briers	Warrington Wolves	8
Bobbie Goulding	Salford City Reds	8
Graham Holroyd	Salford City Reds	7
Paul Sculthorpe	St Helens	6
Jason Smith	Hull FC	5
Ben Kusto	Huddersfield Giants	5

Tommy Martyn	St Helens	5
Iestyn Harris	Leeds Rhinos	4
Adrian Lam	Wigan Warriors	4
Steve McNamara	Huddersfield Giants	4
Gavin Clinch	Halifax Blue Sox	4

MARKER TACKLES
Tony Grimaldi	Hull FC	121
Malcolm Alker	Salford City Reds	106
Danny Nutley	Warrington Wolves	..103
David Atkins	Huddersfield Giants	..96
Mick Cassidy	Wigan Warriors	89
Steele Retchless	London Broncos	86
Nathan Sykes	Castleford Tigers	84
Shayne McMenemy	Halifax Blue Sox	79
Tim Jonkers	St Helens	79
Mike Wainwright	Salford City Reds	78

TRY ASSISTS
Adrian Lam	Wigan Warriors	21
Andy Farrell	Wigan Warriors	19
Gavin Clinch	Halifax Blue Sox	18
Kevin Sinfield	Leeds Rhinos	15
Brad Davis	Wakefield Wildcats	15
Dennis Moran	London Broncos	15
Jason Smith	Hull FC	14
Allan Langer	Warrington Wolves	13
Henry Paul	Bradford Bulls	12
Paul Sculthorpe	St Helens	11
Bobbie Goulding	Salford City Reds	11
Lee Briers	Warrington Wolves	11
Michael Withers	Bradford Bulls	11

GOALS KICKED *(% Accuracy)*
Andy Farrell	Wigan Warriors	......84.7
Henry Paul	Bradford Bulls	......83.7
Iestyn Harris	Leeds Rhinos	..........80.9
Lee Briers	Warrington Wolves	..80.0
Tony Martin	London Broncos	....78.1
Danny Tickle	Halifax Blue Sox	....76.3
Steve McNamara	Huddersfield Giants	76.1
Jamie Bloem	Halifax Blue Sox	....75.9
Paul Sculthorpe	St Helens	................75.5
Steve Prescott	Hull FC	....................74.6

AVERAGE GAIN PER CARRY
Leon Pryce	Bradford Bulls	........11.4
Mick Higham	St Helens	................10.7
Michael Withers	Bradford Bulls	........10.0
Paul Newlove	St Helens	....................9.9
Lee Gilmour	Bradford Bulls	..........9.9
Brett Dallas	Wigan Warriors	........9.9
Chris Langley	Huddersfield Giants	..9.6
Nathan McAvoy	Bradford Bulls	..........9.5
Keith Senior	Leeds Rhinos	..........9.5
Tevita Vaikona	Bradford Bulls	..........9.5

Stuart Fielden dives over to score against Wigan in the Grand Final. The Bulls scored more tries in Super League VI than any other team

SUPER LEAGUE VI AVERAGES PER MATCH

TACKLES		MISSED TACKLES		CARRIES		METRES	
London Broncos	276	Castleford Tigers	34	Wigan Warriors	177	Bradford Bulls	1482
Huddersfield Giants	252	Halifax Blue Sox	30	Bradford Bulls	176	Wigan Warriors	1393
Hull FC	247	Wakefield Wildcats	28	St Helens	168	St Helens	1270
Wakefield Wildcats	245	London Broncos	28	Hull FC	168	Leeds Rhinos	1212
Salford City Reds	243	Salford City Reds	28	London Broncos	167	Hull FC	1195
Wigan Warriors	237	Huddersfield Giants	25	Castleford Tigers	164	London Broncos	1186
Leeds Rhinos	237	Warrington Wolves	25	Wakefield Wildcats	161	Castleford Tigers	1174
Halifax Blue Sox	237	Hull FC	23	Leeds Rhinos	160	Wakefield Wildcats	1147
Bradford Bulls	234	St Helens	23	Salford City Reds	159	Salford City Reds	1128
St Helens	234	Leeds Rhinos	22	Warrington Wolves	156	Huddersfield Giants	1104
Warrington Wolves	233	Wigan Warriors	21	Huddersfield Giants	153	Halifax Blue Sox	1100
Castleford Tigers	230	Bradford Bulls	18	Halifax Blue Sox	152	Warrington Wolves	1092

CLEAN BREAKS		OFFLOADS		TACKLE BUSTS		DUMMY HALF RUNS	
Bradford Bulls	13	St Helens	22	Bradford Bulls	32	St Helens	31
Wigan Warriors	12	Bradford Bulls	21	St Helens	32	Salford City Reds	24
St Helens	11	Wigan Warriors	18	Wigan Warriors	28	Wakefield Wildcats	24
Hull FC	9	London Broncos	17	Leeds Rhinos	28	Halifax Blue Sox	23
Leeds Rhinos	9	Salford City Reds	17	Castleford Tigers	24	Wigan Warriors	21
London Broncos	8	Hull FC	15	Huddersfield Giants	24	Huddersfield Giants	21
Castleford Tigers	8	Castleford Tigers	15	Hull FC	23	Hull FC	19
Warrington Wolves	7	Halifax Blue Sox	15	London Broncos	23	London Broncos	19
Salford City Reds	7	Leeds Rhinos	14	Wakefield Wildcats	23	Bradford Bulls	17
Wakefield Wildcats	7	Wakefield Wildcats	14	Halifax Blue Sox	21	Leeds Rhinos	16
Huddersfield Giants	7	Huddersfield Giants	12	Warrington Wolves	20	Warrington Wolves	14
Halifax Blue Sox	6	Warrington Wolves	10	Salford City Reds	20	Castleford Tigers	12

SUPER LEAGUE VI TRIES SCORED/CONCEDED

TOTAL TRIES SCORED		TOTAL TRIES CONCEDED		TRIES SCORED (KICKS)		TRIES CONCEDED (KICKS)	
Bradford Bulls	183	Huddersfield Giants	163	Halifax Blue Sox	22	St Helens	27
St Helens	166	Salford City Reds	161	Wigan Warriors	21	Huddersfield Giants	23
Wigan Warriors	163	Warrington Wolves	143	Salford City Reds	21	Warrington Wolves	20
Leeds Rhinos	134	Wakefield Wildcats	141	Hull FC	19	Salford City Reds	17
Hull FC	134	Halifax Blue Sox	140	Huddersfield Giants	19	Leeds Rhinos	17
Warrington Wolves	115	Castleford Tigers	131	Warrington Wolves	17	Halifax Blue Sox	16
London Broncos	107	St Helens	125	Leeds Rhinos	16	Wakefield Wildcats	15
Halifax Blue Sox	105	Leeds Rhinos	122	Wakefield Wildcats	16	Wigan Warriors	15
Huddersfield Giants	103	Hull FC	109	London Broncos	15	London Broncos	14
Salford City Reds	100	London Broncos	102	Castleford Tigers	13	Castleford Tigers	13
Castleford Tigers	100	Wigan Warriors	82	Bradford Bulls	9	Hull FC	11
Wakefield Wildcats	87	Bradford Bulls	78	St Helens	9	Bradford Bulls	9

BRADFORD BULLS

TEAM TOTALS
Tackles	6090
Misses	511
Carries	4940
Metres	41498
Clean Breaks	366
Offloads	599
Handling Errors	362
Penalties conceded	194
Tackle busts	906
Runs from dummy half	472
40/20s	3
Try Savers	17

TACKLES
James Lowes	695
Mike Forshaw	559
Henry Paul	530
Jamie Peacock	500
Stuart Fielden	469

CARRIES
Tevita Vaikona	377
Jamie Peacock	360
Brian McDermott	358
Stuart Fielden	340
Mike Forshaw	321

METRES
Tevita Vaikona	3587
Jamie Peacock	2965
Stuart Fielden	2892
Michael Withers	2818
Paul Anderson	2668

CLEAN BREAKS
Michael Withers	42
Robbie Paul	37
Tevita Vaikona	36
Leon Pryce	27
Henry Paul	25

OFFLOADS
Mike Forshaw	79
Tevita Vaikona	66
Jamie Peacock	58
Joe Vagana	39
Henry Paul	38
Robbie Paul	38

TACKLE BUSTS
Tevita Vaikona	100
Leon Pryce	74
Michael Withers	68
Robbie Paul	67
Henry Paul	65

MARKER TACKLES
James Lowes	71
Henry Paul	50
Jamie Peacock	49
Stuart Fielden	48
Brian McDermott	45
Robbie Paul	45

AVERAGE SEASON INDEX
Tevita Vaikona	920
Michael Withers	850
Henry Paul	792
Jamie Peacock	774
Mike Forshaw	710

TRY ASSISTS
Henry Paul	12
Michael Withers	11
Robbie Paul	9
Paul Deacon	8
Daniel Gartner	5
Graham Mackay	5
Mike Forshaw	5

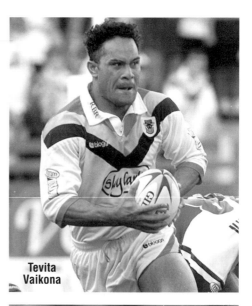

Tevita Vaikona

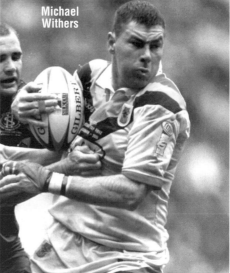

Michael Withers

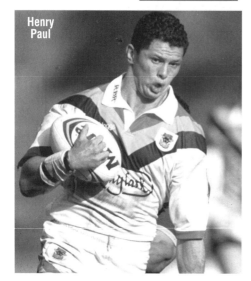

Henry Paul

TOP 5 OPTA INDEX PERFORMERS
	Vaikona	Withers	H Paul	Peacock	Forshaw
Matches	25	24	27	24	24
Tackles	64	208	530	500	559
Misses	12	21	53	31	37
Carries	377	283	310	360	321
Metres	3587	2818	2207	2965	2105
Clean Breaks	36	42	25	14	16
Offloads	66	30	38	58	79
Tackle Busts	100	68	65	54	60
Opta Index	23004	20406	21374	18570	17050

CASTLEFORD TIGERS

TEAM TOTALS
Tackles............................6212
Misses 944
Carries 4581
Metres 32866
Clean Breaks 217
Offloads 424
Handling Errors 352
Penalties conceded 177
Tackle busts....................666
Runs from dummy half ..349
40/20s 12
Try Savers 17

TACKLES
Darren Shaw 619
Nathan Sykes.................604
Dale Fritz 585
Dean Sampson 545
Lee Harland 423

CARRIES
Michael Smith 445
Dean Sampson 318
Dale Fritz 293
Nathan Sykes.................282
Jon Wells........................264

METRES
Michael Smith 3578
Dale Fritz 2461
Dean Sampson 2262
Jon Wells......................2059
Nathan Sykes...............1878

CLEAN BREAKS
Danny Orr 20
Michael Smith 19
Mark Lennon 17
Darren Rogers 16
Michael Eagar 15

OFFLOADS
Dean Sampson 61
Michael Smith 60
Danny Orr 39
Lee Harland 37
Dale Fritz 24

TACKLE BUSTS
Michael Smith 120
Danny Orr 51
Lee Harland 49
Dale Fritz 43
Mark Lennon 43

MARKER TACKLES
Nathan Sykes...................84
Dale Fritz 62
Dean Sampson 59
Darren Shaw 54
Lee Harland 44

AVERAGE SEASON INDEX
Michael Smith 859
Danny Orr 740
Dean Sampson 669
Nathan Sykes.................604
Dale Fritz 561

TRY ASSISTS
Danny Orr 9
Adrian Vowles 7
Mitch Healey 5
Mark Lennon 5
Jonathan Roper 4

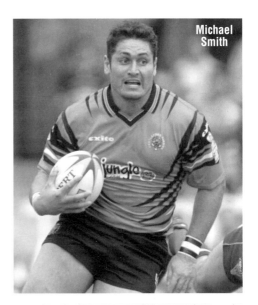

Michael Smith

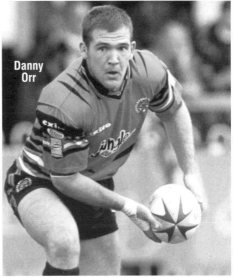

Danny Orr

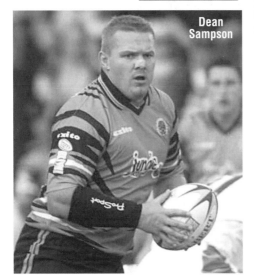

Dean Sampson

TOP 5 OPTA INDEX PERFORMERS

	M Smith	Orr	Sampson	Sykes	Fritz
Matches	26	18	23	21	27
Tackles	385	299	545	604	585
Misses	21	51	50	41	97
Carries	445	166	318	282	293
Metres	3578	1129	2262	1878	2461
Clean Breaks	19	20	8	3	13
Offloads	60	39	61	16	24
Tackle Busts	120	51	35	25	43
Opta Index	22346	13328	15384	12676	14580

249

HALIFAX BLUE SOX

TEAM TOTALS
Tackles..........................6627
Misses 848
Carries 4267
Metres 30812
Clean Breaks 166
Offloads 410
Handling Errors 297
Penalties conceded 242
Tackle busts 592
Runs from dummy half ..649
40/20s 7
Try Savers 18

TACKLES
Johnny Lawless..............712
Shayne McMenemy 671
Jim Gannon 625
Gavin Clinch 449
Danny Tickle 415

CARRIES
Jim Gannon 431
Brett Goldspink 342
Shayne McMenemy 335
Oliver Marns 279
Paul Davidson 275

METRES
Jim Gannon 2847
Brett Goldspink 2707
Shayne McMenemy 2523
Paul Davidson 2361
Damian Gibson 2078

CLEAN BREAKS
Daryl Cardiss....................17
Oliver Marns 16
Damian Gibson 14
Paul Davidson 13
Stuart Donlan 13

OFFLOADS
Brett Goldspink 58
Jim Gannon 52
Shayne McMenemy 44
Paul Davidson 41
Andrew Dunemann 33

TACKLE BUSTS
Daryl Cardiss...................67
Shayne McMenemy 59
Damian Gibson 55
Oliver Marns 48
Jamie Bloem 48

MARKER TACKLES
Shayne McMenemy 79
Danny Tickle 62
Johnny Lawless...............61
Stuart Donlan 60
Jamie Bloem 59

AVERAGE SEASON INDEX
Andrew Dunemann 765
Shane McMenemy..........744
Jim Gannon 616
Daryl Cardiss.................578
Damian Gibson 566

TRY ASSISTS
Gavin Clinch 18
Andrew Dunemann 7
Shayne McMenemy 6
Martin Moana 4
Johnny Lawless.................3

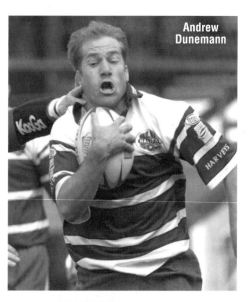

Andrew
Dunemann

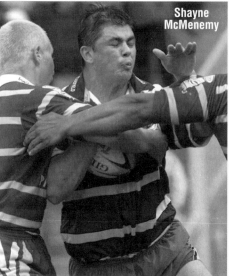

Shayne
McMenemy

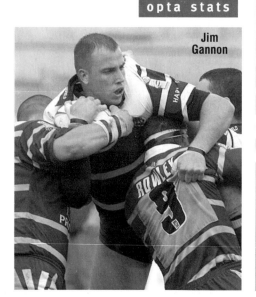

Jim
Gannon

TOP 5 OPTA INDEX PERFORMERS

	Dunemann	McMenemy	Gannon	Cardiss	Gibson
Matches	15	26	26	23	27
Tackles	284	671	625	178	278
Misses	19	30	78	33	37
Carries	161	335	431	224	255
Metres	936	2523	2847	1637	2078
Clean Breaks	9	11	2	17	14
Offloads	33	44	52	5	18
Tackle Busts	19	59	14	67	55
Opta Index	10712	19356	16014	13294	15276

HUDDERSFIELD GIANTS

TEAM TOTALS
Tackles...........................6804
Misses 687
Carries 4288
Metres 30925
Clean Breaks 184
Offloads 331
Handling Errors 315
Penalties conceded 241
Tackle busts...................667
Runs from dummy half ..593
40/20s 13
Try Savers 31

TACKLES
David Atkins 824
Steve McNamara 598
Paul Rowley....................586
Richard Marshall 582
David Lomax 581

CARRIES
Brandon Costin 326
David Atkins 322
Andrew Frew 287
Martin Gleeson 266
David Lomax 257

METRES
Andrew Frew 2377
David Atkins 2300
Brandon Costin 2178
Paul Reilly 1944
Martin Gleeson 1826

CLEAN BREAKS
Brandon Costin 20
Andrew Frew 18
Ben Kusto 15
Stanley Gene 15
Paul Reilly 14

OFFLOADS
David Lomax 31
Stanley Gene 31
Brandon Costin 25
Steve McNamara 24
Chris Thorman.................23

TACKLE BUSTS
Paul Reilly 83
Andrew Frew 65
Martin Gleeson 61
Stanley Gene 60
Brandon Costin 45

MARKER TACKLES
David Atkins 96
Richard Marshall 66
David Lomax 65
Steve McNamara 64
Brandon Costin 63

AVERAGE SEASON INDEX
Paul Reilly 902
Brandon Costin 728
David Atkins 646
Stanley Gene 625
Andrew Frew 575

TRY ASSISTS
Steve McNamara 7
Ben Kusto 6
Brandon Costin 6
Stanley Gene 5
Andrew Frew 4
Chris Thorman...................4

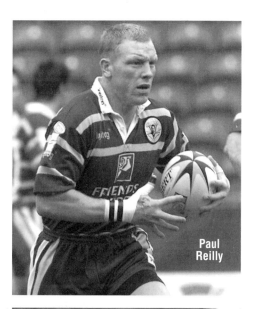

Paul
Reilly

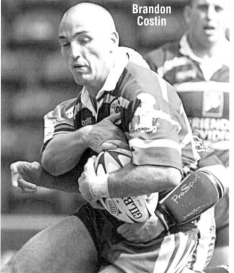

Brandon
Costin

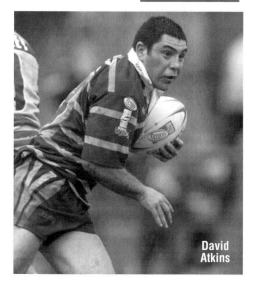

David
Atkins

TOP 5 OPTA INDEX PERFORMERS

	Reilly	Costin	Atkins	Gene	Frew
Matches	14	25	27	13	26
Tackles	85	538	824	180	113
Misses	19	51	68	27	20
Carries	222	326	322	196	287
Metres	1944	2178	2300	1440	2377
Clean Breaks	14	20	12	15	18
Offloads	13	25	20	31	13
Tackle Busts	83	45	26	60	65
Opta Index	12628	18206	16806	11390	14944

251

HULL F C

HULL F.C.

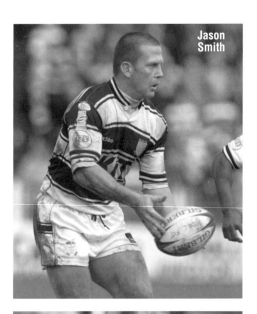

Jason Smith

TEAM TOTALS
Tackles...........................6413
Misses...........................744
Carries.........................4703
Metres 33456
Clean Breaks 255
Offloads 419
Handling Errors 371
Penalties conceded 182
Tackle busts...................631
Runs from dummy half ..541
40/20s 7
Try Savers 19

TACKLES
Tony Grimaldi 887
Luke Felsch 547
Jason Smith 509
Steve Craven 484
Paul Cooke 470

CARRIES
Steve Craven 371
Jason Smith 369
Luke Felsch 341
Deon Bird 299
Steve Prescott 293

METRES
Steve Craven 2809
Jason Smith 2426
Deon Bird 2381
Luke Felsch 2283
Paul Broadbent 2129

CLEAN BREAKS
Deon Bird 27
Steve Prescott 26
Tony Smith 25
Richard Horne 24
Tony Grimaldi 16
Gareth Raynor 16

OFFLOADS
Jason Smith 47
Gareth Raynor 35
Paul Broadbent 35
Tony Grimaldi 29
Deon Bird 29

TACKLE BUSTS
Steve Prescott 68
Richard Horne 59
Gareth Raynor 57
Jason Smith 51
Deon Bird 47

MARKER TACKLES
Tony Grimaldi 121
Paul Cooke 57
Logan Campbell..............54
Luke Felsch 51
Jason Smith 46

AVERAGE SEASON INDEX
Jason Smith 809
Tony Smith 664
Tony Grimaldi 657
Deon Bird 648
Steve Prescott 639

TRY ASSISTS
Jason Smith 14
Richard Horne 10
Paul Cooke 9
Tony Smith 8
Tony Grimaldi 4

opta stats

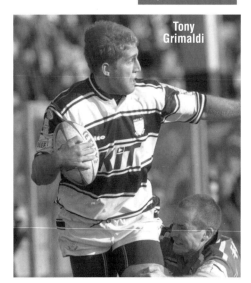

Tony Grimaldi

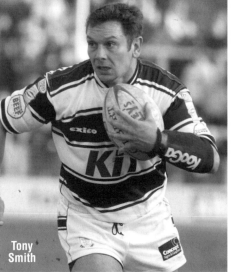

Tony Smith

TOP 5 OPTA INDEX PERFORMERS

	J Smith	T Smith	Grimaldi	Bird	Prescott
Matches	25	23	28	23	23
Tackles	509	239	887	237	148
Misses	39	44	68	57	31
Carries	369	215	275	299	293
Metres	2426	1540	1761	2381	2108
Clean Breaks	12	25	16	27	26
Offloads	47	18	29	29	12
Tackle Busts	51	35	33	47	68
Opta Index	20222	13282	18382	14902	14686

LEEDS RHINOS

TEAM TOTALS
Tackles 6628
Misses 621
Carries 4480
Metres 33930
Clean Breaks 248
Offloads 396
Handling Errors 332
Penalties conceded 204
Tackle busts 778
Runs from dummy half .. 461
40/20s 6
Try Savers 23

TACKLES
Robert Mears 658
Kevin Sinfield 641
Darren Fleary 481
Anthony Farrell 430
Andy Hay 418

CARRIES
Barrie McDermott 352
Andy Hay 298
Kevin Sinfield 297
Francis Cummins 274
Darren Fleary 268

METRES
Barrie McDermott 2762
Keith Senior 2484
Andy Hay 2392
Tonie Carroll 2172
Francis Cummins 2096

CLEAN BREAKS
Keith Senior 42
Iestyn Harris 24
Tonie Carroll 19
Chev Walker 19
Andy Hay 17

OFFLOADS
Barrie McDermott 69
Kevin Sinfield 67
Keith Senior 39
Iestyn Harris 34
Anthony Farrell 26

TACKLE BUSTS
Iestyn Harris 84
Keith Senior 76
Chev Walker 67
Robert Mears 59
Karl Pratt 55

MARKER TACKLES
Kevin Sinfield 63
Robert Mears 56
Anthony Farrell 46
Darren Fleary 40
Andy Hay 37
Jamie Mathiou 37

AVERAGE SEASON INDEX
Iestyn Harris 870
Robert Mears 733
Keith Senior 719
Tonie Carroll 685
Kevin Sinfield 673

TRY ASSISTS
Kevin Sinfield 15
Keith Senior 9
Iestyn Harris 9
Robert Burrow 5
Robert Mears 4
Tonie Carroll 4

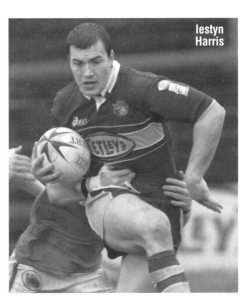

Iestyn Harris

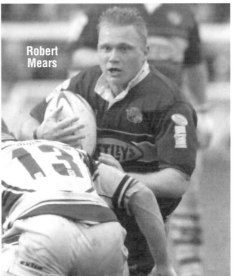

Robert Mears

Keith Senior

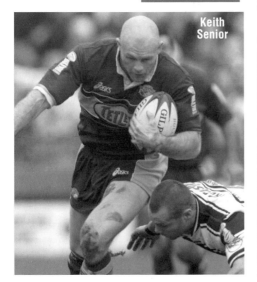

TOP 5 OPTA INDEX PERFORMERS

	Harris	Mears	Senior	Carroll	Sinfield
Matches	18	23	24	23	28
Tackles	252	658	286	292	641
Misses	52	23	27	27	41
Carries	215	179	261	254	297
Metres	1711	1460	2484	2172	1728
Clean Breaks	24	15	42	19	7
Offloads	34	11	39	12	67
Tackle Busts	84	59	76	46	18
Opta Index	15662	16850	17258	15074	18176

LONDON BRONCOS

TEAM TOTALS
Tackles...........................7727
Misses............................783
Carries..........................4662
Metres.........................33219
Clean Breaks 216
Offloads...........................470
Handling Errors 338
Penalties conceded 223
Tackle busts....................646
Runs from dummy half ..544
40/20s 14
Try Savers 21

TACKLES
Steele Retchless 837
Shane Millard 701
Scott Cram 657
Mat Toshack 625
Jim Dymock 565

CARRIES
Shane Millard 423
Justin Dooley...................417
Nigel Roy.........................400
Steele Retchless 343
Jim Dymock 322

METRES
Nigel Roy.......................3263
Shane Millard 2820
Richie Barnett 2806
Justin Dooley................2698
Steele Retchless 2442

CLEAN BREAKS
Richie Barnett 29
Dennis Moran 22
Nigel Roy..........................20
Jim Dymock 15
Greg Fleming 13

OFFLOADS
Shane Millard 72
Jim Dymock 71
Justin Dooley...................56
Nigel Roy..........................38
Richie Barnett 31

TACKLE BUSTS
Richie Barnett 119
Nigel Roy..........................55
Shane Millard 53
Jim Dymock 43
Brett Warton 35

MARKER TACKLES
Steele Retchless 86
Shane Millard 66
Scott Cram 65
Mat Toshack 64
Dennis Moran 60

AVERAGE SEASON INDEX
Richie Barnett 1035
Jim Dymock 775
Shane Millard 756
Nigel Roy.........................730
Dennis Moran 650

TRY ASSISTS
Dennis Moran 15
Jim Dymock 8
Glen Air 4
Shane Millard 4
Rob Parker 2
Justin Dooley.....................2
Richie Barnett 2
Tony Martin 2
Paul Sykes.........................2

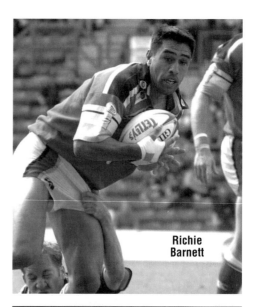

Richie Barnett

Jim Dymock

Shane Millard

TOP 5 OPTA INDEX PERFORMERS

	Barnett	Dymock	Millard	Roy	Moran
Matches	17	26	27	28	27
Tackles	95	565	701	412	496
Misses	23	63	72	25	101
Carries	301	322	423	400	183
Metres	2806	1963	2820	3263	1341
Clean Breaks	29	15	10	20	22
Offloads	31	71	72	38	19
Tackle Busts	119	43	53	55	32
Opta Index	17592	20156	20400	20456	16904

SALFORD CITY REDS

TEAM TOTALS
Tackles...........................6803
Misses.............................778
Carries...........................4439
Metres.........................31590
Clean Breaks..................200
Offloads..........................470
Handling Errors..............313
Penalties conceded........175
Tackle busts.....................570
Runs from dummy half ..679
40/20s................................17
Try Savers..........................21

TACKLES
Malcolm Alker...............1050
Mike Wainwright.............611
Andy Coley......................594
Paul Highton....................526
Damien Driscoll..............423

CARRIES
Andy Coley......................318
Damien Driscoll..............313
Mike Wainwright.............273
Michael Hancock............260
Nick Pinkney...................251

METRES
Andy Coley....................2513
Damien Driscoll............2054
Nick Pinkney.................1976
Stuart Littler..................1904
Michael Hancock...........1885

CLEAN BREAKS
Stuart Littler.....................26
Nick Pinkney....................26
Francis Maloney...............19
Michael Hancock.............14
Martin Offiah...................13

OFFLOADS
Michael Hancock..............86
Andy Coley.......................52
Mike Wainwright..............48
Malcolm Alker..................33
Steve Blakeley.................26

TACKLE BUSTS
Nick Pinkney....................56
Michael Hancock..............52
Andy Coley.......................51
Stuart Littler.....................47
Paul Highton....................40

MARKER TACKLES
Malcolm Alker.................106
Mike Wainwright..............78
Andy Coley.......................53
Paul Highton....................53
Damien Driscoll...............43

AVERAGE SEASON INDEX
Andy Coley......................686
Malcolm Alker.................654
Mike Wainwright.............589
Michael Hancock............578
Gary Broadbent..............569

TRY ASSISTS
Bobbie Goulding...............11
Francis Maloney..................8
Steve Blakeley....................6
Darren Brown......................4
Nick Pinkney.......................4
Graham Holroyd..................4

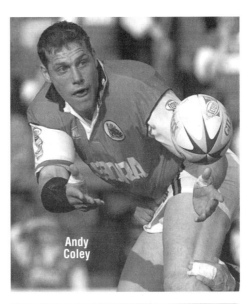

Andy Coley

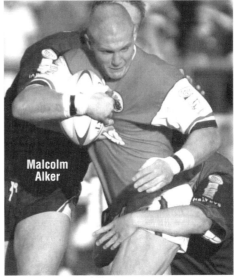

Malcolm Alker

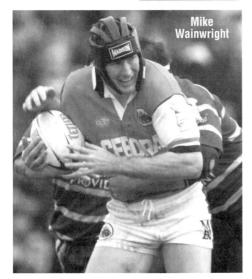

Mike Wainwright

TOP 5 OPTA INDEX PERFORMERS

	Coley	Alker	Wainwright	Hancock	Broadbent
Matches	25	28	24	25	17
Tackles	594	1050	611	470	166
Misses	68	82	60	33	26
Carries	318	211	273	260	237
Metres	2513	1388	1835	1885	1609
Clean Breaks	12	10	6	14	5
Offloads	52	33	48	86	10
Tackle Busts	51	10	22	52	27
Opta Index	17156	18316	14130	13872	9668

ST HELENS

TEAM TOTALS
Tackles	6540
Misses	630
Carries	4692
Metres	35555
Clean Breaks	321
Offloads	604
Handling Errors	378
Penalties conceded	187
Tackle busts	889
Runs from dummy half	856
40/20s	13
Try Savers	20

TACKLES
Tim Jonkers	656
Chris Joynt	640
David Fairleigh	532
Keiron Cunningham	503
Sonny Nickle	488

CARRIES
Paul Sculthorpe	429
Paul Wellens	422
David Fairleigh	408
Keiron Cunningham	366
Sean Hoppe	279

METRES
David Fairleigh	3344
Keiron Cunningham	3160
Paul Sculthorpe	3058
Paul Wellens	2980
Sean Hoppe	2183

CLEAN BREAKS
Keiron Cunningham	34
Paul Sculthorpe	32
Kevin Iro	30
Sean Hoppe	28
Anthony Stewart	21
Paul Newlove	21

OFFLOADS
Keiron Cunningham	77
Peter Shiels	58
David Fairleigh	51
Kevin Iro	40
John Stankevitch	39

TACKLE BUSTS
Keiron Cunningham	129
Paul Wellens	94
David Fairleigh	71
Kevin Iro	70
Paul Sculthorpe	58

MARKER TACKLES
Tim Jonkers	79
Chris Joynt	70
Sonny Nickle	56
Sean Hoppe	53
Paul Sculthorpe	39

AVERAGE SEASON INDEX
Keiron Cunningham	990
Paul Sculthorpe	987
David Fairleigh	826
Paul Wellens	728
Sean Hoppe	658

TRY ASSISTS
Paul Sculthorpe	11
Tommy Martyn	9
Keiron Cunningham	9
John Stankevitch	8
Sean Hoppe	6

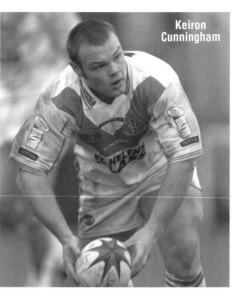

Keiron Cunningham

Paul Sculthorpe

David Fairleigh

TOP 5 OPTA INDEX PERFORMERS
	Cunningham	Sculthorpe	Fairleigh	Wellens	Hoppe
Matches	26	24	25	27	25
Tackles	503	438	532	218	328
Misses	44	42	37	47	38
Carries	366	429	408	422	279
Metres	3260	3058	3344	2980	2183
Clean Breaks	34	32	15	20	28
Offloads	77	37	51	24	14
Tackle Busts	129	58	71	94	47
Opta Index	25730	23686	20658	19650	15782

WAKEFIELD T WILDCATS

TEAM TOTALS
Tackles...........................6847
Misses.............................794
Carries...........................4505
Metres........................32128
Clean Breaks 182
Offloads 390
Handling Errors 303
Penalties conceded 198
Tackle busts....................649
Runs from dummy half ..674
40/20s 5
Try Savers 25

TACKLES
Ryan Hudson..................673
Jamie Field 597
Julian O'Neill 549
Paul Jackson 544
David March 485

CARRIES
Julian O'Neill 382
Waisale Sovatabua..........380
Jamie Field 334
Willie Poching 284
Paul Jackson 278

METRES
Waisale Sovatabua.......2620
Julian O'Neill 2597
Willie Poching 2343
Jamie Field 2183
Paul Jackson 2085

CLEAN BREAKS
Waisale Sovatabua............21
Justin Brooker 20
Neil Law............................14
Ben Westwood..................14
Willie Poching 14

OFFLOADS
Willie Poching 70
Waisale Sovatabua............52
Julian O'Neill 47
Jamie Field 39
David March 22

TACKLE BUSTS
Willie Poching 88
Waisale Sovatabua............76
Justin Brooker 73
Ben Westwood..................48
Paul Jackson 37

MARKER TACKLES
Ryan Hudson....................75
David March 51
Jamie Field 51
Ben Rauter.......................48
Julian O'Neill 47

AVERAGE SEASON INDEX
Waisale Sovatabua..........669
Willie Poching 666
Martyn Holland 658
David March 633
Ryan Hudson...................612

TRY ASSISTS
Brad Davis 15
Dane Dorahy 6
Ryan Hudson......................6
Martin Pearson 5
Willie Poching 4

Waisale Sovatabua

opta stats

Willie Poching

Martyn Holland

TOP 5 OPTA INDEX PERFORMERS

	Sovatabua	Poching	Holland	D March	Hudson
Matches	28	24	15	19	26
Tackles	156	422	132	485	673
Misses	27	66	21	18	58
Carries	380	284	239	147	269
Metres	2620	2343	1702	1037	1862
Clean Breaks	21	14	7	9	12
Offloads	52	70	9	22	15
Tackle Busts	76	88	19	18	21
Opta Index	18740	15986	9874	11394	15914

WARRINGTON WOLVES

TEAM TOTALS

Tackles	6288
Misses	676
Carries	4376
Metres	30578
Clean Breaks	184
Offloads	289
Handling Errors	321
Penalties conceded	232
Tackle busts	551
Runs from dummy half	388
40/20s	8
Try Savers	22

TACKLES

Danny Nutley	726
Jerome Guisset	472
Tawera Nikau	463
Ian Sibbit	421
Gary Mercer	409

CARRIES

Alan Hunte	362
Danny Nutley	357
Tawera Nikau	328
Jerome Guisset	297
Gary Mercer	290

METRES

Alan Hunte	2630
Danny Nutley	2630
Jerome Guisset	2300
Tawera Nikau	1846
Gary Mercer	1816

CLEAN BREAKS

Alan Hunte	26
Toa Kohe-Love	23
Rob Smyth	17
David Kidwell	16
Lee Penny	14

OFFLOADS

David Kidwell	40
Toa Kohe-Love	31
Tawera Nikau	25
Steve McCurrie	20
Gary Mercer	17

TACKLE BUSTS

Alan Hunte	72
Toa Kohe-Love	48
Danny Nutley	41
David Kidwell	36
Rob Smyth	34

MARKER TACKLES

Danny Nutley	103
Gary Mercer	45
Dean Busby	35
Tawera Nikau	34
Ian Sibbit	34

AVERAGE SEASON INDEX

Alan Hunte	663
Danny Nutley	660
Gary Mercer	635
Toa Kohe-Love	588
Dean Busby	560

TRY ASSISTS

Allan Langer	13
Lee Briers	11
Toa Kohe-Love	8
Tawera Nikau	6
David Kidwell	5

opta

opta stats

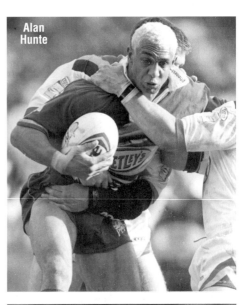

Alan Hunte

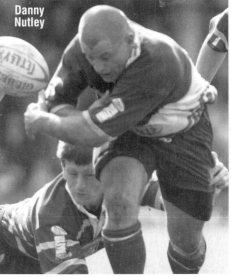

Danny Nutley

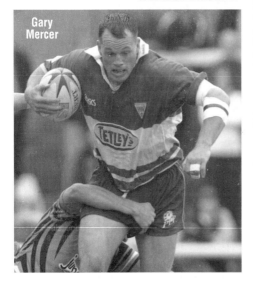

Gary Mercer

TOP 5 OPTA INDEX PERFORMERS

	Hunte	Nutley	Mercer	Kohe-Love	Busby
Matches	26	24	18	21	18
Tackles	156	726	409	239	360
Misses	11	45	37	29	35
Carries	362	357	290	176	208
Metres	2630	2630	1816	1612	1594
Clean Breaks	26	2	3	23	8
Offloads	16	2	17	31	11
Tackle Busts	72	41	27	48	21
Opta Index	17230	15850	11052	12354	10088

WIGAN WARRIORS

TEAM TOTALS
Tackles	6393
Misses	600
Carries	4948
Metres	39009
Clean Breaks	322
Offloads	490
Handling Errors	333
Penalties conceded	203
Tackle busts	773
Runs from dummy half	590
40/20s	5
Try Savers	13

TACKLES
Terry Newton	647
David Furner	637
Mick Cassidy	556
Neil Cowie	549
Terry O'Connor	509

CARRIES
Andy Farrell	492
Terry O'Connor	427
David Furner	359
Neil Cowie	315
Kris Radlinski	305

METRES
Andy Farrell	3811
Terry O'Connor	3689
Kris Radlinski	2651
David Furner	2455
Neil Cowie	2379

CLEAN BREAKS
Kris Radlinski	37
Andy Farrell	35
Steve Renouf	34
Adrian Lam	26
Paul Johnson	25

OFFLOADS
Terry Newton	65
David Furner	65
Terry O'Connor	42
Neil Cowie	39
Andy Farrell	37

TACKLE BUSTS
Andy Farrell	80
David Furner	63
Paul Johnson	57
Brett Dallas	57
Steve Renouf	53

MARKER TACKLES
Mick Cassidy	89
Neil Cowie	72
David Furner	65
Andy Farrell	59
Terry Newton	55

AVERAGE SEASON INDEX
Andy Farrell	995
Kris Radlinski	735
Terry O'Connor	706
David Furner	704
Adrian Lam	680

TRY ASSISTS
Adrian Lam	21
Andy Farrell	19
Kris Radlinski	9
Matthew Johns	8
Terry Newton	7

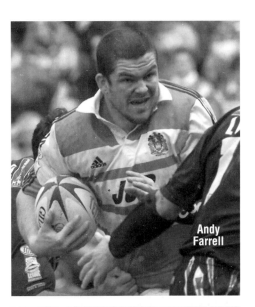

Andy Farrell

Kris Radlinski

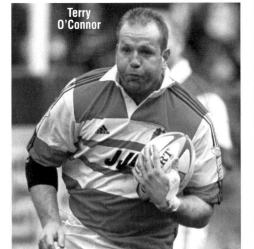

Terry O'Connor

TOP 5 OPTA INDEX PERFORMERS
	Farrell	Radlinski	O'Connor	Furner	Lam
Matches	28	26	25	27	25
Tackles	504	188	509	637	342
Misses	40	23	22	54	44
Carries	492	305	427	359	255
Metres	3811	2651	3689	2455	1643
Clean Breaks	35	37	0	20	26
Offloads	37	12	42	65	23
Tackle Busts	80	49	27	63	44
Opta Index	27862	19102	17648	19010	17016

NORTHERN FORD PREMIERSHIP 2001
Club by Club

BARROW BORDER RAIDERS

DATE	FIXTURE	RESULT	SCORERS	LGE	ATT
3/12/00	Oldham (h)	L16-28	t:Whitehead,Wilson,Rawlinson,Hutton	N/A	1,294
10/12/00	Leigh (a)	L19-8	t:Whitehead g:Holt(2)	17th	2,088
17/12/00	Swinton (a)	L26-24	t:Murray,Rawlinson,A Gardner,Marshall g:Holt(4)	15th	862
24/12/00	Chorley (a)	W24-38	t:Murray(2),Leigh,Burns,Massey,Marshall,Charlton g:Holt(3),Atkinson(2)	14th	488
7/1/01	Whitehaven (h)	W5-4	g:Holt(2) fg:Holt	12th	1,008
28/1/01	Askam (h) (CCR3)	W40-16	t:Hutton(4),Liku,Holt,McDermott g:Holt(6)	N/A	2,092
4/2/01	Widnes (h)	D6-6	t:Whitehead g:Holt	13th	1,116
11/2/01	Halifax (h) (CCR4)	L4-56	g:Holt(2)	N/A	2,160
18/2/01	Batley (a)	W10-18	t:Leigh,A Gardner,Charlton g:Holt(3)	11th	518
25/2/01	Workington (h)	L28-31	t:Murray,Whitehead,Wilson,Holt,Charlton g:Holt(4)	12th	976
4/3/01	Sheffield (a)	L40-16	t:Atkinson,A Gardner g:Holt(4)	12th	838
11/3/01	Doncaster (h)	W18-16	t:Holt,Clark,A Gardner g:Holt(3)	13th	888
18/3/01	Keighley (a)	L60-20	t:Holt(2),Rawlinson,A Gardner g:Holt(2)	14th	2,431
25/3/01	Hunslet (h)	W44-4	t:Atkinson(3),A Gardner(2),Murray,Whitehead,Clark g:Holt(6)	14th	1,042
1/4/01	Dewsbury (a)	L66-10	t:Leigh,Clark g:Atkinson	14th	853
8/4/01	Hull KR (a)	L38-8	t:Charlton g:Kavanagh(2)	14th	1,532
13/4/01	Chorley (h)	W50-18	t:Leigh(3),Whitter,Whitehead,Atkinson,Holt,Rhodes,Murray g:Holt(7)	14th	627
16/4/01	Workington (a)	L29-6	t:Irabor g:Holt	14th	1,103
22/4/01	Gateshead (h)	W20-12	t:Irabor,McDermott,Holt g:Holt(4)	14th	689
6/5/01	Oldham (a)	L36-10	t:McDermott,A Gardner g:Holt	15th	1,554
9/5/01	Featherstone (h)	L22-38	t:McDermott(2),Rawlinson,Murray g:Holt(3)	15th	683
13/5/01	Leigh (h)	L12-28	t:Leigh,Hutton g:Holt(2)	15th	1,080
20/5/01	Swinton (h)	W40-26	t:A Gardner(2),Marshall,Charlton,McDermott,Hutton,Murray g:Holt(6)	14th	602
27/5/01	Whitehaven (a)	L24-0	No Scorers	14th	850
3/6/01	Hunslet (a)	L24-10	t:Irabor,Holt g:Holt	14th	509
10/6/01	York (h)	W60-0	t:Leigh(4),Hutton(2),Marshall(2),Sharp,A Gardner,Irabor g:Holt(8)	14th	655
17/6/01	Gateshead (a)	W14-44	t:A Gardner(3),Hutton(2),Sharp(2),Magorian,Murray,Marshall g:Holt(2)	14th	610
20/6/01	Rochdale (a)	L38-10	t:Hutton,McDermott g:Holt	14th	1,083
24/6/01	Batley (h)	W50-12	t:A Gardner(2),McDermott,Salmon,Whitehead,Burns,Magorian,Irabor,Murray g:Holt(6) fg:Holt(2)	14th	665
1/7/01	Sheffield (h)	W38-14	t:Whitehead(2),Salmon,Murray,Luxon g:Holt(8) fg:Holt(2)	14th	945

	APP		TRIES		GOALS		FG		PTS	
	ALL	NFP	ALL	NFP	ALL	NFP	ALL	NFP	ALL	NFP
Phil Atkinson	20	18	5	5	3	3	0	0	26	26
Clint Barends	6	5	0	0	0	0	0	0	0	0
Willie Burns	11(5)	10(5)	2	2	0	0	0	0	8	8
Gary Charlton	18(3)	17(3)	5	5	0	0	0	0	20	20
Dave Clark	6	6	3	3	0	0	0	0	12	12
Adrian Gardner	29	27	16	16	0	0	0	0	64	64
Paul Gardner	(2)	(2)	0	0	0	0	0	0	0	0
Darren Holt	29	27	8	7	92	84	5	5	221	201
Glen Hutton	15(1)	14(1)	12	8	0	0	0	0	48	32
Shane Irabor	17	17	5	5	0	0	0	0	20	20
Steve Jackson	(16)	(16)	0	0	0	0	0	0	0	0
Paul Jones	(1)	(1)	0	0	0	0	0	0	0	0
Wayne Jones	(1)	(1)	0	0	0	0	0	0	0	0
Mike Kavanagh	5(3)	5(2)	0	0	2	2	0	0	4	4
Matthew Leigh	25	23	11	11	0	0	0	0	44	44
Tau Liku	15(9)	13(9)	1	0	0	0	0	0	4	0
Danny Lockhart	5(1)	5(1)	0	0	0	0	0	0	0	0
Geoff Luxon	16(13)	14(13)	1	1	0	0	0	0	4	4
Stuart Magorian	5	5	2	2	0	0	0	0	8	8
Jamie Marshall	9(9)	8(8)	6	6	0	0	0	0	24	24
Chris Massey	23(2)	21(2)	1	1	0	0	0	0	4	4
Rod Maybon	1	1	0	0	0	0	0	0	0	0
Brett McDermott	27(1)	25(1)	8	7	0	0	0	0	32	28
Anthony Murray	30	28	11	11	0	0	0	0	44	44
Gareth Pratt	3(12)	2(11)	0	0	0	0	0	0	0	0
Ian Rawlinson	16(12)	16(10)	4	4	0	0	0	0	16	16
Stewart Rhodes	5(1)	5(1)	1	1	0	0	0	0	4	4
Paul Salmon	2	2	2	2	0	0	0	0	8	8
Dean Sharp	3(1)	3(1)	3	3	0	0	0	0	12	12
Mike Whitehead	23(7)	22(6)	9	9	0	0	0	0	36	36
Damien Whitter	17(10)	17(8)	1	1	0	0	0	0	4	4
Darren Wilson	9(1)	8(1)	2	2	0	0	0	0	8	8

Adrian Gardner

LEAGUE RECORD
P28-W12-D1-L15
(14th, NFP)
F631, A685, Diff-54
25 points.

CHALLENGE CUP
Round Four

ATTENDANCES
Best - v Halifax (CC - 2,160)
Worst - v Swinton (NFP - 602)
Total (NFP only) - 12,270
Average (NFP only) - 876
(Down by 495 on 2000)

BATLEY BULLDOGS

DATE	FIXTURE	RESULT	SCORERS	LGE	ATT
3/12/00	Sheffield (a)	L34-1	fg:Heptinstall	N/A	1,429
10/12/00	Gateshead (h)	W24-4	t:Lingard,Heptinstall,Gleadhill,Shillabeer g:Price(4)	10th	823
17/12/00	Doncaster (h)	L16-19	t:Heptinstall,Gleadhill,Longo g:Dyson(2)	13th	1,101
26/12/00	Dewsbury (a)	L24-12	t:Hicks,Maun,Jackson	15th	2,520
1/1/01	York (h)	W12-4	t:Longo,Wittenberg g:Dyson(2)	11th	637
7/1/01	Featherstone (h)	L6-37	t:Longo g:Price	14th	1,358
14/1/01	Hunslet (a)	W4-13	t:Longo,Tomlinson g:Price(2) fg:Heptinstall	10th	836
23/1/01	Hull KR (h)	W18-16	t:Shillabeer,Maun,Cass g:Price(3)	8th	574
28/1/01	Heworth (h) (CCR3)	W70-0	t:Lingard(4),Maun(2),Gleadhill,Horsley,Longo,Dyson,Tomlinson, Cass,Price g:Price(9)	N/A	573
11/2/01	London (a) (CCR4)	L44-6	t:Cartledge g:Price	N/A	1,204
18/2/01	Barrow (h)	L10-18	t:Maun,Longo g:Price	10th	518
25/2/01	Keighley (a)	L66-12	t:Lingard,Richards g:Dyson(2)	11th	1,728
11/3/01	Leigh (a)	L34-8	t:Lingard,Gleadhill	14th	2,619
18/3/01	Whitehaven (h)	W18-14	t:Lingard(2),Tomlinson g:Dyson(3)	13th	449
25/3/01	Chorley (a)	W4-39	t:Tomlinson(2),Shillabeer(2),Longo,Cartledge,Lingard g:Dyson(5) fg:Heptinstall	12th	289
1/4/01	Swinton (a)	W12-34	t:Horsley,Gleadhill,Tomlinson,Lingard,Shillabeer,Wittenberg g:Dyson(5)	12th	743
8/4/01	Oldham (a)	L26-8	t:Horsley g:Dyson(2)	12th	1,598
13/4/01	Dewsbury (h)	W14-12	t:Lingard(3) g:Dyson	12th	1,571
16/4/01	York (a)	W6-20	t:Wittenberg(2),Gleadhill,Jackson g:Dyson(2)	12th	498
22/4/01	Oldham (h)	L8-9	t:Shillabeer,Dyson	13th	962
6/5/01	Sheffield (h)	W23-2	t:Lingard(2),Tomlinson,Horsley g:Price(3) fg:Heptinstall	13th	693
13/5/01	Workington (a)	L25-16	t:Lingard(2),Harrison g:Price(2)	13th	832
20/5/01	Doncaster (a)	L36-10	t:Lingard,Simpson g:Price	13th	945
27/5/01	Gateshead (a)	W26-29	t:Dyson,Cartledge,Simpson,Shillabeer,Harrison g:Dyson(3),Price fg:Cass	13th	553
3/6/01	Rochdale (a)	L36-10	t:Harrison,Davis g:Price	13th	1,076
6/6/01	Widnes (h)	L15-36	t:Harrison,Tomlinson g:Dyson(3) fg:Tomlinson	13th	890
10/6/01	Swinton (h)	W38-24	t:Harrison(2),Simpson,Tomlinson,Gleadhill,Wright,Lister g:Dyson(4),Gleadhill	13th	418
17/6/01	Keighley (h)	W16-14	t:Wright(2) g:Dyson(3) fg:Wright,Tomlinson	13th	1,002
24/6/01	Barrow (a)	L50-12	t:Pennington,Cass g:Dyson(2)	13th	665
1/7/01	Rochdale (h)	L10-26	t:Horsley,North g:Dyson	13th	728

	APP		TRIES		GOALS		FG		PTS	
	ALL	NFP	ALL	NFP	ALL	NFP	ALL	NFP	ALL	NFP
Andy Adamson	(1)	(1)	0	0	0	0	0	0	0	0
Chris Beevers	(2)	(2)	0	0	0	0	0	0	0	0
Alan Boothroyd	5(2)	5(2)	0	0	0	0	0	0	0	0
Will Cartledge	22(6)	20(6)	3	2	0	0	0	0	12	8
Mark Cass	6(20)	6(18)	3	2	0	0	1	1	13	9
Jamie Coventry	1(7)	1(6)	0	0	0	0	0	0	0	0
Shelton Davis	(2)	(2)	1	1	0	0	0	0	4	4
Jeremy Dyson	28(1)	26(1)	3	2	40	40	0	0	92	88
Richard Gibson	2(1)	2(1)	0	0	0	0	0	0	0	0
Paul Gleadhill	26	24	7	6	1	1	0	0	30	26
Paul Harrison	10	10	6	6	0	0	0	0	24	24
Andy Heptinstall	28	26	2	2	0	0	4	4	12	12
Paul Hicks	25(4)	23(4)	1	1	0	0	0	0	4	4
Ryan Horsley	30	28	5	4	0	0	0	0	20	16
Simon Jackson	4(6)	4(6)	2	2	0	0	0	0	8	8
Lee Kelly	8(2)	8(2)	0	0	0	0	0	0	0	0
Craig Lingard	24	22	19	15	0	0	0	0	76	60
Paul Lister	5(4)	5(4)	1	1	0	0	0	0	4	4
Davide Longo	20(1)	18(1)	7	6	0	0	0	0	28	24
Danny Maun	21	19	5	3	0	0	0	0	20	12
Chris McWilliam	10	8	0	0	0	0	0	0	0	0
Graham Middleton	(2)	(2)	0	0	0	0	0	0	0	0
Chris North	(1)	(1)	1	1	0	0	0	0	4	4
Rob Padgett	1(3)	1(1)	0	0	0	0	0	0	0	0
Matt Pennington	5	5	1	1	0	0	0	0	4	4
Richard Price	16	14	1	0	29	19	0	0	62	38
Paul Reilly	3(1)	3(1)	0	0	0	0	0	0	0	0
Craig Richards	1(11)	1(11)	1	1	0	0	0	0	4	4
Andy Richardson	5(1)	5(1)	0	0	0	0	0	0	0	0
Gary Shillabeer	22(5)	20(5)	7	7	0	0	0	0	28	28
Roger Simpson	19(1)	19	3	3	0	0	0	0	12	12
Craig Stevens	1(1)	1(1)	0	0	0	0	0	0	0	0
Glen Tomlinson	30	28	9	8	0	0	2	2	38	34
Mark Toohey	(2)	(2)	0	0	0	0	0	0	0	0
Jeff Wittenberg	8(20)	8(19)	4	4	0	0	0	0	16	16
Andy Wray	(5)	(4)	0	0	0	0	0	0	0	0
Craig Wright	4(6)	4(6)	3	3	0	0	1	1	13	13

Glen Tomlinson

LEAGUE RECORD
P28-W13-D0-L15
(13th, NFP)
F452, A618, Diff-166
26 points.

CHALLENGE CUP
Round Four

ATTENDANCES
Best - v Dewsbury (NFP - 1,571)
Worst - v Swinton (NFP - 418)
Total (NFP only) - 11,724
Average (NFP only) - 837
(Up by 37 on 2000)

CHORLEY LYNX

DATE	FIXTURE	RESULT	SCORERS	LGE	ATT
3/12/00	Swinton (h)	L12-30	t:Cookson,Potter g:Fisher(2)	N/A	670
17/12/00	Rochdale (a)	L52-12	t:Fisher,Capewell g:Fisher(2)	18th	745
24/12/00	Barrow (h)	L24-38	t:Capewell(2),Taberner,Fisher,Talbot g:Fisher(2)	18th	488
7/1/01	Leigh (h)	L4-56	t:Taberner	18th	1,382
10/1/01	Whitehaven (a)	L28-4	t:Cookson	18th	638
28/1/01	Woolston (h) (CCR3)	L8-22	t:Talbot g:Capewell(2)	N/A	559
30/1/01	Oldham (a)	L56-2	g:Capewell	18th	1,210
14/2/01	Workington (a)	L42-0	No Scorers	19th	674
18/2/01	Dewsbury (a)	L70-0	No Scorers	19th	725
25/2/01	Widnes (h)	L14-48	t:Prescott,Farrell,Friar g:Fisher	19th	710
4/3/01	Hull KR (h)	L32-54	t:Doherty,Dickinson,Friar,Westwood,Taberner,Prescott g:Fisher(4)	19th	354
11/3/01	Featherstone (a)	L64-6	t:Fisher g:Fisher	19th	1,273
18/3/01	York (h)	W78-8	t:Fisher(5),Farrell(3),Talbot,Brown,Geritas,Taberner,Ramsdale,Maiden,Vincent g:Fisher(9)	18th	254
25/3/01	Batley (h)	L4-39	t:Dickinson	18th	289
31/3/01	Sheffield (a)	L60-4	t:Westwood	18th	870
8/4/01	Gateshead (h)	W19-14	t:Dickinson,Ramsdale,Taberner g:Talbot(3) fg:Lee	17th	356
13/4/01	Barrow (a)	L50-18	t:Maiden,Taberner,Dickinson g:Talbot(3)	17th	627
16/4/01	Whitehaven (h)	L10-42	t:Wilcock,Dickinson g:Talbot	17th	295
22/4/01	Keighley (a)	L60-18	t:Wilcock(2),Dickinson g:Fisher(2),Talbot	17th	1,501
29/4/01	Hull KR (a)	L40-6	t:Talbot g:Talbot	17th	1,314
9/5/01	Doncaster (a)	L56-20	t:Wilcock(3),Bamber g:Talbot(2)	17th	700
13/5/01	Oldham (a)	L10-60	t:Alexander,Tickle g:Talbot	17th	610
20/5/01	Rochdale (h)	L10-66	t:Talbot,Wilcock g:Talbot	18th	311
27/5/01	Leigh (a)	L52-18	t:Dickinson,Birdseye,Prest g:Talbot(2),Birdseye	18th	2,639
3/6/01	Workington (h)	L8-52	t:Harrison g:Talbot(2)	18th	282
10/6/01	Widnes (a)	L72-18	t:Wilcock,Hindle,Dickinson g:Fisher(3)	18th	3,683
17/6/01	Hunslet (a)	L42-24	t:Harrison,Fisher,Vincent,Taberner g:Fisher(4)	18th	441
24/6/01	Dewsbury (h)	L10-50	t:Prescott,Dickinson g:Wilcock	18th	364
1/7/01	Keighley (h)	L10-60	t:Dickinson,Bloor g:Wilcock	18th	704

	APP		TRIES		GOALS		FG		PTS	
	ALL	NFP	ALL	NFP	ALL	NFP	ALL	NFP	ALL	NFP
Neil Alexander	5	5	1	1	0	0	0	0	4	4
Steve Argent	4(1)	4(1)	0	0	0	0	0	0	0	0
Lee Ashton	11(2)	10(2)	0	0	0	0	0	0	0	0
Lee Bamber	10	10	1	1	0	0	0	0	4	4
Lee Bargate	1	1	0	0	0	0	0	0	0	0
Lee Beresford	(1)	(1)	0	0	0	0	0	0	0	0
Lee Birdseye	2(1)	2(1)	1	1	1	1	0	0	6	6
Gary Blood	1(5)	1(4)	0	0	0	0	0	0	0	0
Wayne Bloor	11(1)	11(1)	1	1	0	0	0	0	4	4
Matthew Brown	7(6)	7(6)	1	1	0	0	0	0	4	4
Peter Cahalin	4(1)	4(1)	0	0	0	0	0	0	0	0
Peter Cain	7	6	0	0	0	0	0	0	0	0
Brian Capewell	8	7	3	3	3	1	0	0	18	14
David Cayzer	(1)	(1)	0	0	0	0	0	0	0	0
Gareth Chambers	4	4	0	0	0	0	0	0	0	0
Dale Christy	5(4)	5(3)	0	0	0	0	0	0	0	0
Dean Conway	3	3	0	0	0	0	0	0	0	0
Stuart Conway	(1)	(1)	0	0	0	0	0	0	0	0
Paul Cookson	3(3)	2(3)	2	2	0	0	0	0	8	8
Stuart Dickinson	24	23	10	10	0	0	0	0	40	40
Gary Doherty	8(5)	8(5)	1	1	0	0	0	0	4	4
Michael Donnelly	(3)	(3)	0	0	0	0	0	0	0	0
Mick Farrell	3	3	4	4	0	0	0	0	16	16
Stuart Fisher	24	24	9	9	30	30	0	0	96	96
Andrew Friar	12(1)	12(1)	2	2	0	0	0	0	8	8
Darren Geritas	5	5	1	1	0	0	0	0	4	4
Phil Harrison	24(2)	23(2)	2	2	0	0	0	0	8	8
Warren Hindle	1(8)	1(8)	1	1	0	0	0	0	4	4
Andy Horrobin	(3)	(3)	0	0	0	0	0	0	0	0
Karl Jones	(1)	(1)	0	0	0	0	0	0	0	0
Steve Kelly	(2)	(2)	0	0	0	0	0	0	0	0
Kieran Lacey	(2)	(2)	0	0	0	0	0	0	0	0
Mark Lee	1	1	0	0	0	0	1	1	1	1
Gary Lowe	3	3	0	0	0	0	0	0	0	0
Lee Maiden	15(3)	14(3)	2	2	0	0	0	0	8	8
Ian Marsh	(2)	(1)	0	0	0	0	0	0	0	0
Carl Parker	(1)	(1)	0	0	0	0	0	0	0	0
Gareth Potter	1	1	1	1	0	0	0	0	4	4

	APP		TRIES		GOALS		FG		PTS	
	ALL	NFP	ALL	NFP	ALL	NFP	ALL	NFP	ALL	NFP
Mike Prescott	20(4)	19(4)	3	3	0	0	0	0	12	12
Lee Prest	20(2)	20(1)	1	1	0	0	0	0	4	4
Chris Ramsdale	23(1)	22(1)	2	2	0	0	0	0	8	8
Paul Ridgway	(2)	(2)	0	0	0	0	0	0	0	0
Anthony Roberts	5(3)	4(3)	0	0	0	0	0	0	0	0
Paul Roberts	6	5	0	0	0	0	0	0	0	0
Graham Taberner	23	23	7	7	0	0	0	0	28	28
Ian Talbot	23(3)	22(3)	5	4	17	17	0	0	54	50
Simon Tickle	1(3)	1(3)	1	1	0	0	0	0	4	4
Chris Todd	(1)	(1)	0	0	0	0	0	0	0	0
Chris Tordoff	(1)	(1)	0	0	0	0	0	0	0	0
Rob Verrelli	10(10)	9(10)	0	0	0	0	0	0	0	0
Luke Vincent	12(10)	12(10)	2	2	0	0	0	0	8	8
Dave Wadsley	(1)	(1)	0	0	0	0	0	0	0	0
Simon Warhurst	1	1	0	0	0	0	0	0	0	0
Lee Westwood	11(5)	11(5)	2	2	0	0	0	0	8	8
Paul Wilcock	12(2)	12(2)	8	8	2	2	0	0	36	36
Danny Winrow	3(3)	3(3)	0	0	0	0	0	0	0	0

Phil Harrison

LEAGUE RECORD
P28-W2-D0-L26
(18th, NFP)
F395, A1361, Diff-966
4 points.

CHALLENGE CUP
Round Three

ATTENDANCES
Best - v Leigh (NFP - 1,382)
Worst - v York (NFP - 254)
Total (NFP only) - 7,069
Average (NFP only) - 505
(Up by 31 on 2000)

263

DEWSBURY RAMS

DATE	FIXTURE	RESULT	SCORERS	LGE	ATT
3/12/00	Featherstone (h)	W21-12	t:Flynn,Eaton,Potter g:Eaton(4) fg:Eaton	N/A	2,608
10/12/00	Keighley (a)	L32-6	t:Flynn g:Eaton	11th	2,511
17/12/00	Hull KR (h)	W32-10	t:Ball(2),Godfrey,Potter,Richardson,Baker g:Eaton(4)	8th	2,116
26/12/00	Batley (h)	W24-12	t:Graham(2),Baker,Richardson g:Eaton(4)	6th	2,520
1/1/01	Hunslet (a)	W2-34	t:Tallon(2),Flynn(2),Eaton g:Eaton(7)	3rd	1,260
7/1/01	York (h)	W50-2	t:Ball(2),Flynn(2),Cain,Potter,Eaton,Graham,Kershaw g:Eaton(7)	3rd	1,200
27/1/01	Leigh MR (h) (CCR3)	W48-10	t:Eaton(3),Mycoe,A Spink,Flynn,Baker,Fisher g:Eaton(8)	N/A	1,260
31/1/01	Sheffield (a)	W6-25	t:Baker,Potter,Graham,Cain g:Eaton(3),Ball fg:Ball	3rd	862
11/2/01	Castleford (h) (CCR4)	L4-18	g:Eaton(2)	N/A	3,384
18/2/01	Chorley (h)	W70-0	t:Cain(3),Flynn(3),Pachniuk(3),Potter,Smith,Wood,Richardson g:Mycoe(9)	3rd	725
25/2/01	Gateshead (h)	W54-10	t:Flynn(3),Baker(2),Smith(2),Graham,Mycoe,Godfrey,Ball g:Mycoe(4),Ball	3rd	832
4/3/01	Swinton (a)	W18-20	t:Baker,Smith,Potter,Richardson g:Mycoe,Cain	2nd	846
11/3/01	Oldham (h)	W18-13	t:Pachniuk,Cain,Smith g:Eaton(3)	2nd	1,453
18/3/01	Rochdale (a)	L44-26	t:Pachniuk,Long,Godfrey,K Spink,Potter g:Eaton(2),Cain	3rd	1,195
1/4/01	Barrow (h)	W66-10	t:Cain(3),Potter(3),Crouthers(2),Flynn(2),K Spink g:Eaton(11)	3rd	853
7/4/01	Widnes (h)	L12-13	t:Flynn g:Eaton(4)	3rd	2,135
13/4/01	Batley (a)	L14-12	t:Flynn,Fisher g:Eaton(2)	3rd	1,571
16/4/01	Gateshead (a)	W22-33	t:Crouthers(2),Ball,Graham,Eaton,Baker g:Eaton(4) fg:Eaton	2nd	469
22/4/01	Leigh (a)	L32-18	t:Potter,A Spink,Flynn,Baker g:Eaton	3rd	3,126
29/4/01	Workington (h)	L16-22	t:Pachniuk,Flynn g:Eaton(4)	5th	736
6/5/01	Featherstone (a)	L23-15	t:Cain,Hughes,Crouthers g:Mycoe fg:Mycoe	6th	1,945
13/5/01	Keighley (h)	W19-9	t:Flynn(2),Crouthers g:Eaton(3) fg:Lawford	6th	1,052
20/5/01	Hull KR (a)	L12-6	t:Crouthers g:Eaton	7th	1,645
27/5/01	York (a)	W6-68	t:Eaton(4),Baker(3),Potter(2),Pachniuk,Leatham,Griffin g:Eaton(10)	7th	425
3/6/01	Whitehaven (a)	L18-17	t:Crouthers,Potter,Griffin g:Eaton(2) fg:Lawford	8th	725
10/6/01	Sheffield (h)	W28-16	t:Jowitt,Ball,Flynn,Baker,Potter g:Eaton(3) fg:Eaton(2)	8th	700
17/6/01	Doncaster (h)	W32-16	t:Graham,Potter,Eaton,Baker,Leatham g:Eaton(6)	6th	826
24/6/01	Chorley (a)	W10-50	t:Griffin(3),Flynn(2),Potter,Pachniuk,Graham,Crouthers g:Eaton(7)	6th	364
27/6/01	Doncaster (a)	W12-13	t:Crouthers g:Eaton(4) fg:Lawford	6th	1,047
1/7/01	Swinton (h)	L16-42	t:Pachniuk(2),Griffin g:Eaton(2)	6th	853
8/7/01	Hull KR (h) (ESF)	L6-19	t:Eaton g:Eaton	N/A	1,576

	APP		TRIES		GOALS		FG		PTS	
	ALL	NFP	ALL	NFP	ALL	NFP	ALL	NFP	ALL	NFP
Richard Agar	7	6	0	0	0	0	0	0	0	0
Richard Baker	24(1)	22(1)	14	13	0	0	0	0	56	52
Damian Ball	25(1)	24(1)	7	7	2	2	1	1	33	33
Danny Burton	4(2)	4(2)	0	0	0	0	0	0	0	0
Mark Cain	17(10)	16(9)	10	10	2	2	0	0	44	44
Kevin Crouthers	16	16	10	10	0	0	0	0	40	40
Barry Eaton	28(1)	26(1)	13	10	110	100	4	4	276	244
Andy Fisher	20(3)	18(3)	2	1	0	0	0	0	8	4
Adrian Flynn	31	29	24	23	0	0	0	0	96	92
Alex Godfrey	14	12	3	3	0	0	0	0	12	12
Nathan Graham	26(2)	24(2)	8	8	0	0	0	0	32	32
Matthew Griffin	12(1)	12(1)	6	6	0	0	0	0	24	24
Simon Hicks	1(8)	1(7)	0	0	0	0	0	0	0	0
Ian Hughes	9(2)	9(2)	1	1	0	0	0	0	4	4
Robin Jowitt	24(4)	23(4)	1	1	0	0	0	0	4	4
Billy Kershaw	(5)	(5)	1	1	0	0	0	0	4	4
Dean Lawford	5(2)	5(2)	0	0	0	0	3	3	3	3
Jim Leatham	4(2)	4(2)	2	2	0	0	0	0	8	8
Matthew Long	8(4)	8(3)	1	1	0	0	0	0	4	4
Ryan McDonald	5(23)	5(21)	0	0	0	0	0	0	0	0
David Mycoe	8(7)	7(7)	2	1	15	15	1	1	39	35
Richard Pachniuk	28	27	10	10	0	0	0	0	40	40
Dan Potter	27(1)	25(1)	17	17	0	0	0	0	68	68
Sean Richardson	16	14	4	4	0	0	0	0	16	16
Matthew Roberts	(3)	(3)	0	0	0	0	0	0	0	0
Paul Smith	20	19	5	5	0	0	0	0	20	20
Andrew Spink	10(10)	9(9)	2	1	0	0	0	0	8	4
Kevin Spink	4(6)	3(6)	2	2	0	0	0	0	8	8
Liam Tallon	1(8)	1(7)	2	2	0	0	0	0	8	8
Shayne Williams	4(3)	3(3)	0	0	0	0	0	0	0	0
Gavin Wood	5(7)	5(6)	1	1	0	0	0	0	4	4

Adrian Flynn

LEAGUE RECORD
P28-W18-D0-L10
(6th, NFP/Elimination Semi Finalists)
F801, A438, Diff+363
36 points.

CHALLENGE CUP
Round Four

ATTENDANCES
Best - v Castleford (CC - 3,384)
Worst - v Sheffield (NFP - 700)
Total (NFP, inc play-offs) - 20,185
Average (NFP, inc play-offs) - 1,346
(Down by 520 on 2000)

DONCASTER DRAGONS

DATE	FIXTURE	RESULT	SCORERS	LGE	ATT
3/12/00	York (a)	W8-26	t:Tawhai,Stott,Weston,Edwards g:Weston(3),Irving(2)	N/A	1,251
10/12/00	Hunslet (h)	W36-8	t:Mansson(2),Wilson,Bennett,Crouthers,Conway,Hepi g:Weston(4)	2nd	1,305
17/12/00	Batley (a)	W16-19	t:Mansson(2),Hepi g:Irving(3) fg:Tawhai	2nd	1,101
26/12/00	Sheffield (h)	W22-2	t:Stott,Irving,Mansson,Bunyan g:Irving(2) fg:Mansson,Edwards	2nd	1,970
1/1/01	Featherstone (a)	L34-4	t:Bunyan	5th	2,363
7/1/01	Gateshead (a)	W8-27	t:Hall,Weston,Garcia,Mansson,Tawhai g:Bunyan(3) fg:Tawhai	4th	675
14/1/01	Hull KR (a)	W0-30	t:Tawhai(2),Hepi,Hall,Mansson g:Cook(5)	3rd	2,257
28/1/01	Siddal (h) (CCR3)	W44-14	t:Tawhai(2),David,Weston,Garcia,Bunyan,Cook,Atter g:Cook(6)	N/A	1,341
30/1/01	Keighley (h)	L17-23	t:Crouthers,Irving,Weston g:Cook(2) fg:Cook	3rd	1,691
11/2/01	Sheffield (h) (CCR4)	W14-12	t:Edwards,Atter g:Cook(3)	N/A	1,344
18/2/01	Rochdale (a)	L26-6	g:Irving(3)	6th	1,058
25/2/01	Huddersfield (a) (CCR5)	L38-24	t:Weston,Stott,Mansson,Tawhai g:Irving(4)	N/A	2,176
11/3/01	Barrow (a)	L18-16	t:Mansson,Lawton,Weston g:Irving(2)	8th	888
18/3/01	Widnes (a)	W10-18	t:Fella,Bennett,Garcia g:Weston(2),Irving	7th	3,209
25/3/01	Leigh (h)	W16-11	t:Garcia,Mansson,Woodcock g:Weston(2)	5th	1,630
1/4/01	Whitehaven (h)	W28-24	t:Bennett,Woodcock,Garcia,Handley,Edwards g:Irving(4)	5th	1,093
13/4/01	Sheffield (a)	L28-4	t:Irving	9th	1,632
16/4/01	Featherstone (h)	L15-21	t:Lawton,Edwards g:Irving(3) fg:Mansson	11th	1,426
22/4/01	Swinton (a)	L19-18	t:Edwards,Irving,Maher g:Irving(3)	12th	674
25/4/01	Oldham (a)	L23-4	t:Atter	12th	1,171
6/5/01	York (h)	W82-4	t:Maher(2),Handley(2),David,Edwards,Hall,Mansson,T Miller,Lawton,Hepi, Ramskill,Woodcock,Forsyth g:Irving(13)	11th	741
9/5/01	Chorley (h)	W56-20	t:Mansson(3),Hall(2),Edwards(2),Coult,Irving,Handley,Woodcock g:Irving(5),Mansson	10th	700
13/5/01	Swinton (h)	W27-26	t:Mansson(2),Edwards,Woodcock g:Irving(3),Mansson(2) fg:Irving	9th	819
20/5/01	Batley (h)	W36-10	t:Mansson(2),Garcia(2),Atter,Lawton g:Woodcock(6)	8th	945
23/5/01	Workington (h)	W21-10	t:Hall(2),Woodcock g:Woodcock(3) fg:Conway(3)	6th	783
3/6/01	Hull KR (h)	L16-18	t:Hall,Coult,Garcia g:Woodcock(2)	9th	1,378
10/6/01	Keighley (a)	L52-12	t:Lawton,Ellis g:Ellis(2)	9th	1,697
17/6/01	Dewsbury (a)	L32-16	t:Coulton,Hall,Lawton g:Woodcock(2)	10th	826
24/6/01	Rochdale (h)	L22-34	t:Woodcock,Fella,David,Hall g:Woodcock(2),Coult	12th	899
27/6/01	Dewsbury (h)	L12-13	t:Garcia,Conway g:Woodcock(2)	12th	1,047
1/7/01	Workington (a)	L34-16	t:Mansson,Ramskill,Garcia g:W Green(2)	12th	993

	APP		TRIES		GOALS		FG		PTS	
	ALL	NFP	ALL	NFP	ALL	NFP	ALL	NFP	ALL	NFP
Chris Allen	(1)	(1)	0	0	0	0	0	0	0	0
Asa Amone	11(2)	10(1)	0	0	0	0	0	0	0	0
Tony Atter	8(14)	8(12)	4	2	0	0	0	0	16	8
Neil Bennett	13(3)	13(1)	3	3	0	0	0	0	12	12
Joe Berry	7	6	0	0	0	0	0	0	0	0
James Bunyan	12	9	3	2	3	3	0	0	18	14
Billy Conway	5(10)	5(9)	2	2	0	0	3	3	11	11
Paul Cook	5	3	1	0	16	7	1	1	37	15
Mick Coult	12(2)	12(2)	2	2	1	1	0	0	10	10
Dean Coulton	1(3)	1(3)	1	1	0	0	0	0	4	4
Kevin Crouthers	11	9	2	2	0	0	0	0	8	8
Maea David	23(5)	20(5)	3	2	0	0	0	0	12	8
Peter Edwards	31	28	9	8	0	0	1	1	37	33
St John Ellis	2	2	1	1	2	2	0	0	8	8
Tony Fella	13(4)	13(4)	2	2	0	0	0	0	8	8
Jamie Fielden	(6)	(5)	0	0	0	0	0	0	0	0
Craig Forsyth	(5)	(5)	1	1	0	0	0	0	4	4
Anton Garcia	22(6)	20(6)	10	9	0	0	0	0	40	36
Peter Green	4(11)	4(11)	0	0	0	0	0	0	0	0
Wayne Green	2(1)	2(1)	0	0	2	0	0	0	4	0
Carl Hall	24	22	10	10	0	0	0	0	40	40
Paddy Handley	12	12	4	4	0	0	0	0	16	16
Chris Hannah	(1)	(1)	0	0	0	0	0	0	0	0
Brad Hepi	22(2)	20(1)	4	4	0	0	0	0	16	16
Simon Irving	20	18	5	5	48	44	1	1	117	109
Troy Kini	(2)	(2)	0	0	0	0	0	0	0	0
Alan Langham	1(7)	1(7)	0	0	0	0	0	0	0	0
Craig Lawton	18(6)	18(4)	6	6	0	0	0	0	24	24
Lee Maher	6	6	3	3	0	0	0	0	12	12
Paul Mansson	23	22	19	18	3	3	2	2	84	80
Shane Miller	4	4	0	0	0	0	0	0	0	0
Tony Miller	18(6)	16(5)	1	1	0	0	0	0	4	4
Carl Oakes	1	1	0	0	0	0	0	0	0	0
John Okul	1(1)	(1)	0	0	0	0	0	0	0	0
Ian Ramskill	4(8)	4(8)	2	2	0	0	0	0	8	8
Gary Smith	(1)	(1)	0	0	0	0	0	0	0	0
Lynton Stott	10	7	3	2	0	0	0	0	12	8
Latham Tawhai	12	9	7	4	0	0	2	2	30	18
Jimmy Walker	(1)	(1)	0	0	0	0	0	0	0	0
Craig Weston	18	15	6	4	11	11	0	0	46	38
Phil White	3(7)	2(7)	0	0	0	0	0	0	0	0
Rob Wilson	9	7	1	1	0	0	0	0	4	4
Johnny Woodcock	15(1)	15(1)	7	7	17	17	0	0	62	62

Paul Mansson

LEAGUE RECORD
P28-W14-D0-L14
(12th, NFP)
F622, A532, Diff+90
28 points.

CHALLENGE CUP
Round Five

ATTENDANCES
Best - v Sheffield (NFP - 1,970)
Worst - v Chorley (NFP - 700)
Total (NFP only) - 16,427
Average (NFP only) - 1,173
(Down by 503 on 2000)

FEATHERSTONE ROVERS

DATE	FIXTURE	RESULT	SCORERS	LGE	ATT
3/12/00	Dewsbury (a)	L21-12	t:Lowe g:Rooney(4)	N/A	2,608
10/12/00	Sheffield (h)	L12-15	t:Rhodes,Stokes g:Rooney(2)	12th	2,359
17/12/00	Gateshead (h)	W68-6	t:Stokes(3),Simpson(2),Lowe,Chapman,Bramald,Rhodes,Clarkson, Dickens,Morgan,Rooney g:Rooney(8)	10th	1,717
26/12/00	Hull KR (a)	D6-6	t:Bramald g:Rooney	10th	2,384
1/1/01	Doncaster (h)	W34-4	t:Rooney(2),Swinson,Chapman,Stokes,Bramald g:Rooney(5)	7th	2,363
7/1/01	Batley (a)	W6-37	t:Bramald(2),Rooney(2),Stokes,Morgan g:Rooney(6) fg:Rooney	6th	1,358
14/1/01	Keighley (a)	D22-22	t:Lowe,Dooler,Evans,Stokes g:Rooney(3)	5th	3,269
28/1/01	Eccles (h) (CCR3)	W56-0	t:Chapman(3),Morgan(2),Bramald,Rooney,Stokes,Swinson,Darley g:Gibson(5),Rooney(3)	N/A	1,045
31/1/01	Hunslet (h)	W26-14	t:Bramald(2),Chapman,Rooney g:Rooney(5)	5th	1,292
4/2/01	York (a)	W6-37	t:Bramald,Darley,Lowe,Stokes,Simpson,Chapman,Bastow g:Rooney(4) fg:Rooney	3rd	704
11/2/01	Huddersfield (a) (CCR4)	L28-6	t:Chapman g:Dickens	N/A	2,527
18/2/01	Leigh (h)	L20-30	t:Bramald,Spurr,Chapman,Jones g:Dickens,Chapman	4th	2,683
7/3/01	Whitehaven (a)	L19-10	t:Stokes,Turner g:Dickens	5th	927
11/3/01	Chorley (h)	W64-6	t:Thaler(2),Chapman(2),Stokes(2),Darley,Simpson,Rooney,Morgan, Lowe,Gibson g:Rooney(8)	5th	1,273
18/3/01	Swinton (a)	L28-25	t:Thaler(2),Rooney,Chapman,Jones g:Rooney(2) fg:Rooney	5th	947
25/3/01	Oldham (h)	W22-8	t:Rhodes,Thaler,Bramald,Swinson g:Rooney(3)	4th	1,966
8/4/01	Workington (h)	W24-4	t:Bramald(3),Evans,Chapman g:Rooney fg:Rooney(2)	6th	1,656
13/4/01	Hull KR (h)	W23-16	t:Lowe(2),Stokes,Dooler g:Rooney(3) fg:Rooney	4th	2,065
16/4/01	Doncaster (a)	W15-21	t:Bramald(2),Lowe,Stokes g:Rooney(2) fg:Rooney	4th	1,426
22/4/01	Rochdale (h)	L18-20	t:Lowe,Turner,Bramald g:Rooney(3)	5th	1,746
29/4/01	Gateshead (a)	W7-38	t:Thaler(2),Rooney(2),Lowe,Helliwell,Booth g:Rooney(5)	4th	487
6/5/01	Dewsbury (h)	W23-15	t:Seal(2),Evans,Morgan g:Rooney(3) fg:Rooney	4th	1,945
9/5/01	Barrow (a)	W22-38	t:Chapman(2),Rooney(2),Jackson,Bastow g:Rooney(5)	3rd	683
13/5/01	Sheffield (a)	W14-28	t:Seal,Rhodes,Stokes,Chapman g:Rooney(6)	3rd	1,296
20/5/01	Widnes (a)	L25-22	t:Morgan,Bramald,Stokes g:Rooney(5)	4th	4,372
3/6/01	Keighley (h)	W42-0	t:Rhodes(2),Bramald,Jackson,Chapman,Morgan,Darley,Lowe g:Rooney(5)	4th	1,735
10/6/01	Hunslet (a)	W8-24	t:Rhodes(2),Morgan,Bastow g:Rooney(4)	4th	909
17/6/01	York (h)	W92-2	t:Stokes(3),Jackson(2),Evans(2),Swinson(2),Spurr(2),Bastow, Chapman,Morgan,Lowe,Dooler,Bramald g:Rooney(12)	4th	1,347
24/6/01	Leigh (a)	L38-17	t:Morgan g:Rooney(6) fg:Rooney	5th	2,842
1/7/01	Whitehaven (h)	L20-24	t:Stokes(2),Lowe,Bramald g:Rooney(2)	5th	1,550
8/7/01	Keighley (h) (ESF)	W28-24	t:Rooney(2),Swinson,Spurr,Chapman g:Rooney(4)	N/A	1,710
15/7/01	Leigh (a) (MiSF)	L26-10	t:Bastow,Thaler g:Rooney	N/A	3,236

	APP		TRIES		GOALS		FG		PTS	
	ALL	NFP	ALL	NFP	ALL	NFP	ALL	NFP	ALL	NFP
Gary Barnett	2(7)	1(6)	0	0	0	0	0	0	0	0
Andy Bastow	31(1)	29(1)	5	5	0	0	0	0	20	20
Craig Booth	15(4)	15(4)	1	1	0	0	0	0	4	4
Matt Bramald	32	30	21	20	0	0	0	0	84	80
Richard Chapman	32	30	19	15	1	1	0	0	78	62
Micky Clarkson	4(5)	4(3)	1	1	0	0	0	0	4	4
Paul Darley	27(1)	25(1)	4	3	0	0	0	0	16	12
Stuart Dickens	19(11)	17(11)	1	1	3	2	0	0	10	8
Steve Dooler	21(7)	19(7)	3	3	0	0	0	0	12	12
Danny Evans	19(9)	18(8)	5	5	0	0	0	0	20	20
Richard Gibson	3(3)	3(1)	1	1	5	0	0	0	14	4
Ricky Helliwell	11(18)	10(17)	1	1	0	0	0	0	4	4
Simon Jackson	7(3)	7(3)	4	4	0	0	0	0	16	16
Stephen Jones	1(5)	1(5)	2	2	0	0	0	0	8	8
Gary Lord	20(1)	20(1)	0	0	0	0	0	0	0	0
Neil Lowe	27(5)	25(5)	13	13	0	0	0	0	52	52
Gavin Morgan	6(26)	4(26)	11	9	0	0	0	0	44	36
Michael Rhodes	26(1)	25(1)	9	9	0	0	0	0	36	36
Jamie Rooney	29	28	15	14	121	118	9	9	311	301
James Rushforth	4	4	0	0	0	0	0	0	0	0
Danny Seal	3(1)	3(1)	3	3	0	0	0	0	12	12
Nick Simpson	12(2)	11(1)	4	4	0	0	0	0	16	16
Chris Spurr	11	11	4	4	0	0	0	0	16	16
Jamie Stokes	31	29	21	20	0	0	0	0	84	80
Wayne Sutcliffe	(1)	(1)	0	0	0	0	0	0	0	0
Gavin Swinson	10(10)	8(10)	6	5	0	0	0	0	24	20
Richard Thaler	8(4)	8(4)	8	8	0	0	0	0	32	32
Matt Turner	5	5	2	2	0	0	0	0	8	8
Lee Williamson	(2)	(2)	0	0	0	0	0	0	0	0

Jamie Stokes

LEAGUE RECORD
P28-W17-D2-L9
(5th, NFP/Minor Semi Finalists)
F825, A401, Diff+424
36 points.

CHALLENGE CUP
Round Four

ATTENDANCES
Best - v Leigh (NFP - 2,683)
Worst - v Eccles (CC - 1,045)
Total (NFP, inc play-offs) - 27,407
Average (NFP, inc play-offs) - 1,827
(Down by 99 on 2000)

GATESHEAD THUNDER

DATE	FIXTURE	RESULT	SCORERS	LGE	ATT
3/12/00	Hull KR (h)	L0-18	No Scorers	N/A	2,332
10/12/00	Batley (a)	L24-4	t:Gambles	18th	823
17/12/00	Featherstone (a)	L68-6	t:McGibbon g:Hall	19th	1,717
24/12/00	Keighley (h)	L0-52	No Scorers	19th	1,052
7/1/01	Doncaster (h)	L8-27	t:Derose g:Hall(2)	19th	675
24/1/01	Sheffield (a)	L38-12	t:Gambles g:Hall(4)	19th	753
28/1/01	Wigan St J (h) (CCR3)	W34-20	t:Hall,Dyson,Thorman,Rutherford,Mervill,Williamson g:Hall(5)	N/A	501
4/2/01	Hunslet (h)	L12-26	t:Williamson,Rutherford,Derose	19th	464
14/2/01	Whitehaven (h) (CCR4)	L0-56	No Scorers	N/A	377
18/2/01	Oldham (a)	L52-6	t:Carlton g:Hall	18th	1,451
22/2/01	York (a)	L21-4	t:Grundy	18th	426
25/2/01	Dewsbury (a)	L54-10	t:Briggs,Derose g:Hall	18th	832
7/3/01	Widnes (h)	L18-30	t:Mervill,Field,Johnson g:Hall(3)	18th	517
11/3/01	Whitehaven (h)	L4-23	t:Dyson	18th	532
18/3/01	Leigh (a)	L52-4	t:McGibbon	19th	2,242
25/3/01	Workington (h)	L8-34	t:Southernwood,Williamson	19th	617
1/4/01	Rochdale (h)	L15-40	t:Grundy,Field,Thorman g:Briggs fg:Briggs	19th	387
8/4/01	Chorley (a)	L19-14	t:Lloyd(2),Briggs g:Briggs	19th	356
16/4/01	Dewsbury (h)	L22-33	t:Barron,Lloyd,Carlton,Field g:Briggs(3)	19th	469
22/4/01	Barrow (a)	L20-12	t:Thorman,Callaghan g:Briggs(2)	19th	689
29/4/01	Featherstone (h)	L7-38	t:Briggs g:Briggs fg:Briggs	19th	487
6/5/01	Swinton (a)	L20-8	t:Callaghan g:Briggs(2)	19th	614
9/5/01	Widnes (a)	L72-4	t:Thorman	19th	3,105
13/5/01	Hunslet (a)	W12-40	t:Carlton(3),Johnson(2),Dyson,Thorman g:Briggs(6)	19th	607
20/5/01	York (h)	W30-12	t:Thorman(2),Parker,Johnson,Williamson,Briggs g:Briggs(3)	17th	675
27/5/01	Batley (h)	L26-29	t:Williamson(2),Garside,Thorman,Johnson g:Briggs(3)	17th	553
3/6/01	Oldham (h)	L20-50	t:Williamson(2),Briggs(2) g:Briggs(2)	17th	743
10/6/01	Hull KR (a)	L30-16	t:Rutherford,McGibbon,Gambles g:Briggs(2)	17th	1,653
17/6/01	Barrow (h)	L14-44	t:Carlton,Thorman,Lloyd g:Briggs	17th	610
24/6/01	Whitehaven (a)	L52-22	t:Carlton(3),Johnson g:Briggs(3)	17th	848

	APP		TRIES		GOALS		FG		PTS	
	ALL	NFP	ALL	NFP	ALL	NFP	ALL	NFP	ALL	NFP
Richard Arrowsmith	4	4	0	0	0	0	0	0	0	0
Gareth Barron	10(7)	10(6)	1	1	0	0	0	0	4	4
Stephen Bradley	10(2)	10(2)	0	0	0	0	0	0	0	0
Carl Briggs	23	23	6	6	30	30	2	2	86	86
Matthew Brown	3(1)	3(1)	0	0	0	0	0	0	0	0
Darren Callaghan	7	7	2	2	0	0	0	0	8	8
Jim Carlton	26(2)	24(2)	9	9	0	0	0	0	36	36
Darrell Derose	14(2)	13(1)	3	3	0	0	0	0	12	12
Scott Dyson	21	19	3	2	0	0	0	0	12	8
Andy Field	16(3)	15(3)	3	3	0	0	0	0	12	12
Martin Gambles	9(8)	7(8)	3	3	0	0	0	0	12	12
Lee Garside	11(15)	11(14)	1	1	0	0	0	0	4	4
Andy Grundy	23(1)	21(1)	2	2	0	0	0	0	8	8
Steve Hall	22(4)	20(4)	1	0	17	12	0	0	38	24
Michael Johnson	20	20	6	6	0	0	0	0	24	24
Paul Lister	11(6)	10(5)	0	0	0	0	0	0	0	0
Gareth Lloyd	10	10	4	4	0	0	0	0	16	16
Wes McGibbon	24(1)	22(1)	3	3	0	0	0	0	12	12
Richard Mervill	13(5)	12(4)	2	1	0	0	0	0	8	4
Kevin Neighbour	(2)	(2)	0	0	0	0	0	0	0	0
Chris Parker	22(4)	20(4)	1	1	0	0	0	0	4	4
Matthew Roberts	5(10)	5(8)	0	0	0	0	0	0	0	0
Stephen Rutherford	8(11)	6(11)	3	2	0	0	0	0	12	8
Paul Sebine	3(18)	2(17)	0	0	0	0	0	0	0	0
Darren Simpson	5	5	0	0	0	0	0	0	0	0
Roy Southernwood	23(1)	22(1)	1	1	0	0	0	0	4	4
Richard Spence	3(4)	3(4)	0	0	0	0	0	0	0	0
Paul Thorman	15(6)	13(6)	9	8	0	0	0	0	36	32
Mark Wilkinson	2(4)	2(4)	0	0	0	0	0	0	0	0
Leon Williamson	29	27	8	7	0	0	0	0	32	28

Jim Carlton

LEAGUE RECORD
P28-W2-D0-L26
(17th, NFP)
F346, A990, Diff-644
4 points.

CHALLENGE CUP
Round Four

ATTENDANCES
Best - v Hull KR (NFP - 2,332)
Worst - v Whitehaven (CC - 377)
Total (NFP only) - 10,113
Average (NFP only) - 722

HULL KINGSTON ROVERS

DATE	FIXTURE	RESULT	SCORERS	LGE	ATT
3/12/00	Gateshead (a)	W0-18	t:Kitching,Smith,Chambers,Dunham g:Yeaman	N/A	2,332
10/12/00	York (h)	W2-0	g:Charles	5th	2,110
17/12/00	Dewsbury (a)	L32-10	t:Taewa,Yeaman g:Charles	9th	2,116
26/12/00	Featherstone (h)	D6-6	g:Charles(3)	7th	2,384
3/1/01	Keighley (a)	L24-8	t:Wilkins g:Charles(2)	8th	2,150
7/1/01	Hunslet (h)	W40-12	t:Taewa(2),Sodje,Callaghan,Andrews,Smith,Bovill g:Charles(6)	7th	1,953
14/1/01	Doncaster (h)	L0-30	No Scorers	7th	2,257
23/1/01	Batley (a)	L18-16	t:Taewa(2),Everitt g:Everitt,Charles	9th	574
28/1/01	Toulouse (h) (CCR3)	W44-0	t:Andrews(2),Taewa,Everitt,Walker,Charles,Kitching g:Charles(8)	N/A	1,649
4/2/01	Sheffield (a)	W11-12	t:Everitt,Sodje g:Charles(2)	8th	1,081
13/2/01	Oldham (a) (CCR4)	L17-6	t:Sodje g:Charles	N/A	2,008
18/2/01	Whitehaven (h)	D10-10	t:Molloy,Charles g:Charles	9th	1,385
4/3/01	Chorley (a)	W32-54	t:Walker(3),Taewa(2),Rob Wilson(2),McLarron,Aston,Everitt,Dixon g:Everitt(5)	8th	354
11/3/01	Swinton (h)	W32-6	t:Walker(2),Everitt,Slater,Fletcher g:Everitt(6)	6th	1,536
25/3/01	Rochdale (h)	W12-6	t:Fletcher g:Everitt(4)	7th	1,513
1/4/01	Workington (a)	L24-18	t:Molloy,Everitt,Schultz g:Charles(3)	10th	1,064
8/4/01	Barrow (h)	W38-8	t:Dixon(3),Everitt(2),Kitching,Yeaman g:Charles(5)	9th	1,532
13/4/01	Featherstone (a)	L23-16	t:Charles,Everitt,Walker g:Charles(2)	10th	2,065
16/4/01	Keighley (h)	W17-10	t:Kitching,Walker,Blanchard g:Charles(2) fg:Walker	9th	1,910
22/4/01	Widnes (a)	L28-0	No Scorers	10th	3,726
29/4/01	Chorley (h)	W40-6	t:McLarron(4),Taewa(2),Carter,Anderson g:Charles(4)	9th	1,314
6/5/01	Leigh (a)	L58-10	t:Rob Wilson,Carter g:Charles	9th	3,410
9/5/01	Rochdale (a)	L32-10	t:Taewa,Cochrane g:Charles	11th	1,102
13/5/01	York (a)	W8-56	t:Godfrey(3),Rob Wilson(2),Everitt,Fletcher,Dunham,Murdock,Blanchard g:Charles(8)	10th	656
20/5/01	Dewsbury (h)	W12-6	t:Carter,Godfrey g:Charles(2)	10th	1,645
27/5/01	Hunslet (a)	W6-32	t:Taewa(2),Cochrane,Godfrey,Luckwell g:Charles(6)	9th	725
3/6/01	Doncaster (a)	W16-18	t:Walker,Kitching,Godfrey g:Charles(3)	6th	1,378
10/6/01	Gateshead (h)	W30-16	t:Taewa(2),Charles,McLarron,Fletcher,Kitching g:Charles(3)	6th	1,653
17/6/01	Sheffield (a)	L14-18	t:Everitt,Charles g:Charles(3)	7th	1,625
1/7/01	Oldham (h)	W24-4	t:McLarron,Hayes,Rob Wilson,Walker g:Charles(4)	7th	2,537
8/7/01	Dewsbury (a) (ESF)	W6-19	t:Everitt(2),Dixon g:Charles(3) fg:Kitching	N/A	1,576
15/7/01	Rochdale (a) (MiSF)	L21-14	t:Walker,Taewa,Slater g:Charles	N/A	2,252

	APP		TRIES		GOALS		FG		PTS	
	ALL	NFP	ALL	NFP	ALL	NFP	ALL	NFP	ALL	NFP
Richard Anderson	2(1)	2(1)	1	1	0	0	0	0	4	4
Dean Andrews	12(5)	10(5)	3	1	0	0	0	0	12	4
Jon Aston	17(12)	15(12)	1	1	0	0	0	0	4	4
Graeme Barber	1(1)	1(1)	0	0	0	0	0	0	0	0
Mark Blanchard	3(8)	3(8)	2	2	0	0	0	0	8	8
Jamie Bovill	1(8)	1(7)	1	1	0	0	0	0	4	4
Darren Callaghan	6(1)	6	1	1	0	0	0	0	4	4
Colin Carter	9	9	3	3	0	0	0	0	12	12
Anthony Chambers	6	6	1	1	0	0	0	0	4	4
Chris Charles	28(1)	26(1)	5	4	77	68	0	0	174	152
Steve Cochrane	11(1)	11(1)	2	2	0	0	0	0	8	8
Mick Crane	6(3)	6(3)	0	0	0	0	0	0	0	0
Mike Dixon	21	19	5	5	0	0	0	0	20	20
Allan Dunham	1(16)	1(14)	2	2	0	0	0	0	8	8
Bob Everitt	29	27	13	12	16	16	0	0	84	80
Paul Fletcher	17(15)	15(15)	4	4	0	0	0	0	16	16
Alex Godfrey	10	10	6	6	0	0	0	0	24	24
Rich Hayes	26(1)	24(1)	1	1	0	0	0	0	4	4
Chris Kitching	19(7)	18(6)	6	5	0	0	1	1	25	21
David Luckwell	3(15)	3(15)	1	1	0	0	0	0	4	4
Alisdair McLarron	10(4)	10(4)	7	7	0	0	0	0	28	28
Gavin Molloy	9	9	2	2	0	0	0	0	8	8
Craig Murdock	11	11	1	1	0	0	0	0	4	4
Matt Schultz	13	13	1	1	0	0	0	0	4	4
Richard Slater	25(2)	24(2)	2	2	0	0	0	0	8	8
Andy Smith	16	14	2	2	0	0	0	0	8	8
Bright Sodje	12	10	3	2	0	0	0	0	12	8
Whetu Taewa	32	30	16	15	0	0	0	0	64	60
Andrew Taylor	3	3	0	0	0	0	0	0	0	0
Jimmy Walker	17(3)	15(3)	11	10	0	0	1	1	45	41
Jon Wilkins	4(2)	4(1)	1	1	0	0	0	0	4	4
Richard Wilson	16(7)	16(5)	0	0	0	0	0	0	0	0
Rob Wilson	9(5)	9(5)	6	6	0	0	0	0	24	24
Scott Yeaman	9(5)	9(5)	2	2	1	1	0	0	10	10

Whetu Taewa

LEAGUE RECORD
P28-W16-D2-L10
(7th, NFP/Minor Semi Finalists)
F555, A450, Diff+105
34 points.

CHALLENGE CUP
Round Four

ATTENDANCES
Best - v Oldham (NFP - 2,537)
Worst - v Chorley (NFP - 1,314)
Total (NFP only) - 25,354
Average (NFP only) - 1,811
(Down by 410 on 2000)

HUNSLET HAWKS

DATE	FIXTURE	RESULT	SCORERS	LGE	ATT
3/12/00	Keighley (h)	L12-44	t:Roberts,Ross g:Ross(2)	N/A	1,404
10/12/00	Doncaster (a)	L36-8	t:Campbell,N Dobson	19th	1,305
17/12/00	Sheffield (h)	W14-0	t:Higgins,Wainwright g:Ross fg:Roberts(3),Vassilakopoulos	13th	856
26/12/00	York (a)	D20-20	t:Coyle(2),Raynor g:Ross(3) fg:Roberts(2)	11th	698
1/1/01	Dewsbury (h)	L2-34	g:Ross	12th	1,260
7/1/01	Hull KR (a)	L40-12	t:Ross(2) g:Ross(2)	15th	1,953
14/1/01	Batley (h)	L4-13	g:Ross(2)	15th	836
28/1/01	Thornhill (h) (CCR3)	W38-6	t:Raynor,N Dobson,Wainwright,Jessey,Ross,Redfearn g:Ross(7)	N/A	629
31/1/01	Featherstone (a)	L26-14	t:Maher,Jessey,Campbell g:Robinson	16th	1,292
4/2/01	Gateshead (a)	W12-26	t:Bates(2),Maher,Higgins,Campbell g:Ross(3)	14th	464
13/2/01	Rochdale (a) (CCR4)	L38-4	t:Wainwright	N/A	605
18/2/01	Swinton (h)	W26-16	t:Raynor(3),Higgins,Wainwright g:Vassilakopoulos(2),Robinson	12th	666
11/3/01	Rochdale (h)	L20-42	t:North,Kershaw,Ibbotson g:Robinson(4)	15th	746
18/3/01	Workington (a)	L60-10	t:Coyle,Maher g:Robinson	16th	826
25/3/01	Barrow (a)	L44-4	t:Higgins	16th	1,042
28/3/01	Oldham (a)	L58-4	t:Skerrett	16th	1,038
1/4/01	Widnes (a)	L64-4	t:Robinson	16th	3,253
8/4/01	Leigh (h)	L6-50	t:Wainwright g:Naylor	16th	1,274
13/4/01	York (h)	W30-14	t:Ibbotson,Adams,Howcroft,Wainwright,Atha g:Robinson(5)	16th	612
22/4/01	Whitehaven (h)	L50-10	t:Coleman,Morphet g:Robinson	16th	785
6/5/01	Keighley (a)	L26-24	t:Howcroft(2),Naylor(2),Raynor g:Robinson(2)	16th	1,465
9/5/01	Leigh (a)	L68-4	t:Higgins	16th	1,951
13/5/01	Gateshead (h)	L12-40	t:Ibbotson,Coyle g:Robinson,Higgins	16th	607
20/5/01	Sheffield (a)	L40-10	t:Coleman,Raynor g:Higgins	16th	1,154
27/5/01	Hull KR (h)	L6-32	t:Raynor g:Ross	16th	725
3/6/01	Barrow (h)	W24-10	t:Wainwright(2),Coyle,N Dobson g:Ross(4)	16th	509
10/6/01	Featherstone (h)	L8-24	t:Wainwright g:Ross(2)	16th	909
17/6/01	Chorley (h)	W42-24	t:Higgins,Coyle,Howcroft,Banks,Adams,Wainwright,Naylor g:Ross(4),Robinson(3)	16th	441
24/6/01	Swinton (a)	L30-20	t:Raynor(2),Thompson,Higgins g:Coleman(2)	16th	823
1/7/01	Widnes (h)	L4-42	t:Thompson	16th	1,498

	APP		TRIES		GOALS		FG		PTS	
	ALL	NFP	ALL	NFP	ALL	NFP	ALL	NFP	ALL	NFP
Guy Adams	22(1)	20(1)	2	2	0	0	0	0	8	8
Andy Atha	3(9)	3(8)	1	1	0	0	0	0	4	4
Michael Banks	19(5)	17(5)	1	1	0	0	0	0	4	4
David Bates	6(6)	6(4)	2	2	0	0	0	0	8	8
Neil Bradbrook	6(2)	6(2)	0	0	0	0	0	0	0	0
Danny Briggs	1(1)	1(1)	0	0	0	0	0	0	0	0
Aaron Campbell	11(1)	9(1)	3	3	0	0	0	0	12	12
Jermaine Coleman	14(2)	14(2)	2	2	2	2	0	0	12	12
Mick Coyle	25	23	6	6	0	0	0	0	24	24
Danny Dobson	6(2)	6(2)	0	0	0	0	0	0	0	0
Nicky Dobson	13(13)	11(13)	3	2	0	0	0	0	12	8
Mick Dowds	1	1	0	0	0	0	0	0	0	0
Junior Henderson	2(5)	2(5)	0	0	0	0	0	0	0	0
Chris Heywood	9(4)	9(4)	0	0	0	0	0	0	0	0
Iain Higgins	30	28	7	7	2	2	0	0	32	32
Tony Howcroft	14(2)	14(2)	4	4	0	0	0	0	16	16
Craig Ibbotson	14(2)	14(2)	3	3	0	0	0	0	12	12
Dave Jessey	15(8)	15(6)	2	1	0	0	0	0	8	4
Billy Kershaw	3	3	1	1	0	0	0	0	4	4
Lee Maher	7(1)	6(1)	3	3	0	0	0	0	12	12
Adam Moore	1(2)	1(2)	0	0	0	0	0	0	0	0
Craig Morphet	4(1)	4(1)	1	1	0	0	0	0	4	4
Steve Morton	4	4	0	0	0	0	0	0	0	0
Hamish Munton	8(9)	8(9)	0	0	0	0	0	0	0	0
Gareth Naylor	12(7)	12(7)	3	3	1	1	0	0	14	14
Chris North	4(5)	3(5)	1	1	0	0	0	0	4	4
David Plange	2(1)	2(1)	0	0	0	0	0	0	0	0
Steve Pryce	(1)	(1)	0	0	0	0	0	0	0	0
George Raynor	29	27	10	9	0	0	0	0	40	36
Chris Redfearn	8	6	1	0	0	0	0	0	4	0
Damian Reed	1	1	0	0	0	0	0	0	0	0
Robert Roberts	10(1)	8(1)	1	1	0	0	5	5	9	9
Craig Robinson	20(2)	19(1)	1	1	19	19	0	0	42	42
Chris Ross	14(1)	13	4	3	32	25	0	0	80	62
Ben Skerrett	7(15)	7(14)	1	1	0	0	0	0	4	4
Ben Thompson	7(2)	7(2)	2	2	0	0	0	0	8	8
Marcus Vassilakopoulos	8	6	0	0	2	2	1	1	5	5
Michael Wainwright	30	28	10	8	0	0	0	0	40	32

George Raynor

LEAGUE RECORD
P28-W6-D1-L21
(16th, NFP)
F380, A959, Diff-579
13 points.

CHALLENGE CUP
Round Four

ATTENDANCES
Best - v Widnes (NFP - 1,498)
Worst - v Chorley (NFP - 441)
Total (NFP only) - 12,343
Average (NFP only) - 882
(Down by 86 on 2000)

KEIGHLEY COUGARS

DATE	FIXTURE	RESULT	SCORERS	LGE	ATT
3/12/00	Hunslet (a)	W12-44	t:Lee(3),Seal(2),Lord,Leatham,Carter g:Wood(6)	N/A	1,404
10/12/00	Dewsbury (h)	W32-6	t:Rushforth(2),Hughes,Seal,Horne,Antonik g:Wood(4)	1st	2,511
17/12/00	York (a)	W14-48	t:Lee(2),Wood,Horne,Rushforth,Harrison,Seal,M Walker g:Wood(6),Lee(2)	1st	943
24/12/00	Gateshead (a)	W0-52	t:Lee(3),Carter(2),Ramshaw,Harrison,Seal,Antonik,Horne g:Wood(6)	1st	1,052
3/1/01	Hull KR (h)	W24-8	t:Lee,Harrison,Rushforth,Carter g:Wood(4)	1st	2,150
7/1/01	Sheffield (a)	W16-52	t:Horne(2),Seal(2),Lee(2),Harrison,Antonik,Carter g:Wood(8)	1st	1,642
14/1/01	Featherstone (h)	D22-22	t:Ramshaw,Lee,Rushforth,Seal g:Wood(3)	1st	3,269
28/1/01	Rochdale M (h) (CCR3)	W76-0	t:M Walker(4),Horne(2),Tomlinson(2),Leatham,Hooson,Antonik, Pickles,Wood,Seal g:Wood(9),Antonik	N/A	1,764
30/1/01	Doncaster (a)	W17-23	t:Horne(2),Lee,Rushforth g:Hallas(2),Wood fg:Ramshaw	1st	1,691
11/2/01	Hull (h) (CCR4)	L20-34	t:Lee(2),Harrison,Horne g:Wood(2)	N/A	4,401
25/2/01	Batley (h)	W66-12	t:Seal(3),Antonik(3),Rushforth(2),Boothroyd,Hallas,Hughes g:Wood(11)	2nd	1,728
7/3/01	Rochdale (h)	L20-23	t:Antonik,Wood,Lee,Hughes g:Wood(2)	3rd	1,533
11/3/01	Workington (a)	W4-32	t:Rushforth(2),Seal,Hughes,Hallas,Lee g:Wood(4)	3rd	1,099
18/3/01	Barrow (h)	W60-20	t:Horne(3),Wood,Hallas,Harrison,Ramshaw,Seal,Antonik,Rushforth g:Wood(10)	2nd	2,431
25/3/01	Widnes (a)	W19-22	t:Harrison(2),Ramshaw,Antonik g:Hallas(2),Wood	2nd	3,469
1/4/01	Leigh (h)	L6-16	t:Seal g:Hallas	2nd	3,727
8/4/01	Whitehaven (a)	L17-4	t:Seal	2nd	895
13/4/01	Swinton (h)	L22-26	t:Lee,Robinson,Hallas,Leatham g:Lee(3)	2nd	1,719
16/4/01	Hull KR (a)	L17-10	t:Harrison,Antonik g:Lee	3rd	1,910
22/4/01	Chorley (h)	W60-18	t:Hooson(3),Murdock(2),Hughes(2),Rushforth,Harrison,Seal,D Best g:J Walker(5),Lee(3)	2nd	1,501
29/4/01	Oldham (a)	L38-4	t:Davies	3rd	1,815
6/5/01	Hunslet (h)	W26-24	t:Hooson(2),Ramshaw,Ashton,Smith g:Holker(2),Ashton	3rd	1,465
9/5/01	Whitehaven (h)	L4-30	t:Hooson	5th	1,208
13/5/01	Dewsbury (a)	L19-9	t:Holker g:Holker(2) fg:Holker	5th	1,052
27/5/01	Sheffield (h)	W26-14	t:Hogg(2),Sanchez,Tomlinson g:Ashton(5)	6th	1,471
30/5/01	Leigh (h) (TPCF)	L0-36	No Scorers	N/A	2,626
3/6/01	Featherstone (a)	L42-0	No Scorers	7th	1,735
10/6/01	Doncaster (h)	W52-12	t:Ashton(2),Rivett(2),Smith,Antonik,Ramshaw,Hooson,Stephenson g:Ashton(8)	7th	1,697
17/6/01	Batley (a)	L16-14	t:Tomlinson,Wilkes,Ashton g:Ashton	8th	1,002
24/6/01	Oldham (h)	L16-26	t:Antonik,Roberts,Wilkes g:Ashton(2)	8th	2,225
1/7/01	Chorley (a)	W10-60	t:Ramshaw(3),Roberts,Rice,Hayes,Ashton,Wilkes,Foster,Rushforth, Tomlinson g:Roberts(5),Ashton(3)	8th	704
8/7/01	Featherstone (a) (ESF)	L28-24	t:Roberts(2),Ashton,Ramshaw g:Ashton(4)	N/A	1,710

	APP		TRIES		GOALS		FG		PTS	
	ALL	NFP	ALL	NFP	ALL	NFP	ALL	NFP	ALL	NFP
Nathan Antonik	25	22	13	12	1	0	0	0	54	48
Paul Ashton	10	9	6	6	24	24	0	0	72	72
David Best	8(4)	8(2)	1	1	0	0	0	0	4	4
Jason Best	(2)	(2)	0	0	0	0	0	0	0	0
Alan Boothroyd	11(4)	10(4)	1	1	0	0	0	0	4	4
Lee Bowyer	(1)	(1)	0	0	0	0	0	0	0	0
Craig Brown	(1)	(1)	0	0	0	0	0	0	0	0
Darren Carter	4(11)	3(10)	5	5	0	0	0	0	20	20
Gareth Davies	1	1	1	1	0	0	0	0	4	4
Matthew Foster	7	6	1	1	0	0	0	0	4	4
Jon Gwilliam	(2)	(2)	0	0	0	0	0	0	0	0
Graeme Hallas	18	17	4	4	5	5	0	0	26	26
Chris Hannah	5	4	0	0	0	0	0	0	0	0
Paul Harrison	19	18	10	9	0	0	0	0	40	36
Adam Hayes	3(1)	3(1)	1	1	0	0	0	0	4	4
Gareth Hobson	7	6	0	0	0	0	0	0	0	0
Chris Hogg	8(1)	7(1)	2	2	0	0	0	0	8	8
Mark Holker	3	3	1	1	4	4	1	1	13	13
Gareth Hooson	12(3)	11(2)	8	7	0	0	0	0	32	28
Craig Horne	18	16	13	10	0	0	0	0	52	40
Ian Hughes	15(1)	14(1)	6	6	0	0	0	0	24	24
Kris Kirk	4(3)	4(2)	0	0	0	0	0	0	0	0
Jim Leatham	8(12)	7(11)	3	2	0	0	0	0	12	8
Jason Lee	19	18	18	16	9	9	0	0	90	82
Gary Lord	1(5)	(5)	1	1	0	0	0	0	4	4
Craig Morphet	4(6)	4(5)	0	0	0	0	0	0	0	0
Craig Murdock	4(2)	3(2)	2	2	0	0	0	0	8	8
Steve Pickles	1(1)	0	1	0	0	0	0	0	4	0
Daio Powell	8	6	0	0	0	0	0	0	0	0
Jason Ramshaw	29	28	10	10	0	0	1	1	41	41
Andy Rice	4	4	1	1	0	0	0	0	4	4
Andy Richardson	(4)	(4)	0	0	0	0	0	0	0	0
Leroy Rivett	2(1)	2(1)	2	2	0	0	0	0	8	8
Robert Roberts	7(1)	6(1)	4	4	5	5	0	0	26	26
Chris Robinson	2	2	1	1	0	0	0	0	4	4
Chris Ross	(1)	(1)	0	0	0	0	0	0	0	0
James Rushforth	21(3)	20(3)	13	13	0	0	0	0	52	52

	APP		TRIES		GOALS		FG		PTS	
	ALL	NFP	ALL	NFP	ALL	NFP	ALL	NFP	ALL	NFP
Carlos Sanchez	3(4)	2(4)	1	1	0	0	0	0	4	4
Danny Seal	16(4)	15(3)	17	16	0	0	0	0	68	64
Luke Sellars	1	1	0	0	0	0	0	0	0	0
Andy Senior	(2)	(1)	0	0	0	0	0	0	0	0
Graeme Shaw	5(2)	5(2)	0	0	0	0	0	0	0	0
James Simeunovich	6(4)	5(4)	0	0	0	0	0	0	0	0
Michael Slicker	17	16	0	0	0	0	0	0	0	0
Karl Smith	24(2)	22(2)	2	2	0	0	0	0	8	8
Phil Stephenson	11(18)	10(17)	1	1	0	0	0	0	4	4
Martin Taylor	(3)	(3)	0	0	0	0	0	0	0	0
Max Tomlinson	12	10	5	3	0	0	0	0	20	12
James Walker	2(3)	1(3)	0	0	5	5	0	0	10	10
Matt Walker	11(9)	10(8)	5	1	0	0	0	0	20	4
Liam Walsh	1	1	0	0	0	0	0	0	0	0
Oliver Wilkes	3(1)	3(1)	3	3	0	0	0	0	12	12
Johnny Williams	2	2	0	0	0	0	0	0	0	0
Martin Wood	15	13	4	3	77	66	0	0	170	144

Jason Ramshaw

LEAGUE RECORD
P28-W16-D1-L11
(8th, NFP/Elimination
Semi Finalists)
F810, A498, Diff+312
33 points.

CHALLENGE CUP
Round Four

ATTENDANCES
Best - v Hull (CC - 4,401)
Worst - v Whitehaven
(NFP - 1,208)
Total (NFP only) - 28,635
Average (NFP only) - 2,045
(Down by 7 on 2000)

LEIGH CENTURIONS

DATE	FIXTURE	RESULT	SCORERS	LGE	ATT
10/12/00	Barrow (h)	W19-8	t:Fairclough,Anderson,Svabic g:Svabic(3) fg:Svabic	8th	2,088
17/12/00	Whitehaven (a)	W8-30	t:Hadcroft(2),Anderson,Baldwin,Turley g:Svabic(5)	4th	1,061
26/12/00	Widnes (a)	W20-25	t:Turley,Baldwin,Svabic,Kendrick g:Svabic(4) fg:Svabic	3rd	6,644
1/1/01	Swinton (h)	W46-4	t:Turley(3),Whittle,Hamilton,Hadcroft,Jones,Anderson g:Svabic(6),Turley	2nd	2,881
7/1/01	Chorley (a)	W4-56	t:Turley(5),Hamilton,Hadcroft,Street,Bowker,Anderson g:Turley(8)	2nd	1,382
14/1/01	Oldham (a)	W18-44	t:Fairclough(2),Turley,Svabic,Anderson,Hamilton,Bradbury,Watts g:Svabic(5),Turley	2nd	4,747
28/1/01	West Hull (h) (CCR3)	W28-5	t:Johnson(2),Fairclough,Whittle,Anderson,Sanderson g:Svabic,Sanderson	N/A	1,547
31/1/01	Workington (h)	W70-0	t:Turley(6),Ingram,Duffy,Bretherton,Hadcroft,Whittle,Svabic g:Svabic(11)	2nd	2,149
4/2/01	Rochdale (h)	W48-0	t:Anderson(2),Watts,Whittle,Turley,Bretherton,Svabic,Hadcroft,Baldwin g:Svabic(6)	1st	2,568
11/2/01	Salford (h) (CCR4)	W16-12	t:Anderson,Turley,Bristow g:Svabic(2)	N/A	6,408
18/2/01	Featherstone (a)	W20-30	t:Turley,Kendrick,Baldwin,Fairclough,Morley g:Svabic(5)	1st	2,683
25/2/01	Warrington (a) (CCR5)	L20-10	t:Anderson g:Svabic(3)	N/A	8,844
8/3/01	York (a)	W12-84	t:Turley(4),Johnson(2),Swann(2),Svabic(2),Bretherton,Roden,Jones,Anderson g:Svabic(14)	1st	428
11/3/01	Batley (h)	W34-8	t:Anderson(2),Bradbury(2),Gass,Watts g:Svabic(5)	1st	2,619
18/3/01	Gateshead (h)	W52-4	t:Kendrick(3),Turley(3),Watts(2),Bretherton,Johnson g:Svabic(5),Turley	1st	2,242
25/3/01	Doncaster (a)	L16-11	t:Turley g:Svabic(3) fg:Svabic	1st	1,630
1/4/01	Keighley (h)	W6-16	t:Hamilton,Baldwin,Turley g:Svabic(2)	1st	3,727
8/4/01	Hunslet (a)	W6-50	t:Kendrick(2),Johnson(2),Ingram(2),Svabic,Morley,Turley,Whittle g:Svabic(5),Turley	1st	1,274
13/4/01	Widnes (h)	W26-22	t:Morley,Baldwin,Bristow,Turley g:Svabic(5)	1st	4,914
15/4/01	Swinton (a)	W0-40	t:Baldwin,Swann,Norman,Jones,Bretherton,Kendrick,Roden,Turley g:Svabic(4)	1st	1,892
22/4/01	Dewsbury (h)	W32-18	t:Kendrick,Whittle,Turley,Morley,Ingram g:Svabic(6)	1st	3,126
29/4/01	Sheffield (a)	W28-34	t:Bretherton,Duffy,Bristow,Bradbury,Swann,Hamilton g:Svabic(5)	1st	1,614
6/5/01	Hull KR (h)	W58-10	t:Ingram(4),Turley(3),Kendrick(2),Morley,Anderson g:Svabic(7)	1st	3,410
9/5/01	Hunslet (h)	W68-4	t:Sanderson(4),Turley(3),Ingram(2),Anderson(2),Swann,Bretherton g:Svabic(5),Sanderson(3)	1st	1,951
13/5/01	Barrow (a)	W12-28	t:Turley(2),Bradbury,Street,Watts g:Svabic(4)	1st	1,080
20/5/01	Whitehaven (h)	W42-4	t:Morley(3),Watts,Baldwin,Anderson,Duffy g:Sanderson(4),Bretherton(3)	1st	2,409
27/5/01	Chorley (h)	W52-18	t:Turley(2),Kendrick,Bradbury,Bretherton,Street,Bristow,Hadcroft,Swann g:Sanderson(8)	1st	2,639
30/5/01	Keighley (a) (TPCF)	W0-36	t:Turley(2),Anderson(2),Swann,Bretherton,Baldwin g:Svabic(4)	N/A	2,626
10/6/01	Workington (a)	W17-18	t:Fairclough,Hadcroft,Anderson g:Svabic(3)	1st	1,114
17/6/01	Rochdale (a)	L36-4	t:Kendrick	1st	2,473
24/6/01	Featherstone (h)	W38-17	t:Turley(5),Johnson g:Svabic(6),Turley	1st	2,842
1/7/01	York (h)	W84-1	t:Turley(3),Kendrick(2),Watts(2),Street(2),Ingram(2),Swann,Fairclough,Morley,Cross g:Svabic(8),Street(4)	1st	2,433
8/7/01	Oldham (h) (PSF)	L14-15	t:Turley,Anderson,Watts g:Svabic	N/A	3,436
15/7/01	Featherstone (h) (MiSF)	W26-10	t:Bristow,Bradbury,Turley g:Svabic(7)	N/A	3,236
22/7/01	Widnes (h) (MaSF)	L18-26	t:Morley,Hadcroft,Kendrick g:Svabic(3)	N/A	6,399

	APP		TRIES		GOALS		FG		PTS	
	ALL	NFP	ALL	NFP	ALL	NFP	ALL	NFP	ALL	NFP
Paul Anderson	29(1)	25(1)	21	16	0	0	0	0	84	64
Simon Baldwin	29(1)	26(1)	9	8	0	0	0	0	36	32
Radney Bowker	(1)	(1)	1	1	0	0	0	0	4	4
David Bradbury	19(11)	17(10)	7	7	0	0	0	0	28	28
Liam Bretherton	26(6)	24(4)	9	8	3	3	0	0	42	38
Adam Bristow	31(1)	28(1)	5	4	0	0	0	0	20	16
Alan Cross	1(2)	1(2)	1	1	0	0	0	0	4	4
John Duffy	9(17)	9(13)	3	3	0	0	0	0	12	12
Andy Fairclough	20(1)	17(1)	7	6	0	0	0	0	28	24
Jamie Gass	2(3)	1(3)	1	1	0	0	0	0	4	4
Alan Hadcroft	19(1)	17(1)	9	9	0	0	0	0	36	36
John Hamilton	23(9)	20(9)	5	5	0	0	0	0	20	20
David Ingram	19(2)	15(2)	12	12	0	0	0	0	48	48
Jason Johnson	6(8)	5(8)	8	6	0	0	0	0	32	24
David Jones	11(1)	10(1)	3	3	0	0	0	0	12	12
Phil Kendrick	18(11)	15(10)	16	16	0	0	0	0	64	64
Andy Leatham	11(15)	11(12)	0	0	0	0	0	0	0	0
Chris Morley	26(2)	24(2)	10	10	0	0	0	0	40	40
Paul Norman	6(11)	6(10)	1	1	0	0	0	0	4	4
Kieron Purtill	6(1)	5(1)	0	0	0	0	0	0	0	0
Martin Roden	5(4)	4(4)	2	2	0	0	0	0	8	8
Lee Sanderson	3(2)	3(1)	5	4	16	15	0	0	52	46
Tim Street	18(7)	15(7)	5	4	4	4	0	0	28	28
Simon Svabic	32	28	8	8	153	143	3	3	341	321
Willie Swann	18(6)	16(5)	8	7	0	0	0	0	32	28
Neil Turley	31	28	55	52	12	12	0	0	244	232
Michael Watts	22	20	10	10	0	0	0	0	40	40
David Whittle	15(15)	13(13)	6	5	0	0	0	0	24	20

Neil Turley

LEAGUE RECORD
P28-W26-D0-L2
(1st, NFP/Major Semi Finalists)
F1139, A321, Diff+818
52 points.

CHALLENGE CUP
Round Five

ATTENDANCES
Best - v Salford (CC - 6,408)
Worst - v West Hull (CC - 1,547)
Total (NFP, inc play-offs) - 51,342
Average (NFP, inc play-offs) - 3,020
(Up by 380 on 2000)

OLDHAM

DATE	FIXTURE	RESULT	SCORERS	LGE	ATT
3/12/00	Barrow (a)	W16-28	t:Sibson,D Gibbons,Roden,A Gibbons,Hough g:Rich(4)	N/A	1,294
17/12/00	Workington (a)	W6-22	t:Roden(2),Cross,Sibson g:Rich(2) fg:Roden(2)	5th	1,295
24/12/00	Rochdale (a)	W6-10	t:D Gibbons g:Rich(3)	4th	3,402
1/1/01	Widnes (h)	W20-12	t:Arnold(2),Lacey g:Rich(3) fg:Roden,Ford	4th	3,471
14/1/01	Leigh (h)	L18-44	t:Arnold,Hough,Sibson g:Rich(3)	6th	4,747
28/1/01	Queensbury (h) (CCR3)	W64-0	t:Sibson(4),D Gibbons(3),Arnold,P Farrell,C Farrell,Dodd,Norton g:Rich(8)	N/A	1,559
30/1/01	Chorley (h)	W56-2	t:D Gibbons(4),Procter(2),Cross(2),Roden,Sibson g:Rich(8)	5th	1,210
13/2/01	Hull KR (h) (CCR4)	W17-6	t:Barber,D Gibbons g:Rich(4) fg:Roden	N/A	2,008
18/2/01	Gateshead (h)	W52-6	t:Sibson(3),Roden(3),Dodd,D Gibbons,Lacey g:Rich(8)	5th	1,451
25/2/01	Wakefield (h) (CCR5)	L6-26	t:Rich g:Rich	N/A	3,071
11/3/01	Dewsbury (a)	L18-13	t:D Gibbons,Norton g:Rich(2) fg:Roden	7th	1,453
14/3/01	Whitehaven (h)	L8-19	t:Rich g:Rich(2)	7th	1,179
18/3/01	Sheffield (h)	W24-16	t:Rich,D Gibbons,Roden g:Rich(6)	6th	1,503
25/3/01	Featherstone (a)	L22-8	t:Dodd g:Rich(2)	9th	1,966
28/3/01	Hunslet (h)	W58-4	t:Barrow(2),Hayes(2),Mannion(2),Rich,Hough,Roden,D Gibbons g:Rich(9)	5th	1,038
1/4/01	York (a)	W6-70	t:Barrow(3),A Gibbons(3),Clegg,Rich,D Gibbons,Hayes,Roden,Lacey,Dodd g:Rich(9)	4th	514
8/4/01	Batley (h)	W26-8	t:Hough,A Gibbons,Norton,P Farrell g:Rich(5)	4th	1,598
13/4/01	Rochdale (h)	L10-38	t:P Farrell g:Rich(3)	5th	2,398
16/4/01	Widnes (a)	L34-16	t:A Gibbons,Dodd,D Gibbons g:Rich(2)	7th	4,072
22/4/01	Batley (a)	W8-9	t:Brennan g:Rich(2) fg:Dodd	7th	962
25/4/01	Doncaster (h)	W23-4	t:McNicholas(2),Roden,Sinfield g:Rich(3) fg:Brennan	4th	1,171
29/4/01	Keighley (h)	W38-4	t:Brennan(2),A Gibbons(2),Dodd,Mannion g:Rich(7)	2nd	1,815
2/5/01	Swinton (a)	W10-33	t:Mannion(2),Rich,McNicholas,Dodd,Roden g:Rich(4) fg:Roden	2nd	1,014
6/5/01	Barrow (h)	W36-10	t:Mannion,Lacey,A Gibbons,Henare,P Farrell,D Gibbons g:Rich(6)	2nd	1,554
9/5/01	Swinton (h)	W22-20	t:McNicholas,P Farrell,Henare,A Gibbons g:Rich(3)	2nd	1,360
13/5/01	Chorley (a)	W10-60	t:Sibson(3),Roden(2),McNicholas(2),Rich,Henare,Clegg,C Farrell g:Rich(8)	2nd	610
20/5/01	Workington (h)	W24-18	t:Sibson(2),Brennan,Lacey g:Rich(4)	2nd	1,276
3/6/01	Gateshead (a)	W20-50	t:Brennan(3),A Gibbons(2),McNicholas,Roden,Henare,Clegg g:Rich(7)	2nd	743
17/6/01	Whitehaven (a)	W15-16	t:Sibson,Brennan,A Gibbons g:Rich(2)	2nd	1,027
24/6/01	Keighley (a)	W16-26	t:Brennan(2),Hayes,Casey,Roden g:Rich(3)	2nd	2,225
1/7/01	Hull KR (a)	L24-4	t:Hayes	4th	2,537
8/7/01	Leigh (a) (PSF)	W14-15	t:Hough,Sibson g:Rich(3) fg:Brennan	N/A	3,436
22/7/01	Rochdale (a) (MaSF)	W32-39	t:Henare(2),Brennan,Casey,McNicholas g:Rich(9) fg:Ford	N/A	4,153
28/7/01	Widnes (GF)	L14-24	t:Brennan,Ford,Mannion g:Rich	N/A	8,974

	APP		TRIES		GOALS		FG		PTS	
	ALL	NFP	ALL	NFP	ALL	NFP	ALL	NFP	ALL	NFP
Danny Arnold	10(1)	9(1)	4	3	0	0	0	0	16	12
Gareth Barber	4(3)	2(3)	1	0	0	0	0	0	4	0
Warren Barrow	5	5	5	5	0	0	0	0	20	20
Keith Brennan	16(1)	16(1)	12	12	0	0	2	2	50	50
Leo Casey	20(2)	18(2)	2	2	0	0	0	0	8	8
Jason Clegg	20(13)	19(11)	3	3	0	0	0	0	12	12
Dean Cross	7	5	3	3	0	0	0	0	12	12
Gavin Dodd	12(4)	11(3)	7	6	0	0	1	1	29	25
Lee Doran	(7)	(6)	0	0	0	0	0	0	0	0
Chris Farrell	7(19)	6(18)	2	1	0	0	0	0	8	4
Phil Farrell	34	31	5	4	0	0	0	0	20	16
Mike Ford	8(12)	8(10)	1	1	0	0	2	2	6	6
Anthony Gibbons	32	30	13	13	0	0	0	0	52	52
David Gibbons	29(1)	26(1)	17	13	0	0	0	0	68	52
Danny Guest	1(25)	(24)	0	0	0	0	0	0	0	0
Joey Hayes	10	10	5	5	0	0	0	0	20	20
Bryan Henare	10(1)	10(1)	6	6	0	0	0	0	24	24
John Hough	21(6)	18(6)	5	5	0	0	0	0	20	20
Gavin Johnson	(1)	(1)	0	0	0	0	0	0	0	0
Daryl Lacey	20(4)	19(4)	5	5	0	0	0	0	20	20
Kevin Mannion	18(9)	16(8)	7	7	0	0	0	0	28	28
Shayne McMenemy	1	1	0	0	0	0	0	0	0	0
Joe McNicholas	14	14	8	8	0	0	0	0	32	32
Paul Norton	24(7)	24(4)	3	2	0	0	0	0	12	8
Andy Procter	11(9)	9(9)	2	2	0	0	0	0	8	8
Pat Rich	34	31	7	6	146	133	0	0	320	290
Neil Roden	34	31	16	16	0	0	6	5	70	69
Mark Sibson	22(1)	19(1)	18	14	0	0	0	0	72	56
Ian Sinfield	18(7)	15(7)	1	1	0	0	0	0	4	4

Pat Rich

LEAGUE RECORD
P28-W21-D0-L7
(4th, NFP/Grand Final Runners Up)
F780, A416, Diff+364
42 points.

CHALLENGE CUP
Round Five

ATTENDANCES
Best - v Leigh (NFP - 4,747)
Worst - v Hunslet (NFP - 1,038)
Total (NFP only) - 25,771
Average (NFP only) - 1,841
(Down by 356 on 2000)

ROCHDALE HORNETS

DATE	FIXTURE	RESULT	SCORERS	LGE	ATT
3/12/00	Workington (a)	L18-8	t:Sculthorpe g:Wood(2)	N/A	1,384
10/12/00	Widnes (h)	L14-24	t:Wood,Fearon,Miller g:Wood	15th	1,547
17/12/00	Chorley (h)	W52-12	t:Coates(2),Bunce(2),Mayberry(2),Wood,Larder,Miller,Fearon g:Wood(6)	11th	745
24/12/00	Oldham (h)	L6-10	t:Stephenson g:Wood	12th	3,402
7/1/01	Swinton (a)	W4-8	t:Ayres g:Wood(2)	10th	1,153
27/1/01	Wigan RB (h) (CCR3)	W52-0	t:Watson(2),Wood(2),Rogers(2),Stephenson,Owen,Billy,Newall g:Coates(5),Wood	N/A	731
31/1/01	Whitehaven (a)	L13-4	t:O'Meara	12th	641
4/2/01	Leigh (a)	L48-0	No Scorers	16th	2,568
13/2/01	Hunslet (h) (CCR4)	W38-4	t:Billy(2),Robinson,Watson,O'Meara,Calland,Larder g:Wood(3),Robinson,Coates	N/A	605
18/2/01	Doncaster (h)	W26-6	t:Robinson,Wood,Calland g:Wood(5)	13th	1,058
25/2/01	Villeneuve (h) (CCR5)	L19-26	t:O'Meara,Billy,Robinson g:Wood(3) fg:Coates	N/A	817
7/3/01	Keighley (h)	W20-23	t:Billy(2),McHugh g:Wood(5) fg:Sculthorpe	11th	1,533
11/3/01	Hunslet (a)	W20-42	t:Billy(2),Owen,Robinson,Ayres,Larder,Wood g:Wood(7)	11th	746
18/3/01	Dewsbury (h)	W44-26	t:Watson(2),Robinson,Billy,Larder,Owen,McHugh,Ayres g:Wood(6)	11th	1,195
25/3/01	Hull KR (a)	L12-6	t:O'Meara g:Wood	11th	1,513
1/4/01	Gateshead (a)	W15-40	t:Bunyan(2),Billy(2),Tawhai,Robinson,Owen,O'Meara g:Wood(3),Ayres	11th	387
8/4/01	York (h)	W98-0	t:Billy(5),O'Meara(4),Robinson(3),Cooper,Watson,Bunce,Larder,Owen,Wood,Bunyan g:Wood(11)	11th	762
13/4/01	Oldham (a)	W10-38	t:Watson(2),Bunyan,Cooper,Calland,Owen g:Wood(7)	8th	2,398
17/4/01	Sheffield (h)	W46-8	t:Robinson(2),Tawhai,Bunyan,Watson,Wood,Billy g:Wood(9)	6th	1,101
22/4/01	Featherstone (a)	W18-20	t:Ireland,Sculthorpe,Calland,Billy g:Wood(2)	6th	1,746
6/5/01	Workington (h)	W38-16	t:Billy(2),Larder,Sculthorpe,Calland,Tawhai,Robinson g:Wood(5)	7th	1,067
9/5/01	Hull KR (h)	W32-10	t:Billy(2),Calland,Bunyan,Owen,Cooper g:Wood(4)	6th	1,102
13/5/01	Widnes (a)	L44-18	t:Stephenson(2),Calland,Bunyan g:Gartland	7th	3,860
20/5/01	Chorley (a)	W10-66	t:Owen(3),Berry(3),Larder(2),Gartland(2),Wood,Tawhai,McHugh g:Wood(7)	5th	311
27/5/01	Swinton (h)	W32-9	t:Wood,O'Meara,Calland,Cooper,Gartland,Berry g:Wood(3),Gartland	4th	1,116
3/6/01	Batley (h)	W36-10	t:Wood(2),McHugh(2),O'Meara,Calland,Bunyan,Cooper g:Wood(2)	5th	1,076
10/6/01	Whitehaven (h)	W34-24	t:Billy(2),Cooper,Sculthorpe,Watson,Berry g:Wood(3),Gartland(2)	5th	1,190
17/6/01	Leigh (h)	W36-4	t:Calland(2),Billy,Robinson,Wood,McHugh g:Wood(6)	5th	2,473
20/6/01	Barrow (h)	W38-10	t:Cooper(2),O'Meara,Bunyan,McHugh,Robinson,Billy g:Wood(5)	4th	1,083
24/6/01	Doncaster (a)	W22-34	t:Billy,Robinson,Rogers,Wood,O'Meara,Calland g:Wood(5)	4th	899
1/7/01	Batley (a)	W10-26	t:Billy(2),Robinson,Berry g:Wood(5)	3rd	728
8/7/01	Widnes (a) (PSF)	L34-24	t:Robinson(2),Stephenson,Owen g:Wood(4)	N/A	4,202
15/7/01	Hull KR (h) (MiSF)	W21-14	t:Cooper,Billy,Bunyan,Wood g:Wood(2) fg:Sculthorpe	N/A	2,252
22/7/01	Oldham (h) (MaSF)	L32-39	t:Sculthorpe,Cooper,Robinson,Billy,Calland,Wood g:Wood(4)	N/A	4,153

	APP		TRIES		GOALS		FG		PTS	
	ALL	NFP	ALL	NFP	ALL	NFP	ALL	NFP	ALL	NFP
Neil Alexander	1(2)	1(2)	0	0	0	0	0	0	0	0
Paul Ashton	1	1	0	0	0	0	0	0	0	0
Warren Ayres	11(7)	10(7)	3	3	1	1	0	0	14	14
Joe Berry	(14)	(14)	6	6	0	0	0	0	24	24
Marlon Billy	33	30	31	27	0	0	0	0	124	108
Martin Bunce	8(14)	6(14)	3	3	0	0	0	0	12	12
James Bunyan	16(7)	16(7)	10	10	0	0	0	0	40	40
Matt Calland	23(1)	22	13	12	0	0	0	0	52	48
Steve Campbell	(7)	(6)	0	0	0	0	0	0	0	0
Mick Coates	11	8	2	2	6	0	1	0	21	8
Sean Cooper	27(2)	24(2)	10	10	0	0	0	0	40	40
Mickey Edwards	(3)	(3)	0	0	0	0	0	0	0	0
Danny Fearon	4(1)	4(1)	2	2	0	0	0	0	8	8
Steve Gartland	2(11)	2(11)	3	3	4	4	0	0	20	20
Rob Hall	(1)	(1)	0	0	0	0	0	0	0	0
Andy Ireland	31(3)	29(2)	1	1	0	0	0	0	4	4
Matt Knowles	2(4)	2(4)	0	0	0	0	0	0	0	0
David Larder	12(9)	11(8)	8	7	0	0	0	0	32	28
Mick Martindale	1(3)	(1)	0	0	0	0	0	0	0	0
Casey Mayberry	1(5)	1(3)	2	2	0	0	0	0	8	8
Wayne McHugh	9(3)	8(3)	7	7	0	0	0	0	28	28
Marlon Miller	5	5	2	2	0	0	0	0	8	8
Chris Newall	(3)	(2)	1	0	0	0	0	0	4	0
Brendan O'Meara	33	30	13	11	0	0	0	0	52	44
Paul Owen	33	30	11	10	0	0	0	0	44	40
Mark Powell	(1)	(1)	0	0	0	0	0	0	0	0
Dave Radley	(2)	(1)	0	0	0	0	0	0	0	0
Neil Ramsden	(1)	(1)	0	0	0	0	0	0	0	0
Darren Robinson	22(2)	20(2)	20	18	1	0	0	0	82	72
Wes Rogers	17(10)	15(9)	3	1	0	0	0	0	12	4
Danny Sculthorpe	33	30	5	5	0	0	2	2	22	22
Ben Simpson	(7)	(6)	0	0	0	0	0	0	0	0
David Stephenson	24(6)	21(6)	5	4	0	0	0	0	20	16
Latham Tawhai	20	20	4	4	0	0	0	0	16	16
Dave Watson	30	28	10	7	0	0	0	0	40	28
Danny Wood	33	30	16	14	130	123	0	0	324	302

Marlon Billy

LEAGUE RECORD
P28-W21-D0-L7
(3rd, NFP/Major Semi Finalists)
F865, A433, Diff+432
42 points.

CHALLENGE CUP
Round Five

ATTENDANCES
Best - v Oldham (MaSF - 4,153)
Worst - v Hunslet (CC - 605)
Total (NFP, inc play-offs) - 25,322
Average (NFP, inc play-offs) - 1,583
(Up by 408 on 2000)

SHEFFIELD EAGLES

DATE	FIXTURE	RESULT	SCORERS	LGE	ATT
3/12/00	Batley (h)	W34-1	t:Brent(2),Goddard,Briggs,Judge g:Goddard(7)	N/A	1,429
10/12/00	Featherstone (a)	W12-15	t:Wells g:Goddard(5) fg:Robinson	3rd	2,359
17/12/00	Hunslet (a)	L14-0	No Scorers	6th	856
26/12/00	Doncaster (a)	L22-2	g:Goddard	9th	1,970
7/1/01	Keighley (h)	L16-52	t:I Brown(2),Brent g:Goddard(2)	13th	1,642
24/1/01	Gateshead (h)	W38-12	t:Thompson(2),Rhodes(2),Kite,Goddard g:Goddard(7)	10th	753
28/1/01	East Leeds (h) (CCR3)	W42-0	t:Kite(3),Rhodes,Walker,Hewitt,Thompson g:Goddard(6),G Brown	N/A	778
31/1/01	Dewsbury (h)	L6-25	t:Goddard g:Goddard	10th	862
4/2/01	Hull KR (h)	L11-12	t:Walker,Poynter g:G Brown fg:Robinson	10th	1,081
11/2/01	Doncaster (a) (CCR4)	L14-12	t:I Brown g:Goddard(4)	N/A	1,344
18/2/01	Workington (a)	L15-12	t:Goddard,Thompson g:Goddard(2)	14th	990
25/2/01	York (a)	W6-48	t:Goddard(2),Wright,Poynter,Thompson,I Brown,Flynn,Walker g:Goddard(8)	10th	455
4/3/01	Barrow (h)	W40-16	t:Goddard(2),Chapman(2),Walker,Bruce,Speak g:Goddard(6)	10th	838
11/3/01	Widnes (h)	W26-17	t:Goddard,Chapman,Judge,Rhodes g:Goddard(5)	9th	1,560
18/3/01	Oldham (a)	L24-16	t:Walker,Poynter g:Goddard(4)	10th	1,503
25/3/01	Whitehaven (a)	W12-18	t:Kite,Poynter,Wells g:Goddard(3)	10th	865
31/3/01	Chorley (h)	W60-4	t:Kite(2),Poynter(2),Walker(2),Tillyer,Brent,Thompson,Speak,Wells g:Goddard(7),G Brown	9th	870
8/4/01	Swinton (a)	W22-23	t:Wells,Goddard,Thompson,Poynter g:Goddard(3) fg:Goddard	7th	715
13/4/01	Doncaster (h)	W28-4	t:Kite(2),Rhodes,Chapman,Walker g:Goddard(4)	6th	1,632
17/4/01	Rochdale (a)	L46-8	t:Hewitt g:Goddard(2)	8th	1,101
29/4/01	Leigh (h)	L28-34	t:Chapman(2),Flynn,Wright,Sodje g:Goddard(2),G Brown(2)	11th	1,614
6/5/01	Batley (a)	L23-2	g:Goddard	12th	693
13/5/01	Featherstone (h)	L14-28	t:Flynn,Kite g:Goddard(3)	12th	1,296
20/5/01	Hunslet (h)	W40-10	t:Hill,Sodje,Brent,Aston,Hewitt,Wells,Poynter g:Goddard(3),G Brown(3)	12th	1,154
27/5/01	Keighley (a)	L26-14	t:Judge,Hewitt,I Brown g:Goddard	12th	1,471
3/6/01	York (h)	W56-0	t:Wells(2),Brent(2),Rhodes,Hewitt,Chapman,Poynter,Goddard,Howieson g:Goddard(5),G Brown	12th	1,008
10/6/01	Dewsbury (a)	L28-16	t:G Brown,Goddard,Howieson g:Goddard(2)	12th	700
17/6/01	Hull KR (a)	W14-18	t:I Brown,Thompson,Goddard g:Goddard(3)	12th	1,625
24/6/01	Workington (h)	W34-26	t:Hewitt(2),Dobson,Kershaw,Poynter,Goddard g:Goddard(5)	11th	1,259
1/7/01	Barrow (a)	L38-14	t:Wells,G Brown g:G Brown(2),Goddard	11th	945

	APP		TRIES		GOALS		FG		PTS	
	ALL	NFP	ALL	NFP	ALL	NFP	ALL	NFP	ALL	NFP
Mark Aston	9(12)	9(10)	1	1	0	0	0	0	4	4
Lee Bettinson	(2)	(2)	0	0	0	0	0	0	0	0
Andy Brent	7(16)	6(15)	7	7	0	0	0	0	28	28
Carl Briggs	5	5	1	1	0	0	0	0	4	4
Gavin Brown	19(1)	17(1)	2	2	13	12	0	0	34	32
Ian Brown	6(16)	6(14)	6	5	0	0	0	0	24	20
Jon Bruce	16(5)	15(4)	1	1	0	0	0	0	4	4
Chris Chapman	18(4)	16(4)	7	7	0	0	0	0	28	28
Heath Cruckshank	13(1)	11(1)	0	0	0	0	0	0	0	0
Gareth Dobson	11	11	1	1	0	0	0	0	4	4
Wayne Flynn	20	19	3	3	0	0	0	0	12	12
Matthew Foster	2(1)	2(1)	0	0	0	0	0	0	0	0
Richard Goddard	30	28	14	14	103	93	1	1	263	243
Gareth Hewitt	14(6)	13(6)	7	6	0	0	0	0	28	24
Steve Hill	21(3)	20(3)	1	1	0	0	0	0	4	4
Jack Howieson	(7)	(7)	2	2	0	0	0	0	8	8
Chris Judge	10(2)	10(2)	3	3	0	0	0	0	12	12
Billy Kershaw	5(7)	5(7)	1	1	0	0	0	0	4	4
Neil Kite	29	27	10	7	0	0	0	0	40	28
Andy Poynter	23(1)	23(1)	10	10	0	0	0	0	40	40
Scott Rhodes	17(7)	16(6)	6	5	0	0	0	0	24	20
Chris Robinson	8(1)	7(1)	0	0	0	0	2	2	2	2
Bright Sodje	4	4	2	2	0	0	0	0	8	8
Andy Speak	17	15	2	2	0	0	0	0	8	8
Darren Summerill	5(8)	5(8)	0	0	0	0	0	0	0	0
Ian Thompson	26(1)	24(1)	8	7	0	0	0	0	32	28
Simon Tillyer	(7)	(6)	1	1	0	0	0	0	4	4
Steve Walker	17(3)	15(3)	8	7	0	0	0	0	32	28
Paul Wells	21(5)	20(5)	8	8	0	0	0	0	32	32
Ricky Wright	17(3)	15(3)	2	2	0	0	0	0	8	8

Richard Goddard

LEAGUE RECORD
P28-W14-D0-L14
(11th, NFP)
F637, A543, Diff+94
28 points.

CHALLENGE CUP
Round Four

ATTENDANCES
Best - v Keighley (NFP - 1,642)
Worst - v Gateshead (NFP - 753)
Total (NFP only) - 16,998
Average (NFP only) - 1,214
(Up by 38 on 2000)

SWINTON LIONS

DATE	FIXTURE	RESULT	SCORERS	LGE	ATT
3/12/00	Chorley (a)	W12-30	t:Nanyn(2),P Loughlin,Smith,Cheetham,Crossland g:Nanyn(3)	N/A	670
10/12/00	Whitehaven (a)	W4-8	t:Cheetham,Smith	4th	1,138
17/12/00	Barrow (h)	W26-24	t:Russell,English,Nanyn,Mead,Smith g:Nanyn(3)	3rd	862
1/1/01	Leigh (a)	L46-4	t:Cushion	6th	2,881
7/1/01	Rochdale (h)	L4-8	t:Nanyn	9th	1,153
25/1/01	Widnes (a)	L16-8	t:Bateman g:Nanyn(2)	11th	3,004
28/1/01	N Earswick (h) (CCR3)	W44-12	t:Nanyn(2),Stazicker(2),Cheetham(2),Napolitano,Bateman,Peet g:Nanyn(4)	N/A	478
4/2/01	Workington (h)	L20-29	t:Veivers,Smith,Hudson,Cheetham g:P Loughlin,Nanyn	11th	630
11/2/01	Leeds (h) (CCR4)	L10-106	t:P Loughlin,Smith g:Nanyn	N/A	3,239
18/2/01	Hunslet (h)	L26-16	t:P Loughlin(2),Nanyn g:Nanyn(2)	15th	666
4/3/01	Dewsbury (h)	L18-20	t:Smith(2),Veivers g:Nanyn(3)	15th	846
11/3/01	Hull KR (a)	L32-6	t:Doherty g:Nanyn	16th	1,536
18/3/01	Featherstone (h)	W28-25	t:Hudson(2),Nanyn,Barraclough,Mead g:Nanyn(4)	15th	947
25/3/01	York (h)	W74-0	t:Nanyn(3),Veivers(2),Hudson(2),Smith(2),Holdstock(2),Furey, Evans,Bateman g:Nanyn(9)	15th	545
1/4/01	Batley (h)	L12-34	t:Bateman(2) g:Nanyn(2)	15th	743
8/4/01	Sheffield (h)	L22-23	t:Smith(2),Nanyn,Napolitano g:Nanyn(3)	15th	715
13/4/01	Keighley (a)	W22-26	t:Smith,Cushion,Cheetham,Bateman g:Nanyn(4) fg:Waring(2)	15th	1,719
15/4/01	Leigh (h)	L0-40	No Scorers	15th	1,892
22/4/01	Doncaster (h)	W19-18	t:Napolitano,Nanyn,Bateman,Russell g:Nanyn fg:Evans	15th	674
2/5/01	Oldham (h)	L10-33	t:Furey,Waring g:Nanyn	15th	1,014
6/5/01	Gateshead (h)	W20-8	t:Cheetham(2),Smith,Doherty g:Nanyn(2)	14th	614
9/5/01	Oldham (a)	L22-20	t:Mead,Doherty,Cheetham g:Nanyn(4)	14th	1,360
13/5/01	Doncaster (a)	L27-26	t:Smith(2),Doherty,Gallagher g:Nanyn(5)	14th	819
20/5/01	Barrow (a)	L40-26	t:English,Bateman,Waring,Barraclough,Smith g:Nanyn(3)	15th	602
27/5/01	Rochdale (a)	L32-9	t:Holdstock g:Nanyn(2) fg:Waring	15th	1,116
3/6/01	Widnes (h)	L0-62	No Scorers	15th	1,761
10/6/01	Batley (a)	L38-24	t:Bateman(2),Chambers,Evans,Nanyn g:Nanyn(2)	15th	418
17/6/01	Workington (a)	L34-10	t:Woods,Gallagher g:Nanyn	15th	737
24/6/01	Hunslet (h)	W30-20	t:Woods(2),Chambers,Bateman,Doherty,Mead g:Nanyn(2),Doherty	15th	823
1/7/01	Dewsbury (a)	W16-42	t:English(2),Woods,Veivers,Nanyn,Evans,Butler g:Nanyn(7)	15th	853

	APP		TRIES		GOALS		FG		PTS	
	ALL	NFP	ALL	NFP	ALL	NFP	ALL	NFP	ALL	NFP
Rob Barraclough	29	27	2	2	0	0	0	0	8	8
Tony Barrow	2(5)	(5)	0	0	0	0	0	0	0	0
Matt Bateman	25	23	11	10	0	0	0	0	44	40
Danny Butler	1(17)	1(17)	1	1	0	0	0	0	4	4
Nick Cammann	2(9)	1(9)	0	0	0	0	0	0	0	0
Gareth Chambers	4	4	2	2	0	0	0	0	8	8
Andy Cheetham	14(4)	12(4)	9	7	0	0	0	0	36	28
Paul Crossland	1(3)	(3)	1	1	0	0	0	0	4	4
Phil Cushion	22	21	2	2	0	0	0	0	8	8
Jon-Paul Doherty	15(9)	14(9)	5	5	1	1	0	0	22	22
Wayne English	15(3)	14(2)	4	4	0	0	0	0	16	16
Jim Evans	14(6)	14(5)	3	3	0	0	1	1	13	13
Shaun Furey	15(2)	15(2)	2	2	0	0	0	0	8	8
Rob Gallagher	5(4)	5(4)	2	2	0	0	0	0	8	8
Lee Hansen	26(1)	25	0	0	0	0	0	0	0	0
Dale Holdstock	13(4)	13(4)	3	3	0	0	0	0	12	12
Lee Hudson	11(3)	10(2)	5	5	0	0	0	0	20	20
Wayne Jackman	1(1)	1(1)	0	0	0	0	0	0	0	0
Ian Lewis	(5)	(5)	0	0	0	0	0	0	0	0
Mike Loughlin	7(4)	7(4)	0	0	0	0	0	0	0	0
Paul Loughlin	10(1)	9(1)	4	3	1	1	0	0	18	14
Adrian Mead	16(4)	16(4)	4	4	0	0	0	0	16	16
Mick Nanyn	29	27	15	13	72	67	0	0	204	186
Carlo Napolitano	7(8)	6(7)	3	2	0	0	0	0	12	8
Jonathan Neill	6	6	0	0	0	0	0	0	0	0
Chris Newall	4(5)	4(5)	0	0	0	0	0	0	0	0
Kelvin Peet	7	5	1	0	0	0	0	0	4	0
Robert Russell	5(3)	4(2)	2	2	0	0	0	0	8	8
Paul Smith	23(3)	22(2)	16	15	0	0	0	0	64	60
Ryan Stazicker	5(8)	4(8)	2	0	0	0	0	0	8	0
Phil Veivers	20(1)	19	5	5	0	0	0	0	20	20
Phil Waring	19(2)	18(2)	2	2	0	0	3	3	11	11
Mike Woods	4	4	4	4	0	0	0	0	16	16

Rob Barraclough

LEAGUE RECORD
P28-W10-D0-L18
(15th, NFP)
F538, A711, Diff-173
20 points.

CHALLENGE CUP
Round Four

ATTENDANCES
Best - v Leeds (CC - 3,239)
Worst - v New Earswick (CC - 478)
Total (NFP only) - 13,219
Average (NFP only) - 944
(Down by 160 on 2000)

WHITEHAVEN

DATE	FIXTURE	RESULT	SCORERS	LGE	ATT
3/12/00	Widnes (a)	L22-14	t:Seeds,Kiddie g:O'Neill(3)	N/A	3,864
10/12/00	Swinton (h)	L4-8	t:Walsh	13th	1,138
17/12/00	Leigh (h)	L8-30	t:Miller g:O'Neill(2)	16th	1,061
4/1/01	Workington (a)	L31-10	t:Wignall g:Kirkbride(3)	17th	2,460
7/1/01	Barrow (a)	L5-4	t:Walsh	17th	1,008
10/1/01	Chorley (h)	W28-4	t:C Campbell,Morton,Kiddie,Lester,Seeds g:Kirkbride(3),Wilson	16th	638
28/1/01	Oldham S A (h) (CCR3)	W34-16	t:Miller(2),Hill,Walsh,Seeds,Morton,C Campbell g:Kirkbride(3)	N/A	616
31/1/01	Rochdale (h)	W13-4	t:Morton,Lester g:Kirkbride(2) fg:Kirkbride	15th	641
14/2/01	Gateshead (a) (CCR4)	W0-56	t:Seeds(4),Jackson(2),Morton,C Campbell,Joe,Nelson g:Kirkbride(8)	N/A	377
18/2/01	Hull KR (a)	D10-10	t:Miller g:Kirkbride(3)	16th	1,385
25/2/01	St Helens (h) (CCR5)	L22-34	t:Lester,Cox,Seeds g:Kirkbride(5)	N/A	4,750
7/3/01	Featherstone (h)	W19-10	t:Jackson(2),Wignall g:Jackson(3) fg:Joe	13th	927
11/3/01	Gateshead (a)	W4-23	t:Lester(2),Wignall,Joe g:Jackson(3) fg:Joe	12th	532
14/3/01	Oldham (a)	W8-19	t:O'Neill,Hill,Seeds g:Jackson(3) fg:Jackson	11th	1,179
18/3/01	Batley (a)	L18-14	t:Joe,Wignall,Hill g:O'Neill	12th	449
25/3/01	Sheffield (h)	L12-18	t:Seeds(2) g:O'Neill(2)	13th	865
1/4/01	Doncaster (a)	L28-24	t:Seeds,C Campbell,Joe,Devlin g:O'Neill(3) fg:Kiddie,Joe	13th	1,093
8/4/01	Keighley (h)	W17-4	t:Wignall,Lester,Devlin g:Kirkbride(2) fg:Kirkbride	13th	895
13/4/01	Workington (h)	W38-18	t:Hill(3),Miller(2),O'Neill,Lester g:Kirkbride(5)	13th	1,795
16/4/01	Chorley (a)	W10-42	t:Seeds(2),Joe(2),Kiddie,Devlin,Hill,Kirkbride g:O'Neill(4),Kirkbride	13th	295
22/4/01	Hunslet (h)	W50-10	t:Lester(3),Joe(2),Hill(2),O'Neill,Wallace g:O'Neill(7)	13th	785
29/4/01	York (a)	W6-54	t:Kirkbride(2),Lester(2),Wallace(2),Sherwen,R Purdham,O'Neill,Seeds g:O'Neill(7)	10th	314
6/5/01	Widnes (h)	L14-16	t:Lester,Wallace,Miller g:Kirkbride	10th	1,239
9/5/01	Keighley (a)	W4-30	t:R Purdham(2),Joe,Kirkbride,Devlin g:Kirkbride(5)	9th	1,208
20/5/01	Leigh (a)	L42-4	t:G Purdham	11th	2,409
27/5/01	Barrow (h)	W24-0	t:Devlin,Lester,O'Neill,Seeds g:Kirkbride(4)	11th	850
3/6/01	Dewsbury (h)	W18-17	t:Lester,G Purdham,Sherwen g:Kirkbride(2) fg:Kirkbride(2)	11th	725
10/6/01	Rochdale (a)	L34-24	t:R Purdham,Seeds,Wallace,Hill g:Kirkbride(4)	11th	1,190
17/6/01	Oldham (h)	L15-16	t:Roach(2),R Purdham g:Kirkbride fg:R Purdham	11th	1,027
24/6/01	Gateshead (h)	W52-22	t:Seeds(4),R Purdham(3),Wallace,Vaughan g:Kirkbride(7),R Purdham	10th	848
1/7/01	Featherstone (a)	W20-24	t:Lester,Kirkbride,Sherwen g:Kirkbride(5) fg:Kirkbride(2)	10th	1,550

	APP		TRIES		GOALS		FG		PTS	
	ALL	NFP	ALL	NFP	ALL	NFP	ALL	NFP	ALL	NFP
Alan Bone	(4)	(4)	0	0	0	0	0	0	0	0
Chris Campbell	15(1)	12(1)	4	2	0	0	0	0	16	8
Ryan Campbell	1(6)	1(6)	0	0	0	0	0	0	0	0
Craig Chambers	5	5	0	0	0	0	0	0	0	0
Mark Cox	28(1)	25(1)	1	0	0	0	0	0	4	0
Jason Critchley	6	6	0	0	0	0	0	0	0	0
Tony Cunningham	(2)	(2)	0	0	0	0	0	0	0	0
Ian Devlin	9(12)	8(10)	5	5	0	0	0	0	20	20
David Fatialofa	15(2)	12(2)	0	0	0	0	0	0	0	0
Paul Graham	(1)	(1)	0	0	0	0	0	0	0	0
Howard Hill	21(6)	18(6)	10	9	0	0	0	0	40	36
Marc Jackson	6(10)	6(7)	4	2	9	9	1	1	35	27
Leroy Joe	16(3)	14(2)	9	8	0	0	3	3	39	35
Lee Kiddie	13(6)	12(6)	3	3	0	0	1	1	13	13
Darren King	(1)	(1)	0	0	0	0	0	0	0	0
Steve Kirkbride	21(2)	18(2)	5	5	64	48	6	6	154	122
Aaron Lester	30	27	16	15	0	0	0	0	64	60
Stephen McCourt	(1)	(1)	0	0	0	0	0	0	0	0
Spencer Miller	28(3)	25(3)	7	5	0	0	0	0	28	20
Graeme Morton	11	8	4	2	0	0	0	0	16	8
Andrew Nelson	4(1)	1(1)	1	0	0	0	0	0	4	0
Paul O'Neill	21(3)	20(3)	5	5	29	29	0	0	78	78
Garry Purdham	21(4)	19(3)	2	2	0	0	0	0	8	8
Robert Purdham	12(10)	12(10)	8	8	1	1	1	1	35	35
Jason Roach	6	6	2	2	0	0	0	0	8	8
David Seeds	30	27	21	15	0	0	0	0	84	60
Phil Sherwen	10(13)	10(11)	3	3	0	0	0	0	12	12
Gary Smith	8(12)	8(12)	0	0	0	0	0	0	0	0
Dean Vaughan	17(14)	17(11)	1	1	0	0	0	0	4	4
Mark Wallace	12	12	6	6	0	0	0	0	24	24
Craig Walsh	8	7	3	2	0	0	0	0	12	8
Jonathan Wignall	13	13	5	5	0	0	0	0	20	20
Wesley Wilson	17	15	0	0	1	1	0	0	2	2

Aaron Lester

LEAGUE RECORD
P28-W15-D1-L12
(10th, NFP)
F608, A419, Diff+189
31 points.

CHALLENGE CUP
Round Five

ATTENDANCES
Best - v St Helens (CC - 4,750)
Worst - v Oldham S A (CC - 616)
Total (NFP only) - 13,434
Average (NFP only) - 960
(Up by 106 on 2000)

WIDNES VIKINGS

DATE	FIXTURE	RESULT	SCORERS	LGE	ATT
3/12/00	Whitehaven (h)	W22-14	t:Coussons,Forster,Martin,Munro,Demetriou g:Hammond	N/A	3,864
10/12/00	Rochdale (a)	W14-24	t:Cantillon,Martin,Coussons,Crompton g:Hammond(4)	6th	1,547
26/12/00	Leigh (h)	L20-25	t:Coussons,Percival,Gee,Argent g:Jones(2)	8th	6,644
1/1/01	Oldham (a)	L20-12	t:Coussons,Munro,Crompton	9th	3,471
7/1/01	Workington (h)	W26-16	t:Munro(2),Forster,Holgate,McKinney,Cantillon g:Watson	8th	3,312
25/1/01	Swinton (h)	W16-8	t:Cantillon,Munro g:Watson(4)	6th	3,004
28/1/01	Wigan St Pats (h) (CCR3)	W70-2	t:Cantillon(4),Percival(3),Munro(2),Jones,Gee,Coussons,Faimalo g:Watson(9)	N/A	2,465
4/2/01	Barrow (a)	D6-6	t:Percival g:Watson	7th	1,116
11/2/01	Bradford (a) (CCR4)	L54-10	t:Hodgkinson,Crompton g:Watson	N/A	7,760
18/2/01	York (h)	W90-6	t:Cantillon(7),Gee(2),Coussons,Percival,Demetriou,Munro,Hill,Hammond, Forster g:Watson(13)	7th	2,941
25/2/01	Chorley (a)	W14-48	t:Knox(3),Coussons(2),Demetriou(2),Munro,Argent g:Watson(6)	4th	710
7/3/01	Gateshead (a)	W18-30	t:Hammond,Cantillon,Crouthers,Demetriou,Knox g:Watson(5)	4th	517
11/3/01	Sheffield (a)	L26-17	t:Cantillon(2),Cook g:Watson(2) fg:Hammond	4th	1,560
18/3/01	Doncaster (h)	L10-18	t:Coussons,Cantillon g:Cook	4th	3,209
25/3/01	Keighley (h)	L19-22	t:Holgate(2),Cantillon g:Watson(3) fg:Watson	8th	3,469
1/4/01	Hunslet (h)	W64-4	t:Demetriou(2),Long(2),Cantillon(2),Munro(2),Atcheson,Knox,Coussons, Crompton g:Watson(6),Agar(2)	7th	3,253
7/4/01	Dewsbury (a)	W12-13	t:Demetriou,Cantillon g:Watson(2) fg:Watson	5th	2,135
13/4/01	Leigh (a)	L26-22	t:Richardson,Atcheson,Crompton g:Watson(5)	7th	4,914
16/4/01	Oldham (h)	W34-16	t:Cantillon(2),Demetriou,Gee,Percival,Agar g:Agar(5)	5th	4,072
22/4/01	Hull KR (h)	W28-0	t:Cantillon(2),Crompton,Coussons,Munro g:Jones(3),Agar	4th	3,726
6/5/01	Whitehaven (a)	W14-16	t:Coussons,Demetriou,Munro g:Watson,Agar	5th	1,239
9/5/01	Gateshead (a)	W72-4	t:Cantillon(4),Coussons,Weston(2),Percival(2),Faimalo,Demetriou, Munro,Jones g:Watson(8)	4th	3,105
13/5/01	Rochdale (h)	W44-18	t:Percival(3),Long(2),Munro,Cantillon,Weston g:Weston(6)	4th	3,860
20/5/01	Featherstone (h)	W25-22	t:Munro,Weston,Demetriou,McKinney g:Weston(4) fg:Agar	3rd	4,372
27/5/01	Workington (a)	W6-25	t:Cantillon,Holgate,Percival,Munro g:Weston(4) fg:Agar	3rd	1,341
3/6/01	Swinton (a)	W0-62	t:Cantillon(5),Long(2),Weston,Agar,McKinney,Munro g:Weston(9)	3rd	1,761
6/6/01	Batley (a)	W15-36	t:Cantillon(2),Knox,Munro,Richardson,Craig g:Weston(6)	3rd	890
10/6/01	Chorley (h)	W72-18	t:Cantillon(3),Craig(3),Richardson(2),Coussons(2),Jones,Demetriou, Munro,Gee g:Jones(8)	2nd	3,683
24/6/01	York (a)	W11-66	t:Cantillon(3),Richardson(2),Craig(2),Percival,Crompton,Munro,Weston, Long g:Watson(5),Weston(4)	3rd	952
1/7/01	Hunslet (a)	W4-42	t:Crompton(2),Gee,Cantillon,Weston,Knox,Munro g:Weston(7)	2nd	1,498
8/7/01	Rochdale (h) (PSF)	W34-24	t:Long(2),Demetriou,Atcheson,Craig,Cantillon g:Agar(4),Weston	N/A	4,202
22/7/01	Leigh (a) (MaSF)	W18-26	t:Percival(2),Munro(2),McKinney g:Weston(2) fg:Agar,Knox	N/A	6,399
28/7/01	Oldham (GF)	W14-24	t:Demetriou(2),Gee,Cantillon,Munro g:Weston(2)	N/A	8,974

	APP		TRIES		GOALS		FG		PTS	
	ALL	NFP	ALL	NFP	ALL	NFP	ALL	NFP	ALL	NFP
Richard Agar	13(3)	13(3)	2	2	13	13	3	3	37	37
Steve Argent	1(6)	1(5)	2	2	0	0	0	0	8	8
Paul Atcheson	14	14	3	3	0	0	0	0	12	12
Lee Birdseye	1	1	0	0	0	0	0	0	0	0
Phil Cantillon	33	31	48	44	0	0	0	0	192	176
Paul Cook	3(1)	3(1)	1	1	1	1	0	0	6	6
Phil Coussons	23(2)	21(2)	16	15	0	0	0	0	64	60
Andy Craig	2(4)	2(4)	7	7	0	0	0	0	28	28
Martin Crompton	25(3)	23(3)	9	8	0	0	0	0	36	32
Kevin Crouthers	3(1)	3(1)	1	1	0	0	0	0	4	4
Jason Demetriou	29(3)	27(3)	16	16	0	0	0	0	64	64
Joe Faimalo	12(16)	11(15)	2	1	0	0	0	0	8	4
Mark Flanagan	1	1	0	0	0	0	0	0	0	0
Chris Foran	(2)	(2)	0	0	0	0	0	0	0	0
Mark Forster	13(4)	13(2)	3	3	0	0	0	0	12	12
Steve Gee	22(7)	20(7)	8	7	0	0	0	0	32	28
Gareth Haggerty	1	1	0	0	0	0	0	0	0	0
Karle Hammond	7(3)	6(2)	2	2	5	5	1	1	19	19
Mike Hill	1(10)	1(9)	1	1	0	0	0	0	4	4
Tommy Hodgkinson	31(1)	30	1	0	0	0	0	0	4	0
Stephen Holgate	23(3)	22(3)	4	4	0	0	0	0	16	16
David Hulme	(1)	(1)	0	0	0	0	0	0	0	0
Liam Jones	9(1)	7(1)	3	2	13	13	0	0	38	34
Eddie Kilgannon	1	1	0	0	0	0	0	0	0	0
Simon Knox	28(2)	27(2)	7	7	0	0	1	1	29	29
Matthew Long	2(16)	2(16)	9	9	0	0	0	0	36	36
Scott Martin	3	3	2	2	0	0	0	0	8	8
Chris McKinney	10(16)	8(16)	4	4	0	0	0	0	16	16
David Mills	(1)	(1)	0	0	0	0	0	0	0	0
Damian Munro	29(4)	27(4)	25	23	0	0	0	0	100	92
Chris Percival	28(2)	26(2)	16	13	0	0	0	0	64	52
Stewart Rhodes	9(7)	8(6)	0	0	0	0	0	0	0	0
Sean Richardson	16	16	6	6	0	0	0	0	24	24
Alan Shea	1(1)	1(1)	0	0	0	0	0	0	0	0
Ian Watson	22(3)	20(3)	0	0	72	62	2	2	146	126
Craig Weston	11(1)	11(1)	7	7	45	45	0	0	118	118

Jason Demetriou

LEAGUE RECORD
P28-W21-D1-L6
(2nd, NFP/Grand Final Winners,
Champions)
F961, A377, Diff+584
43 points.

CHALLENGE CUP
Round Four

ATTENDANCES
Best - v Leigh (NFP - 6,644)
Worst - v Wigan St P (CC - 2,465)
Total (NFP, inc play-offs) - 56,716
Average (NFP, inc play-offs) - 3,781
(Up by 409 on 2000)

WORKINGTON TOWN

DATE	FIXTURE	RESULT	SCORERS	LGE	ATT
3/12/00	Rochdale (h)	W18-8	t:Sturm,Lewthwaite,L Smith g:Hetherington(3)	N/A	1,384
17/12/00	Oldham (h)	L6-22	t:Lewthwaite g:J Smith	12th	1,295
4/1/01	Whitehaven (h)	W31-10	t:Okesene,Samuel,McGrady,J Smith g:Manihera(7) fg:J Smith	9th	2,460
7/1/01	Widnes (a)	L26-16	t:Lewthwaite,Savelio,Hoyles g:Hetherington,Manihera	11th	3,312
28/1/01	Cas Lock Lane (h) (CCR3)	W38-0	t:Lewthwaite(2),Sini,Sice,Frazer,Hoyles,Stoddart g:J Smith(4),Stoddart	N/A	867
31/1/01	Leigh (a)	L70-0	No Scorers	14th	2,149
4/2/01	Swinton (a)	W20-29	t:Samuel,Beaumont,Sice,Lewthwaite,Rumney g:Manihera(4) fg:Manihera	12th	630
11/2/01	Wakefield (h) (CCR4)	L6-56	t:Lewthwaite g:Manihera	N/A	1,710
14/2/01	Chorley (h)	W42-0	t:Beaumont(2),Blackburn(2),Okesene,Sini,McGrady,Lewthwaite g:Manihera(4),Rumney	9th	674
18/2/01	Sheffield (h)	W15-12	t:Lewthwaite(2),J Smith g:Hetherington fg:Hetherington	8th	990
25/2/01	Barrow (a)	W28-31	t:J Smith(2),Frazer,Sice,Lewthwaite g:Hetherington(5) fg:Manihera	8th	976
11/3/01	Keighley (h)	L4-32	t:Lewthwaite	10th	1,099
18/3/01	Hunslet (h)	W60-10	t:Lewthwaite(3),Sini(2),Frazer,Samuel,Savelio,Beaumont,Sturm,Blackburn g:Manihera(8)	9th	826
25/3/01	Gateshead (a)	W8-34	t:Lewthwaite(2),Williamson,Okesene,Rumney,Sini g:Manihera(5)	6th	617
1/4/01	Hull KR (h)	W24-18	t:Heaney,Stott,Manihera g:Manihera(6)	6th	1,064
8/4/01	Featherstone (a)	L24-4	t:Samuel	10th	1,656
13/4/01	Whitehaven (a)	L38-18	t:L Smith,Williamson,Stott g:Manihera(3)	11th	1,795
16/4/01	Barrow (h)	W29-6	t:Lewthwaite(2),Stott,Hetherington g:Manihera(5),Hetherington fg:Manihera	10th	1,103
22/4/01	York (a)	W10-60	t:Lewthwaite(5),Heaney(2),L Allen,Frazer,Beaumont,Hetherington g:Manihera(8)	8th	395
29/4/01	Dewsbury (a)	W16-22	t:L Allen,Beaumont,Sini,Hetherington g:Manihera(3)	6th	736
6/5/01	Rochdale (a)	L38-16	t:Lewthwaite(2),Hetherington g:Hetherington(2)	8th	1,067
13/5/01	Batley (h)	W25-16	t:Lewthwaite(2),Woodcock,Sice g:Hetherington(4) fg:Stott	8th	832
20/5/01	Oldham (a)	L24-18	t:Hetherington,Lewthwaite,Sice g:Manihera(3)	9th	1,276
23/5/01	Doncaster (a)	L21-10	t:Manihera,Lewthwaite g:Manihera	9th	783
27/5/01	Widnes (h)	L6-25	t:Beaumont g:Hetherington	10th	1,341
3/6/01	Chorley (a)	W8-52	t:Stott(2),Sice(2),Woodcock,Hetherington,Hoyles,Sturm,Lewthwaite g:Hetherington(5),Wood(3)	10th	282
10/6/01	Leigh (a)	L17-18	t:J Allen,Hoyles g:Hetherington(4) fg:Stott	10th	1,114
17/6/01	Swinton (h)	W34-10	t:Sice(2),Stott,Okesene,Williamson,Frazer g:Hetherington(5)	9th	737
24/6/01	Sheffield (a)	L34-26	t:Hoyles,Woodcock,Frazer,Savelio,Hetherington g:Manihera(3)	9th	1,259
1/7/01	Doncaster (h)	W34-16	t:Lewthwaite(2),Beaumont(2),Hoyles,Stott g:Manihera(5)	9th	993

	APP		TRIES		GOALS		FG		PTS	
	ALL	NFP	ALL	NFP	ALL	NFP	ALL	NFP	ALL	NFP
John Allen	6(3)	6(3)	1	1	0	0	0	0	4	4
Lee Allen	8	8	2	2	0	0	0	0	8	8
Craig Barker	(1)	(1)	0	0	0	0	0	0	0	0
Jamie Beaumont	19(6)	19(4)	9	9	0	0	0	0	36	36
William Blackburn	3(10)	2(9)	3	3	0	0	0	0	12	12
Gary Charlton	3	3	0	0	0	0	0	0	0	0
Scott Chilton	(3)	(3)	0	0	0	0	0	0	0	0
Adam Coulson	1	1	0	0	0	0	0	0	0	0
Craig Fisher	2(1)	2(1)	0	0	0	0	0	0	0	0
David Fletcher	(1)	(1)	0	0	0	0	0	0	0	0
Neil Frazer	27(2)	25(2)	6	5	0	0	0	0	24	20
Richard Haile	1	1	0	0	0	0	0	0	0	0
Jonathan Heaney	9(1)	9(1)	3	3	0	0	0	0	12	12
Kevin Hetherington	19(2)	19(2)	7	7	32	32	1	1	93	93
Micky Horner	8	6	0	0	0	0	0	0	0	0
Anthony Horton	(1)	(1)	0	0	0	0	0	0	0	0
Stuart Hoyles	14(8)	12(8)	6	5	0	0	0	0	24	20
David Humes	(2)	(2)	0	0	0	0	0	0	0	0
Graeme Lewthwaite	29	27	33	30	0	0	0	0	132	120
Tane Manihera	21(2)	20(2)	2	2	67	66	3	3	145	143
Steve McGrady	7	6	2	2	0	0	0	0	8	8
Jamie Nixon	(6)	(5)	0	0	0	0	0	0	0	0
Hitro Okesene	25(2)	24(2)	4	4	0	0	0	0	16	16
Craig Rumney	9(4)	8(4)	2	2	1	1	0	0	10	10
Anthony Samuel	30	28	4	4	0	0	0	0	16	16
Lokeni Savelio	17(13)	15(13)	3	3	0	0	0	0	12	12
Carl Sice	13(10)	11(10)	9	8	0	0	0	0	36	32
Fata Sini	11(7)	10(6)	6	5	0	0	0	0	24	20
Jamie Smith	10(1)	8(1)	4	4	5	1	1	1	27	19
Leigh Smith	13(3)	11(3)	2	2	0	0	0	0	8	8
Steve Stoddart	1(1)	1	1	0	1	0	0	0	6	0
Lynton Stott	17	17	7	7	0	0	2	2	30	30
Matt Sturm	30	28	3	3	0	0	0	0	12	12
Matthew Tunstall	7(17)	7(15)	0	0	0	0	0	0	0	0
Owen Williamson	17(3)	17(3)	3	3	0	0	0	0	12	12
Kevin Wilson	(1)	(1)	0	0	0	0	0	0	0	0
Steve Wood	6(2)	6(2)	0	0	3	3	0	0	6	6
Matthew Woodcock	7(2)	7(2)	3	3	0	0	0	0	12	12

Tane Manihera

LEAGUE RECORD
P28-W16-D0-L12
(9th, NFP)
F681, A568, Diff+113
32 points.

CHALLENGE CUP
Round Four

ATTENDANCES
Best - v Whitehaven (NFP - 2,460)
Worst - v Chorley (NFP - 674)
Total (NFP only) - 15,912
Average (NFP only) - 1,137
(Up by 278 on 2000)

YORK

DATE	FIXTURE	RESULT	SCORERS	LGE	ATT
3/12/00	Doncaster (h)	L8-26	t:Allen g:Benn(2)	N/A	1,251
10/12/00	Hull KR (a)	L2-0	No Scorers	16th	2,110
17/12/00	Keighley (h)	L14-48	t:M Smith(2),Pallister g:Austerfield	17th	943
26/12/00	Hunslet (h)	D20-20	t:Benn,Handley,Allen,McKenzie g:Benn(2)	16th	698
1/1/01	Batley (a)	L12-4	g:Benn(2)	16th	637
7/1/01	Dewsbury (a)	L50-2	g:Benn	16th	1,200
28/1/01	Oulton (h) (CCR3)	W24-12	t:Lloyd,Handley,Darling,Allen g:Oulton(4)	N/A	914
4/2/01	Featherstone (h)	L6-37	t:Darling g:Oulton	17th	704
11/2/01	Villeneuve (h) (CCR4)	L8-22	t:Handley,Austerfield	N/A	471
18/2/01	Widnes (a)	L90-6	t:Moore g:Oulton	17th	2,941
22/2/01	Gateshead (h)	W21-4	t:Dobson,Mulholland,Rumford,Allen g:Waite(2) fg:Waite	17th	426
25/2/01	Sheffield (h)	L6-48	t:Dobson g:Waite	17th	455
8/3/01	Leigh (h)	L12-84	t:Judson,Moore g:Oulton(2)	17th	428
18/3/01	Chorley (a)	L78-8	t:A Hutchinson,Lloyd	17th	254
25/3/01	Swinton (a)	L74-0	No Scorers	17th	545
1/4/01	Oldham (h)	L6-70	t:Dobson g:Oulton	17th	514
8/4/01	Rochdale (a)	L98-0	No Scorers	18th	762
13/4/01	Hunslet (a)	L30-14	t:Acklam,Bardauskas,Moore g:Waite	18th	612
16/4/01	Batley (h)	L6-20	t:Moore g:Oulton	18th	498
22/4/01	Workington (h)	L10-60	t:Austerfield,Hagan g:Roberts	18th	395
29/4/01	Whitehaven (h)	L6-54	t:R Hall g:Oulton	18th	314
6/5/01	Doncaster (a)	L82-4	t:Musgrove	18th	741
13/5/01	Hull KR (h)	L8-56	t:Wray,Dooley	18th	656
20/5/01	Gateshead (a)	L30-12	t:Ramsden,Pallister g:Oulton(2)	19th	675
27/5/01	Dewsbury (h)	L6-68	t:M Hall g:Waite	19th	425
3/6/01	Sheffield (a)	L56-0	No Scorers	19th	1,008
10/6/01	Barrow (a)	L60-0	No Scorers	19th	655
17/6/01	Featherstone (a)	L92-2	g:Oulton	19th	1,347
24/6/01	Widnes (h)	L11-66	t:Pallister,Oulton g:Oulton fg:Precious	19th	952
1/7/01	Leigh (a)	L84-1	fg:Oulton	19th	2,433

	APP		TRIES		GOALS		FG		PTS	
	ALL	NFP	ALL	NFP	ALL	NFP	ALL	NFP	ALL	NFP
Scott Acklam	3(1)	3(1)	1	1	0	0	0	0	4	4
Chris Allen	10(1)	9(1)	4	3	0	0	0	0	16	12
Shaun Austerfield	11(1)	9(1)	2	1	1	0	0	0	10	6
Lee Bardauskas	6(2)	6(2)	1	1	0	0	0	0	4	4
Barrington Barnett	(1)	(1)	0	0	0	0	0	0	0	0
Jamie Benn	5	5	1	1	7	7	0	0	18	18
Luke Billyeald	2(2)	2(2)	0	0	0	0	0	0	0	0
Dave Birdsall	1(1)	1(1)	0	0	0	0	0	0	0	0
Adam Briggs	1(6)	1(6)	0	0	0	0	0	0	0	0
Carl Bristow	6(2)	6(2)	0	0	0	0	0	0	0	0
Paul Butterfield	9	7	0	0	0	0	0	0	0	0
Aaron Campbell	3	3	0	0	0	0	0	0	0	0
Shane Cochrane	4(4)	4(4)	0	0	0	0	0	0	0	0
Chris Cooney	(2)	(2)	0	0	0	0	0	0	0	0
Paul Couch	(2)	(2)	0	0	0	0	0	0	0	0
Darren Crake	17(3)	15(3)	0	0	0	0	0	0	0	0
Lee Crooks	(2)	(2)	0	0	0	0	0	0	0	0
Rich Darling	6	4	2	1	0	0	0	0	8	4
Gareth Dobson	13(4)	12(3)	3	3	0	0	0	0	12	12
Mark Dooley	8(1)	8(1)	1	1	0	0	0	0	4	4
Craig Forsyth	12(1)	10(1)	0	0	0	0	0	0	0	0
Jason Gatus	3	3	0	0	0	0	0	0	0	0
Jon Gwilliam	(1)	(1)	0	0	0	0	0	0	0	0
Mick Hagan	11(6)	10(5)	1	1	0	0	0	0	4	4
Mike Hall	10	10	1	1	0	0	0	0	4	4
Ricky Hall	1(2)	1(2)	1	1	0	0	0	0	4	4
Paddy Handley	12	10	3	1	0	0	0	0	12	4
Ryan Hardy	2	2	0	0	0	0	0	0	0	0
Spencer Hargrave	4(1)	3	0	0	0	0	0	0	0	0
Neil Harmon	5	5	0	0	0	0	0	0	0	0
Paul Harper	1	1	0	0	0	0	0	0	0	0
Andy Hill	2	2	0	0	0	0	0	0	0	0
Charles Hoggard	(2)	(1)	0	0	0	0	0	0	0	0
Darren Hughes	5	5	0	0	0	0	0	0	0	0
Martyn Hunt	2	2	0	0	0	0	0	0	0	0
Andy Hutchinson	15(1)	15(1)	1	1	0	0	0	0	4	4
Lee Hutchinson	(2)	(1)	0	0	0	0	0	0	0	0
Andy Innes	7(4)	7(4)	0	0	0	0	0	0	0	0
Callum Irving	5(1)	5(1)	0	0	0	0	0	0	0	0
Luke Judson	3(1)	3(1)	1	1	0	0	0	0	4	4
Steve Lamb	(1)	(1)	0	0	0	0	0	0	0	0
Gareth Lloyd	11	9	2	1	0	0	0	0	8	4
Glen Matsell	2	2	0	0	0	0	0	0	0	0
Leroy McKenzie	6(1)	6	1	1	0	0	0	0	4	4
Lee McNichol	1(1)	1(1)	0	0	0	0	0	0	0	0
Gavin Molloy	6	6	0	0	0	0	0	0	0	0
Craig Moore	15(1)	13(1)	4	4	0	0	0	0	16	16
Matthew Mulholland	17(4)	17(4)	1	1	0	0	0	0	4	4
Phil Musgrove	6(1)	6(1)	1	1	0	0	0	0	4	4
Gareth Oulton	17(7)	15(7)	1	1	15	11	1	1	35	27
Alan Pallister	21(2)	19(2)	3	3	0	0	0	0	12	12
Nathan Pincher	13(7)	13(7)	0	0	0	0	0	0	0	0
Andy Precious	4(1)	4(1)	0	0	0	0	1	1	1	1
Richard Punchard	(1)	(1)	0	0	0	0	0	0	0	0
Mick Ramsden	14	14	1	1	0	0	0	0	4	4
Robert Roberts	2	2	0	0	1	1	0	0	2	2
Steve Robinson	(5)	(5)	0	0	0	0	0	0	0	0
Tim Rumford	8(3)	8(3)	1	1	0	0	0	0	4	4
Carl Sayer	(2)	(2)	0	0	0	0	0	0	0	0
Gavin Smith	1(1)	1(1)	0	0	0	0	0	0	0	0
Michael Smith	6	6	2	2	0	0	0	0	8	8
Mark Spears	6	6	0	0	0	0	0	0	0	0
Gareth Stephens	4	2	0	0	0	0	0	0	0	0
Steve Thickbroom	(1)	(1)	0	0	0	0	0	0	0	0
Lee Turnbull	1(1)	1(1)	0	0	0	0	0	0	0	0
Danny Waite	11(5)	11(4)	0	0	5	5	1	1	11	11
Andrew Webster	2	2	0	0	0	0	0	0	0	0
John Williams	1	1	0	0	0	0	0	0	0	0
Simon Wray	11	11	1	1	0	0	0	0	4	4

Gareth Dobson

LEAGUE RECORD
P28-W1-D1-L26
(19th, NFP)
F193, A1499, Diff-1306
3 points.

CHALLENGE CUP
Round Four

ATTENDANCES
Best - v Doncaster
(NFP - 1,251)
Worst - v Whitehaven
(NFP - 314)
Total (NFP only) - 8,659
Average (NFP only) - 619
(Down by 154 on 2000)

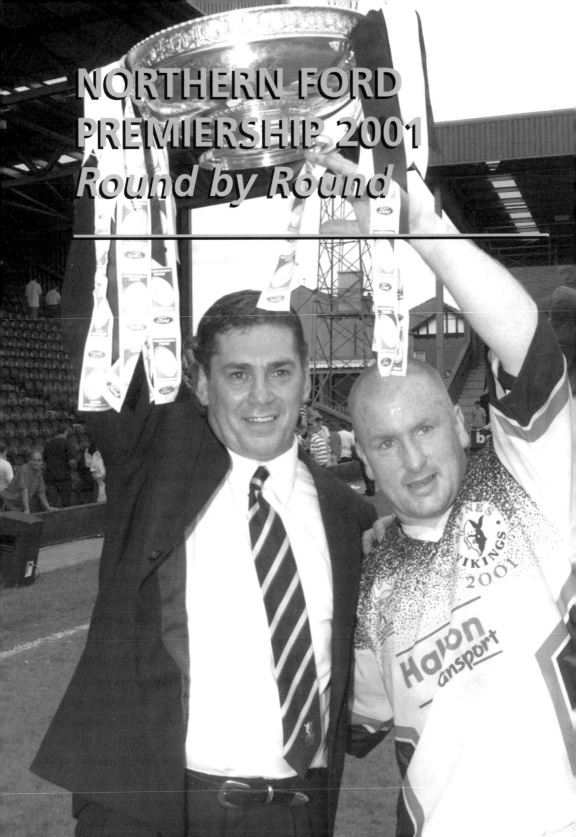

NORTHERN FORD
PREMIERSHIP 2001
Round by Round

Northern Ford Premiership 2001 - Round by Round

WEEK 1

Sunday 3rd December 2000

BARROW BORDER RAIDERS 16 OLDHAM 28

BORDER RAIDERS: 1 Rod Maybon; 2 Glen Hutton; 3 Phil Atkinson; 4 Darren Wilson; 5 Adrian Gardner; 6 Clint Barends; 7 Darren Holt; 8 Damien Whitter; 9 Anthony Murray; 10 Willie Burns; 11 Mike Whitehead; 12 Gareth Pratt; 13 Matthew Leigh. Subs: 14 Chris Massey for Maybon (67); 15 Steve Jackson for Whitter (23); 16 Ian Rawlinson for Pratt (18); 17 Wayne Jones for Pratt (75); Whitter for Jackson (48); Pratt for Burns (52).
Tries: Whitehead (36), Wilson (41), Rawlinson (52), Hutton (60).
OLDHAM: 1 Mark Sibson; 2 Dean Cross; 3 Anthony Gibbons; 4 Pat Rich; 5 Warren Barrow; 6 David Gibbons; 7 Neil Roden; 8 Andy Procter; 9 John Hough; 10 Jason Clegg; 11 Phil Farrell; 12 Shayne McMenemy; 13 Ian Sinfield. Subs: 14 Mike Ford for Roden (70); 15 Leo Casey for Clegg (22); 16 Danny Guest for Procter (35); 17 Chris Farrell for McMenemy (55); Procter for Guest (55).
Tries: Sibson (4), D Gibbons (12), Roden (18), A Gibbons (50), Hough (75); **Goals:** Rich 4.
League Express Men of the Match:
Border Raiders: Mike Whitehead; *Oldham:* Neil Roden.
Penalty count: 5-2; **Half-time:** 4-16; **Referee:** Richard Silverwood (Dewsbury); **Attendance:** 1,294.

CHORLEY LYNX 12 SWINTON LIONS 30

LYNX: 1 Paul Roberts; 2 Paul Cookson; 3 Lee Maiden; 4 Graham Taberner; 5 Gary Doherty; 6 Gareth Potter; 7 Stuart Fisher; 8 Dean Conway; 9 Ian Talbot; 10 Mike Prescott; 11 Luke Vincent; 12 Peter Cain; 13 Dale Christy. Subs: 14 Stuart Conway for D Conway (30BB, rev 39); 15 Kieran Lacey for D Conway (51); 16 Chris Ramsdale for Christy (41); 17 Dave Wadsley for Doherty (64); D Conway for Prescott (60); Christy for Lacey (71); Doherty for Roberts (78).
Tries: Cookson (5), Potter (54); **Goals:** Fisher 2.
Sin bin: Fisher (61) - tripping.
LIONS: 1 Wayne English; 2 Adrian Mead; 3 Mick Nanyn; 4 Paul Loughlin; 5 Matt Bateman; 6 Phil Veivers; 7 Kelvin Peet; 8 Jonathan Neill; 9 Rob Barraclough; 10 Lee Hansen; 11 Phil Cushion; 12 John-Paul Doherty; 13 Paul Smith. Subs: 14 Andy Cheetham for Bateman (14); 15 Tony Barrow for Hansen (42BB); 16 Jim Evans for Mead (41); 17 Paul Crossland for Doherty (46); Mead for Cheetham (64).
Tries: P Loughlin (15), Smith (26), Cheetham (29), Nanyn (50, 70), Crossland (79); **Goals:** Nanyn 3.
League Express Men of the Match:
Lynx: Dean Conway; *Lions:* Wayne English.
Penalty count: 6-6; **Half-time:** 6-18;
Referee: John Farrell (Widnes); **Attendance:** 670.

DEWSBURY RAMS 21 FEATHERSTONE ROVERS 12

RAMS: 1 Nathan Graham; 2 Alex Godfrey; 3 Gavin Wood; 4 Dan Potter; 5 Adrian Flynn; 6 Richard Agar; 7 Barry Eaton; 8 Andy Fisher; 9 Richard Pachniuk; 10 Robin Jowitt; 11 Sean Richardson; 12 Paul Smith; 13 Damian Ball. Subs: 14 Liam Tallon for Wood (61); 15 Billy Kershaw for Richardson (75); 16 Andrew Spink for Fisher (65); 17 Ryan McDonald for Jowitt (48); Richardson for Spink (74).
Tries: Flynn (28), Eaton (34), Potter (60);
Goals: Eaton 4; **Field goal:** Eaton.
On report: Agar (39) – foul.
ROVERS: 1 Michael Rhodes; 2 Jamie Stokes; 3 Chris Spurr; 4 Nick Simpson; 5 Matt Bramald; 6 Andy Bastow; 7 Jamie Rooney; 8 Stuart Dickens; 9 Richard Chapman; 10 Craig Booth; 11 Danny Evans; 12 Neil Lowe; 13 Steve Dooler. Subs: 14 Gavin Swinson for Dooler (70BB); 15 Gary Barnett for Bastow (65); 16 Ricky Helliwell for Evans (50); 17 Gavin Morgan for Booth (19BB); Evans for Chapman (78).
Try: Lowe (62); **Goals:** Rooney 4.
Sin bin: Chapman (29) – dissent.
League Express Men of the Match:
Rams: Damian Ball; *Rovers:* Neil Lowe.
Penalty count: 10-16; **Half-time:** 12-8; **Referee:** Steve Nicholson (Whitehaven); **Attendance:** 2,608.

WIDNES VIKINGS 22 WHITEHAVEN 14

VIKINGS: 1 Damian Munro; 2 Phil Coussons; 3 Chris Percival; 4 Scott Martin; 5 Mark Forster; 6 Karle Hammond; 7 Lee Birdseye; 8 Simon Knox; 9 Phil Cantillon; 10 Stephen Holgate; 11 Joe Faimalo; 12 Chris McKinney; 13 Tommy Hodgkinson. Subs: 14 Martin Crompton for Birdseye (48); 15 Stewart Rhodes for McKinney (77); 16 Jason Demetriou for Knox (58); 17 Steve Gee for Hammond (58); Hammond for Hodgkinson (71).
Tries: Coussons (15), Forster (19), Martin (52), Munro (60), Demetriou (77); **Goal:** Hammond.
WHITEHAVEN: 1 Paul O'Neill; 2 Wesley Wilson; 3 David Seeds; 4 Craig Walsh; 5 Jonathan Wignall; 6 Robert Purdham; 7 Lee Kiddie; 8 Mark Cox; 9 Aaron Lester; 10 David Fatialofa; 11 Craig Chambers; 12 Graeme Morton; 13 Howard Hill. Subs: 14 Ryan Campbell not used; 15 Garry Purdham for Vaughan (70); 16 Spencer Miller for Morton (9); 17 Dean Vaughan for Cox (22).
Tries: Seeds (47), Kiddie (56); **Goals:** O'Neill 3.
League Express Men of the Match:
Vikings: Martin Crompton; *Whitehaven:* David Fatialofa.
Penalty count: 11-6; **Half-time:** 8-2;
Referee: Nick Oddy (Halifax); **Attendance:** 3,864.

WORKINGTON TOWN 18 ROCHDALE HORNETS 8

TOWN: 1 Neil Frazer; 2 Fata Sini; 3 Kevin Hetherington; 4 Leigh Smith; 5 Graeme Lewthwaite; 6 Micky Horner; 7 Tane Manihera; 8 Matt Sturm; 9 Carl Sice; 10 Hitro Okesene; 11 Jamie Beaumont; 12 Lokeni Savelio; 13 Anthony Samuel. Subs: 14 William Blackburn for Savelio (47); 15 Matthew Tunstall for Okesene (21); 16 Stuart Hoyles for Beaumont (66); 17 Scott Chilton for Lewthwaite (66); Okesene for Tunstall (53); Savelio for Sturm (75).
Tries: Sturm (8), Lewthwaite (58), L Smith (70);
Goals: Hetherington 3.
HORNETS: 1 Paul Owen; 2 Marlon Miller; 3 Danny Wood; 4 Brendan O'Meara; 5 Marlon Billy; 6 Neil Alexander; 7 Mick Coates; 8 Danny Sculthorpe; 9 Darren Robinson; 10 Andy Ireland; 11 Martin Bunce; 12 David Larder; 13 Danny Fearon. Subs: 14 Sean Cooper for O'Meara (32); 15 Chris Newall for Larder (62); 16 Mickey Edwards for Sculthorpe (22); 17 David Stephenson for Alexander (ht); Sculthorpe for Ireland (47); Alexander for Edwards (64).
Try: Sculthorpe (79); **Goals:** Wood 2.
League Express Men of the Match:
Town: Matt Sturm; *Hornets:* Danny Sculthorpe.
Penalty count: 8-7; **Half-time:** 10-2;
Referee: Paul Lee (Leigh); **Attendance:** 1,384.

YORK 8 DONCASTER DRAGONS 26

YORK: 1 Jamie Benn; 2 Paul Butterfield; 3 Darren Hughes; 4 Gareth Lloyd; 5 Leroy McKenzie; 6 Paddy Handley; 7 Gareth Dobson; 8 Andy Precious; 9 Alan Pallister; 10 Craig Forsyth; 11 Michael Smith; 12 Craig Moore; 13 Spencer Hargrave. Subs: 14 Chris Allen for Pallister (49); 15 Shaun Austerfield for Forsyth (34); 16 Matthew Mulholland for Lloyd (53); 17 Mick Hagan for Precious (2); Forsyth for Hagan (49).
Try: Allen (53); **Goals:** Benn 2.
Sin bin: Hargrave (40) - interference at the play the ball.
DRAGONS: 1 Lynton Stott; 2 Kevin Crouthers; 3 Craig Weston; 4 Carl Hall; 5 Neil Bennett; 6 Paul Mansson; 7 Latham Tawhai; 8 Asa Amone; 9 Peter Edwards; 10 Joe Berry; 11 Rob Wilson; 12 James Bunyan; 13 Simon Irving. Subs: 14 Jimmy Walker for Bunyan (63); 15 Billy Conway for Irving (38); 16 Maea David for Berry (27); 17 Ian Ramskill for Amone (49); Berry for Ramskill (64); Amone for Wilson (76).
Tries: Tawhai (6), Stott (43), Weston (47), Edwards (66);
Goals: Irving 2, Weston 3.
Sin bin: Crouthers (30) - obstruction;
David (63) - lying on in the tackle.
League Express Men of the Match:
York: Craig Forsyth; *Dragons:* Peter Edwards.
Penalty count: 11-9; **Half-time:** 2-8; **Referee:** Ronnie Laughton (Barnsley); **Attendance:** 1,251.

SHEFFIELD EAGLES 34 BATLEY BULLDOGS 1

EAGLES: 1 Andy Poynter; 2 Paul Wells; 3 Neil Kite; 4 Wayne Flynn; 5 Ian Thompson; 6 Carl Briggs; 7 Chris Robinson; 8 Jon Bruce; 9 Andy Speak; 10 Steve Hill; 11 Chris Judge; 12 Heath Cruckshank; 13 Richard Goddard. Subs: 14 Steve Walker for Brent (59); 15 Andy Brent for Bruce (23); 16 Chris Chapman for Judge (31); 17 Ian Brown for Thompson (66); Bruce for Hill (55); Judge for Robinson (71); Hill for Cruckshank (76BB).
Tries: Goddard (25), Brent (36, 42), Briggs (75), Judge (77); **Goals:** Goddard 7.
BULLDOGS: 1 Craig Lingard; 2 Roger Simpson; 3 Danny Maun; 4 Davide Longo; 5 Paul Gleadhill; 6 Richard Price; 7 Glen Tomlinson; 8 Jeff Wittenberg; 9 Andy Heptinstall; 10 Chris McWilliam; 11 Gary Shillabeer; 12 Rob Padgett; 13 Ryan Horsley. Subs: 14 Jeremy Dyson for Simpson (53); 15 Paul Hicks for Shillabeer (36); 16 Craig Richards for McWilliam (68); 17 Andy Richardson for McWilliam (28); McWilliam for Wittenberg (57).
Field goal: Heptinstall.
League Express Men of the Match:
Eagles: Richard Goddard; *Bulldogs:* Craig Lingard.
Penalty count: 5-6; **Half-time:** 14-1;
Referee: Peter Taberner (Wigan); **Attendance:** 1,429.

GATESHEAD THUNDER 0 HULL KINGSTON ROVERS 18

THUNDER: 1 Darren Simpson; 2 Richard Arrowsmith; 3 Wes McGibbon; 4 Steve Hall; 5 Leon Williamson; 6 Scott Dyson; 7 Martin Gambles; 8 Paul Lister; 9 Roy Southernwood; 10 Andy Grundy; 11 Jim Carlton; 12 Matthew Roberts; 13 Darrell Derose. Subs: 14 Paul Sebine for Southernwood (34); 15 Lee Garside for Lister (13); 16 Andy Field not used; 17 Chris Parker for Roberts (27); Lister for Grundy (23); Grundy for Garside (54); Southernwood for McGibbon (65).
ROVERS: 1 Andrew Taylor; 2 Anthony Chambers; 3 Chris Kitching; 4 Whetu Taewa; 5 Mark Blanchard; 6 Darren Callaghan; 7 Scott Yeaman; 8 Rich Hayes; 9 Steven Cochrane; 10 Jon Aston; 11 Andy Smith; 12 Richard Slater; 13 Chris Charles. Subs: 14 Dean Andrews for Blanchard (58); 15 Allan Dunham for Cochrane (63); 16 Paul Fletcher for Aston (25); 17 David Luckwell for Hayes (26); Aston for Luckwell (54).
Tries: Kitching (42), Smith (59), Chambers (69), Dunham (78); **Goal:** Yeaman.
League Express Men of the Match:
Thunder: Scott Dyson; *Rovers:* Andy Smith.
Penalty count: 8-10; **Half-time:** 0-0; **Referee:** Colin Morris (Huddersfield); **Attendance:** 2,332.

HUNSLET HAWKS 12 KEIGHLEY COUGARS 44

HAWKS: 1 Hamish Munton; 2 Chris Heywood; 3 Iain Higgins; 4 Michael Wainwright; 5 Aaron Campbell ; 6 George Raynor; 7 Chris Ross; 8 Adam Moore; 9 Nicky Dobson; 10 Guy Adams; 11 Mick Coyle; 12 Dave Jessey; 13 Gareth Naylor. Subs: 14 Robert Roberts for Dobson (20); 15 Chris North for Heywood (66); 16 David Bates for Moore (ht); 17 Ben Skerrett for Jessey (58); Dobson for Naylor (ht).
Tries: Roberts (59), Ross (78); **Goals:** Ross 2
COUGARS: 1 James Rushforth; 2 Craig Horne; 3 Karl Smith; 4 Graeme Hallas; 5 Jason Lee; 6 Martin Wood; 7 Nathan Antonik; 8 Michael Slicker; 9 Jason Ramshaw; 10 James Walker; 11 Paul Harrison; 12 Ian Hughes; 13 Danny Seal. Subs: 14 Gary Lord for Slicker (18); 15 Jim Leatham for Hughes (31); 16 Phil Stephenson for Walker (18); 17 Darren Carter for Ramshaw (57); Walker for Harrison (62).
Tries: Seal (27, 44), Lee (41, 69, 74), Lord (56), Leatham (65), Carter (73); **Goals:** Wood 6.
League Express Men of the Match:
Hawks: Chris Ross; *Cougars:* Danny Seal.
Penalty count: 6-5; **Half-time:** 0-6;
Referee: Ian Smith (Oldham); **Attendance:** 1,404.

WEEK 2

Sunday 10th December 2000

BATLEY BULLDOGS 24 GATESHEAD THUNDER 4

BULLDOGS: 1 Craig Lingard; 2 Jeremy Dyson; 3 Danny Maun; 4 Davide Longo; 5 Paul Gleadhill; 6 Richard Price; 7 Glen Tomlinson; 8 Chris McWilliam; 9 Andy Heptinstall; 10 Andy Richardson; 11 Gary Shillabeer; 12 Paul Hicks; 13 Ryan Horsley. Subs: 14 Simon Jackson for Price (70); 15 Jeff Wittenberg for Richardson (20); 16 Craig Richards for McWilliam (50); 17 Will Cartledge for Heptinstall (72).
Tries: Lingard (6), Heptinstall (17), Gleadhill (40), Shillabeer (67); **Goals:** Price 4.
THUNDER: 1 Darren Simpson; 2 Richard Arrowsmith; 3 Wes McGibbon; 4 Steve Hall; 5 Leon Williamson; 6 Scott Dyson; 7 Martin Gambles; 8 Paul Lister; 9 Roy Southernwood; 10 Andy Grundy; 11 Jim Carlton; 12 Matthew Roberts; 13 Darrell Derose. Subs: 14 Paul Sebine for Southernwood (18); 15 Lee Garside for Lister (20); 16 Chris Parker for Roberts (25); 17 Andy Field for Arrowsmith (11).
Try: Gambles (73).
League Express Men of the Match:
Bulldogs: Chris McWilliam; *Thunder:* Andy Grundy.
Penalty count: 5-7; **Half-time:** 16-0;
Referee: Julian King (St Helens); **Attendance:** 823.

DONCASTER DRAGONS 36 HUNSLET HAWKS 8

DRAGONS: 1 Lynton Stott; 2 Neil Bennett; 3 Craig Weston; 4 Carl Hall; 5 Kevin Crouthers; 6 Paul Mansson; 7 Latham Tawhai; 8 Asa Amone; 9 Peter Edwards; 10 Joe Berry; 11 Rob Wilson; 12 James Bunyan; 13 Brad Hepi. Subs: 14 Billy Conway for Stott (ht); 15 Maea David for Amone (27); 16 Tony Atter for David (65); 17 Jamie Fielden for Bunyan (18); Amone for Fielden (50); Fielden for Berry (71).
Tries: Wilson (25), Bennett (28), Mansson (46, 72), Crouthers (61), Conway (69), Hepi (80); **Goals:** Weston 4.
HAWKS: 1 George Raynor; 2 Chris North; 3 Iain Higgins; 4 Michael Wainwright; 5 Aaron Campbell; 6 Chris Redfearn; 7 Chris Ross; 8 Guy Adams; 9 Gareth Naylor; 10 David Bates; 11 Mick Coyle; 12 Dave Jessey; 13 Robert Roberts. Subs: 14 Adam Moore for Bates (51); 15 Nicky Dobson for Ross (1); 16 Chris Heywood for Redfearn (31BB, rev 50); 17 Ben Skerrett for Naylor (45); Bates for Jessey (61); Heywood for Redfearn (77).
Tries: Campbell (7), N Dobson (33).
League Express Men of the Match:
Dragons: Brad Hepi; *Hawks:* David Bates.
Penalty count: 2-6; **Half-time:** 10-8;
Referee: Ian Smith (Oldham); **Attendance:** 1,305.

FEATHERSTONE ROVERS 12 SHEFFIELD EAGLES 15

ROVERS: 1 Michael Rhodes; 2 Jamie Stokes; 3 Chris Spurr; 4 Nick Simpson; 5 Matt Bramald; 6 Andy Bastow; 7 Jamie Rooney; 8 Stuart Dickens; 9 Richard Chapman; 10 Craig Booth; 11 Danny Evans; 12 Neil Lowe; 13 Steve Dooler. Subs: 14 Gavin Swinson for Chapman (68); 15 Gary Barnett for Bastow (65); 16 Ricky Helliwell for Lowe (29BB, rev 45); 17 Gavin Morgan for Booth (37); Helliwell for Evans (64); Booth for Dickens (61); Dickens for Morgan (75).
Tries: Rhodes (6), Stokes (57); **Goals:** Rooney 2.
EAGLES: 1 Andy Poynter; 2 Paul Wells; 3 Neil Kite; 4 Wayne Flynn; 5 Ian Thompson; 6 Carl Briggs; 7 Chris Robinson; 8 Jon Bruce; 9 Andy Speak; 10 Steve Hill; 11 Chris Judge; 12 Heath Cruckshank; 13 Richard Goddard. Subs: 14 Steve Walker for Judge (50); 15 Andy Brent for Bruce (22); 16 Chris Chapman for Hill (33); 17 Ian Brown for Briggs (72); Bruce for Chapman (53); Briggs for Speak (73).
Try: Wells (60); **Goals:** Goddard 5; **Field goal:** Robinson.
Sin bin: Judge (3 & 39) – late tackles; Goddard (53) - interference at the play the ball.
On report: Judge (3 & 39) – late tackles.
League Express Men of the Match:
Rovers: Jamie Rooney; *Eagles:* Richard Goddard.
Penalty count: 14-11; **Half-time:** 8-6; **Referee:** Richard Silverwood (Dewsbury); **Attendance:** 2,359.

HULL KINGSTON ROVERS 2 YORK 0

ROVERS: 1 Andrew Taylor; 2 Anthony Chambers; 3 Chris Kitching; 4 Whetu Taewa; 5 Bright Sodje; 6 Darren Callaghan; 7 Scott Yeaman; 8 Jon Aston; 9 Steven

Cochrane; 10 Rich Hayes; 11 Andy Smith; 12 Richard Slater; 13 Chris Charles. Subs: 14 Dean Andrews for Slater (59); 15 Allan Dunham for Cochrane (54); 16 Paul Fletcher for Smith (20); 17 David Luckwell for Hayes (26); Smith for Taewa (31); Hayes for Aston (69).
Goal: Charles.
YORK: 1 Jamie Benn; 2 Paul Butterfield; 3 Shaun Austerfield; 4 Gareth Lloyd; 5 Leroy McKenzie; 6 Chris Allen; 7 Paddy Handley; 8 Michael Smith; 9 Allan Pallister; 10 Craig Forsyth; 11 Andy Hill; 12 Darren Hughes; 13 Spencer Hargrave. Subs: 14 Matthew Mulholland for Austerfield (34); 15 Mick Hagan for Forsyth (43); 16 Gareth Dobson for Allen (34); 17 Adam Briggs not used.
League Express Men of the Match:
Rovers: Jon Aston; *York:* Leroy McKenzie.
Penalty count: 5-0; **Half-time:** 0-0;
Referee: Peter Taberner (Wigan); **Attendance:** 2,110.

KEIGHLEY COUGARS 32 DEWSBURY RAMS 6

COUGARS: 1 James Rushforth; 2 Craig Horne; 3 Karl Smith; 4 Graeme Hallas; 5 Jason Lee; 6 Martin Wood; 7 Nathan Antonik; 8 Michael Slicker; 9 Jason Ramshaw; 10 Matt Walker; 11 Paul Harrison; 12 Ian Hughes; 13 Danny Seal. Subs: 14 Gary Lord for Slicker (27); 15 Jim Leatham for Walker (27); 16 Darren Carter for Ramshaw (57); 17 Phil Stephenson for Hughes (47); Walker for Harrison (68); Slicker for Leatham (72).
Tries: Hughes (11), Rushforth (26, 66), Seal (30), Horne (50), Antonik (59); **Goals:** Wood 4.
Sent off: Lord (38) - high tackle on Smith.
RAMS: 1 Nathan Graham; 2 Alex Godfrey; 3 Gavin Wood; 4 Dan Potter; 5 Adrian Flynn; 6 Richard Agar; 7 Barry Eaton; 8 Matthew Long; 9 Richard Pachniuk; 10 Robin Jowitt; 11 Sean Richardson; 12 Paul Smith; 13 Damian Ball. Subs: 14 Liam Tallon for Ball (52); 15 Billy Kershaw for Richardson (60); 16 Andrew Spink for Jowitt (31); 17 Ryan McDonald for Long (22); Long for McDonald (65).
Try: Flynn (70); **Goal:** Eaton.
Sent off: Smith (38) - retaliation.
League Express Men of the Match:
Cougars: James Rushforth; *Rams:* Richard Pachniuk.
Penalty count: 4-8; **Half-time:** 18-2;
Referee: Nick Oddy (Halifax); **Attendance:** 2,511.

LEIGH CENTURIONS 19 BARROW BORDER RAIDERS 8

CENTURIONS: 1 Neil Turley; 2 Alan Hadcroft; 3 Paul Anderson; 4 Andy Fairclough; 5 David Ingram; 6 Simon Svabic; 7 John Duffy; 8 Tim Street; 9 Martin Roden; 10 Paul Norman; 11 Phil Kendrick; 12 Simon Baldwin; 13 Adam Bristow. Subs: 14 Chris Morley for Ingram (57); 15 David Bradbury for Street (31); 16 Andy Leathem for Norman (21); 17 John Hamilton for Roden (27); Street for Leathem (67); Roden for Hamilton (74).
Tries: Fairclough (15), Anderson (51), Svabic (79);
Goals: Svabic 3; **Field goal:** Svabic.
BORDER RAIDERS: 1 Chris Massey; 2 Glen Hutton; 3 Phil Atkinson; 4 Darren Wilson; 5 Adrian Gardner; 6 Clint Barends; 7 Darren Holt; 8 Damien Whitter; 9 Anthony Murray; 10 Willie Burns; 11 Gareth Pratt; 12 Mike Whitehead; 13 Matthew Leigh. Subs: 14 Jamie Marshall for Hutton (44); 15 Ian Rawlinson for Pratt (22); 16 Steve Jackson for Whitter (20); 17 Geoff Luxon for Jackson (53); Whitter for Rawlinson (68).
Try: Whitehead (46); **Goals:** Holt 2.
League Express Men of the Match: *Centurions:* Simon Svabic; *Border Raiders:* Matthew Leigh.
Penalty count: 8-11; **Half-time:** 10-2; **Referee:** Steve Nicholson (Whitehaven); **Attendance:** 2,088.

ROCHDALE HORNETS 14 WIDNES VIKINGS 24

HORNETS: 1 Paul Owen; 2 Marlon Miller; 3 Danny Wood; 4 Sean Cooper; 5 Marlon Billy; 6 Dave Watson; 7 Mick Coates; 8 Danny Sculthorpe; 9 Darren Robinson; 10 Andy Ireland; 11 Martin Bunce; 12 David Larder; 13 Danny Fearon. Subs: 14 Casey Mayberry for Robinson (71); 15 Steve Campbell for Sculthorpe (47BB, rev 63); 16 Mickey Edwards for Ireland (21); 17 David Stephenson for Fearon (67); Ireland for Edwards (56).
Tries: Wood (2), Fearon (26), Miller (39); **Goal:** Wood.
VIKINGS: 1 Damian Munro; 2 Phil Coussons; 3 Chris Percival; 4 Scott Martin; 5 Mark Forster; 6 Karle Hammond; 7 Martin Crompton; 8 Simon Knox; 9 Phil Cantillon; 10 Stephen Holgate; 11 Chris McKinney; 12 Joe Faimalo; 13 Tommy Hodgkinson. Subs: 14 Mike Hill for McKinney (70); 15 Stewart Rhodes for Knox (59); 16 Jason Demetriou for Martin (49); 17 Steve Gee for Holgate (60); Martin for Crompton (64BB, rev 70).
Tries: Cantillon (13), Martin (21), Coussons (49), Crompton (64); **Goals:** Hammond 4.
League Express Men of the Match:
Hornets: Paul Owen; *Vikings:* Tommy Hodgkinson.
Penalty count: 5-3; **Half-time:** 14-12;
Referee: Paul Lee (Leigh); **Attendance:** 1,547.

WHITEHAVEN 4 SWINTON LIONS 8

WHITEHAVEN: 1 Paul O'Neill; 2 Wesley Wilson; 3 David Seeds; 4 Craig Walsh; 5 Jonathan Wignall; 6 Robert Purdham; 7 Lee Kiddie; 8 Mark Cox; 9 Aaron Lester; 10 David Fatialofa; 11 Craig Chambers; 12 Graeme Morton; 13 Howard Hill. Subs: 14 Ryan Campbell for Seeds (76); 15 Garry Purdham not used; 16 Spencer Miller for Morton (51); 17 Dean Vaughan for Cox (74).
Try: Walsh (67).
LIONS: 1 Wayne English; 2 Adrian Mead; 3 Mick Nanyn; 4 Paul Loughlin; 5 Andy Cheetham; 6 Phil Veivers; 7 Kelvin Peet; 8 Jonathan Neill; 9 Rob Barraclough; 10 Lee Hansen; 11 Phil Cushion; 12 John-Paul Doherty; 13 Paul Smith. Subs: 14 Sean Furey for Peet (ht); 15 Tony Barrow for Neill (50); 16 Ryan Stazicker for Doherty (27); 17 Paul Crossland not used; Neill for Hansen (74).
Tries: Cheetham (5), Smith (75).
League Express Men of the Match:
Whitehaven: Aaron Lester; *Lions:* Wayne English.
Penalty count: 6-7; **Half time:** 0-4; **Referee:** Ronnie Laughton (Barnsley); **Attendance:** 1,138.

WEEK 3

Sunday 17th December 2000

BATLEY BULLDOGS 16 DONCASTER DRAGONS 19

BULLDOGS: 1 Craig Lingard; 2 Jeremy Dyson; 3 Danny Maun; 4 Davide Longo; 5 Paul Gleadhill; 6 Simon Jackson; 7 Glen Tomlinson; 8 Chris McWilliam; 9 Andy Heptinstall; 10 Andy Richardson; 11 Paul Hicks; 12 Gary Shillabeer; 13 Ryan Horsley. Subs: 14 Jamie Coventry for Jackson (58); 15 Jeff Wittenberg for McWilliam (39); 16 Andy Wray for Richardson (38); 17 Cartledge for Shillabeer (22).
Tries: Heptinstall (5), Gleadhill (11), Longo (66);
Goals: Dyson 2.
DRAGONS: 1 Kevin Crouthers; 2 Carl Hall; 3 Craig Weston; 4 James Bunyan; 5 Neil Bennett; 6 Paul Mansson; 7 Latham Tawhai; 8 Asa Amone; 9 Peter Edwards; 10 Joe Berry; 11 Rob Wilson; 12 Brad Hepi; 13 Simon Irving. Subs: 14 Anton Garcia for Okul (57); 15 John Okul for Hall (15); 16 Maea David for Bunyan (40); 17 Jamie Fielden for Bennett (22); Bennett for Weston (62).
Tries: Hepi (22), Mansson (57, 73); **Goals:** Irving 3;
Field goal: Tawhai.
League Express Men of the Match:
Bulldogs: Ryan Horsley; *Dragons:* Paul Mansson.
Penalty count: 7-7; **Half-time:** 12-8; **Referee:** Steve Nicholson (Whitehaven); **Attendance:** 1,101.

DEWSBURY RAMS 32 HULL KINGSTON ROVERS 10

RAMS: 1 Nathan Graham; 5 Alex Godfrey; 4 Dan Potter; 3 Adrian Flynn; 2 Richard Baker; 6 Richard Agar; 7 Barry Eaton; 8 Matthew Long; 9 Richard Pachniuk; 10 Robin Jowitt; 11 Sean Richardson; 12 Paul Smith; 13 Damian Ball. Subs: 14 Liam Tallon for Potter (41); 15 Billy Kershaw for Richardson (63); 16 Andrew Spink for McDonald (63); 17 Ryan McDonald for Long (30); Long for Jowitt (57); Richardson for Smith (68).
Tries: Ball (4, 62), Godfrey (6), Potter (22), Richardson (44), Baker (80); **Goals:** Eaton 4.
ROVERS: 1 Andrew Taylor; 2 Anthony Chambers; 3 Chris Kitching; 4 Whetu Taewa; 5 Bright Sodje; 6 Darren Callaghan; 7 Scott Yeaman; 8 Jon Aston; 9 Steven Cochrane; 10 Rich Hayes; 11 Andy Smith; 12 Richard Slater; 13 Chris Charles. Subs: 14 Dean Andrews for Taylor (74); 15 Allan Dunham for Cochrane (46); 16 Paul Fletcher for Slater (23); 17 David Luckwell for Aston (35); Aston for Luckwell (55); Slater for Kitching (63).
Tries: Taewa (12), Yeaman (18); **Goal:** Charles.
League Express Men of the Match:
Rams: Richard Pachniuk; *Rovers:* Chris Charles.
Penalty count: 4-4; **Half-time:** 16-10;
Referee: Ian Smith (Oldham); **Attendance:** 2,116.

FEATHERSTONE ROVERS 68 GATESHEAD THUNDER 6

ROVERS: 1 Michael Rhodes; 2 Jamie Stokes; 3 Chris Spurr; 4 Nick Simpson; 5 Matt Bramald; 6 Andy Bastow; 7 Jamie Rooney; 8 Gavin Morgan; 9 Richard Chapman; 10 Craig Booth; 11 Steve Dooler; 12 Neil Lowe; 13 Paul Darley. Subs: 14 Gavin Swinson for Darley (54); 15 Danny Evans for Lowe (48); 16 Stuart Dickens for Morgan (19); 17 Micky Clarkson for Booth (19); Morgan for Dickens (62); Booth for Clarkson (62).
Tries: Simpson (4, 31), Lowe (9), Chapman (11), Bramald (16), Rhodes (19), Stokes (24, 44, 74), Clarkson (38), Dickens (52), Morgan (69), Rooney (77);
Goals: Rooney 8.
THUNDER: 1 Steve Hall; 2 Andy Field; 3 Wes McGibbon; 4 Darren Simpson; 5 Leon Williamson; 6 Scott Dyson; 7 Martin Gambles; 8 Lee Garside; 9 Paul Sebine; 10 Andy Grundy; 11 Jim Carlton; 12 Chris Parker; 13 Darrell Derose. Subs: 14 Matthew Brown for Simpson (37); 15 Matthew Roberts for Carlton (19); 16 Richard Mervill for Parker (19); 17 Stephen Rutherford for Derose (19); Derose for Dyson (57).
Try: McGibbon (50); **Goal:** Hall.
League Express Men of the Match:
Rovers: Jamie Stokes; *Thunder:* Martin Gambles.
Penalty count: 6-3; **Half-time:** 40-0; **Referee:** Ronnie Laughton (Barnsley); **Attendance:** 1,717.

ROCHDALE HORNETS 52 CHORLEY LYNX 12

HORNETS: 1 Paul Owen; 2 Marlon Miller; 3 Danny Wood; 4 Brendan O'Meara; 5 Marlon Billy; 6 Dave Watson; 7 Mick Coates; 8 Danny Sculthorpe; 9 Warren Ayres; 10 Andy Ireland; 11 Martin Bunce; 12 David Larder; 13 Danny Fearon. Subs: 14 Sean Cooper for Miller (64); 15 Steve Campbell for Ireland (25); 16 Casey Mayberry for O'Meara (50); 17 David Stephenson for Sculthorpe (41); Ireland for Fearon (57); Fearon for Bunce (74); O'Meara for Mayberry (75BB).
Tries: Wood (6), Coates (12, 36), Bunce (24, 40), Larder (27), Miller (38), Mayberry (61, 68), Fearon (76);
Goals: Wood 6.
LYNX: 1 Paul Roberts; 2 Lee Maiden; 3 Lee Bargate; 4 Graham Taberner; 5 Gary Doherty; 6 Anthony Roberts; 7 Stuart Fisher; 8 Mike Prescott; 9 Ian Talbot; 10 Dean Conway; 11 Phil Harrison; 12 Peter Cain; 13 Brian Capewell. Subs: 14 Carl Parker for A Roberts (14); 15 Paul Cookson for Vincent (47); 16 Dale Christy for Harrison (56); 17 Luke Vincent for Conway (28); Conway for Doherty (47); Doherty for Bargate (53BB, rev 59); Harrison for Conway (69).
Tries: Fisher (17), Capewell (70); **Goals:** Fisher 2.
League Express Men of the Match:
Hornets: Dave Watson; *Lynx:* Stuart Fisher.
Penalty count: 5-5; **Half-time:** 36-6;
Referee: John Farrell (Widnes); **Attendance:** 745.

SWINTON LIONS 26 BARROW BORDER RAIDERS 24

LIONS: 1 Wayne English; 2 Adrian Mead; 3 Mick Nanyn; 4 Paul Loughlin; 5 Andy Cheetham; 6 Phil Veivers; 7 Sean Furey; 8 Jonathan Neill; 9 Rob Barraclough; 10 Lee Hansen; 11 Robert Russell; 12 Ryan Stazicker; 13 Paul Smith. Subs: 14 Jim Evans for Russell (27); 15 Tony Barrow for Neill (35); 16 Nick Camman for Cheetham (25); 17 Paul Crossland for Stazicker (63); Neill for Hansen (51); Hansen for Barrow (72).
Tries: Russell (1), English (11), Nanyn (21), Mead (29), Smith (35); **Goals:** Nanyn 3.
BORDER RAIDERS: 1 Chris Massey; 2 Jamie Marshall; 3 Phil Atkinson; 4 Darren Wilson; 5 Adrian Gardner; 6 Clint Barends; 7 Darren Holt; 8 Damien Whitter; 9 Anthony Murray; 10 Willie Burns; 11 Ian Rawlinson; 12 Mike Whitehead; 13 Matthew Leigh. Subs: 14 Brett McDermott for Wilson (22); 15 Steve Jackson for Whitter (22); 16 Geoff Luxon for Rawlinson (32); 17 Gary Charlton for Burns (40); Rawlinson for Jackson (65); Whitter for Luxon (66); Burns for Charlton (74).
Tries: Murray (14), Rawlinson (25), A Gardner (51), Marshall (56); **Goals:** Holt 4.
League Express Men of the Match:
Lions: Wayne English; *Border Raiders:* Darren Holt.
Penalty count: 2-2; **Half-time:** 26-12;
Referee: Colin Morris (Huddersfield); **Attendance:** 862.

WHITEHAVEN 8 LEIGH CENTURIONS 30

WHITEHAVEN: 1 Paul O'Neill; 2 Wesley Wilson; 3 David Seeds; 4 Craig Walsh; 5 Chris Campbell; 6 Aaron Lester; 7 Lee Kiddie; 8 Mark Cox; 9 Garry Purdham; 10 David Fatialofa; 11 Craig Chambers; 12 Graeme Morton; 13 Howard Hill. Subs: 14 Stephen McCourt for Purdham (33); 15 Alan Bone for Morton (55); 16 Spencer Miller for Chambers (49); 17 Dean Vaughan for Cox (49); Cox for Fatialofa (78).
Try: Miller (60); **Goals:** O'Neill 2.
CENTURIONS: 1 Neil Turley; 2 Alan Hadcroft; 3 Paul Anderson; 4 Andy Fairclough; 5 David Jones; 6 Simon Svabic; 7 Liam Bretherton; 8 Tim Street; 9 John Hamilton; 10 David Bradbury; 11 Simon Baldwin; 12 Chris Morley; 13 Adam Bristow. Subs: 14 Phil Kendrick for Bristow (66); 15 Paul Norman for Bradbury (57); 16 David Whittle for Street (28); 17 Martin Roden for Hamilton (35); Street for Baldwin (78).
Tries: Anderson (12), Hadcroft (16, 45), Baldwin (35), Turley (71); **Goals:** Svabic 5.
League Express Men of the Match:
Whitehaven: David Fatialofa; *Centurions:* Neil Turley.
Penalty count: 4-8; **Half-time:** 2-16; **Referee:** Richard Silverwood (Dewsbury); **Attendance:** 1,061.

WORKINGTON TOWN 6 OLDHAM 22

TOWN: 1 Neil Frazer; 2 Fata Sini; 3 Kevin Hetherington; 4 Leigh Smith; 5 Graeme Lewthwaite; 6 Micky Horner; 7 Tane Manihera; 8 Matt Sturm; 9 Carl Sice; 10 Hitro Okesene; 11 Jamie Beaumont; 12 Lokeni Savelio; 13 Anthony Samuel. Subs: 14 William Blackburn for Okesene (32); 15 Matthew Tunstall for Beaumont (55); 16 Stuart Hoyles for Savelio (55); 17 Jamie Smith for Hetherington (44); Okesene for Sturm (75).
Try: Lewthwaite (61); **Goal:** J Smith.
OLDHAM: 1 Mark Sibson; 2 Dean Cross; 3 Anthony Gibbons; 4 Pat Rich; 5 Daryl Lacey; 6 David Gibbons; 7 Neil Roden; 8 Andy Procter; 9 John Hough; 10 Leo Casey; 11 Phil Farrell; 12 Paul Norton; 13 Ian Sinfield. Subs: 14 Mike Ford for Norton (71); 15 Jason Clegg for Casey (21); 16 Danny Guest for Procter (33); 17 Chris Farrell for Sinfield (52); Procter for Clegg (63); Casey for Guest (63).
Tries: Roden (6, 73), Cross (36), Sibson (42);
Goals: Rich 2; **Field goals:** Roden 2.
League Express Men of the Match:
Town: Carl Sice; *Oldham:* Neil Roden.
Penalty count: 8-13; **Half-time:** 0-10;
Referee: Nick Oddy (Halifax); **Attendance:** 1,295.

YORK 14 KEIGHLEY COUGARS 48

YORK: 1 Chris Allen; 2 Paul Butterfield; 3 Shaun Austerfield; 4 Gareth Lloyd; 5 Leroy McKenzie; 6 Paddy Handley; 7 Gareth Dobson; 8 Michael Smith; 9 Alan Pallister; 10 Craig Forsyth; 11 Andy Hill; 12 Darren Hughes; 13 Mick Ramsden. Subs: 14 Matthew Mulholland for Austerfield (26); 15 Tim Rumford for Mulholland (58); 16 Adam Briggs for Pallister (66); 17 Mick Hagan for Hughes (8BB, rev 15); Hagan for Hughes (20); Austerfield for Hill (35).
Tries: Pallister (45), M Smith (54, 67); **Goal:** Austerfield.
COUGARS: 1 James Rushforth; 2 Craig Horne; 3 Karl Smith; 4 Graeme Hallas; 5 Jason Lee; 6 Martin Wood; 7 Nathan Antonik; 8 Michael Slicker; 9 Jason Ramshaw; 10 Matt Walker; 11 Paul Harrison; 12 Jim Leatham; 13 Danny Seal. Subs: 14 Gary Lord for Walker (23); 15 Darren Carter for Hallas (60); 16 Phil Stephenson for Slicker (32); 17 Craig Brown for Lord (57); Slicker for Wood (63); Walker for Stephenson (71).
Tries: Lee (4, 13), Wood (17), Horne (22), Rushforth (29), Harrison (59), Seal (74), M Walker (80);
Goals: Wood 6, Lee 2.
League Express Men of the Match:
York: Michael Smith; *Cougars:* Martin Wood.
Penalty count: 7-7; **Half-time:** 0-30;
Referee: Paul Lee (Leigh); **Attendance:** 943.

HUNSLET HAWKS 14 SHEFFIELD EAGLES 0

HAWKS: 1 George Raynor; 2 David Plange; 3 Iain Higgins; 4 Michael Wainwright; 5 Aaron Campbell; 6 Marcus Vassilakopoulos; 7 Chris Ross; 8 Guy Adams; 9 Nicky Dobson; 10 David Bates; 11 Mick Coyle; 12 Dave Jessey; 13 Robert Roberts. Subs: 14 Adam Moore for Munton (57BB, rev 63); 15 Ben Skerrett for Bates (21); 16 Tony Howcroft for Dobson (53); 17 Hamish Munton for Plange (32); Plange for Higgins (71).
Tries: Higgins (1), Wainwright (34); **Goal:** Ross; **Field goals:** Roberts 3, Vassilakopoulos.
EAGLES: 1 Andy Poynter; 2 Paul Wells; 3 Neil Kite; 4 Wayne Flynn; 5 Ian Thompson; 6 Carl Briggs; 7 Chris Robinson; 8 Jon Bruce; 9 Andy Speak; 10 Ricky Wright; 11 Chris Judge; 12 Heath Cruckshank; 13 Richard Goddard. Subs: 14 Steve Walker for Thompson (59); 15 Ian Brown for Wright (26); 16 Steve Hill for Bruce (19); 17 Andy Brent for Judge (56); Wright for Brent (67); Bruce for Hill (64).
League Express Men of the Match:
Hawks: Robert Roberts; *Eagles:* Andy Speak.
Penalty count: 3-3; **Half-time:** 12-0;
Referee: Peter Taberner (Wigan); **Attendance:** 856.

WEEK 4

Sunday 24th December 2000

GATESHEAD THUNDER 0 KEIGHLEY COUGARS 52

THUNDER: 1 Matthew Brown; 2 Andy Field; 3 Wes McGibbon; 4 Steve Hall; 5 Leon Williamson; 6 Scott Dyson; 7 Martin Gambles; 8 Richard Mervill; 9 Roy Southernwood; 10 Andy Grundy; 11 Jim Carlton; 12 Chris Parker; 13 Darrell Derose. Subs: 14 Matthew Roberts for Mervill (46); 15 Lee Garside for Grundy (23); 16 Stephen Rutherford for Derose (32); 17 Paul Thorman for Southernwood (53); Derose for Brown (59); Southernwood for Dyson (72).
COUGARS: 1 James Rushforth; 2 Craig Horne; 3 Karl Smith; 4 Graeme Hallas; 5 Jason Lee; 6 Martin Wood; 7 Nathan Antonik; 8 Michael Slicker; 9 Jason Ramshaw; 10 Matt Walker; 11 Paul Harrison; 12 Ian Hughes; 13 Danny Seal. Subs: 14 Darren Carter for Rushforth (ht); 15 Jim Leatham for Hughes (67); 16 Phil Stephenson for Walker (28); 17 Alan Boothroyd for Slicker (30); Walker for Harrison (65); Slicker for Stephenson (72).
Tries: Lee (3, 38, 68), Ramshaw (5), Harrison (19), Seal (24), Antonik (42), Carter (51, 77), Horne (79); **Goals:** Wood 6.
League Express Men of the Match:
Thunder: Leon Williamson; *Cougars:* Jason Lee.
Penalty count: 6-1; **Half-time:** 0-26;
Referee: Peter Taberner (Wigan); **Attendance:** 1,052.

ROCHDALE HORNETS 6 OLDHAM 10

HORNETS: 1 Paul Owen; 2 Marlon Miller; 3 Danny Wood; 4 Brendan O'Meara; 5 Marlon Billy; 6 Dave Watson; 7 Mick Coates; 8 Danny Sculthorpe; 9 Warren Ayres; 10 Andy Ireland; 11 Martin Bunce; 12 David Stephenson; 13 Danny Fearon. Subs: 14 Casey Mayberry for Owen (11BB, rev 27); 15 Steve Campbell for Ireland (27); 16 Darren Robinson not used; 17 Mickey Edwards for Fearon (33); Ireland for Campbell (62); Fearon for Edwards (67); Mayberry for Sculthorpe (70); Sculthorpe for Edwards (75).
Try: Stephenson (29); **Goal:** Wood.
OLDHAM: 1 Danny Arnold; 2 Dean Cross; 3 Anthony Gibbons; 4 Pat Rich; 5 Daryl Lacey; 6 David Gibbons; 7 Neil Roden; 8 Andy Procter; 9 John Hough; 10 Leo Casey; 11 Phil Farrell; 12 Paul Norton; 13 Ian Sinfield. Subs: 14 Mike Ford for Clegg (56); 15 Jason Clegg for Procter (23); 16 Danny Guest for Casey (23); 17 Kevin Mannion for Norton (8BB, rev 20); Mannion for Sinfield (50); Casey for Guest (54); Clegg for Casey (75).
Try: D Gibbons (15); **Goals:** Rich 3.
League Express Men of the Match:
Hornets: David Stephenson; *Oldham:* Paul Norton.
Penalty count: 3-11; **Half-time:** 6-10;
Referee: Colin Morris (Huddersfield); **Attendance:** 3,402.

CHORLEY LYNX 24 BARROW BORDER RAIDERS 38

LYNX: 1 Paul Roberts; 2 Gary Doherty; 3 Brian Capewell; 4 Chris Ramsdale; 5 Graham Taberner; 6 Lee Ashton; 7 Stuart Fisher; 8 Mike Prescott; 9 Lee Maiden; 10 Phil Harrison; 11 Peter Cain; 12 Dale Christy; 13 Ian Talbot. Subs: 14 Kieran Lacey for Harrison (64); 15 Luke Vincent for Christy (20); 16 Paul Cookson for Doherty (51); 17 Anthony Roberts for Ashton (67); Harrison for Prescott (68).
Tries: Capewell (22, 77), Taberner (34), Fisher (47), Talbot (59); **Goals:** Fisher 2.
Sin bin: Vincent (52) - tripping.
BORDER RAIDERS: 1 Chris Massey; 2 Jamie Marshall; 3 Phil Atkinson; 4 Brett McDermott; 5 Adrian Gardner; 6 Clint Barends; 7 Darren Holt; 8 Damien Whitter; 9 Anthony Murray; 10 Willie Burns; 11 Matthew Leigh; 12 Mike Whitehead; 13 Gary Charlton. Subs: 14 Ian Rawlinson for Whitter (22); 15 Geoff Luxon for Whitehead (56); 16 Gareth Pratt for Holt (67); 17 Tau Liku for Rawlinson (38); Whitter for Liku (60); Rawlinson for Leigh (65).
Tries: Leigh (9), Murray (13, 18), Burns (27), Massey (37), Marshall (62), Charlton (65); **Goals:** Holt 3, Atkinson 2.
League Express Men of the Match:
Lynx: Ian Talbot; *Border Raiders:* Mike Whitehead.
Penalty count: 7-5; **Half-time:** 10-26;
Referee: Julian King (St Helens); **Attendance:** 488.

Tuesday 26th December 2000

DEWSBURY RAMS 24 BATLEY BULLDOGS 12

RAMS: 1 Nathan Graham; 2 Alex Godfrey; 4 Dan Potter; 3 Adrian Flynn; 5 Richard Baker; 6 Richard Agar; 7 Barry Eaton; 8 Matthew Long; 9 Richard Pachniuk; 10 Robin Jowitt; 11 Sean Richardson; 12 Paul Smith; 13 Damian Ball. Subs: 14 Liam Tallon for Potter (32); 15 Billy Kershaw not used; 16 Andrew Spink for Richardson (58); 17 Ryan McDonald for Long (22); Long for Jowitt (51).
Tries: Baker (24), Graham (38, 79), Richardson (45); **Goals:** Eaton 4.
Sent off: Agar (53) - kicking.
BULLDOGS: 1 Craig Lingard; 2 Jeremy Dyson; 3 Danny Maun; 4 Davide Longo; 5 Paul Gleadhill; 6 Simon Jackson; 7 Glen Tomlinson; 8 Jeff Wittenberg; 9 Andy Heptinstall; 10 Andy Richardson; 11 Gary Shillabeer; 12 Paul Hicks; 13 Ryan Horsley. Subs: 14 Jamie Coventry for Jackson (50); 15 Craig Richards not used; 16 Andy Wray for Wittenberg (34); 17 Will Cartledge for Hicks (61); Wittenberg for Richardson (50); Richardson for Wray (61); Jackson for Coventry (77).
Tries: Hicks (14), Maun (17), Jackson (80).
On report: An alleged biting incident on Potter (27) and the events prior to Agar's dismissal (53).
League Express Men of the Match:
Rams: Ryan McDonald; *Bulldogs:* Ryan Horsley.
Penalty count: 5-6; **Half-time:** 14-8;
Referee: Paul Lee (Leigh); **Attendance:** 2,520.

DONCASTER DRAGONS 22 SHEFFIELD EAGLES 2

DRAGONS: 1 Lynton Stott; 2 Kevin Crouthers; 3 Craig Weston; 4 Carl Hall; 5 Neil Bennett; 6 Paul Mansson; 7 Latham Tawhai; 8 Asa Amone; 9 Peter Edwards; 10 Joe Berry; 11 James Bunyan; 12 Brad Hepi; 13 Simon Irving. Subs: 14 Anton Garcia for Hall (34); 15 Maea David for Amone (ht); 16 Craig Lawton for Bunyan (62); 17 Jamie Fielden for Berry (32); Berry for Fielden (59); Amone for Hepi (71); Bunyan for Garcia (75).
Tries: Stott (5), Irving (8), Mansson (70), Bunyan (78); **Goals:** Irving 2; **Field goals:** Mansson, Edwards.
EAGLES: 1 Andy Poynter; 2 Paul Wells; 3 Neil Kite; 4 Steve Walker; 5 Ian Thompson; 6 Richard Goddard; 7 Chris Robinson; 8 Jon Bruce; 9 Carl Briggs; 10 Steve Hill; 11 Ian Brown; 12 Heath Cruckshank; 13 Wayne Flynn. Subs: 14 Scott Rhodes for Briggs (52); 15 Gareth Hewitt for Walker (65); 16 Ricky Wright for Bruce (21); 17 Darren Summerill for Hill (47); Walker for Poynter (74).
Goal: Goddard.
League Express Men of the Match:
Dragons: James Bunyan; *Eagles:* Heath Cruckshank.
Penalty count: 10-8; **Half-time:** 11-0; **Referee:** Richard Silverwood (Dewsbury); **Attendance:** 1,970.

HULL KINGSTON ROVERS 6 FEATHERSTONE ROVERS 6

ROBINS: 1 Bob Everitt; 2 Anthony Chambers; 3 Chris Kitching; 4 Whetu Taewa; 5 Bright Sodje; 6 Darren Callaghan; 7 Scott Yeaman; 8 Jon Aston; 9 Mike Dixon; 10 Rich Hayes; 11 Andy Smith; 12 Richard Slater; 13 Chris Charles. Subs: 14 Dean Andrews for Kitching (33); 15 Allan Dunham not used; 16 Paul Fletcher for Yeaman (33); 17 Jamie Bovill for Aston (63); Kitching for Callaghan (50).
Goals: Charles 3.
ROVERS: 1 Michael Rhodes; 2 Jamie Stokes; 3 Chris Spurr; 4 Nick Simpson; 5 Matt Bramald; 6 Andy Bastow; 7 Jamie Rooney; 8 Stuart Dickens; 9 Richard Chapman; 10 Micky Clarkson; 11 Steve Dooler; 12 Neil Lowe; 13 Paul Darley. Subs: 14 Gavin Swinson for Simpson (63); 15 Danny Evans not used; 16 Ricky Helliwell for Dooler (50); 17 Gavin Morgan for Clarkson (28).
Try: Bramald (23); **Goal:** Rooney.
League Express Men of the Match:
Robins: Chris Charles; *Rovers:* Jamie Rooney.
Penalty count: 10-8; **Half-time:** 4-6;
Referee: Nick Oddy (Halifax); **Attendance:** 2,384.

WIDNES VIKINGS 20 LEIGH CENTURIONS 25

VIKINGS: 1 Damian Munro; 2 Phil Coussons; 3 Chris Percival; 4 Scott Martin; 5 Mark Forster; 6 Jason Demetriou; 7 Martin Crompton; 8 Simon Knox; 9 Phil Cantillon; 10 Stephen Holgate; 11 Joe Faimalo; 12 Chris McKinney; 13 Tommy Hodgkinson. Subs: 14 Liam Jones for Martin (17); 15 Stewart Rhodes for McKinney (62); 16 Steve Gee for Argent (62); 17 Steve Argent for Holgate (22); Argent for Knox (70); McKinney for Hodgkinson (72).
Tries: Coussons (2), Percival (60), Gee (64), Argent (79); **Goals:** Jones 2.
Sin bin: Knox (41) - late tackle.
CENTURIONS: 1 Neil Turley; 2 Alan Hadcroft; 3 Paul Anderson; 4 Andy Fairclough; 5 David Ingram; 6 Simon Svabic; 7 Liam Bretherton; 8 David Bradbury; 9 Martin Roden; 10 David Whittle; 11 Simon Baldwin; 12 Chris Morley; 13 Adam Bristow. Subs: 14 Tim Street for Whittle (23); 15 Andy Leathem for Street (70); 16 Phil Kendrick for Hadcroft (70); 17 John Hamilton for Roden (62); Whittle for Bradbury (73).
Tries: Turley (7), Baldwin (43), Svabic (49), Kendrick (69); **Goals:** Svabic 4; **Field goal:** Svabic.
Sin bin: Bradbury (35) - lying on.
On report: Bradbury (22) - high tackle.
League Express Men of the Match:
Vikings: Simon Knox; *Centurions:* Simon Svabic.
Penalty count: 8-7; **Half-time:** 6-9; **Referee:** Steve Nicholson (Whitehaven); **Attendance:** 6,644.

YORK 20 HUNSLET HAWKS 20

YORK: 1 Chris Allen; 2 Jamie Benn; 3 Paul Butterfield; 4 Craig Moore; 5 Leroy McKenzie; 6 Paddy Handley; 7 Gareth Oulton; 8 Mick Hagan; 9 Gareth Dobson; 10 Craig Forsyth; 11 Darren Hughes; 12 Michael Smith; 13 Mick Ramsden. Subs: 14 Tim Rumford for Oulton (27); 15 Matthew Mulholland for Hagan (59); 16 Alan Pallister for Ramsden (27); 17 Adam Briggs not used; Oulton for Dobson (79).
Tries: Benn (28), Handley (40), Allen (56), McKenzie (80); **Goals:** Benn 2.
HAWKS: 1 George Raynor; 2 David Plange; 3 Iain Higgins; 4 Michael Wainwright; 5 Aaron Campbell; 6 Marcus Vassilakopoulos; 7 Chris Ross; 8 Guy Adams; 9 Nicky Dobson; 10 David Bates; 11 Mick Coyle; 12 Dave Jessey; 13 Robert Roberts. Subs: 14 Chris North for Plange (ht); 15 Michael Banks for Jessey (28); 16 Tony Howcroft not used; 17 Ben Skerrett for Banks (55); Banks for Bates (72).
Tries: Raynor (6), Coyle (45, 66);
Goals: Ross 3; **Field goals:** Roberts 2.
League Express Men of the Match:
York: Paddy Handley; *Hawks:* Robert Roberts.
Penalty count: 9-8; **Half-time:** 10-6;
Referee: Julian King (St Helens); **Attendance:** 698.

WEEK 5

Monday 1st January 2001

BATLEY BULLDOGS 12 YORK 4

BULLDOGS: 1 Craig Lingard; 2 Jeremy Dyson; 3 Danny Maun; 4 Davide Longo; 5 Roger Simpson; 6 Simon Jackson; 7 Glen Tomlinson; 8 Craig Richards; 9 Andy Heptinstall; 10 Andy Richardson; 11 Gary Shillabeer; 12 Will Cartledge; 13 Ryan Horsley. Subs: 14 Jamie Coventry for Shillabeer (ht); 15 Mark Cass for Heptinstall (57); 16 Andy Wray for Richardson (20); 17 Jeff Wittenberg for Richards (15).
Tries: Longo (5), Wittenberg (68); **Goals:** Dyson 2.
YORK: 1 Jamie Benn; 2 Matthew Mulholland; 3 Chris Allen; 4 Paul Butterfield; 5 Leroy McKenzie; 6 Paddy Handley; 7 Gareth Oulton; 8 Mick Hagan; 9 Gareth Dobson; 10 Craig Forsyth; 11 Craig Moore; 12 Darren Hughes; 13 Michael Smith. Subs: 14 Tim Rumford for Mulholland (40); 15 Adam Briggs for Hughes (60); 16 Alan Pallister for Hagan (68); 17 Trialist not used.
Goals: Benn 2.
League Express Men of the Match:
Bulldogs: Ryan Horsley; *York:* Jamie Benn.
Penalty count: 5-5; **Half-time:** 4-4;
Referee: John Farrell (Widnes); **Attendance:** 637.

FEATHERSTONE ROVERS 34 DONCASTER DRAGONS 4

ROVERS: 1 Michael Rhodes; 2 Jamie Stokes; 3 Steve Dooler; 4 Nick Simpson; 5 Matt Bramald; 6 Andy Bastow; 7 Jamie Rooney; 8 Stuart Dickens; 9 Richard Chapman; 10 Micky Clarkson; 11 Danny Evans; 12 Neil Lowe; 13 Paul Darley. Subs: 14 Gavin Swinson for Dooler (32BB, rev 45); 15 Gary Barnett for Bastow (67); 16 Ricky Helliwell for Evans (25); 17 Gavin Morgan for Clarkson (23); Clarkson for Morgan (56); Evans for Dickens (65); Swinson for Darley (68).
Tries: Rooney (26, 43), Swinson (34), Chapman (38), Stokes (52), Bramald (66); **Goals:** Rooney 5.
DRAGONS: 1 Craig Weston; 2 Neil Bennett; 3 Kevin Crouthers; 4 James Bunyan; 5 Anton Garcia; 6 Paul Mansson; 7 Latham Tawhai; 8 Asa Amone; 9 Peter Edwards; 10 Joe Berry; 11 Rob Wilson; 12 Brad Hepi; 13 Simon Irving. Subs: 14 Tony Miller for Hepi (41); 15 Maea David for Amone (24); 16 Craig Lawton for David (63); 17 Jamie Fielden for Berry (24); Amone for Fielden (62); Berry for Wilson (63).
Try: Bunyan (14).
League Express Men of the Match:
Rovers: Jamie Rooney; *Dragons:* Peter Edwards.
Penalty count: 7-8; **Half-time:** 16-4;
Referee: Ian Smith (Oldham); **Attendance:** 2,363.

LEIGH CENTURIONS 46 SWINTON LIONS 4

CENTURIONS: 1 Neil Turley; 2 Alan Hadcroft; 3 Paul Anderson; 4 Andy Fairclough; 5 David Jones; 6 Simon Svabic; 7 Liam Bretherton ; 8 Andy Leathem; 9 John Hamilton; 10 David Whittle; 11 Simon Baldwin; 12 Chris Morley; 13 Adam Bristow. Subs: 14 Phil Kendrick for Bristow (53); 15 Paul Norman for Whittle (30); 16 John Duffy for Hamilton (35); 17 David Bradbury for Norman (50); Hamilton for Svabic (65); Whittle for Bradbury (72).
Tries: Whittle (19), Hamilton (23), Hadcroft (24), Jones (30), Turley (35, 37, 79), Anderson (52);
Goals: Svabic 6, Turley.
Sin bin: Morley (9) - fighting.
LIONS: 1 Wayne English; 2 Adrian Mead; 3 Mick Nanyn; 4 Paul Loughlin; 5 Lee Hudson; 6 Phil Waring; 7 Kelvin Peet; 8 Jonathan Neill; 9 Rob Barraclough; 10 Lee Hansen; 11 Phil Cushion; 12 Paul Smith; 13 Phil Veivers. Subs; 14 Andy Cheetham for Hudson (31); 15 John-Paul Doherty for Peet (51); 16 Carlo Napolitano for Loughlin (36); 17 Ryan Stazicker for Hansen (65); Hansen for Napolitano (68).
Try: Cushion (64).
Sin bin: Neill (9) - fighting.
League Express Men of the Match:
Centurions: Simon Baldwin; *Lions:* Phil Veivers.
Penalty count: 5-6; **Half-time:** 34-0;

Referee: Peter Taberner (Wigan); **Attendance:** 2,881.

OLDHAM 20 WIDNES VIKINGS 12

OLDHAM: 1 Mark Sibson; 2 Danny Arnold; 3 Anthony Gibbons; 4 Pat Rich; 5 Daryl Lacey; 6 David Gibbons; 7 Neil Roden; 8 Leo Casey; 9 John Hough; 10 Paul Norton; 11 Phil Farrell; 12 Ian Sinfield; 13 Kevin Mannion. Subs: 14 Mike Ford for Roden (56); 15 Jason Clegg for Norton (23BB, rev 49); 16 Danny Guest for Casey (25); 17 Chris Farrell for Sinfield (56); Casey for Guest (51); Clegg for Casey (67).
Tries: Lacey (12), Arnold (73, 79); **Goals:** Rich 3;
Field goals: Roden, Ford.
VIKINGS: 1 Damian Munro; 2 Phil Coussons; 3 Chris Percival; 4 Eddie Kilgannon; 5 Mark Forster; 6 Jason Demetriou; 7 Martin Crompton; 8 Simon Knox; 9 Phil Cantillon; 10 Stewart Rhodes; 11 Joe Faimalo; 12 Chris McKinney; 13 Tommy Hodgkinson. Subs: 14 Liam Jones not used; 15 Stephen Holgate for Argent (49); 16 Mike Hill for Rhodes (72); 17 Steve Argent for Knox (27).
Tries: Coussons (21), Munro (33), Crompton (51).
League Express Men of the Match:
Oldham: David Gibbons; *Vikings:* Martin Crompton.
Penalty count: 6-5; **Half-time:** 11-8; **Referee:** Richard Silverwood (Dewsbury); **Attendance:** 3,471.

HUNSLET HAWKS 2 DEWSBURY RAMS 34

HAWKS: 1 George Raynor; 2 Iain Higgins; 3 Chris Redfearn; 4 Michael Wainwright; 5 Aaron Campbell; 6 Marcus Vassilakopoulos; 7 Chris Ross; 8 Michael Banks; 9 Nicky Dobson; 10 David Bates; 11 Mick Coyle; 12 Guy Adams; 13 Robert Roberts. Subs: 14 David Plange for Campbell (66); 15 Chris North not used; 16 Tony Howcroft for Ross (51); 17 Dave Jessey for Bates (41); Ross for Raynor (55); Bates for Coyle (57).
Goal: Ross.
RAMS: 1 Nathan Graham; 2 Alex Godfrey; 3 Liam Tallon; 4 Paul Smith; 5 Adrian Flynn; 6 Richard Agar; 7 Barry Eaton; 8 Matthew Long; 9 Richard Pachniuk; 10 Robin Jowitt; 11 Sean Richardson; 12 Andrew Spink; 13 Damian Ball. Subs: 14 Mark Cain for Pachniuk (48); 15 Billy Kershaw for Ball (41); 16 Ryan McDonald for Jowitt (30); 17 Simon Hicks for Long (36); Jowitt for McDonald (67).
Tries: Tallon (20, 62), Flynn (32, 40), Eaton (58);
Goals: Eaton 7.
Sent off: Hicks (73) - punch on Ross.
League Express Men of the Match:
Hawks: Guy Adams; *Rams:* Barry Eaton.
Penalty count: 8-4; **Half-time:** 2-22; **Referee:** Ronnie Laughton (Barnsley); **Attendance:** 1,260.

Wednesday 3rd January 2001

KEIGHLEY COUGARS 24 HULL KINGSTON ROVERS 8

COUGARS: 1 James Rushforth; 2 Craig Horne; 3 Karl Smith; 4 Graeme Hallas; 5 Jason Lee; 6 Martin Wood; 7 Nathan Antonik; 8 Michael Slicker; 9 Jason Ramshaw; 10 Matt Walker; 11 Paul Harrison; 12 Ian Hughes; 13 Danny Seal. Subs: 14 Darren Carter for Seal (54); 15 Jim Leatham for Hughes (48); 16 Phil Stephenson for Walker (26); 17 Alan Boothroyd for Slicker (26); Slicker for Boothroyd (64); Walker for Stephenson (65).
Tries: Lee (27), Harrison (54), Rushforth (60), Carter (71); **Goals:** Wood 4.
Sin bin: Hallas (37) - dissent.
ROVERS: 1 Bob Everitt; 2 Dean Andrews; 3 Andy Smith; 4 Whetu Taewa; 5 Bright Sodje; 6 Chris Kitching; 7 Anthony Chambers; 8 Jon Aston; 9 Mike Dixon; 10 Rich Hayes; 11 Jon Wilkins; 12 Paul Fletcher; 13 Chris Charles. Subs: 14 Scott Yeaman for Chambers (40); 15 Allan Dunham for Wilkins (50); 16 Mark Blanchard for Andrews (62); 17 Jamie Bovill for Aston (33); Aston for Bovill (54); Chambers for Yeaman (74).
Tries: Wilkins (40); **Goals:** Charles 2.
Sin bin: Chambers (17) - dissent;
Smith (50) - professional foul.
League Express Men of the Match:
Cougars: Jason Ramshaw; *Rovers:* Rich Hayes.
Penalty count: 10-3; **Half-time:** 8-8; **Referee:** Steve Nicholson (Whitehaven); **Attendance:** 2,150.

Thursday 4th January 2001

WORKINGTON TOWN 31 WHITEHAVEN 10

TOWN: 1 Jamie Smith; 2 Neil Frazer; 3 Fata Sini; 4 Steve McGrady; 5 Graeme Lewthwaite; 6 Tane Manihera; 7 Micky Horner; 8 Lokeni Savelio; 9 Carl Sice; 10 Hitro Okesene; 11 Matt Sturm; 12 Anthony Samuel; 13 Stuart Hoyles. Subs: 14 William Blackburn for Savelio (52); 15 Matthew Tunstall for Savelio (9BB, rev 24); 16 Owen Williamson for Sice (71); 17 Jamie Nixon for Sini (52); Tunstall for Okesene (62); Savelio for Sturm (76).
Tries: Okesene (8), Samuel (25), McGrady (30), J Smith (76); **Goals:** Manihera 7; **Field goals:** J Smith.
Sin bin: Sturm (40) - interference in an offside position.
WHITEHAVEN: 1 Wesley Wilson; 2 Chris Campbell; 3 David Seeds; 4 Craig Walsh; 5 Jonathan Wignall; 6 Lee Kiddie; 7 Steve Kirkbride; 8 Mark Cox; 9 Aaron Lester; 10 David Fatialofa; 11 Craig Chambers; 12 Graeme Morton; 13 Spencer Miller. Subs: 14 Marc Jackson for Chambers (43); 15 Alan Bone for Miller (69); 16 Howard Hill for Morton (54); 17 Dean Vaughan for Cox (30); Cox for Fatialofa (69).
Tries: Wignall (78); **Goals:** Kirkbride 3.
Sent off: Lester (42) - head shot.
League Express Men of the Match:
Town: Tane Manihera; *Whitehaven:* Lee Kiddie.
Penalty count: 7-7; **Half-time:** 20-4; **Referee:** Colin Morris (Huddersfield); **Attendance:** 2,460.

WEEK 6

Sunday 7th January 2001

BARROW BORDER RAIDERS 5 WHITEHAVEN 4

BORDER RAIDERS: 1 Chris Massey; 2 Glen Hutton; 3 Phil Atkinson; 4 Brett McDermott; 5 Adrian Gardner; 6 Clint Barends; 7 Darren Holt; 8 Damien Whitter; 9 Anthony Murray; 10 Willie Burns; 11 Matthew Leigh; 12 Mike Whitehead; 13 Gary Charlton. Subs: 14 Geoff Luxon for Atkinson (60); 15 Ian Rawlinson for Burns (45); 16 Steve Jackson for Liku (ht); 17 Tau Liku for Whitter (26); Whitter for Jackson (63).
Goals: Holt 2; **Field goal:** Holt.
WHITEHAVEN: 1 Wesley Wilson; 2 Craig Walsh; 3 David Seeds; 4 Ian Devlin; 5 Chris Campbell; 6 Lee Kiddie; 7 Steve Kirkbride; 8 Mark Cox; 9 Aaron Lester; 10 David Fatialofa; 11 Craig Chambers; 12 Graeme Morton; 13 Spencer Miller. Subs: 14 Gary Purdham not used; 15 Alan Bone for Morton (68); 16 Howard Hill for Chambers (ht); 17 Dean Vaughan for Fatialofa (50); Fatialofa for Cox (63).
Try: Walsh (29).
League Express Men of the Match: *Border Raiders:* Brett McDermott; *Whitehaven:* Aaron Lester.
Penalty count: 7-7; **Half-time:** 2-4; **Referee:** Richard Silverwood (Dewsbury); **Attendance:** 1,008.

BATLEY BULLDOGS 6 FEATHERSTONE ROVERS 37

BULLDOGS: 1 Craig Lingard; 2 Jeremy Dyson; 3 Danny Maun; 4 Davide Longo; 5 Roger Simpson; 6 Richard Price; 7 Glen Tomlinson; 8 Chris McWilliam; 9 Andy Heptinstall; 10 Andy Richardson; 11 Gary Shillabeer; 12 Paul Hicks; 13 Ryan Horsley. Subs: 14 Jamie Coventry for Price (60); 15 Mark Cass for Heptinstall (ht); 16 Will Cartledge for Richardson (33); 17 Jeff Wittenberg for McWilliam (23).
Try: Longo (44); **Goal:** Price.
ROVERS: 1 Michael Rhodes; 2 Jamie Stokes; 3 Steve Dooler; 4 Nick Simpson; 5 Matt Bramald; 6 Andy Bastow; 7 Jamie Rooney; 8 Stuart Dickens; 9 Richard Chapman; 10 Micky Clarkson; 11 Danny Evans; 12 Neil Lowe; 13 Paul Darley. Subs: 14 Gavin Swinson for Darley (ht); 15 Gary Barnett for Dooler (64); 16 Ricky Helliwell for Evans (30); 17 Gavin Morgan for Clarkson (27).
Tries: Bramald (5, 52), Rooney (35, 65), Stokes (50), Morgan (79); **Goals:** Rooney 6; **Field goal:** Rooney.
League Express Men of the Match:
Bulldogs: Paul Hicks; *Rovers:* Jamie Rooney.
Penalty count: 7-9; **Half-time:** 2-12; **Referee:** Colin Morris (Huddersfield); **Attendance:** 1,358.

CHORLEY LYNX 4 LEIGH CENTURIONS 56

LYNX: 1 Paul Roberts; 2 Stuart Dickinson; 3 Brian Capewell; 4 Chris Ramsdale; 5 Graham Taberner; 6 Lee Ashton; 7 Stuart Fisher; 8 Mike Prescott; 9 Lee Maiden; 10 Dean Conway; 11 Phil Harrison; 12 Peter Cain; 13 Ian Talbot. Subs: 14 Anthony Roberts for P Roberts (51); 15 Gary Doherty for Dickinson (63); 16 Dale Christy for Harrison (25); 17 Luke Vincent for Prescott (65); Harrison for Conway (34); Conway for Cain (65).
Try: Taberner (58).
CENTURIONS: 1 Neil Turley; 2 Alan Hadcroft; 3 Phil Kendrick; 4 Andy Fairclough; 5 David Jones; 6 John Duffy; 7 Liam Bretherton; 8 Tim Street; 9 John Hamilton; 10 Andy Leathem; 11 Simon Baldwin; 12 Chris Morley; 13 Adam Bristow. Subs: 14 Paul Anderson for Duffy (53); 15 Martin Roden for Hamilton (41); 16 Radney Bowker for Baldwin (30); 17 David Whittle for Leathem (28); Baldwin for Hadcroft (65); Leathem for Street (70).
Tries: Turley (10, 30, 69, 78, 80), Hamilton (16), Hadcroft (22), Street (40), Bowker (56), Anderson (64);
Goals: Turley 8.
League Express Men of the Match:
Lynx: Graham Taberner; *Centurions:* Neil Turley.
Penalty count: 4-8; **Half-time:** 0-26; **Referee:** Ronnie Laughton (Barnsley); **Attendance:** 1,382.

DEWSBURY RAMS 50 YORK 2

RAMS: 1 Nathan Graham; 2 Alex Godfrey; 3 Gavin Wood; 4 Dan Potter; 5 Adrian Flynn; 6 Richard Agar; 7 Mark Cain; 8 Matthew Long; 9 Barry Eaton; 10 Robin Jowitt; 11 Sean Richardson; 12 Paul Smith; 13 Damian Ball. Subs: 14 Andrew Spink for Richardson (55); 15 Billy Kershaw for Smith (ht); 16 Ryan McDonald for Jowitt (25); 17 Simon Hicks for Long (27); Long for McDonald (67); Jowitt for Hicks (67).
Tries: Cain (11), Ball (33, 54), Potter (37), Eaton (49), Graham (55), Flynn (64, 66), Kershaw (75);
Goals: Eaton 7.
YORK: 1 Jamie Benn; 2 Matthew Mulholland; 3 Paul Butterfield; 4 Gareth Lloyd; 5 Leroy McKenzie; 6 Paddy Handley; 7 Gareth Stephens; 8 Michael Smith; 9 Alan Pallister; 10 Craig Forsyth; 11 Craig Moore; 12 Shaun Austerfield; 13 Chris Allen. Subs: 14 Gareth Oulton for Mulholland (55); 15 Gareth Dobson for Forsyth (15); 16 Charles Hoggard for Austerfield (63); 17 Adam Briggs for Forsyth (5BB, rev 9); Briggs for Pallister (ht); Forsyth for Briggs (57).
Goal: Benn.
League Express Men of the Match:
Rams: Damian Ball; *York:* Gareth Stephens.
Penalty count: 5-2; **Half-time:** 18-2; **Referee:** Steve Nicholson (Whitehaven); **Attendance:** 1,200.

HULL KINGSTON ROVERS 40 HUNSLET HAWKS 12

ROVERS: 1 Bob Everitt; 2 Dean Andrews; 3 Andy Smith; 4 Whetu Taewa; 5 Bright Sodje; 6 Chris Kitching; 7 Darren Callaghan; 8 Jon Aston; 9 Mike Dixon; 10 Rich Hayes; 11 Jon Wilkins; 12 Paul Fletcher; 13 Chris Charles. Subs: 14 Scott Yeaman for Everitt (59); 15 Allan Dunham for Wilkins (50); 16 Mark Blanchard for Fletcher (23); 17 Jamie Bovill for Aston (32); Wilkins for Hayes (68); Everitt for Callaghan (79).
Tries: Sodje (8), Callaghan (29), Andrews (34), Smith (50), Bovill (55), Taewa (58, 76); **Goals:** Charles 6.
HAWKS: 1 George Raynor; 2 Iain Higgins; 3 Chris Redfearn; 4 Michael Wainwright; 5 Chris Heywood; 6 Marcus Vassilakopoulos; 7 Chris Ross; 8 Michael Banks; 9 Nicky Dobson; 10 David Bates; 11 Mick Coyle; 12 Guy Adams; 13 Robert Roberts. Subs: 14 David Plange not used; 15 Chris North for Higgins (44); 16 Andy Atha not used; 17 Dave Jessey for Banks (22); Banks for Bates (75).
Tries: Ross (20, 63); **Goals:** Ross 2.
League Express Men of the Match:
Rovers: Rich Hayes; *Hawks:* Chris Ross
Penalty count: 3-3; **Half-time:** 16-6;
Referee: Ian Smith (Oldham); **Attendance:** 1,953.

SWINTON LIONS 4 ROCHDALE HORNETS 8

LIONS: 1 Wayne English; 2 Adrian Mead; 3 Mick Nanyn; 4 Andy Cheetham; 5 Lee Hudson; 6 Phil Veivers; 7 Phil Waring; 8 Jonathan Neill; 9 Rob Barraclough; 10 Lee Hansen; 11 Phil Cushion; 12 Ryan Stazicker; 13 Paul Smith. Subs: 14 Jim Evans for Barraclough (53); 15 Tony Barrow for Neill (ht); 16 Robert Russell for Stazicker (28); 17 John-Paul Doherty for Hansen (ht); Neill for Barrow (71); Hansen for Doherty (71).
Try: Nanyn (62).
HORNETS: 1 Dave Watson; 2 Marlon Miller; 3 Danny Wood; 4 Brendan O'Meara; 5 Marlon Billy; 6 Paul Owen; 7 Mick Coates; 8 Danny Sculthorpe; 9 Warren Ayres; 10 Andy Ireland; 11 Martin Bunce; 12 David Larder; 13 David Stephenson. Subs: 14 Sean Cooper for Miller (21); 15 Steve Campbell for Larder (18BB, rev 19); 16 Wes Rogers for Stephenson (14); 17 Darren Robinson for Rogers (58); Campbell for Ireland (51); Ireland for Sculthorpe (68).
Try: Ayres (47); **Goals:** Wood 2.
League Express Men of Match:
Lions: Phil Cushion; *Hornets:* Danny Sculthorpe.
Penalty count: 7-6; **Half-time:** 0-0;
Referee: Julian King (St Helens); **Attendance:** 1,153.

WIDNES VIKINGS 26 WORKINGTON TOWN 16

VIKINGS: 1 Damian Munro; 2 Phil Coussons; 3 Jason Demetriou; 4 Mark Flanagan; 5 Mark Forster; 6 Martin Crompton; 7 Ian Watson; 8 Stewart Rhodes; 9 Phil Cantillon; 10 Stephen Holgate; 11 Joe Faimalo; 12 Chris McKinney; 13 Tommy Hodgkinson. Subs: 14 Karle Hammond for Hodgkinson (46); 15 Steve Gee for Faimalo (34); 16 Chris Percival for Demetriou (56); 17 Alan Shea for Rhodes (70); Faimalo for McKinney (45).
Tries: Forster (1), Holgate (10), Munro (13, 59), McKinney (27), Cantillon (69); **Goal:** Watson.
TOWN: 1 Jamie Smith; 2 Neil Frazer; 3 Kevin Hetherington; 4 Steve McGrady; 5 Graeme Lewthwaite; 6 Tane Manihera; 7 Micky Horner; 8 Lokeni Savelio; 9 Carl Sice; 10 Hitro Okesene; 11 Matt Sturm; 12 Anthony Samuel; 13 Stuart Hoyles. Subs: 14 William Blackburn for Okesene (70); 15 Matt Tunstall for Savelio (50); 16 Owen Williamson for Sice (78); 17 Jamie Nixon for Hetherington (12); Hetherington for McGrady (60).
Tries: Lewthwaite (5), Savelio (24), Hoyles (38);
Goals: Hetherington, Manihera.
League Express Men of the Match:
Vikings: Joe Faimalo; *Town:* Tane Manihera.
Penalty count: 5-2; **Half-time:** 16-16;
Referee: Peter Taberner (Wigan); **Attendance:** 3,312.

SHEFFIELD EAGLES 16 KEIGHLEY COUGARS 52

EAGLES: 1 Andy Poynter; 2 Paul Wells; 3 Neil Kite; 4 Steve Walker; 5 Ian Brown; 6 Carl Briggs; 7 Chris Robinson; 8 Jon Bruce; 9 Andy Speak; 10 Ricky Wright; 11 Wayne Flynn; 12 Heath Cruckshank; 13 Richard Goddard. Subs: 14 Andy Brent for Wright (24); 15 Scott Rhodes for Briggs (30); 16 Darren Summerill for Speak (54); 17 Gareth Hewitt for Cruckshank (59); Wright for Bruce (68); Bruce for Poynter (77).
Tries: I Brown (42, 75), Brent (61); **Goals:** Goddard 2.
Sin bin: Poynter (26) - holding down.
COUGARS: 1 James Rushforth; 2 Craig Horne; 3 Darren Carter; 4 Graeme Hallas; 5 Jason Lee; 6 Martin Wood; 7 Nathan Antonik; 8 Michael Slicker; 9 Jason Ramshaw; 10 Matt Walker; 11 Paul Harrison; 12 Ian Hughes; 13 Danny Seal. Subs: 14 Gary Lord for Harrison (51); 15 Jim Leatham for Hughes (48); 16 Phil Stephenson for Walker (36); 17 Alan Boothroyd for Slicker (29); Walker for Stephenson (54BB, rev 66); Harrison for Boothroyd (70); Hughes for Seal (74).
Tries: Harrison (5), Horne (17, 79), Seal (23, 53), Antonik (27), Lee (35, 71), Carter (40); **Goals:** Wood 8.
League Express Men of the Match:
Eagles: Richard Goddard; *Cougars:* Nathan Antonik.
Penalty count: 4-9; **Half-time:** 0-36;
Referee: Nick Oddy (Halifax); **Attendance:** 1,642.

GATESHEAD THUNDER 8 DONCASTER DRAGONS 27

THUNDER: 1 Matthew Brown; 2 Andy Field; 3 Wes McGibbon; 4 Steve Hall; 5 Leon Williamson; 6 Scott Dyson; 7 Martin Gambles; 8 Richard Mervill; 9 Roy Southernwood; 10 Andy Grundy; 11 Jim Carlton; 12 Chris Parker; 13 Darrell Derose. Subs: 14 Paul Sebine for Southernwood (40BB, rev 56); 15 Paul Lister for Grundy (23); 16 Lee Garside for Mervill (32); 17 Matthew Roberts for Lister (45); Grundy for Garside

(58); Sebine for Dyson (62BB, rev 69); Mervill for Parker (61); Sebine for Gambles (76).
Try: Derose (27); **Goals:** Hall 2.
DRAGONS: 1 Craig Weston; 2 Carl Hall; 3 Simon Irving; 4 James Bunyan; 5 Kevin Crouthers; 6 Paul Mansson; 7 Latham Tawhai; 8 Asa Amone; 9 Billy Conway; 10 Joe Berry; 11 Rob Wilson; 12 Maea David; 13 Peter Edwards. Subs: 14 Anton Garcia for Conway (ht); 15 Tony Miller for David (ht); 16 Phil White for Wilson (69); 17 Tony Atter not used; David for Berry (72).
Tries: Hall (23), Weston (44), Garcia (53), Mansson (59), Tawhai (62); **Goals:** Bunyan 3; **Field goal:** Tawhai.
League Express Men of the Match:
Thunder: Darrell Derose; *Dragons:* Latham Tawhai.
Penalty count: 6-5; **Half-time:** 8-6;
Referee: Paul Lee (Leigh); **Attendance:** 675.

Wednesday 10th January 2001

WHITEHAVEN 28 CHORLEY LYNX 4

WHITEHAVEN: 1 Wesley Wilson; 2 Craig Walsh; 3 David Seeds; 4 Ian Devlin; 5 Chris Campbell; 6 Lee Kiddie; 7 Steve Kirkbride; 8 Mark Cox; 9 Aaron Lester; 10 David Fatialofa; 11 Howard Hill; 12 Graeme Morton; 13 Spencer Miller. Subs: 14 Leroy Joe for Kirkbride (ht); 15 Alan Bone for Morton (50); 16 Garry Purdham for Lester (75); 17 Dean Vaughan for Cox (26).
Tries: C Campbell (10), Morton (14), Kiddie (16), Lester (63), Seeds (75); **Goals:** Kirkbride 3, Wilson.
LYNX: 1 Paul Roberts; 2 Paul Cookson; 3 Brian Capewell; 4 Chris Ramsdale; 5 Graham Taberner; 6 Anthony Roberts; 7 Stuart Fisher; 8 Mike Prescott; 9 Lee Maiden; 10 Phil Harrison; 11 Dale Christy; 12 Peter Cain; 13 Ian Talbot. Subs: 14 Lee Ashton for Roberts (17); 15 Gary Blood for Capewell (75); 16 Luke Vincent for Ramsdale (65); 17 Gary Doherty for Christy (30); Christy for Prescott (71).
Try: Cookson (49).
Sin bin: Fisher (15) – dissent.
League Express Men of the Match:
Whitehaven: David Fatialofa; *Lynx:* Stuart Fisher.
Penalty count: 8-4; **Half time:** 18-0;
Referee: Paul Lee (Leigh); **Attendance:** 638.

WEEK 7

Sunday 14th January 2001

HULL KINGSTON ROVERS 0 DONCASTER DRAGONS 30

ROVERS: 1 Bob Everitt; 2 Dean Andrews; 3 Andy Smith; 4 Whetu Taewa; 5 Bright Sodje; 6 Chris Kitching; 7 Darren Callaghan; 8 Jon Aston; 9 Mike Dixon; 10 Paul Fletcher; 11 Jon Wilkins; 12 Richard Slater; 13 Chris Charles. Subs: 14 Scott Yeaman for Everitt (52); 15 Allan Dunham for Wilkins (23); 16 Mark Blanchard for Andrews (20BB, rev 25); 17 Jamie Bovill for Dunham (52); Blanchard for Smith (34); Everitt for Kitching (65).
Sin bin: Slater (45) - fighting.
DRAGONS: 1 Lynton Stott; 2 Paul Cook; 3 Carl Hall; 4 Simon Irving; 5 Kevin Crouthers; 6 Craig Weston; 7 Latham Tawhai; 8 Asa Amone; 9 Peter Edwards; 10 Maea David; 11 James Bunyan; 12 Rob Wilson; 13 Paul Mansson. Subs: 14 Anton Garcia for Hall (59); 15 Tony Miller for Edwards (57); 16 Brad Hepi for Wilson (19); 17 Tony Atter for Amone (28); Amone for David (55); David for Atter (59).
Tries: Tawhai (11, 33), Hepi (22), Hall (51), Mansson (77); **Goals:** Cook 5.
Sin bin: Stott (45) - fighting.
League Express Men of the Match:
Rovers: Mike Dixon; *Dragons:* Latham Tawhai.
Penalty count: 9-5; **Half time:** 0-18; **Referee:** Richard Silverwood (Dewsbury); **Attendance:** 2,257.

KEIGHLEY COUGARS 22 FEATHERSTONE ROVERS 22

COUGARS: 1 James Rushforth; 2 Craig Horne; 3 Darren Carter; 4 Graeme Hallas; 5 Jason Lee; 6 Martin Wood; 7 Nathan Antonik; 8 Jim Leatham; 9 Jason Ramshaw; 10 Matt Walker; 11 Paul Harrison; 12 Ian Hughes; 13 Danny Seal. Subs: 14 Gary Lord for Hughes (54); 15 Karl Smith for Ramshaw (78); 16 Phil Stephenson for Leatham (25); 17 Alan Boothroyd for Walker (25); Leatham for Harrison (63); Walker for Stephenson (70).
Tries: Ramshaw (32), Lee (40), Rushforth (45), Seal (80); **Goals:** Wood 3.
ROVERS: 1 Michael Rhodes; 2 Jamie Stokes; 3 Steve Dooler; 4 Gavin Swinson; 5 Matt Bramald; 6 Andy Bastow; 7 Jamie Rooney; 8 Stuart Dickens; 9 Richard Chapman; 10 Micky Clarkson; 11 Danny Evans; 12 Neil Lowe; 13 Paul Darley. Subs: 14 Nick Simpson for Bramald (15); 15 Gary Barnett for Darley (71); 16 Ricky Helliwell for Evans (49); 17 Gavin Morgan for Clarkson (33); Clarkson for Morgan (67).
Tries: Lowe (19), Dooler (23), Evans (28), Stokes (56);
Goals: Rooney 3.
League Express Men of the Match:
Cougars: Nathan Antonik; *Rovers:* Richard Chapman.
Penalty count: 10-2; **Half-time:** 10-16;
Referee: Ian Smith (Oldham); **Attendance:** 3,269.

OLDHAM 18 LEIGH CENTURIONS 44

OLDHAM: 1 Mark Sibson; 2 Danny Arnold; 3 Anthony Gibbons; 4 Pat Rich; 5 Daryl Lacey; 6 David Gibbons; 7 Neil Roden; 8 Andy Procter; 9 John Hough; 10 Leo Casey; 11 Phil Farrell; 12 Paul Norton; 13 Kevin Mannion. Subs: 14 Mike Ford for Lacey (1BB, rev 15); 15 Jason Clegg for Casey (25); 16 Danny Guest for Procter (47); 17 Ian Sinfield for Clegg (65); Ford for Lacey (47); Casey for Guest (65); Procter for Norton (72).
Tries: Arnold (18), Hough (61), Sibson (64);
Goals: Rich 3.
Sent off: A Gibbons (18) - retaliation.
CENTURIONS: 1 Neil Turley; 2 Michael Watts; 3 Paul Anderson; 4 Andy Fairclough; 5 David Jones; 6 Simon Svabic; 7 Liam Bretherton; 8 Tim Street; 9 John Hamilton; 10 David Bradbury; 11 Simon Baldwin; 12 Chris Morley; 13 Adam Bristow. Subs: 14 David Whittle for Bradbury (22BB, rev 51); 15 Phil Kendrick for Morley (26); 16 Andy Leathem for Bradbury (71); 17 John Duffy for Hamilton (52); Morley for Kendrick (67); Hamilton for Svabic (77).
Tries: Turley (2), Svabic (8), Anderson (37), Fairclough (46, 75), Hamilton (52), Bradbury (66), Watts (78);
Goals: Svabic 5, Turley.
Sent off: Street (18) - use of knees.
League Express Men of the Match:
Oldham: John Hough; *Centurions:* Simon Baldwin.
Penalty count: 11-5; **Half-time:** 6-14;
Referee: Nick Oddy (Halifax); **Attendance:** 4,747.

HUNSLET HAWKS 4 BATLEY BULLDOGS 13

HAWKS: 1 George Raynor; 2 Iain Higgins; 3 Michael Wainwright; 4 Chris Redfearn; 5 Aaron Campbell; 6 Marcus Vassilakopoulos; 7 Chris Ross; 8 Michael Banks; 9 Nicky Dobson; 10 Guy Adams; 11 Mick Coyle; 12 Dave Jessey; 13 Robert Roberts. Subs: 14 David Bates for Banks (20); 15 Chris North for Campbell (58); 16 Andy Atha for Coyle (71); 17 Lee Maher for Campbell (33); Campbell for Jessey (ht); Bates for Banks (65).
Goals: Ross 2.
BULLDOGS: 1 Craig Lingard; 2 Jeremy Dyson; 3 Danny Maun; 4 Davide Longo; 5 Paul Gleadhill; 6 Richard Price; 7 Glen Tomlinson; 8 Chris McWilliam; 9 Andy Heptinstall; 10 Paul Hicks; 11 Gary Shillabeer; 12 Will Cartledge; 13 Ryan Horsley. Subs: 14 Jamie Coventry for Price (74); 15 Mark Cass for Heptinstall (62); 16 Andy Wray for Wittenberg (53); 17 Jeff Wittenberg for McWilliam (26); McWilliam for Hicks (57); Hicks for Wray (70BB); Wittenberg for McWilliam (71).
Tries: Longo (8), Tomlinson (40); **Goals:** Price 2;
Field goal: Heptinstall.
League Express Men of the Match:
Hawks: Nicky Dobson; *Bulldogs:* Craig Lingard.
Penalty count: 4-5; **Half-time:** 2-13;
Referee: Paul Lee (Leigh); **Attendance:** 836.

WEEK 8

Tuesday 23rd January 2001

BATLEY BULLDOGS 18 HULL KINGSTON ROVERS 16

BULLDOGS: 1 Craig Lingard; 2 Jeremy Dyson; 3 Danny Maun; 4 Davide Longo; 5 Paul Gleadhill; 6 Richard Price; 7 Glen Tomlinson; 8 Chris McWilliam; 9 Andy Heptinstall; 10 Paul Hicks; 11 Gary Shillabeer; 12 Will Cartledge; 13 Ryan Horsley. Subs: 14 Jamie Coventry for Price (65); 15 Mark Cass for Heptinstall (52); 16 Rob Padgett for Shillabeer (52); 17 Jeff Wittenberg for McWilliam (27).
Tries: Shillabeer (2), Maun (21), Cass (53);
Goals: Price 3.
ROVERS: 1 Bob Everitt; 2 Anthony Chambers; 3 Mark Blanchard; 4 Whetu Taewa; 5 Gavin Molloy; 6 Mick Crane; 7 Scott Yeaman; 8 Jon Aston; 9 Mike Dixon; 10 Jamie Bovill; 11 Andy Smith; 12 Paul Fletcher; 13 Jon Wilkins. Subs: 14 Jimmy Walker for Crane (53); 15 Allan Dunham for Blanchard (48); 16 Chris Charles for Wilkins (23); 17 Richard Slater for Bovill (7); Bovill for Slater (59).
Tries: Taewa (8, 24) Everitt (71); **Goals:** Everitt, Charles.
League Express Men of the Match:
Bulldogs: Craig Lingard; *Rovers:* Mike Dixon.
Penalty count: 4-7; **Half-time:** 10-10;
Referee: Ronnie Laughton (Barnsley); **Attendance:** 574.

Wednesday 24th January 2001

SHEFFIELD EAGLES 38 GATESHEAD THUNDER 12

EAGLES: 1 Steve Walker; 2 Ian Brown; 3 Neil Kite; 4 Wayne Flynn; 5 Ian Thompson; 6 Gavin Brown; 7 Scott Rhodes; 8 Jon Bruce; 9 Andy Speak; 10 Richard Wright; 11 Andy Brent; 12 Chris Chapman; 13 Richard Goddard. Subs: 14 Heath Cruckshank for Bruce (34); 15 Mark Aston for Speak (55); 16 Gareth Hewitt for Flynn (ht); 17 Paul Wells for Chapman (68); Bruce for Wright (66); Wright for Brent (74).
Tries: Kite (10), Goddard (36), Thompson (50, 80), Rhodes (54, 63); **Goals:** Goddard 7.
Sin bin: G Brown (25) - fighting.
THUNDER: 1 Matthew Brown; 2 Andy Field; 3 Wes McGibbon; 4 Steve Hall; 5 Leon Williamson; 6 Scott Dyson; 7 Martin Gambles; 8 Richard Mervill; 9 Roy Southernwood; 10 Andy Grundy; 11 Jim Carlton; 12 Chris Parker; 13 Darrell Derose. Subs: 14 Paul Sebine for Brown (60); 15 Paul Lister for Grundy (26); 16 Lee Garside for Mervill (35); 17 Matthew Roberts for Derose (50); Grundy for Garside (58); Mervill for Carlton (66).
Try: Gambles (76); **Goals:** Hall 4.
Sin bin: Dyson (25) - fighting.
League Express Men of the Match:
Eagles: Richard Goddard; *Thunder:* Andy Grundy.
Penalty count: 6-6; **Half-time:** 14-4;
Referee: Colin Morris (Huddersfield); **Attendance:** 753.

Thursday 25th January 2001

WIDNES VIKINGS 16 SWINTON LIONS 8

VIKINGS: 1 Damian Munro; 2 Phil Coussons; 3 Chris Percival; 4 Jason Demetriou; 5 Mark Forster; 6 Karle Hammond; 7 Ian Watson; 8 Steve Argent; 9 Phil Cantillon; 10 Stephen Holgate; 11 Joe Faimalo; 12 Alan Shea; 13 Martin Crompton. Subs: 14 Steve Gee for Watson (48BB, rev 63); 15 Stewart Rhodes for Knox (55); 16 Simon Knox for Argent (19); 17 Chris McKinney for Shea (40); Gee for Faimalo (72).
Tries: Cantillon (46), Munro (74); **Goals:** Watson 4.
LIONS: 1 Wayne English; 2 Matt Bateman; 3 Mick Nanyn; 4 Paul Loughlin; 5 Jim Evans; 6 Phil Veivers; 7 Kelvin Peet; 8 Jonathan Neill; 9 Rob Barraclough; 10 Lee Hansen; 11 Phil Cushion; 12 John-Paul Doherty; 13 Paul Smith. Subs: 14 Phil Waring for Barraclough (48); 15 Tony Barrow for Hansen (31); 16 Ryan Stazicker for Doherty (47); 17 Andy Cheetham for Bateman (71); Hansen for Neill (56); Barraclough for Veivers (68).
Try: Bateman (10); **Goals:** Nanyn 2.
League Express Men of the Match:
Vikings: Joe Faimalo; *Lions:* Kelvin Peet.
Penalty count: 11-5; **Half-time:** 2-6; **Referee:** Steve Nicholson (Whitehaven); **Attendance:** 3,004.

WEEK 9

Tuesday 30th January 2001

OLDHAM 56 CHORLEY LYNX 2

OLDHAM: 1 Mark Sibson; 2 Dean Cross; 3 David Gibbons; 4 Pat Rich; 5 Daryl Lacey; 6 Gareth Barber; 7 Neil Roden; 8 Andy Procter; 9 John Hough; 10 Leo Casey; 11 Phil Farrell; 12 Ian Sinfield; 13 Kevin Mannion. Subs: 14 Keith Brennan for Roden (48); 15 Jason Clegg for Casey (25); 16 Lee Doran for Sinfield (54); 17 Paul Norton for Procter (41); Roden for Clegg (72).
Tries: Procter (12, 32), D Gibbons (20, 29, 34, 58), Roden (36), Cross (44, 71), Sibson (75); **Goals:** Rich 8.
LYNX: 1 Stuart Dickinson; 2 Chris Ramsdale; 3 Brian Capewell; 4 Andrew Friar; 5 Gary Blood; 6 Anthony Roberts; 7 Lee Ashton; 8 Mike Prescott; 9 Ian Talbot; 10 Lee Prest; 11 Peter Cain; 12 Gareth Chambers; 13 Dale Christy. Subs: 14 Paul Cookson for Talbot (62); 15 Ian Marsh for Prescott (41); 16 Phil Harrison for Prest (22); 17 Rob Verrelli for Cain (33); Prest for Harrison (65); Cain for Marsh (72).
Goal: Capewell.
League Express Men of the Match:
Oldham: David Gibbons; *Lynx:* Dale Christy.
Penalty count: 2-4; **Half-time:** 36-2;
Referee: Colin Morris (Huddersfield); **Attendance:** 1,210.

DONCASTER DRAGONS 17 KEIGHLEY COUGARS 23

DRAGONS: 1 Paul Cook; 2 Anton Garcia; 3 Carl Hall; 4 Simon Irving; 5 Kevin Crouthers; 6 Craig Weston; 7 Latham Tawhai; 8 Maea David; 9 Peter Edwards; 10 Brad Hepi; 11 James Bunyan; 12 Tony Miller; 13 Paul Mansson. Subs: 14 Neil Bennett for Garcia (ht); 15 Billy Conway for Fielden (61); 16 Tony Atter for Bunyan (57); 17 Jamie Fielden for Mansson (24); Bunyan for David (69).
Tries: Crouthers (22), Irving (52), Weston (78);
Goals: Cook 2; **Field goal:** Cook.
COUGARS: 1 James Rushforth; 2 Craig Horne; 3 Karl Smith; 4 Graeme Hallas; 5 Jason Lee; 6 Martin Wood; 7 Nathan Antonik; 8 Michael Slicker; 9 Jason Ramshaw; 10 Alan Boothroyd; 11 Paul Harrison; 12 Ian Hughes; 13 Danny Seal. Subs: 14 Matt Walker for Slicker (27); 15 Jim Leatham for Smith (48); 16 Phil Stephenson for Boothroyd (27); 17 Darren Carter for Wood (45).
Tries: Horne (27, 30), Lee (32), Rushforth (44);
Goals: Wood, Hallas 2; **Field goal:** Ramshaw.
League Express Men of the Match:
Dragons: Brad Hepi; *Cougars:* Craig Horne.
Penalty count: 8-4; **Half-time:** 7-17; **Referee:** Steve Nicholson (Whitehaven); **Attendance:** 1,691.

Wednesday 31st January 2001

FEATHERSTONE ROVERS 26 HUNSLET HAWKS 14

ROVERS: 1 Michael Rhodes; 2 Jamie Stokes; 3 Nick Simpson; 4 Gavin Swinson; 5 Matt Bramald; 6 Andy Bastow; 7 Jamie Rooney; 8 Stuart Dickens; 9 Richard Chapman; 10 Gavin Morgan; 11 Danny Evans; 12 Neil Lowe; 13 Steve Dooler. Subs: 14 Ricky Helliwell for Evans (19BB, rev 49); 15 Gary Barnett for Rhodes (34); 16 Micky Clarkson for Morgan (25); 17 Stephen Jones for Evans (73); Morgan for Dickens (54); Helliwell for Lowe (67).
Tries: Chapman (19), Rooney (39), Bramald (48, 55);
Goals: Rooney 5.
HAWKS: 1 George Raynor; 2 Lee Maher; 3 Iain Higgins; 4 Michael Wainwright; 5 Aaron Campbell; 6 Chris Redfearn; 7 Chris Ross; 8 Michael Banks; 9 Nicky Dobson; 10 Guy Adams; 11 Mick Coyle; 12 Dave Jessey; 13 Robert Roberts. Subs: 14 Andy Atha for Banks (80); 15 David Bates for Banks (20); 16 Craig Robinson for Ross (43); 17 Ben Skerrett for Jessey (49); Ross for Maher (63); Banks for Coyle (64).
Tries: Maher (31), Jessey (45), Campbell (74);
Goal: Robinson.
League Express Men of the Match:
Rovers: Richard Chapman; *Hawks:* Guy Adams.
Penalty count: 11-6; **Half-time:** 12-4;
Referee: Nick Oddy (Halifax); **Attendance:** 1,292.

LEIGH CENTURIONS 70 WORKINGTON TOWN 0

CENTURIONS: 1 Neil Turley; 2 David Ingram; 3 Paul Anderson; 4 Kieron Purtill; 5 Alan Hadcroft; 6 Simon Svabic; 7 Liam Bretherton; 8 David Bradbury; 9 John

Duffy; 10 Andy Leathem; 11 Simon Baldwin; 12 Adam Bristow; 13 Andy Fairclough. Subs: 14 David Whittle for Leathem (25); 15 Willie Swann for Purtill (25); 16 Paul Norman for Bradbury (36); 17 John Hamilton for Duffy (33); Purtill for Swann (57); Bradbury for Bristow (66).
Tries: Ingram (4), Turley (15, 24, 45, 51, 56, 65), Duffy (20), Bretherton (32), Hadcroft (37), Whittle (53), Svabic (74); **Goals:** Svabic 11.
TOWN: 1 Steve Stoddart; 2 Neil Frazer; 3 Adam Coulson; 4 Leigh Smith; 5 Graeme Lewthwaite; 6 Craig Rumney; 7 Mickey Horner; 8 Lokeni Savelio; 9 Carl Sice; 10 Matt Sturm; 11 Jamie Beaumont; 12 Anthony Samuel; 13 Stuart Hoyles. Subs: 14 Jamie Nixon for Rumney (18); 15 Matthew Tunstall for Sice (29); 16 Scott Chilton for Coulson (37); 17 Craig Barker for Savelio (67); Rumney for Chilton (53).
League Express Men of the Match:
Centurions: Neil Turley; *Town:* Anthony Samuel.
Penalty count: 2-2; **Half-time:** 36-0; **Referee:** Richard Silverwood (Dewsbury); **Attendance:** 2,149.

SHEFFIELD EAGLES 6 DEWSBURY RAMS 25

EAGLES: 1 Steve Walker; 2 Paul Wells; 3 Neil Kite; 4 Gareth Hewitt; 5 Ian Thompson; 6 Gavin Brown; 7 Scott Rhodes; 8 Jon Bruce; 9 Andy Speak; 10 Ricky Wright; 11 Andy Brent; 12 Heath Cruckshank; 13 Richard Goddard. Subs: 14 Ian Brown for Wright (61); 15 Mark Aston for Speak (54); 16 Simon Tillyer for Brent (79); 17 Darren Summerill for Bruce (14); Speak for Summerill (78).
Try: Goddard (17); **Goal:** Goddard.
RAMS: 1 Nathan Graham; 2 Alex Godfrey; 3 Dan Potter; 4 Adrian Flynn; 5 Richard Baker; 6 Mark Cain; 7 Barry Eaton; 8 Matthew Long; 9 David Mycoe; 10 Robin Jowitt; 11 Sean Richardson; 12 Andrew Spink; 13 Damian Ball. Subs: 14 Gavin Wood for Baker (78); 15 Andy Fisher for Jowitt (6BB, rev 30); 16 Kevin Spink for Mycoe (73); 17 Simon Hicks for Long (30); Fisher for Hicks (67); Long for Jowitt (69); Mycoe for Eaton (79).
Tries: Baker (19), Potter (51), Graham (60), Cain (80); **Goals:** Eaton 3, Ball; **Field goal:** Ball.
League Express Men of the Match:
Eagles: Heath Cruckshank; *Rams:* Mark Cain.
Penalty count: 4-6; **Half-time:** 6-4;
Referee: Paul Lee (Leigh); **Attendance:** 862.

WHITEHAVEN 13 ROCHDALE HORNETS 4

WHITEHAVEN: 1 Wesley Wilson; 2 Craig Walsh; 3 David Seeds; 4 Howard Hill; 5 Chris Campbell; 6 Leroy Joe; 7 Steve Kirkbride; 8 Mark Cox; 9 Aaron Lester; 10 David Fatialofa; 11 Garry Purdham; 12 Graeme Morton; 13 Spencer Miller. Subs: 14 Andrew Nelson for Walsh (15); 15 Marc Jackson for Joe (42); 16 Phil Sherwen for Morton (62); 17 Dean Vaughan for Cox (56).
Tries: Morton (2), Lester (46); **Goals:** Kirkbride 2;
Field goal: Kirkbride.
HORNETS: 1 Dave Watson; 2 Sean Cooper; 3 Brendan O'Meara; 4 Matt Calland; 5 Marlon Billy; 6 Paul Owen; 7 Mick Coates; 8 Danny Sculthorpe; 9 Warren Ayres; 10 Andy Ireland; 11 Wes Rogers; 12 David Larder; 13 David Stephenson. Subs: 14 Neil Alexander for Owen (18); 15 Steve Campbell for Ireland (20); 16 Mick Martindale for Coates (37BB, rev 50); 17 Ben Simpson for Sculthorpe (26); Sculthorpe for Ayres (52); Martindale for Coates (66).
Try: O'Meara (74).
League Express Men of the Match:
Whitehaven: Aaron Lester; *Hornets:* Matt Calland.
Penalty count: 5-5; **Half-time:** 6-0;
Referee: Colin Morris (Huddersfield); **Attendance:** 641.

WEEK 10

Sunday 4th February 2001

BARROW BORDER RAIDERS 6 WIDNES VIKINGS 6

BORDER RAIDERS: 1 Chris Massey; 2 Glen Hutton; 3 Phil Atkinson; 4 Darren Wilson; 5 Adrian Gardner; 6 Brett McDermott; 7 Darren Holt; 8 Tau Liku; 9 Anthony Murray; 10 Willie Burns; 11 Matthew Leigh; 12 Mike Whitehead; 13 Gary Charlton. Subs: 14 Mike Kavanagh not used; 15 Damien Whitter for Liku (20); 16 Geoff Luxon for Burns (70); 17 Ian Rawlinson for Whitehead (35); Whitehead for Rawlinson (50).
Try: Whitehead (75); **Goal:** Holt.
Sin bin: Leigh (45) - holding down.
VIKINGS: 1 Damian Munro; 2 Phil Coussons; 3 Chris Percival; 4 Jason Demetriou; 5 Liam Jones; 6 Martin Crompton; 7 Ian Watson; 8 Simon Knox; 9 Phil Cantillon; 10 Stewart Rhodes; 11 Steve Gee; 12 Joe Faimalo; 13 Tommy Hodgkinson. Subs: 14 Mark Forster for Demetriou (53); 15 Mike Hill for Gee (50); 16 Mark Flanagan not used; 17 Chris McKinney for Hodgkinson (7BB, rev 24).
Try: Percival (62); **Goal:** Watson.
League Express Men of the Match: *Border Raiders:* Mike Whitehead; *Vikings:* Martin Crompton.
Penalty count: 11-5; **Half-time:** 2-0; **Referee:** Colin Morris (Huddersfield); **Attendance:** 1,116.

LEIGH CENTURIONS 48 ROCHDALE HORNETS 0

CENTURIONS: 1 Neil Turley; 2 Alan Hadcroft; 3 Paul Anderson; 4 Kieron Purtill; 5 Michael Watts; 6 Simon Svabic; 7 Liam Bretherton; 8 Tim Street; 9 John Hamilton; 10 David Whittle; 11 Simon Baldwin; 12 Adam Bristow; 13 Willie Swann. Subs: 14 David Bradbury for Whittle (25); 15 John Duffy for Hamilton (28); 16 Phil Kendrick for Turley (41); 17 Paul Norman for Street (36); Street for Svabic (65); Hamilton for Duffy (72).
Tries: Anderson (6, 76), Watts (16), Whittle (24), Turley (27), Bretherton (30), Svabic (38), Hadcroft (51), Baldwin (60); **Goals:** Svabic 6.
HORNETS: 1 Casey Mayberry; 2 Sean Cooper; 3 Danny Wood; 4 Brendan O'Meara; 5 Marlon Billy; 6 Dave Watson; 7 Mick Coates; 8 Danny Sculthorpe; 9 Darren Robinson; 10 Martin Bunce; 11 Wes Rogers; 12 David Larder; 13 David Stephenson. Subs: 14 Mark Powell for Mayberry (41); 15 Steve Campbell for Sculthorpe (41); 16 Ben Simpson for Rogers (41); 17 Andy Ireland for Bunce (23); Sculthorpe for Coates (60); Rogers for Ireland (60).
League Express Men of the Match:
Centurions: Simon Baldwin; *Hornets:* David Larder.
Penalty count: 4-3; **Half-time:** 34-0; **Referee:** Steve Nicholson (Whitehaven); **Attendance:** 2,568.

SWINTON LIONS 20 WORKINGTON TOWN 29

LIONS: 1 Andy Cheetham; 2 Adrian Mead; 3 Mick Nanyn; 4 Paul Loughlin; 5 Matt Bateman; 6 Phil Veivers; 7 Kelvin Peet; 8 Jon-Paul Doherty; 9 Rob Barraclough; 10 Lee Hansen; 11 Phil Cushion; 12 Carlo Napolitano; 13 Paul Smith. Subs: 14 Phil Waring for Peet (55); 15 Ryan Stazicker for Russell (57); 16 Lee Hudson for Mead (40); 17 Robert Russell for Cushion (37); Russell for Napolitano (71).
Tries: Veivers (6), Smith (29), Hudson (53), Cheetham (66); **Goals:** P Loughlin, Nanyn.
TOWN: 1 Jamie Smith; 2 Neil Frazer; 3 Steve McGrady; 4 Leigh Smith; 5 Graeme Lewthwaite; 6 Tane Manihera; 7 Micky Horner; 8 Lokeni Savelio; 9 Carl Sice; 10 William Blackburn; 11 Matt Sturm; 12 Anthony Samuel; 13 Stuart Hoyles. Subs: 14 Fata Sini for L Smith (30); 15 Matthew Tunstall not used; 16 Craig Rumney for Horner (55); 17 Jamie Beaumont for Savelio (23); Savelio for Blackburn (55); L Smith for McGrady (77).
Tries: Samuel (16), Beaumont (42), Sice (61), Lewthwaite (75), Rumney (80); **Goals:** Manihera 4;
Field goal: Manihera.
League Express Men of the Match:
Lions: Paul Smith; *Town:* Carl Sice.
Penalty count: 3-8; **Half-time:** 10-4;
Referee: Ronnie Laughton (Barnsley); **Attendance:** 630.

YORK 6 FEATHERSTONE ROVERS 37

YORK: 1 Rich Darling; 2 Paul Butterfield; 3 Craig Moore; 4 Gareth Lloyd; 5 Gareth Oulton; 6 Paddy Handley; 7 Gareth Stephens; 8 Mick Hagan; 9 Alan Pallister; 10 Craig Forsyth; 11 Shaun Austerfield; 12 Darren Crake; 13 Spencer Hargrave. Subs: 14 Lee Hutchinson for Forsyth (40); 15 Gareth Dobson for Crake (10); 16 Nathan Pincher for Hagan (26); 17 Adam Briggs not used; Crake for Dobson (20); Dobson for Pallister (40); Forsyth for Stephens (57).
Try: Darling (48); **Goal:** Oulton.
Sin bin: Pallister (5) - late challenge on Rooney.
On report: Pallister (5) - same late challenge.
ROVERS: 1 Richard Gibson; 2 Jamie Stokes; 3 Steve Dooler; 4 Nick Simpson; 5 Matt Bramald; 6 Gary Barnett; 7 Jamie Rooney; 8 Stuart Dickens; 9 Richard Chapman; 10 Gavin Morgan; 11 Ricky Helliwell; 12 Neil Lowe; 13 Paul Darley. Subs: 14 Gavin Swinson for Dickens (68); 15 Danny Evans for Helliwell (55); 16 Andy Bastow for Barnett (64); 17 Micky Clarkson for Darley (68); Barnett for Chapman (75).
Tries: Bramald (13), Darley (21), Lowe (45), Stokes (56), Simpson (64), Chapman (70), Bastow (79);
Goals: Rooney 4; **Field goal:** Rooney.
League Express Men of the Match:
York: Darren Crake; *Rovers:* Jamie Rooney.
Penalty count: 11-7; **Half-time:** 0-10;
Referee: Julian King (St Helens); **Attendance:** 704.

SHEFFIELD EAGLES 11 HULL KINGSTON ROVERS 12

EAGLES: 1 Steve Walker; 2 Andy Poynter; 3 Neil Kite; 4 Gareth Hewitt; 5 Ian Thompson; 6 Gavin Brown; 7 Scott Rhodes; 8 Steve Hill; 9 Andy Speak; 10 Darren Summerill; 11 Andy Brent; 12 Heath Cruckshank; 13 Richard Goddard. Subs: 14 Chris Robinson for Rhodes (20); 15 Mark Aston for Speak (67); 16 Paul Wells for Hill (33); 17 Ian Brown for Summerill (25); Summerill for Goddard (40); Hill for Summerill (62).
Tries: Walker (75), Poynter (79); **Goal:** G Brown;
Field goal: Robinson.
ROVERS: 1 Bob Everitt; 2 Dean Andrews; 3 Andy Smith; 4 Whetu Taewa; 5 Bright Sodje; 6 Mick Crane; 7 Jimmy Walker; 8 Jon Aston; 9 Mike Dixon; 10 Rich Hayes; 11 Allan Dunham; 12 Paul Fletcher; 13 Chris Charles. Subs: 14 Chris Kitching for Crane (37); 15 Jamie Bovill for Wilson (61); 16 Jon Wilkins for Dunham (64); 17 Richard Wilson for Aston (26); Aston for Hayes (62).
Tries: Everitt (13), Sodje (70); **Goals:** Charles 2.
League Express Men of the Match:
Eagles: Ian Thompson; *Rovers:* Mike Dixon.
Penalty count: 3-1; **Half-time:** 3-6;
Referee: Peter Taberner (Wigan); **Attendance:** 1,081.

GATESHEAD THUNDER 12 HUNSLET HAWKS 26

THUNDER: 1 Darrell Derose; 2 Andy Field; 3 Darren Simpson; 4 Steve Hall; 5 Leon Williamson; 6 Carl Briggs; 7 Paul Thorman; 8 Paul Lister; 9 Martin Gambles; 10 Richard Mervill; 11 Jim Carlton; 12 Chris Parker; 13 Stephen Rutherford. Subs: 14 Paul Sebine for Williamson (64); 15 Lee Garside for Barron (45); 16 Matthew Roberts for Mervill (ht); 17 Gareth Barron for Lister (33); Barron for Roberts (71); Roberts for Simpson (73).
Tries: Williamson (22), Rutherford (35), Derose (75).
HAWKS: 1 George Raynor; 2 Lee Maher; 3 Iain Higgins; 4 Michael Wainwright; 5 Aaron Campbell; 6 Chris Redfearn; 7 Chris Robinson; 8 Michael Banks; 9 Chris Ross; 10 Guy Adams; 11 Mick Coyle; 12 Dave Jessey; 13 Robert Roberts. Subs: 14 David Bates for Coyle (17); 15 Ben Skerrett for Maher (53); 15 Andy Atha for Raynor (33); 17 Nicky Dobson not used; Coyle for Banks (26); Banks for Jessey (58).
Tries: Maher (2), Higgins (17), Campbell (27), Bates (65, 78); **Goals:** Ross 3.
League Express Men of the Match:
Thunder: Stephen Rutherford; *Hawks:* Chris Robinson.
Penalty count: 3-3; **Half-time:** 8-14;
Referee: John Farrell (Widnes); **Attendance:** 464.

WEEK 11

Wednesday 14th February 2001

WORKINGTON TOWN 42 CHORLEY LYNX 0

TOWN: 1 Jamie Smith; 2 Fata Sini; 3 Steve McGrady; 4 Leigh Smith; 5 Graeme Lewthwaite; 6 Tane Manihera; 7 Craig Rumney; 8 Hitro Okesene; 9 Carl Sice; 10 Lokeni Savelio; 11 Jamie Beaumont; 12 Matt Sturm; 13 Anthony Samuel. Subs: 14 William Blackburn for Okesene (ht); 15 Matthew Tunstall for Savelio (50); 16 Neil Frazer for L Smith (42BB); 17 Stuart Hoyles for Samuel (54); Okesene for Beaumont (68); L Smith for Manihera (73).
Tries: Okesene (9), Sini (39), Beaumont (53, 57), McGrady (69), Lewthwaite (73), Blackburn (75, 80);
Goals: Manihera 4, Rumney.
LYNX: 1 Stuart Dickinson; 2 Chris Ramsdale; 3 Brian Capewell; 4 Andrew Friar; 5 Graham Taberner; 6 Lee Ashton; 7 Stuart Fisher; 8 Lee Prest; 9 Lee Maiden; 10 Rob Verrelli; 11 Phil Harrison; 12 Gareth Chambers; 13 Ian Talbot. Subs: 14 Anthony Roberts for Talbot (ht); 15 Dale Christy for Verrelli (28); 16 Michael Donnelly for Prest (31); 17 Chris Tordoff for Chambers (73); Prest for Ashton (45); Verrelli for Harrison (72).
Sin bin: Fisher (69) - backchat.
League Express Men of the Match:
Town: Craig Rumney; *Lynx:* Phil Harrison.
Penalty count: 8-12; **Half-time:** 14-0;
Referee: John Farrell (Widnes); **Attendance:** 674.

WEEK 12

Sunday 18th February 2001

BATLEY BULLDOGS 10 BARROW BORDER RAIDERS 18

BULLDOGS: 1 Craig Lingard; 2 Jamie Coventry; 3 Danny Maun; 4 Davide Longo; 5 Roger Simpson; 6 Richard Price; 7 Glen Tomlinson; 8 Chris McWilliam; 9 Andy Heptinstall; 10 Paul Hicks; 11 Gary Shillabeer; 12 Will Cartledge; 13 Ryan Horsley. Subs: 14 Mark Cass for Heptinstall (50); 15 Graham Middleton for Coventry (53); 16 Lee Kelly for Cartledge (40); 17 Jeff Wittenberg for McWilliam (27); McWilliam for Kelly (61); Heptinstall for Hicks (72).
Tries: Maun (34), Longo (52); **Goal:** Price.
Sin bin: Wittenberg (60) - retaliation.
BORDER RAIDERS: 1 Chris Massey; 2 Glen Hutton; 3 Phil Atkinson; 4 Darren Wilson; 5 Adrian Gardner; 6 Brett McDermott; 7 Darren Holt; 8 Tau Liku; 9 Anthony Murray; 10 Willie Burns; 11 Geoff Luxon; 12 Mike Whitehead; 13 Matthew Leigh. Subs: 14 Mike Kavanagh not used; 15 Damien Whitter for Liku (23); 16 Gary Charlton for Liku (55); 17 Ian Rawlinson for Luxon (38); Liku for Whitter (40); Whitter for Rawlinson (70).
Tries: Leigh (17), A Gardner (46), Charlton (68);
Goals: Holt 3.
Sin bin: Rawlinson (60) - foul play.
League Express Men of the Match: *Bulldogs:* Glen Tomlinson; *Border Raiders:* Matthew Leigh.
Penalty count: 3-6; **Half-time:** 4-6;
Referee: Peter Taberner (Wigan); **Attendance:** 518.

DEWSBURY RAMS 70 CHORLEY LYNX 0

RAMS: 1 Nathan Graham; 2 Alex Godfrey; 3 Dan Potter; 4 Adrian Flynn; 5 Richard Baker; 6 Mark Cain; 7 David Mycoe; 8 Andy Fisher; 9 Richard Pachniuk; 10 Matthew Long; 11 Sean Richardson; 12 Paul Smith; 13 Damian Ball. Subs: 14 Gavin Wood for Potter (28BB); 15 Andrew Spink for Ball (43); 16 Robin Jowitt for Long (31); 17 Ryan McDonald for Spink (49); Long for Smith (68).
Tries: Potter (2), Smith (7), Cain (13, 35, 72), Flynn (15, 68, 74), Pachniuk (23, 46, 55), Wood (43), Richardson (58); **Goals:** Mycoe 9.
LYNX: 1 Stuart Dickinson; 2 Chris Ramsdale; 3 Brian Capewell; 4 Andrew Friar; 5 Graham Taberner; 6 Anthony Roberts; 7 Stuart Fisher; 8 Mike Prescott; 9 Lee Maiden; 10 Lee Prest; 11 Phil Harrison; 12 Gareth Chambers; 13 Dale Christy. Subs: 14 Gary Blood for Taberner (40); 15 Michael Donnelly for Prest (28); 16 Rob Verrelli for Friar (40); 17 Ian Talbot for Roberts (15); Prest for Donnelly (62).
League Express Men of the Match:
Rams: Richard Pachniuk; *Lynx:* Ian Talbot.
Penalty count: 8-3; **Half-time:** 32-0; **Referee:** Steve Nicholson (Whitehaven); **Attendance:** 725.

FEATHERSTONE ROVERS 20 LEIGH CENTURIONS 30

ROVERS: 1 Michael Rhodes; 2 Jamie Stokes; 3 Chris Spurr; 4 Nick Simpson; 5 Matt Bramald; 6 Andy Bastow; 7 Richard Gibson; 8 Stuart Dickens; 9 Richard Chapman; 10 Gavin Morgan; 11 Ricky Helliwell; 12 Neil Lowe; 13 Paul Darley. Subs: 14 Richard Thaler for Gibson (60); 15 Danny Evans for Helliwell (40); 16 Gary Lord for Morgan (23); 17 Stephen Jones for Simpson (68); Morgan for

Dickens (55).
Tries: Bramald (22), Spurr (33), Chapman (71), Jones (76); **Goals:** Dickens, Chapman.
CENTURIONS: 1 Neil Turley; 2 Alan Hadcroft; 3 Phil Kendrick; 4 Andy Fairclough; 5 David Ingram; 6 Simon Svabic; 7 Keiron Purtill; 8 Paul Norman; 9 John Duffy; 10 David Bradbury; 11 Simon Baldwin; 12 Chris Morley; 13 Adam Bristow. Subs: 14 Tim Street for Norman (25); 15 John Hamilton for Duffy (21BB, rev 62); 16 Willie Swann for Fairclough (54); 17 Andy Leathem for Bradbury (38); Norman for Street (65); Bradbury for Baldwin (68); Hamilton for Purtill (78).
Tries: Turley (2), Kendrick (38), Baldwin (50), Fairclough (53), Morley (67); **Goals:** Svabic 5.
League Express Men of the Match:
Rovers: Richard Chapman; *Centurions:* Simon Baldwin.
Penalty count: 9-4; **Half-time:** 10-12;
Referee: Ian Smith (Oldham); **Attendance:** 2,683.

HULL KINGSTON ROVERS 10 WHITEHAVEN 10

ROVERS: 1 Bob Everitt; 2 Gavin Molloy; 3 Andy Smith; 4 Whetu Taewa; 5 Bright Sodje; 6 Mick Crane; 7 Jimmy Walker; 8 Jon Aston; 9 Mike Dixon; 10 Rich Hayes; 11 Richard Slater; 12 Paul Fletcher; 13 Chris Charles. Subs: 14 Graeme Barber for Molloy (56); 15 Chris Kitching for Walker (ht); 16 Jamie Bovill for Slater (46); 17 Richard Wilson for Aston (25); Aston for Hayes (46); Slater for Bovill (65).
Tries: Molloy (26), Charles (75); **Goal:** Charles.
WHITEHAVEN: 1 Wesley Wilson; 2 Andrew Nelson; 3 David Seeds; 4 Howard Hill; 5 Chris Campbell; 6 Leroy Joe; 7 Steve Kirkbride; 8 Mark Cox; 9 Aaron Lester; 10 David Fatialofa; 11 Garry Purdham; 12 Graeme Morton; 13 Spencer Miller. Subs: 14 Marc Jackson for Lester (65); 15 Ian Devlin for Wilson (18); 16 Phil Sherwen for Morton (54); 17 Dean Vaughan for Cox (31); Cox for Fatialofa (52); Lester for Purdham (75).
Try: Miller (11); **Goals:** Kirkbride 3.
League Express Men of the Match:
Rovers: Mike Dixon; *Whitehaven:* Garry Purdham.
Penalty count: 7-7; **Half-time:** 4-10;
Referee: Nick Oddy (Halifax); **Attendance:** 1,385.

OLDHAM 52 GATESHEAD THUNDER 6

OLDHAM: 1 Mark Sibson; 2 Anthony Gibbons; 3 David Gibbons; 4 Pat Rich; 5 Gavin Dodd; 6 Gareth Barber; 7 Neil Roden; 8 Jason Clegg; 9 John Hough; 10 Paul Norton; 11 Phil Farrell; 12 Ian Sinfield; 13 Kevin Mannion. Subs: 14 Daryl Lacey for Barber (46); 15 Lee Doran for Norton (56); 16 Danny Guest for Clegg (24); 17 Chris Farrell for P Farrell (44); Clegg for Guest (58); Barber for Sibson (78).
Tries: Sibson (1, 36, 55), Roden (3, 39, 43), Dodd (14), D Gibbons (34), Lacey (74); **Goals:** Rich 8.
THUNDER: 1 Michael Johnson; 2 Andy Field; 3 Wes McGibbon; 4 Steve Hall; 5 Leon Williamson; 6 Scott Dyson; 7 Carl Briggs; 8 Gareth Barron; 9 Roy Southernwood; 10 Richard Mervill; 11 Jim Carlton; 12 Matthew Roberts; 13 Chris Parker. Subs: 14 Martin Gambles for Southernwood (26); 15 Andy Grundy for Barron (20); 16 Paul Lister for Mervill (52); 17 Stephen Rutherford for Roberts (ht); Barron for Carlton (67).
Try: Carlton (27); **Goal:** Hall.
League Express Men of the Match:
Oldham: Neil Roden; *Thunder:* Jim Carlton.
Penalty count: 5-5; **Half-time:** 34-6;
Referee: Paul Lee (Leigh); **Attendance:** 1,451.

ROCHDALE HORNETS 26 DONCASTER DRAGONS 6

HORNETS: 1 Paul Owen; 2 Sean Cooper; 3 Matt Calland; 4 Brendan O'Meara; 5 Marlon Billy; 6 Danny Wood; 7 Mick Coates; 8 Danny Sculthorpe; 9 Darren Robinson; 10 Andy Ireland; 11 David Stephenson; 12 Wes Rogers; 13 Dave Watson. Subs: 14 Wayne McHugh for Calland (74); 15 Dave Radley for Ireland (50); 16 Chris Newall for Watson (17BB); 17 Ben Simpson for Sculthorpe (76).
Tries: Robinson (16, 66), Wood (71), Calland (74);
Goals: Wood 5.
Sin bin: Robinson (44) – late challenge on Tawhai.
DRAGONS: 1 Lynton Stott; 2 Paul Cook; 3 Carl Hall; 4 Kevin Crouthers; 5 Neil Bennett; 6 Simon Irving; 7 Latham Tawhai; 8 Maea David; 9 Peter Edwards; 10 Brad Hepi; 11 Rob Wilson; 12 James Bunyan; 13 Tony Miller. Subs: 14 Anton Garcia for Cook (9); 15 Tony Atter for Hepi (60); 16 Asa Amone for David (28); 17 Craig Lawton for Bennett (70); David for Atter (72); Atter for David (78).
Goals: Irving 3.
League Express Men of the Match:
Hornets: Danny Wood; *Dragons:* Latham Tawhai.
Penalty count: 10-9; **Half-time:** 8-2; **Referee:** Richard Silverwood (Dewsbury); **Attendance:** 1,058.

WIDNES VIKINGS 90 YORK 6

VIKINGS: 1 Damian Munro; 2 Phil Coussons; 3 Chris Percival; 4 Jason Demetriou; 5 Liam Jones; 6 Martin Crompton; 7 Ian Watson; 8 Simon Knox; 9 Phil Cantillon; 10 Stewart Rhodes; 11 Steve Gee; 12 Tommy Hodgkinson; 13 Karle Hammond. Subs: 14 Mark Forster for Percival (45); 15 Mike Hill for Crompton (55); 16 Chris Foran for Munro (60); 17 Steve Argent for Rhodes (30); Rhodes for Knox (60).
Tries: Gee (1, 26), Coussons (5), Cantillon (13, 18, 24, 48, 57, 68, 75), Percival (22), Demetriou (42), Munro (50), Hill (63), Hammond (73), Forster (80);
Goals: Watson 13.
YORK: 1 Rich Darling; 2 Tim Rumford; 3 Craig Moore; 4 Shaun Austerfield; 5 Matthew Mulholland; 6 Paddy Handley; 7 Gareth Oulton; 8 Mick Hagan; 9 Gareth Dobson; 10 Craig Forsyth; 11 Jason Gatus; 12 Nathan Pincher; 13 Adam Briggs. Subs: 14 Danny Waite for Dobson (23); 15 Steve Harris not used; 16 Pat Howdle not used; 17 Lee Crooks for Forsyth (40); Dobson for Briggs (33); Forsyth for Hagan (50); Hagan for Crooks (65).
Try: Moore (29); **Goal:** Oulton.
League Express Man of the Match:
Vikings: Phil Cantillon; *York:* Jason Gatus.
Penalty count: 5-2; **Half-time:** 42-6; **Referee:** Ronnie Laughton (Barnsley); **Attendance:** 2,941.

WORKINGTON TOWN 15 SHEFFIELD EAGLES 12

TOWN: 1 Jamie Smith; 2 Fata Sini; 3 Leigh Smith; 4 Steve McGrady; 5 Graeme Lewthwaite; 6 Kevin Hetherington; 7 Craig Rumney; 8 Hitro Okesene; 9 Carl Sice; 10 Lokeni Savelio; 11 Jamie Beaumont; 12 Matt Sturm; 13 Anthony Samuel. Subs: 14 William Blackburn for Savelio (17); 15 Matthew Tunstall for Blackburn (47); 16 Neil Frazer for McGrady (ht); 17 Stuart Hoyles not used; Savelio for Okesene (54); Okesene for Tunstall (71).
Tries: J Smith (25), Lewthwaite (47, 64);
Goal: Hetherington; **Field goal:** Hetherington.
Sin bin: Savelio (56) - fighting.
EAGLES: 1 Steve Walker; 2 Gareth Hewitt; 3 Neil Kite; 4 Wayne Flynn; 5 Ian Thompson; 6 Mark Aston; 7 Chris Robinson; 8 Steve Hill; 9 Gavin Brown; 10 Ricky Wright; 11 Chris Chapman; 12 Heath Cruckshank; 13 Richard Goddard. Subs: 14 Scott Rhodes for Aston (23); 15 Andy Poynter for Hewitt (50); 16 Ian Brown for Brent (47); 17 Andy Brent for Hill (21); Hill for Cruckshank (66); Aston for G Brown (68).
Tries: Goddard (34), Thompson (39); **Goals:** Goddard 2.
Sin bin: Wright (56) - fighting;
Chapman (60) - persistent holding down.
League Express Men of the Match:
Town: Matt Sturm; *Eagles:* Ricky Wright.
Penalty count: 12-3; **Half-time:** 4-10;
Referee: Colin Morris (Huddersfield); **Attendance:** 990.

HUNSLET HAWKS 26 SWINTON LIONS 16

HAWKS: 1 George Raynor; 2 Lee Maher; 3 Iain Higgins; 4 Michael Wainwright; 5 Aaron Campbell; 6 Marcus Vassilakopoulos; 7 Craig Robinson; 8 Robert Roberts; 9 Guy Adams; 10 David Bates; 11 Michael Banks; 12 Ben Thompson; 13 Mick Coyle. Subs: 14 Dave Jessey for Banks (18); 15 Andy Atha for Coyle (73); 16 Junior Henderson for Maher (5); 17 Danny Briggs for Roberts (21); Banks for Thompson (52); Thompson for Briggs (78).
Tries: Raynor (33, 59, 68), Higgins (44), Wainwright (77); **Goals:** Robinson, Vassilakopoulos 2.
LIONS: 1 Wayne English; 2 Adrian Mead; 3 Mick Nanyn; 4 Paul Loughlin; 5 Matt Bateman; 6 Phil Veivers; 7 Sean Furey; 8 Lee Hansen; 9 Rob Barraclough; 10 Jon-Paul Doherty; 11 Phil Cushion; 12 Carlo Napolitano; 13 Paul Smith. Subs: 14 Danny Butler for Furey (42); 15 Ryan Stazicker for Napolitano (54); 16 Nick Cammann for English (4); 17 Paul Crossland for Doherty (53).
Tries: P Loughlin (26, 79), Nanyn (34); **Goals:** Nanyn 2.
League Express Men of the Match:
Hawks: George Raynor; *Lions:* Lee Hansen.
Penalty count: 6-6; **Half-time:** 4-4;
Referee: Julian King (St Helens); **Attendance:** 666.

Thursday 22nd February 2001

YORK 21 GATESHEAD THUNDER 4

YORK: 1 Matthew Mulholland; 2 Tim Rumford; 3 Gareth Lloyd; 4 Chris Allen; 5 Rich Darling; 6 Paddy Handley; 7 Danny Waite; 8 Mick Hagan; 9 Gareth Dobson; 10 Craig Forsyth; 11 Jason Gatus; 12 Craig Moore; 13 Shaun Austerfield. Subs: 14 Gareth Oulton for Lloyd (73); 15 Nathan Pincher for Crooks (55); 16 Adam Briggs for Austerfield (78); 17 Lee Crooks for Forsyth (40); Forsyth for Hagan (59).
Tries: Dobson (13), Mulholland (21), Rumford (40), Allen (50); **Goals:** Waite 2; **Field goal:** Waite.
THUNDER: 1 Michael Johnson; 2 Andy Field; 3 Wes McGibbon; 4 Steve Hall; 5 Leon Williamson; 6 Scott Dyson; 7 Carl Briggs; 8 Gareth Barron; 9 Roy Southernwood; 10 Andy Grundy; 11 Jim Carlton; 12 Matthew Roberts; 13 Chris Parker. Subs: 14 Martin Gambles for Southernwood (40); 15 Richard Mervill for Barron (15); 16 Paul Lister for Carlton (38); 17 Stephen Rutherford for Roberts (30); Roberts for Parker (77); Southernwood for Dyson (78).
Try: Grundy (34).
League Express Men of the Match:
York: Shaun Austerfield; *Thunder:* Carl Briggs.
Penalty count: 5-7; **Half-time:** 15-4;
Referee: Julian King (St Helens); **Attendance:** 426.

WEEK 13

Sunday 25th February 2001

BARROW BORDER RAIDERS 28 WORKINGTON TOWN 31

BORDER RAIDERS: 1 Chris Massey; 2 Glen Hutton; 3 Phil Atkinson; 4 Darren Wilson; 5 Jamie Marshall; 6 Brett McDermott; 7 Darren Holt; 8 Tau Liku; 9 Anthony Murray; 10 Willie Burns; 11 Matthew Leigh; 12 Mike Whitehead; 13 Gary Charlton. Subs: 14 Shane Irabor not used; 15 Mike Kavanagh not used; 16 Geoff Luxon for Whitehead (40); 17 Damien Whitter for Liku (21); Liku for Whitter (40); Whitter for Liku (53); Whitehead for Luxon (63).
Tries: Murray (9), Whitehead (21), Wilson (28), Holt (53), Charlton (62); **Goals:** Holt 4.
Sin bin: Holt (30) - dissent.
TOWN: 1 Jamie Smith; 2 Fata Sini; 3 Neil Frazer; 4 Steve McGrady; 5 Graeme Lewthwaite; 6 Kevin Hetherington; 7 Craig Rumney; 8 Hitro Okesene; 9 Carl Sice; 10 Lokeni Savelio; 11 Jamie Beaumont; 12 Matt Sturm; 13 Anthony Samuel. Subs: 14 Tane Manihera for Rumney (22); 15 Matthew Tunstall for Okesene (57); 16 John Allen for McGrady (28); 17 Stuart Hoyles for Savelio (50).
Tries: J Smith (6, 37), Frazer (40), Sice (43), Lewthwaite (72); **Goals:** Hetherington 5; **Field goal:** Manihera.
League Express Men of the Match:
Border Raiders: Darren Holt; *Town:* Carl Sice.
Penalty count: 2-1; **Half-time:** 16-18;
Referee: Colin Morris (Huddersfield); **Attendance:** 976.

CHORLEY LYNX 14 WIDNES VIKINGS 48

LYNX: 1 Mick Farrell; 2 Gary Doherty; 3 Chris Ramsdale; 4 Andrew Friar; 5 Graham Taberner; 6 Lee Ashton; 7 Stuart Fisher; 8 Mike Prescott; 9 Lee Maiden; 10 Rob Verrelli; 11 Phil Harrison; 12 Gareth Chambers; 13 Ian Talbot. Subs: 14 Gary Blood for Friar (33); 15 Warren Hindle for Donnelly (70); 16 Michael Donnelly for Verrelli (33); 17 David Cayzer for Taberner (58); Friar for Maiden (49); Verrelli for Ashton (63).
Tries: Prescott (44), Farrell (54), Friar (76); **Goal:** Fisher.
Sin bin: Talbot (22) - dissent.
VIKINGS: 1 Liam Jones; 2 Phil Coussons; 3 Damian Munro; 4 Jason Demetriou; 5 Mark Forster; 6 Martin Crompton; 7 Ian Watson; 8 Simon Knox; 9 Phil Cantillon; 10 Stewart Rhodes; 11 Steve Gee; 12 Tommy Hodgkinson; 13 Karle Hammond. Subs: 14 Chris Foran for Munro (68); 15 David Mills for Rhodes (37); 16 Mike Hill for Argent (55); 17 Steve Argent for Gee (16); Rhodes for Mills (56); Munro for Coussons (69).
Tries: Coussons (13, 47), Munro (15), Demetriou (31, 70), Argent (40), Knox (67, 72, 80); **Goals:** Watson 6.
League Express Men of the Match:
Lynx: Mike Prescott; *Vikings:* Simon Knox.
Penalty count: 11-8; **Half-time:** 0-24;
Referee: Paul Lee (Leigh); **Attendance:** 710.

DEWSBURY RAMS 54 GATESHEAD THUNDER 10

RAMS: 1 Nathan Graham; 2 Alex Godfrey; 3 Dan Potter; 4 Adrian Flynn; 5 Richard Baker; 6 Mark Cain; 7 David Mycoe; 8 Robin Jowitt; 9 Richard Pachniuk; 10 Ryan McDonald; 11 Sean Richardson; 12 Paul Smith; 13 Kevin Spink. Subs: 14 Gavin Wood for Spink (55); 15 Damian Ball for Smith (40); 16 Andy Fisher for Jowitt (40); 17 Matthew Long for McDonald (40).
Tries: Baker (1, 10), Smith (12, 27), Graham (15), Mycoe (40), Flynn (52, 54, 70), Godfrey (60), Ball (64);
Goals: Mycoe 4, Ball.
THUNDER: 1 Wes McGibbon; 2 Andy Field; 3 Paul Sebine; 4 Steve Hall; 5 Leon Williamson; 6 Scott Dyson; 7 Carl Briggs; 8 Paul Lister; 9 Roy Southernwood; 10 Andy Grundy; 11 Matthew Roberts; 12 Chris Parker; 13 Darrell Derose. Subs: 14 Martin Gambles for Southernwood (40); 15 Richard Mervill for Lister (22); 16 Stephen Bradley for Roberts (60); 17 Gareth Barron for Grundy (30); Lister for Dyson (64BB, rev 67); Grundy for Barron (60); Southernwood for Gambles (48).
Tries: Briggs (34), Derose (42); **Goal:** Hall.
League Express Men of the Match:
Rams: Mark Cain; *Thunder:* Carl Briggs.
Penalty count: 3-3; **Half-time:** 34-2;
Referee: Ronnie Laughton (Barnsley); **Attendance:** 832.

KEIGHLEY COUGARS 66 BATLEY BULLDOGS 12

COUGARS: 1 James Rushforth; 2 Craig Horne; 3 Daio Powell; 4 Graeme Hallas; 5 Jason Lee; 6 Martin Wood; 7 Nathan Antonik; 8 Michael Slicker; 9 Jason Ramshaw; 10 Alan Boothroyd; 11 Paul Harrison; 12 Ian Hughes; 13 Danny Seal. Subs: 14 Matt Walker for Boothroyd (46); 15 Jim Leatham for Hughes (49); 16 Phil Stephenson for Slicker (46); 17 Darren Carter for Powell (45); Hughes for Ramshaw (68).
Tries: Seal (6, 71, 74), Antonik (17, 46, 60), Rushforth (36, 62), Boothroyd (39), Hallas (47), Hughes (79);
Goals: Wood 11.
BULLDOGS: 1 Craig Lingard; 2 Jeremy Dyson; 3 Danny Maun; 4 Roger Simpson; 5 Paul Gleadhill; 6 Davide Longo; 7 Glen Tomlinson; 8 Chris McWilliam; 9 Andy Heptinstall; 10 Jeff Wittenberg; 11 Paul Hicks; 12 Gary Shillabeer; 13 Ryan Horsley. Subs: 14 Mark Cass for Wittenberg (61); 15 Simon Jackson for Shillabeer (49); 16 Graham Middleton for McWilliam (23BB, rev 45); 17 Craig Richards for Longo (49); Longo for Hicks (69); Middleton for Dyson (70).
Tries: Lingard (9), Richards (55); **Goals:** Dyson 2.
League Express Men of the Match:
Cougars: Nathan Antonik; *Bulldogs:* Craig Richards.
Penalty count: 12-6; **Half-time:** 26-6;
Referee: Thierry Alibert (France); **Attendance:** 1,728.

YORK 6 SHEFFIELD EAGLES 48

YORK: 1 Matthew Mulholland; 2 Tim Rumford; 3 Chris Allen; 4 Gareth Lloyd; 5 Rich Darling; 6 Paddy Handley; 7 Danny Waite; 8 Mick Hagan; 9 Gareth Dobson; 10 Craig Forsyth; 11 Jason Gatus; 12 Darren Crake; 13 Shaun Austerfield. Subs: 14 Gareth Oulton for Handley (55); 15 Craig Moore for Hagan (40); 16 Dave Birdsall for Forsyth (23); 17 Nathan Pincher for Crake (47); Hagan for Austerfield (52).
Try: Dobson (6); **Goal:** Waite.
EAGLES: 1 Andy Poynter; 2 Paul Wells; 3 Steve Walker; 4 Gareth Hewitt; 5 Ian Thompson; 6 Scott Rhodes; 7 Chris Robinson; 8 Steve Hill; 9 Andy Speak; 10 Ricky

Wright; 11 Richard Goddard; 12 Heath Cruckshank; 13 Wayne Flynn. Subs: 14 Mark Aston for Robinson (17); 15 Ian Brown for Wells (51BB, rev 59); 16 Chris Chapman for Flynn (34); 17 Darren Summerill for Hill (29); Flynn for Rhodes (44); Hill for Chapman (64); Brown for Wells (70).
Tries: Wright (1), Goddard (12, 46), Poynter (44), Thompson (56), I Brown (75), Flynn (77), Walker (80);
Goals: Goddard 8.
League Express Men of the Match:
York: Gareth Lloyd; *Eagles:* Richard Goddard.
Penalty count: 8-9; **Half-time:** 6-14;
Referee: Richard Frileux (France); **Attendance:** 455.

WEEK 14

Sunday 4th March 2001

CHORLEY LYNX 32 HULL KINGSTON ROVERS 54

LYNX: 1 Stuart Dickinson; 2 Gary Doherty; 3 Chris Ramsdale; 4 Andrew Friar; 5 Graham Taberner; 6 Mick Farrell; 7 Stuart Fisher; 8 Rob Verrelli; 9 Lee Maiden; 10 Lee Prest; 11 Phil Harrison; 12 Mike Prescott; 13 Ian Talbot. Subs: 14 Gary Blood for Doherty (29); 15 Lee Ashton for Blood (51); 16 Luke Vincent for Talbot (66); 17 Lee Westwood for Prest (29); Prest for Verrelli (60); Doherty for Ramsdale (73).
Tries: Doherty (14), Dickinson (34), Friar (45), Westwood (68), Taberner (75), Prescott (77);
Goals: Fisher 4.
Sin bin: Vincent (67) - obstruction.
ROVERS: 1 Bob Everitt; 2 Bright Sodje; 3 Chris Kitching; 4 Whetu Taewa; 5 Alasdair McLarron; 6 Jimmy Walker; 7 Colin Carter; 8 Jon Aston; 9 Mike Dixon; 10 Rich Hayes; 11 Andy Smith; 12 Paul Fletcher; 13 Richard Slater. Subs: 14 Mick Crane for Kitching (41); 15 Steve Cochrane for Dixon (49); 16 Rob Wilson for Aston (29); 17 Richard Wilson for Smith (29); Aston for Hayes (61); Smith for McLarron (64BB, rev 71); Dixon for Carter (72).
Tries: Walker (2, 20, 60), Taewa (11, 79), McLarron (26), Aston (28), Rob Wilson (38, 58), Everitt (70), Dixon (80); **Goals:** Everitt 5.
League Express Men of the Match:
Lynx: Lee Westwood; *Rovers:* Jimmy Walker.
Penalty count: 6-8; **Half-time:** 12-28;
Referee: Steve Addy (Huddersfield); **Attendance:** 354.

SWINTON LIONS 18 DEWSBURY RAMS 20

LIONS: 1 Andy Cheetham; 2 Adrian Mead; 3 Mick Nanyn; 4 Matt Bateman; 5 Lee Hudson; 6 Paul Loughlin; 7 Phil Waring; 8 Mike Loughlin; 9 Rob Barraclough; 10 Lee Hansen; 11 Phil Cushion; 12 Paul Smith; 13 Phil Veivers. Subs: 14 Danny Butler for Cheetham (55); 15 Dale Holdstock for P Loughlin (36); 16 Carlo Napolitano for Hansen (51); 17 Jon-Paul Doherty for M Loughlin (16); Hansen for Doherty (67).
Tries: Veivers (11), Smith (57, 66); **Goals:** Nanyn 3.
Sin bin: Cushion (51) - fighting.
RAMS: 1 Nathan Graham; 2 Alex Godfrey; 3 Dan Potter; 4 Adrian Flynn; 5 Richard Baker; 6 Mark Cain; 7 David Mycoe; 8 Andy Fisher; 9 Richard Pachniuk; 10 Ryan McDonald; 11 Sean Richardson; 12 Paul Smith; 13 Kevin Spink. Subs: 14 Barry Eaton for Cain (61); 15 Gavin Wood not used; 16 Matthew Long for Fisher (24); 17 Robin Jowitt for McDonald (24); Fisher for Long (40); McDonald for Jowitt (40).
Tries: Baker (3), Smith (17), Potter (40), Richardson (54); **Goals:** Mycoe, Cain.
Sin bin: Fisher (51) - fighting.
League Express Men of Match:
Lions: Phil Veivers; *Rams:* David Mycoe.
Penalty count: 6-8; **Half-time:** 6-14;
Referee: Paul Lee (Leigh); **Attendance:** 846.

SHEFFIELD EAGLES 40 BARROW BORDER RAIDERS 16

EAGLES: 1 Andy Poynter; 2 Paul Wells; 3 Neil Kite; 4 Steve Walker; 5 Ian Thompson; 6 Richard Goddard; 7 Mark Aston; 8 Steve Hill; 9 Andy Speak; 10 Ricky Wright; 11 Chris Chapman; 12 Heath Cruckshank; 13 Wayne Flynn. Subs: 14 Ian Brown for Brent (47); 15 Andy Brent for Flynn (10); 16 Darren Summerill for Hill (47); 17 Jon Bruce for Wright (4); Hill for Bruce (69); Brent for Goddard (73).
Tries: Walker (1), Goddard (18, 36), Bruce (39), Speak (52), Chapman (64, 67); **Goals:** Goddard 6.
BORDER RAIDERS: 1 Chris Massey; 2 Glen Hutton; 3 Phil Atkinson; 4 Darren Wilson; 5 Adrian Gardner; 6 Brett McDermott; 7 Darren Holt; 8 Tau Liku; 9 Anthony Murray; 10 William Burns; 11 Matthew Leigh; 12 Mike Whitehead; 13 Gary Charlton. Subs: 14 Jamie Marshall for Hutton (20); 15 Gareth Pratt for Burns (61); 16 Geoff Luxon for Liku (23); 17 Paul Gardner for Liku (66); Liku for Luxon (42); Luxon for Whitehead (57).
Tries: Atkinson (73), A Gardner (80); **Goals:** Holt 4.
League Express Men of the Match:
Eagles: Andy Poynter; *Border Raiders:* Anthony Murray.
Penalty count: 7-12; **Half-time:** 22-4;
Referee: Ronnie Laughton (Barnsley); **Attendance:** 838.

Wednesday 7th March 2001

GATESHEAD THUNDER 18 WIDNES VIKINGS 30

THUNDER: 1 Michael Johnson; 2 Andy Field; 3 Wes McGibbon; 4 Steve Hall; 5 Leon Williamson; 6 Scott Dyson; 7 Carl Briggs; 8 Paul Lister; 9 Roy Southernwood; 10 Andy Grundy; 11 Richard Mervill; 12 Chris Parker; 13 Stephen Rutherford. Subs: 14 Paul Thorman for Southernwood (26); 15 Darrell Derose for Thorman (53); 16 Matt Roberts for Grundy (62); 17 Lee Garside for Lister (39BB, rev 61); Grundy for Lister (74); Thorman for Rutherford (75).
Tries: Mervill (50), Field (52), Johnson (78); **Goals:** Hall 3.
VIKINGS: 1 Liam Jones; 2 Phil Coussons; 3 Damian Munro; 4 Jason Demetriou; 5 Mark Forster; 6 Martin Crompton; 7 Ian Watson; 8 Simon Knox; 9 Phil Cantillon; 10 Stewart Rhodes; 11 Steve Gee; 12 Tommy Hodgkinson; 13 Karle Hammond. Subs: 14 Paul Cook for Coussons (49); 15 Mike Hill for Hodgkinson (49); 16 Kevin Crouthers for Jones (31); 17 Steve Argent for Rhodes (22); Rhodes for Knox (51); Knox for Argent (68); Jones for Demetriou (75BB).
Tries: Hammond (5), Cantillon (22), Crouthers (33), Demetriou (56), Knox (75); **Goals:** Watson 5.
League Express Men of the Match:
Thunder: Michael Johnson; *Vikings:* Jason Demetriou.
Penalty count: 9-3; **Half-time:** 0-20;
Referee: Ronnie Laughton (Barnsley); **Attendance:** 517.

KEIGHLEY COUGARS 20 ROCHDALE HORNETS 23

COUGARS: 1 James Rushforth; 2 Craig Horne; 3 Daio Powell; 4 Graeme Hallas; 5 Jason Lee; 6 Martin Wood; 7 Nathan Antonik; 8 Phil Stephenson; 9 Jason Ramshaw; 10 Matt Walker; 11 Paul Harrison; 12 Jim Leatham; 13 Darren Carter. Subs: 14 Danny Seal for Carter (41); 15 Michael Slicker for Walker (41); 16 Alan Boothroyd for Leatham (41); 17 Ian Hughes for Stephenson (41); Leatham for Harrison (69).
Tries: Antonik (43), Wood (52), Lee (73), Hughes (79);
Goals: Wood 2.
Sin bin: Ramshaw (8) - punching.
HORNETS: 1 Paul Owen; 2 Wayne McHugh; 3 Brendan O'Meara; 4 Matt Calland; 5 Marlon Billy; 6 Danny Wood; 7 Paul Ashton; 8 Danny Sculthorpe; 9 Darren Robinson; 10 Andy Ireland; 11 David Stephenson; 12 Wes Rogers; 13 Dave Watson. Subs: 14 Ryan Blake not used; 15 Martin Bunce for Stephenson (60); 16 James Bunyan for O'Meara (33); 17 Ben Simpson for Rogers (73); Stephenson for Ashton (64).
Tries: Billy (38, 68), McHugh (56); **Goals:** Wood 5;
Field goal: Sculthorpe.
League Express Men of the Match:
Cougars: Jason Ramshaw; *Hornets:* Dave Watson.
Penalty count: 5-9; **Half-time:** 0-11;
Referee: Nick Oddy (Halifax); **Attendance:** 1,533.

WHITEHAVEN 19 FEATHERSTONE ROVERS 10

WHITEHAVEN: 1 Paul O'Neill; 2 Jonathan Wignall; 3 Howard Hill; 4 David Seeds; 5 Chris Campbell; 6 Aaron Lester; 7 Leroy Joe; 8 Mark Cox; 9 Marc Jackson; 10 David Fatialofa; 11 Spencer Miller; 12 Phil Sherwen; 13 Garry Purdham. Subs: 14 Robert Purdham for G Purdham (33); 15 Ryan Campbell for Seeds (70); 16 Gary Smith for Sherwen (73); 17 Dean Vaughan for Cox (49); Cox for Fatialofa (64).
Tries: Wignall (30), Jackson (48, 70); **Goals:** Jackson 3;
Field goal: Joe.
ROVERS: 1 Matt Bramald; 2 Jamie Stokes; 3 Neil Lowe; 4 Richard Thaler; 5 Matt Turner; 6 Andy Bastow; 7 Richard Gibson; 8 Stuart Dickens; 9 Richard Chapman; 10 Gary Lord; 11 Danny Evans; 12 Ricky Helliwell; 13 Paul Darley. Subs: 14 Wayne Sutcliffe for Darley (77); 15 Stephen Jones for Helliwell (50); 16 Craig Booth for Dickens (55); 17 Gavin Morgan for Lord (ht); Lord for Evans (75).
Tries: Stokes (25), Turner (76); **Goal:** Dickens.
League Express Men of the Match:
Whitehaven: Marc Jackson; *Rovers:* Richard Chapman.
Penalty count: 7-7; **Half-time:** 6-6;
Referee: Peter Taberner (Wigan); **Attendance:** 927.

Thursday 8th March 2001

YORK 12 LEIGH CENTURIONS 84

YORK: 1 Martyn Hunt; 2 Tim Rumford; 3 Craig Moore; 4 Chris Allen; 5 Andy Innes; 6 Ricky Hall; 7 Gareth Oulton; 8 Mick Hagan; 9 Gareth Dobson; 10 Dave Birdsall; 11 Luke Judson; 12 Darren Crake; 13 Nathan Pincher. Subs: 14 Adam Briggs for Pincher (76); 15 Richard Punchard for Innes (70); 16 Lee Bardauskas for Pincher (27); 17 Andy Hutchinson for Birdsall (24BB, rev 40); Pincher for Judson (49).
Tries: Judson (18), Moore (59); **Goals:** Oulton 2.
CENTURIONS: 1 Neil Turley; 2 Michael Watts; 3 Paul Anderson; 4 Jason Johnson; 5 David Jones; 6 Simon Svabic; 7 Liam Bretherton; 8 Andy Leathem; 9 John Duffy; 10 David Whittle; 11 Simon Baldwin; 12 Chris Morley; 13 Willie Swann. Subs: 14 Jamie Gass for Duffy (21); 15 Martin Roden for Whittle (21); 16 David Bradbury for Leathem (53); 17 Kieron Purtill for Anderson (40); Anderson for Bretherton (60BB); Duffy for Baldwin (66); Leathem for Turley (72).
Tries: Turley (3, 23, 37, 53), Johnson (6, 69), Bretherton (8), Swann (15, 76), Svabic (47, 67), Roden (51), Jones (55), Anderson (64); **Goals:** Svabic 14.
League Express Men of the Match:
York: Andy Innes; *Centurions:* Neil Turley.
Penalty count: 8-5; **Half-time:** 6-36; **Referee:** Richard Silverwood (Dewsbury); **Attendance:** 428.

WEEK 15

Sunday 11th March 2001

BARROW BORDER RAIDERS 18 DONCASTER DRAGONS 16

BORDER RAIDERS: 1 Chris Massey; 2 Jamie Marshall; 3 Phil Atkinson; 4 Brett McDermott; 5 Adrian Gardner; 6 Darren Holt; 7 Anthony Murray; 8 Tau Liku; 9 Dave Clark; 10 Mike Whitehead; 11 Matthew Leigh; 12 Geoff Luxon; 13 Gary Charlton. Subs: 14 Darren Wilson not used; 15 Damien Whitter for Liku (25); 16 Ian Rawlinson for Charlton (21); 17 Gareth Pratt for Rawlinson (50); Liku for Whitter (40); Whitter for Liku (60).
Tries: Holt (42), Clark (55), A Gardner (66); **Goals:** Holt 3.
DRAGONS: 1 Lynton Stott; 2 Anton Garcia; 3 Mick Coult; 4 Simon Irving; 5 Neil Bennett; 6 Craig Weston; 7 Billy Conway; 8 Asa Amone; 9 Peter Edwards; 10 Brad Hepi; 11 Tony Miller; 12 Craig Lawton; 13 Paul Mansson. Subs: 14 Johnny Woodcock for Conway (72); 15 Carl Tower not used; 16 Tony Atter for Amone (40); 17 Ian Ramskill for Atter (70); Amone for Hepi (60).
Tries: Mansson (4), Lawton (32), Weston (74);
Goals: Irving 2.
League Express Men of the Match:
Border Raiders: Matthew Leigh; *Dragons:* Paul Mansson.
Penalty count: 8-6; **Half-time:** 2-10; **Referee:** Steve Nicholson (Whitehaven); **Attendance:** 888.

DEWSBURY RAMS 18 OLDHAM 13

RAMS: 1 Nathan Graham; 2 Richard Baker; 3 Dan Potter; 4 Paul Smith; 5 Adrian Flynn; 6 Barry Eaton; 7 David Mycoe; 8 Andy Fisher; 9 Richard Pachniuk; 10 Robin Jowitt; 11 Sean Richardson; 12 Andrew Spink; 13 Damian Ball. Subs: 14 Gavin Wood for Spink (76); 15 Mark Cain for Pachniuk (25); 16 Ryan McDonald for Long (54); 17 Matthew Long for Jowitt (27); Jowitt for McDonald (68).
Tries: Pachniuk (22), Cain (57), Smith (79);
Goals: Eaton 3.
OLDHAM: 1 Mark Sibson; 2 Daryl Lacey; 3 Anthony Gibbons; 4 Pat Rich; 5 Danny Arnold; 6 David Gibbons; 7 Neil Roden; 8 Jason Clegg; 9 John Hough; 10 Leo Casey; 11 Phil Farrell; 12 Paul Norton; 13 Ian Sinfield. Subs: 14 Mike Ford for Lacey (47); 15 Andy Procter for Casey (28); 16 Chris Farrell for Norton (66); 17 Danny Guest for Clegg (53); Casey for Procter (56).
Tries: D Gibbons (10), Norton (32); **Goals:** Rich 2;
Field goal: Roden.
League Express Men of the Match:
Rams: Sean Richardson; *Oldham:* David Gibbons.
Penalty count: 5-7; **Half-time:** 6-13;
Referee: Colin Morris (Huddersfield); **Attendance:** 1,453.

FEATHERSTONE ROVERS 64 CHORLEY LYNX 6

ROVERS: 1 Matt Bramald; 2 Jamie Stokes; 3 Nick Simpson; 4 Richard Thaler; 5 Matt Turner; 6 Andy Bastow; 7 Jamie Rooney; 8 Stuart Dickens; 9 Richard Chapman; 10 Gary Lord; 11 Danny Evans; 12 Neil Lowe; 13 Paul Darley. Subs: 14 Richard Gibson for Bramald (50); 15 Ricky Helliwell for Chapman (57); 16 Stephen Jones for Evans (50); 17 Gavin Morgan for Dickens (34BB, rev 40); Morgan for Lord (47).
Tries: Darley (9), Thaler (14, 20), Chapman (16, 49), Simpson (24), Stokes (37, 64), Rooney (52), Morgan (60), Lowe (73), Gibson (78); **Goals:** Rooney 8.
LYNX: 1 Stuart Dickinson; 2 Gary Doherty; 3 Graham Taberner; 4 Andrew Friar; 5 Chris Ramsdale; 6 Lee Ashton; 7 Stuart Fisher; 8 Rob Verrelli; 9 Lee Maiden; 10 Lee Prest; 11 Phil Harrison; 12 Lee Westwood; 13 Ian Talbot. Subs: 14 Mike Prescott for Verrelli (21); 15 Warren Hindle for Prest (45); 16 Luke Vincent for Westwood (47BB); 17 Mick Farrell not used; Verrelli for Maiden (53); Prest for Harrison (67).
Try: Fisher (28); **Goal:** Fisher.
League Express Men of the Match:
Rovers: Jamie Rooney; *Lynx:* Ian Talbot.
Penalty count: 5-7; **Half-time:** 32-6; **Referee:** Richard Silverwood (Dewsbury); **Attendance:** 1,273.

HULL KINGSTON ROVERS 32 SWINTON LIONS 6

ROVERS: 1 Bob Everitt; 2 Bright Sodje; 3 Chris Kitching; 4 Whetu Taewa; 5 Gavin Molloy; 6 Jimmy Walker; 7 Mick Crane; 8 Jon Aston; 9 Mike Dixon; 10 Rich Hayes; 11 Richard Slater; 12 Rob Wilson; 13 Colin Carter. Subs: 14 Alasdair McLarron for Sodje (40); 15 Mark Blanchard for Carter (23); 16 Paul Fletcher for Rob Wilson (19); 17 Richard Wilson for Aston (30); Aston for Hayes (50); Carter for Crane (58).
Tries: Everitt (6), Walker (63, 68), Slater (65), Fletcher (74); **Goals:** Everitt 6.
LIONS: 1 Mick Nanyn; 2 Jim Evans; 3 Danny Butler; 4 Matt Bateman; 5 Shaun Furey; 6 Phil Veivers; 7 Phil Waring; 8 Mike Loughlin; 9 Rob Barraclough; 10 Lee Hansen; 11 Phil Cushion; 12 Dale Holdstock; 13 Paul Smith. Subs: 14 Lee Hudson for Napolitano (56); 15 Carlo Napolitano for Holdstock (26); 16 Ryan Stazicker for Cushion (40); 17 Jon-Paul Doherty for Loughlin (20); Loughlin for Hansen (54).
Try: Doherty (27); **Goal:** Nanyn.
League Express Men of the Match:
Rovers: Jimmy Walker; *Lions:* Phil Waring.
Penalty count: 7-6; **Half-time:** 10-6; **Referee:** Ronnie Laughton (Barnsley); **Attendance:** 1,536.

LEIGH CENTURIONS 34 BATLEY BULLDOGS 8

CENTURIONS: 1 Neil Turley; 2 Alan Hadcroft; 3 Paul Anderson; 4 Liam Bretherton; 5 Michael Watts; 6 Simon Svabic; 7 Kieron Purtill; 8 Andy Leathem; 9 John Hamilton; 10 David Bradbury; 11 Simon Baldwin; 12 Chris Morley; 13 Adam Bristow. Subs: 14 Jamie Gass for Leathem (34); 15 Phil Kendrick for Bradbury (70); 16 John Duffy for Hamilton (30); 17 Jason Johnson for Hadcroft (3); Hamilton for Duffy (69); Leathem for Gass (65).
Tries: Anderson (18, 75), Bradbury (42, 51), Gass (46), Watts (69); **Goals:** Svabic 5.

BULLDOGS: 1 Craig Lingard; 2 Jeremy Dyson; 3 Danny Maun; 4 Roger Simpson; 5 Paul Gleadhill; 6 Davide Longo; 7 Glen Tomlinson; 8 Lee Kelly; 9 Andy Heptinstall; 10 Paul Hicks; 11 Will Cartledge; 12 Gary Shillabeer; 13 Ryan Horsley. Subs: 14 Mark Cass for Jackson (59); 15 Simon Jackson for Kelly (11); 16 Jeff Wittenberg for Lingard (71); 17 Craig Richards for Hicks (29); Hicks for Richards (41); Richards for Heptinstall (72).
Tries: Lingard (26), Gleadhill (32).
League Express Men of the Match:
Centurions: David Bradbury; *Bulldogs:* Craig Lingard.
Penalty count: 9-3; **Half-time:** 4-8;
Referee: Nick Oddy (Halifax); **Attendance:** 2,619.

WORKINGTON TOWN 4 KEIGHLEY COUGARS 32

TOWN: 1 Jamie Smith; 2 Fata Sini; 3 Neil Frazer; 4 John Allen; 5 Graeme Lewthwaite; 6 Kevin Hetherington; 7 Tane Manihera; 8 Hitro Okesene; 9 Carl Sice; 10 Lokeni Savelio; 11 Jamie Beaumont; 12 Matt Sturm; 13 Anthony Samuel. Subs: 14 William Blackburn for Savelio (50); 15 Steve McGrady not used; 16 Craig Rumney for Sice (31); 17 Anthony Horton for Okesene (63).
Try: Lewthwaite (67).
COUGARS: 1 James Rushforth; 2 Craig Horne; 3 Karl Smith; 4 Graeme Hallas; 5 Jason Lee; 6 Martin Wood; 7 Nathan Antonik; 8 Michael Slicker; 9 Jason Ramshaw; 10 Alan Boothroyd; 11 Paul Harrison; 12 Ian Hughes; 13 Danny Seal. Subs: 14 Matt Walker for Slicker (51); 15 Darren Carter for Smith (21); 16 Phil Stephenson for Boothroyd (50); 17 Jim Leatham for Horne (43).
Tries: Rushforth (28, 38), Seal (41), Hughes (54), Hallas (55), Lee (78); **Goals:** Wood 4.
League Express Men of the Match:
Town: Graeme Lewthwaite; *Cougars:* Martin Wood.
Penalty count: 2-3; **Half-time:** 0-16;
Referee: Peter Taberner (Wigan); **Attendance:** 1,099.

SHEFFIELD EAGLES 26 WIDNES VIKINGS 17

EAGLES: 1 Andy Poynter; 2 Paul Wells; 3 Neil Kite; 4 Steve Walker; 5 Ian Thompson; 6 Richard Goddard; 7 Mark Aston; 8 Jon Bruce; 9 Andy Speak; 10 Steve Hill; 11 Chris Chapman; 12 Heath Cruckshank; 13 Wayne Flynn. Subs: 14 Scott Rhodes for Aston (68); 15 Ian Brown for Poynter (32); 16 Andy Brent for Hill (27); 17 Chris Judge for Bruce (59); Hill for Brent (42); Bruce for Chapman (74).
Tries: Goddard (48), Chapman (52), Judge (67), Rhodes (76); **Goals:** Goddard 5.
Sin bin: Aston (20) - use of elbow;
Flynn (42) - interference.
VIKINGS: 1 Damian Munro; 2 Phil Coussons; 3 Kevin Crouthers; 4 Jason Demetriou; 5 Paul Cook; 6 Martin Crompton; 7 Ian Watson; 8 Simon Knox; 9 Phil Cantillon; 10 Stewart Rhodes; 11 Steve Gee; 12 Chris McKinney; 13 Tommy Hodgkinson. Subs: 14 Chris Percival for Gee (48); 15 Mike Hill for Hammond (69); 16 Karle Hammond for McKinney (17); 17 Mark Forster not used.
Tries: Cook (5), Cantillon (27, 43); **Goals:** Watson 2;
Field goal: Hammond.
Sent off: Rhodes (34) - high tackle.
Sin bin: Crompton (33) - interference.
League Express Men of the Match:
Eagles: Andy Speak; *Vikings:* Tommy Hodgkinson.
Penalty count: 4-8; **Half-time:** 4-12;
Referee: Paul Lee (Leigh); **Attendance:** 1,560.

GATESHEAD THUNDER 4 WHITEHAVEN 23

THUNDER: 1 Michael Johnson; 2 Paul Thorman; 3 Andy Field; 4 Steve Hall; 5 Leon Williamson; 6 Wes McGibbon; 7 Carl Briggs; 8 Paul Lister; 9 Scott Dyson; 10 Andy Grundy; 11 Richard Mervill; 12 Chris Parker; 13 Darrell Derose. Subs: 14 Richard Spence for Thorman (56); 15 Matt Roberts for Parker (52); 16 Jim Carlton for Grundy (26); 17 Lee Garside for Lister (22); Grundy for Mervill (65); Lister for Garside (66).
Try: Dyson (58).
WHITEHAVEN: 1 Paul O'Neill; 2 Jonathan Wignall; 3 David Seeds; 4 Howard Hill; 5 Chris Campbell; 6 Aaron Lester; 7 Leroy Joe; 8 Mark Cox; 9 Marc Jackson; 10 Dean Vaughan; 11 Spencer Miller; 12 Phil Sherwen; 13 Garry Purdham. Subs: 14 Robert Purdham for G Purdham (44); 15 Ryan Campbell for Lester (75); 16 Gary Smith for Vaughan (71); 17 David Fatialofa for Cox (21).
Tries: Wignall (6), Joe (21), Lester (51, 68);
Goals: Jackson 3; **Field goal:** Joe.
League Express Men of the Match:
Thunder: Carl Briggs; *Whitehaven:* Aaron Lester.
Penalty count: 8-4; **Half-time:** 0-10;
Referee: Julian King (St Helens); **Attendance:** 532.

HUNSLET HAWKS 20 ROCHDALE HORNETS 42

HAWKS: 1 George Raynor; 2 Lee Maher; 3 Iain Higgins; 4 Michael Wainwright; 5 Chris North; 6 Craig Robinson; 7 Nicky Dobson; 8 Michael Banks; 9 Gareth Naylor; 10 Guy Adams; 11 Mick Coyle; 12 Ben Thompson; 13 Billy Kershaw. Subs: 14 Dave Jessey for Thompson (48); 15 Junior Henderson for Banks (63); 16 Craig Ibbotson for Kershaw (63); 17 Jermaine Coleman for Dobson (24).
Tries: North (38), Kershaw (50), Ibbotson (80);
Goals: Robinson 4.
HORNETS: 1 Paul Owen; 2 Wayne McHugh; 3 Brendan O'Meara; 4 Matt Calland; 5 Marlon Billy; 6 Danny Wood; 7 Warren Ayres; 8 Danny Sculthorpe; 9 Darren Robinson; 10 Andy Ireland; 11 David Stephenson; 12 Wes Rogers; 13 Dave Watson. Subs: 14 Neil Ramsden for Stephenson (64); 15 Martin Bunce for Calland (40); 16 James Bunyan for Rogers (25); 17 David Larder for Stephenson (25); Stephenson for Ireland (42); Rogers for Sculthorpe (55).
Tries: Owen (18), Robinson (28), Ayres (30), Billy (34, 71), Larder (45), Wood (60); **Goals:** Wood 7.
League Express Men of the Match:
Hawks: George Raynor; *Hornets:* Danny Wood.
Penalty count: 8-4; **Half-time:** 10-24;
Referee: Graeme Shaw (Wigan); **Attendance:** 746.

Wednesday 14th March 2001

OLDHAM 8 WHITEHAVEN 19

OLDHAM: 1 Gavin Dodd; 2 Dean Cross; 3 Anthony Gibbons; 4 Pat Rich; 5 Danny Arnold; 6 David Gibbons; 7 Mike Ford; 8 Jason Clegg; 9 Neil Roden; 10 Leo Casey; 11 Phil Farrell; 12 Paul Norton; 13 Chris Farrell. Subs: 14 John Hough for Ford (58); 15 Ian Sinfield for C Farrell (60); 16 Andy Procter for Casey (23); 17 Kevin Mannion for Clegg (48); Casey for Proctor (67).
Try: Rich (37); **Goals:** Rich 2.
WHITEHAVEN: 1 Paul O'Neill; 2 Jonathan Wignall; 3 David Seeds; 4 Howard Hill; 5 Chris Campbell; 6 Robert Purdham; 7 Leroy Joe; 8 Dean Vaughan; 9 Marc Jackson; 10 David Fatialofa; 11 Spencer Miller; 12 Phil Sherwen; 13 Garry Purdham. Subs: 14 Ryan Campbell not used; 15 Ian Devlin for G Purdham (67); 16 Gary Smith for Sherwen (65); 17 Mark Cox for Vaughan (33); Vaughan for Fatialofa (63); Sherwen for Jackson (72).
Tries: O'Neill (3), Hill (56), Seeds (64);
Goals: Jackson 3; **Field goal:** Jackson.
League Express Men of the Match:
Oldham: Phil Farrell; *Whitehaven:* Marc Jackson.
Penalty count: 6-5; **Half-time:** 6-8; **Referee:** Richard Silverwood (Dewsbury); **Attendance:** 1,179.

WEEK 16

Sunday 18th March 2001

BATLEY BULLDOGS 18 WHITEHAVEN 14

BULLDOGS: 1 Craig Lingard; 2 Jeremy Dyson; 3 Danny Maun; 4 Roger Simpson; 5 Paul Gleadhill; 6 Davide Longo; 7 Glen Tomlinson; 8 Lee Kelly; 9 Andy Heptinstall; 10 Paul Hicks; 11 Gary Shillabeer; 12 Will Cartledge; 13 Ryan Horsley. Subs: 14 Mark Cass for Horsley (62); 15 Simon Jackson not used; 16 Jeff Wittenberg for Kelly (25); 17 Craig Richards for Shillabeer (48); Horsley for Heptinstall (70); Shillabeer for Richards (73).
Tries: Lingard (2, 53), Tomlinson (51); **Goals:** Dyson 3.
WHITEHAVEN: 1 Paul O'Neill; 2 Jonathan Wignall; 3 David Seeds; 4 Howard Hill; 5 Chris Campbell; 6 Robert Purdham; 7 Leroy Joe; 8 Mark Cox; 9 Aaron Lester; 10 David Fatialofa; 11 Spencer Miller; 12 Phil Sherwen; 13 Garry Purdham. Subs: 14 Lee Kiddie for R Purdham (70); 15 Ian Devlin for Miller (70); 16 Gary Smith for Sherwen (77); 17 Dean Vaughan for Cox (48).
Tries: Joe (21), Wignall (27), Hill (29); **Goal:** O'Neill.
League Express Men of the Match:
Bulldogs: Paul Hicks; *Whitehaven:* Leroy Joe.
Penalty count: 4-4; **Half-time:** 8-14;
Referee: Paul Lee (Leigh); **Attendance:** 449.

CHORLEY LYNX 78 YORK 8

LYNX: 1 Stuart Dickinson; 2 Chris Ramsdale; 3 Darren Geritas; 4 Andrew Friar; 5 Graham Taberner; 6 Mick Farrell; 7 Stuart Fisher; 8 Lee Prest; 9 Lee Ashton; 10 Lee Westwood; 11 Phil Harrison; 12 Mike Prescott; 13 Ian Talbot. Subs: 14 Lee Maiden for Talbot (60); 15 Matthew Brown for Dickinson (8); 16 Rob Verrelli for Prest (24BB, rev 41); 17 Luke Vincent for Harrison (50); Verrelli for Prescott (64).
Tries: Farrell (3, 19, 48), Talbot (22), Fisher (25, 41, 60, 75, 80), Brown (27), Geritas (29), Taberner (45), Ramsdale (56), Maiden (63), Vincent (73);
Goals: Fisher 9.
YORK: 1 Martyn Hunt; 2 Tim Rumford; 3 Craig Moore; 4 Gareth Lloyd; 5 Andy Innes; 6 Chris Allen; 7 Danny Waite; 8 Mick Hagan; 9 Gareth Dobson; 10 Andy Hutchinson; 11 Luke Judson; 12 Darren Crake; 13 Lee Bardauskas. Subs: 14 Ricky Hall for Waite (30); 15 Gareth Oulton for Judson (17); 16 Nathan Pincher for Moore (31); 17 Matthew Mulholland not used; Moore for Crake (47); Crake for Dobson (54).
Tries: A Hutchinson (10), Lloyd (38).
Sent off: Hagan (7) - use of elbow.
League Express Men of the Match:
Lynx: Stuart Fisher; *York:* Andy Hutchinson.
Penalty count: 7-2; **Half-time:** 30-8;
Referee: Ronnie Laughton (Barnsley); **Attendance:** 254.

**KEIGHLEY COUGARS 60
BARROW BORDER RAIDERS 20**

COUGARS: 1 James Rushforth; 2 Craig Horne; 3 Daio Powell; 4 Graeme Hallas; 5 Jason Lee; 6 Martin Wood; 7 Nathan Antonik; 8 Michael Slicker; 9 Jason Ramshaw; 10 Alan Boothroyd; 11 Paul Harrison; 12 Ian Hughes; 13 Danny Seal. Subs: 14 Matt Walker for Hughes (48); 15 Jim Leatham for Slicker (40); 16 Phil Stephenson for Boothroyd (32); 17 Darren Carter for Seal (52); Hughes for Powell (68); Seal for Ramshaw (74).
Tries: Wood (9), Hallas (12), Harrison (20), Ramshaw (25), Horne (45, 56, 68), Seal (47), Antonik (54), Rushforth (75); **Goals:** Wood 10.
BORDER RAIDERS: 1 Chris Massey; 2 Adrian Gardner; 3 Phil Atkinson; 4 Brett McDermott; 5 Jamie Marshall; 6 Darren Holt; 7 Anthony Murray; 8 Damien Whitter; 9 Dave Clark; 10 Tau Liku; 11 Mike Whitehead; 12 Geoff Luxon; 13 Matthew Leigh. Subs: 14 Darren Wilson for McDermott (54); 15 Gareth Pratt for Liku (20); 16 Ian Rawlinson for Whitter (27); 17 Paul Gardner not used; Liku for Rawlinson (40); Rawlinson for Pratt (54); McDermott for Liku (66).
Tries: Rawlinson (30), A Gardner (40), Holt (62, 65);
Goals: Holt 2.
League Express Men of the Match:
Cougars: Craig Horne; *Border Raiders:* Darren Holt.
Penalty count: 5-3; **Half-time:** 24-10;
Referee: Colin Morris (Huddersfield); **Attendance:** 2,431.

LEIGH CENTURIONS 52 GATESHEAD THUNDER 4

CENTURIONS: 1 Neil Turley; 2 David Jones; 3 Jason Johnson; 4 Liam Bretherton; 5 Michael Watts; 6 Simon Svabic; 7 Kieron Purtill; 8 Jamie Gass; 9 Martin Roden; 10 David Bradbury; 11 Phil Kendrick; 12 Adam Bristow; 13 Willie Swann. Subs: 14 David Whittle for Gass (30); 15 Chris Morley for Purtill (41); 16 John Hamilton for Roden (53); 17 David Ingram for Svabic (60); Gass for Morley (68); Roden for Hamilton (70).
Tries: Watts (2, 79), Bretherton (5), Johnson (13), Kendrick (25, 47, 49), Turley (55, 59, 66);
Goals: Svabic 5, Turley.
THUNDER: 1 Michael Johnson; 2 Andy Field; 3 Wes McGibbon; 4 Steve Hall; 5 Leon Williamson; 6 Scott Dyson; 7 Carl Briggs; 8 Paul Lister; 9 Richard Spence; 10 Andy Grundy; 11 Richard Mervill; 12 Chris Parker; 13 Darrell Derose. Subs: 14 Paul Thorman for Dyson (27); 15 Jim Carlton for Lister (34); 16 Lee Garside for Mervill (44); 17 Matt Roberts for Grundy (52); Lister for Garside (71); Grundy for Roberts (74).
Try: McGibbon (17).
League Express Men of the Match:
Centurions: Willie Swann; *Thunder:* Andy Grundy.
Penalty count: 11-4; **Half-time:** 20-4;
Referee: Graeme Shaw (Wigan); **Attendance:** 2,242.

OLDHAM 24 SHEFFIELD EAGLES 16

OLDHAM: 1 Mark Sibson; 2 Daryl Lacey; 3 Anthony Gibbons; 4 Pat Rich; 5 Danny Arnold; 6 David Gibbons; 7 Neil Roden; 8 Jason Clegg; 9 John Hough; 10 Leo Casey; 11 Phil Farrell; 12 Paul Norton; 13 Ian Sinfield. Subs: 14 Gavin Dodd not used; 15 Andy Procter for Casey (49); 16 Chris Farrell for Sinfield (75); 17 Kevin Mannion for Clegg (55); Clegg for Norton (75).
Tries: Rich (44), D Gibbons (50), Roden (77);
Goals: Rich 6.
EAGLES: 1 Andy Poynter; 2 Paul Wells; 3 Neil Kite; 4 Steve Walker; 5 Ian Thompson; 6 Richard Goddard; 7 Mark Aston; 8 Jon Bruce; 9 Andy Speak; 10 Steve Hill; 11 Chris Chapman; 12 Chris Judge; 13 Wayne Flynn. Subs: 14 Scott Rhodes for Aston (21); 15 Ian Brown for Chapman (50); 16 Andy Brent for Judge (53); 17 Ricky Wright for Bruce (24); Bruce for Hill (53); Hill for Wright (73).
Tries: Walker (25), Poynter (54); **Goals:** Goddard 4.
League Express Men of the Match:
Oldham: Neil Roden; *Eagles:* Richard Goddard.
Penalty count: 12-8; **Half-time:** 2-10; **Referee:** Richard Silverwood (Dewsbury); **Attendance:** 1,503.

ROCHDALE HORNETS 44 DEWSBURY RAMS 26

HORNETS: 1 Paul Owen; 2 Wayne McHugh; 3 Matt Calland; 4 Brendan O'Meara; 5 Marlon Billy; 6 Danny Wood; 7 Latham Tawhai; 8 Danny Sculthorpe; 9 Darren Robinson; 10 Andy Ireland; 11 David Stephenson; 12 Wes Rogers; 13 Dave Watson. Subs: 14 Warren Ayres for Robinson (52); 15 David Larder for Stephenson (28); 16 James Bunyan for Rogers (28); 17 Martin Bunce for Ireland (60); Rogers for Tawhai (66); Ireland for Sculthorpe (72).
Tries: Robinson (4), Watson (20, 34), Billy (53), Larder (59), Owen (61), McHugh (69), Ayres (72);
Goals: Wood 6.
RAMS: 1 Nathan Graham; 2 Alex Godfrey; 3 Dan Potter; 4 Adrian Flynn; 5 Richard Baker; 6 Mark Cain; 7 Barry Eaton; 8 Andy Fisher; 9 Richard Pachniuk; 10 Matthew Long; 11 Sean Richardson; 12 Paul Smith; 13 Damian Ball. Subs: 14 David Mycoe for Eaton (67); 15 Gavin Wood for Flynn (60); 16 Kevin Spink for Cain (35); 17 Robin Jowitt for Long (52); Long for Richardson (62); Cain for Ball (72).
Tries: Pachniuk (37), Long (43), Godfrey (74), K Spink (77), Potter (79); **Goals:** Eaton 2, Cain.
Sent off: Fisher (15) - punching.
League Express Men of the Match:
Hornets: Danny Sculthorpe; *Rams:* Richard Pachniuk.
Penalty count: 6-6; **Half-time:** 20-6;
Referee: Nick Oddy (Halifax); **Attendance:** 1,195.

SWINTON LIONS 28 FEATHERSTONE ROVERS 25

LIONS: 1 Jim Evans; 2 Adrian Mead; 3 Mick Nanyn; 4 Matt Bateman; 5 Lee Hudson; 6 Shaun Furey; 7 Phil Waring; 8 Jon-Paul Doherty; 9 Rob Barraclough; 10 Phil Cushion; 11 Dale Holdstock; 12 Paul Smith; 13 Phil Veivers. Subs: 14 Danny Butler for Waring (34); 15 Nick Cammann for Mead (53); 16 Carlo Napolitano for Doherty (59); 17 Ryan Stazicker for Holdstock (62).
Tries: Nanyn (8), Barraclough (17), Hudson (39, 46), Mead (52); **Goals:** Nanyn 4.
Sent off: Stazicker (75) - high tackle.
ROVERS: 1 Michael Rhodes; 2 Matt Bramald; 3 Nick Simpson; 4 Richard Thaler; 5 Matt Turner; 6 Andy Bastow; 7 Jamie Rooney; 8 Stuart Dickens; 9 Richard Chapman; 10 Gary Lord; 11 Danny Evans; 12 Neil Lowe; 13 Paul Darley. Subs: 14 Steve Dooler for Evans (24); 15 Ricky Helliwell for Lowe (24); 16 Stephen Jones for Evans (65); 17 Gavin Morgan for Lord (50); Evans for Helliwell (50).
Tries: Rooney (3), Chapman (28), Thaler (33, 67), Jones

(71); **Goals:** Rooney 2; **Field goal:** Rooney.
League Express Men of the Match:
Lions: Dale Holdstock; *Rovers:* Jamie Rooney.
Penalty count: 7-7; **Half-time:** 16-15; **Referee:** Steve Nicholson (Whitehaven); **Attendance:** 947.

WIDNES VIKINGS 10 DONCASTER DRAGONS 18

VIKINGS: 1 Damian Munro; 2 Phil Coussons; 3 Chris Percival; 4 Kevin Crouthers; 5 Paul Cook; 6 Jason Demetriou; 7 Martin Crompton; 8 Simon Knox; 9 Phil Cantillon; 10 Stewart Rhodes; 11 Steve Gee; 12 Joe Faimalo; 13 Tommy Hodgkinson. Subs: 14 David Hulme for Rhodes (65); 15 Mike Hill for Faimalo (69); 16 Ian Watson for Gee (60); 17 Mark Forster not used.
Tries: Coussons (4), Cantillon (31); **Goal:** Cook.
DRAGONS: 1 Lynton Stott; 2 Neil Bennett; 3 Carl Hall; 4 Simon Irving; 5 Mick Coult; 6 Craig Weston; 7 Paddy Handley; 8 Asa Amone; 9 Peter Edwards; 10 Tony Fella; 11 Tony Miller; 12 Brad Hepi; 13 Paul Mansson. Subs: 14 Anton Garcia for Irving (52); 15 Tony Atter for Bennett (70); 16 Craig Lawton for Miller (65); 17 Ian Ramskill for Amone (36); Amone for Ramskill (56).
Tries: Fella (36), Bennett (63), Garcia (74);
Goals: Weston 2, Irving.
League Express Men of the Match:
Vikings: Jason Demetriou; *Dragons:* Craig Weston.
Penalty count: 6-4; **Half-time:** 10-6;
Referee: Peter Taberner (Wigan); **Attendance:** 3,209.

WORKINGTON TOWN 60 HUNSLET HAWKS 10

TOWN: 1 Jamie Smith; 2 Fata Sini; 3 Neil Frazer; 4 Leigh Smith; 5 Graeme Lewthwaite; 6 Tane Manihera; 7 Craig Rumney; 8 Hitro Okesene; 9 Owen Williamson; 10 Lokeni Savelio; 11 Jamie Beaumont; 12 Matt Sturm; 13 Anthony Samuel. Subs: 14 William Blackburn for Okesene (32); 15 Matthew Tunstall for Beaumont (68); 16 Kevin Hetherington for Lewthwaite (70); 17 John Allen for Samuel (59); Okesene for Savelio (51).
Tries: Lewthwaite (1, 14, 58), Frazer (6), Sini (8, 17), Samuel (11), Savelio (40), Beaumont (48), Sturm (52), Blackburn (72); **Goals:** Manihera 8.
Sin bin: Sturm (78) - holding down.
HAWKS: 1 George Raynor; 2 Lee Maher; 3 Iain Higgins; 4 Michael Wainwright; 5 Chris North; 6 Craig Robinson; 7 Nicky Dobson; 8 Michael Banks; 9 Gareth Naylor; 10 Guy Adams; 11 Mick Coyle; 12 Junior Henderson; 13 Billy Kershaw. Subs: 14 Dave Jessey for North (15); 15 Craig Ibbotson for Banks (ht); 16 Ben Skerrett for Coyle (31); 17 Jermaine Coleman for Dobson (ht); Coyle for Jessey (51).
Tries: Coyle (65), Maher (75); **Goal:** Robinson.
League Express Men of the Match:
Town: Graeme Lewthwaite; *Hawks:* Guy Adams.
Penalty count: 5-6; **Half-time:** 38-0;
Referee: Julian King (St Helens); **Attendance:** 826.

WEEK 17

Sunday 25th March 2001

BARROW BORDER RAIDERS 44 HUNSLET HAWKS 4

BORDER RAIDERS: 1 Darren Wilson; 2 Adrian Gardner; 3 Phil Atkinson; 4 Brett McDermott; 5 Shane Irabor; 6 Darren Holt; 7 Anthony Murray; 8 Tau Liku; 9 Dave Clark; 10 Damien Whitter; 11 Mike Whitehead; 12 Geoff Luxon; 13 Gary Charlton. Subs: 14 Danny Lockhart for Luxon (55); 15 Gareth Pratt for Rawlinson (70); 16 Ian Rawlinson for Liku (25); 17 Chris Massey for Clark (78); Liku for Whitter (40); Whitter for Liku (62).
Tries: Atkinson (8, 39, 70), A Gardner (47, 52), Murray (62), Whitehead (72), Clark (77); **Goals:** Holt 6.
HAWKS: 1 George Raynor; 2 Lee Maher; 3 Iain Higgins; 4 Michael Wainwright; 5 Danny Dobson; 6 Jermaine Coleman; 7 Craig Robinson; 8 Michael Banks; 9 Guy Adams; 10 Craig Ibbotson; 11 Mick Coyle; 12 Billy Kershaw; 13 Gareth Naylor. Subs: 14 Nicky Dobson for Coleman (63); 15 Junior Henderson for Kershaw (40); 16 Ben Skerrett for Ibbotson (20); 17 Hamish Munton for D Dobson (49); Ibbotson for Banks (28); Kershaw for Coyle (50).
Try: Higgins (75).
League Express Men of the Match:
Border Raiders: Phil Atkinson; *Hawks:* Craig Robinson.
Penalty count: 7-7; **Half-time:** 14-0; **Referee:** Richard Silverwood (Dewsbury); **Attendance:** 1,042.

CHORLEY LYNX 4 BATLEY BULLDOGS 39

LYNX: 1 Stuart Dickinson; 2 Chris Ramsdale; 3 Matthew Brown; 4 Andrew Friar; 5 Graham Taberner; 6 Lee Ashton; 7 Stuart Fisher; 8 Lee Prest; 9 Lee Maiden; 10 Lee Westwood; 11 Phil Harrison; 12 Mike Prescott; 13 Ian Talbot. Subs: 14 Gary Doherty for Ashton (53); 15 Warren Hindle for Prescott (74); 16 Luke Vincent for Harrison (32); 17 Rob Verrelli for Prest (32); Prest for Westwood (74).
Try: Dickinson (76).
BULLDOGS: 1 Craig Lingard; 2 Jeremy Dyson; 3 Danny Maun; 4 Roger Simpson; 5 Paul Gleadhill; 6 Davide Longo; 7 Glen Tomlinson; 8 Lee Kelly; 9 Andy Heptinstall; 10 Paul Hicks; 11 Gary Shillabeer; 12 Will Cartledge; 13 Ryan Horsley. Subs: 14 Mark Cass for Simpson (49); 15 Simon Jackson for Tomlinson (66); 16 Jeff Wittenberg for Kelly (20); 17 Craig Richards for Cartledge (47); Cartledge for Hicks (60).
Tries: Tomlinson (2, 58), Shillabeer (26, 65), Longo (29), Cartledge (34), Lingard (72); **Goals:** Dyson 5;
Field goal: Heptinstall.
League Express Men of the Match:
Lynx: Ian Talbot; *Bulldogs:* Glen Tomlinson.
Penalty count: 9-6; **Half-time:** 0-20;
Referee: Julian King (St Helens); **Attendance:** 289.

DONCASTER DRAGONS 16 LEIGH CENTURIONS 11

DRAGONS: 1 Johnny Woodcock; 2 Neil Bennett; 3 Paul Mansson; 4 Mick Coult; 5 Anton Garcia; 6 Craig Weston; 7 Paddy Handley; 8 Asa Amone; 9 Peter Edwards; 10 Maea David; 11 Tony Miller; 12 Tony Fella; 13 Craig Lawton. Subs: 14 Gary Smith not used; 15 Tony Atter for Amone (72); 16 Peter Green for Fella (62); 17 Ian Ramskill for David (59).
Tries: Garcia (41), Mansson (48), Woodcock (77);
Goals: Weston 2.
CENTURIONS: 1 Neil Turley; 2 Michael Watts; 3 Paul Anderson; 4 Jason Johnson; 5 David Ingram; 6 Simon Svabic; 7 Liam Bretherton; 8 David Bradbury; 9 John Hamilton; 10 David Whittle; 11 Simon Baldwin; 12 Phil Kendrick; 13 Adam Bristow. Subs: 14 Jamie Gass for Bradbury (34); 15 Andy Leathem for Whittle (14BB, rev 31); 16 John Duffy for Hamilton (23); 17 Willie Swann for Kendrick (55); Bradbury for Whittle (51BB); Leathem for Gass (65); Whittle for Duffy (65).
Try: Turley (60); **Goals:** Svabic 3; **Field goal:** Svabic.
League Express Men of the Match:
Dragons: Asa Amone; *Centurions:* Simon Svabic.
Penalty count: 5-8; **Half-time:** 0-4;
Referee: Colin Morris (Huddersfield); **Attendance:** 1,630.

FEATHERSTONE ROVERS 22 OLDHAM 8

ROVERS: 1 Michael Rhodes; 2 Jamie Stokes; 3 Steve Dooler; 4 Richard Thaler; 5 Matt Bramald; 6 Andy Bastow; 7 Jamie Rooney; 8 Stuart Dickens; 9 Richard Chapman; 10 Gary Lord; 11 Danny Evans; 12 Neil Lowe; 13 Paul Darley. Subs: 14 Gavin Swinson for Bramald (60); 15 Ricky Helliwell for Lord (63); 16 Gavin Morgan for Dickens (29); 17 Craig Booth for Darley (63); Darley for Bastow (78).
Tries: Rhodes (1), Thaler (29), Bramald (47), Swinson (63); **Goals:** Rooney 3.
OLDHAM: 1 Mark Sibson; 2 Daryl Lacey; 3 Anthony Gibbons; 4 Pat Rich; 5 Danny Arnold; 6 David Gibbons; 7 Neil Roden; 8 Jason Clegg; 9 John Hough; 10 Leo Casey; 11 Phil Farrell; 12 Paul Norton; 13 Ian Sinfield. Subs: 14 Gavin Dodd for Lacey (19BB, rev 29); 15 Andy Procter for Clegg (29); 16 Chris Farrell for Norton (47); 17 Kevin Mannion for Sinfield (23); Dodd for Sibson (ht); Clegg for Casey (54); Norton for P Farrell (75).
Try: Dodd (66); **Goals:** Rich 2.
League Express Men of the Match:
Rovers: Richard Chapman; *Oldham:* Leo Casey.
Penalty count: 8-5; **Half-time:** 12-0;
Referee: Nick Oddy (Halifax); **Attendance:** 1,966.

HULL KINGSTON ROVERS 12 ROCHDALE HORNETS 6

ROVERS: 1 Bob Everitt; 2 Dean Andrews; 3 Chris Kitching; 4 Whetu Taewa; 5 Gavin Molloy; 6 Mick Crane; 7 Jimmy Walker; 8 Jon Aston; 9 Mike Dixon; 10 Rich Hayes; 11 Richard Slater; 12 Paul Fletcher; 13 Colin Carter. Subs: 14 Alasdair McLarron for Andrews (43); 15 Mark Blanchard for Crane (ht); 16 David Luckwell for Fletcher (22); 17 Richard Wilson for Aston (22); Aston for Hayes (54); Fletcher for Luckwell (55).
Try: Fletcher (75); **Goals:** Everitt 4.
HORNETS: 1 Paul Owen; 2 Wayne McHugh; 3 Brendan O'Meara; 4 Matt Calland; 5 Marlon Billy; 6 Danny Wood; 7 Latham Tawhai; 8 Danny Sculthorpe; 9 Darren Robinson; 10 Andy Ireland; 11 David Stephenson; 12 Wes Rogers; 13 Dave Watson. Subs: 14 Warren Ayres for Billy (56); 15 Martin Bunce for Ireland (63); 16 James Bunyan for Stephenson (25); 17 David Larder for Rogers (25); Stephenson for Watson (50); Billy for Robinson (74).
Try: O'Meara (65); **Goal:** Wood.
League Express Men of the Match:
Rovers: Mike Dixon; *Hornets:* Matt Calland.
Penalty count: 7-3; **Half-time:** 2-0;
Referee: Peter Taberner (Wigan); **Attendance:** 1,513.

SWINTON LIONS 74 YORK 0

LIONS: 1 Jim Evans; 2 Adrian Mead; 3 Mick Nanyn; 4 Matt Bateman; 5 Lee Hudson; 6 Shaun Furey; 7 Phil Waring; 8 Jon-Paul Doherty; 9 Rob Barraclough; 10 Phil Cushion; 11 Dale Holdstock; 12 Paul Smith; 13 Phil Veivers. Subs: 14 Danny Butler for Barraclough (33); 15 Carlo Napolitano for Cushion (40); 16 Nick Cammann for Mead (33); 17 Ryan Stazicker for Doherty (46); Doherty for Veivers (67); Veivers for Holdstock (74).
Tries: Veivers (2, 40), Furey (18), Hudson (24, 77), Nanyn (26, 72, 75), Smith (36, 67), Evans (40), Holdstock (46, 48), Bateman (64); **Goals:** Nanyn 9.
YORK: 1 Andy Innes; 2 Tim Rumford; 3 Callum Irving; 4 Gareth Lloyd; 5 Paul Harper; 6 Gareth Oulton; 7 Danny Waite; 8 Mick Hagan; 9 Gareth Dobson; 10 Andy Hutchinson; 11 Luke Judson; 12 Darren Crake; 13 Nathan Pincher. Subs: 14 Adam Briggs for Irving (72); 15 Gavin Smith for Crake (62); 16 Lee McNichol for Rumford (16BB, rev 28); 17 Scott Acklam for Hagan (13); McNichol for Innes (35); Hagan for Hutchinson (45BB, rev 52).
League Express Men of the Match:
Lions: Mick Nanyn; *York:* Gareth Dobson.
Penalty count: 4-5; **Half-time:** 38-0;
Referee: Ronnie Laughton (Barnsley); **Attendance:** 545.

WHITEHAVEN 12 SHEFFIELD EAGLES 18

WHITEHAVEN: 1 Paul O'Neill; 2 Jonathan Wignall; 3 David Seeds; 4 Howard Hill; 5 Chris Campbell; 6 Robert Purdham; 7 Leroy Joe; 8 Mark Cox; 9 Aaron Lester; 10 David Fatialofa; 11 Spencer Miller; 12 Phil Sherwen; 13 Garry Purdham. Subs: 14 Lee Kiddie for R Purdham (ht); 15 Ian Devlin for Sherwen (60); 16 Gary Smith for G Purdham (70); 17 Dean Vaughan for Fatialofa (40); Fatialofa for Cox (60).
Tries: Seeds (40, 42); **Goals:** O'Neill 2.
EAGLES: 1 Andy Poynter; 2 Paul Wells; 3 Neil Kite; 4 Steve Walker; 5 Ian Thompson; 6 Gavin Brown; 7 Scott Rhodes; 8 Steve Hill; 9 Andy Speak; 10 Ricky Wright; 11 Chris Judge; 12 Richard Goddard; 13 Wayne Flynn. Subs: 14 Simon Tillyer for Hill (ht); 15 Darren Summerill for Speak (50); 16 Gavin Hewitt for Poynter (69); 17 Andy Brent for Flynn (35); Flynn for Wright (67).
Tries: Kite (9), Poynter (30), Wells (67); **Goals:** Goddard 3.
Sin bin: Brown (16) - professional foul;
Goddard (75) - professional foul.
League Express Men of the Match:
Whitehaven: Aaron Lester; *Eagles:* Richard Goddard.
Penalty count: 15-5; **Half-time:** 6-12;
Referee: Graeme Shaw (Wigan); **Attendance:** 865.

WIDNES VIKINGS 19 KEIGHLEY COUGARS 22

VIKINGS: 1 Paul Cook; 2 Phil Coussons; 3 Chris Percival; 4 Kevin Crouthers; 5 Mark Forster; 6 Jason Demetriou; 7 Ian Watson; 8 Simon Knox; 9 Phil Cantillon; 10 Stephen Holgate; 11 Tommy Hodgkinson; 12 Joe Faimalo; 13 Martin Crompton. Subs: 14 Damian Munro for Forster (65); 15 Chris McKinney for Holgate (59); 16 Mike Hill not used; 17 Steve Gee for Knox (62); Knox for Faimalo (70); Holgate for McKinney (76).
Tries: Holgate (22, 48), Cantillon (25); **Goals:** Watson 3;
Field goal: Watson.
COUGARS: 1 James Rushforth; 2 Craig Horne; 3 Daio Powell; 4 Graeme Hallas; 5 Jason Lee; 6 Martin Wood; 7 Nathan Antonik; 8 Michael Slicker; 9 Jason Ramshaw; 10 Alan Boothroyd; 11 Paul Harrison; 12 Ian Hughes; 13 Danny Seal. Subs: 14 Matt Walker for Hughes (65); 15 Jim Leatham for Slicker (52); 16 Phil Stephenson for Boothroyd (44); 17 Darren Carter for Powell (17); Powell for Wood (40); Hughes for Harrison (76).
Tries: Harrison (11, 74), Ramshaw (17), Antonik (53);
Goals: Wood, Hallas 2.
League Express Men of the Match:
Vikings: Tommy Hodgkinson; *Cougars:* Nathan Antonik.
Penalty count: 6-3; **Half-time:** 11-10; **Referee:** Steve Nicholson (Whitehaven); **Attendance:** 3,469.

GATESHEAD THUNDER 8 WORKINGTON TOWN 34

THUNDER: 1 Michael Johnson; 2 Richard Arrowsmith; 3 Darren Simpson; 4 Steve Hall; 5 Leon Williamson; 6 Wes McGibbon; 7 Carl Briggs; 8 Paul Lister; 9 Roy Southernwood; 10 Andy Grundy; 11 Jim Carlton; 12 Chris Parker; 13 Darrell Derose. Subs: 14 Andy Field for Simpson (40); 15 Stephen Bradley for Barron (55); 16 Lee Garside for Grundy (35); 17 Gareth Barron for Lister (30); Grundy for Garside (57); Lister for Hall (63).
Tries: Southernwood (15), Williamson (30).
TOWN: 1 Lynton Stott; 2 Fata Sini; 3 Neil Frazer; 4 Leigh Smith; 5 Graeme Lewthwaite; 6 Tane Manihera; 7 Craig Rumney; 8 Hitro Okesene; 9 Owen Williamson; 10 Lokeni Savelio; 11 Jamie Beaumont; 12 Matt Sturm; 13 Anthony Samuel. Subs: 14 William Blackburn for Savelio (16); 15 John Allen for Samuel (67); 16 Carl Sice for Williamson (47); 17 Jonathan Heaney for Smith (57); Savelio for Okesene (52); Okesene for Blackburn (72).
Tries: Williamson (4), Okesene (19), Lewthwaite (26, 53), Rumney (42), Sini (68); **Goals:** Manihera 5.
League Express Men of the Match:
Thunder: Carl Briggs; *Town:* Tane Manihera.
Penalty count: 5-2; **Half-time:** 8-16;
Referee: Paul Lee (Leigh); **Attendance:** 617.

Wednesday 28th March 2001

OLDHAM 58 HUNSLET HAWKS 4

OLDHAM: 1 Gavin Dodd; 2 Joey Hayes; 3 Anthony Gibbons; 4 Pat Rich; 5 Warren Barrow; 6 Neil Roden; 7 Mike Ford; 8 Jason Clegg; 9 John Hough; 10 Leo Casey; 11 Phil Farrell; 12 Paul Norton; 13 David Gibbons. Subs: 14 Danny Guest for Clegg (49); 15 Andy Procter for Casey (49); 16 Chris Farrell for Norton (31); 17 Kevin Mannion for D Gibbons (34BB, rev 47); Mannion for Ford (47); Ford for A Gibbons (73).
Tries: Barrow (18, 67), Hayes (23, 48), Rich (33), Hough (38), Roden (46), Mannion (53, 55), D Gibbons (75);
Goals: Rich 9.
HAWKS: 1 George Raynor; 2 Danny Dobson; 3 Iain Higgins; 4 Michael Wainwright; 5 Hamish Munton; 6 Jermaine Coleman; 7 Craig Robinson; 8 Danny Briggs; 9 Guy Adams; 10 Ben Skerrett; 11 Chris Ibbotson; 12 Michael Banks; 13 Gareth Naylor. Subs: 14 Junior Henderson for Briggs (25); 15 Nicky Dobson for Robinson (15); 16 Chris Heywood for D Dobson (63); 17 Tony Howcroft not used; Robinson for Naylor (31); Naylor for Banks (60).
Try: Skerrett (28).
League Express Men of the Match:
Oldham: Neil Roden; *Hawks:* Nicky Dobson.
Penalty count: 5-3; **Half-time:** 24-4; **Referee:** Steve Nicholson (Whitehaven); **Attendance:** 1,038.

Saturday 31st March 2001

SHEFFIELD EAGLES 60 CHORLEY LYNX 4

EAGLES: 1 Andy Poynter; 2 Paul Wells; 3 Neil Kite; 4 Steve Walker; 5 Ian Thompson; 6 Gavin Brown; 7 Scott Rhodes; 8 Darren Summerill; 9 Andy Speak; 10 Ricky Wright; 11 Chris Judge; 12 Richard Goddard; 13 Wayne Flynn. Subs: 14 Gareth Hewitt for Goddard (41); 15 Ian Brown for Flynn (45); 16 Andy Brent for Summerill (28); 17 Simon Tillyer for Wright (28); Summerill for Judge

(54); Goddard for Poynter (77).
Tries: Kite (7, 23), Poynter (12, 27), Walker (20, 40), Tillyer (30), Brent (36), Thompson (44), Speak (58), Wells (78); **Goals:** Goddard 7, G Brown.
LYNX: 1 Matthew Brown; 2 Chris Ramsdale; 3 Stuart Dickinson; 4 Andrew Friar; 5 Graham Taberner; 6 Ian Talbot; 7 Stuart Fisher; 8 Lee Prest; 9 Lee Maiden; 10 Lee Westwood; 11 Phil Harrison; 12 Rob Verrelli; 13 Luke Vincent. Subs: 14 Paul Wilcock for Fisher (53); 15 Warren Hindle for Harrison (41); 16 Andy Horrobin for Prest (28); 17 Darren Geritas not used; Prest for Verrelli (49); Verrelli for Horrobin (59); Horrobin for Westwood (73).
Try: Westwood (61).
League Express Men of the Match:
Eagles: Scott Rhodes; *Lynx:* Ian Talbot.
Penalty count: 6-6; **Half-time:** 44-0;
Referee: Paul Lee (Leigh); **Attendance:** 870.

WEEK 18

Sunday 1st April 2001

DEWSBURY RAMS 66 BARROW BORDER RAIDERS 10

RAMS: 1 Nathan Graham; 2 Richard Baker; 3 Dan Potter; 4 Kevin Crouthers; 5 Adrian Flynn; 6 Mark Cain; 7 Barry Eaton; 8 Robin Jowitt; 9 Richard Pachniuk; 10 Shayne Williams; 11 Sean Richardson; 12 Andrew Spink; 13 Damian Ball. Subs: 14 David Mycoe for Ball (62); 15 Kevin Spink for McDonald (56); 16 Liam Tallon for Richardson (35); 17 Ryan McDonald for Williams (27); Richardson for Flynn (61).
Tries: Cain (2, 58, 62), Potter (7, 65, 75), Crouthers (23, 38), Flynn (27, 60), K Spink (72); **Goals:** Eaton 11.
BORDER RAIDERS: 1 Danny Lockhart; 2 Adrian Gardner; 3 Phil Atkinson; 4 Brett McDermott; 5 Shane Irabor; 6 Darren Holt; 7 Anthony Murray; 8 Tau Liku; 9 Dave Clark; 10 Damien Whitter; 11 Matthew Leigh; 12 Mike Whitehead; 13 Gary Charlton. Subs: 14 Jamie Marshall not used; 15 Geoff Luxon for Holt (24); 16 Gareth Pratt for Rawlinson (60); 17 Ian Rawlinson for Liku (20); Liku for Whitter (ht); Whitter for Liku (46).
Tries: Leigh (49), Clark (55); **Goal:** Atkinson.
League Express Men of the Match:
Rams: Barry Eaton; *Border Raiders:* Dave Clark.
Penalty count: 9-8; **Half-time:** 32-0; **Referee:** Steve Nicholson (Whitehaven); **Attendance:** 853.

DONCASTER DRAGONS 28 WHITEHAVEN 24

DRAGONS: 1 Johnny Woodcock; 2 Neil Bennett; 3 Carl Hall; 4 Simon Irving; 5 Anton Garcia; 6 Craig Weston; 7 Paddy Handley; 8 Ian Ramskill; 9 Peter Edwards; 10 Maea David; 11 Tony Fella; 12 Craig Lawton; 13 Paul Mansson. Subs: 14 Wayne Green not used; 15 Peter Green for Ramskill (18); 16 Phil White for P Green (64); 17 Tony Atter for Handley (47).
Tries: Bennett (2), Woodcock (11), Garcia (19), Handley (33), Edwards (72); **Goals:** Irving 4.
Sent off: Hall (79) - high tackle.
On report: Bennett (51) - high tackle.
WHITEHAVEN: 1 Paul O'Neill; 2 Jonathan Wignall; 3 David Seeds; 4 Howard Hill; 5 Chris Campbell; 6 Lee Kiddie; 7 Leroy Joe; 8 Mark Cox; 9 Aaron Lester; 10 Dean Vaughan; 11 Gary Smith; 12 Phil Sherwen; 13 Spencer Miller. Subs: 14 Steve Kirkbride for Campbell (52); 15 Robert Purdham for Lester (33); 16 Ian Devlin for Sherwen (34); 17 David Fatialofa for Cox (18); Cox for Fatialofa (39).
Tries: Seeds (6), C Campbell (28), Joe (43), Devlin (47); **Goals:** O'Neill 3; **Field goals:** Kiddie, Joe.
League Express Men of the Match:
Dragons: Simon Irving; *Whitehaven:* Leroy Joe.
Penalty count: 7-7; **Half-time:** 22-12;
Referee: Nick Oddy (Halifax); **Attendance:** 1,093.

KEIGHLEY COUGARS 6 LEIGH CENTURIONS 16

COUGARS: 1 James Rushforth; 2 Craig Horne; 3 Daio Powell; 4 Graeme Hallas; 5 Jason Lee; 6 Karl Smith; 7 Nathan Antonik; 8 Michael Slicker; 9 Jason Ramshaw; 10 Alan Boothroyd; 11 Paul Harrison; 12 Ian Hughes; 13 Danny Seal. Subs: 14 Matt Walker for Ramshaw (41); 15 Craig Murdock for Antonik (2); 16 Phil Stephenson for Boothroyd (35); 17 Jim Leatham for Slicker (33); Ramshaw for Walker (46BB); Walker for Smith (56); Slicker for Stephenson (63).
Try: Seal (16); **Goal:** Hallas.
CENTURIONS: 1 Neil Turley; 2 David Ingram; 3 Paul Anderson; 4 Andy Fairclough; 5 Michael Watts; 6 Simon Svabic; 7 Willie Swann; 8 Andy Leathem; 9 John Hamilton; 10 David Whittle; 11 Simon Baldwin; 12 Adam Bristow; 13 Chris Morley. Subs: 14 Phil Kendrick for Morley (59); 15 David Bradbury for Whittle (25); 16 Liam Bretherton for Fairclough (37); 17 John Duffy for Hamilton (28); Whittle for Leathem (63); Hamilton for Duffy (77).
Tries: Hamilton (27), Baldwin (40), Turley (50);
Goals: Svabic 2.
League Express Men of the Match:
Cougars: Craig Murdock; *Centurions:* Simon Baldwin.
Penalty count: 4-4; **Half-time:** 6-10;
Referee: Peter Taberner (Wigan); **Attendance:** 3,727.

SWINTON LIONS 12 BATLEY BULLDOGS 34

LIONS: 1 Jim Evans; 2 Adrian Mead; 3 Mick Nanyn; 4 Matt Bateman; 5 Andy Cheetham; 6 Shaun Furey; 7 Phil Waring; 8 Jon-Paul Doherty; 9 Rob Barraclough; 10 Lee Hansen; 11 Phil Cushion; 12 Dale Holdstock; 13 Paul Smith. Subs: 14 Danny Butler for Waring (34); 15 Wayne English for Mead (34); 16 Nick Cammann for Napolitano (41BB, rev 56); 17 Carlo Napolitano for Holdstock (20); Cammann for Evans (58); Evans for Cushion (67); Waring for Barraclough (73).
Tries: Bateman (63, 75); **Goals:** Nanyn 2.
BULLDOGS: 1 Craig Lingard; 2 Jeremy Dyson; 3 Danny Maun; 4 Roger Simpson; 5 Paul Gleadhill; 6 Davide Longo; 7 Glen Tomlinson; 8 Lee Kelly; 9 Andy Heptinstall; 10 Paul Hicks; 11 Gary Shillabeer; 12 Will Cartledge; 13 Ryan Horsley. Subs: 14 Mark Cass for Heptinstall (55); 15 Simon Jackson for Longo (56); 16 Jeff Wittenberg for Kelly (24); 17 Craig Richards for Shillabeer (27); Shillabeer for Richards (43); Richards for Wittenberg (67).
Tries: Horsley (5), Gleadhill (8), Tomlinson (14), Lingard (40), Shillabeer (55), Wittenberg (66); **Goals:** Dyson 5.
League Express Men of Match:
Lions: Jon-Paul Doherty; *Bulldogs:* Glen Tomlinson.
Penalty count: 11-5; **Half-time:** 0-24;
Referee: Graeme Shaw (Wigan); **Attendance:** 743.

WIDNES VIKINGS 64 HUNSLET HAWKS 4

VIKINGS: 1 Paul Atcheson; 2 Phil Coussons; 3 Chris Percival; 4 Jason Demetriou; 5 Mark Forster; 6 Martin Crompton; 7 Ian Watson; 8 Simon Knox; 9 Phil Cantillon; 10 Stephen Holgate; 11 Steve Gee; 12 Joe Faimalo; 13 Tommy Hodgkinson. Subs: 14 Damian Munro for Atcheson (55); 15 Stewart Rhodes for Gee (49); 16 Richard Agar for Watson (62); 17 Matthew Long for Knox (25); Knox for Holgate (62); Watson for Hodgkinson (68).
Tries: Atcheson (9), Knox (15), Demetriou (17, 53), Long (43, 48), Cantillon (50, 65), Coussons (57), Munro (60, 70), Crompton (80); **Goals:** Watson 6, Agar 2.
HAWKS: 1 George Raynor; 2 Hamish Munton; 3 Iain Higgins; 4 Michael Wainwright; 5 Danny Dobson; 6 Jermaine Coleman; 7 Craig Robinson; 8 Craig Ibbotson; 9 Tony Howcroft; 10 Ben Skerrett; 11 Michael Banks; 12 Junior Henderson; 13 Gareth Naylor. Subs: 14 Chris Heywood for Naylor (76); 15 Nicky Dobson for D Dobson (40); 16 Craig Morphet for Banks (20); 17 Mick Coyle not used; Banks for Skerrett (34); D Dobson for Raynor (62); Naylor for Robinson (77).
Try: Robinson (76).
League Express Men of the Match:
Vikings: Tommy Hodgkinson; *Hawks:* Craig Robinson.
Penalty count: 5-1; **Half-time:** 16-0; **Referee:** Colin Morris (Huddersfield); **Attendance:** 3,253.

WORKINGTON TOWN 24 HULL KINGSTON ROVERS 18

TOWN: 1 Lynton Stott; 2 Jonathan Heaney; 3 Neil Frazer; 4 Leigh Smith; 5 Graeme Lewthwaite; 6 Tane Manihera; 7 Craig Rumney; 8 Matt Sturm; 9 Owen Williamson; 10 Lokeni Savelio; 11 Jamie Beaumont; 12 William Blackburn; 13 Anthony Samuel. Subs: 14 Carl Sice for Williamson (48); 15 Matthew Tunstall for Savelio (46BB); 16 Fata Sini for Blackburn (58); 17 Hitro Okesene for Savelio (20); Savelio for Sturm (ht); Williamson for Sice (69).
Tries: Heaney (64), Stott (73), Manihera (78);
Goals: Manihera 6.
ROVERS: 1 Bob Everitt; 2 Mark Blanchard; 3 Chris Kitching; 4 Whetu Taewa; 5 Gavin Molloy; 6 Chris Charles; 7 Mick Crane; 8 Richard Wilson; 9 Mike Dixon; 10 Rich Hayes; 11 Richard Slater; 12 Paul Fletcher; 13 Matt Schultz. Subs: 14 Scott Yeaman for Fletcher (ht); 15 Allan Dunham not used; 16 Jamie Bovill for Luckwell (56); 17 David Luckwell for Wilson (19); Wilson for Hayes (43); Hayes for Wilson (48BB, rev 67); Fletcher for Slater (63).
Tries: Molloy (42), Everitt (48), Schultz (58);
Goals: Charles 3.
League Express Men of the Match:
Town: Tane Manihera; *Rovers:* Mike Dixon.
Penalty count: 10-5; **Half-time:** 6-2;**Referee:** Ronnie Laughton (Barnsley); **Attendance:** 1,064.

YORK 6 OLDHAM 70

YORK: 1 Lee Turnbull; 2 Tim Rumford; 3 Lee McNichol; 4 Andrew Webster; 5 Callum Irving; 6 Lee Bardauskas; 7 Gareth Oulton; 8 Scott Acklam; 9 Gareth Dobson; 10 Andy Hutchinson; 11 Gavin Smith; 12 Darren Crake; 13 Nathan Pincher. Subs: 14 Adam Briggs not used; 15 Luke Judson for Smith (46); 16 Luke Billyeald for McNichol (28); 17 Craig Forsyth for Hutchinson (40); McNichol for Rumford (37); Hutchinson for Acklam (54); Rumford for McNichol (62).
Try: Dobson (6); **Goal:** Oulton.
OLDHAM: 1 Gavin Dodd; 2 Joey Hayes; 3 Anthony Gibbons; 4 Pat Rich; 5 Warren Barrow; 6 Neil Roden; 7 Keith Brennan; 8 Andy Procter; 9 John Hough; 10 Jason Clegg; 11 Phil Farrell; 12 Chris Farrell; 13 David Gibbons. Subs: 14 Daryl Lacey for Hayes (25); 15 Lee Doran for Procter (49); 16 Danny Guest for Clegg (49); 17 Kevin Mannion for C Farrell (58).
Tries: Barrow (2, 32, 44); A Gibbons (13, 15, 74), Clegg (19), Rich (25), D Gibbons (56), Hayes (58), Roden (65), Lacey (72), Dodd (78); **Goals:** Rich 9.
League Express Men of the Match:
York: Gareth Dobson; *Oldham:* Anthony Gibbons.
Penalty count: 9-5; **Half-time:** 6-30; **Referee:** Richard Silverwood (Dewsbury); **Attendance:** 514.

GATESHEAD THUNDER 15 ROCHDALE HORNETS 40

THUNDER: 1 Michael Johnson; 2 Richard Arrowsmith; 3 Wes McGibbon; 4 Andy Field; 5 Leon Williamson; 6 Darren Callaghan; 7 Carl Briggs; 8 Paul Lister; 9 Roy Southernwood; 10 Andy Grundy; 11 Jim Carlton; 12 Chris Parker; 13 Darrell Derose. Subs: 14 Paul Thorman for McGibbon (32); 15 Richard Mervill for Lister (30); 16 Lee Garside for Grundy (30); 17 Gareth Barron for Derose (30); Derose for Parker (61); Grundy for Garside (65); Lister for Barron (66BB).
Tries: Grundy (2), Field (35), Thorman (60);
Goal: Briggs; **Field goal:** Briggs.
HORNETS: 1 Paul Owen; 2 Sean Cooper; 3 Brendan O'Meara; 4 Matt Calland; 5 Marlon Billy; 6 Danny Wood; 7 Latham Tawhai; 8 Danny Sculthorpe; 9 Darren Robinson; 10 Andy Ireland; 11 James Bunyan; 12 David Larder; 13 Dave Watson. Subs: 14 Warren Ayres for Tawhai (ht); 15 Martin Bunce for Ireland (43); 16 Wes Rogers for Larder (48); 17 David Stephenson for Calland (48); Larder for Wood (59).
Tries: Bunyan (7, 24), Tawhai (21), Robinson (29), Billy (38, 59), Owen (56), O'Meara (66); **Goals:** Wood 3, Ayres.
League Express Men of the Match:
Thunder: Carl Briggs; *Hornets:* Marlon Billy.
Penalty count: 5-5; **Half-time:** 11-24;
Referee: Julian King (St Helens); **Attendance:** 387.

Saturday 7th April 2001

DEWSBURY RAMS 12 WIDNES VIKINGS 13

RAMS: 1 Nathan Graham; 2 Alex Godfrey; 3 Dan Potter; 4 Kevin Crouthers; 5 Adrian Flynn; 6 Mark Cain; 7 Barry Eaton; 8 Robin Jowitt; 9 Richard Pachniuk; 10 Shayne Williams; 11 Sean Richardson; 12 Andrew Spink; 13 Damian Ball. Subs: 14 Liam Tallon for Hicks (59); 15 David Mycoe for Godfrey (77); 16 Kevin Spink not used; 17 Simon Hicks for Williams (23).
Try: Flynn (65); **Goals:** Eaton 4.
VIKINGS: 1 Paul Atcheson; 2 Phil Coussons; 3 Chris Percival; 4 Jason Demetriou; 5 Mark Forster; 6 Martin Crompton; 7 Ian Watson; 8 Simon Knox; 9 Phil Cantillon; 10 Stephen Holgate; 11 Steve Gee; 12 Chris McKinney; 13 Tommy Hodgkinson. Subs: 14 Damian Munro for Atcheson (71); 15 Stewart Rhodes for Forster (75); 16 Richard Agar for McKinney (61); 17 Matthew Long for Knox (21); Knox for Holgate (66); Holgate for Hodgkinson (79).
Tries: Demetriou (6), Cantillon (39); **Goals:** Watson 2;
Field goal: Watson.
Sin bin: Crompton (31) - obstruction.
League Express Men of the Match:
Rams: Sean Richardson; *Vikings:* Tommy Hodgkinson.
Penalty count: 8-8; **Half-time:** 6-13;
Referee: Steve Presley (Castleford); **Attendance:** 2,135.

WEEK 19

Sunday 8th April 2001

CHORLEY LYNX 19 GATESHEAD THUNDER 14

LYNX: 1 Matthew Brown; 2 Andrew Friar; 3 Darren Geritas; 4 Stuart Dickinson; 5 Graham Taberner; 6 Mark Lee; 7 Chris Ramsdale; 8 Lee Prest; 8 Lee Maiden; 10 Lee Westwood; 11 Phil Harrison; 12 Mike Prescott; 13 Ian Talbot. Subs: 14 Gary Doherty for Geritas (31BB, rev 50); 15 Wayne Bloor for Prest (30); 16 Andy Horrobin for Westwood (56BB, rev 67); 17 Rob Verrelli for Prescott (30); Prest for Verrelli (51BB); Doherty for Friar (63); Prescott for Prest (80).
Tries: Dickinson (3), Ramsdale (10), Taberner (32);
Goals: Talbot 3; **Field goal:** Lee.
THUNDER: 1 Michael Johnson; 2 Paul Thorman; 3 Andy Field; 4 Gareth Lloyd; 5 Leon Williamson; 6 Darren Callaghan; 7 Carl Briggs; 8 Gareth Barron; 9 Roy Southernwood; 10 Andy Grundy; 11 Jim Carlton; 12 Richard Mervill; 13 Darrell Derose. Subs: 14 Stephen Rutherford not used; 15 Paul Lister for Barron (31); 16 Lee Garside for Grundy (64); 17 Chris Parker for Derose (11); Barron for Lister (80); Grundy for Garside (80).
Tries: Lloyd (16, 80), Briggs (20); **Goal:** Briggs.
League Express Men of the Match:
Lynx: Ian Talbot; *Thunder:* Carl Briggs.
Penalty count: 9-5; **Half-time:** 16-10;
Referee: Ian Chatterton (Huddersfield); **Attendance:** 356.

FEATHERSTONE ROVERS 24 WORKINGTON TOWN 4

ROVERS: 1 Michael Rhodes; 2 Jamie Stokes; 3 Steve Dooler; 4 Richard Thaler; 5 Matt Bramald; 6 Andy Bastow; 7 Jamie Rooney; 8 Stuart Dickens; 9 Richard Chapman; 10 Gary Lord; 11 Danny Evans; 12 Neil Lowe; 13 Paul Darley. Subs: 14 Gavin Swinson for Thaler (55); 15 Ricky Helliwell for Evans (58); 16 Gavin Morgan for Lord (22BB); 17 Craig Booth for Morgan (70); Lord for Dickens (49).
Tries: Bramald (9, 63, 78), Evans (30), Chapman (70);
Goal: Rooney; **Field goals:** Rooney 2.
TOWN: 1 Lynton Stott; 2 Jonathan Heaney; 3 Neil Frazer; 4 Leigh Smith; 5 Graeme Lewthwaite; 6 Tane Manihera; 7 Craig Rumney; 8 Hitro Okesene; 9 Owen Williamson; 10 Lokeni Savelio; 11 Matt Sturm; 12 Jamie Beaumont; 13 Anthony Samuel. Subs: 14 Fata Sini for Okesene (60); 15 Matthew Tunstall for Savelio (21); 16 Kevin Hetherington for Rumney (46); 17 Jamie Nixon for Lewthwaite (72); Savelio for Tunstall (70).
Try: Samuel (54).
League Express Men of the Match:
Rovers: Michael Rhodes; *Town:* Lynton Stott.
Penalty count: 6-6; **Half-time:** 9-0;
Referee: Peter Taberner (Wigan); **Attendance:** 1,656.

HULL KINGSTON ROVERS 38 BARROW BORDER RAIDERS 8

ROVERS: 1 Bob Everitt; 2 Gavin Molloy; 3 Chris Kitching; 4 Whetu Taewa; 5 Graeme Barber; 6 Jimmy Walker; 7 Scott Yeaman; 8 Richard Wilson; 9 Mike Dixon; 10 Rich Hayes; 11 Richard Slater; 12 Matt Schultz; 13 Chris Charles. Subs: 14 Mick Crane for Barber (ht); 15 Paul Fletcher for Schultz (21); 16 Jon

Northern Ford Premiership 2001 - Round by Round

Aston for Wilson (21BB, rev ht); 17 David Luckwell for Hayes (28BB, rev ht); Schultz for Slater (ht); Luckwell for Wilson (54); Aston for Hayes (54).
Tries: Kitching (20), Everitt (29, 43), Dixon (35, 38, 59), Yeaman (54); **Goals:** Charles 5.
On report: Aston (68) – dangerous tackle.
BORDER RAIDERS: 1 Danny Lockhart; 2 Adrian Gardner; 3 Phil Atkinson; 4 Brett McDermott; 5 Shane Irabor; 6 Mike Kavanagh; 7 Anthony Murray; 8 Damien Whitter; 9 Dave Clark; 10 Ian Rawlinson; 11 Matthew Leigh; 12 Mike Whitehead; 13 Gary Charlton. Subs: 14 Jamie Marshall not used; 15 Geoff Luxon for Whitter (29); 16 Gareth Pratt for Luxon (64); 17 Paul Gardner for Atkinson (72).
Try: Charlton (47); **Goals:** Kavanagh 2.
Sent off: Rawlinson (17 seconds) – high tackle.
League Express Men of the Match:
Rovers: Mike Dixon; *Border Raiders:* Mike Kavanagh.
Penalty count: 9-8; **Half-time:** 20-2;
Referee: Nick Oddy (Halifax); **Attendance:** 1,532.

OLDHAM 26 BATLEY BULLDOGS 8

OLDHAM: 1 Gavin Dodd; 2 Danny Arnold; 3 Anthony Gibbons; 4 Pat Rich; 5 Warren Barrow; 6 Neil Roden; 7 Keith Brennan; 8 Jason Clegg; 9 John Hough; 10 Leo Casey; 11 Phil Farrell; 12 Chris Farrell; 13 David Gibbons. Subs: 14 Daryl Lacey for Hough (60); 15 Paul Norton for Casey (24BB, rev ht); 16 Danny Guest for Clegg (48); 17 Ian Sinfield for Brennan (63); Norton for Casey (48).
Tries: Hough (23), A Gibbons (42), Norton (51), P Farrell (55); **Goals:** Rich 5.
BULLDOGS: 1 Craig Lingard; 2 Jeremy Dyson; 3 Danny Maun; 4 Roger Simpson; 5 Paul Gleadhill; 6 Davide Longo; 7 Glen Tomlinson; 8 Lee Kelly; 9 Andy Heptinstall; 10 Paul Hicks; 11 Gary Shillabeer; 12 Will Cartledge; 13 Ryan Horsley. Subs: 14 Mark Cass for Heptinstall (56); 15 Simon Jackson for Longo (49); 16 Jeff Wittenberg for Kelly (16BB, rev 33); 17 Craig Richards for Cartledge (52); Wittenberg for Kelly (42).
Try: Horsley (29); **Goals:** Dyson 2.
League Express Men of the Match:
Oldham: Anthony Gibbons; *Bulldogs:* Glen Tomlinson.
Penalty count: 9-7; **Half-time:** 8-8; **Referee:** Ronnie Laughton (Barnsley); **Attendance:** 1,598.

ROCHDALE HORNETS 98 YORK 0

HORNETS: 1 Paul Owen; 2 Sean Cooper; 3 Brendan O'Meara; 4 Matt Calland; 5 Marlon Billy; 6 Danny Wood; 7 Warren Ayres; 8 Danny Sculthorpe; 9 Darren Robinson; 10 Andy Ireland; 11 David Stephenson; 12 James Bunyan; 13 Dave Watson. Subs: 14 Neil Alexander for Stephenson (46); 15 Martin Bunce for Ireland (23); 16 Wes Rogers for Watson (41); 17 David Larder for Sculthorpe (41); Ireland for Bunyan (73).
Tries: Billy (2, 20, 45, 71, 78), Robinson (6, 9, 37), Cooper (14), Watson (18), O'Meara (26, 34, 59, 68), Bunce (29), Larder (49), Owen (57), Wood (61), Bunyan (64); **Goals:** Wood 11.
YORK: 1 Callum Irving; 2 Tim Rumford; 3 Andrew Webster; 4 Luke Billyeald; 5 Andy Innes; 6 Gareth Oulton; 7 Danny Waite; 8 Scott Acklam; 9 Alan Pallister; 10 Andy Hutchinson; 11 Nathan Pincher; 12 Mick Ramsden; 13 Gareth Dobson. Subs: 14 Lee Turnbull for Pincher (55); 15 Steve Lamb for Irving (15); 16 Barrington Barnett for Webster (25); 17 Steve Harris not used; Webster for Lamb (62).
League Express Men of the Match:
Hornets: Paul Owen; *York:* Gareth Oulton.
Penalty count: 3-5; **Half-time:** 54-0;
Referee: Graeme Shaw (Wigan); **Attendance:** 762.

SWINTON LIONS 22 SHEFFIELD EAGLES 23

LIONS: 1 Wayne English; 2 Jim Evans; 3 Mick Nanyn; 4 Matt Bateman; 5 Andy Cheetham; 6 Shaun Furey; 7 Phil Waring; 8 Jon-Paul Doherty; 9 Rob Barraclough; 10 Lee Hansen; 11 Dale Holdstock; 12 Carlo Napolitano; 13 Paul Smith. Subs: 14 Danny Butler for Furey (51); 15 Chris Newall for Holdstock (40); 16 Nick Cammann for Doherty (50); 17 Adrian Mead not used; Doherty for Napolitano (68); Furey for Butler (75).
Tries: Smith (13, 58), Nanyn (19), Napolitano (26);
Goals: Nanyn 3.
EAGLES: 1 Andy Poynter; 2 Paul Wells; 3 Neil Kite; 4 Steve Walker; 5 Ian Thompson; 6 Gavin Brown; 7 Scott Rhodes; 8 Darren Summerill; 9 Andy Speak; 10 Ricky Wright; 11 Chris Judge; 12 Richard Goddard; 13 Wayne Flynn. Subs: 14 Gareth Hewitt for Wells (68); 15 Andy Brent for Summerill (18); 16 Chris Chapman for Judge (40); 17 Billy Kershaw for Wright (45); Summerill for Brent (53); Brent for Rhodes (61).
Tries: Wells (6), Goddard (16), Thompson (34), Poynter (45); **Goals:** Goddard 3; **Field goal:** Goddard.
League Express Men of Match:
Lions: Rob Barraclough; *Eagles:* Richard Goddard.
Penalty count: 6-7; **Half-time:** 16-16;
Referee: Julian King (St Helens); **Attendance:** 715.

WHITEHAVEN 17 KEIGHLEY COUGARS 4

WHITEHAVEN: 1 Wesley Wilson; 2 Jonathan Wignall; 3 David Seeds; 4 Howard Hill; 5 Paul O'Neill; 6 Leroy Joe; 7 Steve Kirkbride; 8 Mark Cox; 9 Aaron Lester; 10 Dean Vaughan; 11 Spencer Miller; 12 Ian Devlin; 13 Garry Purdham. Subs: 14 Lee Kiddie for Wilson (54); 15 Robert Purdham for Devlin (79); 16 Gary Smith for Cox (57); 17 Phil Sherwen for Vaughan (62); Devlin for Seeds (80).
Tries: Wignall (36), Lester (60), Devlin (75);
Goals: Kirkbride 2; **Field goal:** Kirkbride.
COUGARS: 1 James Rushforth; 2 Craig Horne; 3 Daio Powell; 4 Graeme Hallas; 5 Jason Lee; 6 Karl Smith; 7 Craig Murdock; 8 Michael Slicker; 9 Jason Ramshaw; 10 Alan Boothroyd; 11 Paul Harrison; 12 Matt Walker; 13 Danny Seal. Subs: 14 Carlos Sanchez for Seal (72); 15 Chris Ross for Powell (45); 16 Phil Stephenson for Boothroyd (35); 17 Jim Leatham for Slicker (23); Boothroyd for Stephenson (70).
Try: Seal (30).
Sent off: Ross (53) - high tackle.
League Express Men of the Match:
Whitehaven: Aaron Lester; *Cougars:* Craig Murdock.
Penalty count: 10-4; **Half time:** 6-4; **Referee:** Richard Silverwood (Dewsbury); **Attendance:** 895.

HUNSLET HAWKS 6 LEIGH CENTURIONS 50

HAWKS: 1 George Raynor; 2 Hamish Munton; 3 Iain Higgins; 4 Michael Wainwright; 5 Danny Dobson; 6 Jermaine Coleman; 7 Chris Robinson; 8 Michael Banks; 9 Tony Howcroft; 10 Craig Morphet; 11 Neil Bradbrook; 12 Craig Ibbotson; 13 Guy Adams. Subs: 14 Gareth Naylor for Banks (25); 15 Chris Heywood for Munton (45); 16 Junior Henderson for Ibbotson (37); 17 Nicky Dobson for Coleman (11); Ibbotson for Morphet (72); Banks for Howcroft (59).
Try: Wainwright (79); **Goal:** Naylor.
CENTURIONS: 1 Neil Turley; 2 David Ingram; 3 Paul Anderson; 4 Liam Bretherton; 5 David Jones; 6 Simon Svabic; 7 Willie Swann; 8 Andy Leathem; 9 John Duffy; 10 David Whittle; 11 Phil Kendrick; 12 Adam Bristow; 13 Chris Morley. Subs: 14 Tim Street for Whittle (27); 15 Simon Baldwin for Bristow (52); 16 Jason Johnson for Jones (13); 17 Martin Roden for Duffy (31); Duffy for Turley (60); Whittle for Leathem (59).
Tries: Svabic (13), Kendrick (21, 45), Morley (37), Johnson (38, 74), Ingram (47, 62), Turley (52), Whittle (64); **Goals:** Svabic 5.
League Express Men of the Match:
Hawks: Neil Bradbrook; *Centurions:* Phil Kendrick.
Penalty count: 4-12; **Half-time:** 0-20; **Referee:** Steve Nicholson (Whitehaven); **Attendance:** 1,274.

Friday 13th April 2001

BARROW BORDER RAIDERS 50 CHORLEY LYNX 18

BORDER RAIDERS: 1 Danny Lockhart; 2 Adrian Gardner; 3 Phil Atkinson; 4 Brett McDermott; 5 Shane Irabor; 6 Darren Holt; 7 Anthony Murray; 8 Damien Whitter; 9 Dave Clark; 10 Ian Rawlinson; 11 Matthew Leigh; 12 Mike Whitehead; 13 Gary Charlton. Subs: 14 Geoff Luxon for Clark (30); 15 Mike Kavanagh for Rawlinson (25); 16 Tau Liku for Whitter (18); 17 Stewart Rhodes for Whitehead (40); Rawlinson for Luxon (61).
Tries: Whitter (3), Whitehead (7), Atkinson (10), Leigh (15, 57, 75), Holt (18), Rhodes (61), Murray (66);
Goals: Holt 7.
LYNX: 1 Matthew Brown; 2 Gary Doherty; 3 Darren Geritas; 4 Stuart Dickinson; 5 Graham Taberner; 6 Neil Alexander; 7 Chris Ramsdale; 8 Lee Prest; 9 Lee Maiden; 10 Lee Westwood; 11 Phil Harrison; 12 Wayne Bloor; 13 Ian Talbot. Subs: 14 Paul Wilcock for Doherty (23); 15 Luke Vincent not used; 16 Andy Horrobin for Prest (50); 17 Rob Verrelli for Westwood (67).
Tries: Maiden (39), Taberner (40), Dickinson (47);
Goals: Talbot 3.
League Express Men of the Match:
Border Raiders: Matthew Leigh; *Lynx:* Phil Harrison.
Penalty count: 4-2; **Half-time:** 28-12;
Referee: Graeme Shaw (Wigan); **Attendance:** 627.

LEIGH CENTURIONS 26 WIDNES VIKINGS 22

CENTURIONS: 1 Neil Turley; 2 David Ingram; 3 Paul Anderson; 4 Liam Bretherton; 5 Michael Watts; 6 Simon Svabic; 7 Willie Swann; 8 Tim Street; 9 John Hamilton; 10 David Bradbury; 11 Simon Baldwin; 12 Chris Morley; 13 Adam Bristow. Subs: 14 David Whittle for Street (23BB, rev 63); 15 Andy Leathem for Bradbury (52); 16 Phil Kendrick for Morley (55); 17 John Duffy for Hamilton (35); Hamilton for Duffy (68); Morley for Kendrick (73BB).
Tries: Morley (9), Baldwin (37), Bristow (54), Turley (72); **Goals:** Svabic 5.
VIKINGS: 1 Paul Atcheson; 2 Phil Coussons; 3 Chris Percival; 4 Jason Demetriou; 5 Damian Munro; 6 Martin Crompton; 7 Ian Watson; 8 Simon Knox; 9 Phil Cantillon; 10 Stephen Holgate; 11 Steve Gee; 12 Sean Richardson; 13 Tommy Hodgkinson. Subs: 14 Richard Agar for Watson (64); 15 Chris McKinney for Hodgkinson (64); 16 Joe Faimalo for Gee (55); 17 Matthew Long for Knox (31); Knox for Long (56).
Tries: Richardson (2), Atcheson (67), Crompton (75);
Goals: Watson 5.
League Express Men of the Match:
Centurions: Adam Bristow; *Vikings:* Sean Richardson.
Penalty count: 13-8; **Half-time:** 14-12;
Referee: Nick Oddy (Halifax); **Attendance:** 4,914.

OLDHAM 10 ROCHDALE HORNETS 38

OLDHAM: 1 Danny Arnold; 2 Joey Hayes; 3 Anthony Gibbons; 4 Pat Rich; 5 Warren Barrow; 6 David Gibbons; 7 Neil Roden; 8 Jason Clegg; 9 John Hough; 10 Leo Casey; 11 Phil Farrell; 12 Paul Norton; 13 Ian Sinfield. Subs: 14 Gavin Dodd for Barrow (41); 15 Daryl Lacey for Hough (55); 16 Chris Farrell for Sinfield (41); 17 Andy Procter for Casey (27); Sinfield for Clegg (55); Clegg for Procter (72).
Try: P Farrell (74); **Goals:** Rich 3.
HORNETS: 1 Paul Owen; 2 Sean Cooper; 3 Brendan O'Meara; 4 Matt Calland; 5 Marlon Billy; 6 Danny Wood; 7 Latham Tawhai; 8 Danny Sculthorpe; 9 Darren Robinson; 10 Andy Ireland; 11 David Stephenson; 12 James Bunyan; 13 Dave Watson. Subs: 14 Warren Ayres for Billy (55); 15 Martin Bunce for Ireland (30); 16 Wes Rogers for Calland (49); 17 David Larder for Stephenson (14); Ireland for Watson (62BB); Stephenson for Sculthorpe (68).
Tries: Watson (9, 27), Bunyan (40), Cooper (43), Calland (45), Owen (62); **Goals:** Wood 7.
League Express Men of the Match:
Oldham: Jason Clegg; *Hornets:* Danny Sculthorpe.
Penalty count: 7-5; **Half-time:** 4-22;
Referee: Steve Presley (Castleford); **Attendance:** 2,398.

WHITEHAVEN 38 WORKINGTON TOWN 18

WHITEHAVEN: 1 Paul O'Neill; 2 Jonathan Wignall; 3 David Seeds; 4 Howard Hill; 5 Mark Wallace; 6 Leroy Joe; 7 Steve Kirkbride; 8 Mark Cox; 9 Aaron Lester; 10 Dean Vaughan; 11 Gary Smith; 12 Ian Devlin; 13 Spencer Miller. Subs: 14 Lee Kiddie for Joe (37); 15 Robert Purdham for Devlin (59); 16 Ryan Campbell for Seeds (78); 17 Phil Sherwen for Cox (54).
Tries: Hill (5, 15, 60), Miller (20, 35), O'Neill (63), Lester (77); **Goals:** Kirkbride 5.
TOWN: 1 Lynton Stott; 2 Jonathan Heaney; 3 Neil Frazer; 4 Leigh Smith; 5 Graeme Lewthwaite; 6 Tane Manihera; 7 Lee Allen; 8 Hitro Okesene; 9 Owen Williamson; 10 Matt Sturm; 11 Jamie Beaumont; 12 Anthony Samuel; 13 Kevin Hetherington. Subs: 14 Fata Sini for Hetherington (57); 15 Matthew Tunstall for Smith (62); 16 Lokeni Savelio for Okesene (30); 17 Craig Rumney for Williamson (62); Okesene for Savelio (70); Smith for Heaney (72).
Tries: L Smith (41), Williamson (47), Stott (71);
Goals: Manihera 3.
League Express Men of the Match:
Whitehaven: Dean Vaughan; *Town:* Tane Manihera.
Penalty count: 5-4; **Half time:** 24-0;
Referee: Julian King (St Helens); **Attendance:** 1,795.

BATLEY BULLDOGS 14 DEWSBURY RAMS 12

BULLDOGS: 1 Craig Lingard; 2 Jeremy Dyson; 3 Danny Maun; 4 Roger Simpson; 5 Paul Gleadhill; 6 Andy Heptinstall; 7 Glen Tomlinson; 8 Lee Kelly; 9 Andy Heptinstall; 10 Paul Hicks; 11 Gary Shillabeer; 12 Will Cartledge; 13 Ryan Horsley. Subs: 14 Mark Cass for Simpson (68); 15 Craig Wright for Richards (58); 16 Jeff Wittenberg for Kelly (22); 17 Craig Richards for Hicks (44); Hicks for Wright (72).
Tries: Lingard (45, 49, 61); **Goal:** Dyson.
RAMS: 1 Nathan Graham; 2 Richard Baker; 3 Gavin Wood; 4 Kevin Crouthers; 5 Adrian Flynn; 6 Mark Cain; 7 Barry Eaton; 8 Robin Jowitt; 9 Richard Pachniuk; 10 Ryan McDonald; 11 Andy Fisher; 12 Andrew Spink; 13 Damian Ball. Subs: 14 David Mycoe for Cain (62); 15 Matthew Griffin for Graham (68); 16 Kevin Spink not used; 17 Simon Hicks for McDonald (30).
Tries: Flynn (13), Fisher (21); **Goals:** Eaton 2.
League Express Men of the Match:
Bulldogs: Craig Lingard; *Rams:* Barry Eaton.
Penalty count: 10-3; **Half-time:** 0-12;
Referee: Paul Lee (Leigh); **Attendance:** 1,571.

FEATHERSTONE ROVERS 23 HULL KINGSTON ROVERS 16

ROVERS: 1 Michael Rhodes; 2 Jamie Stokes; 3 Steve Dooler; 4 Gavin Swinson; 5 Matt Bramald; 6 Andy Bastow; 7 Jamie Rooney; 8 Craig Booth; 9 Richard Chapman; 10 Gary Lord; 11 Danny Evans; 12 Neil Lowe; 13 Paul Darley. Subs: 14 Richard Thaler for Swinson (33); 15 Stuart Dickens for Booth (23); 16 Gavin Morgan for Lord (25); 17 Ricky Helliwell for Evans (50); Lord for Morgan (57).
Tries: Stokes (6), Lowe (26, 64), Dooler (46);
Goals: Rooney 3; **Field goal:** Rooney.
ROBINS: 1 Bob Everitt; 2 Chris Kitching; 3 Paul Fletcher; 4 Whetu Taewa; 5 Gavin Molloy; 6 Jimmy Walker; 7 Scott Yeaman; 8 Richard Wilson; 9 Mike Dixon; 10 Rich Hayes; 11 Richard Slater; 12 Matt Schultz; 13 Chris Charles. Subs: 14 Mick Crane for Dixon (ht); 15 Allan Dunham for Schultz (34); 16 Jon Aston for Wilson (19BB); 17 David Luckwell for Hayes (50).
Tries: Charles (29), Everitt (56), Walker (59);
Goals: Charles 2.
On report: Incident (62) - late tackle on Rooney.
League Express Men of the Match:
Rovers: Jamie Stokes; *Robins:* Chris Charles.
Penalty count: 6-5; **Half-time:** 10-6; **Referee:** Steve Nicholson (Whitehaven); **Attendance:** 2,065.

HUNSLET HAWKS 30 YORK 14

HAWKS: 1 George Raynor; 2 Hamish Munton; 3 Iain Higgins; 4 Michael Wainwright; 5 Chris Heywood; 6 Jermaine Coleman; 7 Craig Robinson; 8 Michael Banks; 9 Tony Howcroft; 10 Craig Morphet; 11 Neil Bradbrook; 12 Craig Ibbotson; 13 Guy Adams. Subs: 14 Gareth Naylor for Heywood (56); 15 Ben Skerrett for Banks (26); 16 Andy Atha for Coleman (50); 17 Nicky Dobson for Adams (ht); Adams for Bradbrook (40BB, rev 61); Adams for Bradbrook (71).
Tries: Ibbotson (5), Adams (9), Howcroft (32), Wainwright (60), Atha (80); **Goals:** Robinson 5.
YORK: 1 Matthew Mulholland; 2 Simon Wray; 3 Craig Moore; 4 Luke Billyeald; 5 Phil Musgrove; 6 Mark Spears; 7 Danny Waite; 8 Scott Acklam; 9 Alan Pallister; 10 Andy Hutchinson; 11 Ryan Hardy; 12 Darren Crake; 13 Mick Ramsden. Subs: 14 Gareth Oulton not used; 15 John Williams for Pallister (25); 16 Lee Bardauskas for Billyeald (7); 17 Nathan Pincher for Acklam (27); Billyeald for Crake (73).
Tries: Acklam (16), Bardauskas (24), Moore (55);
Goal: Waite.

Sin bin: Pallister (61) - lying on.
League Express Men of the Match:
Hawks: Craig Ibbotson; *York:* Mark Spears.
Penalty count: 11-5; **Half-time:** 18-10;
Referee: Steve Addy (Huddersfield); **Attendance:** 612.

KEIGHLEY COUGARS 22 SWINTON LIONS 26

COUGARS: 1 James Rushforth; 2 Craig Horne; 3 Gareth Hooson; 4 Graeme Hallas; 5 Jason Lee; 6 Craig Murdock; 7 Chris Robinson; 8 Michael Slicker; 9 Jason Ramshaw; 10 Alan Boothroyd; 11 Paul Harrison; 12 Jim Leatham; 13 Danny Seal. Subs: 14 Matt Walker for Harrison (30); 15 Karl Smith for Horne (47); 16 Phil Stephenson for Boothroyd (48); 17 James Walker for Slicker (50); Harrison for Ramshaw (60); Boothroyd for Stephenson (75).
Tries: Lee (5), Robinson (21), Hallas (44), Leatham (53); **Goals:** Lee 3.
LIONS: 1 Wayne English; 2 Matt Bateman; 3 Mick Nanyn; 4 Andy Cheetham; 5 Jim Evans; 6 Phil Waring; 7 Shaun Furey; 8 Jon-Paul Doherty; 9 Rob Barraclough; 10 Lee Hansen; 11 Phil Cushion; 12 Carlo Napolitano; 13 Paul Smith. Subs: 14 Danny Butler for Hansen (68); 15 Chris Newall for Napolitano (35); 16 Adrian Mead for Bateman (70); 17 Dale Holdstock for Doherty (55); Doherty for Furey (68); Bateman for Nanyn (78).
Tries: Smith (2), Cushion (28), Cheetham (30), Bateman (64); **Goals:** Nanyn 4; **Field goals:** Waring 2.
League Express Men of the Match:
Cougars: Jim Leatham; *Lions:* Mick Nanyn.
Penalty count: 5-3; **Half-time:** 10-18;
Referee: Colin Morris (Huddersfield); **Attendance:** 1,719.

SHEFFIELD EAGLES 28 DONCASTER DRAGONS 4

EAGLES: 1 Andy Poynter; 2 Paul Wells; 3 Neil Kite; 4 Steve Walker; 5 Ian Thompson; 6 Gavin Brown; 7 Scott Rhodes; 8 Steve Hill; 9 Andy Speak; 10 Darren Summerill; 11 Chris Chapman; 12 Richard Goddard; 13 Wayne Flynn. Subs: 14 Mark Aston for Brown (70); 15 Andy Brent for Summerill (25); 16 Billy Kershaw for Thompson (28); 17 Jack Howieson for Hill (54).
Tries: Kite (2, 52), Rhodes (33), Chapman (59), Walker (77); **Goals:** Goddard 4.
DRAGONS: 1 Lee Maher; 2 Carl Hall; 3 Paul Mansson; 4 Simon Irving; 5 Anton Garcia; 6 Craig Weston; 7 Paddy Handley; 8 Ian Ramskill; 9 Peter Edwards; 10 Maea David; 11 Tony Miller; 12 Tony Fella; 13 Craig Lawton. Subs: 14 Chris Allen for Miller (60); 15 Alan Langham for Atter (55); 16 Tony Atter for Ramskill (26); 17 Dean Coulton for Edwards (68); Ramskill for David (72).
Try: Irving (21).
League Express Men of the Match:
Eagles: Gavin Brown; *Dragons:* Paddy Handley.
Penalty count: 3-4; **Half-time:** 12-4; **Referee:** Richard Silverwood (Dewsbury); **Attendance:** 1,632.

WEEK 20

Sunday 15th April 2001

SWINTON LIONS 0 LEIGH CENTURIONS 40

LIONS: 1 Wayne English; 2 Matt Bateman; 3 Mick Nanyn; 4 Jim Evans; 5 Adrian Mead; 6 Phil Waring; 7 Shaun Furey; 8 Jon-Paul Doherty; 9 Rob Barraclough; 10 Lee Hansen; 11 Phil Cushion; 12 Carlo Napolitano; 13 Paul Smith. Subs: 14 Danny Butler for Evans (50); 15 Dale Holdstock for Napolitano (28); 16 Chris Newall for Holdstock (37); 17 Nick Cammann for Mead (63); Evans for Furey (57); Napolitano for Doherty (58); Doherty for Smith (67BB).
CENTURIONS: 1 Neil Turley; 2 Michael Watts; 3 Paul Anderson; 4 Liam Bretherton; 5 David Jones; 6 Simon Svabic; 7 Willie Swann; 8 Tim Street; 9 Martin Roden; 10 David Whittle; 11 Simon Baldwin; 12 Phil Kendrick; 13 Adam Bristow. Subs: 14 Paul Norman for Whittle (30); 15 John Hamilton for Roden (24); 16 David Bradbury for Street (24); 17 Jason Johnson for Swann (54); Street for Norman (61); Roden for Hamilton (65).
Tries: Baldwin (25), Swann (29), Norman (34), Jones (53), Bretherton (57), Kendrick (64), Roden (70), Turley (75); **Goals:** Svabic 4.
League Express Men of the Match:
Lions: Wayne English; *Centurions:* David Bradbury.
Penalty count: 6-12; **Half-time:** 0-14;
Referee: Graeme Shaw (Wigan); **Attendance:** 1,892.

Monday 16th April 2001

DONCASTER DRAGONS 15 FEATHERSTONE ROVERS 21

DRAGONS: 1 Lee Maher; 2 Carl Hall; 3 Craig Weston; 4 Simon Irving; 5 Anton Garcia; 6 Paul Mansson; 7 Paddy Handley; 8 Ian Ramskill; 9 Peter Green; 10 Maea David; 11 Tony Miller; 12 Craig Lawton; 13 Peter Edwards. Subs: 14 Mick Coult for Lawton (67); 15 Tony Fella for Ramskill (28); 16 Alan Langham for Fella (61); 17 Tony Atter not used.
Tries: Lowe (5), Edwards (29); **Goals:** Irving 3; **Field goal:** Mansson.
ROVERS: 1 Michael Rhodes; 2 Jamie Stokes; 3 Steve Dooler; 4 Matt Turner; 5 Matt Bramald; 6 Andy Bastow; 7 Jamie Rooney; 8 Gary Lord; 9 Richard Chapman; 10 Craig Booth; 11 Danny Evans; 12 Neil Lowe; 13 Paul Darley. Subs: 14 Richard Thaler for Dooler (44); 15 Ricky Helliwell for Evans (53); 16 Gavin Morgan for Lord (28); 17 Stuart Dickens for Booth (26); Dooler for Turner (49BB, rev 53); Booth for Morgan (68); Evans for Darley (79).
Tries: Lowe (22), Bramald (40, 51), Stokes (70); **Goals:** Rooney 2; **Field goal:** Rooney.
League Express Men of the Match:
Dragons: Paul Mansson; *Rovers:* Neil Lowe.
Penalty count: 13-10; **Half-time:** 12-12;
Referee: Colin Morris (Huddersfield); **Attendance:** 1,426.

HULL KINGSTON ROVERS 17 KEIGHLEY COUGARS 10

ROVERS: 1 Bob Everitt; 2 Gavin Molloy; 3 Chris Kitching; 4 Whetu Taewa; 5 Richard Anderson; 6 Jimmy Walker; 7 Scott Yeaman; 8 Jon Aston; 9 Steve Cochrane; 10 Rich Hayes; 11 Richard Slater; 12 Paul Fletcher; 13 Chris Charles. Subs: 14 Mick Crane not used; 15 Mark Blanchard for Kitching (67); 16 Allan Dunham for Luckwell (56); 17 David Luckwell for Aston (18); Luckwell for Fletcher (71).
Tries: Kitching (3), Walker (33), Blanchard (76); **Goals:** Charles 2; **Field goal:** Walker.
COUGARS: 1 James Rushforth; 2 Gareth Hooson; 3 Karl Smith; 4 Ian Hughes; 5 Jason Lee; 6 Chris Robinson; 7 Nathan Antonik; 8 Michael Slicker; 9 Jason Ramshaw; 10 Alan Boothroyd; 11 Paul Harrison; 12 Jim Leatham; 13 Matt Walker. Subs: 14 Danny Seal for Rushforth (18BB, rev 40); 15 Craig Murdock for Robinson (50); 16 Phil Stephenson for Slicker (54); 17 James Walker for Boothroyd (56); Seal for Leatham (53).
Tries: Harrison (12), Antonik (24); **Goal:** Lee.
Sin bin: Smith (55) - holding down.
League Express Men of the Match:
Rovers: Rich Hayes; *Cougars:* Nathan Antonik.
Penalty count: 7-3; **Half-time:** 12-10; **Referee:** Karl Kirkpatrick (Warrington); **Attendance:** 1,910.

WIDNES VIKINGS 34 OLDHAM 16

VIKINGS: 1 Paul Atcheson; 2 Phil Coussons; 3 Chris Percival; 4 Jason Demetriou; 5 Mark Forster; 6 Richard Agar; 7 Martin Crompton; 8 Simon Knox; 9 Phil Cantillon; 10 Stephen Holgate; 11 Steve Gee; 12 Sean Richardson; 13 Tommy Hodgkinson. Subs: 14 Damian Munro for Forster (40); 15 Chris McKinney for Gee (19); 16 Joe Faimalo for Knox (55); 17 Matthew Long for Holgate (18); Gee for McKinney (65); Knox for Long (70).
Tries: Cantillon (25, pen, 65), Demetriou (45), Gee (50), Percival (53), Agar (57); **Goals:** Agar 5.
OLDHAM: 1 Gavin Dodd; 2 Joey Hayes; 3 Anthony Gibbons; 4 Pat Rich; 5 Daryl Lacey; 6 Neil Roden; 7 Mike Ford; 8 Jason Clegg; 9 John Hough; 10 Paul Norton; 11 Phil Farrell; 12 Ian Sinfield; 13 David Gibbons. Subs: 14 Gareth Barber for Ford (71); 15 Danny Arnold for Hough (48); 16 Chris Farrell for Clegg (62); 17 Andy Procter for Norton (35); Clegg for Sinfield (69).
Tries: A Gibbons (5), Dodd (19), D Gibbons (37); **Goals:** Rich 2.
League Express Men of the Match:
Vikings: Richard Agar; *Oldham:* Neil Roden.
Penalty count: 7-7; **Half-time:** 6-16; **Referee:** Steve Nicholson (Whitehaven); **Attendance:** 4,072.

WORKINGTON TOWN 29 BARROW BORDER RAIDERS 6

TOWN: 1 Lynton Stott; 2 Jonathan Heaney; 3 Neil Frazer; 4 Kevin Hetherington; 5 Graeme Lewthwaite; 6 Tane Manihera; 7 Lee Allen; 8 Matthew Tunstall; 9 Owen Williamson; 10 Hitro Okesene; 11 Jamie Beaumont; 12 Matt Sturm; 13 Anthony Samuel. Subs: 14 Fata Sini for Savelio (64); 15 Lokeni Savelio for Tunstall (21); 16 Leigh Smith for Stott (ht); 17 Craig Rumney for Allen (74); Tunstall for Okesene (51); Okesene for Sturm (74).
Tries: Stott (11), Lewthwaite (14, 75), Hetherington (24); **Goals:** Manihera 5, Hetherington; **Field goal:** Manihera.
BORDER RAIDERS: 1 Danny Lockhart; 2 Adrian Gardner; 3 Phil Atkinson; 4 Brett McDermott; 5 Shane Irabor; 6 Darren Holt; 7 Anthony Murray; 8 Damien Whitter; 9 Mike Kavanagh; 10 Ian Rawlinson; 11 Matthew Leigh; 12 Stewart Rhodes; 13 Gary Charlton. Subs: 14 Jamie Marshall for Lockhart (ht); 15 Geoff Luxon for Rawlinson (26); 16 Tau Liku for Whitter (ht); 17 Mike Whitehead for Atkinson (26); Whitter for Liku (55).
Try: Irabor (65); **Goal:** Holt.
Sin bin: Charlton (69) - persistent holding down.
League Express Men of the Match:
Town: Anthony Samuel; *Border Raiders:* Darren Holt.
Penalty count: 12-8; **Half-time:** 21-2; **Referee:** Richard Silverwood (Dewsbury); **Attendance:** 1,103.

YORK 6 BATLEY BULLDOGS 20

YORK: 1 Matthew Mulholland; 2 Simon Wray; 3 Craig Moore; 4 Ryan Hardy; 5 Aaron Campbell; 6 Mark Spears; 7 Danny Waite; 8 Neil Harmon; 9 Alan Pallister; 10 Andy Hutchinson; 11 Mick Ramsden; 12 Darren Crake; 13 Robert Roberts. Subs: 14 Gareth Oulton for Waite (46); 15 Jon Gwilliam for Pallister (20); 16 Paul Couch for Hutchinson (26); 17 Mick Hagan not used; Hutchinson for Crake (49); Pallister for Gwilliam (56); Crake for Harmon (64).
Try: Moore (73); **Goal:** Oulton.
BULLDOGS: 1 Craig Lingard; 2 Jeremy Dyson; 3 Danny Maun; 4 Simon Jackson; 5 Paul Gleadhill; 6 Richard Price; 7 Glen Tomlinson; 8 Lee Kelly; 9 Andy Heptinstall; 10 Paul Hicks; 11 Gary Shillabeer; 12 Will Cartledge; 13 Ryan Horsley. Subs: 14 Mark Cass for Heptinstall (57); 15 Craig Wright for Hicks (45); 16 Davide Longo for Jackson (62); 17 Jeff Wittenberg for Kelly (27); Kelly for Cartledge (68).
Tries: Gleadhill (5), Jackson (18), Wittenberg (43, 64); **Goals:** Dyson 2.
Sin bin: Shillabeer (69) – holding down.
League Express Men of the Match:
York: Neil Harmon; *Bulldogs:* Glen Tomlinson.
Penalty count: 12-8; **Half-time:** 0-8;
Referee: Ian Chatterton (Huddersfield); **Attendance:** 498.

GATESHEAD THUNDER 22 DEWSBURY RAMS 33

THUNDER: 1 Michael Johnson; 2 Paul Thorman; 3 Wes McGibbon; 4 Gareth Lloyd; 5 Leon Williamson; 6 Darren Callaghan; 7 Carl Briggs; 8 Gareth Barron; 9 Roy Southernwood; 10 Andy Grundy; 11 Jim Carlton; 12 Richard Mervill; 13 Chris Parker. Subs: 14 Stephen Rutherford for Grundy (37); 15 Andy Field for Southernwood (42); 16 Lee Garside for Barron (32); 17 Paul Sebine for Lloyd (59); Grundy for Garside (65); Barron for Carlton (69).
Tries: Barron (13), Lloyd (24), Carlton (26), Field (60); **Goals:** Briggs 3.
RAMS: 1 Matthew Griffin; 2 Richard Baker; 3 Gavin Wood; 4 Kevin Crouthers; 5 Adrian Flynn; 6 Mark Cain; 7 Barry Eaton; 8 Ryan McDonald; 9 Richard Pachniuk; 10 Simon Hicks; 11 Andy Fisher; 12 Andrew Spink; 13 Damian Ball. Subs: 14 David Mycoe for Cain (71); 15 Shayne Williams for McDonald (25); 16 Kevin Spink for Crouthers (ht); 17 Nathan Graham for Wood (25).
Tries: Crouthers (31, 78), Ball (33), Graham (35), Eaton (55), Baker (70); **Goals:** Eaton 4; **Field goal:** Eaton.
League Express Men of the Match:
Thunder: Richard Mervill; *Rams:* Kevin Crouthers.
Penalty count: 7-7; **Half-time:** 16-10;
Referee: Ronnie Laughton (Barnsley); **Attendance:** 469.

CHORLEY LYNX 10 WHITEHAVEN 42

LYNX: 1 Neil Alexander; 2 Paul Wilcock; 3 Darren Geritas; 4 Stuart Dickinson; 5 Graham Taberner; 6 Chris Ramsdale; 7 Stuart Fisher; 8 Rob Verrelli; 9 Lee Ashton; 10 Lee Westwood; 11 Phil Harrison; 12 Wayne Bloor; 13 Ian Talbot. Subs: 14 Lee Maiden for Taberner (17); 15 Luke Vincent for Talbot (39BB, rev 48); 16 Mike Prescott for Harrison (31); 17 Lee Prest for Verrelli (24BB); Verrelli for Westwood (52); Westwood for Verrelli (61BB); Vincent for Geritas (62); Harrison for Prest (69); Geritas for Maiden (73).
Tries: Wilcock (47), Dickinson (55); **Goal:** Talbot.
WHITEHAVEN: 1 Paul O'Neill; 2 Jonathan Wignall; 3 David Seeds; 4 Howard Hill; 5 Mark Wallace; 6 Lee Kiddie; 7 Steve Kirkbride; 8 Mark Cox; 9 Aaron Lester; 10 Dean Vaughan; 11 Gary Smith; 12 Ian Devlin; 13 Spencer Miller. Subs: 14 Leroy Joe for Kirkbride (25); 15 Robert Purdham for Miller (58); 16 Ryan Campbell for Devlin (68); 17 Phil Sherwen for Vaughan (34); Vaughan for Cox (54); Kirkbride for Kiddie (72).
Tries: Kiddie (16), Seeds (26, 41), Devlin (36), Joe (44, 62), Hill (67), Kirkbride (74); **Goals:** O'Neill 4, Kirkbride.
League Express Men of the Match:
Lynx: Wayne Bloor; *Whitehaven:* Leroy Joe.
Penalty count: 2-5; **Half-time:** 0-12;
Referee: Paul Lee (Leigh); **Attendance:** 295.

Tuesday 17th April 2001

ROCHDALE HORNETS 46 SHEFFIELD EAGLES 8

HORNETS: 1 Paul Owen; 2 Sean Cooper; 3 Brendan O'Meara; 4 Matt Calland; 5 Marlon Billy; 6 Danny Wood; 7 Latham Tawhai; 8 Danny Sculthorpe; 9 Darren Robinson; 10 Andy Ireland; 11 David Larder; 12 James Bunyan; 13 Dave Watson. Subs: 14 Warren Ayres for Robinson (70); 15 Martin Bunce for Ireland (31); 16 Wes Rogers for Watson (56); 17 Ben Simpson for O'Meara (68); Ireland for Sculthorpe (64).
Tries: Tawhai (9), Bunyan (20), Robinson (31, 53), Watson (50), Wood (70), Billy (80); **Goals:** Wood 9.
EAGLES: 1 Andy Poynter; 2 Paul Wells; 3 Neil Kite; 4 Steve Walker; 5 Gareth Hewitt; 6 Gavin Brown; 7 Scott Rhodes; 8 Steve Hill; 9 Gareth Dobson; 10 Darren Summerill; 11 Chris Chapman; 12 Richard Goddard; 13 Wayne Flynn. Subs: 14 Mark Aston for Rhodes (41); 15 Matthew Foster for Poynter (37); 16 Billy Kershaw for Hill (24); 17 Jack Howieson for Summerill (24); Hill for Howieson (56); Summerill for Foster (68).
Try: Hewitt (45); **Goals:** Goddard 2.
League Express Men of the Match:
Hornets: Latham Tawhai; *Eagles:* Richard Goddard.
Penalty count: 10-8; **Half-time:** 20-4;
Referee: Nick Oddy (Halifax); **Attendance:** 1,101.

WEEK 21

Sunday 22nd April 2001

BARROW BORDER RAIDERS 20 GATESHEAD THUNDER 12

BORDER RAIDERS: 1 Danny Lockhart; 2 Adrian Gardner; 3 Matthew Leigh; 4 Brett McDermott; 5 Shane Irabor; 6 Chris Massey; 7 Darren Holt; 8 Damien Whitter; 9 Anthony Murray; 10 Ian Rawlinson; 11 Geoff Luxon; 12 Stuart Rhodes; 13 Gary Charlton. Subs: 14 Mike Kavanagh for Lockhart (35); 15 Willie Burns for Luxon (61); 16 Steve Jackson for Whitter (26); 17 Mike Whitehead for Charlton (45); Whitter for Jackson (50); Charlton for Whitehead (55).
Tries: Irabor (12), McDermott (67), Holt (73); **Goals:** Holt 4.
THUNDER: 1 Michael Johnson; 2 Andy Field; 3 Wes McGibbon; 4 Gareth Lloyd; 5 Leon Williamson; 6 Darren Callaghan; 7 Carl Briggs; 8 Gareth Barron; 9 Roy Southernwood; 10 Andy Grundy; 11 Jim Carlton; 12 Richard Mervill; 13 Chris Parker. Subs: 14 Paul Thorman for Southernwood (40); 15 Stephen Rutherford for McGibbon (55); 16 Lee Garside for Grundy (24); 17 Paul Sebine for Mervill (35).
Tries: Thorman (52), Callaghan (61); **Goals:** Briggs 2.
League Express Men of the Match:
Border Raiders: Damien Whitter; *Thunder:* Gareth Lloyd.

Penalty count: 6-3; **Half-time:** 8-0;
Referee: Paul Lee (Leigh); **Attendance:** 689.

BATLEY BULLDOGS 8 OLDHAM 9

BULLDOGS: 1 Craig Lingard; 2 Jeremy Dyson; 3 Danny Maun; 4 Davide Longo; 5 Paul Gleadhill; 6 Richard Price; 7 Glen Tomlinson; 8 Lee Kelly; 9 Mark Cass; 10 Paul Hicks; 11 Gary Shillabeer; 12 Will Cartledge; 13 Ryan Horsley. Subs: 14 Paul Reilly for Price (60); 15 Craig Wright for Kelly (40); 16 Jeff Wittenberg for Hicks (32); 17 Craig Richards for Kelly (20BB, rev 39); Hicks for Shillabeer (57); Price for Gleadhill (74).
Tries: Shillabeer (35), Dyson (54).
Sin bin: Longo (11) - holding down.
OLDHAM: 1 Gavin Dodd; 2 Joey Hayes; 3 Anthony Gibbons; 4 Pat Rich; 5 Daryl Lacey; 6 Neil Roden; 7 Mike Ford; 8 Andy Procter; 9 Keith Brennan; 10 Jason Clegg; 11 Phil Farrell; 12 Ian Sinfield; 13 David Gibbons. Subs: 14 Lee Doran for Guest (65); 15 Kevin Mannion for Dodd (62); 16 Chris Farrell not used; 17 Danny Guest for Proctor (32).
Try: Brennan (20); **Goals:** Rich 2; **Field goal:** Dodd.
League Express Men of the Match:
Bulldogs: Jeff Wittenberg; *Oldham:* Mike Ford.
Penalty count: 7-2; **Half-time:** 4-9;
Referee: Graeme Shaw (Wigan); **Attendance:** 962.

FEATHERSTONE ROVERS 18 ROCHDALE HORNETS 20

ROVERS: 1 Michael Rhodes; 2 Jamie Stokes; 3 Richard Thaler; 4 Matt Turner; 5 Matt Bramald; 6 Andy Bastow; 7 Jamie Rooney; 8 Gary Lord; 9 Richard Chapman; 10 Craig Booth; 11 Danny Evans; 12 Neil Lowe; 13 Paul Darley. Subs: 14 Steve Dooler for Thaler (74); 15 Stuart Dickens for Evans (73); 16 Gavin Morgan for Booth (24); 17 Ricky Helliwell for Lord (14BB); Lord for Morgan (73); Booth for Darley (76).
Tries: Lowe (36), Turner (41), Bramald (45);
Goals: Rooney 3.
HORNETS: 1 Paul Owen; 2 Sean Cooper; 3 Brendan O'Meara; 4 Matt Calland; 5 Marlon Billy; 6 Danny Wood; 7 Latham Tawhai; 8 Danny Sculthorpe; 9 Darren Robinson; 10 Andy Ireland; 11 David Larder; 12 James Bunyan; 13 Dave Watson. Subs: 14 Warren Ayres not used; 15 Martin Bunce for Ireland (26); 16 Wes Rogers not used; 17 Rob Hall for Sculthorpe (76); Ireland for O'Meara (36).
Tries: Ireland (8), Sculthorpe (16), Calland (21), Billy (58); **Goals:** Wood 2.
On report: Calland (39) - high tackle.
League Express Men of the Match:
Rovers: Richard Chapman; *Hornets:* David Larder.
Penalty count: 9-5; **Half-time:** 8-16;
Referee: Peter Taberner (Wigan); **Attendance:** 1,746.

KEIGHLEY COUGARS 60 CHORLEY LYNX 18

COUGARS: 1 James Rushforth; 2 Gareth Hooson; 3 Karl Smith; 4 Graeme Hallas; 5 Jason Lee; 6 Matt Walker; 7 Craig Murdock; 8 Michael Slicker; 9 Jason Ramshaw; 10 Alan Boothroyd; 11 Paul Harrison; 12 Ian Hughes; 13 Jim Leatham. Subs: 14 Danny Seal for Slicker (24); 15 David Best for Rushforth (47); 16 Phil Stephenson for Boothroyd (26); 17 James Walker for Leatham (47); Boothroyd for J Walker (75).
Tries: Rushforth (13), Hooson (25, 47, 65), Murdock (29, 77), Hughes (36, 67), Harrison (54), Seal (59), D Best (61); **Goals:** Lee 3, J Walker 5.
LYNX: 1 Matthew Brown; 2 Simon Warhurst; 3 Darren Geritas; 4 Stuart Dickinson; 5 Paul Wilcock; 6 Chris Ramsdale; 7 Stuart Fisher; 8 Lee Prest; 9 Lee Ashton; 10 Rob Verrelli; 11 Mike Prescott; 12 Luke Vincent; 13 Ian Talbot. Subs: 14 Warren Hindle for Prest (55); 15 Phil Harrison for Verrelli (28BB); 16 Karl Jones for Ramsdale (6BB, rev 21); 17 Lee Maiden for Ashton (75); Jones for Ramsdale (48); Prest for Fisher (69).
Tries: Wilcock (39, 46), Dickinson (80);
Goals: Fisher 2, Talbot.
League Express Men of the Match:
Cougars: Jason Ramshaw; *Lynx:* Paul Wilcock.
Penalty count: 4-2; **Half-time:** 22-6;
Referee: Julian King (St Helens); **Attendance:** 1,501.

LEIGH CENTURIONS 32 DEWSBURY RAMS 18

CENTURIONS: 1 Neil Turley; 2 David Ingram; 3 Paul Anderson; 4 Phil Kendrick; 5 Michael Watts; 6 Simon Svabic; 7 Willie Swann; 8 Andy Leathem; 9 John Hamilton; 10 David Bradbury; 11 Simon Baldwin; 12 Chris Morley; 13 Adam Bristow. Subs: 14 Tim Street for Whittle (75); 15 David Whittle for Leathem (11); 16 Liam Bretherton for Svabic (58); 17 John Duffy for Hamilton (27); Svabic for Anderson (71).
Tries: Kendrick (13), Whittle (30), Turley (32), Morley (53), Ingram (73); **Goals:** Svabic 6.
Sin bin: Kendrick (50) - fighting.
RAMS: 1 Nathan Graham; 2 Richard Baker; 3 Dan Potter; 4 Kevin Crouthers; 5 Adrian Flynn; 6 David Mycoe; 7 Barry Eaton; 8 Andy Fisher; 9 Richard Pachniuk; 10 Robin Jowitt; 11 Paul Smith; 12 Andrew Spink; 13 Damian Ball. Subs: 14 Mark Cain for Mycoe (40); 15 Kevin Spink not used; 16 Simon Hicks for McDonald (55); 17 Ryan McDonald for Jowitt (22); Jowitt for Fisher (69); McDonald for Ball (75).
Tries: Potter (47), A Spink (56), Flynn (65), Baker (77);
Goal: Eaton.
Sin bin: Eaton (50) - fighting.
League Express Men of the Match:
Centurions: Simon Svabic; *Rams:* Barry Eaton.
Penalty count: 9-2; **Half-time:** 22-0;
Referee: Colin Morris (Huddersfield); **Attendance:** 3,126.

SWINTON LIONS 19 DONCASTER DRAGONS 18

LIONS: 1 Wayne English; 2 Matt Bateman; 3 Mick Nanyn; 4 Robert Russell; 5 Andy Cheetham; 6 Jim Evans; 7 Phil Waring; 8 Jon-Paul Doherty; 9 Rob Barraclough; 10 Lee Hansen; 11 Phil Cushion; 12 Carlo Napolitano; 13 Chris Newall. Subs: 14 Danny Butler for Evans (31); 15 Mike Loughlin for Hansen (51); 16 Adrian Mead for Russell (61BB, rev 73); 17 Dale Holdstock for Napolitano (48); Napolitano for Cushion (55); Evans for Butler (60); Hansen for Loughlin (71).
Tries: Napolitano (18), Nanyn (25), Bateman (33), Russell (38); **Goal:** Nanyn; **Field goal:** Evans.
DRAGONS: 1 Lee Maher; 2 Mick Coult; 3 Anton Garcia; 4 Simon Irving; 5 Johnny Woodcock; 6 Craig Weston; 7 Paddy Handley; 8 Tony Fella; 9 Peter Edwards; 10 Maea David; 11 Tony Miller; 12 Craig Lawton; 13 Paul Mansson. Subs: 14 Peter Green for White (68); 15 Tony Atter for David (26); 16 Phil White for Miller (34); 17 Alan Langham for Fella (62).
Tries: Edwards (12), Irving (56), Maher (79);
Goals: Irving 3.
Sent off: Atter (72) - high tackle.
League Express Men of the Match:
Lions: Phil Waring; *Dragons:* Paul Mansson.
Penalty count: 9-5; **Half-time:** 18-8; **Referee:** Steve Nicholson (Whitehaven); **Attendance:** 674.

WHITEHAVEN 50 HUNSLET HAWKS 10

WHITEHAVEN: 1 Paul O'Neill; 2 Jonathan Wignall; 3 David Seeds; 4 Howard Hill; 5 Mark Wallace; 6 Lee Kiddie; 7 Leroy Joe; 8 Mark Cox; 9 Aaron Lester; 10 Dean Vaughan; 11 Gary Smith; 12 Ian Devlin; 13 Spencer Miller. Subs: 14 Steve Kirkbride for Joe (65); 15 Robert Purdham for Smith (58); 16 Garry Purdham for Devlin (22); 17 Phil Sherwen for Vaughan (32); Vaughan for Cox (65).
Tries: Joe (14, 55), Hill (31, 50), Lester (59, 73, 77), O'Neill (64), Wallace (68); **Goals:** O'Neill 7.
HAWKS: 1 George Raynor; 2 Chris Heywood; 3 Iain Higgins; 4 Michael Wainwright; 5 Hamish Munton; 6 Jermaine Coleman; 7 Craig Robinson; 8 Michael Banks; 9 Tony Howcroft; 10 Craig Morphet; 11 Neil Bradbrook; 12 Craig Ibbotson; 13 Guy Adams. Subs: 14 Gareth Naylor for Munton (48); 15 Ben Skerrett for Ibbotson (18); 16 Andy Atha for Bradbrook (56); 17 Nicky Dobson for Wainwright (65); Ibbotson for Banks (26); Banks for Morphet (56).
Tries: Coleman (17), Morphet (44); **Goal:** Robinson.
League Express Men of the Match:
Whitehaven: Garry Purdham; *Hawks:* Craig Robinson.
Penalty count: 8-2; **Half time:** 10-6;
Referee: Ronnie Laughton (Barnsley); **Attendance:** 785.

WIDNES VIKINGS 28 HULL KINGSTON ROVERS 0

VIKINGS: 1 Damian Munro; 2 Phil Coussons; 3 Chris Percival; 4 Jason Demetriou; 5 Liam Jones; 6 Richard Agar; 7 Martin Crompton; 8 Simon Knox; 9 Phil Cantillon; 10 Stephen Holgate; 11 Steve Gee; 12 Sean Richardson; 13 Tommy Hodgkinson. Subs: 14 Ian Watson for Crompton (56); 15 Chris McKinney for Hodgkinson (40); 16 Joe Faimalo for Knox (53); 17 Matthew Long for Holgate (19); Holgate for Long (63); Knox for Gee (70).
Tries: Crompton (14), Coussons (30), Munro (59), Cantillon (63, 73); **Goals:** Jones 3, Agar.
ROVERS: 1 Bob Everitt; 2 Jimmy Walker; 3 Matt Schultz; 4 Whetu Taewa; 5 Gavin Molloy; 6 Colin Carter; 7 Scott Yeaman; 8 Richard Wilson; 9 Mike Dixon; 10 Rich Hayes; 11 Richard Slater; 12 Paul Fletcher; 13 Chris Charles. Subs: 14 Richard Anderson for Carter (45); 15 Alasdair McLarron for Molloy (40); 16 Allan Dunham for Slater (60); 17 David Luckwell for Wilson (27); Wilson for Luckwell (63); Slater for Fletcher (70).
League Express Men of the Match:
Vikings: Simon Knox; *Rovers:* Mike Dixon.
Penalty count: 10-13; **Half-time:** 10-0;
Referee: Nick Oddy (Halifax); **Attendance:** 3,726.

YORK 10 WORKINGTON TOWN 60

YORK: 1 Matthew Mulholland; 2 Simon Wray; 3 Shaun Austerfield; 4 Craig Moore; 5 Aaron Campbell; 6 Robert Roberts; 7 Danny Waite; 8 Neil Harmon; 9 Alan Pallister; 10 Mick Hagan; 11 Mick Ramsden; 12 Darren Crake; 13 Lee Bardauskas. Subs: 14 Gareth Oulton for Pincher (60); 15 Paul Couch for Austerfield (52); 16 Luke Billyeald for Moore (52); 17 Nathan Pincher for Hagan (34).
Tries: Austerfield (2), Hagan (22); **Goal:** Roberts.
TOWN: 1 Lynton Stott; 2 Jonathan Heaney; 3 Neil Frazer; 4 Kevin Hetherington; 5 Graeme Lewthwaite; 6 Tane Manihera; 7 Lee Allen; 8 Matthew Tunstall; 9 Owen Williamson; 10 Hitro Okesene; 11 Jamie Beaumont; 12 Matt Sturm; 13 Anthony Samuel. Subs: 14 Fata Sini for Sturm (40); 15 Lokeni Savelio for Tunstall (24); 16 Stuart Hoyles for Samuel (60); 17 Leigh Smith for Stott (53); Tunstall for Okesene (64); Stott for Manihera (76).
Tries: L Allen (15), Frazer (28), Lewthwaite (32, 41, 50, 59, 80), Heaney (36, 61), Beaumont (38), Hetherington (47); **Goals:** Manihera 8.
League Express Men of the Match:
York: Lee Bardauskas; *Town:* Tane Manihera.
Penalty count: 6-7; **Half-time:** 10-32;
Referee: Steve Addy (Huddersfield); **Attendance:** 395.

Wednesday 25th April 2001

OLDHAM 23 DONCASTER DRAGONS 4

OLDHAM: 1 Gavin Dodd; 2 Joe McNicholas; 3 Anthony Gibbons; 4 Pat Rich; 5 Daryl Lacey; 6 Neil Roden; 7 Mike Ford; 8 Andy Procter; 9 Keith Brennan; 10 Jason Clegg; 11 Phil Farrell; 12 Ian Sinfield; 13 David Gibbons. Subs: 14 Chris Farrell for Sinfield (54); 15 Paul Norton for Procter (40); 16 Danny Guest for Clegg (51); 17 Kevin Mannion for Ford (40); Procter for Guest (72); Sinfield for Brennan (77).
Tries: McNicholas (30, 63), Roden (47), Sinfield (78);
Goals: Rich 3; **Field goal:** Brennan.
DRAGONS: 1 Lee Maher; 2 Anton Garcia; 3 Craig Lawton; 4 Simon Irving; 5 Johnny Woodcock; 6 Paul Mansson; 7 Paddy Handley; 8 Ian Ramskill; 9 Peter Edwards; 10 Maea David; 11 Tony Fella; 12 Tony Atter; 13 Brad Hepi. Subs: 14 Billy Conway for Handley (69); 15 Peter Green for Atter (52); 16 Alan Langham for Hannah (58); 17 Chris Hannah for Ramskill (23); Ramskill for David (69); Atter for Fella (74).
Try: Atter (1).
League Express Men of the Match:
Oldham: Keith Brennan; *Dragons:* Paul Mansson.
Penalty count: 5-4; **Half-time:** 4-4;
Referee: Steve Ganson (St Helens); **Attendance:** 1,171.

WEEK 22

Sunday 29th April 2001

DEWSBURY RAMS 16 WORKINGTON TOWN 22

RAMS: 1 Nathan Graham; 2 Richard Baker; 3 Dan Potter; 4 Kevin Crouthers; 5 Adrian Flynn; 6 David Mycoe; 7 Barry Eaton; 8 Robin Jowitt; 9 Richard Pachniuk; 10 Ryan McDonald; 11 Andrew Spink; 12 Paul Smith; 13 Kevin Spink. Subs: 14 Mark Cain for Mycoe (47); 15 Liam Tallon for K Spink (47); 16 Andy Fisher not used; 17 Simon Hicks for McDonald (25); McDonald for Hicks (61).
Tries: Pachniuk (57), Flynn (61); **Goals:** Eaton 4.
TOWN: 1 Lynton Stott; 2 Craig Fisher; 3 Neil Frazer; 4 Kevin Hetherington; 5 Fata Sini; 6 Tane Manihera; 7 Lee Allen; 8 Matthew Tunstall; 9 Owen Williamson; 10 Hitro Okesene; 11 Jamie Beaumont; 12 Matt Sturm; 13 Anthony Samuel. Subs: 14 Jamie Nixon for Sini (70); 15 Lokeni Savelio for Tunstall (23); 16 Stuart Hoyles for Beaumont (62); 17 Richard Bell not used; Tunstall for Savelio (62); Beaumont for Manihera (79).
Tries: L Allen (35), Beaumont (40), Sini (46), Hetherington (55); **Goals:** Manihera 3.
League Express Men of the Match:
Rams: Paul Smith; *Town:* Tane Manihera.
Penalty count: 10-4; **Half-time:** 4-14;
Referee: Steve Presley (Castleford); **Attendance:** 736.

HULL KINGSTON ROVERS 40 CHORLEY LYNX 6

ROVERS: 1 Bob Everitt; 2 Richard Anderson; 3 Matt Schultz; 4 Whetu Taewa; 5 Alasdair McLarron; 6 Jimmy Walker; 7 Colin Carter; 8 David Luckwell; 9 Mike Dixon; 10 Richard Wilson; 11 Rob Wilson; 12 Paul Fletcher; 13 Chris Charles. Subs: 14 Scott Yeaman for Carter (52); 15 Allan Dunham for Rob Wilson (29); 16 Richard Slater for Schultz (59); 17 Rich Hayes for Richard Wilson (35BB, rev 50); Rob Wilson for Fletcher (52); Fletcher for Dixon (67).
Tries: McLarron (6, 34, 63, 68), Carter (9), Anderson (28), Taewa (47, 57); **Goals:** Charles 4.
LYNX: 1 Matthew Brown; 2 Paul Wilcock; 3 Gary Lowe; 4 Stuart Dickinson; 5 Lee Bamber; 6 Neil Alexander; 7 Stuart Fisher; 8 Lee Prest; 9 Ian Talbot; 10 Mike Prescott; 11 Phil Harrison; 12 Luke Vincent; 13 Wayne Bloor. Subs: 14 Danny Winrow for Fisher (70); 15 Simon Tickle for Brown (30); 16 Warren Hindle for Harrison (20); 17 Rob Verrelli not used.
Try: Talbot (39); **Goal:** Talbot.
League Express Men of the Match:
Rovers: Alasdair McLarron; *Lynx:* Ian Talbot.
Penalty count: 6-4; **Half-time:** 20-6; **Referee:** Ronnie Laughton (Barnsley); **Attendance:** 1,314.

GATESHEAD THUNDER 7 FEATHERSTONE ROVERS 38

THUNDER: 1 Michael Johnson; 2 Andy Field; 3 Wes McGibbon; 4 Gareth Lloyd; 5 Leon Williamson; 6 Darren Callaghan; 7 Carl Briggs; 8 Gareth Barron; 9 Roy Southernwood; 10 Lee Garside; 11 Jim Carlton; 12 Stephen Bradley; 13 Chris Parker. Subs: 14 Paul Thorman for Southernwood (54); 15 Stephen Rutherford for Barron (47); 16 Paul Sebine for Garside (52); 17 Steve Hall for Williamson (71); Barron for Bradley (70); Garside for Rutherford (78).
Try: Briggs (20); **Goal:** Briggs; **Field goal:** Briggs.
ROVERS: 1 Michael Rhodes; 2 Jamie Stokes; 3 Steve Dooler; 4 Richard Thaler; 5 Matt Bramald; 6 Andy Bastow; 7 Jamie Rooney; 8 Craig Booth; 9 Richard Chapman; 10 Gary Lord; 11 Danny Evans; 12 Neil Lowe; 13 Paul Darley. Subs: 14 Stuart Dickens for Booth (28); 15 Ricky Helliwell for Evans (67); 16 Gavin Morgan for Lord (28); 17 Matt Turner not used; Booth for Morgan (67).
Tries: Thaler (5, 36), Rooney (15, 74), Lowe (50), Helliwell (70), Booth (78); **Goals:** Rooney 5.
League Express Men of the Match:
Thunder: Carl Briggs; *Rovers:* Jamie Rooney.
Penalty count: 11-8; **Half-time:** 7-16;
Referee: Nick Oddy (Halifax); **Attendance:** 487.

YORK 6 WHITEHAVEN 54

YORK: 1 Mike Hall; 2 Simon Wray; 3 Matthew Mulholland; 4 Shaun Austerfield; 5 Aaron Campbell; 6 Mark Spears; 7 Danny Waite; 8 Neil Harmon; 9 Alan Pallister; 10 Andy Hutchinson; 11 Mick Ramsden; 12 Darren Crake; 13 Lee Bardauskas. Subs: 14 Gareth Oulton for Waite (47); 15 Shane Cochrane for

Hutchinson (34); 16 Ricky Hall for Pallister (34); 17 Nathan Pincher for Crake (24); Hutchinson for Cochrane (55).
Try: R Hall (50); **Goal:** Oulton.
WHITEHAVEN: 1 Wesley Wilson; 2 Paul O'Neill; 3 David Seeds; 4 Howard Hill; 5 Mark Wallace; 6 Leroy Joe; 7 Steve Kirkbride; 8 Phil Sherwen; 9 Aaron Lester; 10 Dean Vaughan; 11 Spencer Miller; 12 Gary Smith; 13 Garry Purdham. Subs: 14 Lee Kiddie for Joe (50); 15 Robert Purdham for G Purdham (11); 16 Ryan Campbell for Miller (70); 17 Tony Cunningham for Vaughan (26).
Tries: Sherwen (4), Kirkbride (8, 45), R Purdham (17), Lester (22, 54), Wallace (30, 40), O'Neill (57), Seeds (68); **Goals:** O'Neill 7.
League Express Men of the Match:
York: Andy Hutchinson; *Whitehaven:* Phil Sherwen.
Penalty count: 9-9; **Half-time:** 0-32;
Referee: Graeme Shaw (Wigan); **Attendance:** 314.

OLDHAM 38 KEIGHLEY COUGARS 4

OLDHAM: 1 Gavin Dodd; 2 Joe McNicholas; 3 Anthony Gibbons; 4 Pat Rich; 5 Daryl Lacey; 6 David Gibbons; 7 Neil Roden; 8 Andy Procter; 9 Keith Brennan; 10 Jason Clegg; 11 Phil Farrell; 12 Ian Sinfield; 13 Kevin Mannion. Subs: 14 Gareth Barber for D Gibbons (64); 15 Paul Norton for Clegg (48); 16 Danny Guest for Procter (33); 17 Chris Farrell for Sinfield (48); Procter for Guest (68); Clegg for Norton (71BB); Sinfield for Brennan (75).
Tries: Brennan (4, 40), Dodd (53), A Gibbons (58, 68), Mannion (70); **Goals:** Rich 7.
COUGARS: 1 Gareth Davies; 2 Gareth Hobson; 3 Gareth Hooson; 4 Karl Smith; 5 Kris Kirk; 6 Mark Holker; 7 Jason Ramshaw; 8 Phil Stephenson; 9 Liam Walsh; 10 David Best; 11 James Simeunovich; 12 Luke Sellars; 13 Carlos Sanchez. Subs: 14 Martin Taylor for Sellars (4); 15 Lee Bowyer for Hobson (63); 16 Jason Best for Taylor (23); 17 Nathan Antonik not used; Taylor for Stephenson (57BB, rev 63); Taylor for Walsh (71).
Try: Davies (29).
Sin bin: Ramshaw (24) - dissent.
League Express Men of the Match:
Oldham: Keith Brennan; *Cougars:* Phil Stephenson.
Penalty count: 11-3; **Half-time:** 14-4;
Referee: Colin Morris (Huddersfield); **Attendance:** 1,815.

SHEFFIELD EAGLES 28 LEIGH CENTURIONS 34

EAGLES: 1 Matthew Foster; 2 Paul Wells; 3 Neil Kite; 4 Chris Campbell; 5 Bright Sodje; 6 Gavin Brown; 7 Scott Rhodes; 8 Steve Hill; 9 Gareth Dobson; 10 Ricky Wright; 11 Billy Kershaw; 12 Richard Goddard; 13 Wayne Flynn. Subs: 14 Mark Aston for Rhodes (45); 15 Chris Judge for Kershaw (23); 16 Ian Brown for Hill (32BB, rev 60); 17 Andy Brent for Wright (22); Kershaw for Goddard (61); Wright for Brent (62); I Brown for Dobson (76).
Tries: Chapman (11, 29), Flynn (45), Wright (65), Sodje (73); **Goals:** Goddard 2, G Brown 2.
CENTURIONS: 1 Liam Bretherton; 2 David Jones; 3 Jason Johnson; 4 Phil Kendrick; 5 Michael Watts; 6 Simon Svabic; 7 Willie Swann; 8 Tim Street; 9 John Duffy; 10 David Whittle; 11 David Bradbury; 12 Chris Morley; 13 Adam Bristow. Subs: 14 Paul Norman for Street (27); 15 John Hamilton for Duffy (27); 16 Lee Sanderson for Svabic (59); 17 Alan Cross for Jones (62); Street for Norman (69); Duffy for Whittle (70).
Tries: Bretherton (3), Duffy (15), Bristow (23), Bradbury (33), Swann (40), Hamilton (57); **Goals:** Svabic 5.
League Express Men of the Match:
Eagles: Bright Sodje; *Centurions:* David Whittle.
Penalty count: 8-7; **Half-time:** 10-30; **Referee:** Richard Silverwood (Dewsbury); **Attendance:** 1,614.

Wednesday 2nd May 2001

SWINTON LIONS 10 OLDHAM 33

LIONS: 1 Wayne English; 2 Matt Bateman; 3 Mick Nanyn; 4 Robert Russell; 5 Andy Cheetham; 6 Phil Waring; 7 Shaun Furey; 8 Jon-Paul Doherty; 9 Rob Barraclough; 10 Lee Hansen; 11 Phil Cushion; 12 Dale Holdstock; 13 Paul Smith. Subs: 14 Jim Evans for Furey (28BB, rev 36); 15 Mike Loughlin for Doherty (28); 16 Chris Newall for Holdstock (24BB); 17 Carlo Napolitano for Loughlin (60); Evans for Russell (41); Doherty for Newall (66).
Tries: Furey (17), Waring (50); **Goal:** Nanyn.
OLDHAM: 1 Gavin Dodd; 2 Joe McNicholas; 3 Anthony Gibbons; 4 Pat Rich; 5 Daryl Lacey; 6 David Gibbons; 7 Neil Roden; 8 Jason Clegg; 9 Keith Brennan; 10 Paul Norton; 11 Phil Farrell; 12 Kevin Mannion; 13 Chris Farrell. Subs: 14 John Hough for Brennan (32); 15 Andy Procter for Norton (24); 16 Danny Guest for Procter (50); 17 Ian Sinfield for Mannion (59); Norton for Clegg (50); Clegg for Guest (74); Procter for C Farrell (74BB).
Tries: Mannion (8, 37), Rich (14), McNicholas (29), Dodd (58), Roden (74); **Goals:** Rich 4; **Field goal:** Roden.
League Express Men of the Match:
Lions: Lee Hansen; *Oldham:* Neil Roden.
Penalty count: 4-2; **Half-time:** 4-21;
Referee: Peter Taberner (Wigan); **Attendance:** 1,014.

WEEK 23

Sunday 6th May 2001

BATLEY BULLDOGS 23 SHEFFIELD EAGLES 2

BULLDOGS: 1 Craig Lingard; 2 Jeremy Dyson; 3 Danny Maun; 4 Davide Longo; 5 Paul Reilly; 6 Richard Price; 7 Glen Tomlinson; 8 Alan Boothroyd; 9 Andy Heptinstall; 10 Paul Hicks; 11 Paul Harrison; 12 Will Cartledge; 13 Ryan Horsley. Subs: 14 Mark Cass for Heptinstall (68); 15 Craig Wright for Boothroyd (27); 16 Jeff Wittenberg for Cartledge (32); 17 Paul Lister for Wittenberg (47); Wittenberg for Hicks (53); Hicks for Lister (64BB, rev 76); Cartledge for Maun (66).
Tries: Tomlinson (3), Lingard (21, 39), Horsley (80);
Goals: Price 3; **Field goal:** Heptinstall.
EAGLES: 1 Matthew Foster; 2 Paul Wells; 3 Neil Kite; 4 Chris Chapman; 5 Bright Sodje; 6 Gavin Brown; 7 Mark Aston; 8 Steve Hill; 9 Gareth Dobson; 10 Ricky Wright; 11 Chris Judge; 12 Richard Goddard; 13 Wayne Flynn. Subs: 14 Ian Thompson for Wells (12); 15 Andy Brent for Hill (24BB, rev 52); 16 Jon Bruce for Wright (40); 17 Billy Kershaw for Brown (53); Wells for Foster (60); Wright for Bruce (67); Brown for Judge (74).
Goal: Goddard.
League Express Men of the Match:
Bulldogs: Craig Lingard; *Eagles:* Ian Thompson.
Penalty count: 7-14; **Half-time:** 16-2; **Referee:** Steve Nicholson (Whitehaven); **Attendance:** 693.

DONCASTER DRAGONS 82 YORK 4

DRAGONS: 1 Lee Maher; 2 Johnny Woodcock; 3 Carl Hall; 4 Simon Irving; 5 Anton Garcia; 6 Paul Mansson; 7 Paddy Handley; 8 Maea David; 9 Peter Edwards; 10 Tony Fella; 11 Tony Miller; 12 Craig Lawton; 13 Brad Hepi. Subs: 14 Wayne Green for Mansson (53); 15 Peter Green for Forsyth (50); 16 Craig Forsyth for David (24); 17 Ian Ramskill for Fella (38); David for Edwards (50); Forsyth for Ramskill (62).
Tries: David (2), Maher (11, 64), Edwards (15), Handley (18, 59), Hall (24), Mansson (45), T Miller (49), Lawton (50), Hepi (53), Ramskill (61), Woodcock (69), Forsyth (78); **Goals:** Irving 13.
YORK: 1 Mike Hall; 2 Simon Wray; 3 Lee Bardauskas; 4 Mark Spears; 5 Phil Musgrove; 6 Mark Dooley; 7 Danny Waite; 8 Neil Harmon; 9 Alan Pallister; 10 Andy Hutchinson; 11 Carl Bristow; 12 Nathan Pincher; 13 Mick Ramsden. Subs: 14 Matthew Mulholland not used; 15 Ricky Hall not used; 16 Shane Cochrane for Pincher (ht); 17 Darren Crake for Hutchinson (23); Pincher for M Hall (62).
Try: Musgrove (34).
League Express Men of the Match:
Dragons: Craig Lawton; *York:* Neil Harmon.
Penalty count: 6-7; **Half-time:** 32-4;
Referee: Paul Lee (Leigh); **Attendance:** 741.

FEATHERSTONE ROVERS 23 DEWSBURY RAMS 15

ROVERS: 1 Michael Rhodes; 2 Jamie Stokes; 3 Steve Dooler; 4 James Rushforth; 5 Matt Bramald; 6 Andy Bastow; 7 Jamie Rooney; 8 Craig Booth; 9 Richard Chapman; 10 Gary Lord; 11 Danny Evans; 12 Neil Lowe; 13 Paul Darley. Subs: 14 Richard Thaler for Dooler (40); 15 Ricky Helliwell for Darley (67); 16 Danny Seal for Lord (17); 17 Gavin Morgan for Booth (27); Dooler for Thaler (65); Lord for Evans (65).
Tries: Evans (15), Seal (55, 59), Morgan (65);
Goals: Rooney 3; **Field goal:** Rooney.
RAMS: 1 Matthew Griffin; 2 Richard Baker; 3 Dan Potter; 4 Kevin Crouthers; 5 Adrian Flynn; 6 Mark Cain; 7 Barry Eaton; 8 Andy Fisher; 9 Richard Pachniuk; 10 Robin Jowitt; 11 Ian Hughes; 12 Paul Smith; 13 Jim Leatham. Subs: 14 David Mycoe for Eaton (20); 15 Andrew Spink for McDonald (50); 16 Ryan McDonald for Jowitt (20); 17 Kevin Spink not used; Jowitt for Fisher (61).
Tries: Cain (26), Hughes (39), Crouthers (77);
Goal: Mycoe; **Field goal:** Mycoe.
League Express Men of the Match:
Rovers: Danny Seal; *Rams:* David Mycoe.
Penalty count: 8-4; **Half-time:** 4-10;
Referee: Steve Presley (Castleford); **Attendance:** 1,945.

KEIGHLEY COUGARS 26 HUNSLET HAWKS 24

COUGARS: 1 Kris Kirk; 2 Gareth Hobson; 3 Gareth Hooson; 4 Karl Smith; 5 Max Tomlinson; 6 Mark Holker; 7 Paul Ashton; 8 Phil Stephenson; 9 Jason Ramshaw; 10 Chris Hannah; 11 James Simeunovich; 12 David Best; 13 Johnny Williams. Subs: 14 Jason Best for Tomlinson (58); 15 Martin Taylor for Hannah (52); 16 Lee Bowyer not used; 17 Chris Hogg for Williams (25); Hannah for Stephenson (61); Williams for Holker (63); Tomlinson for D Best (67).
Tries: Hooson (2, 41), Ramshaw (24), Ashton (46), Smith (80); **Goals:** Holker 2, Ashton.
HAWKS: 1 George Raynor; 2 Chris Heywood; 3 Iain Higgins; 4 Michael Wainwright; 5 Hamish Munton; 6 Jermaine Coleman; 7 Craig Robinson; 8 Michael Banks; 9 Tony Howcroft; 10 Craig Morphet; 11 Mick Coyle; 12 Craig Ibbotson; 13 Guy Adams. Subs: 14 Ben Thompson for Banks (21); 15 Dave Jessey for Coyle (31BB, rev 47); 16 Andy Atha for Morphet (57); 17 Gareth Naylor for Adams (47BB); Jessey for Coyle (55); Banks for Ibbotson (53); Ibbotson for Banks (69); Banks for Jessey (72).
Tries: Raynor (9), Howcroft (17, 57), Naylor (66, 74);
Goals: Robinson 2.
League Express Men of the Match:
Cougars: Jason Ramshaw; *Hawks:* Tony Howcroft.
Penalty count: 6-6; **Half-time:** 10-10; **Referee:** Ronnie Laughton (Barnsley); **Attendance:** 1,465.

LEIGH CENTURIONS 58 HULL KINGSTON ROVERS 10

CENTURIONS: 1 Neil Turley; 2 David Ingram; 3 Paul Anderson; 4 Phil Kendrick; 5 Michael Watts; 6 Simon Svabic; 7 Willie Swann; 8 Tim Street; 9 John Hamilton; 10 David Bradbury; 11 Simon Baldwin; 12 Chris Morley; 13 Adam Bristow. Subs: 14 David Whittle for Street (26); 15 Andy Leathem for Bradbury (31); 16 John Duffy for Hamilton (29); 17 Liam Bretherton for Swann (55); Street for Morley (61); Bradbury for Baldwin (70).
Tries: Ingram (3, 38, 46, 75), Morley (17), Turley (23, 30, 48), Kendrick (40, 56), Anderson (68); **Goals:** Svabic 7.
ROVERS: 1 Bob Everitt; 2 Dean Andrews; 3 Jimmy Walker; 4 Whetu Taewa; 5 Alasdair McLarron; 6 Craig Murdock; 7 Colin Carter; 8 David Luckwell; 9 Mike Dixon; 10 Richard Wilson; 11 Richard Slater; 12 Paul Fletcher; 13 Chris Charles. Subs: 14 Allan Dunham for Dixon (15); 15 Chris Kitching for Fletcher (49); 16 Rob Wilson for Luckwell (23); 17 Jon Aston for Slater (23); Slater for Andrews (49); Fletcher for Carter (60).
Tries: Rob Wilson (34), Carter (53); **Goal:** Charles.
League Express Men of the Match:
Centurions: Simon Baldwin; *Rovers:* Chris Charles.
Penalty count: 5-1; **Half-time:** 34-4;
Referee: Peter Taberner (Wigan); **Attendance:** 3,410.

OLDHAM 36 BARROW BORDER RAIDERS 10

OLDHAM: 1 Gavin Dodd; 2 Joe McNicholas; 3 Anthony Gibbons; 4 Pat Rich; 5 Daryl Lacey; 6 David Gibbons; 7 Neil Roden; 8 Jason Clegg; 9 Keith Brennan; 10 Paul Norton; 11 Phil Farrell; 12 Kevin Mannion; 13 Chris Farrell. Subs: 14 Mark Sibson for Dodd (56); 15 Ian Sinfield for C Farrell (64); 16 Danny Guest for Clegg (53); 17 Bryan Henare for Norton (32); Norton for Mannion (71); Clegg for Henare (75).
Tries: Mannion (12), Lacey (28), A Gibbons (35), Henare (55), P Farrell (74), D Gibbons (78); **Goals:** Rich 6.
Sin bin: Guest (60) – late tackle on Holt.
On report: Guest (60) – same late tackle.
BORDER RAIDERS: 1 Chris Massey; 2 Adrian Gardner; 3 Matthew Leigh; 4 Brett McDermott; 5 Shane Irabor; 6 Darren Holt; 7 Mike Kavanagh; 8 Ian Rawlinson; 9 Anthony Murray; 10 Willie Burns; 11 Geoff Luxon; 12 Stewart Rhodes; 13 Gary Charlton. Subs: 14 Glen Hutton not used; 15 Damien Whitter for Burns (22); 16 Mike Whitehead for Rawlinson (26); 17 Steve Jackson for Whitter (69); Rawlinson for Luxon (47); Burns for Whitehead (64).
Tries: McDermott (42), A Gardner (52); **Goal:** Holt.
On report: Rhodes (8) – spear tackle.
League Express Men of the Match:
Oldham: Neil Roden; *Border Raiders:* Anthony Murray.
Penalty count: 7-7; **Half-time:** 14-2;
Referee: Julian King (St Helens); **Attendance:** 1,554.

ROCHDALE HORNETS 38 WORKINGTON TOWN 16

HORNETS: 1 Paul Owen; 2 Sean Cooper; 3 Brendan O'Meara; 4 Matt Calland; 5 Marlon Billy; 6 Danny Wood; 7 Latham Tawhai; 8 Danny Sculthorpe; 9 Darren Robinson; 10 Andy Ireland; 11 David Stephenson; 12 James Bunyan; 13 Dave Watson. Subs: 14 Steve Gartland for Billy (60); 15 Joe Berry for Ireland (29); 16 Wes Rogers for Calland (65); 17 David Larder for Robinson (23); Robinson for Stephenson (49); Ireland for Sculthorpe (70).
Tries: Larder (25), Sculthorpe (29), Calland (36), Billy (48, 59), Tawhai (51), Robinson (65); **Goals:** Wood 5.
TOWN: 1 Lynton Stott; 2 Jonathan Heaney; 3 Neil Frazer; 4 Kevin Hetherington; 5 Graeme Lewthwaite; 6 Craig Fisher; 7 Lee Allen; 8 Matthew Tunstall; 9 Owen Williamson; 10 Hitro Okesene; 11 Jamie Beaumont; 12 Matt Sturm; 13 Anthony Samuel. Subs: 14 Leigh Smith for Fisher (41); 15 Lokeni Savelio for Tunstall (29); 16 Stuart Hoyles for Okesene (60); 17 David Fletcher for Beaumont (70); Fisher for Williamson (69); Tunstall for Savelio (70).
Tries: Hetherington (7), Lewthwaite (55, 68);
Goals: Hetherington 2.
League Express Men of the Match:
Hornets: Latham Tawhai; *Town:* Graeme Lewthwaite.
Penalty count: 4-9; **Half-time:** 16-6;
Referee: Ian Smith (Oldham); **Attendance:** 1,067.

SWINTON LIONS 20 GATESHEAD THUNDER 8

LIONS: 1 Wayne English; 2 Andy Cheetham; 3 Mick Nanyn; 4 Matt Bateman; 5 Lee Hudson; 6 Phil Waring; 7 Shaun Furey; 8 Lee Hansen; 9 Rob Barraclough; 10 Phil Cushion; 11 Dale Holdstock; 12 Carlo Napolitano; 13 Paul Smith. Subs: 14 Rob Gallagher for Furey (58); 15 Jon-Paul Doherty for Napolitano (51); 16 Danny Butler for Barraclough (65); 17 Chris Newall for Cushion (54); Napolitano for Holdstock (72); Cushion for Hansen (78).
Tries: Smith (24), Cheetham (29, 78), Doherty (59);
Goals: Nanyn 2.
Sin bin: Holdstock (47) - off the ball incident.
THUNDER: 1 Michael Johnson; 2 Paul Thorman; 3 Wes McGibbon; 4 Gareth Lloyd; 5 Leon Williamson; 6 Darren Callaghan; 7 Carl Briggs; 8 Gareth Barron; 9 Roy Southernwood; 10 Lee Garside; 11 Jim Carlton; 12 Stephen Bradley; 13 Chris Parker. Subs: 14 Paul Sebine for Parker (65); 15 Stephen Rutherford for Southernwood (70); 16 Steve Hall for Garside (54); 17 Mark Wilkinson for Barron (36).
Try: Callaghan (72); **Goals:** Briggs 2.
League Express Men of the Match:
Lions: Rob Barraclough; *Thunder:* Carl Briggs.
Penalty count: 6-10; **Half-time:** 10-0;
Referee: Steve Addy (Huddersfield); **Attendance:** 614.

WHITEHAVEN 14 WIDNES VIKINGS 16

WHITEHAVEN: 1 Wesley Wilson; 2 Paul O'Neill; 3 David Seeds; 4 Howard Hill; 5 Mark Wallace; 6 Leroy Joe; 7 Steve Kirkbride; 8 Mark Cox; 9 Aaron Lester; 10 Dean Vaughan; 11 Spencer Miller; 12 Gary Smith; 13 Garry Purdham. Subs: 14 Lee Kiddie for Kirkbride (66); 15 Robert Purdham for Seeds (64BB, rev 76); 16 Ian Devlin for Hill (20); 17 Phil Sherwen for Cox (50); Kirkbride for Joe (66); Joe for Seeds (78); Cox for Vaughan (78).
Tries: Lester (12), Wallace (28), Miller (65);

Goal: Kirkbride.
VIKINGS: 1 Damian Munro; 2 Phil Coussons; 3 Chris Percival; 4 Jason Demetriou; 5 Mark Forster; 6 Richard Agar; 7 Ian Watson; 8 Simon Knox; 9 Phil Cantillon; 10 Stephen Holgate; 11 Steve Gee; 12 Sean Richardson; 13 Tommy Hodgkinson. Subs: 14 Craig Weston for Percival (58); 15 Mike Hill not used; 16 Joe Faimalo for Gee (62); 17 Matthew Long for Holgate (26); Percival for Watson (65).
Tries: Coussons (2), Demetriou (45), Munro (75);
Goals: Watson, Agar.
League Express Men of the Match:
Whitehaven: Wesley Wilson; *Vikings:* Ian Watson.
Penalty count: 10-4; **Half time:** 8-4;
Referee: Colin Morris (Huddersfield); **Attendance:** 1,239.

Wednesday 9th May 2001

BARROW BORDER RAIDERS 22 FEATHERSTONE ROVERS 38

BORDER RAIDERS: 1 Chris Massey; 2 Adrian Gardner; 3 Matthew Leigh; 4 Brett McDermott; 5 Shane Irabor; 6 Darren Holt; 7 Mike Kavanagh; 8 Tau Liku; 9 Anthony Murray; 10 Ian Rawlinson; 11 Stewart Rhodes; 12 Mike Whitehead; 13 Gary Charlton. Subs: 14 Glen Hutton not used; 15 Damien Whitter for Liku (19); 16 Geoff Luxon for Rawlinson (31); 17 Steve Jackson for Rhodes (52); Rawlinson for Whitter (52); Rhodes for Luxon (67).
Tries: McDermott (14, 32), Rawlinson (56), Murray (67);
Goals: Holt 3.
ROVERS: 1 Michael Rhodes; 2 Jamie Stokes; 3 Simon Jackson; 4 James Rushforth; 5 Matt Bramald; 6 Andy Bastow; 7 Jamie Rooney; 8 Gary Lord; 9 Richard Chapman; 10 Craig Booth; 11 Danny Evans; 12 Paul Darley; 13 Danny Seal. Subs: 14 Ricky Helliwell for Dickens (60); 15 Neil Lowe for Evans (34); 16 Gavin Morgan for Lord (24); 17 Stuart Dickens for Booth (24); Lord for Morgan (68); Booth for Darley (70).
Tries: Jackson (4), Chapman (8, 80), Rhodes (20), Rooney (22, 77), Bastow (29); **Goals:** Rooney 5.
League Express Men of the Match:
Border Raiders: Brett McDermott; *Rovers:* Jamie Rooney.
Penalty count: 6-4; **Half-time:** 10-24;
Referee: Graeme Shaw (Wigan); **Attendance:** 683.

DONCASTER DRAGONS 56 CHORLEY LYNX 20

DRAGONS: 1 Lee Maher; 2 Johnny Woodcock; 3 Carl Hall; 4 Simon Irving; 5 Anton Garcia; 6 Paul Mansson; 7 Paddy Handley; 8 Tony Fella; 9 Peter Edwards; 10 Tony Atter; 11 Tony Miller; 12 Craig Lawton; 13 Brad Hepi. Subs: 14 Mick Coult for Maher (15); 15 Billy Conway for Irving (65); 16 Phil White for Hepi (62); 17 Alan Langham for Atter (51); Atter for Fella (69).
Tries: Mansson (8, 41, 68), Hall (25, 74), Edwards (30, 62), Coult (34), Irving (48), Handley (58), Woodcock (71); **Goals:** Irving 5, Mansson.
LYNX: 1 Lee Bamber; 2 Paul Wilcock; 3 Matthew Brown; 4 Stuart Dickinson; 5 Gary Doherty; 6 Neil Alexander; 7 Stuart Fisher; 8 Lee Prest; 9 Chris Ramsdale; 10 Mike Prescott; 11 Phil Harrison; 12 Wayne Bloor; 13 Ian Talbot. Subs: 14 Danny Winrow for Ramsdale (41); 15 Luke Vincent for Fisher (52); 16 Lee Beresford for Harrison (62); 17 Steve Kelly for Prest (35); Prest for Kelly (59); Fisher for Prescott (69).
Tries: Wilcock (3, 12, 18), Bamber (44); **Goals:** Talbot 2.
League Express Men of the Match:
Dragons: Paul Mansson; *Lynx:* Paul Wilcock.
Penalty count: 3-8; **Half-time:** 20-16;
Referee: Colin Morris (Huddersfield); **Attendance:** 700.

KEIGHLEY COUGARS 4 WHITEHAVEN 30

COUGARS: 1 Chris Hogg; 2 Gareth Hobson; 3 Gareth Hooson; 4 Karl Smith; 5 Max Tomlinson; 6 Paul Ashton; 7 Jason Ramshaw; 8 Phil Stephenson; 9 Johnny Williams; 10 Chris Hannah; 11 David Best; 12 Kris Kirk; 13 James Simeunovich. Subs: 14 Andy Richardson for Kirk (25); 15 Craig Morphet for Stephenson (30); 16 Carlos Sanchez for Best (34); 17 Jon Gwilliam for Williams (50); Best for Richardson (53); Stephenson for Hannah (57); Kirk for Hogg (62BB).
Try: Hooson (4).
WHITEHAVEN: 1 Lee Kiddie; 2 Paul O'Neill; 3 Robert Purdham; 4 Ian Devlin; 5 Ryan Campbell; 6 Leroy Joe; 7 Steve Kirkbride; 8 Mark Cox; 9 Aaron Lester; 10 Dean Vaughan; 11 Spencer Miller; 12 Phil Sherwen; 13 Garry Purdham. Subs: 14 Paul Graham for Joe (73); 15 Darren King for Lester (76); 16 Tony Cunningham for Vaughan (74); 17 Gary Smith for Cox (55).
Tries: R Purdham (29, 50), Joe (32), Kirkbride (72), Devlin (79); **Goals:** Kirkbride 5.
League Express Men of the Match:
Cougars: Jason Ramshaw; *Whitehaven:* Leroy Joe.
Penalty count: 8-6; **Half-time:** 4-12; **Referee:** Richard Silverwood (Dewsbury); **Attendance:** 1,208.

LEIGH CENTURIONS 68 HUNSLET HAWKS 4

CENTURIONS: 1 Neil Turley; 2 David Ingram; 3 Paul Anderson; 4 Liam Bretherton; 5 Alan Cross; 6 Simon Svabic; 7 Lee Sanderson; 8 Andy Leathem; 9 John Hamilton; 10 Paul Norman; 11 Simon Baldwin; 12 Chris Morley; 13 Willie Swann. Subs: 14 Tim Street for Norman (28); 15 Jason Johnson for Svabic (50); 16 David Jones for Hamilton (65); 17 David Whittle for Leathem (31); Norman for Baldwin (72); Hamilton for Cross (74).
Tries: Ingram (10, 78), Anderson (14, 18), Sanderson (27, 37, 40, 50), Swann (43), Turley (54, 56, 62), Bretherton (65); **Goals:** Svabic 5, Sanderson 3.
HAWKS: 1 Michael Wainwright; 2 Chris Heywood; 3 Iain Higgins; 4 Dave Jessey; 5 Damian Reed; 6 Nicky Dobson; 7 Craig Robinson; 8 Mick Dowds; 9 Tony Howcroft; 10 Ben Skerrett; 11 Craig Ibbotson; 12 Andy Atha; 13 Mick Coyle. Subs: 14 George Raynor not used; 15 Gareth Naylor for Dowds (23); 16 Hamish Munton for Reed (41); 17 Ben Whiteman not used.
Try: Higgins (22).
League Express Men of the Match:
Centurions: Lee Sanderson; *Hawks:* Craig Ibbotson.
Penalty count: 4-5; **Half-time:** 32-4;
Referee: Nick Oddy (Halifax); **Attendance:** 1,951.

ROCHDALE HORNETS 32 HULL KINGSTON ROVERS 10

HORNETS: 1 Paul Owen; 2 Sean Cooper; 3 Brendan O'Meara; 4 Matt Calland; 5 Marlon Billy; 6 Danny Wood; 7 Latham Tawhai; 8 Danny Sculthorpe; 9 Warren Ayres; 10 Andy Ireland; 11 David Stephenson; 12 James Bunyan; 13 Dave Watson. Subs: 14 Steve Gartland for Calland (65); 15 Joe Berry for Ireland (23); 16 Wes Rogers for Ayres (57); 17 David Larder for Stephenson (23); Stephenson for Bunyan (33BB); Ireland for Sculthorpe (52); Ayres for Billy (71).
Tries: Calland (6), Billy (13, 39), Bunyan (20), Owen (22), Cooper (70); **Goals:** Wood 4.
ROVERS: 1 Bob Everitt; 2 Alex Godfrey; 3 Paul Fletcher; 4 Whetu Taewa; 5 Alasdair McLarron; 6 Chris Kitching; 7 Craig Murdock; 8 David Luckwell; 9 Steve Cochrane; 10 Richard Wilson; 11 Richard Slater; 12 Rob Wilson; 13 Chris Charles. Subs: 14 Dean Andrews for Rob Wilson (50); 15 Mark Blanchard not used; 16 Allan Dunham for Slater (39BB); 17 Jon Aston for Luckwell (23); Slater for Richard Wilson (63); Rob Wilson for Dunham (63).
Tries: Taewa (9), Cochrane (73); **Goal:** Charles.
League Express Men of the Match:
Hornets: Paul Owen; *Rovers:* Steve Cochrane.
Penalty count: 8-3; **Half-time:** 26-4;
Referee: Peter Taberner (Wigan); **Attendance:** 1,102.

WIDNES VIKINGS 72 GATESHEAD THUNDER 4

VIKINGS: 1 Damian Munro; 2 Phil Coussons; 3 Chris Percival; 4 Craig Weston; 5 Liam Jones; 6 Richard Agar; 7 Ian Watson; 8 Matthew Long; 9 Phil Cantillon; 10 Stephen Holgate; 11 Joe Faimalo; 12 Sean Richardson; 13 Tommy Hodgkinson. Subs: 14 Jason Demetriou for Coussons (59); 15 Simon Knox for Long (30); 16 Mike Hill for Holgate (40); 17 Steve Gee for Faimalo (65); Long for Knox (55); Holgate for Hodgkinson (72).
Tries: Coussons (1, 38), Cantillon (3, 58, 73, 79), Weston (6, 49), Faimalo (14), Percival (29, 35), Demetriou (62), Munro (70), Jones (77); **Goals:** Watson 8.
THUNDER: 1 Michael Johnson; 2 Paul Thorman; 3 Wes McGibbon; 4 Steve Hall; 5 Leon Williamson; 6 Darren Callaghan; 7 Carl Briggs; 8 Lee Garside; 9 Richard Spencer; 10 Andy Grundy; 11 Jim Carlton; 12 Stephen Bradley; 13 Mark Wilkinson. Subs: 14 Stephen Rutherford for Callaghan (32); 15 Paul Sebine for Briggs (53); 16 Roy Southernwood for Spencer (69); 17 Chris Parker for Grundy (32); Grundy for Williamson (69).
Try: Thorman (42).
League Express Men of the Match:
Vikings: Phil Cantillon; *Thunder:* Andy Grundy.
Penalty count: 6-5; **Half-time:** 36-0;
Referee: Paul Lee (Leigh); **Attendance:** 3,105.

OLDHAM 22 SWINTON LIONS 20

OLDHAM: 1 Mark Sibson; 2 Joe McNicholas; 3 Anthony Gibbons; 4 Pat Rich; 5 Daryl Lacey; 6 David Gibbons; 7 Neil Roden; 8 Paul Norton; 9 Keith Brennan; 10 Bryan Henare; 11 Phil Farrell; 12 Ian Sinfield; 13 Kevin Mannion. Subs: 14 Gavin Dodd not used; 15 Chris Farrell for Sinfield (45); 16 Andy Procter for Guest (59); 17 Danny Guest for Henare (36); Henare for Brennan (48); Sinfield for Henare (78); Guest for Norton (79).
Tries: McNicholas (6), P Farrell (10), Henare (26), A Gibbons (52); **Goals:** Rich 3.
LIONS: 1 Wayne English; 2 Adrian Mead; 3 Mick Nanyn; 4 Matt Bateman; 5 Lee Hudson; 6 Phil Waring; 7 Shaun Furey; 8 Lee Hansen; 9 Rob Barraclough; 10 Phil Cushion; 11 Dale Holdstock; 12 Ryan Stazicker; 13 Chris Newall. Subs: 14 Danny Butler for Furey (71); 15 Jon-Paul Doherty for Stazicker (34); 16 Andy Cheetham for English (27); 17 Nick Cammann for Hudson (53); Stazicker for Newall (58); Newall for Holdstock (69); English for Mead (74BB).
Tries: Mead (37), Doherty (48), Cheetham (61);
Goals: Nanyn 4.
League Express Men of the Match:
Oldham: David Gibbons; *Lions:* Jon-Paul Doherty.
Penalty count: 5-8; **Half-time:** 16-8;
Referee: Julian King (St Helens); **Attendance:** 1,360.

WEEK 24

Sunday 13th May 2001

BARROW BORDER RAIDERS 12 LEIGH CENTURIONS 28

BORDER RAIDERS: 1 Chris Massey; 2 Adrian Gardner; 3 Matthew Leigh; 4 Brett McDermott; 5 Shane Irabor; 6 Mike Kavanagh; 7 Darren Holt; 8 Tau Liku; 9 Anthony Murray; 10 Ian Rawlinson; 11 Stewart Rhodes; 12 Mike Whitehead; 13 Gary Charlton. Subs: 14 Glen Hutton for Kavanagh (38); 15 Geoff Luxon for Whitehead (13); 16 Steve Jackson for Liku (20); 17 Gareth Pratt for Luxon (78); Whitehead for Rawlinson (36); Rawlinson for Jackson (53).
Tries: Leigh (14), Hutton (73); **Goals:** Holt 2.
Sin bin: Holt (22) - punching;
Irabor and Holt (79) - fighting.
On report: Rawlinson (56) - fighting.
CENTURIONS: 1 Neil Turley; 2 David Ingram; 3 Paul Anderson; 4 Phil Kendrick; 5 Michael Watts; 6 Simon Svabic; 7 Liam Bretherton; 8 Tim Street; 9 John Hamilton; 10 David Bradbury; 11 Simon Baldwin; 12 Chris Morley; 13 Adam Bristow. Subs: 14 Andy Leathem for Street (25BB, rev 40); 15 Willie Swann for Bretherton (2BB, rev 18); 16 Jason Johnson for Morley (66); 17 Paul Norman for Bradbury (34); Swann for Turley (58BB, rev 70); Bradbury for Street (61).
Tries: Turley (12, 41), Bradbury (25), Street (60), Watts (77); **Goals:** Svabic 4.
Sin bin: Baldwin (53) - punching; Turley (79) - fighting.
On report: Street (56) - fighting.
League Express Men of the Match:
Border Raiders: Darren Holt; *Centurions:* Liam Bretherton.
Penalty count: 9-14; **Half-time:** 6-12; **Referee:** Steve Nicholson (Whitehaven); **Attendance:** 1,080.

CHORLEY LYNX 10 OLDHAM 60

LYNX: 1 Lee Bamber; 2 Paul Wilcock; 3 Gary Lowe; 4 Stuart Dickinson; 5 Graham Taberner; 6 Neil Alexander; 7 Stuart Fisher; 8 Lee Prest; 9 Chris Ramsdale; 10 Lee Westwood; 11 Mike Prescott; 12 Luke Vincent; 13 Ian Talbot. Subs: 14 Lee Birdseye for Dickinson (28); 15 Simon Tickle for Vincent (48); 16 Steve Argent for Prescott (38BB); 17 Paul Ridgway for Prest (28); Vincent for Ramsdale (56); Prest for Westwood (60); Dickinson for Taberner (72).
Tries: Alexander (14), Tickle (79); **Goal:** Talbot.
OLDHAM: 1 Mark Sibson; 2 Joe McNicholas; 3 Anthony Gibbons; 4 Pat Rich; 5 Daryl Lacey; 6 David Gibbons; 7 Neil Roden; 8 Jason Clegg; 9 John Hough; 10 Paul Norton; 11 Phil Farrell; 12 Bryan Henare; 13 Chris Farrell. Subs: 14 Gavin Dodd for D Gibbons (41); 15 Lee Doran for Clegg (38BB); 16 Danny Guest for C Farrell (33); 17 Ian Sinfield for P Farrell (48); C Farrell for A Gibbons (59); P Farrell for Henare (68).
Tries: Roden (3, 46), Rich (10), Henare (18), McNicholas (31, 52), Clegg (37), Sibson (39, 49, 77), C Farrell (61); **Goals:** Rich 8.
League Express Men of the Match:
Lynx: Paul Ridgway; *Oldham:* Neil Roden.
Penalty count: 5-6; **Half-time:** 4-30;
Referee: Julian King (St Helens); **Attendance:** 610.

DEWSBURY RAMS 19 KEIGHLEY COUGARS 9

RAMS: 1 Matthew Griffin; 2 Richard Baker; 3 Dan Potter; 4 Kevin Crouthers; 5 Adrian Flynn; 6 Dean Lawford; 7 Barry Eaton; 8 Andy Fisher; 9 Richard Pachniuk; 10 Jim Leatham; 11 Ian Hughes; 12 Paul Smith; 13 Damian Ball. Subs: 14 Mark Cain for Pachniuk (59); 15 Gavin Wood for Crouthers (79); 16 Ryan McDonald for Leatham (23); 17 Shayne Williams for Fisher (31); Fisher for Williams (54).
Tries: Flynn (37, 47), Crouthers (78); **Goals:** Eaton 3;
Field goal: Lawford.
COUGARS: 1 Chris Hogg; 2 Max Tomlinson; 3 Karl Smith; 4 Matthew Foster; 5 Gareth Hobson; 6 Mark Holker; 7 Gareth Hooson; 8 Craig Morphet; 9 Jason Ramshaw; 10 Chris Hannah; 11 David Best; 12 Kris Kirk; 13 James Simeunovich. Subs: 14 Jon Gwilliam for Holker (61); 15 Graeme Shaw for Kirk (30); 16 Andy Richardson for Shaw (53); 17 Carlos Sanchez for Morphet (20); Shaw for Hannah (58BB); Kirk for Best (69); Holker for Hogg (73).
Try: Holker (2); **Goals:** Holker 2; **Field goal:** Holker.
League Express Men of the Match:
Rams: Kevin Crouthers; *Cougars:* Mark Holker.
Penalty count: 6-5; **Half-time:** 6-8;
Referee: Peter Taberner (Wigan); **Attendance:** 1,052.

DONCASTER DRAGONS 27 SWINTON LIONS 26

DRAGONS: 1 Johnny Woodcock; 2 Mick Coult; 3 Carl Hall; 4 Simon Irving; 5 Anton Garcia; 6 Paul Mansson; 7 Paddy Handley; 8 Maea David; 9 Peter Edwards; 10 Tony Fella; 11 Tony Miller; 12 Craig Lawton; 13 Brad Hepi. Subs: 14 Peter Green for Hepi (26); 15 Phil White for Miller (63); 16 Tony Atter for David (8BB, rev 19); 17 Ian Ramskill for Fella (57BB, rev 65); Atter for Irving (42).
Tries: Mansson (28, 30), Edwards (55), Woodcock (80);
Goals: Irving 3, Mansson 2; **Field goal:** Irving.
On report: Mansson (75) - high tackle.
LIONS: 1 Andy Cheetham; 2 Lee Hudson; 3 Mick Nanyn; 4 Matt Bateman; 5 Nick Cammann; 6 Phil Waring; 7 Shaun Furey; 8 Jon-Paul Doherty; 9 Rob Barraclough; 10 Lee Hansen; 11 Ryan Stazicker; 12 Dale Holdstock; 13 Chris Newall. Subs: 14 Danny Butler for Waring (18); 15 Rob Gallagher for Furey (49); 16 Paul Smith for Holdstock (30); 17 Mike Loughlin for Stazicker (45); Holdstock for Newall (65); Stazicker for Smith (74).
Tries: Doherty (4), Smith (50, 65), Gallagher (73);
Goals: Nanyn 5.
League Express Men of the Match:
Dragons: Paul Mansson; *Lions:* Paul Smith.
Penalty count: 10-7; **Half-time:** 14-10;
Referee: Ronnie Laughton (Barnsley); **Attendance:** 819.

WIDNES VIKINGS 44 ROCHDALE HORNETS 18

VIKINGS: 1 Paul Atcheson; 2 Damian Munro; 3 Craig Weston; 4 Jason Demetriou; 5 Chris Percival; 6 Richard Agar; 7 Martin Crompton; 8 Simon Knox; 9 Phil Cantillon; 10 Stephen Holgate; 11 Steve Gee; 12 Sean Richardson; 13 Tommy Hodgkinson. Subs: 14 Ian Watson for Crompton (33); 15 Chris McKinney for Demetriou (49); 16 Joe Faimalo for Knox (37); 17 Matthew Long for Holgate (29); Holgate for Hodgkinson (59); Knox for Long (63).
Tries: Munro (3), Percival (20, 47, 75), Cantillon (26), Long (29, 62), Weston (52); **Goals:** Weston 6.
HORNETS: 1 Paul Owen; 2 Sean Cooper; 3 Brendan O'Meara; 4 Matt Calland; 5 Marlon Billy; 6 Danny Wood;

7 Latham Tawhai; 8 Danny Sculthorpe; 9 Warren Ayres; 10 Andy Ireland; 11 David Stephenson; 12 James Bunyan; 13 Dave Watson. Subs: 14 Steve Gartland for Stephenson (32); 15 Joe Berry for Wood (70); 16 Danny Fearon for Billy (55); 17 David Larder for Ayres (25); Wood for Bunyan (77).
Tries: Stephenson (16, 47), Calland (66), Bunyan (72); **Goal:** Gartland.
League Express Men of the Match:
Vikings: Chris Percival; *Hornets:* David Stephenson.
Penalty count: 6-9; **Half-time:** 24-4;
Referee: Steve Presley (Castleford); **Attendance:** 3,860.

WORKINGTON TOWN 25 BATLEY BULLDOGS 16

TOWN: 1 Lynton Stott; 2 Jonathan Heaney; 3 Neil Frazer; 4 John Allen; 5 Graeme Lewthwaite; 6 Kevin Hetherington; 7 Lee Allen; 8 Matthew Tunstall; 9 Owen Williamson; 10 Hitro Okesene; 11 Jamie Beaumont; 12 Matt Sturm; 13 Anthony Samuel. Subs: 14 Stuart Hoyles for Tunstall (34); 15 Lokeni Savelio for Okesene (23); 16 Carl Sice for Williamson (51); 17 Matthew Woodcock for Allen (40); Okesene for Savelio (66); Tunstall for Sturm (70).
Tries: Lewthwaite (7, 42), Woodcock (47), Sice (67);
Goals: Hetherington 4; **Field goal:** Stott.
BULLDOGS: 1 Craig Lingard; 2 Jeremy Dyson; 3 Paul Reilly; 4 Davide Longo; 5 Paul Gleadhill; 6 Richard Price; 7 Glen Tomlinson; 8 Craig Wright; 9 Andy Heptinstall; 10 Paul Hicks; 11 Paul Harrison; 12 Will Cartledge; 13 Ryan Horsley. Subs: 14 Mark Cass for Lingard (73); 15 Gary Shillabeer for Cartledge (48); 16 Jeff Wittenberg for Wright (26); 17 Paul Lister for Wright (67); Wright for Hicks (51).
Tries: Lingard (27, 67), Harrison (75); **Goals:** Price 2.
League Express Men of the Match:
Town: Anthony Samuel; *Bulldogs:* Glen Tomlinson.
Penalty count: 8-5; **Half-time:** 8-6;
Referee: Graeme Shaw (Wigan); **Attendance:** 832.

YORK 8 HULL KINGSTON ROVERS 56

YORK: 1 Mike Hall; 2 Simon Wray; 3 Matthew Mulholland; 4 Mark Spears; 5 Phil Musgrove; 6 Mark Dooley; 7 Gareth Oulton; 8 Darren Crake; 9 Alan Pallister; 10 Andy Hutchinson; 11 Carl Bristow; 12 Nathan Pincher; 13 Mick Ramsden. Subs: 14 Danny Waite for Pallister (40); 15 Chris Cooney for Mulholland (70); 16 Andy Innes for Pincher (59); 17 Shane Cochrane for Hutchinson (25); Hutchinson for Crake (32); Crake for Bristow (52); Pallister for Oulton (66BB).
Tries: Wray (48), Dooley (55).
ROVERS: 1 Bob Everitt; 2 Dean Andrews; 3 Matt Schultz; 4 Whetu Taewa; 5 Alex Godfrey; 6 Colin Carter; 7 Craig Murdock; 8 Richard Wilson; 9 Steve Cochrane; 10 Jon Aston; 11 Richard Slater; 12 Rob Wilson; 13 Chris Charles. Subs: 14 Mark Blanchard for Schultz (21); 15 Allan Dunham for Luckwell (62); 16 Paul Fletcher for Rob Wilson (26); 17 David Luckwell for Aston (26); Rob Wilson for Slater (52); Aston for Richard Wilson (60BB).
Tries: Godfrey (12, 17, 75), Everitt (30), Rob Wilson (34, 51), Fletcher (41), Dunham (65), Murdock (68), Blanchard (71); **Goals:** Charles 8.
League Express Men of the Match:
York: Andy Hutchinson; *Rovers:* Rob Wilson.
Penalty count: 8-10; **Half-time:** 0-24;
Referee: Nick Oddy (Halifax); **Attendance:** 656.

HUNSLET HAWKS 12 GATESHEAD THUNDER 40

HAWKS: 1 Michael Wainwright; 2 Chris Heywood; 3 Iain Higgins; 4 Dave Jessey; 5 George Raynor; 6 Nicky Dobson; 7 Craig Robinson; 8 Michael Banks; 9 Tony Howcroft; 10 Ben Skerrett; 11 Craig Ibbotson; 12 Andy Atha; 13 Mick Coyle. Subs: 14 Ben Thompson for Atha (19); 15 Hamish Munton for Howcroft (39BB, rev 53); 16 Gareth Naylor for Jessey (3); 17 Steve Pryce for Skerrett (32); Munton for Robinson (63); Skerrett for Pryce (55); Pryce for Ibbotson (70).
Tries: Ibbotson (21), Coyle (61);
Goals: Robinson, Higgins.
Sent off: Banks (12) - headbutting.
THUNDER: 1 Michael Johnson; 2 Paul Thorman; 3 Wes McGibbon; 4 Gareth Lloyd; 5 Leon Williamson; 6 Scott Dyson; 7 Carl Briggs; 8 Lee Garside; 9 Roy Southernwood; 10 Andy Grundy; 11 Jim Carlton; 12 Stephen Bradley; 13 Chris Parker. Subs: 14 Stephen Rutherford for Carlton (49); 15 Paul Sebine for Southernwood (55); 16 Steve Hall for Parker (ht); 17 Mark Wilkinson for Grundy (25); Carlton for Garside (66).
Tries: Carlton (10, 31, 47), Johnson (13, 54) Dyson (59), Thorman (80); **Goals:** Briggs 6.
League Express Man of the Match:
Hawks: Craig Ibbotson; *Thunder:* Jim Carlton.
Penalty count: 3-4; **Half-time:** 6-18;
Referee: Martin Dawber (Wigan); **Attendance:** 607.

SHEFFIELD EAGLES 14 FEATHERSTONE ROVERS 28

EAGLES: 1 Andy Poynter; 2 Bright Sodje; 3 Neil Kite; 4 Gareth Hewitt; 5 Ian Thompson; 6 Gavin Brown; 7 Scott Rhodes; 8 Jon Bruce; 9 Gareth Dobson; 10 Ricky Wright; 11 Chris Chapman; 12 Richard Goddard; 13 Wayne Flynn. Subs: 14 Mark Aston for Dobson (66); 15 Steve Hill for Wright (27); 16 Paul Wells for Chapman (30); 17 Billy Kershaw for Flynn (22); Wright for Kershaw (68).
Tries: Flynn (6), Kite (68); **Goals:** Goddard 3.
Sent off: Wright and Sodje (80) - fighting.
ROVERS: 1 Michael Rhodes; 2 Jamie Stokes; 3 Simon Jackson; 4 James Rushforth; 5 Matt Bramald; 6 Andy Bastow; 7 Jamie Rooney; 8 Craig Booth; 9 Richard Chapman; 10 Gary Lord; 11 Steve Dooler; 12 Ricky Helliwell; 13 Danny Seal. Subs: 14 Danny Evans for Lord (61); 15 Paul Darley for Helliwell (51); 16 Neil Lowe for Jackson (42); 17 Gavin Morgan for Booth (22); Booth for Morgan (72); Lord for Evans (76).
Tries: Seal (24), Rhodes (42), Stokes (55), Chapman (66); **Goals:** Rooney 6.
League Express Men of the Match:
Eagles: Jon Bruce; *Rovers:* Jamie Rooney.
Penalty count: 7-7; **Half-time:** 10-6;
Referee: Colin Morris (Huddersfield); **Attendance:** 1,296.

WEEK 25

Sunday 20th May 2001

BARROW BORDER RAIDERS 40 SWINTON LIONS 26

BORDER RAIDERS: 1 Jamie Marshall; 2 Glen Hutton; 3 Adrian Gardner; 4 Brett McDermott; 5 Shane Irabor; 6 Chris Massey; 7 Darren Holt; 8 Tau Liku; 9 Anthony Murray; 10 Ian Rawlinson; 11 Matthew Leigh; 12 Geoff Luxon; 13 Gary Charlton. Subs: 14 Gareth Pratt for Luxon (73); 15 Damien Whitter for Liku (20); 16 Steve Jackson for Rawlinson (30); 17 Mike Whitehead for Luxon (35); Luxon for Jackson (65).
Tries: Marshall (3), A Gardner (15, 79), Charlton (45), McDermott (49), Hutton (54), Murray (67); **Goals:** Holt 6.
LIONS: 1 Wayne English; 2 Jim Evans; 3 Mick Nanyn; 4 Matt Bateman; 5 Lee Hudson; 6 Phil Waring; 7 Shaun Furey; 8 Jon-Paul Doherty; 9 Rob Barraclough; 10 Lee Hansen; 11 Phil Cushion; 12 Dale Holdstock; 13 Phil Veivers. Subs: 14 Chris Newall for Cushion (37); 15 Rob Gallagher for English (50); 16 Paul Smith for Holdstock (25); 17 Mike Loughlin for Doherty (28).
Tries: English (6), Bateman (19), Waring (37), Barraclough (62), Smith (76); **Goals:** Nanyn 3.
League Express Men of the Match:
Border Raiders: Anthony Murray; *Lions:* Rob Barraclough.
Penalty count: 3-6; **Half-time:** 12-18;
Referee: Julian King (St Helens); **Attendance:** 602.

CHORLEY LYNX 10 ROCHDALE HORNETS 66

LYNX: 1 Lee Bamber; 2 Paul Wilcock; 3 Gary Lowe; 4 Stuart Dickinson; 5 Graham Taberner; 6 Lee Birdseye; 7 Stuart Fisher; 8 Lee Prest; 9 Peter Cahalin; 10 Steve Argent; 11 Phil Harrison; 12 Luke Vincent; 13 Wayne Bloor. Subs: 14 Simon Tickle for Vincent (60); 15 Ian Talbot for Bloor (31BB); 16 Lee Westwood for Argent (8BB, rev 16); 17 Paul Ridgway for Harrison (9); Westwood for Prest (34); Bloor for Ridgway (57); Prest for Argent (67); Vincent for Dickinson (72).
Tries: Talbot (39), Wilcock (65); **Goal:** Talbot.
HORNETS: 1 Paul Owen; 2 Sean Cooper; 3 Brendan O'Meara; 4 Wayne McHugh; 5 Marlon Billy; 6 Danny Wood; 7 Latham Tawhai; 8 Danny Sculthorpe; 9 David Stephenson; 10 Andy Ireland; 11 Wes Rogers; 12 David Larder; 13 Steve Gartland. Subs: 14 Warren Ayres for Stephenson (41); 15 Joe Berry for Ireland (21); 16 James Bunyan for Rogers (21); 17 Martin Bunce for Ireland (70); Ireland for Sculthorpe (60); Rogers for O'Meara (67).
Tries: Owen (10, 34, 55), Larder (15, 37), Berry (28, 45, 59), Gartland (33, 42), Wood (68), Tawhai (75), McHugh (78); **Goals:** Wood 7.
League Express Men of the Match:
Lynx: Peter Cahalin; *Hornets:* Latham Tawhai.
Penalty count: 8-6; **Half-time:** 6-32;
Referee: Ronnie Laughton (Barnsley); **Attendance:** 311.

DONCASTER DRAGONS 36 BATLEY BULLDOGS 10

DRAGONS: 1 Johnny Woodcock; 2 Mick Coult; 3 Carl Hall; 4 Anton Garcia; 5 Shane Miller; 6 Paul Mansson; 7 Paddy Handley; 8 Maea David; 9 Peter Edwards; 10 Tony Fella; 11 Tony Atter; 12 Craig Lawton; 13 Brad Hepi. Subs: 14 Billy Conway for Edwards (61); 15 Peter Green for Hepi (11BB, rev 25); 16 Gary Smith for Hall (67); 17 Craig Forsyth for David (56); Green for Hepi (61).
Tries: Mansson (6, 22), Garcia (17, 41), Atter (33), Lawton (73); **Goals:** Woodcock 6.
BULLDOGS: 1 Craig Lingard; 2 Jeremy Dyson; 3 Paul Reilly; 4 Roger Simpson; 5 Paul Gleadhill; 6 Richard Price; 7 Glen Tomlinson; 8 Alan Boothroyd; 9 Andy Heptinstall; 10 Paul Hicks; 11 Paul Harrison; 12 Gary Shillabeer; 13 Ryan Horsley. Subs: 14 Mark Cass for Reilly (19); 15 Craig Wright for Boothroyd (28); 16 Jeff Wittenberg for Shillabeer (28); 17 Will Cartledge for Wright (62); Shillabeer for Harrison (76).
Tries: Lingard (40), Simpson (59); **Goal:** Price.
Sin bin: Heptinstall (41) - interference at the play the ball; Tomlinson (47) - dissent; Dyson (64) - obstruction.
On report: Price (47) - late tackle.
League Express Men of the Match:
Dragons: Paul Mansson; *Bulldogs:* Craig Lingard.
Penalty count: 13-10; **Half-time:** 22-6;
Referee: Nick Oddy (Halifax); **Attendance:** 945.

HULL KINGSTON ROVERS 12 DEWSBURY RAMS 6

ROVERS: 1 Bob Everitt; 2 Alex Godfrey; 3 Dean Andrews; 4 Whetu Taewa; 5 Alasdair McLarron; 6 Colin Carter; 7 Craig Murdock; 8 Rich Hayes; 9 Steve Cochrane; 10 Richard Wilson; 11 Richard Slater; 12 Rob Wilson; 13 Chris Charles. Subs: 14 Mark Blanchard for McLarron (39); 15 Jon Aston for Richard Wilson (29); 16 Paul Fletcher for Slater (30); 17 David Luckwell for Hayes (46); Slater for Rob Wilson (34); Richard Wilson for Cochrane (74).
Tries: Carter (60), Godfrey (69); **Goals:** Charles 2.
RAMS: 1 Matthew Griffin; 2 Richard Baker; 3 Dan Potter; 4 Kevin Crouthers; 5 Adrian Flynn; 6 Dean Lawford; 7 Barry Eaton; 8 Andy Fisher; 9 Richard Pachniuk; 10 Jim Leatham; 11 Ian Hughes; 12 Paul Smith; 13 Damian Ball. Subs: 14 Mark Cain for Lawford (55BB, rev 64); 15 Ryan McDonald for Fisher (30); 16 Robin Jowitt for Spink (71); 17 Andrew Spink for Smith (36); Fisher for Leatham (48); Cain for Ball (70).
Try: Crouthers (7); **Goal:** Eaton.
Sin bin: Flynn (13) – dissent.
League Express Men of the Match:
Rovers: Bob Everitt; *Rams:* Dean Lawford.
Penalty count: 7-3; **Half-time:** 2-6; **Referee:** Steve Nicholson (Whitehaven); **Attendance:** 1,645.

LEIGH CENTURIONS 42 WHITEHAVEN 4

CENTURIONS: 1 David Ingram; 2 Alan Hadcroft; 3 Paul Anderson; 4 Phil Kendrick; 5 Michael Watts; 6 Liam Bretherton; 7 Lee Sanderson; 8 Paul Norman; 9 John Hamilton; 10 David Whittle; 11 Simon Baldwin; 12 Chris Morley; 13 Adam Bristow. Subs: 14 John Duffy for Hamilton (31); 15 Jason Johnson for Baldwin (67); 16 Andy Fairclough for Ingram (63); 17 David Bradbury for Norman (29); Hamilton for Sanderson (60); Norman for Whittle (67).
Tries: Morley (13, 34, 75), Watts (43), Baldwin (50), Anderson (67), Duffy (72);
Goals: Sanderson 4, Bretherton 3.
WHITEHAVEN: 1 Wesley Wilson; 2 Paul O'Neill; 3 David Seeds; 4 Robert Purdham; 5 Mark Wallace; 6 Lee Kiddie; 7 Steve Kirkbride; 8 Mark Cox; 9 Aaron Lester; 10 Dean Vaughan; 11 Spencer Miller; 12 Phil Sherwen; 13 Garry Purdham. Subs: 14 Marc Jackson for Campbell (41); 15 Chris Campbell for Wilson (8); 16 Ian Devlin for Kirkbride (41); 17 Gary Smith for Cox (34); Wilson for Miller (60); Kirkbride for Kiddie (72).
Try: G Purdham (54).
League Express Men of the Match:
Centurions: Chris Morley; *Whitehaven:* Spencer Miller.
Penalty count: 6-3; **Half-time:** 12-0;
Referee: Colin Morris (Huddersfield); **Attendance:** 2,409.

OLDHAM 24 WORKINGTON TOWN 18

OLDHAM: 1 Mark Sibson; 2 Joe McNicholas; 3 Anthony Gibbons; 4 Pat Rich; 5 Daryl Lacey; 6 Neil Roden; 7 Mike Ford; 8 Jason Clegg; 9 Keith Brennan; 10 Paul Norton; 11 Phil Farrell; 12 Bryan Henare; 13 Kevin Mannion. Subs: 14 John Hough for Ford (48); 15 Chris Farrell for Mannion (72); 16 Danny Guest for Clegg (52); 17 Ian Sinfield for Henare (79); Ford for Brennan (66); Clegg for Guest (73).
Tries: Sibson (19, 33), Brennan (22), Lacey (28);
Goals: Rich 4.
TOWN: 1 Lynton Stott; 2 Jonathan Heaney; 3 Neil Frazer; 4 Kevin Hetherington; 5 Graeme Lewthwaite; 6 Tane Manihera; 7 Lee Allen; 8 Matthew Tunstall; 9 Owen Williamson; 10 Hitro Okesene; 11 Stuart Hoyles; 12 Matt Sturm; 13 Anthony Samuel. Subs: 14 Steve Wood for Allen (66); 15 Lokeni Savelio for Tunstall (26); 16 Carl Sice for Williamson (53); 17 Matthew Woodcock for Heaney (35); Heaney for Lewthwaite (57BB, rev 73); Tunstall for Savelio (77).
Tries: Hetherington (14), Lewthwaite (49), Sice (60);
Goals: Manihera 3.
League Express Men of the Match:
Oldham: Paul Norton; *Town:* Lynton Stott.
Penalty count: 8-7; **Half-time:** 24-8;
Referee: Karl Kirkpatrick (Warrington);
Attendance: 1,276 *(at Spotland, Rochdale).*

WIDNES VIKINGS 25 FEATHERSTONE ROVERS 22

VIKINGS: 1 Paul Atcheson; 2 Damian Munro; 3 Craig Weston; 4 Jason Demetriou; 5 Chris Percival; 6 Richard Agar; 7 Ian Watson; 8 Simon Knox; 9 Phil Cantillon; 10 Stephen Holgate; 11 Steve Gee; 12 Sean Richardson; 13 Tommy Hodgkinson. Subs: 14 Phil Coussons for Munro (70); 15 Chris McKinney for Hodgkinson (55); 16 Joe Faimalo for Knox (48); 17 Matthew Long for Holgate (30); Knox for Long (57).
Tries: Munro (15), Weston (21), Demetriou (55), McKinney (65); **Goals:** Weston 4; **Field goal:** Agar.
ROVERS: 1 Michael Rhodes; 2 Jamie Stokes; 3 Simon Jackson; 4 James Rushforth; 5 Matt Bramald; 6 Andy Bastow; 7 Jamie Rooney; 8 Gary Lord; 9 Richard Chapman; 10 Craig Booth; 11 Steve Dooler; 12 Ricky Helliwell; 13 Danny Seal. Subs: 14 Danny Evans for Seal (40); 15 Neil Lowe for Dooler (34); 16 Stuart Dickens for Booth (25); 17 Gavin Morgan for Lord (25); Booth for Evans (74).
Tries: Morgan (45), Bramald (65), Stokes (71);
Goals: Rooney 5.
League Express Men of the Match:
Vikings: Simon Knox; *Rovers:* Richard Chapman.
Penalty count: 9-8; **Half-time:** 13-4;
Referee: Peter Taberner (Wigan); **Attendance:** 4,372.

SHEFFIELD EAGLES 40 HUNSLET HAWKS 10

EAGLES: 1 Andy Poynter; 2 Bright Sodje; 3 Neil Kite; 4 Gareth Hewitt; 5 Ian Thompson; 6 Gavin Brown; 7 Mark Aston; 8 Jon Bruce; 9 Gareth Dobson; 10 Steve Hill; 11 Chris Judge; 12 Billy Kershaw; 13 Richard Goddard. Subs: 14 Paul Wells for Kershaw (40); 15 Ricky Wright for Bruce (29); 16 Andy Brent for Hill (26); 17 Ian Brown for Goddard (40); Bruce for Brent (63); Hill for Wright (69).
Tries: Hill (8), Sodje (23), Brent (28), Aston (43), Hewitt (51), Wells (62), Poynter (65);
Goals: Goddard 3, G Brown 3.
HAWKS: 1 George Raynor; 2 Danny Dobson; 3 Iain Higgins; 4 Michael Wainwright; 5 Hamish Munton; 6 Jermaine Coleman; 7 Gareth Naylor; 8 Michael Banks; 9 Tony Howcroft; 10 Ben Skerrett; 11 Ben Thompson; 12

Andy Atha; 13 Mick Coyle. Subs: 14 Nicky Dobson for Howcroft (26); 15 Aaron Campbell for Atha (37BB, rev 53); 16 Neil Bradbrook for Atha (22); 17 Chris Heywood not used; Atha for Banks (35); Banks for Skerrett (58); Campbell for D Dobson (66).
Tries: Coleman (39), Raynor (45); **Goal:** Higgins.
League Express Men of the Match:
Eagles: Mark Aston; *Hawks:* Jermaine Coleman.
Penalty count: 8-6; **Half-time:** 18-4;
Referee: Graeme Shaw (Wigan); **Attendance:** 1,154.

GATESHEAD THUNDER 30 YORK 12

THUNDER: 1 Michael Johnson; 2 Paul Thorman; 3 Wes McGibbon; 4 Gareth Lloyd; 5 Leon Williamson; 6 Scott Dyson; 7 Carl Briggs; 8 Lee Garside; 9 Roy Southernwood; 10 Andy Grundy; 11 Jim Carlton; 12 Stephen Bradley; 13 Chris Parker. Subs: 14 Stephen Rutherford for McGibbon (68); 15 Paul Sebine for Wilkinson (72); 16 Steve Hall for Southernwood (56); 17 Mark Wilkinson for Grundy (52); Grundy for Garside (74); Wilkinson for Lloyd (77).
Tries: Parker (23), Johnson (43), Thorman (58, 64), Williamson (73), Briggs (79); **Goals:** Briggs 3.
YORK: 1 Mike Hall; 2 Matthew Mulholland; 3 Craig Moore; 4 Mark Spears; 5 Phil Musgrove; 6 Mark Dooley; 7 Gareth Oulton; 8 Neil Harmon; 9 Alan Pallister; 10 Andy Hutchinson; 11 Simon Wray; 12 Mick Ramsden; 13 Lee Bardauskas. Subs: 14 Danny Waite for Innes (65); 15 Darren Crake for Mulholland (52); 16 Andy Innes for Dooley (62); 17 Shane Cochrane for Hutchinson (28); Mulholland for Oulton (70).
Tries: Ramsden (10), Pallister (15); **Goals:** Oulton 2.
League Express Men of the Match:
Thunder: Michael Johnson; *York:* Mick Ramsden.
Penalty count: 6-4; **Half-time:** 6-12;
Referee: Paul Lee (Leigh); **Attendance:** 675.

Wednesday 23rd May 2001

DONCASTER DRAGONS 21 WORKINGTON TOWN 10

DRAGONS: 1 Johnny Woodcock; 2 Neil Bennett; 3 Mick Coult; 4 Anton Garcia; 5 Shane Miller; 6 Carl Hall; 7 Paddy Handley; 8 Maea David; 9 Peter Edwards; 10 Tony Fella; 11 Tony Atter; 12 Craig Lawton; 13 Brad Hepi. Subs: 14 Billy Conway for Handley (43); 15 Tony Miller for Edwards (51); 16 Peter Green for Hepi (67); 17 Craig Forsyth for Atter (57); Atter for Lawton (77).
Tries: Woodcock (20), Hall (31, 44);
Goals: Woodcock 3; **Field goals:** Conway 3.
TOWN: 1 Lynton Stott; 2 Jonathan Heaney; 3 Neil Frazer; 4 Matthew Woodcock; 5 Graeme Lewthwaite; 6 Tane Manihera; 7 Lee Allen; 8 Matthew Tunstall; 9 Owen Williamson; 10 Hitro Okesene; 11 Stuart Hoyles; 12 Matt Sturm; 13 Anthony Samuel. Subs: 14 Steve Wood for Allen (56); 15 Lokeni Savelio for Tunstall (23); 16 Carl Sice for Frazer (50); 17 Jamie Beaumont for Williamson (50); Tunstall for Savelio (67).
Tries: Manihera (27), Lewthwaite (61); **Goal:** Manihera.
League Express Men Of the Match:
Dragons: Carl Hall; *Town:* Hitro Okesene.
Penalty count: 8-10; **Half-time:** 12-6;
Referee: Steve Presley (Castleford); **Attendance:** 783.

WEEK 26

Sunday 27th May 2001

KEIGHLEY COUGARS 26 SHEFFIELD EAGLES 14

COUGARS: 1 Chris Hogg; 2 Gareth Hobson; 3 Gareth Hooson; 4 Karl Smith; 5 Max Tomlinson; 6 Paul Ashton; 7 Nathan Antonik; 8 Phil Stephenson; 9 Jason Ramshaw; 10 Chris Hannah; 11 David Best; 12 James Simeunovich; 13 Carlos Sanchez. Subs: 14 Craig Morphet for Hannah (52); 15 Graeme Shaw for Hannah (12BB, rev 23); 16 Robert Roberts for Best (27); 17 Kris Kirk for Ashton (72); Shaw for Stephenson (56); Best for Sanchez (74).
Tries: Sanchez (36), Hogg (46, 66), Tomlinson (69);
Goals: Ashton 5.
EAGLES: 1 Andy Poynter; 2 Paul Wells; 3 Neil Kite; 4 Gareth Hewitt; 5 Ian Thompson; 6 Gavin Brown; 7 Mark Aston; 8 Jon Bruce; 9 Gareth Dobson; 10 Andy Brent; 11 Chris Judge; 12 Chris Chapman; 13 Richard Goddard. Subs: 14 Scott Rhodes for G Brown (73); 15 Steve Hill for Brent (22); 16 Jack Howieson for Bruce (29); 17 Ian Brown for Judge (68); Bruce for Howieson (55); Brent for Hill (68); G Brown for Dobson (74BB).
Tries: Judge (24), Hewitt (42), I Brown (78);
Goal: Goddard.
League Express Men of the Match:
Cougars: Robert Roberts; *Eagles:* Richard Goddard.
Penalty count: 9-4; **Half-time:** 8-6;
Referee: Steve Ganson (St Helens); **Attendance:** 1,471.

LEIGH CENTURIONS 52 CHORLEY LYNX 18

CENTURIONS: 1 Neil Turley; 2 Alan Hadcroft; 3 Andy Fairclough; 4 Phil Kendrick; 5 David Jones; 6 Liam Bretherton; 7 Lee Sanderson; 8 Paul Norman; 9 John Duffy; 10 David Bradbury; 11 Adam Bristow; 12 Chris Morley; 13 Willie Swann. Subs: 14 Tim Street for Bradbury (24); 15 John Hamilton for Duffy (41); 16 Jason Johnson for Morley (51); 17 David Whittle for Norman (27); Norman for Bristow (60); Bradbury for Street (67).
Tries: Kendrick (3), Bradbury (7), Bretherton (26), Turley (29, 48), Street (39), Bristow (43), Hadcroft (53), Swann (68); **Goals:** Sanderson 8.
LYNX: 1 Lee Bamber; 2 Paul Wilcock; 3 Simon Tickle; 4 Stuart Dickinson; 5 Graham Taberner; 6 Lee Birdseye; 7 Stuart Fisher; 8 Lee Prest; 9 Chris Ramsdale; 10 Steve Argent; 11 Luke Vincent; 12 Wayne Bloor; 13 Ian Talbot. Subs: 14 Mike Prescott for Prest (28); 15 Peter Cahalin for Fisher (41); 16 Lee Westwood for Argent (47); 17 Rob Verrelli for Talbot (65); Prest for Prescott (70).
Tries: Dickinson (11), Birdseye (32), Prest (75);
Goals: Talbot 2, Birdseye.
League Express Men of the Match:
Centurions: Neil Turley; *Lynx:* Lee Birdseye.
Penalty count: 5-5; **Half-time:** 28-12;
Referee: Graeme Shaw (Wigan); **Attendance:** 2,639.

ROCHDALE HORNETS 32 SWINTON LIONS 9

HORNETS: 1 Paul Owen; 2 Sean Cooper; 3 Brendan O'Meara; 4 Matt Calland; 5 Marlon Billy; 6 Danny Wood; 7 Latham Tawhai; 8 Danny Sculthorpe; 9 David Stephenson; 10 Andy Ireland; 11 Wes Rogers; 12 David Larder; 13 Dave Watson. Subs: 14 Steve Gartland for Wood (41); 15 Joe Berry for Ireland (23); 16 James Bunyan for Rogers (23); 17 Martin Bunce for Calland (62); Wood for Billy (53); Rogers for Stephenson (79); Ireland for O'Meara (79BB).
Tries: Wood (5), O'Meara (29), Calland (32), Cooper (42), Gartland (61), Berry (75); **Goals:** Wood 3, Gartland.
Sin bin: Berry (34) – intervention in fight.
LIONS: 1 Jim Evans; 2 Adrian Mead; 3 Mick Nanyn; 4 Robert Russell; 5 Matt Bateman; 6 Phil Waring; 7 Shaun Furey; 8 Mike Loughlin; 9 Rob Barraclough; 10 Lee Hansen; 11 Dale Holdstock; 12 Chris Newall; 13 Phil Veivers. Subs: 14 Danny Butler for Holdstock (47); 15 Ian Lewis for Newall (35); 16 Rob Gallagher for Evans (41); 17 Nick Cammann for Mead (58); Holdstock for Russell (54); Mead for Furey (77).
Try: Holdstock (21); **Goals:** Nanyn 2; **Field goal:** Waring.
League Express Men of the Match:
Hornets: Danny Sculthorpe; *Lions:* Dale Holdstock.
Penalty count: 4-7; **Half-time:** 16-9;
Referee: Steve Presley (Castleford); **Attendance:** 1,116.

WHITEHAVEN 24 BARROW BORDER RAIDERS 0

WHITEHAVEN: 1 Wesley Wilson; 2 Jason Roach; 3 David Seeds; 4 Jason Critchley; 5 Mark Wallace; 6 Lee Kiddie; 7 Steve Kirkbride; 8 Mark Cox; 9 Aaron Lester; 10 Dean Vaughan; 11 Spencer Miller; 12 Ian Devlin; 13 Garry Purdham. Subs: 14 Paul O'Neill for G Purdham (70); 15 Marc Jackson for Lester (30BB, rev 40); 16 Robert Purdham for Kiddie (13); 17 Gary Smith for Devlin (37); Jackson for R Purdham (58); G Purdham for Vaughan (75).
Tries: Devlin (15), Lester (66), O'Neill (74), Seeds (80);
Goals: Kirkbride 4.
BORDER RAIDERS: 1 Jamie Marshall; 2 Glen Hutton; 3 Adrian Gardner; 4 Brett McDermott; 5 Shane Irabor; 6 Chris Massey; 7 Darren Holt; 8 Tau Liku; 9 Anthony Murray; 10 Ian Rawlinson; 11 Geoff Luxon; 12 Matthew Leigh; 13 Gary Charlton. Subs: 14 Dean Sharp for Rawlinson (70); 15 Gareth Pratt for Charlton (40); 16 Steve Jackson for Liku (19); 17 Mike Whitehead for Rawlinson (22); Rawlinson for Luxon (32).
League Express Men of the Match: *Whitehaven:* Robert Purdham; *Border Raiders:* Anthony Murray.
Penalty count: 10-2; **Half-time:** 6-0;
Referee: Peter Taberner (Wigan); **Attendance:** 850.

WORKINGTON TOWN 6 WIDNES VIKINGS 25

TOWN: 1 Steve Wood; 2 Matthew Woodcock; 3 Neil Frazer; 4 Kevin Hetherington; 5 Graeme Lewthwaite; 6 Tane Manihera; 7 Lynton Stott; 8 Matt Sturm; 9 Owen Williamson; 10 Hitro Okesene; 11 Jamie Beaumont; 12 Stuart Hoyles; 13 Anthony Samuel. Subs: 14 Kevin Wilson for Manihera (33); 15 Lokeni Savelio for Okesene (24); 16 Carl Sice for Williamson (49); 17 Matthew Tunstall for Hoyles (35BB, rev 58); Okesene for Savelio (55); Savelio for Hoyles (70).
Try: Beaumont (36); **Goal:** Hetherington.
VIKINGS: 1 Paul Atcheson; 2 Damian Munro; 3 Craig Weston; 4 Jason Demetriou; 5 Chris Percival; 6 Richard Agar; 7 Ian Watson; 8 Simon Knox; 9 Phil Cantillon; 10 Stephen Holgate; 11 Steve Gee; 12 Sean Richardson; 13 Tommy Hodgkinson. Subs: 14 Phil Coussons for Percival (73); 15 Chris McKinney for Richardson (57); 16 Joe Faimalo for Knox (27); 17 Matthew Long for Holgate (14BB, rev 47); Knox for Faimalo (51); Richardson for Gee (68); Faimalo for Hodgkinson (77).
Tries: Cantillon (10), Holgate (56), Percival (69), Munro (79); **Goals:** Weston 4; **Field goal:** Agar.
League Express Men of the Match:
Town: Anthony Samuel; *Vikings:* Ian Watson.
Penalty count: 5-4; **Half-time:** 6-6;
Referee: Julian King (St Helens); **Attendance:** 1,341.

YORK 6 DEWSBURY RAMS 68

YORK: 1 Mike Hall; 2 Phil Musgrove; 3 Callum Irving; 4 Matthew Mulholland; 5 Gavin Molloy; 6 Mark Dooley; 7 Gareth Oulton; 8 Andy Hutchinson; 9 Alan Pallister; 10 Shane Cochrane; 11 Darren Crake; 12 Nathan Pincher; 13 Mick Ramsden. Subs: 14 Danny Waite for Oulton (23); 15 Steve Robinson for Pallister (55); 16 Carl Bristow for Cochrane (29); 17 Andy Innes for Musgrove (64); Cochrane for Pincher (61); Pallister for Hutchinson (70).
Try: M Hall (24); **Goal:** Waite.
RAMS: 1 Matthew Griffin; 2 Richard Baker; 3 Nathan Graham; 4 Dan Potter; 5 Adrian Flynn; 6 Mark Cain; 7 Barry Eaton; 8 Andy Fisher; 9 Richard Pachniuk; 10 Robin Jowitt; 11 Ian Hughes; 12 Jim Leatham; 13 Damian Ball. Subs: 14 Kevin Crouthers not used; 15 Ryan McDonald for Jowitt (22); 16 Danny Burton for Ball (36); 17 Andrew Spink for Leatham (63); Jowitt for Fisher (68); Ball for Hughes (70).
Tries: Eaton (28, 53, 66, 69), Pachniuk (41), Baker (47, 51, 72), Potter (57, 80), Leatham (62), Griffin (75);
Goals: Eaton 10.
League Express Men of the Match:
York: Andy Hutchinson; *Rams:* Barry Eaton.
Penalty count: 6-9; **Half-time:** 6-6;
Referee: Nick Oddy (Halifax); **Attendance:** 425.

GATESHEAD THUNDER 26 BATLEY BULLDOGS 29

THUNDER: 1 Michael Johnson; 2 Paul Thorman; 3 Steve Hall; 4 Gareth Lloyd; 5 Leon Williamson; 6 Scott Dyson; 7 Carl Briggs; 8 Lee Garside; 9 Roy Southernwood; 10 Andy Grundy; 11 Jim Carlton; 12 Stephen Bradley; 13 Chris Parker. Subs: 14 Martin Gambles for Southernwood (60); 15 Paul Sebine for Grundy (57); 16 Stephen Rutherford not used; 17 Gareth Barron for Garside (48); Garside for Barron (71); Grundy for Sebine (71).
Tries: Garside (9), Thorman (22), Johnson (34), Williamson (50, 76); **Goals:** Briggs 3.
Sin bin: Grundy (26) - lying on.
BULLDOGS: 1 Craig Lingard; 2 Jeremy Dyson; 3 Ryan Horsley; 4 Roger Simpson; 5 Paul Gleadhill; 6 Richard Gibson; 7 Richard Price; 8 Jeff Wittenberg; 9 Andy Heptinstall; 10 Paul Hicks; 11 Paul Harrison; 12 Will Cartledge; 13 Glen Tomlinson. Subs: 14 Mark Cass for Heptinstall (58); 15 Alan Boothroyd for Wittenberg (30); 16 Gary Shillabeer for Lingard (14); 17 Paul Lister for Hicks (54BB, rev 78); Wittenberg for Harrison (55); Harrison for Gibson (60).
Tries: Dyson (15), Cartledge (26), Simpson (54), Shillabeer (63), Harrison (68); **Goals:** Price, Dyson 3;
Field goal: Cass.
League Express Men of the Match:
Thunder: Carl Briggs; *Bulldogs:* Glen Tomlinson.
Penalty count: 4-10; **Half-time:** 16-8;
Referee: Steve Addy (Huddersfield); **Attendance:** 553.

HUNSLET HAWKS 6 HULL KINGSTON ROVERS 32

HAWKS: 1 George Raynor; 2 Danny Dobson; 3 Iain Higgins; 4 Michael Wainwright; 5 Chris Heywood; 6 Chris Ross; 7 Craig Robinson; 8 Ben Thompson; 9 Tony Howcroft; 10 Craig Ibbotson; 11 Mick Coyle; 12 Dave Jessey; 13 Jermaine Coleman. Subs: 14 Hamish Munton for Heywood (40); 15 Ben Skerrett for Thompson (65); 16 Neil Bradbrook for Ibbotson (17); 17 Andy Atha for Jessey (34); Ibbotson for Bradbrook (43); Heywood for Dobson (68); Jessey for Atha (38BB, rev 40).
Try: Raynor (58); **Goal:** Ross.
ROVERS: 1 Bob Everitt; 2 Alex Godfrey; 3 Matt Schultz; 4 Whetu Taewa; 5 Alasdair McLarron; 6 Colin Carter; 7 Craig Murdock; 8 Rich Hayes; 9 Steve Cochrane; 10 Richard Wilson; 11 Richard Slater; 12 Rob Wilson; 13 Chris Charles. Subs: 14 Chris Kitching for Carter (40); 15 Jon Aston for Richard Wilson (21); 16 Paul Fletcher for Slater (30); 17 David Luckwell for Hayes (53); Slater for Rob Wilson (53); Richard Wilson for Cochrane (70).
Tries: Cochrane (23), Godfrey (42), Luckwell (55), Taewa (70, 79); **Goals:** Charles 6.
League Express Men of the Match:
Hawks: Jermaine Coleman; *Rovers:* Rich Hayes.
Penalty count: 11-11; **Half-time:** 0-6;
Referee: Ronnie Laughton (Barnsley); **Attendance:** 725.

Wednesday 30th May 2001

TRANS-PENNINE CUP FINAL

KEIGHLEY COUGARS 0 LEIGH CENTURIONS 36

COUGARS: 1 Chris Hogg; 2 Gareth Hobson; 3 Gareth Hooson; 4 Karl Smith; 5 Max Tomlinson; 6 Paul Ashton; 7 Nathan Antonik; 8 Phil Stephenson; 9 Jason Ramshaw; 10 Chris Hannah; 11 Robert Roberts; 12 James Simeunovich; 13 Carlos Sanchez. Subs: 14 Craig Morphet for Sanchez (26); 15 Kris Kirk for Hobson (60); 16 Andrew Senior for Stephenson (54); 17 David Best for Hannah (50); Sanchez for Simeunovich (56); Stephenson for Morphet (75).
Sin bin: Sanchez (68) – interference at the play the ball; Ramshaw (74) – fighting.
On report: Brawl incident (74).
CENTURIONS: 1 Neil Turley; 2 David Ingram; 3 Paul Anderson; 4 Andy Fairclough; 5 Michael Watts; 6 Simon Svabic; 7 Willie Swann; 8 Tim Street; 9 John Hamilton; 10 David Whittle; 11 Simon Baldwin; 12 Phil Kendrick; 13 Adam Bristow. Subs: 14 Andy Leathem for Whittle (24BB, rev 64); 15 David Bradbury for Street (16BB, rev 28); 16 John Duffy for Hamilton (28); 17 Liam Bretherton for Kendrick (57); Bradbury for Street (54BB); Hamilton for Duffy (66); Kendrick for Bristow (78).
Tries: Turley (2, 65), Anderson (20, 27), Swann (34), Bretherton (70), Baldwin (74); **Goals:** Svabic 4.
Sent off: Whittle (79) – striking.
Sin bin: Whittle (68) – striking; Anderson (74) – fighting.
On report: Brawl incident – (74).
League Express Men of the Match:
Cougars: Jason Ramshaw; *Centurions:* Simon Baldwin.
Penalty count: 8-9; **Half-time:** 0-20; **Referee:** Richard Silverwood (Dewsbury); **Attendance:** 2,626.

WEEK 27

Sunday 3rd June 2001

CHORLEY LYNX 8 WORKINGTON TOWN 52

LYNX: 1 Lee Bamber; 2 Paul Wilcock; 3 Luke Vincent; 4 Stuart Dickinson; 5 Graham Taberner; 6 Chris Ramsdale; 7 Stuart Fisher; 8 Lee Prest; 9 Peter Cahalin; 10 Steve Argent; 11 Phil Harrison; 12 Wayne Bloor; 13 Ian Talbot. Subs: 14 Matthew Brown for Ramsdale (43); 15 Mike Prescott for Argent (38); 16 Lee Westwood for Prest (28); 17 Rob Verrelli for Talbot (78); Argent for Westwood (59).

Try: Harrison (28); **Goals:** Talbot 2.
Sent off: Prescott (70) - high tackle.
Sin bin: Taberner (69) - dissent; Fisher (73) - dissent.
TOWN: 1 Steve Wood; 2 Richard Haile; 3 Matthew Woodcock; 4 John Allen; 5 Graeme Lewthwaite; 6 Kevin Hetherington; 7 Lynton Stott; 8 Matt Sturm; 9 Carl Sice; 10 Lokeni Savelio; 11 Jamie Beaumont; 12 Stuart Hoyles; 13 Anthony Samuel. Subs: 14 Craig Fisher for Hetherington (75); 15 Matthew Tunstall for Savelio (33); 16 Owen Williamson for Sice (41); 17 Hitro Okesene for Beaumont (22); Savelio for Tunstall (55); Sice for Stott (76).
Tries: Woodcock (4), Stott (14, 64), Hetherington (17), Hoyles (36), Sturm (49), Lewthwaite (73), Sice (79, 80);
Goals: Hetherington 5, Wood 3.
Sin bin: Savelio (70) - retaliation.
League Express Men of the Match:
Lynx: Wayne Bloor; *Town:* Lynton Stott.
Penalty count: 10-10; **Half-time:** 8-22;
Referee: Steve Addy (Huddersfield); **Attendance:** 282.

DONCASTER DRAGONS 16
HULL KINGSTON ROVERS 18

DRAGONS: 1 Johnny Woodcock; 2 St John Ellis; 3 Mick Coult; 4 Anton Garcia; 5 Shane Miller; 6 Carl Hall; 7 Billy Conway; 8 Maea David; 9 Peter Edwards; 10 Tony Fella; 11 Tony Atter; 12 Craig Lawton; 13 Brad Hepi. Subs: 14 Gary Smith not used; 15 Peter Green for Hall (67); 16 Tony Miller for Atter (31); 17 Craig Forsyth for Fella (45); Atter for David (59); David for Forsyth (73).
Tries: Hall (24), Coult (69), Garcia (72);
Goals: Woodcock 2.
ROVERS: 1 Bob Everitt; 2 Alex Godfrey; 3 Chris Kitching; 4 Whetu Taewa; 5 Alasdair McLarron; 6 Jimmy Walker; 7 Craig Murdock; 8 Rich Hayes; 9 Steve Cochrane; 10 Richard Wilson; 11 Richard Slater; 12 Matt Schultz; 13 Chris Charles. Subs: 14 Rob Wilson for Richard Wilson (25); 15 Jon Aston for Cochrane (25); 16 Paul Fletcher for Walker (25); 17 David Luckwell for Hayes (49); Cochrane for Fletcher (64); Walker for McLarron (70BB); Fletcher for Cochrane (73).
Tries: Walker (15), Kitching (43), Godfrey (48);
Goals: Charles 3.
League Express Men of the Match:
Dragons: Tony Atter; *Rovers:* Paul Fletcher.
Penalty count: 10-7; **Half-time:** 6-8;
Referee: Steve Presley (Castleford); **Attendance:** 1,378.

FEATHERSTONE ROVERS 42 KEIGHLEY COUGARS 0

ROVERS: 1 Michael Rhodes; 2 Jamie Stokes; 3 Simon Jackson; 4 Chris Spurr; 5 Matt Bramald; 6 Andy Bastow; 7 Jamie Rooney; 8 Craig Booth; 9 Richard Chapman; 10 Gary Lord; 11 Steve Dooler; 12 Ricky Helliwell; 13 Paul Darley. Subs: 14 Danny Evans for Chapman (41); 15 Neil Lowe for Dooler (29); 16 Stuart Dickens for Lord (29); 17 Gavin Morgan for Booth (9); Lord for Morgan (64); Dooler for Evans (68); Morgan for Bramald (75BB).
Tries: Bramald (15), Jackson (21), Chapman (24), Rhodes (29, 53), Morgan (33), Darley (49), Lowe (78);
Goals: Rooney 5.
COUGARS: 1 Chris Hogg; 2 Gareth Hobson; 3 Gareth Hooson; 4 Karl Smith; 5 Max Tomlinson; 6 Paul Ashton; 7 Nathan Antonik; 8 Phil Stephenson; 9 Jason Ramshaw; 10 David Best; 11 Craig Morphet; 12 Graeme Shaw; 13 Robert Roberts. Subs: 14 Carlos Sanchez for Best (29); 15 James Simeunovich for Shaw (26); 16 Kris Kirk for Stephenson (54); 17 Andy Senior for Roberts (50BB, rev 60); Shaw for Morphet (46); Senior for Ramshaw (63); Best for Shaw (68).
League Express Men of the Match:
Rovers: Andy Bastow; *Cougars:* Phil Stephenson.
Penalty count: 5-6; **Half-time:** 26-0;
Referee: Julian King (St Helens); **Attendance:** 1,735.

ROCHDALE HORNETS 36 BATLEY BULLDOGS 10

HORNETS: 1 Paul Owen; 2 Sean Cooper; 3 Brendan O'Meara; 4 Matt Calland; 5 Wayne McHugh; 6 Danny Wood; 7 Latham Tawhai; 8 Danny Sculthorpe; 9 Warren Ayres; 10 Andy Ireland; 11 Wes Rogers; 12 James Bunyan; 13 Dave Watson. Subs: 14 Steve Gartland for Wood (55); 15 Joe Berry for Sculthorpe (21); 16 David Stephenson for Ayres (64); 17 Martin Bunce for Calland (55); Wood for O'Meara (73).
Tries: Wood (9, 74), O'Meara (12), Calland (27), Bunyan (39), McHugh (44, 54), Cooper (68); **Goals:** Wood 2.
BULLDOGS: 1 Richard Gibson; 2 Jeremy Dyson; 3 Ryan Horsley; 4 Roger Simpson; 5 Paul Gleadhill; 6 Richard Price; 7 Glen Tomlinson; 8 Jeff Wittenberg; 9 Andy Heptinstall; 10 Paul Hicks; 11 Gary Shillabeer; 12 Will Cartledge; 13 Paul Harrison. Subs: 14 Mark Cass for Heptinstall (51); 15 Alan Boothroyd for Cartledge (29); 16 Paul Lister for Hicks (62); 17 Shelton Davis for Dyson (48); Dyson for Price (60); Cartledge for Gibson (67).
Tries: Harrison (48), Davis (59); **Goal:** Price.
League Express Men of the Match:
Hornets: Brendan O'Meara; *Bulldogs:* Jeff Wittenberg.
Penalty count: 5-5; **Half-time:** 20-0; **Referee:** Steve Nicholson (Whitehaven); **Attendance:** 1,076.

SWINTON LIONS 0 WIDNES VIKINGS 62

LIONS: 1 Rob Gallagher; 2 Jim Evans; 3 Mick Nanyn; 4 Matt Bateman; 5 Lee Hudson; 6 Phil Veivers; 7 Phil Waring; 8 Mike Loughlin; 9 Rob Barraclough; 10 Lee Hansen; 11 Dale Holdstock; 12 Gareth Chambers; 13 Paul Smith. Subs: 14 Danny Butler for Barraclough (61); 15 Ian Lewis for Loughlin (26); 16 Adrian Mead for Hudson (33); 17 Nick Cammann for Holdstock (54); Loughlin for Lewis (61); Barraclough for Waring (75).
Sent off: Nanyn (34) – high tackle.
VIKINGS: 1 Paul Atcheson; 2 Damian Munro; 3 Craig Weston; 4 Jason Demetriou; 5 Chris Percival; 6 Richard Agar; 7 Ian Watson; 8 Simon Knox; 9 Phil Cantillon; 10 Stephen Holgate; 11 Steve Gee; 12 Sean Richardson; 13 Tommy Hodgkinson. Subs: 14 Martin Crompton not used; 15 Chris McKinney for Hodgkinson (40); 16 Joe Faimalo for Knox (33); 17 Matthew Long for Holgate (26); Holgate for Long (60).
Tries: Weston (4), Agar (21), Cantillon (27, 38, 55, 60, 65), Long (44, 53), McKinney (57), Munro (78);
Goals: Weston 9.
League Express Men of the Match:
Lions: Lee Hansen; *Vikings:* Phil Cantillon.
Penalty count: 9-10; **Half-time:** 0-20;
Referee: Graeme Shaw (Wigan); **Attendance:** 1,761.

WHITEHAVEN 18 DEWSBURY RAMS 17

WHITEHAVEN: 1 Wesley Wilson; 2 Jason Roach; 3 David Seeds; 4 Jason Critchley; 5 Mark Wallace; 6 Robert Purdham; 7 Steve Kirkbride; 8 Mark Cox; 9 Aaron Lester; 10 Dean Vaughan; 11 Spencer Miller; 12 Gary Smith; 13 Garry Purdham. Subs: 14 Paul O'Neill for Wallace (75); 15 Marc Jackson for Smith (55); 16 Howard Hill for Smith (17BB, rev 40); 17 Phil Sherwen for Vaughan (25); Vaughan for Cox (67); Hill for Seeds (70).
Tries: Lester (20), G Purdham (33), Sherwen (36);
Goals: Kirkbride 2; **Field goals:** Kirkbride 2.
RAMS: 1 Matthew Griffin; 2 Richard Baker; 3 Nathan Graham; 4 Kevin Crouthers; 5 Adrian Flynn; 6 Dean Lawford; 7 Barry Eaton; 8 Andy Fisher; 9 Richard Pachniuk; 10 Robin Jowitt; 11 Ian Hughes; 12 Danny Burton; 13 Damian Ball. Subs: 14 Mark Cain for Lawford (47); 15 Dan Potter for Hughes (35); 16 Ryan McDonald for Jowitt (35); 17 Kevin Spink for Burton (73); Jowitt for Fisher (63); Hughes for McDonald (71).
Tries: Crouthers (11), Potter (56), Griffin (62);
Goals: Eaton 2; **Field goal:** Lawford.
League Express Men of the Match:
Whitehaven: Aaron Lester; *Rams:* Dean Lawford.
Penalty count: 5-3; **Half-time:** 16-7;
Referee: Colin Morris (Huddersfield); **Attendance:** 725.

SHEFFIELD EAGLES 56 YORK 0

EAGLES: 1 Andy Poynter; 2 Paul Wells; 3 Neil Kite; 4 Gareth Hewitt; 5 Ian Thompson; 6 Gavin Brown; 7 Scott Rhodes; 8 Jon Bruce; 9 Gareth Dobson; 10 Steve Hill; 11 Andy Brent; 12 Chris Chapman; 13 Richard Goddard. Subs: 14 Mark Aston for Goddard (65); 15 Jack Howieson for Bruce (22); 16 Simon Tillyer for Chapman (26); 17 Billy Kershaw for Hill (33); Bruce for Howieson (69); Chapman for Tillyer (69).
Tries: Rhodes (5), Hewitt (8), Wells (12, 39), Chapman (20), Poynter (23), Goddard (29), Howieson (54), Brent (56, 70); **Goals:** Goddard 5, G Brown 3.
YORK: 1 Mike Hall; 2 Simon Wray; 3 Matthew Mulholland; 4 Gavin Molloy; 5 Andy Innes; 6 Mark Dooley; 7 Danny Waite; 8 Andy Hutchinson; 9 Alan Pallister; 10 Shane Cochrane; 11 Carl Bristow; 12 Nathan Pincher; 13 Mick Ramsden. Subs: 14 Callum Irving for Cooney (26); 15 Steve Robinson for Pallister (69); 16 Chris Cooney for Innes (14); 17 Darren Crake for Cochrane (44); Cochrane for Pincher (74); Pincher for Hutchinson (80).
League Express Men of the Match:
Eagles: Andy Brent; *York:* Mick Ramsden.
Penalty count: 4-7; **Half-time:** 38-0;
Referee: Mike Dawber (Wigan); **Attendance:** 1,008.

GATESHEAD THUNDER 20 OLDHAM 50

THUNDER: 1 Michael Johnson; 2 Paul Thorman; 3 Stephen Rutherford; 4 Steve Hall; 5 Leon Williamson; 6 Scott Dyson; 7 Carl Briggs; 8 Lee Garside; 9 Roy Southernwood; 10 Andy Grundy; 11 Jim Carlton; 12 Stephen Bradley; 13 Richard Mervill. Subs: 14 Martin Gambles for Southernwood (59); 15 Paul Sebine for Mervill (40); 16 Richard Spence for Dyson (65); 17 Gareth Barron for Garside (32); Garside for Barron (65).
Tries: Williamson (3, 22), Briggs (8, 25); **Goals:** Briggs 2.
OLDHAM: 1 Mark Sibson; 2 Joe McNicholas; 3 Anthony Gibbons; 4 Pat Rich; 5 Daryl Lacey; 6 David Gibbons; 7 Neil Roden; 8 Jason Clegg; 9 Keith Brennan; 10 Paul Norton; 11 Phil Farrell; 12 Bryan Henare; 13 Kevin Mannion. Subs: 14 Lee Doran for Norton (65); 15 Leo Casey for Clegg (32); 16 Gareth Barber for Lacey (58); 17 Gavin Johnson for D Gibbons (49); Clegg for Casey (60); Lacey for Brennan (68).
Tries: Brennan (12, 39, 78), McNicholas (15), A Gibbons (32, 35), Roden (45), Henare (67), Clegg (73);
Goals: Rich 7.
League Express Men of the Match:
Thunder: Roy Southernwood; *Oldham:* Keith Brennan.
Penalty count: 6-4; **Half-time:** 20-28;
Referee: Ronnie Laughton (Barnsley); **Attendance:** 743.

HUNSLET HAWKS 24 BARROW BORDER RAIDERS 10

HAWKS: 1 Michael Wainwright; 2 George Raynor; 3 Iain Higgins; 4 Dave Jessey; 5 Chris Heywood; 6 Chris Ross; 7 Craig Robinson; 8 Neil Bradbrook; 9 Tony Howcroft; 10 Craig Ibbotson; 11 Mick Coyle; 12 Gareth Naylor; 13 Jermaine Coleman. Subs: 14 Nicky Dobson for Higgins (33); 15 Hamish Munton for D Dobson (80); 16 Danny Dobson for Heywood (5); 17 Ben Skerrett for Naylor (41); Naylor for Skerrett (50); Skerrett for Bradbrook (53); Bradbrook for Coyle (69BB).
Tries: Coyle (10), Wainwright (21, 65), N Dobson (40);
Goals: Ross 4.
Sin bin: Coyle (44) - fighting.
BORDER RAIDERS: 1 Jamie Marshall; 2 Glen Hutton; 3 Adrian Gardner; 4 Brett McDermott; 5 Shane Irabor; 6 Chris Massey; 7 Darren Holt; 8 Tau Liku; 9 Anthony Murray; 10 Ian Rawlinson; 11 Mike Whitehead; 12 Geoff Luxon; 13 Matthew Leigh. Subs: 14 Gareth Pratt for Rawlinson (75); 15 Steve Jackson for Liku (22); 16 Damien Whitter for Luxon (22); 17 Gary Charlton for Whitehead (53); Luxon for Jackson (52); Liku for Whitter (68).
Tries: Irabor (28), Holt (80); **Goal:** Holt.
Sin bin: McDermott (44) - fighting;
Murray (55) - punching; Rawlinson (58) - fighting.
League Express Men of the Match:
Hawks: Dave Jessey; *Border Raiders:* Damien Whitter.
Penalty count: 10-7; **Half-time:** 18-6;
Referee: Paul Lee (Leigh); **Attendance:** 509.

Wednesday 6th June 2001

BATLEY BULLDOGS 15 WIDNES VIKINGS 36

BULLDOGS: 1 Jeremy Dyson; 2 Roger Simpson; 3 Ryan Horsley; 4 Matt Pennington; 5 Paul Gleadhill; 6 Glen Tomlinson; 7 Mark Cass; 8 Alan Boothroyd; 9 Andy Heptinstall; 10 Paul Lister; 11 Jeff Wittenberg; 12 Will Cartledge; 13 Paul Harrison. Subs: 14 Chris Beevers for Gleadhill (75); 15 Lee Kelly for Boothroyd (75); 16 Paul Hicks for Lister (26); 17 Mark Toohey for Cartledge (60); Lister for Hicks (63).
Tries: Harrison (18), Tomlinson (48); **Goals:** Dyson 3;
Field goal: Tomlinson.
VIKINGS: 1 Paul Atcheson; 2 Damian Munro; 3 Craig Weston; 4 Jason Demetriou; 5 Chris Percival; 6 Richard Agar; 7 Ian Watson; 8 Simon Knox; 9 Phil Cantillon; 10 Stephen Holgate; 11 Chris McKinney; 12 Sean Richardson; 13 Tommy Hodgkinson. Subs: 14 Martin Crompton for Watson (48); 15 Joe Faimalo for McKinney (58); 16 Andy Craig for Atcheson (56); 17 Matthew Long for Holgate (26); Holgate for Long (61).
Tries: Cantillon (12, 20), Knox (59), Munro (75), Richardson (78), Craig (80); **Goals:** Weston 6.
League Express Men of the Match:
Bulldogs: Paul Hicks; *Vikings:* Sean Richardson.
Penalty count: 7-7; **Half-time:** 9-14;
Referee: Graeme Shaw (Wigan); **Attendance:** 890.

WEEK 28

Sunday 10th June 2001

BARROW BORDER RAIDERS 60 YORK 0

BORDER RAIDERS: 1 Dean Sharp; 2 Glen Hutton; 3 Stuart Magorian; 4 Adrian Gardner; 5 Shane Irabor; 6 Chris Massey; 7 Darren Holt; 8 Damien Whitter; 9 Anthony Murray; 10 Ian Rawlinson; 11 Geoff Luxon; 12 Matthew Leigh; 13 Brett McDermott. Subs: 14 Jamie Marshall for Massey (60); 15 Steve Jackson for Whitter (54); 16 Mike Whitehead for Luxon (50); 17 Tau Liku for Rawlinson (43).
Tries: Leigh (2, 47, 54, 60), Sharp (17), Hutton (25, 38), A Gardner (58), Marshall (61, 73), Irabor (63);
Goals: Holt 8.
YORK: 1 Mike Hall; 2 Simon Wray; 3 Matthew Mulholland; 4 Gavin Molloy; 5 Andy Innes; 6 Mark Dooley; 7 Gareth Oulton; 8 Andy Hutchinson; 9 Alan Pallister; 10 Shane Cochrane; 11 Carl Bristow; 12 Darren Crake; 13 Nathan Pincher. Subs: 14 Phil Musgrove for Wray (27); 15 Steve Robinson for Innes (65); 16 Mick Hagan for Precious (45); 17 Andy Precious for Hutchinson (25); Hutchinson for Cochrane (35).
League Express Men of the Match:
Border Raiders: Darren Holt; *York:* Mike Hall.
Penalty count: 7-5; **Half-time:** 22-0;
Referee: Steve Addy (Huddersfield); **Attendance:** 655.

BATLEY BULLDOGS 38 SWINTON LIONS 24

BULLDOGS: 1 Jeremy Dyson; 2 Roger Simpson; 3 Ryan Horsley; 4 Matt Pennington; 5 Paul Gleadhill; 6 Glen Tomlinson; 7 Mark Cass; 8 Paul Lister; 9 Andy Heptinstall; 10 Paul Hicks; 11 Jeff Wittenberg; 12 Will Cartledge; 13 Paul Harrison. Subs: 14 Shelton Davis for Simpson (59); 15 Craig Wright for Wittenberg (8); 16 Mark Toohey for Adamson (32); 17 Andy Adamson for Hicks (12).
Tries: Harrison (35, 50), Simpson (45), Tomlinson (51), Gleadhill (72), Wright (75), Lister (79);
Goals: Dyson 4, Gleadhill.
LIONS: 1 Rob Gallagher; 2 Jim Evans; 3 Mick Nanyn; 4 Matt Bateman; 5 Mike Woods; 6 Phil Waring; 7 Shaun Furey; 8 Mike Loughlin; 9 Rob Barraclough; 10 Lee Hansen; 11 Paul Smith; 12 Gareth Chambers; 13 Phil Veivers. Subs: 14 Danny Butler for Barraclough (40); 15 Jon-Paul Doherty for Loughlin (58); 16 Wayne Jackman for Furey (20); 17 Ian Lewis for Chambers (71).
Tries: Chambers (30), Bateman (33, 54), Evans (42), Nanyn (55); **Goals:** Nanyn 2.
League Express Men of the Match:
Bulldogs: Glen Tomlinson; *Lions:* Lee Hansen.
Penalty count: 3-4; **Half-time:** 6-12;
Referee: Colin Morris (Huddersfield); **Attendance:** 418.

DEWSBURY RAMS 28 SHEFFIELD EAGLES 16

RAMS: 1 Matthew Griffin; 2 Richard Baker; 3 Nathan Graham; 4 Kevin Crouthers; 5 Adrian Flynn; 6 Dean Lawford; 7 Barry Eaton; 8 Andy Fisher; 9 Richard Pachniuk; 10 Robin Jowitt; 11 Ian Hughes; 12 Dan Potter; 13 Damian Ball. Subs: 14 Mark Cain for Fisher (63); 15 Jim Leatham for Crouthers (17); 16 Ryan McDonald for Jowitt (23); 17 Kevin Spink for Hughes (25); Crouthers for Ball (73).
Tries: Jowitt (13), Ball (31), Flynn (39), Baker (43), Potter (59); **Goals:** Eaton 3; **Field goals:** Eaton 2.

EAGLES: 1 Andy Poynter; 2 Paul Wells; 3 Neil Kite; 4 Gareth Hewitt; 5 Ian Thompson; 6 Gavin Brown; 7 Scott Rhodes; 8 Jon Bruce; 9 Gareth Dobson; 10 Steve Hill; 11 Andy Brent; 12 Chris Chapman; 13 Richard Goddard. Subs: 14 Mark Aston for Dobson (66); 15 Jack Howieson for Bruce (25); 16 Simon Tillyer for Howieson (66); 17 Billy Kershaw for Brent (60); Bruce for Hill (29BB, rev 48); Bruce for Hill (66); Howieson for Hewitt (66).
Tries: G Brown (47), Goddard (53), Howieson (71); **Goals:** Goddard 2.
League Express Men of the Match:
Rams: Adrian Flynn; *Eagles:* Gavin Brown.
Penalty count: 6-5; **Half-time:** 19-0;
Referee: Julian King (St Helens); **Attendance:** 700.

HULL KINGSTON ROVERS 30 GATESHEAD THUNDER 16

ROVERS: 1 Bob Everitt; 2 Alex Godfrey; 3 Matt Schultz; 4 Whetu Taewa; 5 Alasdair McLarron; 6 Chris Kitching; 7 Craig Murdock; 8 Rich Hayes; 9 Steve Cochrane; 10 Richard Wilson; 11 Richard Slater; 12 Rob Wilson; 13 Chris Charles. Subs: 14 Jimmy Walker for McLarron (ht); 15 Paul Fletcher for Slater (25); 16 Jon Aston for Richard Wilson (25); 17 David Luckwell for Hayes (ht); Richard Wilson for Cochrane (62); Slater for Rob Wilson (62).
Tries: Charles (2), McLarron (20), Taewa (33, 52), Fletcher (55), Kitching (63); **Goals:** Charles 3.
THUNDER: 1 Michael Johnson; 2 Paul Thorman; 3 Steve Hall; 4 Gareth Lloyd; 5 Wes McGibbon; 6 Scott Dyson; 7 Carl Briggs; 8 Lee Garside; 9 Roy Southernwood; 10 Gareth Barron; 11 Jim Carlton; 12 Stephen Bradley; 13 Stephen Rutherford. Subs: 14 Martin Gambles for Garside (25); 15 Paul Sebine for Barron (21); 16 Richard Spence for Southernwood (58); 17 Kevin Neighbour for McGibbon (58); Garside for Carlton (37); Barron for Lloyd (68).
Tries: Rutherford (14), McGibbon (46), Gambles (71); **Goals:** Briggs 2.
League Express Men of the Match:
Rovers: Whetu Taewa; *Thunder:* Michael Johnson.
Penalty count: 4-3; **Half-time:** 16-6; **Referee:** Ronnie Laughton (Barnsley); **Attendance:** 1,653.

KEIGHLEY COUGARS 52 DONCASTER DRAGONS 12

COUGARS: 1 Chris Hogg; 2 Gareth Hooson; 3 Karl Smith; 4 Matthew Foster; 5 Max Tomlinson; 6 Paul Ashton; 7 Nathan Antonik; 8 Phil Stephenson; 9 Jason Ramshaw; 10 David Best; 11 Craig Morphet; 12 Graeme Shaw; 13 Robert Roberts. Subs: 14 Andy Richardson for Stephenson (2BB, rev 12); 15 James Rushforth for Ramshaw (57); 16 Leroy Rivett for Hogg (50); 17 James Simeunovich for Best (28); Best for Shaw (ht); Richardson for Morphet (66); Hogg for Best (70); Morphet for Stephenson (72BB).
Tries: Smith (12), Antonik (15), Ramshaw (22), Hooson (34), Ashton (50, 72), Stephenson (54), Rivett (64, 70); **Goals:** Ashton 8.
DRAGONS: 1 St John Ellis; 2 Johnny Woodcock; 3 Mick Coult; 4 Anton Garcia; 5 Shane Miller; 6 Carl Hall; 7 Billy Conway; 8 Maea David; 9 Peter Edwards; 10 Tony Atter; 11 Tony Miller; 12 Craig Lawton; 13 Brad Hepi. Subs: 14 Peter Green for Hepi (46); 15 Phil White for T Miller (59); 16 Tony Fella for Atter (23); 17 Craig Forsyth for David (36); T Miller for Hall (60BB); Atter for T Miller (70); David for Forsyth (75).
Tries: Lawton (7), Ellis (58); **Goals:** Ellis 2.
League Express Men of the Match:
Cougars: Paul Ashton; *Dragons:* Peter Edwards.
Penalty count: 5-4; **Half-time:** 22-6; **Referee:** Steve Nicholson (Whitehaven); **Attendance:** 1,697.

ROCHDALE HORNETS 34 WHITEHAVEN 24

HORNETS: 1 Paul Owen; 2 Sean Cooper; 3 Brendan O'Meara; 4 Matt Calland; 5 Marlon Billy; 6 Danny Wood; 7 Latham Tawhai; 8 Danny Sculthorpe; 9 David Stephenson; 10 Andy Ireland; 11 Wes Rogers; 12 James Bunyan; 13 Dave Watson. Subs: 14 Warren Ayres for Stephenson (28); 15 Joe Berry for Ireland (28); 16 Steve Gartland for Wood (70); 17 Wayne McHugh not used; Ireland for Sculthorpe (49); Stephenson for Ayres (58); Sculthorpe for Ireland (75).
Tries: Billy (4, 32), Cooper (7), Sculthorpe (15), Watson (75), Berry (80); **Goals:** Wood 3, Gartland 2.
Sin bin: O'Meara (22) - deliberate offside.
WHITEHAVEN: 1 Wesley Wilson; 2 Jason Roach; 3 David Seeds; 4 Jason Critchley; 5 Mark Wallace; 6 Robert Purdham; 7 Steve Kirkbride; 8 Mark Cox; 9 Aaron Lester; 10 Dean Vaughan; 11 Spencer Miller; 12 Gary Smith; 13 Garry Purdham. Subs: 14 Paul O'Neill for Wallace (67); 15 Marc Jackson for Cox (59); 16 Howard Hill for Miller (33); 17 Phil Sherwen for Vaughan (33); Miller for Smith (59); Vaughan for G Purdham (59).
Tries: R Purdham (19), Seeds (43), Wallace (59), Hill (69); **Goals:** Kirkbride 4.
League Express Men of the Match:
Hornets: Matt Calland; *Whitehaven:* Aaron Lester.
Penalty count: 6-5; **Half-time:** 22-8;
Referee: Steve Presley (Castleford); **Attendance:** 1,190.

WIDNES VIKINGS 72 CHORLEY LYNX 18

VIKINGS: 1 Damian Munro; 2 Phil Coussons; 3 Andy Craig; 4 Jason Demetriou; 5 Liam Jones; 6 Richard Agar; 7 Ian Watson; 8 Matthew Long; 9 Phil Cantillon; 10 Mike Hill; 11 Steve Gee; 12 Sean Richardson; 13 Tommy Hodgkinson. Subs: 14 Martin Crompton for Watson (41); 15 Chris McKinney for Hodgkinson (47); 16 Joe Faimalo for Demetriou (16); 17 Stephen Holgate for Long (30); Watson for Agar (45); Long for Holgate (59).
Tries: Jones (4), Demetriou (5), Richardson (6, 30), Cantillon (8, 24, 27), Coussons (20, 78), Munro (36), Craig (42, 46, 75), Gee (70); **Goals:** Jones 8.
LYNX: 1 Lee Bamber; 2 Danny Winrow; 3 Luke Vincent; 4 Stuart Dickinson; 5 Andrew Friar; 6 Paul Wilcock; 7 Stuart Fisher; 8 Lee Prest; 9 Peter Cahalin; 10 Lee Westwood; 11 Phil Harrison; 12 Mike Prescott; 13 Wayne Bloor. Subs: 14 Matthew Brown for Prest (30); 15 Warren Hindle for Brown (49); 16 Ian Talbot for Friar (59); 17 Rob Verrelli for Westwood (30); Prest for Prescott (49); Westwood for Harrison (55).
Try: Wilcock (32), Hindle (55), Dickinson (63); **Goals:** Fisher 3.
League Express Men of the Match:
Vikings: Phil Cantillon; *Lynx:* Paul Wilcock.
Penalty count: 5-4; **Half-time:** 46-6;
Referee: Paul Lee (Leigh); **Attendance:** 3,683.

WORKINGTON TOWN 17 LEIGH CENTURIONS 18

TOWN: 1 Steve Wood; 2 Matthew Woodcock; 3 Neil Frazer; 4 John Allen; 5 Graeme Lewthwaite; 6 Kevin Hetherington; 7 Lynton Stott; 8 Matt Sturm; 9 Owen Williamson; 10 Hitro Okesene; 11 Stuart Hoyles; 12 Anthony Samuel; 13 Gary Charlton. Subs: 14 Scott Chilton for Lewthwaite (78); 15 Lokeni Savelio for Okesene (50); 16 Carl Sice for Williamson (50); 17 David Humes for Hoyles (71); Okesene for Savelio (74); Hoyles for Charlton (76).
Tries: J Allen (19), Hoyles (23); **Goals:** Hetherington 4; **Field goal:** Stott.
CENTURIONS: 1 Neil Turley; 2 Alan Hadcroft; 3 Paul Anderson; 4 Andy Fairclough; 5 Michael Watts; 6 Simon Svabic; 7 Liam Bretherton; 8 Paul Norman; 9 John Duffy; 10 David Whittle; 11 Simon Baldwin; 12 Chris Morley; 13 Adam Bristow. Subs: 14 David Bradbury for Norman (19); 15 Willie Swann for Bretherton (57); 16 John Hamilton for Duffy (26); 17 Andy Leathem for Whittle (30); Whittle for Leathem (53); Duffy for Hamilton (73).
Tries: Fairclough (34), Hadcroft (42), Anderson (75); **Goals:** Svabic 3.
League Express Men of the Match:
Town: Matt Sturm; *Centurions:* Simon Baldwin.
Penalty count: 13-6; **Half-time:** 14-6;
Referee: Nick Oddy (Halifax); **Attendance:** 1,114.

HUNSLET HAWKS 8 FEATHERSTONE ROVERS 24

HAWKS: 1 Michael Wainwright; 2 George Raynor; 3 Iain Higgins; 4 Dave Jessey; 5 Steve Morton; 6 Chris Ross; 7 Craig Robinson; 8 Neil Bradbrook; 9 Tony Howcroft; 10 Craig Ibbotson; 11 Mick Coyle; 12 Gareth Naylor; 13 Jermaine Coleman. Subs: 14 Michael Banks for Bradbrook (17); 15 Hamish Munton for Wainwright (59); 16 Ben Skerrett for Ibbotson (32); 17 Nicky Dobson for Howcroft (58); Bradbrook for Jessey (74).
Try: Wainwright (37); **Goals:** Ross 2.
ROVERS: 1 Michael Rhodes; 2 Jamie Stokes; 3 Simon Jackson; 4 Chris Spurr; 5 Matt Bramald; 6 Andy Bastow; 7 Jamie Rooney; 8 Stuart Dickens; 9 Richard Chapman; 10 Gary Lord; 11 Ricky Helliwell; 12 Neil Lowe; 13 Paul Darley. Subs: 14 Danny Evans for Helliwell (34); 15 Steve Dooler for Darley (65); 16 Gavin Swinson for Jackson (29); 17 Gavin Morgan for Lord (26).
Tries: Morgan (50), Bastow (54), Rhodes (65, 74); **Goals:** Rooney 4.
League Express Men of the Match:
Hawks: Iain Higgins; *Rovers:* Neil Lowe.
Penalty count: 5-10; **Half-time:** 8-0;
Referee: Graeme Shaw (Wigan); **Attendance:** 909.

WEEK 29

Sunday 17th June 2001

BATLEY BULLDOGS 16 KEIGHLEY COUGARS 14

BULLDOGS: 1 Jeremy Dyson; 2 Roger Simpson; 3 Ryan Horsley; 4 Matt Pennington; 5 Paul Gleadhill; 6 Glen Tomlinson; 7 Mark Cass; 8 Alan Boothroyd; 9 Craig Stevens; 10 Paul Lister; 11 Craig Wright; 12 Will Cartledge; 13 Paul Harrison. Subs: 14 Chris Beevers for Gleadhill (54); 15 Paul Hicks for Richards (44); 16 Gary Shillabeer for Boothroyd (56); 17 Craig Richards for Lister (25); Gleadhill for Beevers (58); Lister for Wright (69).
Tries: Wright (11, 16); **Goals:** Dyson 3; **Field goals:** Wright, Tomlinson.
COUGARS: 1 Chris Hogg; 2 Leroy Rivett; 3 Karl Smith; 4 Matthew Foster; 5 Max Tomlinson; 6 Paul Ashton; 7 Nathan Antonik; 8 Phil Stephenson; 9 Jason Ramshaw; 10 Craig Morphet; 11 Graeme Shaw; 12 Andy Rice; 13 Robert Roberts. Subs: 14 Adam Hayes for Roberts (30BB, rev 48); 15 Oliver Wilkes for Morphet (20); 16 James Rushforth for Hogg (57); 17 Gareth Hooson for Smith (72); Hayes for Rice (51); Morphet for Stephenson (54).
Tries: Tomlinson (4), Wilkes (22), Ashton (40); **Goal:** Ashton.
League Express Men of the Match:
Bulldogs: Craig Wright; *Cougars:* Paul Ashton.
Penalty count: 9-5; **Half-time:** 14-14;
Referee: Nick Oddy (Halifax); **Attendance:** 1,002.

DEWSBURY RAMS 32 DONCASTER DRAGONS 16

RAMS: 1 Matthew Griffin; 2 Richard Baker; 3 Nathan Graham; 4 Kevin Crouthers; 5 Adrian Flynn; 6 Mark Cain; 7 Barry Eaton; 8 Andy Fisher; 9 Richard Pachniuk; 10 Robin Jowitt; 11 Ian Hughes; 12 Dan Potter; 13 Damian Ball. Subs: 14 David Mycoe for Leatham (40); 15 Ryan McDonald for Jowitt (27); 16 Jim Leatham for Crouthers (27); 17 Matthew Roberts for Fisher (62); Crouthers for Hughes (73); Fisher for Ball (76BB).
Tries: Graham (9), Potter (12), Eaton (28), Baker (33), Leatham (37); **Goals:** Eaton 6.
Sin bin: Pachniuk (50) - retaliation; McDonald (65) - deliberate offside.
DRAGONS: 1 Johnny Woodcock; 2 Mick Coult; 3 Carl Hall; 4 Craig Lawton; 5 Anton Garcia; 6 Wayne Green; 7 Billy Conway; 8 Maea David; 9 Peter Green; 10 Brad Hepi; 11 Tony Fella; 12 Tony Miller; 13 Peter Edwards. Subs: 14 Dean Coulton for W Green (35); 15 Phil White for Miller (67); 16 Tony Atter for Hepi (37); 17 Ian Ramskill for Edwards (60BB, rev 65); Hepi for Fella (58); Ramskill for David (76).
Tries: Coulton (45), Hall (66), Lawton (69); **Goals:** Woodcock 2.
Sin bin: Edwards (50) - offence in the tackle.
League Express Men of the Match:
Rams: Dan Potter; *Dragons:* Dean Coulton.
Penalty count: 6-5; **Half-time:** 30-0;
Referee: Steve Presley (Castleford); **Attendance:** 826.

FEATHERSTONE ROVERS 92 YORK 2

ROVERS: 1 Simon Jackson; 2 Jamie Stokes; 3 Gavin Swinson; 4 Chris Spurr; 5 Matt Bramald; 6 Andy Bastow; 7 Jamie Rooney; 8 Stuart Dickens; 9 Richard Chapman; 10 Gary Lord; 11 Danny Evans; 12 Neil Lowe; 13 Paul Darley. Subs: 14 Steve Dooler for Chapman (52); 15 Craig Booth for Evans (26); 16 Lee Williamson for Lord (21); 17 Gavin Morgan for Dickens (21); Dickens for Morgan (56); Evans for Booth (65).
Tries: Jackson (3, 37), Evans (7, 73), Bastow (10), Swinson (17, 20), Stokes (24, 46, 58), Chapman (28), Morgan (32), Spurr (42, 65), Lowe (51), Dooler (68), Bramald (76); **Goals:** Rooney 12.
YORK: 1 Mike Hall; 2 Phil Musgrove; 3 Matthew Mulholland; 4 Gavin Molloy; 5 Andy Innes; 6 Mark Dooley; 7 Gareth Oulton; 8 Andy Precious; 9 Alan Pallister; 10 Shane Cochrane; 11 Carl Bristow; 12 Darren Crake; 13 Nathan Pincher. Subs: 14 Steve Thickbroom for Pallister (ht); 15 Steve Robinson for Dooley (70); 16 Carl Sayer for Cochrane (22); 17 Steve Harris not used; Cochrane for Sayer (52); Pallister for Crake (72); Sayer for Cochrane (72).
Goal: Oulton.
Sin bin: Bristow (34) - holding down.
On report: Crake (26) - high tackle on Rooney.
League Express Men of the Match:
Rovers: Andy Bastow; *York:* Alan Pallister.
Penalty count: 9-8; **Half-time:** 52-2; **Referee:** Ronnie Laughton (Barnsley); **Attendance:** 1,347.

HULL KINGSTON ROVERS 14 SHEFFIELD EAGLES 18

ROVERS: 1 Bob Everitt; 2 Alex Godfrey; 3 Andy Smith; 4 Whetu Taewa; 5 Alasdair McLarron; 6 Chris Kitching; 7 Craig Murdock; 8 Rich Hayes; 9 Steve Cochrane; 10 Richard Wilson; 11 Matt Schultz; 12 Rob Wilson; 13 Chris Charles. Subs: 14 Jimmy Walker for McLarron (46); 15 Jon Aston for Richard Wilson (26); 16 Paul Fletcher for Schultz (26); 17 David Luckwell for Hayes (48); Schultz for Smith (57).
Tries: Everitt (63), Charles (78); **Goals:** Charles 3.
EAGLES: 1 Andy Poynter; 2 Ian Brown; 3 Neil Kite; 4 Gareth Hewitt; 5 Ian Thompson; 6 Mark Aston; 7 Scott Rhodes; 8 Jon Bruce; 9 Gareth Dobson; 10 Steve Hill; 11 Billy Kershaw; 12 Chris Chapman; 13 Richard Goddard. Subs: 14 Lee Bettinson for Dobson (78); 15 Jack Howieson for Bruce (30); 16 Simon Tillyer for Chapman (70); 17 Darren Summerill for Howieson (50); Bruce for Hill (64).
Tries: I Brown (15), Thompson (33), Goddard (45); **Goals:** Goddard 3.
League Express Men of the Match:
Rovers: Bob Everitt; *Eagles:* Richard Goddard.
Penalty count: 5-2; **Half-time:** 2-12;
Referee: Colin Morris (Huddersfield); **Attendance:** 1,625.

ROCHDALE HORNETS 36 LEIGH CENTURIONS 4

HORNETS: 1 Paul Owen; 2 Sean Cooper; 3 Brendan O'Meara; 4 Matt Calland; 5 Marlon Billy; 6 Danny Wood; 7 Latham Tawhai; 8 Danny Sculthorpe; 9 Warren Ayres; 10 Andy Ireland; 11 Wes Rogers; 12 James Bunyan; 13 Dave Watson. Subs: 14 Wayne McHugh for Watson (72); 15 Joe Berry for Ireland (31); 16 Darren Robinson for Ayres (31); 17 Martin Bunce for Rogers (64); Ireland for Sculthorpe (72).
Tries: Billy (6), Robinson (44), Calland (51, 55), Wood (71), McHugh (80); **Goals:** Wood 6.
CENTURIONS: 1 Neil Turley; 2 David Ingram; 3 Paul Anderson; 4 Andy Fairclough; 5 Alan Hadcroft; 6 Simon Svabic; 7 Liam Bretherton; 8 Tim Street; 9 John Hamilton; 10 David Bradbury; 11 Simon Baldwin; 12 Phil Kendrick; 13 Willie Swann. Subs: 14 David Whittle for Bradbury (ht); 15 Adam Bristow for Bretherton (ht); 16 John Duffy for Hamilton (ht); 17 Paul Norman for Street (33BB, rev 67); Bradbury for Fairclough (66); Bretherton for Swann (69); Norman for Baldwin (76).
Try: Kendrick (30).
League Express Men of the Match:
Hornets: Matt Calland; *Centurions:* David Bradbury.
Penalty count: 7-8; **Half-time:** 6-4;
Referee: Peter Taberner (Wigan); **Attendance:** 2,473.

WHITEHAVEN 15 OLDHAM 16

WHITEHAVEN: 1 Paul O'Neill; 2 Jason Roach; 3 David Seeds; 4 Jason Critchley; 5 Mark Wallace; 6 Robert Purdham; 7 Steve Kirkbride; 8 Mark Cox; 9 Marc Jackson; 10 Dean Vaughan; 11 Spencer Miller; 12 Garry Purdham; 13 Aaron Lester. Subs: 14 Ian Devlin for G Purdham (65); 15 Howard Hill for Miller (48); 16 Gary

Smith for Vaughan (65); 17 Phil Sherwen for Cox (30); G Purdham for Jackson (70).
Tries: R Purdham (12), Roach (16, 20);
Goal: Kirkbride; **Field goal:** R Purdham.
OLDHAM: 1 Mark Sibson; 2 Joe McNicholas; 3 Anthony Gibbons; 4 Pat Rich; 5 Daryl Lacey; 6 David Gibbons; 7 Neil Roden; 8 Leo Casey; 9 Keith Brennan; 10 Paul Norton; 11 Phil Farrell; 12 Bryan Henare; 13 Kevin Mannion. Subs: 14 Mike Ford for D Gibbons (65); 15 Jason Clegg for Casey (21); 16 Chris Farrell for Brennan (56); 17 Danny Guest for Clegg (57); Clegg for Guest (70).
Tries: Sibson (25), Brennan (35), A Gibbons (50);
Goals: Rich 2.
League Express Men of the Match:
Whitehaven: Phil Sherwen; *Oldham:* Keith Brennan.
Penalty count: 9-4; **Half-time:** 14-12;
Referee: Julian King (St Helens); **Attendance:** 1,027.

WORKINGTON TOWN 34 SWINTON LIONS 10

TOWN: 1 Steve Wood; 2 Matthew Woodcock; 3 Neil Frazer; 4 John Allen; 5 Graeme Lewthwaite; 6 Kevin Hetherington; 7 Lynton Stott; 8 Matt Sturm; 9 Owen Williamson; 10 Hitro Okesene; 11 Stuart Hoyles; 12 Anthony Samuel; 13 Gary Charlton. Subs: 14 Tane Manihera for Frazer (ht); 15 Lokeni Savelio for Okesene (22); 16 Carl Sice for Williamson (21); 17 David Humes for Hoyles (68BB); Okesene for Savelio (63); Williamson for Charlton (71BB); Frazer for Allen (71).
Tries: Stott (42), Sice (59, 79), Okesene (64), Williamson (72), Frazer (75); **Goals:** Hetherington 5.
LIONS: 1 Wayne Jackman; 2 Adrian Mead; 3 Mick Nanyn; 4 Matt Bateman; 5 Mike Woods; 6 Rob Gallagher; 7 Phil Veivers; 8 Mike Loughlin; 9 Rob Barraclough; 10 Lee Hansen; 11 Phil Cushion; 12 Gareth Chambers; 13 Paul Smith. Subs: 14 Danny Butler for Jackman (71); 15 Jon-Paul Doherty for Hansen (25); 16 Jim Evans for Bateman (53); 17 Ian Lewis for Chambers (74); Hansen for Loughlin (55); Bateman for Nanyn (73).
Tries: Woods (24), Gallagher (39); **Goal:** Nanyn.
League Express Men of the Match:
Town: Gary Charlton; *Lions:* Paul Smith.
Penalty count: 3-8; **Half-time:** 0-10;
Referee: Paul Lee (Leigh); **Attendance:** 737.

GATESHEAD THUNDER 14
BARROW BORDER RAIDERS 44

THUNDER: 1 Michael Johnson; 2 Paul Thorman; 3 Steve Hall; 4 Gareth Lloyd; 5 Leon Williamson; 6 Scott Dyson; 7 Carl Briggs; 8 Lee Garside; 9 Richard Spence; 10 Gareth Barron; 11 Jim Carlton; 12 Stephen Bradley; 13 Stephen Rutherford. Subs: 14 Martin Gambles for Spence (55); 15 Paul Sebine for Barron (32); 16 Wes McGibbon for Hall (72); 17 Mark Wilkinson for Garside (46).
Tries: Carlton (24), Thorman (34), Lloyd (41);
Goal: Briggs.
BORDER RAIDERS: 1 Dean Sharp; 2 Glen Hutton; 3 Stuart Magorian; 4 Adrian Gardner; 5 Shane Irabor; 6 Chris Massey; 7 Darren Holt; 8 Damien Whitter; 9 Anthony Murray; 10 Ian Rawlinson; 11 Geoff Luxon; 12 Mike Whitehead; 13 Brett McDermott. Subs: 14 Jamie Marshall for Massey (67); 15 Willie Burns for Rawlinson (50); 16 Steve Jackson for Whitter (59); 17 Tau Liku for Luxon (63).
Tries: A Gardner (2, 56, 67), Hutton (11, 28), Magorian (37), Sharp (59, 65), Murray (74), Marshall (79);
Goals: Holt 2.
League Express Men of the Match: *Thunder:* Michael Johnson; *Border Raiders:* Adrian Gardner.
Penalty count: 4-5; **Half-time:** 8-16;
Referee: Mike Dawber (Wigan); **Attendance:** 610.

HUNSLET HAWKS 42 CHORLEY LYNX 24

HAWKS: 1 Michael Wainwright; 2 George Raynor; 3 Iain Higgins; 4 Dave Jessey; 5 Steve Morton; 6 Chris Ross; 7 Craig Robinson; 8 Neil Bradbrook; 9 Tony Howcroft; 10 Ben Thompson; 11 Mick Coyle; 12 Ben Skerrett; 13 Jermaine Coleman. Subs: 14 Guy Adams for Ross (27); 15 Gareth Naylor for Coyle (ht); 16 Michael Banks for Bradbrook (24); 17 Hamish Munton for Higgins (49); Ross for Howcroft (ht); Bradbrook for Banks (64BB, rev 71); Howcroft for Ross (73).
Tries: Higgins (4), Coyle (13), Howcroft (15), Banks (35), Adams (48), Wainwright (37), Naylor (76);
Goals: Robinson 3, Ross 4.
LYNX: 1 Lee Bamber; 2 Danny Winrow; 3 Luke Vincent; 4 Stuart Dickinson; 5 Graham Taberner; 6 Paul Wilcock; 7 Stuart Fisher; 8 Lee Prest; 9 Peter Cahalin; 10 Steve Argent; 11 Rob Verrelli; 12 Phil Harrison; 13 Wayne Bloor. Subs: 14 Matthew Brown for Wilcock (76); 15 Andrew Friar for Dickinson (57); 16 Warren Hindle for Verrelli (37); 17 Lee Westwood for Prest (33); Prest for Argent (57); Argent for Westwood (70).
Tries: Harrison (18), Fisher (52), Vincent (59), Taberner (78); **Goals:** Fisher 4.
League Express Men of the Match:
Hawks: Craig Robinson; *Lynx:* Stuart Fisher.
Penalty count: 8-10; **Half-time:** 30-6; **Referee:** Steve Nicholson (Whitehaven); **Attendance:** 441.

Wednesday 20th June 2001

ROCHDALE HORNETS 38
BARROW BORDER RAIDERS 10

HORNETS: 1 Paul Owen; 2 Sean Cooper; 3 Brendan O'Meara; 4 Wayne McHugh; 5 Marlon Billy; 6 Danny Wood; 7 Latham Tawhai; 8 Danny Sculthorpe; 9 Darren Robinson; 10 Andy Ireland; 11 Wes Rogers; 12 James Bunyan; 13 Dave Watson. Subs: 14 Steve Gartland for Watson (56); 15 Joe Berry for Ireland (21); 16 Matt Knowles for Rogers (21); 17 Martin Bunce for Tawhai (68); Rogers for Berry (64); Ireland for Sculthorpe (65).
Tries: Cooper (27, 42), O'Meara (33), Bunyan (45), McHugh (65), Robinson (68), Billy (72); **Goals:** Wood 5.
BORDER RAIDERS: 1 Dean Sharp; 2 Glen Hutton; 3 Stuart Magorian; 4 Adrian Gardner; 5 Shane Irabor; 6 Chris Massey; 7 Darren Holt; 8 Damien Whitter; 9 Anthony Murray; 10 Ian Rawlinson; 11 Geoff Luxon; 12 Mike Whitehead; 13 Brett McDermott. Subs: 14 Jamie Marshall for Massey (59); 15 Willie Burns for Luxon (ht); 16 Steve Jackson for Rawlinson (48); 17 Tau Liku for Whitter (62).
Tries: Hutton (20), McDermott (24); **Goal:** Holt.
League Express Men of the Match: *Hornets:* Latham Tawhai; *Border Raiders:* Brett McDermott.
Penalty count: 10-10; **Half-time:** 12-10;
Referee: Steve Presley (Castleford); **Attendance:** 1,083.

WEEK 30

Sunday 24th June 2001

BARROW BORDER RAIDERS 50 BATLEY BULLDOGS 12

BORDER RAIDERS: 1 Paul Salmon; 2 Glen Hutton; 3 Stuart Magorian; 4 Adrian Gardner; 5 Shane Irabor; 6 Phil Atkinson; 7 Darren Holt; 8 Damien Whitter; 9 Anthony Murray; 10 Ian Rawlinson; 11 Geoff Luxon; 12 Mike Whitehead; 13 Brett McDermott. Subs: 14 Paul Jones for Hutton (65); 15 Willie Burns for Rawlinson (47); 16 Steve Jackson for Whitter (59); 17 Tau Liku for Luxon (57).
Tries: McDermott (4), Salmon (22), A Gardner (26, 77), Whitehead (32), Burns (60), Magorian (62), Irabor (68), Murray (71); **Goals:** Holt 6; **Field goals:** Holt 2.
BULLDOGS: 1 Jeremy Dyson; 2 Roger Simpson; 3 Ryan Horsley; 4 Matt Pennington; 5 Paul Gleadhill; 6 Glen Tomlinson; 7 Mark Cass; 8 Alan Boothroyd; 9 Andy Heptinstall; 10 Paul Lister; 11 Craig Wright; 12 Will Cartledge; 13 Paul Harrison. Subs: 14 Craig Stevens for Heptinstall (50); 15 Paul Hicks for Cartledge (26); 16 Gary Shillabeer for Boothroyd (46); 17 Jeff Wittenberg for Lister (26).
Tries: Pennington (16), Cass (38); **Goals:** Dyson 2.
League Express Men of the Match:
Border Raiders: Paul Salmon; *Bulldogs:* Mark Cass.
Penalty count: 4-3; **Half-time:** 21-12;
Referee: Paul Lee (Leigh); **Attendance:** 665.

CHORLEY LYNX 10 DEWSBURY RAMS 50

LYNX: 1 Lee Bamber; 2 Andrew Friar; 3 Luke Vincent; 4 Stuart Dickinson; 5 Graham Taberner; 6 Paul Wilcock; 7 Stuart Fisher; 8 Mike Prescott; 9 Chris Ramsdale; 10 Lee Westwood; 11 Phil Harrison; 12 Warren Hindle; 13 Wayne Bloor. Subs: 14 Danny Winrow for Friar (22); 15 Matthew Brown for Fisher (41); 16 Rob Verrelli for Westwood (34); 17 Lee Prest not used; Westwood for Prescott (55); Prescott for Harrison (61); Harrison for Verrelli (73).
Tries: Prescott (67), Dickinson (75); **Goal:** Wilcock.
RAMS: 1 Matthew Griffin; 2 Kevin Crouthers; 3 Nathan Graham; 4 Dan Potter; 5 Adrian Flynn; 6 Mark Cain; 7 Barry Eaton; 8 Shayne Williams; 9 Richard Pachniuk; 10 Robin Jowitt; 11 Ian Hughes; 12 Danny Burton; 13 Damian Ball. Subs: 14 Matthew Roberts for Ball (46); 15 Dean Lawford for Pachniuk (26); 16 Andy Fisher for Hughes (29); 17 Ryan McDonald for Williams (21); Hughes for Burton (56); Williams for Jowitt (72).
Tries: Flynn (12, 30), Griffin (15, 45, 60), Potter (21), Pachniuk (25), Graham (41), Crouthers (80);
Goals: Eaton 7.
League Express Men of the Match:
Lynx: Wayne Bloor; *Rams:* Matthew Griffin.
Penalty count: 7-4; **Half-time:** 0-26;
Referee: Graeme Shaw (Wigan); **Attendance:** 364.

DONCASTER DRAGONS 22 ROCHDALE HORNETS 34

DRAGONS: 1 Dean Coulton; 2 Neil Bennett; 3 Anton Garcia; 4 Mick Coult; 5 Johnny Woodcock; 6 Carl Hall; 7 Brad Hepi; 8 Maea David; 9 Peter Green; 10 Tony Atter; 11 Tony Miller; 12 Craig Lawton; 13 Peter Edwards. Subs: 14 Troy Kini for Woodcock (66); 15 Phil White for Fella (62); 16 Tony Fella for Edwards (13); 17 Alan Langham for Atter (38); Atter for David (61); David for Langham (75).
Tries: Woodcock (3), Fella (25), David (28), Hall (65);
Goals: Woodcock 2, Coult.
HORNETS: 1 Paul Owen; 2 Sean Cooper; 3 Brendan O'Meara; 4 Matt Calland; 5 Marlon Billy; 6 Danny Wood; 7 Latham Tawhai; 8 Danny Sculthorpe; 9 Darren Robinson; 10 Matt Knowles; 11 David Stephenson; 12 James Bunyan; 13 Steve Gartland. Subs: 14 Wayne McHugh not used; 15 Andy Ireland for Knowles (31); 16 Joe Berry for Sculthorpe (20); 17 Wes Rogers for Stephenson (22); Stephenson for Bunyan (44BB, rev 49); Knowles for Berry (60); Stephenson for Bunyan (60); Bunyan for Rogers (69BB); Berry for Ireland (74).
Tries: Billy (6), Robinson (31), Rogers (36), Wood (51), O'Meara (67), Calland (75); **Goals:** Wood 5.
League Express Men of the Match:
Dragons: Maea David; *Hornets:* Danny Wood.
Penalty count: 10-9; **Half-time:** 14-18;
Referee: Karl Kirkpatrick (Warrington); **Attendance:** 899.

KEIGHLEY COUGARS 16 OLDHAM 26

COUGARS: 1 James Rushforth; 2 Leroy Rivett; 3 Karl Smith; 4 Matthew Foster; 5 Max Tomlinson; 6 Paul Ashton; 7 Nathan Antonik; 8 Graeme Shaw; 9 Adam Hayes; 10 David Best; 11 Andy Rice; 12 Oliver Wilkes; 13 Robert Roberts. Subs: 14 Andy Richardson for Best (24); 15 Craig Morphet for Wilkes (30BB, rev 52); 16 Gareth Hooson for Rivett (52); 17 James Simeunovich for Shaw (24); Shaw for Roberts (58); Best for Richardson (61); Roberts for Hayes (71).
Tries: Antonik (28), Roberts (38), Wilkes (65);
Goals: Ashton 2.
OLDHAM: 1 Mark Sibson; 2 Joey Hayes; 3 Anthony Gibbons; 4 Pat Rich; 5 Joe McNicholas; 6 Neil Roden; 7 Keith Brennan; 8 Leo Casey; 9 John Hough; 10 Paul Norton; 11 Phil Farrell; 12 Bryan Henare; 13 Kevin Mannion. Subs: 14 Mike Ford for McNicholas (49BB, rev 54); 15 Jason Clegg for Casey (8); 16 Chris Farrell for P Farrell (62); 17 Danny Guest for Clegg (33); Casey for Guest (49BB, rev 63); Clegg for Norton (59); Casey for Guest (70BB, rev 78); Norton for Clegg (72).
Tries: Brennan (2, 18), Hayes (12), Casey (57), Roden (70); **Goals:** Rich 3.
Sin bin: Brennan (35) - holding down.
League Express Men of the Match:
Cougars: Oliver Wilkes; *Oldham:* Keith Brennan.
Penalty count: 7-6; **Half-time:** 10-14;
Referee: Colin Morris (Huddersfield); **Attendance:** 2,225.

LEIGH CENTURIONS 38 FEATHERSTONE ROVERS 17

CENTURIONS: 1 Neil Turley; 2 Alan Hadcroft; 3 Paul Anderson; 4 Andy Fairclough; 5 Michael Watts; 6 Simon Svabic; 7 Liam Bretherton; 8 Andy Leathem; 9 John Hamilton; 10 David Bradbury; 11 Simon Baldwin; 12 Chris Morley; 13 Adam Bristow. Subs: 14 Tim Street for Leathem (27); 15 David Ingram for Svabic (69); 16 Jason Johnson for Norman (58); 17 Paul Norman for Bradbury (33); Leathem for Morley (58); Bradbury for Street (67).
Tries: Turley (24, 42, 49, 61, 77), Johnson (65);
Goals: Svabic 6, Turley.
Sin bin: Anderson (34) - foul.
ROVERS: 1 Michael Rhodes; 2 Jamie Stokes; 3 Gavin Swinson; 4 Chris Spurr; 5 Matt Bramald; 6 Andy Bastow; 7 Jamie Rooney; 8 Stuart Dickens; 9 Richard Chapman; 10 Gary Lord; 11 Ricky Helliwell; 12 Neil Lowe; 13 Paul Darley. Subs: 14 Simon Jackson for Bastow (46); 15 Steve Dooler for Swinson (59); 16 Lee Williamson for Dickens (50); 17 Gavin Morgan for Lord (25); Lord for Williamson (71).
Try: Morgan (56); **Goals:** Rooney 6; **Field goal:** Rooney.
League Express Men of the Match:
Centurions: Neil Turley; *Rovers:* Jamie Rooney.
Penalty count: 9-8; **Half-time:** 8-10;
Referee: Steve Ganson (St Helens); **Attendance:** 2,842.

SWINTON LIONS 30 HUNSLET HAWKS 20

LIONS: 1 Jim Evans; 2 Adrian Mead; 3 Mick Nanyn; 4 Matt Bateman; 5 Mike Woods; 6 Rob Gallagher; 7 Phil Veivers; 8 Lee Hansen; 9 Rob Barraclough; 10 Mike Loughlin; 11 Phil Cushion; 12 Gareth Chambers; 13 Paul Smith. Subs: 14 Danny Butler for Veivers (74); 15 Jon-Paul Doherty for Loughlin (31); 16 Dale Holdstock for Chambers (47); 17 Ian Lewis for Hansen (67); Loughlin for Doherty (68); Chambers for Cushion (73).
Tries: Woods (9, 60), Chambers (20), Bateman (22), Doherty (41), Mead (55); **Goals:** Nanyn 2, Doherty.
HAWKS: 1 Michael Wainwright; 2 George Raynor; 3 Iain Higgins; 4 Dave Jessey; 5 Steve Morton; 6 Jermaine Coleman; 7 Craig Robinson; 8 Ben Thompson; 9 Tony Howcroft; 10 Craig Ibbotson; 11 Mick Coyle; 12 Gareth Naylor; 13 Guy Adams. Subs: 14 Nicky Dobson for Robinson (17); 15 Michael Banks for Naylor (20); 16 Ben Skerrett for Ibbotson (35); 17 Danny Dobson for Morton (68); Ibbotson for Banks (53); Naylor for Howcroft (69).
Tries: Raynor (25, 77), Thompson (35), Higgins (47);
Goals: Coleman 2.
League Express Men of the Match:
Lions: Jim Evans; *Hawks:* Jermaine Coleman.
Penalty count: 6-5; **Half-time:** 16-10;
Referee: Julian King (St Helens).
Attendance: 823 *(at The Willows, Salford).*

WHITEHAVEN 52 GATESHEAD THUNDER 22

WHITEHAVEN: 1 Paul O'Neill; 2 Jason Roach; 3 David Seeds; 4 Jason Critchley; 5 Mark Wallace; 6 Robert Purdham; 7 Steve Kirkbride; 8 Mark Cox; 9 Marc Jackson; 10 Dean Vaughan; 11 Spencer Miller; 12 Garry Purdham; 13 Aaron Lester. Subs: 14 Ian Devlin for Wallace (45); 15 Howard Hill not used; 16 Gary Smith for Vaughan (33); 17 Phil Sherwen for Cox (20); Wallace for G Purdham (75).
Tries: Seeds (8, 33, 62, 74), Wallace (12), Vaughan (19); R Purdham (29, 48, 57); **Goals:** Kirkbride 7, R Purdham.
THUNDER: 1 Michael Johnson; 2 Paul Thorman; 3 Steve Hall; 4 Mark Wilkinson; 5 Leon Williamson; 6 Scott Dyson; 7 Carl Briggs; 8 Lee Garside; 9 Roy Southernwood; 10 Gareth Barron; 11 Jim Carlton; 12 Stephen Bradley; 13 Stephen Rutherford. Subs: 14 Martin Gambles for Dyson (36); 15 Paul Sebine for Bradley (42); 16 Richard Spence for Barron (25); 17 Kevin Neighbour for Williamson (59); Barron for Garside (50); Bradley for Spence (64); Garside for Hall (70BB).
Tries: Carlton (2, 15, 79), Johnson (45); **Goals:** Briggs 3.
League Express Men of the Match:
Whitehaven: Robert Purdham; *Thunder:* Jim Carlton.
Penalty count: 4-12; **Half time:** 28-10;
Referee: Nick Oddy (Halifax); **Attendance:** 848.

YORK 11 WIDNES VIKINGS 66

YORK: 1 Mike Hall; 2 Simon Wray; 3 Callum Irving; 4 Gavin Molloy; 5 Matthew Mulholland; 6 Gareth Oulton; 7 Glen Matsell; 8 Andy Hutchinson; 9 Alan Pallister; 10 Andy Precious; 11 Carl Bristow; 12 Nathan Pincher; 13

Mick Ramsden. Subs: 14 Mark Dooley for Irving (43); 15 Andy Innes for Matsell (73); 16 Carl Sayer for Hutchinson (53); 17 Mick Hagan for Bristow (27); Bristow for Ramsden (50); Hutchinson for Precious (75).
Tries: Pallister (32), Oulton (76); **Goal:** Oulton; **Field goal:** Precious.
VIKINGS: 1 Paul Atcheson; 2 Damian Munro; 3 Craig Weston; 4 Andy Craig; 5 Chris Percival; 6 Ian Watson; 7 Martin Crompton; 8 Simon Knox; 9 Phil Cantillon; 10 Gareth Haggerty; 11 Steve Gee; 12 Sean Richardson; 13 Tommy Hodgkinson. Subs: 14 Stephen Holgate for Gee (48); 15 Chris McKinney for Weston (51); 16 Joe Faimalo for Knox (24); 17 Matthew Long for Haggerty (23); Haggerty for Long (59).
Tries: Percival (1), Richardson (8, 50), Crompton (10), Munro (38), Weston (41), Long (53), Craig (63, 71), Cantillon (65, 68, 74); **Goals:** Weston 4, Watson 5.
League Express Men of the Match:
York: Alan Pallister; *Vikings:* Sean Richardson.
Penalty count: 8-12; **Half-time:** 7-20; **Referee:** Steve Nicholson (Whitehaven); **Attendance:** 952.

SHEFFIELD EAGLES 34 WORKINGTON TOWN 26

EAGLES: 1 Andy Poynter; 2 Ian Brown; 3 Neil Kite; 4 Gareth Hewitt; 5 Ian Thompson; 6 Mark Aston; 7 Scott Rhodes; 8 Steve Hill; 9 Gareth Dobson; 10 Ricky Wright; 11 Billy Kershaw; 12 Chris Chapman; 13 Richard Goddard. Subs: 14 Gavin Brown for Aston (57); 15 Simon Tillyer not used; 16 Jon Bruce for Hill (28); 17 Darren Summerill for Wright (28); Hill for Bruce (57); Wright for Summerill (57).
Tries: Hewitt (7, 71), Dobson (11), Kershaw (34), Poynter (40), Goddard (65); **Goals:** Goddard 5.
TOWN: 1 Steve Wood; 2 Matthew Woodcock; 3 Neil Frazer; 4 Kevin Hetherington; 5 Graeme Lewthwaite; 6 Tane Manihera; 7 Lynton Stott; 8 Matt Sturm; 9 Owen Williamson; 10 Hitro Okesene; 11 John Allen; 12 Stuart Hoyles; 13 Anthony Samuel. Subs: 14 Matthew Tunstall not used; 15 Lokeni Savelio for Okesene (27); 16 Carl Sice for Williamson (55); 17 Jamie Beaumont for Allen (ht); Allen for Sturm (68).
Tries: Hoyles (20), Woodcock (28), Frazer (50), Savelio (74), Hetherington (77); **Goals:** Manihera 3.
League Express Men of the Match:
Eagles: Andy Poynter; *Town:* Lynton Stott.
Penalty count: 3-5; **Half-time:** 22-10; **Referee:** Steve Presley (Castleford); **Attendance:** 1,259.

Wednesday 27th June 2001

DONCASTER DRAGONS 12 DEWSBURY RAMS 13

DRAGONS: 1 Johnny Woodcock; 2 Neil Bennett; 3 Carl Hall; 4 Anton Garcia; 5 Mick Coult; 6 Paul Mansson; 7 Brad Hepi; 8 Maea David; 9 Peter Edwards; 10 Tony Atter; 11 Phil White; 12 Craig Lawton; 13 Tony Miller. Subs (all used): 14 Billy Conway; 15 Tony Fella; 16 Peter Green; 17 Alan Langham.
Tries: Garcia (5), Conway (76); **Goals:** Woodcock 2.
RAMS: 1 Matthew Griffin; 2 Kevin Crouthers; 3 Dan Potter; 4 Nathan Graham; 5 Adrian Flynn; 6 Mark Cain; 7 Barry Eaton; 8 Andy Fisher; 9 Richard Pachniuk; 10 Robin Jowitt; 11 Ian Hughes; 12 Paul Smith; 13 Danny Burton. Subs (all used): 14 Richard Baker; 15 Dean Lawford; 16 Matthew Roberts; 17 Ryan McDonald.
Try: Crouthers (23); **Goals:** Eaton 4; **Field goal:** Lawford.
League Express Men of the Match:
Dragons: Anton Garcia; *Rams:* Barry Eaton.
Penalty count: 12-11; **Half-time:** 4-8; **Referee:** Nick Oddy (Halifax); **Attendance:** 1,047.

WEEK 31

Sunday 1st July 2001

BARROW BORDERS RAIDERS 38 SHEFFIELD EAGLES 14

BORDER RAIDERS: 1 Paul Salmon; 2 Adrian Gardner; 3 Stuart Magorian; 4 Phil Atkinson; 5 Shane Irabor; 6 Chris Massey; 7 Darren Holt; 8 Damien Whitter; 9 Anthony Murray; 10 Ian Rawlinson; 11 Geoff Luxon; 12 Mike Whitehead; 13 Brett McDermott. Subs: 14 Jamie Marshall for Magorian (ht); 15 Willie Burns for Luxon (53); 16 Steve Jackson for Rawlinson (59); 17 Tau Liku for Whitter (67).
Tries: Salmon (7), Whitehead (25, 80), Murray (40), Luxon (50); **Goals:** Holt 8; **Field goals:** Holt 2.
EAGLES: 1 Andy Poynter; 2 Ian Brown; 3 Neil Kite; 4 Gareth Hewitt; 5 Ian Thompson; 6 Gavin Brown; 7 Scott Rhodes; 8 Steve Hill; 9 Gareth Dobson; 10 Ricky Wright; 11 Billy Kershaw; 12 Chris Chapman; 13 Richard Goddard. Subs: 14 Lee Bettinson for Rhodes (50); 15 Jack Howieson for Wright (25); 16 Jon Bruce for Hill (15); 17 Paul Wells for Goddard (ht); Hill for Bruce (32); Wright for Howieson (60).
Tries: Wells (52), G Brown (62); **Goals:** G Brown 2, Goddard.
League Express Men of the Match:
Border Raiders: Damien Whitter; *Eagles:* Gavin Brown.
Penalty count: 8-7; **Half-time:** 22-2; **Referee:** Ronnie Laughton (Barnsley); **Attendance:** 945.

BATLEY BULLDOGS 10 ROCHDALE HORNETS 26

BULLDOGS: 1 Jeremy Dyson; 2 Roger Simpson; 3 Ryan Horsley; 4 Matt Pennington; 5 Paul Gleadhill; 6 Glen Tomlinson; 7 Mark Cass; 8 Paul Lister; 9 Andy Heptinstall; 10 Paul Hicks; 11 Jeff Wittenberg; 12 Craig Wright; 13 Paul Harrison. Subs: 14 Richard Gibson for Dyson (51); 15 Will Cartledge for Lister (54); 16 Gary Shillabeer for Hicks (46); 17 Chris North for Gleadhill (57); Lister for Wittenberg (63); Gleadhill for Heptinstall (63); Heptinstall for Tomlinson (70BB).
Tries: Horsley (22), North (67); **Goal:** Dyson.
HORNETS: 1 Paul Owen; 2 Sean Cooper; 3 Brendan O'Meara; 4 Wayne McHugh; 5 Marlon Billy; 6 Danny Wood; 7 Latham Tawhai; 8 Matt Knowles; 9 Darren Robinson; 10 Andy Ireland; 11 Wes Rogers; 12 James Bunyan; 13 Dave Watson. Subs: 14 Steve Gartland for Watson (60); 15 Joe Berry for Knowles (20); 16 Ben Simpson for Rogers (51); 17 David Stephenson for Knowles (51); Knowles for Ireland (21); Knowles for Berry (72).
Tries: Billy (8, 62), Robinson (53), Berry (60); **Goals:** Wood 5.
League Express Men of the Match:
Bulldogs: Glen Tomlinson; *Hornets:* Joe Berry.
Penalty count: 5-5; **Half-time:** 6-10; **Referee:** Steve Nicholson (Whitehaven); **Attendance:** 728.

CHORLEY LYNX 10 KEIGHLEY COUGARS 60

LYNX: 1 Lee Bamber; 2 Paul Wilcock; 3 Luke Vincent; 4 Stuart Dickinson; 5 Graham Taberner; 6 Wayne Bloor; 7 Danny Winrow; 8 Lee Prest; 9 Chris Ramsdale; 10 Lee Westwood; 11 Phil Harrison; 12 Rob Verrelli; 13 Mike Prescott. Subs: 14 Matthew Brown for Winrow (20); 15 Steve Kelly for Westwood (69); 16 Gary Doherty for Verrelli (52); 17 Chris Todd for Bloor (71).
Tries: Dickinson (11), Bloor (42); **Goal:** Wilcock.
COUGARS: 1 Chris Hogg; 2 Gareth Hooson; 3 Karl Smith; 4 Matthew Foster; 5 Max Tomlinson; 6 Paul Ashton; 7 Nathan Antonik; 8 Phil Stephenson; 9 Jason Ramshaw; 10 Oliver Wilkes; 11 Andy Rice; 12 Robert Roberts; 13 Adam Hayes. Subs: 14 James Simeunovich for Ashton (53); 15 Craig Morphet for Best (55); 16 James Rushforth for Hogg (41); 17 David Best for Stephenson (28); Stephenson for Wilkes (63); Wilkes for Hayes (74).
Tries: Roberts (3), Rice (6), Hayes (16), Ashton (18), Wilkes (23), Foster (28), Ramshaw (54, 67, 78), Rushforth (64), Tomlinson (75);
Goals: Ashton 3, Roberts 5.
League Express Men of the Match:
Lynx: Wayne Bloor; *Cougars:* Jason Ramshaw.
Penalty count: 10-6; **Half-time:** 4-30; **Referee:** Nick Oddy (Halifax); **Attendance:** 704.

DEWSBURY RAMS 16 SWINTON LIONS 42

RAMS: 1 Matthew Griffin; 2 Richard Baker; 3 Nathan Graham; 4 Kevin Crouthers; 5 Adrian Flynn; 6 Dean Lawford; 7 Barry Eaton; 8 Andy Fisher; 9 Richard Pachniuk; 10 Robin Jowitt; 11 Dan Potter; 12 Paul Smith; 13 Damian Ball. Subs: 14 Mark Cain for Ball (40); 15 Ian Hughes for Jowitt (23); 16 Danny Burton for Smith (31); 17 Ryan McDonald for Fisher (23); Smith for McDonald (64).
Tries: Griffin (11), Pachniuk (56, 78); **Goals:** Eaton 2.
LIONS: 1 Jim Evans; 2 Adrian Mead; 3 Mick Nanyn; 4 Matt Bateman; 5 Mike Woods; 6 Rob Gallagher; 7 Phil Veivers; 8 Mike Loughlin; 9 Rob Barraclough; 10 Lee Hansen; 11 Phil Cushion; 12 Dale Holdstock; 13 Paul Smith. Subs: 14 Danny Butler for Cushion (71); 15 Shaun Furey for Gallagher (64); 16 Wayne English for M Loughlin (30); 17 Paul Loughlin for Bateman (18); Bateman for Holdstock (47); M Loughlin for Hansen (58).
Tries: Woods (4), Veivers (13), English (33, 46), Nanyn (64), Evans (71), Butler (79); **Goals:** Nanyn 7.
League Express Men of the Match:
Rams: Dean Lawford; *Lions:* Phil Veivers.
Penalty count: 5-4; **Half-time:** 6-18; **Referee:** Peter Taberner (Wigan); **Attendance:** 853.

FEATHERSTONE ROVERS 20 WHITEHAVEN 24

ROVERS: 1 Simon Jackson; 2 Jamie Stokes; 3 Gavin Swinson; 4 Chris Spurr; 5 Matt Bramald; 6 Andy Bastow; 7 Jamie Rooney; 8 Craig Booth; 9 Richard Chapman; 10 Gary Lord; 11 Stephen Jones; 12 Steve Dooler; 13 Paul Darley. Subs: 14 Michael Rhodes for Jackson (29); 15 Stuart Dickens for Lord (20); 16 Neil Lowe for Dooler (22); 17 Gavin Morgan for Booth (20); Dooler for Jones (ht); Lord for Dickens (69).
Tries: Lowe (24), Bramald (35), Stokes (59, 78);
Goals: Rooney 2.
WHITEHAVEN: 1 Paul O'Neill; 2 Mark Wallace; 3 David Seeds; 4 Jason Critchley; 5 Jason Roach; 6 Robert Purdham; 7 Steve Kirkbride; 8 Phil Sherwen; 9 Marc Jackson; 10 Dean Vaughan; 11 Spencer Miller; 12 Garry Purdham; 13 Aaron Lester. Subs: 14 Ryan Campbell not used; 15 Gary Smith for Vaughan (36); 16 Howard Hill for G Purdham (25); 17 Ian Devlin for Wallace (ht); Vaughan for Sherwen (51); G Purdham for Jackson (57); Sherwen for Smith (68).
Tries: Lester (50), Kirkbride (53), Sherwen (74);
Goals: Kirkbride 5; **Field goals:** Kirkbride 2.
League Express Men of the Match:
Rovers: Neil Lowe; *Whitehaven:* Aaron Lester.
Penalty count: 7-10; **Half-time:** 10-4; **Referee:** Colin Morris (Huddersfield); **Attendance:** 1,550.

HULL KINGSTON ROVERS 24 OLDHAM 4

ROVERS: 1 Bob Everitt; 2 Alex Godfrey; 3 Andy Smith; 4 Whetu Taewa; 5 Alasdair McLarron; 6 Jimmy Walker; 7 Craig Murdock; 8 Rich Hayes; 9 Mike Dixon; 10 Richard Wilson; 11 Richard Slater; 12 Matt Schultz; 13 Chris Charles. Subs: 14 Chris Kitching not used; 15 Rob Wilson for Schultz (24); 16 Paul Fletcher for Slater (ht); 17 Jon Aston for Richard Wilson (24); Richard Wilson for Hayes (50); Schultz for Fletcher (60).
Tries: McLarron (12), Hayes (37), Rob Wilson (47), Walker (69); **Goals:** Charles 4.
OLDHAM: 1 Mark Sibson; 2 Joey Hayes; 3 Anthony Gibbons; 4 Pat Rich; 5 Joe McNicholas; 6 Neil Roden; 7 Keith Brennan; 8 Leo Casey; 9 John Hough; 10 Paul Norton; 11 Phil Farrell; 12 Bryan Henare; 13 Kevin Mannion. Subs: 14 Mike Ford for Brennan (44); 15 Jason Clegg for Casey (20); 16 Chris Farrell for Guest (70); 17 Danny Guest for Clegg (50).
Try: Hayes (74).
Sin bin: A Gibbons (15) - professional foul.
League Express Men of the Match:
Rovers: Mike Dixon; *Oldham:* Kevin Mannion
Penalty count: 7-9; **Half-time:** 12–0;
Referee: Steve Presley (Castleford); **Attendance:** 2,537.

LEIGH CENTURIONS 84 YORK 1

CENTURIONS: 1 Neil Turley; 2 David Ingram; 3 Phil Kendrick; 4 Andy Fairclough; 5 Michael Watts; 6 Simon Svabic; 7 Willie Swann; 8 Tim Street; 9 John Hamilton; 10 David Whittle; 11 Adam Bristow; 12 Chris Morley; 13 Jason Johnson. Subs: 14 Andy Leathem for Whittle (24); 15 Alan Hadcroft for Turley (61); 16 Alan Cross for Bristow (48); 17 Paul Norman for Street (33); Street for Hamilton (55); Whittle for Svabic (68).
Tries: Kendrick (2, 47), Turley (6, 24, 28), Watts (17, 33), Swann (23), Fairclough (51), Morley (53), Street (60, 72), Ingram (64, 74), Cross (78);
Goals: Svabic 8, Street 4.
YORK: 1 Mike Hall; 2 Matthew Mulholland; 3 Simon Wray; 4 Gavin Molloy; 5 Mark Dooley; 6 Gareth Oulton; 7 Glen Matsell; 8 Andy Hutchinson; 9 Alan Pallister; 10 Andy Precious; 11 Darren Crake; 12 Nathan Pincher; 13 Mick Ramsden. Subs: 14 Andy Innes not used; 15 Carl Sayer not used; 16 Carl Bristow for Crake (32); 17 Steve Robinson for Matsell (52); Crake for Bristow (76).
Field goal: Oulton.
League Express Men of the Match:
Centurions: Tim Street; *York:* Andy Precious.
Penalty count: 5-4; **Half-time:** 38-0;
Referee: Ben Thaler (Wakefield); **Attendance:** 2,433.

WORKINGTON TOWN 34 DONCASTER DRAGONS 16

TOWN: 1 Steve Wood; 2 Matthew Woodcock; 3 Neil Frazer; 4 Lynton Stott; 5 Graeme Lewthwaite; 6 Tane Manihera; 7 Kevin Hetherington; 8 Matt Sturm; 9 Owen Williamson; 10 Hitro Okesene; 11 Stuart Hoyles; 12 Anthony Samuel; 13 Gary Charlton. Subs: 14 Matthew Tunstall for Sturm (59); 15 Lokeni Savelio for Okesene (25); 16 Carl Sice for Williamson (50); 17 Jamie Beaumont for Charlton (ht); Okesene for Tunstall (60BB); Sturm for Savelio (69); Williamson for Sice (72).
Tries: Hoyles (5), Stott (16), Lewthwaite (20, 38), Beaumont (42, 71); **Goals:** Manihera 5.
DRAGONS: 1 Wayne Green; 2 Johnny Woodcock; 3 Craig Lawton; 4 Anton Garcia; 5 Carl Oakes; 6 Paul Mansson; 7 Brad Hepi; 8 Maea David; 9 Peter Edwards; 10 Alan Langham; 11 Phil White; 12 Peter Green; 13 Tony Miller. Subs: 14 Billy Conway for Lawton (39); 15 Dean Coulton for Woodcock (60); 16 Troy Kini for White (50); 17 Ian Ramskill for Langham (ht); White for Ramskill (50BB, rev 59).
Tries: Mansson (62), Ramskill (69), Garcia (76);
Goals: W Green 2.
League Express Men of the Match:
Town: Matt Sturm; *Dragons:* Maea David.
Penalty count: 7-7; **Half-time:** 22-0;
Referee: Robert Connolly (Wigan); **Attendance:** 993.

HUNSLET HAWKS 4 WIDNES VIKINGS 42

HAWKS: 1 Michael Wainwright; 2 George Raynor; 3 Iain Higgins; 4 Gareth Naylor; 5 Steve Morton; 6 Jermaine Coleman; 7 Craig Robinson; 8 Ben Thompson; 9 Tony Howcroft; 10 Craig Ibbotson; 11 Mick Coyle; 12 Dave Jessey; 13 Guy Adams. Subs: 14 Michael Banks for Jessey (18); 15 Ben Skerrett for Howcroft (ht); 16 Hamish Munton for Morton (53); 17 Nicky Dobson for Coyle (53); Jessey for Ibbotson (58BB, rev 63); Coyle for Thompson (61).
Try: Thompson (39).
VIKINGS: 1 Paul Atcheson; 2 Damian Munro; 3 Craig Weston; 4 Jason Demetriou; 5 Chris Percival; 6 Ian Watson; 7 Martin Crompton; 8 Simon Knox; 9 Phil Cantillon; 10 Stephen Holgate; 11 Steve Gee; 12 Sean Richardson; 13 Tommy Hodgkinson. Subs: 14 Andy Craig for Watson (51); 15 Chris McKinney for Hodgkinson (51); 16 Joe Faimalo for Holgate (27); 17 Matthew Long for Knox (24); Knox for Gee (60).
Tries: Gee (12), Crompton (19, 78), Cantillon (22), Weston (53), Knox (68), Munro (74); **Goals:** Weston 7.
League Express Men of the Match:
Hawks: Craig Ibbotson; *Vikings:* Craig Weston.
Penalty count: 4-8; **Half-time:** 4-18;
Referee: Paul Lee (Leigh); **Attendance:** 1,498.

PLAY-OFFS

Sunday 8th July 2001

PRELIMINARY SEMI-FINALS

LEIGH CENTURIONS 14 OLDHAM 15

CENTURIONS: 1 Neil Turley; 2 Alan Hadcroft; 3 Paul Anderson; 4 Andy Fairclough; 5 Michael Watts; 6 Simon Svabic; 7 Liam Bretherton; 8 Tim Street; 9 John Hamilton; 10 David Bradbury; 11 Simon Baldwin; 12 Chris Morley; 13 Adam Bristow. Subs: 14 David Whittle for Street (25); 15 Willie Swann not used; 16 John Duffy for Hamilton (31); 17 Andy Leathem for Bradbury (40); Hamilton for Duffy (64); Bradbury for Whittle (67); Street for Leathem (70).

Tries: Turley (44), Anderson (53), Watts (63); Goal: Svabic.
Sin bin: Turley (28) - holding down.
OLDHAM: 1 Mark Sibson; 2 Joey Hayes; 3 Anthony Gibbons; 4 Pat Rich; 5 Joe McNicholas; 6 Neil Roden; 7 Mike Ford; 8 Leo Casey; 9 Keith Brennan; 10 Paul Norton; 11 Phil Farrell; 12 Bryan Henare; 13 Kevin Mannion. Subs: 14 John Hough for Brennan (26); 15 Jason Clegg for Norton (50); 16 Chris Farrell for Henare (76); 17 Danny Guest for Casey (45); Norton for Guest (70); Brennan for Hough (74).
Tries: Hough (30), Sibson (64); Goals: Rich 3;
Field goal: Brennan.
Sin bin: Ford (57) - late tackle.
On report: Casey (38) - tripping.
League Express Men of the Match:
Centurions: Neil Turley; Oldham: Mike Ford.
Penalty count: 9-5; Half-time: 0-9;
Referee: Colin Morris (Huddersfield); Attendance: 3,436.

WIDNES VIKINGS 34 ROCHDALE HORNETS 24

VIKINGS: 1 Paul Atcheson; 2 Damian Munro; 3 Craig Weston; 4 Jason Demetriou; 5 Chris Percival; 6 Richard Agar; 7 Martin Crompton; 8 Simon Knox; 9 Phil Cantillon; 10 Stephen Holgate; 11 Steve Gee; 12 Sean Richardson; 13 Tommy Hodgkinson. Subs: 14 Andy Craig for Weston (16); 15 Chris McKinney for Crompton (71); 16 Joe Faimalo for Knox (37); 17 Matthew Long for Holgate (29); Knox for Faimalo (61).
Tries: Demetriou (7), Atcheson (22), Craig (33), Long (40, 65), Cantillon (70); Goals: Weston, Agar 3.
HORNETS: 1 Paul Owen; 2 Sean Cooper; 3 Brendan O'Meara; 4 Matt Calland; 5 Marlon Billy; 6 Danny Wood; 7 Latham Tawhai; 8 Danny Sculthorpe; 9 Darren Robinson; 10 Andy Ireland; 11 David Stephenson; 12 James Bunyan; 13 Dave Watson. Subs: 14 Steve Gartland for Watson (71); 15 Joe Berry for Ireland (29); 16 Matt Knowles for Stephenson (65); 17 Wes Rogers for Bunyan (29); Ireland for Sculthorpe (73).
Tries: Stephenson (11), Robinson (15, 42), Owen (76);
Goals: Wood 4.
League Express Men of the Match:
Vikings: Martin Crompton; Hornets: Darren Robinson.
Penalty count: 12-6; Half-time: 22-14; Referee: Karl Kirkpatrick (Warrington); Attendance: 4,202.

ELIMINATION SEMI-FINALS

FEATHERSTONE ROVERS 28 KEIGHLEY COUGARS 24

ROVERS: 1 Michael Rhodes; 2 Jamie Stokes; 3 Gavin Swinson; 4 Chris Spurr; 5 Matt Bramald; 6 Andy Bastow; 7 Jamie Rooney; 8 Gary Lord; 9 Richard Chapman; 10 Ricky Helliwell; 11 Craig Booth; 12 Neil Lowe; 13 Paul Darley. Subs: 14 Simon Jackson for Chapman (77); 15 Steve Dooler for Spurr (50); 16 Stuart Dickens for Helliwell (38); 17 Gavin Morgan for Lord (31); Lord for Morgan (68).
Tries: Rooney (15, 34), Swinson (21), Spurr (27), Chapman (62); Goals: Rooney 4.
On report: Rhodes (68) - incident following Keighley try.
COUGARS: 1 James Rushforth; 2 Matthew Foster; 3 Karl Smith; 4 Andy Rice; 5 Max Tomlinson; 6 Paul Ashton; 7 Nathan Antonik; 8 Phil Stephenson; 9 Jason Ramshaw; 10 Graeme Shaw; 11 Oliver Wilkes; 12 Robert Roberts; 13 Adam Hayes. Subs: 14 Craig Morphet for Stephenson (50); 15 Danny Horne not used; 16 Andy Richardson not used; 17 Martin Taylor for Shaw (45); Stephenson for Taylor (62); Shaw for Wilkes (76).
Tries: Roberts (24, 77), Ashton (41), Ramshaw (67);
Goals: Ashton 4.
On report: Roberts (64) - high tackle on Chapman.
League Express Men of the Match:
Rovers: Jamie Rooney; Cougars: Oliver Wilkes.
Penalty count: 7-5; Half-time: 22-8;
Referee: Peter Taberner (Wigan); Attendance: 1,710.

DEWSBURY RAMS 6 HULL KINGSTON ROVERS 19

RAMS: 1 Matthew Griffin; 2 Richard Baker; 3 Dan Potter; 4 Kevin Crouthers; 5 Adrian Flynn; 6 Mark Cain; 7 Barry Eaton; 8 Andy Fisher; 9 Richard Pachniuk; 10 Robin Jowitt; 11 Danny Burton; 12 Paul Smith; 13 Damian Ball. Subs: 14 Nathan Graham for Ball (44); 15 Ian Hughes for Smith (48); 16 Shayne Williams for Jowitt (30BB, rev 41); 17 Ryan McDonald for Jowitt (49); Ball for Griffin (65); Smith for Cain (54).
Try: Eaton (66); Goal: Eaton.
Sin bin: Fisher (38) - punching.
ROVERS: 1 Bob Everitt; 2 Dean Andrews; 3 Andy Smith; 4 Whetu Taewa; 5 Alex Godfrey; 6 Jimmy Walker; 7 Craig Murdock; 8 Rich Hayes; 9 Mike Dixon; 10 Richard Wilson; 11 Richard Slater; 12 Matt Schultz; 13 Chris Charles. Subs: 14 Chris Kitching for Walker (51); 15 Rob Wilson for Smith (39); 16 Paul Fletcher for Slater (49); 17 Jon Aston for Richard Wilson (24); Richard Wilson for Hayes (54); Slater for Fletcher (68).
Tries: Dixon (4), Everitt (11, 42); Goals: Charles 3;
Field goal: Kitching.
Sin bin: Andrews (38) - retaliation.
League Express Men of the Match:
Rams: Danny Burton; Rovers: Chris Charles.
Penalty count: 9-6; Half-time: 2-10;
Referee: Nick Oddy (Halifax); Attendance: 1,576.

Sunday 15th July 2001

MINOR SEMI-FINALS

LEIGH CENTURIONS 26 FEATHERSTONE ROVERS 10

CENTURIONS: 1 Neil Turley; 2 Alan Hadcroft; 3 Paul Anderson; 4 Andy Fairclough; 5 Michael Watts; 6 Simon Svabic; 7 Willie Swann; 8 Tim Street; 9 John Hamilton;

Widnes' Joe Faimalo takes on Oldham duo Danny Guest and Mike Ford during the NFP Grand Final at Spotland

10 Andy Leatham; 11 Simon Baldwin; 12 Chris Morley; 13 Adam Bristow. Subs: 14 David Whittle for Leatham (1); 15 David Bradbury for Whittle (27); 16 Liam Bretherton for Turley (41); 17 Phil Kendrick for Morley (56); Whittle for Bradbury (70); Morley for Bristow (79).
Tries: Bristow (17), Bradbury (34), Turley (39);
Goals: Svabic 7.
Sent off: Street (5) - fighting.
ROVERS: 1 Michael Rhodes; 2 Jamie Stokes; 3 Gavin Swinson; 4 Richard Thaler; 5 Matt Bramald; 6 Andy Bastow; 7 Jamie Rooney; 8 Gary Lord; 9 Richard Chapman; 10 Ricky Helliwell; 11 Craig Booth; 12 Neil Lowe; 13 Paul Darley. Subs: 14 Simon Jackson for Darley (56); 15 Steve Dooler for Lowe (47); 16 Stuart Dickens for Helliwell (41); 17 Gavin Morgan for Lord (51); Lord for Morgan (65).
Tries: Bastow (43), Thaler (61); Goal: Rooney.
Sent off: Booth (5) - fighting.
League Express Men of the Match:
Centurions: Adam Bristow; Rovers: Jamie Rooney.
Penalty count: 9-5; Half-time: 22-0;
Referee: Nick Oddy (Halifax); Attendance: 3,236.

ROCHDALE HORNETS 21 HULL KINGSTON ROVERS 14

HORNETS: 1 Paul Owen; 2 Sean Cooper; 3 Brendan O'Meara; 4 Matt Calland; 5 Marlon Billy; 6 Danny Wood; 7 Latham Tawhai; 8 Danny Sculthorpe; 9 Darren Robinson; 10 Andy Ireland; 11 David Stephenson; 12 Wes Rogers; 13 Dave Watson. Subs: 14 Steve Gartland for Watson (67); 15 Joe Berry for Ireland (18BB); 16 James Bunyan for Stephenson (32); 17 Matt Knowles for Berry (24); Stephenson for Rogers (46); Berry for Knowles (60); Ireland for Sculthorpe (54).
Tries: Cooper (16), Billy (47), Bunyan (61), Wood (68);
Goals: Wood 2; Field goal: Sculthorpe.
ROVERS: 1 Bob Everitt; 2 Dean Andrews; 3 Matt Schultz; 4 Whetu Taewa; 5 Alex Godfrey; 6 Jimmy Walker; 7 Craig Murdock; 8 Rich Hayes; 9 Mike Dixon; 10 Richard Wilson; 11 Richard Slater; 12 Rob Wilson; 13 Chris Charles. Subs: 14 Chris Kitching for Schultz (30BB, rev ht); 15 Alasdair McLarron for Andrews (63); 16 Paul Fletcher for Slater (49); 17 Jon Aston for Richard Wilson (23); Richard Wilson for Hayes (49); Kitching for Walker (63); Slater for Rob Wilson (69).
Tries: Walker (30), Taewa (75), Slater (78);
Goal: Charles.
League Express Men of the Match:
Hornets: Danny Wood; Rovers: Craig Murdock.
Penalty count: 6-7; Half-time: 4-4;
Referee: Robert Connolly (Wigan); Attendance: 2,252.

Sunday 22nd July 2001

MAJOR SEMI-FINALS

LEIGH CENTURIONS 18 WIDNES VIKINGS 26

CENTURIONS: 1 Liam Bretherton; 2 Alan Hadcroft; 3 Paul Anderson; 4 Andy Fairclough; 5 Michael Watts; 6 Simon Svabic; 7 Willie Swann; 8 Tim Street; 9 John Hamilton; 10 David Whittle; 11 Simon Baldwin; 12 Chris Morley; 13 Adam Bristow. Subs: 14 Phil Kendrick for Hadcroft (55); 15 John Duffy for Hamilton (31); 16 David Bradbury for Street (24); 17 Andy Leatham for Bradbury (55); Hamilton for Duffy (52); Street for Whittle (69).
Tries: Morley (3), Hadcroft (24), Kendrick (73);
Goals: Svabic 3.
VIKINGS: 1 Paul Atcheson; 2 Damian Munro; 3 Craig Weston; 4 Jason Demetriou; 5 Chris Percival; 6 Richard Agar; 7 Martin Crompton; 8 Simon Knox; 9 Phil Cantillon; 10 Stephen Holgate; 11 Steve Gee; 12 Sean Richardson; 13 Tommy Hodgkinson. Subs: 14 Andy Craig not used; 15 Chris McKinney for Gee (62); 16 Joe Faimalo for Knox (37); 17 Matthew Long for Holgate (24); Holgate for Faimalo (73).
Tries: Percival (19, 61), Munro (49, 66), McKinney (78);
Goals: Weston 2; Field goals: Agar, Knox.
League Express Men of the Match:
Centurions: Liam Bretherton; Vikings: Sean Richardson.
Penalty count: 5-4; Half-time: 12-4;
Referee: Ian Smith (Oldham); Attendance: 6,399.

ROCHDALE HORNETS 32 OLDHAM 39

HORNETS: 1 Paul Owen; 2 Sean Cooper; 3 Brendan O'Meara; 4 Matt Calland; 5 Marlon Billy; 6 Danny Wood; 7 Latham Tawhai; 8 Danny Sculthorpe; 9 Darren Robinson; 10 Andy Ireland; 11 David Stephenson; 12 James Bunyan; 13 Dave Watson. Subs: 14 Steve Gartland for Watson (65); 15 Joe Berry for Ireland (30); 16 Wayne McHugh for Cooper (10BB); 17 Matt Knowles for Stephenson (59); Ireland for Sculthorpe (71); Sculthorpe for Knowles (76).
Tries: Sculthorpe (25), Cooper (28), Robinson (23), Billy (32), Calland (35), Wood (52); Goals: Wood 4.
Sin bin: O'Meara (51) - fighting.
OLDHAM: 1 Mark Sibson; 2 Joey Hayes; 3 Anthony Gibbons; 4 Pat Rich; 5 Joe McNicholas; 6 Neil Roden; 7 Mike Ford; 8 Leo Casey; 9 Keith Brennan; 10 Paul Norton; 11 Phil Farrell; 12 Bryan Henare; 13 Kevin Mannion. Subs: 14 David Gibbons for Ford (37); 15 Jason Clegg for Casey (27BB, rev 53); 16 John Hough for Brennan (47); 17 Danny Guest for Norton (61); Ford for Mannion (63); Norton for Casey (74BB).
Tries: Brennan (16), Casey (68), McNicholas (71), Henare (73, 80); Goals: Rich 9; Field goal: Ford.
Sin bin: A Gibbons (57) - fighting.
League Express Men of the Match:
Hornets: Matt Calland; Oldham: Mike Ford.
Penalty count: 6-13; Half-time: 24-12;
Referee: Steve Ganson (St Helens); Attendance: 4,153.

Saturday 28th July 2001

GRAND FINAL

OLDHAM 14 WIDNES VIKINGS 24

OLDHAM: 1 Mark Sibson; 2 Joey Hayes; 3 Anthony Gibbons; 4 Pat Rich; 5 Joe McNicholas; 6 David Gibbons; 7 Neil Roden; 8 Leo Casey; 9 Keith Brennan; 10 Paul Norton; 11 Phil Farrell; 12 Bryan Henare; 13 Kevin Mannion. Subs: 14 Mike Ford for Mannion (27); 15 Jason Clegg for Casey (18); 16 John Hough for Brennan (44); 17 Danny Guest for Norton (40BB, rev 54); Mannion for Henare (66); Guest for Clegg (73).
Tries: Brennan (9), Ford (74), Mannion (80); Goal: Rich.
VIKINGS: 1 Paul Atcheson; 2 Damian Munro; 3 Craig Weston; 4 Jason Demetriou; 5 Chris Percival; 6 Richard Agar; 7 Martin Crompton; 8 Simon Knox; 9 Phil Cantillon; 10 Stephen Holgate; 11 Steve Gee; 12 Sean Richardson; 13 Tommy Hodgkinson. Subs: 14 Andy Craig for Percival (59); 15 Chris McKinney for Gee (41); 16 Joe Faimalo for Knox (32); 17 Matthew Long for Holgate (23); Knox for Long (49BB, rev 61); Holgate for Long (74).
Tries: Gee (17), Demetriou (38, 60), Cantillon (50), Munro (69); Goals: Weston 2.

CHALLENGE CUP 2001
Round by Round

ROUND 3

Friday 26th January 2001

HALTON SIMMS CROSS 10 VILLENEUVE LEOPARDS 42

SIMMS CROSS: 1 Keiron Kavanagh; 2 Paul Walsh; 3 Kel McGeiver; 4 Dave Myers; 5 Mike Yearsley; 6 Neil Percival; 7 Mark Shepperd; 8 Carl Burns; 9 Mark O'Connor; 10 Peter Grady; 11 Neil Highfield; 12 John Bowles; 13 Jim Cassidy. Subs (all used): 14 Peter Worthington; 15 Lee Swain; 16 Matt Carmichael; 17 Darren O'Brien.
Tries: Kavanagh (35), Cassidy (80); **Goal:** Percival.
LEOPARDS: 1 Michael Van Snick; 2 Ludovic Perolari; 3 Gilles Cornut; 4 Daniel Vergniol; 5 Chad Dillinger; 6 Laurent Frayssinous; 7 Frederic Banquet; 8 Grant Doorey; 9 Vincent Wulf; 10 Dragan Durdevic; 11 Brock Mueller; 12 Romain Sort; 13 Laurent Carrasco. Subs (all used): 14 David Collado; 15 Christophe Canal; 16 Nicolas Hermet; 17 Jérôme Hermet.
Tries: Perolari (1), Wulf (18), Doorey (22), J Hermet (60), Van Snick (68), Vergniol (72), Frayssinous (77); **Goals:** Banquet 7.
League Express Men of the Match:
Simms Cross: Jim Cassidy; *Leopards:* Grant Doorey.
Penalty count: 7-10; **Half-time:** 6-18;
Referee: Karl Kirkpatrick (Warrington);
Attendance: 809 *(at Auto Quest Stadium, Widnes).*

Saturday 27th January 2001

ROCHDALE HORNETS 52 WIGAN ROSE BRIDGE 0

HORNETS: 1 Dave Watson; 2 Sean Cooper; 3 Danny Wood; 4 Brendan O'Meara; 5 Marlon Billy; 6 Paul Owen; 7 Mick Coates; 8 Danny Sculthorpe; 9 Warren Ayres; 10 Andy Ireland; 11 Wes Rogers; 12 David Stephenson; 13 Mick Martindale. Subs: 14 Matt Calland for Watson (45); 15 Steve Campbell for Ireland (22); 16 Chris Newall for Stephenson (52); 17 Ben Simpson for Sculthorpe (25); Ireland for Rogers (70); Stephenson for Ayres (76).
Tries: Watson (4, 32), Wood (18, 25), Stephenson (21), Owen (28), Rogers (35, 59), Billy (47), Newall (66); **Goals:** Coates 5, Wood.
ROSE BRIDGE: 1 Damien Cleary; 2 Ben Molyneux; 3 Lee Jones; 4 Andrew Moncrief; 5 Barry Sharman; 6 Stuart Cassidy; 7 Carl Roden; 8 Peter Valentine; 9 Lee Cassidy; 10 Andy Eatock; 11 Neil Jukes; 12 Kevin Shepherd; 13 Wes Else. Subs: 14 Mark Whitefield for Sharman (61); 15 Peter Fairhurst for Else (41); 16 Alan Wood for Eatock (30); 17 Mark Matthews for Valentine (3BB, rev 5); Matthews for Valentine (21); Eatock for Matthews (56); Matthews for Fairhurst (75).
League Express Men of the Match:
Hornets: Paul Owen; *Rose Bridge:* Stuart Cassidy.
Penalty count: 9-5; **Half-time:** 36-0;
Referee: Julian King (St Helens); **Attendance:** 731.

DEWSBURY RAMS 48 LEIGH MINERS RANGERS 10

RAMS: 1 Nathan Graham; 2 Alex Godfrey; 3 Dan Potter; 4 Adrian Flynn; 5 Richard Baker; 6 Mark Cain; 7 Barry Eaton; 8 Andy Fisher; 9 David Mycoe; 10 Shayne Williams; 11 Sean Richardson; 12 Andrew Spink; 13 Kevin Spink. Subs: 14 Liam Tallon for Flynn (54); 15 Gavin Wood for Potter (54); 16 Ryan McDonald for Williams (23); 17 Simon Hicks for McDonald (52); Williams for Fisher (71).
Tries: Eaton (9, 59, 79), Mycoe (13), A Spink (28), Flynn (44), Baker (48), Fisher (63); **Goals:** Eaton 8.
MINERS RANGERS: 1 Matt Irwin; 2 Steve Clark; 3 Mark Hudspith; 4 Mark Sarsfield; 5 Paul Shepherd; 6 Mick Warburton; 7 Scott Hilton; 8 Danny Flannery; 9 Roy Stott; 10 Johnny Light; 11 Chris Flynn; 12 Steve Flannery; 13 Tommy Goulding. Subs: 14 Sean Phoenix for Warburton (47); 15 Alan Coleman for Hilton (38); 16 Lee Lomax for Stott (37); 17 Lewis Waterworth for D Flannery (27); Stott for Flynn (54); D Flannery for Waterworth (54).
Tries: Hudspith (22), Clark (77); **Goal:** Hudspith.
League Express Men of the Match:
Rams: Barry Eaton; *Miners Rangers:* Tommy Goulding.
Penalty count: 12-6; **Half-time:** 18-6;
Referee: Nick Oddy (Halifax); **Attendance:** 1,260.

Sunday 28th January 2001

BARROW BORDER RAIDERS 40 ASKAM 16

BORDER RAIDERS: 1 Chris Massey; 2 Glen Hutton; 3 Phil Atkinson; 4 Brett McDermott; 5 Adrian Gardner; 6 Clint Barends; 7 Darren Holt; 8 Tau Liku; 9 Anthony Murray; 10 Gareth Pratt; 11 Matthew Leigh; 12 Geoff Luxon; 13 Gary Charlton. Subs: 14 Ian Rawlinson for Liku (40); 15 Mike Whitehead for Pratt (40); 16 Damien Whitter for Luxon (40); 17 Jamie Marshall for Atkinson (75).
Tries: Liku (11), Hutton (38, 43, 53, 79), Holt (65), McDermott (76); **Goals:** Holt 6.
ASKAM: 1 Neil Atkinson; 2 Dave Tippett; 3 Mike Wilson; 4 Tom Butler; 5 Craig Regan; 6 Paul Tyson; 7 Paul Jones; 8 Stuart Quayle; 9 Chris Moralee; 10 Martin Porter; 11 Steve Jackson; 12 Mike Bolton; 13 Gary Dixon. Subs: 14 Steve Thomson for Porter (26); 15 Jamie Butler for Quayle (40); 16 Glen Courts for Regan (40); 17 Steve Rowley for Jackson (58).
Tries: Jones (15), T Butler (58); **Goals:** Atkinson 4.
League Express Men of the Match:
Border Raiders: Glen Hutton; *Askam:* Paul Jones.
Penalty count: 7-5; **Half time:** 14-8;
Referee: Grant Maxwell (Wigan); **Attendance:** 2,092.

BATLEY BULLDOGS 70 HEWORTH 0

BULLDOGS: 1 Craig Lingard; 2 Jeremy Dyson; 3 Danny Maun; 4 Davide Longo; 5 Paul Gleadhill; 6 Richard Price; 7 Glen Tomlinson; 8 Chris McWilliam; 9 Andy Heptinstall; 10 Paul Hicks; 11 Gary Shillabeer; 12 Will Cartledge; 13 Ryan Horsley. Subs: 14 Jamie Coventry for Heptinstall (40); 15 Mark Cass for Horsley (27); 16 Rob Padgett for Cartledge (40); 17 Andy Wray for Hicks (48); Cartledge for McWilliam (57).
Tries: Gleadhill (2), Horsley (10), Longo (11), Lingard (18, 62, 67, 72), Maun (34, 73), Dyson (42), Tomlinson (45), Cass (53), Price (78); **Goals:** Price 9.
HEWORTH: 1 Kevin Gott; 2 Neil Stephenson; 3 Gavin Grant; 4 Wayne Foster; 5 Andy Mercer; 6 Stuart Watson; 7 Chris Hammerton; 8 Jason Gatus; 9 Liam Cochrane; 10 Steve Barnard; 11 Sam Clarke; 12 Dan Briggs; 13 Carl Potter. Subs: 14 Jimmy Rothwell for Cochrane (53); 15 Simon Harrison for Briggs (6); 16 Scott Wrigglesworth for Barnard (32); 17 John Coulson for Gott (53); Barnard for Clarke (65); Gott for Mercer (68).
League Express Men of the Match:
Bulldogs: Craig Lingard; *Heworth:* Jason Gatus.
Penalty count: 3-3; **Half-time:** 28-0;
Referee: Ian Chatterton (Huddersfield); **Attendance:** 573.

CHORLEY LYNX 8 WOOLSTON ROVERS 22

LYNX: 1 Stuart Dickinson; 2 Paul Cookson; 3 Brian Capewell; 4 Anthony Roberts; 5 Chris Ramsdale; 6 Lee Ashton; 7 Paul Roberts; 8 Mike Prescott; 9 Lee Maiden; 10 Phil Harrison; 11 Rob Verrelli; 12 Peter Cain; 13 Ian Talbot. Subs: 14 Gary Blood for Cookson (29); 15 Lee Prest for Harrison (33); 16 Dale Christy for Verrelli (49); 17 Ian Marsh for Cain (67); Harrison for Prest (55); Prest for Prescott (62BB); Cookson for Capewell (76).
Try: Talbot (9); **Goals:** Capewell 2.
ROVERS: 1 Mark Wallington; 2 Mark Cosgrove; 3 Tim Iddon; 4 Darren Geritas; 5 Mark Moran; 6 Nigel Quarmby; 7 Steve Martin; 8 Mark Shephard; 9 Drew Povey; 10 Lee Westwood; 11 Stewart Cash; 12 Dave Patterson; 13 Danny Heaton. Subs: 14 Peter Livett for Iddon (62); 15 Shaun Geritas for Shephard (35); 16 Phil Dermott for Povey (23); 17 Graham Muckalt for Cash (65); Povey for Dermott (71); Shephard for S Geritas (75).
Tries: Patterson (24), D Geritas (47), Wallington (65), Cosgrove (77); **Goals:** Martin 3.
League Express Men of the Match:
Lynx: Ian Talbot; *Rovers:* Lee Westwood.
Penalty count: 10-5; **Half-time:** 8-6;
Referee: Robert Connolly (Wigan); **Attendance:** 559.

DONCASTER DRAGONS 44 SIDDAL 14

DRAGONS: 1 Paul Cook; 2 Anton Garcia; 3 Lynton Stott; 4 James Bunyan; 5 John Okul; 6 Craig Weston; 7 Latham Tawhai; 8 Maea David; 9 Peter Edwards; 10 Joe Berry; 11 Phil White; 12 Brad Hepi; 13 Tony Miller. Subs: 14 Neil Bennett for Weston (27); 15 Billy Conway for Hepi (31); 16 Tony Atter for Fielden (40BB, rev 41); 17 Jamie Fielden for Berry (1); Weston for Okul (39); Okul for Edwards (62).
Tries: David (5), Tawhai (8, 44), Weston (20), Garcia (46), Bunyan (56), Cook (61), Atter (77); **Goals:** Cook 6.
Sin bin: Fielden (42) - fighting.
SIDDAL: 1 Darren Phillips; 2 David Holmes; 3 Damieon Pickles; 4 Steve Gracey; 5 Shaun Blackburn; 6 Craig Turner; 7 Richard Wilde; 8 Gary Lewis; 9 Mick Shaw; 10 Ian Muirhead; 11 Wayne Graham; 12 Rick Holroyd; 13 Martin Scrimshaw. Subs: 14 Nick Smith for Lewis (49); 15 Matthew Smith for Phillips (26); 16 Simeon Hoyle for Muirhead (18); 17 Mark Sutcliffe for M Smith (62).
Tries: Holmes (14), Pickles (50), Blackburn (69);
Goal: Holmes.
Sin bin: Scrimshaw (42) - fighting.
League Express Men of the Match:
Dragons: Latham Tawhai; *Siddal:* Mick Shaw.
Penalty count: 6-4; **Half-time:** 18-4;
Referee: Peter Taberner (Wigan); **Attendance:** 1,341.

FEATHERSTONE ROVERS 56 ECCLES 0

ROVERS: 1 Matt Bramald; 2 Jamie Stokes; 3 Steve Dooler; 4 Gavin Swinson; 5 Nick Simpson; 6 Andy Bastow; 7 Jamie Rooney; 8 Stuart Dickens; 9 Richard Chapman; 10 Gavin Morgan; 11 Danny Evans; 12 Neil Lowe; 13 Paul Darley. Subs: 14 Richard Gibson for Stokes (47); 15 Gary Barnett for Rooney (19); 16 Ricky Helliwell for Evans (30); 17 Micky Clarkson for Dickens (19); Dickens for Darley (72).
Tries: Chapman (3, 10, 54), Morgan (7, 75), Bramald (16), Rooney (18), Stokes (32), Swinson (58), Darley (69); **Goals:** Gibson 5, Rooney 3.
ECCLES: 1 Dave Hedgecock; 2 Dave Ratcliffe; 3 Jason Viller; 4 Paul Smith; 5 John Basson; 6 Chris Couelle; 7 John McAtee; 8 Paul Viller; 9 Lee Billingham; 10 Neil McPherson; 11 Paul Raftrey; 12 Kris Smith; 13 Steve Fearnley. Subs: 14 Alan Evans for Couelle (40); 15 Steve Allinson for McPherson (26); 16 Steve Morley for Hedgecock (40); 17 Mark Maudsley for P Viller (26); McPherson for Maudsley (50).
League Express Men of the Match:
Rovers: Richard Chapman; *Eccles:* Paul Smith.
Penalty count: 8-3; **Half-time:** 30-0;
Referee: Paul Lee (Leigh); **Attendance:** 1,045.

HULL KINGSTON ROVERS 44 TOULOUSE SPACERS 0

ROVERS: 1 Bob Everitt; 2 Dean Andrews; 3 Andy Smith; 4 Whetu Taewa; 5 Bright Sodje; 6 Jimmy Walker; 7 Mick Crane; 8 Jon Aston; 9 Mike Dixon; 10 Rich Hayes; 11 Richard Slater; 12 Paul Fletcher; 13 Chris Charles. Subs: 14 Chris Kitching for Andrews (21BB, rev 33); 15 Allan Dunham for Fletcher (18); 16 Jamie Bovill for Wilson (55); 17 Richard Wilson for Aston (26); Fletcher for Slater (34); Aston for Hayes (47); Kitching for Crane (50); Wilson for Fletcher (70BB).
Tries: Taewa (7), Everitt (11), Walker (25), Charles (50), Kitching (54), Andrews (68, 76); **Goals:** Charles 8.
SPACERS: 1 Jean Frison; 2 Olivier Janzac; 3 Jean-Emmanuel Cassin; 4 Frederic Zitter; 5 Peter Lima; 6 Simon Dorrell; 7 Sean Mullins; 8 Olivier Pramil; 9 Ahmed Harrat; 10 Paul Mills; 11 Abderazak El Khalouki; 12 Jerome Vincent; 13 Andre Olari. Subs: 14 Laurent Lucchese for El Khalouki (55); 15 Eric Frayssinet for Bouche (53); 16 Sebastien Raguin for Mills (17); 17 Sebastien Bouche for Pramil (12); Mills for Raguin (50).
League Express Men of the Match:
Rovers: Chris Charles; *Spacers:* Simon Dorrell.
Penalty count: 6-3; **Half-time:** 18-0; **Referee:** Steve Nicholson (Whitehaven); **Attendance:** 1,649.

KEIGHLEY COUGARS 76 ROCHDALE MAYFIELD 0

COUGARS: 1 Matthew Foster; 2 Craig Horne; 3 Karl Smith; 4 Daio Powell; 5 Max Tomlinson; 6 Martin Wood; 7 Craig Murdock; 8 James Walker; 9 Nathan Antonik; 10 Gary Lord; 11 Matt Walker; 12 Jim Leatham; 13 Darren Carter. Subs: 14 Gareth Hooson for Powell (12); 15 Danny Seal for Murdock (29); 16 Dave Best for J Walker (40); 17 Steve Pickles for Smith (15); J Walker for Carter (55).
Tries: M Walker (8, 14, 30, 60), Leatham (10), Horne (19, 72), Hooson (22), Antonik (34), Pickles (37), Wood (47), Seal (55), Tomlinson (76, 79);
Goals: Wood 9, Antonik.
MAYFIELD: 1 Richard Yeomans; 2 Craig Diggle; 3 Chris Hilton; 4 Lee Durrant; 5 Les Salisbury; 6 John Thirsk; 7 Chris Wilkinson; 8 Emon Ratu; 9 Neil Ramsden; 10 Dave Harmer; 11 Danny Kelly; 12 Tony Hilton; 13 Carl Platt. Subs: 14 Adam Brown for Platt (36); 15 Steve Lett for T Hilton (28); 16 Mick Wilson not used; 17 Leon Ashworth for Kelly (63); T Hilton for Harmer (58); Kelly for T Hilton (72); Platt for Ratu (72).
League Express Men of the Match:
Cougars: Matt Walker; *Mayfield:* Neil Ramsden.
Penalty count: 4-5; **Half-time:** 38-0;
Referee: Ronnie Laughton (Barnsley); **Attendance:** 1,764.

LEIGH CENTURIONS 28 WEST HULL 5

CENTURIONS: 1 David Ingram; 2 Michael Watts; 3 Jason Johnson; 4 Paul Anderson; 5 David Jones; 6 Simon Svabic; 7 Willie Swann; 8 Jamie Gass; 9 Martin Roden; 10 David Whittle; 11 Andy Fairclough; 12 Phil Kendrick; 13 Kieron Purtill. Subs: 14 Paul Norman for Gass (58); 15 John Duffy for Roden (27); 16 Liam Bretherton for Svabic (75); 17 Lee Sanderson for Purtill (66); Gass for Whittle (68); Roden for Duffy (70).
Tries: Fairclough (31), Whittle (35), Anderson (39), Johnson (60, 74) Sanderson (79);
Goals: Svabic, Sanderson.
WEST HULL: 1 Lee Moreton; 2 Glyn Jones; 3 Albert Rounding; 4 Carl Moore; 5 Stuart Leake; 6 Brian Newby; 7 Mark Harris; 8 Lee Horsfield; 9 Peter Stephenson; 10 Mark Johnson; 11 Lee Roberts; 12 Gavin Last; 13 Wayne Harris. Subs: 14 Danny Marquez-Laynez for Richardson (44); 15 Paul Roberts for L Roberts (79); 16 Mark Cook for Last (72); 17 Steve Richardson for Johnson (23); Johnson for Stephenson (76).
Goals: W Harris 2; **Field goal:** W Harris.
League Express Men of the Match:
Centurions: Andy Fairclough; *West Hull:* Wayne Harris.
Penalty count: 8-8; **Half-time:** 14-3;
Referee: Russell Smith (Castleford); **Attendance:** 1,547.

OLDHAM 64 QUEENSBURY 0

OLDHAM: 1 Mark Sibson; 2 Danny Arnold; 3 David Gibbons; 4 Pat Rich; 5 Dean Cross; 6 Gareth Barber; 7 Neil Roden; 8 Jason Clegg; 9 John Hough; 10 Danny Guest; 11 Phil Farrell; 12 Ian Sinfield; 13 Chris Farrell. Subs: 14 Gavin Dodd for Sibson (46); 15 Kevin Mannion for P Farrell (ht); 16 Lee Doran for Guest (24); 17 Paul Norton for Clegg (58); Sibson for Roden (50); P Farrell for Sinfield (64BB, rev 69); P Farrell for C Farrell (71).
Tries: Arnold (7), Sibson (10, 25, 57, 78), D Gibbons (16, 20, 72), P Farrell (32), C Farrell (42), Dodd (48), Norton (74); **Goals:** Rich 8.
QUEENSBURY: 1 Steve Eyles; 2 Lee Barron; 3 Martin Potts; 4 Trevor Stead; 5 Jason Pell; 6 Johnny Feather; 7 Carl Smith; 8 Craig Winnard; 9 Steve Senior; 10 Andrew Senior; 11 Nathan Varley; 12 Matthew Galtress; 13 Lee Charlton. Subs: 14 Andrew Barraclough for Pell (58); 15 Kristian Freibach for Charlton (49); 16 Gary Prentice for Winnard (17); 17 Andrew Cannon for Prentice (52); Winnard for Galtress (70); Prentice for A Senior (73).
League Express Men of the Match:
Oldham: Mark Sibson; *Queensbury:* Carl Smith.
Penalty count: 5-3; **Half-time:** 30-0;
Referee: Colin Morris (Huddersfield); **Attendance:** 1,559.

SWINTON LIONS 44 NEW EARSWICK ALL BLACKS 12

LIONS: 1 Andy Cheetham; 2 Nick Cammann; 3 Mick Nanyn; 4 Matt Bateman; 5 Lee Hudson; 6 Phil Waring; 7 Kelvin Peet; 8 Paul Crossland; 9 Rob Barraclough; 10 Tony Barrow; 11 Robert Russell; 12 Carlo Napolitano; 13 Ryan Stazicker. Subs: 14 Wayne English for Hudson (4BB, rev 9); 15 Phil Veivers for English (35); 16 Paul Smith for Stazicker (50); 17 Lee Hansen for Crossland (50); English for Bateman (28).
Tries: Nanyn (6, 76), Stazicker (19, 37), Napolitano (24), Bateman (27), Cheetham (41, 80), Peet (68);
Goals: Nanyn 4.
ALL BLACKS: 1 Dave Carling; 2 Dan Wellard; 3 Carl Pallister; 4 Jez Petch; 5 Gary Isles; 6 Lee Paterson; 7

Mick Harrison; 8 Richard Harrison; 9 Martin McTigue; 10 James Daniel; 11 Nigel Wilson; 12 Trevor Sadler; 13 Lee McTigue. Subs: 14 Simon Mullarkey for Martin McTigue (25); 15 Paul Booth for Daniel (25); 16 Andy Innes for Wellard (62); 17 Mick McTigue for Sadler (40); Daniel for R Harrison (58); Martin McTigue for Wilson (65).
Tries: Mullarkey (30), Paterson (63); **Goals:** Carling 2.
League Express Men of Match:
Lions: Rob Barraclough; *All Blacks:* Lee Paterson.
Penalty count: 3-4; **Half-time:** 22-6;
Referee: John Farrell (St Helens); **Attendance:** 478.

WHITEHAVEN 34 OLDHAM ST ANNES 16

WHITEHAVEN: 1 Wesley Wilson; 2 Craig Walsh; 3 David Seeds; 4 Ian Devlin; 5 Chris Campbell; 6 Lee Kiddie; 7 Steve Kirkbride; 8 Mark Cox; 9 Aaron Lester; 10 David Fatialofa; 11 Howard Hill; 12 Graeme Morton; 13 Spencer Miller. Subs: 14 Leroy Joe for Kiddie (34); 15 Marc Jackson for Lester (66); 16 Garry Purdham for Devlin (40); 17 Dean Vaughan for Fatialofa (30); Fatialofa for Cox (50); Cox for Morton (75).
Tries: Hill (5), Miller (25, 60), Walsh (38), Seeds (46), Morton (51), C Campbell (72); **Goals:** Kirkbride 3.
ST ANNES: 1 Chris Wright; 2 Lee Charlesworth; 3 Richard Badby; 4 Mick Billington; 5 Steve Deakin; 6 Steve Gartland; 7 Paul Kay; 8 Jason Akeroyd; 9 Steve Crowther; 10 Martin Taylor; 11 Michael Deakin; 12 Steve Mills; 13 Martin Kay. Subs: 14 Ian Schifilitti for Cashin (52); 15 Craig Milner for S Deakin (60); 16 Jason Best for Taylor (22); 17 Michael Cashin for Akeroyd (19); Taylor for M Deakin (65).
Tries: Billington (11, 15), Charlesworth (31);
Goals: Badby 2.
Sin bin: Mills (50) - high tackle.
League Express Men of the Match:
Whitehaven: Leroy Joe; *St Annes:* Mick Billington.
Penalty count: 6-8; **Half-time:** 12-16;
Referee: Darren Gillespie (Halifax); **Attendance:** 616.

WIDNES VIKINGS 70 WIGAN ST PATRICKS 2

VIKINGS: 1 Damian Munro; 2 Phil Coussons; 3 Chris Percival; 4 Jason Demetriou; 5 Liam Jones; 6 Karle Hammond; 7 Ian Watson; 8 Simon Knox; 9 Phil Cantillon; 10 Stephen Holgate; 11 Steve Gee; 12 Chris McKinney; 13 Martin Crompton. Subs: 14 Mark Forster for Hammond (40); 15 Stewart Rhodes for Knox (45); 16 Tommy Hodgkinson for Crompton (23); 17 Joe Faimalo for McKinney (28); Crompton for Cantillon (57); Cantillon for Coussons (73).
Tries: Munro (2, 49), Cantillon (5, 27, 42, 80), Jones (17), Gee (21), Percival (26, 31, 56), Coussons (46), Faimalo (78); **Goals:** Watson 9.
ST PATRICKS: 1 Damien Charnock; 2 Barry Burgess; 3 Gary Lowe; 4 Rob McLoughlin; 5 Jason Fishwick; 6 Shaun Boylan; 7 Joe Parkinson; 8 Sean Mullaney; 9 Shaun Bannister; 10 Michael Sharkey; 11 Mike McDonnell; 12 David Hales; 13 Mick Daniels. Subs: 14 Mark Meehan for Lowe (28); 15 Nick Joynt for Fishwick (22); 16 Gary Robinson for Daniels (40); 17 Robert Gallagher for Hales (27); Hales for McDonnell (57); Daniels for McLoughlin (74).
Goal: Fishwick.
League Express Men of the Match:
Vikings: Phil Cantillon; *St Patricks:* Shaun Bannister.
Penalty count: 5-3; **Half-time:** 38-2; **Referee:** Richard Silverwood (Dewsbury); **Attendance:** 2,465.

WORKINGTON TOWN 38 CASTLEFORD LOCK LANE 0

TOWN: 1 Jamie Smith; 2 Neil Frazer; 3 Fata Sini; 4 Leigh Smith; 5 Graeme Lewthwaite; 6 Craig Rumney; 7 Micky Horner; 8 Lokeni Savelio; 9 Carl Sice; 10 William Blackburn; 11 Matt Sturm; 12 Anthony Samuel; 13 Stuart Hoyles. Subs: 14 Jamie Nixon for Sini (ht); 15 Matthew Tunstall for Savelio (46); 16 Stephen Stoddart for Rumney (55); 17 Jamie Beaumont for Hoyles (15BB, rev 44); Beaumont for Sturm (46); Savelio for Blackburn (62); Rumney for J Smith (72).
Tries: Sini (9), Lewthwaite (23, 66), Sice (29), Frazer (51), Hoyles (68), Stoddart (79);
Goals: J Smith 4, Stoddart.
LOCK LANE: 1 Martyn Hunt; 2 Paul Couch; 3 Mick Johnson; 4 Ryan Hardy; 5 Steve Penney; 6 Mark Spears; 7 Dave Wolford; 8 Dave Birdsall; 9 Chris Watson; 10 Lee Partridge; 11 Steve Greatbatch; 12 Stuart Arundel; 13 Lee Hughes. Subs: 14 Steve Thickbroom for Watson (60); 15 Lee Riding for Partridge (48); 16 Jason Heptinstall for Penney (39); 17 Peter Steels for Birdsall (26); Birdsall for Greatbatch (64); Partridge for Steels (64).
On report: An incident in a tackle on L Smith (75).
League Express Men of the Match:
Town: Carl Sice; *Lock Lane:* Martyn Hunt.
Penalty count: 6-8; **Half-time:** 18-0;
Referee: Mike Dawber (Wigan); **Attendance:** 867.

YORK 24 OULTON RAIDERS 12

YORK: 1 Rich Darling; 2 Gareth Oulton; 3 Chris Allen; 4 Gareth Lloyd; 5 Paul Butterfield; 6 Paddy Handley; 7 Gareth Stephens; 8 Mick Hagan; 9 Alan Pallister; 10 Craig Forsyth; 11 Craig Moore; 12 Darren Crake; 13 Shaun Austerfield. Subs: 14 Lee Hutchinson for Austerfield (78); 15 Leroy McKenzie for Butterfield (35); 16 Gareth Dobson for Pallister (40); 17 Spencer Hargrave for Forsyth (27); Forsyth for Hagan (56); Hagan for Moore (60).
Tries: Lloyd (29), Handley (32), Darling (39), Allen (60);
Goals: Oulton 4.
Sin bin: Hargrave (50) - persistent offside.
RAIDERS: 1 Chris Owen; 2 Gary Robb; 3 Neil Bradbrook; 4 Stephen Jakeman; 5 Lee Hall; 6 Paul Halloran; 7 Rob Moules; 8 Lynton Morris; 9 Neil Horton; 10 Danny Burton; 11 Sasch Brook; 12 Mark Longley; 13 Mick Bamford. Subs: 14 Phil Swallow for Jakeman (40); 15 Lee Denton for Brook (69); 16 Steve Holmes for Morris (40); 17 Rob Ward for Longley (5); Jakeman for Halloran (56); Morris for Ward (68).
Tries: Robb (13), Brook (43), Hall (48).
League Express Men of the Match:
York: Gareth Stephens; *Raiders:* Danny Burton.
Penalty count: 4-8; **Half-time:** 18-4;
Referee: Paul Carr (Castleford); **Attendance:** 914.

Leigh's Tim Street feels the force of Salford's Darren Brown during the Centurions' upset Round Four win over the City Reds

SHEFFIELD EAGLES 42 EAST LEEDS 0

EAGLES: 1 Steve Walker; 2 Paul Wells; 3 Neil Kite; 4 Gareth Hewitt; 5 Ian Thompson; 6 Gavin Brown; 7 Scott Rhodes; 8 Jon Bruce; 9 Andy Speak; 10 Ricky Wright; 11 Chris Chapman; 12 Heath Cruckshank; 13 Richard Goddard. Subs: 14 Mark Aston for Speak (32); 15 Simon Tillyer for Bruce (27); 16 Andy Brent for Goddard (40); 17 Ian Brown for Wright (52); Bruce for Chapman (63); Speak for Rhodes (66).
Tries: Kite (19, 38, 58), Rhodes (25), Walker (34), Hewitt (49), Thompson (76); **Goals:** Goddard 6, G Brown.
Sin bin: Brent (47) - fighting.
EAST LEEDS: 1 Philip Robinson; 2 Russell Lancaster; 3 Alex Croll; 4 Paul Hasty; 5 Gary Dibnah; 6 Simon Price; 7 Phil Hasty; 8 Lee Fisher; 9 Craig Walton; 10 James Crawford; 11 Anthony Gregg; 12 Barry Simpson; 13 Craig Waite. Subs: 14 Philip Hall for Walton (27); 15 Mick Keeligan for Fisher (40); 16 David Collier for Simpson (27BB, rev 55); 17 Andy Corbett for Waite (36); Fisher for Crawford (63); Waite for Gregg (66); Gregg for Dibnah (73).
Sin bin: Price (47) - fighting.
League Express Men of the Match:
Eagles: Neil Kite; *East Leeds:* Phil Hasty.
Penalty count: 13-9; **Half-time:** 28-0;
Referee: Steve Addy (Huddersfield); **Attendance:** 778.

GATESHEAD THUNDER 34 WIGAN ST JUDES 20

THUNDER: 1 Darrell Derose; 2 Paul Thorman; 3 Wes McGibbon; 4 Steve Hall; 5 Leon Williamson; 6 Scott Dyson; 7 Martin Gambles; 8 Paul Lister; 9 Roy Southernwood; 10 Andy Grundy; 11 Jim Carlton; 12 Chris Parker; 13 Stephen Rutherford. Subs: 14 Paul Sebine for McGibbon (18); 15 Richard Mervill for Grundy (26); 16 Matthew Roberts for Southernwood (40); 17 Gareth Barron for Lister (54); Grundy for Carlton (64); Lister for Barron (73).
Tries: Hall (3), Dyson (36), Thorman (44), Rutherford (48), Mervill (54), Williamson (64); **Goals:** Hall 5.
ST JUDES: 1 Ian Thompson; 2 Kevin Oakes; 3 Gavin Corfield; 4 Danny Jones; 5 Paul McCormack; 6 Darren Jones; 7 John McMullen; 8 Danny Ashton; 9 Shaun Hilton; 10 Ian Dunn; 11 Brendan Barr; 12 Keiron Wallace; 13 Milton Finney. Subs: 14 Phil Liptrot for Wallace (37); 15 Craig Kay for Dunn (50); 16 Tommy Porter for McMullen (67); 17 Phil Roby for Finney (77).
Tries: Thompson (18), Danny Jones (61), Hilton (67);
Goals: McMullen 3, Danny Jones.
League Express Men of the Match:
Thunder: Scott Dyson; *St Judes:* Shaun Hilton.
Penalty count: 6-10; **Half time:** 14-10;
Referee: Steve Ganson (St Helens); **Attendance:** 501.

HUNSLET HAWKS 38 THORNHILL TROJANS 6

HAWKS: 1 George Raynor; 2 Chris North; 3 Iain Higgins; 4 Michael Wainwright; 5 Aaron Campbell; 6 Chris Redfearn; 7 Chris Ross; 8 Michael Banks; 9 Nicky Dobson; 10 Guy Adams; 11 Mick Coyle; 12 Robert Roberts; 13 Marcus Vassilakopoulos. Subs: 14 David Bates for Banks (18); 15 Dave Jessey for Higgins (40); 16 Andy Atha for Coyle (56); 17 Craig Robinson for North (46); Banks for Bates (56); Coyle for Roberts (70).
Tries: Raynor (1), N Dobson (4), Wainwright (36), Jessey (44), Ross (68), Redfearn (76); **Goals:** Ross 7.
TROJANS: 1 Richard Bainton; 2 Rob Copley; 3 Ben Copley; 4 Phil Hepworth; 5 Abe Phillips; 6 Martin Fox; 7 Jason Firth; 8 Adam Hoyle; 9 Rob Simpson; 10 Paul Goodhall; 11 Chris Haigh; 12 Anthony Broadhead; 13 Sean James. Subs: 14 Andy Smith for Simpson (52); 15 Steve Naylor for Hoyle (21); 16 Richard Sedgewick for Fox (27); 17 Vinny Johnson for Goodhall (60); Fox for Sedgewick (40); Sedgewick for Broadhead (68).
Try: Broadhead (42); **Goal:** Fox.
League Express Men of the Match:
Hawks: Chris Ross; *Trojans:* Jason Firth.
Penalty count: 7-13; **Half-time:** 22-0;
Referee: Ben Thaler (Castleford); **Attendance:** 629.

ROUND 4

Saturday 10th February 2001

ST HELENS 22 WIGAN WARRIORS 8

SAINTS: 1 Paul Wellens; 2 Sean Hoppe; 3 Kevin Iro; 4 Paul Newlove; 5 Anthony Sullivan; 20 Tommy Martyn; 7 Sean Long; 10 David Fairleigh; 9 Keiron Cunningham; 12 Sonny Nickle; 11 Chris Joynt (C); 8 Peter Shiels; 13 Paul Sculthorpe. Subs: 15 Tim Jonkers for Sculthorpe (18); 17 Steve Hall for Long (76); 18 John Stankevitch for Fairleigh (48BB, rev 61); 19 Anthony Stewart for Nickle (30); Nickle for Shiels (53BB, rev 62); Stankevitch for Joynt (68); Joynt for Jonkers (77).
Tries: Sullivan (13), Joynt (17), Jonkers (65), Stewart (72); **Goals:** Long 3.
WARRIORS: 1 Kris Radlinski; 2 Brett Dallas; 4 Gary Connolly; 3 Steve Renouf; 15 Paul Johnson; 6 Matthew Johns (D); 7 Adrian Lam (D); 8 Terry O'Connor; 9 Terry Newton; 10 Neil Cowie; 14 David Furner (D); 12 Denis Betts; 13 Andy Farrell (C). Subs: 11 Mick Cassidy for O'Connor (31); 16 Simon Haughton for Betts (49); 20 Harvey Howard (D) for Cowie (25); 18 Wes Davies for Radlinski (41); O'Connor for Howard (64); Cowie for Cassidy (68).
Try: Connolly (20); **Goals:** Farrell 2.
On report: Howard (53) - high shot on Shiels.
League Express Men of the Match:
Saints: Chris Joynt; *Warriors:* David Furner.
Penalty count: 7-7; **Half-time:** 12-6;
Referee: Stuart Cummings (Widnes); **Attendance:** 13,593.

Sunday 11th February 2001

LEIGH CENTURIONS 16 SALFORD CITY REDS 12

CENTURIONS: 1 Neil Turley; 2 Alan Hadcroft; 3 Paul Anderson; 4 Andy Fairclough; 5 David Ingram; 6 Simon Svabic; 7 Liam Bretherton; 8 Tim Street; 9 John Hamilton; 10 David Bradbury; 11 Simon Baldwin; 12 Adam Bristow; 13 Chris Morley. Subs: 14 David Whittle for Bradbury (25); 15 John Duffy for Hamilton (29); 16 Phil Kendrick for Morley (44); 17 Andy Leathem for Street (29); Bradbury for Whittle (68); Hamilton for Duffy (78).
Tries: Anderson (55), Turley (60), Bristow (71);
Goals: Svabic 2.
Sin bin: Baldwin (78) - fighting.
CITY REDS: 1 Gary Broadbent; 2 Nick Pinkney; 3 Francis Maloney (D); 4 Michael Hancock (D); 5 Martin Offiah; 6 Steve Blakeley; 7 Graham Holroyd; 20 Andy Coley (D); 9 Malcolm Alker; 10 Paul Southern; 11 Warren Jowitt (D); 12 Darren Brown (C); 23 Mike Wainwright. Subs: 13 Paul Highton for Brown (54); 8 Neil Baynes for Coley (21); 18 Stuart Littler not used; 17 Craig Makin for Southern (69); Brown for Southern (55); Southern for Baynes (66); Baynes for Highton (67).
Tries: Jowitt (5, 28); **Goals:** Blakeley 2.
Sin bin: Alker (78) - fighting.
League Express Men of the Match:
Centurions: Simon Baldwin; *City Reds:* Mike Wainwright.
Penalty count: 9-6; **Half-time:** 0-12;
Referee: Russell Smith (Castleford); **Attendance:** 6,408.

WORKINGTON TOWN 6 WAKEFIELD TRINITY WILDCATS 56

TOWN: 1 Jamie Smith; 2 Neil Frazer; 3 Steve McGrady; 4 Leigh Smith; 5 Graeme Lewthwaite; 6 Tane Manihera; 7 Micky Horner; 8 Hitro Okesene; 9 Carl Sice; 10 Lokeni Savelio; 11 Matt Sturm; 12 Anthony Samuel; 13 Stuart Hoyles. Subs: 14 William Blackburn for Okesene (28); 15 Matthew Tunstall for Hoyles (66); 16 Fata Sini for McGrady (51); 17 Jamie Beaumont for Savelio (40); McGrady for Lewthwaite (57).
Try: Lewthwaite (37); **Goal:** Manihera.
Sent off: L Smith (59) - kicking out.
WILDCATS: 1 Martyn Holland; 2 Neil Law; 3 Richard Smith (D); 4 Justin Brooker (D); 5 Waisale Sovatabua (D); 6 Martin Pearson (D); 7 Brad Davis (D2); 10 Frank Watene; 9 David March; 16 Julian O'Neill (D); 11 Jamie Field; 13 Gary Price; 12 Willie Poching (C); Subs: 8 Paul Jackson for Watene (30); 15 Ryan Hudson for Price (49); 25 Tom Haughey (D) for Smith (54); 22 Keith Mason for O'Neill (30); Watene for Mason (61); O'Neill for Poching (71).
Tries: Price (8), Poching (16), Davis (18), Holland (27), Sovatabua (29, 67), N Law (32, 76), Field (53), Brooker (70); **Goals:** Pearson 8.
League Express Men of the Match:
Town: Matt Sturm; *Wildcats:* Brad Davis.
Penalty count: 4-7; **Half-time:** 6-30;
Referee: Paul Lee (Leigh); **Attendance:** 1,710.

BARROW BORDER RAIDERS 4 HALIFAX BLUE SOX 56

BORDER RAIDERS: 1 Chris Massey; 2 Jamie Marshall; 3 Phil Atkinson; 4 Darren Wilson; 5 Adrian Gardner; 6 Brett McDermott; 7 Darren Holt; 8 Tau Liku; 9 Anthony Murray; 10 William Burns; 11 Geoff Luxon; 12 Mike Whitehead; 13 Matthew Leigh. Subs: 14 Mike Kavanagh for Marshall (67); 15 Damien Whitter for Liku (27); 16 Gareth Pratt for Burns (35); 17 Ian Rawlinson for Luxon (15); Luxon for Rawlinson (46); Burns for Whitter (65).
Goals: Holt 2.
BLUE SOX: 1 Daryl Cardiss; 2 Jamie Bloem; 3 Damian Gibson; 4 Adam Hughes (D); 5 Lee Greenwood; 6 Andrew Dunemann; 7 Gavin Clinch (D2); 8 Andy Hobson; 9 Johnny Lawless (D2); 10 Jim Gannon; 11 Gary Mercer; 12 Shayne McMenemy (D); 13 Martin Moana (C); Subs: 14 Danny Tickle for Davidson (60); 15 Paul Davidson (D) for Gannon (30); 23 Brett Goldspink for Hobson (26); 16 Jamie Thackray for Mercer (60); Hobson for McMenemy (52); Gannon for Goldspink (57).
Tries: Hughes (10, 24, 65), Cardiss (12, 35, 75), McMenemy (15, 31), Davidson (38), Greenwood (46), Bloem (79); **Goals:** Hughes 6.
League Express Men of the Match: *Border Raiders:* Anthony Murray; *Blue Sox:* Andrew Dunemann.
Penalty count: 9-3; **Half-time:** 4-36; **Referee:** Richard Silverwood (Dewsbury); **Attendance:** 2,160.

BRADFORD BULLS 54 WIDNES VIKINGS 10

BULLS: 28 Stuart Spruce; 2 Tevita Vaikona; 20 Scott Naylor; 5 Michael Withers; 14 Lee Gilmour (D); 6 Henry Paul; 1 Robbie Paul (C); 22 Brian McDermott; 9 James Lowes; 29 Stuart Fielden; 19 Jamie Peacock; 11 Daniel Gartner (D); 12 Mike Forshaw. Subs: 7 Paul Deacon for R Paul (59); 15 Shane Rigon (D) for Gartner (50); 10 Paul Anderson for McDermott (21); 8 Joe Vagana (D) for Fielden (21); Fielden for Vagana (50); McDermott for Anderson (53).
Tries: Withers (1, 19, 32), Vaikona (6), Naylor (9, 51), Spruce (21), Lowes (42), McDermott (66), Anderson (78); **Goals:** H Paul 7.
VIKINGS: 1 Damian Munro; 2 Phil Coussons; 3 Jason Demetriou; 4 Chris Percival; 5 Liam Jones; 6 Martin Crompton; 7 Ian Watson; 8 Stewart Rhodes; 9 Phil Cantillon; 10 Joe Faimalo; 11 Steve Gee; 12 Chris McKinney; 13 Tommy Hodgkinson. Subs: 14 Mark Forster for Jones (52); 15 Mike Hill for Cantillon (37BB, rev 40); 16 Karle Hammond for Gee (21); 17 Steve Argent for Rhodes (31); Rhodes for Faimalo (40); Gee for McKinney (53); Hill for Cantillon (65).
Tries: Hodgkinson (40), Crompton (46); **Goal:** Watson.
League Express Men of the Match:
Bulls: Michael Withers; *Vikings:* Martin Crompton.
Penalty count: 6-4; **Half-time:** 32-4;
Referee: Ian Smith (Oldham); **Attendance:** 7,760.

DEWSBURY RAMS 4 CASTLEFORD TIGERS 18

RAMS: 1 Nathan Graham; 2 Alex Godfrey; 3 Dan Potter; 4 Adrian Flynn; 5 Richard Baker; 6 Richard Agar; 7 Barry Eaton; 8 Andy Fisher; 9 Richard Pachniuk; 10 Robin Jowitt; 11 Sean Richardson; 12 Paul Smith; 13 Damian Ball. Subs: 14 Mark Cain for Flynn (24); 15 Andrew Spink for Ball (40); 16 Matthew Long for Fisher (30); 17 Ryan McDonald for Jowitt (37); Fisher for Smith (57BB, rev 62); Jowitt for McDonald (72).
Goals: Eaton 2.
TIGERS: 22 Mark Lennon (D); 5 Darren Rogers; 3 Michael Eagar; 4 Barrie-Jon Mather; 2 Jon Wells; 6 Danny Orr; 7 Mitch Healey (D); 10 Dean Sampson; 9 Aaron Raper; 17 Andy Lynch; 16 Ian Tonks; 11 Lee Harland; 13 Adrian Vowles (C). Subs: 15 Darren Shaw for Handford (30); 8 Nathan Sykes for Raper (22); 18 Jonathan Roper (D) for Harland (40); 19 Gareth Handford (D) for Lynch (20); Handford for Tonks (55); Tonks for Handford (65).
Tries: Healey (14), Sampson (70), Orr (72); **Goals:** Orr 3.
League Express Men of the Match:
Rams: Paul Smith; *Tigers:* Dean Sampson.
Penalty count: 5-5; **Half-time:** 4-6; **Referee:** Karl Kirkpatrick (Warrington); **Attendance:** 3,384.

DONCASTER DRAGONS 14 SHEFFIELD EAGLES 12

DRAGONS: 1 Lynton Stott; 2 Paul Cook; 3 Carl Hall; 4 Simon Irving; 5 Kevin Crouthers; 6 Craig Weston; 7 Latham Tawhai; 8 Maea David; 9 Peter Edwards; 10 Brad Hepi; 11 Rob Wilson; 12 James Bunyan; 13 Tony Miller. Subs: 14 Anton Garcia not used; 15 Asa Amone for Weston (22); 16 Tony Atter for David (53); 17 Craig Lawton for Amone (67); David for Wilson (74).
Tries: Edwards (26), Atter (60); **Goals:** Cook 3.
EAGLES: 1 Steve Walker; 2 Wayne Flynn; 3 Neil Kite; 4 Chris Chapman; 5 Ian Thompson; 6 Gavin Brown; 7 Chris Robinson; 8 Steve Hill; 9 Andy Speak; 10 Ricky Wright; 11 Andy Brent; 12 Heath Cruckshank; 13 Richard Goddard. Subs: 14 Scott Rhodes for Speak (12); 15 Mark Aston for G Brown (62); 16 Ian Brown for Wright (51); 17 Jon Bruce for Hill (27); Hill for Bruce (62).
Try: I Brown (66); **Goals:** Goddard 4.
League Express Men of the Match:
Dragons: Carl Hall; *Eagles:* Ricky Wright.
Penalty count: 6-6; **Half-time:** 6-4;
Referee: John Farrell (Widnes); **Attendance:** 1,344.

HUDDERSFIELD GIANTS 28 FEATHERSTONE ROVERS 6

GIANTS: 21 Graham Appo (D); 2 Andrew Frew (D); 3 Martin Gleeson; 4 Dale Cardoza; 25 Ben Cooper; 6 Chris Thorman; 7 Ben Kusto (D); 8 Steve Molloy; 9 Paul Rowley (D); 10 Dale Laughton (C); 11 David Lomax; 13 David Atkins (D); 26 Steve McNamara (D). Subs: 12 Richard Marshall for McNamara (63); 17 Mark Moxon for Kusto (56); 18 Chris Molyneux for Molloy (24); 16 Oliver Wilkes for Laughton (27); Molloy for Lomax (56).
Tries: Frew (32), McNamara (36), Kusto (41), Appo (55), Cardoza (74); **Goals:** McNamara 3, Thorman.
Sin bin: Kusto (29) - late tackle.
On report: Kusto (29) - same late tackle.
ROVERS: 1 Michael Rhodes; 2 Jamie Stokes; 3 Steve Dooler; 6 Gary Barnett; 5 Matt Bramald; 4 Andy Bastow; 9 Gavin Swinson; 8 Stuart Dickens; 7 Richard Chapman; 10 Gavin Morgan; 11 Ricky Helliwell; 12 Neil Lowe; 13 Paul Darley. Subs: 14 Nick Simpson for Lowe (63); 15 Richard Gibson for Clarkson (34); 16 Danny Evans for Rhodes (24BB, rev 29); 17 Micky Clarkson for Morgan (24); Evans for Barnett (60); Morgan for Gibson (65); Barnett for Rhodes (67BB, rev 78); Gibson for Dooler (74).
Try: Chapman (68); **Goal:** Dickens.
League Express Men of the Match:
Giants: Chris Thorman; *Rovers:* Stuart Dickens.
Penalty count: 4-5; **Half-time:** 8-0;
Referee: Steve Ganson (St Helens); **Attendance:** 2,527.

KEIGHLEY COUGARS 20 HULL FC 34

COUGARS: 1 James Rushforth; 2 Craig Horne; 3 Daio Powell; 4 Graeme Hallas; 5 Jason Lee; 6 Martin Wood; 7 Nathan Antonik; 8 Michael Slicker; 9 Steve Pickles; 10 Alan Boothroyd; 11 Paul Harrison; 12 Ian Hughes; 13 Danny Seal. Subs: 14 Matt Walker for Boothroyd (27); 15 Jim Leatham for Hughes (55); 16 Phil Stephenson for Slicker (27); 17 Darren Carter for Pickles (58); Slicker for Stephenson (66); Boothroyd for Walker (72).
Tries: Harrison (5), Lee (39, 61), Horne (65);
Goals: Wood 2.
HULL: 1 Steve Prescott (D2); 2 Chris Smith (D); 6 Richard Horne; 4 Deon Bird; 5 Matt Crowther (D); 14 Stanley Gene; 7 Tony Smith (C) (D); 8 Paul Broadbent; 9 Lee Jackson (D2); 10 Luke Felsch; 11 Adam Maher; 3 David Maiden; 13 Jason Smith (D). Subs: 23 Logan Campbell (D2) for Prescott (27); 20 Garreth Carvell (D) for Maher (58); 18 Steve Craven for Felsch (47); 15 Paul King for Broadbent (31); Broadbent for King (69); Felsch for J Smith (76).
Tries: Crowther (11), Prescott (13, 25), Bird (48), Campbell (57), Gene (74); **Goals:** Prescott 2, Crowther 3.
Sent off: T Smith (3) - high tackle on Horne.
League Express Men of the Match:
Cougars: Martin Wood; *Hull:* Jason Smith.
Penalty count: 5-5; **Half-time:** 12-16;
Referee: Robert Connolly (Wigan); **Attendance:** 4,401.

LONDON BRONCOS 44 BATLEY BULLDOGS 6

BRONCOS: 4 Greg Fleming; 5 Brett Warton; 3 Tony Martin (D2); 2 Nigel Roy (D); 28 Marvin Golden (D); 27 Michael Gillett (D); 7 Dennis Moran (D); 18 Justin Dooley; 9 Jason Hetherington (C) (D); 10 Scott Cram; 11 Shane Millard; 12 Steele Retchless; 6 Jim Dymock (D). Subs: 13 Mat Toshack for Dooley (26); 17 Glen Air for Moran (73); 20 Steffan Hughes for Millard (26); 21 Jon Clarke for Hetherington (35); Dooley for Dymock (60); Millard for Retchless (77).
Tries: Roy (2, 29), Martin (9), Dymock (46), Gillett (55), Golden (64), Toshack (67), Retchless (70);
Goals: Warton 6.
On report: Brawl (78).
BULLDOGS: 1 Craig Lingard; 2 Jeremy Dyson; 3 Danny Maun; 4 Davide Longo; 5 Paul Gleadhill; 6 Richard Price; 7 Glen Tomlinson; 8 Chris McWilliam; 9 Andy Heptinstall; 10 Paul Hicks; 11 Gary Shillabeer; 12 Will Cartledge; 13 Ryan Horsley. Subs: 14 Roger Simpson for Lingard (62); 15 Mark Cass for Heptinstall (26); 16 Rob Padgett for Dyson (58); 17 Jeff Wittenberg for Hicks (25); Hicks for McWilliam (50).
Try: Cartledge (53); **Goal:** Price.
On report: Brawl (78).
League Express Men of the Match:
Broncos: Steele Retchless; *Bulldogs:* Glen Tomlinson.
Penalty count: 5-9; **Half-time:** 18-0;
Referee: Steve Addy (Huddersfield);
Attendance: 1,204 *(at Broadfield Stadium, Crawley).*

SWINTON LIONS 10 LEEDS RHINOS 106

LIONS: 1 Wayne English; 2 Matt Bateman; 3 Mick Nanyn; 4 Paul Loughlin; 5 Andy Cheetham; 6 Phil Veivers; 7 Kelvin Peet; 8 Lee Hansen; 9 Rob Barraclough; 10 Tony Barrow; 11 Phil Cushion; 12 John-Paul Doherty; 13 Paul Smith. Subs: 14 Jim Evans for Peet (39); 15 Lee Hudson for Cheetham (47); 16 Robert Russell for Barrow (49); 17 Carlo Napolitano for Doherty (33); Peet for Loughlin (56); Doherty for Napolitano (65).
Tries: P Loughlin (11), Smith (60); **Goal:** Nanyn.
RHINOS: 6 Brett Mullins (D); 2 Karl Pratt; 3 Tonie Carroll (D); 4 Keith Senior; 5 Francis Cummins; 1 Iestyn Harris (C); 7 Ryan Sheridan; 8 Darren Fleary; 9 Robert Mears (D); 10 Barrie McDermott; 11 Andy Hay; 17 Anthony Farrell; 13 Kevin Sinfield. Subs: 14 Marcus St Hilaire for Mears (39); 15 Chev Walker for Sinfield (53); 12 Bradley Clyde (D) for McDermott (26); 20 Jamie Mathiou for Fleary (23); McDermott for Hay (48); Sinfield for Sheridan (65).
Tries: Farrell (5, 80), Mears (14), Hay (18, 31), Mullins (26, 74), Sinfield (28, 38), Sheridan (34, 45), Harris (43), St Hilaire (52, 71), Senior (54), McDermott (64), Pratt (66), Clyde (76); **Goals:** Harris 17.
League Express Men of the Match:
Lions: Rob Barraclough; *Rhinos:* Iestyn Harris.
Penalty count: 3-2; **Half-time:** 6-46;
Referee: Colin Morris (Huddersfield); **Attendance:** 3,239.

WARRINGTON WOLVES 48 WOOLSTON ROVERS 6

WOLVES: 1 Lee Penny; 2 Rob Smyth; 16 Ian Sibbit; 3 David Kidwell (D); 5 Jamie Stenhouse; 14 Kevin Walters (D); 7 Allan Langer (C); 18 Martin Masella (D); 15 Steve Georgallis (D); 10 Danny Nutley; 19 Ian Knott; 20 Dean Busby; 13 Tawera Nikau. Subs: 17 David Alstead for Penny (40); 12 Jerome Guisset for Nutley (15BB, rev 40); 21 Paul Wood for Guisset (63); 24 Paul Noone for Knott (30); Guisset for Nutley (55); Guisset for Busby (75); Nutley for Masella (78).
Tries: Sibbit (7, 13, 25), Knott (20), Stenhouse (48), Nikau (62), Walters (64), Kidwell (77), Noone (79);
Goals: Smyth 6.
ROVERS: 1 Mark Wallington; 2 Mark Cosgrove; 3 Peter Livett; 4 Darren Geritas; 5 Mark Moran; 6 Nigel Quarmby; 7 Steve Martin; 8 Mark Shephard; 9 Drew Povey; 10 Lee Westwood; 11 Graham Muckalt; 12 Shaun Geritas; 13 Danny Heaton. Subs: 14 Paul Fiddler for Livett (54); 15 Dave Kelly for Martin (59); 16 Phil Dermott for Povey (25); 17 Mark Pendleton for Westwood (34); Povey for Pendleton (45BB, rev 69); Westwood for Shephard (57); Livett for S Geritas (65).
Try: Martin (39); **Goal:** Martin.
League Express Men of the Match:
Wolves: Ian Sibbit; *Rovers:* Steve Martin.
Penalty count: 4-4; **Half-time:** 20-6; **Referee:** Steve Nicholson (Whitehaven); **Attendance:** 6,008.

YORK 8 VILLENEUVE LEOPARDS 22

YORK: 1 Rich Darling; 2 Paul Butterfield; 3 Shaun Austerfield; 4 Gareth Lloyd; 5 Gareth Oulton; 6 Paddy Handley; 7 Gareth Stephens; 8 Darren Crake; 9 Alan Pallister; 10 Craig Forsyth; 11 Spencer Hargrave; 12 Craig Moore; 13 Gareth Dobson. Subs: 14 Danny Waite for Stephens (77); 15 Mick Hagan for Crake (25); 16 Lee Hutchinson not used; 17 Charles Hoggard for Forsyth (60BB, rev 65); Crake for Pallister (50); Hoggard for Hargrave (70).
Tries: Handley (43), Austerfield (72).
LEOPARDS: 1 Michael Van Snick; 2 Ludovic Perolari; 3 Gilles Cornut; 4 Daniel Vergniol; 5 Chad Dillinger; 6 Laurent Frayssinous; 7 Frederic Banquet; 8 Grant Doorey; 9 Vincent Wulf; 10 Dragan Durdevic; 11 Artie Shead; 12 Brock Mueller; 13 Laurent Carrasco. Subs: 14 David Collado for Shead (30); 15 Romain Sort for Mueller (22BB, rev 40); 16 Jérôme Hermet for Perolari (66); 17 Jamal Faqir for Sort (75); Sort for Doorey (65); Doorey for Durdevic (70).
Tries: Cornut (27), Doorey (33), Vergniol (52, 62);
Goals: Banquet 3.
League Express Men of the Match:
York: Gareth Lloyd; *Leopards:* Dragan Durdevic.
Penalty count: 8-5; **Half-time:** 0-12;
Referee: Julian King (St Helens); **Attendance:** 471.

Tuesday 13th February 2001

ROCHDALE HORNETS 38 HUNSLET HAWKS 4

HORNETS: 1 Paul Owen; 2 Sean Cooper; 3 Matt Calland; 4 Brendan O'Meara; 5 Marlon Billy; 6 Danny Wood; 7 Mick Coates; 8 Danny Sculthorpe; 9 Darren Robinson; 10 Martin Bunce; 11 David Stephenson; 12 David Larder; 13 Dave Watson. Subs; 14 Casey Mayberry for Robinson (63); 15 Wes Rogers for Stephenson (48); 16 Andy Ireland for Bunce (14); 17 Mick Martindale for Sculthorpe (51); Stephenson for Mayberry (69).
Tries: Billy (20, 40), Robinson (26), Watson (45), O'Meara (51), Calland (65), Larder (80);
Goals: Wood 3, Robinson, Coates.
Sin bin: Wood (17) - fighting.
HAWKS: 1 George Raynor; 2 Lee Maher; 3 Iain Higgins; 4 Michael Wainwright; 5 Aaron Campbell; 6 Chris Redfearn; 7 Craig Robinson; 8 Michael Banks; 9 Nicky Dobson; 10 Guy Adams; 11 Mick Coyle; 12 Robert Roberts; 13 Marcus Vassilakopoulos. Subs; 14 David Bates for Banks (21); 15 Dave Jessey for Skerrett (61); 16 Ben Skerrett for Adams (41); 17 Chris Ross for Robinson (38); Robinson for Redfearn (39); Banks for Bates (55).
Try: Wainwright (68).
Sin bin: Coyle (17) - fighting.

League Express Men of the Match:
Hornets: Darren Robinson; *Hawks:* George Raynor.
Penalty count: 9-11; **Half-time:** 18-0;
Referee: Nick Oddy (Halifax); **Attendance:** 605.

OLDHAM 17 HULL KINGSTON ROVERS 6

OLDHAM: 1 Mark Sibson; 2 Dean Cross; 3 Anthony Gibbons; 4 David Gibbons; 5 Pat Rich; 6 Gareth Barber; 7 Neil Roden; 8 Andy Procter; 9 John Hough; 10 Leo Casey; 11 Phil Farrell; 12 Ian Sinfield; 13 Kevin Mannion. Subs: 14 Mike Ford for Barber (3BB, rev 9); 15 Jason Clegg for Procter (24); 16 Paul Norton for Sinfield (53); 17 Danny Guest for Casey (31); Procter for Guest (58); Casey for Clegg (58); Ford for Hough (68).
Tries: Barber (34), D Gibbons (48); **Goals:** Rich 4; **Field goal:** Roden.
ROVERS: 1 Bob Everitt; 2 Dean Andrews; 3 Chris Kitching; 4 Whetu Taewa; 5 Bright Sodje; 6 Mick Crane; 7 Jimmy Walker; 8 Jon Aston; 9 Mike Dixon; 10 Rich Hayes; 11 Andy Smith; 12 Paul Fletcher; 13 Chris Charles. Subs: 14 Darren Callaghan for Crane (58); 15 Allan Dunham for Kitching (64); 16 Jon Wilkins for Dixon (72); 17 Richard Wilson for Aston (25); Aston for Hayes (54).
Try: Sodje (19); **Goal:** Charles.
League Express Men of the Match:
Oldham: Phil Farrell; *Rovers:* Jon Aston.
Penalty count: 5-4; **Half-time:** 8-6;
Referee: Peter Taberner (Wigan); **Attendance:** 2,008.

Wednesday 14th February 2001

GATESHEAD THUNDER 0 WHITEHAVEN 56

THUNDER: 1 Wes McGibbon; 2 Andy Field; 3 Paul Sebine; 4 Steve Hall; 5 Leon Williamson; 6 Scott Dyson; 7 Paul Thorman; 8 Richard Mervill; 9 Martin Gambles; 10 Andy Grundy; 11 Jim Carlton; 12 Chris Parker; 13 Stephen Rutherford. Subs: 14 Lee Garside for Grundy (29); 15 Paul Lister for Mervill (31); 16 Darrell Derose for Thorman (46); 17 Matthew Roberts for Garside (50); Mervill for Dyson (50); Grundy for Rutherford (70).
WHITEHAVEN: 1 Wesley Wilson; 2 Andrew Nelson; 3 David Seeds; 4 Howard Hill; 5 Chris Campbell; 6 Leroy Joe; 7 Steve Kirkbride; 8 Mark Cox; 9 Aaron Lester; 10 David Fatialofa; 11 Garry Purdham; 12 Graeme Morton; 13 Spencer Miller. Subs: 14 Ian Devlin for Purdham (66); 15 Marc Jackson for Lester (63); 16 Phil Sherwen for Morton (50); 17 Dean Vaughan for Cox (31); Cox for Fatialofa (63); Purdham for Miller (75).
Tries: Morton (11), C Campbell (17), Joe (44), Seeds (46, 49, 74, 79), Nelson (62), Jackson (66, 69);
Goals: Kirkbride 8.
League Express Men of the Match:
Thunder: Wes McGibbon; *Whitehaven:* Leroy Joe.
Penalty count: 5-8; **Half-time:** 0-12;
Referee: Ronnie Laughton (Barnsley); **Attendance:** 377.

ROUND 5

Saturday 24th February 2001

CASTLEFORD TIGERS 12 LEEDS RHINOS 42

TIGERS: 1 Richard Gay; 5 Darren Rogers; 3 Michael Eagar; 4 Barrie-Jon Mather; 2 Jon Wells; 6 Danny Orr; 9 Aaron Raper; 10 Dean Sampson; 15 Darren Shaw; 17 Andy Lynch; 16 Ian Tonks; 11 Lee Harland; 13 Adrian Vowles (C). Subs: 8 Nathan Sykes for Lynch (22); 23 Michael Smith (D2) for Harland (22); 22 Mark Lennon for Shaw (54); 19 Gareth Handford for Sykes (37); Harland for Tonks (52); Sykes for Handford (60).
Tries: Sykes (26), Rogers (42, 64).
Sent off: Sampson (73) – high tackle.
Sin bin: Gay (10) – obstruction.
RHINOS: 6 Brett Mullins; 2 Karl Pratt; 3 Tonie Carroll; 4 Keith Senior; 5 Francis Cummins; 1 Iestyn Harris (C); 7 Ryan Sheridan; 8 Darren Fleary; 23 Matthew Diskin (D); 10 Barrie McDermott; 11 Andy Hay; 17 Anthony Farrell; 13 Kevin Sinfield. Subs: 14 Marcus St Hilaire for Mullins (31); 15 Chev Walker for Farrell (53); 22 David Wrench for Hay (63); 20 Jamie Mathiou for McDermott (27); McDermott for Fleary (55).
Tries: Senior (1), Carroll (15), Sinfield (21, 46), McDermott (57), Harris (68, 77), Pratt (73);
Goals: Harris 5.
On report: Sheridan (24) – late, high challenge.
League Express Men of the Match:
Tigers: Adrian Vowles; *Rhinos:* Iestyn Harris.
Penalty count: 9-8; **Half-time:** 4-16;
Referee: Robert Connolly (Wigan); **Attendance:** 11,418.

Sunday 25th February 2001

HALIFAX BLUE SOX 18 BRADFORD BULLS 68

BLUE SOX: 1 Daryl Cardiss; 2 Jamie Bloem; 3 Damian Gibson; 4 Adam Hughes; 5 Lee Greenwood; 6 Andrew Dunemann; 7 Gavin Clinch; 8 Andy Hobson; 9 Johnny Lawless; 10 Jim Gannon; 11 Gary Mercer; 12 Shayne McMenemy; 13 Martin Moana (C); Subs: 17 Sean Penkywicz for Lawless (32); 15 Paul Davidson for McMenemy (28); 16 Jamie Thackray for Moana (49); 23 Brett Goldspink for Hobson (25); McMenemy for Gannon (46); Hobson for Davidson (55).
Tries: Mercer (31), Dunemann (54), Clinch (69);
Goals: Bloem 3.
Sin bin: Hobson (63) - foul play.
BULLS: 28 Stuart Spruce; 2 Tevita Vaikona; 20 Scott Naylor; 5 Michael Withers; 14 Lee Gilmour; 6 Henry Paul; 1 Robbie Paul (C); 8 Joe Vagana; 9 James Lowes; 22 Brian McDermott; 11 Daniel Gartner; 19 Jamie Peacock; 12 Mike Forshaw. Subs: 7 Paul Deacon for R Paul (40); 10 Paul Anderson for Vagana (25); 15 Shane Rigon for Forshaw (54); 29 Stuart Fielden for McDermott (25); McDermott for Anderson (59); R Paul for H Paul (68); Vagana for Fielden (64).
Tries: Lowes (7), R Paul (10), Forshaw (22), Gartner (26), Gilmour (35), Naylor (42, 64), Spruce (67), Vaikona (74, 79), Withers (80); **Goals:** H Paul 9, Deacon 3.
On report: McDermott - high tackle.
League Express Men of the Match:
Blue Sox: Andrew Dunemann; *Bulls:* Henry Paul.
Penalty count: 7-10; **Half-time:** 6-32;
Referee: Russell Smith (Castleford); **Attendance:** 6,129.

HUDDERSFIELD GIANTS 38 DONCASTER DRAGONS 24

GIANTS: 21 Graham Appo; 2 Andrew Frew; 3 Martin Gleeson; 4 Dale Cardoza; 25 Ben Cooper; 6 Chris Thorman; 7 Ben Kusto; 8 Steve Molloy; 9 Paul Rowley; 10 Dale Laughton (C); 11 David Lomax; 13 David Atkins; 26 Steve McNamara. Subs: 12 Richard Marshall for Laughton (33); 17 Mark Moxon for Appo (64); 18 Chris Molyneux for Molloy (29); 15 Darren Turner for Atkins (53); Laughton for Lomax (55); Atkins for Molyneux (70).
Tries: Rowley (13), Kusto (24), Appo (32), Frew (45, 48, 63, 72); **Goals:** McNamara 5.
DRAGONS: 1 Lynton Stott; 2 Anton Garcia; 3 Carl Hall; 4 Simon Irving; 5 Kevin Crouthers; 6 Craig Weston; 7 Latham Tawhai; 8 Asa Amone; 9 Peter Edwards; 10 Maea David; 11 Rob Wilson; 12 James Bunyan; 13 Paul Mansson. Subs: 14 Neil Bennett for Crouthers (49); 15 Tony Miller for Wilson (49); 16 Brad Hepi for Amone (40); 17 Craig Lawton for Hall (68); Amone for David (73).
Tries: Weston (21), Stott (28), Mansson (54), Tawhai (79); **Goals:** Irving 4.
League Express Men of the Match:
Giants: Andrew Frew; *Dragons:* Paul Mansson.
Penalty count: 9-6; **Half-time:** 16-14;
Referee: Ian Smith (Oldham); **Attendance:** 2,176.

HULL FC 30 LONDON BRONCOS 20

HULL: 4 Deon Bird; 5 Matt Crowther; 6 Richard Horne; 23 Logan Campbell; 2 Chris Smith; 16 Paul Cooke; 7 Tony Smith; 8 Paul Broadbent; 9 Lee Jackson; 15 Paul King; 11 Adam Maher; 12 Tony Grimaldi (C); 13 Jason Smith. Subs: 14 Stanley Gene for Maher (52); 20 Garreth Carvell for Craven (64); 3 David Maiden for Grimaldi (66); 18 Steve Craven for King (23); King for Broadbent (50).
Tries: Cooke (28), Jackson (31, 74), Campbell (34, 50);
Goals: Crowther 5.
BRONCOS: 4 Greg Fleming; 5 Brett Warton; 3 Tony Martin; 2 Nigel Roy; 28 Marvin Golden; 27 Michael Gillett; 7 Dennis Moran; 18 Justin Dooley; 9 Jason Hetherington (C); 10 Scott Cram; 11 Shane Millard; 12 Steele Retchless; 6 Jim Dymock. Subs: 23 Richie Barnett (D) for Fleming (67); 8 Tony Mestrov (D2) for Dooley (33BB, rev 47); 21 Jon Clarke for Cram (61); 13 Mat Toshack for Millard (52); Cram for Hetherington (76).
Tries: Moran (6), Golden (14), Millard (19), Gillett (55);
Goals: Warton 2.
Sin bin: Martin (13) - offside.
League Express Men of the Match:
Hull: Lee Jackson; *Broncos:* Michael Gillett.
Penalty count: 6-3; **Half-time:** 18-16;
Referee: Stuart Cummings (Widnes); **Attendance:** 6,701.

OLDHAM 6 WAKEFIELD TRINITY WILDCATS 26

OLDHAM: 1 Mark Sibson; 2 Daryl Lacey; 3 Anthony Gibbons; 4 Pat Rich; 5 Gavin Dodd; 6 David Gibbons; 7 Neil Roden; 8 Andy Procter; 9 John Hough; 10 Leo Casey; 11 Phil Farrell; 12 Ian Sinfield; 13 Kevin Mannion. Subs: 14 Mike Ford for Roden (51); 15 Jason Clegg for Casey (22); 16 Paul Norton for Procter (22); 17 Chris Farrell for Sinfield (51); Casey for Clegg (62); Procter for Norton (69).
Try: Rich (75); **Goal:** Rich.
WILDCATS: 1 Martyn Holland; 2 Neil Law; 3 Richard Smith; 4 Justin Brooker; 5 Waisale Sovatabua; 6 Martin Pearson; 7 Brad Davis; 10 Frank Watene; 9 David March; 16 Julian O'Neill; 11 Jamie Field; 13 Gary Price (C); 18 Ben Rauter (D). Subs: 15 Ryan Hudson for O'Neill (31); 8 Paul Jackson for Watene (18); 25 Tom Haughey for March (48); 21 Tony Tatupu for Smith (ht); O'Neill for Davis (66); Watene for Price (69).
Tries: Field (23), Pearson (47), Tatupu (61), Sovatabua (65, 68); **Goals:** Pearson 3.
League Express Men of the Match:
Oldham: John Hough; *Wildcats:* Martin Pearson.
Penalty count: 7-8; **Half-time:** 2-6;
Referee: Nick Oddy (Halifax); **Attendance:** 3,071.

ROCHDALE HORNETS 19 VILLENEUVE LEOPARDS 26

HORNETS: 1 Paul Owen; 2 Wayne McHugh; 3 Sean Cooper; 4 Brendan O'Meara; 5 Marlon Billy; 6 Danny Wood; 7 Mick Coates; 8 Danny Sculthorpe; 9 Darren Robinson; 10 Andy Ireland; 11 Martin Bunce; 12 Wes Rogers; 13 David Stephenson. Subs: 14 Casey Mayberry for McHugh (57); 15 David Larder for Stephenson (51); 16 Dave Radley for Ireland (51); 17 Mick Martindale for Sculthorpe (60); Ireland for Bunce (71).
Tries: O'Meara (8), Billy (40), Robinson (47);
Goals: Wood 3; **Field goal:** Coates.
LEOPARDS: 1 Michael Van Snick; 2 Ludovic Perolari; 3 Gilles Cornut; 4 Daniel Vergniol; 5 Chad Dillinger; 6 Laurent Frayssinous; 7 Frederic Banquet; 8 Grant Doorey; 9 Vincent Wulf; 10 Dragan Durdevic; 11 Artie Shead; 12 Brock Mueller; 13 Laurent Carrasco. Subs: 14 Romain Sort for Shead (27); 15 David Collado for Doorey (41); 16 Jérôme Hermet not used; 17 Jamal Faqir for Collado (79); Shead for Durdevic (57); Doorey for Sort (65); Durdevic for Shead (71).
Tries: Vergniol (30, 35), Shead (62), Dillinger (65), Cornut (74); **Goals:** Banquet 3.
League Express Men of the Match:
Hornets: Brendan O'Meara; *Leopards:* Artie Shead.
Penalty count: 4-2; **Half-time:** 10-10;
Referee: Peter Taberner (Wigan); **Attendance:** 817.

WARRINGTON WOLVES 20 LEIGH CENTURIONS 10

WOLVES: 1 Lee Penny; 2 Rob Smyth; 16 Ian Sibbit; 3 David Kidwell; 5 Jamie Stenhouse; 14 Kevin Walters; 7 Allan Langer (C); 18 Martin Masella; 9 David Highton; 10 Danny Nutley; 11 Steve McCurrie; 20 Dean Busby; 13 Tawera Nikau. Subs: 4 Toa Kohe-Love for Kidwell (40); 15 Steve Georgallis for Busby (75); 12 Jerome Guisset for Masella (34); 6 Lee Briers for Stenhouse (31).
Tries: Langer (50), McCurrie (65, 69), Guisset (74);
Goals: Briers 2.
Sin bin: Nutley (4) - fighting.
On report: Penny (42) - high tackle;
Kidwell (61) - high tackle.
CENTURIONS: 1 Neil Turley; 2 Alan Hadcroft; 3 Paul Anderson; 4 Phil Kendrick; 5 David Ingram; 6 Simon Svabic; 7 Liam Bretherton; 8 Tim Street; 9 John Hamilton; 10 David Bradbury; 11 Simon Baldwin; 12 Chris Morley; 13 Adam Bristow. Subs: 14 Andy Leathem for Bradbury (60); 15 David Whittle for Street (28); 16 John Duffy for Hamilton (32); 17 Willie Swann for Bristow (33).
Try: Anderson (80); **Goals:** Svabic 3.
Sin bin: Street (4) - fighting.
League Express Men of the Match:
Wolves: Allan Langer; *Centurions:* Simon Svabic.
Penalty count: 6-8; **Half-time:** 0-4;
Referee: Steve Ganson (St Helens); **Attendance:** 8,844.

WHITEHAVEN 22 ST HELENS 34

WHITEHAVEN: 1 Paul O'Neill; 2 Andrew Nelson; 3 Howard Hill; 4 David Seeds; 5 Chris Campbell; 6 Leroy Joe; 7 Steve Kirkbride; 8 Mark Cox; 9 Aaron Lester; 10 David Fatialofa; 11 Spencer Miller; 12 Graeme Morton; 13 Garry Purdham. Subs: 14 Ian Devlin for Nelson (34); 15 Marc Jackson for Lester (60); 16 Phil Sherwen for Morton (6); 17 Dean Vaughan for Cox (60); Lester for Purdham (70).
Tries: Lester (6), Cox (55), Seeds (78); **Goals:** Kirkbride 5.
SAINTS: 1 Paul Wellens; 17 Steve Hall; 19 Anthony Stewart; 4 Paul Newlove; 5 Anthony Sullivan; 20 Tommy Martyn; 21 Dwayne West; 16 Vila Matautia; 24 Mick Higham (D); 14 Wayne McDonald (D); 11 Chris Joynt (C); 18 John Stankevitch; 15 Tim Jonkers. Subs; 23 Mike Bennett for Newlove (74); 27 Bryan Henare for Stankevitch (53); 12 Sonny Nickle for McDonald (50); 26 Mark McCully (D) for West (53); McDonald for Joynt (68); West for Martyn (70).
Tries: Higham (12), Joynt (23), Wellens (26), Newlove (36), Hall (60), Martyn (65), McDonald (70);
Goals: Martyn 3.
Sent off: Matautia (47) - high tackle.
League Express Men of the Match:
Whitehaven: Leroy Joe; *Saints:* Tommy Martyn.
Penalty count: 6-5; **Half time:** 10-20; **Referee:** Karl Kirkpatrick (Warrington); **Attendance:** 4,750.

QUARTER FINALS

Friday 9th March 2001

ST HELENS 54 HUDDERSFIELD GIANTS 16

SAINTS: 1 Paul Wellens; 17 Steve Hall; 2 Sean Hoppe; 4 Paul Newlove; 5 Anthony Sullivan; 20 Tommy Martyn; 7 Sean Long; 12 Sonny Nickle; 9 Keiron Cunningham; 10 David Fairleigh; 8 Peter Shiels; 11 Chris Joynt (C); 15 Tim Jonkers. Subs: 25 Mark Edmondson for Long (62); 18 John Stankevitch for Long (39BB, rev 41); 19 Anthony Stewart for Martyn (18); 14 Wayne McDonald for Nickle (26); Stankevitch for Newlove (50); Nickle for Fairleigh (62).
Tries: Wellens (2, 57), Martyn (16), Joynt (20), Long (43, 53), Cunningham (49), Hall (65), Jonkers (69), Edmondson (75); **Goals:** Long 7.
GIANTS: 1 Paul Reilly; 2 Andrew Frew; 3 Martin Gleeson; 4 Dale Cardoza; 25 Ben Cooper; 6 Chris Thorman; 7 Ben Kusto; 8 Steve Molloy; 9 Paul Rowley; 10 Dale Laughton (C); 11 David Lomax; 13 David Atkins; 26 Steve McNamara. Subs: 18 Chris Molyneux for Laughton (35); 17 Mark Moxon for Reilly (37BB, rev 39); 12 Richard Marshall for Lomax (51); 15 Darren Turner for Molloy (23); Moxon for Thorman (45); Laughton for Atkins (67); Thorman for Reilly (67BB); Molloy for Molyneux (71).
Tries: Frew (6), Molloy (12), Rowley (78);
Goals: McNamara 2.
League Express Men of the Match:
Saints: Sean Long; *Giants:* Chris Thorman.
Penalty count: 9-2; **Half-time:** 18-10; **Referee:** Karl Kirkpatrick (Warrington); **Attendance:** 7,899.

Saturday 10th March 2001

HULL FC 18 LEEDS RHINOS 20

HULL: 4 Deon Bird; 2 Chris Smith; 6 Richard Horne; 23 Logan Campbell; 5 Matt Crowther; 16 Paul Cooke; 7 Tony Smith; 8 Paul Broadbent; 9 Lee Jackson; 10 Luke Felsch; 11 Adam Maher; 12 Tony Grimaldi (C); 13 Jason Smith. Subs: 14 Stanley Gene for Maher (47); 3 David

St Helens' Vila Matautia gets the ball away under pressure from Bradford's Michael Withers during the Challenge Cup Final

Maiden for Grimaldi (47); 15 Paul King for Broadbent (23); 18 Steve Craven for King (39BB, rev 62); Broadbent for Felsch (60).
Tries: Horne (3), T Smith (8), C Smith (74);
Goals: Crowther 3.
Sin bin: Broadbent (64) – fighting.
On report: T Smith (75) – late high tackle.
RHINOS: 6 Brett Mullins; 2 Karl Pratt; 3 Tonie Carroll; 4 Keith Senior; 5 Francis Cummins; 13 Kevin Sinfield; 1 Iestyn Harris (C); 8 Darren Fleary; 23 Matthew Diskin; 10 Barrie McDermott; 12 Bradley Clyde; 17 Anthony Farrell; 11 Andy Hay. Subs: 15 Chev Walker for Farrell (26); 16 Mark Calderwood for Mullins (50); 22 David Wrench for Hay (70); 20 Jamie Mathiou for McDermott (24); Farrell for Clyde (57); McDermott for Fleary (62).
Tries: Pratt (18, 27), Clyde (43, 46); **Goals:** Harris 2.
Sin bin: Walker (64) – fighting.
League Express Men of the Match:
Hull: Lee Jackson; *Rhinos:* Bradley Clyde.
Penalty count: 10-8; **Half-time:** 12-8; **Referee:** Russell Smith (Castleford); **Attendance:** 10,123.

Sunday 11th March 2001

WARRINGTON WOLVES 32 VILLENEUVE LEOPARDS 0

WOLVES: 6 Lee Briers; 2 Rob Smyth; 3 David Kidwell; 16 Ian Sibbit; 22 Alan Hunte; 14 Kevin Walters; 7 Allan Langer (C); 8 Andrew Gee; 9 David Highton; 12 Jerome Guisset; 15 Steve Georgallis; 20 Dean Busby; 13 Tawera Nikau. Subs: 21 Paul Wood for Gee (25BB, rev 31); 11 Steve McCurrie for Busby (44); 24 Paul Noone for Nikau (67); 5 Jamie Stenhouse for Sibbit (61); Wood for Guisset (41); Guisset for Gee (49BB, rev 55).
Tries: Smyth (15, 75), Briers (40, 73, 79), Kidwell (45), Langer (60); **Goals:** Briers 2.
LEOPARDS: 1 David Despin; 2 Michael Van Snick; 3 Gilles Cornut; 4 Daniel Vergniol; 5 Chad Dillinger; 6 Laurent Frayssinous; 7 Frederic Banquet; 8 Grant Doorey; 9 Vincent Wulf; 10 Dragan Durdevic; 11 Artie Shead; 12 Brock Mueller; 13 Laurent Carrasco. Subs: 14 David Collado for Durdevic (30); 15 Romain Sort for Shead (41); 16 Christophe Canal for Carrasco (67); 17 Ludovic Perolari for Dillinger (70); Durdevic for Collado (54); Shead for Mueller (60); Carrasco for Frayssinous (74BB).
League Express Men of the Match:
Wolves: Lee Briers; *Leopards:* Frederic Banquet.
Penalty count: 7-7; **Half-time:** 10-0;
Referee: Robert Connolly (Wigan); **Attendance:** 4,805.

WAKEFIELD TRINITY WILDCATS 0 BRADFORD BULLS 38

WILDCATS: 1 Martyn Holland; 3 Richard Smith; 21 Tony Tatupu; 4 Justin Brooker; 5 Waisale Sovatabua; 6 Martin Pearson; 14 Paul March; 16 Julian O'Neill; 18 Ben Rauter; 8 Paul Jackson; 11 Jamie Field; 13 Gary Price (C); 25 Tom Haughey. Subs: 15 Ryan Hudson for

Haughey (17); 10 Frank Watene for O'Neill (25); 17 Graham Law for Field (48); 19 Gareth Ellis for Brooker (63); Haughey for Price (62); O'Neill for Watene (68).
BULLS: 28 Stuart Spruce; 2 Tevita Vaikona; 20 Scott Naylor; 15 Shane Rigon; 5 Michael Withers; 6 Henry Paul; 7 Paul Deacon; 10 Paul Anderson; 9 James Lowes (C); 22 Brian McDermott; 19 Jamie Peacock; 11 Daniel Gartner; 12 Mike Forshaw. Subs: 1 Robbie Paul for H Paul (60); 8 Joe Vagana for Anderson (13); 29 Stuart Fielden for McDermott (24); 14 Lee Gilmour for Naylor (51); Anderson for Vagana (28); Naylor for Withers (66).
Tries: Lowes (8, 62), H Paul (16), Withers (20, 43), Spruce (50), Gartner (72); **Goals:** H Paul 4, Deacon.
League Express Men of the Match:
Wildcats: Frank Watene; *Bulls:* Henry Paul.
Penalty count: 6-9; **Half-time:** 0-16; **Referee:** Stuart Cummings (Widnes); **Attendance:** 6,500.

SEMI FINALS

Saturday 31st March 2001

LEEDS RHINOS 22 ST HELENS 27

RHINOS: 6 Brett Mullins; 5 Francis Cummins; 3 Tonie Carroll; 15 Chev Walker; 16 Mark Calderwood; 1 Iestyn Harris (C); 2 Karl Pratt; 8 Darren Fleary; 23 Matthew Diskin; 10 Barrie McDermott; 17 Anthony Farrell; 11 Andy Hay; 13 Kevin Sinfield. Subs: 14 Marcus St Hilaire for Carroll (27); 12 Bradley Clyde for Farrell (27); 20 Jamie Mathiou for McDermott (32); 27 Jason Netherton not used; McDermott for Fleary (56); Fleary for Mathiou (63); Carroll for St Hilaire (68).
Tries: Calderwood (14), Pratt (41), Sinfield (54), Mullins (63); **Goals:** Harris 3.
Sin bin: Fleary (34) – fighting.
SAINTS: 1 Paul Wellens; 2 Sean Hoppe; 3 Kevin Iro; 4 Paul Newlove; 5 Anthony Sullivan; 20 Tommy Martyn; 7 Sean Long; 12 Sonny Nickle; 9 Keiron Cunningham; 10 David Fairleigh; 11 Chris Joynt (C); 8 Peter Shiels; 13 Paul Sculthorpe. Subs: 16 Vila Matautia for Nickle (22); 15 Tim Jonkers for Shiels (23BB); 18 John Stankevitch for Fairleigh (37); 19 Anthony Stewart for Joynt (72); Fairleigh for Stankevitch (40); Stankevitch for Matautia (58); Matautia for Fairleigh (74).
Tries: Sculthorpe (7, 80), Long (26), Martyn (40), Newlove (61); **Goals:** Long 3; **Field goal:** Martyn.
Sin bin: Matautia (34) – fighting.
League Express Men of the Match:
Rhinos: Karl Pratt; *Saints:* Sean Long.
Penalty count: 8-10; **Half-time:** 6-16;
Referee: Russell Smith (Castleford);
Attendance: 16,416 (at JJB Stadium, Wigan).

Sunday 1st April 2001

BRADFORD BULLS 39 WARRINGTON WOLVES 22

BULLS: 28 Stuart Spruce; 2 Tevita Vaikona; 20 Scott Naylor; 15 Shane Rigon; 5 Michael Withers; 6 Henry Paul; 7 Paul Deacon; 22 Brian McDermott; 9 James Lowes (C); 8 Joe Vagana; 18 Lee Radford; 19 Jamie Peacock; 12 Mike Forshaw. Subs: 1 Robbie Paul for Deacon (32); 10 Paul Anderson for Vagana (25); 29 Stuart Fielden for McDermott (25); 3 Leon Pryce for Vaikona (41); Vagana for Anderson (52); McDermott for Peacock (62); Anderson for Vagana (70).
Tries: Withers (5), R Paul (33, 79), Peacock (56), Spruce (71), Naylor (74); **Goals:** H Paul 7;
Field goal: H Paul.
WOLVES: 22 Alan Hunte; 2 Rob Smyth; 4 Toa Kohe-Love; 16 Ian Sibbit; 5 Jamie Stenhouse; 6 Lee Briers; 7 Allan Langer (C); 8 Andrew Gee; 9 David Highton; 18 Martin Masella; 20 Dean Busby; 13 Tawera Nikau; 15 Steve Georgallis. Subs: 3 David Kidwell for Stenhouse (75); 10 Danny Nutley for Masella (9); 11 Steve McCurrie for Busby (9BB, rev 33); 12 Jerome Guisset for Busby (62BB); Masella for Nutley (28); McCurrie for Georgallis (50); Nutley for Masella (57BB).
Tries: Smyth (11), Briers (16, 60, 80); **Goals:** Briers 3.
League Express Men of the Match:
Bulls: Henry Paul; *Wolves:* Lee Briers.
Penalty count: 10-7; **Half-time:** 12-12;
Referee: Stuart Cummings (Widnes); **Attendance:** 13,856 (at McAlpine Stadium, Huddersfield).

FINAL

Saturday 28th April 2001

BRADFORD BULLS 6 ST HELENS 13

BULLS: 5 Michael Withers; 2 Tevita Vaikona; 20 Scott Naylor; 15 Shane Rigon; 3 Leon Pryce; 6 Henry Paul; 1 Robbie Paul (C); 8 Joe Vagana; 9 James Lowes; 22 Brian McDermott; 19 Jamie Peacock; 11 Daniel Gartner; 12 Mike Forshaw. Subs: 10 Paul Anderson for Vagana (19); 29 Stuart Fielden for McDermott (23); 14 Lee Gilmour for Naylor (62); 7 Paul Deacon for Lowes (70); McDermott for Gartner (50); Vagana for Anderson (57).
Goals: H Paul 3.
Sin bin: Rigon (10) - obstruction off the ball on Martyn.
SAINTS: 1 Paul Wellens; 2 Sean Hoppe; 3 Kevin Iro; 4 Paul Newlove; 5 Anthony Sullivan; 20 Tommy Martyn; 7 Sean Long; 12 Sonny Nickle; 9 Keiron Cunningham; 10 David Fairleigh; 11 Chris Joynt (C); 8 Peter Shiels; 13 Paul Sculthorpe. Subs: 16 Vila Matautia for Nickle (20); 15 Tim Jonkers for Fairleigh (33); 17 Steve Hall for Newlove (52); 19 Anthony Stewart not used; Nickle for Matautia (33BB, rev 37); Fairleigh for Matautia (47BB).
Tries: Martyn (12), Cunningham (26); **Goals:** Long 2;
Field goal: Martyn.
League Express Men of the Match:
Bulls: Mike Forshaw; *Saints:* Sean Long.
Penalty count: 9-10; **Half-time:** 4-13;
Referee: Russell Smith (Castleford);

INTERNATIONAL SCOREBOARD

STATE OF ORIGIN SERIES

ORIGIN I

QUEENSLAND 34...**NEW SOUTH WALES 16**
Qld: T - Darren Lockyer, Darren Smith, Carl Webb, John Doyle, John Buttigieg, Chris Walker; G - Darren Lockyer 5
NSW: T - Matthew Gidley, Brad Fittler, Trent Barrett; G - Michael De Vere 2

Qld: Darren Lockyer (Broncos), Wendell Sailor (Broncos), Paul Bowman (Cowboys), Darren Smith (Bulldogs), Lote Tuqiri (Broncos), Daniel Wagon (Eels), Paul Green (Roosters); John Buttigieg (Cowboys), Shane Webcke (Broncos), Petero Civoniceva (Broncos), Gorden Tallis (Broncos) (c), Brad Meyers (Broncos), Kevin Campion (Warriors). Interchange: John Doyle (Cowboys), Chris Walker (Broncos), Chris Beattie (Sharks), Carl Webb (Broncos). Coach: Wayne Bennett.

NSW: Mark Hughes (Knights), Adam MacDougall (Knights), Michael De Vere (Broncos), Matthew Gidley (Knights), Jamie Ainscough (Dragons), Brad Fittler (Roosters) (c), Brett Kimmorley (Eagles), Jason Stevens (Sharks), Luke Priddis (Broncos), Robbie Kearns (Storm), Nathan Hindmarsh (Eels), Bryan Fletcher (Roosters), Jason Croker (Raiders). Interchange: Trent Barrett (Dragons), Michael Vella (Eels), Ben Kennedy (Knights), Rodney Howe (Storm). Coach: Wayne Pearce.

Referee: Bill Harrigan
Video referee: Eddie Ward
Half-time: Queensland 16-4
Man of the Match: Gorden Tallis (Qld)
Attendance: 38,909 at Suncorp Stadium (Lang Park), Sunday, May 6, 2001

Andrew Johns (Knights), Ryan Girdler (Panthers) and David Peachey (Sharks) were ruled out of the NSW side through injury before selection. Also chosen in the provisional Queensland squad were Shaun Berrigan (Broncos), Dane Carlaw (Broncos), Nathan Fein (Cowboys), Shannon Hegarty (Roosters), Martin Lang (Sharks), Scott Logan (Roosters), Chris McKenna (Sharks), Steve Price (Bulldogs) and Clinton Schifcofske (Canberra Raiders). Berrigan, Carlaw and McKenna were not considered for final selection because of injury.

ORIGIN II

NEW SOUTH WALES 26...**QUEENSLAND 8**
NSW: T - Brad Fittler 2, Luke Ricketson, Jamie Ainscough, Trent Barrett; G - Ryan Girdler 3
Qld: T - Chris Walker; G - Darren Lockyer 2

NSW: Mark Hughes (Knights), Jamie Ainscough (Dragons), Ryan Girdler (Panthers), Matthew Gidley (Knights), Adam MacDougall (Knights), Brad Fittler (Roosters) (c), Trent Barrett (Dragons); Jason Stevens (Sharks), Luke Priddis (Broncos), Mark O'Meley (Eagles), Bryan Fletcher (Roosters), Adam Muir (Eagles), Luke Ricketson (Roosters). Interchange: Craig Gower (Panthers), Michael Vella (Eels), Matt Adamson (Panthers), Andrew Ryan (Eels). On report & suspended for one match for contrary conduct (lifting knees): Adam MacDougall.

Qld: Darren Lockyer (Broncos) (c), Lote Tuqiri (Broncos), Darren Smith (Bulldogs), Paul Bowman (Cowboys), Wendell Sailor (Broncos), Daniel Wagon (Eels), Paul Green (Roosters), Shane Webcke (Broncos), Kevin Campion (Warriors), Russell Bawden (Storm), Petero Civoniceva (Broncos), Dane Carlaw (Broncos), Brad Meyers (Broncos). Interchange: Nathan Fien (Cowboys), Chris Walker (Broncos), Chris Beattie (Sharks), Carl Webb (Broncos).

Referee: Bill Harrigan
Video referee: Mick Stone
Half-time: NSW 6-2
Man of the Match: Trent Barrett (NSW)
Attendance: 70,249 at Stadium Australia, Sunday, June 10, 2001

Gorden Tallis (Broncos) was unavailable for the Queensland sides in Origin II and III because of injury. For the Queensland Origin II side, John Doyle (Cowboys) was not considered because of injury and John Buttigieg (Cowboys) was unavailable through suspension. Rodney Howe (Storm) was not considered for NSW because of injury and Robbie Kearns (Storm) was chosen but withdrew injured.

ORIGIN III

QUEENSLAND 40...**NEW SOUTH WALES 14**
Qld: T - Chris Walker 2, Paul Bowman 2, Dane Carlaw, Darren Lockyer, Allan Langer; G - Darren Lockyer 4
NSW: T - Ryan Girdler; G - Ryan Girdler 3

Qld: Darren Lockyer (Broncos), Wendell Sailor (Broncos), Chris Walker (Broncos), Paul Bowman (Cowboys), Lote Tuqiri (Broncos), Daniel Wagon (Eels), Allan Langer (Warrington Wolves), Shane Webcke (Broncos), Paul Green (Roosters), John Buttigieg (Cowboys), Brad Meyers (Broncos), Petero Civoniceva (Broncos), Darren Smith (Bulldogs). Interchange: John Doyle (Cowboys), Kevin Campion (Warriors), Carl Webb (Broncos), Dane Carlaw (Broncos).

NSW: Mark Hughes (Knights), Adam MacDougall (Knights), Ryan Girdler (Panthers), Matthew Gidley (Knights), Jamie Ainscough (Dragons), Brad Fittler (Roosters) (c), Brett Kimmorley (Eagles), Jason Stevens (Sharks), Luke Priddis (Broncos), Mark O'Meley (Eagles), Bryan Fletcher (Roosters), Adam Muir (Eagles), Andrew Ryan (Eels). Interchange: Craig Gower (Panthers), Michael Vella (Eels), Matt Adamson (Panthers), Steve Menzies (Eagles).

Referee: Bill Harrigan
Video referee: Chris Ward
Half-time: Queensland 28-8
Man of the Match: Darren Lockyer (Qld)
Attendance: 49,441 (Record Qld Origin crowd) at ANZ Stadium, Sunday, July 1, 2001

Chris McKenna (Sharks) was unavailable for Qld selection because of injury. Luke Ricketson (Roosters) and Jason Croker (Raiders) were unavailable through injury for the NSW team. Trent Barrett (Dragons) was chosen for NSW but withdrew through injury and was replaced by Kimmorley. Clinton Schifcofske (Raiders) had been on stand-by should Lockyer withdraw from the Queensland side.

PLAYER OF THE SERIES: Darren Lockyer (Qld)

COUNTRY ORIGIN v SYDNEY ORIGIN

COUNTRY 42...**CITY 10**
Country: T - Scott Hill 2, Darren Britt, Brett Kimmorley, Josh Perry, Chris Hicks, Danny Buderus, Nathan Blacklock; G - Chris Hicks 5
City: T - Anthony Minichiello, Mark Gasnier; G - Hazem El Masri

Country: Jason Moodie (Eels), Nathan Blacklock (Dragons), Chris Hicks (Panthers), Timana Tahu (Knights), Darren Albert (Knights), Scott Hill (Storm), Brett Kimmorley (Storm); Darren Britt (Bulldogs), Danny Buderus (Knights), Jason Ryles (Dragons), Ian Hindmarsh (Eels), Glenn Morrison (Cowboys), Ben Kennedy (Knights), Jason Croker (Raiders). Subs: Mark McLinden (Raiders), Craig Fitzgibbon (Roosters), Steve Simpson (Knights), Josh Perry (Knights). Coach: Brian Smith.

City: Brett Hodgson (Eels), Hazem El Masri (Bulldogs), Colin Best (Sharks), Mark Gasnier (Dragons), Anthony Minichiello (Roosters), Adam Dykes (Sharks), Matt Orford (Storm); Ian Rubin (Roosters), Brad Drew (Eels), Jason Cayless (Eels), Jody Gall (Panthers), Lance Thompson (Dragons), Steve Menzies (Eagles). Subs: Barry Ward (Bulldogs), Colin Ward (Dragons), Brett Galea (Tigers), Craig Wing (Roosters). Coach: Graham Murray.

Referee: Paul Simpkins; **Half-time:** Country 22-10
Man of the Match: Brett Kimmorley (Country)
Attendance: 8,872 at Carrington Park, Bathurst, Friday, June 8, 2001

Ben Kennedy (Knights) was chosen for Country but withdrew through injury and was replaced by Fitzgibbon.

NRL PREMIERSHIP *(for Telstra Cup)*

FINAL PREMIERSHIP TABLE

	P	W	D	L	F	A	Pts
Eels	26	20	2	4	839	406	42
Bulldogs	26	17	3	6	617	568	37
Knights	26	16	1	9	782	639	33
Sharks	26	15	2	9	594	513	32
Broncos	26	14	1	11	696	511	29
Roosters	26	13	1	12	647	589	27
Dragons	26	12	2	12	661	573	26
Warriors	26	12	2	12	638	629	26
Storm	26	11	1	14	704	725	23
Eagles	26	11	1	14	603	750	23
Raiders	26	9	1	16	600	623	19
Tigers	26	9	1	16	474	746	19
Cowboys	26	6	2	18	514	771	14
Panthers	26	7	-	19	521	847	14

(As Minor Premiers, Parramatta Eels won JJ Giltinan Shield)

QUALIFYING FINALS

SHARKS 22 ....BRISBANE BRONCOS 6
Sharks: T - Paul Mellor 3, Andrew Pierce; G - Mat Rogers 3
Broncos: T - Shaun Berrigan; G- Darren Lockyer
Half-time: Sharks 12-6
Referee: Steve Clark
Attendance: 15,508 at Toyota Park, Friday, September 7, 2001

NEWCASTLE KNIGHTS 40 ....SYDNEY ROOSTERS 6
Knights: T - Matthew Gidley, Andrew Johns, Timana Tahu, Adam
MacDougall, Ben Kennedy; G - Andrew Johns 7, Glen Grief
Roosters: T - Anthony Minichiello; G - Craig Fitzgibbon
Half-time: Knights 18-6
Referee: Bill Harrigan
Attendance: 22,016 at Marathon Stadium, Saturday, September 8, 2001

BULLDOGS 22 ....ST GEO-ILLAWARRA DRAGONS 23
Bulldogs: T - Hazem El Masri, Braith Anasta, Glen Hughes;
G - Hazem El Masri 5
Dragons: T - Matt Cooper 2, Amos Roberts, Nathan Blacklock;
G - Mark Riddell 3; FG - Willie Peters
Half-time: Bulldogs 14-12
Referee: Paul Simpkins
Attendance: 17,975 at Sydney Showground, Saturday, September 8, 2001

PARRAMATTA EELS 56 ....AUCKLAND WARRIORS 12
Eels: T - Daniel Wagon 2, Brett Hodgson 2, Ian Hindmarsh, David
Vaealiki, Jamie Lyon, Jason Taylor, Luke Burt;
G - Jason Taylor 7, Luke Burt 3
Warriors: T - Motu Tony, Wairangi Koopu: G - Ivan Cleary 2
Half-time: Eels 24-6
Referee: Tim Mander
Attendance: 17,336 at Parramatta Stadium, Sunday, September 9, 2001

(Roosters & Warriors eliminated)

SEMI-FINALS

BRISBANE BRONCOS 44 ....ST GEO-ILLAWARRA DRAGONS 28
Broncos: T - Wendell Sailor 4, Petero Civoniceva 2, Chris Walker 2;
G - Darren Lockyer 6
Dragons: T - Mark Gasnier 2, Andrew Hart, Nathan Blacklock, Jason
Ryles; G - Mark Riddell 2, Wayne Bartrim 2
Half-time: Broncos 26-12
Referee: Paul Simpkins
Attendance: 19,259 at SFS, Saturday, September 15, 2001

SHARKS 52 ....BULLDOGS 10
Sharks: T - Preston Campbell 2, Jason Ferris 2, Nick Graham, Mat
Rogers, Martin Lang, Colin Best, Luke Stuart;
G - Mat Rogers 7, Adam Dykes
Bulldogs: T - Willie Talau, Steve Price; G - Hazem El Masri
Half-time: Sharks 24-4
Referee: Bill Harrigan
Attendance: 21,507 at SFS, Sunday, September 16, 2001

(Bulldogs & Dragons eliminated)

PRELIMINARY FINALS

NEWCASTLE KNIGHTS 18 ....SHARKS 10
Knights: T - Ben Kennedy 2, Mark Hughes; G - Andrew Johns 3
Sharks: T - Mat Rogers, David Peachey; G - Mat Rogers
Half-time: Sharks 10-6
Referee: Paul Simpkins
Attendance: 31,438 at SFS, Saturday, September 22, 2001

PARRAMATTA EELS 24 ....BRISBANE BRONCOS 16
Eels: T - Jason Moodie 2, PJ Marsh, Jamie Lyon; G - Jason Taylor 4
Broncos: T - Dane Carlaw, Shaun Berrigan, Lote Tuqiri;
G - Darren Lockyer 2
Half-time: Parramatta 14-12

Referee: Bill Harrigan
Attendance: 34,184 at Stadium Australia, Sunday, September 23, 2001

(Sharks & Broncos eliminated)

GRAND FINAL

NEWCASTLE KNIGHTS 30......................................PARRAMATTA EELS 24

EELS: 1 Brett Hodgson; 2 Luke Burt; 3 Jamie Lyon; 4 David Vaealiki; 5
Jason Moodie; 6 Michael Buettner; 7 Jason Taylor; 8 Nathan Cayless (c);
9 Brad Drew; 10 Michael Vella; 11 Nathan Hindmarsh; 12 Ian Hindmarsh;
13 Daniel Wagon. Subs: 14 PJ Marsh; 15 Andrew Ryan; 16 Alex Chan; 17
David Solomona
Tries: Hodgson (57, 79), Lyon (66, 72); **Goals:** Burt 4.

KNIGHTS: 1 Robbie O'Davis ; 2 Timana Tahu ; 3 Matthew Gidley; 4 Mark
Hughes; 5 Adam MacDougall ; 6 Sean Rudder; 7 Andrew Johns (c); 8
Josh Perry; 9 Danny Buderus; 10 Matt Parsons; 11 Steve Simpson; 12
Ben Kennedy; 13 Bill Peden. Subs: 14 Paul Marquet; 15 Clinton O'Brien;
16 Glenn Grief; 17 Daniel Abraham
Tries: Peden (4, 21), Simpson (7), Kennedy (31), Tahu (63);
Goals: Johns 5

League Express Men of the Match
Eels: Nathan Hindmarsh; *Knights:* Andrew Johns.
Half-time: 0-24
Referee: Bill Harrigan
Video referees: Chris Ward & Mick Stone
Attendance: 90,414 at Stadium Australia on Sunday, September 30, 2001
Clive Churchill Medal: Andrew Johns (Newcastle)

TOP POINTSCORERS

	T	G	FG	Pts
Andrew Johns (Knights)	14	110	3	279
Ben Walker (Eagles)	18	103	1	279
Hazem El Masri (Bulldogs)	19	97	-	270
Jason Taylor (Eels)	8	116	1	265
Clinton Schifcofske (Raiders)	10	102	1	245
Matt Orford (Storm)	15	78	-	216
Michael De Vere (Broncos)	2	99	-	206
Craig Fitzgibbon (Roosters)	10	78	-	196
Ivan Cleary (Warriors)	3	80	1	173
Julian O'Neill (Cowboys)	11	56	-	156

TOP TRYSCORERS

Nathan Blacklock (Dragons)	27
Lote Tuqiri (Broncos)	21
Hazem El Masri (Bulldogs)	19
Wendell Sailor (Broncos)	18
Timana Tahu (Knights)	18
Ben Walker (Eagles)	18
Preston Campbell (Sharks)	17
Brett Hodgson (Eels)	17
Ben Kennedy (Knights)	17
Chris Walker (Broncos)	17

DALLY M PLAYER OF THE YEAR - Final Points

Preston Campbell (Sharks)	29
Andrew Johns (Knights) ●	28
Stacey Jones (Warriors)	27
Adam Dykes (Sharks)	23
Matt Orford (Storm)	23
Glenn Morrison (Cowboys)	21
Darren Lockyer (Broncos)	20
Jason Taylor (Eels)	19

(● ineligible through suspension)

MOST POINTS IN A GAME
34 by Andrew Johns (Knights) v Raiders, Marathon Stadium.

MOST TRIES IN A GAME
4 by Aaron Moule (Storm) v Eagles, Colonial Stadium; 4 by Adam
MacDougall (Knights) v Warriors, Ericsson Stadium; 4 by Andrew Johns
(Knights) v Raiders, Marathon Stadium;
4 by Wendell Sailor (Broncos) v Dragons, SFS.

MOST GOALS IN A GAME
11 by Jason Taylor (Eels) v Tigers, Leichhardt Oval.

BIGGEST WIN
Storm 64 d Tigers 0 at Colonial Stadium.

FASTEST TRY
53sec by Anthony Colella (Raiders) v Knights, Marathon Stadium.

International Scoreboard

QUEENSLAND CUP *(For the Bundy Gold Cup)*

FINAL TABLE

	P	W	D	L	B	F	A	Pts
Toowoomba Clydesdales	20	18	1	1	2	794	310	41
Burleigh Bears	20	15	1	4	2	660	401	35
Redcliffe Dolphins	20	14	-	6	2	617	393	32
Norths Devils	20	11	3	6	2	558	446	29
East Coast Tigers	20	12	-	8	2	501	450	28
Wynnum Seagulls	20	8	3	9	2	445	546	23
Central Qld Comets	20	7	3	10	2	468	517	21
Ipswich Jets	20	6	3	11	2	447	536	19
Logan City Scorpions	20	4	1	15	2	385	581	13
Wests Panthers	20	4	1	15	2	392	798	13
Souths Magpies	20	3	-	17	2	388	677	10

QUALIFYING FINALS

EAST COAST TIGERS 52 ....NORTHS DEVILS 10

REDCLIFFE DOLPHINS 40.....................................BURLEIGH BEARS 8

SEMI-FINALS

BURLEIGH BEARS 30 ....EAST COAST TIGERS 23

REDCLIFFE DOLPHINS 20 ....TOOWOOMBA CLYDESDALES 10

PRELIMINARY FINAL

TOOWOOMBA CLYDESDALES 34 ....BURLEIGH BEARS 20

GRAND FINAL

TOOWOOMBA CLYDESDALES 28 ....REDCLIFFE DOLPHINS 26
Clydesdales: T - Michael Ryan, Tony Duggan, Kirk Reynoldson, Casey McGuire, Damien Quinn; G - Damien Quinn 4
Dolphins: T - Jason Webber, Craig O'Dywer, George Wilson, Andrew Wynyard, Luke Scott; G - Michael Roberts 3
Referee: Rob Alexander
At Dolphin Oval, Brisbane, Saturday, September 15, 2001

NEW ZEALAND

BARTERCARD CUP

FINAL TABLE

	P	W	D	L	F	A	Pts
Hibiscus Coast Raiders	22	17	1	4	673	395	35
Eastern Tornadoes	22	14	3	5	573	464	31
Canterbury Bulls	22	14	1	7	748	471	29
Otahuhu Leopards	22	14	1	7	567	484	29
Manurewa Marlins	22	13	1	8	539	465	27
Northcote Tigers	22	11	1	10	528	574	23
Wainuiomata Lions	22	11	1	10	524	585	23
Glenora Bears	22	10	-	12	572	609	20
Marist/Richmond	22	8	2	12	527	617	18
Mt Albert Lions	22	9	-	13	368	614	18
Porirua Pumas	22	5	1	16	391	792	11

QUALIFYING FINALS

MANUREWA MARLINS 43...................................OTAHUHU LEOPARDS 42
(after extra time; 42-all after 80 minutes)

CANTERBURY BULLS 12.................................EASTERN TORNADOES 10

SEMI-FINALS

EASTERN TORNADOES 24...............................MANUREWA MARLINS 20

HIBISCUS COAST RAIDERS 48 ....CANTERBURY BULLS 16

PRELIMINARY FINAL

EASTERN TORNADOES 38.................................CANTERBURY BULLS 30

GRAND FINAL

HIBISCUS COAST RAIDERS 28 ....EASTERN TORNADOES 18
Raiders: T - Regan Wigg 2, Mikio Filitonga, Shane Ata, Daniel Floyd; G - Daniel Floyd 4
Tornadoes: T - Corey Palmer, Jeremiah Pai, Phillip Leuluai; G - Joe Flavell 3
Half-time: Tornadoes: 18-12
Referee: Andy Cook.
Attendance: 6,000 at Carlaw Park, Auckland, Sunday, September 16, 2001

PAPUA NEW GUINEA

SP CUP

FINAL TABLE: Rabaul Island Gurias 22; Goroka Lahanis 18; Enga Mioks 18; Lae Bombers 16; Mendi Muruks 13; Port Moresby Vipers 13; Waghi Tumbe 8; Kundiawa Warriors 4.

SEMI-FINALS

RABAUL ISLAND GURIAS 23 ....GOROKA LAHANIS 18

ENGA MIOKS 26 ....LAE BOMBERS 12

PRELIMINARY FINAL

GOROKA LAHANIS 30 ....ENGA MIOKS 20

GRAND FINAL

RABAUL ISLAND GURIAS 16 ....GOROKA LAHANIS 8
Gurias: T - Giamuku Tau, Lucas Samak, Chris Purkikil; G - Normyle Eremas 2
Lahanis: T - Tarzan Malaguna; G - Fatty Buka, Nime Kapo
Half-time: 6-all
At Lloyd Robson Oval, Port Moresby, Sunday, September 16, 2001
Man of the Match: Michael Marum (Gurias)

TONGA

GRAND FINAL

MU'A SAINTS 28 ....KOLOMAI WARRIORS 8
Man of the Match: Samiuela Fukofuka (Saints)
On Saturday, August 25, 2001

FRANCE

FRENCH CHAMPIONSHIP *(For Max Roussie Shield)*

FINAL TABLE

	P	W	D	L	F	A	Pts
Villeneuve	22	20	-	2	714	242	62
Saint-Gaudens ●	22	16	-	6	605	374	53
Toulouse	22	15	-	7	667	319	52
UTC	22	14	1	7	721	316	51
Pia	22	14	-	8	583	502	50
Grand Avignon	22	11	1	10	444	888	45
Limoux	22	11	-	11	433	486	44
Saint-Cyprien ●●	22	10	2	10	423	483	42
Lezignan	22	7	1	14	432	588	37
Villefranche	22	7	-	15	380	592	35
Carcassonne	22	4	-	18	353	655	30
Lyon-Villerbanne	22	-	1	21	241	964	23

● one point deducted for not fielding an Espoirs team
●● one point deducted for not fielding an Espoirs team & one point deducted for fielding an ineligible player

QUARTER-FINALS (Home and away)

Villeneuve d Saint-Cyprien on 118-28 aggregate
Saint-Gaudens d Limoux on 58-44 aggregate
Toulouse d Grand Avignon on 70-34 aggregate
UTC d Pia on 113-36 aggregate

SEMI-FINALS (Home and away)

Toulouse d Saint-Gaudens on 43-32 aggregate
Villeneuve d UTC on 49-26 aggregate

FINAL

VILLENEUVE LEOPARDS 32 ....TOULOUSE SPACERS 20
Villeneuve: T - Daniel Vergniol, Ludovic Perolari, Dragan Durdevic, Michael van Schnick, Brock Mueller, Vincent Wulf; G - Freddy Banquet 3; FG - Laurent Frayssinous, Freddy Banquet
Toulouse: T - Yannick Cazemajou, Ptrice Benausse, Sebastien Raguin; G - Simon Dorrell 4
Half-time: Villeneuve 11-8
Referee: Richard Frileux
Man of the Match: Freddy Banquet (Villeneuve)
Attendance: 8,000 at Stade Sept Deniers, Toulouse, on Saturday, May 19, 2001

COUPE DE FRANCE *(for Lord Derby Cup)*

FINAL

UNION TRIEZISTE CATALANE 38 ....LIMOUX 17
UTC: T - Florent Lopez 2, Maxime Greseque 2, David Berthezene, Gael Tallec; G - Maxime Greseque 6, Florent Gomez
Limoux: T - Paea Kailea, David Cenet; G - Cedric Jalibert 4; FG - Nicolas Piccolo
Half-time: UTC 12-7
Referee: Thierry Ailbert
Man of the Match: Maxime Greseque (UTC)
Attendance: 8,000 at Stade de l'Amitie, Narbonne, on Sunday, May 27, 2001

2002 FIXTURES

ROUND 1

Friday 1 March
Wigan Warriors v Bradford Bulls
Leeds Rhinos v London Broncos
Saturday 2 March
Widnes Vikings v St Helens
Sunday 3 March
Salford City Reds v Hull
Wakefield Wildcats v Castleford Tigers
Warrington Wolves v Halifax Blue Sox

ROUND 2

Friday 8 March
Hull v Leeds Rhinos
Bradford Bulls v Warrington Wolves
St Helens v Salford City Reds
Saturday 9 March
London Broncos v Wigan Warriors
Sunday 10 March
Castleford Tigers v Widnes Vikings
Halifax Blue Sox v Wakefield Wildcats

ROUND 3

Friday 22 March
Warrington Wolves v Leeds Rhinos
St Helens v Hull
Saturday 23 March
Wakefield Wildcats v Salford City Reds
Sunday 24 March
Castleford Tigers v London Broncos
Halifax Blue Sox v Wigan Warriors
Widnes Vikings v Bradford Bulls

ROUND 4

Thursday 28 March
London Broncos v St Helens
Friday 29 March – Good Friday
Bradford Bulls v Hull
Leeds Rhinos v Halifax Blue Sox
Salford City Reds v Warrington Wolves
Widnes Vikings v Wakefield Wildcats
Wigan Warriors v Castleford Tigers

ROUND 5

Monday 1 April – Easter Monday
Castleford Tigers v Leeds Rhinos
St Helens v Wigan Warriors
Halifax Blue Sox v Salford City Reds
Hull v London Broncos
Wakefield Wildcats v Bradford Bulls
Warrington Wolves v Widnes Vikings

ROUND 6

Friday 5 April
Wigan Warriors v Hull
Saturday 6 April
St Helens v Leeds Rhinos
Sunday 7 April
London Broncos v Bradford Bulls
Salford City Reds v Castleford Tigers
Wakefield Wildcats v Warrington Wolves
Widnes Vikings v Halifax Blue Sox

TETLEY'S
SUPER LEAGUE 2002

ROUND 7

Friday 19 April
Salford City Reds v Widnes Vikings
Leeds Rhinos v Wakefield Wildcats
Wigan Warriors v Warrington Wolves
Saturday 20 April
Bradford Bulls v St Helens
Sunday 21 April
Hull v Castleford Tigers
London Broncos v Halifax Blue Sox

ROUND 8

Monday 29 April
Bradford Bulls v Salford City Reds
Castleford Tigers v St Helens
Halifax Blue Sox v Hull
Leeds Rhinos v Widnes Vikings
Wakefield Wildcats v Wigan Warriors
Warrington Wolves v London Broncos

ROUND 9

Friday 3 May
St Helens v Halifax Blue Sox
Saturday 4 May
Castleford Tigers v Bradford Bulls
Sunday 5 May
Hull v Warrington Wolves
Salford City Reds v Leeds Rhinos

Wakefield Wildcats v London Broncos
Widnes Vikings v Wigan Warriors

ROUND 10

Friday 10 May
Wigan Warriors v Salford City Reds
Saturday 11 May
Leeds Rhinos v Bradford Bulls
Sunday 12 May
Halifax Blue Sox v Castleford Tigers
Hull v Wakefield Wildcats
London Broncos v Widnes Vikings
Warrington Wolves v St Helens

ROUND 11

Friday 17 May
Bradford Bulls v Halifax Blue Sox
Saturday 18 May
Wigan Warriors v Leeds Rhinos
Sunday 19 May
Castleford Tigers v Warrington Wolves
Salford City Reds v London Broncos
Wakefield Wildcats v St Helens
Widnes Vikings v Hull

ROUND 12

Friday 24 May
Bradford Bulls v Wigan Warriors
St Helens v Widnes Vikings
Saturday 25 May
Halifax Blue Sox v Warrington Wolves
Sunday 26 May
Castleford Tigers v Wakefield Wildcats
Hull v Salford City Reds
London Broncos v Leeds Rhinos

ROUND 13

Friday 31 May
Leeds Rhinos v Hull
Wigan Warriors v London Broncos
Saturday 1 June
Salford City Reds v St Helens
Sunday 2 June
Wakefield Wildcats v Halifax Blue Sox
Warrington Wolves v Bradford Bulls
Widnes Vikings v Castleford Tigers

ROUND 14

Friday 7 June
Bradford Bulls v London Broncos
Leeds Rhinos v St Helens
Saturday 8 June
Hull v Wigan Warriors
Sunday 9 June
Castleford Tigers v Salford City Reds
Halifax Blue Sox v Widnes Vikings
Warrington Wolves v Wakefield Wildcats

ORIGIN WEEK

Friday 14 June Origin One
Tuesday 18 June Origin Two

ROUND 15

Friday 21 June
St Helens v Castleford Tigers
Wigan Warriors v Wakefield Wildcats
Saturday 22 June
Widnes Vikings v Leeds Rhinos
Sunday 23 June
Hull v Halifax Blue Sox
London Broncos v Warrington Wolves
Salford City Reds v Bradford Bulls

ROUND 16

Friday 28 June
St Helens v Bradford Bulls
Saturday 29 June
Warrington Wolves v Wigan Warriors
Sunday 30 June
Castleford Tigers v Hull
Halifax Blue Sox v London Broncos
Wakefield Wildcats v Leeds Rhinos
Widnes Vikings v Salford City Reds

ROUND 17

Friday 5 July
Bradford Bulls v Widnes Vikings
Leeds Rhinos v Warrington Wolves
Wigan Warriors v Halifax Blue Sox
Saturday 6 July
London Broncos v Castleford Tigers
Sunday 7 July
Hull v St Helens
Salford City Reds v Wakefield Wildcats

Friday 12 July
Australia v Great Britain

ROUND 18

Friday 12 July
Bradford Bulls v Wakefield Wildcats
Leeds Rhinos v Castleford Tigers
Wigan Warriors v St Helens
Sunday 14 July
London Broncos v Hull
Salford City Reds v Halifax Blue Sox
Widnes Vikings v Warrington Wolves

ROUND 19

Friday 19 July
St Helens v London Broncos
Saturday 20 July
Castleford Tigers v Wigan Warriors
Sunday 21 July
Halifax Blue Sox v Leeds Rhinos
Hull v Bradford Bulls
Wakefield Wildcats v Widnes Vikings
Warrington Wolves v Salford City Reds

ROUND 20

Friday 26 July
Halifax Blue Sox v St Helens
Bradford Bulls v Castleford Tigers
Leeds Rhinos v Salford City Reds
Wigan Warriors v Widnes Vikings
Saturday 27 July
Warrington Wolves v Hull
Sunday 28 July
London Broncos v Wakefield Wildcats

ROUND 21

Friday 2 August
Bradford Bulls v Leeds Rhinos
Saturday 3 August
St Helens v Warrington Wolves
Sunday 4 August
Castleford Tigers v Halifax Blue Sox
Salford City Reds v Wigan Warriors
Widnes Vikings v London Broncos
Wakefield Wildcats v Hull

ROUND 22

Friday 9 August
St Helens v Wakefield Wildcats
Leeds Rhinos v Wigan Warriors
Saturday 10 August
Halifax Blue Sox v Bradford Bulls
Sunday 11 August
Hull v Widnes Vikings
London Broncos v Salford City Reds
Warrington Wolves v Castleford Tigers

ROUND 23

Friday 16 August
Bradford Bulls v St Helens
Leeds Rhinos v Hull
Wigan Warriors v London Broncos
Sunday 18 August
Halifax Blue Sox v Castleford Tigers
Salford City Reds v Wakefield Wildcats
Widnes Vikings v Warrington Wolves

ROUND 24

Friday 23 August
St Helens v Halifax Blue Sox
Sunday 25 August
Castleford Tigers v Bradford Bulls
Hull v Salford City Reds
London Broncos v Widnes Vikings
Wakefield Wildcats v Leeds Rhinos
Warrington Wolves v Wigan Warriors

ROUND 25

Friday 30 August
Bradford Bulls v London Broncos
St Helens v Leeds Rhinos
Sunday 1 September
Castleford Tigers v Wakefield Wildcats
Halifax Blue Sox v Warrington Wolves
Hull v Wigan Warriors
Widnes Vikings v Salford City Reds

ROUND 26

Friday 6 September
Leeds Rhinos v Bradford Bulls
Wigan Warriors v St Helens
Sunday 8 September
London Broncos v Hull
Salford City Reds v Halifax Blue Sox
Wakefield Wildcats v Widnes Vikings
Warrington Wolves v Castleford Tigers

ROUND 27

Friday 13 September
Bradford Bulls v Wigan Warriors
St Helens v Hull
Leeds Rhinos v London Broncos
Sunday 15 September
Castleford Tigers v Widnes Vikings
Halifax Blue Sox v Wakefield Wildcats
Warrington Wolves v Salford City Reds

ROUND 28

Friday 20 September
Wigan Warriors v Leeds Rhinos
Sunday 22 September
Hull v Bradford Bulls
London Broncos v St Helens
Salford City Reds v Castleford Tigers
Wakefield Wildcats v Warrington Wolves
Widnes Vikings v Halifax Blue Sox

*All fixtures are subject to change. Check the
Tetley's Super League Website
www.superleague.co.uk*

*Please note these fixtures remain the property
of Super League (Europe) Limited and must
not be reproduced without permission.*

NORTHERN FORD
PREMIERSHIP 2002

SUNDAY 2 DECEMBER 2001
Chorley Lynx v Featherstone Rovers
Dewsbury Rams v Keighley Cougars
Gateshead Thunder v Doncaster Dragons
Hull Kingston Rovers v Hunslet Hawks
Leigh Centurions v Barrow Raiders
Oldham v Swinton Lions
Rochdale Hornets v Batley Bulldogs
Workington Town v Sheffield Eagles
York v Whitehaven

SUNDAY 9 DECEMBER 2001
Barrow Raiders v York
Batley Bulldogs v Leigh Centurions
Doncaster Dragons v Huddersfield Giants
Featherstone Rovers v Workington Town
Hunslet Hawks v Rochdale Hornets
Keighley Cougars v Chorley Lynx
Sheffield Eagles v Gateshead Thunder
Swinton Lions v Hull Kingston Rovers
Whitehaven v Dewsbury Rams

SUNDAY 16 DECEMBER 2001
Chorley Lynx v Whitehaven
Dewsbury Rams v Barrow Raiders
Gateshead Thunder v Featherstone Rovers
Huddersfield Giants v Sheffield Eagles
Hull Kingston Rovers v Oldham
Leigh Centurions v Hunslet Hawks
Rochdale Hornets v Swinton Lions
Workington Town v Keighley Cougars
York v Batley Bulldogs

SUNDAY 23 DECEMBER 2001
Barrow Raiders v Chorley Lynx
Sheffield Eagles v Doncaster Dragons
Oldham v Rochdale Hornets

WEDNESDAY 26 DECEMBER 2001
Batley Bulldogs v Dewsbury Rams
Featherstone Rovers v Huddersfield Giants
Hunslet Hawks v York
Keighley Cougars v Gateshead Thunder
Swinton Lions v Leigh Centurions
Whitehaven v Workington Town

SUNDAY 30 DECEMBER 2001
Chorley Lynx v Batley Bulldogs
Leigh Centurions v Oldham
Rochdale Hornets v Hull Kingston Rovers

MONDAY 31 DECEMBER 2001
Workington Town v Barrow Raiders

TUESDAY 1 JANUARY 2002
Dewsbury Rams v Hunslet Hawks
Doncaster Dragons v Featherstone Rovers
Gateshead Thunder v Whitehaven
Huddersfield Giants v Keighley Cougars
York v Swinton Lions

SUNDAY 6 JANUARY 2002
Barrow Raiders v Gateshead Thunder
Batley Bulldogs v Workington Town
Featherstone Rovers v Sheffield Eagles
Hull Kingston Rovers v Leigh Centurions
Hunslet Hawks v Chorley Lynx
Keighley Cougars v Doncaster Dragons
Oldham v York
Swinton Lions v Dewsbury Rams
Whitehaven v Huddersfield Giants

SUNDAY 13 JANUARY 2002
Chorley Lynx v Swinton Lions
Dewsbury Rams v Oldham
Doncaster Dragons v Batley Bulldogs
Gateshead Thunder v Batley Bulldogs
Huddersfield Giants v Barrow Raiders
Leigh Centurions v Rochdale Hornets
Sheffield Eagles v Keighley Cougars
Workington Town v Hunslet Hawks
York v Hull Kingston Rovers

SUNDAY 20 JANUARY 2002
Barrow Raiders v Doncaster Dragons
Batley Bulldogs v Huddersfield Giants
Hull Kingston Rovers v Dewsbury Rams
Hunslet Hawks v Gateshead Thunder
Keighley Cougars v Featherstone Rovers
Oldham v Chorley Lynx
Rochdale Hornets v York
Swinton Lions v Workington Town
Whitehaven v Sheffield Eagles

SUNDAY 27 JANUARY 2002
Challenge Cup - Third Round

WEDNESDAY 30 JANUARY 2002
Leigh Centurions v Oldham

SUNDAY 3 FEBRUARY 2002
Chorley Lynx v Hull Kingston Rovers
Dewsbury Rams v Rochdale Hornets
Doncaster Dragons v Batley Bulldogs
Featherstone Rovers v Whitehaven
Gateshead Thunder v Swinton Lions
Huddersfield Giants v Hunslet Hawks
Sheffield Eagles v Barrow Raiders
Workington Town v Oldham
York v Leigh Centurions

SUNDAY 10 FEBRUARY 2002
Challenge Cup - Fourth Round

SUNDAY 17 FEBRUARY 2002
Barrow Raiders v Featherstone Rovers
Batley Bulldogs v Sheffield Eagles
Hull Kingston Rovers v Workington Town
Hunslet Hawks v Doncaster Dragons
Leigh Centurions v Dewsbury Rams
Oldham v Gateshead Thunder
Rochdale Hornets v Chorley Lynx
Swinton Lions v Huddersfield Giants
Whitehaven v Keighley Cougars

SUNDAY 24 FEBRUARY 2002
Challenge Cup - Fifth Round

SUNDAY 3 MARCH 2002
Chorley Lynx v Leigh Centurions
Dewsbury Rams v York
Doncaster Dragons v Swinton Lions
Featherstone Rovers v Batley Bulldogs
Gateshead Thunder v Hull Kingston Rovers
Huddersfield Giants v Oldham
Keighley Cougars v Barrow Raiders
Sheffield Eagles v Hunslet Hawks
Workington Town v Rochdale Hornets

SUNDAY 10 MARCH 2002
Barrow Raiders v Whitehaven
Batley Bulldogs v Keighley Cougars
Hull Kingston Rovers v Huddersfield Giants
Hunslet Hawks v Featherstone Rovers
Leigh Centurions v Workington Town
Oldham v Doncaster Dragons
Rochdale Hornets v Gateshead Thunder
Swinton Lions v Sheffield Eagles
York v Chorley Lynx

FRIDAY 15 MARCH 2002
Sheffield Eagles v Oldham

SUNDAY 17 MARCH 2002
Challenge Cup - Sixth Round

Chorley Lynx v Dewsbury Rams
Doncaster Dragons v Hull Kingston Rovers
Featherstone Rovers v Swinton Lions
Gateshead Thunder v Leigh Centurions
Huddersfield Giants v Rochdale Hornets
Keighley Cougars v Hunslet Hawks
Whitehaven v Batley Bulldogs
Workington Town v York

SUNDAY 24 MARCH 2002
Batley Bulldogs v Barrow Raiders
Dewsbury Rams v Workington Town
Hull Kingston Rovers v Sheffield Eagles
Hunslet Hawks v Whitehaven
Leigh Centurions v Huddersfield Giants
Oldham v Featherstone Rovers
Rochdale Hornets v Doncaster Dragons
Swinton Lions v Keighley Cougars
York v Gateshead Thunder

SUNDAY 14 APRIL 2002
Challenge Cup Semi Finals

Hull Kingston Rovers v York

SATURDAY 27 APRIL 2002
Challenge Cup Final

SUNDAY 12 MAY 2002
National League Cup Quarter Finals

SUNDAY 19 MAY 2002
National League Cup Semi Finals

SUNDAY 26 MAY 2002
National League Cup Final

WEDNESDAY 29 MAY 2002
Gateshead Thunder v Sheffield Eagles
Hunslet Hawks v Huddersfield Giants
Rochdale Hornets v Barrow Raiders
Workington Town v Whitehaven

SUNDAY 2 JUNE 2002
Barrow Raiders v Hunslet Hawks
Doncaster Dragons v Leigh Centurions
Featherstone Rovers v Hull Kingston Rovers
Gateshead Thunder v Dewsbury Rams
Huddersfield Giants v York
Keighley Cougars v Oldham
Sheffield Eagles v Rochdale Hornets
Whitehaven v Swinton Lions
Workington Town v Chorley Lynx

SUNDAY 9 JUNE 2002
Chorley Lynx v Gateshead Thunder
Dewsbury Rams v Huddersfield Giants
Hull Kingston Rovers v Keighley Cougars
Hunslet Hawks v Batley Bulldogs
Leigh Centurions v Sheffield Eagles
Oldham v Whitehaven
Rochdale Hornets v Featherstone Rovers
Barrow Raiders v Swinton Lions
York v Doncaster Dragons

SUNDAY 16 JUNE 2002
Barrow Raiders v Oldham
Batley Bulldogs v Swinton Lions

Doncaster Dragons v Dewsbury Rams
Featherstone Rovers v Leigh Centurions
Gateshead Thunder v Workington Town
Huddersfield Giants v Chorley Lynx
Keighley Cougars v Rochdale Hornets
Sheffield Eagles v York
Whitehaven v Hull Kingston Rovers

SUNDAY 23 JUNE 2002
Chorley Lynx v Doncaster Dragons
Dewsbury Rams v Sheffield Eagles
Hull Kingston Rovers v Barrow Raiders
Leigh Centurions v Keighley Cougars
Oldham v Batley Bulldogs
Rochdale Hornets v Whitehaven
Swinton Lions v Hunslet Hawks
Workington Town v Huddersfield Giants
York v Featherstone Rovers

SUNDAY 30 JUNE 2002
Barrow Raiders v Rochdale Hornets
Batley Bulldogs v Hull Kingston Rovers
Doncaster Dragons v Workington Town
Featherstone Rovers v Dewsbury Rams
Huddersfield Giants v Gateshead Thunder
Hunslet Hawks v Oldham
Keighley Cougars v York
Sheffield Eagles v Chorley Lynx
Whitehaven v Leigh Centurions

SUNDAY 7 JULY 2002
Swinton Lions v Barrow Raiders
Dewsbury Rams v Chorley Lynx
Featherstone Rovers v Rochdale Hornets
Huddersfield Giants v Whitehaven
Hull Kingston Rovers v Gateshead Thunder
Hunslet Hawks v Sheffield Eagles
Keighley Cougars v Batley Bulldogs
Oldham v Leigh Centurions
Workington Town v Doncaster Dragons

SUNDAY 14 JULY 2002
Batley Bulldogs v Featherstone Rovers
Chorley Lynx v Oldham
Doncaster Dragons v Barrow Raiders
Keighley Cougars v Hull Kingston Rovers
Leigh Centurions v Whitehaven
Rochdale Hornets v Dewsbury Rams
Sheffield Eagles v Workington Town
Swinton Lions v Gateshead Thunder
York v Hunslet Hawks

SUNDAY 21 JULY 2002
Barrow Raiders v Dewsbury Rams
Batley Bulldogs v Hunslet Hawks
Doncaster Dragons v York
Featherstone Rovers v Keighley Cougars
Gateshead Thunder v Chorley Lynx
Huddersfield Giants v Swinton Lions
Leigh Centurions v Hull Kingston Rovers
Rochdale Hornets v Sheffield Eagles
Whitehaven v Oldham

FRIDAY 26 JULY 2002
Sheffield Eagles v Batley Bulldogs

SUNDAY 28 JULY 2002
Chorley Lynx v York
Dewsbury Rams v Doncaster Dragons
Gateshead Thunder v Keighley Cougars
Hunslet Hawks v Barrow Raiders
Oldham v Huddersfield Giants
Swinton Lions v Featherstone Rovers
Whitehaven v Rochdale Hornets
Workington Town v Leigh Centurions

SUNDAY 4 AUGUST 2002
Batley Bulldogs v Whitehaven
Chorley Lynx v Workington Town
Dewsbury Rams v Gateshead Thunder
Hull Kingston Rovers v Rochdale Hornets
Keighley Cougars v Huddersfield Giants
Leigh Centurions v Featherstone Rovers
Oldham v Hunslet Hawks
Swinton Lions v Doncaster Dragons
York v Sheffield Eagles

SUNDAY 11 AUGUST 2002
Batley Bulldogs v Oldham
Doncaster Dragons v Sheffield Eagles
Featherstone Rovers v Hunslet Hawks
Huddersfield Giants v Hull Kingston Rovers
Keighley Cougars v Swinton Lions
Leigh Centurions v Chorley Lynx
Rochdale Hornets v Workington Town
Whitehaven v Barrow Raiders
York v Dewsbury Rams

SUNDAY 18 AUGUST 2002
Barrow Raiders v Leigh Centurions
Huddersfield Giants v Batley Bulldogs
Hull Kingston Rovers v Featherstone Rovers
Rochdale Hornets v Oldham
Sheffield Eagles v Dewsbury Rams
Swinton Lions v Chorley Lynx
Whitehaven v Doncaster Dragons
Workington Town v Gateshead Thunder
York v Keighley Cougars

SUNDAY 25 AUGUST 2002
Barrow Raiders v Hull Kingston Rovers
Chorley Lynx v Rochdale Hornets
Dewsbury Rams v Batley Bulldogs
Doncaster Dragons v Keighley Cougars
Featherstone Rovers v York
Gateshead Thunder v Huddersfield Giants
Hunslet Hawks v Leigh Centurions
Oldham v Workington Town
Sheffield Eagles v Swinton Lions

SUNDAY 1 SEPTEMBER 2002
Batley Bulldogs v Gateshead Thunder
Doncaster Dragons v Rochdale Hornets
Featherstone Rovers v Barrow Raiders
Huddersfield Giants v Dewsbury Rams
Hunslet Hawks v Hull Kingston Rovers
Keighley Cougars v Workington Town
Leigh Centurions v Swinton Lions
Whitehaven v Chorley Lynx
York v Oldham

SUNDAY 8 SEPTEMBER 2002
Barrow Raiders v Batley Bulldogs
Chorley Lynx v Hunslet Hawks
Dewsbury Rams v Leigh Centurions
Gateshead Thunder v York
Hull Kingston Rovers v Doncaster Dragons
Oldham v Keighley Cougars
Sheffield Eagles v Huddersfield Giants
Swinton Lions v Whitehaven
Workington Town v Featherstone Rovers

NATIONAL LEAGUE CUP

CENTRAL

GOOD FRIDAY, 29 MARCH 2002
Dewsbury Rams v Batley Bulldogs
Huddersfield Giants v Hunslet Hawks
Rochdale Hornets v Oldham

EASTER MONDAY, 1 APRIL 2002
Batley Bulldogs v Huddersfield Giants
Hunslet Hawks v Keighley Cougars
Oldham v Dewsbury Rams

SUNDAY 7 APRIL 2002
Dewsbury Rams v Rochdale Hornets
Huddersfield Giants v Oldham
Keighley Cougars v Batley Bulldogs

SUNDAY 14 APRIL 2002
Batley Bulldogs v Hunslet Hawks
Oldham v Keighley Cougars
Rochdale Hornets v Huddersfield Giants

SUNDAY 21 APRIL 2002
Huddersfield Giants v Dewsbury Rams
Hunslet Hawks v Oldham
Keighley Cougars v Rochdale Hornets

MONDAY 29 APRIL 2002
Batley Bulldogs v Rochdale Hornets

Hunslet Hawks v Dewsbury Rams
Keighley Cougars v Huddersfield Giants

SUNDAY 5 MAY 2002
Dewsbury Rams v Keighley Cougars
Oldham v Batley Bulldogs
Rochdale Hornets v Hunslet Hawks

WEST

GOOD FRIDAY, 29 MARCH 2002
Chorley Lynx v Barrow Raiders
Leigh Centurions v Swinton Lions
Workington Town v Whitehaven

EASTER MONDAY, 1 APRIL 2002
Barrow Raiders v Workington Town
Whitehaven v Leigh Centurions

SUNDAY 7 APRIL 2002
Barrow Raiders v Swinton Lions
Chorley Lynx v Whitehaven
Leigh Centurions v Workington Town

SUNDAY 14 APRIL 2002
Swinton Lions v Chorley Lynx

SUNDAY 21 APRIL 2002
Leigh Centurions v Chorley Lynx
Whitehaven v Barrow Raiders
Workington Town v Swinton Lions

SUNDAY 5 MAY 2002
Barrow Raiders v Leigh Centurions
Chorley Lynx v Workington Town
Swinton Lions v Whitehaven

EAST

GOOD FRIDAY, 29 MARCH 2002
Doncaster Dragons v Sheffield Eagles
Gateshead Thunder v Hull Kingston Rovers
York v Featherstone Rovers

EASTER MONDAY, 1 APRIL 2002
Featherstone Rovers v Doncaster Dragons
Hull Kingston Rovers v York
Sheffield Eagles v Gateshead Thunder

SUNDAY 7 APRIL 2002
Gateshead Thunder v Featherstone Rovers
Hull Kingston Rovers v Sheffield Eagles
York v Doncaster Dragons

SUNDAY 21 APRIL 2002
Doncaster Dragons v Gateshead Thunder
Featherstone Rovers v Hull Kingston Rovers
Sheffield Eagles v York

SUNDAY 5 MAY 2002
Doncaster Dragons v Hull Kingston Rovers
Gateshead Thunder v York
Sheffield Eagles v Featherstone Rovers

SUNDAY 12 MAY 2002
National League Cup Quarter Finals

SUNDAY 19 MAY 2002
National League Cup Semi Finals

SUNDAY 26 MAY 2002
National League Cup Final

SUPER LEAGUE DREAM TEAM 2001

KRIS RADLINSKI
(Wigan Warriors)
TEVITA VAIKONA
(Bradford Bulls)
TONIE CARROLL
(Leeds Rhinos)
STEVE RENOUF
(Wigan Warriors)
BRETT DALLAS
(Wigan Warriors)
PAUL SCULTHORPE
(St Helens)
ADRIAN LAM
(Wigan Warriors)
DAVID FAIRLEIGH
(St Helens)
KEIRON CUNNINGHAM
(St Helens)
TERRY O'CONNOR
(Wigan Warriors)
DAVID FURNER
(Wigan Warriors)
JAMEI PEACOCK
(Bradford Bulls)
ANDY FARRELL
(Wigan Warriors)

NORTHERN FORD PREMIERSHIP ALL-STARS 2001

NEIL TURLEY
(Leigh Centurions)
MARLON BILLY
(Rochdale Hornets)
BRENDAN O'MEARA
(Rochdale Hornets)
MICK NANYN (Swinton Lions)
GRAEME LEWTHWAITE
(Workington Town)
SIMON SVABIC
(Leigh Centurions)
JAMIE ROONEY
(Featherstone Rovers)
DANNY SCULTHORPE
(Rochdale Hornets)
PHIL CANTILLON
(Widnes Vikings)
SIMON KNOX
(Widnes Vikings)
PHIL FARRELL (Oldham)
SIMON BALDWIN
(Leigh Centurions)
RICHARD GODDARD
(Sheffield Eagles)

2001 SEASON AWARD WINNERS

SUPER LEAGUE MAN OF STEEL, SUPER LEAGUE PLAYERS' PLAYER OF THE YEAR
PAUL SCULTHORPE
(St Helens)

SUPER LEAGUE COACH OF THE YEAR
IAN MILLWARD (St Helens)
Nominees:
BRIAN NOBLE (Bradford Bulls),
SHAUN McRae (Hull FC)

SUPER LEAGUE YOUNG PLAYER OF THE YEAR
ROB BURROW (Leeds Rhinos)
Nominees: MARK LENNON
(Castleford Tigers),
RICHARD HORNE (Hull FC)

SUPER LEAGUE HIT MAN
MALCOLM ALKER
(Salford City Reds)

SUPER LEAGUE METRE MAKER
ANDY FARRELL
(Wigan Warriors)

SUPER LEAGUE REFEREE OF THE YEAR
RUSSELL SMITH

NFP PLAYER OF THE YEAR, NFP YOUNG PLAYER OF THE YEAR, NFP PLAYERS' PLAYER OF THE YEAR
NEIL TURLEY
(Leigh Centurions)
Nominees: Player of the Year:
PHIL CANTILLON (Widnes

Vikings), DANNY SCULTHORPE
(Rochdale Hornets)
Young Player:
PHIL FARRELL (Oldham),
MICK NANYN (Swinton Lions)

NFP COACH OF THE YEAR
PAUL TERZIS
(Leigh Centurions)
Nominees: MIKE FORD (Oldham),
MARTIN HALL (Rochdale Hornets)

NFP CLUB OF THE YEAR
Sheffield Eagles

NFP REFEREE OF THE YEAR
Richard Silverwood
Nominees: COLIN MORRIS,
PETER TABERNER

SUPER LEAGUE

(Play-offs in brackets, inc. in totals)

TRIES
1. Kris Radlinski
   Wigan 30 (3)
2. Michael Withers
   Bradford 25 (3)
3. Paul Sculthorpe
   St Helens 24 (4)
4. Tevita Vaikona
   Bradford 22 (0)
   Tonie Carroll
   Leeds 22 (0)
6. Robbie Paul
   Bradford 20 (2)
   Keiron Cunningham
   St Helens 20 (3)
   Steve Renouf
   Wigan 20 (1)
9. Francis Maloney
   Salford . . . . .19 (-)
10. Tony Smith
    Hull 18 (0)

GOALS
1. Henry Paul
   Bradford 178 (13)
2. Andy Farrell
   Wigan 176 (16)
3. Paul Sculthorpe
   St Helens 82 (8)
4. Lee Briers
   Warrington . . . . .79 (-)
5. Iestyn Harris
   Leeds 76 (0)
6. Matt Crowther
   Hull 69 (6)
7. Steve McNamara
   Huddersfield . . . . .66 (-)
8. Martin Pearson
   Wakefield . . . . .60 (-)
9. Danny Tickle
   Halifax . . . . .58 (-)
10. Danny Orr
    Castleford . . . . .57 (-)

POINTS
1. Andy Farrell
   Wigan 425 (37)
2. Henry Paul
   Bradford 392 (27)
3. Paul Sculthorpe
   St Helens 260 (32)
4. Lee Briers
   Warrington . . . . .186 (-)
5. Iestyn Harris
   Leeds 185 (0)
6. Matt Crowther
   Hull 178 (12)
7. Steve Prescott
   Hull 167 (0)
8. Danny Orr
   Castleford . . . . .150 (-)
9. Steve McNamara
   Huddersfield . . . . .136 (-)
10. Martin Pearson
    Wakefield . . . . .135 (-)

PREMIERSHIP

(Play-offs in brackets, inc. in totals)

TRIES
1. Neil Turley
   Leigh 52 (2)
2. Phil Cantillon
   Widnes 44 (2)
3. Graeme Lewthwaite
   Workington . . . . .30 (-)
4. Marlon Billy
   Rochdale 27 (2)
5. Adrian Flynn
   Dewsbury 23 (0)
   Damian Munro
   Widnes 23 (3)
7. Matt Bramald
   Featherstone 20 (0)
   Jamie Stokes
   Featherstone 20 (0)
9. Danny Seal
   Featherstone 19 (0)
   (includes 16 for Keighley)
10. Paul Mansson
    Doncaster . . . . .18 (-)
    Darren Robinson
    Rochdale 18 (3)

GOALS
1. Simon Svabic
   Leigh 143 (11)
2. Pat Rich
   Oldham 133 (13)
3. Danny Wood
   Rochdale 123 (10)
4. Jamie Rooney
   Featherstone 118 (5)
5. Barry Eaton
   Dewsbury 100 (1)
6. Richard Goddard
   Sheffield . . . . .93 (-)
7. Darren Holt
   Barrow . . . . .84 (-)
8. Chris Charles
   Hull KR 68 (4)
9. Mick Nanyn
   Swinton . . . . .67 (-)
10. Tane Manihera
    Workington . . . . .66 (-)
    Martin Wood
    Keighley 66 (0)

POINTS
1. Simon Svabic
   Leigh 321 (22)
2. Danny Wood
   Rochdale 302 (28)
3. Jamie Rooney
   Featherstone 301 (18)
4. Pat Rich
   Oldham 290 (26)
5. Barry Eaton
   Dewsbury 244 (6)
6. Richard Goddard
   Sheffield . . . . .243 (-)
7. Neil Turley
   Leigh 232 (8)
8. Darren Holt
   Barrow . . . . .201 (-)
9. Mick Nanyn
   Swinton . . . . .186 (-)
10. Phil Cantillon
    Widnes 176 (8)

CHALLENGE CUP

TRIES
1. Michael Withers
   Bradford 7
2. Andrew Frew
   Huddersfield 6
   Lee Briers
   Warrington 6
   David Seeds
   Whitehaven 6
5. Scott Naylor
   Bradford 5
   Karl Pratt
   Leeds 5
   Kevin Sinfield
   Leeds 5
   Daniel Vergniol
   Villeneuve 5

GOALS
1. Henry Paul
   Bradford 30
2. Iestyn Harris
   Leeds 27
3. Steve Kirkbride
   Whitehaven 16
4. Sean Long
   St Helens 15
5. Frederic Banquet
   Villeneuve 13
   Pat Rich
   Oldham 13
7. Matt Crowther
   Hull 11
   Martin Pearson
   Wakefield 11
   Martin Wood
   Keighley 11

POINTS
1. Iestyn Harris
   Leeds 66
2. Henry Paul
   Bradford 65
3. Sean Long
   St Helens 42
4. Lee Briers
   Warrington 38
5. Barry Eaton
   Dewsbury 32
   Steve Kirkbride
   Whitehaven 32
7. Pat Rich
   Oldham 30
8. Michael Withers
   Bradford 28

Kris Radlinski

Simon Svabic

Michael Withers

ALL COMPETITIONS

TRIES

1	Neil Turley	
	Leigh	.55
2	Phil Cantillon	
	Widnes	.48
3	Graeme Lewthwaite	
	Workington	.33
4	Michael Withers	
	Bradford	.32
5	Marlon Billy	
	Rochdale	.31
6	Kris Radlinski	
	Wigan	.30
7	Paul Sculthorpe	
	St Helens	.27
8	Tevita Vaikona	
	Bradford	.25
	Damian Munro	
	Widnes	.25
10	Adrian Flynn	
	Dewsbury	.24

GOALS

1	Henry Paul	
	Bradford	.208
2	Andy Farrell	
	Wigan	.178
3	Simon Svabic	
	Leigh	.153
4	Pat Rich	
	Oldham	.146
5	Danny Wood	
	Rochdale	.130
6	Jamie Rooney	
	Featherstone	.121
7	Barry Eaton	
	Dewsbury	.110
8	Richard Goddard	
	Sheffield	.103
	Iestyn Harris	
	Leeds	.103
10	Darren Holt	
	Barrow	.92

POINTS

1	Henry Paul	
	Bradford	.457
2	Andy Farrell	
	Wigan	.429
3	Simon Svabic	
	Leigh	.341
4	Danny Wood	
	Rochdale	.324
5	Pat Rich	
	Oldham	.320
6	Jamie Rooney	
	Featherstone	.311
7	Barry Eaton	
	Dewsbury	.276
8	Paul Sculthorpe	
	St Helens	.273
9	Richard Goddard	
	Sheffield	.263
10	Iestyn Harris	
	Leeds	.251

TABLES & ATTENDANCES

SUPER LEAGUE

	P	W	D	L	F	A	D	PTS
Bradford	28	22	1	5	1120	474	646	45
Wigan	28	22	1	5	989	494	495	45
Hull	28	20	2	6	772	630	142	42
St Helens	28	17	2	9	924	732	192	36
Leeds	28	16	1	11	774	721	53	33
London	28	13	1	14	644	603	41	27
Warrington	28	11	2	15	646	860	-214	24
Castleford	28	10	1	17	581	777	-196	21
Halifax	28	9	0	19	630	819	-189	18
Salford	28	8	0	20	587	956	-369	16
Wakefield●	28	8	0	20	529	817	-288	14
H'dersfield	28	6	1	21	613	926	-313	13

● *Deducted two points for breach of salary cap*

	2001 Avg	2000 Avg	Diff
Leeds	12,881	12,740	+141
Bradford	12,379	15,350	-2,971
Wigan	11,795	11,329	+466
St Helens	8,779	8,830	-51
Castleford	7,102	7,975	-873
Hull	6,710	5,943	+767
Warrington	6,422	6,872	-450
Halifax	4,832	5,714	-882
Salford	4,170	4,448	-278
Huddersfield	3,681	3,422	+259
Wakefield	3,651	4,615	-964
London	3,177	3,419	-242

'01 Avg 7,223 / **'00 Avg** 7,555 / **Diff** -332

BEST CROWDS

60,164	Bradford v Wigan *(GF)*	.13/10/01
21,073	Wigan v St Helens *(R5)*	.13/4/01
19,260	Wigan v St Helens *(FE)*	.6/10/01
18,242	Leeds v Bradford *(R10)*	.11/5/01
16,572	Bradford v St Helens *(R1)*	.4/3/01
16,247	Bradford v Wigan *(R6)*	.16/4/01
15,702	Leeds v St Helens *(R9)*	.4/5/01
15,235	Wigan v St Helens *(R28)*	.14/9/01
15,106	Bradford v Leeds *(R20)*	.22/7/01
15,052	Wigan v Bradford *(R26)*	.31/8/01

WORST CROWDS

1,800	London v Huddersfield *(R25)*	.26/8/01
2,126	London v Wakefield *(R23)*	.12/8/01
2,153	London v Wakefield *(R18)*	.8/7/01
2,235	Huddersfield v London *(R16)*	.24/6/01
2,342	London v Castleford *(R21)*	.28/7/01
2,376	Wakefield v Salford *(R24)*	.19/8/01
2,547	Wakefield v London *(R7)*	.22/4/01
2,584	London v Halifax *(R12)*	.27/5/01
2,618	Salford v London *(R26)*	.2/9/01
2,717	Wakefield v Warrington *(R21)*	.29/7/01

CHALLENGE CUP

BEST CROWDS

68,250	Bradford v Leeds *(F)*	.28/4/01
16,416	Leeds v St Helens *(SF)*	.31/3/01
13,856	Bradford v Warrington *(SF)*	.1/4/01
13,593	St Helens v Wigan *(R4)*	.10/2/01
11,418	Castleford v Leeds *(R5)*	.24/2/01
10,123	Hull v Leeds *(QF)*	.10/3/01
8,844	Warrington v Leigh *(R5)*	.25/2/01
7,899	St Helens v Huddersfield *(QF)*	.9/3/01
7,760	Bradford v Widnes *(R4)*	.11/2/01
6,701	Hull v London *(R5)*	.25/2/01

WORST CROWDS

377	Gateshead v Whitehaven *(R4)*	.14/2/01
471	York v Villeneuve *(R4)*	.11/2/01
478	Swinton v New Earswick *(R3)*	.28/1/01
501	Gateshead v Wigan St J *(R3)*	.28/1/01
559	Chorley v Woolston *(R3)*	.28/1/01
573	Batley v Heworth *(R3)*	.28/1/01
605	Rochdale v Hunslet *(R4)*	.13/2/01
616	Whitehaven v Oldham St A *(R3)*	.28/1/01
629	Hunslet v Thornhill *(R3)*	.28/1/01
731	Rochdale v Wigan R Bridge *(R3)*	27/1/01

PREMIERSHIP

	P	W	D	L	F	A	D	PTS
Leigh	28	26	0	2	1139	321	818	52
Widnes	28	21	1	6	961	377	584	43
Rochdale	28	21	0	7	865	433	432	42
Oldham	28	21	0	7	780	416	364	42
F'therstone	28	17	2	9	825	401	424	36
Dewsbury	28	18	0	10	801	438	363	36
Hull KR	28	16	2	10	555	450	105	34
Keighley	28	16	1	11	810	498	312	33
Workington	28	16	0	12	681	568	113	32
Whitehaven	28	15	1	12	608	419	189	31
Sheffield	28	14	0	14	637	543	94	28
Doncaster	28	14	0	14	622	532	90	28
Batley	28	13	0	15	452	618	-166	26
Barrow	28	12	1	15	631	685	-54	25
Swinton	28	10	0	18	538	711	-173	20
Hunslet	28	6	1	21	380	959	-579	13
Gateshead	28	2	0	26	346	990	-644	4
Chorley	28	2	0	26	395	1361	-966	4
York	28	1	1	26	193	1499	-1306	3

	2001 Avg	2000 Avg	Diff
Widnes	3,781	3,372	+409
Leigh	3,020	2,640	+380
Keighley	2,045	2,052	-7
Oldham	1,841	2,197	-356
Featherstone	1,827	1,926	-99
Hull KR	1,811	2,221	-410
Rochdale	1,583	1,175	+408
Dewsbury	1,346	1,866	-520
Sheffield	1,214	1,176	+38
Doncaster	1,173	1,676	-503
Workington	1,137	859	+278
Whitehaven	960	854	+106
Swinton	944	1,104	-160
Hunslet	882	968	-86
Barrow	876	1,371	-495
Batley	837	800	+37
Gateshead	722	N/A	N/A
York	619	773	-154
Chorley	505	474	+31

'01 Avg 1,456 / **'00 Avg** 1,525 / **Diff** -69

BEST CROWDS

8,974	Oldham v Widnes *(GF)*	.28/7/01
6,644	Widnes v Leigh *(W4)*	.26/12/00
6,399	Leigh v Widnes *(MaSF)*	.22/7/01
4,914	Leigh v Widnes *(W19)*	.13/4/01
4,747	Oldham v Leigh *(W7)*	.14/1/01
4,372	Widnes v Featherstone *(W25)*	.20/5/01
4,202	Widnes v Rochdale *(PSF)*	.8/7/01
4,153	Rochdale v Oldham *(MaSF)*	.22/7/01
4,072	Widnes v Oldham *(W20)*	.16/4/01
3,864	Widnes v Whitehaven *(W1)*	.3/12/00

WORST CROWDS

254	Chorley v York *(W16)*	.18/3/01
282	Chorley v Workington *(W27)*	.3/6/01
289	Chorley v Batley *(W17)*	.25/3/01
295	Chorley v Whitehaven *(W20)*	.16/4/01
311	Chorley v Rochdale *(W25)*	.20/5/01
314	York v Whitehaven *(W22)*	.29/4/01
354	Chorley v Hull KR *(W14)*	.4/3/01
356	Chorley v Gateshead *(W19)*	.8/4/01
364	Chorley v Dewsbury *(W30)*	.24/6/01
387	Gateshead v Rochdale *(W18)*	.1/4/01

Neil Turley

Henry Paul